National Intelligencer Newspaper Abstracts 1847

Joan M. Dixon

HERITAGE BOOKS
2007

HERITAGE BOOKS
AN IMPRINT OF HERITAGE BOOKS, INC.

Books, CDs, and more—Worldwide

For our listing of thousands of titles see our website
at
www.HeritageBooks.com

Published 2007 by
HERITAGE BOOKS, INC.
Publishing Division
65 East Main Street
Westminster, Maryland 21157-5026

International Standard Book Number: 978-0-7884-4475-3

NATIONAL INTELLIGENCER NEWSPAPER WASHINGTON, D C 1847

TABLE OF CONTENTS

Daily National Intelligencer, Washington, D C, 1847: pg 1

Appointments & promotions-Army: 35; 43; 45; 70; 98; 105-114; 117; 119-120; 246-250; 538-549
Army-Tampico: 90
Barque Iduna collision: 349
Buena Vista: see index
Battle of: Vera Cruz: 152; 322
Tabasco: 320-321
Columbian College Alumni: 313
Commencements: Columbian College: 83; 303-304
St Joseph's Academy, Emmitsburg, Md: 310
St Mary's Female Institution, Chas Co, Md: 340-341
Concord Academy, Caroline Co, Va: 567
Deserters: 460-461
Government of the U S-1789: 68
Heirs of John Paul Jones: 81-82
Licenses-Wash, D C: 54-59; 91-94; 163-164; 225-228; 266-267; 428-430
Mexico: battles; killed & wounded: see index
Marine Corps: 120
Naval Academy: 345
Naval force-Gulf of Mexico: 132
Navy news: 161
Ship Mamlouk disaster: 359-360
Twelve month volunteers: 230
War Dept: see index
Washington City in 1800: 350
Washington City tax sale: 380-387
Index: pg 569

Dedicated to the memory of: Thos [J Thos] Dixon:
b. 1770 St Mary's Co, Md d. Feb 5, 1826, Gtwn, D C.
mrd-1: 1804 ca Catherine Kaldenbach
b 1790 Md; d May 13, 1819, Gtwn, D C
mrd-2: Aug 22, 1820 Mary C Young
b 1788 Montgomery Co, Md d. Jul 16, 1859 Gtwn, D C
[G G Grandfather of Roland C Dixon]

PREFACE

Daily National Intelligencer Newspaper Abstracts
1847
Joan M Dixon

The National Intelligencer & Washington Advertiser is hereafter the Daily National Intelligencer. It was the first newspaper printed in Washington, D C; Samuel H Smith, the originator. The same was transferred to Jos Gales, jr on Aug 31, 1810; on Nov 1, 1812, the paper was under the firm of Jos Gales, sr, & Wm W Seaton. The Library of Congress has microfilm of the paper from the first issue of Oct 31, 1800 thru Jan 8, 1870, the final paper. The Evening Star Newspaper of Jan 10, 1870 reports: The Intelligencer is discontinued: the proprietor, Mr Alex Delmar, says that having lost several thousand dollars, & being in poor health, he has resolved to discontinue its publication.

Included in the abstracts are advertisements; appointments by the President; Hse o/Rep petitions; passed Acts; legal notices; marriages; deaths; mscl notices; social events; tax lists; military promotions; court cases; deaths by accident; prisoners; & maritime information-crews. Items or events which might be a clue as to the location, age or relationship of an individual are copied.

No attempt has been made to correct the spelling. Due to the length of some articles, it was necessary to present only the highlights of same. Chancery and Equity records are copied as written.

The index contains all surnames and ***tracts of lands/places***. **Maritime vessels** are found under barge, boat, brig, frig, schn'r, ship, sloop, steamboat, tugboat, yacht or vessel.

ABBREVIATIONS:

AA CO	ANNE ARUNDEL COUNTY
CO	COMPANY/COUNTY
CMDER	COMMANDER
CMDOR	COMMODOR
D C	DISTRICT OF COLUMBIA
ELIZ	ELIZABETH
ELIZA	ELIZA
MONTG CO	MONTGOMERY COUNTY
PG CO	PRINCE GEORGES CO
WASH	WASHINGTON
WASH, D C	WASHINGTON, DISTRICT OF COLUMBIA

BOOKS IN THE NATIONAL INTELLIGENCER NEWSPAPER SERIES-:
1800-1805/1806-1810/1811-1813/1814-1817/1818-1820/1821-1823/1824-1826/1827-1829/1830-1831/1832-1833/1834-1835/1836-1837/1838-1839/1840/1841/1842/1843/1844/1845/1846/1847/
SPECIAL: CIVIL WAR 2 VOLS, 1861-1865

DAILY NATIONAL INTELLIGENCER NEWSPAPER 1847

FRI JAN 1, 1847

The Balt Btln in Mexico. We have seen a letter from an ofcr of the Balt & Wash Btln, now at Monterey, dated 9th of last month, which says: "We have lost a great many men by deaths & discharge. The aggregate of our btln is only 377, having lost 206 men since we arrived at the Brasos. -Balt Sun

New Orleans Commercial Times: unparalleled munificence. The late Mr Isaac Franklin, of Sumner Co, Tenn, died on Apr 27 last, on a plantation which belonged to him, in the Parish of West Feliciana, leaving, at the usually vigorous age of 55, a fortune amounting to nearly a million of dollars. He bequeathed the principal part of his property toward bldg & endowing an institution of learning in Sumner Co, Tenn, his native State, for the use of the necessitous children living there. Mr Franklin's parents, Jas Franklin & Mary Lauderdale, were from Va; he being a native of Mecklenburg, she of Botetourt. They were married just at the breaking out of the war of Independence, & emigrated to east Tennessee in 1776, where they set up their household goods in Holston, slenderly provided with this world's wealth. In 1789 they moved further west, & for a year resided at the Fort in Manco's Lick. When they, with the remainder of the people thereon, were obliged to decamp by the hostile Indians. They took refuge in Nashville, then the stronghold of West Tenn. Mr Jas Franklin while here performed military service in protecting the young settlement, until 1784, by which he became entitled to 640 acres of land, by pre-emption claim, on the West Ford of Station Camp creek, whither, in 1784, he removed, & where Mr Isaac Franklin, the subject of this memoir, was born on May 26, 1789. In his 18th year, Isaac was associated with his elder brothers, John & Jas, as their agent for transporting on the Mississippi the surplus products of the country of New Orleans, & bringing back merchandise. Mr Isaac Franklin, in the river trade, laid the foundation of his fortune. Mrs Franklin, at the decease of her husband, voluntarily relinquished her legal rights, & renounced the whole of what she might most equitably have claimed, thereby donating a sum of no less than $150,000 to aid in the founding & endowing of the institution. The public are greatly indebted to the Rev O B Hays, the father of Mrs Franklin, for the cheerful acquiescence he gave to her preconceived intentions regarding the carrying out of her husband's will. Mr John Armfield, the partner & bosom friend of Mr Franklin, has also a large claim on the gratitude of the public for the zealous care he has shown in the management of the estate destined to form the seminary in Tenn. Mr Hays & Mr Armfield are the excs to Mr Franklin's will.

Laws of the U S, passed at 2nd Session of 28th Congress: Official Publication. Act for the admission of the State of Iowa into the Union. Approved, Dec 28, 1846. Jas K Polk

Mrd: on Thu, by Rev John C Smith, Jas M McKnight to Miss Anna E, daughter of the late Anthony Preston, all of Wash City.

Died: on Dec 24, at Bloomingdale, near Wash City, "Old Aunt Peggy", late the property of Mrs Emily Beale. She was born in Virginia, & claimed to be 120 years old, retaining a vivid recollection of many interesting facts connected with the history of Lower Virginia for a considerable period previous to the Revolutionary war. The unshaken fidelity with which this ancient servant clung to several generations of the family in which she was born deserves this passing tribute to her memory.

Lt Chas Hoskins was a native of Edenton, N C: graduated at the Military Academy in 1836, & immediately joined his company in the Cherokee Nation. In 1839 he moved with the regt to ***Fort Gibson***, Ark; his regt made a tour in Florida in the winter of 1841. While at the barracks, he became attached & betrothed to an accomplished & amiable lady, residing at Potosi, Missouri. To consummate this union, he obtained the only leave of absence, excepting for a short buffalo excursion in 1841, that he asked for during an active service of more than 10 years. His regt was his only home, its ofcrs his kindred. His wife returned with him to ***Fort Scott***, & he was happily enjoying the choicest blessings which life could afford when the Mexican difficulty carried his regt to Corpus Christi in 1845, & separated him from his family forever. Lt Hoskins was still the adjutant at Monterey. His regt was posted on the night of Sep 20 to cover a mortar battery established in a hollow, within range of the fire from the Mexican citadel, & was more or less exposed all night. The following morning it was directed to storm a fort on the left & at the outskirts of the town. Three companies advanced to the charge: Maj Allen, [now of the 2nd Infty,] Lt Hoskins & Lt Graham since dead. When within a 100 yards, the fire became horribly destructive. Lt Hoskins was shot through the heart by a ball from an escopet, & died without uttering a word. His arm stiffened, with a finger pointing to his wound. Lts Graham & Woods, & 35 men, more than one-third the entire number, fell at the same moment. The record of Hoskins' fate had been brief-an insertion of his name in the list of the killed, often misspelt, occasionally attached to another regt than his own. Even in the only history of the affairs of the 8th & 9th of May, he is designated Lt A Haskins.

Close of the Van Ness Case-Wed. The Jury asked the Court if 11 jurors could make a verdict. The Court said they could not. Mr Easby was then allowed to retire from the jury-box, & the remaining 11 jurors returned to the Court a paper, stating, in the form of a verdict, that, under the instructions, they find "that Mrs Mary Ann Van Ness is not the widow of John P Van Ness." Thus, for the present, ends this case. [Jan 2nd newspaper: As counsel, of Mary A Van Ness, in the case just tried & decided against her, it is her determination, under our advice, to prosecute an appeal from this decision to the Supreme Court. -Brent & May]

Circuit Court of Wash Co, D C-in Chancery. Jas Dundas et al vs Jos Forrest's reps et al. Ratify sale of parts of lots 13 & 14 in square 80, in Wash City, with the appurtenances, to Bladen Forrest, for $350. -W Brent, clerk

Circuit Court of Wash Co, D C-in Chancery. Wm H Thomas, vs Susan Littledeer, alias Susan Kilchula, John W Maury, & Richd Smith. In substance, Thompson Kilchula & Susan Littledeer, alias Susan Kilchula, of Cherokee Co, N C, being Cherokee Indians, having certain claims againt the U S Gov't, &, being indebted to plntf, gave him a power of atty to recover & receive the money for said claims, with the express understanding that he should retain of said money enough to repay himself what they then did owe, or might become indebted for, to him, besides his fees & charges for collection; that they then owed him a considerable sum, & have since become indebted to him on other several accounts; that, after plntf obtained a favorable award on said claims, &, without his knowledge or consent, said Thompson & Susan gave another power of atty to John H Eaton, who received said money, & deposited the same in the Bank of the Metropolis to the credit of said Susan Littledeer. The bill states that Thompson & Susan became citizens of the U S by virtue of the Cherokee treaties, & they lived together as man & wife, after the usage & customs of the Cherokee Indians, but were never married in manner as required by the laws of N C; that said Thompson Kilchula is dead, & no exc or administrator has been appointed to administer to his effects. The bill prays an injunction to restrain the Pres & Cashier of the Bank of the Metropolis from paying out said money until further direction of this Court in the premises, which having been granted, & it having been made to appear to the Court that said Susan Littledeer resides beyond the jurisdiction of this Court. The absent dfndnt is to appear in person or by solicitor, in this Court, on or before the first Monday in May next. -W Brent, clerk

SAT JAN 2, 1847

Mary A Van Ness, vs Cornelius P Van Ness, adm of John P Van Ness, deceased. We the undersigned Jurors, in our opinion, there was nothing in the testimony to impeach in the least the credibility of Miss Serena Conner, of Miss Virginia Fowler, or of Mrs Eliz Fowler, witnesses examined in this cause; or to implicate them or either of them in any charge of fraud, conspiracy, forgery, or perjury.

Thos P Orme, Foreman
J Hepburn
Thos J Triplitt
Z Jones
Henry Trunnel
Wm Bird
Wm Easby
Wm Henry Craig
Peter Hepburn
Geo W Stewart
John Suter

Jonathan Thompson, formerly for many years Collector of the Port of N Y, & lately Pres of the Manhattan Co, died in N Y C, Wed last, at an advanced age. He was a man of great probity & universally respected.

Confectionary, household & kitchen furniture at auction: on Jan 5, at the residence of Mr Barnes, corner of 9th & I sts, his entire stock of Confectionary, shop fixtures, & furniture. -A Green, auctioneer

Mrd: on Dec 31, by Rev G W Samson, Thos H Barron to Miss Catherine Doniphin, all of Wash City.

Died: on Jan 1, at the Navy Yard, in Wash City, after a short & painful illness, Lewis A Newman, aged 41 years, leaving a wife & 3 children to mourn their irreparable loss. His funeral is tomorrow at 2 o'clock, from his late residence, near the Navy Yard.

Died: on Dec 31, Chas Samson, son of Fred'k & Eliza Cudlipp, aged 3 years & 9 months. His funeral is Sunday, at half-past 3 o'clock, from the residence of his parents on Pa ave.

MON JAN 4, 1847

Mr Denton Offutt, the Horse Trainer, has returned to Wash City for a few days, & may be seen at the Md House, on Pa ave, or, during the sittings of the 2 Houses of Congress, in the Rotundo of the Capitol.

Dr Robt Arthur, Surgeon Dentist, having determined to make Wash his permanent residence, offers his professional services to the public. Ofc, Pa ave, between 11th & 12th.

Wash Co, D C: I certify that Robt McChesney, of said county, brought before me, as an estray trespassing on his enclosures, a black buffalo Cow; & a red buffalo Cow.
-C H Wiltberger, J P [Owner to prove their property, pay charges, & take them away. Robt McChesney, living on B O Tayloe's farm, adjoining the turnpike gate of the Wash & Rockville Turnpike.]

The frig **Cumberland**, which arrived at Norfolk last week from the Gulf of Mexico, brought home the body of Lt Morris, son of Com Morris, who was killed in the attack on Tabasco.

A late arrival at Wilmington, N C, reports the death, on Dec 9, of Mr Nicholl, the American Consul at Cardenas.

The gentleman mentioned as having been recommended as Colonel of the Balt Btln, vice Col Watson, deceased, is not B Buchanan, but Maj Robt C Buchanan, son of the late Andrew Buchanan, long a distinguished merchant of Balt. This ofcr was brevetted for his good conduct at Palo Alto & Resaca de la Palma, & serving with some distinction in the Florida campaign. -Balt American

The Marlborough Gaz states that an aged lady, Eliz Burnell, came to an untimely death during the Christmas holydays, at the residence of Smith Martin, in PG Co, by the accidental discharge of a gun in the hands of Martin, while he was laboring under excessive intoxication.

Louis G De Russy, a graduate of West Point, has been chosen Colonel of the new regt of volunteers from Louisiana, & Francis Rigault, Major. The Lt Col is yet to be appointed.

Naval: Ofcrs attached to the U S ship **Ohio**, Dec 19, 1846:
Capt, Silas H Stringham; Cmder, L M Goldsborough
Lts-9:
Wm C Whittle
F A Deas
E L Handy
Jos F Green
J B Marchand
J J Almy
H Eld, jr
P U Murphy
J N Brown
Masters, C Ap R Jones, W E Boudinot
Surgeon, B Washington
Assist Surgeons, E J Bee, R T Macown
Purser, John D Bree
Capt of Marines, T S English
Lt of Marines, C G Grayson
Chaplain, P G Clark
Passed Midshipmen-3: J C Beaumont; M K Warrington; J P Hall
Midshipmen-3: Greenleaf Cilley; Robt Stuart; Edw Renshaw
Acting Midshipmen-9:
D H Lynch
J P Foster
E O Carnes
A B Gherardi
Jas Bredin
F W Robinson
Beverly Kennon
A N Lodge
P C Johnson
Capt's Clerk, Hallett
Cmder's Clerk, Cobb
Purser's Clerk, E W Parks
Boatswain, [acting,] Simpson
Gunner, J W Pennington
Carpenter, Patrick Dee
Sailmaker, Jas Ferguson

The Marlborough Gaz states that an aged lady, Eliz Burnell, came to an untimely death during the Christmas holydays, at the residence of Smith Martin, in PG Co, by the accidental discharge of a gun in the hands of Martin, while he was laboring under excessive intoxication.

House of Reps: 1-Memorial of Geo F Warfield & others, & of Marianne Champagne, praying indemnity for French spoliations prior to 1800. 2-Ptn of Mary Anne O'Brien, widow of the late Lucius O'Brien, of the U S army, asking for a pension. 3-Ptn of Benj Blagge, of N Y, for indemnity for French spoliations prior to 1800. 4-Memorial of the heirs of the late David Henshaw, praying for relief for French spoliations. 5-Memorial of Richd M Thomas, Annetta M Fairlamb, & Theresa M Downing, heirs at law of Jos J Miller, deceased, praying indemnity for French spoliations prior to 1800. 6-Memorial of Peter King, trustee of Mary Whitesides, excx of Peter Whitesides, asking indemnity for French spoliations prior to 1800. 7-Ptn of Chas G Loring, Chas Brown, & Michl Whitney, excs, for the payment of the French indemnities. 8-Ptn of Sarah Chase, praying indemnity for French spoliations prior to 1800.

Mrd: by Rev J B Smith, Dr E W Taylor to Miss Mary T Gibbon, all of Seaford, Delaware. [No date given-appears recent.]

Died: on Sat, in his 64th year, Edw Stephens, a native of Dublin, Ireland, & for upwards of 35 years a resident of Wash City. His funeral will take place from the residence of Mrs E James, corner of I & 10th sts, this morning, at 11 o'clock.

TUE JAN 5, 1847

Senate: 1-Ptn of Rev Thos F Mulledy, Pres, the Rev Jas A Ward, Vice Pres, & the Professors of Gtwn College, in D C, praying a modification of the tariff law of the last session of Congress so as to exempt from duty all instruments & books imported for the use of the college. 2-The ptn of the heirs of the late Gen E Ripley was taken from the files & referred to the Cmte of Claims. 3-The ptn of Gillis Thompson, the rep of the estate of the late Capt Thompson, of the U S Navy, was taken from the files & referred to the Cmte on Foreign Relations. 4-Ptn for the relief of Ralph Tompkins & others, children & heirs at law of the late Danl D Tompkins, deceased. 5-Cmte on Public Lands: bill for the relief of Geo Gordon, of Randolph Co, Ill. 6-Cmte on the Post Ofc & Post Roads: bill for the relief of Thos Rhodes. Same cmte-bill for the relief of Nathl Kuykendall. 7-Cmte on Naval Affairs: bill for the relief of Jos Wilson, & a bill for the relief of Thos Brownell. 8-Resolved: that the Cmte on Naval Affairs inquire into paying a balance claimed by Walter R Johnson to be due him for his services & payments made by him for the U S. Same cmte: to inquire into allowing Hans Nelson a claim against the U S, for his services in the U S Navy during the last war. 9-Bill for the relief of Joshua Dodge: engrossed for a 3rd reading. 10-Joint resolution for the relief of Wm H Thomas: passed over informally.

Mrd: on Dec 16, at ***Planta Place***, the residence of Mrs Ann Minnick, near Nashville, by Judge Green, of the Supreme Court of Tenn, Col J P Campbell, of Columbia, to Rebecca Watson, daughter of Walter Sims, of Nashville.

Died: on Sunday last, after a few days' illness, Walter B Hamilton, in his 21st year. His funeral is this day at 12 o'clock, from the residence of his mother, on Pa ave.

Mr Reese, of Pottsville, was found on Thu near his own residence dead, having apparently been shot through the head with a pistol, & a pickaxe afterwards driven through his skull.

Teacher wanted: the Trustees of a district school in Chas Co, Md, wish to employ a teacher capable of teaching English, Math, Latin & Greek. Apply to Hon John Matthews, of the Senate, at Annapolis, to the Hon John G Chapman, House of Reps, Wash, or to Geo W Matthews, Port Tobacco, Md.

Notice: I forewarn all person from trading or buying notes of mine, given to Robt Brown, Nov 30, 1844, for certain lands in Montg Co, Md, as I do not intend to pay them, owing to a mortgage on the land prior to the time the notes were given. -Jas Gill, his X mark.

WED JAN 6, 1847

Mrd: on Jan 4, by Rev J C Smith, Wm C Greenleaf to Mrs Mary Brightwell, all of Wash City.

Yesterday afternoon, in Wash City, Dr John Wickham, of Richmond, Va, put a period to his life. He was practicing in a public pistol gallery on La ave, &, as we learn, had fired 8 or 9 shots, when he suddenly placed a pistol to the side of his head, & shot himself through the brain. He expired in about an hour.

Meeting of the Medical Class of the Columbian College, Jan 4, 1847, John J Dyer, in the chair: Resolution: sympathy to the afflicted family of the late Walter B Hamilton, esteemed friend & classmate, unexpectedly called from our midst. -Wm H Saunders, sec

The Lexington Observer gives the following extract of a letter from a gentleman in Donaldsonville to Gen Leslie Combs, dated Dec 2, 1846. The fiend O'Blennis, who murdered your gallant son 2 years ago, & has so far escaped punishment for that horrid deed, has at length met his deserts, having been shot by some Mexicans at Matamoros, where he had settled himself as a trader. Just before his death he had murdered a gentleman of the name of Townsend, who had a claim against him, & it was from Townsend's brother that I derived the above information.

Meeting of the Ohio Delegation in Congress, held Jan 4, 1847, at the Capitol in Wash, to express sentiments on the occasion of the death of Brig Gen Thos L Hamer, of Ohio, at Monterey, Mexico. He leaves his wife, children, & numerous friends to mourn his loss. Gen Hamer emigrated to Ohio from the State of Pa when quite young. [Headquarters Army of Occupation, Camp near Monterey, Dec 3, 1846. He expired on Dec 2, 1846, after a short but severe illness. He will be interred at 10 a m tomorrow with the honors due to his rank. Brig Gen Quitman, commanding the volunteer division, will conduct the funeral ceremonies. -W W S Bliss, Assist Adj Gen. Official-J Hooker, Acting Assist Adj Gen.
+
Ofcrs of the 1st regt of Ohio volumteers & of Capt Webster's artl company, being part of the 1st field brig, 2nd division, U S army, commanded by the late Brig Gen Thos L Hamer, convened Dec 4 at the headquarters of the regt. Present were: Maj Giddings; Capt Webster, Long, Harmell, Hamilton, John B Armstrong, Bradley, Miller, Vandevere; 1st Lts Donaldson, Maloney, Kline, Kidd, Beaugrand, Fyffe, Becker, Oakland, Moore; 2nd Lts Bowen, Shearer, Allen, Kriecht, Hall, Cooke, Kneller, Knaneally, McCarter, White, Kochreiser, Boyle, Colville, Smead, Kendall, Vischer, & Longley.

Senate: 1-Ptn from Jas W Schaumburg, asking to be recognized as an ofcr of the army & for promotion. 2-Ptn from Rezin Tevis, asking land & additional pay for services in the Revolutionary war. 2-Ptn from Thos Ap Catesby Jones, asking to be restored to the invalid navy pension list. 3-Ptn from W Hogan, adm of M Hogan, asking payment of a claim certified by a jury to be due him. 4-Ptn from John Martin, an ofcr in the last war, asking arrears of pension. 5-Ptn from Wm A Christian, a purser in the navy, asking certain credits for payments made to forward ofcrs holding acting appointments on board the steamer **Princeton**. Also, ptn from Wm D Crosby, a purser, asking the same for payments on board the U S ship **Ontario**. 6-Ptn from Thos Bideswell, asking payment for money advanced for medical services rendered to the ofcrs & seamen at Sackett's Harbor. 7-Ptn from Eliz Allen, asking a pension as a widow of a Revolutionary soldier. 8-Additional documents in relation to the claim of the heirs of the late Jas Rumney. 9-Ptn from Ed Dennison, asking to be relieved from an error in the description of land settled by him. 10-Bill brought in to compromise the claim of the heirs of John Smith T, under a Spanish grant. 11-Cmte on Foreign Relations: bill for the relief of the heirs of Wm A Slacum, deceased. 12-Cmte of Claims: unfavorable report on the ptn of Jos de La Francis: which was ordered to be printed. 13-Cmte on Public Lands: bill for the relief of Madison Allen. 14-Bill for the relief of Mary McRae, widow of Lt Col Wm McRae. Mr Calhoun: it was proposed to give to the widow of an ofcr of the army, who died while in service, but not in battle, a pension for life. It was an entirely novel application to ask for a pension for a widow under such circumstances; & it was an application which, if allowed, would lead to extensive innovation. The case of Mary McRae might be a meritorious one, but a case of this kind would become a precedent, & would draw after it numerous other cases. Bill to lie on the table & be taken up in the future.

Died: on Jan 5, Edw Gallagher, aged 83 years. His funeral is this day, at 3 o'clock, from his late residence, 13th st, near the corner of G st.

Valuable lot of land at Public sale, within one mile of the City Limits: by deed of trust, to me, dated Jun 24, 1845, & recorded in liber W B 117, folios 310, 311, & 312, of the land records of Wash Co, D C: sale on Feb 5, of that lot containing 16 acres of land, with improvements of 2 good dwlgs,: abounded by the lands of Geo Taylor & the estate of Hoban & Mr Cox, at the Toll-gate, on the Wash & Rockville road, & is also bound by the Rock Creek Church road. -R L Ross, trustee

THU JAN 7, 1847

Senate: 1-Cmte on the Judiciary: asking to be discharged from the further consideration of the ptn of Jas W Schaumburg, & that it be transferred to the executive jurnal. Same cmte: asking to be discharged from the further consideration of the bill for the relief of Clemants, Bryan & Co: that it be referred to the Cmte of Claims. 2-Cmte on the Judiciary: bill for the relief of Peter Capella, adm of Andrew Capella, & for the relief of John Capo. 3-Cmte on Private Land Claims: bill for the relief of Shadrach Gillett & others, without amendment. Same cmte: bill for the relief of Jacques Moulon. 4-Cmte on Pensions: Bill for the relief of Francis Summuraner. Same cmte: bill for the relief of Peter Frost, with a report in each case. 5-Bill introduced on leave: bill to provide for the final settlement of the accounts of John Spencer, late receiver of public moneys in Indiana.

A Court of Inquiry was ordered to assemble on board the U S ship **Pennsylvania** on Jan 4, to inquire into the loss of the U S ship **Boston**, the Court to be composed of the following ofcrs: Cmdor Jesse Wilkinson, Pres; Cmdor Chas W Skinner, Capt W D Salter, members; & Lt Geo P Upshur, Judge Advocate.

The Mountaineer is the title of a new paper printed in Cumberland, Md, the first number of which had been received. It is to be neutral in politics, & devoted to literature & general news.

At Brooklyn, N Y, on Fri last, at the house of Peter Heslin, a large number of persons had gathered for the purpose of raising a hickory tree, when after it had been elevated some of the blocks or tackling gave way, & the massive piece of timber fell, crushing beneath it & instantly killing Mr Owen Flood, an aged man well & favorably known, who was an Irishman by birth. -Advertiser

The Rotundo of the Capitol is adorned with a very large & beautiful Painting, which attracts all eyes & receives general admiration. The subject is Ruth & her dghts, Naomi & Orpah, at the time described in the 1st chapter of Ruth, 14th & 15th verses. The artist is Mr Rossiter, of N Y, from Conn, who has passed some time in Italy. The painting belongs to Mr Parker, of N Y.

Mrd: by Rev Smith Pyne, Rector of St John's Church, T Harman Patterson, U S Navy, to Maria Montresor, 2nd daughter of the late Col R D Wainwright, U S Marine Corps. [No date-appears lately.]

To the honorable the Senate & House of Reps of the U S of America in Congress assembled. Your petitioner, Leslie Combs, of the State of Ky, represents that the late Republic of Texas is justly indebted to him in the sum of $39,200 principal, with interest at the rate of 10% per annum on the sum of $59,000 from Mar 1, 1839, till paid, & with like interest on the sum of $10,000 from Apr 1, 1841, till paid; all which will appear by reference to the books of the Treas Dept of said Republic, as well as by the bonds now in the possession of your petitioner, which he is ready to exhibit when required to do so. As one of the consequences of the annexation of Texas & her adoption into the Federal Union, the Gov't of the U S has taken possession of her custom-houses, & thus deprived her of her most important & reliable source of annual income, the proceed of which had been previously appropriated & "set apart," by law & by express contract with your petitioner, for the payment of the interest on his bonds. He is therefore impelled by every motive of self preservation to ask you to pay what is due him.
-Leslie Combs, Dec 7, 1846.

Appointments by the Pres:
Saml H Montgomery, of Pa, to be Assist Quartermaster, with the rank of Captain
John W Shugart, of Pa, to be Assist Commissary, with the rank of Captain
Benj S Muhlemberg, of Pa, to be Surgeon
Geo Dock, of Pa, to be Assist Surgeon
Saml McGowan, of S C, to be Assist Quartermaster, with the rank of Captain
Jas D Blaiding, of S C, to be Assist Commissary, with the rank of Captain
John Davis, of S C, to be Surgeon
Elbert Bland, of S C, to be Assist Surgeon

By virtue of an order of distress, to me directed, against the goods & chattels of Josiah Dixon, I have taken sundry goods-a counter, set of shelves, glass cases, furniture, vest pattern, remnants of cloth, counter brush, a sign, & hat racks; which will be sold on Jan 9, opposite the Centre Market, to satisfy house rent due in arrears to Saml S Coleman.
-Jas M Wright, bailiff

FRI JAN 8, 1847

Register's Ofc, Wash, Jan 5, 1847. The following named persons have taken out licenses under the laws of the Corp during the month of Dec, 1846.

Adams, Nace: Hack
Boteler & McGregor: Hardware
Barnes, Elias: Shop
Brown, John: Porter
Branner, B & Son: Hardware
Bronaugh, J M: Lottery
Blanford, O A: Retail
Burford, Elim: Retain
Birch, Fielder: Ten pins
Brodbent, G: Dry goods
Beers,Isaac: Hack
Boteler, Philip: Hack
Bignem, Wm: Hack
Bush, Wm : Hack
Callan, Lawrence: Retail
Caton, Michl: Retail
Costigan, J: Retail
Costigan, J: Boots & shoes
Cromwell, Saml: Stage
Clarke, Cornell: Hack
Davis, Jas: Shop
Duckworth, M: Groceries
Donovan, John: Tavern
Drury, Terrence: Retail
Drury, W P: Dry Goods
David, J B: Boots & shoes
Davis, Jas R: Hack
Dumphy, Thos: Hack
Dettro, Thos: Hack
Estep, Hooe & Co: Dry goods
Feeny, Wm: Shop
Fowler, J E Boots & shoes
Frank, Jos: Retail
Foote, Andrew: Hack
Ford, Fred'k: Hack
Greenleaf, W H: Medicines
Gibbs, J H: Dry goods
Gibbs, J H: Hardware
Gibson, John: Shop
Gadsby, Wm: Tavern
Golden, Jno: Tavern
Galt, J & M W: Hardware
Goathard, Saml : Hack
Golden, W L: Stage
Hillyard, C: Retail
Hayden, C W: Hardware
Holmes, S: Grocery
Harkness, J C: Grocery
Howe, John: Retail
Harper, W & Co: Dry goods
Harrison, E: Dry goods
Jackson, Susan: Retail
Jenkins, A J: Hack
Kenney, Jeremiah: Shop
Kraff, Geo: Confectioner
King, Martin: Retail
Knott, J H: blank
Kilmiste, M: Theatre
Leary & Co: Hats
Lucas, Eliz: Stage
Lee, Wm: Hack
McKnight, J W: Dry goods
Middleton & Beall: Retail
Maxwell & Sears: Dry goods
Magee, Owen: Retail
Marceron, J L: Retail
Mann, Wm: Boots & shoes
Merritt, Isaac: Shaking
Morse, J E: Shop
Morse, J E: Billiards
Middleton, L J: Retail
McBlair, J H: Retail

Massoletti, L I: Medicines
McNamara, J: Hack
Mullen, Wm: Hack
Moren, Jas: Hack
Nailor, Dickerson: Retail
Nailor, Allison: Stages
Nailor, Allison: Hack
Nailor, Allison: Hack
Pettigrew, W T: Shop
Pittman & Phillips: Dry goods
Powell, Abraham: Hack
Riley, John: Shop
Rochat, Henry: Retail
Rogers, J C: Retail
Rives, C: Retail
Radcliff, J R: Grocery
Senelan, Francis: Dry goods
Stepper, Andrew: Retail
Stephen, E B: Slave man
Smith, Thos: Hacks
Smith, A Thomas: Hack
Thomas, Jos: Shop
Thompson, J R: Dry goods
Tonge, R: Hardware
Turner, Henry: Hack
Turner, Galen: Hack
Venable, T P: Confectioner
Waters, D S: Retail
Wilson, Patrick: Retail
Walker, Henry: Retail
Weatherby & Bates: Medicine
Welsh, Thos: Hack
Young & Steer: Dry goods
-C H Wiltberger, Register

Senate: 1-Ptn from Benj Wheeler, asking indemnity for French spoliations prior to 1800. 2-Ptn from Wm F Price & others, temporary clerks in the Treas Dept, asking payment for their services. 3-Ptn from Thos C Sheldon, late receiver of public moneys at Kalamazoo, Mich, asking reimbursement of money advanced for extra clerk hire in the sales of public lands. 4-Ptn from I S K Reeves, lt of artl & adjutant of U S Military Academy, asking to be allowed the same pay as adjutants of dragoons in the army of the U S. 5-Ptn from the heirs of Abraham Varick, asking indemnity for spoliations prior to 1800. 6-Ptn of Joshua Barney & others, for indemnity for spoliations prior to 1800. 7-Cmte on Indian Affairs: bill for the relief of Elijah White, with a report: ordered to be printed.

From Calif: 1-Appointments by the cmder of the Northern District Headquarters at San Francisco: E M Kern, to command at ***Sutter's Fort***. E J Sutter, Lt of the fort. Lt J M Revere, U S N, Cmder of the Sonoma District, with 50 mounted men. J H Warbough, U S N, Cmder at Santa Clara. Lt W Bartlett, U S N, to the civil magistracy of the District of San Francisco-ofc in Yerba Buena. Stephen Smith, magistrate at Bodega. Geo Hyde, civil magistrate for the district of Santa Clara-ofc at the Pueblo de San Jose. Capt Mervin notifies all ofcrs & soldiers, late of Gen Castro's army, to present themselves & give their parole; & others who have been paroled to come in & give additional pledges. 2-Capt Mervine, cmder of the U S forces in Monterey, offers a reward of $50 for the apprehension of Wm Parkes, a deserter. Also a notice from Mr Alcaldo Colton, prohibiting the sale of intoxicating liquor, on penalty of fine, imprisonment, & forfeiture. Shopkeepers & keepers of public houses are forbidden to have liquors or wines in their possession.

Wm Brent appointed by the Hon Judge Cranch, Clerk of the District Court of D C, vice Cassius F Lee, resigned. Ofc in the City Hall.

Gtwn improvements: a large rolling factory is nearly completed, adjoining the aqueduct. The cotton factory will be in operation in 2 or 3 weeks. The Canal is now great & rapidly increasing, & there is now a fair prospect of its completion to Cumberland.

Wash City: 1st Ward: a new Methodist Church has been erected on 20th st, between H st & Pa ave. 2nd Ward: a German Hall has been erected on 11th st, between F & G sts. 3rd Ward: a neat & very convenient Market on K st, between 7th & 8th sts, with brick pavement on the south front. A large bldg for a Temperance Hall erected on E st, between 9th & 10th sts. 4th Ward: On 5th st, between G & H sts, has been erected a German Catholic Church; Washington Hall, 4 stories, corner of Pa ave & 6th st; improvements made on the Four-&-a half street Presbyterian Church by a portico & steeple. 5th Ward: a Methodist Protestant Church was erected in 1845. 7th Ward: the new Methodist Church on south D & 10th sts has been finished & occupied.

Anacostia Fire Co elected for the ensuing year:
Thos Kelly, Pres
Hugh Pritchard, Vice Pres
Chas Gordon, Sec
Jas A Gordon, Treas
John Simmons, Steward

A letter dated Parras, Mexico, Dec 9, says: "Col Yell, Lt Col Roane, & Maj Borland are under arrest for positive disobedience of orders. The 'old war horse' [Gen Wool] has ordered a court martial."

Nanny, about 6 years old, youngest daughter of Col Balie Peyton, was killed instantly by a kick received upon her head from a Mexican pony on Dec 25, at the Colonel's farm, in Sumner Co. -Nashville Whig

Mrd: on Jan 5, by Rev S D Finckel, of the First Ward, Wash, Mr Andrew Eichler to Miss Sophia Keiser, both of Wash City.

Mrd: on Jan 5, by Rev S K Cox, Edgar A Richardson, of Fairfax Co, Va, to Eliz A Emerson, of Alexandria, Va.

Died: on Jan 5, at his residence on ***Elk Ridge***, Anne Arundel Co, Md, Gen Chas Sterett Ridgely, in his 65th year. He was the father of Capt Randolph Ridgely, who so highly distinguished himself in the recent battles in Mexico, & who recently died at Monterey in consequence of a fall from his horse.

The Lexington [Ky] Observer notes the death of Jos Brown, jr, of that city, who was suffocated by smoke whilst lying in his bed. A settee took fire while he was asleep.

SAT JAN 9, 1847

Miniature Painting & Instruction in Drawing: Miss Eliz Milligan, Miniature Painter: enlarging the class now receiving lessons at her residence, near the State Dept, one door east of the corner house on N Y ave & 15th st west.

The subscribers have this day entered into copartnership, under the firm of Walker & Peck, for the purpose of carrying on the victualling business in all its branches.
-John Walker, Jos Peck

Valuable lands & slaves at auction: by deed of trust, dated Feb 12, 1840, recorded in Liber W B 77, folios 51 to 58 of the land records in Wash Co, D C, & in liber __, #10, folios 151 to 155 of the land records of Montgomery Co, Md: sale on the premises of ***Delacarlia***, containing about 282 acres or land, lying partly in each of the above counties. Improvements comprise a comfortable farm house, gardener's house, negro quarters, meat-house, & all necessary out-bldgs. The walls also remain of the former mansion house, which was burnt a few years since, & can be repaired at a moderate expense. After the sale of the land, we shall sell at auction about 15 valuable house & farm servants, men, women, & children, slaves for life, under the positive restriction of not being removed from D C or the State of Md. -John Kurtz, Clement Cox, Trustees. -Edw S Wright, auct

Hurricane in Huntingdon, Pa, on Sun last. Miss Malinda Staley was very severely injured; Mrs Burbank was badly cut under her chin; her dght had her left arm broken; Mr Stover's dght had her ancle dislocated. They were all at Duncanvsille in the Baptist meeting-house where the roof was entirely lifted off.

Mrd: on Jan 6, in Wash City, by Rev O Ege, the Rev Newton Heston, of the Phil Conference, Methodist Episcopal Church, to Miss Eliz Sheperd Beck, daughter of Jos W Beck, of Wash City.

U S Army: <u>Recruiting Service</u>: Wanted, for the U S Army, able-bodied men between the ages of 18 & 35 years, being above 5 feet 3 inches high, of good character, & of respectable standing among their fellow citizens. Rates per month: [A bounty of $20 will be paid to each recruit.]
Privates-$7/pay of Dragoon soldiers when mounted-$8
Artificers: $11
Furriers & Blacksmiths: $11
Musicians: $8
Buglers: $8/pay of Dragoon soldiers when mounted-$9
Cpls: $9/pay of Dragoon soldiers when mounted-$10
Ordnance Sgt: $18
All other Sgts: $13

Died: on Jan 8, Chas Edw, aged 19 months & 14 days, youngest child of John N & Ann Lovejoy. His funeral at 3 o'clock this afternoon, from the corner of 12th & I sts.

Died: on Dec 20 last, at Weybridge, Vt, Mrs Eleanor Wright, widow of the late Silas Wright, of that place, & mother of Gov Wright, at the advanced age of 85 years. The husband, father of Gov Wright, died at the same place in May, 1843, aged 84 years, the couple having lived together as husband & wife 61 years.

Died: on Mon last, at the residence of her husband, in PG Co, Md, Mrs Mary Ann Cox, widow of Mr Geo Cox, in her 28th year.

MON JAN 11, 1847

House of Reps: 1-Cmte of Claims: bill for the relief of Wm Culver: ordered to be printed. 2-Ptn of John Ross, a Revolutionary soldier, praying Congress to allow him a pension for his services during the war of the Revolution. 3-Ptn of Benj G Perkins, praying allowance of a pension as an invalid in consideration of disabilities incurred during his services in the U S Army. 4-Ptn of the excs of Capt Judah Alden for commutation. 5-Ptn of Antoine Dupre, praying for confirmation of a tract of land. 6-Ptn of Robt Butler, of Florida, praying compensation for certain losses. 7-Ptn & accompanying papers of L P Cheatham. 8-Ptn of S F Read & accompanying papers. 9-Ptn of the heirs of Peter Dominick Robert, with accompanying papers. 10-Ptn of Saml Graves, with accompanying papers. 11-Memorial of the heirs of Nathl Tracy, for the payment of outstanding loan ofc certificates. 12-Ptn of Wm Wickham. 13-Ptn of J W Nye. 14-Memorial of the heirs of Capt John Thomas, of the Virginia State navy during the war of the Revolution, asking pay & relief. 15-Memorial of Wm & Richd A Reeder, for property destroyed by the enemy in the war of 1812. 16-Ptn of the reps of Col Udney Hay, for payment of lost loan ofc certificates. 17-Memorial of Geo Africanus O'Brien, praying to be indemnified for French spoliations prior to 1800 on the property of his father, Richd O'Brien. 18-Memorial of Jacob Idler, of Phil, in relation to his claim upon the Gov't of Venezuela, & for relief. 19-Ptn of W B Edwards, late an invalid soldier, praying for a pension. 20-Ptn of Jos W Cross, of West Boylston, Mass, praying for the restoration of peace. 21-Cmte on Revolutionary Pensions: adverse reports on the cases of:

Nancy Martin
Alex'r Bills
Jesse Roberts
Lyddal Estas
Magdalena Moore
David Pugh
John Stout
Sophia Albrecht
Mary Hicks
Jas Green
Grace Hudnut
Sarah Knight
John Blair Finley
Mary Andrews
Geo Alford
Nicholas Siscoe
Wm Vice
Eleanor Wills
Lucy Clarke
Hannah J Wick
Freelove Waid
Nancy J Armstrong
Heirs of Robt Allison, dec'd

By deed of trust from Mary Haugh to the subscriber, dated Feb 26, 1846, recorded in Liber W B 126, folios 99 thru 101, of the land records of Wash Co, D C: sale on the premises, on Jan 20: a parcel of ground in said city, being part of lot 7 in square 456, on E st, with the improvements thereon. -Sylvanus Holmes, trustee -A Green, auct

Late papers from the Island of Jamaica announce the death, at Spanish-Town, of a black man named John Crawford Ricketts, at the extraordinary age of 142 years.

Belair [Md] Republican: Mr Jos Edwards, his son, & 2 nephews, were out hunting on Sat, pursing a rabbit, & Mr Edwards' gun, being cocked, went off, killing his son almost instantly & seriously wounding both of his nephews, one of whom has since had his arm amputated.

Died: on Jan 3, in Wash City, Winfield Scott, son of Benj H & Esther E Cowles, formerly of Balt, Md, aged 7 months & 10 days.

Trenton State Gaz announces the death of Mrs Garrett D Wall, the wife of the ex-Senator.

The Life of Lord Stirling-prepared by the Hon Wm A Duer, a grandson of that gallant soldier of our Revolution-is now in press, & is shortly to be published by the Historical Society of N J.

TUE JAN 12, 1847

The nomination of R P Lemington, of Pa, to be Charge d'Affaires of the U S to Denmark, was yesterday confirmed by the Senate.

Balt: Mr John Thos Sims is an independent candidate for the Legislature, at the special election which takes place in Fred'k, Md, on Jan 14.

Senate: 1-Cmte on Patents: bill for the relief of Thos Blanchard. 2-Cmte of Claims: bill for the relief of the widow of Wm B Cheever, deceased. 3-Cmte of Claims: adverse report on the ptn of Harvey Wright, adm of Wm Bunce. Same cmte: asking to be discharged from further consideration of the memorial of Lloyd Slummer, & that it be referred to the Cmte on Naval Affairs. 4-Cmte on Military Affairs: House bill for the relief of W P S Sanger & Geo F de la Roche, without amendment. Same cmte: bill for the relief of Thos S Brownell, accompanied by a report. 5-Cmte of Claims: adverse report on the claim of Jas Leander Cathcart. Same cmte: bill for the relief of Alex'r Watson, accompanied by a report. Same cmte: bill for the relief of Susan E Gordon, accompanied by a report.

WED JAN 13, 1847

Wash Corp: 1- Ptn of Eve Ruppert, praying remission of a fine: referred to the Cmte of Claims. 2-Cmte of Claims: bill for the relief of Wm B Lewis. Same cmte: asked to be discharged from the further consideration of the ptns of Wm Cross, of Ann Lucker, & of Thos N Davis. 3-Bill for the relief of H R Maryman, late police ofcr, was referred to the Cmte of Claims.

Theatre: Mr Chas Burke, of comic celebrity, made a very successful hit at the Odeon last Mon, in the diverting characters of Dickory & Ebenezer Calf. The latter is a Yankee character. Mrs Mossop & Mr G F Brown elicited enthusiastic applause.

Howard District Press: Saml Brown, jr, Reg/o Wills for Howard District, Md, & for many years Reg/o Wills of Anne Arundel Co, died lately. He was about 65 years of age.

The Hon Isaac S Pennybacker, one of the Senators from Virginia, is no more; age less than 42 years, snatched away from his labors almost before he had begun. He was born in Shanandoah Co, Va. He leaves his wife & children to mourn his loss. [Another notice in the same paper: not yet 50 years of age; funeral is today.]

Naval: Ofcrs attached to the U S store ship **Fredonia**, about to sail from Boston for Vera Cruz: Chas W Chauncey, Lt commanding; Benj S Gantt, Master; Isaac N Morris, passed Midshipmen; Joel S Rennard, passed Midshipman; Geo S Ransom, passed Midshipman; R LeRoy Parker, Capt's Clerk. Passengers to join the Gulf Squadron: Lts H Ingersoll & A L Cass; acting Midshipman Chas B Smith.

House of Reps: 1-Ptn of Augustus Ford, praying for the refunding $63.15, erroneously paid into the Treasury. 2-Ptn of the heirs of Jos Marguard, dec'd, late of Newburyport, Mass, praying the allowance of payment of his share of the forfeitures incurred in the seizure & condemnation of certain goods illegally imported during the war with Great Britain. 3-Ptn of Wm Wickham, of Sodus, N Y, praying to be indemnified for a dwlg-house burnt by the British troops in 1813. 4-Ptn of Jacob Kerr, of Seneca Falls, N Y, for compensation for 4 Revolutionary bounty land warrants erroneously patented to another. 5-Claim of Robt Abbott, for depredations committed by the Potawatamie & Ottawa Indians. 6-Claim of Conrad Ten Eyck, for allowancy at treaty with the Potawatamie Indians. 7-Memorial of volunteers in Capt Gillespie's company of Texas, for losses in the present war. 8-Papers in the case of Gardner Herring, for an invalid pension. 9-Papers in the case of Jas Coe, for an invalid pension. 10-Ptn of Mrs Sarah Chace, of Somerset, Mass, for the payment of the French indemnities. 11-Ptn of John P Andrews, of Salem, Mass, for the settlement of our differences with Mexico. 12-Ptn of E N Vernon & others, praying indemnity for French spoliations. 13-Memorial of Thos D Hogg, as one of the heirs of John Hogg, praying indemnification for spoliations committed by France prior to 1800. 14-Ptn of Reuben Taylor, heir of Ezekiel Taylor, of Chicago, Ill, praying remuneration for services rendered by said Ezekiel Taylor in the Revolutionary war. 15-Ptn of Wm Hogan, administrator, for payment of debt due from U S. 16-Memorial of Thos D Hogg, as one of the heirs of John Hogg, praying indemnity for French spoliations prior to 1800. 17-Ptn of Jas Oldham, of the city of Balt, a Revolutionary soldier, for a pension. 18-Memorial of Mrs Susan Caustin, widow of Isaac Caustin, for indemnity for French spoliations prior to 1800. 19-Ptn of the children of Mrs Margaret Henderson, of Carlisle, Pa, for arrears of pension due their mother. 20-Memorial of Wm M Walker, Robt E Johnson, Jas Alden, John B Dale, Edwin J DeHaven, A S Baldwin, Geo T Sinclair, Wm Reynolds, Simon F Blunt, Wm May, Jos P Sanford, Geo Colvocoressis, Lts, & Jas Blair, Passed Midshipman, ofcrs of the late U S Exploring Expedition, complaining that in the narrative published by authority of Congress various statements & allegations are made affecting their professional honor & character, & asking Congress for redress. The memorial was referred to the Cmte on the Library, & ordered to be printed.

A son of Mr McCauley, Cashier of the Camden Bank, Camden, N J, fell on Sat from bars erected in his father's yard for gymnastic exercises, dislocated his neck, & died instantly.

Mrd: on Dec 29, at ***Walnut Grove***, Wash Co, Va, by Rev J H Wallace, Jas B Craighead, of Marengo Co, Ala, to Miss Jane Preston, daughter of Col John Preston, of former place.

Just arrived-Northern Horses, at the Wash Livery Stables, 8th st. -B O Shekell & Co

Senate: 1-Ptn from Eliphalet Grover, for a pension for injuries received while keeping a lighthouse. 2-Ptn from the heirs of Wm Dickey, from Rebecca Robosson, & from Jemima Duval, asking to be allowed pensions. 3-Ptn from Aaron Legget, of N Y, in relation to his claims against Mexico. 4-Ptn from John Morrison, for a pension. 5-Ptn from the heirs of John Patrick, deceased, asking indemnity for spoliations prior to 1800. 6-Ptn from Mrs Bass, asking a reconsideration of the report of the Senate made in her case. 7-Ptn from David Butler, asking allowance to be made for service as Paymaster at the Mount Vernon Arsenal. 8-Ptn from Robt Sewalls, asking indemnity for property destroyed during the late war with Great Britain.

Orphans Court of Wash Co, D C. Letters of administration on the personal estate of Cmdor John B Nicolson, of the U S Navy, dec'd. -Thos L Smith, adm

Country residence for rent: ***Claremont***, about 2½ miles from Balt, the residence of the late Capt Robt T Spence. Apply to Carroll Spence, Atty at Law, at Fayette st, Balt, Md.

For rent: a genteel residence, either furnished or unfurnished, on B st south, Capitol Hill. Inquire on the premises, or at the Genr'l Post Ofc, of N C Towle.

THU JAN 14, 1847

N Y Courier & Enquiries: Wm B Reed, of Phil placed in our hands a manuscript Journal & Order Book, belonging to Gen Saml B Webb, of the Revolutionary Army, commencing Jun 1, 1776. This journal became separated from the papers of Gen Webb, & Mr Reed found it in Pa, when in pursuit of records relating to the services of his grandfather, Gen Reed, & was by him restored to the writer as the rightful owner. Wm B Reed is probably as intimately familiar with the history of the Revolutionary war as any man living. Gen Webb was born in Wethersfield, Conn, in 1753, & in Jun, 1775, then 22, marched to Boston as the 1st lt of a light infty company: engaged in the battle of Bunker Hill, was wounded in the arm. He was appointed the aid-de-camp of Gen Putnam. Letter written by him to his stepfather, Silas Deane, describing the battle of Bunker Hill, had been, we believe, recently deposited with the Historical Society of Hartford. In Jun, 1776, he was appointed the aid-de-camp of Washington, & in 1778 took command of the 3rd regt. In crossing to Long Island, with Gen Parson's expedition, in 1779, he, with most of the command, were captured by the British fleet, in consequence of becoming dispersed in a dense fog. He remained in prison until 1782, when he was promoted to the command of the light infty of the army upon the retirement of Baron Steuben. He was wounded in the battle of White Plains, & was slightly wounded at the battle of Trenton, & was engaged in the battle of Brandywine. He resided in this city from 1782 to 1789, when he removed to Claverack, Columbia Co, where he died in 1807. Orders found in the manuscript: Headquarters, N Y, Jun 21, 1776. Parole-Albany. Counter sign-Bedford. All ofcrs & soldier belonging to either of the regts serving in Canada are to apply immediately to Maj Gen Gates, who will give them orders for repairing to their respective detachments. The Gen has been pleased to appoint Richd Cary & Saml B Webb, his aid-de-camps, & Alex'r Countee Hanson, assist sec. Brig for the day-Gen Lord Sterling; Field ofcrs for the piquet-Col Baldwin, Lt Col Clap, & Maj Knoulton; Brig Maj for the day-Henly. Headquarters, N Y, Jun 22, 1776. Parole-Brunswick Countersign-Cumberland. Aaron Burr is appointed aid-de-camp to Gen Putnam, in the room of Maj Webb, promoted. Brig for the day-Gen Heath; Field ofcrs for the piquet-Col McDougall, Lt Col Durkee, & Maj Sherman; Brig Maj of the day-Trumbull. Remarks: Jun 21, 1776: Some days since, the General received information that a most horrid plot was on foot by the vile Tories of this place; precautions were taken a number of the ofcrs & guards went to different places & took up many of their principals; among whom was David Matthews, Mayor of the city, & 5 or more of the General's Life Guard to be accomplices to assassinate his Excellency & other ofcrs. Thank God they were discovered. Jun 22, 1776: On Jun 2 Gen Thompson, at the head of 1,500 men attacked the enemy at Trios Rivieres, supposing their number to be about 500; but, unluckily for us, they numbered about 4,000 men, with Gen Burgoyne at their head, by which means Gen Thompson was defeated & obliged to retreat. When the express came away Gen Sullivan, with the remaining part of our army about 2,500 men, was fortifying themselves at the Sorrell. Jun 23 1776: the detachment under Col Jacobs is to go on fatigue near King's Bridge. At 11o'clock this evening a detachment of 250, under Majors [blank] ___ & Livingston marched to rout a number of Tories in the swamps on Long Island. Jun 28, 1776: Our cruisers on the back of Long or Nassau Island have retaken 4 prizes, which the man-of war **Greyhound** had a few day before taken. The sailors inform that Gen Howe was on board the **Greyhound**. Agreeably to yesterday's orders, Thos Hickey was hanged in the presence of most of the army; he seemed much more penitent than he was at first. Jul 1, 1776: a reinforcement of 500 men were sent over to reinforce the troops on Long Island under Gen Greene. Jul 3, 1776: This day arrived in camp Brig Gen Mercer, from Va, being appointed & ordered here by the honorable Continental Congress; likewise Gen Herd, with the militia from N J, by order of his Excellency Gen Washington. N Y Jul 9, 1776: Agreeably to this day's orders the declaration of Independence was read at the head of each brigade, & was received by three huzzas from the troops, every one seeming highly pleased we were separated from a king who was endeavoring to enslave his once loyal subjects. God grant us success in this our new character. Jul 10, 1776: Last night the statue of George III was tumbled down & beheaded. [In order that the reader at this distant day may judge of the severity of the censure of the Cmder-in -Chief for the destruction of the statue of George III, we give the order referred to in the journal:] Headquarters, N Y, Jul 20, 1776. Parole-Ogden Countersign-Phil. Genr'l Heath's brig, instead of repairing to their alarm posts tomorrow morning, to hold themselves in readiness to march. They will receive their orders from the Brig Gen on the parade at 4 o'clock. The brig will attend at headquarters this afternoon for orders. Though the Genr'l doubts not the persons who pulled down & mutilated the statue in the Broadway last night were actuated by zeal in the public cause, yet it has so much the appearance of riot & want of order in the army, that he disapproved the manner, & directs that in future these things shall be avoided by the soldiery, & left to be executed by proper authority.

John B Brooke, Atty at Law, Upper Marlborough, PG Co, Md, will practice in the Courts of PG & adjoining counties, & attend promptly to any business entrusted to his care.

Appointments by the Pres: 1-Robt P Flenniken, of Pa, to be Charge d'Affaires of the U S near the Gov't of Denmark, vice Wm W Irwin, at his own request recalled. 2-Burrill B Taylor, of Ohio, to be U S Consul for the port of Buenos Ayres, vice Jas H Tate, resigned. 3-Wm G Moorhead, of Ohio, to be U S Consul for the port of Valparaiso, vice Eben R Dorr, recalled. 4-P S Loughborough, to U S Atty for the district of Ky, from & after Feb 2 next, when his present commission will expire. 5-Duncan K McRae, to the U S Atty for the district of N C, from & after Mar 2 next, when his present commission will expire.

The Misses Schnebly's Boarding & Day School, at their residence, 308 Chestnut st, Phil, Pa, will commence on Feb 1. Pupils will be received at any time & charged accordingly.

Aris Throckmorton begs to acquaint his friends that he is again lessee of the Galt House, in the city of Louisville, Ky, & hopes to meet all his old friends.

Mrd: on Jan 12, in Wash City, by Rev G W Samson, Mr John C Baum to Miss Emeline Larcombe, both of Wash.

Mrd: on Jan 7, at Alexandria, by Rev John L Pascoe, Mr Fred'k Studds to Miss Harriet Virginia Benter, all of this place.

Mrd: on Dec 22, in Huntersville, Pocahontas Co, Va, Dr G B Moffitt, formerly of Augusta Co, Va, to Miss Margaret E Beall, of that place.

Died: on Jan 3, at Waterloo, in Chas Co, Md, in his 40th year, Dr Benj T Johns. In the bloom of life & health, he with his lady started to attend their church. They were seated in their vehicle. The horse took fright & ran, the carriage was overturned, Mrs Johns was thrown to a considerable distance from her husband & was little hurt; he was killed upon the spot. Dr Johns for 16 years followed his profession in PG Co, Chas Co, & St Mary's Co, & reaped a measure of professional reputation of no frequent acquisition at his age. A widow & 5 young children mourn, as do members of the Medical profession & the people.

Died: on Jan 12, Benj Cowles, formerly of Balt, but recently of Wash City, age 28 years. His funeral is today, at 2 P M, from his residence on D st, between 6th & 7th sts.

Died: on Jan 3, at his late residence, near the Great Mills, St Mary's Co, Jas Hebb, in his 65th year.

Orphans Court of Wash Co, D C. Ordered that notice be given for 3 weeks, of the application of Henry Ould to have letters of administration granted to him on the estate of Eliz Pierce, dec'd. -Nathl Pope Causin. -Ed N Roach, Reg/o wills

FRI JAN 15, 1847

Wash City: one of the most striking improvements in this metropolis is that of Mr Crutchett, who has not merely lighted up North Capitol st by the introduction of 9 solar gas burners between his residence & the Capitol gate, but illuminated Capitol Hill by these incomparably beautiful & splendid lights. Compared with these gas lights, the lamps around the Capitol appear quite dim. The beautiful cottage of Mr Crutchett is entirely lighted with solar gas, rendering the whole most beautiful either externally or internally.

Annual meeting of the Columbia Topographical Society, held on Jan 2, 1847: elected for the present year:

Chas F Lowry, Pres
Jas D Chedal, Vice Pres
Michl Caton, Treas
Patrick H Brooks, Corr Sec
Thos Rice, Rec Sec

Cmte of Arrangements:

Chas F Lowry
Patrick H Brooks
Thos W Howard
Wm E Kennaugh
Geo W Cochran
John H Thorn
Thos Caton

Senate: 1-Ptn from Rodolphino Claxton, asking a renewal of pension. 2-Cmte of Claims: adverse on the ptn of John P Baldwin. Same cmte: bill for the relief of Holson Johns. Also, a bill for the relief of Wm E Davis, & Mary Ann, his wife. Also, adverse reports on the ptns of Danl Homans, & on the ptn of the sureties of Wm Estis. 2-Cmte on Indian Affairs: bill for the relief of Saml W Bell, a native of the Cherokee Nation. Also, same cmte, adverse report on the ptn of Benj Crawford. 3-Cmte on Public Lands: bill to compromise the claim of the heirs & legal reps of John Smith T, under a Spanish grant, with a report. 4-Cmte on Naval Affairs: bill for the relief of the heirs of John Paul Jones. 5-Cmte on the Judiciary: bill for the relief of the heirs & legal reps of Galphin Milledge. 6-Cmte on Indian Affairs: House bill for the relief of Dr Clarke Lillybridge, without amendment. 7-Cmte of Claims: asking to be discharged from the further consideration of the claim of Haym M Saloman, & that it be referred to the Cmte on Revolutionary Claims. Same cmte: bill authorizing the payment of a sum of money to Robt Purkis, with a report. Same cmte: bill for the relief of Erskine & Eichelberger, with a report. 8-Bill for the relief of Benj Metayer & Francoise Gaiennie, dec'd: introduced.

Mrd: on Jan 12, at Gtwn, by Rev Mr Varden, Richd E Booth to Eliz, eldest daughter of Wm & Rosanna Cunningham, all of Gtwn.

For sale: to close a concern, Lot 7 in square 382, fronting on the Canal upwards of 100 feet, on La ave about 100 feet, & on 10th st about 40 feet. -E Lindsley, Pa ave

Latest from Monterey: Remains of the valiant dead: Lt Mills brought over in the steamer **Alabama** the remains of the lamented ofcrs & soldiers: Col Watson, Capt Ridgely, Lt R H Graham, late of the 4th Regt of Infty; Herman Thomas, of the Texan Rangers; & Geo W Pearson, of the Wash & Balt btln. The remains of Capt Holmes, of Ga, & Capt Gillespie, of the Texan Rangers, were also brought up on the **Alabama**.

+

Lt Boyle,of the Washington Volunteers, was found dead in his berth on board the steamer **Alabama** yesterday. His berth was in the same state-room in which Lt Mills slept, but the latter knew nothing of the sickness of his room-mate. He was found dead in the morning, & is supposed to have died of apoplexy.

+

Purser A H Crosby, of the ship **Mississippi**, was killed by falling from aloft on board the ship **Vixen**, which vessel he was assisting to pilot over the bar at Laguna, on the occasion of the attack on that place.

Circuit Court of Wash Co, D C-in Chancery. Henry Northrup, cmplnt, vs Thos J Boyd, Thos Ramsey, Jos I Ramsey, Jas Ramsey, Arhart I Simmerman & Mahala his wife; Peter R Straw & Polly his wife; Jos McCamant, J H Price, & Thos Green, dfndnts. Bill states that the plntf, Henry Northup, was employed by Jos Ramsey, in his lifetime, to obtain for him his bounty-land warrant from the State of Va, for the services of said Jos Ramsey, as an ofcr of Va in the Illinois regt, commanded by Gen Geo Rogers Clark; that said Jos agreed to give said Northup the one half of the land warrant that should be obtained, & executed an obligation to that effect to said Northup; that said Northup did take the evidence & file it in the ofc at Richmond, Va, to support the right of said Jos; &, upon the evidence so procured, the land warrant issued to said Jos Ramsey in his lifetime, for 2,666 acres of land. That Saml McCamant & J H Price, with notice of the said contract, & of the evidence taken by said Northup, entered into a contract with said Jos Ramsey, not only to procure his land warrant, but also his half pay, & did draw from the U S Treas the half pay of said Jos, by which proceeding in drawing the half pay, the said Jos was involved in a suit with the U S, as plntfs, to recover back the money; whereby the issuing of the land scrip of the U S for the land warrant was delayed until the satisfaction of the decree in favor of the U S against said Jos Ramsey; that, after the death of said Jos, his heirs employed Thos J Boyd, who is about to withdraw from the Land Ofc & Treas Dept of the U S the land scrip for the said warrant. The object of the bill is to enjoin the one half of said land scrip, & to have relief & decree for the said moiety, as being due to said Northup upon his contract with said Ramsey in his lifetime. And it appearing to the satisfaction of the Court, by the return of the process, that the dfndnts, Thos J Ramsey, Jos J Ramsey, Jas Ramsey, Arhart Simmerman & Mahala his wife; Peter R Straw & Polly his wife; Jos McCamant, & J H Price, are not within the District of Columbia, but residing abroad, & absentees, so that the process of this Court cannot be served on them personally; therefore, on motion of the plntf, by his counsel, Geo M Bibb, it is ordered that the said absentees do appear, on or before the third Mon of May, 1847, & answer the said bill, or, on failure so to do that the allegations of said bill, as against those so failing, will be taken pro confesso, & the matters of said bill & prayers for relief will be decreed accordingly. -W Cranch, W Brent,clerk

We noticed on Wed last a new & remarkably complete war saddle, manufactured by Mr Danl Campbell, on Pa ave. It is one of the sort intended for the Texas mounted riflemen, under the command of Capt Saml H Walker, who is now in Wash City waiting for equipments & accoutrements for his brave companions in arms, to take with him to the seat of war.

For rent; upper part of my house over my Clothing Store, on north side of Pa ave: possession immediately. Also, for rent or sale: two 3 story houses on the south side of Pa ave. Inquire of J M Johnson.

Died: on Jan 13, in Wash City, Mr Jos Martin, aged 65 years, for several years past a resident of Wash. His funeral is this morning, at half past 10 o'clock, from the residence of Henry Polkinhorn, 7th, near F st south.

Died: on Jan 11, in his 68th year, John Little, formerly of Gettysburg, Pa, but for the last 21 years a resident of Washington.

Obit-died: on Jan 13, at the residence of her father, Jos Harbaugh,of Wash City, Mrs Eliza C Mayo, consort of Dr Robt Mayo, formerly of Virginia, in her 44th year, after a painful illness of nearly 3 months, which she endured with a Christian fortitude. She was a member of the Catholic Church, she was eminently pious, a kind neighbor, charitable to the poor, greatly beloved by all who knew her, the most affectionate mother, wife, daughter, & sister. Her funeral is from the residence of her father's, in 7th st, near the General Post Ofc, this afternoon, at 3 o'clock.

SAT JAN 16, 1847
Alexandria [Va] Headquarters for rent: this property is extensive, consisting of a handsome Restaurant, a splendid saloon of 2 bowling alleys, a large ice-house, a green house, bath house, with some 20 rooms, handsomely finished, with balconies annexed to 2 large parlors. -R B Loyd

Wanted, negroes in families: a planter from the South wishes to purchase from 15 to 25 negroes, in families, for his own use. He would prefer most of them to be children or young women. A letter, stating ages & prices of those offered, address to J H West, will meet prompt attention.

Notice: several pleasant rooms can be had, with or without board, at Mrs Widdicombe's, on F st, near the Treas Dept, & next door to Mr Pairo's exchange ofc. Parlor & chamber attached.

MON JAN 18, 1847 Coroner's inquest was held on the body of a white man named Wm Simmons, about 40 years of age, a plaster by trade, & known to be an excellent workman, although unhappily addicted to intemperance, was found drowned last Sat in the Washington Canal.

Appointed managers of the Wash City Orphan Asylum on Jan 12th:

Mrs Hawley, 1st Directress	Mrs Luce
Mrs Laurie, 2nd Directress	Mrs Shubrick
Miss Smith, Treas	Mrs R S Coxe
Miss Taylor, Sec	Mrs Richd Smith
Mrs Lear	Mrs Tucker
Mrs Henderson	Mrs Gilliss
Mrs Brown	Miss Bingham
Mrs Washington	Mrs Geo Totten
Mrs Stone	

The alarm of fire yesterday was caused by the burning of the dwlg of John Cox, late Mayor of Gtwn. His residence was a beautiful site, near the Convent of the Sisters of the Visitation, & the bldg, which was a handsome one, was entirely consumed. Mrs Cox, who was lying ill in the house at the time the fire broke out, has since expired in consequence of the alarm occasioned by the sudden conflagration. [Jan 20th newspaper: Mrs Cox, although not dead, was lying in a very dangerous & hopeless condition.]

Senate: 1-Ptn from the heirs of John Riggs, asking to be allowed commutation pay. 2-Additional documents relating to the claim of the widow of Lt Graham. 3-Cmte on the Judiciary: bill for the relief of Richd Bloss & others. 4-Cmte on Pensions: bill for the relief of Eliz Pistole. 5-Cmte of Claims: bill for the relief of Chas M Gibson. 6-Cmte on Pensions: bill for the relief of Fred'k Hopkins, of Chenango Co, N Y. Same cmte: bill granting a pension to Patrick Kelly. Same cmte: bill for the relief of Zachariah Simmons, of the State of Tenn. 7-Ptn from Ichabod Jordan, collector at Saco, Maine, asking an increase of salary. 8-Ptn from Wm H Prentiss, asking compensation for services rendered as clerk while holding the appointment of assistant messenger. 9-Ptn from Abigail Garland, widow of a Revolutionary soldier, asking a pension. 10-Ptn from E Bernner, asking indemnity for spoliations prior to 1800. 11-Ptn from John F Mullowny, late Consul at Tangier, asking to be indemnified for losses sustained in consequence of a U S ofcr refusing to convey him to his destination. 12-Cmte of Claims: adverse report on the ptn of the legal reps of Geo Mayo. Also, from the same cmte, adverse report on the ptn of Richd Dove. Same cmte: bill for the relief of Thos H Noble. 13-Cmte on Military Affairs: House bill for the relief of Joshua Shaw. 14-Cmte on Revolutionary Claims: House bill for the relief of the heirs of Sgt Maj John Champe.

Northern Market: the new market-house, at the intersection of N Y ave & 7th st, has been very well supplied with all kinds of country produce, butchers' meat, game & poultry.

On Wed, at about 4 o'clock, Wm Parsons, while in a counting-room in the business part of Boston, complained of a sudden dizziness, fell upon the floor, & immediately expired. He was the son of the late Chief Justice Parsons, a most respectable citizen, & who at the time of his death was the Pres of the Massachusetts Bank.

The Nashville Whig comes to us in mourning on account of the death of Jos Norvell, the founder of that paper, & an old & highly respectable citizen of Nashville.

John L Davis, LL D, [the predecessor of Peleg Sprague on the bench of the U S District Court at Boston,] departed this life very suddenly on Thu, at his residence in Boston, at the venerable age of 86 years. He was out but 2 days before, & his sudden decease was produced from a complaint of the intestines.

The Albany papers of Mon announce the death of Capt Richd Winslow, Cmdor of the steam navigation of the Hudson. He expired at his residence in Albany on Sat, after a short illness, in his 76th year. Capt Winslow was a native of Conn, removed to Albany in 1800. Nearly half a century ago he was engaged in the river navigation; engaged in the mercantile pursuits, & at the period of his death had been several years retired from business.

Wiley Williams has been elected Mayor of the city of Columbus, Ga. The compliment was due to him as a true native Georgian, a moderate politician, & a gentleman of liberal views. -Savannah Republican

New Orleans Picayune, of Jun 7. Announcement of the death, on board the steamship **Alabama**, of one of our fellow-citizens, Lt Eugene Boyle, who had, although unknown to him, been commissioned as Capt, to take rank from Nov 23, 1846. He died suddenly, on board the **Alabama**, on her passage from Brasos Santiago to New Orleans. Lt Boyle was of the Balt & District of Columbia Btl of Volunteers. He had distinguished himself in the recent battle of Monterey;.

U S District Court for the N Y District, on Tue last, Wm H Wisner, clerk in the post ofc at Port Jarvis, who had pleaded guilty to 2 indictments for robbing the mail, was arraigned & sentenced to 20 years in prison, being the shortest time allowed by law. He was conducted back to prison, & will be sent to Sing Sing.

Deserters. By last news from Monterey, from the Louisville Courier, information that Robt Hawley, & another named Smith, both belonging to the Montgomery Guards, of that city, deserted, but were pursued, & Smith was caught about 100 miles on the road to Camargo. The court martial was trying him & one named Cassady, of the Wash Blues, for the same offence. It was thought that both would be ordered to be shot.

Killed, on Jan 7, by an injury received from his horse, the Rev John Dangerfield, of Mathews Co, Va.

Mrd: on Jan 5, by Rev Wm H Foote, Mr John B Sherrard to Miss Susan A Gibson, daughter of David Gibson, all of Hampshire Co, Va.

Mrd: on Jan 14, by Rev Mr Matthews, Danl R Clarke to Anne M, daughter of Wm McL Cripps, all of Wash City.

Mrd: on Jan 12, by Rev Mr Smith, Henry Frazier to Miss Columbia Ray, both of Montg Co, Md.

Mrd: on Jan 12, by Rev H Holland, Capt Geo Rhinehart, of Middletown Valley, Fred'k Co, Md, to Miss Sophia Catharine, daughter of Mr Danl Hauptman, of Wash City.

Mrd: on Jan 14, in Balt, by Rev Dr Morris, Fred'k F Green to Margaret Louisa, only daughter of Jas Brown, all of Balt.

Died: on Jan 12, at her residence, in Troy, N Y, Mrs Eliza Dickinson, relict of the late Hon J D Dickinson, formerly Rep in Congress from the State of N Y.

Died: on Sat last, Mary, w/o Thos A Hawke, in her 40th year, leaving a disconsolate husband & 5 children to deplore their loss. Mrs Hawke was reared in the boson of the Roman Catholic Church; lived up to its precepts with undeviating promptitude, & adorned the doctrine of God her Saviour in all things.

Obit-died: on Jan 5, at Burlington, Anne Maria, the w/o Gen Garret D Wall, late Senator of the U S. Mrs Wall, though a native of Scotland, had so indentified herself with the interests & reputation of the city of her adoption, during her residence here of 30 years, as to feel herself as in heart & hand a Burlingtonian. The last time she left her house was in attendance at the worship, from which she was never willingly absent. She rest now in the graveyard of St Mary's Church. -G W D

By writ of fieri facias, I shall expose to public sale, at the intersection of P st, on the Eastern Branch, on Jan 22, the schnr **Sally**, of Fredericksburg & Wash, with all her sails, masts, anchor, stove, & oyster tongs, seized & taken as the property of Wm Craig & Thos Marshall, both of said county, & will be sold to satisfy a judgment in favor of Wm Morders, use of Fielder Magruder. -John Magar, constable

On the arrival of Gen La Vega at Vera Cruz on Dec 15, all the prisoners from the squadron in the hands of the Mexicans were released. Midshipman Rodgers was at Vera Cruz. He had been tried as a spy by the civil & military tribunals, & had been acquitted by the former, but found guilty by the latter. It was believed that the more favorable verdict would prevail, & that he would be liberated.

Orphans Court of Wash Co, D C. Letters of administration on the personal estate of Richd H Graham, late of the U S Army, dec'd. -Geo W Graham, adm

House of Reps: 1-Ptn of John D D Rossett, of Va, praying indemnification for losses by French spoliations prior to 1800. 2-Ptn of Ambrose S Bramlette, praying a pension for the Revolutionary services of Thos Elliot. 3-Memorial of Mrs Mary D Adam, in behalf of Jas, Robt, Wm, & Saml Dunlap, of S C, heirs of John Dunlap,of the house of Dunlap & Irwin, for indemnity for French spoliations prior to 1800. 4-Ptn of Saml Lasley, Geo

Lasley, & Wm Johnson, for remission of certain judgments & costs. 5-Sundry affidavits in support of the ptn of John Russell for an invalid pension. 6-Ptn of Jacob Harshamn, of Montg Co, Ohio, praying for an act to authorize the issuing to him of scrip for 500 acres of land in lieu of Va Military Land Warrant #8,696, for that quantity. 7-Memorial of S H Walker, on the subject of arming & equipping the first rifle regt. 8-Ptn of John Bennett, of Cleveland Co, N C, asking a pension for services in the Revolutionary war. 9-Ptn of Eve Oury, for a pension. 10-Two memorials from the heirs of Fielder Dorsett, of Md, for indemnity for French spoliations. 11-Ptn of the heirs & reps of Ferdinand Hopkins, dec'd, praying for remuneration for Revolutionary services, moneys advanced for Gov't, & depredations committed during the Revolutionary war. 12-Ptn of Wm H Mason, Jas McMullin, & others, for a mail route from Delta, Coahoma Co, Miss, to Panola, Miss. 13-Ptn of Jas Crutchett, praying Congress to examine & report upon the propriety of lighting the Capitol with solar gas. 14-Ptn of Jehiel Tuttle.

TUE JAN 19, 1847

Senate: 1-Ptn from Geo W Edgerby, for clothing lost by his father in the destruction of the U S ship **Adams**. 2-Cmte on Naval Affairs: bill for the relief of Capt Jesse D Elliot. Same cmte: unfavorable report on the ptn of Hans Nelson. 3-Cmte on the Judiciary: bill for the relief of Thos Talbot & others, with a report: ordered to be printed. 4-Cmte on Pensions: bill for the relief of Geo Roush, with a report: ordered to be printed. 5-Cmte on Naval Affairs: bill for the relief of Jas McIntosh, with a report: ordered to be printed.

House & lot for sale: by decree made by the Orphans Court of Wash Co, D C, & approved by the Circuit Court: sale on Feb 4, at public auction, if not sold before at private sale, lot 5 with improvements thereon, in square 576, fronting on 2nd st west. Call at my ofc, in the west wing of the City Hall. -John A Linton, Atty for petitioners. -C W Boteler, jr, auctioneer

Dissolution of copartnership of the firm of J & H Douglas, Florist & Seedsmen, this day, by mutual consent. Henry Douglass will continue the business, at the Greenhouse, G & 15th sts. -J & H Douglas

The trial of Calvin Buss, for the murder of his wife, was terminated on Sat, in N Y, by a verdict of murder in the 1st degree. The unfortunate criminal was immediately sentenced to death, the execution to take place on Mar 12.

Massachusetts Volunteers: meeting last Fri: elected field ofcrs: Caleb Cushing, Col; Isaac H Wright, Lt Col; & E W Abbott, Major.

The American is the title of a handsomely printed paper, commenced last week in Wash City by Messrs J N Davis & Columbus Drew. We wish the publishers success.

For sale: from 18 to 20 young negroes. Inquire of Robt W Dyer, Pa ave.

Died: on Jan 16, in her 50th year, Mrs Frances Ann Radcliff, consort of Jos Radcliff. Her funeral is from her late residence on Gay st, Gtwn, this afternoon, at half past 2 o'clock.

The Trustees of the Female Seminary of Berlin, Md, wish to procure a music teacher: salary will be $300 per annum. -John P Pitts, Zadok D Henry, John S Purnell

In St Mary's Co Court, as a Court of Equity; Dec Term, 1846. Levi Nutwell vs Ann Edwards & others. The bill in this case states that Levi Nutwell, cmplnt, Ann Edwards, Richd Johnson, Raphael Johnson, Catharine Drury, John Jarboe, Basil Jarboe, Wm Jarboe, Geo Jarboe, Mary Jarboe, & Eliz Jarboe, are seised in fee as tenants in common of a certain tract of land in said county; that the widows' dower in one- half of the said land, & an undivided tenth part thereof, belongs to the cmplnt in this cause; that one undivided tenth part of said land belongs to Ann Edwards, one undivided tenth part thereof belongs to Richd Johnson, one undivided tenth part thereof belongs to Raphael Johnson, & one undivided tenth part thereof belongs to Catharine Drury; that one undivided 12th part belongs to each of the other dfndnts in this cause respectively. The bill further states that it will be to the interest & advantage of the said parties to sell said land, & divide the proceeds among the said parties, agreeably to their several proportions; that Eliz Jarboe is an infant under the age of 21 years. The bill asks for a sale of said real estate, & further states that the said Ann Edwards, Richd Johnson, Raphael Johnson, & Catharine Drury, are residents of the State of Ky. It is ordered that they appear in this court on the 1st Mon of May next, either by atty or in proper person. -Peter W Crain.
-Wm Z Maddox, Clerk St Mary's Co Court

WED JAN 20, 1847

House of Reps: 1-Ptn of Jas W Ward & 94 others, of Abington, Mass, for peace with Mexico. 2-Memorial from Rev Thos C Benning & Jas C Demarest, of Savannah, Ga, praying Congress to grant to them the right of pre-emption to a certain quarter section of the public lands in Florida. 3-Ptn of E P Guion & B McLaughlin, of N C, praying compensation for carrying the mail. 4-Ptn of Jos W Knife, a soldier in the last war, praying for a pension. 5-Ptn of Edw Quinn for a pension. 6-Ptn of Lt W A C Farragut, praying to be promoted to the rank of captain. 7-Ptn of Danl McKenny, of Summit Co, Ohio, asking a pension for Revolutionary services. 8-Ptn of Giles S Boggus, praying remuneration for losses sustained by him as express mail contractor on routes 11 & 12, in 1836.

Wash Corp: 1-Ptn of John U Moulder, praying to be refunded for a certain license: referred to the Cmte of Claims. 2-Ptns of Michl Talty; of Thos Turner; of Jas Burch; & of Jas Gates, praying remission of fines: referred to the Cmte of Claims.

Mrd: on Jan 19, by Rev Mr Sprole, Mr Geo D Taff to Miss Mary E Griffith, both of Wash.

Mrd: on Jan 17, by Rev V Palen, Mr Peter Jackson, of N J, to Mrs Sarah Duling, of Wash.

Mrd: on Jan 14, by Rev V Palen, Mr Robt Long to Miss Eliza Butler, all of Wash.

Mrd: on Jan 18, at the Wesley Chapel Parsonage, by Rev H Slicer, Mr Jas C Greer to Miss Henrietta Irwin, all of Wash City.

Mrd: on Jun 12, in Pittsburg, by Rev Dr Upfold, Henry B Foster, of Wash, to Mary, only daughter of the late John Burgess, of the former city.

Died: on Mon, after a long & severe illness, in full assurance of a blissful immortality, Robt Rose, aged 78 years. His funeral is on Jan 21, at 2 o'clock, from his daughter's residence.

Died: on Jan 18, after a painful illness of about 10 weeks, Sarah, w/o Joshua Gibson, & eldest daughter of the late Jos & Eliz Holroyd, aged about 35 years. She leaves a husband & 5 children to mourn their irreparable loss. Her funeral is this afternoon at 2 o'clock, from the residence of her husband, on K st, between 10th & 11th.

Senate: 1-Ptn from T F Gordon, asking compensation for compiling the Revenue laws of the U S, by direction of the Sec of the Treas. 2-Ptn from Susan Coody & other Cherokee Indians, asking indemnity for property destroyed by U S troops. 3-Additional documents in relation to the claim of Ishael Canfield. 4-Ptn from Ed Martin & others, asking indemnity for French spoliations prior to 1800. 5-Cmte on Pensions: bill for the relief of Peter Engles, senior. 6-Cmte on Foreign Relations: adverse report on the claim of Wm M Blackford, late Charge to New Grenada. 7-Cmte on Claims: bill to authorize the settlement of the accounts of Jos Nourse, dec'd. 8-Cmte on Patents: adverse report on the ptn of Ross Winans. 9-Cmte on the Post Ofc & Post Roads: bill for the relief of Jos F Caldwell.

Died: suddenly, yesterday, Geo S Hough, late of Alexandria, in his 63rd year.

Died: on Jan 12, at the residence of her son, Dr H Edelen, near Piscataway, PG Co, Md, Mrs Catharine A Edelen, in her 77th year, widow of the late Jos Edelen, of the same county.

Munificence. The Milwaukee Sentinel says that, with a view of founding a Literary Institution in Wisconsin, Mr Amos A Lawrence, of Boston, has offered to give the sum of $20,000, provided a like amount, in lands or money, be contributed there. The necessary amount will doubtless be immediately raised, & the Institution will be called the Lawrence Institute. -Boston Journal

The Ohio papers state that the Pres had decided not to appoint a Brig Gen in place of Gen Hamer, dec'd, as the Ohio volunteers have only a few months more to serve.

THU JAN 21, 1847

Senate: 1-Ptn from Fred'k Dawson, Jas Schott, & E D Whitney, asking the fulfillment of a contract made with the Gov't of Texas prior to annexation with the U S for supplying that Republic with a naval armament. 2-Ptn from Danl Vann & Wm P Ross, delegates of the Cherokee Indians, asking balance due those Indians under the treaty of 1835, & compensation for surrender of their lands east of the Mississippi. 3-Ptn from Robt Owen, asking an investigation of a mode discovered by him for the improving the condition of society. 4-Ptn from L Stone, for indemnity for spoliations prior to 1800. 5-Ptn from The Society of Friends, asking the adoption of measures for the speedy termination of the war with Mexico. 6-Ptn from Ann Anderson, widow of a seaman, asking for a pension. 7-Cmte on Indian Affairs: bill for the relief of Wm Marvin, with a report: ordered to be printed. 8-Cmte of Commerce: asking to be discharged from the further consideration of the memorial of E P Calkins & Co, & that it be referred to the Cmte on the Judiciary. 9-Cmte on Pensions: to inquire into granting a pension to John Ellis, of Vt, for services as a soldier in the war of the Revolution.

House of Reps: 1-Cmte of Claims: bill for the relief of David Thomas: committed. Same cmte: bill for the relief of the heirs & legal reps of Nathl Cox, dec'd, formerly navy agent at New Orleans: committed. 2-Resolved, that the Cmte of Ways & Means be discharged from the consideration of the memorials of Peter King, trustee of Mary Whiteside, excx of Peter Whiteside, & of Richd M Thomas, Annette M Farland, & Theresa M Downing, heirs at law of Jas J Miller, dec'd, & that they be referred to the Cmte on Forreign Affairs. 3-Cmte on Public Lands: bill for the relief of the heirs of Archibald Laughrey, dec'd: committed. 4-Cmte on the Judiciary: bill for the relief of John P Skinner & the legal rep of Isaac Green, dec'd: committed. 5-Cmte on Revolutionary Claims: bill for the relief of Nancy Haggard, daughter of Wm Grymes: committed. Same cmte: report on the claim of Geo Brent, dec'd, with a bill: committed. Same cmte: discharged from the ptn of citizens of Livingston Co, N Y, for interest on commutation pay to Maj Moses Van Campen, & the ptn was laid on the table. 6-Cmte on Private Land Claims: bill for the relief of Frederick Durrine: committed. 7-Cmte on Naval Affairs: bills for the relief of Saml Graves; relief of Stephan Champlin; relief of Jas Jones; & relief of Jos Bryan: all committed. 8-Cmte on Revolutionary Pensions: adverse reports on the cases of Jane DeGraff, widow of Lt Michl DeGraff, & of the heirs of Thos Reed, dec'd: laid on the table. Same cmte: adverse reports on the ptns of the heirs of John Ferguson, of Ada Smith, widow of Jas Smith, & of Hannah Stevenson, widow of Fred'k P Stevenson: reports were laid on the table. Same cmte: adverse reports on the ptn of Eliz Pain; ptn of Catrina Mickle, widow of Geo Mickle, dec'd; & ptn of Polly Thomas: all laid on the table. 9-Cmte on the Judiciary: bill to refund to the heirs of Thos Cooper, a fine imposed under the sedition law: committed. 10-Cmte on Private Land Claims: bill for the relief of Francois Gramillion, dec'd: committed. 11-Cmte on Patents: joint resolution for the relief of John & Chas Bruce: to be engrossed for a 3rd reading. 12-Cmte on Patents: bill for the relief of Calvin Emmons: committed.

Aston Ridge Seminary for Young Ladies: instructors-Mrs Huntington & Miss McClean: located in Delaware Co, Pa, 2 hours' ride from Phil, via Chester. Recommended by Rt Rev Bishop Alonzo Potter, Phil. Address Rev B S Huntingtn, Village Green, Dela Co, Pa.

Franklin House, 105 Chestnut st, Phil: establishment passed into the hands of the subscriber, in Jun last. -D K Minor, of N Y, Proprietor. Jas M Sanderson, of Phil, & Geo P Burnam, of Boston, assistants.

Hon John Banks, formerly a member of Congress, has been elected State Treasurer of the State of Pennsylvania.

Hon Wm L Goggin has been unanimously nominated as a Whig candidate for Congress in the Albemarle district of Virginia.

Reuben Davis had been elected Colonel of the new regt of Mississippi Volunteers.

On Jan 12, at Columbia, S C, M Edouart, a well-known daguerreotypist & silhouethte, hung himself. A person who had called accidentally to visit him found him dead.

By virtue of a writ of fieri facias, at the suit of T M Milburn, against the goods & chattels of Abel Griggs: sale of 26 pairs of window blinds, the property of said Griggs: sale for cash, at public auction, on Jan 23. -J F Wollard, Bailiff

Mrd: on Jan 14, in Winchester, by Rev Robt S Bell, Andrew Aldridge, of Loudoun Co, Va, to Margarette Irene, 2nd daughter of the late Col Jas Green, of Rappahannock Co, Va.

Mrd: on Jan 13, at Shellfield, Westmoreland Co, Va, by Rev Mr Walke, Feilding Lewis to Kate D, daughter of the late Saml Lewis.

Died: in Balt, after a brief illness, in her 44th year, Mrs Jane Sweeny, consort of Geo Sweeny, of Wash City. Her funeral is today, at 11 o'clock, from the residence of her husband. [No death date given.]

Died: on Jan 18, in Wash City, of paralysis, in his 69th year, Francis Doyle, a native of Ireland, but for many years a resident of Gtwn, D C.

Some of the men saved from the wreck of the brig **Somers**, by drifting ashore on spars: Wm W Cardy, Wm W Powers, John Boyce, Lewis Johnson, Jas Fennel, Mathias Gravel, & Dennis Kelley.

The rumor that Col Jas Gadsden, of S C, had been appointed Brig Gen of Volunteers, & would command the Va, S C, & N C Regts, turns out to be unfounded, the appointment not having not yet been made.

FRI JAN 22, 1847
Mrd: on Thu, by Rev Jas R Donelan, Mr Thos Wilson, of Balt, to Mrs Mary Ann Daly, of Wash City.

The Legislature of Va, on Wed, had 5 votes, without making any choice, for a U S Senator to supply the vacancy caused by the death of Mr Pennybacker. The votes were as follows:

1st Vote:
Geo W Summers, 66
John W Jones, 36
Jas McDowell, 27
Jas M Mason, 18
Geo W Hopkins, 8
Geo H Lee, 1
Thos Richie, sen, 1
Green B Samuels, 1

2nd vote:
Summers, 45
Jones, 41
McDowell, 35
Mason, 29
scattering, 1

3rd Vote:
Jones, 43
McDowell, 45
Jones, 40
scattering, 28

4th Vote:
Mason, 52
McDowell, 45
Jones, 40
scattering, 19

5th Vote:
Mason, 54
McDowell, 45
Jones, 33
Summers, 22
scattering, 2

[Jan 23rd newspaper: Jas M Mason was, on Thu last, elected by the Legislature of Va, a Senator in Congress from that State, to fill the vacancy occasioned by the death of Mr Pennybacker. The voting continued for 2 days. The 9th & last ballot was: Mason, 97, McDowell, 19, Samuels, 19, (all Democrats,) scattering 24.]

During the severe gale on Sat the new & elegant ball room at Boston, built & owned by Geo W Warren, & occupied by Mr F L Raymond, was totally demolished by the falling of the roof, rendering the bldg a perfect wreck. The family of Mr Raymond resided in the back of the tenement, otherwise the most serious consequences would have ensued. -Boston Journal of Mon

Senate: 1-Ptn from L Marchand, praying indemnity for spoliations prior to 1800. 2-Cmte of Claims: bill for the relief of the heirs & legal reps of Robt Sewell. 3-Bills passed: bill to create ofc of Surveyor Genr'l of the public lands in the Territory of Oregon, & to grant donation-rights to settler thereon; bill for the relief of Wm B Keene; relief of the heirs of Lt Crocker Sampson, dec'd; relief of Richd S Coxe; & House bill for the relief of Julius Eldred, Elisha Eldred, & Francis E Eldred, for expenses & services in removing the copper rock from Lake Superior.

Died: in Wash City, Albert Marrion Harrvell, in his 4th year, son of Emerick W & Eliz Harrvell. [No date-recent.]

Mr H H Cunningham, one of those who perished on the steamboat **Atlantic**, had insured his life of $5,000, but his relatives have not yet been able to discover in what office the insurance was effected. Information on this subject will be thankfully received, & may be left with the City Editor of the N Y Tribune.

Com'rs' sale of that portion of Geo Semmes' real estate remaining unsold on Jan 19th will be offered for public sale on Jan 30th, on the premises: so well known as the ***Head of Frazier***, contains 5 acres. -Zach Walker, David Barry, Jas C Barry, Benj T Smith, & Thos Jenkins, Com;rs]

Appointments by the Pres:
Henry P Robinson, to be a Lt in the Navy, from Aug 14, 1846, at which time he was promoted to fill a vacancy occasioned by the dismission of Lt John A Russ.
Isaac N Brown & R Delancy Izard, to be Lts in the Navy, from Oct 31, 1846, at which time they were promoted to fill vacancies, occasioned by the death of Lt Geo M Bache, & the resignation of Lt Henry L Chipman.
Napoleon Collins, to be Lt in the Navy, from Nov 6, 1846, at which time he was promoted to fill the vacancy occasioned by the death of Lt Wm B Beverly.
John L Worden, to be Lt in the Navy, from Nov 30, 1846, at which time he was promoted to fill a vacancy occasioned by the death of Lt Chas W Morris.
Randolph F Mason, of Va, to be Assist Surgeon in the Navy, from Aug 29, 1846, at which time he was appointed to fill a vacancy occasioned by the death of Assist Surgeon John T Barton.
Edw D Reynolds, of Ill, to be Purser in the Navy, from Oct 16, 1846, at which time he was appointed to fill a vacancy occasioned by the death of Purser Thos Breese.
Levi D Slamm, of N Y, to be a Purser in the Navy, from Nov 30, 1846, at which time he was appointed to fill a vacancy occasioned by the death of Purser R R Waldron.
Robt Woodworth, to be a Surgeon in the Navy, from Dec 1, 1846, to fill a vacancy occasioned by the death of Surgeon A Hassler.
Joshua Huntington, to be an Assist Surgeon in the Navy, to fill the vacancy occasioned by the promotion of Robt Woodworth.

Trustee's sale of a valuable stock of Staple & Fancy Dry Goods, by deed of trust executed & delivered by Richd C Washington, dated Mar 31, 1846: sale to be continued this morning, at the store lately occupied by R C Washington, in Wash City.
-J M Carlisle, Trustee -C W Boteler, jr, auctioneer

SAT JAN 23, 1847

The death of Peter R Livingston, on Tue, at Rhinebeck, in his 81st year, is announced in the N Y papers. He was for some years a member of the N Y Senate; had a seat in the council of appointment in 1817; was a delegate to the convention which formed the State Constitution of 1821; member of the House of Assembly, of which he was made Speaker.

Senate: 1-Ptn from Mary Chenung, asking a pension for services of her husband, who was crippled, in 1792, at St Clair's defeat. 2-Ptn from L Stone, aged 96 years, asking indemnity for spoliations prior to 1800. 3-Papers relating to the claim of Jos Ratcliffe: presented. 4-Cmte on the Post Ofc & Post Roads: bill for the relief of Wm B Stokes, surviving partner of John N C Stockton & Co. Same cmte: bill for the relief of Wade Allen. 4-Cmte on Public Lands: bill to provide for the settlement of the accounts of Thos C Sheldon, late receiver of public moneys at Kalamazoo, Mich.

House of Reps: 1-Bill for the relief of Alvan C Goell: motion to amend it, by striking out the sum of $20,000 & inserting $5,000. Amendment agreed to. 2-Bill authorizing the issue of patents to Geo Ramsey & Thos T January, for certain lands entered in St Louis Co, Missouri, was indefinitely postponed. 3-Bills for the relief of the heirs of Lt Thos Wishart, of John Ericsson, of the legal reps of Simon Spaulding, dec'd, & of Andrew A Jones, were taken up, & severally objected to. 4-Bills passed & sent to the Senate for concurrence: for the relief of:

Geo B Russell & others
Susan Brum
Isaac Guess
Wm Causey
Wilfred Knott
Jas Williams
Barnard O'Neil
John Pickett & others
heirs of Stephen Johnson, dec'd
heirs of Hyacinth Laselle
Eliz Adams
Thos M Newell
Henry La Reintree
Harvey Reynolds
Catharine Stevenson
Edith Ramey
Ann Clayton
Jas Green
John C Stewart & others
legal reps of John Lawson, dec'd
John C Stewart & others
Jas H Conley
Wm T Walthall
Eliz Fitch
Thankful Reynolds
Jonathan Hoyt
John Van Slyck
Harrison Whitson
widow & heirs of John B Chaudonia
Eliz Calkins, widow of Silas Winans
widow of Elijah Bragdon, dec'd
Benj Metoyer & Francois Gaiennie, dec'd
legal reps of John Lawson, dec'd
settlement of the accounts of Purser G R Barry
administrators of Jos Edson, dec'd, late marshal of the district of Vt
Final settlement of the accounts of John Spencer, late receiver of public moneys at ***Fort Wayne***, Indiana.
heirs of Gassaway Watkins, an ofcr of the Md Continental line in the war of the Revolution
granting a pension to Silas Chatfield.

Land for sale: Farm containing 100 acres, formerly the residence of John S Bogan: adjoins Col J Jackson, Mr Jas Crawford, & Rev F S Evans, & is located 9 miles north of Wash. Much valuable timber on the premises; also, a new dwlg-house containing 5 rooms, & a new kitchen. Inquire of B L Bogan, M & 8th sts.

The Regt of N C Volunteers is complete, & the following have been appointed field ofcrs: Robt T Paine, Col; John A Fagg, Lt Col; & Montford F Stokes, Major.

Mrd: on Jan 21, by Rev W T Sprole, Mr Geo J Hall, formerly of Alexandria, to Miss Margaret, daughter of Mr Geo Hercus, of Wash.

Died: in Nov last, in Smyrna, Asia Minor, David W Offley, U S Consul at that place.

Died: on Jan 21, in Gtwn, D C, of consumption, Mrs Christiana Armstrong, only daughter of Dr Wm Sothoron. Her funeral is this afternoon at 3 o'clock, from the residence of her father, on Bridge st, Gtwn.

Died: on Jan 5, at Burlington, Iowa, of congestive fever, after 24 hours' illness, Frederick G, youngest child of Abram B & Sarah J Lindsley, aged 9 years & 8 months-a boy of much promise,
& late of Wash City.

To let, the commodious double-front Brick House, lately occupied by Capt Jas Edelen, corner of Pa ave 7 2nd st east. Apply to the subscriber, near the Navy Yard-M King.

The Sec of the Navy has informed Lt Geo S Blake, who commanded the U S brig **Perry** when she went ashore near Key West, that he does not deem it necessary to institute an inquiry into the circumstances of the disaster. The evidence on the records of the Dept justifies me in declaring your claims to the character of a skilful & zealous ofcr are elevated rather than depressed by your conduct in the perilous circumstances.

MON JAN 25, 1847

House of Reps: 1-Ptn of Dorcas Seavey, widow of Ebenezer Seavey, late of Brownfield, Maine, dec'd, praying the allowance of a pension on account of wounds & diabilities received by her husband in the last war with Great Britain. 2-Ptn of & documents of Nathl Bailey, a Revolutionary soldier, for a pension. 3-Ptn of Timothy Savage, of Middletown, Conn, asking indemnity for French spoliations. 4-Ptn of L Stone, of Derby Court, [who has reached the age of 96,] asking indemnity for French spoliations. 5-Memorial & ptn of Orazio de Atellia Santangelo, for indemnity for claims against Mexico. 6-Ptn of Mrs Priscilla Scott, widow of Jos Scott, deceased, praying for a Revolutionary pension. 7-Memorial of Caleb D Owings, C H Owings, T Griffith, heirs of Nicholas Owens, deceased, & others, praying indemnity for French spoliations prior to 1800. 8-Act of the relief of Wm B Keene; an act for the relief of the heirs of Crocker Sampson, dec'd; & an act for the relief of Richd S Coxe: appropriately referred.

Notice of partnership: under the style of Yerby & Brother, for the sale of Foreign & Domestic Staple & Fancy Dry Goods. They have taken the store #6, Centre Market space, between 7th & 8th sts, recently occupied by P H Hooe & Co.
-Albert F Yerby, A L Yerby

Mrd: on Jan 14, by Rev Mr Wickes, Mr Jas M Brown, of Spottsylvania Co, Va, to Miss Mary E, daughter of the late John G Hedgman, of Stafford.

Died: on Sat, at his residence in Wash City, in his 74th year, Dr Fred'k May. He was one of the oldest & most deservedly respected inhabitants of Wash, of which he had been a resident for nearly 50 years, having been for many years the oldest Physician in Wash City. He leaves a family of sons & dghts grown up to manhood & maturity, to whom he was one of the most devoted fathers that ever lived.

Died: on Jan 24, after a long & painful illness, Mr Danl Page, a native of PG Co, Md, but for the last 47 years a resident of the eastern part of Wash City. He was an exemplary member of the Methodist Episcopal Church for 40 years. His funeral is on Tue, at 2 o'clock, from his late residence, near the Baptist Church, Navy Yard.

Died: on Jan 23, after a long & painful illness, Catharine Simm, consort of Mr John Waters, in her 59th year, leaving a large family to mourn their irreparable loss.

A Naval General Court Martial is ordered to convene this day on board the U S ship **Pennsylvania**, at Norfolk, for the trial of Cmders Carpender & Pearson, & such others as may be brought before it. The Court will be composed of: Cmdor Stewart, Pres; Com Downes & Com Turner; Capts Storer, Dulany, Mayo, & Armstrong, members. Gen Blow, Judge Advocate. -Norfolk Herald

Appointments by the Pres: In the Regular Army. Assist Quartermasters with the rank of Captain: 1st Lt J P J O'Brien, 4th Artl; 1st Lt M R Patrick, 2nd Infty; 1st Lt Wm M Shover, 3rd Artl; 1st Lt Arthur B Lansing, 2nd Artl
Medical Dept: Dr Israel Moses, to be Assist Surgeon
In the U S military service, under the act of Jun 18, 1846.
Chas M Price, of Mississippi, to be Assist Quartermaster, with rank of Captain.
Robt Josselyn, of Mississippi, to be Assist Commissary, with rank of Captain, vice Kemp S Holland, dec'd.
Wm Barksdale, of Mississippi, to be Assist Commissary, with the rank of Captain.
Chas R Webster, of N Y, to be Assist Quartermaster, with the rank of Captain.
Jas F Hutton, of N Y, to be Assist Quartermaster, with the rank of Captain.
F N Mioton, of La, to be Assist Quartermaster, with the rank of Captain
Chas E Carr, of La, to be Assist Quartermaster, with the rank of Captain.
Jos L Hasbrouck, of N Y, to be Surgeon.
Benj K Hart, of Ill, to be Surgeon, vice R F Richardson, who declines to accept the appointment.
Luther F Dashiel, of La, to be Assist Surgeon.
Fred'k W Miller, of Pa, to be Assist Surgeon, vice Geo Dock, who declines to accept the appointment.
Miria B Halstead, of N Y, to be Assist Surgeon.

For rent: a very desirable house on 6th st, adjoining the residence of Gen Roger Jones. Apply for key & terms at Dr B Washington's, nearly opposite.

Several papers stated that Mr Augustus Edouard committed suicide in Columbia, S C, on Jan 12. We have seen a letter from him, dated at that place Jan 16th, consequently the report cannot be true. -N Y Express

From Texas: Dr J G Chalmers, [brother of the Senator from Mississippi,] was killed in Austin, the capital of Texas, about 10 days since, by a Mr Holden. The difficulty grew out of a dispute about some property, when the Dr drew his pistol. Mr Holden, with his knife, inflicted a wound which resulted in the instant death of Mr Chalmers.

TUE JAN 26, 1847

Orphans Court of Wash Co, D C, Jan 22, 1847. In the case of Lewis Johnson & Abner B Procter, excs of Henry Smith, dec'd: the excs & the Court have appointed Feb 12th next, for the settlement of the estate. -Ed N Roach, Reg/o wills

H H Fenton will open on Tue, at Mrs Stetson's, 6 doors east of Coleman's Hotel, a fresh supply of rich Parisian Goods.

WED JAN 27, 1847

House of Reps: 1-Ptn of Mary E Edes & 89 others, ladies of West Medway, Mass, for peace with Mexico. 2-Ptn of Eli R N Ross & wife, praying for confirmation of a tract of land. 3-Ptn of Willis S Center, praying increased pay as contractor on route #5,233, leading from Knoxville to Sparta, Tenn. 4-Ptn of Nicholas Edmunds & Henry Edmunds, excs of Thos Edmunds, dec'd, praying for relief for French spoliations prior to 1800. 5-Ptn of Benj Cresey for a pension as an invalid seaman from wounds & disabilities received during the late war with Great Britain. Ptn of Lot Davis, for the same. Ptn of Wm Gaul, for the same. 6-Ptn of Ephraim Clark for his share of prize money due from Denmark for captures in 1779. 7-Ptn of the heirs of Joshua Trafton, of the army of the Revolution, praying for commutation pay. 8-Ptn of the heirs of Peleg Wardsworth, of the army of the Revolution, for commutation pay. 9-Ptn of F Whittle, administrator of Conway Whittle, dec'd, praying indemnity for French spoliations prior to 1800. 10-Ptn of Christopher Slocum & 74 others, of West Medway, Mass, for peace with Mexico. 11-Ptn of C C Beatty, administrator of Jas Vanuxem, dec'd, late of Phil, praying indemnity for French spoliations prior to 1800.

Washington, Jan 25, 1847. As the remains of the late Lt Richd H Graham, of the 4th Infty, who died last Oct from wounds received in the battle of Monterey, will soon reach this city, it is the proper time to say a few words about that gallant ofcr. Lt Graham was the son of the Hon John Graham, formerly U S Minister to the Court of Brazil; he was born in this city, & received his education at West Point. His bereaved mother is now a resident of our city. His conduct was the admiration of the whole army.

The Hon Jas W Bates, the first Delegate of Arkansas in Congress, & subsequently one of the Judges of the Supreme Court of the Territory, died recently at his residence in Van Buren.

Wash Corp: 1-Ptn from Lawrence Callan, for the remission of a fine. 2-Ptn from Jonathan Chapman, for the remission of a fine. 3-Ptn of Dennis Boon, for the remission of a fine. 4-Cmte of Claims: Act for the relief of O J Prather: passed. Same cmte: ptn of Elias Barnes-asked to be discharged from further consideration.

Senate: 1-Ptn from John B Cooper, asking indemnity for French spoilations prior to 1800. Ptn of Caleb Gardner, in relation to the same. 2-Additional documents in the case of Sarah E Graham. 3-Ptn from Peter Von Schmidt, asking an examination into the merits of his process for mineralizing timber. 4-Bill granting a pension to Bethiah Healy. 5-Cmte on Pensions: adverse report on the ptn of Naomi Davis: ordered to be printed. Same cmte: bill for the relief of Andrew Moore. 6-Cmte of Claims: bill for the relief of the heirs & legal reps of Lewis De La Housaye. 7-Bill for the relief of Elijah White: passed. 8-Ptn from Robt Munsen Harrison, U S Consul at Kingston, Jamaica, asking to be indemnified as security for a citizen of the U S who failed to appear. 9-Cmte on Naval Affairs: bill directing that the Sec of the Navy purchase from De Jas P Espy his patent right for the conical ventilator for the use of the U S.

Indian Massacre: from the St Louis Republican of Jan 7: battle between the Omaha & Sioux Indians, near Council Bluffs: it turned out to be a cold blooded butchery of women & children, in the absence of all the warriors of the village. On Jan 12, war party of Yancton Sioux Indians defeated & destroyed 14 lodges of the Omaha tribe of Indians, located at the time at Wood's Bluffs. Two men made their escape; one of them, Jos Lafleche, a trader in the employ of Mr Peter A Sarpy, ran from the scene of blood, barefooted, & arrived at Belleview with both feet frozen. Mr Sarpi & Maj Miller, the present agent, dispatched a party of men who confirmed on their return, the report of Lafleche.

Died: on Jan 26, at his residence in Wash City, Jane Lynch, w/o Mr Ambrose Lynch, in her 64th year. She was a native of the county Meath, Ireland, but for the last 30 years a resident of this city. Her funeral is tomorrow in St Patrick's Church, at 10:30 o'clock.

Died: on Jan 26, in her 74th year, Mrs Ann Edwards, formerly of Balt, but for several years a resident of Wash City. Her funeral is from the residence of her brother, Wm Gordon, on 19th & I sts, tomorrow, at half past 3 o'clock.

Died: on Jan 14, at Lafayette, Indiana, Mrs Nancy G Ellsworth, w/o the Hon H L Ellsworth, late Com'r of Patents. Her death, which resulted from a fractured limb, was calm, peaceful, & resigned to the will of Him who thus suddenly recalled her to himself.

Died: on Jan 23, Clarance, infant son of John L & Rebecca M Smith, aged 10 months & 15 days.

THU JAN 28, 1847
Land for sale: the farm on which the subscriber resides, containing 294 acres, 5 miles from Upper Marlboro, in the Forest, adjoining the lands of Messrs Chas Hill, Thos Duckett, S L Brooke, & Wm I Berry. The dwlg contains 7 rooms, with all necessary out houses. Very convenient is an Episcopal Church, a good school for young ladies, & a mill near.
-G W Bowie, Upper Marlboro, PG Co, Md.

Senate: 1-Cmte on Naval Affairs: house bill for the relief of Jas Jones, of the city of Brooklyn, without amendment. 2-Cmte on the District of Columbia: bill to provide a free communication across the Eastern Branch of the river Potomac, in the District of Columbia.

A Jersey Blue of a Century. The Monmouth Inquirer announces the death, at the residence of his dght, at ***Point Pleasant***, in that county, on Jan 15, of John Chamberlain, in his 105th year. He was a Revolutionary pensioner, & raised 11 children, whose offspring amount to 175 children, grand, great, & great grand.

Mrd: on Nov 29 last, at Phil, by Rev F J Barbelin, Mr Fred'k Ringgold, of Wash Co, Md, to Miss Deborah Louisa Adamson, of Brooklyn, N Y.

Mrd: on Jan 19, at Leesburg, Va, by Rev A H H Boyd, Chas M Faultleroy, U S Navy, to Janet P, only child of Thos P Knox.

Trustee's sale of a valuable 2 story brick house: by virtue of a deed of trust, executed by Brooke M Berry, of record in Liber W B #94, folios 421 thru 423, a land record of Wash Co: sale on Jan 30, lot 16 in square #686, subject to the widow's dower. Property is on Capitol Hill, fronting on the west side of 1st st east, between B & C sts north, with a well finished 2 story brick house, which was occupied by the Hon Mr Holmes, of S C, during the last session of Congress, & now in the possession of Brooke M Berry. The title is indisputable. -John B Magruder, Trustee -A Green, auctioneer

FRI JAN 29, 1847
Cumberland Civilian: John Barrett, assist engineer of the Iron Works at Lonaconing, was instantly killed on Thu by the engine being started while he was on the inside of the cylinder cleaning out the flues. The chief engineer is charged with criminal carelessness in starting the engine.

Died: Jan 27, in Gtwn, Mrs Mary T White, consort of John B White, & daughter of the late Wm O'Brien, of Gtwn.

Died: on Jan 17, in Cincinnati, Ohio, Thos Shreve, in his 77th year. The deceased was born in Burlington Co, N J, in 1770, removed to Alexandria, Va, in 1795, & to Cincinnati in 1827. He was a Minister in the Society of Friends for about 40 years.

We notice at the Franklin Engine House a handsome funeral car, which has been prepared to the order of the Franklin Fire Co, by Mr J E W Thompson, of Wash City. It is intended to be used at the funeral of Capt Eugene Boyle, who was an esteemed member of that fire company. The platform of the car on which the coffin will rest is covered with black velvet-the sides & end are appropriately ornamented with mourning emblems. The car is surmounted with a canopy of black velvet & crape. In front appears the American flag, over which an eagle is perched with extended wings.

Dr Saml Simons, a Rep in the last Congress from the State of N Y, died at his residence in that State on Jan 13, in his 70th year.

Senate: 1-Ptn from Jas Maher, the public gardener, asking his ofc may be rendered independent of the Com'r of Public Bldgs, & stating that he thinks his long experience in his profession better qualifies him to give satisfaction to all concerned. 2-Ptn from John McClintic: asking Congress to purchase for the Gov't the right to use his invention for the making of gun carriages. 3-Cmte on Naval Affairs, without amendment, the following House bill: for the relief of: legal reps of :

Elisha Adams	Thos N Newell	Thos Shields
Susan Brown	Jas H Conley	
Henry La Reintree	Wm T Walthall	

4-Bill for the settlement of the accounts of Purser R Barry.

SAT JAN 30, 1847

Senate: 1-Ptn from Geo Peters, asking a pension. 2-Cmte of Claims: bill for the relief of Jacob L Vance. Same cmte: bill for the relief of Josiah Haskell. 3-Cmte on the Public Lands: House bill for the relief of the widow & heirs of John P Chaudonia. Same cmte: House bill for the relief of the children of Stephen Johnson, dec'd.

Household & kitchen furniture at auction: on Feb 3, at the house occupied by Mrs A Ricketts, on G st, between 17th & 18th sts. -A Green, auctioneer

Fountain Hotel, Light st, Balt, Jan 27, 1847. Arthur L Fogg & Phineas Thurston, Proprietors. Succeeded the late firm of Dix & Fogg. Recently constructed a new Ladies' Ordinary, & also a private sitting room for gentlemen.

Mrd: on Jan 27, by Rev Jas Laurie, D D, Lemuel C Wheat, of Weldon, N C, to Annie Henderson, daughter of Mr Leonard Adams, of Wash City.

Died: Jan 27, at Balt, Mary L, wife of Lt Walbach, U S Army, & daughter of F Lucas, jr.

MON FEB 1, 1847

For rent: those handsome rooms over Geo Krafft's Bakery, corner of 18th st & Pa ave. -Geo Krafft

House of Reps: 1-Ptn of the heiress of Fred'k Leigle. 2-Ptn of J V Kerr, of N Y, asking remuneration for lands, of right his, improperly conveyed to others. 3-Ptn of Nathl S Ruggles & others, praying that no alteration be made in the law in relation to pilots. 4-Memorial of D Klaener, agent for the association for the protection of German emigrants to Texas, praying remission of duties. 5-Ptn of Eliz H Baldwin, widow of Isaac Baldwin, for continuance of a pension heretofore allowed her. 6-Ptn of Wm Blanchard for the repeal of such acts of Congress as authorize the sale of free persons of color into slavery within the District of Columbia. 7-Ptn of John Littlejohn, praying compensation for certain work done by him as contractor upon the public works of Harper's Ferry, Va.

Mrd: on Jan 28, by Rev Dr Morgan, at the residence of her father, in reading, Berks Co, Pa, J Murray Rush, of Phil, son of the Hon Richd Rush, to Eugenia, daughter of John S Heister.

Mrd: on Jan 26, by Rev W J Clark, Mr Fitzhugh Coyle to Miss Mary A, daughter of John Farr, of Phil.

Rev C P Krauth, of Balt, will deliver a Lecture on the Augustan Age, in the Methodist Protestant Church, 9th st, on Feb 2. Admittance free.

The once famous Monroe Edwards, confined in Sing Sing prison for forgery, is said to be in the last stage of quick consumption. [Feb 2nd newspaper: Monroe Edwards died on Fri last in the hospital of the Sing Sing Prison. He was a man of talents & might have attained to an enviable distinction. -Evening Post]

A letter from Hong Kong, China, brings the intelligence of the death of Mrs Devan, after an illness which had continued for some time. She was a daughter of Mr David Hall, of the N Y Journal of Commerce.

On Fri last the house of John Connor, in the township of Lanark, Canada, was burnt to the ground. He perished in the flames, with his wife, 5 children, & a servant girl.

Senate: 1-Ptn from Sarah G Underwood, widow of a naval ofcr, asking a pension. 2-Documents presented in relation to the claim of Jas S Conway. 3-Cmte of Claims: adverse report on the ptn of Jacob Hauseman, to be indemnified for property destroyed by the Indians on Indian Key. 4-Cmte on Pensions: joint resolution for the relief of Sarah Ann Linton.

TUE FEB 2, 1847

Senate: 1-Cmte on Naval Affairs: bill for the relief of Rodolphine Claxton, widow of Alex'r Claxton, late cmder in the navy. Same cmte: unfavorable report on the ptn of Josiah Colton. 2-Cmte on Finance: asking to be discharged from the further consideration of the memorial of Wm H Prentiss, & that it be referred to the Cmte of Claims.

Mrs Wilmer's School, Alexandria, Va, will resume on Feb 15, 1847. She has removed to a larger house.

The remains of Capt Boyle & Lt Graham arrived in Wash City last night by the cars from Balt. An immense body of citizens followed the honored remains from the Depot.

Shocking accident at Mount Savage Iron Works on Wed killed Thos Davis instantly, by being caught in the large fly-wheel of the rolling mill. -Cumberland [Md] Mountaineer

For rent: 2 story brick house near corner of 5th & G sts. Inquire at Mr John Caton's Grocery store, 5th & G.

Mrd: on Feb 1, in Wash City, by Rev J W French, Rector of the Church of the Epiphany, Edw C Stout, U S Navy, to Julia, eldest daughter of Capt John H Aulick, of the U S Navy.

Died: on Feb 1, after a long & painful illness, Charlotte J, consort of John Sioussa, aged 49 years. Her funeral will take place today at 3 P M, from her late residence on N Y ave.

Died: on Jan 21, at ***Belpark***, his residence, in Caroline Co, Va, Mr Lawrence Battaile, sen, in his 81st year. His great characteristics were those of the most devout Christian; talents of a high order enabled him to do & greatly profit by.

Died: on Jan 26, of pulmonary consumption, in his 27th year, Henry S Trevor, eldest son of J B Trevor, Cashier of the Phil Bank.

The funeral of Eugene Boyle will take place, from the residence of his father, today at 1 o'clock. [Feb 3rd newspaper: the military companies marched along Pa ave to the residence of John Boyle, on 10th st, father of the dec'd; the funeral procession of volunteer companies & a vast body of citizens formed into line. Capt Boyle was borne by 6 of the Franklin Fire Co in the splendid funeral car provided by that company for the solemn occasion. The procession moved from 10th st, along Pa ave, to St Patrick's burial ground. The funeral services were performed by Rev W Mathews & Rev Jas B Donelan.]

The remains of Lt Graham, U S Army, will be removed for interment, at 10 o'clock, this morning, from the residence of his mother, corner of H & 15th sts, to St Patrick's Church. Friends of the family & the public are respectfully invited to attend. [Feb 3rd newspaper: the remains of Lt Graham were deposited in the vault attached to St Patrick's Church; Rev W Matthews & Rev Jas B Donelan performed the funeral services; Rev Mr Verhagen delivered a funeral address.]

Balt, Feb 1. The military of our city are now escorting the remains of the illustrious dead, Col Watson, Capt Ridgely, & others, whose bodies were brought here yesterday. Capt Ridgely is to be buried, at the request of his family, without show or parade. Col Watson's body has been escorted to his late residence.

The printers of Western N Y celebrated the anniversary of the birthday of Franklin at Rochester on Jan 18. A C Dauby, of Utica, the first printer of Rochester, presided at the table.

WED FEB 3, 1847

Wash Corp: 1-Cmte of Police: ptn of Uriah B Mitchell, praying the appointment of an additional police constable for the 7th Ward, asked to be discharged from its further consideration. 2-Bill for the relief of O J Prather was referred to the Cmte on Improvements.

A letter from Victoria, dated Jan 7, says that Adj F B Schaeffer, of Balt, has been unanimously elected to the captaincy of company D, one of the companies of this District belonging to the Balt Btln.

Mrd: on Feb 2, by Rev Dr Horatio Potter, Rector of St Peter's Church, Albany, N Y, Dr R A Lacy to Blanche, daughter of Mr Jas Ferguson, all of Wash City.

Mrd: on Feb 2, by Rev J H Van Horseigh, Maj Nicholson, of the Marine Corps, to Sarah, daughter of Danl Carroll, of Duddington.

Senate: 1-Ptn of Ezekiel Potter, asking compensation for services during the last war with Great Britain. 2-Cmte on Foreign Relations: bill for the relief of Robt M Harrison, U S Consul at Jamaica. 3-Cmte on Public Lands: bill granting compensation to John Moore, with a report which was ordered to be printed. 4-Cmte on the Post Ofc & Post Roads: bill for the relief of Creed Taylor. 5-Cmte on Pensions: House bill for the relief of Silas Chatfield, without amendment. 6-Cmte on Military Affairs: bill for the relief of John Stockton, late a Lt in the U S Navy. 7-Cmte on Patents: bill for the relief of the heirs of Jethro Wood. -S S Coleman, Chas Stott, trustees -A Green, auctioneer

By virtue of a deed of trust, we will sell at public auction, for cash, all the remaining stock of Dry Goods, with the store fixtures, & stove, of S W Tucker, on 6th st, near Pa ave. -S S Coleman, Chas Stott, trustees -A Green, auctioneer

House of Reps: 1-Ptn of David Melville, administrator of the estate of Benj Fry, dec'd, asking indemnity for French spoliations. 2-Ptn of Eliot Boss & others, asking indemnity for French spoliations. 3-Memorial of Nathan Fuller & others, for indemnity for French spoliations prior to 1800. 4-Memorial of Robt Hystop, in relation to French spoliations prior to 1800. 5-Ptn of Chas Anthony, heir of Jacob Dick, asking a half section of land in lieu of a like quantity granted to said Dick, on White river, in Indiana. 6-Testimony in relation to the claims of the heirs of the Baron de Kalb.

Balt, Feb 2. The funeral of the late Col Watson will take place on Feb 8. The body of young Herman S Thomas is to be interred on Tue next, at Spesusia Church, in Harford Co, a short distance from Perrymansville. The mortal remains of Capt Ridgely are to be deposited in the Mausoleum, Greenmount Cemetery, on Feb 8.

Appointments by the Pres:
1st Lt John B Magruder, to be Captain, Jun 18, 1849, vice Irwin, assist quartermaster, who, under the 7th section of the Act of Jun 18, 1846, elects to vacate his regimental commission.
2nd Lt Saml K Dawson, to be 1st Lt, Jun 18, 1846, vice Magruder, promoted.
Brevet 2nd Lt Henry Copper, of the 2nd Regt of Artl, to be 2nd Lt, Jun 18, 1846, vice Dawson, promoted.
Adj General's Dept:
1st Lt Wm W Mackall, of the 1st Regt of Artl, to be assist adj general, with the brevet rank of Captain, Dec 29, 1846, vice Prentiss, assist adj general, who vacates his staff commission.
1st Lt Geo Deas, of the 5th Regt of Infty, to be assist adj general, with the brevet rank of Captain, Dec 29, 1846, vice Ridgely, dec'd.
Appointments in accordance with the provisions of the Act of Jun 18, 1846, agreeably to their nominations respectively, viz:
Jas L Kemper, of Va, to be assist quartermaster, with the rank of Captain.
Henry Erskin, of Va, to be assistant commissary, with the rank of Captain.
John Miller Bell, of Va, to be assistant Surgeon.

THU FEB 4, 1847
The owners of farms & estates that are for sale near & within a day's ride of Wash City are invited to leave descriptions of their lands & improvements with the subscribers, who will offer them to purchasers. -David A Hall, Robt A Parrish: ofc in Concert Hall, Wash.

Senate: 1-Mr Johnson, of La, presented the credentials of Mr Pierre Soule, Senator elect from the State of La, to supply the vacancy occasioned by the death of Mr Alex'r Barrow. 2-Ptn from Martin Renehan, doorkeeper at the Pres' house, asking to be allowed the same compensation as is given for similar duties in the Executive Dept.

Through the solicitation of friends, I have concluded to continue the business which has been conducted for the last 12 years by my dec'd husband; that is, of a retail grocery business, at the corner of F & 10th sts. I have for rent a handsome 2 story frame house, containing 9 rooms in all. To a good tenant the rent will be moderate. Apply to me at the store, F & 10th sts, opposite St Patrick's Church. -Eliz A Laub

The subscriber has removed from his old stand, on 8th st, to one on Pa ave, over Hall & Brother's Dry Goods Store, where he is ready at all times to make up work in a style not to be surpassed. Gentlemen desirous of obtaining a beautiful garment are to give him a trial. -Jno Riggles, Draper & Tailor

House for rent: brick dwlg on La ave, fronting the west wing of the City Hall, 2nd east of 4½ st. Apply to Mr A Baldwin, who resides a few doors east.

We regret that information has been received by John Minor Botts, of the death of his son, Lt Archibald B Botts, of the U S Army. Lt Botts graduated at West Point in Jun last, & but recently joined his regt in Mexico. -Richmond Republican

Thirteen houses were consumed by fire in Lewisville, Henry Co, Indiana, on Jan 23. Mr Eli Davis, merchant, is the principal sufferer; his loss is $5,000. No insurance.

Trustee's sale of house & lot: by deed of trust from Patrick Goings, dated Oct 28, 1842, recorded in Liber W B #98, folios 385 thru 388, of the land records of Wash Co, D C: public auction on Mar 8, of the eastern part of lot 8 in square 80, with a good 2 story frame house, with back bldgs. -Wm H Prentiss, trustee -R W Dyer, auct

Died: on Feb 2, Julia Crawford, aged 18, eldest daughter of Chas & Julia Gordon, of Wash City. Her funeral will take place from the residence of her father, on I st, between 17th & 18th sts, on Fri, at 3 o'clock.

Died: suddenly, yesterday, Mrs Eliza Dale, w/o Geo Dale. Her funeral is this morning, at half past 9 o'clock, from her late residence on 11th st.

Died: on Feb 2, in her 17th year, Mary Rochester A, consort of O Bedingfield Queen, & only daughter of the late Lt John T Ritchie, U S Navy, leaving an infant but a few days old. She leaves her bereaved husband & friends. Her funeral is from the Catholic Church, in Gtwn, this morning, at 11 o'clock.

A Card-John Boyle & his family, impressed with sentiments of profound gratitude, desire publicly to tender thanks, which they now do, with heartfelt emotions to their fellow-citizens, civil & military, in New Orleans, Balt, Alexandria, Gtwn, & Wash. The distinguished respect shown by the citizens of all these places in honor of the memory of Capt Eugene Boyle, has awakened feelings which shall be cherished & held, while life endures, in grateful remembrance.

Saml W Tucker, Merchant Tailor, made an assignment of his effects to us for the benefit of such creditors as shall within 60 days from Feb 1, 1847, release & discharge him from their respective debts & claims. -Saml S Colemen, Chas Stott, Assignees

FRI FEB 5, 1847

Martin Javelli, who was for many years in the Ravel Family, the celebrated ballet & pantomine company, died in New Orleans on Jan 20 of consumption.

The steamship **Giraffe** under the command of Capt A H Eldridge, was lost near Brasos Santiago on Jan 7th. Four of the hands perished.

Mrd: on Feb 2, by Rev Mr Donelan, Mr Wilfred Young, of Wash, to Miss Eliz A Boarman, of the same place, & daughter of the late Aloysius Boarman, of Chas Co, Md.

Mrd: on Feb 2, at ***Mount Repose***, Balt Co, Md, by Rev Mr Pendleton, John D McPherson, of Wash, to Eliz Thornburgh, 2nd daughter of the late John Skinner Webster.

Died: yesterday, at Gtwn, Mrs Jane Cox, w/o Col John Cox. Her funeral is tomorrow, at 3 o'clock, from the residence of Clement Cox.

Senate: 1-Ptn from Jane Sprotson, asking for a renewal of her pension. 2-Cmte on Pensions, the following House bills without amendment: relief of Harvey Reynolds; of Catharine Stephenson; of Ann Clayton; of Eliz Fitch; of Thankful Reynolds; of Eliz Calkins, widow of S Winans. House bills for the relief of Jonathan Hoyt, & to increase the pension of Roswell Hale, without amendment. 3-Cmte of Claims: bill for the relief of John Bronson. Same cmte: bill for the relief of Ray Tompkins & others, children & heirs of the late Danl D Tompkins. 4-Bill for the relief of Shadrach Gillet & others: passed. Mr Jarnagin moved to amend the bill by inserting the following: To Walter S Adair $450, to Thos F Taylor $450, & to Wm L Holt $800, to defray their expenses visiting Washington last winter, in an honorable effort to reconcile the different parties in the Cherokee nation. Question was taken on the amendment, & decided in the negative. 5-Passed: bill for the relief of Thos Douglass, late U S Atty for East Florida; relief of Geo Gordon; relief of Nathl Kuykendall; relief of Thos Rhodes; relief of Jos Wilson; relief of Thos Brownell; relief of personal reps of Wm A Slacum, dec'd; relief of Orlando Saltmarsh & Wm Fuller; relief of Madison Allen; relief of Francis Summeraner; relief of Peter Frost; legal reps of Jacques Moulon. Also, bill for the relief of Peter Capella, administrator of Andrew Capella, dec'd, & for the relief of John Capo. 6-The bill to allow arrearages of pension to Hugh W Dobbin, an ofcr in the late war, was laid on the table. 7-Bill for the relief of Thos Blanchard: ordered to be engrossed for a 3rd reading. 8-Bill for the relief of Jeannette C Huntington, widow & sole survivor of Wm D Chever, dec'd, was considered in Cmte of the Whole.

Appointments by the Pres:
Cade D Strickland, jr, Reg of Land Ofc at Greensburg, La, vice Richmond Dennis, dec'd.
John F Payne, Reg of Land Ofc at Natchitoches, La, vice Wm T Walmsley, resigned.
Exum L Whitaker, of N C, to be Assist Commissary, with the rank of Captain.
Wm L Dancy, of N C, to be Assist Quartermaster, with the rank of Captain.
Gaston D Cobbs, of N C, to be Surgeon.
Jas A MacRae, of N C, to be Assist Surgeon
Thos N Love, of Mississippi, to be Surgeon.
Henry Field, of Mississippi, to be Assist Surgeon.
Wm H J Anson, of Va, to be Surgeon.
Jas L Kemper, of Va, to be Assist Quartermaster, vice Wm S Kemper, erroneously named & transmitted to the Senate on Jan 7.

Coroner Woodward yesterday held 2 inquests, one over the body of a white man named John Smith, who was found dead at Gtwn; the other over a colored man, Geo Foster, belonging to Wash City. Both deaths were caused by intemperance & consequent exposure to the weather.

In the N Y Express of Jan 20th there is a report of a special meeting of the N Y Historical Society, at which an interesting paper was read by J B Varnum, upon the Federal Seat of Gov't. One of the requisites for the seat of Gov't was centrality.

Balt, Feb 4. Dr Louis O'Donnell, son of distinguished citizen, Gen Columbus O'Donnell, died last night from a severe attack of smallpox, which he contracted while attending a patient.

On Thu last week there was argued before the Court of Common Pleas, at East Cambridge, the amount of damages which should be paid to Dr Harris, of Ashland, by John Gibson, of Hopkinton, for not turning out of the road when Dr Harris passed, & which occasioned the breaking of his sulkey. The jury decided that Gibson should pay $27 & costs, amounting in all to upwards of $100. The verdict so distressed Mr Gibson, who is 73 years of age, that on Sat, he took a rope & fastened it around the neck of his wife, & then attached it to the bed post. The noise produced by the stangulation caused one of the family to enter the room, & in time to save the life of Mrs Gibson, who, we are informed, has been an invalid for a number of years. As the door was opened, Mr Gibson immediately went to the barn, where he was in about 5 minutes found dead, hanging by the neck. The inquest was rendered by Coroner Mirick. -Boston Traveller

Birthnight Ball at Jackson Hall, Feb 22nd, following elected Managers:

Hon-

Geo M Dallas	Jas Thompson	J W Tibbatts
Jas Buchanan	John W Houston	B Martin
John Y Mason	Reverdy Johnson	E A Hannegan
Nathan Clifford	A A Chapman	S A Douglass
Geo Evans	Geo E Badger	D R Atchison
C G Atherton	Isaac E Holmes	A H Sevier
S S Phelps	T B King	Lewis Cass
Danl Webster	J D Westcott	Saml Houston
Jas Dixon	F W Bowdon	S C Hastins
H Y Cranston	Jacob Thompson	M L Martin
W W Woodworth	I E Morse	
Wm Wright	Wm Allen	

Messrs:

S L Gouverneur	Richd D Cutts	F T Lally
A G Southall	J B Gluch	John B Sullivan
Robt A Lacey	Clement Marsh	J Knox Walker
Saml Humes Porter	J Hall Adams	W W Seaton
John Potts	Benj E Green	Thos Ritchie

R C Weightman	P Barton Key	Com L Warrington
Jos H Bradley	Wm Medill	Capt C S McCauley
Chas K Gardner	N P Trist	Com'r T A Dornin
John C Rives	Edmund Burke	Gen Geo Gibson
J W McCulloch	J R Goldsborough	Col H Stanton
Wm Collins	J H Patterson	Maj J D Graham
J M McCalla	S Nicholson	Capt W H Swift
R H Gillet	L P Calhoun	Lt Josiah Watson
Jas H Piper	Wm B Scott	

Ball of the Perserverance Fire Co: on Feb 15, at the Odd Fellow Hall, for the purpose of aiding them to defray the necessary expenses of repairs of apparatus & house.

Exec Cmte:

C Buckingham	Henry Lyles	Edmund J Ellis
Henry Hay	John D Thompson	

Managers:

W W Seaton	Hiram Richey	Jas Foy
John W Maury	Thos Sessford	Wm A Kennedy
Walter Lenox	John T Towers	Wm Lord
Jas L White	Thos Williams	T W Osgodby
Saml Bacon	R C Weightman	W M Perry
B F Beers	S P Franklin	John Sessford
T H Filions	Alex'r Lee	Richd Touge
W H Harrover	Jos H Bradley	Thos V Hyde
Thos Lewis	Dr Jos Borrows	
Francis B Lord, jr	John E Buckingham	

Coroner Woodward yesterday held 2 inquests, one over the body of a white man named John Smith, who was found dead at Gtwn; the other over a colored man, Geo Foster, belonging to Wash City. Both deaths were caused by intemperance & consequent exposure to the weather.

SAT FEB 6, 1847

Senate: 1-Cmte on Public Lands: bill from the House to provide for the final settlement of the accounts of John Spencer, late receiver of public moneys at ***Fort Wayne***, Indiana, without amendment. 2-Cmte of Claims: joint resolution for the relief of John Devlin. Same cmte: bill for the relief of Pearson Cogswell. Same cmte: bill for the relief of Fred'k Dawson, John Schott, & E D Whitney, creditors of the late Republic of Texas. 3-Cmte on Pensions: asking to be discharged from the further consideration of the papers of Sarah E Graham, & that they be referred to the Cmte on Naval Affairs: agreed to. 4-Leave obtained to bring in a bill for the relief of the heirs & legal reps of Pierre Dufresne.

New Orleans "Tropic" of Jan 28: Gen Chas Fenton Mercer, who has been long & seriously ill in that city, is recovering his health.

Died: yesterday, after a long & severe illness, Mrs Sophia Frost, w/o John T Frost. Her funeral is on Sunday at 3 o'clock, from her late residence.

MON FEB 8, 1847

House of Reps: 1-Ptn of Clara R Cobb, asking for a pension. 2-Ptn of Trefphey Campbell, praying for the benefit of the acts of Congress granting half-pay pensions to the widows of Revolutionary soldiers. 3-Ptn of Isaac Barnes, for pre-emption of lands in Oregon. 4-Ptn of Jno Harrigan, claiming an invalid pension.

Senate: 1-Ptn from Jean R Beaubion, asking confirmation to his land title. 2-Cmte on Claims: joint resolution for the relief of Caleb Green. Same cmte: bill for the relief of Jos Watson. Also, from the same cmte, House bill for the relief of the estates of Benj Metayer & Francois Gaiennie, dec'd, & for the relief of John C Stewart & others, without amendment. 3-Cmte on Pensions: a bill granting a pension to Abigail Garland, widow of Jacob Garland, dec'd. 4-Cmte of Claims: bill for the relief of Jas S Conway. Same cmte: bill for the relief of Jas F Sothoron.

More murders by Volunteers: one, a Spaniard, named John Leborio, who had just returned from a fishing excursion, & on refusing to give up some fish to some volunteers, was shot dead by one of the party. The other, a slave of Madame Vean, in Ferdinand st, was brutally stabbed so that he died yesterday. -New Orleans Times

Wash Assemblies: 3rd Assembly will take place at Jackson Hall, Feb 8, 1847. Managers:

Hon Geo M Dallas	Richd D Cutts	Gen Geo Gibson, U S A
Hon John Y Mason	Geo Thom, U S A	Maj J D Graham, U S A
Hon E A Hannegan	J H Patterson	Capt Chas Wilkes, USN
Hon Wm Wright	Benj E Green	S L Gouverneur
Hon Ed W Hubard	J Nicholson	Ed de Stoekl
Com L Warrington-USN	Hon Jas Buchanan	J R Goldsborough
Col J G Totten, U S A	Hon Danl Webster	Dr R A Lacey
Capt w H Swift, U S A	Hon T Butler King	A L McCrea
N P Trist	Hon s A Douglass	Dr Robt Ritchie

The Rochester Daily Democrat exposes to public abhorrence a rascal by the name of Danl G Unthank, who, within some 14 years, had married, & successively abandoned, at least 3, & it is said 5 wives. His last victim was Miss Lydia Bush, of Rochester. He had lived in Ohio, Detroit, Canada, & Chautauque Co. He was last seen in Canada. He is 38 years of age, light complexion, about 5 feet 9 inches in height, thick set, about 160 pounds, with black eyes, a blacksmith by trade.

Suffocation from Coal Gas, occurred at Boston on Thu. Mrs Mary Emerson, together with her dght, 20 years of age, & her son, aged 12 years, retired to bed on Wed. In the morning Mrs Emerson was quite dead. The dght was senseless, her limbs very much swollen, & doubtful whether she will recover. The boy is quite ill, but it is thought not dangerously.

Coincidental death of a husband & wife. Sabrine Daly, aged about 40, residing in N Y, died in that city on Wed morning. During her illness her husband was indefatigable in his attentions to her, & seldom left her bedside. The moment she expired he left her room, evincing great agony of mind, & went into another & lay down on the bed, & expressed a wish that he also might die immediately & be buried along with his wife; & in 10 minutes after he also was a corpse. An inquest was held & the surgeon who examined it was of opinion that the cause of his death was congestion of the brain.
-N Y Journal of Commerce

Francis McLaughlin, one of the Keepers on Blackwell's Island, who brought over the prisoners of N Y C to vote at the last election, has been convicted & sentenced to a fine of $150 & 30 days' imprisonment in the City Prison.

Nathan Beman, a Revolutionary hero, died at Chateaugay, Franklin Co, N Y, on Jan 22, in his 90th year. The Albany Evening Journal says: Mr Beman was Ethan Allen's guide at the capture of Ticonderoga. He was intimate in the fort, & conducted Allen directly to Capt De la Place's room. He was at Allen's side when he told the astounded ofcr by whose authority he demanded the surrender of the fort.

Washington Monument Fund: J B H Smith, Treasurer: total in fund: $55,359.66
Cmte: Thos Carbery, Thos Munroe.

For rent: large fire-proof brick Warehouse on 6th st, near Coleman's Nat'l Hotel.
-B H Cheever, at Mrs Macdaniel's, 4½ st.

For rent: convenient 2 story brick house on 17th st, between Pa ave & H st. Apply to Saml Redfern.

Super Valentines & all kinds in the stationery way: W F Bayly, Pa ave, between 11th & 12th sts.

Balt, Feb 6. The mortal remains of Herman S Thomas, the gallant young Texan ranger, who met his death at the battle of Monterey, were conveyed to his original home, near Perrymansville, Harford Co, today, by our military & a large number of citizens, & buried.

A verdict of $5,000 has been obtained in Benton, Missouri, by Mary Jane Robinson against John Jackson, for slander.

Relief of Ireland: the undersigned, in view of the fearful ravages of the famine now prevailing in Ireland, hereby call a public meeting of members of Congress & all others at the seat of Gov't who will co-operate in the movement, for the purpose of devising some general efficient plan whereby the charities of the people of the U S may be concentrated for the relief of that unhappy country from the horrors of death by starvation:

G M Dallas	Thos Corwin	Jos Cilley
Thos J Rusk	Reverdy Johnson	A C Greene

Willie P Magnum	C J Ingersoll	Jas B Bowlin
H Johnson	Howell Cobb	R F Simpson
Danl Webster	Orville Dewey	J D Cummins
E A Hannegan	W W Seaton	J C Dobbin
Lewis Cass	Saml K Cox	J R Giddings
D S Dickinson	J R Ingersoll	Danl P King
John McLean	Abner Lewis	Geo Ashmun
John M Clayton	Thos J Henley	Thos C Ripley
Jos W Chalmers	Jas McDowell	Luther Severance
Wm Allen	Jas Johnson	Alfred Dockery
Robt Dale Owen	Geo Sykes	J A McClernand
I E Holmes	H S Clark	John Wentworth
Geo S Houston	H T Ellett	Thos Ritchie
Jas J Faran	E S Dargan	
R Chapman	Watkins Ligon	

Mobile Register: the steamboat **Tuskaloosa**, which left that city on Jan 28, burst 2 of her boilers. Many of the passengers managed to get ashore before the boat was consumed by fire & were taken on board the ship **Jas Hewitt** & returned to the city. The body of Lt Inge was on board & lost. Following is an imperfect list of those who were lost & injured: Passengers & Crew lost: Wm Tannehill, C Chiles, P F Beasly, & Abraham Flynn, of Eutaw; W R Hassel, of Greensboro; Blauvault Pasteur, 2nd clerk; Clark, 1st mate; Arthur McCoy, 2nd engineer; Hoffman, of Tuskaloosa; Pleasant Hill, of S C. Scalded: Capt Geo Kirk, severely; E P Oliver, 1st clerk, severely; Maj J M Winston, of Eutaw, severely; Capt Hamlett, of Green Co, severely; Capt Asa White, of Eutaw, slightly; Lipscomb, badly; Col Wm Armstead, badly; T J Goldsby, of Dallas, slightly; Ward, pilot, slightly.

Mrd: on Thu, at St John's Church, Gtwn, by Rev J Shiras, Robt Peter, of Montg Co, Md, to Roberta, 2nd daughter of Geo Johnson, of Wash.

Mrd: on Jan 28, by Rev Dr McCullough, Baring Powell, of Phil, to Caroline Bayard, daughter of Hon Richd K Bayard, of Wilmington, Delaware.

Mrd: on Feb 2, in Fred'k, Md, by Rev Mr Stonestreet, Henry Jerningham Boone, M D, to Mary Jane, youngest daughter of Col G M Eichelberger, all of that city.

Died: on Feb 6, after a few day's illness of paralysis, Emelio Franzoni, in his 34th year. His funeral is from the residence of his sister, on Capitol Hill, this morning, at 11 o'clock.

Died: on Feb 6, Brooke M Berry, in his 52nd year. His funeral is from his late residence on Capitol Hill this day, at 12 o'clock.

Died: on Feb 7, Jas Galt, in his 68th year, a native of Carroll Co, Md, but for the last 46 years a resident of this District. His funeral will take place from his late residence, Pa ave, between 9th & 10th sts, tomorrow, at one o'clock.

TUE FEB 9, 1847
By application to Miss Sarah Foster, Principal of the Female Seminary at Washington, Pa, a few young ladies can be obtained well qualified as teachers in Female Seminaries or private families. Reference can be had to J H Ewing, member of Congress from this district, or to the Principal.

Senate: 1-Cmte on Naval Affairs: bill for the relief of the heirs of Andrew D Crosby. Same cmte: bill for the relief of Wm A Christian. 2-Bill for the relief of Thos Blanchard was amended.

WED FEB 10, 1847
Wash Corp: 1-Ptn of Patrick Flemming: referred to the Cmte of Claims. 2-Bill for the relief of O J Prather: passed. 3-Ptn of John Fletcher, praying payment for work done in front of square 427: referred to the Cmte on Improvements. 4-Ptn of Jas Cooper for remission of certain fines & costs alleged to have been illegally imposed on him: referred to the Cmte of Claims.

Paris Press of Jan 2 devotes a column to the necrology of 1846. We make a few extracts: Death has made cruel ravages in the course of the year, which has just expired. Europe has lost Pope Gregory XVI, Francis IV, Duke of Modena, & Prince Louis, ex-King of Holland. Also, the Earl of Granville, for a long time the Ambassador of England in Paris; Baron Bulow, late Prussian Minister of State; Count Tornelli di Vergano, once Viceroy of Sardinia; Lord Metcalf, Govn'r of Canada; the last of the family of Ypsilanti, & the Prince of Mingrelia. Also, the elegant Swiss writer Toppfer, Monsieur de Senancourt, the author of Oberman, & the young Spanish poet Nicholas de Castro. The political press lost the Zoll-verein, Frederic List. We have to enumerate the astronomer Damoiseau, 2 Russian navigators, Krusenstern & Kotzebue; the English chemist Marsh, & our own chemist Chas Deroane. The German astrnometers Besel & Beuzenburg, & the 2 entomologists Dupouchel & Samuel. -Boston Atlas

I hereby caution & forewarn all persons from crediting any person on my account without my written order or the order of my book-keeper, as I am determined not to pay any bills that may be taken up, if any, without the foregoing requisites. -Alfred Lee, Gtwn

Obit-died: on Feb 5, at ***Dunblane***, her late residence in PG Co, Md, Miss Eleanor W Magruder, in her 56th year. The disease of which she died was of a complicated & most painful nature. Brought up in retirement, she shunned the allurements of the world, despised its frivolities & follies, & avoided its temptations & pleasures as uncongenial to her nature. In all the relations of dght, sister, mistress & friend, she was exemplary. All who knew her loved & esteemed her, & her servants, whom she had manumitted, & whom, while living, she treated with singular kindness & humanity, wept bitterly over her lifeless remains. She was buried in the family burial ground, a few rods from the mansion in which she was born, & her dust will soon commingle with that of her kindred & of her who gave her birth.

Died: on Feb 4, in Gtwn, Mrs Jane Cox, w/o Col John Cox. After 20 months of incessant & most wretching suffering, this estimable lady, the last of an old & honorable house, has found repose in death.

Died: on Feb 7, at Gtwn, after a sudden & short illness, Mrs Ann O Marbury, in her 77th year.

Died: on Feb 6, in Phil, M F Peale, eldest daughter of T R Peale, of Wash.

Died: on Feb 8, Louisa Brown Duvall, daughter of A J & Eliza Duvall, aged 18 months & 9 days.

Mrd: on Feb 4, at St Patrick's Church, by Rev Mr Mathews, August A Von Schmidt to Sarah Virginia, eldest daughter of Mr Henry N Young, all of Wash City.

Rooms for rent: on 18th st, near the War & Navy Depts. Apply to Edw Hawkins, on the premises.

Orphans Court of Wash Co, D C. Letters of administration on the personal estate of Robt Wallace, late of said county, dec'd. -Richd W Wallace, adm

Senate: 1-Ptn from John R Goodenough, asking to be allowed bounty land for the services of his father in the Revolutionary war. 2-Ptn from Thos P McBlair, asking that the accounting ofcrs of the Treasury may settle his accounts for payments made the forward ofcrs on board the ship **Princeton**. 3-Ptn from J Dandeger, for a naval pension. 4-Cmte on Public Lands: bill to grant a right of pre-emption to Phillip H Deering & Robt H Champion. Adverse reports made in the cases of Hans Nelson, Josiah Nelson, & the admx of Josiah Houseman.

House of Reps: 1-Ptn of Curtis Hodges, asking for lands in lieu of those he owned in Missouri, & was driven from by the authorities of the State of Missouri. 2-Memorial of Chas F Jones, of Boston, for the payment of the French indemnities. 3-Ptn of John Ferguson, of Alleghany Co, Pa, for a pension. 4-Ptn of Henry Shaffer, of Alleghany Co, Pa, asking for a pension.

Balt, Feb 8. The last sad funeral solemnities of the gallant Col Watson & Capt Ridgely, who nobly fell in the service of their country, took place today.

For rent: well furnished convenient house, at present occupied by Hon Wm S Miller, M C, of N Y: on G st, & in full view of the Pres' house. -D A Gardner, on 12th st, opposite Buist's flower garden.

THU FEB 11, 1847
Senate: 1-Cmte on Private Land Claims: House bill for the relief of Isaac Guess, without amendment. Same cmte: House bill for the relief of the heirs of Hyacinth Lasselle, without amendment.

Mr Jas Roosevelt, of N Y C, died at age 88 years, on Thu last. He had felt none of the infirmities of age until that evening when he was seized with a paralysis. For many years he owned the largest Sugar Finery estate in the city; acquired an ample fortune, & for many years since retired from the active pursuits of life, residing in the summer season at his country seat near Poughkeepsie, & in the winter in his house in N Y C. He was a gentleman of the old school, upright in all his dealings. -N Y Express

Rev Mr Tatam, of Brookfield, Mass, has recovered a verdict of $400 against Mr Adams, of that town, in an action of slander, the latter having accused the former of improper conduct with young ladies connected with his congregation.

Seneca Stewart, who not many years ago was a wealthy merchant in N Y C, was found dead in his room, 21 Bowery, on Sat. He died in utter & wretched poverty.

Cornelius W Terhune, counselor of law, was sentenced on Sat at N Y, in the General Sessions, to 30 days in prison, & to have his name struck from the roll of the court. Wm Davis, a highwayman, was at the same time sentenced to 10 years & 6 months in the State prison.

A y/son of Capt Wiswall, of N Y C, was drowned at Bellville, N J, on Feb 1. In crossing a pond, the ice gave way. The body was recovered in about 15 minutes, but it was too late.

The subscriber is selling off to close out his stock of goods below cost.
-G Broadbent's, La ave & 7th st.

Dissolution of the partnership between Ward & Lenman by mutual consent. -Ward & Lenman [The business will hereafter be carried on at the old stand on 12th st, near the canal, by Ulysses Ward & Son.]

FRI FEB 12, 1847
House of Reps: 1-Ptn of John Adolphus Etzler, of Phil, asking the appointment of a cmte to examine certain valuable inventions which propose an immense saving of power, money, & time in many of the arts. 2-Ptn of Barbara Lancaster, for bounty land due her late husband. 3-Ptn of Jas B Behn, of New Orleans, son & heir of John H Behn, dec'd, praying for remuneration for losses sustained by the seizure & condemnation of his property by the French Gov't.

Chesapeake & Ohio Canal Co: election held Feb 9: the late Board of Pres & Dirs were unanimously re-elected, viz: Pres, Jas M Coale. Dirs: Danl Burkhart, John O Wharton, Robt W Bowie, Frisby Tilghman, Wm Price, John P Ingle

Register's Ofc, Wash, Feb 5, 1847. The following have taken out licenses under the law of the Corp during the month of Jan, 1847.

Alger, J E & Bro: Retail
Ailer & Thyson: Dog
Adams, Washington: Dog
Adams, Jas: Dog
Aigler, Jacob: Dog
Abbot, Jos: Dog
Buckley, T R: Shop
Bayliss & Skidmore: Huckster
Bradley & Bitzel: Huckster
Bank, Joshua: Huckster
Brown, Chas: Huckster
Brown, Reuben: Huckster
Brown, Henry: Huckster
Bohlayer, John jr: Butcher
Bohlayer, John: Butcher
Bihler, G: Butcher
Barber, Geo: Butcher
Berkley, Enos: Butcher
Bihler, G: Huckster
Berkeley, Enos: Butcher
Beasley, Jo: Hack
Blake, J B: Dog
Buckley, J: Dog
Bradey, Peter: Dog
Brown, Wm: Dog
Butler, Jas: Dog
Brown, Wm: Dog
Byrne, Theresa: Dog
Brown, Simon: Dog
Burr, H A: Dog
Borland, Jo: Dog
Berryman, Wm: Dog
Burch, Thos: Dog
Brown, Chas: Dog
Bowie, Arn: Dog
Briscoe, Wm: Dog
Bogan, B L: Dog
Begnam, Gep: Dog-2
Beasly, Jos: Dog
Bihler, G: Dog
Bell, Ellen: Dog
Brown, Basil: Dog
Bronaugh, J W: Dog
Beardsley, Jos: Dog
Bradley, Chas: Dog
Bates, F: Dog
Brashears, Wm: Dog
Butler, Ab: Dog
Birch, Fielder: Dog
Boyle, John: Dog
Cuthbert, Jas: Tavern
Caruthers, Andrew: Retail
Combs, M R: Retail
Cruitt, Jas: Huckster
Cunningham, W: Huckster
Crockett, Davy: Hack
Costin, W C P: Hack
Cripps, Wm McL: Dog
Coyle, Randolph: Dog
Clitz, F: Dog
Caden, Jas: Dog
Coumbe, J T: Dog
Clarke, W H: Dog
Crocket, Davy: Dog
Coyle, Fitzhugh: Dog
Clements, A H: Dog
Calvert, Betsey: Dog
Cassanave, Peter: Dog
Cornish, Wm: Dog
Conian, Peter: Dog
Creutzfeldt, Wm: Dog-2
Coltman, C L: dog
Callan, Lawrence: Shop
Dyer, Giles, 2 slaves
Dowling, Wm: Shop
Dulany, C: Huckster
Digges, Judson, Hack
Dyson, Chas: Dog
Donovan, Wm: Dog
Dove, Wm: Dog
Dyer, Giles: Dog
Doemer, Chas: Dog
Davis, J Y: Dog
Dorsey, Isaac: Dog
Duvall, Geo: Dog
DeSaules, P A: Dog

Dent, Bruce: Dog
Dunwell, Saml: Dog
Dawes, Fred: Dog
Dewdney, J: Dog
Eversfield, E: Male slaves
Eichorn, Geo: Huckster
Eichorn, R: Huckster
Emmerson, G: Butcher
Edmonston, J: Dog
Eckloff, Wm: Dog
Edelin, Jas: Dog
Ennis, Philip: Dog
Earle, Robt: Dog
Evans, F S: Dog
Emert, Henry: Dog
Eichorn, Geo: Dog
Eaton, John H: Dog
Funk, F: Grocery
Frailer, C: Retail
Fischer, Wm: Hardware
Fuller, F W: Medicines
Fowler, W R: Huckster
Farquhar, T C & Co: Medicines
Frank, Jacob: Huckster
Fister, John: Butcher
Fleming, John: Hack
Fowler, John L: Hack
Frailer, Chas: Dog
Ford, Wm: Dog
Forrest, Steph'y: Dog-2
Fries, John: Dog
Follansbeel, Jo: Dog
Francis, Betsey: Dog
Fletcher, John: Dog
Fitnam, Thos: Dog
Finkman, C: Dog
Ferguson, Jo: Dog
Fiser, John: Dog
Green, Amon: Auction
Gordon, D S: Huckster
Guyer, Benedict: Butcher-3
Gibson, John: Hack
Group, Wm: Dog
Goddard, Thos: Dog-2
Gillott, Jos: Dog
Goodall, Thos: Dog
Gunton, Thos: Dog
Godfrey, L: Dog
Gardner, J B: Dog
Guists, M A: Dog
Green, Mantroy: Dog
Gunnell, J L: Dog
Goldsborough, Thos: Dog
Gardner, C K: Dog
Gardner, C K: Dog
Gess, John G: Dog-2
Hawkins, E: Huckster
Hawkins, Peter: Huckster
Haines, Washington: Huckster
Harper, W C: Retail
Howell, John H: Huckster
Howell, W P: Huckster
Homiller, Wm: Butcher
Hoover, Saml: Butcher
Hagar & Henry: Butcher
Hoover, John: Butcher-3
Howard, John: Butcher
Homiller, Chas: Butcher-2
Hoover, Wm: Butcher
Hoover, Saml: Butcher
Harrington, Richd: Stage
Hickerson, Wm: Hack
Harrison, Richd: Dog
Hanger, J R: Dog
Hall, Edw: Dog
Hess, Jacob: Dog
Hickman, J L: Dog
Heitmiler, A: Dog-2
Herold, A H: Dog-2
Holland, Isaac: Dog-2
Hess, Paul: Dog-2
Hunter, Wm: Dog
Hobbie, S R: Dog
Hanly, Jane: Dog
Haliday, Henry: Dog
Homans, Benj: Dog
Heyden, C W: Dog
Herbert, Wm: Dog
Hawkins, M: Dog
Horstkamp, Henry: Dog

Henning, Stephen: Dog
Hickman, Jas: Dog
Hicks, Chas: Dog
Hagar & Henry: Dog-2
Jillard, J & Son: Hardware
Johnstone, Thos: Huckster
Jenkins, David: Huckster
Johnson, W C: Huckster
Johnson, D R: Dog-3
Jackson, B & Bro: Dog
Jones, John B: Dog
Jones, Alfred: Dog
Jennings, Polly: Dog
Jordan, Harriet: Dog-2
Jost, B: Dog
Johnson, Lewis: Dog
Jones, Raphael: Dog
Ingle, John P: Dog
Jackson, Susan: Dog
Kilmiste, M: Theatrical-4
Kingman, E: Male slave
Knott, J H: Boots & shoes
Keating, Geo W: Butcher-3
Kidwell, A C: Dog
Krafft, C: Dog
Kingman, E: Dog
Kirby, Saml: Dog
Kuhl, Henry: Dog
Krafft, J M: Dog
Leddy, Owen, Huckster
Lowe, M: Huckster
Lane, John: Huckster
Lefler, John: Huckster
Lewis, Benj: Huckster
Lavender, Jas: Huckster
Lisha & Laskey: Huckster
Little, John: Butcher-4
Little, Saml: Butcher-3
Lancaster, C: Dog
Landrick, H: Dog
Larned, Jas: Dog
Laub, John Y: Dog
Lord, Wm: Dog
Lambell, K H: Dog
Landrick, J: Dog
Lavender, J: Dog
Leddy, Owen: Dog
Lewis, Saml: Dog
Lewis, Saml: Dog
Law, J G: Dog
Lamright, Geo: Dog
Morgan, T P: Medicine
Maguire, J: Hats
McDevitt, J: Grocery
Mudd, Edw: Huckster
Morgan, Wm: Retail
Moore, H W: Huckster
Mankins, Wash: Huckster
Mortimer & Birch: Huckster
Miller, Chas: Butcher
Muse, Lindsay, Dog
Magruder, R: Dog
Mankin, J: Dog
McCoy, S: Dog
Mason, John: Dog
Martin, J W: Dog
Marks, S A HP Dog
McCormick, A T: Dog
McIntire, Alex: Dog
Moore, Wm: Dog
McCleary, J: Dog
Marshall, Wm: Dog
Meehan, C H W: Dog
Masi, F & Co: Dog-2
Muller, Bazil: Dog
Merelesh, Chas: Dog
Mohler, F: Dog
Miller, Chas: Dog-2
Nourse, John: Dog
Nichols, Thos: Dog
Nichols, J N: Dog
Nugent, Eli: Dog
Norbeck, Geo: Dog
Oyster, J H: Huckster
Otterback, Philip: Butcher-3
Owner, Jas: Dog
Ober & Ryon: Dog
Orr, Sarah: Dog
Otterback, Philip: Dog-2
Plant, J W: Grocery

Paxton, John: Huckster
Pumphrey, L: Dog-2
Pursell, Thos: Dog
Peirce, J M: Dog
Plant, J K: Dog
Peck, Jos: Dog
Powell, Thos: Dog
Peterson, Wm: Dog
Phillips, Reuben: Dog
Pepper, John P: Dog
Pleasants, S: Dog
Prather, Alfred: Dog
Prather, O J: Dog
Peirce, Jas M: Huckster
Robertson, Danl: Grocery
Rived, Cort'y: Huckster
Ricketts, A: Huckster
Richardson, C T E: Huckster
Robinson & Burns: Dog
Rhodes, Jas: Butcher-3
Rawlings, David: Butcher
Roth, A: Dog
Roberts, J M: Dog-2
Robertson, Henry: Dog-2
Rochat, Henry: Dog
Riddall, W C: Dog
Randall, H K: Dog
Riordan, Jas: Dog
Ritter, H G: Dog
Rutherford, A: Dog
Redfern, Saml: Dog
Rives, John C: Dog-2
Shad & Heisler: Retail
Sisson, John A: Huckster
Stoops, Richd: Retail
Shreve, John: Huckster
Shreve, Saml: Huckster
Shreve, Caleb: Huckster
Shaw, John: Huckster
Spignall, W B: Huckster
Shedd, J J: Butcher
Spicer, Fred'k: Butcher-3
Stepper, Andrew: Butcher
Shedd, J J: Butcher
Spicer, Fred'k: Butcher
Shaffer, Jonathan: Stage
Sheckell, B O: Hack
Stewart, J C: Dog
Sewall, Richd: Dog
Seaton, W W: Dog
Stewart, Geo: Dog
Sengstack, C P: Dog
Sanders, Hart: Dog
Spignal, Wm: Dog
Shorter, Bazil: Dog
Sweeny, Geo: Dog
Sweeny, H B: Dog
Stott, Saml: Dog
Smith, Thos: Dog-2
Scott, Stephen: Dog
Simms: Ann: Dog
Shepherd, Peter: Dog
Sweeny, Ed: Dog
Shinn, Michl: Dog
Simms, Eleanor: Dog
Sweeting, H W: Dog
Spicer, Fred'k: Dog
Sioussi, John, jr: Dog
Tenant, John: Huckster
Tucker, Jas: Butcher
Thoms, Chas: Butcher-2
Tastet, Nicholas: Dog
Tchiffely, F: Dog
Tonge, J T: Dog
Taylor, R A: Dog
Tinney, Pompey: Dog
Taylor, A S: Dog
Taylor, Hudson: Dog
Thomas, Chas: Dog-2
Upsher, John: Dog
Van Zandt, N B: Dog
Upperman, C E: Dog
Wilson, John: Female slave
Wise, Wm: Retail
Wilson, Thos C: Retail
Whittlesey, O: Hardware
Wallace, Jas: Huckster
Williams, H: Huckster
Wilson, J L: Huckster
Walker & Peck: Butcher-3

Wilson, Wm: Butcher
Walker, Lewis: Butcher-2
Weaver, David: Butcher-2
Weaver, David: Butcher
Walker & Peck: Butcher
Weaver, Henry: Butcher
Williams, T J: Dog
Wheat, Mary: Dog
Washburn, Ann: Dog-2
Whitwell, J C : Dog
Wood, Wm: Dog
Winston, J W: Dog-2
Wright, Henry: Dog
Williams, Z: Dog
Weber, Chris: Dog
Werner, J H T: Dog
Warrington, L: Dog
Wilson, John D: Dog
Wallace, Wm: Dog
Willett, V: Dog
Yerby & Brother: Dry goods
Young, A H: Huckster
Yeabower, Chris: Butcher-3
Young, A H: Dog
Person fined: Funk, N: Confectioner. Person fined: Tuner, Galen: Hack
Fined during Dec & Jan for failing to procure their licenses & selling without:
Beneget, H: Hack
Brown, Benton: Hack
Boone, M: Huckster
Bean, Geo: Huckster
Brown, Wm: Dog
Brown, Henson: Dog
Persons fined:
Callan Lawrence-$20
Diggs, Judson: Hack
Jenkins, A D: Hack
Knott, J H: Groceries
McBlair, J H: Retail
Morgan, Thos P: Medicine
McKnight, Mrs: Huckster
Paris, A: Hack
Riggs, W: Hack
Roberts, John: Groceries
Weatherby & Bates: Medicine
Welsh, Thos: Shop
Williams, Zad: [blank]

I certify that Mrs Sarah Naylor, of Wash Co, D C, brought before me as an estray trespassing on her enclosure for the last 12 or 18 months, a red & white heifer.
-H Naylor, J P [Owner to come forward, prove property, pay charges, & take her away.
-Sarah Naylor.]

Senate: 1-Ptn from F A Parker, U S Navy, asking to be allowed incidental expenses incurred in conveying the American mission to China. 2-Ptn from G W Fulton, in relation to his improvement for propelling vessels by steam. 3-Ptn from Jas Pennoyer, asking compensation for injuries done to his vessel in rescuing the U S brig **Porpoise**. 4-Ptn from David N Smith, asking a pension. 5-Ptn from the legal reps of Chas Porterfield, asking to be allowed bounty land & commutation pay. 6-Cmte on Public Lands: adverse report on the memorial of John E Caro, keeper of the public archives in Florida. 7-Cmte on Patents: joint resolution for the relief of John & Chas Bruce, with out amendment.

During the late severe gale at New Orleans a seaman fell overboard from the barque **Rothschild**, & Jack Jones, a Welchman plunged into the river to rescue him. He rescued the sailor, but Jones sunk & drowned.

SAT FEB 13, 1847
Senate: 1-Cmte on Military Affairs: bill for the relief of Gen Robt Armstrong: ordered to a 3rd reading. 2-Bill for the relief of John More: passed.

House of Reps: 1-Bills/Acts referred to appropriate cmtes: relief of: Jos Wilson; Shadrack Gillet & others; Thos Brownwell; Thos Douglas, late U S Atty for East Florida; legal reps of Jaques Moulon; Geo Gordon; Nathl Kuykendall; Thos Rhodes; personal rep of Wm A Slacum, dec'd; Madison Allen; Peter Capello, administrator of Andrew Capello, dec'd, & for the relief of John Capello; Francis Summeraner; Peter Frost; Orlando Saltmarsh & Wm Fuller. Pension to John Clark; & to Jos Morrison.

Mrd: on Feb 10, by Rev Dr Dewey, Francis Schroeder to Carolina Seaton, daughter of W W Seaton, Mayor of Washington.

Died: on Feb 11, in Wash City, Mr Henry Bowen, aged 26 years. His funeral is this morning, at 11 o'clock, from the residence of Mr Geo W Stewart, corner of 12th & H sts.

Died: on Feb 12, after a long & painful illness, Isaac T Ellwood, in his 38th year, formerly of N Y, but for the last 16 years a resident of Wash City. His funeral is from his late residence at the corner of B & 6th sts north, on Sunday next at 2 o'clock.

The Very Rev P Verhaegan, Provincial of the Society of Jesuits, will preach at St Peter's Church, Capitol Hill, tomorrow, at 11 o'clock.

Trustee's sale of lot, by deed of trust from Jos Marteni to the subscriber, lot 12 in square 818, fronting on 5th st east, between A & B sts south. -Nicholas Callan, Trustee
-R W Dyer, auct

MON FEB 15, 1847
Senate: 1-Cmte on Naval Affairs: bill for the relief of the heirs of Andrew D Crosby. Same cmte: bill for the relief of Wm A Christian. 2-Bill for the relief of Thos Blanchard was amended.

Jas Gartland, an Irishman, about 35 years of age, is now in our City Infirmary, as a person of unsound mind. Since his stay at the infirmary he is much better in the mind. It is hoped to call the attention of the Phil press of this distressing situation. He says he had a brother, John Gartland, who lives in Schuylkill, 2nd st, & a wife living at the corner of 7th & Lombard sts.

House of Reps: 1-Memorial of Thos Lloyd Halsey et al, asking indemnity for French spoliations.

Miss Heaney's Academy-Capitol Hill, Wash: Miss Heaney, Principal. This Institution, re-established in a very healthful residence near the Capitol, & is designed for the education of a small number of boarding & day scholars.

Orphans Court of Wash Co, D C. Letters of administration on the personal estate of Eliz Pierce, late of said county, dec'd. -Henry Ould, adm

Mr Halse has recovered $10,000 damages against Jos Prigg, of Phil, for malicious arrest in 1843. Mr Halse was just starting from Boston in the steamer for England, & for a time his credit was seriously injured.

Lost on Feb 12, between the store of the subscriber, on Bridge st, near High, & the Treasury bldg, Wash, a Cameo Breastpin, with a female bust. Suitable reward by leaving it at the store. -Wm J Stoops

Mr Stephen Stilwell, one of the oldest & most respectable inhabitants of N Y C, died on Fri, aged 87. He was a native of Jamaica, L I, but was a resident of N Y for nearly the whole of his life. He resided there before the war of the Revolution, when the city was but a handful of people. He witnessed the battles of Long Island, & the retreat of Gen Washington & his army through the city. He was twice taken prisoner by the Hessians. He became a merchant in Pearl st, & afterwards a custom-house ofcr. He died of a sound mind till the close of life. -Express

Strayed, on Feb 10, a black Newfoundland Dog, about 8 months old, answers to the name of Zarrass. Libery reward for return of said dog to A N Von Schmidt, on F st, between 9th & 10th sts.

Died: on Feb 13, in Gtwn, Mr Peter Ritter, in his 80th year, a native of Gundishwyle, Canton of Berne, Switzerland, & for the last 45 years a resident of Gtwn.

TUE FEB 16, 1847

Norfolk Herald brings the news of the death of John Cowper, in his 84th year. This venerable citizen from 1804 to 1815 was the editor of the political newspaper, entitled the Public Ledger. [No date-current item.]

Mrs Sarah Underwood, of N Y, is now in this city, having in her possession, & intending to make a public exhibition of them, the original papers found upon the person of Maj Andre, when arrested as a spy during the Revolutionary war. The historical interest of these papers, in connexion with the treason of Arnold & the melancholy fate of Andre, makes them objects of great curiosity.

Senate: 1-Ptn from Chas Stearns, asking to be reimbursed for certain costs to which he was subjected in a certain suit against him by the U S. 2-Ptn from Thos P Harrison, asking confirmation to a certain tract of land. 3-Cmte on pensions: House bills for the relief of Jas Green, of Fauquier Co, Va, & for the relief of Wilfred Kisote, without amendment. 4-Cmte of Claims: House bill for the relief of Jno Pickett & others, without amendment.

Orphans Court of PG Co, Md. Letters testamentary on the estate of Eleanor W Magruder, late of said county, dec'd. -C B Hamilton, exc

Balt, Feb 15, 1847. The jury who had charge of the case of the State vs Geo Campbell, Geo James, & Robt Perry, indicted for having defrauded a young man of this city, Isaac Jones, out of $10,500, by means of gambling, brought into court this morning a verdict of guilty. The penalty for the offence is a fine & imprisonment in the common jail for from 1 to 10 years.

Valuable Paper Mill, with machinery, & dwlg house, at Manayune, for sale: on Mar 9, at the Phil Exchange. The dwlgs are of stone & are on the westerly side of the Schuylkill river. -M Thomas & Son, auctioneers, 93 Walnut st, Phil, Pa.

Household & kitchen furniture at auction: on Feb 19, at the residence of Mrs Henry, on 12th st, between I & E Sts, near Franklin row. -A Green, auctioneer

WED FEB 17. 1847

Wash Corp: 1-Ptn from Wm D Bell for the remission of a fine: referred to the Cmte of Claims. Same for Timothy K Buckley. 2-Statement from Richd Butt in relation to the report of the Select Cmte for the Asylum. 3-Ptn from W C Johnson, in relation to a stall purchased by him in the Northern Market: referred to the Cmte of Claims.

Chas Coffin Jewett, now librarian & professor of modern language in Brown Univ, has lately received the appointment of Assist Secretary & Librarian of the Smithsonian Institute. He is a Massachusetts man, the son of a highly respectable clergyman formerly settled in Scituate. He was educated at Brown Univ.

House of Reps:;1-Resolved that the manuscript work embracing the public accounts from Mar 4, 1789 to 1829, purchased by order of the House of Henry Elliot at the last session of Congress, & now in possession of the Clerk of this House, if conducive to the public interest that the same be printed. 2-Cmte on Military Affairs: reported a bill for the relief of Titian R Peale; which bill was committed. Same cmte: Senate bill for the relief of Jos Wilson: Committed. Same cmte: bill for the relief of Thos Ap C Jones: committed. Same cmte: bill for the relief of Edw Quinn: committed. 3-Cmte on Patents: bill for the relief of Elisha H Holmes: committed. 4-Cmte of Claims: bill for the relief of Barcley & Livingston & Smith, Thurger & Co: committed. 5-Cmte of Ways & Means was discharged from the consideration of the ptns of Chas Blakslee & of S S Bowen, & laid on the table.
6-Cmte on Revolutionary Claims: bill from the Senate for the relief of the heirs of Crocker Sampson, dec'd: committed. 7-Cmte on Private Land Claims: bill for the relief of Wm Triplet, of Missouri: Committed. 8-Cmte on Public Lands: Senate bill for the relief of Madison Allen; committed.

Senate: 1-Ptn from Johnson Lykins, asking compensation for attending certain Indians as their physician. 2-Ptn from the heirs of Arnold D Crosby, for a pension.

The remains of Brig Gen Thos L Hamer, of the Ohio volunteers, who lately died at Monterey, were received at Cincinnati on Thu last, on their way to his late residence in Gtwn, Ohio, where they are to be interred with public honors.

Sale of personal property: in virtue of authority vested in him by the last will & testament of Eleanor W Magruder, late of PG Co, Md, the subscriber will proceed to sell, at the late residence of the dec'd, on Mar 1, all such articles of personal property as the will directs to be sold, consisting of horses, hogs, sheep, cattle, instruments of agriculture, tobacco, together with the corn & bacon belonging to the estate. -C B Hamilton, exc

Mrd: on Mon, by Rev John C Smith, Mr John Hamilton to Mrs Ann McFarley, all of Wash City.

Mrd: on Feb 14, in Wash City, by Rev Mr Sprole, Geo F Reed, of West Stockbridge, Mass, to Jane C Thorp, eldest daughter of the late Robt A Thorp, of Perth Amboy, N J.

THU FEB 18, 1847

To let: a 3 story brick house & back bldgs, on south side of Pa ave, between 9th & 10th sts. Apply to Jno Alexander, Agent, Pa ave, between 12th & 13th sts.

Saml Stettinius, Magistrate, Notary Public, Conveyancer, & Genr'l Agent, has opened an ofc on La ave, Wash City, where he is ready to attend to any business which may be confied to him in the above lines.

Orphans Court of Wash Co, D C. Letters of administration on the personal estate of Isaac T Elwood, late of said county, dec'd. -Edn N Roach, adm

Attention Ironmongers & Capitalist. Public sale of valuable furnace property & lands: pursuant to a decree of the Circuit Superior Court of Law & Chancery for Shenandoah Co, Va, in the suit of Ball & others, against Jas Sterrett's administrator & others, I shall offer for sale on Mar 20 next, at the Furnace on Wait's Run, in Hardy Co, Va, near Wardensville, the lands descended from Jas Sterrett, dec'd, to his heirs, consisting of the ***Furnace Tract*** of 124 acres & various other tracts of land. Also, the interest of said heirs in a tract of land of 100 acres held jointly with Alex'r M Sterrett, & in one of 76 acres, owned jointly with Moses Wilson. Information given by John Leggit, near Wardensville, or by Robt J Tilden, at Morsefield. -Jas Wetten, Sheriff of Hardy, Com'r

John McDevitt, informs his friends & the public that he has taken out an auction license for the purpose of selling real & personal property, & hopes to obtain a share of public patronage. Store on La ave & 7th st.

Mrd: Feb 14, by Rev Mr Carr, Mr Wm N Burch to Miss Eliz M Baden, all of PG Co, Md.

I caution all persons from harboring or trusting my son Wm on my account, as I am determined not to pay any debts of his contracting. -T Collins

Senate: 1-Ptn from Saml P Armstrong & others, of Lewis Co, Ky, asking that a pension may be granted to Arthur Stevenson. 2-Ptn from the legal reps of the late Cmdor Dale, of Phil, who was a lt with the celebrated John Paul Jones. Resolved: that the Cmte on Pensions inquire into the expediency of granting a pension to Arthur Stevenson. 3-Cmte on Patents: bill to extend a patent heretofore granted to Bancroft Woodcock. 4-Following bills were read a 3rd time & passed: relief of Jeanette C Huntington, widow & sole executrix of Wm D Cheever, dec'd. Relief of: Thos Brownell; Susan E Gordon; Wm G Davis & Mary Ann, his wife; Hobson Johns; Saml Bell, a native of the Cherokee nation; heirs of John Paul Jones; Milledge Galphin, exc of the last will & testament of Geo Galphin, dec'd; Chas M Gibson; Eliz Pistole, widow of Chas Pistole, dec'd; Richd Bloss & others; Joshua Shaw; Thos H Noble; Jas McIntosh; Geo Roush; Fernando Fillany; Jos F Caldwel; Peter Engels, sr. 5-Bill to compromise the claims of the heirs or legal reps of John Smith T, under a Spanish grant: passed. 6-Bill providing for the payment of the claim of Walter R Johnson against the U S: passed. 7-Settlement of the accounts of Jos Nourse, dec'd: passed. 8-Payment of a sum of money to Robt Purkis: passed. 9-Act granting a pension to Patrick Kelley: passed. 10-Bill for the relief of Capt Jesse D Elliot was considered in Cmte of the Whole.

Died: on Feb 17, Geo Abbott, son of J A M & Martha Duncanson, aged 2 years & 11 months. His funeral will take place tomorrow at 12 o'clock.

Died: on Feb 9, at his residence in Monroe Co, Va, the Hon Hugh Caperton, aged 67 years. He was an honored Rep in Congress from his state about the period of the last war.

Died: on Feb 6, at his residence in PG Co, Md, Ebsworth Bayne, aged 79 years. He was extensively known in the community which he was so long a member. After a severe struggle with disease, which lasted several weeks, he died amidst sorrowing friends & affectionate relatives, who followed his remains to the grave in unusual numbers & solemnity.

C W Feeks will reopen his School on Feb 18, in the room over Messrs Walker & Kimmell's ofc, on C st, between 4½ & 6th sts.

Land for sale: tract called the ***Forest***, in Montg Co, Md, on the main road leading from Gtwn to Rockville: contains about 250 acres. Apply to the subscriber, on the premises, or to J M Maccubbin, Alexandria. -Zach Maccubbin

FRI FEB 19, 1847

New Hardware Store: at our new Granite Front Warehouse, sign of the Gilt Plane, s e corner of Bridge & High sts. Entrance 1st door from the corner in either st.
-Muncaster & Dodge, Gtwn

Public sale: on Feb 24, on the premises, near Capitol Hill Market-house, one small brick house on square 787, being part of lot 5, seized & taken as the property of the late Mrs Martin, to satisfy ground rent due in arrears to Henry Bradley. -Hanson Brown, Bailiff

House of Reps: 1-Ptn of the heirs & reps of Oliver Keating, late of Boston, for the payment of the French indemnities. 2-Ptn of Pelham Holmes & others, praying indemnity for spoliations by France prior to 1800. 3-Memorial of Jas Owen, of Wilmington, N C, [by his atty, Geo Little,] as legal rep of Jas Porterfield. 4-Ptn of John T Ball, of Indiana, for further allowance. 5-Presented: the drawing & documents of Thos Gregg, of Fayette Co, Pa, in relation to a ball-proof steamer as invented by him.

Lt Col Fremont, the distinguished young ofcr, we believe, a native of Charleston, the citizens are about to present him with a sword as a mark of their respect & admiration.

Senate: 1-Cmte on Private Land Claims: bill confirming the claim of the heirs & legal reps of Pierre Dufresne to a tract of land, without amendment. 2-Cmte on Patents: bill for the relief of the legal reps of Uri Emmons. Same cmte: bill for the relief of Oliver C Harris. 3-Bill for the relief of Wm Marvin, in confirming the title to a tract of land in Florida, granted by the Spanish Gonv't to Bernando Segui on Dec 20, 1815. 4-Bill to authorize the issuing of a new register for the American barque **Pons**, of Phil, by the name of the barque **Cordelia**. 5-Right of pre-emption to Philip F Dering & Robt H Champlin to a tract of mineral land: passed. 6-Bill directing the Sec of the Navy to purchase from Dr Jas P Espy his patent right for the conical ventilator for the use of the U S Navy: passed. 7-Bill to provide for the final settlement of the accounts of Thos C Sheldon, late receiver of public moneys at Kalamazoo, Michigan: passed. 8-Relief of the heirs & reps of the late Robt Sewell: passed. 9-Relief of Ray Tompkins & others, children & heirs at law of the late Danl D Tompkins: passed. 10-Bill confirming the title of a tract of land to the heirs & legal reps of Pierre Dufresne: passed. 11-Bill for the relief of Gen Robt Armstrong was taken up, &, after having been debated at length, was finally laid on the table. 12-Pension to Abigail Garland, widow of Jacob Garland, dec'd: passed. 13-Pension to Bethia Healy, widow of Geo Healy, dec'd: passed. 14-Following bills were passed: <u>relief of:</u>

Wade Allen
Andrew Moore
Alfred White
Mary Ann Linton
Robt M Harrison
Creed Taylor
Hiers of Jethro Wood
John Bronson
John Devlin
Pearson Cogswell
Caleb Green
Jos Watson
Jas S Conway
Jas F Sothron
Wm A Christian
John & Chas Bruce
John R Williams
Heirs of Andrew D Crosby
Heirs of Louis de la Houssaye

Dr Edson, the living skeleton, who has been recently exhibited at the Museum in N Y, died in that city on Saturday of some pulmonary affection. His brother, Calvin Edson, wasted away so that he, like the Dr, became literally nothing but skin & bones. The other members of the family were rather fleshy.

$10 reward: stolen on Feb 18, from the boarding house of Mrs Wise, on 13th st, a gilt silver Watch, Lepine, with enamel dial & Roman figures. There was attached to it a gold vest-chain of round French manufacture & a silk guard. -John B Gluok

Lawrie Spence, a "nice young man", who made a business of raising money for his own private purse by representing himself as an indigent theological student, has been sentenced to the State prison for one year by the Boston Municipal Court.

Pocket book lost yesterday: containing a note drawn by J Mason, payable to & endorsed by J M Mason, payable at the Bank of the Metropolis, dated Feb, 1847, 90 days, for $1,500. A note drawn by Geo C Bomford, dated Gtwn, Nov 14, 1846, at 4 months, in favor of M Mason, for $200. A note drawn by W W Hunter, dated Washington, Jun, 1846, 12 months, in favor of M Mason, for $170 or $180. A reward will be given for book & contents. Inquire at the Union Hotel, Gtwn.
-Maynadier Mason

Lawrie Spence, a "nice young man", who made a business of raising money for his own private purse by representing himself as an indigent theological student, has been sentenced to the State prison for one year by the Boston Municipal Court.

$10 reward: stolen on Feb 18, from the boarding house of Mrs Wise, on 13th st, a gilt silver Watch, Lepine, with enamel dial & Roman figures. There was attached to it a gold vest-chain of round French manufacture & a silk guard.
-John B Gluok

By virtue of 3 writs of venditoni exponas: I will expose for sale at public auction on the premises, on Mar 20, for cash, all the right, title, interest, & estate in & to lots 1 & 2 in square 405, with improvements, in Washington City, D C, the property of Owen Connolly, seized & taken in execution at the suit of Chas W Boteler, John M Donn, & Nicholas McGregor, late trading under the firm of Boteler, Donn & McGregor, in two of the cases, & one in Chas W Boteler, John M Donn, & Chas W Boteler, jr, late trading under the firm of Boteler, Donn & Co, all for the use of Chas W Boteler & Nicholas McGregor, trading under the firm of Boteler & McGregor.
-H R Maryman, Constable

Trustee's sale of valuable property: by deed of trust from John Young, dated Nov 4, 1839, recorded in Liber W B 82, folios 302 thru 305, one of the land records of Wash Co: sale on Mar 22, of part of lot 9 in square 290, with a 2 story brick & frame house. Property is on 13th, between E & F sts. -Henry Naylor, Trustee -R W Dyer, auct

By writ of venditioni exponas: I will expose to sale, at public auction, on the premises, on Mar 20, on the premises, all the right, title, & interest in & to one 2 story brick dwlg house, on the east side of 5th st west, the 2nd door from the corner of H st north, in Wash City, the property of Thos W Burche, seized & taken in execution at the suit of Hilary C Spalding. -H R Maryman, Constable

Mrd: yesterday, by Rev John C Smith, Mr John T Coombs to Miss Ann Matilda Kendrick, all of Wash City.

By virtue of 2 orders of distrain for rent due to Zackariah Hazell by John A Casper, & to me directed, I will expose at public sale on Feb 23, for cash, on the premises occupied by the said John A Casper, on 2nd st east, near Md ave, Capitol Hill, in Wash City, the goods & chattels, to wit: 2 clocks, 1 bureau, 2 stoves, 1 desk, 4 tables, 7 pieces of tinware, 12 chairs, a lot of earthen & crockeryware, 1 silver watch, 1 iron pot, 2 looking glasses, 1 gun, 1 washstand, bowl, & pitcher, 1 box, 1 triangle or stand, 5 window curtains, 1 carryall, 1 buggy, 1 cartbody, 1 wagon-body, 2 wheels, & 1 wheelbarrow.
-H R Maryman, Bailiff

SAT FEB 20, 1847
Shannondale Springs for sale: lying in Jefferson Co, Va, about 5 miles from Charlestown, the county town: large Boarding House of brick & frame, 133 feet by 30, well finished: nearly 200 acres. Property will be exposed at publics sale, on Mar 15 next, at the Court-house in Charlestown, Jefferson Co, Va. -Bushrod C Washington, Pres of S S Co. Andrew Kennedy, Sec. Feb 18, 1847

House of Reps: 1-Bills for the relief of Robt T Norris, & for the relief of the heirs of the Marshal de Rochambeau, were acted on, & ordered to be reported to the House with the recommendation that they do not pass. 2-Bill for the relief of the heirs of John Paul Jones was taken up. Mr Yost moved to extend the distribution of the prize-money to the ofcrs, seamen, & marines of the squadron under his [John Paul Jones'] command, who are citizens of the U S, or their reps: agreed to. Mr Daniel moved to cut off the interest: agreed to. 3-Bill taken up for the relief of: heirs of Tarlton Woodson, dec'd: laid on the table. 4-Bills taken up & passed: relief of: Eliz Converse, widow of Josiah Converse; of the legal reps of the late Jos E Primeau & Thos J Chapman; of the heirs of Silas Duncan, dec'd; of Jos Gideon; of David Myerle; of Capt Jas Pennoyer; of Lewis C Sartori; of the legal reps of Simon Spaulding, dec'd; of the legal reps of Wm Bunce, dec'd; joint resolution for the relief of M A Price & E A White. 5-Bill to grant a pre-emption right to the heirs or legal reps of John Smith T, which had been reported by the Cmte of the Whole with an amendment. The amendment was read as follows: And provided that if any private rights exist to any part of said location adverse to that of the claimants herein, the same shall be reserved, & saved to said adverse claimants. Agreed to. 6-Bill for the relief of Martha Clark: laid on the table. 7-Engrossed bill for the relief of the legal reps of Jas H Clark: passed. 8-Bill for the relief of Thos Wishart: rejected. 9-Bill for the relief of John Ericson: laid on the table. 10-Bill for the relief of the legal reps of Jos E Primeau & Thos J Chapman: passed. 11-Bills for the relief of the heirs of the Marshal de Rochambeau, & for the relief of Robt T Norris: said bills stand rejected. 12-Bill for the relief of John Paul Jones: passed. 13-Act for the relief of Fernando Fillany: referred. 13-Act to authorize the Sec of the Treas to purchase for the U S the interest of Balie Peyton in the tract of land upon which the lighthouse stands at the Southwest Pass, at the mouth of the Mississippi river. 14-Act for the relief of Jeanette C Huntington, widow & sole executrix of Wm D Cheever, dec'd: referred. 15-Act for the relief of Thos Brownwell; of Susan E Gordon; of

Wm G Davis & Mary Ann, his wife; of Saml W Bell, a native of the Cherokee nation; of Hobson Johns: all referred to appropriate cmte. 16-Bills referred: Act for the relief of Milledge Galphin, exc of the last will & testament of Goe Galphin, dec'd. Act to authorize the payment of a sum of money to Robt Purkis. Act for the relief of: Chas M Gibson; of Eliz Pistole, widow of Chas Pistole, dec'd. Act for the relief of Richd Bloss & others: of Thos H Noble; of Jas McIntosh; of Geo Roush; of Jos F Caldwell; of Peter Engls, sen. 17-Act to authorize the settlement of the account of Jos Nourse, dec'd: referred. 18-Bill from the Senate for the relief of the heirs of Jethro Wood was taken up: laid on the table.

An advertisement of my property at a constable's sale having appeared in the papers, to take place Mar 2 next, to satisfy several executions, it has become my unpleasant duty to inform the public that the debts for which those executions have been rendered were not created by me as principal, but as endorser for Wm Cleary, a clerk in the ofc of the Solicitor of the Treasury, who is not now prepared to meet his obligations. Yet I am determined to satisfy them myself. The claimants gave no order to the constable to pursue the course which he has thought fit to adopt in the premises. -Owen Connolly

Cedar & locust timber: to be delivered at the landing in the town of Port Royal, on the Rappahannock river. Address to J H Banning.

Household & kitchen furniture at auction: on Feb 26, at the residence of the Hon W J Brown, corner of 7th D sts. -A Green, auctioneer

Senate: 1-Cmte of Commerce: adverse report on the ptn of Robt Dedrick. Same cmte: ptn of Ichabod Jordan: Sec of Treas to report his reasons for any modifications of the law in relation to collectors. 2-Cmte of Claims: bill for the relief of Ann B Carr. Same cmte: bill for the relief of Elisha N Keene.

Mrd: on Feb 18, by Rev Mr Eggleston, Mr Jos B Stanley to Miss Susannah, daughter of Mr Jas Jack, all of Wash City.

Died: on Feb 7, at New Lisbon, Ohio, Caroline, youngest daughter of Jacob Janney, late of Wash, in her 19th year.

Died: on Feb 18, at Upper Marlborough, after a severe illness of 10 days, in her 24th year, Zeleima F, consort of Danl C Digges, & daughter of the late David M Forrest. Her funeral is on Feb 20 from her late residence, at 12 o'clock.

MON FEB 22, 1847

Senate: 1-Ptn from John Hagan, E Lackett, & Therman Johnson, citizens of Louisiana, asking compensation for slaves liberated by the British authorities at Nassau, N P, when an American vessel put in there in distress. 2-Ptn from Rachael Maule, asking indemnity for French spoliations prior to 1800. 3-Cmte of Claims: Bill for the relief of Wm H Prentiss. Same cmte: bill for the relief of Hola to Emathala & other Seminole Indians.

4-Cmte on the Judiciary: memorial of Edmond J Forstall, in behalf of Hope & Co, of Amsterdam, & others, submitted a report, with a resolution directing the Sec of Treas & the Atty Gen to examine into the case fully: to be printed. 5-Cmte on Pensions: bill for the relief of David N Smith. 6-Cmte of Claims: bill for the relief of Jas Pennoyer.

On Apr 30, 1789, the Constitutional Gov't of the U S began, by the inauguration of Geo Washington as Pres of the U S, in N Y C. Osgood's house, a mansion of very moderate extent, was fixed upon as the residence of the Chief Magistrate: situated in Cherry st. The Pres' family consisted of Mrs Washington, the 2 adopted children, Mr Lear, as principal secretary, Col Humphreys, with Messrs Lewis & Nelson, secretaries, & Maj Wm Jackson, aid-de-camp. In the Senate were several members of the Congress of 1776 & signers of the Declaration of Independence-Richd Henry Lee, who moved the Declaration, John Adams, who seconded it, with Sherman, Morris, & Carroll. Mrs Washington's drawing-rooms, on Fri nights, were attended by the grace & beauty of N Y. Owing to the lowness of the ceiling, the ostrich feathers in the head dress of Miss McIlver, a belle of N Y, took fire from the chandelier, to the no small alarm of the company. Maj Jackson clapped the burning plumes between his hands, extinguishing the flame. Washington rose at 4 o'clock & retired to bed at 9. Bishop, the celebrated body servant of Braddock, was the master of Washington's stables. The Pres' stables in Phil were under the direction of German John. There was but one theatre in N Y in 1789, in John st. It was in the theatre that the now national air of Hail Columbis, then called the Pres' March, was first played. It was composed by a German musician, named Fyles, the leader of the orchestra, in compliment to the Pres. While residing in Cherry st, the Pres was attacked by a severe illness, that required a surgical operation. He was attended by the older & younger Drs Bard. The younger Dr Bard performed the operation, which proved successful. The mansion in Cherry st proved so very inconvenient, induced the French Ambassador to give up his establishment, McComb's new house in Broadway-for the accommodation of the Pres. It was from this house in 1790 that Washington took his final departure from N Y. When near to Phil, the Pres was met by Govn'r Mifflin & a brilliant cortege of ofcrs; among the Govnr's suite was Gen Walter Stewart, a son of Erin, & a gallant & distinguished ofcr of the Pa line. Mifflin, small in stature, was active, alert, very inch a soldier. The Pres left his carriage & mounted the white charger, & proceeded to the City Tavern in 3rd st, where quarters were prepared for him. After remaining a short time in Phil, the Pres speeded on his journey to that home where he ever found rest from his labors, & enjoyed the sweets of rural & domestic happiness amid his farms & his fireside of ***Mount Vernon***.

Mrd: on Feb 11, by Rev G D Chenowith, Mr Andrew J Rock to Miss Angeline Cooke, of Washington.

Mrd: on Jan 26, by Rev Mr Sullivan, Mr Wm J Darden, jr, late of Wash, to Miss Fanny Amelia Dixon, daughter of Gen Moseley Baker, of Houston, Texas.

Mrd: on Feb 10, at Detroit, Mich, Mr Frank Larned Hunt, late of Wash, to Miss Eliza A Knapp, of the former place.

Information received of the murder of Mr B B Hussey, for many years a respectable & much esteemed inhabitant of Charleston, S C, but who for some time past has been engaged in traveling in the Western States as the general agent of several periodicals. He was murdered at Dublin, Geo, by a person by the name of John W Gibbs. Mr Hussey stopped on the night of Feb 22 at Dublin, on his way to Augusta. He had given Gibbs, who was on foot, a ride in his vehicle, & volunteering to pay the tolls & a portion of the other expenses. On arriving at Dublin they took lodgings at the same hotel & roomed together. During the night Gibbs stabbed Hussey 18 times with a large dirk knife. -Charleston News

Fatal accident in the village of Herkimer, on Fri, from the practice of riding down on hand-sleds. A daughter of Mr Sullivan Davis, about 11 years old, in the absence of her parents, took out her little brother, Wilis, aged 2 years & 5 months, to ride with her down a declivity near her father's residence. Placing the infant on the sled, the girl was preparing to seat herself with him, when her foot slipped, giving the sled a start, which escaped from her, & ran with the child directly down into the canal, where he was drowned.

The partnership existing under the firm of T J Magruder & Co is this day dissolved by mutual consent. -Baruch Hall, Isaac Hall, T J Magruder. [T J Magruder will continue the business at the old stand, opposite Centre Market, between 8th & 9th sts, where may be had a general assortment of Boots & Shoes.]

Died: Feb 21, Mary E Sandford, after a painful & lingering illness, which she bore with Christian fortitude. Her funeral will be from Nathl Plant's, on Feb 22, at 3 o'clock.

Died: on Fri last, in Wash City, Sarah Eliz, infant child of Wm W Moore, aged between 4 & 5 years.

House of Reps: 1-Cmte on Public Lands: Act to compensate John M Moore: without amendment. 2-<u>Referred to appropriate cmtes</u>: act for the relief of John Stockton, late a lt in the army of the U S. Act for the relief of Wm Marvin, in confirming his title to a tract of land in Florida, granted by the Spanish Gov't to Bernardo Segui on Dec 10, 1815. Acts referred to the appropriate cmte: for the relief of the heirs & reps of the late Robt Sewell; relief of Wade Allen; relief of Andrew Moore; of the heirs of Louis de la Houssaye, dec'd; of Alfred White; of Robt M Harrison; of Creed Taylor; of John Bronson; of Pearson Cogswell; of Jos Watson; of Jas S Conway; of Jas F Sothoron; of Andrew D Crosby; of Wm A Christian. Also, granting a pension to Abigail Garland, widow of Jacob Garland, dec'd. Also, pension to Bethia Healy, widow of Geo Healy, dec'd. Also, act directing the Sec of the Navy to purchase a patent right from Dr Jas P Espy. Act for the final settlement of the account of Thos C Sheldon, late receiver of public moneys in Kalamazoo, Mich. 3-Act for the relief of the heirs of John Paul Jones: laid on the table. 4-Memorial of David Taylor, asking for an appropriation to pay a settled account against the U S.

I certify that John Cooper, of PG Co, Md, brought before as an estray, trespassing upon his enclosures, near Bladensburg, a sorrel mare. -Benj O Lowndes, J P [Owner to come forward, prove property, pay charges, & take her away. -John Cooper, near Bladensburg, Md.]

Maj Trenor, of the 1st Regt U S Dragoons, died at his father's residence in N Y on Tue evening last.

Tampico, Jan 28, 1847. I learned last night that Lt Ritchie, of the 4th Infty, was assassinated at Villa Grande by a Mexican. He was on his way to Victoria, escorted by a company of Ky cavalry. Gen Taylor encamped there for the night, & the Lt was sauntering about the town when it happened. The next morning the Genr'l had arrested the alcalde, but I do not know where he was taken. At $20 per month there are at least 100 Mexicans working on the fortifications here.

TUE FEB 23, 1847

Orphans Court of Wash Co, D C. Letters testamentary on the personal estate of Robt Rose, late of saied county, dec'd. -Maria A Lindsay, Adam L Rose, excs

Correction of what be a mistake. The Wm Cleary spoken of in the advertisement of Mr Owen Connolly, is not the subscriber, formerly of Va, & who now lives on H st, between 9th & 10th sts. I have never been an applicant for, nor a recipient of Gov't favors. -Wm Cleary, H st, between 9th & 10th sts.

Miss Julia A Dorrell, Fashionable Dressmaker, has removed to D st, between 6th & 7th sts, where she will be pleased to make up in a superior style any articles in her line of business in accordance with the latest fashion, & at the most reasonable rates.

WED FEB 24, 1847

Senate: Cmte on Pensions: House bills for the relief of John Van Slyck & for the relief of Wm Causey, without amendment. Same cmte: adverse reports on the ptns of Isaac Davenport, Nehemiah Brush, & Geo Petty: ordered to be printed. 2-Cmte of Claims: House bill for the relief of the legal reps of Wm Bunce, dec'd. 3-Cmte of Finance: asked to be discharged from the further consideration of the ptn of Martin Renehan, & that it be referred to the Cmte of Claims.

Appointments by the Pres:
Franklin Pierce, of N H, to be Colonel of Infty.
Timothy P Andrews, of D C, to be Colonel of Infty.
Abner B Thompson, of the State of Maine, to be Lt Col of Infty.
Jos E Johnston, of the Corps of Topographical Engineers, to be Lt Col of Infty.
Trueman B Ranson, of the State of Vermont, to be Major of Infty.

The late European steamer brings news of the death of Capt Rathbone, of the packet ship **Columbia**, of N Y; who, with his 1st & 2nd mates, 5 seamen, & a boy, were washed overboard in a gale on Jan 13.

A letter in the New Orleans Delta from Tampico, states that Lt Sturges, who commanded Col May's rear-guard at the time of the capture of the Mexicans, has been triumphantly acquitted by a court martial of the charges of misconduct which were brought against him.

The N C Newbernian states that the gentleman whose marriage & death on the same day are related in the following notices, was formerly a highly respected citizen of Lenoir Co, N C. Mrd: at 7 o'clock a m, on Nov 11, 1846, in Pensacola, Florida, Mortimer Bright to Miss Rebecca Simpson. Died: on the same day, at half past 7 p m, in Pensacola, Mortimer Bright, aged 42 years & 5 months.

Aaron W Musick received a severe cut on the head on Sat while fixing a portion of the machinery of Patton's Plaining Mills, on Coates st wharf, Phil. He was taken to the hospital, & soon after died, leaving a wife & 7 children.

Henry Baily, an extensive & fashionable hat dealer, in Boston, committed suicide in that city on Sat last by taking prussic acid. He was a young man, & left a wife & family. Embarrassed circumstances are given as the cause.

Coroner's Inquest: was held on the body of Benj E Horton, who died the previous night. Horton was confined at the Wash Asylum in a state of derangement for about 8 days; he was removed to the Wash Infirmary, Medical Hospital, on Feb 18, & received every attention while there. He died on Feb 21, 1847.

Wash Corp: 1-Ptn of L H Berryman: referred to the Cmte of Claims. 2-Ptns of Garret Anderson; of L Hoking; of W H Mortimer; of Harrison Cross: all for remission of a fine: referred to the Cmte of Claims. 3-Ptn of T H Brightwell & others, for the improvement of the road leading to Bealiss' Bridge: referred to the Cmte on Improvement. 4-Ptn of J J Fowler & others, praying the curbstone to be set on the south front of square 462, on Md ave, between 6th & 7th sts: referred to the Cmte on Improvements. 5-Cmte on Improvements: ptn of John Fletcher: asked to be discharged from the further consideration of the same: agreed to.

Catalogue sale of old wines, brandies & whiskey, belonging to the private stock of the late Col Chas Simms Oliver, dec'd, of PG Co, Md. -R W Dyer, auct

House of Reps: 1-Ptn of Richd Street & others, in relation to public lands. 2-Ptn of John Montgomery & 57 other citizens of Medina Co, Ohio, to grant a tract of land for bldg a railroad to Oregon.

Died: on Feb 23, in Annapolis, in her 17th year, Fanny Rebecca, eldest daughter of Jos H Nicholson, & grand-daughter of P Hagner, of Wash.

Senate: 1-Ptn from Bryan Gallaghan for compensation for goods destroyed at San Antonio, in Texas, by order of an ofcr of the U S: referred. 2-Ptn from Moses E Levy, asking to be allowed to locate on the public land in Florida the quantity claimed by him under a Spanish grant: referred. 3-Ptn from John Skirving, stating the terms of which he will ventilate the Senate chamber. 4-Ptn from Jacob Kern, asking indemnity for French spoliations prior to 1800. 5-Cmte on the Judiciary: House bill for the relief of the administrators of Jos Edson, dec'd, late marshal of the district of Vermont. 6-Cmte on Naval Affairs: House bills for the relief of Lewis Satori & of Jos Gideon, without amendment. Same cmte: House bill for the relief of the widow & heirs of the late Silas Duncan, with a recommendation that it do not pass. 7-Bill introduced to provide for the purchase of the manuscript papers of the late Jas Madison, former Pres of the U S. 8-The first subject for consideration before the Senate was the reception of the ptn of John A Barry, an alien: laid on the table for the present.

A young lady by the name of Richley, committed suicide at Ashbury, Warren Co, N J, on Sat week. She was engaged to be married to a gentleman, but continued to flirt with another, which offended her intended husband, & he refused to have any more to do with her. She jumped into a mill pond, & when her body was recovered, life was extinct.

The coroner held an inquest at the house of J Chesterman, 710 Broadway, on the body of a young girl named Margaret Cray, a servant in his family, who came to her death by taking laudanum. The day before her death she had received a cruel valentine from one she had looked upon as her lover. -N Y Express

John L Vantine, a jeweler of Phil, weathly & formerly respected, had been sentenced to the Penitentiary for 3 years. He did not resist the indictment, & gave up considerable stolen property.

Danl Aiken died in Wexford, Canada West, a few weeks since, aged 120 years. He had during his life contracted 7 marriages, & had 570 grand-children & great-grand-children-370 boys & 200 girls.

We are requested to state that the subscribers obtained by Mr J Hersman to The Southerner, printed at Richmond, will fine the first numbers at Mr Wm Adams' Periodical Agency, on Pa ave, & hereafter they will be found at the post ofc.

THU FEB 25, 1847
Supreme Court of the U S: Feb 24, 1847. #170: Wm H Irwin, appellant, vs Geo O & John A Dixon. Appeal from the Circuit Court U S, for Alexandria, D C. The cause re-entered on the calendar, the appellant having filed his record in conformity to the rules of this Court.

Henry Addison was on Mon last re-elected Mayor of the city of Gtwn.

Casualties at Sea. The ship **Eliza Warwick**, from N Y, met with a disaster on Jan 12th, by which Capt Loring & 2 of his crew lost their lives, when swept overboard.

Senate: 1-Cmte on Naval Affairs: bill for the relief of Monmouth B Hart, Joel Kelly, & Wm Chase, securities for the late Benj F Hart, a purser in the U S Navy. 2-Cmte of Claims: bill for the relief of Ed Bolun. Same cmte: bill for the relief of Bryan Callaghan.

A court martial is in session at the Brasos to try Col Harney for disobedience of orders. Gen Worth is president of the court.

Mrd: on Feb 21, by Rev J W French, Mr E Evans to Miss Catherine E Cruit, all of Wash City.

Died: on Feb 19, Dr Jas Stewart, of Princess Anne, Md, in his 60th year.

Died: on Feb 9, at the Academy of the Visitation, in Balt, Miss Emily, daughter of Col Wm Coad, of St Mary's Co, in her 15th year.

FRI FEB 26, 1847
Mr Haven, conductor of the gravel train on the Boston & Worcester road, while riding on a snow plough clearing the track, on Mon, was thrown upon the track & instantly killed at Westboro, Mass.

Tampico, Feb 6, 1847. I am sorry to inform you of the loss of the fine ship **Ondiaka**, that had on board some of the Lousiaian volunteers, under Col De Russy. She went ashore about a week ago 40 miles to the southward of this place, & is a total wreck. Lt Miller, of the 4th Artl, with about 40 men, started from her a few days ago to the assistance of the wrecked party. Tampico, Feb 8, 1847. The plot thickens. I think there might be something in the report about the Mexicans having attacked Col De Russy. We learn that Mr John C Howard, who came passenger on the ship **St Paul**, that as the vessel was coming over the bar on the 9th, the propellar **James Cage** was seen returning from the wreck of the **Ondiaka**. The ships **Statesman**, **Prentice**, & **Catharine** were off the bar of Tampico on the 9th, all filled with troops. The 2nd Regt of Mississippi volunteers, on board the ship **Statesman**, were suffering terribly by sick; they were dying in great numbers daily. The New Yorkers, on board the ship **Catharine**, are particularly spoken as a fine-looking set of fellows.

Sale of valuable household & kitchen furniture: by deed of trust from Cyrus J McClellan, will offer at public auction, on Mar 9, all the furniture of the St Charles Hotel.
-Richd Wallach, trustee

Private sale of 2 very superior rifles, with fixtures complete, one made to order by E Tryon, of Phil; the owner having removed from the country, has no further use for it; the other is one of Colt's patent revolvers, in perfect order, with apparatus complete.
-A Green, Auctioneer & Com Merchant

Letter from Brazos: Capture of a detachment of troops under Majors Borland & Gaines, & Capt Cassius M Clay, near Saltillo. Camp of the Rio Grande, near Palo Alto, Jan 30, 1847. Lt Mackall has been promoted, & will act as assistant adjutant general, with Gen Worth, with the rank of brevet captain. Lt Geo Deas, adjutant of the 5th Infty, has received a similar commission, & is ordered to report to Gen Wool. Mouth of the Rio Grande, Feb 3, 1847. On Jan 11 I met Lt Ritchie of the 4th Infty, but then acting with the 2nd Dragoons, on his way from Satillo, with 10 Dragoons, to Victoira, with dispatches to Gen Taylor, from Gen Scott & others. While on the road, the party was attacked, young Ritchie was lassoed & dragged across a cornfield, & the dispatches carried off. The 10 Dragoons were either killed or taken prisoners. Lt Ritchie was one of the most distinguished & excellent young ofcrs in the army. There is little or no doubt of his death, still, there is hope. A few days ago, an ofcr of the 2nd Regt, Lt Miller, is believed to be his name, was murdered at Chichironi, & awfully mutilated. Mouth of the Rio Grande, Feb 4, 1847. There is no doubt about the death of Lt Ritchie. After being dragged across the field, full speed, he was then murdered & stripped. The court martial recently held at Brasos for the trial of Col Harney has ordered him to be released from arrest & reprimanded. We learn that Gen Scott has remitted the latter part of this sentence, but has reiterated his former order to Col Harney.

The pork warehouse of Mr Wallace Sigerson, at Cincinnati, Ohio, was destroyed by fire on Feb 16, with its contents estimated at 200,000 pounds of meat.

Before going into Executive session, the Senate voted to pass the bill authorizing the purchase of the papers of the late Jas Madison, from Mrs D P Madison. The bill give $5,000 in hand, & authorizes the issue of scrip for $20,000, at an interest of 6%-which cannot be sold or disposed of. The bill for the benefit of an elderly lady, who was in very destitute circumstances, the bill for the relief of Mrs Mary McCrae, widow of Col McCrae: read a 3rd time & passed. The Senate adjourned.

Masonic-special meeting of Columbia Royal Arch Chapter at their hall, E & 10th sts, on Feb 26. -Calhoun M Deringer, Sec Col R A Chapter

Extensive sale of household furniture: deed of trust from R C Nichols, to be subscriber, will be sold at auction, at the American Hotel, on Mar 4 next, all the furniture of the Hotel. Also, the Kitchen furniture, most of which is of copper. Johnson Hellen, Trustee -R W Dyer, auct

Mrs E Crampsey has on hand a large assortment of ladies' fancy Corsets & Gentlemen's Shoulder Braces & Russian Girths. -Mrs E Champsey, F st, one door east of 11th st.

Dissolution of the copartnership existing under the name of Estep, Hooe & Co. -Rezin Estep, P H Hooe & Co. [Mr Rezin Estep having withdrawn from the late firm of Estep, Hooe & Co, the subscribers will continue the business at the old stand. -P H Hooe & Co.]

Senate: 1-Ptn from Seth M Leavenworth, asking the passage of an act directing the Postmast Gen to execute a joint resolution which passed at the last session of Congress for the relief of B Leavenworth. 2-Ptn from Jas Crutchett, asking an examination into the propriety of purchasing the right to use solar gas for the use of the Capitol & public bldgs in Wash. 3-Cmte on the Judiciary: asking to be discharged from the further consideration of the following memorials: from Solomon Calvert Ford, Aaron Weeks, the heirs of A L Duncan, & Wm H Basset. Also, from the same cmte, a report, with a resolution, on the claim of Leslie Combs. 4-Cmte on Indian Affairs: asking to be discharged from further consideration of the memorials of Susan Coody & others, Cherokees, & from the memorial of the Cherokee Indians residing in N C. Same cmte: House bill for the relief of Geo B Russell & others, & for the relief of the legal reps of the late Jos E Primeau & Thos J Chapman, without amendment. Same cmte: adverse report on the memorial of Preston Starret & other Cherokees. 5-Cmte on the Judiciary: bill to refund to the legal reps of Thos Cooper a fine imposed under the sedition law. Same cmte: asking to be discharged from the further consideration of the ptn of Robt Owen. 6-Cmte on Revolutionary Claims: House bill for the relief of the legal reps of Simeon Spalding, without amendment.

Runaway apprentices: ranaway from the subscriber, on Sep 12, 1845, John McPherson, an indented apprentice to the coach painting, & Jas Collins on Feb 10, 1847, an indented apprentice to coach wood work. All persons are forewarned from harboring or employing them, as persons so doing will be dealth with according to law. Any persons bringing home said apprentices will receive the sum of ten cents for each, & no expenses.
-Michl McDermott

SAT FEB 27, 1847

The original papers found upon Major Andre are now exhibited at Plumbe's Gallery, a few doors west of Brown's Hotel; &, certainly, if any relic of the war of the Revolution can be of interest to the present generation, those papers are. They are undoubtedly genuine, & their preservation in their actual good condition to the present day is attributed to their having been in the possession of Govn'r Clinton, during his life, &, since his death, in that of his descendants, who have taken great care of them.

Died: on Thu last, Mrs Eliza Cox, w/o J Florentius Cox, of ***Meridian Hill***, leaving a disconsolate husband & family, to deplore the loss of an excellent wife & mother. Her funeral is today at 1 o'clock. [Mar 6th newspaper: died: on Feb 25, Mrs Eliza Cox, aged 56 years, w/o J Florentius Cox, & daughter of Maj Thos S Lansdale, of ***Mount Willow***, PG Co, Md, of the Revolutionary army. A Christian woman, patient, forgiving, retiring. She leaves her husband & children to mourn her loss.]

Lost, on Thu last, in the 1st Ward, the free papers of John Turfley, of Orange Co, Va, with the usual certificate of the Corp of Washington. The finder will receive a reward by delivering them to the subscriber, on the south side of D st, next house to the corner of 8th st. -John Turfley

S W Tucker announces that he is still a candidate for their patronage. Corpulent men will do well to have his made of drawers, as they will act as abdominal supporters. He makes all kinds of gentlemen's clothing. His residence & place of business is on C st, adjoining the exchange Hotel. Terms cash.

MON MAR 1, 1847
Mrs Blagrove, of Richmond, Va, aged about 60 years, was so much injured on Tue last by her clothes taking fire that she died the next day. No one was in the room with her at the time of the accident.

Two powder mills at Lowell, owned by Messrs Whipples, were blown up on Feb 23.

On Feb 17, in Ridgefield, Conn, the 13 year old son of Keeler St John was killed when he crept under a water-wheel to search for something he had lost. The wheel started & caught his head. He died in a few hours.

The friends of Rev Dr Baird will be happy to learn that he returned to this country in the vessel **Cambria**, after an absence of 9 months, & is in fine health.

Col Jonathan P Miller, whose mission to Greece during the struggle of that ill-fated country for freedom will be remembered by all, died at Montpelier, Vt, on Feb 17. -Tribune

A fire in West Gardiner, on Tue last, consumed the house of Deacon Jas Lord, & the Deacon, age 83 years, perished in the flames. He led the devotional exercises of the family before retiring the previous evening.

Dr Jas F Clark, an eminent physician of Trenton, N J, was taken down with apoplexy on Sat, & expired. He was recovering from a severe attack of gout, & fell in his chamber.

Site of the Smithsonian Institution: settled definitively, & without chance of change, on the Mall. It is comprised in the southern half of so much of that reservation as lies between 9th & 12th sts, & contains between 18 & 19 acres.

Mrd: on Feb 25, by Rev Mr Gillis, Mr Ferdinand R Baare to Miss Eliza Fisher, all of Wash City.

Montreal papers of the 19th ult announce the death on the 17th, of the Hon Jos Remi Vallieres de St Real, Chief Justice of Montreal, in his 60th year. He was eminent both at the bar & on the bench.

Mr Jos Davis, of Morristown, N J, has hired 30 Germans from among the paupers in the almhouse, N Y, to work upon his farms. A most essential service has been rendered to many able bodied persons who desire employment, but cannot command the means of obtaining it. -Com Adv

Lt Gibson, of the 2nd Artl, died of fever at Tampico on the night of Feb 6.

We learn that Mr Hosea Hildreth Smith, a member of the Wash Bar, was arrested last Fri, under charge of a criminal offence-that of obtaining from the U S three several sums of money, amounting to $1,297.50, upon certain papers which appear to have been forged, said money being the property of the U S. The arrest of Mr Smith, who has heretofore maintained a good reputation in our community, has caused no little surprise amongst the members of the Bar & the friends of the accused.

Once cent reward for Jas Westly, [colored,] an indented boy, who ran away Jan 26. All persons are forbid harboring or trusting him. The reward will be paid for his apprehension, but no charges. -H B Sawyer

The little girl, the grand-dght of Mr Payne, residing near Good Hope Tavern, on the Eastern Branch, was burnt to death a few days ago. The child's clothes caught fire as she was playing with another little girl in the yard, & before assistance could be had the poor sufferer expired.

Balt, Feb 27. 1-Trial of Rev Mr Trapnell concluded, but the cmte have not yet decided. 2-The four gamblers, Robt Perry, Wm James Geo James, & Geo Campbell, convicted in our Court some days ago of defrauding Isaac H Jones out of $10,000, were sentenced today to 2 years' imprisonment in the jail & a fine of $1,000 each. [Mar 2nd newspaper: the Ecclesiastical Council to whom was referred the case of the Rev Jos Trapnall have decided that, on the first charge, that of having refused to permit Bishop Whittingham to administer the communion, the Bishop claiming to do so by right of ofc, he was innocent. On the 2nd charge, that of having used language disrespectful to his Bishop, in a printed pamphlet, he was pronounced guilty.] Note-2 spellings of Trapnell/Trapnall.

Circuit Court-Wash. The important cause of the U S vs Francis Thomas, ex-Govn'r of Md, is fixed for trial today.

Dissolution of the partnership under the firm of Gault & Emery, on Mar 25, by mutual consent. -Matthew Gault, Matthew G Emery. Mr M G Emery, having bought out the interest of his late partner, will continue the business in his own name, at the old stand near the railroad depot. He intends to keep constantly on hand a supply of Granite, dressed & otherwise; blue stone stepping & N Y flagging.

For rent: comfortable 2 story dwlg near the corner of C & 10th sts. Inquire of Edwin Green, 11th & Pa ave.

The subscribers have this day entered into copartnership, for carrying on the Housefurnishing Business, under the firm of T M & B Milburn. -Thos M Milburn, Benedict Milburn [T M Milburn, East side of 7th st, has associated his brother, Benedict Milburn, in business, in house furnishings. -T M Milburn]

House of Reps: 1-Cmte of Claims: bill for the relief of Noah A Phelps: committed. 2-Cmte of Claims: bill from the Senate for the relief of Hobson Johns: committed without amendment. 3-Cmte of Claims was discharged from the further consideration of the ptn of Solomon Payne: laid upon the table. 4-Cmte on Commerce: Senate bill to authorize the issuing of a register to the brig **Ocean Queen**, reported the same without amendment: bill was passed. Same cmte: was discharged from the further consideration of the ptn of John H Baker: laid on the table. 5-Cmte on Public Lands: bill for the relief of Geo Gordon, without amendment: passed. Same cmte: Senate bill to grant a right of pre-emption to Philip F Derring & Robt H Champion to a tract of mineral land, reported the same without amendment: passed. 6-Cmte on Revolutionary Pensions: was referred the joint resolution of the Senate to correct an error in the act of Jun 17, 1844, for the relief of Mary Ann Linton, reported the same without amendment: resolution was read a 3rd time & passed. Same cmte: was referred the Senate bill for the relief of Geo Roush, without amendment: passed. 7-Cmte on Invalid Pensions: Senate bill to grant a pension to Jos Morrison: passed. 8-Cmte on the Judiciary: Senate bill for the relief of Jas S Conway: passed. 9-Cmte of the Post Ofc & Post Roads: Senate resolution in favor of David Shaw & Solomon F Corser: committed. Same cmte: Senate bill for the relief of Wade Allen: committed. Same cmte: Senate bill for the relief of Nathl Kuykendall: committed. 10-Cmte on the Judiciary reported the following bills from the Senate, without amendment-committed: relief of Richd S Coxe; relief of Jeanette C Huntingdon, widow of Wm D Cheever; of Thos Douglass, late U S atty for East Florida. 11-Act for the relief of Peter Capello, administrator of Andrew Capello, dec'd, & for the relief of John Capo; laid on the table. 12-Act for the relief of Millidge Galphin, exc of Geo Galphin, dec'd: laid on the table. 13-Cmte on the Judiciary: Senate bill for the relief of Richd Bloss & others: committed. 14-Cmte on Naval Affairs: Senate bill for the relief of Jas M McIntosh: committed. Same cmte: Senate bill providing for the payment of the claim of Walter R Johnson against the U S: committed. Same cmte: Senate bill to purchase the patent right of the conical ventilator from Dr Jas P Espy: committed. Same cmte: Senate bill for the relief of Thos Brownell: committed. Same cmte: Senate bill for the relief of Wm A Christian: committed. The same cmte was referred the Senate bill for the relief of the heirs of Andrew D Crosby: committed. 15-Cmte on Foreign Affairs: Senate bill for the relief of the reps of Wm A Slacum, dec'd: reported the same without amendment. Senate bill for the relief of Joshua Dodge, with an amendment. These bills were committed to a Cmte of the Whole House. 16-Cmte on Foreign Affairs: be discharged from the further consideration of the memorials of Jacob Isler, of Phil, & the memorial of Bogert & Kneeland, Benj L Swann, & Thaddeus Phelps, of N Y C, & that the same be referred to the Sec of State. 17-Cmte on Revolutionary Pensions: bill from the Senate granting a pension to Bethiah Healy, widow of Geo Healy, dec'd: committed. Same cmte: Senate bill for the relief of Eliz Pistole, widow of Chas Pistole, dec'd; & Senate bill granting a pension to Abigail Garland, widow of Jacob Garland, dec'd: committed. 18-Cmte in Invalid Pensions: Senate bill granting a pension to John Clark: committed. Same cmte: Senate bill for the relief of Francis Summeraner, reported the same without amendment. 19-Cmte on Indian Affairs: Senate bill for the relief of Saml W Bell, a native of the Cherokee nation: laid on the table. 20-Cmte on the Judiciary: bill for the relief of Geo B Didlake: committed. 21-Cmte of Claims: discharged from the further consideration of the ptn of Allan Gorham: laid on the table. 22-Cmte on Revolutionary Pensions, made adverse reports on the cases of John Millett & of the heirs of Jehoakim Van Valkenberg: laid on the table. Same cmte: bill for the relief of Jonathan Brown: committed. 23-Cmte on Revolutionary Pensions: discharged from the ptns of Catharine Adair, Benj Johnson, Sarah Miles, & John Wallace: laid on the table. Same cmte: bill for the relief of Flora Boyd, widow of Jas Boyd, dec'd: committed. 24-Cmte on Invalid Pensions was discharged from the ptns of Warren Raymond, Thos Badger, Nehemiah Halliday, Susanna Prentiss, Levi M Roberts, Seth Morton, Sarah Hildreth, Stacy Lanphier, J W Knipe, Asa Hall, Hannah Duboise, Carle Dingie, Roswell Bates, Danl Wilson, & Benj Loomis: laid on the table. Same cmte: bill for the relief of Silas Waterman: committed. Same cmte: adverse report on the ptn of Jesse Rose: laid on the table. 25-Cmte on Patents: bill for the relief of E G Smith: committed. Same cmte: bill for the relief of Edw Clark: committed. 26-Cmte on Private Land Claims: bill for the relief of Nicholas E Thouron: committed. 27-Cmte on Revolutionary Claims: bill for the relief of the reps of Nathl Tracy, dec'd: committed. Same cmte: adverse report on the ptn of the reps of Nathl Tracy, dec'd: read twice & committed. 28-Cmte on Indian Affairs: discharged from the ptn of Conrad Ten Eyck: laid on the table. 29-Cmte on Accounts: resolved that the Speaker of this House be directed to pay to S Clinton Hastings & Shepherd Leffler, members of this House from the State of Iowa, $176 each, it being their per diem from the first day of this session to the day on which they took their seats as members, they having attended on the first day of the session. 30-Cmte on Invalid Pension: bill for the relief of Mary Legar & for the relief of Elisha Denison, administrator of Phenix Carpenter Ellit: passed. 31-Ptn of John D D Rosset, of Va, in relation to immigration of foreigners. 32-Ptn of David Waldo, for the payment of services in the war of the Revolution. 33-Ptn of Amanda Fax, administratrix, for compensation for losses sustained in the late war with Great Britain. 34-Memorial of the Legislature of Wisconsin for the indemnification of Elbert Dickinson.

Wash City lots for sale: Dr Van Patten has several bldg lots on the "island," fronting on 3rd 4th & 5th sts, & on Md ave; also 2 lots near the new market, Northern Liberties, & 2 lots near the Capitol. Ofc next door to Todd's hat store, Pa ave.

Senate: 1-Cmte on Commerce: bill to authorize the issuing a register to the brig **Leveret**. 2-Cmte on Private Land Claims: bill for the relief of Nathl Hoggart. 3-Ptn from Russell Sturgis, asking that a register may be issued for a British vessel purchased by him & repaired in the U S. 4-Documents presented in relation to the claim of Amos Holton. 5-Ptn from Wm T Sayward & others, praying that a register may be issued for the barque **Canton**, a vessel wrecked on the coast of the U S. 6-Ptn from Harvey Shepherd, asking a pension. 7-Ptn from John Lorimer Graham, late postmaster of N Y, asking that authority may be given to the Auditor of the Post Ofc to settle his claims on principles of equity & justice. 8-Cmte on Pensions: asking to be discharged from the further consideration of the memorial of Mrs Clara M Pike, widow of Gen Pike; & also from the further consideration of the ptn of David Whelply: & that they have leave to withdrawn their papers. 9-Cmte on the Judiciary: adverse report on the memorial of Wm Hogan, administrator of Michl Hogan, dec'd. Same cmte: bill for the relief of the estates of Benj Metayer & Francis Gaiennie, dec'd, with a recommendation that it do not pass. Same cmte: adverse report on the memorial of Chas Stearns. 10-Cmte on Indian Affairs: asking to be discharged from the further consideration of the ptn of H H Hildreth. 11-Documents relating to the claim of Elisha K Kane for medical services to the Chinese mission in the years 1843 & 1844: presented. 12-Ptn from Phoebe Wood & Sylvia Ann Wood, remonstrating against the provisions of a bill for the relief of the heirs of Jethro Wood. 13-Ptn from the legal reps of Miller & Robinson, late merchants at Charleston, asking indemnity for French spoliations prior to 1800. 14-Ptn from Bassett Edwards Potter, setting forth strong reasons for the speedy termination of the war with Mexico, & asking 100,000 copies of Senator Corwin's speech may be printed at the public expense to enlighten the people on the subject. 15-Cmte on Naval Affairs: House bill for the relief of David Myerlee, without amendment. Same cmte: House bill for the relief of the legal reps of Jas H Clark, without amendment. Same cmte: House bill for the relief of John Paul Jones, with an amendment. [The amendment consisted of a slight change, such as giving to the heirs at law of said John Paul Jones a pro rata allowance provided they came forward & proved their heirship within 2 years from the passage of the bill.] The amendment was concurred in, the bill was read a 3rd time & passed.

For sale: a Carriage, pair of iron gray Horses, & Harness. Call at Walker & Kimmel's Livery Stable C st, rear of Coleman's Hotel.

Cloths, shirtings, vestings, & ready made clothing at auction: order of the Orphans Court: sale on Mar 4, at the store lately occupied by Isaac T Elwood, dec'd, on Pa ave, between 6th & 7th sts. -R W Dyer, auct

TUE MAR 2, 1847

The Maysville Herald is a new tri-weekly paper, edited & published by J S Chambers, at Maysville, Ky. Mr Chambers is a son of Ex-Govn'r Chambers. It advocates the Whig party.

Died: on Sunday last, Mrs Catharine Foxall, relict of the late Rev Henry Foxall, of Gtwn. Her funeral is tomorrow at 3 o'clock, from her late residence at ***Spring Hill***, near Gtwn.

Died: on Feb 27, in Gtwn, Mr Thos Holtzman, in his 45th year, after a long illness, which he bore with Christian fortitude. His funeral is this evening from his late residence, High st, at 3 o'clock.

Died: on Feb 25, at the residence of his son, B B Pleasants, near Brookeville, Md, Jas B Pleasants, in his 86th year. The dec'd was born, & spent the earlier part of his life, in Goochland Co, Va, but for the last 50 years had resided in Md.

Died: on Feb 16, in consequence of a fall from his horse, Maj Jas F Sothoron, of St Mary's Co, Md, aged 63 years. He was the native of the county which now holds his mortal remains: wealthy, occupying the highest social position; as a neighbor he was matchless; he knew not a solitary enemy. As a parent he was the adviser & companion of his children.

The sum of $2 will be paid to any citizen, non-commissioned ofcr, or soldier who shall bring to the rendezvous an able-bodied recruit, who shall be regularly enlisted. The citizen should present his recruit to the Lt or Capt, & not to the Recruiting Sgts. -Jas D Blair, Capt U S A, Recruiting Ofcr, Wash: Feb 26, 1847. Rendezvous: Haslup's bldg, at the west end of Centre Market, & between La ave & C st.

Valuable improved property for sale at public auction: on Mar 15, on the premises: on the road leading from the toll-gate on Balt turnpike to the Anacostia bridge, 65 acres, with a small frame house & other out-bldgs. -John A Bartruff -R W Dyer, auct

Criminal Court for this District was opened yesterday: the Hon Judge Crawford took his seat: the following gentlemen were summoned to serve on the Grand Inquest during the present Mar term:

John W Maury	Hamilton Loughborough	Judson Mitchell
John Kurtz	G C Grammer	Jonathan Prout
John Mason, jr	H C Matthews	Geo W Phillips
John C Rives	Thos Blagden	Zachariah Walker
Thos Brown	John C Harkness	Geo Parker
Wm Gunton	Henry Haw	Thos Fenwick
John F Cox	Isaac Clarke	Andrew Coyle
Henry McPherson	Benj K Morsell	

Claim of the heirs of John Paul Jones: the bill, as it passed the House, comprised all the claimants of the squadron under the command of Paul Jones who were citizens of the U S. The Senate amended the bill by limiting the presentation of their claims to 2 years, & by providing for a distribution of the value of the prizes pro rata among all of those American citizens of the squadron, or their heirs at law, who should prove themselves to be such within that period. The report of a prior administration on the estate of Paul Jones by John H Sherburne: no such administration by that person exists. Early in 1839 Mr Sherburne, in defiance of the wishes of the heirs, obtained from the Orphans Court of this city letters of administration on the estate of Paul Jones. These letters were, under a caveat entered by a niece of Paul Jones, revoked by the Court in July of the same year. The writer is the sole administrator of the estate, & acts as atty for the whole heirs. Not a dollar arising from the Bergen prizes has been ever received by them or by Mr Sherburne-Denmark still failing to pay the same. The captors of the prizes: Paul Jones, in a letter dated N Y, Jun 27, 1787, addressed to the Board of Treasury: It was not my intention to order the prizes in question to a port of Denmark, but the Captain of the **Alliance** took upon himself to give his particular orders to the prizemasters to that effect; &, as this was done in my presence, though without my knowledge or permission, they were separated from the squadron in the night. Thus they were, in Bergen, said to be prizes taken or sent in [which had an equal construction] by the frig **Alliance**. The truth is, they were the prizes of the squadron acting in concert, which the King of France had put under the American flag, & under my command; & the ship **Union**, a ship of more value than the other 2 prizes together, struck her colors under the guns of Bon Homme Richard, after I had hailed her. I, however, have never had the folly to make a distinction on that account.

These have no reference to previous prizes adjudicated in France & paid in like manner to all the captors of the squadron-not to one vessel alone. The heirs of John Paul Jones ask no partial legislation; they have desired investigation, & have relied on the merits of their claims for the same justice which have been awarded to others. -Geo L Lowden, nearest male heir & administrator of the estate of John Paul Jones. Washington, Mar 1, 1847.

House of Reps: 1-Senate bill for relief of Elijah White: passed. 2-Cmte of Claims: Senate bill for relief of the heirs & reps of the late Robt Sewall & a bill for relief of Jas F Sothoron: reported the same without amendment: bills committed. Same cmte: bill for relief of Wm Greer: committed. 3-Cmte of Claims: discharged from the ptn of J W Nye: ordered to be printed. 4-Cmte on Private Land Claims: Senate bills for relief of Wm B Keene; of the heirs of Louisde la Hongsage, dec'd; bill confirming the claim of the heirs & legal reps of Pierre Dufresne to a tract of land, reported same without amendment: passed.

Senate: 1-Joint resolution for the settlement of the accounts of Purser G R Barry: passed. 2-The credentials of Mr R M T Hunter, Senator elect from the State of Va, for 6 years from Mar 4 next, were presented.

WED MAR 3, 1847

The solar gas lights were introduced on Mon night into the Senate Chamber, which was most brilliantly illuminated by these splendid & beautiful gas lights of Mr Crutchfield. It is probable that Congress will adopt them at the Capitol.

Wash Corp: 1-Ptn from Jesse Brown: referred to the Cmte on Improvements.
2-The Guardians of the Poor, in relation to a sum of money left by John Laughan, who died whilst an inmate of the Asylum, is now in the hands of one of the Guardians as administrator of the said John Laughan: referred to the Cmte on the Asylum.
3-The nomination of Henry D Gunnell, as Intendant of the Wash Asylum: rejected.
4-Nomination of Benj E Gittings as Intendant of the Wash Asylum: decided in the affirmative. 5-Ptn of Wm Campbell, for remission of a fine: referred to the Cmte of Claims. 6-Ptn of Jas B Clarke, praying to be refunded a certain amount erroneously paid for a license: referred to the Cmte of Claims. 7-Cmte of Police asking to be discharged from the further consideration of the ptn of Wm B Mitchell: agreed to.

Charleston, S C papers mention the death of John S Cogdell, a gentleman who had held many ofcs of honor & trust, & had been faithful in their discharge: Alderman, Pres of many Companies, Grand Master of the Masons, & Pres of a Bank. He was also an artist of some eminence. He painted & presented to St Mary's Church, in that city, the "Crucifixion."

Geo P Manouvrier, the American Consul at Pernambuco, died there last Jan.

The Alabama Journal records the recent death of the Hon Reuben Saffold, who was for a long time on the Supreme Bench of the State.

The steamboat **Atlantic's Bell**, which tolled so long & dolefully over the sad scene of the wreck, has been purchased for an Episcopal Floating Chapel. It is standing at the corner of Broadway & Murray st, N Y.

Mr J R Ackland, a worthy & industrious mechanic, was found dead one morning last week in the yard of Parker's Hotel, at Norfolk. It is supposed he made the fatal leap from the attic window of his hotel, a height of 45 or 50 feet from the ground, in a state of sleep or somnambulism.

Among the 3,000 foreigners now confined in the Almshouse of N Y C, is a learned German, Dr Heidelberg, who was once a preacher, then a professor in the Berlin & Halle Universities, an author, a doctor of philosophy, a rationalist, & now [almost of course] a pauper. He came to this country about 2 years ago, where he supposed his great learning would find a market. He is a master of many languages, a bitter reviler of the Christian religion, & at the same time the object of Christian charity. It is said he had been brought to his present condition by the united influence of his infidel principles-& the worst species of intemperance. -Express

The Rt Rev John Johns, Assist Bishop of Va, has been elected Pres of Wm & Mary College, in the place of the late Thos R Dew.

Mrd: on Mar 1, by Rev G D Chenoweth, Mr Giles Worster to Miss Mary Usher, of Wash.

Died: on Feb 12, at Marshall, Missouri, of scarlet fever, Caroline Manning Stansbury, infant daughter of Chas Fred'k & Lucy Stansbury, aged 13 months.

By virtue of a deed of trust, recorded in Liber W B 106, folios 218 et sequence, one of the land records of Wash Co, I shall proceed to sell, on Apr 18: part of lot 4 in square 405, in Wash City. The improvements are valuable, & readily command a tenant.
-W Lenox, Trustee -A Green, auctioneer

THU MAR 4, 1847

Senate: 1-Confirmation of David Tod, of Ohio, as Minister to Brazil, vice Henry A Wise. 2-Rejection of Chas J Ingersoll as Minister of France, & the subsequent nomination & confirmation of Richd Rush for the same appointment. 3-Rejection of nomination of Andrew Beaumont as Com'r of Public Bldgs, & the subsequent nomination & confirmation of Chas Douglass, of Conn, for the same ofc. 4-The amendment of the House to the bill for the relief of the heirs of John Paul Jones was concurred in.

Annual Commencement of the Medical Dept of Columbian College was held yesterday in the E st Baptist Chruch. The degree of M D was confirmed on: Oscar G Mix & Alex'r Chapman, of Va, Francis Mills & Geo Harris, of Md, Nathan Tompkins, of Indiana, & John J Dyer, of D C. The German Band played several excellent pieces of music during the ceremonies. Dr Riley delivered an appropriate address.

List of Acts: which have passed at the Session of Congress that has just closed. Bills which originated in the Senate. 1-Act granting a pension to: Jos Morrison. 2-Joint resolution to correct an error in the act of Jun 17, 1844, for the relief of Mary Ann Linton. 3-Act to grant a right of pre-emption to Philip F Dering & Robt H Champion to a tract of mineral land. 4-Act confirming the claim of the heirs & legal reps of Pierre Dufresne to a tract of land. 5-Act to issue a new register for the American barque **Pons**, of Phil, by the name of barque **Cordelia**. 6-Act issuing a register to the brig **Ocean Queen**. 6-The following were "acts for the relief of:" John Stockton, late a lt in the U S Army; heirs of

Louis de la Houssaye, dec'd;
Thos Boronell
Wm B Keene
Geo Gordon
Peter Frost
Elijah White & others
Thos Blanchard
Hobson Johns
Geo Roush
Jas S Conway
Francis Sommerauer
Andrew Moore

List of Acts: which have passed at the Session of Congress that has just closed. Bills which originated in the House: 1-Act for the relief of Ray Tompkins & others, the children & heirs at law of the late Danl D Tompkins. 2-Act granting a pension to Patrick Kelly; to Silas Chatfield; increase the pension of Roswell Hale. 3-Acts for the relief of:

Joshua Shaw
Jos Warren Newcomb
Susan Brum
Eliz Adams
Dr Clarke Lillybridge
Thos N Newell
Henry La Reintree
Jas H Conley
Wm N Walthall
Jacob L Vance
Josiah Haskell
Isaac Guess
Jonathan Hoyt
Edith Ramey
Harvey Reynolds
Catharine Stevenson
Ann Clayton
Eliz Fitch
Wilfred Knott
Bernard O'Neill
John Pickett & others
Harrison Whitson
Job Hawkins
John Speakman
Wm Causey
John Van Slyck
Lewis C Satori
Capt Jas Pennoyer
Legal reps of John Lanson, dec'd
Legal reps of Wm Bunce
Administrators of Jos Edson
Jos Gideon
Thankful Reynolds
Heirs of Hyacinth Lasselle
Zachariah Simmons, of Tenn
Heirs of John Paul Jones
Eliz Calkins, the widow of Silas Winans
John & Chas Bruce
Estates of Benj Metoyer & Francois Gaiennie, dec'd.
Jas Green of Fauquier Co, Va
Legal reps of Thos Shields, dec'd
John C Stewart & others
Heirs of Sgt Maj John Champe
Jas Jones, of the city of Brooklyn
W P S Sanger & Geo De la Roche

Widow & heirs of John B Chaudonia
4-Act for the relief of Julius Eldred, Elisha Eldred, & Francis E Eldred, for removing the copper rock from Lake Superior. 5-Act for the relief of Fred'k Hopkins, of Chenango Co, N Y. 6-Act for the benefit of Jas Williams. 7-Act for the pre-emption right to the heirs & legal reps of John Smith T. 8-Act for the relief of the legal reps of Simon Spalding, dec'd; of the legal reps of Jos E Primeau & Thos J Chapman; of the legal reps of Jas H Clark. 9-Act for the relief of Mary Segar, & for the relief of Elisha Dennison, administrator of Phenix Carpenter Ellis. 10-Resolution for the relief of Wm B Stokes, surviving partner of John N C Stockton & Co. 11-Joint resolution for the relief of the children of Stephen Johnson, dec'd. 12-Joint resolution for the relief of M A Price & E A White. 13-Resolution directing the examination of the settlement of the claims of Alex'r M Cumming. 14-Joint resolution for the settlement of the accounts of Purser G R Barry. 15-Joint resolution of thanks to Maj Gen Zachary Taylor, the ofcrs & soldiers under his command, for their conduct in storming the city of Monterey.

House of Reps: 1-Bill for the relief of the heirs of John Paul Jones was taken up. The question was put on concurring with the Senate in their amendment, & disagreed to. 2-Mr Payne called up the resolution authorizing the Clerk to pay John Lee a certain amount [sum not known] for services as hostler & keeper of the public stables. Resolution was amended by an additional resolution authorizing & directing the Clerk to pay to the ofcrs, messengers, pages, & laborers the same amount allowed & paid by the Senate to their ofcrs, for special services at the close of the present session. 3-Bill for the relief of Thos Rhodes: agreed to.

FRI MAR 5, 1847
Trustee's sale of coach, harness, & 1 pair of horses: by deed of trust from Robt McGowan: sale on Mar 16, opposite Gadsby's Hotel, on Pa ave. Terms of sale cash. -John McDermott, trustee

$200 reward for runaway negro boys, Washington Johnson, about 20, & Bill Diggs, about 18. Johnson has relations in Montg Co. -W F Berry, PG Co, Md

Latest from the Brasos: from the New Orleans Picayune of Feb 25. We have before us another list of the captured, which includes the names of Capt Albert Pike, of Arkansas, & Capt Wm Heady, of Ky. Capt Heady was captured 2 days after Maj Borland's party by a party of rancheros. His fate is uncertain. Reports say that Capt C M Clay wished to break the ranks, but could not induce others to assent to it, finding the Mexicans so outnumbered them. Dan Henrie, well known as a Mier prisoner, who acted as an interpreter to the Arkansas troops, made his escape from the Mexican camp on Maj Gaines' horse. The guard fired upon him, but he escaped uninjured.

Appointments by the Pres: John R Clay, Charge d'Affaires at Peru. Geo W Hopkins, of Va, Charge d'Affaires of the U S to the Queen of Portugal.
Maj Genrl: Thos Hart Benton, of Missouri; Wm Cumming, of Georgia
Brig Genrl: Geo Cadwallader, of Pa; Enos D Hopping, of N Y; Franklin Pierce, of N H

The Hon Richd M Young, of Ill, appointed Com'r of the Genrl Land Ofc, vice Jas Shields, resigned, has arrived in Wash & entered upon the duties of his ofc.

Criminal Court -Wash: yesterday Arthur P Brown was found guilty of stealing watches & jewelry from the store of Mr Geo Brower, at the Navy Yard. He was sentenced to 3 years imprisonment in the penitentiary.

SAT MAR 6, 1847

We regret to announce the death of Saml Purviance, of Balt. He was found in his room on Mon, having been seized during the night with a severe attack of paralysis, from which he died yesterday. The dec'd was a brother of Judge Purviance, of the Balt Co Court.

Beautiful country seat at private sale: by virtue of a deed of trust, executed to the subscriber for certain purposes therein mentioned, & which is recorded in Liber I N #2, one of the land record books of Wash Co, Md, I will sell that elegant Mansion House, & improvements, lately erected by J Kip Anderson, to which is attached 17+ acres. It is in Wash Co, Md, about 6 miles south of Hagerstown. The dwlg house is of brick & is rough cast; front bldg is 2 stories high, with a broad pizzas running around 3 sides of it. Also, all other necessary out-bldgs. The title is indisputable. Apply to John B Hall, trustee, Hagerstown, Md.

The North American records the death of John Latour, one of our most eminent French merchants, who for nearly half a century has stood prominent in the Phil mercantile community. We believe he was almost 80 years old.

Mrd: on Mar 4, by Rev G D Chenoweth, Mr Chas B Church to Miss Matilda S Harris, both of Wash City.

Mrd: on Mar 5, by Rev V Palen, Mr John Skidmore to Miss Mary E Lighter, all of Wash City.

Died: on Mar 5, at the Almshouse, in Wash City, Miss Fanny Ann Mattingly, in her 78th year, after a long & painful illness. Her funeral is from the residence of Mrs Rebecca Bright, near the Navy Yard, on Sunday at 2 p m.

Died: on Feb 28, in Gtwn, after a long & protracted illness, Wm Edw Stroud, in his 19th year, son of Jas & Mary Stroud.

Died: on Mar 2, at the residence of her brother, Wm B Scott, in Wash City, after a short illness, Mrs Eliza C Rankin, in her 65th year, consort of the late Capt Robt Rankin, of the U S Marine Corps, & eldest daughter of the late Gustavus Scott.

Died: on Feb 25, in Wash City, after a short & severe illness, Mrs Gracy Ann Tippett, in her 42nd year, wife of Edw D Tippett.

Died: on Mar 5, Mrs Margaret Smith, consort of John H Smith, of Wash City, & daughter of the late Anthony Buck, of Fredericksburg, Va.

Died: on Monday last, in Phil, after a short & severe illness, John Farr, in his 56th year. A meeting of the Vestry of St Paul's Church, Phil was held on Mar 2, in memory of beloved friend & brother, John Farr, the Senior Warden of this Church. -John W Thomas, sec

House for rent: the dwlg now in the occupancy of Mrs Isabella Walker, on Pa ave, & 7th st, above my store. Will be vacated on Apr 1. -Geo Stettinius, agent for the estate of John Stettinius, dec'd.

Orphans Court of Wash Co, D C. Ordered that Stanislaus Murray, exc of Mary C Hamilton, dec'd, give notice to the heirs of Edw H Hamilton, that they are entitled to a legacy under the will of Mary C Hamilton, dec'd, & which he is now ready to pay. -Nathl Pope Causin -Ed N Roach, Reg/o wills

MON MAR 8, 1847

Perseverance Fire Co election of ofcrs on Thu last:
Geo S Gideon, Pres; Dr Jos Borrows, Vice Pres; V Harbaugh, Sec; Sylas H Hill, Treas; Hiram Richey, Capt Enginemen; Henry Hay, Capt Hoseman. Mr C Buckingham, the old & respected Pres of the Company, declined a further re-election.

The last detachment of the Va Regt of Volunteers left Hampton Roads for Mexico in the transport **Sophia Walker**, on Mon last. The vessel is bound to Point Isabel, & has on board the companies of Capts Preston, Robertson, & Archer. On Thu previous the brig **Saml N Gott** left Wilmington for Brasos Santiago, with 3 companies of the N C Regt on board, under the command of Capts Roberts, Shive, & Blalock; & on Tue the schnr **Harrison** departed from the same place with 2 more companies of the same regt, commanded by Capts Price & Kilpatrick, leaving behind only 2 companies, to follow their companions in 2 or 3 days.

Criminal Court-Wash: 1-Jacob Jones was convicted of petit larceny, & sentenced to 2 months in the county jail.

Laws of the U S passed at the 2nd Session of the 29th Congress: 1-For the execution of an historical painting for the rotundo of the Capitol, by Wm H Powell, in place of the one contracted for with Henry Inman, dec'd, under the joint resolution of Jun 23, 1836: $6,000; & the Library Cmte is directed to contract with the said Wm H Powell to execute the said painting on the same terms as were made with the said Inman. 2-For the payment of bill of John Skirving for extra work done in the Capitol during the year 1846: $321.82. 3-To pay Swann & Palmer for work executed by them at "***Twin island***," on the Ohio river, above the falls, $6,479.25. 4-For settling the claims of the late Republic of Texas, according to principles of justice & equity, for disarming a body of Texan troops under the command of Col Snively; & for entering the custom-house at Bryarly's Landing, & taking certain goods therefrom: a sum not exceeding $30,000.

By virtue of an order of distrain, for house rent due to Miss A E Lindenberger, by Mr Hulbert, I will expose at public sale for cash, on Mar 11, in front of Centre Market-house, in Wash City, the following goods & chattels, to wit: 2 bureaus, 1 clock, 1 round table, 12 chairs, 8 pictures in frames, 1 pine table, 1 stove, 1 map, & 2 pieces of ironware.
-H R Maryman, Bailiff

By virtue of an order of distrain for house rent due Miss A E Lindenberger by Mrs Raynor, I will expose at Public sale, on Mar 11, in front of Centre Market-house, the following goods & chattels, to wit: 1 mahogany table, 3 tables, 4 stands, 2 lamps, carpeting, 2 washstands, 16 chairs, 1 pair of brass andirons, books, 3 pieces of ironware, 6 curtains, 1 toilet glass, candlestick, 1 stove, 1 bedstead, 2 mantel ornaments, 1 lamp, 1 shovel & tongs, & 1 bowl & pitcher. -H R Maryman, Bailiff

Balt, Mar 6. We learn that our respected townsman, Col Solomon Hillen, late Mayor of Balt, is now lying dangerously ill, all hopes of his recovery having been given up.

Died: on Feb 10, at the Planters' House, St Louis, Alice Graham, youngest daughter of Col R B Mason, U S A, & Margaret Mason, aged 4 years. By a deplorable accident, the sweet little creature was scalded so severely that, after 6 days' severe suffering, she expired.

Executor's sale of the effects of the late Cmdor J B Nicolson, of the U S Navy. Sale at my auction room, Concert Hall, on Mar 12, of: a fine gold watch & diamond breastpin; sword & superb new epaulets; writing desk & trunks; also, his personal wardrobe. By order of the Executor. -A Green, auctioneer

For sale: a 2 story brick rough-cast house on N Y ave, in full view of the Potomac, between 17th & 18th sts, on square 170. Also, lot 16 in square 79, eligibly situated on H st, near Gen Eaton's, in the 1st Ward. Apply to Chas De Selding, #11 Todd's Bldg, Pa ave, Wash.

Wm Morgan, 13 years of age, was crushed & killed in Phil last Wed, when he attempted to get between 2 cars of the train, when the engine was reversed.

TUE MAR 9, 1847

Died: on Mar 8, in Wash City, Mr Wm Chas Wright, [printer,] of consumption, in his 22nd year. His funeral will be from his late residence, G st, between 2nd & 3rd sts, Tue at 2 P M.

Died: Mar 5, in Chas Co, Md, after a long illness, Mary Emeline, consort of Levi Semmes, in her 41st year.

Dr John C Warren, who resigned his professorship in the Massachusette Medical College was alluded to last week, delivered his valedictory on Mon. The chair has been occupied by father & son from the first organization of the medical dept in Harvard Univ.
-Boston Med & Surgical Journal

U S vs Francis Thomas: 2 years have elapsed since the publication of the obnoxious paper on which this indictment was instituted: the gentleman prosecuted is a man of many virtues: while the general powers of his mind are unimpaired, there is a morbid delusion traceable of a diseased condition of the mind on this particular subject which cannot be questioned. We see that, while he entertained for his wife the most doting affection, his mind vacillated between it & this particular subject. We withdraw all participation of our part as counsel for the dfndnt, in any line of defence promulgated in or inferred from the paper whereon he stands indicted, against his former wife, the present Mrs Sally C P McDowell. The shocking suspicions entertained by the dnfnt of her purity, originated, beyond any rational doubt, & there is no evidence to justify them; the suspicions originated in an unhappy delusion, destitute of all real foundation.
-Walter Jones, Otho Scott, Wm P Maulsby
+
Mr Preston, after the termination of the cause, read the following: My appearance on the part of the prosecution was for the purpose of vindicating the character of Mrs Sally C P McDowell from all charges & imputations at any time made, & for the purpose of putting her innocence & purity before the court & country. I consider my functions in it at an end. -Wm C Preston
+
Paper by Thos H Benton: I have to say that this indictment was not instituted by me with any view to obtain redress for injury done to myself or my wife in the publication of the letter complained of as libellous, but exclusively to get an opportunity of trying the truth of the accusations made by Francis Thomas, in his pamphlet of 1845, against his then wife, the niece of my wife. This indictment on the letter was instituted Mar, 1845, when the pamphlet was published; the letter itself having been published nearly one year before that time. I have no desire to proceed further with the case. -Thos H Benton
+
The Court directed the nolle prosequi to be entered, & the several papers offered by Gen Jones, Mr Preston, & the District of Atty to be filed.

Land at auction: by decree of the Circuit Superior Court of Law & Chancery, on Oct 17, 1846, in the chancery case of Fitzhugh against Fitzhugh, the undersigned, com'rs appointed for that purpose, will, on Apr 16, 1847, at Auburn in Fauquier Co, sell the real estate in said decree, to wit: the tract of land which was allotted to the heirs of Susannah Dade, dec'd, in the division of the estate of Thos Fitzhugh, dec'd, made under a decree of the Circuit Superior Court of Fauquier Co, in the said case of Fitzhugh against Fitzhugh, being the middle lot of the ***Pageland*** farm formerly the property of Thos Fitzhugh, dec'd, containing by survey 461 acres & 11 poles. -Saml Chilton, Wm A Bowen, Com'rs

Nat'l Intelligencer: Mr Israel E James is our collecting agent in the Southern Atlantic States, assisted by Jas K Whipple, Wm H Weld, O H P Stem, John B Weld, T S Waterman, Reuben A Henry, John Collins, Jas Deering, Isaac D Guyer, & John W Wightman. Mr C W James is our traveling agent for Ohio, Indiana, Ill, Missouri, Iowa, & Wisconsin, assisted by Jas R Smith, J T Dent, E Y Jennings, T G Smith, & Fred'k J Hawse.

Died: on Mar 8, at his residence in Wash City, Col Jas M Selding, naval storekeeper. His funeral is today at 4 o'clock, at the place where he died, near the Capitol.

Headquarters of the Army, Tampico, Feb 18, 1847. The Gen-in-Chief announces to the army the staff ofcrs who are attached to genr'l headquarters in the field.
Dept of Orders: 1st Lt H L Scott, 5th Infty, aid-de-camp & acting assist adj gen; 1st Lt T Williams, 4th Artl, aid-de-camp; 1st Lt E P Scammon, Topographical Engineers, acting aid-de-camp; & 2nd Lt G W Lay, 6th Infty, military secretary.
General Staff Ofcrs: Lt Col E A Hitchcock, 3rd Infty, acting inspector genr'l; Capt Jas Monroe, 6th Infty, acting assist inspector genr'l; Col J G Totten, chief of Corps of Engineers; Maj W Turnbull, acting chief of Topographical Engineers; Capt B Huger, acting chief of Ordnance; Maj S McRee, acting chief of the Quartermaster's Dept; Capt J B Grayson, acting chief of the Subsistence Dept; Maj E Kirby, acting chief of the Pay Dept; & Surgeon Gen T Lawson, chief of the Medical Dept. The senior ofcr of Artl, Col J Bankhead, 2nd Artl, will enter upon the duties of chief of Artl as soon as there shall be occasion for planting heavy batteries. All general staff ofcrs will be mainly employed in their respective depts of duty, & any orders that any chief of dept may give in relation to his peculiar duties in the name & by the authority of the genr'l-in-chief of the army, will be promptly obeyed. By command of Maj Gen Scott: H L Scott, A A A G

WED MAR 10, 1847
For rent: house recently occupied by Mrs France as a milliner's shop, on Pa ave, between 8th & 9th sts. Apply to Geo W Adams.

On Feb 23: 2 brothers, Uris & Wm Garreau, engaged in re-shingling a 4 story bldg in St Louis, fell from the roof to the pavement & both were killed-the eldest immediately, & the other surviving about an hour.

Wash Corp: 1-Cmte of Claims: asking to be discharged from the further consideration of the ptn of Robt Cunningham & of David S Waters: agreed to. 2-Memorial of Lucy Harrison Randolph: referred to the Cmte on Schools. 3-Ptn of J W Beck & others, for a gravel footwalk on East Capitol st: referred to the Cmte on Improvements. 4-Ptns of Adam Dulany, Dickerson Nailor, & Wm Nailor, for remission of fines: referred to the Cmte of Claims. 5-Cmte of Claims: act for the relief of John Burch: passed. 6-Bill for the relief of Caroline H Sanderson, passed with an amendment.

Notice: I have appointed Robt W Latham, of Wash, my agent & collector. -Jno Withers

The case of Joshua Owings & others, caveators against the will of Miss Mary Moxley, came up for argument before the Orphans' Court of Howard District, Md, on Sat. The caveat contained 9 allegations against the will; all of which were withdrawn except the one charging insanity in the testrix. At the close of the argument, the court immediately decided in favor of the will. -Patriot

The First Baptist Church in the town of Swanzey, Mass, was originally constituted in Wales. It was reorganized in Swanzey in 1663, & is the oldest Baptist Church in the Commonwealth of Massachusetts.

By order of distrain for house rent, due to Geo W Adams by Lewis France, I will expose at public sale for cash, on Mar 13, 1847, in front of the Centre Market-house, Wash City: furniture & sundry articles including washstand, 2 clothes-horses, shelving, crockery ware, 1 pair of girandoles, & tinware. -H R Maryman, Bailiff [Same sale advertised in the Mar 19th newspaper.]

Register's Ofc, Wash, Mar 3, 1847. Persons who have taken out licenses under the laws of the Corp during the month of Feb, 1847.

Dog License:

Allen, G F
Anderson, Garret
Atkins, Davy
Boyle, J F
Bohlayer, Jno
Brent, Elton
Branson, B
Barcroft, Maria
Benter, Wm
Barber, Geo
Burr, T S
Boss, J W
Boarman, S B
Bozz, Martin
Boyd, J R
Brooks, R J
Briel, Conrad-2
Bassett, Davig
Brent, Wm-2
Bach, T C
Beall, Robt
Bully, A
Cooper, Wm
Casparis, J
Caster, J H
Cook, J F
Coombe, R M
Campben, W
Catalano, A
Clarke, H A
Callan, H C
Cox, Wm
Cohen, Robt
Cookendorfe, T
Cochran, Geo
Cillion, Jno
Caldwell, J F
Clarke, Wm-2
Choppin, Wm
Carothers, Andrew
Downer, Joel
Downs, S
Dement, Richd
Duvall, Andrew
Duckett, A
Duncanson, H
Deeble, J A
Doyle, Geo
Douglass, Wm
Delany, Caleb
Dulany, Adam
Eckhardt, H
Eberbach, J H
Elliot, W P
Edwards, Geo
Ellie, Jonas
Evans, Edw
Favier, A
Fitzpatrick, Jas
Force, Peter
Fisher, T J
Fearson, J C
Force, Peter
Golding, R R
Gibson, Saml
Grainger, J
Gunnell, W H
Griffith, W T
Grey, H W
Grayson, Wm
Gannon, J P-3
Harris, Angelo
Hall, H C
Harvey, J L
Handy, S W
Hill, R S
Howle, Park G
Hollidge, J
Horning, G D
Hamilton, Wm
Hitz, John
Hooper, Saml
Jones, W T
Isaacs, Hester
Jameison, J M
Jenkins, David
Johnson, Jas
Jillard, Wm
Jenifer, Robt
Krafft, Peter
Kaufman, Geo
Kepler, Henry
Keyworth, R-2
King, Martin
Kurtz, Danl
Lauxman, M

Lee, A
Lusby, John
Laskey, R H
Lee, Josiah
Moran, Patrick
Moran, W P-2
Muller, Jo
Mills, Wm
Marr, J H
Merchant, Ann
Maryman, H R
McNorton, Geo
McDonald, W J
Magruder, t C
Martin, Wm
Mills, R T
Martin, L J
Meigle, Jacob
Nipp, Danl
Nugent, E E
Newton, Benj
Noland, Philip
Noerr, And
Neale, John E
Nokes, Jas-2
Nailor, Dickerson
Nailor, Thompson
Neale, Horatio
Owens, B
Owens, Thos-2
O'Donoghue, P-2
Owens, Benj
Pittibone, Wm
Poston, F B
Parker, G & T
Preston, A J
Pulizze, V
Pettibone, J
Page, Geo
Pettit, Chas
Rupert, Eva
Ross, J W-2
Reed, B W
Reeder, Richd
Roane, J J
Rice, Edm
Rhodes, Jas
Rawlings, D
Sprigg, T B
Stewart, F A
Shedd, W P
Slight, Pringle
Scott, S E
Scott, W B
Scaggs, Susan-2
Smith, Wilfred
Schwettzer, A-2
Smith, J C
Seifferly, G J
Smoot, John H
Sprigman, J M
Sanderson, Carol
Stubbs, W E
Simms, Basil
Shirley, Jesse
Smith, Jerry-2
Smith, G B
Stanley, J T
Speaks, Letitia
Stewart, Donald
Taylor, Sophia
Thompson, J R
Travers, Elias
Talbert, Adel
Thomas, J H
Tait, Jas A
Tanner, Lethe
Tucker, E
Tucker, Jas
Van Reswick, T
Uttermuhle, Geo
Walker, Wm
Wagner, J
Wadsworth, A
Williams, J A
Weyrich, J
Watterston, Geo
Winchester, R
Wenderlich, John
Young, John M
Young, Forrester

<u>Butcher License:</u>

Berkley, J T
Boother, R E
Brown, C H
Berry, John
Bell, Wm D
Bohlayer, John
Dowell, Jno-2
Eggleston, M
Emerson, G W
Ennis, John
Gatrell, Otho
Gatrell, A M
Garrett, Milton
Hoover, Michl
Linkins, Wm
Little, Sam J
Linkins, Wm
Murphy, John
Miller, Jo
Murphy, John
Prather, Alfred
Prather, Jos-2
Rawlings, David
Shedd, W P-2
Walker, Henry-2
Weaver, Henry-2
Weaver, Saml-2

<u>Huckster License:</u>

Atkins, Davy
Brichsler, John
Berryman, L H
Butler, J A W
Buckley, T R
Dulany, Adam
Ellis, Richd
Golding, R R
Garrett, Milton-3

Goodwin, Peter	Meashrell, Richd	Simpson, Wm
Harris, Morgan	Palmer, John	Triplett, T J
Mullikin, J W	Sullivan, Patrick	Taylor, J H

Hardware License: Anderson, Garret; Quirk, Thos
Hack License: Kimmell & Walker; Page, Geo; Smith, Wm; Turner, Henry; Welch, Thos
Grocery License: Bird, Wm; Howard, Jos
Dry Goods License: Clarke, J B, agent; Evans, John; Hills, J B
Medicines License: Tyson, S E-transfer
Concert License: Davis, J S-5
Tavern License: Hall, J S-transfer
Retail License: Huggins, T B; Laub, E A; Robey, J W
Theatre License: Kilmiste, M-2
Jewelry License: Keyworth, R
Brokers License: Latham, R W & Co
Auction License: McDevitt, John
Female Slave License: Noland, Caroline; Richards, J R
Male Slave License: Walker,Wm
Shop License: Pestorias, Fred
The following persons have been fined during the month of Feb for failing to procure their licenses, as per returns of the 2nd 3rd & 4th ward magistrates-the 1st 5th 6th & 7th Wards not returned.
Fined for no Dog License:

Anderson, Garret	Johnson, John	Maguire, Thos
Clagett, Darius	Lewis, Wm B	Moran, Patrick
Campbell, Wm	Lindsley, John	Nailor, Dickerson
Dermott, Ann	McNair, W W	Stettinius, Geo
Force, Peter	Merland, P H	Seifferly, J
Holmes, Sylvanus	Mesheral, Richd	Weeden, Susan
Huggins, F B	Mortimer, W H	Wilner, Geo

Fined for no Huckster License:

Berryman, L H	Colward, John	Fitzgerald, John
Birkley, Tim	Colward, Armsted	Harris, H
Bede, Geo	David, August	Sherwood, A
Cruit, Richd	Dunnington, J F	Thomkins, Richd
Cammack, Wm	Delany, Adam	
Cross, Harrison	Fleming, Patrick	

Fined for no Retail License: Adams, Wm; Hilyard, Mrs

Connecticut: annual election takes place in Apr. Clark Bissell, of Norwalk, is the Whig candidate for Govn'r. The nominations for Congress are as follows: [All Whigs]
1-Hartford & Tolland: Jas Dixon
2-New Haven & Middlesex: Saml D Hubbard
3-New London & Windham: John A Rockwell
4-Fairfield & Litchfield: Truman Smith

We understand that the Hon Thos H Benton declines the appointment of Maj Gen in the Army, tendered to him by the Pres & Senate.

N Y, Mar 6. Yesterday the funeral procession of the remains of the late Capts Morris, Williams, & Fields took place in St Paul's Church. They were taken to City Hall & escorted to a steamboat which was to convey them to Bridgeport, & thence, by the Housatonic Railroad, to Albany.

The Ladies of the Union Benevolent Society gratefully acknowledge the receipt of $50 from Maj Heiss, 10 cords of wood & $10 from W W Corcoran, $20 from Dr Gunton, $20 from Dr J C Hall, & $20 from an unknown friend; besides several minor donations, for which the thanks of the Society are due.

Mr Jonathan Hunt, of N Y, about Jan 15 last, traveled to the South; reached Charleston & left the Charleston Hotel at night; since when there had been no intelligence of him.

<u>The Navy-Official Appointments by the Pres, by & with the advice & consent of the Senate.</u>

Cmder Chas Ganntt, to be captain, vice Jesse D Elliot, dec'd.
Cmder Wm Ramsay, to be a captain, vice Wm M Crane, dec'd.
Cmder Henry Henry, to be a captain, vice Jas Renshaw, dec'd.
Cmder Saml W Downing, to be a captain, vice John B Nicolson, dec'd.
Lt Henry Pinkney, to be a cmder, vice Wm C Wetmore, dec'd.
Lt Wm M Glendy, to be a cmder, vice Chas Ganntt, promoted.
Lt Geo P Upshur, to be a cmder, vice Wm Ramsay, promoted
Lt Geo S Blake, to be a cmder, vice Henry Henry, promoted.
Lt Zachariah F Johnston, to be a cmder, vice Saml W Downing, promoted
Master Wm L Blanton, to be a lt, vice Henry Pinkney, promoted.
Master Benj S Gantt, to be a lt, vice John Graham, dec'd.
Master Henry A Wise, to be a lt, vice Wm M Glendy, promoted.
Master Callender St Geo Noland, to be a lt, vice Richd C Cogdell, resigned.
Master Edw C Anderson to be a lt, vice Geo P Upshur, promoted.
Passed Midshipman Reed Werden, to be a Lt, vice Geo S Blake, promoted
Passed Midshipman Wm H Macomb, to be a lt, vice Zachariah F Johnston, promoted
Passed Midshipman Stephen D Trenchard, to be a lt, vice Richd S Trapier, resigned.
Passed Midshipman Wilson R McKinney, to be lt, vice Wm A Wurts, dec'd.
Thos Coke Stanley, of Alabama, to be a chaplain in the navy, vice Wm Ryland, dec'd.
Edwin Eaton, of Ohio, to be a chaplain in the navy, vice Geo W Latham, dec'd.
John L Lenhart, of N J, to be a chaplain in the navy, vice Chas H Alden, dec'd.
John Blake, of Maine, to be a chaplain in the navy, vice Nathan C Fletcher, resigned.
1st Assist Engineer Alex'r Birbeck, jr, to be a chief engineer in the navy.
John M Bell, to be a navy agent for the port of New Orleans, La.
Thos O Larkin, to be temporary navy agent for the northwest coast of North America.

Marine Corps:
Jos L C Hardy, Geo F Lindsay, Landon N Carter, & John G Reynolds, now 1st lts, to be captains in the Marine Corps.
Josiah Watson, Henry B Watson, Thos A Brady, Isaac T Doughty, Wm A T Maddox, Wm B Slack, John S Devlin, & Algernon S Taylor, now 2nd lts, to be 1st lts in the Marine Corps.
Jas H Jones, of Dela; Edw McD Reynolds,of N Y; Wm Butterfield, of Ill; Henry Welch, of Pa; Wm F Perry, of N Y; Jos K McRae, of Indiana; Thos Y Field, of Pa; Chas G McCauley, of Louisiana; Jas A Buchanan, of Tenn; Israel Green, of Wisconsin; Freeman Norvell, of Mich; Jacob Read, of Georgia: to be 2nd Lts in the Marine Corps.

THU MAR 11, 1847

The Patapsco Institute near Balt, Md, offers advantages for the education of Young Ladies seldom found united. It is located in the mountainous region of Elkridge, within a few minutes' walk of the depot of the Cumberland Railroad at ***Ellicott's Mills***. Its commodious bldgs afford private apartments for elder pupils. It grounds, laid out in gardens, afford the pupils an opportunity for the cultivation of flowers. A large establishment of professors, teachers, & domestic superintendents secures to the pupils an amount of instruction & care seldom to be met with in any institution of the kind. At present there are 14 professors & teachers. The Rev Mr Clarke, resident chaplain, a graduate of Yale College, is Professor of Mental Philosophy. Miss Brown is Vice Principal. Mrs Lincoln Phelps is the Principal, who passed many years as Vice Principal & Principal of the long-established Troy Seminary, founded by her sister, Mrs Emma Willard. Associated with his wife is the Hon John Phelps, formerly a distinguished lawyer & Senator of Vt. Summer session will commence on May 5.

Ecole Francaise, Pour des Jeunes Demoiselles: Madame Dorman, well known in Wash City as an efficient teacher of the French Language in French Seminaries, intends opening a School at her residence, H st, between 9th & 10th sts, opposite the Protestant Asylum.

Appointments by the President, by & with the advice & consent of the Senate.
Wm Marvin, U S district judge for the southern district of Florida
Jos B Brown, U S marshal of the southern district of Florida.
Robt Myers, U S marshal for the northern district of Florida.
J Windsor Smith, U S atty for the souther district of Florida.
Isaac M Preston, U S atty for the district of Iowa
John J Dyer, judge of the district court of the U S for the district of Iowa.
Gideon S Bailey, U S marshal for the district of Iowa.
Geo Latimer, of Pa, U S consul for the port of St John's, in the island of Puerto Rico, vice Henry G Hubbard, dec'd.
Tobias Beehler, of Pa, U S consul for Stuttgard, in the kingdom of Wurtemburg, vice Fred'k List, dec'd.
Washington Greenhow, of Va, to be U S consul for the port of Buenos Ayres, vice Burrill B Taylor, resigned.

C G Salinas, of S C, to be U S consul for the port of Pernambuco, Brazil, vice Geo P Manouvrier, dec'd.
Edw Weld, of N Y, to be U S consul for the island T___ffe, vice Jos Cullen, dec'd.
August Furaldo, U S consul for the port of Bayonne, France.
Christopher Hempstead, of N Y, to be U S consul for the port of Balize, Honduras.
Wm P Pierce, of Mass, to be U S consul for the port of Macao.
Robt Dubs, of Pa, to be U S consul for the port of Maracaibo, vice Robt Hutton, resigned.
Horace Hawes, of Pa, to be U S consul for the Society Island, vice Aza P Ladd, resigned.
C Frank Powell, of N Y, to be U S consul at Muscat, vice Seyd Ben Calfaun, dec'd.
Chas Douglass, of Conn, to be Com'r of Public Bldgs.
Craven P Ashford & Wm R Woodward, justices of the peace for Wash Co, D C.
John Brooks, coiner of the mint at New Orleans, vice Philos B Tyler, resigned.
Gideon C Matlock, Indian agent for the tribes of Indians on the Upper Missouri, vice Thos P Moore, appointed lt-colonel of dragoons.
Land Ofcrs:
Reuben H Boone, register, Grenada, Miss, vice Thos B Ives, resigned.
John Barton, reappointed register, Genesee, Mich.
Isaac D G Nelson, reappointed receiver, Fort Wayne, Indiana.
Robt Benguerel, reappointed receiver, Opelousas, La.
Edw B Randolph, reappointed receiver, Columbus, Miss.
Wm H Simmons, reappointed receiver, St Augustine, Florida.
John F Meade, register, Green Bay, Wisconsin, vice John S Horner, removed.
Custom-house ofcrs:
H C V Dashiel, deputy collector for the port of Sabine, Texas.
John T Stephens, to be surveyor of the port of Capano, in the west collection district of Texas.
Danl Emery, collector of the customs for the port of Bangor, Maine.
Benj Wormstead, reappointed surveyor, Marblehead, Mass.
Danl Foster, reappointed surveyor, Beverly, Mass.
Elisha Atkins, surveyor, Newport, R I, vice Wm G Hammond, whose commission expired.
Benj Pomery, collector, Stonington, Conn, vice Ezra Chesebro, removed.
Saml Harris, surveyor, Velasco, Texas, vice Robt S Herndon, dec'd.
Peleg B Phelps, surveyor, city of Lafayette, La, vice Danl Clark, jr, resigned.
Thos W Kellum, surveyor, Madisonville, La, vice Thos Addison, who did not qualify.

Died: on Mar 2, at Huntington, Suffolk Co, the Hon Silas Wood, aged 78 years. He had in his time been prominently before the public of Long Island as one of the leading men in political life. He is known as the author of a history of Long Island, which was published about 20 years ago; & was for several years a Rep in Congress.

Died: on Mar 2, Mrs E J Sterne, consort of Mr Wm Sterne, of Stafford Co, Va, in her 59th year.

Died: on Mar 7, in Wash City, Saml Judson, 5th son of Mrs Eliz Ann & the late Edmund Coolidge, aged 10 months & 20 days. "Suffer little children to come unto me, & forbid them not, for such is the Kingdom of Heaven."

John M Allen, U S Marshal for Texas, died suddenly on the night of Feb 19.

Died: on Mar 10, Mrs Dolly Thornton, aged about 65 years, for many years a faithful & valued domestic in the family of Peter Lenox, dec'd. Her friends, those her children, & the societies of which she was a member, are invited to attend her funeral on Fri, at 3 o'clock, from the residence of Mrs Lenox, on E between 10th & 11th sts.

The two Quaker sisters, Hannah Gillaspy & Lucy Elkinton, who have for many years lived together in a house in Almond st, Phil, expired about noon on Mon, almost at the same instant. The former was in her 90th & the latter in her 86th year.

I offer for sale, a great bargain, 100 acres of land in Alexandria Co, within 2 miles of the Long Bridge; also 18 acres within one mile of Alexandria. Inquire of Swann & Swann, Attys at Law, Wash. -G B Alexander, King Geo Co, Va.

Orphans Court of Wash Co, D C. Letters of administration on the personal estate of Mary A Cooper, late of said county, dec'd. -Christopher Cammack, adm

Balt, Mar 10. In the case of the State vs Richd J Turner, charged with defrauding the Mechanic's Bank of Balt out of a large sum of money, the impression is that the State cannot obtain a conviction. [Mar 19th newspaper: jury rendered a verdict of acquittal in the case of Richd J Turner, tried for defrauding the Mechanics' Bank.]

H V Hill informs the public that his house is ready for Boarders: located adjacent to the Capitol grounds.

Brookeville Academy: Mr Elisha John Hall & Rev Orlando Hutton, A M: Principals. Trustees: Allen B Davis, Pres; Remus Riggs; W B Magruder, M D; Thos J Bowie; B B Pleasants; Hon Wm Lingan Gaither. Located in the village of Brookeville, Montg Co, Md, 20 miles distant from Wash. The sale of all spirituous liquors is prohibited within 2 miles of the village. The boarders will reside in the families of the instructors. The course of instruction embraces the usual branches of a complete academical education. The principals refer to the following gentlemen, some of whom have pupils in the institution: Rev Dr Wyatt, N C Brooks, M A, Principal of the High School, John Carrere, John G Proud, Thos E Hambleton, John Orndorff: Balt. Messrs Gales & Seaton, Dr Flodoardo Howard, A Green: Wash. Rev Wm Pinkney, A M, Bladensburg; Dr R H Hewett, Sykesville, Md; Rev Ignatius Waters, Fred'k Co; John O'Donnell, Howard District; Caleb Dorsey, Howard District; Thos Lansdale, Ellicott's Mills.

Just arrived, 19 head of Virginia Horses: can be found at the Franklin Livery Stable, corner of D & 8th sts. -Jacob Rowles, Proprietor

Household & kitchen furniture at auction: on Mar 11, at the residence of R H Clements, on C st, between 3rd & 4½ sts: by order of distrain: his entire lot of furniture.
-R R Burr, Bailiff -A Green, auctioneer

Household & kitchen furniture at auction: on Mar 11, at the residence of R H Clements, on C st, between 3rd & 4½ sts: by order of distrain: his entire lot of furniture.
-R R Burr, Bailiff -A Green, auctioneer

Teacher wanted at the Female Seminary in Chestertown. A married gentleman, whose wife would be competent to assist him & teach music, would be preferred. Appy to Geo B Westcott, Chestertown, Md.

Army Gen'l Order: War Dep, Adj Gen Ofc: Wash, Mar 4, 1847. Ofcrs appointed, & the 10 companies of Infty to be recruited in N Y [7] & N J [3] will constitute the 10th Regt of Infty, under Col Robt E Temple: Headquarters at N Y. ***Fort Hamilton & Fort Layafette*** will be receiving depots for this requirement. The ofcrs appointed, & the 10 companies of Infty to be recruited in Pa, [6] Delaware, [1] Va [3] will constitute the 11th Regt of Infty under Col Albert C Ramsey: Headquarters at Balt. The ofcrs appointed, & the 10 companies of Infty to be recruited in N C, [2] S C, [2] Texas, [2] Arkansas, [2] & Missouri [2] will constitute the 12th regt of Infty, under Col Louis D Wilson: Headquarters at New Orleans. The ofcrs appointed, & the 10 companies of Infty to be raised in Va, [1] Ga, [4] Alabama, [4] & Florida [1] will constitute the 13th Regt of Infty, under Col Robt M Echols: Headquarters at New Orleans. The ofcrs appointed, & the 10 companies of Infty to be raised in La, [5] Tenn, [4] & Ill [1] will constitute the 14th regt of Infty under Col Wm Trousdale: Headquarters at New Orleans. The ofcrs appointed, & the 10 companies of Infty to be raised in Ohio, [5] Mich, [3] Iowa, [1] & Wisconsin [1] will constitute the 15th Regt of Infty under Col Geo W Morgan: Headquarters at Cincinnati. The ofcrs appointed, & the 10 companies of Infty to be raised in Ky, [4] Indiana, [4] Ill [2] will constitute the 16th Regt of Infty under Col J W Tibbatts: Headquarters at Newport, Ky. The ofcrs appointed, & the 10 designated companies to be raised in Pa, [2] Md, [3] Va, [2] Miss, [1] Ga, [1] & Ky [1] will constitute The Regt of Voltigeurs, under Col T P Andrews: Headquarters for the present at Wash, D C. The Third Regt of Dragoons is to be raised in the following States: Mich, N Y, Pa, Md, N C, S C, Ala, La, Ky, & Indiana-in each one company; Col Edw G W Butler: Headquarters at New Orleans.
-R Jones, Adj Gen

FRI MAR 12, 1847

Mrs Brauner has several pleasant rooms vacant, & will be pleased to accommodate permanent or transient Boarders.

House of Reps: 1-Ptn of Chas Packard & others of Lancaster, Mass, & of Benj F Wood & others, of Westminster, Mass, praying that an end may be put to the unfortunate war in which we are engaged. 2-Ptn of Robt Falkner & others, inhabitants of Lexington, Greene Co, N Y, praying for the freedom of the public lands. 3-Memorial of Jos Kelley, praying for an invalid pension. 4-Ptn of Luther Pratt, of N J, praying for an alteration of postage.

Supreme Court of the U S. #37: Wharton Jones, plntf, vs John Van Zandt, on a certificate of division in opinion between the judges of the Circuit Court of the U S for Ohio. Mr Justice Woodbury delivered the opinion of this Court, that under the 4th section of the act of Feb 12, 1793, respecting fugitives from justice & persons escaping from the service of their masters, on a charge for harboring & concealing fugitives from labor, that notice in writing by the claimant or his agent, or general notice to the public in a newspaper, is not necessary; that clear proof of the knowledge of the dfndnt that he knew the colored person was a slave & fugitive from labor is sufficient to charge him with notice; that a claim of the fugitive from labor need not precede or accompany the notice; that any overt act, so marked in its character as to show an intention to elude the vigilance of the master or his agent, is calculated to attain such an object, is a harboring of the fugitive within the statute; & that the said act of Congress of Feb 12, 1793, is not repugnant either to the Constitution of the U S or to the ordinance of Congress adopted Jul, 1787, for the gov't of the territory of the U S northwest of the river Ohio.

Mrd: on Feb 21, at Gtwn, D C, by Rev Mr Tarring, Mr Jas G Smith to Miss Ann Eliza Stillings, both of the Navy Yard, Wash.

The admirable portrait of Judge McLean, of the U S Supreme Court, which was recently painted by Matthew Wilson, has elicited such warm & general commendation, that it has been brought to this city, & may be seen at the store of Mr Cariss, 140 Balt st.
-Balt American

The steam saw-mill of Mr John s Walter, Wilmington, Delaware, was burnt to the ground on Thu night. The loss is to be $15,000. The sash manufactory of Messrs Mitchell & McFarlan was also destroyed.

Orphans Court of Montg Co, Md: held on Mar 9, 1847, were present, Geo W Dawson & Otho Magruder, Justices; Wm O Chappell, Sheriff; Henry Harding, Register. Upon application of John T Vinson & Harriet E Vinson, his wife, to the Orphans Court of Montg Co, praying that letters of administration on the personal estate of Joshua Chilton, late of said county, dec'd, may be granted to them, it is, Mar 9, 1847, ordered by the Court that letters of administrationon the personal estate of the said Joshua Chilton be granted to the said John T Vinson & Harriet E Vinson, his wife, unless cause to the contrary be shown to the Court on or before the first Tue of May next.
-Geo W Dawson, Otho Magruder -Henry Harding, Reg/o wills

Died: on Mar 11, Mr Thos I Mudd, in his 72nd year. His funeral will take place today at 4 o'clock, at his late residence, on 10th st.

Wash Co, D C. I hereby certify that Danl W Calclazer brought before as an estray a red & white cow. -T C Donn, J P [Owner to come forward, prove property, pay charges, & take her away. -D W Calclazer, on 7th st turnpike.]

Auction Notice: to Hotel properitors, steamboat owners, & dealers. $10,000 worth of Mason's White Patent Iron Stone China will be sold at auction, by Jacob S Platt, in the large room over the auction store #23 Platt, corner of Gold st, N Y.
-Wm W Shirley, salesman

SAT MAR 13, 1847
Orphans Court of Wash Co, D C. Letters of administration de bonis non with the will annexed, on the personal estate of Henry Thompson, late of said county, dec'd.
-B F Middleton, adm de bonis non W A

The Will of a Clergyman. Rev Mr Cooper, of the Phil Conference of the Methodist Episcopal Church, who died in Phil last week, left a will, in his own handwriting, covering 9 close written pages, in which he states he was born in Caroline Co, Md, in 1763, & at age 21 entered the ministry. He requests to be interred in front of St George's Methodist Episcopal Church, Phil, in consideration of which he leaves the corporation $1,000 to be used in the purchse of wood for the poor of that church. To the Methodist Book Concern in N Y he leaves $1,000, to be used in printing the Bible. Ten annual ground rents of $30, the principal sum being $5,000 he devises for the benefit of worn out preachers & their families, & $1,000 to various Methodist Churches in Phil. He gives to each of his nephews & nieces, whose name is Ezekiel Cooper, [with or without a middle name,] named for & after him, the sum of $100. To each & every child or person, the children of friends & acquaintances, who are named Ezekiel Cooper after him, with or without middle or additional names, a neat octavo Bible. After specific devises of personal property to various persons, the residue of the property is to be divided between his nephews & nieces, & their children. Rev Jas Smith, Peter L Cooper, & Ignatius T Cooper, of Kent Co, Delaware, are nominated executors. It is supposed that the value of his estate is from $150,000 to $200,000.

The U S schnr **On-Ka-Hy-e**, Lt Berryman, arrived at Pensacola on Mar 2, from Chargres, after a very boisterous passage of 14 days. She brings no news of moment.

The Union states that Mr Hampton C Williams, of Wash City, has been appointed by the Sec of the Navy naval storekeeper in place of Jas M Selden, dec'd.

The brig **Aetna** & the brig **Stromboli**, recently fitted out at the Charlestown Navy Yard, near Boston, are ready for sea, to sail on Thu for the Gulf. The **Aetna** is commanded by Com G J Van Brunt, & the **Stromboli** by Com Wm S Walker. Their guns were cast by Alger, at South Boston, weigh each about 1,500 pounds, & will carry a shell weighing some 85 pounds. It is stated that these guns will carry at least half a mile further than those at the castle of San Juan.

Household & kitchen furniture at auction: on Mar 16, at the residence of Miss Shounand, on Pa ave, between 3rd & 4½ sts: an extensive & excellent lot of furniture.
-A Green, auctioneer

Midwifery: Mrs Moenster, having qualified herself by a course of professional study, & improved by many years' experience in a lying-in institution in Copenhagen, has emigrated to Wash City, which she intends to make her future residence, & offers her professional services. Her testimonials, certified by the American Minister at Copenhagen, will satisfy every one of the reality of her pretensions. Her residence in on 13th st, west side, 3 doors from the corner of F st.

Mrd: on Mar 11, by Rev Jas Laurie, D D, the Rev Wm A Westcott, M D, of Goshen, Orange Co, N Y, to Miss Sarah R Stott, of Wash.

Died: on Thu, Mary Jane, daughter of Lemuel & Caroline Williams, aged 3 years & 4 months. Her funeral is from the residence of Mr Williams, Pa ave, near 17th st, today at 4 o'clock.

Died: on Mar 7, in Wash City, Susan Stoddert, w/o Thos Milstead, in her 51st year.

Just finished & for rent: one of those fine 4 story brick houses on 13th st west, between E & F sts north, & one square north of Pa ave, belonging to Geo R Gaither, of Balt. Inquire of Chas Bradley, at Franklin Ins Ofc, 7th st, Wash.

Boarding: Mrs R Smith, corner of Missouri ave & 3rd st, can accommodate a few boarders.

MON MAR 15,1847

The Elmira Gaz announces the death, on Mar 1, of David Petriken, formerly a Rep in Congress from Pa.

Mrd: on Mar 11, by Rev V Palen, Mr John L Fowler to Miss Eliza Jordan, both of Wash.

Mrd: on Mar 11, by Rev Van Horseigh, Mr Chas C M Walter to Miss Ellen C Mohun, all of Wash City.

Died: on Mar 10, at his residence in Wash Co, Mr Richd Lawrence, about 60 years of age. He was formerly of Fredericktown, Md.

Died: on Feb 10, in Auburn, Macon Co, Ala, Austin Woolfolk, aged 50 years, on his way from Balt to his home & family in Louisiana.

Criminal Court-Wash. John Barnard, guilty of an assault with an intent to kill Jas S Hall, was sentenced to suffer imprisonment in the penitentiary for 3 years. The Judge expressed his deep regret at seeing a young man, so respectably connected & well educated, brought into such a painful & distressing situation. [Mar 20th newspaper: John Barnard was yesterday pardoned by the President.]

The case of Dougherty, enlisted in Capt Chas J Biddle's company of Voltigeurs, under act of Feb 11, 1847, was decided by Judge Parsons, in the Court of Common Pleas for Phil Co, on a writ of habeas corpus. Minors could not be enlisted, without the consent of their parents, guardians, or masters; but in this case the recruit being 19 years of age, of intelligence, he could leave it to his own deliberate choice. The recruit expressing a desire to continue in the service, was remanded to the charge of his ofcr. -Pennsylvanian [Mar 17th newspaper: The Court overruled the decision of his Hon Judge Parsons. His discharge was asked by his parents. The laws of the U S give no authority to enlist minors. He was discharged from the custody of Capt Biddle by the Court. -Philadelphia Ledger]

Edw Lucas has received the appointment of paymaster of the U S armory at Harper's Ferry, vice Richd Parker, resigned.

Teacher wanted for the Primary School District #7, residing in Anne Arundel Co, Md. Direct your letter to West river. -Plummer J Drury, Edw McCeney, Jas Higgins, Trustee

Obit-died: on Mar 13, in Wash City, Mrs Effie McArthur Allen, w/o the Hon Wm Allen, Senator from Ohio. She was seized with a pleurisy about the time of the adjournment of Congress, & at last sunk under its violence, notwithstanding the skill of physicians & the devoted attention of her husband. Her relatives are at a distance; her home is in the West. Mrs Allen was the daughter of the late Govn'r McArthur, of Ohio, & was 40 years of age. She leaves but one child by her present marriage, an infant dght, 13 months old-too young to know its loss. Her funeral will take place at 12 o'clock this day, from the ladies' apartments of Brown's Hotel to the <u>Congressional Burying Ground</u>, whence, in a few days thereafter, the body will be interred in Ohio. [Mar 17th newspaper: the funeral of Mrs Allen was attended by the Pres of the U S & Members of the Cabinet, & by the Senators & Reps remaining in the city. Among the pall-bearers were Senators Webster, Benton, & Begby.]

Sheet Brass: 10,000 pounds just received & for sale by Wm Spears, #40 Lombard st, Balt.

TUE MAR 16, 1847

The Boston Relief Cmte have accepted the offer of Capt R B Forbes to convey their contributions to Ireland with the U S ship **Jamestown**.

Criminal Court-Wash. U S vs W H Wall, guilty of stealing a promissory note for $147, the property of Richd N Johnson. He was taken into the custody of the Deputy Marshal. Mr Bradley moved for a new trial, on the ground of newly discovered evidence. [Jul 28th newspaper: <u>nolle prosequi</u> in the case of the U S vs Wall: prisoner was discharged from imprisonment.]

Valuable library of the late Rev Henry Foxall at auction: on Mar 17, at the store on the corner of Bridge & Congress sts. Terms at sale. -Edw S Wright, auctioneer

Mr Walter Urquhart & wife recently instituted in one of the Court of New Haven a suit against the Connecticut River Steamboat Co for injuries sustained by the latter on board one of their steamboats, in 1845. Mrs Urquhart had her arm broken, & had other injuries, whilst being landed at night in a small boat. The evidence showed negligence on the part of the ofcrs, & the jury gave a veridict for the plntf for $1,575.

Valuable property for sale: a very valuable water power, about one mile from the depot at Bladensburg, 19 feet fall, on a never failing stream. Also, about 90 acrs of land about 5 miles from Wash. The property will be exchanged for Wash City property, at a fair price. Inquire of Geo A Digges, near Bladensburg.

Important sale: the Catharine Furnace, with dwlg, 4,648 acres of land: public auction on Jun 1, 1847: located in Spottsylvania Co, Va. The stack was built by Mark McAfee in 1837. Application for private sale may be made to Dr Wm N Wellford, Fredericksburg, Va. -Wm N Wellford, Exc of John S Wellford. -Ed H Carmichael
-R H Cunningham, Trustee of F B Dean, jr

To the heirs of Rebecca White, the w/o Jas White, of the State of Georgia. The subscriber has been appointed by the Orphans Court of Chester Co, Pa, auditor to distribute $1,225.95, arising from the estate of Rachel Brownback, late of the township of East Vincent, in said county, dec'd, to & amongst the heirs of said dec'd; & whereas the said Rebecca White, formerly Parker, was a sister of the said Rachael Brownback, & removed with her husband from Chester Co, Pa, to the State of Georgia about 60 years ago, & her children, if living, are entitled to a portion of said fund. The auditor ofc is in Westchester, Chester Co, Pa. -Washington Townsend, auditor

Mrd: on Mar 8, at the residence of Mr John H Zimmerman, Fairfax Co, Va, by the Rev John L Pascoe, Lovell Middleton to Miss Susan Robey, all of Loudoun Co, Va.

WED MAR 17, 1847

Graceful lines from the pen of Mrs Mary W Thompson, the widow of the late Col Thompson, of the U S Infty, who was killed at the head of his regt in the Florida war.
"The Fallen Heroes of Monterey*:*" by Mrs Mary W Thompson
Soft swells the bugle's note,
Low rolls the muffled drum,
Measured, and slow, the heavy tread,
That bears them to their home.
The battle's din had ceased,
Proud victory's shout is hush'd,
But sorrow mingles in that joy,
For many a hope is crush'd.

Strew'd o're that warring field,
Mangled, and cold, there lay
The brave-the young-our country's boast-

Ah, fearful was the fray!
Late, and amidst those line,
We saw the phalanx stand,
With waving banners-lances high-
Impatient in command

There was no heart that quailed-
No steel remained unclasped;
But every eye flashed forth its zeal,
And every hilt was grasped!
Amidst that deadly strife
They fell, as warriors fall!
Their life was to their country pledged,
Its banner is their pall!

With love like that which glows
Within a brother's breast,
Their comrades seek their loved remains
And bring them here to rest.
Oh, 'twas a mournful task
To seek the gallant dead,
To lift again the clay-cold form,
And fresh warm tears to shed.

Hang up their honored sword
Enwreathed with laurel bough-
And on their breast the olive lay,
For they sleep peaceful now.

Died: on Mon, after a long & painful illness, Mrs Mary Smallwood, wife of Mr John Smallwood, in her 45th year. Her funeral is today, at half past 2 o'clock, from her late residence, on 7th st, near the Navy Yard.

Wash Corp: 1-Ptn of Danl B Clarke: referred to the Cmte on Improvements. 2-Ptns for relief of Henry L Cross; of John Burch; of Jas B Clarke; of Caroline H Sanderson: all referred to the Cmte of Claims. 3-Ptn of Jas Laurie: referred to the Cmte on Improvements. 4-Ptn of Andrew Doig, praying payment for a balance due him for paving a gutter across Mass ave, on 6th st west: referred to the Cmte on Improvements. 5-Ptn of Mrs Matilda Radcliff, praying to be refunded a certain amount erroneously paid for taxes: referred to the Cmte on Improvements. 6-Ptn of Jas B Davis for remission of a fine: referred to the Cmte on Claims. 7-Ptn of Chas F Wood & others, praying the improvement of 9th st west, between E & F sts north: referred to the Cmte on Improvements. 8-Cmte of Claims: act for the relief of Michl Talty: passed. Same cmte: relief of Thos Dumphy: postponed. Same cmte: asked to be discharged from the further consideration of the ptn of L M Deppel.

For sale: a single horse & carriage. Inquire of Ben E Green, ofc on F st, opposite Dr Laurie's Church.

Reporters wanted: the undersigned wants to secure the services of several experienced Stenographers during the next session of Congress. Address to Dr J A Houston, N Y. -Jas A Houston, Stenographer of the U S Senate, Wash, Mar 15, 1847.

Trustee's sale: by deed of trust from Mr Jas B Clarke to Richd G Briscoe, dated Feb 8, 1847, recorded in the Clerk's ofc of Wash Co, D C, in book W B #129, folios 47 to 82: public auction at the store lately occupied by the said Clarke, on Pa ave, between Brown's Hotel & 7th sts, all the goods & merchandise comprising his late stock in trade: articles usually found in a retail dry goods store. -R W Dyer, auct

Oregon Mail: mail will be dispatched to Oregon, under charge of Mr J M Shively, from Independence, Missouri, on Apr 15 next. Persons desirous of sending letters to Oregon will forward them to Independence, Missouri. -C Johnson, Postmaster Genr'l

Just in time-now landing, a small cargo of Anthracite Coal: apply at the Lumber yard on 7th st, near the market, where is kept all kinds of bldg materials. -John Purdy, 7th st, near Market & Canal

THU MAR 18, 1847

Insurrection at Taos of the Mexicans: all the Spaniards who evinced any sympathy with the American cause were compelled to escape. Gov Bent, Stephen Lee, Acting Sheriff, Gen Elliot Lee, Henry Leal, & 20 other Americans, were killed & their families despoiled; the Chief Alcalde was also killed. This all took place on Jan 19. Govt Bent had gone up to Toas a few days before to look after a farm which he owned in that vicinity. The Americans at Sante Fe had there only about 400 effective men; the rest were on the sick list, or had left to join Col Doniphan. Letters received at St Louis state that Col Cooke & the Mormon battalion were 350 miles beyond Santa Fe. They were progressing slowly. A letter from Lt Abert, of the U S Topographical Engineers, of a later date, confirms all the above. [See Mar 19th newspaper on Taos.]

Official.

Promotions & appointments in the army of the U S: Gen Orders #10, War Dept, Adj Gen Ofc, Wash, Mar 12, 1847. Promotions: Adj Gen Dept.

Brevet Maj Saml Cooper, Assist Adj Gen, to be Assist Adj Gen with rank of Lt Col, Mar 3, 1847.

Brevet Capt Wm G Freeman, Assist Adj Gen, to be Assist Adj Gen with the Brevet rank of Maj, Mar 3, 1847, vice Cooper promoted.

Quartermaster's Dept:

Capt Geo H Crosman, Assist Quartermaster, to Quartermaster with rank of Maj, Mar 3, 1847.

Capt Saml B Dusenbery, Assist Quartermaster, to Quartermaster with rank of Maj, Mar 3, 1847.

Capt David H Vinton, Assist Quartermaster, to Quartermaster with rank of Maj, Mar 3, 1847.
Medical Dept:
Assist Surgeon John M Cuyler, to be Surgeon, Mar 3, 1847.
Assist Surgeon Madison Milles, to be Surgeon, Mar 3, 1847.
Corps of Topographical Engineers: all promotions as of Mar 3, 1847:
1st Lt Thos J Lee, to be Capt.
1st Lt Jas M Morgan, to be Capt.
2nd Lt Alex'r B Dyer, to be 1st Lt, vice Talcott, appointed Maj of Infty.
2nd Lt Alex'r H Dearborn, to be 1st Lt, vice Lee, promoted
2nd Lt Franklin D Callender, to be 1st Lt, vice Morgan, promoted
2nd Lt Thos L Ringgold, to be 1st Lt.
2nd Lt Chas P Kingsbury, to be 1st Lt.
2nd Lt John McNutt, to be 1st Lt.
Brevet 2nd Lt Josiah Gorgas, to be 1st Lt.
Brevet 2nd Lt Thos J Rodman, to be 1st Lt.
Brevet 2nd Lt Theodore T S Laidley, to be 1st Lt.
Brevet 2nd Lt Jas G Benton, to be 2nd Lt, vice Dyer, promoted.
Brevet 2nd Lt Geo Deshon, to be 2nd Lt, vice Dearborn, promoted.
Brevet 2nd Lt Thos J Brereton, to be 2nd Lt, vice Callender, promoted.
Brevet 2nd Lt Chas P Stone, to be 2nd Lt.
Brevet 2nd Lt Jesse L Reno, to be 2nd Lt.
Brevet 2nd Lt Thos M Whedbee, to be 2nd Lt.
1st Regt of Dragoons: all promotions as of Feb 16, 1847:
Capt Nathan Boone, to be Major
Brevet Maj Benj L Beall, Capt 2nd Dragoons, to be Major, vice Trenor, dec'd.
1st Lt Philip Kearny, to be Capt, vice Boone, promoted.
1st Lt Robt H Chilton, to be Capt, vice Cooke, promoted to 2nd Dragoons.
2nd Lt Abraham Buford, to be 1st Lt, vice Kearny, promoted.
2nd Lt Patrick Noble, to be 1st Lt, vice Chilton, promoted.
Brevet 2nd Lt Clarendon J L Wilson, to be 2nd Lt, vice Buford, promoted
Brevet 2nd Lt John Adams, to be 2nd Lt, vice Noble, promoted
2nd Regt of Dragoons:
Capt Philip St Geo Cooke, of the 1st Dragoons, to Major, Feb 16, 1847.
1st Lt Henry H Sibley, to Capt, Feb 16, 1847, vice Beall, promoted to 1st Dragoons.
2nd Lt Danl G Rogers, to 1st Lt, Feb 16, 1847, vice Sibley, promoted.
2nd Lt Philip W McDonald, to 1st Lt, Mar 3,1 847, vice Hamilton, appointed Major of Infty.
Regt of Mounted Riflemen: all promotions as of Feb 16, 1847:
Capt Wm W Loring, to be Major.
1st Lt Benj S Roberts, to be Capt, vice Loring, promoted.
2nd Lt Thos Claiborne, to be 1st Lt, vice Roberts, promoted.
Brevet 2nd Lt Danl M Frost, to be 2nd Lt, vice Claiborne, promoted.
1st Regt of Artl:
Brevet Lt Col Thos Childs, Capt of the 3rd Artl, to be Major, Feb 16, 1847.

1st Lt Erastus A Capron, to be Capt, Feb 16, 1847, vice Porter, promoted to 4th Artl.
1st Lt Geo G Waggaman, to be Capt, Mar 3, 1847, [Co M.]
2nd Lt Jas G Martin, to be 1st Lt, Feb 16, 1847, vice Capron, promoted, [Co L.]
2nd Lt Jos F Irons, to be 1st Lt, Mar 3, 1847, vice Waggaman, promoted, [Co M.]
2nd Lt Saml Jones, to be 1st Lt, Mar 3, 1847, vice Burke, promoted.
2nd Lt John W Brannan, to be 1st Lt, Mar 3, 1847, [Co L.]
2nd Lt Isaac Bowen, to be 1st Lt, Mar 3, 1847, [Co M.]
2nd Lt Seth Williams, to be 1st Lt, Mar 3, 1847, [Co I]
2nd Lt Abner Doubleday, to be 1st Lt, Mar 3, 1847, [Co H]
Brevet 2nd Lt Edw C Boynton, of 2nd Artl, to be 2nd Lt, Feb 16, 1847, vice Martin, promoted.
Brevet 2nd Lt Thos J Jackson, to be 2nd Lt, Mar 3, 1847, vice Irons, promoted.
Brevet 2nd Lt Truman Seymour, to be 2nd Lt, Mar 3, 1847, vice Jones, promoted.
2nd Regt of Artl:
Capt Patrick H Galt, of 4th Artl, to be Major, Feb 16, 1847.
1st Lt Roland A Luther, to be Captain, Mar 3, 1847, [Co L.]
1st Lt John F Roland, to be Captain, Mar 3, 1847, [Co M.]
2nd Lt Wm Hays, to be 1st Lt, Mar 3, 1847, vice Luther, promoted, [Co L.]
2nd Lt Harvey A Allen, to be 1st Lt, Mar 3, 1847, vice Roland, promoted, [Co M.]
2nd Lt Saml S Anderson, to be 1st Lt, Mar 3, 1847, [Co L.]
2nd Lt Jas Totten, to be 1st Lt, Mar 3, 1847, [Co M.]
2nd Lt Roswell S Ripley, to be 1st Lt, Mar 3, 1847, [Co K.]
2nd Lt John J Peck, to be 1st Lt, Mar 3, 1847, [Co B.]
Brevet 2nd Lt Thos B J Weld, 1st Artl, to be 2nd Lt, vice David Gibson, dec'd, to date from Feb 16, 1847.
Brevet 2nd Lt Henry B Sears, to be 2nd Lt, Mar 3, 1847, vice Hays, promoted.
Brevet 2nd Lt Marcus D L Simpson, to be 2nd Lt, Mar 3, 1847, vice Allen, promoted.
Brevet 2nd Lt Richd H Rush, to be 2nd Lt, Mar 3,1847.
3rd Regt of Artl:
Capt John M Washington, of 4th Artl, to be Major, Feb 16, 1847.
1st Lt Geo Taylor, to be Captain, Feb 16, 1847, vice Childs, promoted to 1st Artl.
1st Lt Edw J Steptoe, to be Captain, Mar 3, 1847, [Co L.]
1st Lt Francis O Wyse, to be Captain, Mar 3, 1847, [Co M.]
2nd Lt Chas L Kilburn, to be 1st Lt, Feb 16, 1847, vice Taylor, promoted, [Co L.]
2nd Lt Hachaliah Brown, to be 1st Lt, Mar 3, 1847, vice Steptoe, promoted, [Co M.]
2nd Lt Lucein Loeser, to be 1st Lt, Mar 3, 1847, vice Wyse, promoted.
2nd Lt Isaac F Quinby, to be 1st Lt, Mar 3, 1847, [Co L.]
2nd Lt Jos J Reynolds, to be 1st Lt, Mar 3, 1847, [Co M.]
2nd Lt Jas A Hardie, to be 1st Lt, Mar 3, 1847, [Co A.]
2nd Lt Saml G French, to be 1st Lt, Mar 3, 1847, [Co H.]
Brevet 2nd Lt Geo P Andrews, to be 2nd Lt, Feb 16, 1847, vice Kilburn, promoted.
Brevet 2nd Lt Colville J Minor, to be 2nd Lt, Mar 3, 1847, vice Brown, promoted.
Brevet 2nd Lt Hamilton L Shields, to be 2nd Lt, Mar 3, 1847, vice Loeser, promoted.
4th Regt of Artl:
Capt Giles Porter, of 1st Artl, to be Major, Feb 16, 1847.

1st Lt Saml C Ridgely, to be Capt, Feb 16, 1847, vice Galt, promoted to 2nd Artl.
1st Lt Edw Deas, to be Capt, Feb 16, 1847, vice Washington, promoted to 3rd Artl.
1st Lt John H Miller, to be Capt, Mar 3, 1847, [Co L.]
1st Lt Alex'r E Shiras, to be Capt, Mar 3, 1847, [Co M.]
2nd Lt Mansfield Lovell, to be 1st Lt, Feb 16, 1847, vice Ridgely, promoted, [Co L.]
2nd Lt Calvin Benjamin, to be 1st Lt, Mar 3, 1847, vice Deas, promoted, [Co M.]
2nd Lt Henry M Whiting, to be 1st Lt, Mar 3, 1847, vice Miller, promoted.
2nd Lt Geo W Rains, to be 1st Lt, Mar 3, 1847, vice Shiras, promoted.
2nd Lt Danl H Hill, to be 1st Lt, Mar 3, 1847, [Co L.]
2nd Lt John H Greland, to be 1st Lt, Mar 3, 1847, [Co M.]
2nd Lt Saml Gill, to be 1st Lt, Mar 3, 1847, [Co C.]
2nd Lt Thos J Curd, to be 1st Lt, Mar 3, 1847, [Co D.]
Brevet 2nd Lt Edmund Hayes, of 3rd Artl, to be 2nd Lt, Feb 16, 1847, vice Lovell, promoted.
Brevet 2nd Lt Darius N Couch, to be 2nd Lt, Feb 16, 1847, vice Benjamin, promoted.
Brevet 2nd Lt John A Brown, to be 2nd Lt, Mar 3, 1847, vice Whiting, promoted.
Brevet 2nd Lt Albert L Magilton, to be 2nd Lt, Mar 3, 1847, vice Rains, promoted.
Brevet 2nd Lt Henry A Ehninger, to be 2nd Lt, Mar 3, 1847.
1st Regt of Infty:
Capt Edgar S Hawkins, of 7th Infty, to be Major, Feb 16, 1847.
2nd Regt of Infty:
Capt Wm M Graham, of 4th Infty, to be Major, Feb 16, 1847.
Capt Washington Sewall, of 7th Infty, to be Major, Mar 3, 1847, vice Grahan, appointed Lt Col of 11th Infty.
1st Lt Henry W Wessells, to be Capt, Feb 16, 1847, vice Barnum, promoted to 3rd Infty.
1st Lt Jas W Anderson, to be Capt, Feb 16, 1847, vice Waite, promoted to 8th Infty.
2nd Lt Bryant P Tilden, jr, to be 1st Lt, Feb 16,1847, vice Wessells, promoted.
2nd Lt Nathl Lyon, to be 1st Lt, Feb 16, 1847, vice Anderson, promoted.
Brevet 2nd Lt Thos Easly, of 8th Infty, to be 2nd Lt, Feb 16, 1847, vice Tilden, promoted.
Brevet 2nd Lt Nelson H Davis, of 3rd Infty, to be 2nd Lt, Feb 16, 1847, vice Lyon, promoted.
Brevet 2nd Lt Wm M Gardner, of 1st Infty, to be 2nd Lt, vice Thorn, appointed in 3rd Dragoons.
3rd Regt of Infty:
Capt Ephraim K Barnum, of 2nd Infty, to Major, Feb 16, 1847.
1st Lt Stephen D Dobbins, to Capt, Feb 16, 1847, vice Bainbridge, promoted to 4th Infty.
2nd Lt Andrew J Williamson, to 1st Lt, Feb 16, 1847, vice Dobbins, promoted.
Brevet 2nd Lt Jos N G Whistler, of 8th Infty, to 2nd Lt, Jan 7, 1847, vice Rhea, dec'd.
4th Regt of Infty:
Capt Francis Lee, of 7th Infty, to Major, Feb 16, 1847.
1st Lt Abraham C Myers, to Capt, Feb 16, 1847, vice Graham, promoted.
2nd Lt Christopher R Perry, to 1st Lt, Feb 16, 1847, vice Myers, promoted.
Brevet 2nd Lt Thos R McConnell, of 3rd Infty, to 2nd Lt, Feb 16, 1847, vice Perry, promoted.
5th Regt of Infty: Capt Dixon S Miles, of 7th Infty, to Major, Feb 16, 1847.

6th Regt of Infty:
Capt Henry Bainbridge, of 3rd Infty, to be Major, Feb 16, 1847.
1st Lt Seneca G Simmons, to be Capt, Feb 16, 1847, vice Hawkins, promoted to 1st Infty.
1st Lt Forbes Britton, to be Capt, Feb 16, 1847, vice Lee, promoted to 4th Infty.
1st Lt Alex'r Montgomery, to be Capt, Feb 16, 1847, vice Miles, promoted to 5th Infty.
1st Lt Chas Hanson, to be Capt, Mar 3, 1847, vice Seawell, promoted to 2nd Infty.
2nd Lt Levi Gantt, to be 1st Lt, Feb 16, 1847, vice Simmons, promoted.
2nd Lt Napoleon J T Dana, to be 1st Lt, Feb 16, 1847, vice Britton, promoted.
2nd Lt Lafayette McLaws, to be 1st Lt, Feb 16, 1847, vice Montgomery, promoted.
2nd Lt Saml B Hayman, to be 1st Lt, Mar 3, 1847, vice Hanson, promoted.
Brevet 2nd Lt Matthew R Stevenson, of 1st Infty, to be 2nd Lt, Feb 16, 1847, vice Gantt, promoted.
Brevet 2nd Lt Wm H Tyler, of 5th Infty, to be 2nd Lt, Feb 16, 1847, vice Dana, promoted.
Brevet 2nd Lt Cadmus M Wilcox, of 4th Infty, to be 2nd Lt, Feb 16, 1847, vice McLaws, promoted.
Brevet 2nd Lt Edmund Russell, of 6th Infty, to be 2nd Lt, vice Hayman, promoted.
8th Regt of Infty:
Capt Carlos A Waite, of 2nd Infty, to be Major, Feb 16, 1847.
1st Lt Geo Lincoln, to be Capt, Feb 16, 1847, vice Gwynne, promoted to 6th Infty.
Brevets,
"For gallant or meritorious conduct in the battles of Palo Alto & Resaca de la Palma, in Texas, on the 8th & 9th of May, 1846, & in the defence of ***Fort Brown***, Texas, during its bombardment from 3rd to the 9th of May, 1846."
To date from May 9, 1846-by Brevet.
Lt Col John Garland, 4th Infty, to be Colonel.
Capt Thos Childs, 3rd Artl, Lt Col by Brevet, to be Col by Brevet.
Maj Thos Staniford, 5th Infty, to be Lt Col.
Capt Geo W Allen, 4th Infty, Major by Brevet, to be Lt Col by Brevet.
Capt Allen Lowd, 2nd Artl, to be Major.
Capt Martin Scott, 5th Infty, to be Major.
Capt Lewis N Morris, 3rd Infty, to be Major.
Capt Dixon S Miles, 7th Infty, to be Major.
Capt Chas F Smith, 2nd Artl, to be Major.
Capt Wm R Montgomery, 8th Infty, to be Major.
Capt John B Scott, 4th Artl, to be Major.
Capt Lawrence P Graham, 2nd Dragoons, to be Major.
1st Lt Benj Alvord, 4th Infty, to be Capt.
1st Lt Collinson R Gates, 8th Infty, to be Capt.
1st Lt Braxton Bragg, 3rd Arl, to be Capt.
1st Lt Geo Lincoln, 8th Infty, to be Capt.
2nd Lt Francis N Page, [Adj,] 7th Infty, to be 1st Lt.
2nd Lt Chas D Jordan, 8th Infty, to be 1st Lt.
2nd Lt Alfred Pleasanton, 2nd Dragoons, to be 1st Lt.

Brevets:

"For gallant & meritorious conduct in the several conflicts of Monterey, Mexico, on the 21st, 22nd, & 23rd of Sep, 1846.

To date from Sep 23, 1846.

Col Wm J Worth, 8th Infy, Brig Gen by Brevet, to be Maj Gen by Brevet.
Col Persifor F Smith, Regt of Mounted Riflemen, to be Brig Gen by Brevet.
Lt Col Henry Wilson, 1st Infty, to be Col.
Maj Henry K Craig, Ordnance Dept, to be Lt Col.
Capt John J Abercrombie, 1st Infty, Major by Brevet, to be Lt Col by Brevet.
Maj John Munroe, 2nd Artl, to be Lt Col.
Maj Martin Scott, 5th Infty, to be Lt Col.
Capt Dixon S Miles, 7th Infty, Major by Brevet, to be Lt Col by Brevet.
Capt Jos K F Mansfield, Corps of Engineers, Maj by Brevet, to be Lt Col by Brevet.
Capt Chas F Smith, 2nd Artl, Maj by Brevet, to be Lt Col by Brevet.
Capt John R Vinton, 3rd Artl, to be Major.
Capt Lucien B Webster, 1st Artl, to be Major.
Capt Albert S Miller, 1st Infty, to be Major.
Capt Electus Backus, 1st Infty, to be Major.
Capt Jos H Lamotte, 1st Infty, to be Major.
Capt John Sanders, Corps of Engineers, to be Major.
Capt Theopilus H Holmes, 7th Infty, to be Major.
Capt Braxton Bragg, 3rd Artl, to be Major.
Capt John M Scott, 1st Infty, to be Major.
Capt Jos H Eaton, 3rd Infty, to be Major.
1st Lt John R Roland, 2nd Artl, to be Capt.
1st Lt Jas L Donaldson, 1st Artl, to be Capt.
1st Lt Jos Hooker, 1st Artl, to be Capt.
1st Lt Wm H Shover, 3rd Artl, to be Capt.
1st Lt Jeremiah M Scarritt, Corps of Engineers, to be Capt.
1st Lt John C Pemberton, 4th Artl, to be Capt.
1st Lt Geo H Thomas, 3rd Artl, to be Capt.
1st Lt Wm A Nicholas, [Adj,] 2nd Artl, to be Capt.
1st Lt Geo W Ayers, 3rd Artl, to be Capt.
1st Lt Robt S Garnett, 4th Artl, to be Capt.
2nd Lt Geo Meade, Corps of Topographical Engineers, to be 1st Lt.
2nd Lt Isaac Bowen, 1st Artl, to be 1st Lt.
2nd Lt Geo W Lay, 6th Infty, to be 1st Lt.
2nd Lt Franklin Gardner, 7th Infty, to be 1st Lt.
2nd Lt John Pope, Corps of Topographical Engineers, to be 1st Lt.
2nd Lt Lafayette B Wood, 8th Infty, to be 1st Lt.

Appointments:

Genr'l Ofcrs:-effective Mar 3, 1847.

Thos H Benton, of Missouri, to be Maj Gen.
Wm Cumming, of Georgia, to be Maj Gen.
Franklin Pierce, of N H, Col 9th Infty, to be Brig Gen.

Geo Cadwalader, of Pa, to be Brig Gen.
Enos D Hopping, of N Y, to be Brig Gen.

Adj Gen's Dept:

1st Lt Jos Hooker, 1st Artl [late adj,] to Assist Adj Gen with Brvt rank of Capt, Mar 3, 1847.

1st Lt Edw R S Canby, Adj 2nd Infty, to Assist Adj Gen with Brvt rank of Capt, Mar 3, 1847.

Quartermaster's Dept:

Henry Smith, of Mich, to be Quartermaster with the rank of Major, Mar 3, 1847.

To be Assist Quartermaster with the rank of Captain:

1st Lt John P J O'Brien, 4th Artl, Jan 18, 1847.
1st Lt Marsena R Patrick, 2nd Infty, Jan 18, 1847.
1st Lt Wm H Shover, 3rd Artl, Jan 18, 1847.
1st Lt Arthur B Lansing, 2nd Artl, Jan 18, 1847.
1st Lt Wm H Churchill, 3rd Artl, Mar 3, 1847.
1st Lt Jas L Donaldson, 1st Artl, Mar 3, 1847.
1st Lt Langdon C Easton, 6th Infty, Mar 3,1847.
1st Lt Thos L Brent, 4th Artl, Mar 3,1847.
1st Lt Geo W F Wood, 1st Infty, Mar 3, 1847.
1st Lt Justus McKinstry, 2nd Infty, Mar 3, 1847.
1st Lt Fred'k H Masten, 1st Infty, Mar 3, 1847.
1st Lt Chas Hanson, 7th Infty, Mar 3, 1847.
1st Lt Danl H Rucker, 1st Dragoons, Mar 3, 1847.
1st Lt Edw G Elliott, 4th Infty, Mar 3, 1847.
1st Lt Sewall L Fremont, 3rd Artl, Mar 3, 1847.
1st Lt Thos Jordan, 3rd Infty, Mar 3, 1847.
1st Lt Albert Lowry, 2nd Dragoons, Mar 10, 1847.

Medical Dept: to be Assist Surgeons:

Israel Moses, of N Y, Jan 18, 1847.
John F Hammond, of S C, Feb 16, 1847.
Josephus M Steiner, Ohio, Feb 16, 1847.
Robt C Wickham, of Va, Feb 16, 1847.
Chas P Dyerle, of Va, Feb 16, 1847.
Elisha J Bailey, of Pa, Feb 16, 1847.

Pay Dept:

Benj F Larned, Paymaster in the Army, to be Deputy Paymaster Genr'l, Mar 3, 1847.
Thos J Leslie, Paymaster in the Army, to be Deputy Paymaster Genr'l, Mar 3, 1847.
Andrew J Coffee, of Alabama, additional Paymaster, to be Paymaster, Feb 23, 1847.

To be Paymaster, Mar 3, 1847.

Saml S Stacy, of N H.
Joc C Pattridge, of N Y.
Chas Bedine, of N J.
Wm A Spark, of Va.
Benj W Brick, of Ohio.
Felix G Bosworth, of La.
Robt B Reynolds, ot Tenn.
Peter T Crutchfield, of Ark.
Wm Singer, of Wisc.
Noah Johnston, of Ill.

1st Regt of Artl:

Lewis O Morris, to be 2nd Lt, Mar 8, 1847.
Satterlee Hoffman, to be 2nd Lt, Mar 8, 1847.
John B Gibson, to be 2nd Lt, Mar 8, 1847.

2nd Regt of Artl:
Jos S Totten, to be 2nd Lt, Mar 8, 1847.
Anderson Merchant, to be 2nd Lt, Mar 8, 1847.
Julius A d'Lagnel, to be 2nd Lt, Mar 8, 1847.
3rd Regt of Artl:
Geo Andrews, to be 2nd Lt, Mar 8, 1847.
Benj P McNiel, to be 2nd Lt, Mar 8, 1847.
John H Lendrum, to be 2nd Lt, Mar 8, 1847.
4th Regt of Artl:
Gustavus A De Russy, to be 2nd Lt, Mar 8, 1847.
J Spottswood Garland, to be 2nd Lt, Mar 8, 1847.
Saml L Gouverneur, to be 2nd Lt, Mar 8, 1847.
5th Regt of Infty:
Clinton W Lear, to be 2nd Lt, Mar 3, 1847.
Reappointment:
8th Regt of Infty:
Grafton D Hanson, late of the 8th Infty, to be 1st Lt, to date from Dec 31, 1845.
Appointments in the Quartermaster's, Commissary's, & Medical Depts, under the 5th section of the Act supplemental to an act entitled An act providing for the prosecution of the existing war between the U S & the Republic of Mexico, & for other purposes, approved Jun 18, 1846.
Quartermaster's Dept:
Rank-Quartermasters with the rank of Major:
1-John M Sharp, of Miss, Mar 3, 1847, vice Bobbett, resigned.
2-John C Mason, of Ky, Mar 10, 1847.
Assist Quartermasters with the rank of Captain:
1-Saml H Montgomery, of Pa, Jan 4, 1847.
2-Saml McGowan, of S C, Jan 4, 1847.
3-Chas M Prive, of Miss, Jan 18, 1847.
4-Chas R Webster, of N Y, Jan 18, 1847.
5-Chas E Carr, of Louisiana, Jan 18, 1847.
6-Jas L Kemper, of Va, Jan 30, 1847.
7-Paul R George, of N H, Feb 23, 1847.
8-Solomon Pender, jr, of N C, Mar 3, 1847.
9-Jas Vaughn, of Tenn, Mar 3, 1847, vice Robt B Reynolds, appointed Paymaster.
Commissary's Dept:
Assist Commissaries with rank of Captain:
1-Jas D Blaiding, of S C, Jan 4, 1847.
2-John W Shugart, of Pa, Jan 4, 1847.
3-Robt Josselyn, of Miss, Jan 18, 1847, vice Kemp S Holland, dec'd.
4-Wm Barksdale, of Miss, Jan 18, 1847.
5-Jas F Hutton, of N Y, Jan 18, 1847.
6-Francis S Minton, of Louisiana, Jan 18, 1847.
7-Henry Erskin, of Va, Jan 30, 1847.
8-Exum L Whitaker, of N C, Feb 2, 1847.

9-Stephen Hoyt, of Mass, Feb 16, 1847.
10-Thos M Jones, of Ky, Mar 3, 1847, vice Wm Garrard, resigned.
11-Wm Duerson, of Ky, Mar 3, 1847.
Medical Dept. Surgeons:
1-Benj S Muhlenberg, of Pa, Jan 4, 1847.
2-Jas Davis, of S C, Jan 4, 1847.
3-Luther F Dashiel, of Lousiana, Jan 18, 1847.
4-Jos L Hasbrouck, of N Y, Jan 18, 1847.
5-Wm H I Anson, of Va, Feb 2, 1847.
6-Thos N Love, of Miss, Feb 2, 1847.
7-Gaston D Cobbs, of N C, Feb 2, 1847.
8-Otis Hoyt, of Mass, Feb 16, 1847.
9-Gustavus Holland, of Ky, Feb 25, 1847.
10-John B Smith, of Illinois, Mar 3, 1847.
Assist Surgeons:
1-Elbert Bland, of S C, Jan 4, 1847.
2-Fred'k W Miller, of Pa, Jan 18, 1847.
3-Mina B Halstead, of N Y, Jan 18, 1847.
4-Jas M Bell, of Va, Jan 30, 1847.
5-Jas A Mackae, of N C, Feb 2, 1847.
6-Henry Field, of Miss, Feb 2, 1847.
7-Timothy Childs, of Mass, Feb 16, 1847.
Order of rank & precedence of the ofcrs of the Quartermaster's & Commissary's Depts, appointed under the 5th section of the act, approved Jun 18, 1846.
Assist Quartermasters & Assistant Commissaries, with the rank of Capt:
1-Saml H Montgomery, Assist Quartermaster
2-Jas D Blaiding, Assist Commissary
3-John W Shugart, Assist Commissary
4-Saml McGowan, Assist Quartermaster
5-Chas M Price, Assist Quartermaster
6-Robt Josselyn, Assist Commissary
7-Wm Barksdale, Assist Commissary
8-Chas R Webster, Assist Quartermaster
9-Jas F Hutton, Assist Commissary
10-Francis N Mioton, Assist Commissary
11-Chas E Carr, Assist Quartermaster
12-Henry Erskin, Assist Commissary
13-Jas L Kemper, Assist Quartermaster
14-Exum L Whitaker, Assist Commissary
15-Stephen Hoyt, Assist Commissary
16-Paul R George, Assist Quartermaster
17-Solomon Pender, Assist Quartermaster
18-Thos M Jones, Assist Commissary
19-Jas Vaughn, Assist Quartermaster
20-Wm Duerson, Assist Commissary

Casualties
Resignation-1: Capt Ripley A Arnold, 2nd Dragoons, as Assist Quartermaster, [only,] Mar 10, 1847.
Commissions, declined-2: Maj Gen Thos H Benton; Maj Gen Wm Cumming
Deaths-5:
Maj Eustace Trenor, 1st Dragoons, N Y, Feb 18, 1847.
2nd Lt David Gibson, 2nd Artl, Tampico, Mexico, Feb 6, 1847.
2nd Lt John A Richey, 5th Infty, Villa Gran, Mexico, Jan 13, 1847. [Murdered by the Mexicans.]
2nd Lt Wm Rhea, 3rd Infty, Monterey, Mexico, Jan 7, 1847.
Brevet 2nd Lt A B Botts, 4th Infty, Camargo, Mexico, Jan 1, 1847.
Volunteer Service.
Resignations:
Additional Paymaster David W Stone, Dec 30, 1846.
Capt Robt B Reynolds, Assist Quartermaster, Mar 3, 1847, [appointed Paymaster.]
Capt Wm Garrard, Assist Quartermaster, date not known.
Declined:
Capt Wm L Dancy, Assist Quartermaster
Surgeon Robt F Richardson
Surgeon Benj K Hart
Assist Surgeon John J B Hoxey
Assist Surgeon Geo Dock
The additional companies of Artl will be raised without delay, for which purpose the Captains & subalterns [Companies L & M] of the 1st, 2nd, & 3rd Regts will report in person, for instructions, to Col Crane, Superintendent Genr'l Recruiting Service, at N Y; & those of the 4th to Col Walbach, at ***Fort Monroe***.
Ofcrs promoted & appointed will join their proper regts, companies, & stations, without delay; those on detached service, or acting under special instructions, will report by letter to the commanding ofcrs of their respective regts & corps; & ofcrs of the genr'l staff, serving with the army in Mexico, will report to the Maj Genr'l commanding-in-chief. Acceptances or non-acceptances of appointments will be promptly reported to the Adj Gen of the Army; &, in case of acceptance, the birthplace of the person appointed will be stated. By order: R Jones, Adj Gen

New Orleans Picayune of Mar 7: we learn that Mr Dimond, our former Consul at Vera Cruz, was among the passengers on the English steamer **Tweed**, recently lost on the coast of Yucatan. [Mar 19th newspaper: Mr Dimond, the late American Consul at Vera Cruz was saved, & not lost. The remainder were saved by the Spanish brig **Emilio**, Capt Camp, which arrived at Havana on Mar 3, in 6 days from Sisal, with the passengers & crew of the **Tweed**. Total loss is about one million dollars. Of the 48 passengers, 29 were saved; of the crew of 91, 42 were saved.]

St John's Institute, Mount Alban, D C, will commence on May 1st . Address to Messrs Spencer & McKenney, Mount Alban, near Gtwn, D C. -Rev Jos Spencer, D D. Rev Jas A McKenney

Lands in Hardy Co, Va, for sale, at Public Sale, under a decree of the Circuit Superior Court of Law & Chancery for Hardy Co, Va, pronounced on Sep 22, 1844, in the case of Norman Bruce, cmplnt, against the Potomac & Alleghany Coal & Iron Manufacturing Co, dfndnts: for sale before the door of the court-house in Moorefield, in Hardy Co, on Apr 23rd: 20 tracts of land in said decree mentioned, lying on the Alleghany Mountain, in said county.
400 acres on the east side of Stony river
413 acres on Elk run
400 acres southwest side of Elk run
400 acres near Welton Glade
409 acres on Difficult creek
408 acres on Difficult creek
394 acres known as ***Slate Cabin Tract***
290 acres known as ***Slate Cabin Tract***
2005+ near ***Big Elk Lick***, off F & W Deakin's lands
1001+ acres known as the ***Buffalo Tract***, whereon Spencer Hendrickson now resides
140 acres known as ***Benj Ray Tract***
400/340/1000 acres, out of these 3 tracts 200 acres is excepted, being sold to Wm Shillingburg. Said 3 tracts are on Jonnycake creek, near the turnpike road
1,000 acs-103 excepted, sold to Alex'r Smith, by deed Feb 3, 1817.
240/660/740/360/695 acs-the last 6 tracts were land conveyed by F & W Deakins to John Templeman, by said Templeman to Bruce, & by Bruce to the dfndnts in this decree.
Inquire of Wm Seymour, atty for plntf, or to Jos McNemar, my deputy, Moorefield, who are authorized to give any information in relation to said lands.
-Job Welton, Sheriff of Hardy Co, Va.

For rent: 3 story brick house, now occupied by Rev Mr Sprole, fronting on Missouri ave, between 3rd & 4th sts. Possession may be had Apr 1. Inquire of Susan D Shepherd or H H Dent. -Susan D Shepherd

Trustee's sale: by decree of the Circuit Court of Wash Co, D C, in a cause wherein Sabret E Scott is cmplnt, & John Lynch & others are dfndnts: public auction on Apr 20, on the premises, of the following very valuable lots, to wit: lots 11, 12, & 13, in square 728, together with the bldgs & improvements thereon erected. -Hy, Naylor, Trustee
-R W Dyer, auct

For rent: a 2 story frame house on 12th st west, between N & O sts north, with about an acre of ground. Also, a 3 story brick house on 4½ st west, between N & O sts south, at $100 a year. Inquire of J H Wheat, Gen Post Ofc, or to the undersigned, 2 doors north of the last named house. -Mary Wheat

Sale by order of the Orphans Court of Wash Co, D C: public auction on Mar 22, at the late residence of Mrs M E Cooper, dec'd, on 14th st, near the corner of South B st, opposite the residence of John Pettibone, a good lot of furniture & ladies apparel.
-A Green, auctioneer

Orphans Court of Wash Co, D C. Letters of administration on the personal estate of Peter McCardle, late of said county, dec'd. -Wm B Canfield, adm

FRI MAR 19, 1847

$20 reward for the safe delivery to me of my servant Robt Smith, who absented himself 3 weeks since. He is about 19 years of age, a dark color, & slender frame.
-Richd Davis, Music Store, Pa ave

Mr Austin Barnes, of Bakersfield, Vt, on Feb 23, was cutting down some trees, when a limb broke off & struck him & killed him instantly. He had only been married but 3 short months. -St Albans Messenger

Having disposed of my business to M Shanks & Wm Wall, I take this opportunity to ask all persons indebted to me to settle their accounts immediately, as I shall leave the city in a short time. -Wm Marshall Also, the public is invited to the sale of Clothing & Cloths at my store on Thu.
+
Trustee's sale: by deed of trust to him, from Wm H Wall: sale on Mar 20, on the premises, at the foot of P st south, on the Potomac river, the following: 1 horse, 1 four wheel wagon & harness, [butcher's.] Frame bldg with all the fixtures & appurtenances thereto belonging, in square 505, & fitted up as a slaughter- house.
-J W Jones, Trustee -C W Boteler, jr, auctioneer

Criminal Court -Wash: U S vs W H Wall, who was found guilty of grand larceny on Mon last, was sentenced to 2 years imprisonment at hard labor in the penitentiary, to which an appeal has been taken by Mr Bradley.

This letter is from Lt Abert, of the U S Topographical Engineer Corps, who accompanied Col Fremont on one of his expeditions to the Pacific. Turkey Creek, Feb 20, 1847. On the 10th of last month, Gov Bent, with all the Americans residing in Taos, were cruelly massacred by the New Mexicans. 8 Mexicans have been arrest & imprisoned; the most eminent were Thos Ortiz, 2nd in command under Armijo; Diego Archulette, formerly a member of the Mexican Congress; Nicholas Pino, Santiago Armijo, Manuel Chavez, & others. [See Mar 18th newspaper on Taos.]

Valuable real estate at auction: by decree of Circuit Court of Wash Co, D C, in the cause of John H Farland & Zebulon S Farland, vs Wm Henry Farland, Robt L Farland, & others: sale on Apr 17, at public auction, lot 38 in square 435, fronting 24 feet on 7th st west, between south D & south E sts. Improvements consist of good enclosures & a 2 story brick house. -John H Saunders, Trustee -A Green, auctioneer

Criminal Court -Wash: U S vs W H Wall, who was found guilty of grand larceny on Mon last, was sentenced to 2 years imprisonment at hard labor in the penitentiary, to which an appeal has been taken by Mr Bradley.

We announce the death of Thos Goin, acting master in the U S Navy, & one of the firm of Goin, Pool & Pentz, shipping agents of N Y. Mr Goin was a prominent citizen of Brooklyn, & founder of the Naval Apprentice School system, whose successful operation was terminated by causes growing out of the disastrous event on board the U S brig **Somers**. -Brooklyn Adv [See Dec 10, 1846 newspaper.]

SAT MAR 20, 1847

What are we fighting for? To repeal invasion. The act of Mexico, she having passed the boundary of the U S, invaded our territory, & shed American blood upon American soil.

Congressional nominations in Va:

Whig:

Saml Watts	Wm L Goggin	John S Pendleton
Geo W Bolling	John M Botts	Algernon S Gray
Thos S Flournoy	John J Jones	Wm B Preston
Henry P Irving	W Newton	J M Stephenson

Locofoco:

Archibald Atkinson	Jas A Seddon	Aug A Chapman
Geo C Dromgoole	Thos H Bayly	Fayette McMullen
Wm M Tredway	R T L Beale	Robt A Thompson
Thos S Bocock	Henry Bedinger	Wm G Brown
Shelton F Leake	Jas McDowell	

Mrs Ten Eyck, the beautiful & accomplished lady of our Com'r of the Sandwich Islands, who left our shore last summer to follow the fortunes of her husband, died at Honolulu on Nov 5, at age 31 years. She was the daughter of Rev Mr Fairchild, of Boston, & the centre of many strong & enduring friendships. -Express

Appointments by the Pres: Promotions:

1st Lt Francis C Hall, to be Capt, vice Park G Howle, adj & inspector, who retains his staff appointment.

1st Lt Geo H Terrett, to be Capt, vice Geo W Walker, paymaster, who retains his staff appointment.

1st Lt Wm E Stark, to be Capt, vice Augs A Nicholson, paymaster, who retains his staff appointment.

1st Lt Nathl S Waldron, to be Capt, vice Geo F Lindsay, assist quartermaster, who retains his staff appointment.

2nd Lt Wm L Shuttleworth, to be 1st Lt, vice F C Hall, promoted.

2nd Lt Jos W Curtis, to be 1st Lt, vice W E Stark, promoted.

2nd Lt John C Grayson, to be 1st Lt, vice N S Waldron, promoted.

Appointments:

Chas Alex's Henderson, to be 2nd Lt, vice W L Shuttleworth, promoted.

John Stricker Nicholson, to be 2nd Lt, vice J L Curtis, promoted.

A Satterthwaite Nicholson, to be 2nd Lt, vice R Tansill, promoted.

Geo F Lindsay, jr, to be 2nd Lt, vice J C Grayson, promoted. -Navy Dept, Mar 18, 1847

The dwlg of Hezekiah A Holdridge, in North Blenheim, Schoharie Co, was burnt down on Monday last. Mrs Holdridge & 5 children were burnt to death, & the 6th & only remaining child is not expected to survive. [From a correspondent of the Albany Argus.]

Notice given that on Mar 27, will be offered for sale, at public auction, all the Fish Stands in the Centre Market-house, for a term ending on Mar 31, 1848. -W W Seaton, Mayor

Balt, Mar 19. The brave & gallant old soldier, Alberty Hay, who lost his arm at the battle of Monterey, is not in this city, & has received the appointment of watchman in the Navy Yard at Wash. He has also been put on the pension list. This is well done. The old soldier cannot go unrewarded.

Mrd: on Mar 18, in Wash City, by Rev Mr French, Wm Carey Jones, of New Orleans, to Eliza Preston Carrington Benton, eldest daughter of the Hon Thos H Benton, of Missouri.

Mrd: Mar 18, in Wash City, by Rev G W Samson, Mr John Mullin to Mrs Mary Yeatman, both of Wash.

Died: on Mar 19, Mrs R J Waugh, consort of Townshend Waugh, aged 57 years. Her funeral is on Sat at 3½ o'clock, from her late residence on I st, near Friends Meeting House.

Died: on Fri, at Rock Creek, in his 80th year, Mr Edw Bleckford. His funeral will take place at Rock Creek Church tomorrow at 11 o'clock.

Died: on Thu, Ann Jesup, infant daughter of Lt Jas & Mary Jesup Blair, aged 3 months & 8 days. Her funeral will take place at 1 o'clock today from the residence of Gen Jesup.

Aston Ridge Seminary for Young Ladies commences on May 1 & Nov 1. Instructors: Mrs Huntington, who had resided in Paris for 3 years; & Miss McClean an experienced teacher. Aston Ridge is about 2 hours' ride from Phil via Chester. Per session of 5 months: $112. Recommended by Rt Rev Bishop Alonzo Potter. Address Rev B S Huntington, Village Green, Delaware Co, Pa.

MON MAR 22, 1847

The N Y papers announce the death, by suicide, of Thos R Ludlam, formerly one of the city surveyors. During the last 2 months he had been very much depressed in spirits. Cause unknown.

From the New Orleans Commercial Bulletin of Mar 13. Advance of Santa Anna with 15,000 to 20,000 men-Reported great battle at Saltillo-American loss 2,000 men-Mexican loss 4,000 to 5,000-Retreat of Gen Taylor-His precarious situation-Alarm on the Rio Grande.

Balt Annual Conference of the Methodist Episcopal Church closed its session in Wash City on Sat last. The following are the appointments for this District & adjacent Circuits for the present year:
Potomac District-W Hamilton, P E
Washington: Foundry & Asbury-N J B Morgan & M A Turner.
Wesley Chapel-H Slicer.
Ebenezer, W Prettyman; J M Hanson, supernumerary
McKendree Chapel-T M Reese
Ryland Chapel-to be supplied
Gtwn: Thos Sewall & W Taylor
Alexandria: J Merriken & J H March; D Steele, supernumerary
Fairfax: M G Hamilton & J W Kelly
Leesbrug: J Guest
Loudoun: S S Roszel & T C Hayes

Army Orders. Gen Orders, #19. Headquarters of the Army, Tampico, Feb 18, 1847.
Dept of Orders:
1st Lt H L Scott, 4th Infty, aid-de-camp & acting assist Adj Gen.
1st Lt T Williams, 4th Artl, aid-de-camp.
1st Lt E P Scammon, Topographical Engineers, acting aid-de-camp.
2nd Lt G W Lay, 6th Infty, Military Secretary.
Genr'l Staff Ofcrs:
Lt Col E A Hitchcock, 3rd Infty, Acting Inspector Genr'l.
Capt Jas Monroe, 6th Infty, Acting Assist Inspector Genr'l.
Col J G Totten, chief of Corps of Engineers.
Maj W Turnbull, Acting Chief of Topographical Engineers.
Capt B Huger, Acting Chief of Ordnance.
Maj S McRee, Acting Chief of the Quartermaster's Dept.
Capt J B Grayson, Acting Chief of the Subsistence Dept.
Maj E Kirby, Acting Chief of the Pay Dept.
Surgeon Gen T Lawson, Chief of the Medical Dept.
The senior field ofcr of Artl, Col J Bankhead, 2nd Artl, will enter upon the duties of Chief of Artl as soon as there shall be occasion for planting heavy batteries.
-Winfield Scott. By command of Maj Gen Scott: H L Scott, A A A G

$1,500 reward for Francis D Newcomb, late Surveyor Gen of Louisiana, charged & convicted of forgery & embezzlement, escaped from the Parish Prison in this city during the night of Feb 27. Newcomb is a native of Greenfield, Mass, formerly an ofcr of the U S Army; about 45 years of age, blue eyes, light complexion, light hair & whiskers, stout built, about 5 feet 9 or 10 inches. He has a military walk.
-W G Wagner, U S Marshall District of Louisiana.

TUE MAR 23, 1847
For rent: new brick dwlg house on north side of C st north, east of 4½ st: lodgings for servants over the carriage & wood-house, connected by a covered way with the main bldg. Apply to Mr A Baldwin, residing on the north side of the same square.

U S vs Hosea H Smith, on the indictment charging him with forging a power of atty, in the name of C Ford, was resumed yesterday. Witnesses previously examined: Messrs Gillet & Ingraham, & Mrs Martha A Smith. Jury returned with a verdict of guilty. At the time the jury returned this verdict the prisoner was put upon his trial on a 3rd charge of fraud & forgery in relation to the Shippen papers.

Died: on Mar 10, at Norfolk, Va, in his 38th year, Rev Upton Beall, Rector of Christ Church, in Norfolk. He was a native of PG Co, & for a number of years a resident of Upper Marlboro.

Died: on Mar 9, at Norfolk, Va, Miss Ann Mortimer Barron, daughter of Capt Wm Barron, of the Continental Navy of the U S, aged 68 years.

Official Headquarters of the Marine Corps, Adj & Inspectors Ofc, Wash, Mar 20, 1847.
Promotions:
1st Lt Francis C Hall, to be Capt in the line front Mar 16, 1847, vice Capt Parke G Howle, [the adj & inspector of the corps,] promoted to the rank of Major, having vacated his commission of Capt in the line.
1st Lt Geo H Terrett, to be a Capt in the line from Mar 16, 1847, vice Capt Geo W Walker, [the paymaster of the corps,] promoted to the rank of Major, having vacated his commission of Capt in the line.
1st Lt Wm E Stark, to be a Capt in the line Mar 16, 1847, vice Capt Augs A Nicholson, [the quartermaster of the corps,] promoted to the rank of Major, having vacated his commission of Capt in the line.
1st Lt Nathl S Waldron, to be a Capt in the line from Mar 16, 1847,vice Capt Geo F Lindsay, [the assist quartermaster of the corps,] promoted to the rank of Capt, having vacated his commission of Capt in the line.
2nd Lt Wm L Shuttleworth, to be a 1st Lt from Mar 16, 1847, vice Francis C Hall, promoted Capt.
2nd Lt Jos W Curtis, to be 1st Lt from Mar 16, 1847, vice Geo H Terrett, promoted Capt.
2nd Lt Robt Tansill, to be 1st Lt from Mar 16, 1847, vice W E Stark, promoted Capt.
2nd Lt John C Grayson, to be 1st Lt from Mar 16, 1847, vice Nathan S Waldron, promoted Capt.
Appointments: effective Mar 16, 1847:
Chas Alex'r Hamilton, to be a 2nd Lt, vice Wm L Shuttleworth, promoted.
John Stricker Nicholson, to be a 2nd Lt, vice J W Curtis, promoted.
A Satterthwaite Nicholson, to be a 2nd Lt, vice Robt Tansill, promoted.
Geo F Lindsley, jr, to be a 2nd Lt, vice John C Grayson, promoted.
By order of the Brevet Brig Gen Commandant, Parke G Howle, Adj & Inspector U S Marine Corps.

WED MAR 24, 1847
The Pres of Hayti, Jean Baptiste Riche, died at Port-au-Prince on Feb 27. He arrived there on Feb 23, from his tour through the North. He suffered much from illness during his journey, but attended to affairs till the last. In 2 days he would have completed the 2nd year of his presidency. -New Orleans Picayune, Mar 15.

Wash Corp: 1-Cmte of Claims: bill for the relief of Eliz Moran: passed. 2-Relief of Jas B Clarke: passed. Same cmte, reported without amendment, bill for the relief of Henry L Cross: passed. Same cmte: bill for the relief of Jacob Wachter: laid on the table. Same cmte: bill for the relief of J M Peerce: laid on the table. 3-Ptn of Rodey O'Brien & others for a gravel footwalk on south C st, between 6th & 7th sts: referred to the Cmte on Improvements. 4-Cmte of Claims: asked to be discharged from the further consideration of the ptns of: Allison Nailor; of Caleb Dulany;of Wm R Demptster; of Jas Davis; of John P Stallings; of Henry Baines; of Wm Bagman; of Chas McDonald, & of John J Wilson. 5-Cmte of Police: asked to be discharged from the further consideration of the ptn of Richd Cruit. 5-Bill for the relief of Matilda Ratcliff: read twice. 6-Bill for the relief of Wm Cooper: read twice. 7-Cmte on Wharves: bill for the relief of Henderson Fowler: decided in the negative. 8-Cmte of Claims: asked to be discharged from the further consideration of the ptns of Conrad Finkman & of Jas McColgin: agreed to. Same cmte: bill for the relief of John Burch, without an amendment. 9-Bill for the relief of John B Hilleary: to lie on the table.

For rent: 3 story brick house, #2, in Union Row, F st near 7th. Inquire of the present occupant, of of J Gideon.

Died: on Mar 16, at her residence, in PG Co, Md, Flavilla, consort of Dr Chas Duvall, aged 58 years.

Sale at public auction of lands in Alexandria Co, Va: by deed of trust executed by Robt Widdicomb & wife on Mar 25, 1844, & at the risk & expense of purchasers who have failed to comply with the terms of the former sale: the following tracts of land in Alexandria Co, Va, the same being part of the lands formerly belonging to Gen Mason, & by him conveyed to the Bank of the U S, viz: parts of sections 4, 5, & 9, as surveyed & laid down by Lewis Carbery in 1835 & 1836, containing together about 57 acres; & section 15, laid down as aforesaid, containing about 73 acres, more or less; the whole subject to existing rights of way through them. -Rd Smith, Trustee
-Edw S Wright, Auctioneer, Gtwn

The beautiful residence erected by the taste & liberal expenditure of Jos Bonaparte, at Bordentown, on the Delaware, in N J, is to be sold at auction next Jun. The house, large & spacious, is built of stone & brick. The Park, containing 274 acres, is completely inclosed, & admirably planted.

L F Clark has removed his Paper Hangings & Upholstering establishment to the south side of Pa ave, between 10th & 11th sts, next door to J Miller's confectionary.

THU MAR 25, 1847

Orphans Court of Wash Co, D C. Letters of administration on the personal estate of Peter McCardle, late of said county, dec'd. -Wm S Canfield, adm

Orphans Court of Wash Co, D C. Letters testamentary on the personal estate of Robt Rose, late of said county, dec'd. -Maria A Lindsay, Adam L Rose, excs

Trustee's sale of house & lot in Wash, D C: by virtue of a decree of the Circuit Court of Wash Co, D C, the subscriber will sell at public auction, on Apr 24, part of lot 9 in square 426, in Wash, D C, on which is a 2½ story frame house, nearly new, which was owned & occupied by John W Duley at the time of his death. The lot fronts 25 feet on west side of 7th st. On ratification of the sale, the Trustee is authorized to convey the said premises & all the estate of the said John W Duley, Thos McGill, Josiah Essex, & of Eliz C Duley therein to the purchaser. The title is considered good. -John Marbury, Trustee
-B Homans, auctioneer

Orphans Court of Wash Co, D C. Letters of administration on the personal estate of Mary A Cooper, late of said county, dec'd. -Christopher Cammack, adm

Died: on Mar 24, in Wash City, after a painful illness of 3 years, Mrs Lucy Mitchell, consort of Dr Spencer Mitchell, aged 52 years. Her funeral is this afternoon, at 2 o'clock, from the residence of Dr Spencer Mitchell, 7th st, near N Y ave.

Teacher wanted: the Trustees of a Primary School District in PG Co, Md, are desirous of obtaining a teacher to take charge of the school. Direct letter to Good Luck Post Ofc, PG Co, Md. -Franklin Waters, Nathan Waters, Benj H Beckett

FRI MAR 26, 1847

Foreign Obits. 1-The steamer **Hibernia** brings intelligence of the death of Sharon Turner, an eminent English historian, whose principal works are well known in this country. He died on Feb 13 in the 79th year of his age. 2-Mr Macvey Napier, for 20 years an editor of the Edinburgh Review, a Prof of Conveyancing in the Univ, & editor of the 7th edition of the Encyclopedia Britannica, died on Feb 11. 3-Capt Dillon, a celebrated French navigator, the discoverer of the relics of La Peyrouse & his companions, died a few weeks since.

Mrd: on Mon, at Brooklyn, N Y, the Rev John N Maffitt to Miss Frances Smith, step-dght of Judge Pierce, of that place.

Died: yesterday, Sylvanus N Washburn, aged 36 years, a native of Mass. He had no hope but Christ. His funeral is this afternoon at half past 3 o'clock, from his late residence on 12th st.

For rent: a brick house on 4½ st, between C st & Pa ave, now occupied by Wm Marshall. Possession given on May 1. Apply to Thos Pursell, opposite Brown's Hotel.

The slander suit between David Taylor & wife, of Balt City, & Lewis Shipley, of Carroll Co, which has been in the courts for a space of 4 years or more, has finally been determined in the Howard District Court by a verdict for very heavy damages [$5,000] against Shipley, the dfndnt. The suit originated in Aug, 1842, & was brought by Mrs Taylor, then Miss Martha A Jamison.

By virtue of a writ of fieri facias, at the suit of H C Spalding, against the goods & chattels of J H Poletti, & to me directed, I have seized & taken in execution all the right, title, & interest of said Poletti in sundry acticles. Sale on Apr 1, in front of the Centre Market House.

SAT MAR 27, 1847

Mason & Dixon line: not related to the subject of slavery. At the time that line was established, slavery existed on both sides of it. As early as 1682 a dispute arose between Wm Penn & Lord Baltimore respecting the construction of their respective grants, of what now form the State of Pa, Dela, & Md. Lord Baltimore claimed to & including the 40th degree of north latitude; & Wm Penn mildly, but firmly, resisted the claim. In 1761 Mr Chas Mason, of the Royal Observatory, was sent to Pa, to measure a degree of latitude. That duty he performed, & a report of his proceedings was made to the Royal Society of London, for the year 1767. This Mr Mason & Jeremiah Dixon were appointed to run the line in dispute.

One cent reward for Geo Hall [colored,] an indented apprentice to the Barbering business, who ran away on Mar 25. The above will be paid for his apprehension, but no charges.
-Alfred Jones

Trustee's sale of dwlg house & lots at the corner of 2nd & Fred'k st, Gtwn, D C. By virtue of a deed of the Circuit Court of Wash Co, D C: sale on Apr 27, of lot 141 in Beatty & Hawkins' addition to Gtwn, fronting 75 feet on Fred'k st, & bounding on Second st 96 feet. Also, the south part of lot 142 in the same addition, fronting 50 feet 4 inches on Fred'k st: with a commodious & very convenient 2 story brick dwlg house. The title to all this property is unquestionable. -John Marbury, Trustee
-Edw S Wright, Auctioneer, Gtwn

Bldg materials wanted: proposals will be received by the subscribers, at the ofc of the Smithsonian Institute till Apr 6. -Jas Dixon & Co

For sale: new & elegant 3 story brick house, #1, Phil Row, corner of 11th & H sts. The house contains 10 handsome well-finished rooms. -W Noyes, La ave

For sale: 60 acres of land adjoining the city, about 1 miles n e of the Capitol, & bordering on the new county road leading to Bladensburg. Apply to Wm C Brent, Atty at Law, East wing of the City Hall.

Squares 675 & 676, or near 9 acres, for sale at a reasonable price. The Tiber Creek runs nearly throught the centre of both squares, & the land near that stream abounds in sand & gravel. This property is well suited for a large Tannery, or any purpose requiring a supply of water. Apply at the ofc of H M Morfit, on 4½ st, near the corner of Pa ave.

House for rent: 2 story frame house on I st, between 8th & 9th sts: possession on Apr 1. Apply to the present occupant, J W Moorhead, or the subscriber, Michl Larner.

Died: on Mar 25, John O P Degges, in his 35th year. His funeral is this afternoon at 3 o'clock, from his late residence, corner of G & 20th sts.

The vestry of Trinity Church has erected a beautiful monument to the memory of Capt Jas Lawrence, who fell in the Chesapeake in the engagement with the vessel **Shannon**. They have also erected one in memory of Lt Ludlow, who was killed in the same engagement. -Post

Died: on Mar 19, at ***Fairview***, his place of residence in Culpeper Co, Va, Wm Major, in his 73rd year. He had been for many years past one of the most useful magistrates of his county. For a devotedly attached wife he cherished a warm affection. No father was ever more gentle & tender with his children, & the servants of his household at all times received his superintending care & kindness. The closing scene was one of the most perfect calmness & resignation.

Died: on Mar 24, at Alexandria, Mrs Eleanor R Contee, widow of the late Edmund H Contee, of Chas Co, Md.

MON MAR 29, 1847

I propose to print & publish in Wash City, a new weekly Whig journal to be called the Nat'l Whig. The first number will be issued on the first Sat in May, 1847: price will be $2 per annum. It will be the size of the Phil Sat Courier, 30 inches long & 44 inches wide, & will contain 32 columns of new ready matter every week. It will also be a family newspaper. -Chas W Fenton, Wash, D C.

New Orleans Bulletin, Extra, Mar 20. Repulse of Santa Anna-3 days' fighting-Mexican loss 5,000 men-American loss 1,100. Gen Taylor's loss very severe, one report says 1,100, another 1,700 men.

A Copartnership has been entered into under the firm of Wall & Donn for the carrying on the dry goods business at the old stand of Saml T Wall. -Saml T Wall, Oliver P Donn

Famine in Ireland: Buckley dropped dead on the work, after a journey of 3 miles before day. His wife will make affidavit that he had not sufficient food the night before he died, & that she & the rest of the family lived 36 hours on wild weeds to spare a bit of cake for him. In this case a coroner's verdict was given without a sight of the body. This horrifying economy is practised by scores of families.

City Ordinances-Wash. 1-Act for the relief of Jas B Clarke: to refund to him the sum of $13.80, the same having been erroneously paid for a dry goods license by said Clarke. 2-Act for the relief of Eliz Moran: that the fine imposed on her for the violation of an ordinance in relation to dogs, be remitted.

House for rent: 3 story brick dwlg, on Indiana ave, adjoining the one recently occupied by the Rev H Stringfellow. Apply on the premises, A Baldwin.

Geo Knott informs he has a large supply of Ice from Boston, of which he will be able to supply on the most reasonable terms. -Geo Knott, corner of Green & Dunbarton sts

An Irishman, Jas Malone, committed a murder 36 years ago in Ireland, & eluded justice by escaping to America. He lived in this country for 18 years, returned to Ireland, & after 18 more years in security, he has just been identified as the murderer, & committed for trial. He is now over 70 years of age.

The Montreal stage which left Franklin on Mon, met with an accident the following night, by which 3 lives were lost. One of the passengers who was killed was Capt Leary, of England, who came over in the steamer **Hibernia**, & was on his way to Montreal for the purpose of taking charge of the steamer **John Bunn**. The driver & a lady who was a passenger were also killed.

Household & kitchen furniture at auction: on Mar 29, at the residence of Mr Fleischmann, in Union Row, on F st, near 7th: a splendid lot of furniture. -A Green, auctioneer

TUE MAR 30, 1847

Mr Chas J Ingersoll is writing the 2nd volume of his "Historical Sketch of the War of 1812," to embrace the transactions of 1814. He solicits information from all persons, particularly those employed in the public service-military, naval, or civil, whose suggestions will be thankfully received by him.

The will of the late Judge Martin, of New Orleans, was recently declared null & void, but not, as has been stated, on account of the blindness of the testator. The real ground of the decision was that the testator had attemped a fraud upon the State. In Louisiana there is a probate tax of 10% upon bequests to foreigners. To evade this tax Judge Martin, whose penurious disposition looked even beyond the grave, bequeathed all his property nominally to his brother, a resident of New Orleans, but with a secret understanding that there should be an equal division between all his relatives, most of them being Frenchmen, residing in France. For this attempt to escape the probate tax the will was set aside. The amount of the tax coming to the State will be, it is said, about $30,000.

The Advocate of Mar 4: from the Cherokee Country: Geo Ross was stabbed to death at a dance, without provocation by Thos Welch, who was arrested on the spot. Jos Raper, while attempting to escape from the guard who had him in custody, was shot & mortally wounded.

Mrd: on Mar 29, by Rev Wm Sprole, Lt Edw Harte, U S A, to Miss Rose M, daughter of Jas B Holmead, of Wash City.

Died: yesterday, Sarah Edmonston, in her 54th year, wife of Franklin Edmonston, after an illness of about 5 months. Her funeral is this afternoon at 3 o'clock, from her late residence on I st.

Died: on Mar 29, Mary Ross, daughter of John & Louisa E Potts, aged 3 years. The funeral will take place from the residence of Saml J Potts, at 4 o'clock this day.

John Hands, formerly connected with the firm of Fuller & Co, calls the attention of the Travelling Public to his newly-opened establishment, the Mansion House, which has been fitted up in a style of neatness & comfort. It is situated on Pa ave, within a few rods of the Treas Dept. -John Hands, Wash

Arrest of a fugitive from Europe. A German, Nathan Levy, alias Herman Bondy, a passenger on board the London packet ship **Prince Albert**, which arrived at N Y on Thu last, was immediately arrested on a charge of having embezzled some 40,000 ducats, or about $20,000 from the house of Rothschilds & Co, at Vienna, Austria, with whom the accused was employed as clerk.

Dr J R Piper, Homoeopathic Physician, has removed his ofc to Pa ave, north side, a few doors east of 10th st, over J H Gibb's Fancy Store.

Balt, Mar 29. Capt Eager Howards company of voltigeurs, raised in this vicinity, left here this morning in the cars for Cumberland, en route for the seat of the war. The corps number 102 men, all told, of fine & noble appearance. Their ofcrs are John Eager Howard, Capt; Jas H Woolford, 1st Lt; Jas A Frost & Jas H Smyth, 2nd Lt.

The U S frig **St Lawrence** was launched from the Gosport Navy Yard on Thursday in beautiful style, in the presence of a large concourse of spectators. -Norfolk Beacon

WED MAR 31, 1847

American Ofcrs killed & wounded at the Battle of Buena Vista.

Regulars:

Killed: Col Lincoln, Assist Adj Gen

Wounded: Capt E Stein, 1st Dragoons, severely; Lt S G French, 3rd Artl, severely; Lt J J P O'Brien, 4th Artl, slightly.

Mississippi Rifles:

Killed: Lts R S Moore & F McNulty

Wounded: Col J P Davis, severely; Capt J M Sharpe, severely; Lt A B Corwin, slightly; Lts Pozey & Stockton, slightly.

1st Ky Cavalry:

Killed: Adj Vaughan

Wounded: One Capt & 3 Lts, [no names given.]

Arkansas Cavalry:
Killed: Col A Yell & Capt A Porter
Wounded: Lt S A Redder
2nd Ky Foot Rifles:
Killed: Col McKee & Lt Col J H Clay; Capt O W Morse & Capt W T Willis.
Wounded: Lts E S Barbour, Withers, & Mosier.
Indiana Brig:
Wounded: Gen Lane
2nd Regt:
Killed: Capt Kinder, Capt Walker, & Lt Parr
Wounded: Capts Saunders & Osborn; & Lts Cayen, Pennington, Morse, Lewis, Davis, & Epperson
3rd Regt: Killed: Capt Faggat. Wounded: Maj Gorman & Capt Sleep.
Illinois Brig:
1st Regt:
Killed: Col J J Hardin, commanding; Capt Zabriskie & Lt Haughton
Wounded: Lts J L McConnell & H Adams
2nd regt:
Killed: Caot Woodward; Lts Brunton, Fletcher, Ferguson, Rollins, Bartheson, Athuson, & Price.
Wounded: Capt Coffee & Capt Baker; Lts Pickett, Engelson, Steel, & West, & Adj Whiteside
Texas Co:
Killed: 1st Lt Campbell & 2nd Lt Leonhard
Wounded: Capt Conner

Rev Mr Harvey, an aged Baptist minister, died at Frankfort, N Y, on Mar 18, in the 112th year of his age.

New Orleans Bulletin: Battle of Buena Vista-4,000 Mexicans killed, & only 700 Americans. We shall feel anxiety to hear of the gallant spirits who have fallen on our side, among which is Lt Col Clay, the eldest son of the honored Statesman who left this city but a few days ago. Col McKee, of the same regt, has also fallen.

Delta extra of Mar 23. Gen Taylor maintains his position. Safe arrival of Col Morgan at Monterey. On the 23rd the battle commenced in real earnest. Gen Taylor was every where in the thickest of the fight. He received a ball through his overcoat, but was not injured. Adj Bliss was slightly wounded at his side. Adj Lincoln, also of the General's staff, the intrepid young ofcr who so distinguished himself at Resaca de la Palma, was killed. An exchange of prisoners had taken place, & Old Rough & Ready's, promise to Col Marshall to get back Cassius M Clay & his party, by taking Mexicans prisoners enough to exchange for them, has been fully redeemed. After the battle Gen Taylor demanded of Santa Anna an unconditional surrender of his whole army, which the latter declined. Immortal be the reply of Old Rough & Ready, as delivered by the gallant Lt Crittenden-"GEN TAYLOR NEVER SURRENDERS!"

The revenue cutter **Hamilton**, Capt Josiah Sturgis, returned to Boston on Thu, from her arduous cruise in the bay this past winter. They sailed upwards of 3,000 miles during the cruise & were absent for 71 days.

Died: on Mar 30, in Wash City, after an illness of 4 days, in his 43rd year, Mr Pater Callan, a native of N J, but for 42 years past a resident of Wash. His funeral will take place from his late residence on 8th st, between L & M sts, in the Northern Liberties, this afternoon, at 3 o'clock.

Died: on Mar 30, Mr Thos Cross, an old & much respected citizen of the eastern section of Wash City, in his 72nd year. His funeral is tomorrow, at 2 o'clock, from his late residence near the Navy Yard.

Died: on Mar 29, of consumption, Mrs Mary Cramer, wife of the late Jacob Cramer, in her 58th year. Her funeral is Wed at 2 o'clock, from the residence of her son-in-law, corner of 3rd st & N Y ave.

To rent or lease, that beautifully situated & commodious 2 story frame house, with back kitchen, at the corner of 1st east & north C sts, Capitol Hill, known as the late Mr Greenleaf's residence. Apply to D A Hall, Pa ave, or on the premises.

Among the Mexicans killed on the 22nd & 23rd were Col Francisco Berrs, the lt col of the 1st light infty; Col Pena, of the light cavalry. Another gives the following additional names of ofcrs: Pepe Pronoz, Pepe Bonilla, the major of the regt of Morelia, Asonos, & Luyundo, major of hussars. Wounded were: Gen Lombardini, D Angel Guzman & D Miguel Gonzales.

Household & kitchen furniture at auction: on Apr 2, at the residence of Mr H L Northup, on Pa ave, near the corner of 14th st. -R W Dyer, auct

Wash Corp: 1-Ptn of Rezin Beck & others for certain improvements on 6th st west & F st north: referred to the Cmte on Improvements. 2-Cmte on Public Schools: bill for the relief of L H Randolph: passed. 3-Cmte of Claims: asked to be discharged from the further consideration of the ptn of Jas McColgin: ordered to lie on the table. 4-Ptn of H B Mills & others, for opening 8th st west, from M to P sts: referred to the Cmte on Improvements. 5-Ptn of Rudolph Eikhorn, praying remission of a fine: referred to the Cmte on Improvements. 6-Ptn of Wm B Todd & others, for setting curbstone & paving the footway on west side of 10th st, from B st south, to Md ave: referred to the Cmte on Improvements. 7-Ptn of Rhode O'Brien & others, for making a gravel footwalk on the south side of C st north: read twice. 8-Cmte of Claims: ptn of Timothy Buckley, & the ptn of Adam Dulany: cmte asked to be discharged from further consideration of said ptns: which was agreed to. 9-Cmte of Claims: asked to be discharged from the further consideration of the ptn of John O'Leary: agreed to.

Hydraulic rams & lead pipe: of every caliber & thickness. -Fitzhugh Coyle, Genr'l Commission & Agricultural Warehouse, near the corner of 8th & Pa ave.

Trustee's sale: by virtue of a decree of the Circuit Court of Wash Co, D C, sitting in Chancery, in a cause in which Thos A Dornin is cmplnt & Isabella D Thorburn, Helen M Thorburn, Chas E Thorburn, & Anne M Dornin are dfndnts: I will, on Apr 21, sell at public auction, on the premises, the very valuable property at the corner of I st north & 15th st west, near St John's Church, in Wash City, to wit: lots 1, 2, & 21, in square 199. -A H Lawrence, Trustee -R W Dyer, auct

The new Pres of the Republic of Hayti was chosen & proclaimed by the Senate on Mar 2. His name is Faustin Soulouque, a general ofcr, aged about 50 years; a man of good & amiable character.

THU APR 1, 1847

Wanted to purchase immediately a colored boy, from 16 to 20 years of age, as a house servant. He must be honest & of good habits. -Wm Fischer

General Orders, #13. War Dept, Adj Genrl's Ofc, Wash, Mar 27, 1847. The following, appointed in the 10 additional regts, will immediately report to their respective Colonels, who will assign them to duty on the recruiting service; & at the proper time direct them to join their regts, or detachments thereof, as soon as put in route for the seat of war:
3rd Dragoons: to Col E G W Butler, New Orleans:
Surgeon Edw H Barton
Assist Surgeon F J Robertson
Assist Surgeon Corydon S Abell
Regent Voltigeurs: to Col T P Andrews, Wash:
Surgeon John W Tyler
Assist Surgeon Jas L Clarke
9th Infty: to Col T B Ranson, Boston, Mass:
Surgeon Justin E Stevens
Assist Surgeon John D Walker
Assist Surgeon Francis L Wheaton
10th Infty: to Col R E Temple, N Y C:
Surgeon Thos R Spencer
Assist Surgeon Jets R Riggs
Assist Surgeon John Conger
11th Infty: to Major E W Morgan, sup'g rec'g of Regt Phila:
Surgeon Wm J Barry
Assist Surg John H Weir
12th Infty: to Col M L Bonham, New Orleans:
Surgeon Robt R Ritchie
Assist Surgeon A G Howard
Assist Surgeon Leonard Randall

13th Infty: to Col Robt M Echols, New Orleans:
Surgeon John T Lamar
Assist Surgeon Robt F Gibbs
Assist Surgeon Franklin Malone
14th Infty: to Col Wm Trousdale, New Orleans:
Surgeon Lewis W Jordan
Assist Surgeon Robt H McGinnis
Assist Surgeon Edw B Prince
15th Infty:-to Lt Col J Howard, Cincinnati, Ohio:
Surgeon Jas B Slade
Assist Surgeon Wm D Carlin
Assist Surgeon Chas O Waters
16th Infty: to Col J W Tibbatts, Newport, Ky:
Surgeon Geo Berry
Assist Surgeon Allen T Noe
Assist Surgeon Shepherd Laurie
By order: R Jones, Adj Gen

Teacher wanted to take charge of a school near Millersville, Anne Arundel Co, Md; a middle aged man who can teach the languages would be preferred: salary not less than $350 the first year. -Rev Henry Aisquith, Benj E Gantt, Dr Wm Sands, Trustees

By deed of trust, executed by John B Hilleary, recorded on Sep 30, 1846, in the ofc of the Clerk for Wash Co, D C: I shall offer for sale, on Apr 15, at public auction, lot 6 in square 369, in Wash City: portion of the lot is improved with a 2 story brick house & back bldg. -John H Saunders, Trustee -A Green, auctioneer

Lost-In the Gulf of Mexico, by the wrecking of the British mail-steamer **Tweed**, on Feb 12, in his 31st year, Addison Fox, a native of Fairfax Co, Va, & for several years past a lawyer in Mobile.

Died: yesterday, Jas D Hanson, son of the Rev Jas M Hanson, in his 21st year. Through a protracted illness his characteristics were resignation & fortitude, & a firm faith in the religion which he professed. His funeral will take place from the house of Mrs Vancoble, on 4½ st, near the City Hall, today at 4 o'clock.

Died: yesterday, at the residence of his mother, on C st, between 12th & 13th sts, Mr Jas Delany, aged 26 years. He was a sober & industrious young man, but owing to having contracted a disease terminating in consumption, he had not been able to attend business for 12 months. He has been a most dutiful son & kind friend, & none will feel his loss more than his aged mother. His funeral is today at 4 o'clock.

Died: on Mar 19, at Brooklyn, N Y, in his 80th year, John Clouth, U S Navy, father-in-law of Henry G Wheeler. New Orleans papers please copy.

Mexicans on the Rio Grande. Miss Burns, the young lady who in the 3rd wagon when attacked on the 22nd, remained in the wagon until her father was shot, when she ran to his assistance, but found him dead. She was captured & taken to a ranche, where the women who were there paid her every attention. Her father was a resident of Saltillo, & a man of considerable property. He was on his return from New Orleans, where he had been for the purpose of returning with his dght, who was there at school.

Bent's Fort, Feb 1, 1847. In Taos, Chas Bent, Stephen L Lee, Elliott Lee, & many other Americans were massacred. Chas Town made his escape on a mule, & went to Turley's, 8 miles above, to give the alarm, & has not been heard of, & is presumed dead or to have perished in the mountains. Mr Albert, who lived with Turley, states that an old Frenchman, Chas Ortobus was slain. Geo Long is the only one I know of who escaped. They robbed him of every thing he possessed.

Mrd: on Mar 25, at Claymont, by Rev Mr Dutton, Dr Oscar G Mix, of Wash City, to Miss Catharine Mary Hurst, daughter of Wm Hurst, of Jefferson Co, Va.

Capt John Eagar Howard, just before his departure from Balt city with his company for Mexico, sent a check for $500 to the Sisters of the Visitation Convent on Park st. This is the 2nd donation from this gentleman within the past year to the same institution.

For sale: intending to remove West, I wish to dispose of my very valuable property, on G st, a few doors from the War Dept; part of which is occupied at present by Cmdor Bolton, as a private residence, the other part adjoining, at present occupied by myself, as a residence, grocery store, & a butter depot; the butter vault is one of the best in the city. Also, a lot & improvements on 18th st. Apply to Mr Stanislaus Murray or myself.
-Aquilla Ricketts

In the matter of the division of the real estate of Geo Semmes, dec'd. The Com'rs in this case having reported that they sold the tract of land called ***St Elizabeth***, containing 129 acres, 1 rood & 21 perches, to Thos Blagden, at $35 per acre, amounting to the sum of $4,528.34. Ordered by the Court that the sale be ratified, unless cause be shown to the contrary. -Wm Brent, clerk

FRI APR 2, 1847

The Charleston Theatre was sold on Thu, at public auction for $18,600. W C Gatewood was the purchaser.

Michl Carpenter, while working on a farm at Woodbury, West Jersey, was killed by lightning on Fri, with 2 horses he was driving.

Hon Elisha Allen, late Member of Congress from Maine, has removed from Bangor to Boston, where he will practice law.

Orphans Court of Wash Co, D C. Letters of administration on the personal estate of Richd Lawrence, late of said county, dec'd. -Thos J Barrett, adm

Our Naval force in the Gulf of Mexico:
line ship **Ohio**, Capt Stringham: 74 guns
frig **Potomac**, Capt Aulick: 56 guns
frig **Raritan**, Capt Forrest: 52 guns
sloop of war **John Adams**, Capt McCluney: 20 guns
sloop of war **St Mary's**, Capt Saunders: 20 guns
sloop of war **Germantown**, Com Buchanan: 20 guns
sloop of war **Albany**, Com Breese: 20 guns
sloop of war **Decatur**, Com Pinckney: 16 guns
sloop of war **Saratoga**, Com Farragut: 20 guns
brig of war **Porpoise**, Lt Com Hunt: 10 guns
brig of war **Perry**, Lt Barron: 10 guns
schnr of war **Bonita**, Lt Benham: 1 gun
schnr of war **Reefer**, [blank]: 1 gun
schnr of war **Petrel**, Lt Shaw: 1 gun
schnr of war **Tampico**, Mid Perry: 1 gun
steamer **Mississippi**, Com Perry, [Paixhan,]: 10 guns
steamer **Princeton**, Capt Engle: 9 guns
steamer **Spitfire**, Capt Tatnall: 3 guns
steamer **Vixen**, Capt Sands: 3 guns
steamer **McLean**, Capt Howard: 3 guns
steamer **Union**, Capt Rudd: 4 guns
steamer **Alleghany**, Capt Hunter: 10 guns
steamer **Hunter**, Lt McLaughlin: 6 guns
steamer **Polk**, Capt Ogden: 6 guns
steamer **Petrita**, [blank]: 1 gun
steamer **Scorpion**, Com Bigelow, [64 pr.]: 1 gun
steamer **Scourge**, Lt Hunter: 1 gun
store ship **Relief**, Lt Com Bullus: 6 guns
store ship **Supply**, [blank]: 2 guns
store ship **Fredonia**, Lt Com Chauncey: 2 guns
bomb ketch **Stromboli**, Com Walker [85 pre.]: 1 gun
bomb ketch **Etna**, Com Van Brunt: 1 gun
bomb ketch **Vesuvius**, Capt Magruder: 2 guns
bomb ketch **Hecla**, Lt Fairfax: 1 gun
bomb ketch **Electra**, [blank]: 1 gun
sloop **Mariner**, [blank]: 1 gun
cutter **Foxward**, Capt Nones: 6 guns
cutter **Ewing**, Capt Moore: 6 guns

Mrd: Mar 22, in Kent Co, Md, by Rev Dr C F Jones, Hon Jas Alfred Pearce, U S Senator from Md, to Miss Matilda C, daughter of the late Richd Ringgold, of Kent Co.

Mrd: on Mar 30, by Rev Mr Sprole, J M Shively, of Oregon, to Miss Susan L, youngest daughter of Rezin Elliott, of Fairfax Co, Va.

Mrd: on Mar 28, by Rev Mr Slicer, Mr Jos F Moffett to Miss Esther Chopley.

Mrd: on Mar 30, in Balt, by Rev S Kepler, S Merwin Tucker, of Wash City, to Miss Kate Maxwell, of Balt city.

Died: on Mar 31, after a protracted illness, Mrs Barbara Johnson, aged about 69 years. Her funeral is from her late residence on 7th st on Fri next, at 3 o'clock.

SAT APR 3, 1847

Assist Adj Genrl's Ofc, Army of Occupation, Agua Nueva, Mar 1, 1847. List of the names of the killed, wounded, & missing of the army of occupation in the battle of Buena Vista, Feb 23, 1847.

Genrl Staff-Regulars:

Killed: Capt Geo Lincoln, assist adj gen.

Wounded: 1st Lt Henry W Benham, engineers, very slightly. Brevet 2nd Lt Francis T Bryan, topographical engineers, very slightly.

1st Regt of Dragoons:

Wounded: Capt Enoch Steen, severely; Privates: Holloway, Co E, severely; Anderson, Co E, severely; Sherrod, Co E, slightly; Lanning, Co A, severely; Sweet, Co A, severely; Waggoner, Co A, slightly.

2nd Regt Dragoons:

Wounded: Brevet Lt Col C A May*, severe contusion. Private W F Erbe, Co E, severely. [*We understand that Col May's wound is not at all of a dangerous character, being only a contusion of the leg from a spent ball.]

3rd Regt Artl:

Killed: Private Christian F Waihinger, Co C.

Wounded: 2nd Lt Saml G French, severely; Cpl Robt Garns, Co C, severely. Privates, Wm Hudson, Co C, severely; Jacob Weyer, Co C, slightly. Recruit Jesse Gortner, 3rd Infty, burnt severely by accidental explosion of a cartridge. Orderly Sgt Bowning, Co E, slightly. Cpls: Wolfe, Co E, severely; Boyle, Co E, severely. Musician Tischer, Co E, supposed mortally. Artificer Livingood, Co E, severely. Privates: Bell, Co E, dangerously; Fisk, Co E, slightly; Kemp Co E, slightly; McCray, Co E, slightly; Smith, Co E, severely; Levier, Co E, slightly; Shane, Co E, mortally; Kelsey, Co E, severely; McDonnell, Co E, dangerously; Gillam, Co E, slightly; Kolisher, Co E, slightly.

Missing: Privates: Marcus A Hitchcock, Co C; Youngs, Co E; Morgan, Co E.

4th Regt of Artl: Killed: Privates: Holley, Co B; Weekly, Co B; Kinks, Co B; Doughty, Co B; Green, recruit, 3rd Infty.

Wounded: 1st Lt J P J O'Brien, slightly. Sgt Queen, Co B, slightly. Lance Sgt Pratt, Co B, slightly. Privates: Hannams, Co B, in hospital; Puffer, Co B, mortally; Beagle, Co B, in hospital; Berrier, Co B, in hospital; Floyd, Co B, slightly; Baker, Co B, slightly; Tharman, Co B, in hospital; Brown, Co B, slightly; Birch, Co B, in hospital; Butler, Co B, in hospital; Clark, Co B, in hospital.

Volunteers-Mississippi Rifles:

Killed: 1st Lt R L Moore; 2nd Lt Francis McNulty; Sgt Theodore Ingram, Co A

Pvts:

C O'Sullivan, Co A
L Turberville, Co B
W H Wilkinson, Co B
Wm Couch, Co C
D H Eggleston, Co C
Jas Johnson, Co C
John Preston, Co C
Robt A Joyce, Co E
Wm Sellers, Co E
P Durievant, Co F
Stephen Jones, Co F
Enos Garrett, Co F
Jas H Graves, Co G
J S Bond, Co G
L A Cooper, Co G
W M Seay, Co G
Robt Felts, Co G
Richd E Parr, Co G
W D Harrison, Co H
Patrick Rariden, Co H
Jacob Locke, Co H
H G Trotter, Co I
J S Branch, Co I
John Pease, Co I
A Collingsworth, Co I
J W Vinson, Co I
Seaborn Jones, Co R
Thos H Tirley, Co R

Cpls:

F M Robinson, Co E
Jos C Reville, Co E
Jas W Blakely, Co F
D L Butler, Co F
J M Alexander, Co G

Sgts:

B Higany, Co F
W W Philips, Co E
J H Langford, Co E
Gar Anderson, Co L

Wounded:

Col Jefferson Davis, severely
Capt Jos M Sharp, severely
Capt J P Stockaw, slightly
1st Lt A B Corwine, slightly
1st Lt Garnet Posey, slightly
Sgt D M Hollingsworth, Co A, slightly

Pvts:

Geo Brook, Co A, dangerously
H D Clark, Co A, dangerously
W H Stubblefield, Co A, severely
S P Stubblefield, Co A, slightly
R L Shook, Co A, severely
J M Miller, Co B, severely
G H Jones, Co B, severely
Solomon Newman, Co B, severely
J W Donnelly, Co B, slightly
W A Lawrence, Co B, slightly
J M Barnes, Co C, slightly
J W Cown, Co C, severely
Levi Stevens, Co C, slightly
Richd Claridy, Co E, severely
John Keneday, Co E, slightly
J C Laird, Co E, slightly
A B Puckett, Co E, severely
Robt Fox, Co E, severely
Jas Waugh, Co E, severely
J N Bigby, Co F, dangerously
Thos Courtney, Co F, slightly
J W Morris, Co F, severely
J L Simpson, Co F, severely
T J Malone, Co F, slightly
P Burnit, Co G, slightly
B F Edwards, Co G, severely
J Hammond, Co G, slightly
C W Gibbs, Co G, slightly
A J Neely, Co G, slightly
J Thompson, Co G, slightly
Thos White, Co H, dangerously
Wm Wirrans, Co H, slightly
S D Carson, Co H, slightly
S Edwards, Co H, severely
John Dart, Co H, slightly
Wm H McKinney, Co H, slightly
T D Randolph, Co I, severely
J Hedspeth, Co I, dangerously
T O McClanahan, Co I, slightly

Cpls:

J A McLaughlin, Co C, slightly	A B Atkinson, Co G, slightly
Howard Morris, Co C, severely	P Sinclair, Co G, slightly
Saml C Suit, Co C, slightly	G W Harrison, Co G, slightly
J W Collier, Co C, slightly	Henry Lanel, Co H, severely

Sgts: W H Scott, Co C, slightly; P M Martin, Co I, severely; A M Newman, Co H, slightly

Missing:

Pvt F M Schneider, Co B, supposed prisoner. Cpl J E Stewart, Co H, supposed to be killed.

1st Regt of Illinois Volunteers: Killed:

Col John J Hardin	1st Lt Bryan R Houghton	Principal Musician
Capt Jacob W Zabriskie		Austin W Fay

Pvts:

Francis Carter, Co B	Matthew Dandy, Co H
Merrit Hudson, Co C	Wm Smith, Co H
Augustis Canaught, Co D	Thos J Gilbert, Co H
John Emerson, Co D	John White, Co H
Silas Bedell, Co E	John B Bachman, Co K
Henry H Clark, Co E	Ingharat Claibsottle, Co K
Wm Goodwin, Co E	Courad Burrh, Co K
Jas J Kinman, Co E	John Gable, Co K
Randolph R Martin, Co E	Aaron Kiersted, Co K
Greenbury S Richardson, Co E	Jos Shutt, Co K
Saml W Thompson, Co E	Geo Pitson, Co K
Chas Walker, Co E	Wm Vankleharker, Co K
Elias C Mays, Co H	

Wounded: Pvts:

Michl Fenton, Co B, badly	Jackson Evans, Co H, slightly
Jas T Edson, slightly	Wm Roe, Co H, slightly
Francis Quinn, slightly	Danl Penser, Co H, badly
Potter Clemens, slightly	Geo Slack, Co K, slightly
Jas Robins, Co C, slightly	Fred'k Rekow, Co K, badly
Albert Kershaw, Co D, badly	Cpl: Patrick Mehan, badly
Watson R Richardson, Co E, badly	Sgt: John C Barr, Co D, badly
Wm Stevenson, Co E, badly	2nd Lt Hezekiah Evans, slightly
Job Brown, Co F, slight	1st Lt John L McConnell, slightly

Robins, slightly serving with Co B, 4th Artl, Washington's battery; Brown, slightly, do; Richardson, in hospital, do; Raleo, in hospital, do; Duff, in hospital, do; McLean, in hospital, do; Philips, in hospital, do.

2nd Regt Illinois Volunteers: Killed:

Capt Woodward	Lt Robbins	Lt Atherton
Lt A B Roundtree	Lt T Kelley	Lt Price
Lt Fletcher	Lt Steel	
Lt Ferguson	Lt Bartleson	

Pvts:

Wm Kenyon, Co A
Wm L Smith, Co A
Emerson, Co B
Kizer, Co B
Durock, Co B
Crippers, Co B
Woodling, Co C
Patton, Co C
Therman, Co C
McMichel, Co C
Gable, Co E
D O'Conner, Co E
Lortz, Co H
Couze, Co H
Crursmann, Co H
Schoolcraft, Co H
Lear, Co I
Davis, Co I
Cook, Co I
Bradley, Co I
McCrury, Co I
G Clark, Co I
Hogan, Co I
Squires, Co I
Abernathy, Co K
Bonner, Co K
W M Jones, Co K
Kinsey, Co K
S C Marlow, Co K
Robt Marlow, Co K
Wilkes, Co K
Ragland, Co K
W S Jones, Co K
Jenkins, Co G
Hill, Co G
Cpl: Hibbs, Co C
1st Sgt Faysoux, Co B

Wounded:

Capt Coffee, Co B
Capt Baker, Co B
Lt John A Pickett, Co B
Lt Engleman, Co B
Lt West, Co B
Adj Whiteside, Co B
Sgt J W Farmer, Co A

Pvts:

Auldridge, Co A
Burnet, Co A
Bird, Co A
Cooper, Co A
Cheek, Co A
Dempsey, Co A
Hutchings, Co A
J T Lee, Co A
Manaker, Co A
Pate, Co A
G W Rainy, Co A
Robins, Co A
White, Co A
Burke, Co C
Bryant, Co C
Clarage, Co C
Early, Co C
Feake, Co C
Foills, Co C
Fletcher, Co C
J M Nolland, Co C
Montgomery, Co C
Ricketts, Co C
H C Smith, Co C
Van Camp, Co C
Maxwell, Co C
Dwyer, Co C
Tidd, Co C
Fisher, Co C
Hill, Co E
Riley, Co E
Robinson, Co E
Wright, Co E
Bordaux, Co H
Irriges, Co H
Funk, Co H
Felameir, Co H
Gerhard, Co H
Ledergerber, Co H
Ranneberg, Co H
Talbut, Co H
Traenkle, Co H
Uppman, Co H
Henkler, Co I
White, Co I
Murmert, Co I
Fisher, Co I
Strong, Co I
Kell, Co I
McMurty, Co I
Warcheim, Co I
Hiltonan, Co I
Hamilton, Co K
Hoge, Co K
Kelley, Co K
G T Montage, Co K
R Marlow, Co K
John Ragland, Co K
N Ramsey, Co K
Wiey, Co G
McLain, Co G
Scott, Co B
Goodale, Co B
Sgt Major Ketter
Qrtrmstr Sgt Buckmaster

Missing: Pvt Mellen, Co H; Pvt Sinsel, Co H; Pvt Messenger, Co G

Company Texas Volunteers:
Killed: 1st Lt Campbell; 2nd Lt Leonhard; Cpls Voort & King; Pvts Clark, Doohoe, Froche, Hayes, Godwin, Finney, McLean, Klinge, & Largston.
Wounded: Capt Conner; Pvt Freackind
Missing: Pvts Smith, Larig, Bruno, & Miller; Cpt Brand; Sgt Sonop
Indiana Volunteers-Brig Staff.
Wounded: Brig Gen Jos Lane, slightly
2nd Regt Indiana Volunteers. Killed:
Capts T B Kinder & Wm Walker
2nd Lt Thos C Parr
Sgt McHenry Doxier, Co E
Pvts:
Francis Bailey, Co A
Chas H Goff, Co A
Warren Robinson, Co A
A Stephens, Co A
John Shoultz, Co B
J Lafferty, Co B
A Massey, Co B
D McDonald, Co B
J T Hardin, Co B
M Lee, Co D
W Richardson, Co D
J H Sladen, Co D
W Akin, Co E
J B D Dillon, Co E
H Matthews, Co F
J H Wilson, Co F
H Draper, Co H
R Jenkins, Co H
T Price, Co H
R Havritt, Co I
H M Campbell, Co I
J C Migginbotham, Co K
A Jenkins, Co K
G Chapman, Co K
O Lansburg, Co K
E Wyatt, Co K
T Smith, Co K
J Teasley, Co K
Wounded:
Capt W L Sanderson, slightly
1st Lt S W Cayce, slightly
2nd Lt H Pennington, slightly
D S Lewis, slightly
Capt John Osborn, slightly
2nd Lt J A Epperson, slightly
Cpl E McDonald, Co B, badly
Sgt A H Potts, Co D, slightly
Cpl D C Thomas, Co D, badly
Musician A M Woods, Co D, slightly
Sgt J Carathers, Co F, slightly
Sgt V Vestal, Co F, slightly
Cpl J Bishop, Co F, slightly
Cpl A B Carlton, Co F, slightly
Cpl N B Stevens, Co F, slightly
Cpl H Wilson, Co H, severely
Sgt P D Kelse, Co G, slightly
Sgt E Blalock, Co G, badly
Cpl T Rawlins, Co G, slightly
Cpl H Wilson, Co H, severely
Pvts:
T Goen, Co F, slightly
H Mulvany, Co G, slightly
M Queen, Co G, slightly
J McMilton, Co G, slightly
W Adams, Co H, severely
W Benefiel, Co H, severely
R Colbert, Co H, severely
V Swain, Co H, severely
J Ingle, Co H, slightly
A Smith, Co H, slightly
W D Weir, Co H, slightly
N Rumley, Co I, badly
A C Farris, Co K, badly
G McKnight, Co K, slightly
G Wilhart, Co K, slightly

Missing: Pvts: J Brown, Co B; J H Harrison, Co B; W Spalding, Co D; B Hubbard, Co I

3rd Regt Indiana Volunteers:

Killed: Capt J Taggart

Pvts:

J M Buskirk, Co A
W B Holland, Co A
D J Stout, Co A
J Armstrong, Co C
W Hueston, Co D
D Owens, Co F
W C Good, Co F
J Graham, Co G

Wounded:

Maj W A Gorman, slightly
Capt J M Sleep, slightly
Capt V Conover, slightly
Cpl R K Nelson, Co A, slightly

Pvts:

J S Levo, Co A, severely
W G Applegate, Co A, slightly
J Y Davis, Co A, slightly
J W Pullim, Co A, slightly
J Knight, Co A, slightly
J Faulkner, Co B, dangerously
H Hind, jr, Co B, slightly
H C Hoyt, Co B, slightly
D Conroy, Co B, slightly
T H Bowen, Co B, slightly
J Voight, Co C, dangerously
P Lain, Co C, slightly
M Cole, Co C, slightly
F Aubke, Co C, slightly
A Armstrong, Co C, slightly
J Orchard, Co C, slightly
G Miller, Co C, slightly
T Gustin, Co D, severely
J Hinkle, Co D, slightly
J Rochat, Co D, slightly
E Bright, Co D, slightly
A Merrill, Co D, slightly
J Brown, Co E, severely
M Mathis, Co E, severely
S Fred, Co E, slightly
J G Arter, Co E, slightly
S Stuart, Co E, slightly
J C Burton, Co F, seriously
O Dyer, Co F, slightly
J Inskeep, Co F, slightly
D Hunter, Co F, slightly
D Coughenower, Co F, slightly
H C Riker, Co F, slightly
J Meek, Co G, seriously
E Mace, Co G, slightly
J Patterson, Co G, slightly
J Cain, Co G, slightly
R Benson, Co H, severely
J Kelley, Co H, severely
M Conaway, Co I, slightly
J Hervey, Co K, seriously
M Gray, Co K, slightly
S Bradley, Co K, severely
S Lafollet, Co K, severely
Y Foster, Co K, slightly
Cpl J S Wilson, Co F, slightly
Cpl E Weddel, Co E, severely
Cpl R Torrance, Co D, slightly
Cpl J Gringrich, Co B, slightly
Sgt W Coombes, Co I, mortally
Sgt R McGarvey, Co K, severely
Sgt S P Turney, Co K, slightly

2nd Regt Kentucky Volunteers:

Killed: Col W R McKee; Lt Col Henry Clay, jr; Capt W T Willis

Pvts:

W Smith, Co A
A M Chaudowens, Co A
M Updike, Co B
W Blackwell, Co B
L B Bartlett, Co B
R M Baker, Co C

M Borth, Co C
W Burks, Co C
J Moffitt, Co C
J Walden, Co D
H Jones, Co D
W Harmon, Co D
H Frazier, Co E
J H Harkins, Co E
R McCurdy, Co E
H Snow, Co E
H Trotter, Co F
J A Gregory, Co G
J R Ballard, Co G
W Vest, Co G
J J Waller, Co G
W Gilbert. Co H
W Rham, Co H
J Williams, Co H
J J Thorn, Co I
A Goodparter, Co I
J Layton, Co K
W Bord, Co K
J Johnson, Co K
D Davis, Co K
A Thucker, Co K
W P Reynolds, Co K
J W Watson, Co K
Cpl H Edwards, Co I
Cpl J Q Carlin, Co E
Cpl P Srough, Co D
Cpt S M Williams, Co C
Sgt H Wolke, Co B
Sgt J Kring, Co H
Sgt J M Dunlap, Co H
Musician M Randebaugh, Co E

Wounded:
2nd Lt E L Barber, slightly
2nd Lt Thos W Napier, severely
Acting 2nd Lt W S Withers, Co C, severely
Sgt J Minton, Co A, slightly
Sgt J Wheatley, Co C, slightly
Sgt Sgt J Ward, Co H, mortally
Sgt W Lillard, Co K, severely

Pvts:
E Morris, Co A, slightly
S Wallace, Co A, slightly
R Winlock, Co A, slightly
J Burnett, Co A, slightly
B O Branham, Co B, severely
A Bres, Co B, severely
J Williams, Co B, slightly
W S Bartlett, Co B, slightly
E Burton, Co C, slightly
J Cahill, Co C, slightly
J Crawford, Co C, slightly
M Davidson, Co C, slightly
W D Purcell, Co C, slightly
W Hendron, Co C, mortally
H Burditt, Co D, mortally
P Hamilton, Co D, severely
H Vanfleet, Co D, severely
T Welsh, Co E, severely
J S Vanderier, Co E, severely
J Houk, Co E, slightly
W Park, Co E, slightly
D Walker, Co E, slightly
J Yelton, Co E, slightly
J Hunter, Co F, severely
T J Bruner, Co F, slightly
W Stringer, Co G, severely
T Hughes, Co G, severely
M A Davenport, Co G, slightly
A S Montgomery, Co D, severely
F Oak, Co H, mortally
Wm Daily, Co H, slightly
R Holder, Co H, slightly
J Wellington, Co H, slightly
G Simmons, Co H, slightly
E Scahill, Co I, mortally
J Redman, Co I, slightly
Ed McCullar, Co I, slightly
Wm Blunt, Co I, slightly
W Warford, Co K, mortally
B Perry, Co K, severely

G Searey, Co K, slightly	Cpl T Fox, Co H, slightly
W Howard, Co K, slightly	Cpl H Craig, Co H, slightly
J Montgomery, Co K, slightly	Cpl S Mayhall, Co B, mortally
G W Reed, Co K, slightly	Cpl C C Smedley, Co C, slightly
Cpl J Jennisson, Co E, severely	Cpl J Graig, Co D, slightly

Missing: Pvt J Catlett

Arkansas Cavalry: Killed:

Col Archibald Yell	Cpl R M Sanders	
Capt Andrew R Porter	Cpl W Gomberlin	
Pvts:		
Wm Phipps	J Ray	H Wynn
H Penter	W Robinson	T C Rowland
G H Higgins	D Hogan	Cpl D Stewart
G W Martin	P Williams	
J B Pelham	A Teague	

Wounded:

1st Lt Thos A Reader	Sgt Z D Bogard	Cpl M L Poplin
Sgt G Y Latham	Sgt H L Hamilton	
Pvts:		
M Kelley	A C Harris	W Turner
B F Nicholson	J Wilmouth	J Bigerstaff, slightly
W B Searcy	Franklin W Brown	W Gibson, slightly
Jos Penter	O Jones, slightly	R Arnold, slightly
C Taylor	E McCool	J Lowallen, slightly
L McGruder	J Williams	J Johnson
J F Allen	L B Beckwith	C Sullivan
M Graham	J Ray	Sgt J D Adams
D Logan	L A Twrouski	Sgt Maj B F Ross

Missing: Pvts L Settle, Jos Green, Geo Norwood, M Parker

The Kentucky Cavalry:

Killed: Adj E M Vaughan; Sgt D J Lillard, Co A

Pvts:

Lewis Sanders, C A	J Pomeroy, Co C	E Rouston, Co F
A J Marrin, Co A	A G Morgan, Co E	J M Roulin, Co F
J D Miller, Co B	C Jones, Co E	John Ross, Co F
B Warren, Co B	Wm Tevarts, Co E	E F Lilly, Co F
Jas Seston, Co C	N Ramey, Co E	Thos Wright, Co G
John Sander, Co C	H Carty, Co E	C B Thomson, Co H
John Ellingwood, Co C	W W Bales, Co E	C B Dempst, Co I
D P Rogers, Co D	H Danforth, Co F	Cpl J A Jones, Co D
W McClintock, Co D	J C Martin, Co F	

Wounded: Pvts:

John Walker, Co A	Thos Scandlett, Co A	Jos Murphy, Co B
B Spencer, Co A	John H Cluserlan, Co B	Wm Herndon, Co B
E W Ruson, Co A	Saml Evans, Co B	John Reddish, Co C

B F Pierce, Co C	C H Fowler, Co D	H E Brady, Co I
J K Goodloe, Co C	Chas Shepherd, Co E	Cpl Jas Scooley, Co G
Snodgrass, Co D	J Shepherd, Co E	Sgt S Manahan, Co H
J S Bryam, Co D	M C Callahan, Co E	2nd Lt Thos Con, Co B
W C Parker, Co D	Lerasy, Co E	2nd Lt J H Merrifield, Co H
J M Vanhook, Co D	J S Jackson, Co F	2nd Lt G W Brown, Co G
Geo H Wilson, Co D	Thos Brown, Co F	
Jas Warford, Co D	S Help, Co F	

Appointment by the Pres: Jas Ross Snowden, of Venango Co, Pa, to be Treasurer of the U S Mint at Phil, vice Isaac Roach, removed.

Died: on Fri, at her residence in PG Co, Md, Mrs Lucinda Birch, consort of Thos Birch, sen. Her remains will be taken to St Patrick's Church, Wash, on Sat, at 5 o'clock.

Died: some time last Feb, at Tampico, Upton S Heath, son of Maj Jas P Heath, of Balt.

J Riggles, Merchant Tailor: store on 7th st, a few doors north of Phillips' Dry Goods Store.

Valuable city lot for sale: lot 31 in square 126: on the square of Mrs Gen Macomb's house. It fronts on 17th st. Inquire of John M Wyse, at Mrs Tucker's, C st, or by letter to Pikeville, Md.

R W Latham & Co have associated with them in the Banking & Exchange Business, in Wash, J H Lathrop, late of Buffalo, N Y: under firm of R W Latham & Co.

MON APR 5, 1847

From the Brasos: Capt Lown, of 2nd Artl, has been relieved from the command of ***Fort Brown***, & returns home on account of ill health. He has arrived at New Orleans.

From the Cape of Good Hope. The U S sloop of war **Vincennes** arrived at N Y on Fri from Cape Town, in 54 days. Ofcrs of the **Vincennes**: Cmder, H Paulding

1st Lt S Swartwout — Assist Surgeon, R E Wade
2nd Lt, C F McIntosh — Purser, J Y Mason, jr
3rd Lt, J F Armstrong — Acting Master, D Ameren
4th Lt, J C Williamson — Passed Midshipman, J C Wait
Acting Sureon, A J Bowie
Midshipmen: W C West, A C Semmes, & E W Henry
Capt's Clerk, C Francis — Carpenter, G Henderson
Boatswain, J Shannon — Sailmaker, S C Herbert
Gunner, W Arnold

New Spring Goods: the lastest & most fashionable styles. -Jas M McKnight, Pa ave, 5 doors west of 9th st

The Hon Timothy Barnard, a Revolutionary patriot & pensioner, & father of Danl D Barnard, died at Mendon, Monroe Co, on Mar 29, aged 91 years. He was a resident of Monroe Co for more than 40 years, & long held the ofc of Associate Judge in that & Ontario Co.

From Vera Cruz: 1-The wound of Lt Col Dickson, of the Palmetto Regt, is doing well. No other ofcrs than before mentioned have been killed or wounded. 2-The report of the recapture of Midshipman Rogers was premature. He was still, unfortunately, a prisoner.

Mrd: on Mar 30, at Dumfries, Va, by Rev D Ball, Franklin Ball, of Fairfax Co, Va, to Miss Mary C Dulany, of the former place.

Four houses for sale: 2 fronting on Pa ave, heretofore occupied as ofcs of the Treas Dept. The other 2 are on 17th st west, square 127, south of Mrs Macomb's residence, & west of the British Minister & Mrs Gadsby. -Thos Munroe

$25 reward for runaway negro man, Jas Airs, about 23 years old. -John Mitchell, living near Queen Anne, PG Co, Md.

Very superior mutton sold on Sat, in our Centre Market, by Mr F Speisser, who lately purchased of W D Bowie, of P G Co, Md, a lot of mutton that will not suffer on comparison with the fat mutton raised in Va.

TUE APR 6, 1847

When the news of the glorious but bloody battle of Buena Vista was received in Lexington, the Circuit Court was in session, & Gen Combs moved that it immediately adjourn in respect to the memories of Col McKee, Lt Col Clay, Capt Willis, Adj Vaughn, & other ofcrs & soldiers of Ky whose blood was gallantly shed in battle, & that said names be entered on the records of the Court; which was done.

Well improved farm at auction: by deed of trust executed by Wm S Allison & wife, Aug 11, 1840, recorded among the land records of Montg Co, Md, in Liber B S #10, folios 338 thru 340: sale on May 8, all that parcel of land called ***No Gain***, south of & adjoining to the farms of Judge Dunlop & Mr Greenberry Watkins, it being the same tract of land formerly owned by the late John Laird, & was conveyed by Wm Laird to Jas McVean, by deed dated Oct 2, 1838, & contains 307 acres of land, more or less, & that was conveyed by deed, on Aug 10, 1840, by Jas McVean to Wm S Allison, as by reference to said deeds, both on record among the land records of said county. On each of which parts is a dwlg house, barn, & other farm bldgs. Mr Allison himself, who resides on the premises will show the land. -Wm Jewell, Trustee

For rent: dwlg of the late John Little, situated on 11th st east, Navy Yard Hill. Inquire of Mrs Barbara Little, on the premises; or of D Little, 6th st west, between Mass ave & K st.

Gen Cadwalader has passed through Wheeling on his route to the seat of war.

Battle of Buena Vista: from the New Orleans Delta of Mar 27. Interview yesterday with Maj Coffee, of the Army, who brought over Gen Taylor's dispatches. This gallant ofcr, a son of the distinguished General who fought so bravely on the Plains of Chalmette, & other battles, by the side of the illustrious Jackson-acted as Aid of Gen Taylor in the bloody fight at Buena Vista. At sunrise on Feb 23 the battle begain in earnest. The Ky Infty was attacked at the foot of a hill, in a deep ravine. A large number of the ofcrs were killed here; among them was Col McKee, who fell badly wounded, & was pierced with bayonets as he lay on the ground. Lt Col Clay was shot through the thigh, &, being unable to walk, was taken up & carried some distance by some of his men, but, owing to the steepness of the hill, the men finding it very difficult to carry him, & the enemy in great numbers pressing upon them, the gallant Lt Col begged them to leave him & take care of themselves. The last seen of this noble young ofcr he was lying on his back, fighting with his sword the enemy who were stabbing him with their bayonets. The veteran Capt Wm S Willis, of the same regt, at the head of his company, with 3 stalwart sons, who fought at his side, was badly wounded, but still continued the fight, until he was overcome with the loss of blood. The Indiana brigade, drawn out & ordered to charge the enemy, were seized with a panic, &, displaying some hesitation, Assist Adj Gen Lincoln rushed to their front, &, whilst upbraiding them for their cowardice, was shot-several balls passing through his body. Col Hardin led the Illinoisans, & they fought like lions. Their intrepid colonel fell wounded, & experienced the fate of Cols McKee & Clay, & was killed by the enemy; not, however, before he had killed one of the cowardly miscreants with a pistol, which he fired whilst lying on the ground. Col Yell led, the foremost man, a charge of his mounted volunteers, against a large body of lancers, & was killed by a lance, which entered his mouth & tore off one side of his face. The Mississippians, the heroes of Monterey, delivered a most destructive fire among the crowded columns of cavalry. The enemy was completely repulsed. The distinguished commander of this gallant regt, Col Jefferson Davis, was badly wounded, an escopette ball having entered his foot & passed out of his leg. He was, however, doing well when last heard from. The chivalrous Lt Col McClung was prevented from doing his share by the grievious wound received at the battle of Monterey, which still confines him to his bed. Col Humphrey Marshall's splendid regt of Kentucky cavalry stood their ground against a charge of a force of more than 2,000 lancers & hussars.

Orphans Court of Wash Co, D C: order passed on Jul 5 last: I shall sell all of lot 30 in square 127, & part of lot 31 in square 127, being on 17th st, near the residence of Mrs Macomb. -Sarah Voorhees, Guardian -A Green, auctioneer

For rent: the 2 story frame house at the corner of L st north & 13th st west. Inquire of Luke Richardson, near the premises.

$100 reward for runaway negro man Washington Moreland, aged 23 years old: well acquainted with Chas & PG Counties, having lived there 10 years.
-Kitty Turner, living near Charlotte Hall, St Mary's Co, Md.

WED APR 7, 1847

Lt Col Henry Clay, jr, of the Ky volunteers, who was killed at the recent signal victory at Buena Vista, graduated with great distinction at the Military Academy at West Point in 1831. He remained but a short time in the army, & we believe was for a portion of that time stationed in N Y C, in the staff of Gen Scott, & he subsequently devoted himself in Ky to the profession of the law. The Col of his regt, Col Wm R McKee, fell upon the same field. He also was a graduate from West Point, of the class of 1829, who had resigned from the army & become devoted to civil pursuits in Ky. He was a very distinguished civil engineer. Older than Clay, he was invested with the command of the regt. Col Jefferson Davis, of the Mississippi volunteers, reported as wounded at the battle of Buena Vista, is also a graduate from West Point. He was a distinguished member of the last Congress, & on the breaking out of the war left Washington in Aug last, in time to command his regt & win many laurels at the battles of Monterey. Col Alex'r M Mitchell, a native of N C, who commanded a regt of Ohio volunteers at Monterey, graduated at West Point in 1835. He was wounded at the battle of Sep 21, leading his regt at the bloody charged on the south side of the town, under Maj Gen Butler. Capt Albert G Blanchard, a native of Massachusetts, another graduate, commanded the company of Louisiana volunteers, which accompanied Gen Worth in his brilliant operations in storming the heights in rear of Monterey. These were the only troops from that State engaged in that battle. Although the Louisianians turned out in crowds for the Rio Grande in May, they were mostly discharged in 3 months. The regt of volunteers recently raised from that State is left at Tampico, owing, to its misfortune in being recently wrecked upon the coast. This brings us to add that its cmder, Col L G De Russy, is another graduate from the Military Academy. So also are *Lt Col Jason Rogers, of the La Legion, which was at the battle of Monterey, & Col S R Curtis, commanding one of the Ohio regts, & who, at the last dates, had gone to give battle to Gen Urrea. We close this list, viz: Col Albert G Johnson, of Texas, in the staff of Govn'r Henderson at Monterey, Col W B Burnett, of the regt of N Y volunteers, now at Vera Cruz; Lt Col Henry G Burton, a native of Vt, & Maj Hardie, both in the Calf regt, are 5 other graduates. To this list, perhaps, inferior in rank, could be added Maj Merriwether L Clarke, from St Louis, who raised a btln organized as a battery of volunteer artl, which is now in Santa Fe. Cols Hardin, Yell, & many other gallant spirits have sealed with their lives the evidence of their intrepid & faithful discharge of duty. It is but simple justice to West Point to set forth its share in giving efficiency to the volunteer regts at Monterey & Buena Vista, & to exhibit the usefulness of graduates who have resigned from the army in officering the militia in time of war. [Apr 9th newspaper: Lt Col Jason Rogers is of the Louisville Legion, not the Louisiana Legion.]

New Mexico. The news of the assassination of Govn'r Bent is fully confirmed. 25 other Americans fell at the same time.

The U S brig **Boxer**, J E Bisphan, lt commanding, arrived at Monrovia on Mar 28, in 14 days from Kabenda. The **Boxer** had been employed the last 4 months in cruising on the southern part of the coast, as far as St Paul de Loando, & during that time saw but 2 American vessels.

Rev A W Anderson died on Mar 10 after an illness of 12 hours. He was pastor of the Baptist Church in Caldwell, but resided in Monrovia, & afforded much service in the way of preaching to the church here.

Sale of lots in square 185: lots 5 thru 8, [being subdivisions of lots 7 thru 9,] lots 10 thru 13, & lots 9 thru 11, [being subdivisions of lots 14 & 15;] & also lots 16 & 17, in Wash City. -W Redin, Trustee -B Homans, auctioneer

Valuable lots at auction: on Apr 15, on the premises, by order of the Execs, the following lots belonging to the estate of the late John Gadsby: lots 1 through 12, 19 thru 22, & 28 thru 30, in square 76, fronting on K st north, between 20th & 21st sts. Deeds to be at the expense of the purchaser. -R W Dyer, auct

Farming utensils, horse, wagon, cart, cow, shoes, at auction, on Apr 14, at the residence of Mr John Bartruff, a quarter of a mile from the Toll Gate, on the Balt Turnpike. Also household & kitchen furniture. -R W Dyer, auct

The Tower of London still stands on the same spot as in the time of Wm the Conqueror, 700 years ago. The horse armory, in a room or hall 150 feet in length, presenting a line of equestrian figures, representing the suits of armor associated with the times & the names of several monarchs, from Edward I, in 1272, down to James II, 1685, is very interesting & imposing. The old warders still retain their uniform or apparel worn in the time of Edward VI, the most prominent feature of which is the quaint velvet hat, adorned with pink & blue ribands. The most remarkable works of modern times is the Tunnel under the Thames, extending from Wapping to Rotherhithe, 1,200 feet, beneath the river at the depth of 63 feet. It consists of a double arch, each wide enough for a carriage way & a footpath, & lit with gas. It has already cost L500,000 & is a lasting monument to the skill of the celebrated engineer, Sir J M Brunel.

Wash Corp: 1-Nominations from the Mayor: for Com'rs of the Asylum: Chas A Davis, Leonard Harbaugh, & Jas Marshall. For Physician to the Asylum: Dr Alex'r McWilliams. For Resident Medical Student: Martin H Johnson. The nominations were severally confirmed, except that of Leonard Harbaugh, which was rejected. 2-Ptn of David Rich: referred to the Cmte of Claims. 3-Ptn from Mary W P Handy & Susan D Anderson: referred to the Cmte of Claims. 4-Ptn of Henry M Morfit & others: referred to the Cmte on Improvements. 5-Ptn of J R Grimes, praying payment of a balance due for work done on the 2nd District Public School: referred to the Cmte on Improvements. 6-Ptn of Richd Metherall, praying for a remission of a fine: referred to the Cmte on Improvements. 7-Ptn of Jos Downing & others, for construction of a reservoir in the 3rd Ward: which was withdrawn by him. 8-Cmte of Claims: asking to be discharged from the further consideration of the ptn of John P Stallings: ptn was recommitted with instructions to report a bill for the relief of the petitioner: which motion was agreed to. 9-Bill for the relief of Wm Cooper was taken up, read 3 times, & passed.

At auction on Sat next: the frame house & shed on the corner of 15th & F sts, recently occupied by the late Wm Laub as a grocery store. -R W Dyer, auct

Orphans Court of Wash Co, D C. Letters testamentary on the personal estate of John O P Degges, late of Wash Co, dec'd. -Saml Stott, Chas Abbot, excs

The District Assembly of United Brothers of Temperance will hold their next regular monthly meeting in Gtwn on Apr 8, in the hall of the Vigilant Engine House.
-H W Dowden, R S

Orphans Court of Wash Co, D C. Letters of administration on the personal estate of Kemp S Holland, late of the U S Army, dec'd. -M F Maury, adm

Mrs Patten, on Pa ave, nearly opposite Coleman's, can accommodate families or single gentlemen with board, having 4 or 5 very pleasant commodious rooms vacant. For rent, a fine brick stable for 2 horses. Inquire as above.

For rent: 3 story brick house, belonging to the estate of John Foy, on the north side of Pa ave, near the Capitol. Possession may be had now. -Tho Carbery, Agent

Private sale: good & substantial brick house, on I st, between 9th & 10th sts, containing 10 rooms; carriage house, & stabling for 3 horses. Also for sale 3 good bldg lots on K st, near the corner of 12th st, with small tenement. Inquire of J Thompson, on I st.

For rent: comfortable 2 story brick house, with large lot, on E st, near the Gen Post Ofc. Inquire of R S Patterson.

Soda water fixtures for sale. For further information apply to Saml De Vaughan, 9th st.

Carpeting, straw matting, & oil cloth for sale. -P H Hooe & Co

Hovey's seedling strawberries will be sold at the very low price of $7.50 per thousand. They will be put up so that they may be transported to any distance. Apply at my residence, east of Kalorama, between 20th & 21st sts; or orders may be left at the store of J F Callan, corner of E & 7th sts. -Louis Vivans

THU APR 8, 1847

Coroner John Osborn held an inquest on Mon at the residence of John Flinn, Albany, N Y, on the bodies of his 2 children, John 4 years & Wm 6 years old, who died suddenly the previous night from drinking a large quantity of liquor, which they either procured themselves, or was given them by some person yet unknown.

Michigan & Wisconsin land for sale: selected after actual inspection. Apply to Dr Chas Collins, Parker, Phil, of John D McPherson, Wash.

The sudden death of Geo L Lowden, grand nephew of Cmdor Paul Jones, which took place in Phil a few days ago, was deeply deplored by his numerous friends. The bill for the relief of the heirs of Paul Jones, one of whom was Mr Lowden, passed both houses of the last Congress, on the last night of the late session, was lost on the floor of the Senate by the messenger before it had received the Pres' approval, which it would have obtained had it been presented in time. Mr Lowden, after having labored for years to induce Congress to grant this measure of justice, found his object, when on the eve of consummation, defeated by an accident; still he bore up manfully against adverse circumstances, & left Washington in good health. Almost immediately upon his arrival in this city, he took sick, & died in a few days. It is to be hoped that the next Congress will not hestitate to render justice to the claim for which he labored so long. -Pennsylvanian

House for rent: brick house on 10th st, opposite to Col P Force. Apply to F Masi & Co, Pa ave, between 9th & 10th sts.

J M Breedlove, who was tried upon certain charges of fraud before the U S Circuit Court some years ago, & sentenced to 10 years' imprisonment at hard labor, has been pardoned by the President.

From Vera Cruz, brought by the ship **Oswego**, which sailed thence on the 19th ult. 1-The ship **Yazoo**, with Capt Ker's squadron on board, had been lost on Anton Lizardo. More than 100 horses were lost. 2-The ship **Diadem**, which sailed from this port with 230 horses on board, lost all but 27 before her arrival at Vera Cruz. 3-Col Duncan lost several of his horses in the gale. The loss of horses is severely felt. 4-One Dragoon was drowned from the **Yazoo**, & 3 men from the store-ship **Relief** were drowned in endeavoring to rescue the Dragoons.

For rent: 2 story brick house on Missouri ave, between 3rd & 4½ sts; lately occupied by the Rev Mr Sprole. Apply to Mrs Shepherd, at her residence, on 9th st, opposite the Fourth Presbyterian Church; or to Francis Mohun, at his carpenter shop, on 6th st, near La ave.

Died: on Apr 7, after a few days' illness, in his 72nd year, Mr Jas Glenn, formerly of Balt, Md, but for many years past a resident of this place. His funeral is this afternoon, at 4 o'clock, from the residence of Mrs Shryock, on 7th near E st.

Mrs J B Hills will open Spring Millinery on Sat at 10 o'clock, at her new Millinary establishment, Pa ave, between 9th & 10th sts, immediately opposite Walter Harper's dry goods store.

The copartnership existing under the firm of Wagner & Laub, is this day dissolved by mutual consent. -John Wagner, Francis Lamb. Francis Lamb will continue the business, at the old stand, & make to order all kinds of Ornamented & Plain Portrait & Picture Frames, & Curtain Cornices, on reasonable terms.

Died: on Apr 5, of consumption, Wm Dement, of St Mary's Co, Md, & for the last 2 years a resident of Wash City, in his 27th year.

Fairview for sale or rent: a house containing 9 rooms, in square 315, fronting on M st north, between 4th & 5th sts west, now occupied by Capt Crabb, who will vacate on May 1. -Jas A Kennedy

FRI APR 9, 1847

Maj Gen Wm O Butler left Wash on Mon on his return to his family in Ky. His wound is not yet sufficiently healed to return to the duties of the camp, which he is anxious to rejoin. -Union

The Municipal election at Annapolis, Md, on Monday resulted in the election of the entire Whig ticket. Richd Swann was chosen Mayor, & Wm Tell Claude was chosen Recorder.

A recruiting ofc has been opened in Newport, Ky, by the Hon John W Tibbatts, recently appointed Col in the U S Army. -Ky Reporter

Letter from the Little Rock Democrat of Mar 26. A letter of Apr 14, received from an ofcr in Capt Pike's company, states that the body of a member of Capt Danley's [now Lt Gaines'] company, by the name of McCallaster, from Clark Co, had been found hung a few days previous, with a lasso around his neck. A party of some of his comrades from Lt Gaines' & Capt Hunter's companies had been searching for him for 2 or 3 days, &, when they found him, he was stripped of his clothing & appeared to have been dead 2 or 3 days. Near the spot was a cave with over 100 peons, [laborers,] who, they were satisfied, were the murderers of their comrade. In a moment of excitement, the party fell upon the cowardly wretches, & killed some 27 or 30 of them, & took the residue prisoners & carried them to camp. This act was censured by Gen Taylor, who threatened to send those engaged in it to Camargo & employ them in loading & unloading steamboats. It is hardly probably that the threat was carried into execution.

The Mobile papers of Mar 30th state that the dead body of I Moses, a money-broker of that place, formerly of Phil, was found in the woods, some 4 miles below the city, near the shore of the bay, on Sunday previous. The condition in which his inanimate body was found leaves the manner of his death still conjectural & mysterious, with the exception that there was probably no violence used, unless by his own hand. He had his watch, one or two costly rings, & about $90 in money on his person.

Jos Eaches has been appointed by the County Court of Alexandria, Va, Com'r in Chancery.

Mrd: on Mar 25, in Norfolk, by Rev Mr Jennings, Mr John R Hathaway, formerly of Wash City, to Miss Anna E, only daughter of Geo Kerby, of the former place.

A correspondent of the Nat'l Intelligencer pays what is no doubt a just compliment to the professional skill & industry of Mr John Howlett, whose residence & garden is at the corner of 5th & Mass ave, & describes con amore the very fine snap-beans in full growth, raspberries red & nearly ripe, with many other vegetable varieties, which he found in his garden on Good Friday. We acknowledge the politeness of Mr Ousley, the gardener at the Pres' house, for the very fine cucumbers & lettuce which he sent us today.

West Point further Vindicated. Col Humphrey Marshall, commanding a regt of Ky cavalry at Buena Vista, graduated at West Point in 1832. Also, Lt Col Chas Ruff, of the Missouri Regt of Volunteers in Santa Fe. Col Jason Rogers a graduate of West Point, is of the Louisville, [not Louisiana] Legion.

City Ordinance-Wash. 1-Act for the relief of Henry L Cross: the sum of $3.38 having been erroneously paid by the said Cross to the Corp of Wash relative to the tax sale of lot 4 in square 75, to be refunded.

Balt, Apr 8. Painful accident today to Miss Jacobsen, a beautiful young daughter of Mr Henry Jacobsen, the Danish Consul residing in this city. Miss Jacobsen with several other young ladies, were passing along Balt st, in front of the Museum, where a new warehouse is being erected. An empty cask or nail keg fell from the bldg above & struck her on the head, prostrating her to the pavement, producing a severe contusion. She is very severely but it is hoped not fatally injured.

Died: on Apr 7, after a long & painful illness, at his residence near Wash City, in his 79th year, Jesse Brown, the well known proprietor of the Indian Queen Hotel for the last 26 years. His funeral is this day at 11½ o'clock, from the Hotel.

Died: on Wed, Capt John Peabody, in his 48th year. His funeral is this morning at 10 o'clock, from his late residence on 6th st, between E & F sts.

SAT APR 10, 1847

For sale: the late Chancellor Bland's copy of the Nat'l Intell, from the year 1800 to the present time. 34 volumes, up to 1842, are bound, the remainder in files. The whole in excellent order. Apply to Alex'r Randall, Annapolis, Md.

St Osyth for sale: my plantation, in PG Co, Md: contains 400 acres; with a large 2 story frame dwlg, built in the best manner, a good barn, corn-house, stables, & other out-houses, together with a grist mill, which is profitable. -C A Gantt

Orphans Court of Wash Co, D C. Letters of administration on the personal estate of Peter Callan, late of said county, dec'd. -Rowena Callan, adm

Mrd: on Apr 8, by Rev F S Evans, Mr Geo J Butt to Miss Mary E, daughter of Mr Jacob A Bender, of Wash City.

Whilst the Albany Republican Artl were engaged on Mon in firing a salute in honor of the battle of Buena Vista, Francis Fitzpatrick, a carman, who had drawn one of the pieces used on firing the salute to the ground, received so serious an injury from the discharge of one of the guns that his life is despaired of. While ramming down one of the charges an explosion took place, & the ramrod lacerated one of his arms dreadfully, so that amputation was deemed necessary, He also received a serious injury in the breast.

Died: on Apr 7, at the residence of his mother, in Gtwn, D C, Wm H Taylor, in his 41st year.

Died: on Apr 6, at Bowieville, near Upper Marlboro, PG Co, Md, of consumption, Catherine Lee Comegys, aged 16 years, daughter of the late J B Comegys, of Boston, Mass.

Died: on Mar 29, at the ***Hill-Side***, in Northampton, Co, N C, the residence of Henry K Burgwyn, Miss Jane D Greenough, daughter of the late David S Greenough, of Jamaica Plain, Mass, in her 17th year.

Died: on Apr 30, suddenly, with apoplexy, at his residence in Auburn, Loudoun Co, Va, Ariss Buckner, in his 76th year, after a long & protracted illness.

Died: on Apr 2, at Alexandria, after a lingering illness, Mrs Frances Eliza Cazenove, consort of Louis A Cazenove, leaving 3 small children, an affectionate husband, & a large circle of friends & acquaintances to deplore their irreparable loss.

Died: on Thu last, at the residence of her father, in PG Co, Md, Miss Mary M Bowling, in her 20th year, eldest daughter of Jos H & Mary Rose Bowling.

Notice to the Public. This is positively the last time that General Tom Thumb will ever be seen in Wash, as he retires forever from public life as soon as he has paid a brief visit to the principal cities in the Union.

Spring Fashions: Mrs Speir, D st, in the rear of Harper's store: latest Parisian styles.

Caution. The public are cautioned against purchasing a judgment in favor of Geo L Gilchrist against the undersigned, as I have a good & lawful bar against the payment of the same, being a judgment against Gilchrist in my favor, for the same agreement. The judgment against which the public are cautioned amounts to about $84, & is superseded by Jos Dowling. -Wm Johnson

Mrs Garret Anderson has just received 3 superior Pianos, made of rosewood & mahogany, of superior tone & touch: will be sold at the manufacturer's prices. Located between 11th & 12th sts, Pa ave.

MON APR 12, 1847
A man named Geo Northerman has been arrested in N Y charged with being engaged in counterfeiting bank notes, 2 of his accomplices having been previously arrested in Pa.

Gen Taylor's First Brevet. In Nov, 1812, Pres Madison conferred upon Capt Zachary Taylor the Brevet Major, for his gallant defence of ***Fort Harrison***.

In Portland, Maine, Eliphalet Greely, the Whig candidate for Mayor, was elected by a handsome majority.

A shocking murder was perpetrated upon Mr John B Firbanks, a highly respectable resident of the chapel district, in Talbot Co, Md, on Sat last, by a young man in his employ named Jos Millis. An altercation was heard from the direction of his wheel-wright shop where Millis was then at work. Mr Firbanks was found upon the floor with the back of his head fractured & life entirely extinct. The Sheriff of the county & a numerous posse were early in pursuit of Millis.

Great triumph of the American Arms: on Mar 9 the troops were disembarked by the navy, 4,000 being thrown on shore at the first trip, & took possession of the magazine & the hills around Vera Cruz. On Mar 13 the investment was completed, & 2 mortars landed. On the 17th ten or twelve more mortars landed. On the 18th the trenches were opened at night. On the 22nd the city was summoned to surrender at 2 p m; &, on refusal, a fire was opened from 7 mortars, which was afterwards increased to 9. On the 24th the navy, having landed a battery from the ships of three 32 pounders & three 68 pounder Paixhan guns, opened their fire in the morning. It silenced 3 forts, demolishing 2 of them entirely. On the 25th a battery of four 24 pounders & two 8 inch howitzers opened fire. On the 26th the enemy commenced negotiations for surrender. On the 29th possession was taken of the city of Vera Cruz & Castle of San Juan d'Ulua, the enemy marching out & laying down their arms. The American flag hoisted in the town & castle. The number of prisoners is estimated at 4,000. Our total loss is killed & wounded, from the 9th to the 29th of Mar, is 65; of whom 14 were of the Navy, engaged in serving a shore battery, & 51 of the Army. The ofcrs killed ar Capt John R Vinton, 2nd Artl; Capt Wm Alburtis, 2nd Infty; Midshipman Thos D Shubrick, navy. The ofcrs wounded are Lt Col Dickinson, S C volunteers, Lt Augustus S Baldwin, navy, slightly; Lt Delozier Davidson, 2nd Infty, slightly; Lt Lewis Neill, 2nd Dragoons, severely-all doing well.

The bodies of the ofcrs who fell in the battle of Buena Vista have been placed by their friends in coffins, in which pulverized charcoal was introduced, & the coffins placed temporarily in vaults at Saltillo until removed to their late homes. Major Borland, Maj Gaines, Capt Cassius M Clay, & their commands, about 82 men, who have been prisoners in the castle of Perote, were to be delivered up at Vera Cruz. Capt Heady, from Louisville, of the Ky regt, who, with 18 men, were taken by the enemy some time since, were to be restored to Gen Taylor's encampment.

Edw Wright & Joshua Fort, whilest firing a cannon at Mount Holly, N J, in honor of the victory of American arms at the scene of war, were shockingly injured by the premature explosion of the cannon. -Phil Chronicle

John Moss, of Phil, died on Sun, after a painful sickness. He had been for more than 50 years a resident of Phil, & acquired by his industry & enterprise as a merchant an ample fortune. He has passed from life with a good name & in a good old age. -U S Gaz

Wm Lambert has been re-elected Mayor of the city of Richmond for the ensuing year.

Letter from Santa Anna to Gen Don Circiaco Vasquez: Agua Nueva, Feb 25, 1847.
We have to lament the death of Col Berra, Lt Col Anonos, & the cmders of battalions & squadrons, Luyando, Rios, Pena, besides other ofcrs. Gen Lombardino, Col Brito, Col Rocha, Gen Angel Guzman, Lt Cols Gallozo, Monterdeoca, Andrade, Jicotercal, Ouijano, Basave, Onate, & other chiefs & ofcrs are wounded. I lost my horse by a gunshot in one of the first charges.

Articles of Capitulation of the City of Vera Cruz & the Castle of San Juan d'Ulua. Puente de Hornos, without the walls of Vera Cruz, Sat, Mar 27, 1847. Terms of capitulation ageed upon the by the Com'rs: Gens W J Worth & G J Pillow, & Col J G Totten, Chief Engineer, on the part of Maj Gen Scott, Gen-in-Chief of the armies of the U S; & Col Jose Gutierrez de Villanueva, Lt Col of Engineers Manuel Robles, & Col Pedro de Herrera, com'rs appointed by Gen of Brigade Don Jose Juan Landero, commanding in chief Vera Cruz, the castle of San Juan d'Ulua, & their dependencies, for the surrender to the arms of the U S of the said forts, with their armaments, munitions of war, garrisons, & arms. The whole of the garrison to be surrendered to the arms of the U S as prisoners of war Mar 29. Mexican ofcrs shall preserve their arms & private effects, including horses & horse furniture, & to be allowed, regular & irregular ofcrs, as also the rank & file, 5 days to retire to their respective homes on parole. The Mexican flags of the various forts & stations shall be struck, & immediately thereafter ***Fort Santiago*** & ***Fort Conception*** & the castle of San Juan d'Ulua occupied by the forces of the U S. The rank & file of the regular prisoners to be disposed of, after surrender & parole, as their gen-in-chief may desire, & the irregular permitted to return to their homes. All material of war, & all public property to belong to the U S. The sick & wounded Mexicans to be allowed to remain in the city, with medical attention. Absolute protection is solemnly guarantied to persons in the city. Absolute freedom of religious worship & ceremonies is solemnly guaranteed. [Signed in duplicate.] W F Worth, Brig Gen; Gid J Pillow, Brig Gen; Jos G Totten, Col & Chief Engin'r; Jose Gutierrez de Villanueva; Pedro Manuel Herrera; Manuel Robles

An account of the gallant conduct of one of our young ofcrs in Calif, Lt Talbot, in bravely refusing to surrender to a Mexican force 15 times greater than his own, this fellow-townsman of our own, a son of the late Hon Isham Talbot, formerly an esteemed Senator in Congress from Ky, whose respected widow, the mother of the brave young Lt, now resides in this city. [Wash City.]

Cmte appointed in Wash to make collections for the relief of the suffering Highlanders of Scotland.

Dr W B Magruder
Fred D Stuart
John Douglas, sen
Rev Ninian Bannatyne
John Sessford
David Munroe
W D Breckenridge
Benj Williamson
A B McFarlan
Wm Archer
Andrew Small
Danl Campbell
Robt Brown
Thos Blagden
Wm McDonald
Gen A Henderson
Wm D Acken
A McKim
Simon Frazer
Saml Byington
Pringle Sleight

Scotch Relief Cmte appointed in Balt:

Wm Morris
John M Gordon
Chas Farquharson
Patrick Macaulay
J Mason Campbell
Alex'r Smith
Dr J R W Dunbar
Francis Burns
Wm F Murdoch
Wm W Spence
Judge Alex'r Nisbet
John A Robb
Capt Jas Gibson
Danald McIlvaine
R D Burns
Wm Crichton
Capt Jas Frazer
Geo Duncan
Jas Malcoln
John Boyd

Died: on Apr 10, in Wash City, [at the Farmers' & Virginia house, Henry W Sweeting, proprietor,] Mr Geo Brown, a native of the town of Somers, Westchester Co, N Y. He bore his sufferings, inflammation of the lungs, with Christian fortitude, & his last moments were calm & resigned. Due to the proprietor of the hotel, every comfort was rendered to the stranger, & nothing left undone that could aid him in his sickness.

Died: on Mar 29, at his residence near Shepherdstown, Jefferson Co, Va, Mr Jas Marshall, aged 52 years. His sickness was short & severe.
+
Died: on Mar 29, at the same hour & place, Mrs Jane Turner. She was on a visit to aid in nursing her sister, Mrs Marshall. Her attack was sudden, violent, rapid in its progress, & soon terminated fatally.

TUE APR 13, 1847

Edgar Snowden, the esteemed Editor of the Alexandria Gaz, has been nominated by the Whigs of Alexandria, as a candidate to represent the counties of Fairfax & Alexandria in the Va House of Delegates.

The last number of the Georgia Journal announces the sale of the papers by its late proprietor, & it will be published in Macon in connexion with the Messenger, under the conduct of Messrs Chapman & Rose. -Southern Recorder

The late Mr Geo Holloway, of Abbeville, S C, has bequeathed to the Trustees of Cokesbury School, to become available upon the demise of his widow, an estate will will exceed in value $20,000. The object of this munificent donation is to educate & board at Cokesbury School the sons of dec'd traveling preachers of the Conference who are in necessitous circumstances. -Abbeville Banner

St Mary's School, Raleigh, N C: Rt Rev L S Ives, D D, Visiter. Rev Aldert Smedes, Rector. School will commence on Jun 3 till Nov 9; winter term will commence Nov 10 until Apr 15.

U S steamer **Mississippi**, off Sacrificios Island, Mar 23, 1847. Letter to the Hon John Y Mason, Sec of the Navy, Wash: from M C Perry, Commanding Home Squadron. I regret to announce the loss of the steamer **Hunter**, the particulars of the disaster are detailed in the report of Lt McLaughlin.

Died: on Apr 11, in Wash City, aged 35 years, Mrs Huldah Wilson, consort of Wm Wilson, of the First Ward. She died in the unshaken faith of salvation through the efficacy of the redemption wrought by the death of our blessed Saviour. Her funeral is this afternoon, at 3 o'clock, from her late residence on 20th st, between G & H sts.

Died: on Fri week, in Bladen Co, N C, Mrs McKay, consort of the Hon Jas J McKay, Rep in Congress from the State of N C.

The subscriber has for several years been engaged in school-keeping in Portsmouth, N H, & wishes to procure a situation in Va as a Teacher in a private family. For testimonials of character & ability, refer to Rev Chas Burroughs, D C, of Portsmouth, N H. Please address Mrs M A Richardson, Portsmouth, N H.

For sale or rent: cottage-built brick house & lot on the corner of 13th & M sts. Inquire on the premises. -F A Tschiffely

For sale: the lot of ground commonly known as the Brick Yard establishment of the late Thos Corcoran, with fixtures, machinery, & implements used in the manufacture of brick. Apply to the subscriber, residing in Gtwn. -H C Matthews, Trustee

Household & kitchen furniture at auction: Apr 19, at the residence of W Marshall, on 4½ st. -A Green, auct

WED APR 14, 1847

Richd Barry, well known in Wash City, drowned in the Potomac last Fri. He was in a skiff with Wesley Birch & 2 dogs when the skiff was upset. Birch swam to the bridge & saved himself. Barry was so impeded & weighed down with the dogs & a bag of fish, which was slung across his shoulders, as to sink in 30 feet depth of water. Barry & the dogs drowned.

The house of Mr J P Heiss, on F st, between 13th & 14th sts, was discovered on fire. The flames were subdued without any material injury to the bldg.

By order of the Orphans Court of Wash Co, D C: sale of unimproved real estate in Wash City, whereof Borden M Voorhees died seised: all of lot 30 in square 127, & part of lot 31 in said square: lots are on 17th st west, near the residence of Mrs Macomb. Sale on Apr 17. -Sarah Voorhees, Guardian -A Green, auct

Died: on Mar 18, at Tampico, Mexico, after a short illness, Andrew W Norris, eldest brother of John E Norris, of Wash City. The dec'd was a member of Capt Schaeffer's company, & was in the first day's operations at Monterey, & received a severe wound, from the effects of which he had not wholly recovered up to the time of his disease. Though much enfeebled, he faithfully & zealously performed his duties, till attacked by a violent bilious fever that soon terminated fatally.

Henry Leech, the well-known personifier of the monkey race, under the assumed name of Hervio Nano, died recently at Shoreditch, London. Leech was a native of N J.

Death of a Poetess. The Sandwich Observer chronicles the death of Miss Abigail C Bodfish, of West Barnstable, aged 37. She has long been bereft of reason, & at one time was maintained at the Worcester Asylum. For many preceding years she kept house as an invalid.

We record the death of Mr Elihu Chauncey, a gentleman of great worth & distinction: a native of Connecticut; came early to this city; was for several years was joint editor & proprietor of the U S Gaz; became more intimately connected with the active business of Phil; was brought up in the nurture of New England morals & habits, having enjoyed their benefits through a long life. -U S Gaz of Fri [No death date given.]

THU APR 15, 1847

John H Frick, the proprietor of the American Sentinel, [Phil] gave notice on Sat that his connexion with that paper would cease, he, for some time past, having that other important duties to perform, & that the Sentinel would pass into the hands of Alex'r Cummings, & be blended with & issued under the name of Cummings' Telegrahphic Evening Bulletin, which paper was also issued on Sat.

The stage coach from Columbus, Ohio, to Mount Vernon, on Thu night, was upset some 5 miles from the latter place, by which a Mrs Courtney, of Mass, was killed, & several passengers more or less hurt.

Mr Jos French, of Cabotville, age about 22 years, shot himself with a pistol in the side, on Wed of last week, inflicting a wound that caused his death in about 36 hours. The deed was committed in the presence of his wife & child. He had fallen victim to the insatiable love of strong drink. -Springfield Gaz

Mr Alex'r Rodgers, a daguerreotypist, fell dead in the streets of N Y on Mon. It is supposed his death was superinduced by inhalation from the mercury bath, which he is compelled to use in the practice of his art.

Died: in Wash City, at his brother's residence, on 14th st, Thos Birch, sen, of PG Co, Md, in his 57th year, after a short but painful illness of the quincy, leaving behind 10 children to mourn their untimely loss of an affectionate father. The funeral is this evening at 4 o'clock, at St Patrick's Church, on F st. [No date.]

Died: on Apr 6, in Phil, Mr Thos Nesbit, printer, in his 63rd year. The dec'd formerly resided in Wash City, & here, as elsewhere, was much respected.

Died: on Apr 7, at his residence in Anne Arundel Co, Md, Thos J Dorsett, aged 42 years, after a painful & lingering illness of pulmonary consumption, which he bore with the most exemplary patience.

Valuable lands for sale in Loudoun & Fairfax Counties: by a decree of the Circuit Superior Court of Law & Chancery for Fairfax Co, at its Nov term, 1846, in the suit of R H Cockerille et al against R H Cockerille's heirs et al: sale of 1,200 acres in said county, the residence of the late R H Cockerille, about 4 miles southwest from Dranesville. Also a tract in Loudoun Co containing about 300 acres, about 4 miles east of Gum Spring; a tract of about 320 acres, now in the occupancy of W W Presgraves; a tract of about 140 acres, now occupied by Mr Ellmore; a tract, adjoining the lands of John J Coleman & others, containing about 146 acres; & a tract of 60 acres, adjoining the lands of R M Newman. Apply at the Fairfax Court-house. -H W Thomas, R H Cockerille, Com'rs

During a severe storm on Mar 26 the public house in Southport known as the Farmer's Exchange was struck by lightning, & a young man, Bernard Vankleek, was instantly killed. -Buffalo Com Adv of Sat

For sale: farm in the District of Columbia, adjoining the city of Wash: contains between 40 & 50 acres; has a small dwlg-house. This is the property of a gentleman who has removed from the District. -A C Peachy, Atty at Law: ofc on 6th st, under Coleman's Hotel, 4th door from Pa ave.

FRI APR 16, 1847

Very superior household & kitchen furniture, china & glass ware, table linen, Horses & Phaeton, at auction, on Apr 29, at the residence of the Rt Hon Richd Pakenham, Minister from the Court of St James, on H st, between 16th & 17th sts, his very superior Furniture, all of which is of the best kind, & most of it made in England. -R W Dyer, auct

The Phil papers announce the death of Fred'k Graff, late Superintendent of the Fairmount Water Works, under whose inspection they were originally constructed, & managed ever since.

Appointments by the Pres: 1-Brig Gen Gideon J Pillow, to be Maj Gen in the U S Army, vice Thos H Benton, who declined to accept. 2-Brig Gen John A Quitman, to be Maj Gen in the U S Army, vice Wm Cumming, who declined to accept. 3-Col Caleb Cushing, to be Brig Gen in the U S Army, vice John A Quitman, promoted.

Army ofcrs who left the Narrows [N Y harbor] on the 13th, bound to Point Isabel. They sailed in the brig **Gen Lamar**, & were all of the 10th Regt of Infty.
Lt Col J J Fay, 10th Regt Infty
1st Lt Saml R Dummer, Adj
1st Lt Francis M Cummins, Acting Commissary
Ofcrs of Co C: Capt Jos A Yard, 1st Lt Geo W Taylor, 2nd Lts Isaac W Patton & Benj Yard.
Co A: Capt Alex'r Wilkin, 1st Lt Francis M Cummins, 2nd Lt Peter H Bruyere
Co H: Capt Joshua W Collett, 1st Lt Saml R Dummer
Also, 200 privates

Frederick the V, of Denmark, in his last moment, exclaimed, "It is a great consolation to me in my last hour that I never willfully offended any one, & that there is not a drop of blood on my hands." -P 341, Democratic Review, Apr, 1847.

Appropriations made during the 2nd Session of the 29th Congress:
1-Act for the relief of Joshua Shaw: full compensation for the past & future use of his invention of percussion caps & locks for small arms, & percussion locks & wafer primers, to be applied to the firing of cannon: $25,000.
2-Act for the relief of Ray Tompkins & others, the children & heirs at law of the late Danl D Tompkins, late Govn'r of the State of N Y: $49,785.02
3-Act for the relief of John Stockton, late a Lt in the U S Army: for the release of the judgment rendered in the Circuit Court of the U S in the district of Michigan, in the case of the U S of America vs John Stockton, against the said John Stockton: $707.55
4-Act for the relief of Harrison Whitson: in full satisfaction of his claim for services rendered & supplies furnished, while on the march to be mustered into the U S service, the company of Capt Cornelius Gilliam, of the Missouri volunteers, that served in Florida: $200.
5-Act for the relief of the administrators of Jos Edson, dec'd, late marshal of the district of Vermont: for the amount of fees due him on certain executions in favor of the U S, which were executed by him while marshal aforesaid; & which fees were charged by him in his account, & disallowed by the accounting ofcrs of the Treasury Dept: $424.91
6-Act for the relief of Bernard O'Neill: in full compensation for the use by the Gov't of his land since 1827, & for sand & for wood taken therefrom for the use of the U S; & in full for any other damages at any time heretofore done to said lands by agents of the U S: $2,000.
7-Act for the relief of the legal reps of John Lauson, dec'd: for services rendered as a private in the U S Army, from May 1, 1817, to Mar 13, 1818, the time of the death of the intestate: $55.

8-Act for the relief of Josiah Haskell: for his services on the Sandy Bay breakwater, within the Commonwealth of Mass: $645.30
9-Act for the relief of Henry La Reintree: for his services as an interpreter: $300.
10-Act for the relief of the legal reps of Jas H Clark: in full satisfaction for his claims against the Gov't to Apr, 1830, as exhibited in his statement thereof, as a purser in the navy: $3,060.94
11-Act for the relief of John Speakman: in full compensation for all losses he may have sustained by reason of any action of the Gov't affecting his contract to line gunpowder barrels with India rubber cloth, for the use of the U S: $741.60
12-Act for the relief of John C Stewart & others: for services while employed in the years 1838, 1838, & 1840, to watch the Treasury bldg, & to build & maintain fires in the rooms of the same: $575.
13-Act for the relief of Jas H Conley: in full payment for his services, as acting carpenter on board the U S steamship **Princeton**, from Sep 8, 1843, to Jan 7, 1846: $1,058.96
14-Act for the relief of the legal reps of Wm Bunce, dec'd: in full for the damage sustained by the dec'd, in the burning of his bldgs, on Palm Island, Florida, by the order of the Brig Gen Armistead, of the U S Army: $1,000
15-Act for the relief of the legal reps of the late Jos E Primeau & Thos J Chapman: for spoliations committed on said firm by the Yancton Indians of the Sioux tribe, in the latter part of 1835: $976.91
16-Act for the relief of Jacob L Vance: for a horse lost in 1813, while in the service of the U S: $50. For the use of his team of 4 horses & a wagon 18 days in the year 1813, which said team was employed in conveying flour to the U S Army: $54.
17-Act for the relief of Lewis C Sartori: for his services as professor of mathematics on board the U S frig **Constitution**, from Jul 10, 1839, to Apr 25, 1841: $1,011.87
18-Act of the relief of Jos Gideon: for his services as an acting purser on board the U S brig **Porpoise**, from Apr 27 to Nov 30, 1845: $597.26
19-Act for the relief of Jos Warren Newcomb: the balance due & unpaid, under resolutions of Congress of Jul 1, 1780: $8,321.48
20-Act for the relief of Jas S Conway: for the balance now owing by said Conway, in virtue of a judgment heretofore obtained against him in the district court of the U S for the district of Arkansas: indefinite.
21-Act for the relief of Julius Eldred, Elisha Eldred, & Francis E Eldred, for expenses & services in removing the copper rock from Lake Superior: for their time, services & expenses in purchasing & removing from the Ontonagon river of Lake Superior to Detroit the mass of native copper, commonly called the copper rock, taken from said Eldred & sons, in 1843, by order of the Sec of War, & removed to Wash City: indefinite.
22-Act for the relief of Hobson Johns: for tobacco furnished the navy under his contract with the Dept, in 1845: indefinite.
23-Act for the relief of Elijah White & others: for the value of property forcibly taken from them by the Pawnee Indians at or near the head of Grand Island, on the Platte or Nebraska river: $1,081.
24-Act for the relief of the Bank of Metropolis: for the sum & interest, in an action commenced by the U S, at the instance of the Post Ofc Dept, in the Circuit Court of Wash Co, D C, against the said bank, to recover the money on deposite at the credit of the

Treasurer of the U S, for the service of said Dept, & in which action the said bank filed, by way of set-off, certain demands arising from acceptances of said Dept in favor of certain contractors,discounted & held by the bank, & protested for non-payment; & also a certain demand arising from an overdraft made on said bank by the agent for disbursing the fund appropriated for the contingent expenses of said Post Ofc Dept, which was found by the jury, under instructions from the Court, to be due from the U S to said bank: $5,192.73
For one acceptance in favor of Jas Reeside, contractor, dated Oct 17, 1835, at 90 days, for $4,500, with interest to Oct 10, 1837, & cost of protest: $4,966.75
For one acceptance in favor of Jas Reeside, contractor, dated Oct 20, 1835, at 90 days, for $1,000, with interest to Oct 10, 1837, & cost of protest: $1,105.25
For one acceptance in favor of Jas Reeside, contractor, dated Oct 23, 1835, at 90 days, for $4,500, with interest to Oct 10, 1837, & cost of protest: $4,969.75
For one acceptance in favor of Jas Reeside, contractor, dated Oct 28, 1835, at 90 days, for $3,000, with interest to Oct 10, 1837, & cost of protest: $3,321.25
For one acceptance in favor of Edwin Porter, dated Apr 24, 1835, at 90 days, for $10,000, with interest to Oct 10, 1837, & cost of protest: $11,350.08
For overdraft of Edmund F Brown, agent for disbursing the contingent fund of the Post Ofc Dept: $611.52
25-Act for the relief of the legal reps of Simon Spaulding, dec'd: the the amount of final settlement certificate #167, dated Jul 28, 1783, issued to said Simon Spaulding, for $760, together with interest thereon from Mar 22, 1783: indefinite.
26-Act for the relief of the legal reps of Thos Shields, dec'd: for a pension up to Aug 23, 1842, in conformity with the provisions of the act of Congress approved Mar 3, 1837, entitled "An act for the more equitable administration of the navy pension fund."-indefinite.
27-Act to provide for the final settlement of the accounts of John Spencer, late receiver of public moneys at ***Fort Wayne***, Indiana: to audit & settle his accounts, upon principles of equity & justice: indefinite.
28-Act for the relief of the heirs of Sgt Maj John Champe: the full amount of 5 years' commutation pay of an ensign of infty in the army of the Revolution to the children of Sgt Maj Champe, late of the army of the Revolution, [Lee's Legion.]-indefinite.
29-Act for the relief of Dr Clark Lillybridge: for services performed as physician in the Cherokee emigration: indefinite.
30-Act for the relief of Thos N Newell: the extra expenses incurred by him for board & attendance, incurred between Feb 2 & Apr 6, 1829, in consequence of a wound received on board the frig **Java**, in the discharge of his duty, while at Port Mahon: indefinite.
31-Act for the benefit of Jas Williams: for services rendered & money advanced & paid by Williams while acting as jailor under Henry Ashton, & which had not been paid or credited to the said Ashton: indefinite.
32-Act for the relief of Wm T Walthall: for his services as acting professor of mathematics from May 24, 1843, to Feb 25, 1845, inclusive; & the amounts allowed & paid by the purser of the frig **Brandywine**, on account of his board & medicine & medical attention at Hong Kong, China: indefinite.

33-Act for the relief of Geo B Russell & others: for bread, meat, & clothing furnished the Cherokee Indians, to induce them to accept Ridge's treaty, & under the appointment & authority of Benj F Curry, superintendent of Cherokee removals: indefinite.
34-Act for the relief of Mary Segar, & for the relief of Elisha Denison, administrator of Phenix Carpenter Ellis: to pay Elisha Denison, of N Y, adm of Phenix Carpenter Ellis, dec'd, the amount of pension payable to said Ellis, from Mar 4, 1838, to Dec 7, 1838: indefinite.
35-Act for the relief of W P S Sanger & Geo F de la Roche: for expenses incurred, in obedience to an order from the Navy Dept, dated Oct 30, 1843, directing them to make the surveys & examinations required by the act of Mar 3, 1843, in reference to the construction of a dry-dock at N Y: indefinite.
36-Act for the relif of Capt Jas Pennoyer: as a full & complete compensation for his services in saving the brig **Porpoise**, her ofcrs & crew: indefinite.
37-Act for the relief of the estate of Benj Metoyer & Francois Gaiennie, dec'd: to adjust & settle the claim upon the said estates aforesaid, in behalf of the U S, & to discharge such claims upon such terms as he shall think most for the interest of the U S: indefinite.
38-Joint resolution authorizing & directing the examination & settlement of the claims of Alex'r M Cumming, of N Y, late mail contractor on routes 951 & 952, between Phil & N Y C, between 1835 & 1839: indefinite.
39-Joint resolution for the settlement of the accounts of Purser G R Barry, of the U S ship **Boston**, Capt Pendergrast, & to pass to the credit of the Purser, G R Barry, the items charged to him in the reconciling statement of his accounts: indefinite.
40-Joint resolution for the relief of Wm B Stokes, surviving partner of John N C Stockton & Co: for carrying the mail in 1836, on the lower or Florida route, in consequence of the interruption of the mail by the Creek hostilities on the upper route, such compensation as shall be established to be an adequate remuneration for the same, taking into consideration the value of the services performed, & the loss to the said contractors by the exclusion of passengers, as directed by the then Postmaster General: indefinite.

The piano forte manufactory of D B Grove, of Phil, was destroyed by fire on Tue: 15 pianos were consumed: loss is heavy; insurance, $4,500.

Lot on Pa ave for sale: the east half of lot 3 in square 221, lying between the Banking-house of Messrs Corcoran & Riggs, & the residence of Dr J S Gunnell. Inquire of Dr O G Mix, at Dr J S Gunnell's, near the Pres' house.

By virtue of an order of distrain for house rent due to W Walker by Henry Broadback, I will expose at public sale, on Apr 20, in front of the Centre Market-house, in Wash City, to wit: 1 bureau, 1 glass, 4 pictures in frames, a lot of carpeting, 1 stove, 4 chairs, 1 pair of andirons, 3 flatirons, 1 table, a lot of crockery ware, 4 pieces of iron ware, 2 buckets & a lot of tin ware. -H R Maryman, Bailiff

Suitable reward for return of a white Buffalo Cow that strayed, on Mon last.
-Wm Emmert, Gtwn, D C

Died: Apr 6, in New Orleans, Randolph Gurley, son of Jos & Rachel Etter, in his 5th year.

SAT APR 17, 1847

Boston Journal: Dr Alfred Hitchcock, of Ashby, brother of the late Dr Henry D Hitchcock, of Middleboro, who was killed on Feb 23 last by a collision of cars on the Fall River Railroad, has made an adjustment of the claims of the widow & heirs against said company. The company, through their treasurer, David Anthony, of Fall River, have paid to the legal claimants the sum of $4,500, & have received a discharge from any further liability.

Navy News: Valparaiso, Dec 20, 1846. On Dec 3 the U S ship **Columbus**, Cmdor Biddle, ship **Independence**, Cmdor Shubrick, & ship **Levant**, Cmder Page, were lying in the harbor of Valparaiso. The **Columbus** from Oahu, Sandwich Islands, the Independence from Rio de Janeirio, in 33 days, & the **Levant** from Calif. Lt Stephen Johnson transferred sick to the **Levant** from the **Columbus**, & Lt J B Randolph transferred to fill his place from the **Independence**. Several midshipmen also transferred to the **Levant** for passage home. The **Independence** sailed on Dec 13 for Monterey; & on Dec 20 the **Columbus** sailed for Callao & Calif. The **Levant** is to sail for Norfolk on or about Dec 25. Ofcrs on board the **Columbus**: Cmdor Biddle
T W Wyman, capt
T O Selfridge, commandant
P Drayton, H French, J H Strong, J B Randolph, lts
Madison Rush, acting lt
J M Wainwright, acting master
E T Dunn, purser
B Ticknor, fleet surgeon
T F B Gillon, passed assist surgeon
Danl L Bryan, assist surgeon
J W Newton, chaplain
M Yarnall, prof of mathematics
H B Tyler, capt marines
N S Waldron & J C Cash, lts marines
D McN Fairfax & A J Drake, passed midshipman
Edw Clarke, cmdor's sec
Harrison, Stevenson, Selden, Stewart, Graham, Van Zandt, Young, Luce, & Graham, midshipmen
V R Hall, boatswain
Thos Robinson, gunner
Jonas Dibble, carpenter
R C Rodman, sailmaker
The **Columbus** is short of lts, having lost one by the death of Todd, & several sent home on account of sickness.

Trustee's sale of a stock of boots & shoes at auction: by deed of trust from Jas Jack to J M Carlisle: sale on Apr 23, at the store lately occupied by said Jack, opposite Brown's Hotel. -J M Carlisle, Trustee -C W Boteler, jr, auctioneer

Dry goods at auction: on Mon next: at the store lately occupied by Mr Jas B Clarke, on Pa ave, near Brown's Hotel. -R W Dyer, auct

For rent: 3 story brick house, containing 10 rooms, pantries, closets, & clothes-presses, a good dry cellar, & a pump in the yard: house nearly new. Property near the State Dept, in full view of the Pres' house, on G st, near 15th. -D A Gardiner

Orphans Court of Wash Co, D C. Letters of administration on the personal estate of Jas M Selden, late of said county, dec'd. -Jas Selden, adm

Wash Corp: 1-Communication was received from the Mayor, enclosing a letter from the widow of the late John McLeod, proposing to dispose of the property of the Columbian Academy: which was referred to the Cmte on Public Schools. 2-Ptn of N P Causin & others: asking the opening of the alley in square 319: referred to the Cmte on Improvements. 3-Nomination of Theodore Wheeler as a Com'r of the Asylum, & John Magar as Police & Com'r of the Fish Wharf at 6th st: considered & confirmed. 4-Ptn from John Fletcher, in reference to payment for an improvement on the south side of Mass ave, between, 7th & 8th sts: referred to the Cmte on Improvements. 5-Ptn of S Cunningham, asking the remission of a fine: referred to the Cmte of Claims. 6-Cmte of Claims: bill for the relief of Rudolph Eickhorn: passed. 7-Cmte of Claims: Act for the relief of Eve Rupert: passed. 8-Cmte of Claims: Bill for the relief of John P Stallings: passed.

Father Rey, one of the Catholic Chaplains in the U S Army, left Monterey for Matamoros on Jan 16, & has not been heard from since. He was one of the ablest members of the Society of Jesus in this country, & as the members of that order have been for many years excluded from Mexico, there is too much cause to fear that evil has befallen him.
-N Y Sun

Arrivals from Vera Cruz: Gen Jesup arrived at New Orleans on the 8th instant from Vera Cruz, in the steamer **Alabama**. The following other ofcrs also came by the **Alabama**:

U S Army:

Maj Allen	Lt Van Vliet	Lt Petigru
Maj Sanders	Lt Whittal	Dr Witherspoon
Capt Swartwout	Lt Dobbins	Capt Bowie
Lt Meade	Lt Hawkins	

U S Navy:

Lt McLaughlin	Lt Hooe	Lt Drayton

Mrd: on Apr 7, at the residence of her father, by Rev Mr Lee, Hon S A Douglass, U S Senator, Illinois, to Miss Martha D, only daughter of Col Robt Martin, of Rockingham Co, N C.

The following named persons have taken out licenses under the laws of the Wash Corp during Mar last.

Dog license:

Anderson, Garret
Barrett, Thos J-2
Butler, John
Bayly, Jas
Brown, J H
Barnhill, J L
Brady, Jas
Boarman, S B
Brereton, John
Bowen, F
Butler, Jos
Barnhill, J L
Corcoran, W W
Cook, John F
Coumbe, J T
Carr, Overton
Dixon, W L
Dorly, Michl
Fleming, John
Ferguson, W P
Feslin, M W
Grimes, M H
Green, Solomon
Gaddis, Adam
Grinnell, C
Keef, J P
Little, Peter
Lee, John
Lisles, Thos
Mentzer, Henry
Martin, Annet
McDermott, M
Mustin, Thos
Marshall, Robt
Murphy, John
Maury, J W
Maury, J & C
Maury, C B
Owens, John
Palmer, Henry
Parris, A K
Plumsell, Thos
Pumphrey, J
Reddy, Wm
Radcliff, Jos-2
Ross, Danl
Spicer, John
Stillings, John
Stewart, Jas W-transfer
Spencer, C
Stevens, Ann M
Talburt, Clinton
Tucker, John
Thompson, G W
Wells, Thos C
Ward, Ulysses
West, John-2
Wilcox, A F
White, A S H
Wirt, J L

Hack license: Clarke, Thos;

Huckster license: Henck, Eliz; Moses, John-transfer; Springman & Blunder-transfer

Slave license:

Cooper, Sarah
Chew, M J
Duvall, Mrs
Dorsey, Mrs
Donovan, John
Lee, Alex
Stevens, N C
Smith, Walter
Weems, Mrs

Concert license: David, J S

Retail license:

Adams, Wm
Cheshire, Eph
Hepburn, G S
McGawley, Pat-transfer
Schwartz, Jos-transfer
Young, Wilford

Dry Goods license:

Bragden, J B
King, Thos
Owens, Evans & Co
Schuster, Wm M

Theatrical license: Kilmiste, M-5

Confectioner License: Barber,Eliz

Shop license: Benter, Wm

Slut license: Clarke, M St C; De Selding, Chas; Tyler, Wm; Williams, Zadock

The following persons have been fined, during March, for failing to procure their licenses, as per returns of the 2nd, 3rd, & 5th ward magistrates-the 1st, 4th, 6th, & 7th wards not returned. Slut license: Barker, W N

Retail license: Collings, Thos; Jackson, Eliza; Moore, G F; Smitson, E

Dog license:

Birell, Jos	Barker, W N	Morsell, Robt
Bush, Wm	Gray, H	Wood, H S
Bartlett, Isaac	Harrington, A M	

-C H Wiltberger, Register

Valuable property for sale or lease in Wash City, D C: Carusi's Saloon: situated on 11th st, within half a square of Pa ave, & has been used for the last 20 years for the Assemblies, Balls, Concerts, & Exhibitions which have been given during nearly the whole of the time. The bldg fronts 103 feet on 11th st, & 53 feet on C st. It is located directly opposite the site of the Smithsonian Institution. Title is indisputable. -Lewis Carusi, Wash, D C

Household & kitchen furniture at auction: on Apr 23, at the residence of the late Brooke M Berry, on Capitol Hill, on 1st st east, near the n e corner of Capitol Square: excellent lot of furniture. -A Green, auct

MON APR 19, 1847

Mr Pageot returns his thanks to the Fire Companies of Wash & Gtwn for their very prompt efforts in saving his house yesterday from destruction by fire.

At Louisville, Ky, on Apr 10, Mr Baptiste Irwin was so much injured by the premature explosion of a cannon that he died on the following day.

A letter from Col McClung, who was shockingly wounded at the capture of Monterey, writes from that city under date of Mar 1, stating that when news arrived of the advance of Santa Anna towards Saltillo, with an overwhelming force, Capt Willis, of Ky, was at Monterey, slowing recovering from a violent attack of pneumonia, in which his life was almost despaired of. He set off at once, reached Gen Taylor's camp before the battle came on, & perished in the thickest of the fight. Col McClung says of himself: I am slowly recovering though still unable to sit up.

The Capital of Michigan. The Legislature of Michigan, at its recent session, passed an act removing the seat of Govn't from Detroit to Lansing. We have some knowledge of the State, but we had none of the location of the new capital. [N Y Evangelist: Lansing is located in the n w corner of Ingham Co, & consists of one log-house & one saw-mill. It is far back in the woods, a perfect terra incognita to most of the sovereign people of this fair peninsula. I never heard of the place until I heard it proposed as our capital.]

Mrd: on Apr 18, in Wash City, by Rev Mr Finkel, Mr Wm Rupp, formerly of Balt, to Miss Eliz Kuhl, of Wash City.

W P Ridgeley & D Davis, tried at Lancaster, Pa, for passing counterfeit money, have been convicted, the former plead guilty. Davis was sentenced to 4 years' confinement, at labor in the penitentiary. The sentence of Ridgeley, who is not yet 21 years of age, was suspended at the prequest of the prosecuting atty.

Dissolution of copartnership existing between Perry & Ashby, by mutual consent. -Augustus E Perry, Saml T Ashby. The undersigned have this day associated themselves together, under the style of Perry & Brother. -Augustus E Perry, Thos J S Perry. Domestic Dry Goods, #7, opposite the Centre Market.

Frame shop, cabinetmaker's tools, furniture, lumber, & hearse, at auction: on Fri, at the shop lately occupied by Mr Peter Callan, on 8th st, between G & H sts, the Frame Shop. -R W Dyer, auct

Died: on Apr 15, in Wash City, from the rupture of a blood vessel, Simon Frazer, in his 54th year. A native of Ross Shire, Scotland, but for many years a resident of Wash City, leaving a disconsolate widow & 4 children to lament their loss.

Died: on Apr 1, at her residence in Knoxville, Tenn, Mrs Ann Eliza White, relict of the late Hon Hugh L White, for many years a distinguished member of the U S Senate from that State.

Died: on Apr 16, after a short illness, Chas Edmund, son of Edmund & Eugenia Brooke, of Wash Co, D C, aged 11 months.

TUE APR 20, 1847

Affairs in New Mexico: Correspondence of the Missouri Republican. Santa Fe, Feb 13, 1847. On the 20th information was brought to Col Price by an Indian living 6 miles from town that Gov Bent & several other Americans had been murdered at Taos-that an insurrection was in progress. Jan 24th: As Capt St Vrain approached the creek, he discovered a number of the enemy; he charged upon them & killed 2. The Col ordered Lt Dyer to move his battery within 190 yards of the house & adobe wall, behind which the enemy were posted, & to drive them from their position. This was done. Another house was charged by Capt Angney, of Infty volunteers; & had one man mortally wounded from the hill; but no one was in the house. Lt Irwin, of the infty volunteers, was severely wounded through the leg, & one private killed, & 2 of the enemy were bayoneted on the hill. Among the slain was their Gen Typhoya. Col Price was stuck by a ball in the early part of the action; but his sword-belt probably saved his life, & his wound was only a severe contusion. Jan 28th: Heard of the battle of Moro town, in which Capt Henley, of the volunteers, was killed; & the previous murder of Prewit, Waldo, Culver, & several other Americans at that place. Feb 4th: Col ordered a charge from each side. This charge was made promptly, but unfortunately Capt Burgwin's company of dragoons, with Capt McMillen's company of mounted volunteers, reached the church door before the other party came up; the intended diversion was not effected, & Capt Burgwin's command received the full shock of the enemy's fire for a time. Capt Burgwin had 5 dragoons killed, & 19 severely wounded, several of whom soon died, among them Capt Burgwin. Capt McMillen has 6 severely wounded. Feb 5th: the women came in crowds to the Col, on their knees, with white flags, & crosses, begging for mercy, & very soon the men followed. The Col granted them peace on conditions that they would bring him Tomas, one of the leaders that had fled. This was done. Feb 6th: Montoya, the ringleader, has been delivered to Col Price, by some friendly Mexicans. He was tried by court-martial today & condemned to be hung. Feb 7th: Montoya was executed at 1 p m. He acknowledged his crimes, & asked pardon of the Mexicans, the Americans, & God. Feb 9th: Commenced our homeward march, & arrived in Santa Fe on the 11th.

I will sell at private sale the Farm upon which I now reside, in the Forest of PG Co, Md, adjoining the estates of Gov Saml Sprigg, Dr Benj Lee, Mr Chas Hill, Mr Thos E Berry, & Mr Marsham Waring, containing about 390 acres of land; a comfortable dwlg house, & every other necessary outbldg. -Wm J Belt

Rose Hill for sale: containing 768 acres, the residence of the late Mr Hay Taliaferro, lying on the Rapidan river, in Orange Co, about 34 miles above the town of Fredericksburg; improvements are a commodious dwlg-house, & all necessary outbldgs. Persons wishing to purchase are referred, in my absence, to Lewis B Williams, at Orange Court-house, Va. -D McF Thornton

Boarding for Boys: only $100 per annum: the York Institute, located in the beautiful & healthy borough of York,Pa. Address the Principal, Dr R T Haughey, York, Pa.

St Anne's Female School, Annapolis, Md: trustees:
Rev E M Van Deusen, Rector of St Anne's Parish
Vestrymen of St Anne's Parish:

Hon Chancellor Johnson	Mr Geo G Brewer
A Randall	Mr Jas Sands
R W Gill	Capt P F Voorhees, U S N
Mr Geo E Franklin	D Claude, M D

Ofcrs:
Rev Edwin M Van Deusen, Rector & Visiter
Miss M Miller, Principal
Miss E Converse, Head of the Family
Miss A Strobel, Teacher of French & Music
Miss C L Haven, English Teacher
Rev H Humphreys, D D, Pres of St John's College
St Anne's is a boarding & day school for young ladies, designed for thorough intellectual & religious training. For girls over 12 years of age $200 per scholastic year of 10 months; for girls under 12 years of age $170. A reduction of $25 for each will be made from the above charges when two or more sisters are placed at the school. Entrance fee $25, or bed, bedding, towels, & table napkins may be furnished by the pupil. Vacations August & Sept.

Circuit Court of Wash Co, D C-in Chancery. Ephraim Wheeler et al, vs Stanislaus Murray, exc, & Cornelius Murphy, heir at law of Martin Murphy, dec'd. The creditors of Martin Murphy, dec'd, are to exhibit their claims, properly vouched, to the subscriber, at his ofc, on or before the first Mon of May next. -Clement Cox, Auditor, Gtwn

Circuit Court of Wash Co, D C-in Chancery. Jos L Scholfield & Mary his wife, Jos Scholfield, Sarah Scholfield, Henry Janney & Hannah his wife, cmplnts, against Thos Levering & Rachel Ann his wife, daughter of Jos L Scholfield, Eliz Hopkins, Ann Scholfield, Wm J Scholfield, Lewis Scholfield, children of Mahlon Scholfield, Isaac Hoge & Rachel his wife, daughter of Mahlon Scholfield, Jas Stanton, son-in-law of Issachar Scholfield, Thos M Scholfield, Jonathan T Scholfield, Andrew Scholfield, Wm G Scholfield, children of Issachar Scholfield, Danl Williams & Martha his wife, a child of Issachar, Jos W Beck, exc of Wm A Scott, Mahlon Scholfield & Ann his wife, Edith Scholfield, widow of Issachar, & Benj Waters, adm de bonis non of Andrew Scholfield, dfndnt. The object of this bill is to procure a decree for a trustee & sale of certain lots of ground in Wash City, D C, which, with other property by the last will & testament of Andrew Scholfield, late of Alexandria, D C, were devised to be sold by his excs, Jonthan Scholfield, one of the excs, having renounced his appointment in writing, & Geo Scott, the other, having died before a sale of said lots. The bill in this cause states that Andrew Scholfield, late of Alexandria, D C, died in Oct, 1839, having first duly made his last will & testament, recorded in the Orphans' Court of Alexandria Co, in which he directs that all his estate, except certain specific legacies, should be sold by his excs in such manner as his brother Mahlon Scholfield & his particular friend Benj Waters, or either of them, shall deem most advisable, & out of the proceeds of sale first to pay his debts, then the money legacies, & the rest & residue to be put out on interest well secured; he further directs, after payment of said debts, money legacies, & their delivery to the different legatees, as well as payment of all costs & charges attending the execution of his last will & testament, that the rest & residue of his estate of every description be sold as stated, & the nett proceeds thereof be divided into 15 equal parts, & distributed in the manner & to certain residuary legatees mentioned in said will, as by reference to the bill & exhibit A, will more fully appear. That the said residuary Legatees, or his excs for them, shall pay the interest of their respective portions to their respective parents for & during their natural lives, & after the death of such parents the payment of interest to cease as to such parents, & not before. The bill states that letters testamentary on the estate of the said Andrew Scholfield were granted to Geo Scott, one of the excs named in the will, the other exc, Jonathan Scholfield, having first renounced his appointment in writing, & that the lots of ground which are described in the bill are a part of the real estate to which the Andrew Scholfield died entitled, & that Geo Scott, his exec died on [blank], without having sold the said lots of ground as directed by the will; that the said debts have been paid, & that the cmplnts are entitled to a sale of said lots, & as parents, to the interest of the portions of their respective children; that since the death of Geo Scott there is no one authorized to dispose of the real estate of the said Andrew Scholfield in accordance with the terms of the will, & cannot be until a trustee be appointed for the purpose by the Court, which cmplnts pray may be granted; that all the said dfndnts, except Jos W Beck, reside & are out of D C. Dfndnts to appear in this Court on the 1st Mon of Sep next to answer said bill.
-W Brent, clk

Mrd: on Apr 18, in Wash City, by Rev Mr Van Horseigh, Jas T Finley, of Balt, to Miss Mary E Quigley, of the former place.

Entire fixtures of the late firm of J Robinson & Co, now dissolved, will be sold in front of the Centre Market, on Apr 20: 2 auction bells, 2 show cases, 1 counter, 1 pair steelyards, 1 writing desk, 2 flags & staves, 1 transparent, & all the shelving in the store, 1 coal stove, & 1 glue kettle. -John McDevitt, auct

The death of the late Capt Vinton, gallant ofcr at Vera Cruz. He had serious thought of following the example of his 2 distinguished brothers, Alex'r & Francis, & taking orders in the Episcopal Church. But he was called to take a part in the Florida campaign. My children will reap some of the fruits of my self denial, by the means I shall leave them of living independently & securing a good education.

Obit-died: on Feb 7,1847, at Taos, New Mexico, Capt J H K Burgwin, 1st U S Dragoons. The deceased was shot in the breast with a rifle-ball on Feb 5, in an action with the Pueblo Indians, in their town near Taos, after having gallantly charged & driven them to their houses. He had acted a conspicuous part in the previous engagement, & by his coolness & intrepidity had inspired courage in his men, who were ready to follow him in the thickest of the fight. As an ofcr, Capt Burgwin was a disciplinarian, was punctual, prompt, & every ready for duty, secured the confidence of his men, the love of his brother ofcrs, & the respect of his superiors.

Mrd: on Apr 13, at the Catholic Church, N Y, by the Rt Rev Bishop McClosky, G R Barry, U S Navy, to Agnes, daughter of Thos Glover, of N Y.

From Vera Cruz: some men belonging to the N Y & 1st Pa regts, & 4 sailors from the frig **Potomac**, left the camp at Vera Cruz the 28th ult, & went into the country about 7 miles. Some returned that evening & reported they had been attacked by rancheros, & most of their number killed. Killed: Rev W H T Barnes, of Wilmington, Delaware; Robt Jeff, of Southwark, Pa; Geo W Miller, of Providence, R I, belonging to the Phil Rangers; Benj Fane, of Providence, R I; Hardin, of the Potomac; & 3 belonging to the N Y regt, whose names are not known. A stringent order was issued by Gen Scott on Apr 1, denouncing certain outrages which had been committed by a few worthless soldiers in the army. Soldiers are not allowed to stray from camp without written permission. F M Dimond is appointed collector & Felix Peters inspector of revenue. J P Levy is appointed harbor master. The former alcalde, R P Vela, having declined to continue in ofc, Lt Holzinger is appointed in his place. -Picayune

WED APR 21, 1847

The following military companies reached New Orleans, from Pittsburg, on Apr 12, en route for the seat of war: from Balt: Capt Merrick's company, 82 Dragoons. Capt J E Howard's company, 93 voltigeurs. From Phil: Capt J C Biddle's company, 92 voltigeurs. Capt Bernard's company, 97 voltigeurs. 2 companies of infty, 215 men, under Capt Irwin & Moore,

Situation wanted: a German Gardener, who is well acquainted with all the branches of his profession, & who has been employed for several years in this country, wishes a situation. Please call on W Creutzfeldt, Pa ave, between 17th & 18th sts.

Mrd: Apr 20th, by Rev Jas B Donelan, L C Browne to Clara Virginia, daughter of Geo Mattingly, all of Wash City.

Died: on Sunday, in Phil, suddenly, Thos Sully, jr, painter, in his 36th year.

Wash Corp: 1-Ptn of G W Venable, praying to be refunded for the unexpired term of a license: referred to the Cmte of Claims. 2-Ptn of Wm Lord & others, for a flag footway across 5th st west: passed.

Died: on Apr 19, after a short but painful illness, [inflammation of the lungs,] aged 50 years, Mariana Von Schmidt, consort of Peter Von Schmidt, natives of Russia. Relations & friends are hereby invited to attend the deceased to her last resting place, today, at 4 o'clock, from her residence on F st, between 11th & 12th sts.

Battle of Buena Vista: Gen Taylor's detailed report. Headquarters Army of Occupation. Aqua Nueva, Mar 6, 1847. Capt O'Brien, Lts Brent, Whiting & Couch, 4th Artl, & Bryan, topographical engineers, [slightly wounded,] were attached to Capt Washington's battery. Lts Thomas, Reynolds, & French, 3rd Artl, [severely wounded,] were attached to that of Capt Sherman; & Capt Shover & Lt Kilburn, 3rd Artl, to that of Capt Bragg. Capt Shover, in conjunction with Lt Donaldson, 1st Artl, rendered gallant & important service in repulsing the cavalry of Gen Minon. The regular cavalry, under Lt Col May, with which was associated Capt Pike's squadron of Arkansas horse, rendered useful service in holding the enemy in check. Capt Steen, 1st Dragoons, was severely wounded early in the day while endeavoring, with my authority, to rally the troops which were falling to the rear. The Mississippi riflemen, under Col Davis, were hightly conspicuous for their gallantry & steadiness, & sustained throughout the engagement the reputation of veteran troops. Col Davis, thought severely wounded, remained in the saddle until the close of the action. The 3rd Indiana Regt, under Col Lane, & a fragment of the 2nd, under Col Bowles, were associated with the Mississippi Regt during the greater portion of the day, & acquitted themselves creditably in repulsing the attempts of the enemy. The Ky cavalry, under Col Marshall, rendered good service dismounted, acting as light troops on our left, & afterwards with a portion of the Arkansas Regt, in meeting & dispersing the column of cavalry at Buena Vista. The 1st & 2nd Illinois & the 2nd Ky Regts served immediately under my eye, & I bear a willing testimony to their excellent conduct throughout the day. Capt Conner's company of Texas volunteers, attached to the 2nd Illinois Regt, fought bravely, its capt being wounded & 2 subalterns killed. Col Bissell, the only surviving colonel of these regts, merits notice for his coolness & bravery. After the fall of the field ofcrs of the 1st Illinois & 2nd Ky Regts, the command of the former devolved upon Lt Col Weatherford; that of the latter upon Maj Fry. Regimental commanders & others who have rendered reports, speak in general terms of the good conduct of their ofcrs & men, & have specified many names, but the limits of this report forbid a recapitulation of them here. I may, however, mention Lts Rucker & Campbell, of the dragoons, & Capt Pike, Arkansas cavalry, commanding squadrons; Lt Col Field, Ky cavalry; Lt Col Roane, Arkansas cavalry, upon whom the command devolved after the fall of Capt Yell; Maj Bradford, Capt Sharpe, [severely wounded,] & Adj Griffith, Mississippi Regt; Lt Col Hadden, 2nd Indiana Regt, & Lt Robinson, A D C to Gen Lane; Lt Col Weatherford, 1st Illinois Regt; Lt Col Morrison, Maj Trail, & Adj Whiteside, [severely wounded,] 2nd Illinois Regt; & Maj Fry, 2nd Ky Regt, as being favorably noticed for gallanty & good conduct. Maj McCulloch, quartermaster in the volunteer service, rendered important services before the engagement, in the command of a spy company, & during the affair was associated with the regular cavalry. To Maj Warren, 1st Illinois volunteers, I feel much indebted for his firm & judicious course, while exercising command in the city of Saltillo. The medical staff, under the able direction of Assist Surgeon Hitchcock, were assiduous in attention to the wounded upon the field, & in their careful removal to the rear. Brig Gen Wool speaks in high terms of the ofcrs of his staff: Lt & A D C McDowell, Col Churchill, inspector genr'l, Capt Chapman, assist quartermaster, Lt Sitgreaves, topographical engineers, & Capts Howard & Davis, volunteer service, are conspicuously noticed by the general for their gallanty & good conduct. Messrs March, Addicks, Potts, Harrison, Burgess, & Dusenbery, attached in various capacities to Gen Wool's headquarters, are likewise mentioned for their conveying orders in all parts of the field. Of my own staff, I feel greatly indebted. Maj Bliss, assist adj-gen, Capt J H Eaton, & Lt R S Garnett, aids-de-camp, served near my person, & were prompt & zealous in the discharge of every duty. Maj Munroe, besides rendering valuable service as chief of artl, was instrumental, & were also Cols Churchill & Belknap, inspectors genr'l, in rallying troops & disposing them for the defence of the train & baggage. Col Whiting, quartermaster gen, & Capt Eaton, Chief of subsistence dept, served in my immediate staff on the field. Capt Sibley, Assist quartermaster, was necessarily left with the headquarter camp near town, where his services were highly useful. Mr Mansfield & Lt Beham, engineers, & Capt Linnard & Lts Pope & Franklin, topographical engineers, were employed before & during the engagement in making reconnoissances, & on the field were very active in bringing information & in conveying my orders to distant points. Lt Kingsbury, in addition to his proper duties as ordinance ofcr, Capt Chilton, assist quartermaster, & Majors Dix & Coffee, served also as extra aids-de-camp. Mr Thos L Crittenden, of Ky, though not in my service, volunteered as my aid-de-camp on this occasion & served with credit. Maj Craig, chief of ordnance, & Surgeon Craig, medical director, had been detached on duty from headquarters, & did not reach the ground until the morning of the 24th-too late to participate in the action, but in time to render useful services in their respective depts of the staff. Your obedient servant, Z Taylor, Maj Gen U S Army, commanding. Note: The above are extractions from the three columns of information of reported in this newspaper.

Died: on Apr 19, Jos Hamilton Harbaugh, 3rd child of Valentine & Ellen Harbaugh, in his 6th year. His funeral will take place from the dwlg of his parents, G & 7th sts, today at 4 o'clock.

Died: on Mar 31, at Gelena, Ill, in her 54th year, after a most distressing illness, Mrs Christina J French, consort of D'Arcy A French, formerly of Wash City, & daughter of the late Basil Spalding, of Chas Co, Md.

Died: at the residence of W Hollyday, in the city of Balt, Col Frisby Tilghman, formerly of Wash Co, Md, in his 74th year. [No death date given.]

Fires. The bagging & rope manufactory of Mr Jas Cooney, of Lexington, Ky, was partially destroyed by fire on Apr 11. The stock in the shipyard of Jos R Anderson, near Richmond, was consumed by fire on Sat, together with 7 bldgs. One of the bldgs destroyed was a large warehouse owned by Mr Lewis Webb. The large steam cotton factory of Messrs Allison, Morgan, & Co, near Lebanon, Tenn, was destroyed by fire on Apr 9. Loss is from $40,000 to $60,000.

THU APR 22, 1847

Headquarters Army in New Mexico. Santa Fe, Feb 15, 1847. On Dec 15th I received information of an attempt to excite the people of this territory against the American Gov't. This rebellion was headed by Thos Ortis & Diego Archuleta. On Jan 14 Govn'r Bent left this city for Taos. On Jan 19 this valuable ofcr, with 5 others persons, were seized at Don Fernando de Taos by the Pueblos & Mexicans, & murdered in the most inhuman manner the savages could devise. On the same day 7 Americans were murdered at the Arroya Honda, & 2 others on the Rio Colorado. The persons brutally butchered were: At Don Fernando de Taos: Chas Bent, govn'r; Stephen Lee, sheriff; Jas W Leal, circuit atty; Cornelio Vigil, [a Mexican,] prefect; Narcisus Beaubien, [son of the circuit judge;] Parbleau Harvimeah, [a Mexican.] At the Arroya Hondo: Simeon Turley, Albert Trubush, Wm Hatfield, Louis Tolque, Peter Robert, Jos Marshall, Wm Austin. At the Rio Colorado: Mark Head, & Wm Harwood. The principal leaders in the insurrection were Tafoya, Pablo Chavis, Palbo Montoya, Cortez, & Tomas, a Pueblo Indian. Of these, Tafoya was killed at Canada, Chavis was killed at Pueblo, Montoya was hanged at Don Fernando on the 7th instant, & Tomas was shot by a private while in the guard-room at the latter town. Cortez is still at large. -Sterling Price, Col commanding the army in New Mexico. [To the Adj Gen of the Army, Wash.]

Orphans Court of Wash Co, D C. In the case of Eliz Milligan, admx of Anne Milligan, dec'd. Distribution of the assets in the hands of the admx on Jun 11th next.
-Ed N Roach, Reg/o wills

Yesterday a pardon was received at the clerk's ofc liberating Isaac Robinson from the penitentiary, where he has been confined since the Mar term of the Criminal Court, 1846. Robinson is about 18 years of age. He was convicted of an assault with intent to kill a young man named Young, by which the latter was severely wounded, in a fracas in a refectory. He was sentenced to 3 years' imprisonment. Mr Young himself signed a petition for his pardon at the time of his conviction.

Meridian Hill for sale-well known Mansion & Farm: named from the monument on it marking the meridian line of the U S: the house is of brick & stuccoed, nearly 90 feet front & 54 feet deep, 1½ stories high, with a portico 54 by 12 feet. It was built by the late Cmdor Porter. It stands on a hill at the head of the avenue, directly in front, & about 1 miles from the Pres' house, commanding a most beautiful & extended view of the Potomac river, the city of Wash, Gtwn, Alexandria, & the adjacent country. The farm contains 110 acres, with a commodious farm house & large barn. It fronts on Boundary st, [the city line,] the rear is on a road leading from Gtwn, & can be subdivided into lots. For terms apply to Messrs Soutter & Broughton, Phil: Messrs Soutter, Brothers & Co, N Y, or to the subscriber on the premises. -J Florentius Cox

The Company of Voltigeurs departed on Mon from Wash City for the seat of war. They are under the command of Capt Jas D Blair, with Wm S Walker as 1st Lt & Washington Terrett as 2nd Lt. They are a fine body of young men of this city & its vicinity.

FRI APR 23, 1847

All the inhabitants of Eglesbach, in the Grand Ducy of Hesse Darmstadt, 1,400 in number, have requested permission to be allowed to emigrate to the U S. From Bremen the number of emigrants has been extraordinary, & in Apr & May will be yet greater. Some districts are threatened with complete depopulation. Throughout all Germany, extensive preparations are making for emigration to the States.

Died: on Mar 31, in St Louis, Missouri, after a painful illness of 3 days' duration, Mrs Pink McPheeters, w/o Dr W M McPheeters, & youngest daughter of the late Maj Carey Selden, of Wash City. A communicant of the Episcopal Church, she died, as she had lived, at peace with all the world. She was endearingly known among her familiar friends & schoolmates of this city as Miss Pink Selden.

Died: on Apr 21, Thos P Wilson, aged 3 years & 5 months, son of Patrick & Margaret Wilson. His funeral is today at 4 o'clock, from the residence of the family, at the corner of 6th & G sts.

Died: on Apr 20, in Gtwn, Thos Clayton, y/son of A H & Anna Dodge, aged 3 years.

Mrs Whitwell has re-opened her house for the reception of boarders. Located opposite the east square of the Capitol, south corner of Duff Green's Row.

SAT APR 24, 1847

Lt F Owen, of the Balt Btln, arrived in Balt last night from the seat of the war. He reports the men & ofcrs all well & in good spirits.

Mrs W Mann, formerly of Phil Pl, 11th & H sts, has fitted up that large commodious house on Pa ave, west of Jackson Hall, for the reception of boarders.

Died: at the residence of her father, J H Bowling, of PG Co, Md, Mary Bowling, aged about 17 years: from the seeds of a fatal disease, consumption. A fond & affectionate father, who had watched over her with tenderness & solicitude, now mourns the loss of a dght, & society an ornament. [No death date-current item.]

Died: on Apr 16, at the residence of her father, in Benton, Miss, Sarah Eliz, eldest daughter of Wm S & Letitia E Grayson, in her 10th year.

Orphans Court of Wash Co, D C. Letters of administration on the personal estate of Simon Fraser, late of said county, dec'd. -Wm Bird, adm

Teacher wanted: I wish to engage the services of a Teacher in my family: a gentleman of moral habits will be preferred. Direct, post paid, to Pomonkey Post Ofc, Chas Co, Md. -Pearson Chapman

The Journal of Commerce has received, by way of Panama, full files of The Californian, published at Monterey, Upper Calif, under the editorial supervision of Walter Colton, Alcalde of Monterey & Chaplain of the U S frig **Congress**, to Jan 28 last. Dec 12: the U S ship **Cyane**, Capt S F Dupont, arrived at San Francisco Monday week. Jan 23: on Dec 13, the launch belonging to the U S sloop-of-war **Warren** left Yerba Buena, on the San Francisco, for ***Fort Sacramento***, [Sutter's,] for the purpose of communicating with the commandant of the fort, Capt E M Kern. She was put in charge of Passed Midshipman Wm H Montgomery, acting master of the U S sloop-of-war **Warren**, with Midshipmen Danl O Hugennin, of the U S sloop **Portsmouth**, as pilot, & E M Montgomery, Clerk of Cmder. _____ Montgomery, & a crew of 9 men: Geo Rodman, seaman, coxswain; Anthony Sylvester, Alex'r McDonald, Saml Turner, Saml Lane, Milton Ladd, John W Dawd, Gilman Hilton, & Lawson Lee. After being absent 17 days, fears were entertained for her safety, & Mr R T Ridley was sent in search of her, with the launch Paul Jones, with 4 men, from the **Warren**. Mr Ridley returned after 19 days, having cruised up the San Joaquin & the Sacramento. Nothing was heard from them, & the conclusion is that the launch was lost in the bay.

MON APR 26, 1847

From a correspondent at Allen's Fresh, Md: the elegant & commodious dwlg of Col Wm D Merrick, late Senator of the U S, was destroyed by fire on Thu last, with about half of its valuable contents.

Died: on Apr 10, at the residence of his dght, in Butler, Wayne Co, N Y, Danl Fowler, in his 86th year, formerly of Hudson, N Y, & for several years a resident of Wash City. Maj Fowler entered the army as a volunteer in the service of his country during its Revolutionary struggle. He served under Gen Huntington, & was taken prisoner at Horse Neck, near N Y, where he was confined in the old sugar-house. After enduring a winter of great severity & suffering his release was effected in the spring by an exchange of prisoners.

In the Circuit Court of Montgomery, Ala, on Apr 6, the jury, in a cause between Richd Jones & Co vs Andrew Donnell, returned a verdict for $10,000 damages against the dfndnt. The action was to recover damages for injuries done the business & credit of plntf from the false issue & levy of an attachment on their goods some 2 years since by dfndnt.

Law case tried in Columbiana Co, against Dr Wm Robertson, of Hanover, for malpractice as a surgeon, in which the jury returned a verdict of $1,250 for the plntf. The treatment was for the dislocation of the knee-joint, which resulted in amputation of the limb. -Mahoning [Ohio] Index

The Rights of Authors. A case was tried in Boston, a few days ago, involving important issues as regards the rights of authors. The plntf, Rev John Pierpont, is the author of the popular school books, the First Class Reader & the Nat'l Reader, & assigned to the dfndnt the copyright of these books. At the expiration of 14 years, the copyright was renewed, & the dfndnt has ever since continued to publish the books as his own. The Court decided that the plntf sold only the right existing then, & that the renewed copyright belongs to the author The dfndnt, in the sales he has made, [which it is said amount to $10,000,] is to be regarded as the agent or trustee of the author, & required to account for the same; & the Court directed that he make disclosures of the amount of sales.

Died: on Apr 25, Mrs Sarah Ellen Ferguson, daughter of the late Wm Prather, of Montg Co, Md, & wife of Mr John W Ferguson, of Wash City. Her funeral is today at 3 o'clock, from her late residence on 6th st east, near the Christ Church, Navy Yard.

Robbery of the Dead Letter ofc. Two of the watchmen, Messrs Wm O Jones & R A Hawke, in the confidence of the ofcrs of the Dept, were stationed last Fri night in the room adjoining the dead letter ofc, where they could not be seen. About 9:30 p m, Mr Allen Petticord, also one of the night-watch, entered the room with a light, & soon afterwards heard him opening letters. Mr Jones then called Petticord by name, who immediately answered. Mr Jones then arrested him, taking several letters out of his hands: confessed his guilty & said this was only the second time he had entered the dead-letter room on such an errand. Petticord is about 60 years of age & his reputation for honesty had been good.

Circuit Court of Wash Co, D C-in Chancery. Thos A Dornin vs Isabella d Thorburn, Helen M Thorburn, Chas E Thorburn, & Anne M Dornin. Ratify the sale of Lots 1, 2, & 21 in square 199, in Wash City, to J B H Smith, the highest bidder & purchaser, for the sum of $673.77. -W Brent, clk

The subscriber wishes to purchase 500 cords of Black Oak Bark, for which he will give from $5 to $7 per cord. Deliver at the Old Stone Warehouse & wharf, called Davidson's, near Gtwn, on the Canal. The subscriber will always be found on the premises. -Beeson Crawford

TUE APR 27, 1847

Ann Adelia Moore was on Apr 9, in Dadeville, Tallapoosa Co, Alabama, found guilty of the murder of her husband. The sentence is confinement in the penitentiary for life. While Mr Moore was asleep, she fractured his skull in various places with an axe. He lived some 6 or 8 days, & reiterated that it was his wife that committed the savage act; that he knew of no cause she had for committing the same.

Hon John Cotton, M D, died at his residence in Marion, Ohio, on Apr 2, aged 86 years. He was a lineal descendant from the divine of that name who landed on the rock of Plymouth. He was remarkable for his literary & scientific attainments, & his unobtrusive piety. -Boston Whig

While Mr Levi Slade was riding on horseback in Chelsea, Mass, on Thu, his horse was struck by lightning & instantly killed. Mr Slade was not harmed.

The vote in the town of Alexandria in favor of erecting a new county out of Alexandria Co & a part of Fairfax, Va, was 271, against it 7-showing a majority of 264 in favor of the measure. The vote at Zimmerman's [the other precinct within the limits of the proposed division] showed a majority, also, of about 70 in favor of the new county.

Maj W W S Bliss: This ofcr, whose name is now favorably known over the Union, is a native of N H, & he graduated at West Point, in Jul, 1833, with considerable distinction. In 1834, during the Indian troubles, he was order to ***Fort Mitchell***, but shortly after he returned to West Point, where he remained until 1840, discharging the duties of assist professor of mathematics. He was appointed in 1839 assist adjutant general, & was attached to the staff of Gen Taylor, then stationed upon the Arkansas frontier. His gallantry in all the late battles in Mexico has especially signalized his name. He was but a poor orphan boy when he entered the Military Academy, & who is now, without a single relative in the world. -Louis Jour

Elk Hill & ***Elk Island*** for sale: this estate is the former residence of the late Randolph Harrison, jr, & is on James river, about 50 miles above Richmond, in Goochland Co, Va. It contains about 2,400 acres; the dwlg, recently built of brick & stucco, is large & handsome. The farm bldgs, barns, threshing machines are the best of their kind. The highland & the island are connected by a handsome & durable bridge. Address by letter to Peyton Harrison, Cartersville, Cumberland Co, Va: Agent for H C Harrison, adm of Randolph Harrison. Immediate possession will be given if desired.

Circuit Court of Wash Co, D C-in Chancery. Edw M Linthicum vs Eliz Ann Duly, widow of John W Duly & others. Ratifly sale by John Marbury, trustee in the above cause, of the real estate of said John W Duly: of lot 9 in square 426, in Wash, D C, with frame house thereon, which was owned by said John W Duly at the time of his death, to Eliz A Duly, for the sum of $750, & that the said Eliz hath complied with the terms of the sale.
-Wm Brent, clk

Wash Co, D C: I certify that Henry Nally brought before me as an estray a bay Horse. -Thos C Donn, J P [The owner is to come forward, prove property, pay charges, & take him away. -Henry Nally, Deep Cut, near Railroad.]

New restaurant: The City Lunch, in the basement of the large new brick house erected by Capt Carbery, on Pa ave, between 14th & 15th sts. -Fred'k Lakemeyer

A house-dog stolen for the 3rd time, & it is hoped the last. Stolen [that is taken away] from the ***Eckington Farm***, sometime on Sunday last, a brindle & white Bull-Dog. Reward of $2 for return of the dog; $5 for evidence as may lead to the conviction of the offender. -Edmund Brooke, jr, near the City Boundary.

Mrd: on Apr 26, at the Church of the Ascension, by Rev L J Gilliss, Mr Geo W Anderson, of Richmond, Va, to Miss Margaret L Horn, of Wash City.

Mrd: on Apr 22, at the residence of her father, Danl Gibson, in Hampshire Co, Va, by Rev Wm H Foote, Miss Mary Jane Gibson to Jas K Gibson, of Abington, Va.

Mrd: on Apr 20, at Leigh, Albemarle Co, Va, by Rev Richd K Meade, the Rev Geo T Wilmer, of Botetourt Co, Va, to Mary Peachy, daughter of the late Peachy R Gilmer.

Died: on Apr 20, in his 79th year, Basil Gordon, of Falmouth, long & widely known in that part of Va. The dec'd was born near Dumfries, in Scotland, in 1767, & having emigrated to this country in 1784, established himself shortly after as a merchant in Falmouth, where he continued to reside the rest of his life. He was the last survivor of a race of his countrymen who settled in that vicinity & flourished about the period of the Revolutionary war. During a longer term of life, & one of greater wordly prosperity than is often allotted to men, he ever maintained the highest character as a merchant, a citizen, & philanthropist.

Died: on Apr 26, Charles James, infant son of Saml & Eliz Ann Byington, aged 8 months. His funeral is tomorrow, at 11 a m, from his late residence, ***Greenleaf's Point***.

Bells: the subscriber is prepared to furnish Bells of all sizes from 20 to 15,000 lbs, suitable for Churches, Fire, Factories, & Steamboats. I sold one recently to the Catholic Church at Laurel, Md, & it has been heard 8 miles, & gives entire satisfaction. Orders promptly attend to. -John Haskell, Agent for A Meneely, Balt, Md.

WED APR 28, 1847

Desirable residence for rent in Gtwn: a 2½ story brick house on Gay st, near the dwlg of John Davidson, containing 2 parlors, kitchen, & dining-room, 4 chambers, with smoke-house, milk-house, & a pump of excellent water convenient to the kitchen, stable & cow-houses, & a large productive garden. The house & fencing have just been thoroughly repaired. Apply to J F Callan, corner of E & 7th sts.

Proposals for carrying the mail: Virginia: #2661: from Fairmont, by Jeremiah Hess', to Salem, 30 miles & back, once a week. #2664: From Fredericksburg, to the store of Wm Colton, 12 miles & back, once a week. #2689: from Mechanicsburg, by Jas Davidson's at the Rocky Gap, thence along the valley of the South or Muddy Fork of Wolf creek, & the house of Pleasant Murphy, to Tazewell C H, & to return by the valley of Clear Fork to Wolf creek, & the house of Henry W Dills & Rocky Gap: equal to 40 miles, once a week. North Carolina: #2944: from Albemarle, by Morgan's Mills, to Clear Creek, & to return by Thos Rowland's, once a week. #2947: from Elizabethtown, by Thos Lewis' house, to Gravely Hill, 16 miles, once a week. #2949: from Jefferson, by Helton, to Shadrick Greer's, Grayston Co, Va: once a week. Missouri: #4829: from Cassville, by John B Williams', to Forsyth, 50 miles & back, once a week. #4848: from Washbourn Prairie, by John B King's, to Maysville, Ark, 40 miles & back, once a week. Kentucky: #5132: from Booneville to Levi Pennington's, once a week. #5133: from Caseyville, by Cypress & O P Griswold's, to Providence, 24 miles & back, once a week. #5146: from Rome, by Danl Baker's, to the Steam Mill, in Clay Co, once a week. Tennessee: #5344: from Sparta, up the Calf-killer river to its source, crossing the old Walton road west to Robt Officer's by Jas M Goodbar's & Magnus Looper's to West Fork, 50 miles & back, once a week. #5345: from Spencer, by Wallsbridge, Isaac Miller's, & Flat Shoals, to Smithville, 46 miles & back, once a week. Alabama: #5634: from Tuscaloosa, by Wilson Sheppard's & Isaac Cain's, to Jasper, 55 miles & back. Arkansas: #5970: from Benton C H, by Preston Bland's, to Perryville C H, 40 miles & back, once a week. #5971: from Benton C H, by Joel Browne's Perriman McDaniels, & Keezee's Mill, through Colbreath's settlement, to Warren C H, 90 miles & back, once a week. #5977: from El Dorado, by Wm Chapman's Store, Wm F Bond's Store, Union Parish, La, & Ouachita City, to Monroe, 60 miles & back. #5980: from Chas Hatcher's every Tue at 1 p m, arrived at Gainesville next day by 8 p m. #5985: from Little Rock, by Alex'r Murphy's, & Kinderhook, to Rich Woods', 100 miles & back, once a week. #5986: from Marion, by Jas Deeron's, to Smith's, Poinsett Co, 40 miles & back, once a week. #5993: from Smithville, by Thos Esta's, to Pilot Hill, 50 miles & back, once a week. #5995: from Van Buren, by Jas Gin's, Wm Howard's, Hathaway's Store, & Enos Harris, 60 miles & back, once a week. #5997: from Yellville, by Jos Coker's, to Forsyth, Mo, 66 miles & back, once a week. Louisiana: #6050: from Covington C H, by John Parkins' & Wadsworth's, to Pear River, Parish of St Tammany, 36 miles & back, once a week. Texas: #6165: from Mansfield, La, to Ezekiel Jones', A G Tierney's, Edw Smith's, & John Graves, to Marshall, 60 miles & back, once a week. -C Johnson, Postmaster Genr'l. Post Ofc Dept, Apr 21 1847.

In Chancery: Sabret E Scott, cmplnt, & John Lynch & others, dfndnts. Henry Naylor, trustee, reported the sale of the lots & improvements decreed to be sold in the said cause, Robt Beale became the purchaser of lot 11 & improvements, in square 728, for the sum of $685; & lot 13 in square 728, for the sum of $300, & Sabret E Scott became the purchaser of lot 12 & improvements, in square 728, for the sum of $250, all in Wash City, & the terms of the sale have been complied with. -Wm Brent, clerk

J Fill, after an absence of 3 years, has returned to Wash, & will open an Academy for the young gentlemen on the first Mon in May: City Academy, 10th st, north of the avenue, nearly opposite Col Peter Force's. -J Fill, Principal

Mr Jas McVicker, a native of Connecticut, went from N Y C a few days back to ***Fort Tompkins***, to assist in firing a salute in honor of our victories in Mexico, & while standing before the gun it was accidentally discharged, & the charge struck him & wounded him so severely that he died on Mon.

New regts of additional regular force en route for the army in Mexico.
9th Infty: Col T B Ranson: 1 company: aggregate strength-60.
10th Infty: Col R E Temple: 5 companies: 410.
11th Infty: Col A C Ramsey: 7 companies: 547.
13th Infty: Col R M Echols: 1 company: 90.
14th Infty: Col W Trousdale: 1 company: 90.
15th Infty: Col G W Morgan: 90. [Now in Mexico,] Lt Col Joshua Howard, superintending.
16th Infty: Col J W Tibbatts: 10 companies: 649.
Voltigeurs: Col T P Andrews: 6 companies: 549.
3rd Dragoons: Col E G W Butler: 6 companies: 539.
Col R B Ranson, 9th Infty, reports Apr 12, from Boston: 450 recruits: one company of the 9th will embark from ***Fort Adams***, R I, early in May, & 3 more at least in the course of that month.
Col R E Temple, 10th Infty, reports from N Y, all the companies of his regt will be recruited & enroute for Mexico by May 12. Two additional companies of the 11th Infty, will be en route in early May, making 9. Col J W Tibbatts, 16th Infty, reports on Apr 16, from Newport, Ky, that in 3 weeks from then all the companies of his regt will be filled, when their aggregate strength will probably be 1,000.
Col T P Andrews, of the voltigeurs, in reporting 6 companies en route, adds that the remaining 4 of his regt will probably be recruited, & his entire regt filled & ready for the field by the end of May.
By May 10th, there will be 45 or 50 companies of the 10 new regts en route for the seat of war, the aggregate strength of which will not much fall short of 4,000. It is possible that there are other detachments now en route for the seat of war, in distant parts of the country, which have not yet reached the Adj Genrl's ofc, & that in May near 6,000 troops may be placed on the banks of the Rio Grande.

Mrd: on Apr 27, in Wash City, by Rev Mr Donelan, Mr Hezekiah Brawner to Mrs Ellen Dement, all of Cornwallis' Neck, Chas Co, Md.

THU APR 29, 1847
R P Fleniken, U S Charge d'Afaires to Denmark, left N Y on Monday, in the packet-ship **Liverpool**, for Stockholm.

Martin Brimmer, formerly Mayor of Boston, died suddenly at his residence in Boston, on Sunday.

Lafayette Hubble, Mr Cassell, Mr Coyle, & Mr Nixon, persons that were scalded by the explosion of the steamer **Newark**, near East Liverpool, Ohio, on Apr 16, have since died. -Wheeling Times

Washington Barrow has retired from the editor-ship of the Nashville [Tenn] Republican Banner, & is succeeded by Mr Wm Wales.

The community of Augusta [Ga] was astonished on Wed week with the intelligence that Mr D B Naphew, of that city, was found drowned in the Savannah river, at the foot of Campbell st. He was subject to very severe attacks of vertigo. -Sentinel

At a race on Sunday week, on the Bingaman Course, New Orleans, the chestnut filly Sally Riddlesworth, belonging to Kirkland Harrison, stumbled & rolled over on her rider, injuring him so severely that he died in about 5 hours. He was a fine looking mulatto, aged about 14 years, & cost his owner $2,500.

The cylinder mill at Hobb's Powder Works, in Barre, Vt, was blown up on Thu, & Geo W Nurse, at work in the mill, was killed. -Barre Gaz

An elderly man was killed on the N J Railroad yesterday, when the train hit a covered wagon. The occupants, Gideon Allen, of Scotch Plain, was killed, & Ephraim Ramer, of Short Hill, had his leg broken. The horse was also killed.

The brilliant exploits of Lt C G Hunter, commanding the U S steamer **Scourge**, in obtaining the capitulation of Alvarado & the town of Tlacotalpan, form the topic of conversation, to the exclusion of almost every other subject, among the nation & military circles. The boldeness of the affair, of the cmder of a vessel with a crew of about 100 men, all told, demanding the surrender of a place containing 7,000 inhabitants, in order to avoid unnecessary bloodshed, is only equaled by the saucy & independent manner in which Cmdor Perry beheld the stars & stripes waving over a place which he was arranging to attack, with almost the whole naval force of the country, & a military force of 2,000 men.

New Orleans, Apr 18. Arrival of troops: the steamer **Mountaineer** arrived yesterday from Pittsburg with nearly 400 troops, destined for Point Isabel & Monterey. Capt John Butler's company A, 3rd Dragoons, 140 strong; Capt Carr's company A, 11th Infty, about 70 strong, both from Phil; Capt Edwards' company U S Regt of voltigeurs from Norfolk, 90 strong; & Capt Fairfax's company of Va volunteers from Fairfax Co, about 80 strong, compose the detachment under the command of Capt Butler. -Courier

Wrought iron hand printing presses: recently constructed by Adam Ramage, Phil. They are moderate in price & easy of transportation by sea or land.

For rent: 3 story brick house, with back bldg, on Capitol Hill, adjoining the residence of A Dowson, near the north Capitol gate. Inquire of J P Pepper, for the heirs.

Marshal's sale: by writ of fieri facias, issued from the Clerk's ofc of the Circuit Court of Wash Co, D C: Sale on May 8, at the steamboat Wharf: the steamboat **Osceola**, with her engines, apparatus, & furniture, seized & levied as the property of Jas Mitchell, & sold to satisfy Judicial #9 to Oct Term of said Court, 1847, in favor of Thos W & Richd C Smith.
-Alex'r Hunter, Marshal of D C

Prize Money. Ofcrs, Seamen, Soldiers, & Marines present in the action of Sep 10, 1813, between the British & the U S fleets on Lake Erie, or their heirs, who have not yet applied for the prize money, are to forward their claims, post paid, with the proofs thereof, in due form of law, to the subscriber, who will pay prompt attention to them.
-Saml Hambleton, U S Navy Prize Agent, near St Michael's, Md.

For sale or rent: a 2 story brick house, with attic, adjoining my residence on Pa ave, near 2nd st, with a pump in the yard. At it again!-not being able to sell my stock of Lumber at auction, as advertised, I have determined to continue the Lumber, Lime, & Coal business, at the old stand, market space, 7th st. -John Purdy

Valuable brick house & lot at auction on May 6: being lot 5 of the subdivision of lots 1 & 2 in square 490, on C st, between 4½ & 6th sts. The property is that belonging to Lt W D Porter. -A Green, auctioneer

Valuable brick house & lot at auction on May 6: the desirable property on C st north, next to the corner of 4½ st, adjoining the residence of the late Dr Sewall, being lot 2 of the subdivision of lots 1 & 2, in square 490. The house is well built & in complete repair.
-A Green, auctioneer

Carriages & harness, parts of carriages: auction on May 4: the effects of Wm Marshall.
-A Green, auct

FRI APR 30, 1847
Mr Elijah Fitch fell dead upon the railroad track at Brighton Station, near Boston, Tue. He was at Brighton on business, & about 70 years of age, a worthy & estimable citizen.

Wash Corp: 1-Ptn of Jas Cuthbert: referred to the Cmte of Claims. 2-Ptn from P Thyson & others: referred to the Cmte on Improvements. 3-Bill for the relief of Richd Davis: referred to the Cmte of Claims. 4-Bill for the relief of Matilda Radcliff: passed.

Died: on Apr 29, Wm Wood, aged 58 years, a native of Newburyport, Mass, but for a number of years a resident of Wash City. His funeral is this afternoon at 4 o'clock, from his late residence, Pa ave, south side, between 9th & 10th sts.

Smithsonian Institution: ceremony of laying the Corner Stone: May 1, 1847. Appointed Assistant Marshals, & will each be distinguished by a baton & white scarf, with blue rosettes, viz: Messrs S Humes Porter, Wm Van Voorhies, R S Patterson, G S Gideon, Chas Abert, A H Lawrence, J Carroll Brent. -Wm Beverley Randolph, Marshal-in-Chief.

The killed & wounded at Vera Cruz. The following are the names, as officially reported, killed, wounded, & missing of the U S Army, during the siege of Vera Cruz, commencing Mar 9 & ending Mar 26, 1847:

Killed:

1st Brig of Regulars: Capt J R Vinton, 3rd Artl; privates John Hafner & Nicholas Burns. One marine, name not ascertained.

2nd Brig of Regulars: Capt Wm Alburtis, 2nd Infty; private Timothy Cunningham; sgt Wm R Blake.

Col Harney's Command: Cpl Jas H Nicholson; private Henry Hopkins.

Gen Patterson's Volunteers: privates John Miller & Gothlib Reip, both of the 1st Pa regt.

Wounded:

Col Harney's Command: 2nd Lt Lewis Neill, adj 2nd Dragoons, severely. Privates: Jos Marshall, severely, Edw A Jones, severely; W T Gillespie, Lewis Geisel, John Smith, & Thos Young, guide, a citizen of Texas, all slightly.

1st Brig of Regulars: Privates: Wheeler B Hunt, Emile Voiturat, John Golden, Wm Henderson, Ernest Krimpe, Owen Boate, Wm Carthage, Jos S Hayden, Archibald McFadgen, Martin Dignum, S D Shurtzenback, Edw Flemming: all slightly. Sgt Jas Foster, slightly; private Adolph Meihle, severely.

2nd Brig of Regulars: Sgts: W B Lane & Edmund Harris, severely. Privates: John Teluns & Thos Waller, severely. Privates Fred'k Warsea & Henry Neal, slightly. Musician John Rema, severely. 1st Lt D Davidson, slightly. Private Jas Stephen, badly. Cpl Spencer. [No details on Spencer.]

Gen Patterson's Volunteers: Lt Col J O Dickinson, badly. Privates: Ballard; M Fox, Coker, Phillips, Hickey, Thos I Scott, John G Ewbank, Ovid C Burdin, Wm Vandenbeck, Andrew Krumer, Theodore Thiess, Jas Stevens, Fay, Wm R Ales, Danl Vann, Green Woodly, Hugh Gavin, John Hubbard: slightly. Quartermaster Sgt B F McDonald, severely: Sgt Jos King, severely. Private Henry Lanbeck, severely. Sgts John Henson & R Williamson: slightly. Private David Harkins. [No details on Harkins.]

The U S sloop-of-war **Levant**, Hugh N Page , cmder, 54 days from Rio Janeiro, anchored in Hampton Roads on Tue last. List of her ofcrs: Cmder, Hugh N Page. Lts: 1st, Robt Handy; 2nd, Richd Forrest; 3rd, Jos H Adams; acting Lt, Geo W Hammersly; Purser, J R Rittenhouse; Assist Surgeon, W H Grier; Acting Master, J Dorsey Read; Midshipmen: H A Colborn, Saml R Franklin, W D Whiting, Wm M Gamble, Geo M Dibble, Wm W Low, G W Young, E H Scovell, Chas Wooley; Capt's Clerk, Wm Y Taylor; Gunner, S M Beckwith; Carpenter, John Green. Passengers: Lt Stephen Johnson, Midshipman Dulany Forrest, Midshipman J G Sproston, & H M Hill, citizen. The U S store-ship **Lexington** arrived at Monterey, California, on Jan 27 last. -Norfolk Beacon

The Mary Washington Union #2, Dghts of Temperance, will meet Crystal Fount Division Sons of Temperance room, 12th & Pa ave. By order of the P S. -Mary C Speakes, R S

SAT MAY 1, 1847

Household & kitchen furniture at auction: on May 5, at the boarding house of Mrs Turpin, on the corner of 7th st, fronting Centre Market. -A Green, auctioneer

Orphans Court of Wash Co, D C. Letters of administration on the personal estate of Henry S Fox, late of England, dec'd. -Hugh C Smith, adm Note: Persons having business with the above mentioned estate may apply to the undersigned Atty, at whose ofc the claims of creditors, when duly proven & passed, may be exhibited.
-J M Carlisle, Atty for adm

Dissolution of the copartnership existing in Wash City: by mutual consent. J A Emmons having withdrawn from the firm the business will in the future be continued by M H Stevens. -M H Stevens, J A Emmons

Among the killed at the battle of Vera Cruz was Lt Wm Price, of Illinois, in his 72nd year. He had left his home of affluence & ease with the expressed wish to die in the service of his country.

To the Board of Managers of the Washington Nat'l Monument Society: ***Arlington House***, Sep 18, 1846. I offer to your acceptance, a site for the proposed Monument upon my patrimonial domain of Arlington, where you are invited to choose as much ground as may be requisite for your pious & patriotic purpose, without money & without price. I beg leave to suggest to your notice 2 prominent situations upon the Arlington estate, either of which will be found to be admirably adapted to your wishes, in the erection of the Monument. With sincere consideration & esteem, I have the honor to be, gentlemen, your obedient servant, Geo W Custis Reply to above: Wash, Apr 29, 1847. I am instructed to tender you the sincere thanks of the Board of Managers for your liberal offer. It is in keeping with the adopted son of Washington, & with one who has so long & so affectionately cherished his sacred memory. The Society limited the locale of the monument to the city of Washington, as the capital of the nation, & therefore peculiarly suited for a Nat'l Monument to the memory of the illustrious patriot whose name it bears.
-Geo Watterston, Sec W N M S

Public Baths: the summer season will commence on May 1st & end Sep 30th. Each subscriber to pay $10 & be entitled to one bath per day for themselves, or son or dght, or the lady of the house. Single bath 25 cents. Bath-house on C, between 4½ & 6th st.
-P Aiken

The remains of Lt Archibald B Botts, who died at Camargo, Mexico, of the disease of the climate, on his way to join his regt, having been received at Richmond, Va, were interred in that city with proper funeral honors on Thu last.

Yesterday fire broke out in the extensive bread & biscuit bakery of Mr Thos Brown, at Gtwn, near the aqueduct. It will be remembered that Mr Brown's bakery was entirely destroyed by fire a few years ago.

Force's picture of Washington & Vicinity: with 41 embellishments on steel & lithograph. Strangers will find the following plates: portrait of Washington; old vault & new vault at ***Mount Vernon***; view of Wash City from Giesborough; view of Wash City from the glass-works; East, S W, & S E, views of the Capitol; view of the Capitol from the Va shore of the Potomac; Hall of the Reps; clock in the Reps Hall; Rotundo; Senate Chamber; portrait of Washington in the Senate Chamber; Tympanum of the easter portico of the Capitol; Statue of War; Statue of Peace; Penn's Treaty with the Indians; Boon's Combat with the Indians; rescue of Capt Smith by Pocahontas; landing of the Pilgrims; Statue of Washington; Naval Monument; north & south view of the Pres' House; Statue of Jefferson; view of the Treas Dept, Post Ofc, Patent Ofc, Nat'l Observatory, Navy Yard, Congressional Burial Ground, Gtwn, Heights of Gtwn, Little Falls of Potomac, Alexandria, ***Mount Vernon***, & Bladensburg. Price $1. For sale by Wm Q Force, Pa av & 10th.

Wash Light Infty: will meet at their armory this morning at 9 o'clock, in summer uniform, for parade. -H Richey, 1st Sgt

Columbia Artl: notified to assemble today at City Hall, at 11 o'clock, preparatory to firing a salute on the occasion of laying the corner stone of the Smithsonian Institution.
-C Buckingham, Capt Col Artl

Headquarters Nat'l Blues, to assemble at the armory this morning at 10 A M precisely, in full uniform, in obedience to a resolution of the corps, by which it was agreed to participate in the ceremonies today. By order of Capt F A Tucker.
-Geo Emmerich, 1st Sgt

MON MAY 3, 1847

The Hon Geo C Dromogoole died on Wed night last, of a severe attack of bilious pleurisy. For several years past he was a Rep in Congress from the Brunswick district of Va, & just re-elected to that station in the 30th Congress.

Capt Oden Bowie reached the residence of his father, in PG Co, Md, last week. He had been suffering some time past with fevers contracted in Mexico, & is at this time confined to his bed.

Ladies with letters in the Wash Post Ofc, May 1, 1847.

Allen, Mrs Sarah	Baldwin, Miss S	Berry, Mrs Rachael
Brown, Miss M A	Baldwin, Mrs M S	Brunston, Mrs Jane
Brown, Mrs M E S	Butler, Miss Ann	Bartin, Miss B
Brown, Miss R-2	Briscoe, Mrs S M	Berry, Mrs E C
Butler, Mrs Eliza	Burgewin, Mrs M A	Butler, Miss Maria

Byer, Miss Henriette
Barnes, Miss Hester
Boyd, Miss Eliza
Berdine, Mrs Emma
Baggett, Cecilia Ann
Crips, Jane
Cook, Mrs Francis
Crawford, Miss M
Cummings, Miss A
Carroll, Miss E
Diggs, Miss Anna
Dade, Mrs G
Duncan, Mrs B
Dugans, Mrs C
Davidson, Mary A
Donnelly, Miss W
Dixon, Mrs O
Dancey, Susan
Dana, Mrs Hannah
Easton, Miss Eliza
Evans, Miss Fanny
Eammons, Mrs M E
Fair, Mrs Catharine
Ford, Miss Lucinda
Fagan, Miss A E
Farrel, Mrs Ann
Forteney, Mrs M A
Graham, Mrs
Hall, Miss A C
Hill, Mrs Maria
Harrison, Mrs S
Hunter, Miss C
Heilman, Mrs A S
Harris, Mrs Martha
Hammond, Miss C
Hutchins, Miss E
Hoover, Miss S
Harrison, Miss E
Hutchison, Mary
Kearney, Mrs J A
Lee, Kitty
Lodge, Mrs Salitha
Leach, Mrs A
Lenzing, Mrs E T
Lamkin, Miss C
Langfit, Miss Julia
Mills, Mrs C H
Morris, Mrs Nancy
Martin, Miss M
Murphy, Mrs A E
Maxwell, Miss F
Miller, Eliza & Mary
Morris, Miss A
Magee, Miss Mary
McGill, Miss M L
McCauley, Mrs E
McCabny, Miss J
McKnight, Miss C C
Paine, Miss F
Perkins, Mrs S
Pumphrey, Miss M
Phelan, Mrs
Runyan, Mrs N E
Russell, Miss C
Randal, Mrs N
Sands, Mrs Lt B G
Smith, Mrs
Sands, Miss F R
Sandford, Rebecca
Saddler, Mrs S A
St Clair, Mrs R
Sinclair, Mrs H W
Stewart, Mrs S
Summerville, Mrs Mary A
Stevens, Ellen S
Shorter, Miss E
Sandford, Mrs M
Soper, Miss C A
Tolson, Mrs E
Vodery, Miss Mary J
Wood, Miss C B
Wise, Miss J M
Williams, Miss M
Wheeler, Mrs M
Walker, Mrs
Warker, Miss E
Washington, Miss E
-C K Gardner, P M

Valuable & desirable private residence at auction: on May 21, in front of the premises, east part of lot 167, & west part of lot 168, in Beatty & Hawkins' addition to Gtwn, belonging to the estate of the late Horatio Jones, dec'd, fronting 70 feet on 3rd st, & extending back 150 feet, with the improvements, being a well finished 2 story brick dwlg house, with back bldgs & finished garrets & good cellars. -Edw S Wright, auct

Trustee's sale: by virtue of an act of Congress passed Jul 20, 1840, & of the decree of the Orphans Court of Wash Co, D C, & the Circuit Court of D C, made in the case of Lewis G Davidson's heirs, & by authority from the heirs: sale on May 24, of lots 2, 3, & 4, in square 169, on F st west, in the immediate neighborhood of the Navy Dept. Also lot 8 in square 163. Title indisputable. -Saml G Davidson, Trustee -B Homans, auctioneer

Nathan I Waters was found guilty of manslaughter at the last County Court of PG Co, Md, & sentenced to 2 years' confinement in the penitentiary. -Marlborough Gaz

Orphans Court of Wash Co, D C. Letters testamentary on the personal estate of Jesse Brown, late of said county, dec'd. -Rosanna Brown, Edw C Dale, Tillotson P Brown, excs Note: Walter Lenox, Atty at Law, is fully authorized to act in behalf of the undersigned in the settlement of said estate. -Rosanna Brown, Edw C Dale.
resorted to. -Allgemeine Zeitung

Headquarters Army of Occupation, Camp near Monterey, Mar 22, 1847. We lament the fall of Capt B F Graham, assist quartermaster in the volunteer service, who was killed in action, after behaving in the most gallant manner. I would recommend to particular notice the gallant conduct & energy of Col Morgan throughout these operations. Lt Col Irvin, Maj Wall, & Adj Joline, 2nd Ohio Regt, & Maj Shepherd, are also entitled to notice fo good conduct & valuable services. -Z Taylor, Maj Gen U S Army, commanding
[Capt Graham's loss appears to have been on Apr 25.]

The King of Sardinia's illness has become alarming for the last few days. On the 17th it was found necessary to apply leeches twice. Today he was worse, & bleeding was resorted to. -Allgemeine Zeitung

Col Albert Pike, of the Arkansas cavalry, has published a card disavowing for the squadron under his command all share in the horrible massacre of a number of poor Mexican peasants a few days before the battle of Buena Vista. His command, he says, was 30 miles off at the time.

On Tue a fire broke out in the charcoal collieries near the residence of Dr Saml P Smith, about 4 miles from Cumberland, Md. 3,000 cords of wood were burnt at the collieries. The wind communicated the fire to the woods, until it reached the farm of John Hoye, in the occupancy of Mr Retter, where 4,000 rails were burnt. Mr Jacob Devore, residing on an adjoining farm, also lost several thousand rails. Dr S P Smith's stables were saved by the lulling of the wind at night. -Cumberland Civilian

It is stated that the late Wm Oliver, of Dorchester, left the whole of his property, valued at not less than $100,000, to be divided equally between the Perkins Institution for the Blind, at South Boston, & the McLean Asylum for the Insane, at Somerville. One-third of this sum is to be paid over immediately, & the remainder at the decease of his 2 sisters.

Judge Rolland has been appointed to the ofc of Chief Justice of the Queen's Bench, in Canada, vacant by the death of the late Chief Justice Valliers de St Real. Jas Smith retires from the ofc of Atty Gen East, & replaces the Chief Justice as Puisne Judge.

Mrd: on Apr 29, by Rev Henry Slicer, John Q Willson to Ellen, 2nd daughter of Chas W Boteler, all of Wash City.

Mrd: on Apr 29, in Richmond, Va, by Rt Rev Bishop Johns, W G Cazenove, of Alexandria, to Miss Mary, daughter of the late Judge Stanard, of Richmond.

Died: on Apr 27, at Warrenton, Va, Eliz Edmonds Wallace, after a lingering illness. She was the eldest daughter of the late Jas W Wallace, M D; & had been afflicted with the disease of which she died for many months. She leaves a numerous circle of relatives & friends to deplore her loss.

Died: on Apr 11, at his residence in Newark, Delaware, John Thomson, in his 83rd year. He was the only surviving nephew of the Hon Chas Thomson, Sec of the 1st American Congress.

Died: on Apr 18, at her residence in Boone Co, Ky, after a lingering illness, Mrs Clara H Pike, widow of Gen Zebulon M Pike, in her 65th year.

Died: Apr 7, at his residence in Kansas, Missouri, Col Wm M Chick, formerly a resident of Alexandria, Va.

The Laying of the Corner Stone of the Smithsonian Institution took place on May 1, with appropriate & imposing ceremonies, agreeably to the order prescribed by the Marshal-in-Chief. The volunteer companies under the command of Capt Tucker & Lt Tate formed at their respective parade grounds, near the City Hall. Members of the various Lodges of Fire & Accepted Masons of the District united with the delegations from Md & Pa, & took the station assigned them in the order of the procession by Marshal-in-Chief, Beverley Randolph: procession was unusually grand: the Phil delegation, headed by Col Jas Page, Grand Master of Pa; the Balt delegation, headed by Chas Gilman, Grand Master of Md, & the Wash, Gtwn, & Alexandria delegations, headed by B B French, the popular Grand Master of D C. Dr W B Magruder, spendidly decorated, acted as the Grand Marshal of the Odd Fellows, whose chief ofcrs are Dr Jos Borrows, Grand Master, & Dr Flodoardo Howard, Deputy Grand Master, who appeared in their proper places. The Marine Bank was excellent, & the Nat'l Brass Band, recently formed under Mr Massoletti, played admirable. Garcia's Band, from Alexandria, attracted particular attention by it excellent performances. The column moved down 4½ st to Pa ave, then up the avenue to 7th st, up 7th to E, up E to 11th, up 11th to F, & thence on F to the Presidential Mansion, where the Pres, Heads of Depts, & Diplomatic Corps, were received into the line. The entire column then moved, by Pa ave & 12th st, to the site of the Smithsonian Institution. B B French, the Grand Master, with Jas Page, the Grand Master of the Grand Lodge of Pa, & Chas Gilman, Grand Master of the Grand Lodge of Md, took his stand at the corner stone, & Brother McJilton addressed the Throne of Grace with a prayer. Deposits in the casket were: an elegant copy of the Holy Bible, presented by Rev Chas A Davis, on behalf of the Bible Society of Wash; a stereotype page of Bancroft's History of the U S; Constitution of the Grand Lodge of D C; an impression of its seal in metal; a copy of its proceedings for 1846; a silver plate inscribed with the names of the ofcrs of the Grand & Subordinate Lodges of the District; various coins of the U S; the newspapers of the day; the Constitution of the U S; evidences of the grant & origin of the Smithsonian Institution, & a plate with the following inscription:
On the First day of May, 1847, was laid,
In the city of Washington,

This foundation stone of a building, to be appropriated for the Smithsonian Institution.
Jas K Polk,
President of the United States.
Corporation.
President of the U States,
Secretary of State,
Secretary of War,
Postmaster General,
Vice President of the U States,
Secretary of the Treasury,
Secretary of the Navy,
Attorney General,
Chief Justice of the U States,
Commissioner of Patents,
Mayor of the city of Washington.
Board of Regents.
George M Dallas, Vice President of the United States.
Roger B Taney, Chief Justice.
W W Seaton, Mayor of the city of Washington.
Lewis Cass, United States Senator
Sidney Breese, United States Senator
James A Pearce, United States Senator.
Robert Dale Owen, United States Representative.
William J Hough, United States Representative.
Henry W Hilliard, United States Representative.
Rufus Choate, Massachusetts.
Richard Rush, Pennsylvania.
Gideon Hawley, New York.
William C Preston, South Carolina
A Dallas Bache, National Institute.
Joseph G Totten, National Institute.
Officers.
George M Dallas, Chancellor.
Executive Committee.
W W Seaton, chairman; Jos G Totten, Robt Dale Owen.
Building Committee.
Robt Dale Owen, chairman; Jos G Totten, Wm W Seaton.
Joseph Henry, Secretary. C C Jewett, Assistant Secretary.
Jas Renwick, jr, Architect.
Robt Mills, Assistant Architect & Superintendent.
The Grand Master then applied the square, level, & plumb, & the pronounced the stone squared, duly laid, true & trusty. He placed upon the stone the corn, wine, & oil: bread to feed the hungry, wine to cheer the sorrowful, & oil to heal the wounds. The Grand Master gave 3 raps upon the stone with the gavel of Washington.

Farm for sale: the subscriber offers to sell a portion of that most desirable farm known as ***Langley***, in Fairfax Co, Va, on the Gtwn & Leesburg Turnpike, 6 miles from the former city. The part for sale contains from 250 to 300 acres, fronting upon the road, it runs back to the Potomac river: improvements are a comfortable frame house in good repair, a log stable & corn house, with other out-bldgs. Apply to the subscriber, at Langley, or to Brooke Mackall, Wash. -R Covington Mackall

Died: on Apr 3, at his residence near Staunton, John H Peyton, in his 69th year.

Died: on May 2, Margaret Pyne, daughter of Rev Smith Pyne, aged 6 years & 6 months.

TUE MAY 4, 1847

For rent: a brick dwlg-house, with basement, on 3rd st, adjoining Capt Powel's, formerly occupied by Senator Bagby. Apply to G W Phillips, dry goods merchant.

The Fall Session of W J Bingham's Select School will begin Jul 14. Sessions regulated by those of the Univ of North Carolina. Address the Principal, directing to Hillsborough, N C. Classical Dept: W J Bingham, Principal. Mathematical Dept: David W Kerr.

On Wed last a fire broke out in Mrs Boyle's house, opposite the brick tavern, & destroyed nearly all the houses at the east end of the town. The house of Mr Dunnington; a large 3 story frame with about 30 rooms, belonging to Colquhoun's & Dunnington's heirs; the old baking house, Mrs Waters', Mr Allen's, & several others, in all 18, were consumed. About 40 persons were turned out of their homes. Nearly all the men were absent at the time, engaged in the fisheries on the Potomac. -Dumfries, Va

Mrd: on May 2, at St John's Church, by Rev Mr French, Mr Geo Melling to Miss Jane C Goods, all of Wash City.

Mrd: Thu last, by Rev Jas B Donelan, Mr Robt A Waters to Miss Anna Maria Meckum, all of Wash City.

Mrd: on Apr 15, at Oak Grove, Alabama, by Rev P McMullin, Dr Thos Anderson, of Greene Co, to Ann Romania, 2nd daughter of H G Wilson, of Gtwn, D C.

Died: on Saturday, in Wash City, Mr John Kennedy, in his 79th year.

Died: on May 2, Margaret Pyne, daughter of Rev Smith Pyne. The funeral will take place at half past 4 o'clock this afternoon.

For sale or rent: a very desirable private residence on Capitol Hill, on 1st st east, between B & C sts, the late residence of B M Berry. The title is indisputable. Inquire of Mrs Berry, or Mr Phillips, next door.

The subscriber is disposed to rent the house in which he lives on 9th near L st. It is large & convenient, having 16 rooms, pantry, large china closet, with an excellent paved cellar, & pump in the yard. To a good tenant the rent will be quite moderate. -W Doughty

House & kitchen furniture at auction: on May 10, at the residence of Mrs Mount, at the corner of 4½ st & Pa ave, an elegant assortment of furniture: by deed of trust recorded in Liber 99, folios 237 through 239, of the land records. -A Green, auctioneer

Desirable property for sale or exchange: the subscriber offers the following property, situated in St Mary's Co, Md: a Farm of about 200 acres, with an excellent dwlg, with all the outhouses suitable for a country residence: situated about 2 miles from Leonardtown, the principal village of the county. Adjoining this property, is a valuable Mill Seat of about 60 acres, upon which now stands a grist mill. My present occupation & place of residence make it necessary to part with this property. Property either in Wash or Gtwn would be taken in exchange for a large portion, say one-half, of the purchase money. For further particulars, apply to the subscriber in Gtwn, or to J T Blakistone, Leonardtown, Md. -S Gough

For rent: two very convenient brick dwlgs on 8th st, between G & H sts. Inquire on the premises, or of the subscriber, on 11th between G & H sts. -Margaret Stewart

Columbian Academy: the Classical & Mathematical Dept will be under the care of Mr J Goodier, a graduate of the Wesleyan Univ, Conn, & late a teacher of languages in Whitestown Seminary, N Y. The Academy is on 9th st, Wash.
-Columbus McLeod, J Goodier

Trustee's sale of 2 story frame House & Lot: on May 25, on the premises, by deed of trust from John S James to Thos Blagden, & recorded in Liber W B 123, folios 160 through 162, one of the land records of Wash Co, D C: part of lot 1 in square 516, fronting on north I st, near the corner of 4th st, 18 feet, running back 75 feet, with the improvements- a good 2 story frame house. Terms cash. -Thos Blagden, Trustee
-A Green, auctioneer

WED MAY 5, 1847

For rent: 2 comfortable brick 2 story tenements on 13th st, adjoining Mr Gaither's new block. Also, two frame ones, on the south side of I street north, near 7th st. For the former apply to Mr B Willet, on same st; for the latter to Mr R D Spencer, at his shoe store, on 7th st, between H & I sts.

For sale or rent: one of those desirable bldgs in Franklin Row, #6, with all the ground lying east between my house & the Rev Mr French's dwlg, being a part of 4 lots. Inquire at the corner of H & 12th sts, or to Mr Wm B Cross, on the premises.

$5 reward for return of my mare Rachel: 9 years old: shod a week ago. I turned her out Fri & she has not come back since. -Julius A Peters, Wine Store, Pa ave, near 10th st.

Notice of a change of business: compelled from necessity to change his manner of doing business, it will be conducted exclusively for cash. -Wm Peterson

Thos G Ford, Practical Currier & Leather Dresser, 7th & G st, offers his services to remove the gum from leather tops, which is so injurious to leathers in the sun, & restore them to their original appearance.

Mrd: on Tue, at the Church of the Ascension, by Rev Mr Gilliss, Dr Anthony Holmead to Miss Eliz, eldest daughter of the late Lt J C Smith, of the U S Army.

Died: on May 3, in his 45th year, Richd Joyce, a native of the city of Cork, Ireland, & a resident of this city for the last 29 years. His funeral is today at 10 o'clock, from his late residence on 18th st.

Franklin D Hitchcock was knocked from the top of one of the cars of the freight train from Boston yesterday in passing under a bridge near Westborough, & run over by the remainder of the train. He died soon after. -Worcester Spy

Buena Vista, Feb 25, 1847. We were at the north base of the mountain: we had to fall back and the lancers did make a charge, & we repulsed them & drove them back to the Mexican infty. Here Col Yell gave an unfortunate order. He dismounted Dillard's squadron to fight in a ravine, till aid could come from the right flank of our army. The Mexican infty advanced & we were near being taken prisoners. The Ky cavalry, under Col Marshall shared the day with us, bad as it had been. If balls & lances, sabres, smoke & dust, shouting, growning, & dying compose glory, we were in the midst of it. Not a word was spoken-it was all fighting. Here Col Yell fell, & Capt Parker-& poor John Pelham, the beloved of our regt. The Mexicans tumbled on every side. I saw them struck down with sabres & trampled beneath our horses' feet. I saw them beg with uplifted hands for mercy, but it was remembered that those very hands had driven their lances into the hearts of our countrymen. Other volunteers were in the fight on our right flank. The Illinois volunteers were in the midst of glory. Col Hardin was killed in a charge. He was the bravest of the brave. Col Clay, & several other gallant ofcrs, also fell. Col Yell was fearless to recklessness; Capt Porter was not able to draw his sword in action, having suffered some time from rheumatism. Desha, & the two Searcy's, brothers, of Capt Porter's company, stood & fought in danger wherever it offered, & as long as the battle lasted they were in the field. I must do justice to Col Roane, whom I hate as a politician as much as any one on earth. He was with us, encouraging & managing our affairs with a skill I thought he did not possess. He stood calm & cheered the men when 2 riflemen were shot down on either side of him; when it came to the charge at the ranch, his sabre fell about like a streak of lightning on the Mexicans, & their blood is upon it now. He honored our State by his gallant bearing at Buena Vista. Pike's squadron was attached to Col May's Dragoons, & did not fire a gun during the day. Those who faltered & ran off to town, belong to the rifle companies. It is thought that the names of all those who fled to Saltillo will be published in the Washington papers. -W Quesenbury

The 4th floor of the large flouring mill at Hackettstown, Warren Co, belonging to Mr Clark, gave way on Tue of this week & Peter Rice, a respectable citizen of the place, was caught by the crushing mass & buried, being found dead under some 10 feet of meal. -Newark Daily

On Fri the ferry boat **Sussex**, plying between N Y & Jersey City, was run into by a schnr belonging to Newark. Mrs Dummer, the lady of the Mayor of Jersey City, was badly injured, & Mrs Carter, wife of Mr Carter, of the Phil hotel, was crushed by the bowsprit, & carried through the wheelhouse, & thrown by the wheel under the boat. She was not missed, nor was it known that any fatal injury had been sustained until her mangled body was found in the East River, near the south ferry. The accident is attributed to carelessness on board the schnr. -Courier

THU MAY 6, 1847

Appointed members of the Levy Court of D C: J F Cox, Henry Naylor, Joshua Pierce, Chas R Belt, John Cox, Robt White, & Lewis Carbery.

An inquiry was lately submitted to a jury of 24 citizens of Brooklyn, in relation to the sanity of Cornelius Heany, an elderly gentleman of wealth, from which he has made very liberal gifts to several benevolent institutions. The inquest is held on the motion of his legal heirs. The decision of the jury was in favor of the heirs.

Notice: public sale on Jun 10 next, for ground rent due by S Sryoch & others to Wm A Bradley, the following property: part of square 353, with the bldgs & improvements. -W G Howison, Bailiff

Circuit Court of Wash Co, D C-in Equity, Mar Term, 1847. Benj G Harris, adm de bonis non of John R Plater, vs Wm G Ridgley & others. John Marbury, the trustee in the original decree in this cause, having reported to the Court that he has sold the whole of the real estate required to be sold: lot 141 & part of 142, in Beatty & Hawkins' addition to Gtwn, D C, with the house & improvements thereon, fronting on Fred'k st, to Wm O'Brien, for $2,450. Ratify same. -Wm Brent, clk

Mrd: on May 4, by Rev Mr Morgan, Andrew F Hoover to Miss Julia Barnicloe, all of Wash City.

Mrd: on Jan 5, by Rev Mr Bean, John W Pageot to Mrs E O Talbott, all of Wash City.

Mrd: on Apr 29, by Rev Thos Castleman, Wm Henry Tams & Marie Antoinette, daughter of the Hon Danl Smith, all of Rockingham Co, Va.

Died: on May 5, at his residence in Gtwn, in his 75th year, Gen Walter Smith, for many years among the leading merchants of this District, & widely known & esteemed for his enterprise, public spirit, probity, & philanthropy. His funeral is on May 7, at 4½ o'clock.

Died: on Apr 24, in New Orleans, Capt Alex'r J Swift, of the corps of Engineers, U S Army, aged 37 years. He was the son of Geo Jos G Swift, of N Y, who served with distinction in the last war, & was at one time the chief engineer of the U S Army. Capt Swift entered the Military Academy as a cadet in 1826, at the early age of 16; was graduated in 1830, & in 1838 was promoted to a captaincy. It being contemplated by the War Dept to raise a company of engineer soldiers, he was selected to visit France, in 1840, for the purpose of acquiring, at the French schools of practice, practical information as to the organization & exercises of this, to us, novel description of troops. He accomplished this object & returned to this country in 1841. Capt Swift was unable to reach the army in time for the assault of Monterey; he was at this period attacked with the disease which has been fatal to so many of our troops on the Rio Grande-the dysentery. He nearly recovered when the Vera Cruz expedition offered him an opportunity to display the peculiars qualities of his company, which he could not resist. He landed with the army before Vera Cruz, & became so exhausted, that he never recovered. A severe relapse of his disease was the consequence. He arrived at New Orleans from Vera Cruz on the 9th ult, & his strength rapidly failed him.

N Y: on May 3, Mr Alva Hotchkiss, a respectable gentleman, about 60 years of age, was returning from his store, corner of Hudson & Charlton sts, in N Y C, to his residence in Union st, South Brooklyn, when he was most savagely & murderously & assaulted & robbed in Clinton st, opposite Christ's Church, Dr Stone. He cannot possibly survive. His pockets had been rifled of a gold watch & about $70 in money.

FRI MAY 7, 1847

From the Joliet Signal [Illinois] 2 young ladies, dghts of Mr Tool, of Lockport, were crossing the river on some timber & fell in. One of them was saved by Wm Gatons, age 14 years, who plunged in at the risk of his own life. -Chicago Journal

Died: on May 1, in Gtwn, D C, after a short & painful illness, Mrs Eleanor Adams, in her 76th year.

Died: on May 6, in Gtwn, D C, Mr Thos J Davis, in his 43rd year. His funeral is tomorrow at 11 o'clock, from his late residence on Prospect st.

The death of Mr N P Ames, probably the most distinguished mechanic in the U S, & widely known, is felt as a personal loss to the citizens of Cabotville, Mass. All who knew Mr Ames esteemed & loved him. -Springfield Republican [No date-appears to be recent.]

Late from New Mexico: the accounts from Chihuahua are to Mar 9 & present nothing new except the details of Col Doniphan's recent victory at Sacramento. The names of the killed on our side are Saml C Owens, a trader of Independence, & Sgt Kirkpatrick, a young lawyer of Lexington, Missouri. Lt Dorn had his horse shot from under him by a 9 pound ball when the enemy opened a heavy fire of cannon.

Attention! The company now raised by E W Robinson meet on Sat at 9 o'clock, at their rendezvous, for the purpose of electing their ofcrs.

A company of nearly 50 able-bodied & well looking men, who have enlisted under Capt Dan Drake Henrie, to serve as volunteers in Mexico, paraded yesterday on Pa ave, preceded by the Marine Band.

Meeting of the Board of Trustees of Temperance Hall will be held Sat at 5 o'clock. -J L Henshaw, sec

For rent: a 2 story frame house on M st, between 4th & 5th sts west, near the old Almshouse. Apply to B F Morsell, 7th st.

Excellent furniture, superior buggy & harness, & wines: at auction, May 10, at the residence of Col Pile, on the Tenallytown road, about 1 mile above Gtwn, the balance of his household furniture. -R W Dyer, auct

Niles, Mich, Apr 12, 1847. The Pilot has just left the lock on her first trip with a large company on board, when a movement of the persons on board careened her so that she could not be steered. Chas Kellogg, of the firm of Kellogg & Brothers, of White Pigeon, & 2 others, were drowned. -Detroit Advertiser

Fred'k Reidel, who was lately convicted at Pittsburg of having murdered his wife, committed suicide during the night by breaking glass from a window with which he opened a vein in his arm, & then hanging himself by his blanket, thus ensuring death by the doubles means of strangulation & bleeding, to avoid a public execution.

SAT MAY 8, 1847

Official: Genr'l Orders, #19. War Dept, Adj Gen Ofc, Wash, Apr 28, 1847. Organization of the 10 Regts authorized to be raised by the act entitled "An act to raise for a limited time an additional military force," approved Feb 11, 1847; & order of precedence & relative rank of the ofcrs of each grade, as established by the Pres, according to law.

Names, rank, & date of commission/ Company / Born in/ Appointed from.

3rd Regt U S Dragoons:

Colonel: Edw G W Butler, Apr 9, 1847; former commission, 1st Lt artl; resigned 1831: from-blank: appt'd from La.

Following are dated Apr 9, 1847:

Lt Colonel: Thos P Moore: Va: Ky.

Majors:

1-Lewis Cass, jr: Ohio: Mich.

2-Wm H Emory; former commission, 1st Lt top engineers: Md: M A.

Surgeon: Edw H Barton: Va: La.

Assist Surgeons: 1-F J Robertson: Tenn: Tenn; 2-Corydon S Abell: N Y: Ky.

Captains:

1-Green W Caldwell: Co A: N C: N C.

2-John Butler: Co B: Pa: Pa.
3-Edgar B Gaither: Co C: Ky: Ky.
4-Lemuel Ford: former commission, capt dragoons, resigned 1837: Co D: Va: Ind.
5-Wm H Duff: Co E: Eng: N Y.
6-John S Sitgreaves: Co F: N C: S C.
7-Alphonse M Duperu: Co G: Va: La
8-Richd T Merrick: Co H: Md: Md.
9-Jas Hagan: Co I: Ireland: Mich
10-Andrew T McReynolds: Co K: Ireland: Mich.
1st Lts: dated Apr 9, 1847:
1-Walter H Jenifer: Md: Md.
12-Danl Petigru: S C: S C.
26-Saml B H Vance: Pa: Pa.
32-Rodolphus Schoonover: Pa: Ind.
45-Geo J Adde: Va: La.
54-Jos A Divver: N Y: N Y.
65-Geo E Maney: Tenn: Tenn.
74-John T Brown: blank: Mich.
81-Wm B Cook : Va: Ala.
2nd Lts: dated Apr 9, 1847:
10-Wm Walker: blank: Ala.
15-Hermann Thorn: former commission, 2nd lt infty: N Y: N Y.
24-J C D Williams: Mich: Mich.
37-Jos C Wallace: Pa: Pa.
44-Wm C Wagley: Ky: Ky.
53-Jos H Maddox: Md: Md.
64-John K Harrison: N C: N C.
78-John Merryfield: Ky: Ky.
85-Wm J Magill: S C: S C.
101-Alfred A Norment: N C: N C.
108-Francis Y Gaines: Ala: Ala.
122-Francis Henry: Ill: Wis.
135-Langdon C Johnson: S C: S C.
145-Chas Radzimiski: Poland: La.
157-John V S Haviland: Pa: Pa.
158-Jas J Moore: Ky: Ky.
172-Edw McPherson: Md: Md.
179-Wm Merrihew: Mass: N Y.
183-Wm Blood: N Y: Ind.
9th U S Infty: dated Apr 9, 1847:
Colonel: Trueman B Ransom: Vt: Vt.
Lt Colonel: Abner B Thompson: Mass: Me.
Majors: 1-Thos H Seymour: Conn: Conn; 2-Folliot T Lally: N Y: Me
Surgeon: Justin E Stevens: Mass: Mass.
Assist Surgeons: 1-John B Walker: N H: N H; 2-Francis L Wheaton: R I: R I.

Captains:
1-Jos S Pitman: Co A: N H: R I.
2-Theodore F Rowe: Co B: N H: N H.
3-Stephen Woodman: Co C: Me: Me.
4-E A Kimball: Co D: N H: Vt.
5-Andrew T Palmer: Co E: Me: Me.
6-Nathl S Webb: Co F: Conn: Conn.
7-Jas W Thompson: Co G: N H: Me.
8-Danl Bachelder: Co H: Vt: N H.
9-Lorenzo Johnson: Co I: Conn: Conn.
10-Chas N Bodfish: Co K: Me: Me.
1st Lts:
9-Alex'r Morrow: Me: Me.
14-Lyman Bissell: Conn: Conn.
21-John S Slocum: R I: R I.
39-Chas J Sprague: Me: Mass.
45-Geo Bowers: N H: N H.
60-John H Jackson: N H: N H.
61-Thos J Whipple: N H: N H.
79-Albert Tracy: N Y: Me.
88-Justin Hodge: Conn: Conn.
100-Jas F Bragg: blank: Mr.
2nd Lts:
4-Danl H Cram: N H: N H.
16-Asa A Stoddard: Conn: Conn.
28-Thos P Pierce: N H: N H.
38-Nathl F Swett: Me: Me.
45-Josiah P Chadbourne: Me: Army
57-Jesse A Gove: N H: Vt.
66-Thompson H Crosby: Me: Me.
75-Alpheus T Palmer: Me: Me.
87-Richd C Drum: Pa: Pa.
93-John Glackin: Mass: R I.
100-Edwin A Whitten: Me: Me.
111-Robt Hopkins: Ky: Vt.
124-Geo W May: blank: Army.
133-Chas Simmons: Me: Me.
143: Levi Woodhouse: Conn: Conn.
151-Henry De Wolf: R I: R I.
160-Wm A Newman: Vt: Vt.
168-Jas P Archer: Md: Md.
180-Chas L Low: blank: N H.
193-John M Hathaway: blank: Conn.

10th Regt U S Infty: dated Apr 9, 1847:
Colonel:
Robt E Temple, Apr 9, 1847: former commission 1st lt artl: resigned 1839: Vt: N Y.
Lt Colonel: John J Fay, Apr 9, 1847: N Y: N Y.
Majors:
1-Fowler Hamilton, Apr 9, 1847: former commission 1st lt dragoons: N Y: M A.
2-Justis J McCarty, Apr 9, 1847: N Y: N Y.
Surgeon: Thos R Spencer, Apr 9, 1847: N Y: N Y.
Assist Surgeons: John Conger, Apr 9, 1847: N Y: N Y.
Captains:
1-Mathew S Pitcher: Co A: N Y: N Y.
2-Wm L Walradt: Co B: N Y: N Y.
3-Wm R Andrews: Co C: Conn: N Y
4-Caleb Wilder: Co D: N H: N Y.
5-Saml Dickinson: Co E: N J: N J.
6-Thos Postley: Co F: blank: N Y.
7-Jos Y Yard: Co G: N J: N J.
8-Joshua W Collett: Co H: N J: N J.
9-Wm W Tompkins: former commission capt dragoons, resigned 1838: Co I: N Y: N Y.
10-Alex'r Wilkin: Apr 9, 1847: Co K: N Y: N Y.
1st Lts:
8-Geo W Taylor: N J: N J.
18-Saml R Dummer: N J: N J.
28-Francis M Cummins: N Y: N Y.
38-Robt C Morgan: N Y: N Y.
47-Stephen Powers: Maine: N Y.
53-Jos H Howard: N Y: N Y.
63-Squire Moon: N Y: N Y.
71-Saml Lea: N Y: N Y.
85-Robt A Bouton: N Y: N Y.
2nd Lts:
9-Edw McGarry: N Y: N Y.
12-Lorimer Graham: N Y: N Y.
30-Jas McKown, jr: N Y: N Y.
31-Hiram Russell: N Y: N Y.
48-Benj Yard: N Y: N Y.
58-Peter H Bruyere: N J: N Y.
61-Thos S Griffin: N Y: N Y.
77-Ira S Konover: N J: N J.
83-John S Nevins: N J: N J.
94-Calvin J Mills: N Y: N Y.
99-John Magee: blank: N Y.
116-Edw Harte: N Y: N Y.
126-Chas Bennett: N J: N J.
128-De Witt Clinton: N Y: N Y.

146-Chas A Johnson: N Y: N Y.
154-Chas Van Alen: N Y: N Y.
165-Isaac W Patton: Va: Va.
191-Gersham Mott, jr: N J: N J.
11th Regt U S Infty: dated Apr 9, 1847:
Colonel: Albert C Ramsey: Pa: Pa.
Lt Colonel: Wm M Graham: Va: M A.
Majors:
1-Edwin W Morgan: former commission, 1st lt artl; resigned, 1839: Pa: Pa.
2-John F Hunter: Apr 9, 1847: S C: Pa.
Surgeon: Wm J Barry: Md: Md.
Assist Surgeons:
1-John H Weir: Pa: Pa.
2-Saml D Scott: Pa: Pa.
Captains:
1-Wm B Taliaferro: Co A: Va: Va.
2-Martin M Moore: Co B: Pa: Pa.
3-Elisha W McComas: Co C: Va: Va.
4-Wm H Irwin: Co D: Pa: Pa.
5-Pemberton Waddell: Co E: Pa: Pa.
6-Geo W Chaytor: Co F: Md: Del
7-Lewis Carr: Co G: Pa: Pa.
8-Preslie N Guthrie: Co H: Pa: Pa
9-Arnold Syberg: Co I: Prussia: Pa.
10-Arthur C Cummings: Co K: Va: Va.
1st Lts:
4-John Motz: Han'r: Pa.
13-Chas T Campbell: Pa: Pa.
23-John I Gregg: blank: Pa.
31-Franklin Mehaffy: Pa: Pa.
41-Jos S Hedges: Del: Del.
57-Thos F McCoy: Pa: Pa.
68-Danl S Lee: Va: Va.
76-Marshall Hanson: Pa: Pa
89-Geo Davidson: blank: Ky.
94-Jas E Hamlett: Va: Va.
2nd Lts:
8-Wm H Gray: Pa: Pa.
19-Columbus P Evans: Pa: Del.
25-John Seddon: Va: Va.
40-Jos Samuels: Va: Va.
41-Benj F Harley: Pa: Pa.
54-Horace Haldeman: blank: Pa.
68-Geo C McClelland, Apr 9, 1847: former commission 2nd lt infty: resigned, 1846: Pa: Pa.

Following dated Apr 9, 1847:
74-Weidman Foster: blank: Pa.
86-Andrew H Tippin: Pa: Pa.
91-Alonzo Loring: N Y: Va.
109-Geo B Fitzgerald: Va: Va.
113-Wm H Scott: Va: blank.
125-Washington Meade: Pa: Pa.
131-Mitchell Stever: Pa: Pa.
144-Andrew Ross: blank: Pa.
156-H B Kuhn: blank: Pa.
159-Wm G Mury: blank: Pa.
173-Richd H L Johnston: blank: Pa.
187-Spear Nicholas: Va: Va.
12th Regt U S Infty: dated Apr 9, 1847:
Colonel: Louis D Wilson: blank: N C.
Lt Colonel: Milledge L Bonham: S C: S C.
Majors:
1-Mazey Gregg: S C: S C.
2-Vacancy.
Surgeon: Robt R Ritchie: Va: Va.
Assist Surgeons:
1-Alfred G Howard: S C: S C.
2-Leonard Randall: blank: Texas.
Captains:
1-Edw Manigault: Co A: S C: S C.
2-Nathl B Holden: Co B: blank: Mo.
3-Allen Wood: Co C: Pa: Ark.
4-Oliver P Hamilton: Co D: S C: S C.
5-Jas M Wells, former commission, 1st lt infty; resigned, 1839: Co E: Md: Texas.
6-J B Anthony: blank: Ark.
7-Walter J Clark: Co I: N C: N C.
10-C C Hornsby: Co K: blank: Texas.
1st Lts: dated Apr 9, 1847:
6-John F Hoke: N C: N C.
19-Chas R Jones: Pa: N C.
25-Wash L Wilson: N Y: Ark.
34-John J Martin: blank: S C.
42-A C Jones: blank: S C.
55-Chas Taplin: N Y: Mo.
70-Nathl G Dial: N Y: Texas.
78-John H H Felch: Mass: Ark.
86-John C Howard: blank: Texas.
55-Wm B Giles: Va: Mo. [Note: #55-Taplin & Giles.]

2nd Lts:
6-Chas M Creanor: blank: Texas.
20-Oscar D Wyche: Va: Texas.
26-Thos T Conway: blank: Ark.
33-Abner M Perrin: S C: S C.
50-Edw Cantwell: S C: N C.
56-Jas F Waddell: N C: N C.
62-Christ R P Butler: S C: S C.
79-J P Miller: blank: Ark.
81-Henry Almstedt: Hanov'r: Mo.
97-Wm A Linn: Mo: Mo.
98-Ormsby Blanding: blank: S C.
117-Robt Patton, jr: Va: Texas.
118-John J Wheeden: N C: N C.
130-Lloyd Magruder: blank: Ark.
147-Ed N Saunders: blank: N C.
150-Wm Reese: blank: Texas.
164-Alex'r E Steen: Mo: Mo.
171-John D Otterson: S C: S C.
176-Alden M Woodruff: blank: Ark.
181-John M Bronaugh: D C: Mo.
13th Regt U S Infty: dated Apr 9, 1847:
Colonel: Robt M Echols: Ga: Ga.
Lt Colonel:
Jones M Withers: former commission, 2nd lt dragoons, resigned, 1835: Ala: Ala.
Majors:
1-Jeremiah Clements: Ala: Ala.
2-Allen g Johnston: Ga: Fla.
Surgeon: John T Lamar: blank: Ga.
Assist Surgeons:
1-Robt T Gibbs: Va: Ala.
2-Franklin Malone: Ala: Ala.
Captains:
1-John Wofford: Co A: Tenn: Ga.
2-John Tyler, jr: Co B: Va: Va.
3-Walton Ector: Co C: Ga: Ga.
4-Alex'r Scott: Co D: Md: Ga.
5-John W Rice: Co E: S C: Ala.
6-Hiram H Higgins: Co F: Ky: Ala.
7-John B Campbell: Co G: S C: Ga.
8-Hugh P Watson: Co I: blank: Ala.
10-Henry E W Clarke: Co K: Ga: Fla.
1st Lts:
10-Adam Hawk: blank: Ala.
11-Duncan L Clinch, jr: Fla: Ga.

27-Eli P Howell: N C: Ga.
35-Jos A White: Ga: Ga.
49-Henry C Bradford: Ala: Ala.
58-Jas M Dye: Ga: Ga.
66-Geo W Clutter: Va: Va.
72-Robt S Hayward: Md: Fla.
83-John C Marrast: blank: Ala.
96-John S Hale: Tenn: Ala.
2nd Lts:
7-Nicholas Davis, jr: Ala: Ala.
21-Fitz H Ripley: Ala: blank.
32-Powhattan R Page: Va: Va.
37-John N Perkins: blank: Ala.
52-Danl Kirkpatrick: Ga: Ga.
70-Nathl Grant: Ga: Ga.
80-Edw J Dummett: Fla: Fla.
88-John C Mangham, jr: Ga: Ga.
104-David G Wilds: S C: Ga.
114-Isaac Hulse, jr: Md: Fla.
119-Wm D Grey: S C: Ga.
137-Mann P Hunter: Va: Va.
140-Oliver H Prince: Ga: Ga.
148-John P Wallace: blank: Ala.
166-Oliver Lowell: blank: Ala.
170-Saml H Crump: Ga: Ga.
178-John C Wellborne: blank: Ala.
189-Wm A Morrison: blank: Ala.
190-Marens L McMillion: blank: Ala.
192-John Sims: blank: Ala.
14th Regt U S Infty: dated Apr 9, 1847:
Colonel: Wm Trousdale: N C: Tenn.
Lt Colonel:
Paul O Hebert: former commission, 2nd lt engineers: resigned, 1845: La: La.
Majors:
1-John H Savage: blank: Tenn.
2-John D Wood: Va: Ill.
Surgeon: Lewis W Jordan: Tenn: Tenn.
Assist Surgeons:
1-Robt H McGinnis: Mass: Ohio.
2-Edw B Price: blank: Ill.
Captains:
1-Robt G Beale: Co A: blank: La.
2-Pierce B Anderson: Co B: Tenn: Tenn.
3-Edw F Nichols: Co C: blank: La.
4-Benj F Fulton: Co D: La: La.

5-Edgar Borgardus: Co E: N Y: Ill.
6-Thos Glenn: Co F: Del: La.
7-Jas M Scantland: Co G: blank: Tenn.
8-Julian P Breedlove: Co H: La: La.
9-Jos W Perkins: Co I: Tenn: Tenn.
10-Creed T Huddlestone: Co K: blank: Tenn.
1st Lts:
3-Jas Blackburn: La: La.
20-C M Haile: blank: La.
24-Thos Shields: Mi: La.
33-Philander A Hickman: Va: La.
48-Geo W Morgan: Tenn: Tenn.
59-Henry B Kelly: Ala: La.
67-Robt Humphreys: Tenn: Tenn.
73-Thos Smith: Va: Ill.
84-Nelson McClannahan: blank:Tenn.
91-Preston G Haynes: Tenn: Tenn.
2nd Lts:
1-A J McAllen: Tenn: Tenn.
14-Richd Steele: N Y: La.
22-Richd T Eastin: blank: La.
35-Jas G Fitzgerald: Ky: La.
46-Saml B Davis: La: La.
55-Wm H Seawell: Va: Tenn.
69-Albert G Moon: Va: Tenn.
72-John T Sanford: Va: La.
84-Robt W Bedford: Tenn: Tenn.
92-Saml H Martin: blank: Ill.
106-Hugh C Murray: Mo: Ill.
109-Perrin Watson: Tenn: Tenn.
127-Alex'r C Layne: Va: Va.
129-Andrew J Isaacs: blank: La.
142-John Chester: Tenn: Tenn.
155-Andrew J Hudson: Tenn: Tenn
161-Geo W Cheney: La: La.
185-Chas C Hays: Apr 12, 1847: blank: blank.
188-Saml T Love: Apr 15, 1847: blank: Tenn.
15th Regt U S Infty: dated Apr 9, 1847:
Colonel: Geo W Morgan: blank: Ohio.
Lt Colonel:
Joshua Howard: former commission captain infty; resigned 1835: Mass: Mich.
Majors:
1-Fred'k D Mills: Conn: Iowa.
2-Saml Woods: former commission captain infty: Indiana: M A.
Surgeon: Jas B Slade: N C: La.

Assist Surgeons: 1-Wm D Carlin: Ohio: Ohio; 2-Chas O Waters: blank: Iowa.
Captains:
1-Eugene Van de Venter: Co A: N Y: Mich.
2-Danl Chase: Co B: Conn: Ohio.
3-Jas A Jones: Co C: N Y: Ohio.
4-Edw A King: Co D: N Y: Ohio.
5-Isaac D Toll: Co E: N Y: Mich.
6-Augustus Quarles: Co F: blank: Wis.
7-Frazey M Winans: Co G: N J: Mich.
8-John S Perry: Co H: Ohio: Ohio.
9-Moses Hoagland: Co I: Ohio: Ohio.
10-Edwin Guthrie: Co K: N Y: Iowa.
1st Lts:
2-Geo W Bowie: Md: Iowa.
17-Wm S Tanneyhill: Md: Ohio.
22-Thos H Freelon: Vt: Mich.
36-Thornton F Brodhead: N H: Mich.
50-Diedrich Upman: Hono'r: Wis.
56-Levi Rhoads: N H: Ohio.
64-John B Miller: N Y: Ohio.
75-Ahira G Eastman: blank: Mich.
88-Edw C Marshall: Ky: Ohio.
92-Albert G Sutton: N J: Ohio.
2nd Lts:
5-John B Goodman: Pa: Mich.
17-Wm R Stafford: Md: Ohio.
29-Danl French: Ohio: Ohio.
36-Wm D Wilkins: Pa: Mich.
42-Chas Peternell: Baden: Ohio.
59-Jas W Wiley: N Y: Ohio.
65-Heman M Cady: N Y: Wis.
76-Cornelius Ketchum: N Y: Ohio.
82-Saml E Beach: N Y: Mich.
95-Francis O Beckett: Me: Iowa.
103-Danl McCleary: Ohio: Ohio.
112-Thos B Tilton: N Y: Ohio.
191-Llewellan Boyle: Md: Md.
136-Wm H H Goodloe: Ohio: Ohio.
141-Michl P Doyle: Ireland: Mich.
153-Edwin R Merrifield: N Y: Mich.
163-Abel W Wright: Conn: Wis.
174-Louis W Templeton: Ohio: Ohio.
175-Platt S Titus: N Y: Ohio.
184-John R Bennett: Md: Iowa.

16th Regt U S Infty: dated Apr 9, 1847:
Colonel: J W Tibbatts: Ky: Ky.
Lt Colonel: Henry L Webb: N Y: Ill.
Majors: 1-Ralph G Norvell: Tenn: Ind. 2-Jas M Talbott: Ind: Ind.
Surgeon: Geo Berry: Va: Ind.
Assist Surgeon: 1-Allen T Noe: blank: Ky.
2-Vacancy.
Captains:
1-Leslie H McKenney: Co A: Canada: Ill.
2-Chas Wickliffe: form'r commission, 2nd lt dragoons; out of service, 1842: Co B: Ky: Ky.
3-John A Hendricks: Co C: Ind: Ind.
4-Richd Owen: Co D: Scotl'd: Ind.
5-Theophilus T Garrard: Co E: Ky: Ky.
6-Edw A Graves: Co F: Ky: Ky.
7-Edmund B Bill: Co G: N Y: Ill.
8-Jos P Smith: Co H: N Y: Ind.
9-Thos F Bethell: Co I: Ind: Ind.
10-Jas W Brannon: Co K: Va: Ky.
1st Lts:
7-Patrick H Harris: Ky: Ky.
16-Geo W Singleton: Ky: Ky.
29-Edw Curd: Ky: Ky.
37-John T Hughes: Ky: Ind.
46-David W Scott: Va: Ind.
52-Chas J Helm: N Y: Ky.
69-Jas Hughes: N Y: Ind.
80-Jos Kellogg: blank: Ill.
98-Wm Hamer: blank: Ind.
99-Joab Wilkinson: blank: Ind.
2nd Lts:
2-Henry K Ramsey: Pa: Pa.
18-Orlando B Griffith: blank: Army
23-Jas M Smith: Ky: Ky.
34-Edw C Berry: Ky: Ky.
49-Wm H Slade: Ill: Ill.
60-Wm W Carr: Ind: Ind.
67-Oliver Dieffendorff: N Y: Ill.
71-Burwell B Irvan: Ky: Ky.
90-Alex'r Evans: Ky: Ky.
107-Francis McMordie: Ky: Ky.
110-Wm Cooper: Ind: Ind.
123-Marcellus M Anderson: blank: Va.
134-Barnard H Garrett: Ky: Ky.
139-Thos T Hawkins: blank: Ky.
152-Fred'k A Snyder: Ill: Ill.

167-Saml V Niles: Md: Ill.
186-John A Markley: blank: Ind.
Regt U S Foot Riflemen & Voltigeurs:
Colonel:
Timothy P Andrews: former commission Paymaster U S A: Ireland: D C.
Jos E Johnston, former commission Capt Top Engr: Va: M A.
Majors:
1-Geo A Caldwell: Ky: Ky.
2-Geo H Talcott, former commission 1st Lt Ord: N Y: M A.
Surgeon: dated Apr 9, 1847: John W Tyler: Va: D C.
Assist Surgeons: 1-Jas L Clark: Va: Va; 2-Aaron D Chaloner: blank: Pa.
Captains:
1-Alex P Churchill: Co A: Ky: Ky.
2-Oscar E Edwards: Co B: Va: Va.
3-John Jones: Co C: blank: Ga.
4-Oden Bowie: Co D: blank: Md.
5-Jas D Blair: Co E: Ky: Miss.
6-Chas J Biddle: Co F: Pa: Pa.
7-John E Howard: Co G: Md: Md.
8-Moses J Barnard: Co H: Mass: Pa.
9-Jas J Archer: Co I: Md: Va.
10-Jas H Calwell: Co K: Md: Va.
1st Lts:
5-Jas C Marriott: Md: Md.
15-Birkett D Fry: Va: Va.
30-Jas Tilton: Del: Ind.
40-Leonidas McIntosh: Fla: Ga.
44-Alex'r H Cross: D C: Md.
51-H C Longnecker: Pa: Pa.
62-Jas H Woolford: Md: Md.
77-Wm S Walker: Pa: Miss.
87-John M Blakey: Va: Va.
90-John W Leigh: Va: Va.
2nd Lts:
3-Chas F Vernon: Ky: Ky.
13-Robt C Forsyth: Ga: Ga.
27-Jas A Frost: Md: Md.
39-Theo D Cochran: Del: Pa.
43-Geo W Carr: Va: Va.
51-Jas M Winder: Md: Md.
63-Van Rensselaer Otey: blank: Va.
73-Robt Swan: Md: Md.
87-Gustavus S Kintzing: Pa: Pa.
96-Geo R Kiger: Va: Mi.
105-Wm J Martin: blank: Pa.

115-Jas W Smith: Va: Va.
120-Mich H Hooper: Md: Md.
132-Jas H Smythe: Md: Md.
138-Jas R May: Va: Va.
149-Edwin C Marvin: Conn: Pa.
162-Robt H Archer: Md: Md.
169-Washington Terrett: Va: Va.
177-Frank H Larned: Mich: Mich.
182-Jas E Slaughter: Va: Va.
<u>Relative Rank of Field Ofcrs & Captains: dated Apr 9, 1847:</u>
1-Edw G W Butler: 3rd Dragoons.
2-Timothy P Andrews: Voltigeurs.
3-Geo W Morgan: 15th Infty.
4-Louis D Wilson: 12th Infty.
5-Wm Trousdale: 14th Infty.
6-Albert C Ramsey: 11th Infty.
7-Robt E Temple: 10th Infty.
8-John W Tibbatts: 16th Infty.
9-Robt M Echols: 13th Infty.
10-Truman B Ranson: 9th Infty.
<u>Lt Colonels:</u>
1-Milledge L Bonham: 12th Infty.
2-Thos P Moore: 3rd Dragoons.
3-Wm M Graham: 11th Infty.
4-Jos E Johnston: Voltigeurs.
5-Abner B Thompson: 9th Infty.
6-Jones M Withers: 13th Infty.
7-John J Fay: 10th Infty.
8-Henry L Webb: 16th Infty.
9-Paul O Hebert: 14th Infty.
10-Joshua Howard: 15th Infty.
<u>Majors:</u>
1-Geo A Caldwell: Voltigeurs.
2-Jeremiah Clemens: 13th Infty.
3-Thos H Seymour: 9th Infty.
4-Lewis Cass, jr: 3rd Dragoons.
5-John H Savage: 14th Infty.
6-Edwin W Morgan: 11th Infty.
7-Ralph G Norvell: 16th Infty.
8-Fred'k D Mills: 15th Infty.
9-Fowler Hamilton: 10th Infty.
10-Maxcy Gregg: 12th Infty.
11-Wm H Emory: 3rd Dragoons.
12-Geo H Talcott: Voltigeurs
13-Saml Woods: 15th Infty.

14-Folliot T Lally: 9th Infty.
15-Allen G Johnston: 13th Infty.
16-Justus I McCarty: 10th Infty.
17-John F Hunter: 11th Infty.
18-John D Wood: 14th Infty.
19-Jas M Talbott: 15th Infty.
20-Vacant.
Captains:
1-Edw Manigault: 12th Infty.
2-Wm B Taliaferro: 11th Infty.
3-Leslie H McKenney: 16th Infty.
4-Jos S Pitman: 9th Infty.
5-Matthew S Pitcher: 10th Infty.
6-Green W Caldwell: 3rd Dragoons.
7-Alex'r P Churchill: Voltigeurs.
8-Robt G Beale: 14th Infty.
9-Eugene Van de Venter: 15th Infty.
10-John Wofford: 13th Infty.
11-Chas Wickliffe: 16th Infty.
12-Danl Chase: 15th Infty.
13-Oscar E Edwards: Voltigeurs.
14-John Butler: 3rd Dragoons.
15-Wm L Walradt: 10th Infty.
16-Nathl B Holden: 12th Infty.
17-Theodore F Rowe: 9th Infty.
18-Martin M Moore: 11th Infty.
19-Pierce B Anderson: 14th Infty.
20-John Tyler, jr: 13th Infty.
21-Jas A Jones: 15th Infty.
22-Edw F Nichols: 14th Infty.
23-John Jones: Voltigeurs.
24-Edgar B Gaither: 3rd Dragoons.
25-Wm R Andrews: 10th Infty.
26-Walton Ector: 13th Infty.
27-Stephen W Woodson: 9th Infty.
28-Elisha W McComas: 11th Infty.
29-Allen Wood: 12th Infty.
30-John A Hendricks: 16th Infy.
31-Richd Owen: 16th Infty.
32-Odin Bowie: Voltigeurs.
33-Benj F Fulton: 14th Infty.
34-Oliver P Hamilton: 12th Infty.
35-Alex'r Scott: 13th Infty.
36-Caleb Wilder: 10th Infty.
37-Wm H Irwin: 11th Infty.

38-Edw A King: 15th Infty.
39-Lemuel Ford: 3rd Dragoons.
40-E A Kimball: 9th Infty.
41-Wm H Duff: 3rd Dragoons.
42-John W Rice: 13th Infty.
43-Jas M Wells: 12th Infty.
44-Saml Dickinson: 10th Infty.
45-Theophilus T Garrard: 16th Infty.
46-Edgar Bogardus: 14th Infty.
47-Jas D Blair: Voltigeurs.
48-Pemberton Waddell: 11th Infty.
49-Andrew T Palmer: 9th Infty.
50-Isaac D Toll: 15th Infty.
51-J H Anthony: 12th Infty.
52-Augustus Quarles: 15th Infty.
53-Thos Postley: 10th Infty.
54-Chas J Biddle: Voltigeurs.
55-John S Sitgreaves: 3rd Dragoons.
56-Geo W Chaytor: 11th Infty.
57-Nathl S Webb: 9th Infty.
58-Hiram H Higgins: 13th Infty.
59-Thos Glenn: 14th Infty.
60-Edw A Graves: 16th Infty.
61-John E Howard: Voltigeurs.
62-John B Campbell: 13th Infty.
63-Alphonse M Duperu: 3rd Dragoons.
64-Lewis Carr: 11th Infty.
65-Frazey M Winans: 15th Infty.
66-Edmund B Bill: 16th Infty.
67-Jas W Thompson: 9th Infty.
68-Jas M Scantland: 14th Infty.
69-Walter P Richards: 12th Infty.
70-Jos A Yard: 10th Infty.
71-Hugh L W Clay: 13th Infty.
72-Presley N Guthrie: 11th Infty.
73-Julian P Breedlove: 14th Infty.
74-Richd T Merrick: 3rd Dragoons.
75-Moses J Barnard: Voltigeurs.
76-John S Perry: 15th Infty.
77-Joshua W Collett: 10th Infty.
78-Jos P Smith: 16th Infty.
79-Jas W Denver: 12th Infty.
80-Danl Bachelder: 9th Infty.
81-Thos F Bethell: 16th Infty.
82-Hugh P Watson: 13th Infty.

83-Wm J Clark: 12th Infty.
84-Arnold Syberg: 11th Infty.
85-Jos W Perkins: 14th Infty.
86-Jas Hagan: 3rd Dragoons.
87-Wm W Tompkins: 10th Infty.
88-Jas J Archer: Voltigeurs.
89-Lorenzo Johnson: 9th Infty.
90-Moses Hoagland: 15th Infty.
91-Jas W Branson: 16th Infty.
92-Jas H Calwell: Voltigeurs.
93-Creed T Huddlestone: 14th Infty.
94-Chas N Bodfish: 9th Infty.
95-Andrew T McReynolds: 3rd Dragoons.
96-Edwin Guthrie: 15th Infty.
97-Arthur C Cummings: 11th Infty.
98-Henry E W Clarke: 13th Dragoons.
99-C C Hornsby: 12th Infty.
100-Alex'r Wilkin: 10th Infty.
II-The relative rank of first & second lts is indicated by the number prefixed to the name in each grade respectively.
III-Promotions will be made in the 3rd Regt of Dragoons, the 8 Regts of Infty, & the Regt of Foot Riflemen & Voltigeurs, respectively, according to established rule. Original vacancies will be filled by selection.
IV-On organization of the several regts, the colonels will make the permanent assignment of the subalterns to companies, in such manner as the good of the service may require.
By order: R Jones, Adj Gen.

Shad Fishery for rent: located on the Potomac river, know as Col Fenwick's Bar, or the Bar Landing: in Pomonkey Neck, Chas Co, Md, midway between Craney Island & the White House. Address the undersigned, at Milestown P O, St Mary's Co, Md.
-Edmund L Plowden

Plan del Rio, Apr 17. The division of Gen Twiggs started 2 hours since, & a heavy cannonade has already commenced upon his line from the furthest of the Mexican works. I am going out with Cols Duncan & Bohlan & Cpt Pemberton, to the seat of action. I have just returned from the scene of conflict, & a bloody one it has been. The Rifles under Maj Sumner, & a detachments of artl & infty, charged up the rugged ascent where the enemy was this morning. Maj Sumner was shot in the head by a musket ball-severely but not mortally; Lts Maury & Gibbs, of the Rifles, were wounded, but not severely, as was also Lt Jarvis, of the 2nd Infty. The entire loss on our side, in killed & wounded, is estimated at about 100. -Mr Kendall

Mrd: on Apr 30, at Alexandria, by Rev J T Johnson, Albert H Dowell, of N C, to Miss Rosina Duffey, of Alexandria.

Mrd: on Wed, by Rev John C Smith, J Mortimer Kilgour, of Va, to Miss Martha W, daughter of the late Dr John Wootton, of Rockville, Md.

Mrd: on Thu, by Rev John C Smith, Mr John Pearce to Miss Martha Virginia Peyton, all of Wash City.

Camp near Plan del Rio: Apr 18. Among the prisoners is our old friend La Vega, who fought with his accustomed gallantry. The other generals are Jose Maria Jareno, Luis Pinson, Manuel Uoriaga, & Jose Obando. The loss on both sides has been heavy. The rifles, Col Haskell's Tennessee volunteers, the 1st Artl, the 7th Infty, & Capt Williams' company of Ky volunteers, have perhaps suffered the most. Gen Shields was severely, & I fear mortally wounded, while gallantly leading this brigade to storm one of the enemy's furthest works. Gen Pillow was slightly wounded, while storming a fortification on this side commanded by Gen La Vega. All the field ofcrs of Col Haskell's regt were wounded at the same time, same himself. Of the rifle, Capt Mason has lost a leg, Lt Ewell has been badly wounded, Lt McLane slightly. I think 500 will cover our entire loss.

Public sale of dwlg-house in the Seven Bldgs: by decree of the Circuit Court of Wash Co, D C, passed in a cause wherein John Ham & Mary his wife, & others, are cmplnts, & Judith Ham & Margaret Stoner & others are dfndnts, [heirs at law of Peter Ham, dec'd,] I will sell, at auction, on May 27, part of lot 1 & lot 13 in square 118, in Wash City; with a 3 story brick house. -W Redin, Trustee -B Homans-Auctioneer

Mexican ofcrs captured at Certo Gorda, on Apr 18, who have given their parole of honor to report themselves without delay to the Commandant of theAmerican forces at Vera Cruz as prisoners of war:
Jose Ma Jarero, Brig Gen
Romulo de la Vega, Brig Gen
P Ruiz y Baranda, Capt of Mexican Navy, commanding artl
Vicente Arguelles, Capt Artl
Jose Ma Matz, Capt
Jose Ma Gallegos, commanding Grenadiers
Mariano Camacho, 1st Lt Artl
Barthome Amable, 2nd Lt Artl
Jose R Cobarubiar, 2nd Lt Artl
Jose de Lastor Bras y Soller, Lt Col Btls dee la Libertad
Jose Nunez, Capt 6th Regt Infty
Jose Ma Moreno, Capt 6th Regt Infty
Gregorio del Callejo, Capt 6th Regt Infty
Rafael de Berrabidas, 2nd Lt 6th Regt Infty
Salveio Velez, Adi-de-Camp to Gen Vega
Francisco Fernandez, 1st Lt Mexican Navy
The above prisoners, under the charge of Capt Geo W Hughes, corps of Topographical Engineers, arrived at Vera Cruz on the 21st instant.

By virtue of 2 writs of fieri facias, issued by John L Smith, a justice of the peace in & for Wash Co, against the goods & chattels of Jas English & John Hennon, at the suit of Eleanah Waters, I have seized & taken in execution all the right, title, & interest of the said John Hennon in one long boat, with mast, sails, & rigging in complete order: said boat will be exposed for sale at 14th st bridge on May 11. -J F Wannall, Constable

Died: at N Y, Dr John Revere, a distinguished professor in the medical dept of the University of that city. He was a native of Boston, & formerly a resident of Balt. [No date-appears recent.]

Mrd: on May 5, in Fairfax, by Rev Mr Lockwood, Wm O Slade to Julia A, daughter of M Cook Fitzhugh, all of Fairfax Co, Va.

MON MAY 10, 1847

Land for sale: 20 acres of woodland in D C, 3 miles from Gtwn. Also, a quantity of Blue Granite. Apply on the premises to Mrs Mary A B Cummings, or to Edw S Wright, auct, Gtwn.

Land for sale: 20 acres of woodland in D C, 3 miles from Gtwn; & some Blue Granite. Apply on the premises to Mrs Mary A B Cummings, or to Edw S Wright, auct, Gtwn.

Plan del Rio, Apr 16. The wounds of Capt Johnston are doing well. I regret to state that Gen P F Smith is confined to his bed-utterly unable either to ride or walk. He has a violent inflammation of the right ankle & knee, resembling erysipelas, which, from neglecting several days when he should have remained in his cot, has finally compelled him to lay up. Plan del Rio, Apr 17. The enemy received their heaviest loss, & their Gen Vasquez was killed. Gen Shields was not so fortunate in the battery which he attacked, & which was commanded by Gen La Vega. A heavy fire was opened on him, under which the fort was carried with some loss by the gallant Illinoisians, under Baker & Bennett, supported by the New Yorkers, under Burnett. Among those who fell under this fire was the gallant Gen, who received a grape shot through his lungs, by which he was completely paralyzed, &, at the last accounts, was in a lingering state. A gallant young ofcr named Halzinger, a German by birth, who extorted the admiration of our army in the bombardment of Vera Cruz, by seizing a flag which was cut down by our balls & holding it up in his hand until a staff could be prepared, had been released by Gen Scott without a parole. He was found among the desperately wounded at Cerro Gordo.

The U S ship **Jamestown**, laden with provisions for the relief of the Irish, & commanded by Robt B Forbes, arrived safely at Cork from Boston, after a prosperous & splendid passage of 15 days.

Ad in the N Y C papers which reached here yesterday: "New York, Apr 30, 1847. This is to give notice that John Henry Covill left his bed & board somewhere in the middle of Dec, 1846; &, if he gives no information where he can be heard from within 3 months, I shall get married again & leave the city. Elizabeth Covill."

An attempt was made to tar & feather Wm Burr, living at Gtwn, near Mercer, Pa, some night since. He received warning & with Mr Stanley, prepared a defence. First to arrive was H Wick who received a stroke from an axe which nearly severed his shoulder from his body; Jas Craig was struck on the side, cutting through to the back bone and died soon after. Burr & Stanley were both very severely beaten, & Geo Palm, G Flick, & others of the assailants, were wounded. Burr & his companion fled.

Mr Saml Neeper, a very respectable citizen of Peace Bottom township, in York Co, Pa, committed suicide on Apr 27, by hanging himself in a room of his dwlg. No cause assigned for the melancholy deed.

A large fire at Balt: Sunday: J & J Williams' extensive cabinet warehouse, on South, near Pratt st; Wm Chesnut's large grocery store, Pratt & South sts; Kernan's bakery, adjoining; also, Middleton's tobacco establishment; Jas Dowell's store, & Hamilton's adjoining, were destroyed by fire this afternoon.

Headquarters of the Army, Plan del Rio, 50 miles from Vera Cruz, Apr 19, 1847. Our loss has been serious. Brig Gen Shields, a commander of activity, zeal, & talent, is, I fear, if not dead, mortally wounded. He is some 5 miles from here at the moment. Pillows brigade is near here, & 1st Lt F B Nelson, & 2nd C G Gill, both of the 2nd Tenn foot, [Haskell's Regt,] are among the killed. Among the wounded: the gallant Brig Gen himself has a smart wound in the arm, but not disabled, & Maj R Farqueson, 2nd Tenn; Capt H F Murray, 2nd Lt, G T Sutherland, 1st Lt W P Hale, [adj] all of the same regt, severely, & 1st Lt W Yearwood, mortally wounded. 1st Lt Ewell, of the rifles, if not now dead, mortally wounded, in entering, sword in hand, the entrenchments around the captured tower. 2nd Lt Derby, topo gen, severely wounded. Capt Patten, 2nd U S Infty, lost his right hand. Maj Sumner, 2nd U S Dragoons, was slightly wounded the day before, & Capt Johnston, topo eng,[now lt colonel of infty,] was very severely wounded some days earlier while reconnoitering. Capt Mason & 2nd Lt Davis, both of the rifles, were very severely wounded in storming the same tower. Highest praise is due to Harney, Childs, Plymton, Loring, Alexander, their gallant ofcrs & men, for their brilliant service. Maj Gen Patterson left a sick bed to share in the dangers & fatifues of the day. -Winfield Scott [To the Hon Wm L Marcy, Sec of War.]

A Painting of Wash City: by John Henry Drury: a fellow citizen: this picture is 12 feet by 25 feet: the city appears, extending far away to the Potomac, displaying Pa ave, the Patent & Gen Post Ofcs, Pres' House, City Hall, Churches, the College & steeples of Gtwn, & all that magnificent panorama towards the west & north. Mr Drury intends exhibiting the View of Washington throughout the Western & Southern States.

Obit-died: recently, Wm Wood, one of this community's oldest & most valuable citizens, & one of the Christian Church's brightest members. For many years he was a clerk in the Gen Land Ofc: he was a devoted husband & a kind father; & though his afflictions in his last sickness were most severe, he cast his sufferings on the Lord; looking to the end as a release from all his trials, he waited patiently till his change came.

To let or lease: house on s e corner of F & 12th sts, opposite the drug store of W Elliot, where terms can be ascertained.

Mrd: on Apr 29, at Phil, by Rev Mr Howe, Pastor of St Luke's, Winfield S Belton to Rebecca, daughter of Purser S P Todd, U S Navy.

Died: on May 7, in Wash City, Mrs Mary Ann Groves, consort of W H Groves, & daughter of Remegius Burch, late of Washington, of a long & painful illness, in her 30th year. Blessed are the dead that die in the Lord.

Died: on May 9, Jas Francis, a native of the county of Derry, Ireland, aged about 39 years. He served for several years in the U S Army, & received a wound in his left leg in the Florida war. His funeral is this evening, at 4 o'clock, from his late residence at the Cross Keys.

Died: on May 7, at ***Greenleaf's Point***, after a short illness, Mr Aaron McAlwee, for the last 17 years employed as a mechanic at the U S Arsenal, leaving a wife & a large family of small children dependent on his daily labor for their support. He was an honest man, a kind parent, a faithful friend, & universally esteemed by all who knew him.

TUE MAY 11, 1847

Thos Hunn, for many years Cashier of the Nat'l Bank of N Y, died on Wed, in his 64th year. He was a highly respectable citizen, & enjoyed the general esteem of the community. -Post

Cheap Boot & Shoe Store: opposite Brown's Hotel, & formerly occupied by his father. Having engaged the services of his father to attend the manufacturing branch of the business, he is enabled to sell his own work cheaper than can be bought in the city for cash. -Jas Jack, jr

Orphans Court of PG Co, Md. In the matter of the right of Martha Young, a professed Nun, to administration on Notley Young's personal estate. Ordered by the Court that on the petition of Geo H Smith & Eloise his wife, filed May 8, praying that letters of administration on the personal estate of Notley Young, late of PG Co, may be granted to him or them, that a summons be issued by the Register to Benj F Young, of PG Co, named in said petition, & also Martha Young, stated in said petition to be a dght of said Notley Young & a nun, resident in D C, be notified of the filing of said petition in the usual manner of this Court, in reference to non-residents, by advertisement in some newspaper in D C, notifying them, the said Benj F Young & Martha Young, to appear in this Court on or before May 19, to answer the matter contained in said petition; Messrs C C Magruder & C Cox, gentlemen professing to be her attorneys. -Thos Duckett, Thos J Marshall, Wm B Hill. [I Jas Harper, Reg/o wills for PG Co, do hereby certify that the above order is truly taken & copied from the Court proceedings.
-Jas Harper, Reg/o wills for PG Co]

Lt Julian May, U S Rifles, was slightly wounded at the battle of Cerro Gordo. Ex-Pres Herreta is said to be one of the Mexicans captured at Cerro Gordo. He was discharged on parole of honor with the other generals.

Mrd: May 6, in Wash City, by Rev Mr Van Horseigh, Mr Jos F Little to Miss Mary M Arth, both of Wash.

Mrd: on May 2, at Harper's Ferry, Va, by Rev Nelson Head, Mr Jos R White, formerly of Wash City, to Miss Elilia A Wood, of the former place.

Died: on Apr 20 last, at ***Cedar Hill***, PG Co, Md, after a sudden but severe illness, Mrs Margaret W Bowie, consort of Robt Bowie, of said county.

Died: on Fri last, in Upper Marlborough, Md, Mrs Mary M, consort of Dr Richd K Osborn, & only daughter of Dr Benj B Hodges, in her 18th year.

Died: on May 6, in Richmond, Va, of inflammation of the bowels, Dr Augustus L Warner, Prof of Surgery in the Medical Dept of Hampden Sydney College. He was for several years Prof of Anatomy & Surgery in the Univ of Va, which post he resigned about 9 years since, & removed to Richmond for the purpose of establishing a medical school in the metropolis of Va.

Homicide: Some intoxicated young men attempting, on Sunday night last, to break into a house in the First Ward, where a young man, Geo Usher, was lodging, the latter fired at one of the assailants named Richd Harry, & killed him on the spot. [Jul 4th newspaper: verdict of not guilty.]

Valuable property for sale: the St Charles Hotel, 3rd st & Pa ave: contains about 40 rooms & 6 stores. -Chas Lee Jones

WED MAY 12, 1847

Capt Alex Churchills' company of Voltigeurs were to leave New Orleans on May 2 in the steamer **Telegraph**. Capt Walker's company was to leave on the following day. Gen Brooke yesterday received orders from the War Dept in Wash to muster into service 5 companies of infty & 2 of cavalry from this State, & 5 companies of infty & 1 of cavalry from Alabama.

Valuable brick house & dairy establishment at auction: on May 14, the handsome brick house & lot at the north end of 7th st west, adjoining the farm of J A Smith, containing nearly an acre of ground, with the improvements, which are a well built 2 story brick house & all necessary out bldgs. Also for sale: 1 Organ & 1 Piano Forte, & a lot of Dairy implements. 2 horses, 2 milk carts, 2 sets of gear, 20 cow-chains, patent straw-cutter, & farm articles. -A Green, auctioneer [Also will be sold, a good lot of household & kitchen furniture, the property of Mr Johnson, at the extreme end of 7th st north.
-A Green, auctioneer]

Quaker turned Roman Catholic. On Mar 4 baptism, according to the Roman ritual, was conferred by Dr Brown, of Wales, & afterward confirmation, upon Mr Jabez M Gibson, till then a member of the Society of Friends. Two years since he met at the house of a common friend, near Rome, the present Pope, then Cardinal Archbishop, Bishop of Imola, & discussed with him topics of religion. -N Y Observer

San Diego, Upper California, Dec 12, 1846. I left Santa Fe, New Mexico, on Sep 25, with 306 of the 1st Dragoons, under Maj Sumner. On Oct 6 we met Mr Kit Carson, with a party of 16 men, on his way to Wash City, with a mail & papers, an express from Cmdor Stockton & Lt Col Fremont, reporting the Californians were already in possession of the Americans under their command; that the American flag was flying from every important territory, & that the country was forever free from Mexican control. -J W Kearny, Brig Gen U S Army: to Brig Gen R Jones, Adj Gen U S Army

Lt Moriarty, R N, has been appointed emigration agent for the post of Balt.

The ship **Charles**, Capt Knox, of Boston, has arrived at New Bedford from Honolulu, Dec 26, bringing a million pounds of whalebone & 8,000 hides. On board the ship was Mrs Beck, 34 years of age, widow of Capt Wm Beck, late of the ship **Atlantic** of New London, who took passage at Honolulu, having a few weeks previously sustained the loss of her husband on board the **Atlantic**, whose remains had been committed to the deep with the customary solemnities 4 days before the arrival of the **Atlantic** at that port. On Jan 30th, not appearing in the morning, it was found she had thrown herself from the cabin window & perished. Mrs Beck accompanied her husband on his last voyage from New London, Aug 5, 1845. -Merc

Green-house plants at auction: on May 13, from the celebrated & well-known green-houses of R Halliday & Chas U Stober, of Balt. -A Green, auctioneer

Orphans Court of Wash Co, D C. Letters of administration on the personal estate of John Kennedy, late of said county, dec'd. -Susanna M Kennedy, admx

Wash Corp: 1-Ptn from Christopher C Clement & Wm A Griffith: referred to the Cmte of Claims. 2-Ptn from J & G S Gideon & others: referred to the Cmte on Improvements. 3-Bills for the relief of Jonathan Chapman; of David Rich; & of L H Berryman: passed. 4-Cmte of Claims: discharged from the petitions of Wm D Bell, Jane Fagans, Mary W P Handy & Susan D Anderson, Wm Wesley McNair, F O'Neall, & R R Golden.

$25 reward for runaway negro girl. She has some bumps upon her forehead, & it can be perceived that she is somewhat pregnant. She formerly belonged to H N Young.
-Louis Marceron, Navy Yard

For rent: my former residence, at present occupied by S R Hobbie, on 4½ st, opposite the Presbyterian Church. I also wish to purchase a girl 14 years old, or a woman not exceeding 22 years. I wish her for a relation residing in Md. -W G W White

THU MAY 13, 1847

Murder in Dorchester. Cambridge [Md] Chronicle: a nego man named Denwood Camper committed an atrocious murder on Tue last, near New Market, upon the person of another negro. The murderer dispatched his victim with a grubbing hoe, & afterwards cut off his head. He was arrested & made a full confession. The quarrel originated about parched corn.

An American lady, who received her education in Europe, wishes to enter a private family as Governess. Letters addressed [post paid] to Miss F C Nottingham, PG Co, Md, will meet with prompt attention.

For rent: brick house on D st, between 7th & 8th sts. Apply at Mrs Varnum's, 8th st.

Accident on board the ship **Euphrasia**, Capt Buntin, of & from Boston, for Alexandria, on Sunday, whilst lying at anchor in Washington's Reach, in the Potomac river. Capt Buntin had left the ship to procure a steamer to tow up his vessel. During his absence the pilot, desirous of getting a better anchorage, ordered a boat to carry out a small anchor, with a view of warping off. The boat swamped, & 5 men drowned: the 2nd mate, Mr Richd Lyons Entwistle; seamen, John Cruse, Alex'r Sillan, Jas Brown, place of nativity unknown, & John Hale, of Newburyport. The rest were rescued by a yawl from a vessel at anchor near by.

By wreck of the English mail-steamer **Tweed** the number of passengers lost was 31, crew 42. Saved: passengers 28, crew 52. Most of the passengers lost appear to have been Spaniards. The publication of the following complete list of them may serve to quiet unnecessary fears:

Mr Yurchanote	Mr Fontnha	Gen Chaulier
Mr Escueno	Mr Barrimeria	Mr Robinson
Mr Larado	Mr Meruende	Mr Seidurbergh
Mrs Escudeno-child-& child	Mr Boom	Mr Gartman
	Mr Rermante	Mr Maspule
Mr Serbrau	Mr Guxruga	Mr Vivings
Mr Fox	Mr Portillo	Mr Santo
Mr Cuvill	Mr Gonzales	Mr Ladira
Mr Cofer	Mr Mathias	Mr Fuentes
Mr Torpete	Mrs Jones & son	

The residence of Solomon Danner, at Chambersburg, Indiana, was burnt to the ground on Apr 17. Three of his children were burnt to death.

Died: on May 11, in Gtwn, William Edward, infant son of Jas Gray & Mary Jane Griffith, aged 13 months.

A fire broke out in the shops of Messrs P Hayden & Co, in the Ohio State Prison at Columbus, on May 7, which consumed the entire eastern wing of shops. The convicts labored hard to extinguish the flames.

For rent: a neat Cottage on Capitol Hill, containing 5 bed rooms & 4 parlors, a kitchen on the same floor, & a room for servants, together with a large garden. Inquire of Seth Hyatt.

FRI MAY 14, 1847
The Phil papers announce the death of Dr Geo McClellan, a distinguished Surgeon & Physician of that city. On Sat he was seized with a bilious cholic & died about midnight.

As the train was passing the Centre st railroad depot on Mon, the 13 year old son of Jas Law, of Newark, attempted to jump from the cars to the platform. He fell under the wheels & was instantly killed. -Newark Advertiser

Particulars of the capture of Tuspan: from the Vera Cruz Eagle of Apr 28. The expedition consisted of the steamer **Mississippi**, [flag-ship,] frig **Raritan**, sloop of war **Albany**, ship **John Adams**, ships **Germantown**, **Decatur**, **Spitfire**, **Vixen**, ships **Scourge**, **Vesuvius**, **Hecla**, & ships **Etna**, **Bonita**, **Petrel** & **Reefer**. Among the vessels were distributed 150 men belonging to the ship **Potomac**, & 340 belonging to the ship **Ohio**, both of which remained at this place. Cmdor Perry hoisted his broad pennant on board the **Spitfire**, & at once led the rest of the vessels up the river. A little while and 2 forts were discovered, both of which opened upon the squadron. In a little while another fort opened upon the vessels & barges. This latter fort was promptly attacked, as were the other two. In the course of the contest our were: Capt Tatnall received a ball in the right elbow joint. Lt Jas L Parker, aid to the Cmdor, a severe wound in the upper part of the left breast. Lt Whittle a flesh wound in the right leg, & Lt Haristene a flesh wound in the right wrist & thigh. All are doing well. It may be proper to state that all the forts of the place were destroyed by our forces.

Trustee's sale: by deed of trust from Mathias Jeffers & others to me, dated Jul 25, 1842, & recorded in Liber W B 96, folios 55 through 60 of the Wash Co land records: auction on Jun 10 next, in front of the premises: the west half of lot 5 in square A, of Wash City, with a commodious brick dwlg, 2 stories high, upon it, besides a high basement.
-John Kurtz, Trustee -R W Dyer, auct

Fire on May 6 at Nashville, Tenn, on College st, destroyed the dwlgs of John D Goss, Mrs Harris, Mrs Austin, the cabinet shop of Y S Patton, & the livery stable of Garnet & Singleton.

Mrd: on May 11, in Wash City, by Rev Mr Matthews, of the Presbyterian Church, Mr John C Brooks, of Portland, Maine, to Miss Caroline W Parris, daughter of the 2nd Comptroller of the Treasury.

From the Vera Cruz Eagle of Apr 28. Some of the Mexicans ofcrs, [prisoners,] Maj H G Bennet, Capt Montgomery, Lt Sorvera, & Lt Sanders, 1st Dragoons, came passengers in the ship **New Orleans**, & 150 discharged volunteers & teamsters.

SAT MAY 15, 1847

Naval: Trial, Defence, & repremand of Lt Chas G Hunter before a Naval Court Martial. Charges & Specifications.

Charge 1-Treating with contempt his superior, being in the execution of his ofc.

Specification First: in that Lt Hunter, on Mar 31, 1847, being then in command of the U S steamer **Scourge**, enter the port of Alvarado, & did there arrogate to himself the authority & power that are vested only in the Cmder-in-Chief, by entering into stipulations for, & receiving the surrender of, Alvarado & its dependents.

Specification Second: in that Lt Hunter, on Mar 31, 1847, with the steamer **Scourge** under his command, proceed from Alvarado to Tiscotalpan, without orders or authority, & there demand the surrender of the last named town, although aware of the immediate approach of the Cmder-in-Chief, whom alone such powers are confided.

Specification Third: in that Lt Hunter, did, on Mar 31, 1847, in proceeding from Alvarado to Flacotalpan, capture 4 schnrs, one of which he set on fire & burnt, & another he abandoned, thus substituting his own will for the discretion of the Cmder-in-Chief, who was within a few hours reach of communication.

Charge Second: Disobedience of orders. Specification First: in that he, Lt Hunter, having been ordered to report to Capt Saml L Breese, & to assist in blockading the port of Alvarado, did, in disobedience or disregard of said orders, enter the harbor & take possession of Alvarado.

Specification Second: in that Lt Hunter, having been ordered, on Apr 1, 1847, to report himself in person to the Cmder-in-Chief at his quarters in Alvaraado, did disobey said order. -M C Perry, Commanding Home Squadron.

Defence of Lt Hunter: My first error was one of simple ignorance. In the second specification of the second charge: I was so absorbed by the difficulties that surrounded me that his order to report myself entirely escaped my recollecion. This may seem a lame excuse, but it has at least the merit of truth. I have aimed at nothing but the glory of my country-the honor & dignity of the service to which I belong. I leave my case with perfect confidence in your hands. -C G Hunter, Lt Comd'g

Sentence of the Court: That the accused, Lt Chas G Hunter, U S Navy, be dismissed from the U S Home Squadron, & reprimanded by the cmder-in-chief, which reprimand is to be read on the quarter deck of every vessel of the squadron, in the presence of the ofcrs & crew. -J Bryan, Judge Advocate

Reprimand of Cmdor Perry: U S Flag ship **Mississippi**, Anton Lizardo, Apr 9, 1847. However lenient the sentence in your case may seem to be, I have approved it; as I can conceive of no punishment more severe than a dismissal in time of war from a squadron actively engaged before the enemy. It would be difficult, if not impossible, to point to another instance of similar folly; & that the most charitable construction that can be given to it is, that, in the elation of a first command, you had truly imagined yourself actually in command of the naval & military detachments then approaching & within a short distance of the scene of your exploits. With due respect, M C Perry, Cmder-in-Chief of Home Squardon

Notice: I hereby notify all persons indebted to the late business of Jas B Clarke to come forward & settle their accounts without delay. -Richd G Briscoe, Trustee

Orphans Court of Wash Co, D C. Letters of administration on the personal estate of Thos J Davis, late of said county, dec'd. -Isabella Davis, Wm Winn, adms [John Marbury, of Gtwn, D C, is appointed our atty. -Isabella Davis, Wm Winn, adms]

Col Jas S McIntosh, of the U S Army, who was severely wounded in the battle of Resaca de la Palma, left Savannah on May 5 for Mexico, to resume his duties. One of his arms is yet almost useless from the effects of his wounds. A splendid sword was presented him by the citizens of Savannah for his gallantry. This was done privately, conformly to his wishes.

Col Ormsby, Maj Shepherd, Adj Riddle, Surgeons Caldwell & Matthews, Capts Harper, Bohn, Stewart, Schroeder, Howe, Kim, & Saunders, Lts L White, W White, & Hilton, in all 28 ofcrs, including the Staff, & 405 men, of the Louisville Legion, have arrived at New Orleans from the Brasos. They were mustered out of the service in New Orleans.

A set of dinner china of 45 pieces, 100 years old, & probably older, now held by one of his descendants, is pronounced by Mr Kirk not to have been made within the last 200 years. It was the property of one of the Presidents of the Revolutionary Congress of the U S, who died in 1783, & was married about 1746. No bid under $500 will be attended to. It is of the richest enameled East India fabric. Samples may be seen at Mr Brunner's Book-store. -Balt

$20 reward for runaway negro boy Sandy, aged about 19 years. -Zadock Robinson, living in PG Co, Md, near Piscataway.

Died: on May 8, at his residence in Anne Arundel Co, after a painful illness, Mr Isaac G Magruder, in his 45th year, leaving a widow & 4 children to lament their irreparable loss.

Died: on May 10, at Cornwall Furnace, Lebanon Co, Pa, in the family of her son-in-law, John Reynolds, Mrs Jane Moore, relict of the late Capt Saml Moore, of the Army of the Revolution, in her 79th year.

MON MAY 17, 1847

The Architect of the Smithsonian Bldg has furnished us with the annexed correct list of the articles deposited in the corner stone of the edifice laid on May 1st. The different coins of the U S; report of the Cmte on Organization; the New Testament; Declaration of Independence; Constitution of the U S; Congressional Directory of 1847; bulletins of the Nat'l Institute; report of the first Nat'l Fair at Washington; report of the U S Agent appointed to receive the legacy of Jas Smithson; medal portrait of Jas Smithson; reports

of the Com'r of Patents; journal of the preceedings of the Board of Regents, 1846; an engraved plate, with the following inscription:
following inscription:
On the First day of May, 1847, was laid,
In the city of Washington,
This foundation stone of a building, to be appropriated for the
Smithsonian Institution.
Jas K Polk,
President of the United States.
Corporation.
President of the U States,
Secretary of State,
Secretary of War,
Postmaster General,
Chief Justice
Vice President of the U States,
Secretary of the Treasury,
Secretary of the Navy,
Attorney General,
Commissioner of Patents,
Chief Justice of the U States,
Mayor of the city of Washington.
Board of Regents.
George M Dallas, Vice President of the United States.
Roger B Taney, Chief Justice.
W W Seaton, Mayor of the city of Washington.
Lewis Cass, United States Senator
Sidney Breese, United States Senator
James A Pearce, United States Senator.
Robert Dale Owen, United States Representative.
William J Hough, United States Representative.
Henry W Hilliard, United States Representative.
Rufus Choate, Massachusetts.
Richard Rush, Pennsylvania.
Gideon Hawley, New York.
William C Preston, South Carolina
A Dallas Bache, National Institute.
Joseph G Totten, National Institute.
Officers: George M Dallas, Chancellor.
Executive Committee.
W W Seaton, chairman; Jos G Totten, Robt Dale Owen.
Building Committee.
Robt Dale Owen, chairman; Jos G Totten, Wm W Seaton.
Joseph Henry, Secretary. C C Jewett, Assistant Secretary.
Jas Renwick, jr, Architect.

Robt Mills, Assistant Architect & Superintendent.
James Dixon & Gilbert Cameron, Contractors.
The address of the Chancellor of the Institution on laying the corner stone; astronomical observations made at the Nat'l Observatory; a copy of the directory of the day; the city newspaper of the day; Box deposited by the Freemasons, containing a Bible; a silver plate inscribed with the names of the ofcrs of the Grand Lodge of D C; stereotype plate of the title page of Bancroft's History of the U S; Constitution & By-laws of the Grand Lodge of D C; seal of Federal Lodge of D C. The Grand Master then applied the square, level, & plumb, & the pronounced the stone squared, duly laid, true & trusty. He placed upon the stone the corn, wine, & oil: bread to feed the hungry, wine to cheer the sorrowful, & oil to heal the wounds. The Grand Master gave 3 raps upon the stone with the gavel of Washington.

Reporters wanted: several experienced Stenographers during the next session of Congress. Communications to be post paid, & addressed to Dr J A Houston, N Y.
-Jas A Houston, Stenographer to the U S Senate, Wash, Mar 15, 1847.

City Ordinances-Wash: 1-Act for the relief of Rudolph Eichhorn, that a fine imposes for an alleged violation of a law relative to renting stalls in the market, be remitted: provided he pay the costs of prosecution. 2-Act for the relief of John P Stallings: that the fine imposed, for violating a law relating to pumps, & hydrants; be remitted: provided he pay the cost of prosecution. 3-Act to pay John Fletcher for paving the gutter on square 427: the sum of $31.70, agreeable to the certificate of the Surveyor of Wash, dated Nov 16, 1846. 4-Act to pay John Dove for work done on 7th st: the sum of $34.50. 5-Act for the relief of Eve Rupert: that the fine for an alleged violation relative to taverns & ordinances, be remitted: provided Rupert pay the cost of prosecution. 6-Act for the relief of L H Randolph: to be paid $124, in full for her services as assistant teacher in the second school district.

Dr John Hill, Pres of the Bank of Cape fear, died at his residence in Wilmington, N C, on May 9, aged 51. This event had been expected for some time from the precarious state of his health.

The killed, wounded, & missing at Cerro Gordo: of the 2nd Division of Regulars, commanded by Gen David E Twiggs. List forwarded by Mr Kendall. First Brig, consisting of the 1st Artl, the Rifles, & the 7th Infty, all under Col Harney.

<u>Ofcrs wounded:</u>

Maj E V Sumner	Lt Thos Davis	Lt Alfred Gibbs
Capt Stevens T Mason	Lt Geo McLane	Lt N J T Dana
Lt Thos Ewell	Lt Dabney H Maury	

<u>Rank & file killed:</u>

Jas Harbison	Dabney Ware	Wm McDonald
Th J Pointer	Chas Willis	C Armstrong
Benj McGee	Wm Cooper	Saml M Roberts
Conrad Kuntz	Geo Collins	Michl Dailey

Robt Wright
Edm Foley
Wm Myers
Lewis Bolio
Jas McDerby
John M Seaton
John Lynch
Francis O'Neill
Isaac Dolen
Griffin Budd
Patrick Casey
Danl Dolay
A Hartzman
Chas Skinner
Jos Wood
Francis Perrod

<u>Rank & file wounded:</u>

Jeremiah Beck
Lewis P Arnold
John McCormick
Wm W Miller
John McCauly
Thos G Hester
David Kealing
Ransom Ross
Saml N Bitner
Wm F Ford
Ebenr N Brown
John Samson
W W Breeden
Edw Allen
Alex'r Evans
Wm Butterfield
Jacob Myers
Darw Carpenter
Thos Sloan
Geo W Gillespie
John Raney
Jos Windle
H Zimmerman
Thos Goslin
Jas McGowan
Wm A Miller
Chas Jones
Wm J Scrivener
Carter L Vizers
Jas A Adams
Geo Sampson
David Bear
Wm Hammerly
W R Leechman
Saml Gilman
John M Robinson
H Louis Brown
Justus Freeman
Adam Ryan
John Hooker
Lindsey Hooker
John Walker
Hezekiah Hill
Wm Higgin
Wm Forbes
Ira White
Geo Tucker
Chas H W Boln
Chas A Alburn
Hiram Bell
Wm H Preston
Wm Scheder
John Lipp
Jos Vogle
John Spencer
Thos Conway
Adams L Ogg
Calvin Bruner
Thos Workman
Ferd Littlebrand
Hiram Melvin
Marinus Lang
David Ferguson
Chas Foster
Gottl'b Bacumlo
Geo Bryding
Stephen Rennison
Julius Schramm
Fred'k Moil
Nat J Campbell
Thos Williams
Patrick Anthony
Anthony Bracklin
Saml Downey
Matthew Eugan
Geo Hamlin
Michl Harley
Jas Keegan
Orin Lawton
John Rooney
John S Sloan
Wm H Webber
John Woolley
Jas Burnet
Thos Lynes
Andrew Wright
John Heynes
John Teahan
John Bandorf
Adam Kock
Patrick Kane
A R Huntington
Nicholas Griffin
Jas West
Jas M Holden
Thos Sullivan
H J Manson
Saml Cline
R S Cross
Jonathan Marsh
Jas Eccles
John Crangle
John Brayman
Nicholas Bradley
John Carter
Patrick Dunighan
Jas Garard
John Jones
Jacob Halpin
Denis McCrystal
Encas Lyons
Edw Peters
Christopher Elliott
Jas Godfrey

C S Hopner	John Sheehan	Walter Root
Wm Langwell	John Barnes	David Radd
John Gillighin	Neill Donelly	Peter McCabe
Chas Johnson	Parick Healy	__ Thompson
Jas Joice	Danl Downs	Aaron Hansford
John Lee	John Frunks	Jas Hanner
John McMahan	Saml Ratcliffe	Wm Sprague
Thos O'Callaghan	Peter Maloney	David Whipple
Wm Robinson	John Davidson	Paul McCrae
John Smith	Michl Dwyer	Jos Bruner
Geo Wakeford	Jas Flynn	Conrad Fischer
Chas Bierwith	Michl Ryan	

Missing: Lewis Monroe

Second Brigade, consisting of the 4th Artl & 2nd & 3rd Infty, under Col Riley:

Ofcrs wounded: Capt Geo W Paten

Lt Chas E Jarvis	Lt J N Ward	Lt B E Bee

Rank & file killed:

Jas Olsted	Wm Turner	Jas Conway
John Schenecke	Jas Mellish	Giles Ischam
Michl Christal	Wm Scott	
Andrew Divin	Jas Wilson	

Rank & file wounded:

Francis A Dona	Alpheus Russell	John D Son
Wm Pollock	Henry Carleton	J B Bichardson
Danl Hogan	Geo Dunn	Wm Kenney
Patrick Sheridan	Robt Foulder	Chas Smith
Jacob Carr	Richd Vickers	Laurence Matten
Geo M Deny	Gustavus Miller	Silas Chappel
Jas Harper	John Wallace	Andrew Munsch
Henry Quill	GeoW Stacey	John Gallin
Richd Crangle	Danl Tenatt	Geo Reed
Morris Welsh	Michl Madigan	Levi S Cory
Lyman Hodgden	Wm Van Tassel	Almon E Marsh
Timothy Burn	David Kerr	John McCenvill
Jas McCullough	Nicholas Tyant	Stephen Garber

Light Co 1st Artl:

Wounded: Chas Kallmyer; Geo Campbell

Racket & Howitzer Battery:

Wounded: Lt Geo H Gordon; Pvt Moses L Kinney

Detachment:

Wounded: Lt Col Jos E Johnston- severely; Graff

Killed: Croley

3rd Brig, consisting of the N Y Volunteers & 3rd & 4th Illinois Volunteers, under Gen Shields:

Ofcr Killed: Lt G M Cowarden

Ofcrs wounded:

Gen Jas Shields	Lt Robt C Scott	Lt Chas Malthy
Capt ___ Pearson	Lt S J Johnson	
Lt Richd Murphy	Lt Andrew Froman	

Rank & file killed:

N H Melton	Jos Neuman	Benj Merritt

Rank & file wounded:

Wm Allen	Uriah Davenport	Thos Tenney
J F Thomasson	J B Anderson	John Price
Andrew Browning	Thos Hessey	Jos Sharp
Geo W Haley	Geo W Nelson	Irwin Becker
John Roe	Jas A Bauch	J J D Todd
Levi Card	Jas Deheid	Chas Fanning
Henry Dimond	John Walker	Fred'k Branched
Stephen White	Wm B Lee	S Brown
Alex McCollum	Jas Malsen	Wm Morris
A C H Ellis	John Arahood	Ebenezer Cook
Geo Hammond	Laban Chamber	Richd Hendrick
Thos Harlan	Geo Carvell	John Stiver
Saml Bullock	Ethridge Rice	Henry Hereran
John Millburn	Jas Shepherd	Christopher Newman
John Maulding	David Haffman	
J M Handshy	Robt Jackson	
J D Lander	Leroy Thunley	

The killed & wounded of Capt Magruder's company 1st Artl is not included in this return, the company being detached since the action. 12 non-commissioned ofcrs & privates of Co F [Illinois] are known to have been either killed or wounded; as the company has been detached since the action, details cannot be furnished at this date.

To the above we add, from the same paper, a list of the killed or wounded in the brigade under Gen Pillow:

Ofcrs killed: Lts F B Allen; Lt C G Gill

Ofcrs wounded:

Gen J G Pillow	Capt Maulding	Lt J T Sutherland
Lt Col D W Cumming	Lt Heman	
Maj R Farquharson	Lt Wm Yeawon	
Capt Murry	Lt Jas Forrest	

Rank & file killed:

S Lauderdale	Saml Floyd	T Griffin
H L Byruirn	W England	R Kierman
F Willis	G W Keeny	E Price
W F Brown	C A Sampson	M M Durham
W O Shebling	R L Rohanon	A Hatton
Franklin Elkin	J N Gunter	

Rank & file wounded:

__ __ Johnson	S G Steamers	M Burns

W F McCrory
S W Garnet
___ Carson
T R Bradley
E H McAdde
G A Smith
John Conart
E T Mockabee
H Mowry
A Dockery
P Wheeler
A Copps
S G Williams
J Kent
M Brewer
B F Bibb
W Bennett
S Davis
J N Greeham
L L Jones
E A Ross
B O'Harrs
J Prescott
E G Roberson
R Plunket
J N Isler
A Gregory
John Gregory
L W Russell
John Burns
E Johnson
J Whittington
Alonzo White
J Cloud
J M Allison
J Wood
J L Dearmar
H Brusoer
N W Keith
J J Langston
M S Smith
J F Storm
H Williams
J Muir
Wm Cheeson
W F Martin
T Hans
F H Boyd
N Morse
J Lyndhurst
D Lindsay
Albert Cudney
J R Davis
C F Keyser
John Sheleen
G Sutton
A Lovier
D B Kitchen
D R Norison
John Smith
A Roland
J Shultz
Jno Chambers
Jacob Simons
Ed Cruse
Jacob Miller
D M Dandron
Wm Wilhelm
F Somers
Jas Shaw
Thos Hunt
Josiah Horn

Mr John C Martin, of Dublin, Ireland, died at the City Hotel in Lexington, Mo, a few days ago from Lockjaw. He imprudently bathed his neck & arms in cold water.

On Apr 22, the house of Mr Stephen Ingram, near Lancaster, Schuyler Co, N Y, was discovered to be on fire. The alarm was given by Mrs Ingram. Everything was on fire. They agreed that Mr Ingram should open a hole & jump out, & that the wife should hand out the children, 6 in number. But, as soon as air was given, the whole house enveloped in flames. Only one scream was heard, which was when the mother roused the children from their sleep. Mr Ingram was unable to render any assistance, & the mother & children all sunk together, under their mother's outstretched arms. The fire is supposed to have communicated to some shavings from ashes which were thrown under the house. A more distressing calamity has rarely been witnessed.

Capture of Tuspan: U S Flag ship **Mississippi**, at sea, off Vera Cruz, Apr 24, 1847. Killed in the assault: Lewis Clayton, Antonio Francis & John Griffin, all seamen. Wounded: Cmder Tatnall, Cmder Mackenzie, [accidentally,] Lt Jas L Parker, Lt Whittel, Lt Hartstene, & seamen Jas McCann, Hiram Townsend, Andrew Sweeny, Henry O Hart, Jas McCullen, & John Monroe.

Capt Flowery, who was convicted at Boston in May, 1845, of fitting out the schnr **Spitfire** for the slave trade, & sentenced to a fine of $2,000, & 5 years' imprisonment, has been pardoned by the Pres. The principal reason given by the Pres in his proclamation is the health of the prisoner has become impaired, & should his imprisonment continue, death or incurable disease may be the result.

Register's Ofc, Wash, May 10, 1847. The following have taken out licenses under the laws of the Corp during the month of Apr last.

Dog license:

Brooke, Thos H	Jones, Levi	Prather, Hugh
Cryer, B	Jones, J W	Rining, C
Cross, Robt	Ingraham, Wash	Seitz, Geo
Douglass, Henry	Kaiser, Adam	Steiger, W T
Ford, J N	Leech, Wm	Sheckell, Owen
Goodrich, J	May, Henry	Tilghman, R
Gladman, Asa	Miller, Jas	Thompson, Eliz
Goodyear, C	Middleton, D W	Whyte, Fred
Guyer, B	Noble, M	Williams, J C
Jones, Henry	Peel, Rezin	Wilson, Thos C
Jones, W B	Parsons, Jas	

Shop:

Black, Saml	Lakemeyer, Fred-transfer	Rupp, W
Holle, D H-transfer		Ruppel, G

Retail:

Lepreux, L & A	Wallace & Warring-transfer
Magee, Pat-transfer	

Huckster:

Bell John	Cooper, Wm	Scott, E P

Slave: Brown, J R

Slave woman:

Emerson, G W	Mattingly, F
Hill, Matilda	Pumphrey, J H

Dry goods: Benedict, A; Brown & Hyatt-transfer

Cart:

Bateman, Alex	Ben, Allen	Davis, H C
Bayliss, Thos	Bates & Bro-2	Devers, Wm
Bruce, Chas	Barrett, Thos J	Dent, Benj
Boyle, John	Chew, John	Dent, Bruce
Black, J M	Chew, Philip	Dick, Moses
Barr, Wm	Casanave, Peter-2	Downing, Jos
Brooks, Hanson	Cissell, Geo W	Delany, Caleb
Bean, Geo	Cross, R	Datcher, Thos
Bean, C	Collins, Wm	Day, D G
Brown, A	Conlan, Peter	Dodd, Reuben
Boone, J B	Casey, Pat-2	Davis, Elias

Easby, Wm-2
Ford, Wm
Green, Patrick
Givney, Bernard
Gunnell, W H
Graham, Guy
Green, Mantroy
Garner, Primus
Hagerty, Wm
Hill, Isaac
Harrison, Chas
Hicks, Chas
Harvey, T J & Co-2
Hill, Isaac
Haitmiller, Anton
Haslip, Henry
Hughes, G W
Hagar, Christ'r-2
King, Martin
Lucas, Henry
Lusby, S
Linkins, Walter
Lord, Wm
Landrick, John
Lyons, Chas-2
Leddy, Owen
Linkins, Danl
Loveless, John
Prather, O J-2
Peterson, Henry
Purdy, John-2
Pumphrey, Jackson
Resin, Chas
Read, Jas
Rining, Conrad
Rittenhouse, B F
Redfern, Saml
Riley, Thos W
Richardson, Luke
Raidy, John
Redin, David
Stott, Saml
Simmons, John
Stephenson, J
Scott, E P
Smoot, Sam & Son-2
Stepper, And
Seytes, Geo
Selby, Thos
Shreve, Saml
Shepherd, Peter
Thomas, Saml
Tinkler, Saml
Unisck, John
Woods, John
Waters, Gustavus
Wilson, John
Warder, Walter-2
Walker, John T
Ward, Enoch
Waters, Elkanah-2
Ward, Helen
Williams, Zad
Ward, Enoch

Grocery: Wannall, C P; Walvaner, J C

Wagon:

Brown, Thos
Briscoe, Henry
Bates & Bro
Dunlop, W H
Gunnell, W H
Green, Edwin
Guyer, Benedict
Haitmiller, Anton
Havenner, T & Son
Hands, John
Harvey & Lloyd
Heitre, Uriah
Hines, Ann
Horning, G W
Jones, Alfred-2
Isaacks, Hunter
Johnson, Jas
Ingraham, Wash
Key, Saml
Miller, Jos
Magee, Saml
Milburn, T M & B
Noble, Martha
O'Donoghue, P & T
Purdy, John-2
Pywell, R R
Rosenthal, Chas
Stephenson, J
Simms, Basil
Sardel, Edwin
Slade, Wm
Tinkler, Saml
Thoms, Chas
Tyler, Washington
Wonderlich, John
Wagner, John
Walker, Wm
Wilson, Wm A
Walker, John T
Young, John

Dray:

Bacon, S & Co
Jackson, B L & Bro
Lowry, Geo
Moorhead & Brown
O'Brien, J
Ober & Ryan
Ryon, J T
Stephenson, J
Simpson, Presley

Public Show: Thumb, Gen Tom

Wild Animals: Van Amburgh

Lumber: Van Reswick & Jones

Lottery: France, John
Tavern: Dorsey, P H
Negro: Davis, C E
Hack:: Sebastian, Caleb
Hardware: Lewis, Saml
Wood & Coal: Harvey, J S & Co
Concerts: Hunt, Danl
Equestrian: Welch & Delavan-2
Following named persons have been fined, during April, for failing to procure their licenses:
Dog license:
Griffith, W A
Humphreys, Walter
Norton, Fortune
O'Neale, H G
Slut license: Humphreys, Walter

Mrd: on May 9, by Rev Henry Slicer, Mr Geo Mantz to Miss Sarah Ann White, all of Wash City.

Mrd: on Thu last, in Wash City, by Rev Thos M Reese, Mr Wm H Dibble to Miss Eliz Jane Longdon, eldest daughter of the late Chas Longdon.

Mrd: on May 12th, by the Rev Mr French, Green H Barton to Miss Lizzie, daughter of Basil Waring, all of Wash City.

TUE MAY 18, 1847
Shannondale Springs, near Charlestown, Jefferson Co, Va: J J Abell, proprietor. I have leased for a term of years this delightful Watering Place, & will have it open for the reception of company on Jun 1.

Fauquier White Sulphur Springs: will be opened for the reception of visiters on Jun 1: situated 50 miles from Alexandria, in one of the most healthy & delightful climates of Va. -Danl Ward

From Matamoros: of the 28th ult: the present disposition of troops is: Col Wm Davenport, 1st Regt U S Infty, is commandant of the post; Capt Merchant, 2nd Regt U S Artl, is in command of ***Fort Brown***; Maj Abbott, 1st Regt Mass Infty, is in command of 9 companies of this regt in garrison at Matamoros; Lt Adams, with a company of Tenn cavalry, is posted in the Calle de Cos; Capt Nichols, Co G 1st Regt Mass Infty, is in command of ***Fort Paredes***. Capt Edw Webster, 1st company Mass Volunteers, who had been for several week confined to his quarters by sickness, is fast recovering, & expects soon to appear on drill with his command.

For sale: a fine bay Horse, warranted sound, equally good for saddle or harness. Can be seen at Robt Earl's Livery Stable, H st, between 20th & 21st sts.

It is due to Mr Bodisco that we should place in our columns the following correction of a statement copied some days ago from a Phil paper:
Correspondence of the N Y Commercial Advertiser. Wash, May 11. Among the various statements sometimes made from this city, I have seen one purporting to be a detail of a certain conversation held between the Russian Minister & the Sec of State, wherein the former was represented to have said: "Do what you please with Mexico, gentlemen, Russia will not interfere: put her in your pocket, if you choose." To say nothing of the indelicacy of introducing private conversation of such a character in public journals, I must protest against garbled & misinterpreted portions being used for political effect, particularly when it is calculated to place one of the parties in a false position. The elevated position of Mr Bodisco, & the estimation in which he is held in the diplomatic & social circles of Wash, attach more or less importance to his remarks, however casually they may be made. Mr Bodisco has said, that his Gov't would not interfere, as it had never recognized the independence of Mexico, & that it was for the U S to do as they pleased so far as Russia was concerned: but at the same time he has never failed to speak of the war with great regret.

The steamboat **Eureka**, from Columbus, arrived yesterday, reports the death, at his residence in that city, of the Hon Jesse Speight, U S Senator from Mississippi. -Mobile Advertiser, May 10. [May 22nd newspaper: An attack of erysipelas about the close of the last session detained Speight in this city, & he was imperfectly recovered when he set out on his return home. He was a native of N C; of the Democratic party; died in the meridian of life; & formerly represented in the House of Reps for a considerable time the Newbern district of N C.]

Trustee's sale of household & kitchen furniture: on May 20, at the residence of Capt Crabb, on M st, between 4th & 5th st, in the house known as Mr Kennedy's cottage: sold by virtue of a deed of trust from Horatio N Crabb to me, recorded in Liber W B 127.
-J M Carlisle, Trustee -A Green, auctioneer

Sale of valuable leasehold premises on Pa ave: by deed of trust from Isaac Kell, recorded in Liber W B 119, folio 295: the leasehold premises of lot 34 in square or reservation B, in Wash City, upon which is a large 3 story brick house, lately erected & occupied by said Kell for the manufacture of tin ware. The lease is for 7 years from May 20, 1836, at an annual rent of $219.75, payable quarterly. -Jos H Bradley, Trustee
-A Green, auctioneer

Executor's sale of brick house & lot & bldg lots at auction: on May 27, on the premises the following propery belonging to the estate of Wm A Scott, dec'd, viz: one 2 story house at L & 20th sts. Lot 8 in square 685, fronting on North Capitol st. Lots 1, 2, & 18, in square 798. -Jos W Beck, exc -A Green, auctioneer

Dr Francis M Gunnell tenders his professional services to the citizens of Wash. Ofc on 9th st, between I st & N Y ave.

Valuable Farm for sale: the subscriber offers at private sale his Farm in PG Co, Md, on the Potomac river, nearly opposite ***Mount Vernon***, & adjoining the lands of Wm Bryan, Wm Lyles, & John H Clagett, & containing about 500 acres. There are on this farm a comfortable dwlg-house, 2 tobacco houses, & all necessary outhouses. Will be shown by R W Dyer, auctioneer. Apply to the subscriber at Chaptico, St Mary's Co, Md, or to Thos J Marshall, Piscataway, PG Co, Md. -Zachariah H Sothoron

Splendid Durham Cattle & choice young Swine, from the herds of Jas Gowen, Mont Airey: public sale on May 27, at the Agricultural Exhibition Ground, Rising Sun, on the Germantown road, about 3 miles north of Phil: we will sell a part of Mr Gowen's celebrated stock of Durham Cattle. Also, some choice young Swine, reared for breeding. -C J Wolbert & Co, Auctioneers, Phil, Pa.

Died: on May 8, at his residence in Anne Arundel Co, after a painful illness, Mr Isaac G Magruder, in his 45th year, leaving a widow & 4 children to lament their irreparable loss.

Died: on May 16, after a short but severe illness, Eliz Sandiford, infant daughter of Wm H & Diana Minix, aged 11 months & 18 days. Her funeral is this afternoon at 4 o'clock.

Meeting of the Ofcrs of the U S Coast Survey schnr **Phoenix**, held May 6, Lt Commanding C P Patterson was called to the chair: resolved-that, in the death of Mr Richd Allison, the country has been deprived of the services of an honorable & meritorious ofcr, & his family & friends of one whose many noble points of character endeared him to their hearts. -C P Patterson, Chrmn: Pascagoula, May 6, 1847.

WED MAY 19, 1847

The 12 months' Volunteers: the terms of service will expire at the following dates:
12 months' volunteers under Maj Gen Scott:
Capt Blanchard's company Louisiana volunteers, Jul 30, 1847.
Col Coffee's Alabama regt, between Jun 8th & 29th, 1847.
Col Jackson's Georgia regt, between Jun 10th & 19th, 1847.
Col Forman's 3rd Illinois regt, between Jun 9 & Jul 2, 1847.
Col Baker's 4th Illinois regt, between Jun 9 & Jul 2, 1847.
Balt & D C battalion, between May 30 & Jun 15, 1847.
Col Thomas' Tenn mounted regt, between Jun 6 & 15, 1847.
Col Campbell's 1st Tenn foot, between May 28 & Jun 2, 1847.
Col Haskell's 2nd Tenn regt, between Jun 4 & 18, 1847.
Volunteers under Maj Gen Taylor:
Three regts of Ohio, between Jun 23 & 29, 1847.
Three regts of Indiana, between Jun 18 & 26, 1847.
Two regts of Illinois, between Jun 17 & 30, 1847.
Three regts of Ky, between May 17 & Jun 11, 1847.
Mississippi regt, between Jun 3, & 15, 1847.
Arkansas regt, between Jun 30 & Jul 3, 1847.

The recruiting service: reinforcements ordered to the seat of war: 10 new regts are rapidly filling up, & the following companies of the same are now concentrated at Point Isabel en route for Vera Cruz & that point.
9th Infty, Col Ranson, [aggregate]: 258
10th Infty, Col Temple: 794
11th Infty, Col Ramsey, [companies & detachment of a company]: 633
12th Infty, Col Wilson, [now in Mexico,] Lt Col Bonham, superintending: 110
13th Infty, Col Echols: 280
14th Infty, Col Trousdale: 180
15th Infty, Col Morgan, [now in Mexico,] Lt Col Howard, superintending: 810
16th Infty, Col Tibbatts: 827
Voltigeurs, Col Andrews: 712
3rd Dragoons, Col Butler: 711

Mr Wm Fischer has presented us with a copy of a grand musical fantasie, for the piano, by Mr Chas Grobe, of Balt, descriptive of the Battle of Buena Vista, & dedicated to the brave Gen Z Taylor.

The Cincinnati papers record the death of Mrs Whiteman, the niece & adopted daughter of Gen Jas Findlay, one of the earliest pioneers of that city. "Her first husband, Wm H Harrison, jr, was the son of the lamented Gen Harrison. She accompanied the Gen [a widow at the time] to Wash, & presided at the White House while he occupied it, in which position she was remarkable for her suavity & courtesy of manner. After his death she returned & married one of our most enterprising merchants, Lewis Whiteman, of the firm of Springer & Whitman."

Wm A Glauton, aged about 20, was accidentally killed at Columbus, Indiana, on Apr 28, when loading a rifle.

Before the Sussex Oyer & Terminer last week was Wm Snyder, of Stillwater, for an assault & battery on Miss Phebe L Allen. The essence of the crime is said to be the fact that Snyder is a married man. He was fined $10. -Newark Daily Adv

Wash Corp: 1-Nominations from the Mayor for the Board of Health for the ensuing year: Dr W B Magruder & J D Barclay, 1st Ward. Dr Thos Miller & Jas Larned, 2nd Ward. Dr J C Hall & J Y Bryant, 3rd Ward. Dr J F May & G C Grammer, 4th Ward. Dr J B Gardner & J P Ingle, 5th Ward. Dr Noble Young & Jas Crandell, 6th Ward. Dr Jas E Morgan & J W Jones, 7th Ward. 2-Also nominated: Isaac Stoddard, as Superintendnt of chimney sweeps for the 7th Ward in place of D Westerfield, resigned. 3-Ptn from J S Miller & others, for a bridge across the Canal at 6th st: ordered to lie on the table. 4-Ptn from W P Shedd & others, for remission of a fine: referred to the Cmte of Claims. 5-Ptn from Thos Gattrell & others, for the removal of the vegetable stands from the new wing of the Centre Market: ordered to lie on the table. 6-Ptn of John Cotter, for remission of a fine: referred to the Cmte of Claims. 7-Ptn of Wm Wise & others, that Md ave & 4½ st may be brought to their proper grade: referred to the Cmte on Improvements. 8-Bill to refund Joshua L

Henshaw the amount paid by him for the rent of the lot of ground attached to the school house of the 1st school distict: referred to the Cmte on Public Schools. 9-Bill for the relief of H R Maryman, late police ofcr: referred to the Cmte of Claims. 10-Cmte of Claims: referred the bill for the relief of Jonathan Chapman, & the act for the relief of L H Berryman: passed. 11-Cmte of Claims: ptns of Thos N Davis, of G W Venable, of Dennis Boone, & of Jas B Davis: asked to be discharged from the further consideration of the same: report was agreed to. 12-Cmte of Claims: asking to be discharged from the further consideration of the ptns of Allison Nailor, Caleb Dulany, W R Dempster, Jas Davis, Henry Barnes, Wm Bagman, Chas McDonald, & John L Wilson: agreed to. 13-Cmte of Claims: asking to be discharged from the further consideration of the subject of the resolution directing an inquiry into the conduct of E W Smallwood, police magistrate, & H Y Maryman, police ofcr of the 4th Ward: taken up & agreed to. 14-Ptn of Thos Hurdle, for remission of a fine: referred to the Cmte of Claims. 15-Cmte of Schools: bill for the relief of J R Grymes: passed. 16-Cmte of Claims: bill for the relief of J M Peerce: agreed to. 17-Cmte of Claims: acts for the relief of Thos Baker; of Wm Cooper; & of Michl Talty: reported without amendment. 18-Com'rs elected to hold an election in the several Wards for one member of the Board of Aldermen & 3 members of the Board of Common Council:

Chas A Davis	Danl Homans	Benj S Bayly
Saml Drury	Alfred R Dowson	Wm M Ellis
Wm H Perkins	Elezius Sims	Noble Young
Geo Crandell	Willard Drake	Jas Crandell
Valentine Harbaugh	Wm Fischer	Jas S Harvey
John Boyle	Benj F Middleton	Wm Wise
J T Van Reswick	F A Klopfer	John Van Reswick

Public sale: by decree of the Circuit Court of Wash Co, D C: in a cause wherein Wm & Mary Eliz Hayman are cmplnts, & Anna, Adelaide, Julia, Catherine, & Saml Hayman are dfndnts: sale on Jun 7, in front of the premises, the following parcel of ground, in Wash City: part of lot 20 in square 254, fronting 20 feet on F st, extending back of equal width 159 feet, with the frame tenement thereon now occupied by John Byrne.
-W Redin, Trustee -B Homans, Auctioneer

Letter from the late Gen Dromgoole, written 3 years ago, giving an account of his descent: we copy from the N Y Tribune. Wash, Jan 21, 1844. My parents were not both natives of the Emerald Isle. Mr father, Edw Dromgoole, was born in Sligo. He came to America a poor boy, with religious impressions & a strong desire for religious freedom. He landed in Phil in 1772-came to Balt, & resided there, or its vicinity, with Mr John Haggerty, a tailor by trade, & a man of exemplary piety. Edw Dromgoole had been brought up in Ireland to the trade of a linen weaver. When he came to reside with Mr Haggerty, he assisted him in the business of tailoring. The thimble with which he worked is still carefully preserved in the family. They worked & prayed together, & the survivor, Edw Dromgoole, to the day of his death, cherished the memory of his departed friend. They were disciples, or followers of John Wesley. In 1774 Edw Dromgoole commenced preaching. While residing with Mr Haggerty, he formed a society or class of Methodists,

& held the first Methodist Class Meeting in America. He entered upon the plan of itinerant labor in the ministry. In the very incipiency of the war between the Colonies & Great Britain, he voluntarily repaired to his friend & Christian brother, Robt Jones, a magistrate in Sussex Co, Va, & before him took the oath of fidelity & allegiance: a certificate he continually kept with him. He settled in Brunswick Co, Va, where he resided until his death in 1835, in his 84th year, having been a minister of the gospel for more than 60 years. He intermarried with Rebecca Walton in said county, whose ancestors had early emigrated from England to Va. Whether they descended from the family of the bishop, the author of the Polyglot Bible, or from old Izak the fisherman, is not known, or material. They lived happily together, raised & educated a family of children. I am their youngest child. Very respectfully, Geo C Dromgoole, to Wm L Mackenzie, N Y.

Assignee's sale of household & kitchen furniture at auction: on May 20, at the residence of Elijah Dyer, on 11th & I sts: by deed of assignment recorded May 15, 1847.
-John A Linton, assignee -C Boteler, auct

Italy: a diabolical plot to murder the Pope has been discovered. It was found out by the French ambassador, who revealed the names of the conspirators to the Pope. They were going to assassinate him while giving audience to one of them, who was appointed to kill him. A Capuchin priest presented himself for an audience. His holiness requested his name, which he gave; but, before he was admitted, the Pope looked over the list of conspirators & found the name of the Capuchin. He immediately summoned his guards, who on the Capuchin's entrance seized him, & found a brace of loaded pistols & a poison dagger about his person. The Capuchin was conveyed to prison, & many arrests took place.

Cmder J R Sands, U S steamer **Vixen**, is going to the U S as bearer of dispatches from Cmdor Perry to Washington, & is to have in charge some magnificent cannon of curious workmanship & ancient date [one of A D 1600, another of 1747] taken from the walls of the castle of San Juan d'Ulus, with others taken at Alvarado, to be placed at the disposal of the Pres of the U S on their arrival. -Vera Cruz Eagle

Died: on May 18, in Wash City, Wm Parsons, in his 70th year. His funeral is today at 4 o'clock, from his late residence on 11th st, near the Navy Yard bridge.

THU MAY 20, 1847
For rent: desirable house on the south side of G st: of brick, 2 stories, now occupied by the District Atty, P Barton Key. Apply to A Fuller. Communication left at Mr Hands' Hotel will be attended to. -A Fuller

For rent: desirable house in the 1st Ward. Inquire of Mrs D Walker, or Jos Peck.

Col Jefferson Davis, of Mississippi, has been appointed by the Pres of the U S to be Brig Gen in the Army, in the place of Gen G J Pillow, promoted.

Two dghts of Rev Jas Weatherby, of Holly Springs, Miss, were riding in a buggy with their father, a few days since, when the horses took fright & ran off, killing one & cruelly mangling the other. The father was also injured.

E J Roberts, Clerk of the U S Court at Pittsburg, fell down in an apoplectic fit on Wed, & died in 2 hours.

Mrd: on May 18, at the Church of the Ascension, by Rev L J Gilliss, Andrew M Thomas to Miss Eliz G Webb, all of Wash City.

Mrd: on Thu, by Rev A Empie, Chas C Lee, of Hardy Co, Va, to Miss Lucy P Taylor, eldest daughter of Gen Taylor, of Richmond.

Lt Col Sir Walter Scott, eldest & last surviving son of the great novelist, recently died at the Cape of Good Hope, on his return from Madras, aged 46 years. The baronetcy is extinct, but the Abbotsford property passes to Walter Scott Lockhart, a Cornet in the 16th Lancers, the only son of the editor of the Quarterly Review, & the only grandson of the author of Waverley. The papers also mention the death of the Duke of Argyle, in his 70th year; & Sir Davidge Gould, Senior Admiral of the Red, the last captains who commanded line of battle ship at the battle of the Nile. He died at the age of 90 years. The death of Lord Cowley, at Paris, a younger brother of the Duke of Wellington, is also stated.

Report of Maj Gen Patterson. Headquarters Volunteer Division, Jalapa, Apr 23, 1847. Operations under my command, at the pass of the Cerro Gordo, on Apr 17 & 18. The chiefs of brigade speak in the highest terms of the courage & conduct of the regts under their command, of their personal staffs, viz: Capt O A Winship, Assist Adj Gen; Lt Rains, 4th Artl, Aid-de-Camp; & Lt Anderson, 2nd Tenn Regt, acting Aid-de-Camp to Pillow's brigade; & 1st Lt R P Hammond, 3rd Artl, acting Assist Adj Gen; & Lt G T M Davis, Illinois volunteers, Aid-de-Camp to Shields' brigade. I desire to recommend to the favorable notice of the Gen-in-Chief Dr Wright, Surgeon U S army, medical director; & 1st Lt Beauregard, of the Engineers, on duty with my division; & the ofcrs of my personal staff, Brevet Lt Col Abercrombie, 1st Infty, Aid-de-Camp; 1st Lt Wm H French, 1st Artl, acting Assist Adj Gen; & 1st Lt Seth Williams, 1st Artl, Aid-de-Camp; to each of whom I am under many obligations for valuable service. -R Patterson, Maj Gen U S Army, comd'g Volunteer division. To Capt H L Scott, U S A, Act, Assist Adj Gen.

For rent: the 2 story brick house on 9th st, between H & I sts, in good order. Inquire of the subscriber. -E Ridgway, Slater

Letter dated May 2 from the parish of Sabine: came to Mr Stille, Clerk of the House of Reps, & was written by his brother. A wedding at old Mr Wilkinson's of an orphan girl he raised, at which all the invited guests were poisoned, including the bridesmaid & groomsman. Out of 60 persons poisoned, 30, Dr Sharp says, will certainly die. Ten or twelve are already dead, including 2 sons of preacher Britton, 2 Castleberrys-the one a young man & the other a young woman-one of the Slaughters & his wife. Strange to tell, none of the family were injured, nor yet the bride & groom; yet one of the bridesmaids died in the house. Old Wilkinson has absconded. This portion of Texas is in arms. What I write you is the fact, without exaggeration. It is supposed the negroes were hired to administer the poison in the coffee, or food, by a disappointed suitor, who was present at the wedding. New Orleans Delta, May 11 [Jun 3 newspaper: Dr A C Denson, directly from Cherokee Co, in the vicinity of Shelby, informs us that the wedding party were probably poisoned by accident, the proprietor of the house having given arsenic in the place of salaeratus to make the cakes & pastry. Dr Jas H Starr, of Nacogdoches, stated that 17 of the 54 poisoned had died about the 1st. Our informant learns that 6 others have since died.] [Jun 16th newspaper: Wilkinson was a man of bad character, a notorious hog thief, & Morris, the groom, had been twice whipped in Mississippi for negro stealing. Wilkinson was accused of stealing the hogs of Spot Sanders, & this is how he revenged himself. He sent food to the house of Sanders, enough to last the family a week, all poisoned. Mr Sanders, 3 children, & a negro boy are dead; the other, the only child left, was dying when I was at our friend Ker's. Mr Sanders & 7 negroes are yet sick, & some will die. Mr Sander's mother, age 70 years, was also a victim. Allen Haley lost a negro man, who lost his wife; Mrs Edens, an old lady, was dead, together with her son; Mr Castleberry lost his sister. Old Wilkinson & his wife & Morris' wife were arrested & committed to prison. Chas Alexander bailed the women.]

For rent: 3 story brick house on N J ave, at present occupied by me. Possession may be had immediately. Apply at the premises. -Saml Hanson

FRI MAY 21, 1847

The First in the Field. Illinois Volunteers. The Govnr's Proclamation, in accordance with the requisition of the Pres of the U S for one regt of infty & one company of cavalry, was issued on Apr 29. It was filled on May 8 by the following companies:
Schuyler Co, Cavalry, Capt A Dunlap
Bond Co, Infty, Thos Bond
Marin Co, Infty, C Turner
Williamson Co, Infty, J M Cunningham
Brown Co, Infty, E B W Newby
St Clair Co: Infty, ___ Kerney
LaSalle Co, Infty, H J Reed
Williamson Co, Infty, Jas Hampson
Shelby Co, Infty, R Madison
Pike Co, Infty, J B Donaldson
Four companies, one from Alton, Capt Wheeler; one from Edwardsville, Capt Niles; one from Vandalia, Capt Lee; & one from Green, Capt Bristow, were reported but a few hours after the requisition was filled. -Springfield Juornal, May 13

The Court-house in Dooly Co, Georgia, together with all the records of the Superior, Inferior, & Ordinary Courts, & $11,000 collected from defendants, were destroyed by fire on May 7.

Movement of Troops: A detachment of the 10th regt U S Infty, under command of Lt Col John J Fay, arrived at Brasos Island May 5, & were to leave on May 6 for Camp Palo Alto. The detachment is composed of: Co A, Capt A Wilkins; 1st Lt Francis M Cummins, Acting Assist Commissary; 2nd Lt Peter H Bruyere. Co C, Capt Jos A Yard; 1st Lt Geo W Taylor; 2nd Lt Benj Yard. Co H, Capt J W Collet; 1st Lt Saml R Dummer, Acting Adj; 2nd Lt Isaac W Patton, John Conger Assist Surgeon. Co A is from N Y, Companies C & H from N J. On May 9, the steamboat **George Washington** brought down to New Orleans a detachment of U S troops, consisting of Co A, 15th Infty, 89 men, under Capt J S Perry, 1st Lt L Rhodes, 2nd Lt L W Templeton; Co B, 15th Infty, 78 men, under Capt E King, 1st Lt J B Miller, 2nd Lt T R Tilton; Co G, 7th Infty, 86 men, in charge of Major Lee. On Sunday the steamboat **Talma** arrived at New Orleans from Evansville, Mount Vernon, & Cairo, with 5 companies of Infty, comprising 14 commissioned & 426 non-commissioned ofcrs & privates, under the command of Lt Col H L Webb. The steamboat **James Dick** arrived at New Orleans on May 10 with Lt Manne & 33 men, belonging to the 3rd Dragoons. The steamboat **Saranac**, from Pittsburg, arrived on May 10, with Col T P Andrews, of the U S Voltiguers; Dr J W Tyler; G P Kennett, Quartermaster; Capt J D Blair, Lt W S Walker, Lt W Terrill, Lt A C K Kiger, & 123 men; also, Lt C F Vernon, in charge of 33 men, enroute to Mexico. On May 12, the steamer **Pike No 8**, from Cincinnati, conveyed to New Orleans Capt Reynolds, Lt Brown, Lt Williams, & Lt McHenarie, with 100 men of the 3rd Dragoons, from Michigan; & on the same day the steamer **Lune**, from Louisville, arrived with Lt Curd & 33 recruits of the 16th Regt, from Ky. The following regts have been ordered to join Gen Scott: the 9th, 11th, 12th, 14th, & 15th Regts of Infty, & the Regt of Voltigeurs. Several companies of the voltigeurs have embarked for the Brasos, as this regt was first ordered to join Gen Taylor. Its destination has been changed. The 10th, 13th, & 16th Infty, & the 3rd Dragoons, have been ordered to Gen Taylor.

The Prince de Polignac, the celebrated Minister of Chas X, whose death has been lately announced, belonged to one of the oldest & most celebrated families in France, among whose members were the famous Cardinal de Polignac, a Minister of Louis XIV, & Madame de Polignac, the confidante of Maria Antoinette. The dec'd Prince was born in 1780, & at an early age emigrated with his brothers, to escape the consequences of the French Revolution. In 1804 they re-entered France, committed themselves in a conspiracy against Napoleon, & were punished by a long imprisonment, which terminated on the restoration of the Bourbons. The Prince became an ultra-royalist & the leader of that party during the reign of Louis XVIII. In 1823 he was sent Minister to London, & remained 6 years. In 1829 he became Prince Minister, & was the principal adviser of Chas X in relation to those ordinances which led to the revolution of the 3 days. The Chamber of Peers condemned him to death for treason; but his life was spared, & he was adjudged to perpetual imprisonment in the Castle of Ham. He was then permitted to go into exile, & the family allowed to return to France, with the restriction of not being permitted to enter Paris. He established himself at St Germains, & passed the remainder of his days in ill health. He was twice married, first to Miss Barbara Campbell, & afterwards to Maria Charlotte, daughter of Lord Rancliffe, & widow of the Marquis de Choiseul. He left 6 children & large possessions.

The Little Rock Democrat of May 6 states that on May 5, about 50 miles from this place, the steamboat **New Hampshire** exploded her boilers killing: Geo T Allen & R B Couples, clerks; 2 passengers, one a nephew of E Barinds, of Arkadelphia, the other an elderly gentleman, name unknown; Alex McKinney, pilot; Jas Van Dyke, mate; the 1st engineer; Chas Ratcliff, carpenter; one deck passenger, & 4 deck hands.

By write of fieri facias at the suit of Geo W Phillips, against the goods & chattels of C G McLellan, to me directed, I have seized & taken in execution all the right, title, & interest of said C G McLellan in 8 casks of Wine & 13 dozen bottles of Wine, & will offer same for sale on May 27, in front of the Centre Market-house, Wash City.
-H Y Maryman, constable

Mrd: on May 18, at Clermont, by Rev C B Dana, C C Jamison, of Balt, to Miss Catherine E Mason, daughter of Gen John Mason, of Clermont, Fairfax Co, Va.

SAT MAY 22, 1847
Orphans Court of Wash Co, D C. Letters of administration on the personal estate of Richd Joyce, late of said county, deceased. -Ann Joyce, admx

Reasonable reward for return of a stray cow, that strayed off from the common near the Railroad, in Wash City. She was bought on Apr 1 last, with a calf, from a Mr Bowman, of Shenandoah, Va. -G C Grammer

Valuable servants at auction: on May 27, at the residence of Mrs Jos Smoot, on K st, nearly opposite the Brewery, 1st Ward: a servant woman aged 24 years, & 2 children; a woman age 19 years; a girl age 13 years; a girl aged 9 years. The above servants are slaves for life & are not restricted. -R W Dyer, auct

Household & kitchen furniture at auction: on May 25, by order of the Orphans Court of Wash Co, D C: at the residence of the late Bernard Kelly, at the corner of K st.
-R W Dyer, auct

By virtue of a writ of fieri facias, against the goods & chattels, lands & tenements of Wm M Cannon & Wm Shields, I have seized & taken all the right, title, & interest of Wm M Cannon in one frame cottage built dwlg-house on I st, between 4½ & 6th sts, in square 499, which said house I shall proceed to sell to the highest bidder, for cash, on May 27, on the premises, to satisfy said execution in favor of Thos N Brashear, which sale will be subject to a claim of $50, now due & unpaid on the ground. -Wm Cox, constable

Appointments & changes: Cmdor Chas W Skinner to be Chief of the Bureau of Construction in the Navy Dept, in the place of Cmdor Chas Morris, resigned on account of ill health. Seth Barton, Solicitor of the Treasury, to be Charge d'Affaires to Chili, in the place of Wm Crump. R H Gillet, Register of the Treasury, to be Solicitor of the Treasury, vice Barton.

Gentlemen's Outfitting Store: Brown's Hotel. -M H Stevens, late Fish & Co.

The young men of Shelbyville, Tenn, on May 10, undertook to fire a salute for Gen Scott's late victory. A premature explosion took place, which blew off the hand & arm of Mr A Turrentine, formerly editor of the Shelbyville Whig, & shattered both arms of Mr John Sutton, while Dr Scott, who had charge of the vent, lost the thumb of the right hand. Mr Sutton underwent the amputation of both arms; a similar operation was performed upon Mr Turrentine, which he survived only 20 hours, he receiving several internal injuries.

Persons wishing to see the Model of the Smithsonian Institute can do so by calling at the Picture Gallery of Mr Van Loan, first bldg west of the U S Hotel, where also may be seen some fine specimens of the Daguerreotype art.

N Y, May 20, 1847. The ship fever is increasing in our city: Dr Van Buren, a grandson of Ex-Pres Van Buren, Assist Physician at the Bellevue Hospital, died of this fever on May 19, 1847; he was about 23 years of age, & was shortly to be married to a young lady of this city.

Mt Pleasant Family School, Roxbury, Mass. Address J H Purkitt, Roxbury, Mass.

Mrd: on May 20, at Pleasant Vale, near Washington, by Rev Henry Slicer, S S Williams, Counsellor-at-law, to Maria Scott, eldest daughter of Enoch Tucker.

Mrd: on May 20, at Church of the Epiphany, by Rev Mr French, Dr Alex S Wortherspoon, of the U S Army, to Miss Louisa Adelaide, daughter of the late Jos L Huhn.

Mrd: on May 19, by Rev N J B Morgan, Mr Wm Ebert to Miss Eliz Dye, both of Gtwn.

Mrd: on May 20, by Rev F S Evans, Mr Danl A Smallwood to Miss Mary E Fowler.

Mrd: on May 13, at Harrisburg, by Rev Dr De Witt, Hon Chas Brown, Rep in Congress from the 2nd district of Pa, to Eliz R Shunk, youngest daughter of Francis R Shunk, Govn'r of Pa.

Died: on May 18, in Balt, after a brief illness, Mrs Margaret Zell, loved & revered by all who knew her. A devout Christian, she departed this life in the hope of a blessed immortality.

MON MAY 24, 1847

The Hon Henry Wheaton, late Minister of the U S to Prussia, with his family, arrived at N Y on Fri in the ship **Baltimore**, from Havre.

Mrs Beard, 25, whose relatives reside in Massachusetts, while on her way from Albany to join her husband at Buffalo, was knocked overboard from a canal boat at Utica on Fri, & was crushed to death.

The descendants of Lafayette. The patriotism of the illustrious friend of Washington is descending undiluted to his successors. His son, Geo Washington Lafayette, who inherits the name of one & the virtues of both his namesakes, has long held a seat among the Liberal members of the French Chamber of Deputies, & at the last election, his eldest son, Oscar, at age 30, was elected a Deputy to the same Chamber by the district of Meaux, the same that his grandfather, the Genr'l, formerly represented. -N Y Tribune

Mrd: on May 20, at Ijamsville, Md, by Rev Mr Phillips, Mr Wm S Brown, of King Geo Co, Va, to Miss Josham Ijams, of Fred'k Co, Md.

Died: on May 22, at his residence near Washington, Thos Fenwick, in his 73rd year. His funeral is from his late residence, on May 24, at 10 o'clock.

Died: on Sat last, in Gtwn, Mrs Milicent Waring, relict of the late Henry Waring. Her funeral is today at 9 A M, from her late residence, at the corner of Market & 2nd sts, in that town.

City Ordinances-Wash: 1-Act for the relief of Jonathan Chapman: that the fine imposed for a violation of a law relative to selling fire-crackers be remitted: provided Chapman pay costs of prosecution. 2-Act for the relief of J R Grymes: to be paid the sum of $60.60, being the amount deducted from his bill for furnishing & finishing the school-house in the 2nd school district. 3-Act for the relief of Richd Davis: to pay him the sum of $75, as a full indemnification for the damage sustained by his hack & horses breaking through the bridge over the canal at Md ave. 4-Act for the relief of J M Peerce: that the fine imposed for an alleged violation of an ordnance relative to grocery licenses, be remitted: provided he pay the costs of prosecution. Same for the fine relative to huckstering: be remitted. 5-Act for the relief of L H Berryman: that the fine imposed for a violation of the law relative to huckstering, be remitted: provided he pay the costs of prosecution.

Balt, May 22. A young man, John Trenchard, son of Dr Trenchard, of Kent Co, Md, was drowned this afternoon by falling overboard from the schnr **Millington** in the Chesapeake Bay, off Hawkins' Point.

TUE MAY 25, 1847

The Charleston papers announce the demise of Doddridge Crocker, in his 79th year, & the oldest merchant in Charleston. He was a native of Massachusetts, & arrived in Charleston between 1790 & 1792.

The general agency of the society organized for the purpose of erecting a Nat'l Monument to the Father of his Country has been conferred upon that judicious & excellent man Elisha Whittlesey, of Ohio. The present funds of the society amount to $57,359. -Cinc Gaz

John Hoover & Thos Sewell, jr, have this day entered into copartnership, under the name, firm, & style of Hoover & Sewell: May 25.

Appointment by the Pres. Saml Holmes, Register of the Land Ofc for the district of lands subject to sale at Quincy, Illinois, vice Wm G Flood, resigned.

The last Lynchburg papers announce the sudden death in that place of Capt Ammon Hancock, one of its oldest & most respected citizens. He was found dead on May 18, before the front door of his residence, with his knees on the ground, & his head resting on a railing near the front gate. His death, so sudden, & while he was alone, shocked the community, by whom many warmly beloved him.

For rent: the dwlg-house now occupied by S Holmes, on the corner of 9th & F sts. Possession given Jun 1. Apply on the premises, or to Mr Chas F Wood.

Died: on May 24, near the Navy Yard, Mr Matthew Wright, aged 80 years, a native of the county of Tyrone, Ireland, whence he emigrated in 1795, & became a citizen of Washington in 1804. His funeral will take place from his late residence on 8th st east, tomorrow at 2 o'clock.

Handsome furniture & very superior old Wines at auction: on May 28, at the residence of the late Gen Walter Smith, corner of Fred'k & Prospect sts. -Edw S Wright, auct, Gtwn.

Farm for sale: the undersigned is authorized to dispose of, at private sale, ***Elmwood***, the plantation owned by Mrs Mary Brookes, upon which she now resides, containing 170 acres. It adjoins the estates of Messrs Wm B Bowie, Allen P Bowie, Wm Z Beall, & Fred'k G Skinner, near the stage road leading from Upper Marlboro to that place. The improvements are such as are suited to a place of its magnitude. No other place in the country for its size is more valuable for agricultural pursuits. -Phil Chew

Valuable property at auction: by virtue of a decree of the Circuit Court of Wash Co, D C, in Chancery, in a case in which Ephraim Wheeler et al are cmplnts, & Stanislaus Murray, executor, & Cornelius Murphy, heir at law of Martin Murphy, dfndnts: sale on the premises, on Jun 25, the valuable brick house & lot near the corner of 4½ st, on the north side of Pa ave, being lot 21 in Reservation 10: house contains 12 rooms. This property was owned & occupied by Martin Murphy, dec'd. -S S Williams, trustee -A Green, auct [Jun 28th newspaper: above sale postponed until Jul 1. -A Green, auct] [Oct 23rd newspaper: Henry H Dent became the purchaser of lot 21, in reservation 10, for the sum of $5,050.00, & the terms of sale have been complied with by the purchaser.
-Wm Brent, clk]

Household & kitchen furniture at auction: on May 28, at the residence of S Holmes, who is declining housekeeping, at the corner of F & 9th sts. -A Green, auctioneer

WED MAY 26, 1847

Major Wm H Emory, of the army, who recently arrived in the U S from Calif, is at present on a visit to his family & friends in Queen Anne's Co, in Md.

San Diego, Calif, Dec 21, 1846. Dear Beale: We, your friends & brother ofcrs, have ordered from England a pair epaulets & sword to be presented to you by the hands of Lt Tilghman, in testimony of our admiration of your gallant conduct in the bold & hazardous enterprise of leaving Gen Kearny's encampment after the battles of San Pascual & San Bernardino of Dec 6, 1846, for the purpose of bringing information to the garrison of San Diego, & obtaining relief for the suffering troops.

J W Revere, Lt	Geo Minor, Lt
W B Renshaw, Lt	W H Thompson, Act Mas
Ben F B Hunter, Act'g Lt	Wm Speiden, Purser
N B Harrison, Act'g Mas	C D Maxwell, Pas As Sur
C Eversfield, Assist Surg	J F Stenson, Act'g Master
Jas H Watmough, Purser	J S Missroon, Lt
R L Tilghman, Lt	Saml Mosely, Surgeon
John Guest, Act'g Master	A A Henderson, As Surg
J Zeilin, U S M C	G W Harrison, Lt
H B Watson, U S M C	Ed Higgins, Act Lt

Part of Lt Beale's reply: U S frig **Congress**, Jan 26, 1947. It was with feelings of gratification I find it hard to express that I received your flattering letter of Dec 21. Such a testimonial from ofcrs whose standing & reputation are so well known calls forth all the warmest feelings of my heart. -Edw F Beale. Letter to Messrs R L Tilghman, Lt John Guest, Master.

Hon Saml Church had been elected Chief Justice of Connecticut in place of Judge Williams, whose resignation has been already mentioned.

Liberal reward for return of a strayed dark red Cow. -E H Metcalf, corner of I & 6th sts.

In the matter of the real estate of Lewis G Davidson, dec'd, the Trustee reported the sale on May 24, to Chas H Winder lots 2, 3,& 4, in square 169, for $1,634.95; Jas Carrico lot 8, in square 163, for $94, & the purchasers have complied with the terms of the sale. -Nathl Pope Causin -Ed N Roach, Reg/o wills

Will be launched this day, from Easby's ship-yard, in the First Ward, the schnr **John Y Mason**, built for the coast survey.

Household & kitchen furniture, on May 25, by order of the Orphans Court of Wash Co, D C: the personal effects of John Little, dec'd, at his late residence, near the Anacostia bridge, Navy Yard. Terms cash. -A Green, auctioneer

The proprietor having taken a large house, between 13th & 14th sts, is prepared to accommodate gentlemen, with or without families. -L V Clements

Mrd: on May 18, at Gtwn, D C, by Rev R T Berry, Mr W T Compton, of Martinsburg, Va, to Miss Maria D B French, daughter of the late Geo French, of Gtwn.

Mrd: May 25, at Balt, by Rev S P Hill, Mr Geo E Jillard, of Wash City, to Miss Cordelia M Scott, of Balt.

Died: on May 25, in Gtwn, Mrs Hester Smart, consort of the late Zachary Smart. Her funeral is today at 5 o'clock, from her late residence on Cherry st, Gtwn.

THU MAY 27, 1847

The fine Hotel at the head of Lake George has just been re-opened to the public by Mr John F Sherrill. The steamboat which runs on the lake will commence her trips on Jun 1.

Valuable mill property for sale or rent. The subscriber offers his Mill property, in Brookeville, Md, consisting of a stone mill-house, with one run of French burrs & one of country stones, cast-iron grating, in good order; miller's house & other outhouses, with about 16 or 17 acres of land. This land is in the immediate vicinity of Sandy Spring, Md. Communications addressed to the subscriber, in Alexandria, Va, will be attended to until Jun 6, after which he may be seen at the Mill until the 14th. -Thos McCormick

For rent: 2 large residences in Wash: one of brick on the corner of F & 12th sts. The other of brick, in the First Ward, adjoining the Quaker Meeting-house. Apply to Wm H Ward, near Brown's Hotel.

An act to establish a town at St Marks, Florida: approved on Mar 2, 1833, Jas K Polk, Pres of the U S of America. By the act of Congress the minimum price of each town lot is fixed at $25, & of each out lot at $25 per acre. -Richd M Young, Com'r of the Land Ofc.

Circuit Court of Wash Co, D C-in Chancery. B L Jackson & Bro, vs Administrators & heirs at law of Benj Leddon, dec'd, et al. The creditors of Benj Leddon, dec'd, are warned to exhibit to me, at my ofc in Gtwn, their respective claims, with the vouchers thereof, & evidences of the dates when the same originated, or on before Jun 2 next. -Clement Cox, Auditor N B: Where more convenient to the creditors, they may leave their claims at the law ofc of Messrs Davidge & Semmes, 7th st west, Wash.

Musical Instruction: John Edgar, Professor of Music, will give instruction on the Piano Forte & in Singing, at his residence on G st, between 12th & 13th sts, or at the residence of the pupil. References:

Leonidas Coyle	G C Grammer	John Ferguson
John Underwood	Sidney Porter	John B North
Julius Peters	Major Hobbie	Dr Green
Wm Voss	R H Gillet	Col Gardner, City P M

$5 reward for Edw Nash, an indented apprentice to the Bricklaying business, who left the subscriber without provocation. All persons are forbid harboring or employing said apprentice. -Thos Lewis

The partnership existing under the firm of Berry & Woodward is this day dissolved by mutual consent. P T Berry has purchased the interest of Mr Woodward, & will continue the wholesale Grocery, Flour, & Commission business at the warehouse they formerly occupied. -P T Berry, R Woodward, Gtwn

Proposals will be received at the ofc of the Jas River & Kanawha Co, Richmond, Va, until Jul 15, for the construction of 3 stone dams across Jas river on the line of the Company's canal between Lynchburg & the mouth of North river. -Walter Gwynn, Chief Engineer, Jas River & Kanawha

House in Pollard's Row [or Mechanic's Row,] for rent: the house at present occupied by Mr Wm Thompson, being the 4th house west. -Bates & Bro, G st

A letter from Capt Corse, of Alexandria [Va] Volunteers, dated China, Mexico, Apr 16, announces the death of Lt Benj G Waters, of that company. He died at China on the 15th ult, after an illness of about 12 days. His disease was dysentery, contracted whilst at Camargo, a place that has been the graveyard of many gallant spirits of the army.

University of N Y: in consequence of the decease of Dr Revere, there is a vacancy in the Chair of the Theory & Practice of Medicine in this Institution. All communications must be addressed to the undersigned. -John W Draper, M D, Sec of the Faculty, 364 Fourth st, N Y.

At the late meeting of the Georgia Historical Society, a paper was read on the Etymology & Definition of the names of several places, & towns of Mexico, which have unusual interest at this moment.
Monterey: from the Count of Monterey, who was Viceroy of Mexico before 1600.
The word literally means King's Mountain.
Cumargo derives its name from the Indian historian of Mexico, Diego Munos Camargo, who wrote his work about the middle of the 16th century.
Matamoros means literally Moor Killer, perpetuating the recollection of the wars against the Moors in Spain.
Chihuahua is an Indian name.
Saltillo means the little leap or fall, perhaps from a sudden descent or slope of the country.
Aqua Nueva-new water.
Agua Fria-cold water.
Buena Vista-beautiful view. Bellevue
Encarnacion-incarnation & its holy mystery.
Vera Cruz-the Holy Cross. The present town was founded by the Vicery of Monterey in the latter part of the 16th century. The old town of Vera Cruz, founded by Cortez, was north of the present town at Antigua.

St Juan de Ulua-St John of Ulua or Culuo, an Indian name.
Alvarado-so called from Pedro de Alvarado, one of Cortez's generals.
Sacrificios-the island of Sacrificios received this name from the human sacrifices of the Mexican Indians, indicated by the human bones found there by the Spaniards.
Cerro Gordo-the large hill.
Sierra Madre-the mother mountain range.
Jalapa, or Xalapa-pronounced Halapa-our medicine Jalap is brought from that place.
Mango de Clavo is the name of Santa Anna's vast estate near a Vera Cruz. It means Club-Handle.

Dwlg-house for rent. That commodious brick dwlg recently vacated by Mrs I Walker, being above my store, corner of 7th st & Pa ave. Apply to Geo Stettinius, agent for the estate of John Stettinius, deceased.

Baltimore & North, May 26, 1847. Mr Robt Scott, of the firm of R Scott & Co, Phil, shoe dealers, was killed on the railroad, somewhere near Wilmington, yesterday. He left Phil with a design of visiting Wash.

Chas A Burnett, Gtwn, D C, has for sale a valuable horse for a family, being well broke to the harness.

Mrd: on May 26, by Rev A Shiras, Mr Hilleary L Offutt to Miss Virginia C Baker, all of Gtwn, D C.

Mrd: on May 25, by Rev Chas A Davis, Mr Wm A Rawlings to Miss Ann E Brown, both of this place.

Died: yesterday, in Wash City, Mrs Anna Prentiss Jacobs, wife of Mr Loring Jacobs, in her 40th year. She was a native of Cambridge, Mass, but for several years past a resident of Wash City. Her funeral is this afternoon, at 3 o'clock, from her late residence on M st, near Col Seaton's garden.

Died: on Apr 26, at his residence at ***Spring Grove***, in Westmoreland Co, Va, Dr Robt Murphy, in his 54th year. He departed to that rest which remaineth for the people of God.

FRI MAY 28, 1847
Old things-from the Phil Mercury of 1727 [says the U S Gaz]: 1-Henry Burkard was drowned in the Perkycoming, at Pawlin's Mill, by the stumbling of his horse. 2-One Mark Blake hung himself on a tree. 3-Mr Harrison, of Vine st, London, is mentioned as the father of 3 dozen of legitimate children. He had had 3 wives. 4-The will of Sir John Randolph, Knight, of Va, is published. He had been charged with being an Atheist, Deist, & divers other *ists*, but his will shows him to have been of a very good creed.

Gen Cushing, of the Massachusetts volunteers, met with a serious accident at Matamoros on May 6. He was walking out with a lady & stepped on a loose brick & fell, & broke his left leg just above the ankle.

Final settlement of the estate of the late Gen S F Austin, after 5 years: the title to 3/4ths of the lands of Gen Austin is left to his sister, Mrs J F Perry. This settlement of title to a large amount of the choicest lands in Texas is of great importance to the public.

Battle of Cerro Gordo in the Jalapa Star: Capt Robert's Co A went into action with 41 ofcrs & men. Of the 41, 24 were left dead & wounded on the field. Every ofcr except himself was struck, & 1st Lt Ewell was killed. Those left unhurt were unable to carry off the wounded.

Wanted: a good female servant, capable of doing all kinds of house work, & who can come well recommended. Apply at my residence, on N J ave, next below the residence of T Blagden. -Saml B Beach

American prisoners in Mexico. Mr Kendall's letter of the 11th states, upon Mexican authority, that Majors Gaines & Borland, Capt Clay, Midshipman Rodgers, & other prisoners were at large in the city of Mexico, & treated with civility. It seems to us that Santa Anna's gross violation of his pledge to release these prisoners would justify his outlawry by Gen Scott.

Died: on May 27, in Gtwn, D C, Mrs Henrietta Young, widow of the late Dominick Young, of PG Co, Md. Her funeral is on Sat, at 9 o'clock, from the residence of her father, Henry Waring.

SAT MAY 29, 1847

A son of Mr Jesse Ellersbee, of Bulloch Co, Ohio, put his hand into a hollow of a tree, & immediately withdrew it, saying he had been bitten. He soon after sunk down & died. He had been bitten by a rattlesnake.

Two story frame house & lots at auction: by decree of the Circuit Court of Wash Co, D C, passed in a cause wherein Saml Redfern is cmplnt, & Barbara A Parker & others are dfndnts: sale on Jun 28, on the premises, of lot 3 in square 56, on 23rd st west, near G st, with the improvements, which are 2 nearly new 2 story frame houses.
-John F Ennis, Trustee -A Green, auctioneer

Household furniture at auction: by order of the Trustee, for account of whom is may concern, in the house at present occupied by Mr Jullien, on Pa ave. -R W Dyer, auct

Mrd: on May 26, at St Matthew's Church, Wash, by Rev Mr Donelan, John H Grindall, of Balt, to Miss Eliza McDermot, of the former place.

The funeral obsequies of Mrs Henrietta Young, widow of the late Dominick Young, will take place at St Peter's Church, Capitol Hill, this day, at 10 o'clock.

MON MAY 31, 1847
Notice appears in the Obituary of the London Morning Chronicle of the 30th ult. On the 28th instant, at the house of her son-in-law, the Earl of Ranfurley, 40 Berkley square, the Hon Sophia Margaret Stuart, grand-dght of the celebrated Wm Penn, founder & proprietor of Pennsylvania, & widow of the Hon & Rev W Stuart, D D, late Lord Primate of all Ireland, in the 83rd year of her age.

A singular case of poisoning occurred at Balt on Sat last, in the family of Mr Stephen A Pierce. Dr Pierce, son of the above, ate breakfast, partaking of some pudding. He went out about 10 o'clock. He became very ill & had to be conveyed home in a carriage. At dinner the rest of the family partook of the same pudding, & all were taken sick. Proper medicines were administered & all are in fair recovery. It had been baked in a tinpan, which had been in use only a short time before. It has not yet been ascertained how the poisonous substance became mixed with the pudding.

We learn that the late Matthew Wright bequeathed the interest on the sum of $20,000 to the 2 incorporated Orphan Asylums of Wash City.

Stacy A Paxon, Treasurer of N J, died at Trenton on Wed last.

City Ordinancee-Wash. 1-Act to refund to Joshua L Henshaw the amount paid by him for rent of the lot attached to the school-house in the First School District: the sum of $25: for the year ending Oct, 1846. 2-Act to pay John G Robinson for certain repairs on the City Hall & enclosure: sum of $38.31.

Died: in Jan last, on board the ship **Vesta**, on her voyage to Havre, Benj Lowndes, member of the bar of New Orleans, a gentleman of eminent learning & piety. The dec'd was a native of PG Co, Md.

TUE JUN 1, 1847
Circuit Court of Wash Co, D C-in Chancery. John Ham & Mary his wife, Thos O'Sheets & Eliz his wife, Michl Runner & Sarah his wife, Wm Johnson & Ann Magill his wife, David C Newcomer & Virginia his wife, David L Ham, & Jos Sherrick & Sarah his wife, against Judith Ham, Margaret Stoner, Jacob Harmer & Eliz his wife, Benj Wagoner, Eliz Wagoner, Augustine A Riggs & Margaret his wife, Ann S Wagoner, Amanda S Wagoner, Magdalena Bougher, Peter Ham, John Pursivall & Sarah Jane his wife, Louis Lauck & Emily his wife, Jacqueline Ham, Andrew J Ham, David S Cox & Mary Leight his wife, & Enos Kessinger & Margaret Ann his wife, defendents. Wm Redin, trustee, reported the sale on May 24, of part of lot 1 & lot 13 in square 118, in Wash City, that Thos R Morgan was the highest bidder for the same, for & on account of Robt J Walker, who became the purchaser thereof at the price of $2,000. Same be ratified & confirmed. -Wm Brent, clerk

Farm for sale: my farm on the Northwestern Turnpike, about 1½ miles west of Winchester, containing 376 acres; with a brick dwlg house, large & commodious, now finishing in the best syle. -A S Tidball, Winchester, Va.

Notice: stopped by the subscriber, as an estray, a small black milch cow, which the owner can have by calling on Jas S Buckley, Keeper of the Navy Yard Bridge.

Official Army Appointments & Promotions: Genr'l Orders #20, War Dept, Adj Gen Ofc, Wash, May 26, 1847: made by the Pres since the publication of Apr 28, 1847:
Promotions:
Corps of Engineers:
1st Lt Jas L Mason, to be Capt, Apr 24, 1847, vice Swift, dec'd.
2nd Lt Zealous B Tower, to be 1st Lt, Apr 24, 1847, vice Mason, promoted.
Brevet 2nd Lt Geo B McClellan, to be 2nd Lt, Apr 24, 1847, vice Tower, promoted.
1st Regt of Dragoons:
1st Lt Philip Kearny, to be Captain, Dec 6, 1846, vice Moore, killed in battle.
1st Lt Robt H Chilton, to be Captain, Dec 6, 1846, vice Johnston, killed in battle.
1st Lt Danl H Rucker, to be Captain, Feb 7, 1747, vice Burgwin, dec'd.
1st Lt Andrew J Smith, to be Captain, Feb 16, 1847, vice Boone, promoted.
1st Lt Jas H Carleton, to be Captain, Feb 16, 1847, vice Cooke, promoted to 2nd Dragoons.
2nd Lt Abraham Buford, to be 1st Lt, Dec 6, 1846, vice Kearny, promoted.
2nd Lt Patrick Noble, to be 1st Lt, Dec 6, 1846, vice Chilton, promoted.
2nd Lt Henry W Stanton, to be 1st Lt, Feb 7, 1847, vice Rucker, promoted.
2nd Lt Rufus Ingalls, to be 1st Lt, Feb 16, 1847, vice Smith, promoted.
2nd Lt Cave J Couts, to be 1st Lt, Feb 16, 1847, vice Carleton, promoted.
Brevet 2nd Lt Clarendon J L Wilson, to be 2nd Lt, Dec 6, 1846, vice Buford, promoted.
Brevet 2nd Lt John Adams, to be 2nd Lt, Dec 6, 1846, vice Noble, promoted.
Brevet 2nd Lt Thos F Castor, of the 2nd Dragoons, to be 2nd Lt, Feb 7, 1847, vice Hammond, killed in battle. Brevet 2nd Lt Orren Chapman, of the 2nd Dragoons, to be 2nd Lt, Feb 7, 1847, vice Stanton, promoted.
Brevet 2nd Lt Oliver H P Taylor, to be 2nd Lt, Feb 16, 1847, vice Ingalls, promoted.
Brevet 2nd Lt Saml D Sturgis,of the 2nd Dragoons, to be 2nd Lt, Feb 16, 1847, vice Couts, promoted.
2nd Regt of Dragoons:
Brevet 2nd Lt Thos J Wood, to be 2nd Lt, Dec 2, 1846, the date of 2nd Lt Neill's appointment as Adj.
Regt of Mounted Riflemen:
2nd Lt Thos G Rhett, to be 1st Lt, Apr 18, 1847, vice Ewell, killed in battle.
Brevet 2nd Lt Geo W Hawkins, to be 2nd Lt, Apr 18, 1847, vice Rhett, promoted.
Brevet 2nd Lt John P Hatch, to be 2nd Lt, Apr 18, 1847, vice Davis, killed in battle.
1st Regt of Artl:
1st Lt John S Hatheway, to be Captain, Mar 3,1 847, vice Waggaman, Commissary of Subsistence, who vacates his regimental commission.
2nd Lt John P Johnstone, to be 1st Lt, Mar 3, 1847, vice Hatheway, promoted.

3rd Regt of Artl:
1st Lt Wm H Shover, to be Capt, Mar 22, 1847, vice Vinton, killed in battle.
2nd Lt Francis J Thomas, to be 1st Lt, Mar 22, 1847, vice Shover, promoted.
1st Regt of Infty:
2nd Lt Jas N Caldwell, to be 1st Lt, Mar 31, 1847, vice Barry, resigned.
2nd Regt of Infty:
2nd Lt Alfred Sully, to be 1st Lt, Mar 11, 1847, vice Alburtis, killed in battle.
4th Regt of Infty:
1st Lt Henry L Scott, to be Captain, Feb 16, 1847, vice Myers, Assist Quartermaster, who vacates his regimental commission.
2nd Lt Christopher C Augur, to be 1st Lt, Feb 16, 1847, vice Scott, promoted.
Brevet 2nd Lt Edmund Russell, of the 6th Infty, to be 2nd Lt, Feb 16, 1847, vice Augur, promoted.
7th Regt of Infty:
1st Lt Chas Hanson, to be Captain, Feb 16, 1847, vice Montgomery, Assist Quartermaster, who vacates his regimental commission.
1st Lt John C Henshaw, to be Captain, Mar 3, 1847, vice Seawell, promoted to 2nd Infty.
2nd Lt Saml B Hayman, to be 1st Lt, Feb 16, 1847, vice Hanson, promoted.
2nd Lt Earl Van Dorn, to be 1st Lt, Mar 3, 1847, vice Henshaw, promoted.
Brevet 2nd Lt Wm M Gardner, of the 1st Infty, to be 2nd Lt, Feb 16, 1847, vice Hayman, promoted.
Brevet 2nd Lt Geo E Pickett, of the 8th Infty, to be 2nd Lt, Mar 3, 1847, vice Van Dorn, promoted.
8th Regt of Infty:
1st Lt Augustus L Sheppard, to be Captain, Feb 23, 1847, vice Lincoln, killed in battle.
2nd Lt Jas Longstreet, to be 1st Lt, Feb 23, 1847, vice Sheppard, promoted.
Brevet 2nd Lt Saml B Maxey, of the 7th Infty, to be 2nd Lt, Feb 23, 1847, vice Longstreet, promoted.
14th Regt of Infty:
2nd Lt A J McAllon, to be 1st Lt, May 23, 1847, vice Haile, appointed Captain-original vacancy.
15th Regt of Infty:
2nd Lt John B Goodman, to be 1st Lt, May 31, 1847, vice Eastman, resigned.
Appointments:
General Ofcrs:
Brig Gen Gideon J Pillow, of Tenn, to be Maj Gen, Apr 13, 1847, vice Benton, declined.
Brig Gen John A Quitman, of Miss, to be Maj Gen, Apr 14, 1847, vice Cumming, declined.
Adj General's Dept:
1st Lt Irvin McDowell, 1st Artl, Aid-de-Camp, to be Assist Adj Gen with the brevet rank of Captain, May 13, 1847, vice Lincoln, killed in battle.
1st Lt Francis N Page, Adj 7th Infty, to be Assist Adj Gen with the brevet rank of Captain, May 13, 1847, vice Freeman, promoted.

Quartermaster's Dept:
1st Lt Leslie Chase, 2nd Artl, to be Assist Quartermaster with the rank of Captain, Apr 10, 1847, vice Patrick, declined.
Pay Dept:
Danl Randall, Paymaster, to be Deputy Paymaser Gen, Mar 27, 1847, vice Leslie, declined.
Ordnance Dept:
Edw Lucas, jr, of Va, to be Military Storekeeper, May 12, 1847, vice Parker, resigned.
2nd Regt of Dragoons:
Arthur D Tree, late Sgt Maj, to be 2nd Lt, May 20, 1847.
3rd Regt of Dragoons:
W G Moseley, of Florida, to be 2nd Lt, Apr 12, 1847.
1st Regt of Artl:
Theodore Talbot, of D C, to be 2nd Lt, May 22, 1847.
3rd Regt of Artl:
B F McDonald, of Georgia, to be 2nd Lt, May 22, 1847.
1st Regt of Infty:
Geo D Brewerton, of N Y, to be 2nd Lt, May 22, 1847.
2nd Regt of Infty:
John R Butler, of Ky, to be 2nd Lt, May 22, 1847.
7th Regt of Infty:
Thos Henry, Quartermaster Sgt, to be 2nd Lt, May 20, 1847.
10th Regt of Infty:
Gaylord H Griswold, of N Y, to be 2nd Lt, May 13, 1847.
Abraham Scouten, of N Y, to be 2nd Lt, May 22, 1847: Co D.
Thos Spencer, of N Y, to be Surgeon, May 5, 1847, vice Thos R Spencer, declined.
Wm L Booth, of Louisiana, to be Assist Surgeon, May 22, 1847.
11th Regt of Infty:
Purnell Lofland, of Delaware, to be 2nd Lt, May 4, 1847.
Jos P Thorn, of Va, to be 2nd Lt, May 13, 1847, vice Seddon, resigned.
Jacob Brua, of Pa, to be 2nd Lt, May 25,1847, vice Ross, dec'd. [Co I]
12th Regt of Infty:
John C Simkins, of S C, to be 1st Lt, May 22, 1847, vice A C Jones, declined. [Co D]
13th Regt of Infty:
Chas McClung, of Alabama, to be 2nd Lt, May 5, 1847, vice Lowell, declined. [Co B]
14th Regt of Infty:
Christopher M Haile, of Louisiana, to be Captain, May 22, 1847, vice Nicholls, declined. [Co C]
David St Leon Porter, of Louisiana, to be 2nd Lt, May 22, 1847, vice McAllon, promoted. [Co B]
16th Regt of Infty:
Danl O May, of Indiana, to be 2nd Lt, May 22, 1847. [Co H]
Saml N Whitcomb, of Indiana, to be 2nd Lt, May 22, 1847. [Co H]
Thos M Winston, of Ky, to be 2nd Lt, May 25, 1847. [Co K]
Jas D Stuart, of Ky, to be Assist Surgeon, May 11, 1847.

Regt of Foot Riflemen & Voltigeurs:
Albert G Blanchard, of Louisiana, to be Captain, vice Bowie, declined, to date from Apr 9, 1847, & to take place in the regt next below Capt Jones-relative rank #32. [Co D]
Re-Appointments:
3rd Regt of Infty:
Stephen D Dobbins, late of the 3rd Infty, to be Captain, to date from Feb 16, 1847. [Co F]
6th Regt of Infty:
Geo C Hutter, late of the 6th Infty, to be Captain, to date from May 12, 1847. [Co E]
Appointments in pursuance of the act entitled "An act to provide for the organization of the volunteer forces brought into the service of the U S into brigades & Divisions, & for the appointment of the necessary number of Genr'l Ofcrs to command the same," approved Jun 26, 1846.
Caleb Cushing, of Mass, to be Brig Gen, Apr 14, 1847, vice Pillow, appointed Maj Gen.
Jefferson Davis, of Miss, to be Brig Gen, May 17, 1847, vice Quitman, appointed Maj Gen.
Appointments under the 5th section of the "Act supplemental to an act entitled An act providing for the prosecution of the existing war between the U S & the Republic of Mexico, & for other purposes," approved, Jun 18, 1846.
Commissary's Dept:
Thos D Martin, of Tenn, to be Assist Commissary with rank of Captain, Apr 7, 1847, vice Cherry, resigned.
Medical Dept:
Jas S McFarlane, of Louisiana, to be Surgeon, May 20, 1847, vice Muhlenberg, resigned.
D A Kinchloe, of Miss, to be Assist Surgeon, May 22, 1847, vice Fields, declined.
Appointment in the Pay Dept under the 25th section of the act, approved Jul 5, 1838:
Gaston H Wilder, of N C, to be Additional Paymaster, Jan 30, 1847, vice Stone, resigned.
Casualties: Resignation:
1st Lt Garret Barry, 1st Infty, Mar 31, 1847.
1st Lt Ahira G Eastman, 15th Infty, May 31, 1847.
2nd Lt John Seddon, 11th Infty, May 13, 1847.
Military Storekeeper Richd Parker, Ordnance Dept, May 11, 1847.
Commissions vacated under the provisions of the 7th Section of the Act approved Jun 18, 1846:
Capt A C Myers, 4th Infty, Feb 16, 1847, Assist Quartermaster: Regimental commission [only] vacated.
Capt G G Waggaman, 1st Artl, Mar 3,1 847, Commissary of Subsistence.
Capt A Montgomery, 7th Infty, Feb 16, 1847, Assist Quartermaster: Regimental commission [only] vacated.
Capt R H Chilton, Assist Quartermaster, Dec 6, 1846.
Declined:
Capt Edw F Nicholls, 14th Infty
Capt Odin Bowie, Regt Foot Riflemen & Voltigeurs
1st Lt Marsena R Patrick, 2nd Infty, as Assist Quartermaster
1st Lt A C Jones, 12th Infty
2nd Lt Wm E Reese, 12th Infty

2nd Lt Oliver Lowell, 13th Infty
Paymaster Thos J Leslie, as Deputy Paymaster General
Surgeon Thos R Spencer, 10th Infty
Deaths:
Bvt Maj John R Vinton, 3rd Artl, at siege of Vera Cruz, Mexico, Mar 22, 1847. Killed in battle.
Capt Benj D Moore, 1st Dragoons, at San Pascual, Calif, Dec 6, 1846. Killed in battle.
Capt H K Burgwin, 1st Dragoons, at Pueblo de Taos, New Mexico, Feb 7, 1847. Of wounds received Feb 4, in attack of Pueblo de Taos.
Capt Alex'r J Swift, Corps of Engineers, at New Orleans, La, Apr 24, 1847.
Bvt Capt Wm Alburtis, 2nd Infty, in the investment of Vera Cruz, Mexico, Mar 11, 1847. Killed in battle.
Capt Abraham R Johnston, 1st Dragoons, at San Pascual, Calif, Dec 6, 1846. Killed in battle.
Capt Geo Lincoln, 8th Infty, Assist Adj Gen, at Buena Vista, Mexico, Feb 23, 1847. Killed in battle.
1st Lt Thos Ewell, Mounted Riflemen, at Cerro Gordo, Mexico, Apr 18, 1847. Killed in battle.
2nd Lt Thos C Hammond, 1st Dragoons, at San Pascual, Calif, Dec 6, 1846. Killed in battle.
2nd Lt Thos Davis, Mounted Riflemen, at Cerro Gordo, Mexico, Apr 18, 1847. Killed in battle.
2nd Lt Andrew Ross, 11th Infty, at sea___
Dismissed: Capt Stephen D Dobbins, 3rd Infty, Mar 21, 1847.
Casualties: Volunteer Service: Resignations:
Capt Wm B Cherry, Assist Commissary, Apr 6, 1847
Capt Franklin Smith, Assist Quartermaster, Apr 14, 1847
Capt Nathan Adams, Assist Quartermaster, May 26, 1847
Capt John S Bradford, Assist Commissary, Apr 27, 1847
Surgeon John W Moore, May 4, 1847
Surgeon Abram S Hill, May 26, 1847
Surgeon Benj S Muhlenberg, Apr 30, 1847
Assist Surgeon Wm D Dorris, Arp 6, 1847
Assist Surgeon John W Stout, Apr 27, 1847
Assist Surgeon Enoch P Hale, May 26, 1847
Additional Paymaster Marcus C M Hammond, Apr 15, 1847
Declined: Maj John M Sharp, Quartermaster; Assist Surgeon Henry Fields
Deaths:
Capt Benj F Graham, Assist Quartermaster, of wounds received in action at San Francisco, Mexico, Feb 26, 1847 -By order: R Jones, Adj Gen

Runaway committed to the jail of Wash Co, a negro man, John Thomas, about 27 years old. He says he belongs to Hugh Perry, of PG Co, Md, & was hired to Dr Mackle, of Gtwn, D C. The owner is come & prove his property, pay charges, & take him away, otherwise he will be released according to law. -Thos Martin, Sheriff

Fred'k Co, Md, has appointed the following delegates to the Gubernatorial Convention:

Wm Ross	Peregrine Fitzhugh	J Bartholomew
Maj Richd Coale	David Schley	Dr Chas Baer

The Whigs of Balt Co, appointed the following delegates to the Gubernatorial Convention:

Wm Matthews	John Wethered	Chas A Buchanan
Peter F Cockey	Wm Tagart	Edw Worthington

WED JUN 2, 1847

Potomac Pavilion-Piney Point, Md: the subscribers having taken this popular place of recreation, will be open for reception of visiters on Jun 15. -Kirkwood & Keller

The citizens of Alexandria are about to present a splendid sword to Lt Col Childs, U S Army, as a testimonial of their admiration of his gallant conduct in Mexico. Col Childs was formerly a citizen of Alexandria.

The citizens of Newburgh, N Y, have caused to be made an elegant sword, which they intend to present to Col Belknap, U S Army, as a testimonial of their admiration of his gallantry as a soldier. Col Belknap is a native of Newburgh.

Judge John Schley died on May 26, at his residence in this county, of a disease of the heart, aged 62 years. For several years he occupied the station of Judge of the Supreme Court of the Middle Circuit of Georgia. -Augusta Chronicle

Toronto papers announce the death of Rev Thos Fidler, missionary at Fenelon Falls. His boat, in which were himself & 2 laboring men, was drawn into the current & carried over the Falls, the 3 perishing.

Wash Corp: 1-Cmte of Claims: bill for the relief of Jas McColgon: passed. 2-Passed-act for the relief of Michl Talty; of John B Hilleary; of Thos Baker; of Caroline H Sanderson; & of Wm Cooper. 3-Ptn presented from N Tastet: to lie on the table. 4-Cmte of Claims: asking to be discharged from the further consideration of the ptn of Richd Wetherall: agreed to.

Jalapa, Mexico, May 3, 1847. Gen Quitman's brigade will leave by Tue, which will be followed in a day thereafter by either Gen Pillow's or Shields' brigade, until they have all left. Gen Twiggs' command will then follow. The last authentic information from Santa Anna left him in possession of about 3,000 men, which he expected to augment to 4,000 in a very short time. We have in the hospitals in this city between 300 & 400 wounded, among whom within the last few days there has been quite a number of deaths. The most critical & doubtful case is that of Gen Shields; but from what I ascertained this morning from Capt Davis, his aid-de-camp, he would eventually recover. Gen Scott has nearly recovered. [N B: The contents of this paper have been anticipated by the reception of later dates since the above letter was written.]

Dr Whistler, of Sandy Prairie, Scott Co, Missouri, was shot at & killed while riding, by some one concealed in bushes.

Died: on May 25, at New Market, Md, Abel Russell, aged 66 years.

Large reward for return of strayed or stolen fine young red Milch Cow.
-L M Powell, 3rd st

Valuable lots at auction: by order of the Orphans Court of Wash Co, D C: lot 11 in square 348, fronting on E st, between 10th & 11th sts. Part of lot 12 in square 348, fronting on E st. Lots 7 & 8 in square 316, on the n e corner of 12th & K sts, near Franklin Row.
-B Homans, auctioneer

The Wilkesbarre [Pa] Advertiser states that on May 22, the powder mill in Kingston, belonging to Mr D Schooley, exploded. Silas Lord, a young man, was instantly killed.

Orphans Court of Wash Co, D C. Letters testamentary on the personal estate of Matthew Wright, late of said county, dec'd. -Jas Adams, Matthew Trimble, excs

For rent, a desirable house for a small family, on 12th st, between F & G sts. Inquire at the residence of R M Beall, Pollard's Row, east of the City Hall.

Official: the Volunteer Staff of the Army. Gen Orders, 22: War Dept, Adj Gen's Ofc, Wash, May 29, 1847. The Pres directs that the following ofcrs be retained, to wit:

Quartermasters with the rank of Major:
1-Saml M Mooney
2-Alex'r Dunlap
3-Thos B Eastland
4-Benj McCullough
5-Nathl Anderson

Assist Quartermasters will the rank of Captain:
1-Theodore O'Hara
2-Jos Naper
3-Alanson W Enos
4-Robt R Howard
5-Jos Daniels
6-Geo W Miller
7-Jas H Ralston
8-Geo H Kennerly
9-Jas H Walker
10-Hugh O'Donnell
11-Geo M Lauman
12-Saml H Montgomery
13-Saml McGowan
14-Chas M Price
15-Chas R Webster
16-Chas E Carr
17-Jas L Kemper
18-Paul R George
19-Solomon Pender, jr
20-Jas Vaughan

Commissaries with the rank of Major:
1-Alfred Boyd
2-Alex'r F Morrison
3-Brookens Campbell
4-Richd Roman
5-Fred'k A Churchill

Assist Commissaries with the rank of Captain:

1-Amos F Garrison
2-Wm C McCaudlin
3-Thos P Randle
4-Nehemiah Hayden
5-Robt Fenner
6-Saml Hackelton
7-Wm G Marcy
8-Geo T Howard
9-Francis M Dimond
10-Isaac E Diller
11-Jas D Blaiding
12-John W Shugart
13-Robt Josselyn
14-Wm Barksdale
15-Jas F Hutton
16-Francis M Mioton
17-Henry Erskin
18-Exum L Whitaker
19-Stephen Hoyt
20-Thos D Martin

Surgeons:

1-Edw B Price
2-Seymour Hasley
3-Wm Trevitt
4-E K Chamberlain
5-Caleb V Jones
6-A Parker
7-Geo Penn
8-Ewing H Roane
9-Alex'r Perry
10-John C Reynolds
11-Jas Davis
12-Luther F Dashiel
13-Jos L Hasbrouck
14-Wm H J Anson
15-Thos N Love
16-Gaston D Cobbs
17-Otis Hoyt
18-Jas S McFarlane
19-Wm B Herrick

Assist Surgeons:

1-Danl Turney
2-Robt McNeil
3-John Thompson
4-John G Dunn
5-Jas B Snail
6-C J Clark
7-E Tucker
8-Thos M Morton
9-John W Glenn
10-Geo B Sanderson
11-Wm C Parker
12-Thos C Bunting
13-Elbert Bland
14-Fred'k W Miller
15-Mina B Halstead
16-Jas M Bell
17-Jas A Macrae
18-Timothy Childs
19-D A Kinchloe
20-__ Miller, [of Illinois]

The President directs that all the ofcrs appointed for the volunteer staff, not named in the foregoing list, either in the Quartermaster, Commissary, or Medical Depts, be discharged from the public service on Jun 30 next. W L Marcy, Sec of War
By order: R Jones, Adj Gen

Constable's sale: by virtue of a writ of fieri facias, against the goods & chattels, lands & tenements, rights & credits of Henderson Fowler & John L Fowler, & to me directed, I have seized one brick dwlg-house & part of lot 17, in square 799, in Wash City, & will sell the interest of the said John L Fowler in same, on Jul 1. -Thos Plumsill, Constable

Household & kitchen furniture at auction: on Jun 3, at the residence of Josiah Clements, near the Navy Yard gate. -A Green, auctioneer

THU JUN 3, 1847

Circuit Court of Wash Co, D C-in Chancery, Mar Term, 1847. Thos P Jones, vs Wm Cammack & Allison Nailor. The bill states that the cmplnt in 1841 purchased of the dfndnt Cammack that part of lot 17 in square 253, in Wash City, which had been conveyed to the latter by deed recorded in Liber W B 75, folio 265, land record of Wash Co; that Cammack gave his bond for conveyance of the said lot, on the payment of the purchase money; that the same has been fully paid, but that Cammack has made no conveyance of the said lot, but has left D C & gone to parts unknown to the cmplnt. The bill prays a decree for the conveyance of the said lot to cmplnt, & an order of publication against the said dfndnt Cammack, & also leave to redeem the said lot from a tax sale, & a conveyance thereof to the said Nailor. -Wm Brent, clk

The house of F X Quevillion, of St Lin, Lower Canada, was burnt to the ground on May 6. Madame Quevillion & her 4 children, were burnt to death. Her husband was absent at the time of the accident.

$50 reward for apprehension & securing in jail, in PG Co, Md, so that I get him again, my negro man Philip: about 25 to 30 years of age. I bought him out of the estate of Mr John A Turton, between Nottingham & Piscataway. He may be about that place, or sulking about Dr Edw Eversfield's, near Piscataway, where he is said to have a wife. He left his wife & children at home. -Thos N Baden, near Nottingham, PG Co, Md.

On Sunday last, while a party of friends were passing through a wood in Glenville, near Schenectady, a root, mistaken for spignet, was pulled up & eaten by Eliz A Boyer, which caused her death suddenly & violently, before medical aid could be procured.

In Chancery in Somerset Co Court-May Term, 1847. May 27, 1847. Thos Robertson, vs Isaac Parks, John Parks, Wm Parks, Mary Parks, Hugh Ford & Nancy Ford his wife. The object of this suit is to procure a decree for the sale of the real estate of which Edw Parks died seised for the payment of his debts. The bill states that Edw Parks was in his lifetime indebted to the cmplnt for $235.30 on several judgments rendered in the 3rd District Court of Somerset County; that the said Edw Parks, under the will of his father Wm Parks, was seised of certain real estate in said county, subject to the life estate of his mother Sally Parks, who is still living; that the said Edw Parks died in 1845 intestate, leaving Isaac Parks, John Parks, Wm Parks, Mary Parks, & Nancy Ford, wife of Hugh Ford, his only heirs at law, all of whom are of full age & reside in Somerset Co, except the said John Parks & Wm Parks, who do not reside in Md; that the said Edw Parks at the time of his death was possessed of no personal estate, & that no letters of administration have been granted thereon; that the cmplnt is entitled to have his said claims paid out of the real estate in the hands of his said heirs at law; the bill prays for a sale of said real estate, & for subpoenas against the resident dfndnts & an order of publication as to the non-resident dfndnts to warn them to appear & answer. Notice give to John Parks & Wm Parks to appear in this court, on or before Nov 2. -Wm T G Polk, clerk

The locomotive running on the railroad between Ithica & Owego broke through the bridge on Sat last, near Candor, & killed D C Hatch & A Dickinson, who were on it at the time.

For sale or rent: 3 story brick house on south A st, Capitol Hill, near the south gate of the Capitol square. This house is well calculated for a tavern, store, or boarding house, as it fronts the principal street leading to the Navy Yard. Apply to the subscriber, Mrs A Sweeny.

For rent: 2 story brick dwlg house on 13th st, adjoining Mr Gaither's block. Apply to Mr B Willet, on the west side of the same street, a door or 2 south of Pa ave.

Trustee's sale of valuable property: on Jun 9, under deed of trust from the late Fred'k Chas Erb & his wife, Wilhelmine Erb, to H H Dent, dated Oct 1, 1845, recorded in liber W B 121, folios 35 thru 37, in the land records of Wash Co, D C: lot 10 in square 758, of Wash City, with bldgs & improvements thereon. The property fronts on Md ave.
-H H Dent, Trustee -A Green, auctioneer

FRI JUN 4, 1847
On Sat week a young man, Hamilton Spangler, of East Berlin, Adams Co, Pa, aged 17 years, while in the act of shooting a squirrel, was so severely injured by the kicking of his gun that he soon after died.

The Springfield [Mass] papers announce the death of Rev Dr Wm B O Peabody, well known as an able contributor to the North American Review & other periodicals.
[No date-current news item.]

Lt Geiger, of the Staunton Volunteers, on May 20, was fired on by one of the public guard, & his leg so terribly shattered a few inches above the knee, that immediate amputation of the limb was done. Hopes are entertained of his speedy recovery.

Savannah Republican of May 28. On May 26 Geo Anderson, one our oldest & most respected citizens died. Mr Anderson was born in the city of Savannah, & was at the time of his death 80 years of age. He was one of the most active men in procuring the charters of our banking institutions. Over the fortunes of the Planter's Bank he presided a long time with signal success & credit to himself.

Dr Wm Marbury offers his professional services to the citizens of Gtwn & vicinity. Ofc in the basement of Mr J Ratcliff's dwlg, north side of Gay st, a few door west of Congress st, Gtwn, D C.

$5 reward for lost pocketbook containing a gold pencil, & 7 promissory notes, with some cards & memoranda of no value to any one but the owner. Leave at this ofc-J F May.

New Orleans Picayune of May 27. Gen Shields continues to improve slowly.

Chancery sale: by virtue of a decree of the Circuit Court of Wash Co, D C, as Court of Chancery, made in the cause of Easter, Bro & Co, vs Wm Ward et al, I shall offer at auction, on Jun 25, all the west half part of lot 11 in square A, in Wash City, with a 3 story brick dwlg: fronts on the north side of Missouri st. The creditors of Wm C Orme, dec'd, are warned to exhibit their claims, with the vouchers thereof, in the above cause, on or before the 3rd Mon in Oct next. -Clement Cox, Trustee -R W Dyer, auct

Jalapa, Mexico, May 16, 1847. Capt Mason, of the rifles, died on May 15th. He is to be buried this afternoon with military honors. He was a gallant & most promising young officer, beloved by all.

Orphans Court of Wash Co, D C. Letters of administration on the personal estate of John Little, late of said county, dec'd. -Wm B Jackson, adm

SAT JUN 5, 1847

New Candle & Soap Factory: in warehouse on Lenox's wharf, near Long Bridge.
-Jared Coleman

Divorces-Cincinnati must be a great place for the enjoyment of connubial felicity. Last week the Court of Common Pleas granted 20 divorces to mismatched, dissatisfied couples.

Mrd: on Thu, by Rev John C Smith, Mr Robt T Bassett to Miss Susan Demarest, all of Wash City.

Died: on May 29, at Bladensburg, of consumption, Mr John Cull, in his 39th year. The dec'd was greatly esteemed by his many friends for his mild & amiable qualities.

Clover Hill Coal will be received by the undersigned, agent for the Clover Hill Co, who will furnish to any of the Depts or to families who desire it a sample of the Coal.
-Wm E Stubbs, G st, near 9th st.

Household & kitchen furniture, & servants, at auction by order of the Orphans Court of Wash Co, D C. Sale on Jun 9, at the late residence of Simon Fraser, dec'd, south F st, between 8th & 9th sts west: 2 valuable servants, slaves for life. -A Green, auctioneer

MON JUN 7, 1847

Fresh troops for the war. Maj Savage, Capt Huddleston, Lt Humphreys, Lt Bedford, & Lt Love, with 100 soldiers of Co I, 14th Regt U S Infty, arrived at New Orleans from Nashville on May 28, on their way to the seat of war. The latest accounts from Galveston [to the 26th] state that Col Hays' Regt of volunteers had departed from San Antonio on the 14th for Monterey, intending to cross the Rio Grande at Loredo.

Mr Robt Meldron, an old & respectable citizen residing near Deerfield, Ohio, met his death, when burning brush & trees. A tree fell across his thighs, holding him in that iron vice. He was nearly consumed when his body was found.

The following gentleman are the Directors of the Farmers' Bank of Virginia at Alexandria:

Phineas Janney-Pres	W Fowle	A P Gover
Hugh Smith	G H Smoot	
Wm Gregory	J H Brent	

The Branch went into operation on Fri last. Washington C Paul: Cashier

Albert G Fuqua was shot dead on May 8 by Thos Harper, eldest son of Mr W W Harper, of the parish of Iberville, La. The young man was examined & admitted to bail in the sum of $5,000.

A fatal accident happened at Franklinton, N C, as the Pres of the U S proceeded on to Raleigh. A man named Dancy was instantly killed as the parting salute was fired.

Mrd: on Jun 4, by Rev C A Davis, Mr Henry M Lowry to Miss Mary J Calvert, both of Wash City.

City Ordinances: 1-Act for the relief of R R Burr, & for other purposes: to be paid the sum of $120 for services rendered as acting Intendant of the Asylum for Feb 9 to Mar 4, 1847. Also, to pay to the late Guardians of the Poor, in proportions that may be due to each, the sum of $360; & to the Physicians of the Asylum his half year's salary when due, being to Jun 30th next. 2-Act for the relief of Caroline H Sanderson: fine imposed for the violation of an ordinance relative to the keeping or harboring of dogs, is hereby remitted. 3-Act for the relief of H R Maryman, late Police Ofcr: to be paid $160.58, being the balance due him for workhouse & other fees to Jul 31, 1846. 4-Act for the relief of Jas McColgan: remit fine imposed for an alleged violation in the erection of frame bldgs. 5-Act for the relief of John B Hilleary: fine imposed for alleged violation relative to the keeping of dogs: hereby remitted. 6-Act for the relief of Thos Baker: fine imposed for a violation relative to the keeping open taverns: hereby remitted. 7-Act for the relief of Michl Talty: fine imposed for alleged violation relative to taverns: hereby remitted. 8-Act for the relief of Wm Cooper: fine imposed upon Wm Cooper be remitted, together with the costs of prosecution; the amount of said fine & costs being $19.93.

For rent: desirable brick residence on 3rd st, lately occupied by Gov Bagby. For terms apply to G W Phillips, dry goods merchant.

TUE JUN 8, 1847

Valuable brick house at auction on Jun 15, on the premises, that large & commodious 3 story brick house, owned & occupied by Mr E Guttslich, on La ave, near 6th st. The lot is 25 feet front & 100 feet deep. The property is wholly unincumbered & the title indisputable. -B Homans, auctioneer

Thos A Marshall, of Lexington, has been appointed by the Govn'r to be Chief Justice of Ky, in the place of Ephraim M Ewing, resigned. Jas Simpson, of Clarke Co, to be Judge of the Court of Appeals, in the place of Thos A Marshall, appointed Chief Justice. The Court of Appeals consists of: Hon Thos A Marshall, Chief Justice; Hon Danl Breck & Jas Simpson.

Died: on Jun 3, in the Convent at Gtwn, after a long & painful illness of consumption, Sister Mary Simplecia, youngest daughter of the late Michl Flanagan, in her 24th year.

Balt American of yesterday: we announce the death of our esteemed fellow-citizen, Maj Jas O Law, which took place yesterday. While in the performance of an act of the most charitable devotion, & his unremitted attention to the sick emigrants now at Canton, he contracted the disease which caused his premature death. The dec'd was formerly Mayor of the city, an ofc which he filled with great efficiency; he was also for many years Pres of the Independent Fire Co; &, at the time of his death, was Major of the 53rd Regt Md Volunteers, & held the several ofcs of Treas of the Hibernian Society, Noble Grand of Franklin Lodge I O O F, & Treasurer of Ira Encampment of the same Order. He also held the appointment, under the State Gov't, of Inspector Genr'l of the Fleet. Few men have died more universally regretted by the whole community than Maj Law.

Hon Saml W Morris, of Tioga Co, Pa, died at his residence in Wellsborough on May 25, in his 60th year. He served many years as Judge of the Court in that District, & was afterwards twice elected to Congress.

Wash City election for 1 Alderman & 3 Common Councilmen. The following is the vote:
1st Ward:
For Alderman: Wm B Scott: 105; John D Barclay: 81
For Councilman:

Thos P Morgan: 119	Saml Stott: 106	Wm Easby: 90
Geo J Abbott: 110	Wm Wilson: 99	Scattering: 3

2nd Ward:
For Alderman: John Wilson: 97; Lambert S Tree: 56
For Councilmen:

Lewis Johnson: 104	Nicholas Callan: 73	Geo W Stewart: 11
Jas F Haliday: 80	John A Blake: 65	
Jesse E Dow: 74	John E Norris: 27	

3rd Ward:
For Alderman: Stephen P Franklin: 108
For Councilmen:

Jos Borrows: 84	Jos Bryan: 70
Silas H Hill: 80	John W Moorhead: 57

4th Ward:
For Alderman: John W Maury: 172
For Councilmen:

Richd Wallach: 145	Hugh B Sweeny: 138	Saml Bacon: 92

Thos H Havenner: 71	A H Lawrence: 51	Scattering: 3

5th Ward:

For Alderman: Jas Adams: 96; Peter Brady: 69; Jas Young: 17

For Councilmen:

John Johnson: 75	Richd Dement: 63	Jas B Fugett: 17
C E Tims: 73	Wm W Lowe: 52	John Purdy: 13
E W Smallwood: 68	John L Maddox: 33	___ White: 8
John M Jamieson: 57	Jacob B Gardner: 29	Thos E Mackey: 6

6th Ward:

For Alderman: Robt Clark: 82

For Councilmen:

Jas Cull: 70	John R Queen: 67	Geo H Fulmer: 67

7th Ward:

For Alderman: Ignatius Mudd: 66

For Councilmen:

Wm Lloyd: 57	Wm Ashdown: 41	John W Jones: 15
John T Cassell: 56	Wm Wise: 30	

WED JUN 9, 1847

The New Orleans Picayune states, on the authority of Lt Aiken, of the 2nd Ky Foot, that a most deplorable duel occurred at China, Mexico, about May 21, between 2 Lts in the Va Regt-one of whom was named Mahan, & the other the name not recollected. They fought with muskets loaded with ball & buckshot, & both parties were killed.

Franklin [La] Banner, of May 5: an affray the day before occurred between Mr Jos Hartman, of Bayou Sarah & Mr Alfred Stansberry, a planter of Bayou Chene, in that parish. Stansberry, with his wife & children, stopped at the house of Hartman to dine. A dispute arose & Stansberry called to his son to get him his gun; Hartman went into the house & got a gun & shot Stansberry as he was in the act of rising with his gun. Stansberry died within moments. This occurred in the presence of the wives & children of both parties. Hartman has been lodged in jail.

Pensacola Gaz: ofcrs of the navy, who have been attached to the squadron in the Gulf, relieved to repair their health, arrived there during the past week, viz: Capt Tatnall, Lt R E Hooe, & Lt McBlair. Capt Tatnall appeared to have recovered entirely from his wound received in the capture of Tuspan on Apr 18 last. Lt Hooe had been confined, first at Tampico & then at New Orleans, by extreme ill health, & has returned to Pensacola for treatment in the hospital.

Military Movements. Co F, Lt R P Maclay, 8th Infty, 90 men; Co G, Capt Larkin Smith, 8th Infty, 90 men; Co H, Lt C F Lovell, 2nd Infty, 90 men; & Lt W K Van Bokkelen, 7th Infty, Commissary to the detachment, sailed from N Y for Vera Cruz on Sat.

Orphans Court of Wash Co, D C. Letters of administration on the personal estate of Patrick Crowley, late a private in the U S Marine Corps, dec'd, be granted to Wm I Jeffers, a creditor, unless cause to the contrary be shown on or before Jun 29.
-Ed N Roach, Reg/o wills

On Sat last Mr White, of the firm of White & Headon, of Decatur, Ga, while driving a pair of horses in a barouche from Atlantic to Decatur, the horses took fright, & Miss Stone, daughter of Danl Stone, an old & respectable citizen & clerk of the Superior Court of Decatur, was precipated over the dash board & killed.

$250 reward for the return to her disconsolate parents their dght Mary Fox, or one-half of said reward for information as will lead to her recovery. She left her school on May 20, & has not been seen since. She is only 15 years of age, small features, & quite girlish in appearance. It is strongly suspected that she has been abducted by Michl alias Martin Hare, who absconded about that time from this city, deserting his wife, & leaving her entirely destitute of support. Said Hare is about 28 years of age, & of rather genteel appearance. He was seen lurking in the neighborhood of her school a short time previous, disguised with false whiskers. Communicate [by telegraph, if possible] to Geo W Matzell, Chief of Police, N Y.

Household & kitchen furniture at auction: on Jun 11, at the residence of Jacob Small, near the Navy Yard Market-house, a good lot of furniture. -A Green, auctioneer

For rent or sale, & possession immediately: the commodious 3 story brick dwlg house & premises at the corner of 3rd & D sts. Inquire of Jas Larned, 13th st, for the owner.

THU JUN 10, 1847
For sale: 1,016 acres of land on Ivy creek, Albemarle Co, 5 miles from Charlottesville, on the Staunton turnpike: improvements are a good dwlg house with 8 rooms, & other out bldgs. Also, an estate of 700 acres on James river, Fluvanna Co, at the junction of Hardware with that stream: there are now houses to cure 15 hogsheads, built in the best manner. Direct communications to me at Hardin's tavern, Albemarle Co, Va.
-W W Gilmer

Chancery Sale: by decree of the Circuit Court of Wash Co, D C, sitting as a Court of Chancery, made in the cause of Benj L Jackson & Wm B Jackson, vs Catherine Leddon & Jas S Harvey, adms upon the estate of Benj Leddon, dec'd, et al. Public sale on Jul 7, part of square 353 in Wash City, with a 2 story brick dwlg thereon. The creditors of Benj Leddon, dec'd, are hereby warned to file their claims, with the vouchers thereof, within 2 months from the day of the above sale. -Walter D Davidge, Trustee -R W Dyer, auct

Miss Mary Watson was burnt to death in Southwark, Phil, on Sat, by rashly attempting to fill a burning fluid lamp while it was burning, & her mother & brother severely, & grandmother slightly burnt also, in attempting to extinguish the flames. She lingered in great agony until Sunday.

Medical Dept of the Army: The Army Medical Board, which convened in N Y C for examination of applicants for appointment to the Medical Staff of the Regular Army, adjourned on May 25. Of the candidates who were exaimined the following were approved:

Nicholas L Campbell, N Y
John Campbell, N Y
Saml L Barbour, Ga
John E Summers, Va
Geo Edw Cooper, Pa
Chas H Smith, Va
Ebenezer Swift, Ohio
Washington M Ryer, N Y
John S Battee, Md
P G Stuyvesant Ten Broeck, N Y
Glover Parin, Ohio

Before the same Board, Surgeon John B Wells was examined for promotion to that grade, & was fully approved.

Died: on Jun 8, of consumption, Mary W, w/o Mr Isaac H Wayles, of Wash City, in her 45th year. Her funeral is from her late residence on 10th st, near Md ave, this morning, at 10 o'clock.

Died: on May 31, at Newcastle, Delaware, after a painful illness, Eliz Clayton Young, w/o Maj Nathl Young, & daughter of the Hon Thos Clayton.

Official: Gen orders #23. War Dept, Adj Gen Ofc, Wash, Jun 1, 1847. The Surgeons & Assist Surgeons retained in the service of the U S by the Pres for duty with the Volunteers enrolled for the war with Mexico, are assigned to Regts & Bltns as follows:

Massachusetts Regt, Col ____
Surgeon Otis Hoyt, of Mass
Assist Surgeon Timothy Childs, of Mass
1st N Y Regt, [Col J D Stevenson]
Surgeon Alex'r Perry, of N Y
Assist Surg Wm C Parker, of N Y
2nd N Y Regt, [Col W B Burnett]
Surgeon Jos L Hasbrouck, of N Y
Assist surgeon Min B Halstead, of N Y
1st Pennsylvania Regt, [Col F M Wynkoop]
Surgeon John C Reynolds, of Pa
Assist Surgeon Thos C Bunting, of Pa
2nd Pennsylvania Regt, [Col W B Roberts]
Surgeon Jas S McFarlane, of La
Assist Surgeon Fred'k W Miller, of Pa
Virginia Regt, [Col J F Hamtramck]
Surgeon Wm H J Anson, of Va
Asist Surgeon Jas M Bell, of Va
North Carolina Regt, [Col R T Paine]
Surgeon Gaston D Cobbs, of N C
Assist Surgeon Jas A Macrae, of N C
South Carolina Regt, [Col P M Butler]

Surgeon Jas Davis, of S C
Assist Surgeon Elbert Bland, of S C
Louisiana Regt, [Col L G De Russy]
Surgeon Luther F Dashiel, of La
Assist Surgeon John Thompson, of Miss
Texas Regt of Horse, [Col J C Hays]
Surgeon A Parker, of Texas
Assist Surgeon E Tucker, of Texas
Mississippi Regt, [Col Reuben Davis]
Surgeon Thos N Love, of Miss
Assist Surgeon D A Kinchloe, of Miss
Ohio Regt, [Col ___]
Surgeon E K Chamberlain, of Ohio
Assist Surgeon Robt McNeill, of Ohio
Indiana Regt, [Col___]
Surgeon Caleb V Jones, of Indiana
Assist Surgeon John G Dunn, of Indiana
1st Illinois Regt, [Col____]
Surgeon Wm B Herrick, of Ill
Assist Surgeon Danl Turney, of Ill
Missouri Regt of Horse, [Col ___]
Surgeon Geo Penn, of Mo
Assist Surgeon Thos M Morton, of Mo
Missouri Btln of Horse, [Lt Col ___]
Assistant Surgeon Jas B Snail, of Ky
Missouri Btln of Foot, [Lt Col ___]
Assistant Surgeon Geo B Sanderson, of Mo
Alabama Btln, [Lt Col ___]
Assist Surgeon C J Clarke, of Ala
Louisiana Btln, [Lt Col ___]
Assist Surgeon John W Glenn, of Arkansas
The foregoing assignment embraces all the Medical Ofcrs retained, except Surgeon Seymour Halsey, of Miss, Wm Trevitt, of Ohio, & Ewing H Roane, of Ark. The former will report in person to Maj Gen Scott, the other 2 to Maj Gen Taylor, who will assign them to duty. By order: R Jones, Adj Gen

Lt Julian May: some of the Northern papers have motally wounded this ofcr, & others have actually killed him, at Cerro Gordo. We, therefore, to set matters right, state that his wound was a slight one, & from which he has entirely recovered.

FRI JUN 11, 1847
Troops for Vera Cruz: the barque **Edith** sailed for Vera Cruz on Jun 2, with 2 companies of troops, one under Capt Guthrie, 11th Infty, & one under Capt Casey, 2nd Infty.

For sale or rent the steam-brick press: the proprietor of this well-known establishment offers it for sale. The bldgs are capacious, & the steam machinery being in good order. For full particulars apply to Mr Jos Ingle, who, in the absence of the proprietor, will act as his agent.

1st Ward property for sale: the subscriber, wishing to sell any or all of his property, would like to dispose of: one 2 story house on H st, between 17th & 18th sts, containing 11 rooms. One 3 story brick dwlg & store on Pa ave, between 17th & 18th sts; store occupied by Mr Rawlings, dry goods dealer; dwlg vacant, for rent.
One 2 story frame-house on 19th st, 2nd door south of the Union Engine-house; & one 2 story frame on G st, near 23rd st. Apply to the subscriber, at his residence, on 19th st, 2 doors south of the Union Engine-house. -Jos Fraser

The son of Hon Mr Sawyer, & the son of Mr Vanhorne, of St Mary's, left there about 5 days ago to go to Mr Sawyer's farm, 2 miles from St Mary's, & left the farm, on their return homes, the same afternoon. Since then they have not been heard from. About 400 persons have been searing the woods & creeks. Mr Sawyer offers a reward of $1,000 for their recovery. They are about 10 & 12 years of age. -Cinci Chron

Return of troops: the ship **Remittance**, from Brasos, brought to New Orleans on Jun 2 the following troops: Col Churchill, U S A; Col S D Wilson, 15th Infty; Lt Col Field, commanding a portion of the Ky Cavalry, & 160 non-commissioned ofcrs & privates.

Died: on Jun 9, in Balt, Danl Cover, aged 48 years. His funeral is on Fri, at 4 o'clock, from the residence of Geo Parker, corner of 4½ st & C st, without further notice.

SAT JUN 12, 1847
Capt Edw Webster, at present in New Orleans on leave of absence, has been appointed by Gen Cushing aid-de-camp, with the rank & emoluments of major. He will not come north, but, as soon as his health will permit, intends returning to Matamoros.

Mrd: on Wed last, by Rev Mr Donelan, Mr Chas H Kreamer to Miss Catharine Martin, all of Wash City.

Mrd: on Jun 3, at ***Mount Pleasant***, near Upper Marlboro, by Rev Mr Saunders, O C Magruder to Sally, youngest daughter of Col Waring, late of PG Co, Md.

Died: on Jun 10, at N Y, in her 72nd year, Mrs Helen Macleod, w/o Mr John Macleod, late of Wash City, & formerly of the Gen Post Ofc Dept.

Died: in May, in Brunswick, Va, very suddenly, Mrs Rebeca Sims, w/o Dr Richd Sims. Mrs Sims was sister to the Hon Geo C Dromgoole, dec'd, & mother of the Hon A D Sims, at present a member of the House of Reps in Congress from S C.

Died: on Jun 6, at her residence in Prince Wm Co, Va, after a protracted illness, Mrs Margery Barron, relict of the late Dr Hendly Barron, in her 78th year. The Editors of the Union, Alexandria Gaz, & Port Tobacco Times will please copy.

The undersigned, having sold out his interest in the Lumber Yard adjoining the Centre Market, near the Canal, to Mr Peter M Pearson, has opened a Yard near the Railroad Depot, in the rear of his present dwlg. -John Purdy

MON JUN 14, 1847

Headquarters Army of Occupation, Camp near Monterey, May 9, 1847. Sir: Your letter of the 4th ult, in relation to the remains & effects of your much lamented son, Capt Geo Lincoln, has safely reached me. I beg leave to offer my heartfelt sympathies with you in the death of this accomplished gentleman. In his fall you have been bereaved of a son whom you might be justly proud, while the army has lost one of its most gallants soldiers. I learn upon inquiry, that the body of your son was carefully removed from the field immediately after his death, & that it was decently interred by itself. His effects are understood to have been collected with due care, & are now under the direction of Gen Wool. He will be kind enough to put the remains & effects, carefully prepared for transportation, in route for N Y or Boston, by the first safe opportunity.
-Z Taylor, Maj Gen U S Army to Gov Levi Lincoln, Worcester, Mass.

The Providence Journal announces the death of Hezekiah Williams, Collector of that port. He died on Sunday last.

The daughter of Mr Geo Taylor, near Upper Marlborough, Md, was burnt to death a few days ago by her clothes taking fire. She was about 14 years of age.

Died: on Jun 12, in Wash City, Geo C, 2nd son of Jas & Rosanna B Anderson. His funeral is this morning at 10 o'clock, from the residence of his parents on south side of Pa ave.

Died: on Jun 7, at Woodland, Chas Co, Md, Miss Annie Maria Hamilton, after a protracted illness of several months, in her 29th year.

The Parlor Magazine, J T Headley, Editor. This magazine, formerly under the care of D Mead, commences its 4th Volume under the editorship of J T Headley, author of Napoleon & his Marshals, Washington & his Generals, & Letters from Italy.
-E E Miles, Publisher, 151 Nassau st, N Y

The undersigned informs that after having for a series of years labored for others, & for their benefit, has made a break, & commenced working for himself. So all those who want Lumber, Lime, Cement, or Calcined Plaster, will find themselves accommodated by called at his Lumber Yard, which is the stand vacated by Mr John Purdy, & so long occupied by Alex'r Shepherd, being on 7th st, near the Canal, & adjoining the Centre Market. -P M Pearson

For rent: well finished 2 story brick house, on Missouri st, between 4½ & 6th sts. -E Lindsley

TUE JUN 15, 1847

By virtue of a deed of trust from Andrew Jenkins & Fanny Jenkins, late Fanny Hampton, his wife, dated Jul 5, 1841, recorded in Liber W B 89, folios 189 through 192, one of the land records of Wash Co, D C: sale at auction, on Jul 16, the south half part of lot 23 in square 5 in Wash City, with a small frame house. -Thos Jewell, Trust -B Homans, auct

The Hon Richd Rush, our Minister to France, accompanied by his family, sailed from N Y on Sat in the packet ship **Dutchesse d'Orleans** for Havre.

On the night of Jan 28 last Capt Monroe Quarrier, of the steamer **James Hewitt**, rescued sufferers from the steamboat **Tuscaloosa**, that left Mobile for Tuscaloosa. Her boilers exploded, causing the death of several of the ofcrs, crew, & passengers. The only chance for relief of some of the survivors, was from some passing boat, for all would have perished if compelled to remain many hours in the water. The sufferers were taken on board. After all were safe & comfortable, the **Hewitt** returned to Mobile.

Mr C F Daniels, well known as one of the ablest editors in the U S, has taken charge of the New London [Ct] Morning News. He is a native of that county. -Louisville Journal

The subscribers wish to employ a male Teacher, who is qualified to teach the Latin, Greek, & English languages, to take care of a small School in a healthy neighborhood. Salary will be $300 per annum, paid semi-annually, & board. Apply to W J Hill & W H Anthony, Scotland Neck, N C.

From the Buffalo Commercial Advertiser of Jun 11. Yesterday a fatal collision occurred off Conneaut, between the steamer **Chesapeake**, bound up with passengers & merchandise, & the schnr **J F Porter**, bound down with a cargo of wheat & corn. The only person belonging to the steamer missing is the first enginer. Mr Folsom, of Cleveland, was on board, with his family; his family is safe, but he is among the missing. Capt Warner & his mates are highly spoken up. [Jun 16th newspaper: the collision on Lake Erie of the steamer **Chesapeake** & schnr **J F Porter** was attended with a larger loss of life than was at first supposed. The Cleveland Herald gives the names of the dead of the steamboat **Chesapeake**: passengers-Geo Van Doren, of Lower Sandusky, Ohio; E Cone, of Bellville, Ohio; S York, of Tifflin, Ohio; Mrs Houck, of Watertown, N Y. Crew: R Sutherland, 1st Engineer; O Wait, 2nd porter, & R McMann, deck hand. It is greatly feared that Mr D A Folsom, of Rochester, N Y, formerly of Cleveland, is also among the lost. The passengers lost all their baggage, not a single trunk being saved. The mail to Sandusky city was also lost.]

Mrd: on Jun 14, in Wash City, by Rev Mr Butler, Saml Chase Barney, U S Navy, to Mary Eleanor, only daughter of the late Edw De Krafft.

Died: on Jun 7, at the residence of Maj Chas S Williams, in Chas Co, Md, Miss Annie M Hamilton, aged 25 years. For more than 2 months the deceased had been suffering acutely under the disease which has consigned her to eternity.

Boy lost: Jos Ackles; light hair; fair complexion; 8 or 9 years old. His mother, a stranger here, sent him to a store last week, since then she has not heard of him. Any information will be thankfully received by his disconsolate mother, if addressed to this ofc.

Vera Cruz, May 31. The yellow fever is now getting really serious amongst us. Col Kearney, the Gov't contractor, is now lying in a very dangerous state, & 13 cases terminated yesterday & 3 today.

WED JUN 16, 1847

Dr Ithamer B Crawe, an old resident of Watertown, N Y, distinguished for his zeal & attainments in the natural sciences, was drowned on Wed in Perch Lake, while on a botanizing excursion. The boat, an old one, sunk near the shore. Gould, Mr Eddy, & Dr Crawe made for the shore, but the latter gave out before reaching it.

Col H R Jackson, of the Georgia Regt, has reached his home at Savannah after a year's faithful service in Mexico. The Georgia Regt [but owing to no fault of theirs] had not an opportunity of being engaged in battle during their term of service.

The schnr **Gen Patterson**, which arrived at New Orleans on Jun 5 from Brasos Santiago, brought the honored remains of Col McKee, Lt Col Clay, Capt Willis, Capt Lincoln, Lt Powell, Adj Vaughan, & Private H Trotter, all of whom fell at Buena Vista nobly stemming the tide of battle. Several companies of the 2nd Regt of Kentuckians arrived in the same vessel.

Register's Ofc, Wash, Jun 10, 1847. The following persons have taken out licenses under the laws of the Corporation during the month of May last:

Boots & shoes license: Flenner, Wm; Jack, Jas, jr

Cart license:

Adams, J G	Hopkins, J	Neale, L
Addison & Cockrell-2	Lewis, Thos	Otterback, Phil
Butler & Burns-2	Logan, H	Paine, Saml
Casparis, Jas	Lockey, And	Rhodes, Jas
Downs, Wm	Loveless, Jno	Shroder, Chr
English, Jas	Linkins, J	Sibley, C
Eunis, Philip-2	Little, Peter-2	Speiser, Fred
Fry, J, jr	Miller, Chas	Stewart, Chas-2
Fitzgerald, Jno	Magruder, F	Stewart, Wm
Fletcher, Jno-2	McQuay, B	Simms, J M-2
Fugitt, J	Mohun, Phil	Stewart. Geo-2
Harkness, G W	Martin, W	Taylor, J H
Holmes, S	Murphy, Wm	Thorn, J F

Upperman, C E-2	Wilson, W B	Woods, Dennis
Woods, John	Walker & Peck	

Confectionary license: Saltzer, G & Bro
Dray license: Berry, J W; Middleton & Beall; Parker, G & T
Dry Goods license: Tree, J B & Bro
Grocery license: Cady, Horace-transfer
Hack license: Pursell, Thos
Huckster license: Cartwright, Wm; Dwyer, Pat; Durr, G W
Grocery license: Garner, Cath
Lottery license: France, T E
Lumber license: Fugitt, J; Harvey & Lloyd; Lenman & Bro; Preston, O J & Co
Retail license: Barnes, Elias-transfer; Begnam, Wm; Fitzgerald, David; Moorhead & Brown; Robey, Jane
Slave license: Draine, Wm; Stewart, G W
Shop license: Black, Barbara-transfer
Tavern license: Hands, John
Wagon license:

Addison & Cockrell	Fugitt, J	Moore, John
Bohlayer, Ann	Fitzgerald, D-2	McGarvey & Conner
Barber, Geo	Forsher, M	Otterback, Phil
Burnet, E	Gess, John G	Preston, O J
Bird & Gunnell	Grainger, Jno	Rhodes, Jas
Butler & Burns-2	Hagar & Hanna	Shedd, W P
Bihler, G	Howard, John	Shedd, J J
Beveridge, C C	Hubbard, J T	Speiser, Fred
Cook, L O-2	Heiter, U	Straub, Ja
Colburn, J	Henry, Jas	Shaub, J & Co
Dowell, John	Kraft, J M-2	Tolson, J F
Emerson, G W	Miller, Chas	Wakeling, Ig

Wood license:

Addison & Cockrell	Day, David G-transfer	McCutcheon, Jno
Boone, J B	English, Jas	Magruder, F
Bean, Geo	Haislup, H	Neal, J E
Casanave, P	Hill, Isasc	Rittenhouse, B F
Cockrell, G H	Jolly, John	Thorn, Henry

Wood & Coal license: Warder, Walter
The following have been fined during the month of May for failing to procure their licenses:

Aller, Wm, dog	Hanover, Geo, peddling	Shedd, W R, wagon
Brown, Robt, dog	Jacobs, Henry, cart	Shaw, Richd, cart
Burnett, E, wagon	McQuay, Benj, wagon	Skirving, Jas, wagon
Beverage, C C, wagon	Otterback, Phil, cart	Stewart, And, wagon
Gengeback, Geo, dog	Reily, Jno, cart	Thorn, Henry, cart
Hoover, John, cart	Rawlings, Davis, wagon	Thomas, Lewis, cart
Hager, F, wagon	Rhodes, Jas, wagon	Wheatley, wagon

Died: on Jun 12, in Wash City, Miss Eliz Ewell, y/d o the late Bertrand Ewell, formerly of Belle-Air, Prince Wm Co, Va.

For rent: 2 story brick house on Pa ave, lately occupied by Mr Jullien, & adjoining the house now occupied by Cmdor Smith. -Louis Vivan

A serious affray occurred at Yorktown, Va, on Fri, between P A Southall, formerly Purser in the U S Navy, & Thos Nelson, U S Collector, & Mr Wm A Parker. In the course of the strife Mr Southall shot Mr Nelson with a pistol in the abdomen, inflicting a wound which it is feared will prove fatal. [Jun 21st newspaper: Mr Southall's wound is healing up. Wm Nelson was not seriously hurt. -Norfolk, Beacon]

Patent Ofc, Jun 14, 1847. Ptn of Wm & Thos Schnebly, of Wash Co, Md, for an extension of a patent granted to them for a machine for cutting grain, for 7 years from the expiration of said patent, which takes place of Aug 22, 1847.
-Edmund Burke, Com'r of Patents

THU JUN 17, 1847

Ship Bldg in Cincinnati. On Jun 9, the first brig ever built in the Queen City of the west was launched from the ship-yard of Mr B Hazen.

Ferdinand Gardiner, for many years the able & efficient U S Consul, died at Port Praya, May 6, of the country fever. Cmdor Read found it necessary to appoint an agent in his place, & selected a very capable Portuguese, formerly the British & now the French agent, Wm Peixoto, to act until the Gov't appointment is made.

At Savannah, on Fri last, Capt Jas Buker, while riding along Broad st, was thrown against a tree with such violence that he expired in about 15 minutes. He was a native of Maine, where he has a brother & 2 sisters residing.

Shocco Springs, Warren Co, N C: on the first range of hills, about equidistant from the seaboard to the Mountains: accessible by the Raleigh & Gaston railroad, being within 12 miles of Warrenton Depot: will be open for visiters on Jun 1. Frank Johnson's celebrated Band of Music will be in attendance during the season. -Saml Calvert

Boarding: Mrs M Byrne, having taken that large & commodious house on the corner of 10th st & Pa ave, formerly occupied by Mrs Gassaway.

Maj Gaines, Maj Borland, Capt Cassius M Clay, Midshipman Rogers, & all the other American ofcrs who are prisoners in the city of Mexico, have been given the liberty of the city.

Mrd: on Jun 15, in Wash City, by Rev Mr Shiras, Dr John L Fox, U S Navy, to Eliz A, daughter of Com Chas Morris.

New Orleans Picayune of Jun 9. The steamer **Admiral** arrived this morning & brings intelligence that the steamer **Edna**, Capt Phillips, on her way down from Onachita, had all 4 of her boilers explode, on Jun 4. Passengers saved: John B Lewis, M D, of S C; Col W Evans, of Marion, S C; W Lane, Bastrop, La; J J Stringer, Biloxi, Miss; Mr Simpson, Ouachita, La; F Miller, Farmersville, La; Mrs Goulding; Amelia McDonald, Champagnole, Ark. Passengers lost: Judge Mayo, Harrisonburg, La; Mr Hill, Champagnole, Ark; Mr Odell, Union District, S C; Mr King, Union District, S C; Mr Daly, Clairborne, La; & Mr Jones, Florida. Boat's crew saved: Mr Johnson, clerk; Martin Williams, mate; Wm Goulding, engineer; Mr Switzer, Antony Olen, Edw Carson, Edw Torowny, J McSorley, Owen Riley, Benj Mitchell, 2 cooks, 5 cabin servants & 1 stewardess. Boat's hands lost: Mr Donaldson, Jim Watson, Jim Thompson, Patrick Gorhon, Thos Plunket, D Anderson, Geo ___; barkeeper, name not known; John H Voss; Jas Pool, pilot; Austin Steager; ___ Oliver, engineer, & 2 deck passengers, names not known. Dr John B Lewis, of S C, [for himself & Wm Evans & J J Stringer,] does not hesitate to attribute this disaster mainly to the misconduct of those having charge of the boat. They were in a state of excitement, & were supposed to have been under the influence of ardent spirits.

Maj Gaines, Maj Borland, Capt Cassius M Clay, Midshipman Rogers, & all the other American ofcrs who are prisoners in the city of Mexico, have been given the liberty of the city.

Hanging a son for the murder of his mother. Wm H Stepter, age 17 years, was executed in Greenupsburg, Ky, on Jun 5, for the murder of his mother. Nearly 5,000 persons assembled to witness the closing scene. The father was arrested, & if his son had not come forward, he unquestionably would have been hanged. The son was convicted on his own confession. He was of a very weak mind; occasionally insane, it is said.

Died: on Jun 10, at Orange Courthouse, after a severe affliction of 6 weeks' duration, Mrs Helen Blair, relict of the dec'd Jas Blair, merchant, Fredericksburg, & daughter of the late Andrew Shepherd, of Orange, Va.

FRI JUN 18, 1847

On Jun 8, Wm Lewis, 63 years of age, a resident of Silver st, in South Boston, received a blow in the back from a dirt car as he was standing near the track of the Old Colony Railroad in South Boston. He was taken home & lingered along until Mon, when he died.

On Jun 11, the 3 year old son of Wm H Ulman, blacksmith, of Cottage st, East Boston, fell into a kettle of boiling water, & died on Sunday, after excrutiating sufferings. -Traveller

Mr R B Steel, a student of Lafayette College, & son of the Rev B Steel, of Abington, Pa, was drowned while bathing in the Delaware, on Thu week. He ventured across the river, a feat often successfully attempted before, but within a few feet of the opposite shore, he was heard to cry for aid. A boat was sent out, but too late to render any assistance.

Ex-Adlerman Calvin Balis, of N Y, died on Thu of last week at Oswego, where he had gone in hopes of restoring his impaired health. He was held in high esteem by men of all parties. -N Y Cour & Enq

Smithsonian Institution. We are glad to perceive more hands busily employed in laying the foundation & otherwise engaged workmen & laborers at the Smithsonian Institution. Under the superintendence of Mr Renwick, the able & vigilant architect, the contractor & mechanics will execute their work in a faithful & satisfactory manner. In our last notice under the present head we stated that Mr Cameron was the sole contractor. This was not intended by us to convey any censure upon Mr Dixon. We think this explantation is due to Mr Dixon as well as to ourselves.

Peruvian Indemnity: Atty Gen's Ofc, Wash, Jun 17, 1847. On Aug 14, 1846, the following notice was issued from this ofc: The Atty Gen of the U S having been empowered to adjudicate the claims arising under the convention concluded between the U S & Peru, at Lima, Mar 17, 1841, hereby gives notice of his appointment to perform the duties confided to him, & requires the claimants to present their claims with all dispatch, that he may proceed to execute the law. -Nathan Clifford, Atty Gen Attest: John T Reid, Clerk

Robt Basler, convicted of the murder of Robt Atkinson, in Wyoming Co, Pa, & who escaped from jail in Jan, 1845, has been recaptured at Buena Vista, Mexico. He was attached to the Illinois volunteers, as a teamster, & was recognized by Mr Luther Adkins, of the Ohio volunteers.

Gen R H Hammond, Paymaster of the U S Army, who lately died on his way to New Orleans from Vera Cruz, belonged to Milton, Pa, & was the father of Lt Hammond, of the Army, who was killed in one of Gen Kearny's battles in California.

List of claims not filed, as appears by the papers in the Atty Gen's ofc: brig **Thetis**, of Boston, Henry Parsons master; brig **Elizabeth Ann**, of Phil, Oliver Brooks master.
Beriah Fitch, master of the ship **Flying Fish**, of Boston.
Eliphalet Smith, for any interest he may have in the schnr **Wasp**, of Boston, & in the cargo of the ship **Esther**, of Boston.
Stephen B Howe, for any interest he may have in the cargo of the ship **Esther**, of Boston.
Edw L Scott, for any interest he may have in the schnr **Robinson Crusoe**.
John Huan, for any interest he may have in the cargo of the schnr **Robinson Crusoe**.

SAT JUN 19, 1847
Orphans Court of Wash Co, D C: the case of Jas Burdine, adm of Ann Sheckells, dec'd. The administrator & Court have appointed Jun 22, for the settlement of the said estate. -Ed N Roach, Reg o/wills

For rent or sale: 3 story brick dwlg house & premises at the corner of 3rd & D sts. Inquire of Jas Larned, 13th st, for the owner.

From Europe: 1-Mr O'Connell died at Genoa on May 15. He has directed his heart to be deposited in Rome, & his body to be buried in Ireland. 2-Dr Chalmers, the eminent theologian, died suddenly.

Mrd: on Jun 9, at Raleigh, N C, by Rev Dr Mason, Rector of Christ Church, Mr Chas B Root to Miss Annie Freeman, eldest daughter of Weston R Gales.

Mrd: on Jun 17, by Rev F S Evans, Mr John G Smith to Miss Ann S Cook, daughter of Mr L O Cook, all of Wash City.

Died: on Jun 17, John Joseph, y/son of the late Wm B Laub, aged 18 months & 18 days. His funeral is this afternoon at 4 o'clock, from the residence of his mother, 10th & F sts.

Died: on Jun 18, at the residence of her son-in-law, Cmdor Wadsworth, Mrs Jerusha Denison, in her 85th year, widow of the late Gideon Denison, of Harford Co, Md. Her funeral is this afternoon, from St John's Church, at 5 o'clock.

Died: on May 29 last, in St Louis, Missouri, the Hon Alonzo W Manning, Judge of the Criminal Court of that city, aged 37 years. He was a native of Chas Co, Md, & had been a resident of St Louis for a number of years.

Died: on Jun 15, at her residence, near Beltsville, PG Co, Md, after a brief but severe illness, Mrs Eliz W Hamilton, w/o Col Saml Hamilton, in her 51st year.

Mr John Haven, of West Hartford, attempting some weeks since to slack some lime for whitewash with hot water in a boiler on the stove, had reduced the whole, as he supposed, to a liquid; but, on adding another dipper full of water, the whole exploded, throwing some of it into his face & eyes, destroying both his eyes, & so badly burning him that his life was despaired at the last accounts. -Woodstock Mercury

Messrs, Editors: I was not a little surprised to see in the Intelligencer this morning a notice, signed by Mr Gilbert Cameron, of the dissolution of the copartnership existing between him & myself, as builders of the Smithsonian Institution, accompanied by an affidavit of Mr Gilbert Cameron "that the copartnership had been dissolved on Jun 2," & that the reason that publicity was not given to the fact of such dissolution was an omission on my part to send the notice of the same to some newspaper for publication. It is true that a dissolution of the copartnerhisp was contemplated by Mr Cameron & myself, & a note to that effect in blank form as to date signed by both, with the understanding that it was to be published if & so soon as I should be released from all responsibility to the Bldg Cmte for the faithful performance of the contract made by us, & also from the contract made with Mr John Sniffen, & Mr Cameron should give me sufficient security for the repayment of moneys advanced by me for the purposes of our copartnership. So soon, therefore, as these requisites are complied with, & not until then, I am willing the copartnership existing between Mr Cameron & myself should be dissolved. -Jas Dixon

I have for sale upwards of 15,000 acres of Timber & Iron Land belonging to myself & others, contiguous to the Chesapeake & Ohio Canal & Balt & Ohio Railroad, east of Cumberland, in Allegheny Co, Md. Apply to Jas Smith, Cumberland, Md

Circuit Court of Wash Co, D C-in Chancery. Augustus D Sheele vs John Peter Coulter et al. The object of this suit is to procure a decree for a sale of certain mortgaged premises in said county, which were, on May 19, 1817, mortgaged by one Peter Coulter, since dec'd, to the cmplnt, with the above-named suit. This bill states that on May 19, Coulter conveyed certain real estate, described in the bill, to the cmplnt, by way of mortgage, to secure the payment of the sum of $300, with interest from May 19, 1817, the same to be paid to the cmplnt at the end of 3 years from & after the date of the said mortgage, or that, in default of such payment, the real estate, or so much thereof as might be necessary, would be sold to pay the same; that the cmplnt afterwards assigned, bargained, sold, & conveyed his rights under the said mortgage to one Henry L Clarke, one of the dfndnts in the above suit; that said Clarke afterwards assigned, transferred, & set over all his right & interest in the said mortgage unto one Thos Brownrigg, one of the dfndnts with said suit; that on Oct 9, 1821, Brownrigg assigned, transferred, & set over to the cmplnt all his right, title, & interest in & under the said mortgage. The said mortgage debt has never been paid, but is now due & owing unto the cmplnt. The said Peter Coulter died about 1830, having made his last will & testament, devising the said real estate so mortgaged as foresaid [after limiting a life estate in the same to the use of his widow] to his children, share & share alike, to them, their heirs & assigns forever; that the said widow departed this life some time about Nov 9, 1842. That the children & only heirs & devisees of the said Peter are dfndnts, John Peter Coulter & Margaret Sheele, wife of the cmplnt. That one Michl Weaver, who was appointed sole executor of the said will, duly renounced the said executorship, & that administration of the estate of the said Peter has never been granted to or undertaken by any one. That there is not any personal estate, or other real estate of the said Peter, than the said mortgaged property. That the said property so mortgaged is charged with & liable to be sold for the payment of the aforesaid debt & interest, & the bill prays for such sale & foreclosure of equity of redemption. That the said John Peter Coulter, Henry L Clarke, & Thos Brownrigg reside out of D C. It is ordered that the absent dfndnts are to appear in this Court on or before the 3rd Mon of Oct next. -W Cranch Test: Wm Brent, clk -B P Smith, Solicitor

MON JUN 21, 1847

Correspondence of the N Y Tribune. Sault St Marie, Jun 11, 1847. On Jun 10 a row boat upset in passing down the rapids, & 3 of the 9 men who embarked on it were drowned: Dr Hught T Prouty, of Norwalk, Ohio, here on a tour of observation, accompanied by his wife, leaving several children at home to mourn their sudden bereavement; Thos Riches, engineer of the propeller **Independence** on Lake Superior; & Wm Flynn, an intelligent & worthy laboring man was the third. Mr Seymour, who represented this county in the last Legislature of Mich, narrowly escaped death. He had sunk to rise no more, when an Indian, fishing in the rapids, seeing a man's body at the bottom of a lucid pool, seized a boat-hook & drew him up.

New Troops for the War: the New Orleans papers of Jun 12th chronicle the following arrivals at that place: The U S steamer **Col Yell**, from Pittsburg, brought Capt Taylor, Lt Smith, Lt Hotons, & Lt Keefe, with Co A, Independent Greys, 80 men, from Bedford Co, Pa. Also, Capt Caldwell, Lt McKany, Lt Bowers, & Lt Doyle, with Co B, Wayne Guards, 90 men, from Mifflin Co, Pa. The steamer **Louisiana**, from St Louis, brought Maj J H Savage, Lt A G Moon & Lt W H Seawell, with 100 men of the 14th Regt U S Infty, from Memphis. The steamer **Pontiac**, from Cincinnati, brought Maj Norval, Lt Winston & Lt Perry, with 122 men of the 16th Regt U S Infty.

Died: on Jun 29, in Wash City, Henry W Sweeting, in his 41st year, formerly of Balt, but for many years a resident of Wash City. His funeral will take place from his late residence on C st, today, at 4 o'clock.

Saml Weir, Editor of the Columbia [S C] Chronicle, died on Jun 8, after a most painful & protracted illness.

Died: on Jun 15, at Frostburg, Md, Mr Arthur Lalanne, in his 26th year, brother of Mrs Geo Stettinius, of Wash City. He had been on a visit during the winter in the South for the benefit of his health, & reached Frostburg on his return to his relations here. Being much exhausted by his journey, he left the stage to remain a day to recruit his wasted strength, & in a few hours his spirit calmly passed away. Mr Lalanne was a young gentleman of fine education, & a candidate for orders in the Episcopal Church. [Jun 22nd newspaper: died-suddenly, at Frostburg, Arthur J T Lalanne, formerly a teacher in the College of St James, near Hagerstown. He had long been under the influence of a severe disease.]

On Sat last, about 5 miles from Hagerstown, Md, Mr Wm Schleigh was in the act of mounting his horse, when the stirrup broke & he fell to the ground, the horse falling on him injuring him internally. This accident resulted in his death. He has left a wife & 5 children.

TUE JUN 22, 1847
Mr Jas H Caldwell, of the White Sulphur Springs, Va, has formed a company of Voltigeurs for service in Mexico.

Troops for Mexico: the ship **Charleston** sailed from there on Thu for Vera Cruz with 2 companies of the 12th Infty, U S Army, numbering in all about 200 men, under command of Maj Maxcy Gregg. Also, Capt Sitgreaves' company of Dragoons, about 80 men. The latter will be landed at Brasos. The brig **Paul T Jones** cleared the same day for the Brasos, & was to take out Capt Ecro's company of the 13th Infty, U S Infty, numbering about 190 men. A steamboat from Cincinnati arrived at New Orleans on Jun 12, with companies D & B, belonging to the 3rd Regt, U S Infty, under command of Lts Hart, Schroeder, Travet, & Sheppard.

Mrd: on Jun 10, at Lynchburg, Va, by Rev Mr Kinckle, Dr John Staige Davis, of Charlottesville, to Lucy Landon, daughter of Wm M Blackford.

Died: on Jun 19, Mrs Margaret Fitzpatrick & her infant babe, a native of Dingle, Kerry Co, Ireland, but for the last 16 years a resident of Washington, aged 34 years.

Died: on Jun 21, after a long & painful illness, Mrs Mary B Edmonds, aged 41 years. Her funeral is this afternoon, at 3 o'clock, at her late residence, on 10th, near C st.

Died: on Jun 18, at ***Oak Lodge***, the residence of his father, in PG Co, Chas Parker, aged 2 years & 2 months, son of Clement & Sarah Anne Hill.

Criminal Court-Wash. Following gentlemen were sworn to serve on the Grand Inquest:

Roger C Weightman-Foreman	John Carter	Joshua Pierce
John Boyle	Jacob Gideon	Geo Watterston
Edw M Linthicum	John P Ingle	Geo Sweeny
Saml McKenney	Wm H Gunnell	B F Middleton
John C Rives	Edw Simms	Jesse E Dow
Wm A Bradley	Geo W Young	Thos Thornley
Wm Doughty	Robt White	
Geo Lowry	G Thomas	
	H Addison	

By virtue of a writ of fieri facias, I have levied & taken in execution all the right, title, interest, & estate of Chas Lafon in the leasehold of the subdivision of lot 3 in square 575, with improvements thereon, on Pa ave, in Wash City: will be sold on Jul 1, to pay & satisfy said fieri facias, in favor of Chas Webster. Terms cash. -Jno Waters, Constable

Dissolution of copartnership: existing between Jas Dixon & Gilbert Cameron, contractors for bldg the Smithsonian Institution in Wash City, & known as the firm of Dixon & Cameron, is dissolved by mutual consent. Claims against said firm are to be presented to Gilbert Cameron, at his ofc on the bldg site, who has assumed the contract, & the payment of all the liabilities of the same. -Jas Dixon, Gilbert Cameron

The subscriber offers for sale that very valuable Farm on which he lives, about 4 miles from the Centre Market House, on the Wash & Rockville turnpike, where taxes are merely nominal. It contains about 108 acres, with a new 2 story frame dwlg house, 36 x 25, containing 7 rooms; also all necessary out bldgs. Messrs Causin, Carbery, Clagett, & Blair have each places contiguous. I also offer for sale 3 small parcels of land, one of 2 acres, one of 4 acres, & one of 5 acres. The 2 & 4 acres lots adjoing N Causin; the 5 acre lot is in Montgomery Co. Inquire of A Green, auctioneer, Robt Ould, Gtwn, or on the premises of Henry Ould.

WED JUN 23, 1847

Criminal Court-Wash. 1-U S vs John Krouse, found guilty for an assault with intent to kill Wm Thrift, at Gtwn, by wounding him severely on the head with a stone. It was alleged, & not denied, that Thrift had committed an assault upon the father of the accused, who was a cripple at the time he was so assaulted. [Jun 24th newspaper: on Jun 23, the Court decided to overrule the motion, thereby sustaining the indictment.]

Workmen are now busily employed in pulling down the old edifice in Chestnut st, Phil, recently occupied by the Bank of North America, & found papers stowed away in the garret. We have been furnished with one of these relics of the olden time: the American Weekly Mercury, published at Phil by Andrew Bradford, Nov 28, 1728. We extract the following ad: just arrived from London, in the ship **Borden**, Wm Harbert, cmder, a parcel of young likely Men Servants, consisting of Husbandmen, Joyners, Shoemakers, Weavers, Smiths, Brick-makers, Bricklayers, Sawyers, Taylors, Stay-makers, Butchers, Chair-maker, & several other trades, & are to be sold very reasonable, either for ready Money, Wheat, Bread, or Flour, by Edw Horne, Phil.

Died: last evening, at the residence of her husband, Geo W Dobbin, on the Mall, Mrs Frances Dobbin, aged 24 years. Her funeral is this evening at 5 o'clock, from the same place.

Mrs Bullard, a lady residing near Montgomery, Ala, was killed on Jun 13, by the running away of the horses of her carriage. A young lady who was in the carriage jumped out & was saved.

The Wash Light Infty, commanded by Lt Tate, turned out on Mon to render military honors to the remains of H W Sweeting, their late pioneer, who died at his residence, on C st, early on Sunday. The dec'd being also one of the fraternity of Old-Fellows, had the usual honors paid to his remains by the members of that numerous & respectable brotherhood.

We announce the death of our countryman, Professor Francis Fauvel Gouraud. He arrived in the U S in Dec, 1838, being with him, as its introducer to this country, the magnificent discovery of Daguerre, whose pupil he had been: but Prof Gouraud was to win his fame in another career. He published his work on phreno-mnemotechny, which have been compared by the American press to the most brilliant pages in English literature. As an American orator in a manner so facile & remarkable, he gained $20,000 in a single winter. A long illness deprived him of the power to continue his labors, & he has died in a condition bordering on indigence. -N Y Courier des Etats Unis

Church organ for sale: now standing in St John's Church, in Wash City: it has a mahogany case of 6 stops, & was made by Green, of London. Inquire of the Treasurer of the Church, or of Geo Thompson, the Sexton, at the Topographical Bureau.

Mrs Ann Hart died suddenly on Monday last at 112 Bowery, N Y, having taken a large quantity of laudanum instead of tincture of rhubard. Her grandson was sent to a drug store for the medicine & an apprentice gave him the wrong bottle. She died in the course of a few hours.

Valuable brick houses & lot at auction: on Jun 28: part of lot 19 in square 169, with 2 good well-built 3 story brick houses; also, a good stable for 3 horses. The above property is in the immediate vicinity of the War Dept, known as the property of Aquilla Rickets: lot fronts on G st north, next to the corner of 17th st west. Title indisputable.
-A Green, auctioneer

Died: on Jun 19, at Uniontown, Pa, of consumption, Jas G Sturgeon, in his 33rd year, eldest son of the Hon Danl Sturgeon, Senator from Pa. Mr Sturgeon was appointed by Pres Polk, in May, 1846, military storekeeper of the U S Arsenal at Pittsburg-a post where, it was the hope of himself & friends, that his declining health might be restored. On his return from a Southern tour, which proved of no benefit to his health, he was so much debilitated that he stopped at his father's residence, where, after lingering a few weeks, he died.

THU JUN 24, 1847
The son of the Hon Wm Sawyer, & a son of Mr Van Horn were drowned at St Mary's, Ohio, last week, as supposed. The body of one of them has been found.

Heart-rending accident occurred on the Okaw, in Coles Co, Ill, on May 30: as Mr Chandler, with his wife, his son's wife & child, another son, a dght, & a Mrs Mosely, were on their way to preaching, in a 2 horse wagon, they were overtaken by a terrific storm, which blew down a large tree upon the vehicle, crushing to death Mrs Mosley & the child, & injuring Mrs Chandler who survived only half an hour.

Capt John Poynor, of Dinwiddie Co, Va, came to a sudden & painful death on Thu last: having just a chill, he went into the ofc of his brother-in-law, Dr John H Edwards, to take a dose of quinine. He mistook morphine for quinine, swallowed it, & was, in a very few minutes, numbered among the dead. He was in the bloom of manhood, & has left a widow & 3 little children. -Petersburg Intelligencer

The Donaldsonville papers announce the death of Judge Thos C Nicholls, who died at that place on Jun 12, in his 57th year. He was a Marylander by birth, & has resided in this State for many years, having been for a long time Judge of the 4th District Court, & lately one of the Judges of the Court of Appeals in criminal cases. Judge Nicholls was a veteran of the late war, having been engaged in the operations below New Orleans in 1814 & 1815.
-New Orleans Delta

Robt S Foster, a promising son of Jas H Foster, on Jun 14, in Nashville, Tenn, accidentally shot & killed himself when getting over a fence. His gun went off, & the whole charge lodged in his body.

Return of Volunteers: on Jun 15, 7 companies, [666 men,] of the 1st Regt of Missouri volunteers arrived at New Orleans, under the command of Col A W Doniphan, Lt Col Jackson, & Capts Waldo, Walton, Moss, Reid, Parsons, Hughes, & Rogers. Also, 3 companies of the 2nd Regt Ohio volunteers, under the command of Capts Seifert, Hart, & McGinnis. Also, 2 companies of the 3rd Regt Ohio volunteers, under the command of Capts Noles & Robinson. The 3 other companies of the Missouri volunteers, being those under Capts Stevenson & Hudson, & Capt Weightman's artl company, [being about 250 men in all,] left the Brasos on a schnr prior to their companions, & were hourly expected.

Rev Dr Chalmers, of Glasgow, Scotland, died suddenly in that city about Jun 1. He was a great man-great in his power, in his mental supremacy, & in his moral grandeur. He established the Free Church. He was discovered by his servant sitting up in bed-dead. The reverend doctor has left behind him a widow to lament his loss, & a family, we believe, of 6 dghts, 2 of whom are married, the one to the Rev Mr McKenzie, of Ratho, the other to the Rev Dr Hanna, of Skirkling, editor of the North British Review, & 4 unmarried. Dr Chalmers was a native of Anstruther, Fife; he was born about 1780; died age 67 years old. -British Mail [Edinburgh, May 31: Dr Chalmers died at Morningside, near Edinburgh.]

The undersigned wished to purchase, expressly for his own use, a good Cook, Washer, & Ironer. I want one immediately. -Alex'r Lee

New stores for rent: the subscriber is bldg 2 new stores on Bridge st, Gtwn, next to the store of English & Sons, Hardware Merchants. Inquire at the store of Mrs Ann H Clarke, on Bridge st, Gtwn. -Saml Clarke

Died: on Jun 9, at Chicago, Ill, in her 24th year, Mrs Martha C Sherman, wife of Mr Robt D Sherman, of Chicago, & daughter of Mrs John Moore, of Wash City.

FRI JUN 25, 1847

Property to the amount of $25,000 was destroyed by fire at Maysville, Ky, on Jun 18. The sufferers are: John B McIlvain, Duke & Moody, Conrad Phister, Thos J Pickett, O H Davis, Mooklar & Chiles, & Peter A Claybrook.

For Vera Cruz: the steamer **New Orleans**, which sailed from New Orleans on Jun 16, took out 250 men belonging to the 12th & 16th regts, the former destined for Gen Taylor, & the latter for Gen Scott. She also took over 150 horses & about 100 quartermaster's men. The following were among her passengers: for **Vera Crua**: Sr Atocha, De J S McFarlane, U S Army; Lt Merrifield, 3rd Dragoons; Darius Val, aid to Gen Worth. For **Brasos**: Col J W Tibbatts & son, Maj R J Norvell, Adj J C Helan, Lt Berry, 16th Infty; Lt Winston, do; Lt Hawkins, do; Capt Claiborne, John M Reeves, Col R E Clements, Col J W Kinney, T P Andrews, J E Marks, Assist Surgeon, A E Hughtway, U S Army, Capt C A Coolridge, Mass Volunteers, Lt G W Celly, do, Capt Jesse Gray, Sgt L M Prim, B Cord.

New Orleans Bulletin of Jun 11: Wm Caseman, charged with having cruelly beaten his mother, aged 85, & from the effects of which she died on Thu, was remanded for further examination. He frequently said that she had lived too long & ate too much.

New Orleans, Jun 17. On Jun 14, the towboat **Porpoise**, Capt Disney, near ***Fort Jackson***, burst all her boilers, wounding & killing several persons. She had in tow the ship **Wakona** & the brig **Union**. Mr Francewagh, 1st engineer, killed; C Woolf, fireman, missing, supposed to have been blown overboard; J Stone, fireman, badly wounded; J Kammar & O Hill, deck hands, both badly scalded; J Moss, steerman, & H Christ, firemen, both slightly scalded. The chief mate of the **Wakona**, Robt G Stanwood, was severely scalded, & sent to town for medical aid. The following persons on the brig **Union** were wounded: Miss C Quinn, severely; Mrs Pebo, slightly, & her child, severely; Mr Tobias Alhouse, severely, & 2 of the crew slightly. The brig **Union** was bound to Balt, & the **Wakona** to Bordeaux. -Picayune

The Mormon Temple: this celebrated edifice has been sold to a cmte of the Catholic Church for $75,000. This community also purchased other property at Nauvoo. The last of the Mormons at Nauvoo, consisting of 30 or 40 families under the charge of Danl H Wells, have left Nauvoo to join the Calif expedition. Babbitt & Co still remain at Nauvoo to close up the affairs of the Mormons. -Warsaw Signal

An interesting little girl, about 14 months, daughter of Mr Christian Hershman, residing in the upper part of Catoctin Valley, Md, whilst playing in the dairy, on Jun 11, accidentally fell into the milk trough & was drowned.

Miss Mary Nowlen, daughter of Asa Nowlen, of Avon, died on Mon, from the effects of corrosive sublimate, which she took by mistake on Fri last. -Roch Amer

New Orleans Picayune, Jun 17. C Gaines, of the Mounted Rifles, & John Drew, of Co I, 7th Infty, died on board before the ship **Massachusetts** left Vera Cruz, & were sent on shore for interment on Jun 11. On Jun 12, John Pope, of the Mounted Rifles, & John Smith, of Co C, 7th Infty, died at sea. On Jun 13 J F Carson, S C volunteers, died. On Jun 14, D Scurry, S C volunteers, & H Heck, 2nd Dragoons. On Jun 15 L Grover, Co E, Mounted Rifles. Paymaster Bosworth, who sailed from here on May 18, sickened & died in Vera Cruz of the vomito. His remains were brought back on the Massachusetts in charge of his brother.

Appointments by the Pres: on Jun 18. 1-John B Butler, of Pa, paymaster & military storekeeper, from Jun 30th, in place of Sturgeon, resigned. 2-Victor E Pioletti, Pa, paymaster, in the place of Hammond, deceased. 3-John B Guthrie, pension agent, at Pittsburg, Pa.

A negro woman, belonging to J B Mullikin, in the Forest of PG Co, Md, died a few days ago, supposed to have been at least 110 years old.

Rev Mr Morsell, of West River, Anne Arundel Co, Md, has been invited by the vestry of Trinity Church, Upper Marlborough, to succeed Rev Mr Nelson.

Mrd: on Jun 22, by Rev W French, Hon L H Arnold, a member of the last Congress & formerly Govn'r of the State of R I, to Miss Catharine Shonnard, of Wash City.

Died: on Jun 23, after a short & painful illness, Mrs Julia Herrity, consort of Jas Herrity, in her 25th year. Her funeral is this day, at 4 o'clock, at her residence, on G st, between 2nd & 3rd sts.

Died: on Jun 18, at Laurel, Md, after a severe illness of 21 days, Frances Joanna Clementine, daughter of Jos O D & Eliza Brown, in her 5th year.

$5 reward for bundle of papers lost on Jun 21, consisting of judgments, warrants, which can be of no use to anyone but the undersigned. Return to T C Donn, John L Smith, or either of the Magistrates, for a suitable reward. -Michl Reardon, Constable

Criminal Court-Wash. 1-In the case of the U S vs Enoch Tucker, charged with obstructing a public road near his farm on the Eastern Branch: the case was abandoned. 2-Jos Humphreys, free negro, was found guilty for assaulting his wife with intent to kill her: sentenced to 2 years imprisonment at labor in the Penitentiary for this offence. He was convicted of resisting ofcr Handy while in the discharge of his duty as a constable: for this offence the Court sentenced him to one week in the county jail.

Laurel Hill Cemetery: Phil, Jun 17, 1847. This cemetery is located on the banks of Schuykill. Among the works of rare merit is the tomb of the dght of Fred'k Foering, constructed of marble, with head & foot stones, presenting the appearance of a couch, the mound being strewn with roses. At the pedestal is a lamb, the emblem of innocence & purity, admirable done by Mr Jos Maples. Another work by the same is the monument of Susan R, w/o Jos Bispham, & daughter of the late Hon Ebenezer Tucker, of N Y. The tomb of Cmdor Isaac Hull is copied from that of Scipio Africanus. The American Flag is thrown carelessly over the tomb, & on it perched the American Eagle. The monument of F Rudolph Hassler, late Superintendant of the U S Coast Survey, has a sculptured likeness of the dec'd, done by John Schmidt, of N Y. The monument of Passed Midshipman Stephen Decatur Lavalette, by Krips, is worthy of attention. On the tomb of Jos S Lewis, who projected & superintended the construction of the Fairmount Water Works, & was done by Nutman. The tomb of John A Brown, a wealthy broker, is a Gothic monument. The monument of Wm Young Birch, erected by the Pa Institution for the Blind, is a very clever thing, by Struthers, of purely Grecian architecture, classic & beautiful. One of the most striking, is that erected to the memory of Augusta & Rebecca Richards. Mrs Richards was the daughter of Judge McLean, of Ohio. "My name shall be my epitaph alone." Also worthy of notice: the monuments of Saml Woodward & Dr Swain, both by Maples.

For rent: a 2 story brick dwlg-house, on Mass ave, between 11th & 12th sts. Inquire of Richd Elliott, on N Y ave, between 12th & 13th sts, or of J Goodrich, at the City Post Ofc.

I certify that Wm Major, of Wash Co, brought before me as a stray trespassing upon his enclosures, a gray horse. -Jas Marshall, J P [The owner is to prove property, pay charges, & take him away. -Wm B Major, at the Wash & Rockville Toll-gate.]

$100 reward for runaway negro man Henry, about 18 or 19 years of age. He left home without any provocation. -Wm Clark, near Queen Anne, PG Co, Md

SAT JUN 26, 1847

A special meeting of the Boston Association of the Friends of Ireland, John W James, Pres-chrmn, was held last night, to take suitable notice of the death of Danl O'Connell, the Liberator. -Boston Post, Jun 22

Judiciary of N Y: Court of Appeals:
Freeborn Jewett, 2 years
Greene C Bronson, 4 years
Chas H Ruggles, 6 years
Addison Gardiner, 8 years
Supreme Court: 1st District:
Saml Jones, 2 years
Elisha P Hurlbut, 4 years
John W Edmonds, 6 years
Henry P Edwards, 8 years
2nd District:
Selah B Strong, 2 years
Wm T McCoun, 4 years
Nathan B Morse, 6 years
Seward Barculo, 8 years
3rd District:
Wm B Wright, 2 years
Ira Harris, 4 years
Melbone Watson, 6 years
Amasa J Parker, 8 years
4th District:
Danl Cady, 2 years
Alonzo C Paige, 4 years
John Willard, 6 years
Augustus C Hand, 8 years
5th District:
Chas Gray, 2 years
Danl Pratt, 4 years
Philo Gridley, 6 years
Wm F Allen, 8 years
6th District:
Wm H Shankland, 2 years
Hiram Gray, 4 years
Chas Mason, 6 years
Eben B Morehouse, 8 years
7th District:
Thos S Johnson, 2 years
John Maynard, 4 years
Henry Welles, 6 years
Saml L Seldon, 8 years
8th District:
Jas G Hoyt, 2 years
Jas Mullett, 4 years
Seth E Sill, 6 years
Richd P Marvin, 8 years

The N Y Courier says that the tonnage of the steamer **United States**, now bldg in that city for Chas H Marshall & others, will be 3,081 tons. The length of the spar-deck will 254 feet.

On Sat last, at Gloucester, Mass, two boys, sons of widow Marsh, Geo-10, & Ephraim-7, took their uncle's gun from the house without leave, & the elder boy accidentally shot & killed his brother, Ephraim.

Trustee's sale: by virtue of an act of Congress, passed Jul 20, 1840, & of the decree of the Circuit Court of Wash Co, D C, & the Orphans Court of Wash Co, D C, made in the case of Lewis G Davidson's heirs, & by authority from the heirs: sale on Jul 22, of the following lots in Wash City, viz: lots 1 through 6 in square 170, according to Davidson's subdivision, in the neighborhood of the Navy Dept. Lots 4, 5, & 6 in square 126, according to said subdivision, adjoining Col Abert's, & near the late residence of Gen Macomb. Title indisputable. -Saml G Davidson, trustee -B Homans, auctioneer

Balt, Jun 25. The Locofoco Convention at Annapolis nominated Mr Philip Francis Thomas, of Talbot Co, as the candidate of their party for Govn'r.

For sale: tract of land called ***Muddy Branch***, in Montg Co, Md, containing about 234 acres, lying on both sides of the Chesapeake & Ohio Canal, at the 20 mile stone from Wash. Also, ***New Design***, containing 100 acres, lying near 2 miles north of the Capitol, west of the road leading to Rock Creek Church. And, as executor of Rev John Brackenridge, by order of the Probate Court of Warrick Co, Indiana, for the benefit of the Board of Education of the Presbyterian Church, I will sell for the best price it will bring by Jul 10, that tract of land called ***Mt Ararat***, lying on Rock Creek, 2 miles from Gtwn, containing about 75 acres, & lately occupied by Geo Broadrup as a paper mill. Refer to Clement Cox, Gtwn. -John A Brackenridge

John D Clark, dentist, was arraigned upon & pleaded guilty to an indictment for a constructive larceny. He had fitted a lady with artificial teeth, & when he did not get paid for them, he removed & pocketed them. Her friends went before the Grand Jury, & a bill of larceny was found. -Boston Post

Dissolution of the copartnership between John McDevitt & John Robinson, Auctioneers & Commission Merchants, by mutual consent. Auction store on La ave. -John McDevitt, John Robinson [The subscriber informs that he has again resumed his former business of repairing clocks, watches, jewelry, at the auction store of John McDevitt, the stand of the late firm of McDevitt & Robinson. -John Robinson]

Orphans Court of Wash Co, D C. In the case of Wm J Wheatley, administrator of Jas M Tims, deceased. The Court & administrator have appointed Jul 16 next for the settlement of the estate, & for payment & distribution, of the assets in the hands of the administrator. -Ed N Roach, Reg/o wills

PG Co Court, sitting as a Court of Equity: Apr Term, 1847. Thos B Berry, Saml T Berry, & others, vs Mary Edelen, Jos Hunter & Mary L his wife, Edw L Lanham & Martha Ann his wife. The cmplnts, Thos B Berry & Saml T Berry, & the cmplnt Jane, before her intermarriage with the cmplnt, Wm H Gwynn, recovered judgments in the Chas Co Court, at the Aug term of said Court, in 1833, each for the sum of $2,287.35, with interest from Aug 12, 1833, till paid, & costs, against a certain Edw C Edelen & Mary his wife, being for the distributive share due to the cmplnts of the personal estate of their dec'd father, on whose estate the said Edw C Edelen & wife had administered. That said judgments still remain unpaid & unsatisfied, & that the said Edw C Edelen has departed this life intestate & insolvent, leaving his personal estate insufficient to pay his debts, but dying seised of a tract of land called ***part of Aix, part of Providence Enlarged***, & part of ***McDaniel's Resurvey***, containing 220 acres, lying & being in PG Co, Md. That the said Edw C Edelen left the following reps & heirs at law to inherit the real estate, to wit, Mary Edelen, his widow, who resides in Chas Co, Md, & 2 children, to wit, Mary L Edelen, the w/o Jos Hunter, & Martha Ann, the wife of Edw L Lanham. The two latter, to wit, Edw L Lanham & wife reside in the State of Missouri, beyond the jurisdiction of this Court. The said heirs at law are made parties dfndnts, & the bill prays for subpoenas against those who reside in the State of Md & an order of publication in some newspaper against the said Edw L Lanham & wife, notifying them of the objects & contents of this bill; & prays for a sale of the said real estate for the payment of the balance due on said judgments & claims. Same to appear in this Court on or before the first Mon in Nov next, to answer the said bill. -A C Magruder -J B Brooke,clerk

$400 reward for runaway negroes, Ben & John. Ben is the slave of Robt Beverley, about 30 years of age. John is the property of T Henderson, & is 25 years old. -Robt Beverley, Thos Henderson, The ***Plains***, Fauquier Co, Va.

Vegetable stalls for sale in the Centre Market-house: in the West Market-house; in the Northern Market house; & in the Eastern Branch market-house: for one year, commencing Jul 1. -W W Seaton, Mayor

Lost, a small colored girl, about 6 years of age, named Susan. She left her owner's house on Jun 24, since which time nothing has been heard of her. A liberal reward will be paid for her delivery to her owner. -Mrs W A Roche, 8th st, north of the Patent Ofc

Died: on Jun 25, in Wash City, Mrs Catharine Denham, age 80 years, formerly of Fred'k Co, Va, but for the last 30 years a resident of Wash City. Her funeral is today at 3 o'clock, from her residence on C st, between 13th & 14th sts.

Died: on Jun 25, John, the y/son of Eli & Margaret Davis, aged 7 years & 23 days. His funeral is from the residence of his father, on 12th st, between N Y ave & I st.
[No date or time.]

Died: on Jun 23, of consumption, Mrs Christina Guy, in her 28th year, wife of Wm B Guy, of N H.

Died: on Jun 25, of catarrh fever, Wm Von-Albade, infant son of J B & Jane Innes Wingerd, aged 3 years, 1 month & 28 days. His funeral is this afternoon, at 5 o'clock, from the residence of his grandfather, Mr Wm Anderson.

Died: on Jul 25, suddenly, Robt, only son of Robt & Rose Greenhow, aged 2½ years. His funeral is this afternoon, at 5 o'clock, from their residence, on F st.

Notice is given that application will be made for the payment of the following certificates issued in the name of Isaac Whippo, formerly of N Y, but who died in Rhode Island, viz: certificate of 3% stock for $38,03, due thereon. One certificate deferred 6% stock for $25.35, final dividend: .37. Standing to the credit of the said Isaac Whippo on the books of the treasury, returned from the Rhode Island agency as unpaid. -John Whippo, adm of Isaac Whippo

MON JUN 28, 1847

Wilkinson, who poisoned the wedding party in Texas not long since, has been hanged in due form by the people, under the Lynch code.

Chesapeake & Ohio Canal Co elected Pres & Directors for the ensuing year:
Jas M Coale, Pres
Directors:

John Pickell, of Balt, Md	H Daingerfield, of Alexandria, Va
Saml P Smith, of Alleghany Co, Md	*Wm Cost Johnson, of Montg Co, Md
Wm A Bradley, of Wash, D C	Geo Schley, of Wash Co, Md

*[Jul 3rd newspaper: correction: the residence of Wm Cost Johnson is Fred'k Co, Md.]

The remains of Col McKee, Lt Col Clay, Capt Willis, Adj Vaughan, & private H Trotter, were received at Louisville, Ky, on Jun 21, by the military companies & citizens, with every demonstration of public esteem & honor. Business was entirely suspended, & all the stores closed along the streets through which the funeral procession moved.

Rev Timothy Clowes, LL D, aged 60 years, died at Hempstead, L I, on Jun 16. He was one of the greatest mathematicians of the age: graduated at Columbia College in 1808: in 1821 was Principal of Erasmus Hall, Flatbush: in 1823 chosen Pres of Wash College, Md, & Rector of the church in Chestertown & St Paul's, Kent Co: in 1838 was invited to preside over the Clinton Liberal Institute, Oneida Co, where he remained until the fall of 1842.

Military execution: as the train came down from Monterey that brought us news from there up to May 31, the guard arrested at Ceralvo a Mexican who had become notorious for his daring thefts & murders. Upon being examined, enough was elicited to order his immediate execution. Six soldiers were selected as executioners: he saw the weapons raised, remarking he only had one life to lose while he had taken 40. In another instant he sprang forward a corpse, one ball penetrating his head. Papers found on his dead body revealed he was the brother of the notorious Canales. -N O National

We announce the death of Jas Camak, long & widely known as the editor of the Georgia Journal, as the first Pres of the Central Bank, & of late the editor of the Southern Cultivator. He died on Wed week of disease of the heart. -Georgia Recorder

The new Regt of Indiana Volunteers, raised under the late call of the Pres, are now being mustered into service. Maj Willis A Gorman, who distinguished himself in command of the rifle btln at Buena Vista, has been elected colonel; Ebenezer Dumont, of Dearborn Co, lt colonel; & W W McCoy, of Laporte, major.

A Md Hero. There is now living ½ miles above the toll-gate, Fulton, an old Revolutionary soldier named Benj Yeats. He was born in Balt Co, Md, in 1736, & is therefore 111 years old. He was in the battles of Yorktown, Pauli, Brandywine, & several others. He was present at the taking of Cornwallis. At Yorktown he was wounded in the hip by a shell. This wound is now troublesome; otherwise, the old veteran's health is good. He can see to read, & walks out daily. He is active-exceedingly so for a man of his advanced age.

Geo W Clarke, son of Mr Geo Clarke, of Cumberland, Md, aged about 22 years, came to his death by an accident as he worked in a brickyard on Sat, at Gamble's Furnace, about 4 miles from Cumberland, Hampshire Co, Va. He stuck a very sharp pick into the ground, & placing a shingle upon the upper point, seated himself thereon. The shingle split and the pick pierced his body, causing his death Monday. -Chron

Wm Armstrong, a Deputy Sheriff of Hampshire Co, Va, was killed on Fri last by a man named Roby. He had gone to Roby's house to levy an execution, & was alightning from his horse when he was shot & instantly killed.

In the city of Rochester, N Y, on Tuesday, during a thunder storm of unusual violence, one bolt descended with fatal effect upon the house of Mr Wm Mathews, 28 Wilder st, killing Mr Mathews, his wife & dght. -Rochester Democrat

Mr Herron, who has a private school in the College Bldgs, Cincinnati, took the boys under his charge out to Foster's Crossings on Wed week for recreation. They were prohibited to go bathing, but a son of Mr J Elstner, about 9 or 10, disobeying the injunction, went bathing, & being unable to swim, was drowned.

Rev Dr Tyng, formerly of Phil, arrived safely at Havre, from N Y, in the ship **Arago**, after a passage of 19 days, with health greatly improved by the voyage. After a few days in Paris, he expects to leave on May 18 for Italy.

The following embarked on Mon for Smyrna, in the barque **Catalpa**, Capt Watson, viz: Rev Messrs Cochran, Benson, & Bliss, with their wives, & Miss Rice. Mr & Mrs Cochran & Miss Rice are to proceed to Oroomiah, to join the Nestorian mission. Mr & Mrs Bliss will go with them as far as Erzeroom, where they are to labor in behalf of the Armenians. Mr & Mrs Benton are expected to join the Syria mission. -Boston Traveller

On Jun 11, as John Schelinger was digging a well on the premises of Mr Bennett, Kendall Co, at the depth of 50 feet below the surface, the sides caved in and Mr Schelinger was buried alive. He was not able to be extricated until early evening, when he was taken out dead. -Chicago Democrat

Yesterday fire destroyed the Soap & Candle Factore recently established by Mr Jared Coleman at Lenox's wharf, near the Long Bridge, Wash City. Nothing but the brick walls were left standing. He was insured on his stock & fixtures to the amount of $3,000.

Noah Barlow, formerly proprietor of the City Hotel at Natchez, & noted for his energy & enterprise in business, died recently in that city.

Mr Wm Fischer has just commenced the bldg of an elegant dwlg on the south side of C st, between 3rd & 4½ sts. Mr Curran is the contractor & carpenter; Mr P Hevner is engaged in the brick work. Mr Walter Lenox has commenced the erection of a new store & good brick dwlg near the corner of Pa ave & 9th st. Mr Peter Hevner is to do the brick work.

Died: on Jun 27, Clara Helen, infant & only daughter of John & Martha Wilson, aged 7 months & 24 days. Her funeral is today at 4 o'clock, from the residence of her father, near the corner of N Y ave & 11th st. The friends & acquaintances of her parents are invited to attend the funeral.

TUE JUN 29, 1847

For rent & possession immediately: a large frame house with 9 rooms, on the brow of the Capitol Hill; recently the residence of Jas Greenleaf, & previously to that time had been occupied by Mr Dixon, & the land attached to it, consisting of 30 or more adjoining lots, cultivated by him as a market garden. There is every convenience for a family residence. Apply to Mrs Jonathan Elliot, on the premises, in the rear of the residence of the Hon Judge Cranch.

Mrd: on May 24 last, by Rev Saml C Davis, Mr Chas H Barron, formerly of Wash, to Miss Eliz Ann, daughter of Mr Benj Cockrell, of Randolph Co, Missouri.

Died: on Sunday, in Wash City, of consumption, Jos Beardsley, in his 34th year. He was a native of England, & emigrated to this country early in life. About 15 years since he was initiated a member of the Independent Order of Odd Fellows, in Wash Lodge, #6, of this District. He had died, as he lived, respected & beloved by all who knew him. [Jun 30th newspaper: the remains of the late Jos Beardsley were interred yesterday with the honors of the Order to which he belonged. The procession was a large one, & would probably have been larger if the weather had been favorable.]

J D Blondell, Portrait Painter, can be seen at his studio at Mrs Hamilton, Pa ave, between 4½ & 6th sts.

Mrd: on Jun 24, at Harrisburg, by Rev Dr De Witt, Hon Victor E Piolet to Jane, daughter of the Hon Jesse Miller, late First Auditor of the Treasury.

Died: Jun 14, at Quincy, Illinois, Maria, aged 18 years, youngest daughter of the late F Cornelius De Krafft, of Wash City.

WED JUN 30, 1847

For sale, a Newfoundland dog, 11 months old, 4 feet long, 2½ feet high, possessing great sagacity, susceptible of receiving any training peculiar to that species; he is jet black. Inquire at Mr Maher's Globe Hotel, Wash.

Orphans Court of Wash Co, D C. Letters of administration on the personal estate of Henreitta M S Young, late of PG Co, Md, dec'd. -Geo W Young, adm

Mr Crutchett is busily engaged in preparing to erect the mast, of 100 feet in length, to the top of which his immense gas light lantern is to be affixed. The mast was conveyed to the Captiol grounds on Mon, & will be erected on the Dome of the Capitol.

We do not know how it happens that the death of Reuben G Beasley, the long time respected Consul of the U S at Havre, has not, as far as we have seen, been formally announced by the press.

Mrs Forrest, the mother of the American Tragedian, died at her home in Phil on Jun 24, in her 75th year.

Wm W Birth begs leave to inform his friends & the public that he has purchased of Mr M Caton his entire stock of well-selected Groceries, Wines, & Liquors, west room, Jackson Hall bldg, Pa ave, to which he had made considerable additions & is now prepared to offer for sale.

Died: Jun 25, at New Haven, Conn, Mrs Rebecca Webster, relict of the late Noah Webster, in her 82nd year.

Died: on Jun 28, George Herrick, infant son of Wm F & Margaret Bayly, aged 8 months.

Boston Journal: Dr Fletcher, a young physician of thorough education & great promise, died yesterday of typhoid or ship fever, contracted by attendance upon some Irish emigrants. [No date-current news item.]

The Hon Jas McKown, for many years one of the most prominent citizens of Albany, & at the time of his decease Recorder of the city of Albany, died in that city suddenly on Saturday, aged 58 years.

THU JUL 1, 1847
Came to the subscriber's premises, on Jun 19, a small Red Cow. Owner is to prove property, pay expenses, & take her away. -Mary Huchison, near Navy Yard Bridge

On the 28th ult, Dr Ezra Green, of Dover, N H, [Harvard College, 1765,] completed his 101st year, with his powers of mind scarcely if at all impaired by length of days. He has outlived all his classmates by 16 years; the latest survivor, Andrew Fuller, died at age 88 at Lyndeborough, N H, in April, 1831. Within a fortnight, a second centenarian will be added to the Harvardian roll, the Hon Timothy Farrar, [Harvard College, 1767,] formerly of the Supreme Bench of N H, whose life has been passed at New Ispwich, N H, until about 5 years since, when, for the solace & society of a dght, he removed to Hollis. He was a native of Lincoln, in this vicinity, where he was born Jul 11, 1747.
-Boston Transcript

Dr Henry Tennent, of Thibodeaux, La, & formerly of Delaware, was drowned on Jun 5 at the mouth of Bayou Lafourche. He & a friend were swimming, when the strong ebb tide swept him out into the Gulf, & before assistance could reach him he sunk exhausted.

For sale: a modern light-built Buggy, Harness, & Saddle. Also, a very handsome Horse, about 6 years old, very gentle, & perfectly sound. Inquire of W Voss, Pa ave, near 12th st.

The beautiful grounds & mansion belonging to the estate of the late Jos Napoleon Bonaparte, ex-King of Spain, were on Sat sold at auction for the sum of $30,500. Mr Thos Richards, of Phil, was the purchaser. It is said that the bldgs alone cost $60,000. The paintings brought $10 to $1,050. Two lions & a fawn by Reubens sold for the largest sum. Nativity of our Saviour, by Raphael Mengs, brought $1,000; the portrait of a dog, by Hackets, brought $210. The picture of Napoleon crossing the Alps, by David, the proprietors refused to put up unless the sum of $6,000 was bid for it. As no person present was willing to bid that sum it was passed, & will be sent to Europe.
-Newark Advertiser, Jun 26

A distressing disaster at Kingsland forge, Willsboro, on Tue, by the bursting of a mass of cinder just drawn from the fire: S Whitcomb, John Foster, & a lad named Hamer, were injured. Yesterday it was considered that Foster was past all hope.
-Essex Co, [N Y] Republican

Col J D Edwards, principal of the N J Oil Cloth Manufacturing Co at Elizabethtown, died at Boston on Thu of injuries received on the railroad in the morning. He had stepped upon the platform for an instant at the stopping place at Mansfield, & just as the train started was thrown between the platform & the next car, with his right arm across the track. The cars passed over his arm, cutting it off. He was taken to Boston & conveyed to the Massachusetts Hospital, where proper surgical & medical aid was afforded. He lingered in great agony for 12 hours. Providentially his dght, Mrs Jas W Woodriff, of Elizabethtown, & her son were with him to minister to his necessities in the dreadful extremity.

Public sale of land: by decree of the Circuit Superior Court of Loudoun Co, Va, pronounced at Oct Term, 1846, in the case of Dawson vs Dawson, I shall offer for sale on Jul 24, at Purdom's Tavern, opposite the Point of Rocks, the following: 1-The ***Iron Ore Lot***: 60 acres, more or less: in Loudoun Co, near the Point of Rocks: adjoining the ***Furnace Tract***, on the Potomac river. 2-The Mountain lot of woodland: 15¼ acres, in Loudoun Co; originally a part of the land of Saml Clapham, dec'd, & described, in the division thereof, a ***Woodlot #6***. 3-***Peach Island***: about 10 acres, nearly opposie the Point of Rocks, between the upper point of Kanawha Island & the Virginia shore. 4-***Razor Tract***, the undivided interest of the late Saml Dawson: being seven-elevenths thereof: the whole tract contains about 186 acres, & lies in Loudoun Co, adjoining the lands of B Shreve & Gunnell Saunders. -Chas Gassaway, Com'r

Memphis Enquirer of Jun 16, states that Mr Jos Aiken, a respectable citizen of that place, was stabbed through the heart with a large bowie-knife by a returned volunteer, Nat Ursery, of Capt Cook's company. He died instantly. Ursery was tried before an examining Court, & held to bail in the sum of $5,000, with 2 securities in a like sum, in default of which he was committed to prison.

Died: on Jun 17, in Boone Co, Ky, Silas Dinsmoor, in his 81st year.

The Circuit Superior Court of Law & Chancery for the County of Albemarle & State of Va, pronounced a decree on May 23, 1847, in a chancery cause pending in said Court, in which Jas B Stroud & Mary Stroud are plntfs, & Wm Robinson, administrator of Jas Stroud, dec'd, Saml Harding, Thos Wood, Egbert R Watson & John Ball, administrators of Ann Stroud, dec'd, are dfndnts, by which it was, among other things, ordered that one of the com'rs of said Court "take an account of all claims outstanding against the estate of Jas Stroud, dec'd; before doing so, however, he shall, by advertisement, for at least 2 months, in the Lynchburg Virginian, Nat'l Intelligencer, & some paper published in Newcastle or Wilmington, Delaware, notify all persons holding claims against said estate that unless they present & prove them before him on or before a given day, the Court will proceed to decree a distribution of the assets of the estate, & such notice will be held a bar to any future attempt to assert their claims. And the said advertisement shall contain a similar notice & warning to all persons, other than the parties to this suit, who may claim to be distributes of the estate of the intestate." Sep 21, 1847, has been assigned as the time for the above mentioned. -Wm J Robertson, Com'r of Chancery of Circuit Superior court of Law & Chancery for Albemarle Co, Va.

Died: on May 28, John Augustin, son of Henry M Prevost, aged 18 months.

I am authorized to sell the elegant mansion of the late Gen Van Ness, near the President's House, with spacious & beautiful ornamented grounds attached to the same: 7 acres, enclosed with a brick wall; bldgs alone cost upwards of $50,000; dwlg house is large & well constructed; with all necessary out-bldgs. To a fashionable family a chance is now offered to procure the finest residence in Washington, & at a sum far below its value. -Thos Carbery

For sale: a modern light-built Buggy, Harness, & Saddle. Also, a very handsome Horse, about 6 years old, very gentle, & perfectly sound. Inquire of W Voss, Pa ave, near 12th st.

The subscriber, being about to withdraw from the profession of Teaching, offers for sale the good will & fixtures of the Central Collegiate Institute, #96 Fayette st, Balt, Md, together with 3 separate branches, located in different sections of the city. This Institution has enjoyed ample patronage for the last 3 years. Apply to Rev Wm H Smith, #96 Fayette st, Balt, Md. All communications post paid.

FRI JUL 2, 1847

Wm Duane Wilson, one of the editors & proprietors of the Milwaukie [Wisc] Sentinel, was thrown from a carriage on May 21, & so severely injured as to cause his death. Mr Wilson was associated with Gen Rufus King, formerly of Albany, in conducting the Sentinel, a most valuable newspaper. [Jul 17th newspaper: the copy of the accidental death of Mr Wm Duane Wilson, of Milwaukee, was entirely without foundation. He is still amongst the living, & no such accident occurred to him.]

Mrd: on May 29, by Rev Chas H Hall, of West Point, Mary Louisa, daughter of the late Israel Corse, to Hon Wm H Polk, Charge d'Affaires to Naples.

Wash Corp: 1-Ptn from Stephen Coster & others, for bridges over certain streets: referred to the Cmte on Improvements. 2-Ptn of Elton Brent, for remission of a fine: referred to the Cmte of Claims. 3-Ptn of Jas Crutchett & others, for improvement of North Capitol st & bridge over the same: referred to the Cmte on Improvements. 4-Ptn of John Ball & others, for improvement of G st, between 1st & 2nd sts: referred to the Cmte on Improvements. 5-Ptn of John Fitzgerald, for remission of a fine: referred to the Cmte of Claims. 6-Mr Tims, on leave, introduced a joint resolution of respect to Lt Col Chas A May: we have learned that Lt Col Chas A May, who, more than 10 years ago, at his country's call, abandoned the pleasant & quiet avocations of peaceful life, the luxuries of affluence, & entered her permanent service, during the Seminole war in Florida, where his many acts of heroism & chivalrous bearing as an ofcr gave such flattering promise of his future usefulness in her service, has just returned from the seat of war in Mexico to this his native city. We should tender to him some public token of our approval of his conduct, of welcome to our hospitalities, of our appreciation of his merits, & of our high social regard. Resolution was passed.

As the train from Springfield, Mass, for Cabotville & Chicopee Falls was turning off at the junction on Sat last to go to the village, it ran over & killed Mr Russell Searle, of Southampton, who had attempted to cross the track just as the cars came along. He was about 35 years of age, & has left a family.

Exhibition of the pupils at St Vincent's Female Orphan Asylum: on Wed, amounting to 200, had their usual exhibition, in the presence of a numerous & hightly gratified audience, amongst whom was Fr Mathews, the Rev Jas B Donelan, of St Matthew's Church, & other reverend gentlemen of the Catholic denomination.

Died: on Jul 1, in Wash City, at the residence of her brother-in-law, [Chas De Selden,] Miss Herriott Brown, late of N Y C. Her funeral is from his residence, on 6th st, next to F st, at 4 o'clock today. [Jul 3rd newspaper: correction: Chas De Selding not Selden.]

The village of Romney, Va, was thrown into consternation & overwhelmed with gloom on Sun last, by the intelligence that Wm J Armstrong, estimable fellow-citizen & townsman, had been shot dead on the preceding night, whilst in the command of a patrol, near Ridgeville. Four persons are in custody, charged as principal & accessories, by the verdict of the Coroner's jury.

Jas Campbell, who went down from New Orleans as Clerk of the Paymaster's Dept with Judge Bosworth, died at Vera Cruz of vomito on May 6; & the Judge, [Paymaster,] whose obit we have already published, died on the Wed following.

A lady named Spencer arrived at N Y in the ship **Monongahela** from Liverpool, on Fri, says the Phil Inquirer, & was met at the wharf by her brother-in-law, who conducted her to his residence in Southwark, where, after being welcomed by her sister, she fell over & died almost immediately, Mrs Spencer had not met her sister for about 17 years, & had come to this country at her request.

Mrd: on May 29, by Rev J A Collins, Chas H Tavenner, of Loudoun Co, Va, to Miss Maria, 3rd daughter of Philip Otterback, of Wash City.

SAT JUL 3, 1847

For sale: lot 27 in square 387, & the 2 story frame house thereon: on south D st, near the Ryland Chapel: on Jul 7, at public auction. -Jas S Harvey, Arsenius J Harvery, owners -R W Dyer, auct

Col J P Taulor, Col Craig, Capt L Chase, Lts Wooster, Montgomery, Allen, Mizner, & Dr T C Darley, all of the regular army; also, Adj G N Cardwell, 3rd Regt Ky volunteers, & 40 discharged soldiers arrived at New Orleans from the Rio Grande on the 23rd ult.

The Archduke Charles. This distinguished General, the ablest rival of Napoleon, with the exception of Wellington, & pronounced by Napoleon himself as one of the ablest tacticians of the day, died at Vienna on Apr 29 last: from a severe cold, followed by inflammation of the pleura. He commanded the bloody battle of Wagram, & held for a while the fate of the day even against Napoleon. He also commanded at the battle of Aspern Eesling, in which Marshal Lannes was killed. He was uncle to the present Emperor.

C K Johnson, a distinguished member of the New Orleans bar, was accidentally drowned on Jun 19 by falling from a steamboat on the Mississippi.

Farmers' & Mechanic' Bank, Gtwn, Jul 1, 1847. The Trustees have this day declared a dividend of 2½%. -Alex'r Suter, Cashier

Sir Humphrey Davy, the celebrated chemist & philosopher, when he published his "Elements of Chemical Philosophy," dedicated it not to a prince or powerful nobleman, but to his Wife! "To Lady Davy: There is no individual to whom I can with so much propriety or so much pleasure dedicate this work as to you. ---receive it as a proof of my ardent affection, which must be unalterable, for it is founded upon the admiration of your moral & intellectual qualities. H Davy."

Patriotic Bank of Wash, Jul 1, 1847. This Bank will be closed on Mon, Jul 5.
-C Bestor, Cashier

Ofc Potomac Ins Co, Gtwn, Jul 2, 1847. The Pres & Dirs have this day declared a dividend of 5%, which will be paid to the Stockholders, or their legal reps, on or after Jul 7. -Henry King, Secretary

Bank of the Metropolis, Jul 1, 1847. As the 4th of Jul falls this year on Sunday, this Bank will not be open on Monday, the 5th. -Rd Smith, Cashier

The undersigned, having sold his interest in the business of Walter Harper & Co, has retired from that firm. -Franklin Gardner

Orphans Court of Wash Co, D C. Letters of administration on the personal estate of Jos Beardsley, late of said county, dec'd. -Susannah Beardsley, adms

Dissolution of the copartnership existing under the firm of Hall & Wallace, by mutual consent. John Q Willson is authorized to settle up the business, & intends to continue the Dry Goods Business in the same store occupied by the above firm.
-B Hall, I Hall, John Q Willson

A Dodge, late Postmaster at Frankfort Mills, Maine, was convicted on Jun 26 before the District Court, & sentenced to 10 years' imprisonment in the county jail of Waldo.

Another arrest: John P Chester, another of the active agents of the Post Ofc Dept, has arrested John Carpenter, a stage-driver on the route from Rockford to Talladega, Alabama, who has been committed for trial at Tuscala. -Union

Cape Henlopen: improved & fashionable Watering Place will be opened for visiters the first week in Jul: the Ocean House will accommodate from 150 to 200 persons.
-A W Prettyman, Ocean House, Lewes, Dela

Trustee's sale: by deed of trust from Jas Kelly, dated Nov 30, 1843, recorded in Liber W B 106, folios 476 through 480, one of the land records of Wash Co, D C: sale on Jul 10, in front of the premises: the north 22 feet of lot 28 in square 105, in Wash City, being that part of said lot lying between the south line of lot 27; & the part sold to Chas Sioussa, fronting 22 feet on 18th st west; with bldgs & improvements thereon, being a comfortable 2 story brick house. -E J Middleton, trustee -R W Dyer, auct

Through the carelessness of a driver, on Wed, a horse was permitted to run through Park Row, N Y. He ran upon the sidewalk over Mr Thaddeus C Craft, of Balt, & his wife, to whom he was married on Sunday last, in Roxbury, Mass, knocking them down & injuring them very seriously. They were taken to the house of Mr Mowett, & Dr John Stearns was called, who dressed their wounds, & they are doing as well as the circumstances will permit.

The schnr **George M Bache**, for the U S Coast Survey, will be launched from Easby's ship-yard at 12 o'clock this day.

It is said that Mr Thos Richards, of Phil, who purchased the mansion of the late Jos Bonaparte, at Bordentown, is about to convert it into a manufactory of glass.

Died: on Jul 2, in Wash City, after a long & painful illness of nearly 4 months' duration, of catarrh fever, Henry Clay, y/son of Jas & Deborah Mankin, aged 14 months & 18 days. His funeral is this morning at 10 o'clock, from their residence on 9th st, between H & I sts.

Savannah, Jun 29. Railroad accident on the Central Railroad on Fri last, when the train had to pass over a part of the road at night where the embankment had been washed away, leaving the superstructure without support. The locomotive, followed by its tender & the baggage car, plunged into this chasm: Messrs O B Darby, the fireman, & John Long, a train hand, were killed on the spot, & Mr C F England, a most worthy man, & one of the best engineers of the company, so seriously wounded that he died on Sat. -Republican

Died: on Jun 14, at Green Bay, Wisc, after a protracted & severe illness, Col Alex'r J Irwin, Receiver of the Land Ofc at Green Bay, aged 48.

MON JUL 5, 1847

Capt Weightman, the young ofcr who commanded the artillery at the battle of Sacramento, & who accompanied Col Doniphan throughout his long march, had a fact upon which he may be congratulated almost as much as upon his gallantry in battle. Letter from Capt Weightman, published in the Richmond Republican, says: "I have, as far as I am at this moment informed, to congratulate myself upon a circumstance peculiar to my company. In a campaign of one year, marching as we have a distance of 5,000 miles, I have not lost a man by sickness or from wounds received in battle. I will go home with my whole company, except the arm of one man, amputated in consequence of a wound received in battle." The Captain adds, that his own health is excellent, with the exception of a slight cold, contracted from sleeping under a roof.

The new Indiana Regt commanded by Col Gorman, left their rendezvous opposite Louisville, on Sunday last, for the seat of war.

Wilmington [Del] Gaz: the Sec of War has declined the services of Capt Wm Hemphill Jones' company of volunteers, raised in that place, assigning as a reason that the Dept did not need any more men at present.

Immigrants: the following statistics of emigration from Jan 1 to Jun 30, 1847:
Arrived: 81,954
Died on the passage as reported by captains: 947
Admitted to the marine hospital quarantine: 2,750
Died in hospital: 288
Died with 24 hours of reception: 30
Very few, indeed, were Germans, as ships sailing from German ports are compelled to have sufficient provisions on board. Most of the sick are in a famished condition, many of then in the same clothes in which they came on board the ship, without changing or washing on the voyage, & full of vermin. The disease called ship fever is nothing new, & may be engendered any where under circumstances of filthy confinement. -Jour of Com

The New Orleans Delta: assassination of a father & his son, at Pine Bluffs, Ark, by a Dr Emory. Murdered were Jas De Baun, sr, & Jas De Baun, jr. The Dr had betrayed the dght of Mr De Baun, & hence a state of hostility between the parties, which induced Emory to come into town, & from a window, with a double-barrelled weapon, fired with fatal effect on Mr De Baun & his son. This happened on Jun 15.

A rencontre at New Orleans on Jun 25 between Mr Robt Shortridge, a clerk in the employ of Alfred Penn & Co, & Mr O A Tarbonny, a sampler, at Mr G W Sully's, cotton brokers, which resulted in the death of the Tarbonny. Tarbonny assaulted Shortridge with a cane; shortridge fired 3 shots from his revolver at the assailant, the last of which took fatal effect. Opinion was that he acted in self-defence.

Died: on Jun 28, at ***Tulip Hill***, West River, Md, Mary Maxcy Hughes, only daughter of Lt Col & Mrs Anne Sarah Hughes.

French Variety Store, formerly Guion Bazaar, corner of 4½ st & Pa ave. -T Bastianelli

WED JUL 7, 1847
Capt Wm Armstrong, Indian Superintendent, died at ***Fort Townsend*** on Jun 12.

Died: on Jul 6, [yesterday] Lt John T McLaughlin, of the U S Navy, in his 36th year. His funeral is this day, at 4 o'clock p m, from his late residence, without further notice.

Died: on Jul 6, Beall, infant daughter of B F & Eliz Middleton, aged 6 months. Her funeral is today at 10 o'clock, from the residence of her father on Missouri ave.

Died: on Jun 30, Francis Y, infant son of Francis Y & Ann E Naylor, aged 9 months & 18 days.

Died: on Jul 4, in Wash City, Blanche, infant daughter of R C & Sophia May Washington, aged 9 months.

Mr Thos H Williams & Mr David Watson were killed by lightning near Hickory Wythe, Fayette Co, Tenn, on Jun 16. Others were badly injured at the same time.

Criminal Court:1-Allen Peddicord, formerly a watchman in the Gen Post Ofc, was put on trial charged with stealing a letter from the Gen Post Ofc in Wash City, the property of Hon Cave Johnson, the Postmaster Gen. From the appearances of the prisoner before & during the trial, his counsel urged with great force the plea of insanity in his behalf. The case will probably go to the Jury. [Jul 8th newspaper: verdict-not guilty]

Yesterday the steamboat **Jewess**, Capt Sutton, left Balt with nearly 700 persons, of all ages, & put in at Annapolis. A disturbance took place between the disorderly portion of the Baltimoreans & some of the Annapolitans. A volley of missiles were thrown & young Edw Burrell, of Annapolis, was wounded, & he may now be dead. Also wounded were Mr Brady, Mr McNeir, also a citizen of Annapolis, & a man named Hall, who had 2 of his toes shot off.

THU JUL 8, 1847

In the matter of Smith vs Long Island Railroad Co, for damages for the loss of the services of his dght Almeda, who was killed through the alleged negligence of the railroad agents, Judge Greenwood, as referee, on Thursday rendered a decision in favor of the plntf for $950. -N Y Gaz

Trustee's sale: by virtue of a deed of trust from Wm T Dove, dated Sep 4, 1845, recorded in Liber W B 121, folios 59 thru 61, one of the land records of Wash Co, D C: sale at public auction on Jul 13: lot 4 in square 124. Title indisputable. -R W Dyer, auct

Valuable property at auction; the subscriber, being about to leave the city, is desirous to settle with his creditors, & has determined to sell: lot 10 in square 38, & part of lot 22 in square 77, with the two 3 story brick houses thereon, both of which are in the 1st Ward: the first fronts on 24th st, near Gtwn; the other is near the West Market. -Jos Boulanger
-R W Dyer, auct

Household & kitchen furniture at auction: on Jul 14, at the residence of Mrs Whitwell, on Capitol Hill, in Gen D Green's row: a good assortment of furniture. -A Green, auctioneer

The N Y papers announce the death of Jas Alex'r Brown, aged 24 years, eldest son of Jas Brown, of the firm of Brown, Brothers & Co. His death occurred at the place of Gardiner Howland, of Flushing, on Sat, & was caused by a shot from a small cannon which some lads were firing in celebrating the anniversary of Independence. The young man had only time to tell the boys they had shot him, when he expired. [Jul 9th newspaper: Mr Brown was exercising himself in a swing while 2 sons of G G Howland, aged about 12 & 14 years, were amusing themselves by firing off a small cannon about 3 inches long, mounted on wheels. Mr Brown was the son of Jas Brown, & son-in-law of G G Howland, to whose dght he had been married about 8 months.]

A small boy, John Bride, whilst getting on the Pittsburg train of cars in Market st, Phil, on Fri, fell, & the wheels passed across his legs. He died in about 3 hours after he met with the accident.

A salary of $900 per annum will be paid to a competent person who will employ 2 female assistants & take charge of the Berlin Female Seminary. By order of the Board.
-John R Pitts, Berlin, Worcester Co, Md

The Proprietor of the Virginia Hotel, at Dranesville, Va, informs that the Hotel is open for visiters. Distance from the Big Falls 4 or 5 miles. -Ann M Farr

Mrd: on Jun 24, by Rev R T Brown, the Rev Geo D Cummins, Rector of Christ Church, Norfolk, to Alexandrine Macomb Baleh, youngest daughter of L P W Baleh, of Jefferson Co, Va.

Died: on Jul 7, Silvie, infant daughter of Agricola & Albertine Marchal Favier, aged 17 days.

Died: on Jul 7, Mr Claude Arme Ricard, aged 65 years, a native of Stain, near Paris, France, but for the last 28 years a respected citizen of Wash City. His funeral is on Jul 8, at 5 o'clock, from his late residence, on Boundary, between 17th & 18th sts, near Meridian Hill.

Died: on Jul 4, after a long & painful illness, Mrs Eliz Dement, w/o Chas F Dement, of PG Co, Md, leaving a husband & 2 small children, besides a large circle of relatives & friends to mourn her early death. To her distant friends we can truly say that she died in the full assurance of a happy immortality. -D

FRI JUL 9, 1847

Mr John M Brown, a native of Petersbur, Va, lost his life in Richmond on Jul 4 through the culpable carelessness of one of the members of a volunteer corps of that city, whilst the military were firing a national salute. A musket of one of the Richmond Greys was loaded with a ball cartridge, & the dec'd, who was a spectator, was shot through the head.

Mr Jas C Carter, celebrated for his management of wild beasts, known as the lion-tamer, died at London on Jun 18, after a brief illness.

The Valley Whig of Fri announces the death of Lewis Neal, the delegate elect to the Virginia State Legislature from the election district of Giles & Mercer. He has been in delicate health for some time.

Col J B Thompson, an old & respected citizen of Louisville, Ky, died a few days since. He was on the steamer **Lucy Walker** when the terrible disaster occurred to her some 3 years ago, & has been, from that time until the hour of his death, confined to his bed in consequence of the injuries he then received.

Wm H Hays, son of Michl Hays, of Burlington, N J, recently studied law in the ofc of the Hon Garrett D Wall, was married on Jun 8 to a young lady of Burlington, & with his bride set out on a wedding tour to Niagara & Montreal. Having returned as far as Saratoga Springs he was seized with bilious fever, & on Wed, just 3 weeks from the time he was married, he expired. His parents & sister arrived just in time to see him die, at the early age of 26 years.

For rent: 3 story brick house, being one of the block of bldgs known as Gadsby's Row, now in the occupancy of Capt Chauncey. Possession can be given on Aug 1. Apply to Alex McIntire.

Balt, Jul 8. Judge Jas Harwood died on Jul 7 at his residence in Balt City after a lingering illness. He was for many years Judge of the Orphans Court of Balt City & County.

Mrd: on Jul 4, in King George Co, Va, by Rev Philip Montague, Philibert Louis Rodier, of Gtwn, to Miss Louisa Monroe Rodgers, of King George Co.

Died: yesterday, at his residence in Gtwn, Rev Jas McVean, Principal of the Gtwn Scientific & Classical Academy. His funeral will take place from his late residence, at the corner of Montgomery & Dunbarton sts, this afternoon, at 5 o'clock. [The former pupils of Rev McVean are to meet at the residence of Dr Grafton Tyler, Washington & Gay sts, Gtwn, on Fri at 4 o'clock. -Many of his old scholars]

Died: on Jul 8, in Wash City, Miss Sarah Tenney, late of Newburyport, Mass, aged 62 years. Her funeral is this afternoon at 5 o'clock, from her late residence on G st, near the Observatory.

Died: on Jul 6, in Gtwn, suddenly, in his 26th year, Lt Robt Getty, of the U S Navy. He had labored under a pulmonary affection for a considerable length of time before his decease.

Died: on Jul 8, Mrs Mary Stewart, w/o Wm Stewart, aged 65 years. Her funeral is from her late residence, on 12th st, near G, this morning, at 9 o'clock. The friends & acquaintances of the family, as well as the members of the Ladies' Sodality, are requested to attend.

Died: on Wed, at N Y, in his 63rd year, Thaddeus Phelps.

Valuable house & lots for sale: on Jul 15, on the premises, I shall sell one lot of ground with a frame house of 2 stories & 4 rooms, fronting on 4th st, & one vacant lot adjoining the above. Both lots are in square 513, between M & N sts, west of John Walker's slaughter-house. -John McDevitt, auctioneer

For rent: the new & commodious house on F st west, now occupied by Thos Ritchie. Possession on Jul 20. Inquire of Wm A Gordon, Quartermaster General's Ofc, War Dept.

SAT JUL 10, 1847
$300 reward for runaways from the undersigned, near Mount Jackson, Shenandoah Co, Va, on Jul 3, Ezekiel, a very black negro, about 27 years old. Also, Jack Hays, a bright mulatto, about 25 years old. -John G Meem, A R Rude

The murder at Pine Bluff: Mr De Baun & his son James were walking from his dwlg up to his store, when Dr Embree, who had disguised himself in an old blanket coat & an unusual cap, slipped to the dining room door & shot Mr De Baun down, several shot having struck him in the breast; & then he or his comrade shot his son James, hitting him with 5 buckshot, which wounded him badly, but not mortally. Mr Merrill happening to be close by, ran to Mr De Baun as he lay strangling in death. He died immediately. This is the end of one of the most industrious & business merchants in the Western country. He died with knowing who perpetrated the bloody act. -Little Rock Gazette

Proposals will be received by the subscriber until Jul 19, for constructing a culvert across Mass ave, between 4th & 5th sts. -Fra B Lord, Com'r of the 4th Ward

MON JUL 12, 1847
Marshal Grouchy, who commanded the French corps d'arme, which was destined to employ the Prussian army, while Napoleon attacked the Duke of Wellington at Waterloo, died lately at St Etienne, on the Loire, in his 82nd year.

Col Jos P Taylor, Assist Commissary Genr'l of Subsistence, the only brother of Maj Gen Taylor, [who has been for the last year with the Army in Mexico,] arrived at Cincinnati on a visit to his family, now there.

Miss Rosalie Sully, daughter of our much esteemed townsman, Thos Sully, died yesterday, at her father's residence, after a short but severe attack of brain fever. It is but a few days since we took occasion to notice 2 exquisitely painted miniatures, just completed by this talented young lady. -Phil Chronicle

Our esteemed friend & former fellow-citizen, Capt Wm Jamesson, now in Alexandria, has received orders to take command of the frig **Cumberland**, now fitting out at the Gosport navy yard. -Norfolk Beacon

Albany Evening Journal: Florence Fitzpatrick, a native of Deer Park, Queens Co, Ireland, who, with his 3 children, Thos, aged 12, Mary, aged 10, & Danl aged 4 years, sailed from Liverpool for N Y on Mar 3 last, it is believed, in the ship **Cornelia**. His wife died a short time before he left home. In April last Florence reached Saguerties, where his brother resides, in an exhausted condition from ship fever, delirious, without his children, & unable to give an account of them. In a short time he died. His surviving friends have made every exertion to find the 3 little orphans, thus far without success. If any person can give information of them they will perform an act of the greatest charity. Write-Mr David Nelligan, Emigrant Agent, Albany.

Land for sale in Fairfax Co, Va: the subscriber offers for sale 530 acres, more or less, in the above county, lying its entire length on a main county road leading from Fairfax Courthouse to the Falls Church: land is equally divided in 2 tracts. Apply to Thos R Love, Fairfax C H; or to Edw Pittman, Balt, Md.

Mrd: on Sat, at Coleman's Hotel, by Rev John C Smith, John A Sims to Miss Margaret F Eskridge, both of Mississippi.

Dinner to be tendered to Lt Col Chas A May: cmte of arrangements:

W W Seaton-Chrmn	J Madison Cutts	Jas Adams
R C Weightman	Peter Force	J N Barker
W W Corcoran	John T Towers	John C Brent
W B Scott	J W Moorhead	Thos Blagden
Wm Easby	Silas H Hill	W J McDonald
J B H Smith	R S Patterson	C Tims
Thos P Morgan	J Y Bryant	Peter Brady
Geo Harkness	Geo Sweeny	Dr J B Gardner
S Humes Porter	Geo S Gideon	Thos Thornley
Wm Orme	Walter Lenox	J R Queen
J F Haliday	Richd Wallach	Jas Cull
Robt Farnham	W H Winter	W M Ellis
John C Rives	Jos H Bradley	Henry Otterback
Dr Thos Miller	J P Pepper	S Byington
John P Heiss	Jas H Blake	J T Cassell
John A Blake	John Mills	J W Jones
Lewis Johnson	J B Thomas	Wm Wise
Balaam Burch	Dr J C Boyle	

Criminal Court-Wash: Robt Coltman, convicted of assault upon John Frizzell: fined $50.

TUE JUL 13, 1847

Virginia Bacon Hams, 600 hams, cured at the farms of the Hon John Y Mason, of superior quality, just received & for sale by B L Jackson & Bro.

The Life & Times of Jacques Coeur, the French Argonaut, has recently been published in London.

Two children of Mr Robt Donnell, of Montgomery, Ala, on Fri of last week, overset a kettle of boiling water & the oldest, a boy of about 7 years, was scalded so severely as to cause his death in a few hours. The other, a little girl, was scalded badly about the feet, but will recover. -Journal, Jun 30th

Balt, Jul 12. Robt H Leslie, of Balt, has been appointed Quartermaster of the 10th Rifle Regt, in place of Jas P Delacour, resigned.

The remains of Col Hardin & Capt Zabriskie, of the Illinois volunteers, & of Col Yell & Capt Porter, of the Arkansas volunteers, all of whom were amongst the slain at Buena Vista, have been conveyed to New Orleans by late arrivals from the Rio Grande, on their way to the places of their former residence.

Household & kitchen furniture at auction: on Jul 16, at the residence of Mr Stedman, on C st, between 3rd & 4½ sts, north side, [the flag will designate the house,] a lot of good furniture. -A Green, auctioneer

Mrd: on Feb 10, 1847, in the First German Reformed Church, Balt, by Rev Mr Heiner, Mr Calhoun M Deringer to Miss Martha A Bladen, daughter of the late Thos Bladen, all of Phil.

Mrd: on Jul 11, by Rev N J B Morgan, Mr Jas Thos Waters, of Mobile, Ala, to Miss Jane Margaret Lowry, of Wash City.

Died: on Jul 5, in PG Co, Md, Eliz A Dement, w/o Chas E Dement, aged 27 years.
A violent attack of pneumonia, which baffled all medical skill, terminated in phthisis pulmonalis, of which she died, after a painful & protracted illness of near 6 months. The dec'd has left 2 small children, [dghts] & a circle of relatives & friends to deplore her untimely end.

Died: on Jul 10, Catherine Rebecca Payne, in her 7th year.

Dr D V Quenaudon's Ofc: Pa ave, south side, 2nd door west of 12th st, Washington.

The death of the Hon Richd Biddle is a loss to the city of Pittsburg, of which he was a conspicuous & worthy citizen; an intelligent member of the Bar; & a scholar. Like others of his family, he has been cut off in middle age. He was a brother to Nicholas Biddle, of Phil, & of Col Biddle, of the army. -Pittsburg Gaz
[Current news item-no death date given.]

WED JUL 14, 1847
Sydney C Long, Atty at Law: Princess Anne, Md. Practices in the Courts of Somerset & Worcester Counties. All business entrusted will be promptly & faithfully attended to.

Wash Corp: 1-Ptn of John Mills: referred to the Cmte of Claims. 2-Ptn from Abraham Butler: referred to the Cmte of Claims. 3-Ptn of from B Willet & others: referred to the Cmte on Improvements. 4-Ptn of Thos H Havener & others, praying for the paving of an alley in square 452: referred to the Cmte on Improvements. 5-Ptn of Thos Raleigh, for remission of a fine: referred to the Cmte of Claims.

Brown's Hotel, so long & well conducted by the late proprietor, is now under the direction & in the sole possession of his sons, Messrs Marshall & T P Brown.

Melancholy casualties. Jas H Abbott, son of Mr Aaron Abbott, jr, of New Canaan, Fairfied Co, Conn, aged 13 years, residing with Col J B Abbott, of this village, was drowned in the Chenango river, on Sunday last, while bathing. On Fri week, Mr Chas Witbeck, age 18 years, son of Mr Jacob Witbeck, while bathing in the Claverack creek, at Stockport, was drowned. He had charge of the district school at Stockport, & was a young man of fine promise. A son of Mrs Rensselaer Kip, a lad of 7 or 8 years, was drowned in the Kinderbook creek, at Valatie, on Mon, into which he had gone to bathe with another boy.

Died: yesterday, in Wash City, Mr Patrick Bulger, aged 52 years. He was a native of the county of Wexford, Ireland, but for the last 23 years a resident of Wash City. His funeral is today at 3½ o'clock, from his late residence on Capitol Hill. The members of the Wash Benevolent Society, & of the Union Benevolent Society, are to meet at the Hall on G st for the purpose of attending at the same time.

Died: on Jul 12, of cholera infantum, Robt L Boyd, infant son of John D & Ann E Boyd, aged 10 months.

Dissolution of the copartnership existing between the undersigned, by mutual consent. -Patrick McGarvey, John Connor [Patrick McGarvey will continue the business as usual at the old stand, Pa ave, east of the Railroad Depot, known as the Railroad Hotel.]

Died: on Jul 13, after a short but painful illness, Mrs Ann D Brown, aged 45 years, consort of Richd Brown, formerly of St Mary's, Chas, & PG Counties, Md, leaving a husband & 3 children, besides a large circle of friends, to mourn her early death. Her funeral is today at 2 o'clock.

Died: on Jul 7, at Belleville, N J, at the residence of her grandfather, Rosalie Austin, aged 21 months, youngest child of Silas H & Mary B Hill, of Wash City.

Died: on Jul 10, in her 39th year, Louisa G, wife of Rev Horace Stringfellow, of Petersburg, Va, in the confidence of a certain faith in a blessed immortality.

<u>Articles from the Dead Letter ofc, at auction on Jul 16:</u>

Books	Shirts	Gold plate & teeth
Jewelry	Coats	Children's dresses
Music	Medicines	Silver rifle pistol
Dry goods	Pocket books	-R W Dyer, auct
Pants	Razors & strops	

An estray Cow to my residence last Fri, on ***Greenleaf's Point***, Wash City. Owner will place come forward & take her away. -Thos Miles

$10 reward for a Mocking Bird, of sweet & varied song, stolen from the yard, or escaped from the cage about 3 weeks ago, from the residence of Mrs Lenox, E st, between 10th & 11th sts.

A lot of 30 acres near Gtwn for sale at public auction: by deed of trust, executed by the late Jos Nourse, on Oct 7, 1835, duly recorded: sale on Jul 22: all the land beginning at a stone marked on the north side N, & on the south side T, in the line dividing the tract called ***Weston*** from the lands of the said Jos Nourse, purchased by him of a certain Richd Harrison, at a point on the said line, [being the 13th line of the survey of ***Weston*** as made by Francis Fenwick, according to the plat of said survey,] between the corner of the road leading from Tenallytown to the Rock Creek Mills; & the next corner, designated by a stone marked #11. -Richd Smith, Trustee -E S Wright, auctioneer

THU JUL 15, 1847

Mount St Mary's College, Emmitsburg, Md: commences on Aug 17.
-Jos McCaffrey, Pres

Orphans Court of Wash Co, D C. In the case of John F Callan, adm of Jas Hoban, dec'd: the administrator & Court have appointed Aug 6 next for the distribution of the said estate, of the assets in the hands of said administrator, so far as had been collected & turned into money. -Ed N Roach, Reg/o wills

A son of the Hon Wm Sawyer [living at St Mary's, Ohio] disappeared some weeks since under circumstances which induced the belief that he was drowned. Paternal affection hopes that he yet lives. His name is T Benton Sawyer, & has been missing since May 29 last: he is about 12 years old, small of his age, hair & complexion light, & wore his hair long; his eyes are dark.

Hon John Quincy Adams completed his 80th year on Jul 11. Alexander Hamilton fell by the hands of Aaron Burr, in a duel, on Jul 11, 1806. Hon Timothy Farrar, of Hollis, N H, & Dr Ezra Green, of Dover, N H, both completed their 100th year on Jul 11, & are both graduates of Harvard University.

Appointment by the Pres: Wm J Staples, of N Y, appointed to be Consul for Havre, France, vice Reuben G Beasely, dec'd.

Mrd: on Jul 11, by Rev John C Smith, Mr Wm Campbell to Miss Lucy Virginia Jardine, all of Wash City.

A letter was received by Dr Bishey, of this city, announcing the death of Capt Chas Naylor, of the 2nd Pa Regt. He died in Mexico, from the effects of a brain fever, to which he was subject. The news will indeed be a sudden blow to his numerous friends & relatives in this city. -Phil Bulletin [Jul 17th newspaper: Capt Naylor's death was a premature announcement. We hope to welcome his return, with his gallant companions, when peace shall have been achieved. -Phil North American]

Died: on Jul 14, John Kedglie, a native of Scotland, & long a resident of Wash City. His funeral is today, at 4 o'clock, from his late residence on Capitol Hill.

The Bar-fixtures & Liquors & Furniture of the house known as the Franklin Coffee-House is for private sale. This house is now offered for sale. Apply to the present proprietor. -Thos Baker

FRI JUL 16, 1847

Appointment by the Pres: Saml M Rutherford, of Arkansas, to be Superintendent of Indian Affairs West, vice Wm Armstrong, dec'd.

Mrd: on Thu last, at Balt, by Rev Mr Coskrey, P H King, of Wash City, to Miss Catherine Maria Whelan, of the former place.

Mrd: on Jun 15, in St Louis Co, Missouri, by Rev John N Gilbreath, Henry Barron, of Wash, to Miss Eliz S, daughter of Wm McCutchan, of the former place.

Died: on Jul 14, at Rockville, Harriet Robertson, daughter of the Rev Chas H & Maria Nourse, aged 10 months & 21 days.

The Californian publishes the names of the crew of the launch of the ship **Warren**, lost on the coast, as follows: Passed Midshipman Wm H Montgomery; Midshipman Danl C Hugennin, of the U S sloop **Portsmouth**, pilot; E M Montgomery, clerk to Cmder Montgomery; Geo Rodman, cockswain; Anthony Sylvester, Alex'r McDonald, Saml Turner, Saml Lane, Milton Ladd, John W Dawd, Gilman Hilton, Lawson Lee.

Capt J B Hall, Govn'r of the district of San Francisco, issued an official notice on Feb 17 declaring that martial law was at an end, & that the civil gov't would then resume its functions. Capt Du Pont, of the ship **Cyane**, succeeded Capt Hull, as naval commandant of the district. Edw Bryant was appointed by Gen Kearny alcalde of Yerba Buena, vice Lt W A Bartlett, who returned to his naval duties.

SAT JUL 17, 1847

The staging on which J W Fowler was delivering an oration on Jul 5 at Canajoharie, N Y, broke down, with 6 or 8 underneath it at the time. Mr Fowler was frightfully mangled, & some others were severely injured.

Died: on Jul 7, at the residence of Dr Maurice Beesley, Cape May Co, N J, after a lingering & painful illness, Mr Leaming Moore, merchant, of the late firm of Ellison & Moore, of Phil.

Died: on Jul 9, in Doylestown, Pa, Jos H Pawling. He was a Lt in the U S Army, & served his country in the Florida war. For several years previous to his death he was a Clerk in the ofc of the Engineer dept, in Wash City. He was a graduate of West Point, & held a respectable rank in talents & literature.

The Chicago Convention. The Pres announced the following named gentlemen as composing the cmte to gather statistics & present the same to the consideration of the Congress of the U S:
Mass: Abbott Lawrence, John Mills
N H: Jas Wilson, John Page
N Y: John C Spencer, Saml B Ruggles
Ky: Jas T Morehead, Jas Guthrie
Indiana: Jacob G Sleight, Zebulon Baird
Missouri: Thos Allen, Jos M Converse
R I: Alex'r Duncan, Zachariah Allen
Iowa: Geo C Stone, Wm Ewing
Pa: T J Bingham, S C Johnson
Ohio: Jas Hall, J L Weatherly
Conn: Thos W Williams, Philip Ripley
Wisc: Rufus King, W Woodman
Georgia: Thos Butler King, Wm B Hodgson
Florida: John G Camp
Mich: Jos R Williams, David A Noble
Maine: Chas Javis, Geo Evans
Illinois: Jesse B Thomas, David J Baker
N J: Chas King, R L Colt

Summer Boarding: at the Union Hotel, Fairfax Court-house, Va. -Lewis S Pritchartt

Mrd: on Jul 14, by Rev Mr Dougherty, Wm F Hardey, of La, to Miss Eliz Millard, of Leonardtown, Md.

Died: on Jul 16, Geo McDuell, after a lingering illness, aged 54 years. His funeral is on Sunday, at 2 o'clock, from his late residence on 10th st, between D & E sts.

Died: on Jul 16, Mrs Susan P Burroughs, w/o Wm Burroughs, in her 44th year. Her funeral is today at 4 o'clock.

Died: on Jul 16, George Hay, infant son of Andrew & Laura Duffey, aged 7 months & 16 days. His funeral is today at 3 o'clock.

Died: on Jul 15, in her 39th year, Mrs Anne Eliz Hill, w/o Chas Hill, of PG Co, Md.

Annual Commencement of Columbian College was held in the Baptist Church on E st on Wed last. Amongst the audience we noticed the Pres of the U S, Mr Atty Gen, the Mayor, & several clergymen.
Orations by:
Alfred Bagby, of Stevensville, Va.
Jos Christian, Urbanna, Va.
Wm L Claybrook, Urbanna, Va.
John P Craig, Readfield, Me
Robt French, Gtwn, D C
G W Hervey, South Durham, N Y

Richd James, Phil
Robt H Land, Sussex, Va
Bradford H Lincoln, Hingham, Mass
John R Nunn, Essex, Va
Thos Pollard, Stevensville, Va
Wm Stickney, Bangor, Me
Wm T Hendren, Norfolk, Va
Wm B Webb, Washington

Candidates for the 2nd Degree:
Saml Cornelius, jr, N J
Wm J Darden, Texas
Jas W H Lovejoy, D C
Oscar G Mix, Va
Wm B Webb, D C

MON JUL 19, 1847

Cmder Piercy, of the U S Navy, died on Jul 14, at his residence in Portsmouth, Va. [Jul 20th newspaper: obit for Cmder Wm P Piercey.] [2 splgs of Piercy/Piercey.]

Lt May of the Navy. The New Orleans Bulletin states that it was an error when it stated that Lt May lost an arm in the attack on Alvarado. It should have stated only that his arm was severely shattered.

Col A H Pemberton, the former editor & proprietor of the South Carolinian, died at his residence, near Columbia, Jul 12th, after a protracted illness. He had been connected with the press for a number of years.

On Monday ofcr A M C Smith, of the lower police court, arrested John D Klengden, Commission Merchant, 73 New st, on a warrant issued by Justice Drinker, on a charge of obtaining from Chas Bonnaffi, banker, 4 Hanover st, the sum of $14,250 by false & fraudulent representations. He was held to bail in the sum of $3,000. Yesterday Mr Klengden committed suicide by shooting himself with a pistol, thus furnishing strong evidence of the truth of the charges made against him. -N Y Courier

Died: Jul 11, in Wash City, Miss Hellen Walthen, a native of Chas Co, Md, aged 72 years.

The District Btln: there are now at ***Fort McHenry*** the 6 companies composing the D C Btln, under Lt Col Geo W Hughes, viz. Capts Henrie, Degges, & Barry's companies from Wash, & Capts Dolan, Brown, & Taylor's companies, recruited in Balt. All are to be fully equipped in a few days, ready to sail for the Rio Grande, in the ship **Alexandria**, on Jul 22. They are a fine looking body of men, & will do credit to the place of their nativity.

Notice: the administrator of Nancy Moye requests the original heirs, or their reps, as non-residents, to come forward, in person or by agent, & receive their portions of said estate. Original heirs: Sparkman Britt & wife Martha, Synthy Brooks & wife Vicey, Franklin Moye & wife Lydia, & Churchill Moye. There is other property coming to the same heirs, excluding the first named & the last. -Reuben Guartney, adm: Greenville, Pitt Co, N C, Jul 15, 1847. By writing to me at the above place the said heirs can speedily receive their shares of both kinds of property, in good drafts. Commissions 2½% on sums over $100; 4 on smaller. -Lewis P Olds, Atty at Law

The battalion of volunteers, under the command of Lt Col Hughes, raised mainly from D C & the State of Md, are under orders for immediate transportation to the active seat of war. It is intended that Col Hughes shall open the road from Vera Cruz to Jalapa, & occupy that important town for the purpose of securing Gen Scott's line of operation.

Death from the explosion of spirit gas: on Thu night, the respectable, & beautiful young married woman, Mrs Julia Whiting, wife of Mr J L Whiting, & daughter of Mr L K Henshaw, with whom she resided, at the corner of Front & Gold sts. She had attempted to fill a lamp with the compound burning fluid, but the lamp not having been previously extinguished, exploded. She was instantaneously enveloped in flames. Her screams were heard in the lower part of the house, & her mother attempted to go to her, but fainted on the way. Not a square inch of her person had not been burnt or blackened. She died this morning. She had been married about 18 months, & leaves an infant 6 or 8 months of age, which was sleeping unconsciously in the room at the time of the accident, but escaped all injury. -Brooklyn Advertiser

The copartnership existing between the subscribers has been dissolved by mutual consent. -Jas W Moorhead, Lucien C Brown. [Lucien C Brown will continue the Grocery Business at the old stand occupied by Moorhead & Brown.]

Balt, Jul 17, 1-One of our most venerable citizens, Dr White, died yesterday, after having passed the ripe old age of 90 years. He had been blind for several years. 2-I regret to announce the sudden death of our respected fellow citizen, Col Wm Dickinson, who for a long time [until 2 years before his death] held the ofc of appraiser in the custom-house. He has been in bad health for some years; but only a few moments before his sudden demise was well as usual. He died of heart disease. 3-Mr Henry W Long, of Somerset Co, Md, was killed by lightning on Jul 8 while in a field of his farm.

TUE JUL 20, 1847

Gen Walter Jones has published a pamphlet entitled "The Case of the Battalion Stated; with an exposition of the grounds upon which Chas Lee Jones, expecting to have had the command of the btln [containing 3 companies raised by himself in D C, & 2 to be raised in Md] conferred upon him as of right & justice, due both to him & to the ofcrs & men who had volunteered to serve his command as Lt Col. He tendered his services to Gov't to raise 3 companies in the District; he raised 2 entire companies, & wanted only a few men to complete the 3rd; he had been appointed a commissary, who was recognized by the War Dept; he devoted his time & means [with the full knowledge & approbation of the Gov't] to the procurement of the 3 companies, the command was conferred on a regular ofcr of the army, without any explantation to Mr Jones as to the cause of rejection. -Clipper

The Hon Edw Bates was elected Pres of the Chicago River & Harbor Convention: is a citizen of St Louis; one of the great men of the West; was a Member of Congress some 20 years ago; is now about 55 years of age, & is considered one of the ablest men in Missouri, not second even to Mr Benton.

Died: on Jul 19, John Warren Metamora, infant son of Richd & Lucretia Ann Stoops, aged 1 year, 6 months & 2 days. His funeral is this afternoon at 4 o'clock, from their residence, corner of 12th st & N Y ave.

Spain: The efforts of the Pope's Nuncio & others to effect a reconciliation between the Queen & her consort have failed, & it is feared that by dint of French influence the determination of the Queen to obtain a divorce will be rendered nugatory, & the favorite project of an Orleans dynasty on the throne of Spain accomplished in the persons or descendents of the Duke & Duchess of Montpensier.

Farm for sale: 148 acres, within 4 miles of Wash City, on the District line, in PG Co, Md; improvements consist of a log house, with an excellent well at the door; good storehouse; & a dwlg suitable for a small family on the s e part of it. Inquire of the subscriber, 1 mile beyond Rock Creek Church. -Wm Markward

Trustee's sale of valuable brewery: by deed of trust from Jacob Harman, jr, to John Kurtz, Clement Cox, & others, trustees, dated Aug 27, 1844, recorded in liber W B 113, folios 16 throu 19, of the land records of Wash: auction on Aug 25 of: lots 5 thru 8 in square 4 in Wash City, with the celebrated Brewery thereon, formerly known as Haymam's, & more recently conducted by Harman & Gordon: bldgs are of brick, erected about 17 years ago; in excellent order. The title is believed to be unquestionable & may readily be traced; but, selling as trustees, no warrantly will be given. -R W Dyer, auct

Died: on Jul 14, in Portsmouth, Va, after a long & painful illness, Cmder Wm P Piercey, U S Navy, in his 54th year, leaving a wife & relatives who deeply mourn his loss.

By virtue of a writ of fieri facias, I shall expose to public sale, for cash, on Jul 22, the leasehold estate & interest of Edw Grindall in Lot 1 in the subdivision of the north half of square 436, in Wash City, as made & recorded by Wm A Bradley, seized & taken in execution as the property of Edw Grindall, & will be sold to satisfy a judgment in favor of Wm A Bradley. -R R Burr, Constable

The remains of Col Hardin & Lt B R Houghton reached St Louis on Jul 7, in charge of the returning Illinois volunteers. These brave men were feelingly addressed by John M Eager, who was replied to be Maj Richardson, of the volunteers. The coffins containing the ashes of the gallant dead were borne in procession to the Courthouse, & placed in the rotundo on a catafalque covered with black, relieved at the borders & edges by white lace, & surmounted at the summit with a row of cannon. The assembly was addressed by Rev Mr Van Court & Mr Benton. The procession moved to the river bank, where the remains were committed to the steamboat **Defiance** to be carried to Meredosia, & thence to their last resting place in Jacksonville, Illinois.

WED JUL 21, 1847

The Govn'r appointed Dickinson Woodruff to command of the btln now raising in N J for the Mexican war. Mr W received his commission yesterday. -Trenton State Gaz

Midshipman Rogers, who was taken prisoner by the Mexicans whilst making a reconnaissance of the defences at Vera Cruz, has written to his father, who resides near New Castle, Delaware: dated May 28, city of Mexico. The writer was allowed the liberty of the city. He had not received any support from the Mexican Gov't, & was twice robbed on his way from the seacoast to the city of Mexico.

A sword was presented to Capt Wm H Degges last week by the citizens of the First Ward, through Dr T B J Frye. Its blade is of the best Damascus steel; the scabbard copper covered with black leather. It has a silver plate with the inscription: "Presented to Captain W H Degges, by the citizens of the First Ward," & the date of its being presented. [***Fort McHenry***, Jul 14, 1847. Permit me to acknowledge through you the receipt of a serviceable & suitable sword, presented by my fellow citizens of the First Ward of Washington. -Wm H Degges To Dr T B J Frye, Wash.]

Wash Corp: 1-Cmte of Claims: asked to be discharged from the futher consideration of the ptn of John Mills: which was adopted. 2-Ptn of John Sietz, asking remission of a fine: referred to the Cmte of Claims. 3-Ptn of R J Morsell & others, asking the improvement of Vt ave: referred to the Cmte of Improvements. 4-The nomination of Jacob Klieber as inspector of flour: confirmed. 5-Nomination of Geo W Harkness as the Com'r of the 1st Ward: decided in the negative. 6-Ptn of John Bohlayer, jr, for remission of a fine: referred to the Cmte of Claims. 7-Cmte of Claims: asked to be discharged from the further consideration of the ptn of Eve Rupert.

Balt, Jul 20. Capt John R Kenly, who commanded company Batlimore's Own in the war with Mexico, has received the appointment of Major to the new Btln from Md & the District, now making ready to repair for the seat of war. The ship **Napier** & the ship **Alexandria**, two of our finest vessels, has been chartered by the Gov't to carry out the troops now at ***Fort McHenry***.

The death of Jos C Neal, of Phil, on Sat last, by sudden illness, has produced a sensation in the city of Phil & elsewhere. He was the Editor of Neal's Saturday Gaz. He was seized with sudden illness at his residence in Phil City on Sat morning early, & died 4 o'clock in the afternoon. The disease was congestion of the brain. He was born at Greenland, N H, Feb 3, 1807; his father was for many years the principal of a leading seminary, & afterwards a minister of a Congregational Church. He died when Jos, his only son, was but 2 years old. The subject of our notice resided for several years in Pottsville, but in 1831 he came to Phil, took up his abode, & has lived her every since. He was all gentleness, truth, & honor.

Notice: will be served up today at the City Launch by Fred'k Lakemeyer, Pa ave, between 14th & 15th sts, Green Turtle Soups & Steaks, from a most superb Turtle just received, prepared in the most gastronomic style. N B. Families supplied on reasonable terms.

THU JUL 22, 1847
For sale or rent: beautiful residence, at the north end of 7th st west & adjoining the farm of John A Smith: a well built 2 story brick house, 22 by 32 feet. Apply to Henry Johnson, 7th st, near the boundary line.

$50 reward for the apprehension & confinement of my negro man Chas Herbert, about 24 years old. He has taken up with a free woman lately from Alexandria.
-Richd W Wallace, adm

A meeting of printers was held at Boston last Monday to consider the subject of adopting some measures to honor the memory of Stephen Daye, the first printer in the U S. The meeting was organized by the choice of J T Buckingham, as chrmn, & Geo W Liberty, secretary. Cmte was comprised of: J T Buckingham & T R Marvin, H W Dutton, John Ford, & Wm Nichols.

Northampton, Jul 19. Hiram N Johnson, aged about 17, clerk in the store of L R Lincoln & Co, was instantly killed yesterday by the accidental discharge of a shot-gun in the hands of a young man named Harkness, a student of medicine in the ofc of Thompson & Co of this village. -Springfield Republican

Obit-died: on Jul 18, at the Convent of the Visitation, in Gtwn, Sister Mary Agatha, the Rev Mother Superior of the Sisters of the Visitation, in her 54th year. She was a native of Chas Co, Md, & entered the Convent in Gtwn more than 30 years ago. She was 3 times elevated by her associates to the important ofc of Mother Superior.

FRI JUL 23, 1847
Official accounts of the capture of Tabasco: from Surgeon Barrington's Return to Comm Perry of the killed & wounded on this occasion: U S ship **John Adams**, off Tabasco river, Jun 24, 1847.
Lt May, of the ship **Mississippi**, severe gunshot wound near right elbow.
Patrick Rourke, seaman, of the **Mississippi**, slight gunshot wound near right scapula.
Danl Foley, ordinary seaman, of the **Mississippi**, slight gunshot wound of left arm.
Passed Midshipman Hudson, of the ship **Scorpion**, slight wound of right hand & abdomen, supposed by grape.
Walter Jefferson, ordinary seaman, of the ship **Vesuvius**, severe gunshot wound of left leg.
The body of a seaman, not recognized at the time, was found floating down the river, a day or two after the capture of the place, with marks of injury on the head, as I have been informed.

Accident on the Norwich & Worcester Railroad on Tue: Mr Jos Adams, the engineer of the accommodation train, was instantly killed, & also Mr Stackpole, of Boston, who was standing upon the platform of the forward car.

It is not generally known that B F Ross, Adj of the Arkansas Regt, who fought with such distinguished bravery at Buena Vista, is a Cherokee, & has numerous relations in the Cherokee nation, although he has not lived there for many years, having adopted Arkansas as his home. -N O Delta

The subscriber is authorized to sell those 2 valuable lots, in the 1st Ward of Wash City, fronting on Pa ave & north K st, adjoining the late residence of Hon John Forsyth, being lots 2 & 3 in square 27. These lots will be sold very cheap, & a perfect title conveyed to the purchaser. -Richd Wallach

The U S frig **Potomac** arrived in Hampton Roads on Thu, in 18 days from Vera Cruz: list of her ofcrs: Capt John H Aulick
Lts-5: Edw K Thompson; Richd Meade; Jas H North; Jas Madison Frailey; Abraham D Harrel
Surgeon: Robt I Dodd
Assist Surgeon: Jas Hamilton
Purser: Thos B Nalle
Lt of Marines: Addison Garland
Passed Assist Surgeon: Jas N Minor
Passed Midshipmen-2: Richd M Cuyler; Wm E Hopkins
Midshipmen-4: John P Jones; Allen McLane; Chas C Hunter; Chas B Smith
Capt's Clerk: S T Emmons
Boatswain: Robt Simpson
Purser's Clerk: Chas H Ellis
Carpenter: Jas Magill
Gunner: Archibald S Lewis
Sailmaker: B B Burchstead
Passengers: Capt Abraham N Brevoort; Lt Josiah Watson, U S Marine Corps; Ofcrs & crew all well.

Died: on Jul 21, at Bladensburg, Md, Levi Marmaduke, only child of Dionysius & Margaret D Sheriff, aged 1 year & 21 days.

SAT JUL 24, 1847

Trenton News: on Sun an interesting child of Wm S Hutchinson, of this city, met its death in a singular manner. The mother had carefully laid her infant to sleep on the bed, placing chairs in front to protect it from rolling off. At the foot of the bed stood a bureau a few inches from the rail of the bedstead. The mother found her infant had slipped down, feet foremost, between the foot of the bed & the bureau, where it was hanging & life was extinct.

Letters have been received in this country, announcing the death, at Jerusalem, on May 27, of the Rev Nathan W Fiske, of Amherst College. He died, it is stated, of cholera.

The following 8 Mexican prisoners arrived at New Orleans on Jul 15 from Tampico: John Swegert, John A Scott, A W Holeman, W P O Normandie, Wm Funk, 1st Ky cavalry; Wm Russell, Arkansas cavalry; Robt S Cockrill, John Thomas, 1st Ky infty.

The purchase of the Portsmouth & Roanoke railroad, by David Henshaw & Wm Ward, of Boston, for themselves & their associates, has been finally consummated.

For rent: 3 story dwlg on E st, 4 doors down from 14th st: dwlg is large & commodious. Also, a smaller 3 story dwlg adjoining, with other conveniences. Apply to Balaam Birch, s w corner of 8th & D sts, or to the subscriber, who will be in Wash a few days, at the residence of Wm T Steiger, 8th st, between E & F sts. -Geo W McLean

Mrd: on Jul 19, at the Church of the Epiphany, by Rev J W French, J A Van Zandt, Engineer Corps U S Navy, to Miss Gilbertine Livingston, daughter of G L Thompson, all of Wash City.

Mrd: on Jun 30, at Walscot, Bath, England, W G Villiers Villiers, eldest son of the late G W Villiers Villiers, to Norah Frances Sheridan, youngest daughter of the late Tyrone Power.

For rent, the Union Hotel, Gtwn, D C: was rebuilt in 1838; has 55 rooms; stables for 80 horses. Its situation on the main st of the town, near to Wash, affords the advantages of a residence in the latter city without the annoyances of its heat & dust. Possession given on Nov 1 next. Apply to Mrs L Humphreys, Gtwn, D C.

A visit to St Joseph's Academy: & to the Mother House of the Sisters of Charity, near Emmetsburg, Md. St Joseph's: consisted of massive bldgs, lofty spires, extensive walks & playgrounds, its falls, & gondolier, called the Louis Regis. North of the chapel is a pathway that leads to the cemetery. A small mausoleum of gothic form occupies the centre. Beneath this are the remains of the venerated & illustrious Mother Seton, foundress & first mother of the Sisters in the U S. Around her, still faithful in death, are her early associates in this great & good work; while above them all is seen the cross, the lot of the Sister of Charity through life, her title to a crown beyond the confines of death. A bright day [Jul 1,] ushered in the annual distribution day. The first event was the crowning of 10 young ladies for every virtue that adorns youth & innocence. Their names respectively are: Regina McNeil, Mary E Jenkins, Marion Matthews, Rosalie Keefe, Cecilia Hickey, Jane M Dugan, Eliz Gartland, Eveline Smith, Margaret Lyons, & Sarah Waters. A prose essay by Miss Emily Parrott, of Wash, was a creditable effort; but the sweet little essay on Joan d'Arc, l'Heroine d'Orleans, in French prose, by the same young lady, was her masterpiece. The poetic composition, The Hebrew's Visit to Jerusalem," by Abby Maher, of Gardner, Maine, is unsurpassed for gorgeousness of description, & happy illustration. A prose essay by Miss Regina McNeil, of Phil, & another by Miss Rosalie Keefe, of Norfolk, Va, gave evidence of considerable research. Farewell address was given by Miss Sarah Waters, of Maine. Miss Parrott, of Wash, wrote the Farewell Song. Thus ended the exercises of this joyous day-Jul 1st, 1847.

Died: on Jul 18, in Wash City, Mrs Vanduden, w/o Saml C Wroe, & daughter of Mr John Dodson, of PG Co, Md. Her last illness, which was short, but extremely painful, was borne without a murmur.

Died: this morning, Frank, son of Dr Chas S Frailey, aged 6 months & 23 days.

Died: on Jul 23, after a lingering & painful illness, Addison Armistead Randolph, son of Jas Innes & Susan Randolph, in his 6th year.

Fresh vegetables: at the Provision store of Walker & Peck, on D st, near 7th.
-John M Donn

For sale: that splendid residence at the corner of Vt & Mass ave & 14th st west: the dwlg is built in the best & most substantial manner & with the best materials: situation is one of the most commanding character, being as high as the top of the Capitol, & affords a full view of the city, & of the Potomac as far down as Mt Vernon. It is well known as the residence for some years of the Hon Sec Crawford, & since then of Chas Hill. For terms apply to Nich's Callan, Agent, F st.

Dog lost: a large black Newfoundland Cog. Liberal reward if brought to Michl Connington, C st, between 13th & 14th sts.

MON JUL 26, 1847

Morris Power, formerly resident of N Y, who married the youngest daughter of Hon Brockholst Livingston, it is said, is elected member of Parliament for Cork, in the place of the late Danl O'Connell. This gentleman is the brother of Bishop Power, now at Toronto, Canada, & well known to many of the inhabitants of N Y.

Ofcrs of the frig **Raritan**, who arrived in Hampton Roads on Thu:
Capt, French Forrest; Lts, T R Roots, M G L Claiborne, Wm A Parker, Jas S Biddle Surgeon, Solomon Sharp; Passed Assist Surgeon, J H Wright; Acting Master, Geo H Cooper; Purser, Nat Wilson; Midshipmen, Chas Gray, Francis G Clarke, Wm H Parker Capt's Clerk, H G Weightman; Master's Mate, John M Ballard; Boatswain, John Munro; Carpenter, Amos Chicks; Sailmaker, Thos J Boyce

Passengers:

Cmder Wm McCluney
Cmder Wm S Walker
Cmder Timothy G Benham
Lt Wm C May
Lt M C Marin
Assist Surgeon W Sherman
Midshipmen March & Hodge
Cmder's Clerks Abrams & Watson
Carpenter, C H Boardman

Besides Capt Edson, Capt of Marines, who died of fever at Havana on the 15th, we notice among the deaths the name of Midshipman R B Storer, a son of Capt Geo W Storer, of the Navy. He died on Jul 4th. We were misinformed as to Lt May, of the Navy, who has returned home in the U S ship **Raritan**, having lost his right arm. His wound, in that arm, was a most severe one, & he is yet suffering very painfully under it. It, however, is the opinion of his brother, Dr J F May, an eminent Surgeon of our city, that his arm will be saved, though the process of cure may be tedious & painful.

Troy Post: on Tue Alex Fish, 10 or 12 years of age, a son of Stillman S Fish, was run over by the cars near the railroad bridge, killing him instantly.

The Eastern papers announce the death of the Hon Henry Waggaman Edwards, late Govn'r of Connecticut. He died in New Haven, on Jul 22, aged nearly 68 years. He was a native of this town, son of the late Hon Pierpont Edwards, of the U S District Court, & grandson of the eminent divine, Jonathan Edwards. He graduated at Princeton in 1797: from 1819 to 1823 was a Rep in Congress; from 1823 to 1827 was U S Senator; a member of the State Senate in 1828 & 1829; & in 1830 a Rep from New Haven, & Speaker of the House of Reps: in 1833 he was elected Govn'r, & again in 1835, 1836, & 1837.

Boston Courier. Accident on the Norwich & Worcester railroad on Tue: Mr Jos Lewis Stackpole, of this city, whose wife & children were at Norwich, was struck by a wooden fixture of the tender, which pierced his body, causing his death.

Accident on the eastern Railroad on Mon, by which Mr John W Staniford was very seriously, if not fatally injured. He arrived at Portsmouth, N H, on Sunday, & was returning to his family, who reside in Salem, & on account of the excessive heat was riding outside of the cars, when, he accidentally fell off to the ground. He laid insensible much of the time on Tuesday, & fears are entertained that he will not recover.

Valuable farm in Lousoun Co for sale at public auction: on Aug 9, at the Courthouse door, in Leesburg, that well known farm formerly owned by J L McKenna, & now in the tenancy of Mr Alex'r McFarland, containing 331 acres, bounded on the east by Broad Run, on the south by Kilgore's mill road, on the west by Col Chas Taylor's land, & on the north by that of D G Smith. -Richd Smith , for himself, & as Exec of the late Gen Walter Smith.

The first organized meeting of the Alumni of the Columbian College was held in the Baptist Church on 10th st, in Wash, on Jul 14, 1847. Dr T B J Frye, being the eldest alumni present, convened the meeting. Names & residences of Alumni present:

Rev Eli Ball, Va
S C Smoot, M D, Wash
Rev T S Walthall, Va
Y B J Frye, M D, Wash
E M Chapin, M D, Wash
Rev H W Dodge, Va
Wm Q Force, Wash
Rev T J Shepherd, Va
Rev J B Taylor, Va
Rev A J Huntington, College Hill
H L Chapin, Wash
W B Webb, Wash
J W H Lovejoy, Wash
W L Childs, N Y
R S Haynes, Va
J R Bagby, Va
J Picket, Va
W T Hendren, Va
J P Craig, Maine
J R Nunn, Va
W L Claybrook, Va
B H Lincoln, Mass
T Pollard, Va
J Christian, Va
R H Land, Va
R French, D C
A Bagby, Va

On Thu, Jul 24, a young man named Keating, belonging to the township of Fitzroy, was attacked by a large she-bear, & mutilated so dreadfully, that he died of his wounds. -Ottawa [Canada] Advocate

TUE JUL 27, 1847

Information on the parentage & connexions of Mr Edw Bates of Missouri: he is the son of the late Thos F Bates, of Goochland Co, Va, who was a Whig of the Revolution, a true patriot, of Quaker descent, but who did not permit his sectarian views to hold him back from the service of his country. His brothers have all been men of distinction. He is a cousin of the late Gov Jas Pleasants: his eldest brother, Chas Bates, must be remembered for his legal knowledge, & something of eccentricity of character, especially for his red breeches. His brother, Fred'k Bates was acting Govn'r of Missouri during the absence of Gov Clarke, under the territorial gov't in 1819, & he was elected the 2nd & 3rd Govn'r of the State of Missouri. The Hon Jas W Bates, another brother, was once delegate to Congress from Arkansas, & afterwards Govn'r of Arkansas. Fleming Bates, of Northumberland Co, Va, a member of the late Va convention, was another brother. Edw Bates, of Missouri, emigrated from Va to Missouri, I think, in 1814; he studied law there under Rufus Easton, the predecessor of Hon John Scott, [who was the predecessor of Mr Bates.] He was an active member from St Louis Co in the Convention which framed the Constitution of Missouri in 1820, David Barton, being Pres of it. He was the first Atty Gen of that State under Govn'r McNair. -C

Capt A R Hetzel, of the Army, died at Louisville on Tue last. He had arrived there but a few days previously from Vera Cruz, where he discharged the duties of Assist Quartermaster.

Died: on Jul 17, in Indianapolis, Indiana, after a short illness, Mrs Martha Ann, wife of Gov Whitcomb.

Died: on Jul 25, Henry Clay, son of Jas A & Harriet Ann Wise. His funeral is today at 4 o'clock, from his father's residence on M st, between 7th & 8th sts.

Valuable Albemarle Real Estate for sale: by the last will & testament of John Winn, deceased: sale on Sep 10, that most beautiful farm, ***Belle Mont***, the residence of the late Mr Winn, containing 564 acres, adjoining the town of Charlottesville, within 2 miles of Monticello. Improvements consist of a large & handsome Brick Dwlg, with every convenient out-house attached: all in perfect order. At the same time I offer the block of bldgs in the town of Charlottesville, located upon the Public Square, known as the ***Jefferson House***: wholly of brick, covered with tin, & is 4 stories high; contains 4 commodious stores. Also for sale: the brick tenement, with a tin roof, now occupied as the Advocate ofc, on the cross st leading from the Square to the Monticello Hotel. also, for sale: the wooden house attached to the foregoing tenement, & now occupied by Wm Jeffries as a saddler's shop. Mr B B Winn, residing on the farm, or myself, will show same. -V W Southall, exc of John Winn, dec'd

The remains of the late gallant Capt Geo Lincoln, who fell at the battle of Buena Vista, were interred at Worcester, Mass, on Thu last with military honors. They were conveyed to Worcester from Boston by a military escort & a large number of citizens.

Died: in Greene Co, Ala, at the residence of Jas G Rows, Mr Jas Saunders, eldest son of the Hon R M Saunders, U S Minister to Spain. Mr Saunders had served a short campaign with the army in Mexico under Gen Scott, from which he was honorably discharged, & returned laboring under that severe disease that has proved fatal to so many of our brave volunteers. [No date-current item.]

Houses for rent: 2 story frame house on E st, between 9th & 10th sts. A 2 story frame dwlg house on I st north, near 7th st west. For the former apply to Mr Skirving's, Pa ave & 10th sts, & for the latter at Mr Spencer's Shoe Store, 7th st, between H & I sts.

At auction; a lot of furniture made by M L Tobias, London. Terms cash. John McDevitt, auctioneer

WED JUL 28, 1847

Robt Thom, British Counsul at Ning-Po: died of dropsy, in China, on Sep 14 last, at the age of 39. He was a native of Glasgow, Scotland; went to Caraccas in 1828, afterward to Mexico, next to England, thence to Bordeaux, & finally to China, the language of which, as well as French & Spanish, he spoke with fluency. His brother, Mr David Thom, of Liverpool, has written a remarkable book on theology.

Circuit Court of Wash Co, D C. Insolvent debtor Edw Smith [colored,] has applied to be discharged from imprisonment. -Wm Brent, clerk

Died: on May 21 last, Mrs Helen Steuart, w/o Col Wm Steuart, of Gtwn, D C. Through life beloved & respected by all who knew her. [The above was inadvertently omitted. -A Friend]

Winchester-its Cathedral; ancient city some 15 or 20 miles from Southampton; in early times was the metropolis of the West Saxons; here Egbert was crowned in 827; now has about 8,000 residents; old Isak Walton used to angle in the neighboring streams. Much to be seen: a fine picture by West, the Raising of Lazurus, is over the altar, the highly ornamental monumental chapels of Cardinal Beaufort & Bishop Waynflete, the monument to Wm of Wykeham, the tomb of Wm Rufus, & the 6 mortuary chests which enclose the dust of several Saxon Kings. The cathedral was founded by the first Christian king of the West Saxons A D 634, is 545 feet in length; some of the best of the Norman architecture are found in the transcept of this cathedral. SALISBURY: the Cathedral is the most beautifully proportioned & perfect structure in the Gothic style in Great Britain; founded by Bishop Richd Poore A D 1220 & finished in 1260; its form is that of the Greek cross. Among the many great men whose remains rest beneath the arches of Salisbury Cathedral are those of Jas Harris, author Hermes, & of Dr Young, the immortal poet.

For rent: the dwlg-house on 3rd st, Gtwn, adjoining the residence of Dr Linthicum, & formerly owned & occupied by Horatio Jones. Apply to John Marbury, jr, at the store of E M Linthicum & Co, Gtwn.

Household & kitchen furniture, & shower-bath at auction: on Jul 28, at the residence of Dr Arnold, on 11th st, between F & G sts. -A Green, auctioneer
+
Finding that the ad for the sale of his furniture has created an impression that he was about to remove from the city, the subscriber hastens to announce that such is not his intention. His health being prostracted by the aruous labors of the last year, he is taking a vacation, a tour to the North, intending on his return, in consequence of the feeble condition of his wife's health, to take lodgings for the winter. He hopes to resume the duties of his vocation on Sep 1 ensuing. -Edwin Arnold, Principal, Washington High School

Signification of Mexican names:
Parras, Grape Vines
Buena Vista, Pleasant View
La Encantada, the Enchanted
Palomos, Pigeons
Linares, Fields of Flax
Victoria, Victory
Penasco, Ridge of Rocks
Rinconada, The Corner
Passo del Norte, Pass of the North
Preside del Norte, Northern Fortress
Casas Grandes, Large Houses
Caterce, Fourteen
Canales, Canals
Lobos, Marinos, [under stood,] Sea Wolves
Lagos, Lakes
Roseta, Small Rose
Rose Morada, Scarlet Rose
Aquas Calientes, Warm Waters
Dolores, Sorrows
Los Patos, the Geese
Nombre, Name
Brqazos, Arms
Rio de Conchas, Shell River
Rio de Parras, Vine River
Rio Puerco, Hog River
Rio Balsas, Raft River
-New Orleans paper

Annual Commencement of Gtwn College was held on Jul 27, 1847. The degree of A M was conferred on
John M Heard, of Md
Walter S Cox, of D C
J Theodore Talbot, U S Army
John E Wilson, of Md
Degree of A B was conferred on:
John C Longstreth, of Pa
Jas H Donegan, of Alabama
Chas De Blanc, of Louisiana
Oliveira Andrews, of Va
Richd Rochford, of Ireland
The following students have distinguished themselves in their respective classes, & were awarded with silver medals of premiums:
Longstreth, Donegan, De Blanc, & Andrews-see above, and:
Bernard G Caulfield, of D C
Henry J Forstall, of La
Edmond K Smith, of N Y
John C Riley, of D C
Edmund L Smith, of Pa
Geo Loyall, of Va

Chas H Fulmer, of D C
Edmund A Deslonde, of La
Clement Cox, of D C
J B Adrien Lepretre, of La
Robt C Kent, of Va
Alphonso T Semmes, of Ga
Alexius L Jamison, of Va
Alfred H Byrd, of Va
Edwin F King, of D C
Henry P Tricon, of La
Patrick H Gibson, of Va
Hermogene Dufresne, of La
Matthews F Lancaster, of Md
John C Hamilton, of D C
Ernest L Forstall
Dominick A O'Byrne
Stanislaus Coiron, of La
Geo T May, of D C
Jas B Henry, of Pa
Florence O'Donoghue, of D C
Julius C Eslava, of Ala
Isaac Pritchard, of La
Oscar F Tete, of La
Chas C Longstreth, of Pa
Alex'r A Allemong, of S C
Henry B Leaumont, of La
Richd H Edelen, of Md
Federigo Aldunante, Chili
Roger Semmes, of Ga
Henry W Brent, of Md
Marshall T Polk, of N C
Jos N Young, of D C
John C Hamilton, of D C

Walker K Armistead, of Va
Edwin F King, of D C
Wm H Moore, of Miss
D Clinton Yell, of Ark
Manuel Sorneo, Bolivia, S A
Aristide L Aubert, of Ala
Thos D Brooks, of D C
Julius C Eslava, of Ala
Lewis B France, of D C
Jos W Hickman, of Fla
Celestine C Pendergast, of Md
Jerome A Pendergast, of Md
Horace E Hickman, of Fla
Andrew Canovas, of Fla
Jules M Brou, of La
Robt Patterson, of Md
Louis F Pise, of N Y
Wm Boarman, of Md
J B Adrien Lepretre, of La
Nicholas A Coyeault, of La
Francis Neale, of Md
Aristide L Aubert, of Ala
Peter A Brenner, of D C
Thos H Dawson, of D C
Chas B Rozer, of D C
Wm H Brawner, of D C
Washington A Young, of D C
Eugene de St Romes, of La
Jas Pritchard, of La
L Valery Landry, of La
Michel Lepretre, of La
Zenon Freire, of Chili, S A

Thos J Semmes delivered the address before the Philodemic Society. Address of Mr B G Caulfield, of Wash City, received marked applause: his poem was entitled "The Jamestown, the war-ship of peace." Mr John C Longstreth, of Pa: "Poetry of Life;" & Mr Jas H Donegan, of Ala: "Influence of Knowledge."

The remains of Col Hardin, who fell at Buena Vista, were interred with imposing honors at Jacksonville, Ill, late the place of his residence, on Jul 14. The funeral eulogy was delivered by Richd Yeates. The remains of Cols McKee & Clay, Capts Willis, Vaughan, & of the other gallant Kentuckians recovered from the field of Buena Vista, took place at Frankfort on Tue last. J C Breckenridge pronounced the oration.

Mrd: on Jul 27, in Fred'k, Md, by Rev John Miller, John T Woodside, of Balt, to Margaret, 2nd daughter of Col G M Eichelberger, of the former city.

THU JUL 29, 1847

The New Orleans papers of the 19th announce the death of Sister Ann Barrilia Lynch, a member of the noble Sisterhood of Charity. She died a day or 2 previously in the Charity Hospital of typhus fever, contracted while in the unremitting dischargeof the functions imposed under her order. She was yet in the bloom of youth, aged 24 years.

Andrew Baily, son of Capt John Baily, of Alexandria, accidentally fell from a skiff near Prince st dock on Sat last, & was drowned. His body was found the next day.

Leeds Mercury. Quaker marriage: in Wakefield. John Bright was married to Margaret Eliz Leatham: Mr Geo Bennington read the certificate, or declaration. [No date given.]

A child of Mr Chas Chapman, of Danbury, Conn, was poisoned on Jul 5 by putting a visiting card in its mouth. It died in 48 hours. The enamel or coating on the card was composed of carbonate of lead.

The storm of Thu passed over Danbury, Conn, & Mr Willard Taylor, recently from South America, & on a visit to his mother, standing in the door of her house, was struck by lightning & instantly killed.

Capt E C Carrington, jr, of the Va regt of volunteers, reached Richmond, Va, on Sun. The object of his return from Mexico is to obtain recruits to supply the vacancies in the regt occasioned by deaths & discharge. -Whig

David St Leger Porter, Lt in the U S Army, died at Vera Cruz lately of the vomito. He was a nephew of the late Com Porter.

The Btln of Volunteers raised in Washington by Chas Lee Jones, & of the command of which he was deprived in the most outrageous manner by the Sec of War & the Pres, is to be increased to a regt, to be formed of infty, artl, & mounted men, constituting thus something like a legion. In sympathy with the paternal interest felt by the Pres, we hope Col Hughes will call his regt the Pres' Own. -Lynchburg Virginian

Montreal Herald of Thu: we record, this morning, the death J G McTaviss-we believe the senior ofcr of the Hudson's Bay Co, & for several years past resident in charge of their post at the Lake of Two Mountains. He had long been a resident of Canada, & generally known in Montreal.

For sale: or exchange for property in Wash City, 160 acres of land in Tishimingo Co, Mississippi: southeast quarter, section 21, township 1, range 7 east. Also for rent, a neat 2 story brick house on G st, between 12th & 13th sts. Apply to J E Dow, G st, between 14th & 15th sts.

Mrd: on Jul 15, at Christ Church, Phil, by Rev J Hicks Smith, Hon Edw Joy Morris to Eliz Gatliff, daughter of John Ella, of Phil.

Died: on Jul 22, at Montreal, in the Hospital of the Hotel Dieu, Rev John Richards, Priest & Econome of the Seminary of St Sulpice, aged 60 years. He had caught the ship fever at the emigrant sheds. He was a native of Alexandria, D C, came to Canada 39 years ago, & was a chaplain in the English army at Plattsburgh in 1813. The church employed him to comfort & counsel the Irish immigrants, & while seeking to save the lives of others he lost his own.

Jos S Wright, the Orderly Sgt of Capt L A Besancon's company of mounted volunteers, committed suicide at the Commercial Hotel, New Orleans, on Jul 20th, by cutting his throat with a razor. He is said to have been a temperate man, but during the last few days he was observed to be very melancholy, & down at heart. He was about 35 years of age, & claimed Virginia as his birth place. His effects are in the hands of Coroner Spedden.

Died: on Jul 27, Mr Thos Gibson, aged about 50 years, a native of Yorkshire, England, but for the last 28 years a resident of the U S.

FRI JUL 30, 1847

Collector's certificate lost: application made for the renewal of certificate given by A Rothwell, Collector, to Jas Whitney, for the purchase at tax sale of lot 15 in square 539, on Dec 13, 1843. -J B Morgan

Sale of valuable property in Gtwn: by deed of trust: the following lots of ground:
1-Part of lot 100, in Beatty & Hawkins' addition, at the corner of 1st & Potomac sts, fronting 42 feet on 1st st & 120 feet on Potomac st, with the privilege of an alley. Both streets are paved & gravelled.
2-Part of lot 119, in same addition, at the corner of 2nd & Potomac sts, opposite St John's Church, fronting 25 feet on 2nd & 150 feet on Potomac st. The streets on each front have been recently paved & gravelled.
3-Lot 133, same addition, fronting 70 feet on the north side of 2nd st, nearly opposite the termious of Potomac st, & has 3 small tenements on it.
4-Lot 285, in same addition, fronting on the south side of Madison st.
5-Lot 39, same addition, on the east side of High st, above Road st, 105 feet front on High st, by 150 feet in depth. This lot lies near Mr Adler's property. -John Marbury, Trustee
-Edw S Wright, auctioneer

Potomac land, well covered with White Oak Timber, for sale: 860 acres, located at the head of Monroe's creek, in Westmoreland Co, Va. There is a farm house on it & a tenement rented out for the present year. Address to the subscriber, at ***Oak Grove***, Westmoreland Co, Va; to C W Van Ness, N Y C, or C P Van Ness, Wash.
-G W Lewis, agent for the heirs of Gen John P Van Ness.

Wash Corp: 1-Ptn from M Shanks: referred to the Cmte of Claims. 2-Ptn of Wm P Shedd & others: referred to the Cmte of Claims.

For sale: tract of land containing between 25 & 27 acres, on the heights just without the limits of the corporation of Wash, & within 1 miles of the Capitol. It is bounded on the west by the road leading to Rock Creek Church & Bladensburg; on the north by the estate of Mr Berry; on the east by Mr Gales' estate; & on the south by Mr Keating's estate. Apply to R Dement at the Post Ofc Dept.

An Ofcr of the Navy, in regard to the loss of the U S schnr **Shark**, lately lost in the mouth of the Columbia river, Oregon: This wreck will, I trust, convince the Gov't of the impracticability of her men-of-war entering the Columbia river without a competent pilot. Our cmder, Lt Howison, possesses, in an emiment degree, judgment, coolness, & an accurate knowledge of his profession; but to navigate the Columbia requires the piloting of one who has been familiar with it for years.

Mr John Pettit, the late Member of Congress from Indiana, & a candidate for the next, was thrown from his buggy on the 16th in consequence of his horse taking fright, & broke his leg below the knee. -Union

St John's Herald states of the emigrants, within this year, left Great Britain for Quebec alone, 4,095 never reached their destination, having died at sea or at quarantine. About 600 more perished at sea by shipwreck. Smallpox has again broken out on board H M Troop-ship **Appollo**. One of the Church of England Ministers, Rev W Chaderton, Lt Lloyd, R N, Mr Crispo, Capt Christian, of the ship **Sisters**, & several others are also dead.

Died: on Jul 29, Zachary Taylor, son of John T & Susan B Towers, aged 6 months. His funeral is today at 5 o'clock.

The Capture of Tabasco: extracts of a letter from an ofcr on board the U S steamer **Spitfire** at Tabasco. On Jun 1st weighed anchor; ran down the coast until the 3rd, when we made the mouth of the Tabasco river. A few houses are frame built, covered with tiles. Mr Shields, an English gentleman, is bldg a handsome residence, which reminds me of a Yankee cottage. People of the most part are races of pure Italian or Spanish & Indian blood. On the 12th we returned to Frontera. On the 13th the Grand Mogul the ship **Mississippi** arrived, bringing along the remainder of our attacking squadron. On the 14th everything was arraigned. We weighed anchor. On the 16th, one felt more like dancing than dying. The day was beautiful. The Mexicans formed a bar over which they supposed we could not come. This bar Cmdor Perry ordered to be sounded, having detailed Lt May, Midshipman Wainwright, & a boats' crew. They were fired upon from a concealed breastwork on the bank. Lt May had the misfortune to be severely wounded in the arm whilst writing down the soundings. The landing place of Cmdor Perry was upon the farm of Gen Bruno, a young man of talents, who, devoting his whole time to nautical pursuits, has become an Esau in this land of plenty, & had a good education in the U S, now misapplies his talents & neglects his best interests by devoting himself to revolutionizing this unfortunate country. We struck bottom near the shore, & we jumped overboard & reached the fort, Lt Porter carrying the treasured stars & strips. Midshipman Briceland, master of the ship **Scorpion**, broke a hole through the roof of the Govn'r house, & mounted the flag thereon, amidst a shower of bullets. It is said that Gen Bruno told Gen Garcia to hold on & fight at the fort, whilst he went down to thrash the Cmdor. The city of Tabasco is built of one-story bldgs of stone, & shows melancholy evidence in every part of the bloody internal revolutions. Two of our men have been found killed, one with a lasso around his neck & his face much disfigured. Our scouts found the four quarters of a man hung up. A most horrid sight, but common here. The steamer **Spitfire** expects to go to New Orleans & repair ship, as our noble little craft, from such hard service, leaks 20 inches per hour steadily.

The Hon Jos Durfee, Chief Justice of the Supreme Court, expired yesterday at his residence in Tiverton. He was elected a Rep in Congress in 1821 & again in 1823, & elected Chief Justice in 1825, vice Judge Eddy, who resigned. He was 57 years of age. -Providence Journal of Jul 27.

Dr Ezra Green, of Dover, N H, who completed the 101st year of his age on Jun 28 last, died at his residence on Sunday; consequently the Hon Timothy Farrar, of Hollis, who reached his 100th on Jul 11, is now the oldest living graduate of Harvard Univ. Dr Green belonged to the class of 1765, & Mr Farrar to that of 1767. -Boston Transcript

On Thu last Miss Eliz R, daughter of Jos B Lippincott, of Morristown, N J, arrived at the Falls in company with some friends, & put up at the Eagle Hotel. Her curiosity led her to look at the cataract in all its phases of sublimity, even from behind the magnificent sheet of the Horse Shoe. The excitement & fatigue caused a fatal hemorrhage of the lungs, & she died on Fri. -Buffalo Advertiser of Jul 28.

A large limestone fell from near the top of Coal Hill, above Sligo, on Mon, & rolled against a frame schoolhouse, & instantly killed 5 children, besides wounding 3 others. The children killed were Oliver McAninch, John Cassidy, Morgan Richards, John Davis, & Chas Doran. The teacher, Mr Chiders, narrowly escaped injury. -Pittsburg Gaz of Tue.

Railroad accident on Fri: a brakeman, Lewis Morse, on the freight train from Boston to Worcester, was knocked from the top of one of the cars, in passing under a bridge, & had his arm & foot run over. His arm was amputated. He was removed to the hospital in Boston on Sat, & his recovery is confidently hoped for.

Died: yesterday, at Gtwn College, whilst on a visit to this Institution, in his 25th year, Rev Francis X King, late Pastor of the Catholic congregations of Montgomery Co, Md. Requiescat in pace!

The captain of the schnr **Eleanor Ann**, T Messick, plying between Fredericksburg & Gtwn, D C, was knocked overboard by the main boom, about 12 miles from Fredericksburg, on Jul 22, & drowned.

Fatal accident at Harrisburg, Pa, Thu last, Mr Wm Root, examining the bridge in process of erection over the Susquehanna, lost his balance, & fell 20 feet. He was taken from the water in a state of insensibility, but was soon restored to consciousness, & lingered until Sunday when death ended his sufferings.

Copartnership existing under the firm of Wallace & Warring was this day dissolved by mutual consent. John Waring will hereafter conduct the business.
-W A Wallace, John Waring

Letter from Independence, Wash Co, Pa: Mr Henry Virtu, a highly respectable man with a small family, accidentally discharged his gun, the load passing through his head, killing him instantly.

SAT JUL 31, 1847
St Timothy's Hall, a School for Boys, at Catonsville, 6 miles from Balt, Md. Rev L Van Bokkelen, A M, Rector. Bldgs are complete & ample accommodations for 80 pupils. Terms: $100 per session of 5 months.

Desirable business stand for rent: the 3 story warehouse on Pa ave, between 10th & 11th sts, at present occupied by B Homans, as an auction store. Apply to Chas W Pairo.

Appointment by the Pres: Geo W Clinton, of the State of N Y, to be U S Dist Atty for the northern dist of N Y, vice Wm Allen, elected Justice of the Supreme Court of the State.

Vera Cruz Sun of the 13th instant: the troops under Col De Russey marched within 7 miles of Huejutla on the 12th, when the Mexicans commenced a heavy fire on them. The Americans continued fighting their way along the road toward the river at intervals until the 16th, with a loss of 20 men killed, 10 wounded, & 2 missing. Among the number was Capt Boyd, who fell in the first charge, with 3 balls through his body; also his 1st Lt, who fell mortally wounded, & was left dying on the field. Col De Russy had several balls through his coat; Capt Wise had his horse shot from under him. Lt Whipple, acting adj of the 9th infty, was lassoed by a small party of guerrillos on the 10th, when retiring from the cemetery, within 400 yards of the walls of the city of Vera Cruz. The chaparral has been search for miles around, but his body could not be found. Capt Wm Duff, of the 2nd Dragoons, died of vomito at Vera Cruz, on the 16th.

Meeting in Phil, over which J R Chandler presided, at which it was resolved to erect a monument to the memory of the late Jos C Neal.

Plaquemine Ibervillian of Jul 17th announces the death of Judge Merriam, an old & estimable citizen of Louisiana, at the age of 68 years. He was a native of Lexington, or Concord, Mass, whence he emigrated to La in 1800, & was a successful practioner at the Bar; was Sheriff of Iberville Co, Parish Judge, & State Senator. After the expiration of his term in the Senate, Judge Merriam withdrew from public life.

We heard news yesterday of the loss of the sloop-of-war **Jamestown**, & probably a large portion of her ofcrs & crew. She sailed from Boston for Norfolk on Thu last week, under the command of Lt Thatcher, to complete her equipments for a cruise on the coast of Africa. She was lost on Cape Henry. The schnr **Valante**, Capt Mathias, arrived from N Y, & reports having seen a sloop-of-war, no doubt the **Jamestown**, on her way from Boston, aground in Chinquoteage Shoal. She was observed to be again thumping as if on a bar. Gov't has no steamer here of its own, of sufficient power to go to her relief; & there is not one in private hands to be had for love or money. [Aug 2nd newspaper: the U S sloop-of-war **Jamestown**, Cmder Mercer, reported ashore on Chingoteague Shoal, having got off with little difficulty, arrived at the anchorage on Thu. It was in consequence of a defect in the chart which she was steered by, that the **Jamestown** ran upon the shoal.]

During the thunder storm on Mon last the lightning struck the house of Mr Ezra M Kenny, near the lighthouse, & instantly killed a 4 year old child of Mr Kenny. The electric fluid also passed through both feet of Mr Kenny's sister, tearing & mangling them horribly. The house was injured. -New London News

Mr McKutcheons, of Castalio, accidentally shot & killed himself when out hunting. He was about 26 years of age, & has left a wife. -Sandusky [O] Mir

At Phil, on Wed, Jas McMullen, who was engaged in putting on the cap of a musket, has his whole lower jaw shot away. He died shortly after. A young man, named Balty, was severely wounded.

Jos G Semmes, brought his life to an end by his own hand, on Jul 9, at the house of his brother in Washington, Georgia. He shot himself with a pistol, leaving a note in the form of a certificate, dated Jul 9, 1847, that his death was occasioned by himself, & was brought about either by pistol or razor.

The partnership existing under the firm of Bickley & Tyson, has been dissolved by mutual consent. The business of the late firm will be settled up by the new firm of Tyson & Hewlings. -L W Bickley, J W Tyson The undersigned will continue at the same ofc, on F st, to discount or puchase bills of exchange, drafts, checks, or promissory notes.
-J W Tyson, Edwin P Hewlings

Strayed away from my residence, opposite the Protestant Orphan Asylum, a dark red buffalo Cow: answers to the name of Cherry. All expenses will be cheerfully paid, as she is a great favorite. -Mrs Jane Deneal

Valuable tract of land near Gtwn at auction: on Aug 13, 116 acres lying in Alexandria Co, Va, being the property on which Mr Fredell resides, with a handsome dwlg erected on one of the most beautiful sites, in full view of Wash City & Gtwn. -A Green, auctioneer

MON AUG 2, 1847
Catastrophe at New Brighton. On Thu, as 2 children of Mr B R Winthrop & 2 children of Mr Jos Kernochan, attended by their nurses, a waiter & coachman, were entering a row-boat on the gunwale of the boat, instantly upset the whole company into the water. Through the 2 apprentices, one a mere lad, who were nearby, the lives of all were saved except Mr Winthrop's child aged 6 years, & the nurse of Mr Kernochan. -N Y Post

The U S steamer **Ann Chase**, while off the mouth of the Sabine river, on Jul 12, burst one of her boilers, killing F V Carmichael, a private in the 4th Regt Indiana volunteers, & Jas Dolan, a boat hand, belonging to Pittsburg, & scalding Aaron Lawson, of the Indiana volunteers, & John Brannon & Thos Newland, of Cincinnati. The Indiana troops on board were to be sent to the Rio Grande by a chartered vessel.

Wm Waller, Dealer in Clothing & Furniture, states that he is late salesman in Mr Marshall's store, & now of the firm of Shanks & Wall, in same store, on Pa ave, Wash City, & thinks it proper to state to the public that he has no knowledge or connexion with the Mr Wm H Wall lately arraigned before the Criminal Court of this county. -Wm Wall -M Shanks [Balt Sun & Leesburg, Va papers please copy & send bill to this ofc.]

Died: on Jul 31, in Gtwn, D C, Mrs Eliz M P Darby, aged 62 years, wife of Wm Darby, & sister of Messrs Tanner, engravers. Rest in peace the sacred dust of her who on earth was all that made amiable the dght, sister, wife, & mother!

Died: on Jul 31, Thomas, infant son of Thomas & Eliz Tonge, aged 8 months & 18 days. His funeral will be from his grandfather's residence, on 7th st, next to the Odd Fellows' Hall, this morning, at 10 o'clock.

An interesting son of Mr Wm Cundell, aged about 8 years, was consigned to the grave at Paterson, N J, on Mon, his death having been caused by contact with burning gas. Some inconsiderate person threw the gas in an ignited state in the midst of some boys who had gathered in the street, which set the clothes of the dec'd on fire. The little sufferer bore patiently his pain during 8 days.

Died: on Jul 31, in Wash City, Emma Arianna, daughter of Matthew & Laura C Gault, aged 1 year, 6 months & 15 days.

The Misses Quincy intend opening a boarding school, [for small boys only,] in connexion with their day school for boys & girls. Terms made known at their residence, west end of Franklin Row, K & 13th sts.

The public are notified that the land in Alexandria Co, on which Mr Fredell now resides, advertised for sale, is bound by a deed of trust to secure the subscriber a debt, with interest, amounting to about $300, now due by the terms of the deed, the payment of which will be enforced according to the terms of the deed. -Wm Emmert, Gtwn

Left the subscriber on Jul 16, John Hunt, an indented apprentice to the house-carpentering business. All persons are hereby warned that I will hold liable & prosecute for damages any person who may harbor or employ said boy. -W Mann [Aug 17th newspaper: In reply to the above: I left because I was desirous of acquiring a full knowledge of my trade, & he has failed to furnish such work for a long time past [in fact, not having it] as would enable me to learn my trade. Mr Mann has engaged in the shoe business which absorbs his time & attention. -John Hunt, Wash]

For rent: commodious & pleasant dwlg-house & premises on the corner of 14th & N Y ave, late in the occupancy of Francis H Davidge. Apply to C H James, next door, or to Jas Larnes, 13th st.

TUE AUG 3, 1847

Appointment by the Pres: John Miller, Register of the Land Ofc at Batesville, Ark, vice Henry Niel, removed.

Bar fixtures & Ten-pin alley for sale. The subscriber offers for sale his interest in the house now kept by him on La ave, adjoining Kopp's Bowling Saloon. Inquire on the premises-J Douglas.

Mrd: on Jul 20, at Charlotte Court-house, Va, by Rev Mr Hart, Mr Leonard J Anderson, of Wash City, to Miss Betty, daughter of John Merton.

Died: Aug 2, Phineas, youngest child of P J & Isabella Steer, aged 2 years & 4 months. His funeral is this morning, at 10 o'clock, from the residence of his parents, on I st, between 9th & 10th sts.

Naval: the Norfolk Beacon of Sat says: Capt Thos Crabbe has been appointed to the command of the frig **Brandywine**, lying at the Gosport navy yard, & destined for the coast of Brazil. The U S ordnance transport barque **Electra**, Cmder T A Hunt, arrived at Pensacola on Jul 18 from the Gulf squadron. She brought the following passengers: Com'r Alex Slidell Mackenzie, in charge of ordnance stores; Purser Wm H Kennon, & Midshipman Wm Van Wycke. The U S brig **Perry**, Lt Com'g Barron, sailed from Pensacola on 22nd for the Brazil station. The U S schnr **On-ka-hy-e**, Lt Com'g Berryman, was to sail on the 23rd for Havana, via Key West. The Electro & ship **Supply** will return to Vera Cruz, the latter under the command of Lt DeCamp, as Lt Calhoun returns North on leave. The **Electra** & Supply will return to Vera Cruz, the latter under the command of Lt DeCamp, as Lt Calhoun returns North on leave. The U S storeship **Relief** sailed from Anton Lizardo on Jul 19 for Pensacola. She brought as passengers: Lt John DeCamp & Passed Midshipman E R Calhoun.

Died: on Jul 31, Jos Clinton, youngest child & only son of Jos & Sarah Ann Sessford, aged 3 months.

Died: on Jul 27, at the residence of Mrs Fox, in Fairfax Co, Va, Mr Jesse Ewell, in his 76th year. Mr Ewell was a resident of Prince Wm Co, where he spent the greater part of his life. He left home on Jul 26 for Wash, but became slightly indisposed towards the close of the day as he journeyed on, & called at Mrs Fox's to tarry all night; but ere the sun arose he had passed away from the earth.

Valuable farm at auction: on Aug 16, an excellent tract of land containing 100 acres, lying on the Rock Creek Church road, adjoining the farms of Maj Walker & Messrs Ould & Reys, being a part of the tract formerly belonging to the estate of Alex'r Shepard, dec'd. -A Green, auctioneer

WED AUG 4, 1847

Died: on Jun 27 last, at Santa Fe, near Vera Cruz, Mr Jas Sullivan, formerly of Wash City, aged 25 years.

Died: on Jul 31, Mary Cordelia, aged 18 months, daughter of Robt A & Mary Hawks.

Wash Corp: 1-Ptn from Thos Welch, for remission of a fine: referred to the Cmte of Claims. 2-Nomination of Geo W Harkness as Com'r of the 1st Ward: confirmed. 3-Nomination of John W Dexter, as police constable of the 2nd Ward: confirmed. 4-Ptn of John Mills, to be released from the penalty of a certain bond: referred to the Cmte of Claims. 5-Ptn of Danl Knipple, for remission of a fine: referred to the Cmte of Claims. 6-Ptn of Elisha Lazenby & others, for grading & paving an alley in square 425: referred to the Cmte on Improvements.

<u>Army Order: Genr'l Order #26: War Dept, Adj Gen Ofc, Wash, Jul 23, 1847.</u>
<u>Recruiting for the old Establishment:</u>
Col I B Crane, 1st Artl: Superintendent, Eastern Division-Headquarters, N Y
Lt Col J Erving, 2nd Artl: Superintendent, Western Division-Headquarters, Cincinnati
<u>Recruiting for the 10 additional Regts:</u>
For the 9th & 10th Infty: Col Jas Bankhead, 2nd Artl, Superintendent, Headquarters, N Y
For the 11th Infty & Voltigeurs: Maj E W Morgan, 11th Regt, Superintendent, Baltimore
For the 12th, 13th, & 14th Regts: Brig Gen G M Brooke, commanding Wester Division, [assisted by A G Blanchard, 12th Regt,] Headquarters, New Orleans
For the 15th & 16th Regts: Lt Col J Erving, 2nd Artl, Cincinnati
<u>Recruiting for the Volunteer Regts:</u>
For the Mass, N Y, & N J Volunteers: Col J Bankhead, 2nd Artl, N Y
For the Pa, D C, & Md Volunteers: Maj E W Morgan, 11th Regt, Baltimore
For the Va Volunteers: Col J B Walbach, 4th Artl, ***Fort Monroe***
For the North & South Carolina Volunteers: Col W Whistler, 4th Infty, ***Fort Moultrie***
For the Ga, Ala, Miss, & La Volunteers: Brig Gen G M Brooke, New Orleans
For the Ill & Missouri Volunteers: Lt Col T Staniford, 8th Infty, Jefferson Barracks
For the Indiana & Ohio Volunteers: Lt Col J Erving, 2nd Artl, Cincinnati
By order: R Jones, Adj Gen

Chancery sale: by decree of the Circuit Court of Wash Co, D C, as Court of Chancery, made in the cause of Benj L Jackson & Wm B Jackson vs Catherine Leddon & Jas S Harvey, administrators of the estate of Benj Leddon, dec'd, et al. I shall offer at public sale, on Aug 28, all that part of square 353, in Wash City, with a 2 story brick dwlg upon it. -Walter D Davidge, Trustee -R W Dyer, auct

A wife killed by her husband: on Thu of last week, near Troy, Pa, Mrs Pierce, w/o Dr J B Pierce, had occasion to go to the window of the chamber in which they were sleeping, leaving Dr Pierce asleep. The raising of the window awoke him, & he instantly seized his gun, which was near his bedside, supposing that some one was trying to break into the house. After Mrs Pierce had let down the window, she advanced towards the bed. Dr Pierce called out twice to stop, or he would fire; but she still advanced, & he fired when she was near the muzzle of the gun, & she fell dead on the floor. He then felt in the bed for his wife to tell her he had killed some one; when, not finding her, the truth flashed upon him that he had shot his own wife! We understand that his affliction is great, as they were very warmly attached to each other in life. -Elmira Gaz

THU AUG 5, 1847

Orphans Court of Wash Co, D C. Letters of administration on the personal estate of John T McLaughlin, late of the U S Navy, dec'd. -Saloadora McLaughlin, admx or to her atty, A Thos Smith, ofc on F st, near the Treasury Dept.

By 3 writs of fieri facias, & to me directed: one in favor of Wm H Gunnell & Ira Hayden, trading under the firm of Wm H Gunnell & Co, & 2 in favor of Wm H Gunnell: I have seized & taken in execution all the right, title, & interest of John Gibson, in a 2 story frame house on D st south & 8th st, now occupied by the said John Gibson. -E G Handy, Cnstbl

We announce the death of Col Thos Throop, the Democratic candidate for Congress in the 9th Congressional District of Ky. He died at his residence in the town of Flemingsburg on Fri last, of congestive fever. He was a native of D C, but had resided for many years in Flemingsburg, where he practiced law with distinguished success. Am amiable wife & an interesting family of little children are left to mourn his death. -Ky Commonwealth

Missionaries sailed: Rev Wm Wood, of Henniker, N H, Mrs Wood, of Groton, Mass, & Rev Geo Bowen, of N Y, sailed from Boston on Sat, under the appointment of the American Board of Missions, for the Bombay Mission. In the Switzerland, from Liverpool, was Mr Amos Abbot, wife, & 5 children, of Andover. Mr Abbot has been for the last 13 years a missionary at Bombay.

Lamentable accident on Fri, on the Columbia Railroad, near Lancaster, in which Edw Edwards & Thos Williams, were crushed to death between 2 boat cars, which came violently together by the breaking of an axle, while going at considerable speed. The two men killed belonged to Ohio, & were accompanied by their wives, one of whom had her collar bone broken by the accident.

One cent reward for runaway, Thos Richd Elmer, an indented apprentice to the house painting business. He is 19 or 20 years old, with black hair, answers to the name of Dick. -Geo Harvey

Chancery Sale: by decree of the Court of Chancery, at Nashville, Tenn, at the May term, 1847: public sale on Oct 2, all the property, real, personal, & mixed of Stacker, Woods & Co, in Stewart Co, Tenn. Property consists of 39,000 acres of land, on which is erected one large Rolling Mill. Also, one Steam Blast Furnace, called ***Bear Spring Furnace***, with all the necessary dwlg houses, negro houses, workshops, & stabling. Also included in said sales are 258 Slaves. Also, all the stock of horses, mules, oxen, wagons, carts, & tools. Also, the Merchandise that may be in the store attached to the mill. Also, all the pig metal, blooms, seraps, coal, cord wood, & dug ore. The death of Robt Woods having rendered the sale of the foregoing property necessary to make a proper distribution between his heirs & surviving partners. -E S Hall, Com'r

Ofcrs attached to the U S brig **Perry**, which sailed from Pensacola on Jul 22 for the Brazil station, to relieve the U S brig **Bainbridge**: Saml Barron, commanding
Lts Geo F Sinclair, Jas B Lewis; Acting Master: Chas Deas
Purser: Jos C Eldridge; Assist Surgeon: Edw R Squibb
Midshipmen: W W Holmes, J H Carter, W W Wilkinson
The following are ofcrs of the U S brig **Washington**, now on a surveying cruise in the Gulf stream: Saml P Lee, Lt commanding
Lts: F Sands, J R Mullany, Francis Winslow
Passed Assist Surgeon: L J Williams
Acting Master: Gustavus F Fox
Passed Midshipman: Richd Anlick

Died: on Jul 12, 1847, near Caseyville, Union Co, Ky, Mrs Nancy Casey, widow of Judge Peter Casey, in her 84th year. She was born on Oct 8, 1763, in Spotsylvania Co, Va, & about 2 years afterwards her parents moved to Mill Creek, Berkeley Co, Va. She was the daughter of Maj Andrew Waggener, who was an ofcr [first a captain, then a major] in the continental army of the Revolution. She married Peter Casey about the close of the Revolutionary war, & soon after emigrated to Harrod's Station, now Harrodsburg, Ky. This was then the most exposed point of Indian attack in Ky. The place was besieged again & again. Mr Casey lived in the neighborhood of Harrodsburg until about 1810, when he moved with his family to Union Co, Ky, thinly & rudely settled. She was loved & admired & imitated. She took orphans into her own family, reared them, & treated them as kindly as she did her own children. Her husband died nearly 20 years ago.

Lynchburg Virginian of Mon: On Thu last, discovery of a defalcation in the Branch bank of Va in this place, of some $13,000 or $14,000, in consequence of the improper use of its funds by 2 of the ofcrs, viz: Wm B Averett, teller, & Jas B Green, bookkeeper. The discovery was made at the mother bank. Mr Green was arrested & admitted to bail; Mr Averett left town.

Little Rock Banner, Arkansas: on Thu last, in attempting to serve a peace process, Deputy Sheriff Berchfield, of Saline Co, was killed by the older of the two brothers named Allen, upon whom the writ was to be served. Mr Low, one of the posse, drew a pistol & killed Allen, while the younger Allen fired upon Low, which was also fatal. Some one of the posse shot the surviving Allen. The wound was not mortal, & he made his escape. He will no doubt be overtaken.

Foreign news: Mrs Ruillinan, only daughter of the venerable Poet Laureate, Wordsworth, expired at ***Rydal Mount***, the poet's residence, on Fri week, after many weeks' suffering from pulmonary consumption.

Valuable lands & negroes for sale: having determined to settle permanently in the South, I shall sell, on Sep 15, on the premises, all my Va property lying in Orange Co. The several farms mentioned below are subdivisions of one tract containing about 3,500 acres, 2 miles from Racoon Ford, on the Rapid Ann river.
The ***Meadows*** contains 1,005 acres: with a comfortable dwlg-house.
Winder Tract contains 600 acres next above the Meadows: with a comfortable dwlg-house.
Birchland Tract contains 600 acres.
Independent Tract, contains 468 acres.
Guinea Tract contains 287 acres
Goshen contains 175 acres
Brazier Tract contains 89 acres, adjoining the ***Meadows***.
The lands will be shown by Mr John Newman, living on the premises, or by Philip Mallory, who lives adjoining. My brother, Jeremiah Morton, is fully authorized to act for me. His address is Orange Courthouse. -Jackson Morton

FRI AUG 6, 1847
Mr Alick Smith, an esteemed resident & farmer in Hoppaug, Long Island met an accident, a few days since, which resulted in his death. While at work in the field with a scythe, he accidentally stepped on the snath & the blade turned up in his direction & severely cut him. He died in 2 days.

The Trement Daily News says that a person answering the description of Mr Alex'r St George, whose disappearance was noticed a few days ago since, has been in that city in the past week, with Capt Fatio, & the two departed in company for Princeton.

Sale of valuable household furniture: on Aug 14, by bill of sale, in trust from Louisa Ballard: sale at the house now occupied by said Louisa Ballard, opposite the north gate of the Capitol, certain valuable articles of furniture. -Richd Wallach, trustee

Agency for Claims: John Underwood, late Chief Clerk in the ofc of the 1st Auditor of the Treasury Dept. Ofc on Capitol Hill, 2nd square south of the Capitol.

Reward of $50 is offered in the St Louis Republican for the apprehensionof Wm Osborne, a murderer.

Mr E McFaul, late U S Consul at Laguna, was drowned on his way from Tabasco to his place of residence, leaving at his death a destitute widow, a sister, & 5 small children. The steamer **Vixen** & gun-boat **Petrel** were at Laguna at the time, & the ofcrs & men of those vessels, & subsequently those of the ships **Princeton & Porpoise**, contributed very liberally to the support of Mrs McFaul & her family. On the visit of Cmdor Perry to that place, he started a subscription on board the vessels of the squadron, & a sufficient sum was raised not only to defray all the expenses of the helpless family to their home, at St Louis, Mo, but Mrs McFaul must have had a considerable sum left; reportedly as Lt Commandant Wm E Hunt, of the **Porpoise**, generously gave her a passage to Vera Cruz, at which place she was embarked in an army steamer for New Orleans, & was doubtless conveyed free of charge.

Gerrit L Dox, of Albany, departed this life on Mon, at the residence of his brother-in-law, Mr Mercer, at Waterloo, Seneca Co, N Y. He was a native of Albany, & connected with many of its oldest Dutch families. He held the ofc of Treasurer of the State from 1816 to 1821, & afterwards for several years one of the magistrates in the Justices' Court of Albany.

Mrd: on Aug 4, by Rev Mr Reese, Mr John A Moran, U S N, to Miss Sarah Umberfield, all of Wash City.

Died: on Aug 5, Mrs Ellen Irvin Gillis Klopfer, in her 23rd year, leaving a husband & 2 infant children to mourn her untimely loss. Her funeral is this day, at 4 o'clock, from the residence of her husband, Henry Klopfer, on 6th st, above H st.

Died: on Jul 30, in Wash City, John Henry, eldest son of John & Eliza Hamilton, aged 2 years & 6 months.

Miss A Gusta M Billing, having completed her education at the North, intends to open a School on Sep 1, in the vicinity of her mother's residence, on 9th st, for the instruction of Misses in all the branches of an English education. The location & terms of the school will be announced.

SAT AUG 7, 1847

For rent: furnished or unfurnished rooms, on 7th st, opposite the Odd Fellows' Hall. Inquire of Mr L Harbaugh.

Thos Byrnes & Saml C Wood, eldest sons of Silas Wood, of N Y, drowned in the Ohio river, near Louisville, on Jul 14.

Genteel furniture at auction: on Aug 11, at the residence of Mr Hardbottle, east end of Bridge st, his stock of new & well kept furniture. -Edw S Wright, auctioneer

Mrd: on Thu, in Balt, by Rev John C Smith, of Wash City, Mr Alex'r H Barrow to Miss Isabella, daughter of the late Jonathan Rogers, of Balt.

Died: on Aug 3, at his residence in Clifton, Fairfax Co, Va, Mr David Curtis, formerly of Duchess Co, N Y.

Died: on Jul 13, at Manchester, Ill, Mr Silas Reed, a native of Massachusetts, but for more than 30 years a citizen of Alexandria, Va, in his 62nd year.

MON AUG 9, 1847

The Hon Edw Bradley, a Rep elect to the next Congress from the western district of Michigan, died in N Y C on Thu last.

We regret to record the death of one of our oldest citizens, Solomon Etting. Mr Etting has for a great number of years past been identified with the best interests of the city. -Balt American [No date-current news item.]

Capt Jonathan Winship, extensively known throughout New England as one of the pioneers in the science of horticulture, died at his residence in Brighton on Fri last.

Capt Martin M Moore, of the 11th U S Infty, a native of Pa, died on Jul 25 on board the schnr **Velasco**, on her passage from Tampico to New Orleans. Lt Moore, of the 12th Infty, died at the hospital at San Francisco on Jul 17.

Wash City: the foundation has been laid during the last week of a large brick edifice, at the corner of 17th & F st, intended for public ofcs. The front on F st extends 209 feet & 7 inches; the front on 17th st extends 101 feet. It is to be erected for W H Winder, of Phil, the owner, & he will lease it for 12 years certain to the Gov't, who are anxious to have a suitable fire-proof bldg to be used as ofcs for some of the bureaus of the War & Navy Depts. Mr Chas Coltman is the contractor; Mr Gilpin, of Phil, the architect; Mr Caldwell, of Phil, the carpenter; Mr Thos Lewis, the bricklayer; Mr S H Hutchins, the stone-mason; Mr H D Cooper, is the general superintendent. All the iron castings & furnaces will be done at the Wash Foundry.

Henry Gray & B F Stewart were committed to jail last Fri, to await a requisition of Gov Pratt, for their delivery to the Md authorities. They are charged with stealing a gold watch, the property of Mr Jas C Clark, a merchant of Alexandria. The watch was found on the person of Gray. [Aug 11th newspaper: due to their intoxication at the time, Judge Crawford ordered their discharge: they were set at liberty.]

Died: on Jul 5, in Nashville, Tenn, Saml J Riggs, after a lingering illness of many months. He was born in Gtwn, D C, Aug, 1821, 3 years before the removal of his father, Romulus Riggs, from Gtwn.

Died: on Thu, at his residence in Norfolk, Va, in his 79th year, the Hon Thos Newton, formerly & for 30 consecutive years the Rep of that District in the Congress of the U S. [Aug 10th newspaper: he pursued the profession in the early stage of his life; took his seat in Congress at the opening of the first session under the Administration of Mr Jefferson; his term of representative service continued through the Administrations of Jefferson, Madison, Monroe, John Q Adams, & Jackson; in 1833 he declined being a candidate; was the Recorder of the Hustings Court of the City of Norfolk till his death. -Norfolk Herald]

Died: on Aug 4, at N Y, after a severe illness, Mr Nathl P Bixby, formerly of this District, in his 66th year.

Died: on Aug 4, in Wash City, Geo Alex'r, son of Robt Francis & Mira Catharine Magee, aged 10 months & 21 days.

TUE AUG 10, 1847

Among the passengers in the steamer **Hibernia**, at Boston from Liverpool, was Rev G C Moore, a Baptist clergyman from Sligo Co, Ireland, who comes out by invitation by some gentlemen of N Y.

In consequence of the death of the publisher, the late Gerrit L Dox, the publication of the Statesman, at Albany, has been suspended, at least for the present.

A letter from a member of Capt Merrick's company, at Matamoros, announces the death of Sgt Yates & private Buroughs, both of St Mary's Co.

Naval. The U S sloop-of-war **Albany**, commanded by Saml L Breese, arrived at Hampton Roads on Aug 6. She left the Home Squadron at Anton Lizardo on Jul 10.
Her ofcrs are as follows: Capt, Saml L Breese
Lts, Oliver H Perry, Saml R Knox, Benj S Gantt
Surgeon, Ninian S Pinkney; Purser, J Geo Harris
Master, Thos M Crossan, Jas S Ridgely, [late acting master of the schnr **Reefer**]
Midshipmen, Elijah T Andrews, Wm H Weaver, J B Smith, Henry H Key, Geo W Morris
Capt's Clerk, S J O'Brien; Gunner, Saml Allen; Carpenter, L R Sheffield
Sailmaker, Alex W Cassell
Passengers from the Squadron: Capt Isaac Mayo, Lt Reed Werden, Passed Assist Surgeon S R Addison, Assist Surgeon O F Baxter, Passed Midshipmen Edw Barrett, J S Bohrer, 2nd Assist Engineer Wm H Shock. [The Albany brings home the remains of Midshipman Shubrick, who fell at the navy battery while gallantly doing his duty.] -Norfolk Herald

Mrd: on Aug 5, at Selma, Fred'k Co, Va, the residence of her father, by Rev Wm T Rooker, John Ambler to Anna M, eldest daughter of the Hon Jas M Mason.

Mrd: on Aug 4, in Pittsburg, by Rev Wm Preston, Col Geo W McCook to Miss Margaret Dick Beatty, both of Steubenville, Ohio.

Died: on Aug 4, at Sandy Spring, Montgomery Co, Md, Bernad Gilpin, in his 84th year.

Died: early on Sabbath morning, in Balt, Mrs Maria Rogers, relict of the late Jonathan Rogers, merchant of Balt, & sister of the Rev John C Smith, of Wash City. She feared God from her youth up.

Mail robbers Pettis & Wilson were sentenced on Sat, the former to 10 & the latter to 7 years confinement in the penitentiary.

The College of St James, near Hagerstown, Md. This Institution is the Diocesan College of the Protestant Episcopal Church in Md, but its classes are open to students from any State. The next session opens on Oct 4. Apply to Rev John B Kerfoot, Rector.

Wood & Coal: the subscriber had opened a Wood & Coal Yard on 12th st, south of Pa ave. Orders may be left at the Stationers' Store of Mr Wm F Bayly, Pa ave, between 11th & 12th sts, or at the residence of the subscriber, G st, between 8th & 9th sts. -Wm E Stubbs

$50 reward for runaway negro man Edmund Johnson, who left my residence at the White House, on the Balt & Wash Turnpike Road, on Sun last. He is between 25 & 30 years of age. -J W Brown, near Beltsville, Md.

By virtue of 7 writs of venditioni exponas, I will expose at public auction, on the premises, on Sep 11, for cash, all the right, title, & interest of Henry Wilson in & unto one lot & improvements, consisting of one 2 story brick dwlg house in Wash City, on the east side of 10th st, between H & I sts, late the property of Henry Wilson, & seized & taken in execution at the suit of Wm R Roby. -H R Maryman, Constable

By virtue of 2 writs of venditioni exponas, I will expose to sale at public auction, on Sep 11, on the premises, for cash, one lot & improvements, consisting of one 2 story brick house, with basement, on the east side of 10th st, between H & I sts, late the property of Henry Wilson, seized & taken in execution at the suit of Wm H Gunnell.
-E G Handy, Constable

Mrs A T McCormick having taken the house recently occupied by Mrs Turpin, 7th st & Market space, is prepared for the accommodation of boarders, with or without families.

WED AUG 11, 1847

At the last session of the N Y Legislature a law was passed providing for the registry of births, marriages, & deaths: to include the month & day of the occurrence; names & residents of the persons married or dead; the name of the parents of the children born; the sex, color, & name of the child; name & residence of the ofcr or clergyman solemnizing the marriage; the age of the person married or who have died, with the disease or cause of their death.

By virtue of a writ of venditioni exponas, I will expose to sale at public auction, on Sep 11, on the premises, for cash, all the right, title, & interest of Henry Wilson, in one lot & improvements, consisting of one 2 story brick house, with basement, on the east side of 10th st, between H & I sts, seized & taken in execution at the suit of Raphael Semmes. -Thos Plumsell, Constable

By virtue of 2 writs of venditioni exponas, I will expose to sale at public auction, on Sep 11, on the premises, for cash, all the right, title, & interest of Owen Connolly, in Lot 1 in square 407, with one brick house, on the corner of D & 8th ts, Wash City, seized & taken in execution at the suit of Jos Fugitt & Co. -Thos Plumsell, Constable

The town of Maysville, Ky, was visited by another fire on Wed last, which destroyed property to the amount of nearly $40,000: consumed 3 warehouses of Mr R Collins, & 3 small dwlgs of Mr N Cooper.

Appointment by the Pres: Col Sterling Price, of Missouri, to be Brig Gen, vice Jefferson Davis, declined. There is not a man in Missouri who would believe it: Sterling Price Brig Gen of the Army! Why, it is the most foolish & ridiculous of all the outrageous appointments made by Jas K Polk during the war. Who recommended him? Not those who served under him certainly in New Mexico, nor any body who ever was in Santa Fe, & took note of his inefficiency & misconduct there. Who will say that he has earned such promotion? No one who saw the disorderly & terrible condition of his camp at Santa Fe, the sickness which was superinduced by this neglect of all subordination, & the result which followed, in the death of a fourth of the men composing his regt. This appointment is an insult to the brave ofcrs of Missouri, Illinois, & the other Western & Southern States, who have shown a fitness for command & have also distinguished themselves in battle; & we are much mistaken if any body in this State or elsewhere is found to applaud it. -from the Missouri Republican

Wash Corp: 1-Ptn of Dorcas Galvin: referred to the Cmte of Claims. 2-Ptn of Catharine Adamson: postponed. 3-Ptn of Patrick Goings, for remission of a fine: referred to the Cmte of Claims. 4-Ptn of Maria A Queen, for remission of a fine: referred to the Cmte of Claims.

Died: on Fri last, at Springfield, Mass, David Ames, at the advanced age of 87. He at one period held the ofc of Superintendent of the Armory at Springfield, under the Federal Gov't, with great credit to himself. For more than half a century he has been a manufacturer of paper, & was the first to introduce modern improvements into his mill. Up to a very short period before his death, he was engaged in active business.

Died: on Fri last, at Springfield, Mass, David Ames, at the advanced age of 87. He at one period held the ofc of Superintendent of the Armory at Springfield, under the Federal Gov't, with great credit to himself. For more than half a century he has been a manufacturer of paper, & was the first to introduce modern improvements into his mill. Up to a very short period before his death, he was engaged in active business.

Official: Gen Orders #27: War Dept, Adj Gen Ofc, Wash, Aug 5, 1847.
Promotions: Regt of Mounted Riflemen:
1st Lt Andrew Porter, to be Capt, May 15, 1847, vice Mason, dec'd.
2nd Lt Chas L Denman, to be 1st Lt, May 15, 1847, vice Porter, promoted.
Brevet 2nd Lt Gordon Granger, to be 2nd Lt, May 29, 1847, vice Ragnet, resigned.
4th Regt of Artl: 2nd Lt Fitz-John Porter, to be 1st Lt, May 29, 1847, vice Gill, resigned.
4th Regt of Infty:
1st Lt Carter L Stevenson, to be Capt, Jun 30, 1847, vice Whipple, dec'd.
2nd Lt Chas S Hamilton, to be 1st Lt, Jun 30, 1847, vice Stevenson, promoted.
9th Regt of Infty: Maj Jeremiah Clements, of 13th Infty, to be Lt Col, Jul 16, 1847, vice Thompson, resigned.
11th Regt of Infty:
1st Lt John Motz, to be Capt, Aug 2, 1847, vice Moore, resigned.
2nd Lt Wm H Gray, to be 1st Lt, May 13, 1847, vice Mahaffy, dec'd.
2nd Lt Columbus P Evans, to be 1st Lt, Jul 29, 1847, vice Hamlett, resigned.
2nd Lt Jos Samuels, to be 1st Lt, Aug 2, 1847, vice Motz, promoted.
12th Regt of Infty:
1st Lt John F Hoke, to be Capt, Jun 27, 1847, vice Richards, dec'd.
1st Lt Chas R Jones, to be Capt, Jul 16, 1847, vice Manigault, promoted to 13th Infty.
2nd Lt Chas M Creanor, to be 1st Lt, Jun 27, 1847, vice Hoke, promoted.
2nd Lt Oscar D Wyche, to be 1st Lt, Jul 16, 1847, vice Jones, promoted.
13th Regt of Infty:
Capt Edw Manigault, of the 12th Infty, to be Major, Jul 16, 1847, vice Clemens, promoted to 9th Infty.
1st Lt Adam Hawk, to be Capt, May 28, 1847, vice Tyler, resigned.
1st Lt Duncan L Clinch, to be Capt, Jul 30, 1847, vice Scott, resigned.
2nd Lt Nicholas Davis, to be 1st Lt, May 28, 1847, vice Hawk, promoted.
2nd Lt Fitz H Ripley, to be 1st Lt, Jul 30, 1847, vice Clinch, promoted.
15th Regt of Infty:
2nd Lt Wm R Stafford, to be 1st Lt, ___, 1847, vice Rhoads, dec'd.
16th Regt of Infty:
1st Lt Patrick H Harris, to be Capt, Jun 14, 1847, vice Hendricks, resigned.
2nd Lt Henry K Ramsey, to be 1st Lt, Jun 14, 1847, vice Harris, promoted.
Appointments:
Quartermaster's Dept:
1st Lt Stewart Van Vliet, 3rd Artl, to be Assist Quartermaster with the rank of Capt, Jun 4, 1847, vice Chilton, who vacates his staff commission.
1st Lt Wm Armstrong, 2nd Artl, to be Assist Quartermaster with the rank of Capt, Aug 5, 1847, vice Canby, declined.
1st Lt Alex'r W Reynolds, 1st Infty, to be Assist Quartermaster with the rank of Capt, Aug 5, 1847, vice Hanson, declined.
1st Lt Edw H Fitzgerald, 6th Infty, to be Assist Quartermaster with the rank of Capt, Aug 5, 1847, vice Rucker, declined.
1st Lt Jas G Martin, 1st Artl, to be Assist Quartermaster with the rank of Capt, Aug 5, 1847, vice Hetzel, dec'd.

Pay Dept:
Victor E Piollet, of Pa, to be Paymaster, Jun 17, 1847, vice Hammond, dec'd.
Geo H Ringgold, of D C, [Additional Paymaster,] to be Paymaster, Jul 21, 1847, vice Larned, appointed Deputy Paymaster Genr'l.
Ordnance Dept:
John B Butler, of Pa, [Additional Paymaster,] to be Paymaster & Military Storekeeper, Jun 30, 1847, vice Sturgeon, dec'd.
3rd Regt of Dragoons:
John W Martin, of Va, to be 2nd Lt, Jul 21, 1847, vice Merrifield, dec'd.
Robt E Halitt, of Md, to be 2nd Lt, Jul 21, 1847, vice Haviland, appointed Adjutant.
Regt of Mounted Riflemen:
Christopher Carson, of Missouri, to be 2nd Lt, Jun 9, 1847, vice Denman, promoted.
1st Regt of Artl:
Francis E Patterson, of Pa, to be 2nd Lt, Jun 24, 1847.
Rank: to be 2nd Lt, Jul 1, 1847:
3-Cadet Jos J Woods, Co C
7-Cadet Saml F Chalfin, Co B
2nd Regt of Artl:
4-Cadet Julian McAllister, Co B
6-Cadet Danl T Van Buren, Co E
3rd Regt of Artl:
Brevet 2nd Lt Dabney H Maury, of the Regt of Mounted Riflemen, to be 2nd Lt.
2-Cadet John Hamilton, Co A
9-Cadet John S Mason, Co D
4th Regt of Artl:
1-Cadet John C Symmes, Co I
5-Cadet Geo W Hazzard, Co A
8-Cadet Orlando B Wilcox, Co G
5th Regt of Infty:
19-Cadet Richd H Long, Co C
9th Regt of Infty
John McNabb, Sgt Maj, to be 2nd Lt, Aug 3, 1847, vice Whitten, resigned.
Robt T Spence, of Md, to be Assist Surgeon, Jul 22, 1847, vice Walker, resigned.
11th Regt of Infty:
Jas Elder, of Pa, to be 2nd Lt, Jul 24, 1847, vice Gray, promoted.
John A Bayard,of Pa, to be 2nd Lt, Aug 4,1 847, vice Evans, promoted.
12th Regt of Infty:
Albert G Blanchard, of Louisiana, to be Major, May 27, 1847, original vacancy.
Danl M Short, of Texas, to be 1st Lt, Jun 2, 1847, vice Dial, declined.
Henry R Crosby, of Va, to be 2nd Lt, Jul 21, 1847, vice Reese, declined.
Wm J Coleman, Sgt, Co F, Mounted Riflemen, to be 2nd Lt, Aug 4, 1847, vice Creanor, promoted.
Whitfield B Brookes, of S C, to be 2nd Lt, Aug 4, 1847, vice Wyche, promoted.
John B Butler, of Va, to be Assist Surgeon, Aug 3, 1847, vice Randall, resigned.

13th Regt of Infty:

Egbert I Jones, of Alabama, to be Capt, Jul 22, 1847, vice Watson, declined, Co I
Wm F Rives, of Va, to be 2nd Lt, Jun 8, 1847, vice Davis, promoted.
Reuben T Thorn, of Alabama, to be 2nd Lt, Aug 3, 1847, vice Ripley, promoted.

14th Regt of Infty:

Benj S Mudd, of Louisiana, to be 2nd Lt, Jul 16, 1847, original vacancy.
John E Helms, of Tenn, to be 2nd Lt, Aug 4, 1847, vice Porter, dec'd.

15th Regt of Infty:

Henry H Green, of Ky, to be 2nd Lt, Aug 3, 1847, vice Goodman, promoted.
Saml D Stuart, of Ohio, to be 2nd Lt, Aug 4, 1847, vice McCleary, dec'd.
Geo S Hooper, of Illinois, to be 2nd Lt, Aug 4, 11847, vice Stafford, promoted.

17th Regt of Infty:

John C How, Private of Co H, to be 2nd Lt, Aug 3, 1847, vice Ramsey, promoted.
Alex'r C Hensley, of Ky, to be Assist Surgeon, Jul 7, 1847, vice Noe, resigned.

Regt of Foot Riflemen & Voltigeurs:

Archibald B Campbell, of Pa, to be Assist Surgeon, Jul 12, 1847, vice Chaloner, resigned.

The Following named Cadets, graduates of the Military Academy, are attached to the Army with the brevet of 2nd Lt, in conformity with the 4th section of the act of Apr 29, 1812, to take rank from Jul 1, 1847: Brevet 2nd Lts attached to the Artl Arm:

Rank:

10-Cadet Geo Patten, Co C, 3rd Artl
11-Cadet Joh H Dickerson, Co B, 4th Artl
12-Cadet Danl T Beltzhoover, Co A, 1st Artl
13-Cadet Otis H Tillinghast, Co E, 3rd Artl
14-Cadet Jas B Fry, Co B, 3rd Artl
15-Cadet Ambrose P Hill, Co K, 1st Artl
16-Cadet Anson J Cook, Co A, 2nd Artl
17-Cadet Horatio G Gibson, Co F, 2nd Artl
18-Cadet Ambrose E Burnside, Co G, 2nd Artl
20-Cadet John Gibbon, Co H, 3rd Artl
21-Cadet Clermont L Best, Co E, 1st Artl
22-Cadet Romeyn B Ayres, Co A, 4th Artl
23-Cadet Chas Griffin, Co E, 4th Artl

Brevet 2nd Lts attached to the Infty Arm:

24-Cadet Henry M Black, Co C, 4th Infty
25-Cadet Henry B Hendershott, Co K, 5th Infty
26-Cadet Tredwell Moore, Co F, 8th Infty
27-Cadet Thos H Neill, Co G, 4th Infty
28-Cadet Wm Burns, Co D, 3rd Infty
29-Cadet Edmund F Abbott, Co A, 6th Infty
30-Cadet Egbert L Viele, Co A, 2nd Infty
31-Cadet Washington P Street, Co E, 5th Infty
32-Cadet Montgomery P Harrison, Co B, 7th Infty
33-Cadet Lewis C Hunt, Co F, 3rd Infty
34-Cadet Augustus H Seward, Co I, 8th Infty

35-Cadet Peter W L Plympton, Co K, 7th Infty
36-Cadet John D Russy, Co I, 6th Infty
37-Cadet Edw D Blake, Co K, 2nd Infty
38-Cadet Henry Heth, Co K, 1st Infty
Appointments in pursuance of the act entitled "An act to provide for the organization of the volunteer forces brought into the service of the U S into brigades & divisions, & for the appointment of the necessary number of general ofcrs to command the same," approved Jun 26, 1846.
Sterling Price, of Missouri, to be Brig Gen, Jul 20, 1847, vice Davis, declined.
Appointments in the Quartermaster, Commissary, & Medical Depts:
Quartermaster Dept:
Geo T Howard, of Texas, [Assist Commissary,] to be Quartermaster, with rank of Major, Jun 21, 1847, vice Dunlap, resigned.
Thos B Ives, of Miss, to be Assist Quartermaster with rank of Capt, Jul 9, 1847, vice Price, resigned.
Thos M Gleason, of Alabama, to be Assist Quartermaster with rank of Capt, Jul 14, 1847, vice R R Howard, resigned.
Commissary Dept:
Saml Milligan, of Tenn, to be Commissary with rank of Major, Jul 17, 1847, vice Campbell, resigned.
Jos C Allen, of Tenn, to be Assist Commissary with rank of Capt, Jun 21, 1847, vice G T Howard, appointed Quartermaster.
Wm P Graves, of N C, to be Assist Quartermaster with rank of Capt, Jul 14, 1847, vice Whittaker, dec'd.
Medical Dept:
Wm B Herrick, of Ill, [Assist Surgeon,] to be Surgeon, May 27, 1847, vice Quinn, resigned.
R McMillan, of S C, to be Surgeon, Jun 8, 1847, vice Hill, resigned.
Thos E Massie, of Missouri, to be Surgeon, Jun 21, 1847, vice Penn, resigned.
C J Clark, of Ala, [Assist Surgeon,] to be Surgeon, Jun 28, 1847, vice Davis, resigned.
Danl Turney, of Ill, [Assist Surgeon,] to be Surgeon, Jul 13, 1847, vice Price, resigned.
J L Miller, of Ill, to be Assist Surgeon, May 27, 1847, vice Herrick, appointed Surgeon; & to be Surgeon, Jul 13, 1847, vice Herrick, declined.
Edmund Ravanel, of S C, to be Surgeon, Aug 4, 1847, vice Jones, dismissed.
N H Ash, of Ill, to be Assist Surgeon, Jul 13, 1847, vice Turney, appointed Surgeon.
Jas D Robinson, of Ill, to be Assist Surgeon, Jul 13, 1847, vice J L Miller, appointed Surgeon.
Craven Peyton, of Arkansas, to be Assist Surgeon, Jul 28, 1847, vice Thompson, resigned.
Smyth M Miles, of Ga, to be Assist Surgeon, Aug 4, 1847, vice F W Miller, resigned.
Casualties:
Resignations:
Lt Col Abner B Thompson, 9th Infty, Jul 16, 1847.
Capt Martin M Moore, 11th Infty, Aug 2, 1847.
Capt John Tyler, 13th Infty, May 28, 1847.

Capt John A Hendricks, 16th Infty, Jun 14, 1847.
Capt Alex'r Scott, 13th Infty, Jul 30, 1847.
1st Lt Saml Gill, 4th Artl, May 29, 1847.
1st Lt Jas E Hamlet, 11th Infty, Jul 29, 1847.
2nd Lt Llewellyn Raguet, Mounted Riflemen, May 29, 1847.
2nd Lt Edwin A Whitten, 9th Infty, Aug 3, 1847.
2nd Lt Alfred A Norment, 3rd Dragoons, Aug 5, 1847.
Assist Surgeon John D Walker, 9th Infty, Jun 26, 1847.
Assist Surgeon Leonard Randall, 12th Infty, Aug 3, 1847.
Assist Surgeon Chas O Waters, 15th Infty, Jun 10, 1847.
Assist Surgeon Allen T Noe, 16th Infty, Jul 7, 1847.
Assist Surgeon Aaron D Chaloner, Regt Voltiguers, Jul 12, 1847.
Delined:
Capt Danl H Rucker, 1st Dragoons, as Assist Quartermaster.
Capt Chas Hanson, 7th Infty, as Assist Quartermaster.
Capt Hugh P Watson, 13th Infty.
Capt Albert G Blanchard, Regt Foot Riflemen & Voltigeurs.
1st Lt Nathl G Dial, 12th Infty
Deaths:
Capt Abner R Hetzel, Assist Quartermaster, at Louisville, Ky, Jul 20, 1847.
Capt Stevens T Mason, Mounted Riflemen, at Jalapa, Mexico, May 15, 1847. [Of wounds received Apr 18, 1847, in the battle of Cerro Gordo.]
Capt Jos H Whipple, 5th Infty, at Perote, Mexico, Jun 30, 1847.
Capt Walter P Richards, 12th Infty, at Tampico, Mexico, Jun 27, 1847.
1st Lt Franklin Mehaffy, 11th Infty, at New Orleans, La, Jun 13, 1847.
1st Lt Levi Rhoads, 15th Infty, at Vera Cruz, Mexico, ___ 1847.
2nd Lt John A Merrifield, 3rd Dragoons, near Vera Cruz, Mexico, Jun 29, 1847.
2nd Lt Danl McCleary, 15th Infty, near Vera Cruz, Mexico, Jun 29, 1847.
2nd Lt David St Leon Porter, 14th Infty, near Vera Cruz, Mexico, Jun 30, 1847.
Paymaster Robt H Hammond, at sea, Jun 2, 1847.
Paymaster Felix G Bosworth, at Vera Cruz, Mexico, Jun 9, 1847.
Military Storekeeper, Jas G Sturgeon, Ord Dept, at Alleghany Arsenal, Pa, Jun 19, 1847.
Casualties-Volunteer Service:
Resignations:
Maj Alex'r Dunlap, Quartermaster, Jun 14, 1847.
Maj Brookens Campbell, Commissary, Jul 17, 1847.
Capt Robt R Howard, Assist Quartermaster, Jun 30, 1847.
Capt Geo M Lauman, Assist Quartermaster, Jun 16, 1847.
Capt Chas M Price, Assist Quartermaster, jul 8, 1847.
Surgeon Edw B Price, Jun 30, 1847.
Surgeon Wm M Quinn, May 27, 1847.
Surgeon Geo Penn, Jun 21, 1847.
Surgeon Gideon M Alsup, May 29, 1847.
Surgeon Jas Davis, Jun 28, 1847.
Assist Surgeon John Thompson, Jul 28, 1847.

Assist Surgeon John W Glenn, Jul 9, 1847.
Assist Surgeon Fred'k W Miller, Jul 28, 1847.
Additional Paymaster Nathan Weston, Jun 30, 1847.
Additional Paymaster John B Butler, Jun 30, 1847.
Declined-2: Brig Gen Jefferson Davis; Surgeon Wm B Herrick
Discharged from service, Jun 30, 1847.
Quartermasters with rank of Major-2: John T Arthur; John C Mason
Assist Quartermasters with rank of Capt-9:

Turner S Gilbert
Henry Scott
Stephen H Webb
Geo P Smith
John Neff
Zebulon C Bishop
Horatio M Vandever
Harry Toulmin
Geo V Hebb

Commissary with the rank of Major-1: Pleasant L Ward
Assist Commissaries with the rank of Capt-12:

Joel S Post
Richd D Gholson
John J Clendinin
Christopher C Graham
John Caldwell
McDonough J Bunch
Stephen Z Hoyle
Jas R Copeland
Thos M Jones
Jesse B Stephens
Delany R Eckels
Wm Duerson

Surgeons-10:

Jas Mahon
Alex'r C Hensley
Gustavus Holland
Benj Stone
Danl S Lane
John B Smith
Jas S Athow
David McKnight
Thos L Caldwell
Wm B Washington

Assist Surgeons-8:

P H Mulvaney
A E Heighway
Richd P Ashe
Alex'r M Blanton
John T Walker
John M Leech
Wm Fosdick
John J Mathews

Deaths-1:
Capt Exum L Whittaker, Assist Commissary, at Camargo, Mexico, Jun 2, 1847.
Dismissed-1: Surgeon Caleb V Jones, Aug 4, 1847.
By order: R Jones, Adj Gen

THU AUG 12, 1847

Bethlehem, Aug 7, 1847. On Tue at Bethlehem, Mr E F Bleck, teacher of a private school, went with his pupils to take a bath in the river Lehigh, when Wm Schall, aged 10, from New Orleans, & Chas Brunner, aged 13, from Lehigh Co, Pa, went beyond their depth & drowned. Mr Bleck narrowly escaped the same fate when he made the greatest exertions to save them. Their bodies have been found. -Phil Ledger

For sale: a valuable tract of land in Southwestern Va: I desire to sell my tract of land on Wolf creek, in Giles Co, Va, containing 3,318 acres;there are 2 log dwlg-houses with stone chimneys on the land, & some outhouses; also, 2 or 3 other log cabins, which have been occupied by tenants' families. Information can be had by application to myself at Wytheville, Va, or to my Manager on the land, or to Capt G D French or Saml Pack, at Giles Courthouse. -Thos J Boyd, Wytheville, Va.

For sale: the ***Mount Savage Iron Works***, & Railroad, in Alleghany Co, Md. By virtue of several executions issued upon judgments standing in Alleghany Co Court against the Md & N Y Iron & Coal Co, better known as the ***Mount Savage Iron Co***, & to me directed, one at the suit of John Wright, Robt Saml Palmer, & Chas Weld, trustees for the English bondholders; another at the suit of Wm F Cary & John M Forbes, I have seized & taken all the real & personal property of said company, & I will proceed to sell the same to the highest bidder, at the ofc of the company, Mount Savage, Md, on Oct 7. This property includes the iron works, brickyard, machinery, engines, railroad 9 miles in length, land containing upwards of 4,800 acres, of which 2,062 acres lie adjoining & near the town of Cumberland, & 2,700 acres lie exclusively within the Frostburg basin. For information apply to Manning & Lee, Balt; Cary & Co, N Y; John M Forbes, Boston; J M Hewe & H T Weld, Mount Savage; & S M Semmes, Cumberland. -Moses Rawlings, Sheriff of Alleghany Co. -Cumberland, Aug 9, 1847.

St John's College, Annapolis, Md, will resume on Sep 6. -Hector Humphreys, President

Two young men, Geo Schwartz & Edw Miller, charged with kidnapping Mary Whiting, a free colored woman, from Chambersburg, Pa, were arrested here yesterday & committed to jail for further examination. They had sold the girl for $500 to Mr Hope H Slatter.

Reuben Davis, has resigned his commission as Col of the 2nd Regt Mississippi riflemen in consequence of impaired health & the pressure of private affairs.

Died: on Fri last, in Fredericksburg, Va, Mr John Crump, Flour Inspector in that place, & one of the most aged & respectable citizens.

Died: on Aug 2, at ***Mount View***, King Geo Co, Va, Col Benj D Rust, aged about 50 years. He was kicked by a horse on the leg a week before his death. Believing the injury to be slight, he neglected the wound until too late for the successful administration of the usual remedies.

Two silver crucifixes, about 8 inches by 7, with a few circular devices furnished with rings, & evidently intended for the neck, & bearing an inscription with the name of DeSoto, & dated 1615, have lately been taken from a small Indian mound in Murray Co, Georgia.

FRI AUG 13, 1847

St Mary's Female Institution, near Bryantown, Chas Co, Md, Aug 4, 1847: Annual Exhibition & Distribution of Premiums: Rev Mr Courtney, of Bryantown presented the premiums; Rev J P Donelan, of Balt, & Rev J B Donelan, of Wash, were also present. Successful competitors:

Miss Eleanor Downey
Miss Teresa A Culverwell, of Wash
Miss Ellen M Queen, of Chas Co, Md
Miss Eliza F Dyer, of Wash
Miss Amelia D Thompson, Chas Co, Md
Miss Mary R Bulger, of Wash
Miss Mary H Mitchell, of Chas Co, Md
Miss Anne Downey, of Chas Co, Md
Miss Mary Tennison, of Chas Co
Miss Maria L Hamilton, of Chas Co

Miss Mary Emily Bowling, of PG Co
Miss Mary C Thompson, of Chas Co
Miss Mary J Boarman, of Chas Co
Miss Eleanor R Boarman, of Chas Co
Mss Margaret Queen, of Chas Co
Miss Anna M Bowling, of Chas Co
Miss Mary C Hughes, of Chas Co
Miss Martina H Dyer, of Wash
Miss Mary E Fenwick, of Wash
Miss Maria R Gwynn, of PG Co
Miss Rosalie Boone, of Chas Co
Miss Virginia Gardiner, of Chas Co
Miss Ann F Gardiner, of PG Co
Miss Beatrice Gardiner, of Chas Co
Miss Eliza E Fenwick, of Wash
Miss Josephine Freeman, of Chas Co
Miss Mgt H Gardiner, of PG Co
Miss Mary Clements, of PG Co
Miss Emily Boarman, of Chas Co
Miss Eliz Bowling, of Chas Co
Miss Mary H Mitchell, of Chas Co

At the close of the exercises Rev J P Donelan, of Balt, made a few appropriate remarks, in the course of which he alluded very feelingly to the late lamented Edw Dyer, who was one of the first & most devoted friends of the institute.

Died: on Aug 6, at Brunswick, N J, Col Danl Kemper, in his 98th year. Col Kemper was an ofcr in the war of the Revolution, & his subsequent character, through a long life, has been patriotic & exemplary.

Com'rs sale of that portion of Geo Semmes' real estate remaining unsold: sale on Aug 24, on the premises; the same consisting of that delightful situation nearly opposite Alexandria, containing one of the best landings for taken herring near it; the dwlg house has lately undergone through repair. Sale is made under a decree of the Circuit Court of D C, by the undersigned com'rs. Zach Walker, David Barry, Jas C Barry, Benj T Smith, & Thos Jenkins

Mrd: on Wed last, at the residence of Thos Willson, in Montgomery Co, Md, by Rev Henry Slicer, Mr Geo Smyzer, of Missouri, to Miss Martha A Willson, of Md.

Mrd: on Aug 10, by Rev Mr Reese, Mr John T Stanley to Miss Sarah E De Vaughn, both of Wash City.

Mrd: on Aug 12, by Rev Mr Reese, Mr Alex'r F Forrest to Miss Malvina Essex, all of Wash City.

Died: on Aug 7, at Brunswick, N J, Capt Lewis Johnson, a soldier of the Revolution, in his 87th year.

Died: on Aug 11, in Wash City, John Lewis, only son of Richd B & Eliza A M Owens, aged 2 weeks.

$5 reward for strayed or stolen, from or on my premises, at Capitol Hill, on Sunday last, a blood Bay Mare, blind in the right eye, natural trotter. -Wm Bush

SAT AUG 14, 1847
Madame Adnet, a young Creole lady, having a slight fever, sent for an eminent medical practitioner for advice. The Dr prescribed Morphine, which was intended to be Quinine. She died on Aug 4.

Jefferson College, Pa, will commence on Aug 25. -Jas McCullough, Sec of the Board of Trustees

Died: on Aug 7, at his residence in Dover, Del, Henry Moore Ridgley, aged 69 years. He was one of the oldest, &, for many years, one of the most prominent members of the Delaware Bar, being contemporary with the elder Bayard, the Reads, Rodney, Van Dyke, Robinson, Hall, Clayton, McLane, Black, & other prominent lawyers of that school. He was twice elected a Rep to Congress; on the death of Mr Van Dyke, in 1827, he succeeded him in the Senate of the Union.

$25 reward for runaway negro girl, calling herself Ann Gardner. -Louis Marceron, near the Navy Yard

Died: on Aug 11, at the U S Hotel, N Y, Wm P, only child of Parker P & Mary E Clark, aged 19 months & 12 days, grandson of Wm D Acken, of Wash City.

Lt Tanneyhill, who was severely wounded & taken prisoner in the unlucky affair of Col De Russy, with the Mexicans under Gen Garay, & whose wound was thought to be mortal, was still alive as late as Jul 20, & being cared for by Gen Garay, into whose family he was received.

MON AUG 16, 1847
Mrs Eliza Williams, w/o Rev Gershom Williams, of Scott, Wayne Co, Pa, was murdered on Aug 1, while on her way to a Sabbath school, in which she was a teacher. The murderer is an Englishman, named John Bell, recently liberated from the penitentiary in Phil. This man was immediately apprehended, & confessed that he had strangled her.

The venerable mother of the late Judge Story, widow of Dr Elisha Story, died at East Boston on Monday last, in her 89th year. No one could know this lady & her late distinguished son without perceiving how many of his striking qualities were derived from her.

Fire broke out last Sat in Mr W G Bitner's locksmith's shop, on Pa ve, between 17th & 18th sts. The flames communicated to the grocery store, kept by Mr Jas H McBlair, which, as well as Mr Bitner's shop, was totally consumed.

The body of a white man was found last Sat in the Potomac river. He was a well dressed man, about 35 years of age, & a Catholic prayer book was found in his pocket, with the name of Michl Sexton, thought to be the unfotunate sufferer.

Mr Jos D Gorman, one of the North Carolina volunteers for the Mexican war, returned to Raleigh on Sat week, having been discharged from service on account of bad health. He left Gen Taylor's camp on Jul 1, at which time & place he heard from the North Carolina regt. They were then at Saltillo, where they would remain until Gen Taylor was ready to make his advance upon San Luis Potosi. There have been 125 deaths in the regt, & about 200 on the sick list, many of them dangerously so. -Register

Mantles, Monuments, & Headstones for sale: at Marble Yard on Pa ave, & 11th st.
-Alex Rutherford

Mrd: on Thu last, in Wash City, by Rev Jas B Donelan, Mr John McClelland Roddy, of Alexandria, to Miss Ann McAdams, of Wash City.

For sale or rent: highly finished residence on the heights of Gtwn, opposite Col Robinson's. Inquire of M Duffey, near the premises.

TUE AUG 17, 1847

Portrait frames, curtain cornices: opposite the burnt Theatre, & next door west of the Apollo Hall. Looking-glass plates constantly kept on hand. -Francis Lamb, opposite the Union ofc.

Land for sale: the estate lately the homestead of their father, Wm Penn, near Allen's Fresh, Chas Co, Md: contains about 765 acres; dwlg is elevated & healthy; all necessary family bldgs are in good repair. -Benj Penn, Alex'r Penn

Trustee's sale of real estate: by decree of Chas Co Court, in Equity: public sale in Port Tobacco on Sep 7, all those tracts of land in said county of which Annie M Hamilton, dec'd, late of Chas Co, was seized as tenant in common with Alex'r Hamilton, consisting of a tract of land upon the Potomac river, being part of ***Cornwallis' Neck***, containing 500 acres, more or less, & a tract lying upon Port Tobacco run, composed of certain tracts or parts of tracts called, ***Part of St Matthew***, ***Part of Green Spring***, & ***Part of Carpenter's Square***, containing 180 acres. ***Cornwallis' Neck*** adjoins the farms of Thos Irvin, & Capt Leonard Marbury, & lies between the Potomac river & Mattawoman creek: small dwlg upon the place, also a barn & other out-houses. -John W Mitchell, Trustee

In Kingston, N H, Col Wm Webster, aged 67, married Miss Martha Winslow, aged 19. The bridegroom has married his sister's grand-dght, which makes the bride a wife to her great uncle, sister to her grandfather & grandmother, & aunt to her father & mother, & great aunt to her brothers & sisters. She is stepmother to 5 children, 14 grand children, & one great grand child.

A child of Mr Andrew Howe, of Townsend, Mass, was poisoned week before last with a green card which the child put in its mouth. The fluids of the green pigment dissolved in the child's mouth: antidotes were applied and the child is doing well.

From Tampico: On the 27th a plot was discovered by which some of the privates of the Louisiana regt were found to have been in the habit of stealing cartridges & selling them to the Mexicans. In one Mexican house over 60 pounds were found concealed in a demijohn, & a proportionate quantity of balls. Two men were already in confinement, one belonging to Co D, & one in Co H, & it was supposed more would be implicated, & that it had been going on for some time. The price received was .75 for 6 cartridges, or a bit of a piece.

Chas Co Court, sitting as Court of Equity, Jul Term, 1847. Thos Skinner vs Wm Posey & others. This cause is to obtain a decree for the sale of the real estate of Hendly Posey, late of Chas Co, dec'd. Posey died seized & possessed of certain lands in said county, that he left several heirs at law, the following of whom are non-residentsof this State: Wm Posey, Robt Posey, Middleton Posey, Mary Posey, Thos Posey, & Edw Henderson; that there is no personal property of said Posey out of which said claims may be paid. Non-resident dfndnts to appear in this court on or before the 3rd Mon in Feb next.
-Edmund Key, W Mitchell, clerk

Leesburg Academy, Va, has procured the services of Mr Wm B Benedict as Principal & of Mr John Wildman as Assist Teacher. Mr Benedict has been long engaged as an instructor of youth, & for 7 years last past as Prof of Mathematics in the U S Navy. Mr Wildman graduated at the Virginia Military Institute.

Geo Rapp, the founder of Economy, Pa, & the greatest communitist of the age, is dead. He died on Aug 9, aged 92 years: was a native of Germany, & emigrated to this country half a century ago with a band of followers, with his own peculiar religious, policital, & social views. His niece is his heiress, but, as celibacy is a peculiarity of their creed, the stock will of course soon run out.

Died: at Elizabethtown, N J, Marvin Hale, Proprietor & Editor of the Elizabethtown Journal: his death was caused by lock-jaw, resulting from the injury which he received a few days since on the railroad. He was a gentleman of exceeding amiability, but had suffered several severe misfortunes during his life, among which were deafness & the loss of an eye. [No death date given-recent item.]

Died: on Aug 8, at the residence of his brother, Jedediah Strong, in Chester township, Burlington, Co, N J, Hon Jas Strong, of N Y C, aged 64 years, formerly for several years a Rep in Congress from the State of N Y.

Died: on Aug 4, at his residence in Newcastle, Delaware, Jos Sawyer, in his 84th year. He was born near the village of Port Penn, where he devoted the early years of life to agricultural pursuits. He then entered the revenue service of the U S, in which, for a considerable time, he was employed as a lt, & then as capt of one of the cutters. He retired from that service & was appointed inspector of the port of Newcastle, which ofc he held until the election of Gen Jackson to the Presidency.

Died: on Aug 11, at the residence of her brother, Jacob Hume, Fauquier Co, Va, Miss Jane Hume, in her 55th year. During a long & severe illness she evinced the same gentleness & Christian resignation which had marked her through life.

Trustee's sale of real estate at the Great Falls of the Potomac, including valuable Water Power. By 2 deeds of trust, executed by Chapman S Monroe, dec'd, & Ann his wife, of N Y C, to the undersigned trustees, dated Dec 3, 1845, one of record in the Clerk's ofc of the County Court of Fairfax & State of Va, the other in the Clerk's ofc of Montg Co, Md: sale on Sep 20 next, at the Courthouse of Fairfax Co, Va: one tract of land in Fairfax Co, on the Potomac river at Great Falls, containing 761 acres; one other tract of land in Montg Co, Md, lying in the river Potomac, near the Great Falls, & known as ***Bishop's*** or ***Conn's Island***. The title is believed to be unquestionable. For further information apply to Thos George, Atty at Law, N Y C; to Cmdor Thos Ap C Jones, Prospect Hill, Va, or to either of the trustees. -John Marron, Trustee, Wash, D C; Thos R Love, Trustee, Fairfax Courthouse, Va.

Whereas the Postmaster, Edw D Boon, has been removed from the Post Ofc at Beantown, Chas Co, Md, & without cause or complaint, I hereby request all persons who may correspond with me in any way, [by letters, documents, or otherwise,] to please direct them to Bryantown post ofc, Chas Co, Md. -Geo Gardiner

Alex'r Henry died at Phil on Fri last, in his 82nd year. His long life has been a continued exercise of benevolence, & the sanctity of a bright religious faith ennobled his motives.

WED AUG 18, 1847

Naval Academy: the annual examination of the Midshipmen was closed at Annapolis on Aug 7, & the following is a list of those who have been successfully passed by the Board of Examiners:

John L Davis	Thos Roney	Wm Sharp
W K Bridge	J M Brooke	Robt Selden
W R Thomas	A F Monroe	Thos C Eaton
J S Thornton	W H Fauntleroy	The L Walker
W H Willcox	W W Brodhead	H C Hunter
W H Reily	John Wilkes, jr	S S Bassett
W T Truxtun	W P Buckner	J H Somerville
W Gibson	R J D Price	L H Lyne
R L Law	Thos C Harris	Jos Fry
John T Walker	W H Murdaugh	E D Denny
N T West	M P Jones	John T Barraud
A C Jackson	O C Badger	
J Van McCollan	Jas Armstrong	

These names are given in the order of appointment, & not in the order of merit. The class of 41 is so large that a great part of it will remain to be examined during the coming year.

U S Flag-ship **Mississippi**: Anton Lizardo, Jul 25, 1847. Having this moment returned from Tabasco, I write a brief line to inform the dept: we have had 9 deaths, including Lt Parker, the only ofcr who has died. -M C Perry, Commanding Home Squardron: to Hon J Y Mason, Sec of the Navy, Wash.

A multilated seaman came to see us today. His name is John Mitchell, a native of Kennebunk, Maine: he was a seaman on the U S steamer **Alabama**; but both his arms, one below the elbow & the other above the wrist, were taken off by the accidental discharge of a gun on board the steamer during the celebration of the victories of Gens Scott & Taylor, on May 15 last, in the port of New Orleans. Capt Windle, commanding the steamer **Alabama**, certifies to his being an honest, industrious, & worthy man. He is now regularly discharged from the service of the U S, but he cannot receive a pension, & has been advised to remain in Wash for the purpose of memoralizing Congress at the next session. The poor fellow is helpless; he is unable to dress or undress himself, or feed himself without help. It is hoped that this appeal to the humanity of the citizens of Wash will not be in vain.

Died: on Aug 10, at Hayfield, near Alexandria, Fairfax Co, Va, Rosalie Allen, infant daughter of
H Allen Taylor, aged 13 months.

House in Pollard's Row for sale or rent: lately occupied by Mr W Thompson, containing 9 rooms. -Bates & Brother, G st, Soap & Candle Manufacturers

Zanesville papers: accident on Aug 2, near that place: three persons in a skiff, after passing the steamboat **Mingo Chief**, were swamped by a huge roller. Mr Sanders & his wife & a young man named Steinbrook were drowned. Their bodies were recovered.

A negro man, Richd Bays, was arrested yesterday & committed for trial under the charge of stealing from Mr Chas Horneller, butcher, his coat, gloves, & silk handkerchief, while Mr Horneller was engaged in his stall in the Centre Market.

Quatepec, Jul 19, 1847. At this place I have arrived today, & am to rendezvous at Hualusco until I am exchanged. It is unnecessary to say that Gen Soto has received me with courtesy & assures me I shall be exchanged the first opportunity. He has assigned my residence as above: rendering it peculiarly eligible to a prisoner of war. I was captured in my camp dress; I am in want of clothing. My health is excellent. I beg that in some manner my brother, Dr Alonzo Whipple, Wentworth, Grafton Co, N H, may be informed of my safety & health. -Thos Whipple, 1st Lt & Adj 9th Infty. To his Excellency Gov Wilson.

By virtue of a writ of distrain from C P Van Ness against the goods & chattels of Francis S Murphy, I have levied on the frame shop, on G st, between 6th & 7th sts, on part of lot 5 in square 454, which I shall proceed to sell, according to law, on Aug 24, to the highest bidder for cash, to satisfy a bill of rent due & unpaid. -Danl McPherson

For sale of exchange for well-improved property in Wash City on Pa ave: a tract of land in Alexandria Co, containing about 241 acres, according to survey of Lewis Carbery, made in 1840 by order of Court, in which survey is reported 34½ acres disputed by adjoining land holders, leaving in said report 206½ acres free of dispute. The land is in the Ten Miles Square, about 1½ miles from the Gtwn ferry; with a small wooden tenement, of little value, occupied by Mr Stummond S Crabb, on a few enclosed acres. Inquire of Anthony R Fraser, 1 mile south of the first tollgate on the Columbian Turnpike, leading from the Potomac bridge.

THU AUG 19, 1847

Major Smith, U S Quartermaster at Vera Cruz, died on Jul 24.

The Classical & Military Academy in Raleigh, N C, under the superindendence of Prof T J Lovejoy, is the first school in the State. The military arrangements are similar to those at West Point, & in the classical dept a full collegiate course is taught. The academy at his time numbers about 90 boys.

On Jul 10 there arrived in the village of St Paul, near St Peters & the Falls of St Anthony, on the Upper Mississippi, the most original looking Caravan. There is an isolated settlement of several thousand inhabitants in a high latitiude of British North America, known as the Selkirk Settlement. They are cut off from the commerce of the world, & rely entirely upon their own resources, their farms, their flocks, fishing & hunting, for support. Their chief point of contact was Toronto, but now they trade at St Paul. The caravan was made up of men & boys of all ages; their clothing varied except they all wore moccasins. -Wisconsin Herald

Pursuant to a decree of the Circuit Superior Court of Law & Chancery for Monroe Co, Va, pronounced on May 14, 1847, in the case of Caperton, exc, against John B Lewis & others, dfndnts: & Dunlap against the same dfndnts, the undersigned com'rs will expose to sale, at public auction, to the highest bidder, on the premises, on Sep 30, that beautiful & valuable estate the ***Sweet Springs***, & the lands appertenant thereto, lying in Monroe Co, & extending into Alleghany Co: 23 miles from Covington: on this property is a Brick Hotel & other houses for visiters for the most part cabins: contains 159 acres. Also will be sold, all the Household & Kitchen Furniture belonging to the ***Sweet Springs***.
-Jas L Woodville, Henry Massie, Com'rs

Valuable North Branch of Potomac Lands for sale: by a decree of the Circuit Superior Court of Law & Chancery for Hampshire Co, Va, pronounced on Apr 15, 1847, in the cause of John McDowell & Jas Gibson & Graham & Miller, cmplnts, & the executor, widow, & heirs of Wm Naylor, dec'd, dfndnts, I will sell, on the premises, at public auction, on Aug 31, that valuable farm on the North Branch of Potomac river, 6 miles east of Cumberland, containing 475 acres, a large proportion of which is bottom land.
-John Kern, jr, Special Com'r

Mrd: on Aug 16, at Brown's Hotel, by Rev L J Gilliss, Henry F Thornton to Miss Mary Smith Thornley, of Va.

Died: on Aug 1, at Hamilton Place, Maury Co, Tenn, Mrs Mary Ann Polk, w/o Lucius J Polk, & daughter of the late Wm Eastin, in her 38th year. She was born in Davidson Co, Tenn, on Jul 25, 1810, & married in Washington on Apr 10, 1832.

Died: on Sat last, at Norfolk, of apoplexy, Dr Wm Moseley, who for more than 20 years was one of the most eminent physicians of that borough, & a gentleman highly esteemed for his amiable qualities.

$20 reward for the apprehension of an indented apprentice to the Blacksmith business, who absconded about Jul 9, named Mathew Procter. -Bernard Grason, 12th st, opposite Ward's Lumber Yard

Household & Kitchen furniture at auction on Aug 23, at the residence of the Rev C A Davis, who is declining housekeeping, on H, between 18th & 19th sts.
-A Green, auctioneer

FRI AUG 20, 1847

Farm for sale: on Aug 30, on the premises, that valuable Farm on which Mrs Hodge now resides, containing 125 acres, more or less, lying in PG Co, Md, bordering on the District line, & adjoining the lands of Messrs Sheriff & Darnold. Improvements consist of 2 comfortable tenements, a large barn, nearly new, stables & shed for stock, & other necessary out-bldgs. At the same time will be sold the growing crop, farming utensils, horses & cows, carryall, cart, & harness of all kinds. -Middleton & Beall

The Beaver [Pa] Argus, noticing the death of Geo Rapp, who was so many years the Principal of Economy, states that he came to this country in 1804, & first organized an associtation of Harmony, Butler Co, where the community system, or union of labor & property, was fairly tested.

Wash, Aug 19, 1847. Whereas Messrs Cornelius P Van Ness & others, heirs at law of Gen John P Van Ness, late of Wash City, have, by their deed of indenture, executed on Aug 4, 1847, conveyed to the subscriber all the real estate in D C & in the State of Va, which stood in the name of said John P Van Ness at the time of his death, in trust, for the purposes in said deed mentioned; & whereas it is one of the purposes of said deed that a portion of the real estate should be disposed of, & the proceeds applied to the payment of such unsatisfied claims against the estate of said Van Ness, which had passed the Orphans Court of Wash Co, D C, or which should be passed by said Court by Nov 1 next, & against which there is no offset nor objection: Now this is to give notice to all persons having such claims to present the same to the subscriber, on or before Nov 1 next; otherwise they may be excluded from all benefit or participation in the fund set apart to pay the same. -Rd Smith, Trustee

Died: on Monday last, Richd Hyatt, son of Mr Seth Hyatt, aged 18 years.

From Santa Fe: information received at Bagos, 75 miles this side of Santa Fe, that Lt Brown, attached to Capt Horine's company of volunteers, with privates McClenahan & Quisenberry, & a Mexican guide, had been killed at a small place about 15 miles from Bagos. They had left camp in pursuit of persons who had stolen horses from them, &, not returning, on Jul 5 information was received from a Mexican woman that they had been murdered. Maj Edmonson, on receiving the news, took measures to avenge their deaths. The bodies of 2 of the Americans were burnt, but the body of Lt Brown, who had the emblem of the cross on his neck, supposed to be a Catholic, was hid in the mountains, where it was found. All the houses of the persons concerned in the murder were burnt to the ground by the order of the Major. He marched with some 60 men, & found the men fleeing to the mountains, & killed 6 of them, & took 40 or 50 prisoners. An express reached Bagos on Jul 6, stating that 30 men of Capt Morin's company, a grazing party, belonging to Lt Col Willock's btln, had been attacked by about 200 Mexicans on the Seneca: among the killed were Lt Larkin & privates Owens, Wright, Mason, & Wilson.

Boston papers: loss of life incurred by passengers on board the Swedish barque **Iduna**, from coming in collision at sea with the ship **Shanunga**. The **Iduna** was from Hamburg, bound for N Y, with 206 persons on board. She was commanded by Capt Arnest Andreas Moberg. On Aug 9, the weather foggy, she came in contact with the ship **Shanunga**, Capt Patten, from Liverpool for Boston, & sunk in 30 minutes. 172 perished. Names of those who were saved: Edw Kaiser, cabin passenger; Teresa Lithner, cabin passenger

Steerage passengers:

Carl Lausen
Leohard Rohshuber
A Werster
Fred'k Rohr
Carle Setz & wife
Danl Gunthee
Fred'k Kaseburg
Johanna Wenzel
Heinrich Frohlose & dght
Jos Forster
Johnanna Knight
Gothee Shultz & wife
Anton Buttner
Christopher Glocke
Johnanna Gessner
Fred'k Mahnhort
Andreas Long & son
Heinrich Hoffman
Susannah Schelbecker
Barbara Larkden

Seamen:

P G Wiberg, 1st mate
Hayfroon, 2nd mate
Cloff Soderlann
John Medburg
Elias Lindstron
Peter Carlshorn
Justoff Mohttohon

The passengers of the **Iduna** were industrious Swedes, who were coming to this country with considerable sums of money in their possession, for the purpose of purchasing farms & settling in the West. It is supposed that Capt Moberg, master of the barque, had $1,400 in gold about his person. A little girl, 12 years old, lost her father, mother, brother, & sister.

Died: on Wed, Allen Munro, aged 2 years & 9 months, only child of Geo & Harriet Gregory. His funeral is this morning at 10 o'clock.

For sale or rent, the residence of the late S Humphrey, east end of Gay st, Gtwn. The lot extends to Olive st, upon which there is a carriage-house & stable. Inquire of Mrs L Humphreys, on the premises, Gtwn.

Washington in 1800, with a brief notice of the first session of Congress in that city: by John Cotton Smith. [The first Congress under the Constitution was held in N Y C.] The States of Va & Md ceded to the U S the territory which now constitutes D C, comprising the cities of Alexandria & Gtwn, with the projected city of Washington. I arrived at the end of my journey to Washington, passing through a region less hilly & less smitten with the blight of slavery, particularly 2 plantations, one of which belonged to the Hon John Chew Thomas, then a member of Congress, 18 miles from Wash. One wing of the Capitol only had been erected, which, with the Pres' house, a mile distant from it, both constructed with white sandstone, were shining objects in dismal contrast with the scene around them. Instead of recognizing the avenues & streets portrayed on the plan of the city, not one was visible, unless we except a road with 2 bldgs on each side of it, called the N J ave. The Pennsylvania, leading as laid down on the papers, from the Capitol to the Pres' mansion, was then nearly the whole distance a deep morass, covered with alder bushes, which were cut through the width of the intended ave during the then ensuing winter. Between the Pres' house & Gtwn a block of house had been erected, which bore the name of six bldgs. There were also 2 other blocks consisting of 2 or 3 dwlg houses, in different directions, & now & then an insulated wooden habitation; the intervening spaces, &, indeed the surface of the city generally, being covered with shrub oak bushes on the higher grounds, & on the marshy soil either trees or some sort of shrubbery. There were a number of unfinished edifices at **Greenleaf's Point**, commenced by an individual whose name they bore, but the state of whose funds compelled him to abandon them. There appeared to be but 2 comfortable habitations within the bounds of the city, one of which belonged to Dudley Carroll, & the other to Notley Young, who were the former proprietors of a large proportion of the land appropriated to the city, but who reserved for their own accommodation ground sufficient for gardens & other useful appurtenances. The roads in every direction were muddy & unimproved. Our party took lodgings with a Mr Peacock, in one of the houses on N J ave, with the addition of Senators Tracy, of Conn, & Chipman & Paine, of Vt; & Reps Thomas, of Md, & Dana, Edmond, & Griswold, of Conn. Speaker Sedgwick was allowed a room to himself, the rest of us in pairs. Davenport & myself were allotted a spacious & decently furnished apartment, with separate beds, on the lower floor. A large portion of the Southern members took lodgings at Gtwn. I express my admiration of its local position. From the Capitol you have a distinct view of the fine undulating surface, situated at the confluence of the Potomac & its eastern branch, the wide expanse of that majestic river to the bend at ***Mount Vernon***, the cities of Alexandria & Gtwn, & the cultivated fields & blue hills of Md & Va on either side of the river. The city has delightful water.

$25 reward for runaway negro woman Serena, 30 years of age. She is a mulatto.
-Arundel Smith, near Bladensburg, PG Co, Md

Sumner Hudson, a merchant of Boston, died very suddenly on Saturday night.

A letter from the correspondent of the Missouri Republican, dated Belleville on Aug 9, announced the accidental death of Dr W G Goforth. He was thrown from a horse he was considering buying, when it started at full speed. He was thrown with great force to the ground & lingered until that evening. He served in the last war with Great Britain, & received a wound in the memorable battle of New Orleans.

SAT AUG 21, 1847

A street fight occurred in New Orleans on Aug 12th between M C Edwards & Maj Orran Byrd, in which Maj Byrd was killed, having received 2 wounds from a revolving pistol. [Aug 23rd newspaper: Mr Edwards, on being taken before Recorder Baldwin, gave security for his appearance & was liberated. -Picayune] [Aug 30th newspaper: the case was dismissed on Aug 17, the Recorder being satisfied that Mr Edwards acted purely in self defence.]

Mrd: on Aug 19, by Rev Mr Mathews, Mr John Kerrow to Miss Jane C Whitaker, both of Wash City.

Died: on Aug 12, at his residence, in the town of Falmouth, Va, Dr Alex'r Fitzhugh, in his 61st year. He was a highly educated physician, & at the time of his death one of the oldest practitioners in the State.

One day this week a party of young men from Randolph, left the shore in a skiff for the purpose of boarding a sloop, intending to have a sail on her; but the skiff capsized, & Asa French Thayer, Simeon Smith, & Lewis Smith, were drowned. -Boston Post

Peter G Stuyvesant, an old, respectable, & wealthy citizen of N Y, left that city about a week ago, with his wife & niece, on an excursion to the Lakes, & although at the age of 75, was in the injoyment of excellent health. It appears that at the time of his death he was bathing in the "Plunging Bath" near the hotel, & on search being made found to be dead. He was the lineal descendant of Gov Stuyvesant, & the inheritor of a large portion of the family fortune. Next to Mr Astor he was the wealthiest individual in the city, & probably one of the richest in the country. His possessions in N Y are vast indeed, principally in real estate in the 11th, 16th, & 17th Wards. He has left a wife only, never, we believe, having had children.

Orphans Court of Wash Co, D C. In the case of the estate of Lewis G Davidson, dec'd. Saml G Davidson, Trustee, reported that on Jul 22 be exposed to sale, the following lots, being part of the unimproved & unproductive real estate of the late Lewis G Davidson, & that at such sale Chas H Winder became the purchaser of lots 1 thru 6 in square 170 for $1,893.50; & that Alex'r H Mechlin became the purchaser of lots 5 & 6 in square 126 for $1,096.16, all in Wash City. -Nathl Pope Causin -Ed N Roach, Reg/o wills

For rent: the commodious dwlg house on Bridge st, Gtwn, long the residence of Mrs Gen Forrest. -Dr Bohrer's, Gay st, Gtwn

For rent: the 2 story brick dwlg on 7th st, near I st, next adjoining the residence of Andrew Rothwell. Inquire of R W Dyer, auct, or of the subscriber, on 8th st, between E & F.
-Jane Maria Dyer

MON AUG 23, 1847
Pittsburg American of Aug 18. Died, on board the steamer **Old Hickory**, on its way up the Mississippi, the Hon Thos Butler, aged 64 years. He was the son of Col Thos Butler, one of that military family so famous in the early history of the country. Judge Butler was an eminent planter, a resident of West Felicina, La: at one time a Rep from that State in Congress; a native of Carlisle, Pa, but was brought up & went to school in Pittsburg. He emigrated at an early period to the Southwest.

Naval School: 2 gentlemen of the class of 1840 who were also examined & passed: Colville Terrett, of Indiana, appointed Jan 3, 1840; W F Davidson, of Va, appointed Feb 20, 1840.

Martinsburg Gaz: Fancy Ball at Berkeley Springs, Va, on Aug 11. The hero of the evening was Maj Jack Downing, who had stopped here on his return from Mexico. He wore, during the dance, a remarkably tall cocked hat, with a corresponding plume, & a very long sword. Many persons not acquainted with the Major's phiz mistook him for Gen Pillow, at which he was very indignant.

The funeral of Peter G Stuyvesant was held on Aug 21 at St Mark's Church, where the solemnities of the Episcopal service were performed & the coffin was then deposited in the old Stuyvesant vault, under the church. The present church bldg has been erected about half a century in which Govn't Stuyvesant used to worship, & near by the old pear tree which he planted some 200 years ago, & which still continues to bear fruit, though it is 165 years since the Govn'r himself fell asleep. In the church yard of St Mark's are many family vaults of old & wealthy families, among them I noticed that of Danl D Tompkins, formerly Vice Pres of the U S. After the corpse was deposited, I went into the vault. It now contains 9 coffins of grown persons, & 5 or 6 children. [He had 2 or 3 children by a former wife, but they sleep with their mother in the family vault.] Among them rest the remains of Petrus Stuyvesant, who, though the pen of genius has embalmed his memory in burlesque, was undoubtedly an able & worthy govn'r & a brave & gallant soldier.
Over the entrance of the vault is the inscription: In this vault lies buried /Petrus Stuyvesant, /Late Captain-General & Governor-in-chief of Amsterdam, /in New Netherland, now called New York, /And the Dutch West India Islands. Died in August A D/ 1682, aged 80 years.

Dr Hawkins, of Balt, the senior Surgeon & Medical Director of Tampico, died on Aug 7, after an illness of several days.

On Nov 16, 1847, at 10 o'clock, I will sell, at the ofc of the Clerk of the Corp, at auction, for cash, the following lots & parts of lots of ground, in Gtwn; the same being seized by me for taxes due thereon to the Corp of Gtwn:
All that part of lot 252 in Beatty & Hawkins' addition; as originally laid out by the Rev Stephen Bloomer Balch. Likewise, all that part of lot 13, in said Wilberforestown, as laid out. Both properties being assessed together in the name of Wm Koontz, otherwise Kuhns' heirs. Taxes due: $27.50, for years 1845 thru 1847.
Lot 19, Deakins, Lee, & Casenave's addition. Assessed to Mary G D Ringgold. Taxes due: $1.50, for years 1846 & 1847.
Part of lot 83, Deakins, Lee, & Casenave's addition. Assessed to Tench Ringgold. Taxes due: $6.75, for years 1846 & 1847.
Lot not numbered, in Threlkeld's square, Threlkeld's addition, on the West side of Fayette st, running back of the same to the grounds of Col John Cox; being bounded on the south by Mrs Benj Clarke's lot. Assessed to Ann Cruit. Taxes due: $2.75, for years 1846 & 1847.
Part of lot not numbered, in Threlkeld's square, Threlkeld's addition, on the west side of Fayette st. Assessed to the heirs of Gabriel Duvall. Taxes due: $1.30, for the year 1847.
Lot 39, Holmead's addition. Assessed to Wm S Allison. Taxes due: $1.50, for 1847.
-Wm Jewell, Collector of the Corp of Gtwn

Orphans Court of Wash Co, D C. Ordered that letters of administration on the personal estate of Mary Smith, of Gtwn, D C, dec'd, be granted to Jas P Kerby. -Ed N Roach, Reg/o wills

Later from Vera Cruz. A wagon train of considerable extent left Verz Cruz on Aug 6, with an escort of 1,500 men. It was to have been commanded by Col Louis D Wilson, of N C, but he was taken suddenly ill with the fever on Aug 5, when Major Lally took charge.

The Quartermaster Smith who died of vomito at Vera Cruz on Jul 24, was Capt Henry Smith, an old & cherished friend. He was extensively known & greatly esteemed in this State & in Michigan. Henry Smith was a native of Stillwater, Saratoga Co. In 1812 he was our fellow apprentice in the printing ofc of Messrs Seward & Williams, at Utica. His uncle, Moses Smith, kept a hotel on the corner of Orange & North Market sts. The present war found Capt Smith a private citizen, residing with his family at Monroe, Mich.

TUE AUG 24, 1847
From the Western Plains: from the reports, it seems probable that Kit Carson, who was going out with dispatches to Calif, has lost all his horses & mules. He was seen near the Pawnee Rock, & afterwards heard from by a party who said they had passed him the day following, & that his mules & horses had all been stolen the night previous. From Carson's well known knowledge of the woods & familiarity with the Indian character, the St Louis Republican is disposed to doubt the correctness of the report.

Sealed proposals will be received at the Ofc of the Solicitor of the Treasury until Oct 25, for the purchase of the interest of the U S, at law & in equity, of the property described, upon the terms & conditions mentioned below, to wit:

Lands lying in the State of Mass:

Land acquired from the Commonwealth Bank, Boston, May, 1838: property in South Boston.

Lands lying in the State of Vt:

Land acquired from Nathan B Haswell, Jul, 1816: undivided half of 200 acres: Burlington Co.

Land acquired from Jona M Blaisdell, Sep, 1831: 8 + acres, near St Alban's: Franklin Co

Lands lying in the State of New York:

Land acquired from Saml Swartwout, Jun, 1839: lots in N Y C.

Land acquired from Silas E Burrows, Jan, 1841: lots in the City of Troy.

Land acquired from Chas F Codwise, Oct, 1846: lots in the City of Brooklyn.

Lands lying in the State of N J:

Land acquired from Saml Swartwout, Jun, 1839: tracts of land & Docks in Bergen Co.

Lands lying in the State of Pa:

Land acquired from Benj F Johnson, Apr, 1835: lots in Schuylkill Co.

Lands lying in the State of Md:

Land acquired from Saml Swartwout, Mar, 1842: shares of stock in the Md & N Y Iron & Coal Co.

Lands lying in the State of Virginia:

Land acquired from Wm H Dundas, May, 1839: tracts of land in Randolph Co: Kenawha Co, Fairfax Co, Alexandria Co.

Land acquired from Saml Swartwout, May, 1839: part of a tract of land in Hampshire Co.

Lands lying in the State of Mississippi:

Land acquired from Gordon D Boyd, former owner, Sep 1839: in Attala Co, Choctaw Co.

Land acquired from Zach Rector, former owner, Jun, 1844: in Attala Co, Holmes Co, Carroll Co, Choctaw Co.

Land acquired from Geo B Dameron, former owner, May, 1840: land in Hinds Co.

Land acquired from Danl Fore, former owner: land in Brandon Co.

Lands lying in the State of Louisiana:

Lands acquired from Richd M Carter, Jan, 1843: half part of a tract of land in the Parish of Plaquemines.

Lands lying in Ky:

Land acquired from Jas C Wilson, Apr, 1834: one seventh part of a tract of 11,000 acres, in Mason Co.

Lands lying in the State of Indiana:

Land acquired from Israel T Canby, former owner, Aug, 1833: land near Logansport, in Miami Co, in Wabash Co.

Land acquired from John Milroy, former owner: Dec, 1843: land in Miami Co.

Lands lying in the State of Illinois:

Land acquired from Wm Linn, former owner, Oct, 1843: land in Clarke Co, Effingham Co, Macon Co, Coles Co, Shelby Co, McLean Co, Clay Co, Morgan Co, Fayette Co, town of Vandalia.

Land acquired from the heirs of Jos Duncan, former owner, Aug, 1846: land in Bureau Co, Peoria Co, Starke Co, Henry Co, Fulton Co, Knox Co, McDonough Co, Warren Co, Mercer Co, Henderson Co.
Land acquired from Eli S Prescott, former owner, Jan, 1846: land in Henderson Co.
Land acquired from Geo Abernethy, former owner, Oct, 1846: land in Henderson Co.
Land acquired from J B F Russell, former owner, Apr, 1843: land in Will Co, Grundy Co, Coake Co.
Land acquired from Saml Swartwout, former owner, Nov, 1843: land in La Dalle Co, Grundy Co. Lands were conveyed by Saml Swartwout to Wm Young, late Pres of the Mount Savage Coal & Iron Co.
Lands lying in the State of Missouri:
Land acquired from Wm Rector, former owner, Aug, 1840: land in Linn Co, Chariton Co.
Lands lying in the State of Arkansas:
Land acquired from David Thompson, former owner, Dec, 1845: land on the Mississippi river near the mouth of Scrubgrass.
Land acquired from Wharton Rector, former owner, Mar, 1845: land in Pulaski Co, Jefferson Co.
Land acquired from Laban C Howell & others, former owners, Apr, 1845: land in Pope Co, Johnson Co, town of Clarksville.
Land acquired from Lucius Lyon & Calvin Britain, sureties of Allen Hutchins, former owner, Aug, 1844: lots in village of St Jos, Berrien Co.
Land acquired from Henry R Schoolcraft, former owner, May, 1845: land in Oakland Co, Macomb Co, Barry Co, Saginaw Co.
Land acquired from Allen Hutchins, former owner, Aug, 1842: land in Village of Ionia, Ionia Co, Village of Lyons.
Lands lying in the State of Texas:
Land acquired from Saml Swartwout, former owner, Mar, 1842: tract of land granted by the Republic of Texas to Y Barbos, whose atty was Frost Thorn, which grant is described in a deed made by Vetal Flores, to Barbos, Jun, 1834. Also one certificate of lands issued by John T Mason, Jun, 1834. Lands conveyed by Saml Swartwout to Wm Young, late Pres of the Mount Savage Coal & Iron Co.
Lands lying in the State of Florida:
Land acquired from Lewis H Bryant, et al, former owners, Jan, 1844: town of Jacksonville, Duval Co.
Lands lying in the Terriroty of Wisconsin:
Lands acquired from Thos Lee, former owner, May, 1842: in town of Astor, Brown Co
Lands lying in the State of Iowa:
Land acquired from Benj S Roberts, former owner, Mar, 1845: 2,800 acres; reservation of land conveyed to Roberts by deed, dated May 25, 1837, recorded in Lee Co, in the former Territory of Wisconsin; subject to an agreement made to Mary Roberts to the value of one-twelfth of one entire claim.
-R H Gillet, Solicitor of the Treasury

Died: yesterday, in Wash City, Samuel, son of Saml J & Margaret Little, aged 3 years & 6 months. His funeral is on Aug 25, at 4 o'clock, at the residence of his father, on L st south, near the Navy Yard.

Died: on Aug 23, at Bladensburg, of consumption, Maria Lee Comegys, aged 15 years, youngest daughter of the late J B Comegys, of Boston, Mass.

Meeting on Aug 14, at which Capt E S Harding, U S A, presided, the following preamble & resolutions, reported by Wilson McCandless were unanimously adopted. Lt Parker, whose death we deplore, has left to his family no inheritance but an illustrious name. His wife & children are in our midst. 1-Resolved: that an annuity be purchased for the support of the family & education of the children of Lt Jas Lawrence Parker. 2-Resolved, that a subscription for the above object be commenced forthwith. 3-Resolved, that Hon Harmar Denny, Dr Jos P Gazzam, John H Shoenberger, Jas Ross, jr, Andrew Burke, Col Wm Robinson, & Maj John Sanders, be a cmte to expend the "Parker Fund," in the purchase of an annuity.

WED AUG 25, 1847

Died: yesterday, in Wash City, Samuel, son of Saml J & Margaret Little, aged 3 years & 6 months. His funeral is on Aug 25, at 4 o'clock, at the residence of his father, on L st south, near the Navy Yard. [Repeated same as Aug 24th obituary.]

Meeting on Aug 14, at which Capt E S Harding, U S A, presided, the following preamble & resolutions, reported by Wilson McCandless were unanimously adopted. Lt Parker, whose death we deplore, has left to his family no inheritance but an illustrious name. His wife & children are in our midst. 1-Resolved: that an annuity be purchased for the support of the family & education of the children of Lt Jas Lawrence Parker. 2-Resolved, that a subscription for the above object be commenced forthwith. 3-Resolved, that Hon Harmar Denny, Dr Jos P Gazzam, John H Shoenberger, Jas Ross, jr, Andrew Burke, Col Wm Robinson, & Maj John Sanders, be a cmte to expend the "Parker Fund," in the purchase of an annuity.

Foreign news. The King of Belgium is out of health & out of spirits, but his good father-in-law, Louis Philippe, will not hear of his resignation, & urges him to leave the cares of his kingdom for a time to his wife & son, & pass some months in Italy. Leopold, like an obedient son-in-law, appears desirous of following his advice.

The steam frig **Mississippi** arrived on Aug 14 at Pensacola. Among the sick are Surgeon Lewis Minor & Passed Assist Surgeon John Thornley.

The Hon John Mattocks, ex-Govn'r of Vt, died at his residence in Peacham, Vt, on Sat last, aged 71. No man long in public life could boast of more or warmer friends than John Mattocks.

A splendid sword & epaulets have been presented to Lt Hunter, the victor of Alvarado, by citizens of N Y. The presentation speech was made by Jas T Brady. Many ofcrs of the Army & Navy were present.

The sugar-house of Mr Geo Broom, on Broad st, Phil, was fired by an incendiary on Sat, & entirely consumed. One of the walls fell upon a bldg in the rear of Newlin's brewery, & fell upon the Fairmount & Reliance engines, killing & maiming a number of those at work on them. Killed: Andrew Butler & Chas H Hines. Seriously injured: Elias Reed, Richd Wellington, [leg broken,] Fouden S Carll, Saml Hall, John Delaney, Peter Crouse, Wm Roberts, of N Y, & Jas Brown, of N Y. Less seriously injured: Wm Fitzpatrick, John & Augustus Slubb, Wm Masters, Fred'k Baun, Andrew Juffer, Geo Reese, Geo Brook, Wm Kigler, Geo Hoenhorsen, & John C Shilling. Mr Broom's loss is estimated at about $140,000, one fifth of which was covered by insurance. Mr Newlin's loss is about $25,000, but he was fully insured.

Wash Corp: 1-Memorial of Gilbert Cameron, praying for the privilege of landing the building materials for the Smithsonian Institution in Wash City free of wharfage: referred to the Cmte of Claims.

For rent: a 2 story brick dwlg-house on G st, east of Col T F Andrews'. To a good tenant to be rented for $150 per year. Inquire of Judson Mitchell, Gtwn, or A Ricketts, near the premises.

Notice to Whom it May Concern. The subscribers, trustees appointed by Wm Lorman, dec'd, & the heirs at law of Wm Crawford, dec'd, to hold the Union Tavern property in Gtwn D C, to secure sundry sums of money due to the subscribers to a fund raised to rebuild the said premises, & to sell the same on the failure of the proprietors of the said property to pay said sums of money at a time stipulated in the deed of trust, having, pursuant to the terms of the said deed sold the said premises, are prepared to pay to the subscribers, or to their duly authorized attys or reps, a first dividend of 37% on the amount of their respective subscriptions. The same will be paid by John Kurtz, at the Farmers & Mechanics' Bank of Gtwn, on Oct 4 next. Claimants will be required to produce the evidence of their several demands. -W S Nichols, John Kurtz, E M Linthicum

Numerous lots for sale in Wash City; also, lands in Alexandria Co, Va, known as the ***Glebe*** property, belonging to the estate of the late Gen Van Ness, containing about 1,300 acres; & also 2 valuable tracts of land in Westmoreland Co, Va, containing together about 362 acres, one of which is described in a deed from Isaac Pollock to Marcia Burns, afterwards Marcia Van Ness, dated Nov 16, 1801, & the other is a deed from said Pollock to J P Van Ness, dated Dec 31, 1802-both deeds being duly recorded in Westmoreland Co, Va. -Richd Smith, Trustee

THU AUG 26, 1847

For rent: the dwlg part of my House, over my lottery & exchange ofc, on Pa ave, between 4½ & 6th sts. Apply at my ofc, Alex Lee.

Regarding Mr John Cotton Smith's description of Washington in 1800, published in the Intelligencer of Fri last, I find it necessary to make a few corrects. The surface of the city was not covered with scrub-oak, which was not known to the District. The trees were oak, hickory, walnut, pine, & chestnut. I remember the windings of the picturesque stream called the Tiber, gliding along between magnificent oaks & underwood. This stream was once called ***Goose Creek***, & in the spring & autumn, overspread with wild ducks. It is said to have derived its classical name from a European who owned a farm near the Capitol, & whose name was Pope. But it is called the ***Tiber*** in deeds nearly 2 centuries old. He called his farm ***Rome***, the stream at the bottom of it the ***Tiber***, & the hill above Capitol Hill, on which he is said to have predicted, many years before the event took place, that a magnificent edifice would be erected which would be called the Capitol. Long before 1800 the leading avenues were formed by cutting down the trees in the woods through which they passed, & could be distinctly seen from the Capitol. In 1793 the road leading from the Pres' House [called by the Com'rs the Pres' Palace] to the Capitol, passed near the present Gen Post Ofc bldg, about 2 squares north of the Ave, & the ***Tiber*** was crossed by a rude bridge formed of a single log, & a little above by a few large stones, which, when the water was low, rendered the creek fordable. It was along this road that the procession, headed by Gen Washington passed to lay the corner-stone of the Capitol. The ceremony was concluded by a barbecue. The public road leading into Montg Co wound pass within a few yards of the spring. The old domicil of Mr Carroll was pulled down by Maj L'Infant, the engineer, &, as it would seem, without the orders of the Com'rs, who subsequently dismissed him for it. The only brick bldg on the banks of the Potomac was the one owned & occupied by Mr Notley Young: built of brick imported from England about 50 years before. From the want of a church, this house was occasionally used as a place of worship by the Roman Catholics, & Rev Mr Plunkitt was the officiating priest. Mr Young's house, like Mr Carroll's, was on one of the streets; but, in consequence of the interposition of Gen Washington, who wrote to the Comr's on the subject, it was allowed to stand, but is very different from what it once was. The block of houses spoken of by Mr Smith as being east of the Capitol, was a large brick bldg erected by Mr Danl Carroll, & occupied by Mr Stelle as a tavern, & another was occupied by Mr Tunnecliff, called the City Hotel. There was another block built by Mr Thos Law, on N J ave, called the Ten Bldgs, in which the Nat'l Intell was first issued.

Mrd: on Aug 16, by Rev Mr Jones, at the residence of Mr Nathl Burwell, sr, of Clarke Co, Va, Beverly Randolph, U S N, to Miss Mary C, eldest daughter of the late Dr Philip Grymes Randolph, of Clarke.

For sale: a number of handsome bldg lots in the vicinity of Young's old Mansion & the Steamboat Wharf. Inquire of Benj Young, at Capt Jones' Steamboat Hotel, or Wilfred Young, corner of 12th & C sts south.

Orphans Court of Wash Co, D C. Letters of administration on the personal estate of John Kedglie, late of said county, dec'd. -Geo Watterston, Robt Brown, administrators

Died: on Jul 20, at the residence of her dght, Mary S Lippincott, Moorestown, N J, Jane Hallowell, in her 79th year. The dec'd was the mother of Benj Hallowell, of Alexandria.

Died: on Aug 23, after a short illness, George Felix, infant son of Geo E & Rebecca Jane Kirk, aged 3 months & 6 days.

FRI AUG 27, 1847

A dreadful event took place at Damietta Egypt, in June. The govn'r of the town, Ariff Effonol, kept in his gardens 2 crocidiles he had succeeded in taming. One of the negros, whose duty it was to attend to them, having illtreated one of the animals, its natural ferocity returned, & in its fury sprang on the govnr's son, a youth about 12 years of age, who was walking by the negro's side, & strangled him.

The report that Lt Niles, of the Illinois volunteers, had been drowned in the Mississippi, is incorrect. He was thrown overboard accidentally, but swam ashore.

At Harrisburg, on Sunday last, Mr Christian Carver, with his wife & dght-in-law, were returning from a funeral, & the horse ran off & broke the carriage to atoms, causing the death of Mrs Carver, & leaving little hope of the recovery of Mr Carver, or his dght-in-law, who is a very amiable young lady, & but recently married. Mr Carver belongs to Newmarket, Cumberland Co.

Died: in St Louis, Missouri, in his 26th year, Geo Thos Coote, y/son of Clement T Coote, of Wash City. [No death date given-appears lately.]

Washington & Alexandria Boat: the steamboat **Joseph Johnson** will depart from Alexandria at 7, 9, 11, 2, 4, & 6. Leave Washington at 8, 10, 12, 3, 5, & 7 o'clock.
-Job Corsen, Captain

We regret to announce the wreck of the new ship **Mamlouk**, Capt Christianson, which sailed from N Y for Liverpool on Aug 9, & the loss of 35 steerage passengers & 7 of the crew, all of whom were washed overboard before assistance reached them. The first injury to the ship occurred on Aug 15, in a violent hurricane. On Aug 18 the brig **Belize**, Capt Jas H Dawses, from Boston, bound to Port au Prince rescued the survivors & brought them all safely to this port. Only one steerage passenger, David Howels, was saved. The cabin passengers were all saved, viz: J B Butler, of Brooklyn; Mrs Christianson, [captain's lady,] Miss Floride Patten, & Mr Henry Plant, of Demerara. Persons lost are as follows:

Crew: Wm Howard	Harry Dunham	Wm Miller-[colored]
Jacob Dyer	Robt ___	cook
John Allen		
Passengers:		
John Blaine	Asa Gill	Wm Cornell
Eliz Hoppock	Mr Morris	Hugh Humphrey
Miss Morehead	Mr Green	Mr Mathias

Hugh Hannell	Eliz Masterten	Patrick Dowling, wife & infant
David S Hale	R O'Brien	E Green, wife & 3 children
Mr Taylor & wife	Thos Davis	
John Duncan	John Gormar	
Edw Bishop	Jas Joyce, wife & infant	
Wm Odell	T H Gerry, wife & infant	

The **Mamlouk** was on her first voyage & owned by W Delano. The vessel & freight money were insured in Wall st for about $55,000. The ship cost from $60,000 to $70,000. -Commercial Advertiser

Household & kitchen furniture at auction: on Sep 2, by virtue of a deed of trust: at the residence of Mrs Ballard, opposite the north Capitol gate. -Richd Wallach, trustee
-R W Dyer, auct

The Iron steamer **Water-Witch** sailed yesterday from the Navy Yard for Norfolk, where she is to take in her stores previous to her departure for the Gulf of Mexico. Her ofcrs:

Lt Commanding J G Tooten	J S Walker
Acting Master A J Dallas	Assist Engineers:
Assist Surgeon S G White	John Carroll
1st Assist Engnr J K Matthews	J A Van Zandt
Passed Midshipmen:	Capt's Clerk J M Mechan
W K Bridge	

Asbury Tyler, [colored] who was discharged from the penitentiary about 4 months ago, was arrested for the robbery of the bakery of Messrs Thos Havenner & Son, of a set of harness & a whip, a few nights ago.

SAT AUG 28, 1847

On Aug 10, Mr Jos Passover, who lived about 3 miles from Noblesville, Hamilton Co, Indiana, went into his well for the purpose of cleaning it out. When within a few feet of the top the wall gave way, & he was carried down with it. The neighbors worked all night, but when he was taken out he was dead.

Constable's sale: by 2 writs of fieri facias, I will expose to sale at public auction, for cash, all the right, title, & interest of John W D Gray, in one lot with a 2 story frame dwlg house upon it, on 8th st, between L & M sts, Wash City, late the property of John W D Gray, seized & taken in execution at the suit of Wm R Riley. -J F Wollard, Constable

7 days later from Gen Scott: Gen Scott was still at Puebla on Aug 6. Gen Pierce arrived at Puebla on Aug 6. He lost not a single man on his march, notwithstanding another severe battle with the guerillas. Major Gaines & Passed Midshipman Rogers escaped from the city of Mexico & arrived safely at Gen Scott's headquarters. Mr Kendall writes of the death of Lt Hill, of the 2nd Dragoons, & Dr Hamner, of S C Regt.

Camp at Bridge, 24 miles from Vera Cruz, Aug 11, 1847. The command under Maj Lally was met by the guerillas Aug 10 in force at Paso Oneja: our loss is severe, 2 ofcrs being severely wounded-Capt Jas H Calwell, of the Voltigeurs, & Capt Arthur C Cummins, of the 11th Infty, the former a native of Md, the latter of Va.

Constable's sale: by a writ of venditioni exponas: I will expose to sale at public auction, on the premises, on Sep 28, for cash, all the right, title, & interest of Wm Durr, in & unto lot 23 in square 253, with improvements, a 2 story frame house, on the corner of 13th & G sts, late the property of Wm Durr. Seized & taken at the suit of Henry Lysle.
-J F Wollard, Constable

My school, at my residence on 11th st, between F & G sts, will be reopened on Aug 30.
-John Neely

Hermitage Institute, Montg Co, Md: Mrs General Wheeler informs that she intends opening a Boarding School for Young Ladies, at the residence of the late Dr Bowie, known as the ***Hermitage***, 12 miles on the road from Wash to Brookville. It will be the constant aim of Mrs Wheeler to improve the moral & intellectual powers of her pupils. Mrs Wheeler was educated with the view of being a teacher, & has taught in N Y, also in Mrs Edwards' Seminary, in Leesburg. Address Mrs Wheeler, near Poolesville, Montg Co, Md; after Nov 22, to Colesville, Montg Co, Md.

Mrd: on Aug 26, by Rev Mr Morgan, Mr John Fitzhugh to Miss Martha Ann Taylor, all of Wash City.

Died: on Sunday, Aug 15, in Gtwn, Laura Jane, aged 15 months; & on Friday, Aug 20, Margaret Virginia, aged 2 years & 3 months. Both died of whooping-cough, & are dghts of Jas & Susanna L Coyle.

MON AUG 30, 1847

The Hon Silas Wright, of the State of N Y, died of apoplexy, at his residence in Lawrence Co, N Y, on Aug 27. He was not more than 55 years of age. [Sep 1st newspaper: Mr Wright lives in a small wooden house, in nowise distinguishable from those of his neighbors. I think it cost him some $800. He is about middling size, calm, dignified, & a respectful man. He was married at Canton in the fall of 1833 to the dght of a gentleman in whose family he had always boarded when there. A more attentive, kind, & affectionate husband does not exist. He was born in Amherst, Mass, on May 24, 1795. The subsequent year his father & family removed to Vt. In 1815 he graduated at Middlebury College, Vt.]

Capt McLean, Gov'r of Sierra Leone, & well known as the husband of the dec'd poetess, Miss Landon, died at Capt Coast about Apr 20 last.

Lt Chas Wolcott Chauncey, U S Navy, commanding U S steamer **Spitfire**, died at Anton Lizardo on Aug 10, from the effects of the prevailing epidemic. He was an ofcr of high reputation.

A man named McElroy , with his wife, both of whom were intoxicated] & an infant, aged 10 months, fell into the harbor at Cleveland, Ohio. The wife & child were drowned. The man was saved.

Late from Vera Cruz. Col Louis D Wilson, 12th Infty, died on Aug 12. He was a gallant son of N C. A violent attack of the fever finally terminated in his lamented death. He was one of the strongest Democrats in Edgecome Co, for 20 years a member of the Legislature-& in 1842-3 the Speaker of the Senate. He was a bachelor, & near 60 years of age.

Mr Russell, editor of the Red Lander, was killed a few days ago in San Augustine, Texas, by Mr Kendall,of the San Augustine Shield. A very bitter newspaper controversy had been going on between the parties for several weeks.

Jackson City was founded some 10 or 12 years ago, on the other side of the Potomac, christened, & laid off & the corner stone was laid by Gen Jackson; & G W P Curtis, our good old friend of Arlington, made the corner-stone speech, to a large assemblage of people. Not a single house has been erected in Jackson city since its foundation, not a lot bought by speculators; the cornerstone has been broken into, & the last we hear is that it has been carried up into Fairfax Co, where, at the last advices, an old negro was pounding homminy in it. On Tempora! -Wash Correspondence N Y Herald

A laborer, P Carl, an Englishman, was suffocated in a Wheat Warehouse on Thu last, as Steele & Co were loading a train of cars at Monroeville. He was buried in the mass wheat, & taken out quite dead.

The large Hotel now being erected at the corner of Pa ave & 12th sts for Messrs Fuller & Son, & although unfinished, presents 2 imposing fronts. It will be 4 stories, a basement & attic, which will contain 70 fine spacious rooms. Master builders: Mr B Willett, carpenter; Mr Geo H Plant, bricklayer; Messrs Wilkins & Cassidy, granite cutters; & Mr Sioussa, plasterer.

One day last week a man named John Riley, formerly a hack driver in Wash City, while working in an iron ore mine at Ellicott's Mills, was so severely injured by the caving in of the embankment that he lingered until last Wed & then died of the hurt he had received. The poor man's thigh was fractured, & he was otherwise severely injured.

French & English Boarding & Day School: the Misses Hawley, dghts of the late Rector of St John Church of Wash City, have, with their mother, Mrs Hawley, removed from F st to Pa ave, between 17th & 18th sts, & will resume their School on Sep 13.

Will of Peter G Stuyvesant: deposited in the Surrogate's ofc, N Y:
American Bible Society: $5,000
American Tract Society: $1,000
Institution for the Blind: $3,000
Protestant Half Orphan Asylum: $5,000
To his wife, Helen Stuyvesant, he has bequeathed the house & lot of ground in the 17th Ward of N Y C, where she now resides; also a farm in Harrison, Hudson Co, N J; all his furniture, plate, printed books, wines, pictures, household goods, carriages, horses, & other live stock; also the sum of $12,000 a year, to be paid quarterly. To Margaret S Gibson, the daughter of his dec'd sister, Cornelia Ten Broeck, he left an annuity of $250. To his nieces at law, Julia Stuyvesant, w/o Peter Stuyvesant, Augusta Stuyvesant, w/o Nicholas Wm Stuyvesant, & to his nieces, Catherine Ann Catlin, Helen E Olmstead, Margaret Folsom, Susan Le Roy, Margaret Neilson, Eliz Morris, & his nephews, John R Stuyvesant, Rev Petrus T Ten Broeck, & Benj R Winthrop, & Margaret S Rutherford, one-half of his lands lying in N Y C. To his executors, Hamilton Fish, Gerard Stuyvesant, & Lewis M Rutherford, he has left the remainder of his property,on condition that the last shall make the name of Stuyvesant his surname. His real estate is estimated to be worth $2,000,000, & his personal estate $300,000.

French & English Boarding & Day School: the Misses Hawley, dghts of the late Rector of St John Church of Wash City, have, with their mother, Mrs Hawley, removed from F st to Pa ave, between 17th & 18th sts, & will resume their School on Sep 13.

Died: on Aug 27, at ***Grove Wood***, PG Co, Md, Mary Ellen, infant daughter of Leo Ward & Winifred Harbaugh, aged 6 months & 2 days.

Orphans Court of Wash Co, D C. Letters of administration on the personal estate of Abner R Hetzel, late of the U S Army, dec'd. -Margaret Hetzel, admx

Sale of valuable property: by deed of trust from S Holmes to the subscriber, dated May 7, & recorded May 8, 1846, in Liber W B 122, folios 176 thru 181, in the land records of Wash Co, D C: auction on Sep 29 of lots 14 & 15 in square 297, in Wash City. This property has on it 3 brick dwlg houses & a carpenter's shop; at the corner of 13th & south C sts. -P R Fendall, Trustee -R W Dyer, auct

This is to give notice to the heirs, & creditors, of John Holland, dec'd, that the subscriber, on Sep 20 next, will apply to the Orphans Court of Wash Co, D C, for letters of administration upon the estate of said Holland. -J O'Leary

Mrs Okill, 8 & 10 Clinton Pl, N Y, will reopen her School on Sep 1.

TUE AUG 31, 1847
Household & kitchen furniture, & Carriage at auction: on Sep 3, at the residence of Jas Cathcart, at 17th & H sts, an excellent lot of furniture. -A Green, auctioneer

Public execution of 2 Poles at Lemberg, in Galicia, on Jul 31, on the occasion of the execution of Theophilus Wisniowski & Jos Kapuscinski, declared guilty of high treason against Austria, by the Imperial Courts, on Jul 1, 1847. The execution of the priest who is under sentence of death has been adjourned till further notice.

Balt American, writing from Knightstown, Indiana, under date of Aug 25. Last night, as Messrs Welsh & Delavan's Circus Co were performing at this place, a tremendous hurricane passed over us, upset their canvas tent, & tore parts of it to atoms. At the same time, Mr Levi North, a well known equestrian, was going through his famous 4 horse act, when the horses took fright, & threw him on the planks in the ring, dashing his brains out, & killing him instantly. The ring-master was run over by one of the horses & had his arm broken. Among the spectators, 2 women & a child were killed instantly, & others were injured. [Sep 1st newspaper: Mr North was well on Aug 27th: letter franked by F L Goble, P M, by whom it was purported to have been written. Another company was performing at that time & perhaps the name of the proprietor & performers were mistaken.
-Balt American]

Dissolution of the partnership under the firm of Young & Steer, this day by mutual consent. -A H Young, P J Steer [P J Steer will hereafter continue the business on his own account.]

WED SEP 1, 1847

Tampico, Aug 17, 1847. The war has been the cause of the death of hundreds, but disease of various description, has slain its thousands. This morning 2nd Lt John Evans, of Capt Mace's company of the Louisiana Regt, died of yellow fever; his remains will be sent to your city. New Orleans National

The steamer **Duchess of Kent**, having on board the remains of Mr Danl O'Connell, reached the lighthouse at Southwall on Aug 9. The coffin, preceded by the trades, headed by Mr Thos Reynolds, the City Marshal, followed by Rev Dr Miley as chaplain, by the sons, relatives, & friends, moved through the crowd up Marlborough st, to the church. Rev Mr Cooper assisted by Rev Mr Maher, Rev Mr Mullen, & Rev Mr Smith, met the coffin. The solemn obsequies for Mr O'Connell took place on Wed. Mr Steele, the faithful friend of Mr O'Connell was in the gallery. The funeral took place on Thu.
-Dublin paper

J M G Lescure, one of the publishers of the Harrisburg Union, & holding the ofc of Pa State Printer, died at Harrisburg on Sat.

Chas & Edw Tate, 2 boys, aged 7 & 9 years, while fishing on Sat in a pond west of Broad st, Phil, accidentally fell in & were drowned. This distressing affair had such an overwhelming effect on the father as to produce almost immediate insanity.

London Chronicle of Aug 12. We announce the demise of Don Affonso, [the Imperial Prince of Brazil,] only son of Don Pedro II, & lately heir apparent to the throne of Brazil. In the Journal do Commercio of Rio de Janeiro of Jun 12th, it simply stated the event.

The following vessels were to leave New Orleans on 23rd ult for the seat of war: the steamship **New Orleans**, for Tampico, with 5 companies of the 2nd Regt Ill volunteers, under the command of Lt Col Hicks. The steamship **Mary Kingsland**, for Vera Cruz, with 1 company 2nd Regt Ill volunteers, & Capt Connolly's company of La mounted volunteers. The steamship **Massachusetts** was to leave for the same destination, with the remaining 4 companies of the 2nd Regt Ill volunteers, under the command of Col Collins. Passengers per **New Orleans**: Drs Whitesides & Remes. Per **Mary Kingsland**: Lt Col G W Hughes, commanding the District btln; W H Pease, U S A; Dr Canter, A P Hollister & Mr Farquhar, Quartermaster's Dept, & 70 teamsters.

Dr Upon H Berryman, Senior Physician of the new Marine Hospital at Balt, died on Sat last from the ship fever, contracted while in attendance upon his duties. He was the son of Mr John Berryman, Assist Clerk of Balt County Court. His remains were conveyed from his father's residence to Reisterstown on Sun, where they were interred.

From the Rio Grande. The Matamoros Flag notices recent attacks upon Gov't trains by the guerrilla bands. A scouting party of 27 Texans, commanded by Capt Baylor, & ordered out by Col Abbot, commander at Ceralvo, to scout the country between that post & Monterey, fell in with a large body of Mexicans, & were all killed but 3. Capt Baylor was returning with 3 prisoners, when he was surrounded by some 300 Mexicans who charged upon his little band, killing many of them at the first fire. When Capt Baylor was last seen he was wounded & unhorsed, but still fighting, with only 3 of his men in their saddles.

Dr Upon H Berryman, Senior Physician of the new Marine Hospital at Balt, died on Sat last from the ship fever, contracted while in attendance upon his duties. He was the son of Mr John Berryman, Assist Clerk of Balt County Court. His remains were conveyed from his father's residence to Reisterstown on Sun, where they were interred.

The public are cautioned against receiving a note given by me, in favor of Michl McDermott, for $20, dated Apr 29, 1847, & endorsed by Wm Markward, as the said note was given without consideration, & I will not pay the same. -Martin Buell

Mrd: Aug 10, at Batesville, Arkansas, by Rev Mr Hunter, Lt Lloyd Magruder, U S Army, to Miss Caroline E, youngest daughter of Col Chas H Pelham, all of the above place.

West Street Academy will commence this day, Sep 1. Apply at the Academy or residence of the proprietor, one door east. -Saml Kelly, Pres: Gtwn, D C

City Ordinance: Act for the relief of Abraham Butler, that the fine imposed for an alleged violation of the law relative to the firing of guns in the street, be remitted, together with the costs of prosecution.

Stray cow: strayed on Aug 22: suitable reward for information which may lead to her recovery. -F S McCarthy, on F, between 6th & 7th sts.

THU SEP 2, 1847

Mrs Ellen Jones will reopen her School on the first Monday in Sep, at her residence on F st, between 19th & 20th sts.

Among the passengers on the steamer **Amelia**, from ***Fort Leavenworth***, Aug 25, were Gen S W Kearny, Major P St Geo Cooke, of the 2nd Dragoons; Capt H S Turner, of the 1st Dragoons; Maj T Swords, Quartermaster; Lt Radford, of the Navy; & Mr Bryant, of Lexington, Ky. This party reached ***Fort Leavenworth*** from Calif on Aug 22. In company as far as the Fort were also Lt Col Fremont, Assist Surgeon Sanderson, & the Hon W P Hall, member of Congress elect from this State. Col Mason, 1st Dragoons, was left at Monterey, Govn'r & Cmder-in-chief.

The Hon Nicholas Baylies, an aged & eminent man of Caledonia Co, Vt, died at the residence of his son-in-law, Hon Geo C Cahoun, of Lyndon, on Aug 17, at the age of about 75. -Manchester American

Mrd: on Aug 31, by Rev Mr Allen, W F Wallace, M D, to Ellen Rebecca, eldest daughter of John Purdy, all of Wash City.

Mrd: on Aug 31, by Rev L J Gillis, Mr John S Emmerson to Miss Louisa M Duffey.

Died: on Sep 1, in Wash City, of consumption, Mrs Mary Hardy, w/o Henry Hardy. Whilst on earth, as a child dutiful, as a wife faithful & affectionate, & as a mother devoted, she has gone to that better life

Died: on Aug 25, at ***Linwood***, the residence of S M Ball, near Fairfax Courthouse, in his 66th year, Henry Waring Ball, late of Wash, D C, & the only surviving son of the late Col Spencer M Ball, of Northumberland Co, Va. His illness was of long & painful duration; yet not a murmur escaped him. He breathed his last surrounded by sorrowing friends & relatives, in the full assurance of a blissful immortality.

Jas Minor, a Clerk in Mr Hagner's ofc, assaulted a colored boy named Andrew, belonging to Mr O'Neal, by stabbing him in the leg. This outrage & others were committed by Minor while under the influence of mania potu. He was arrested, no bail having been required in the case.

St Louis Republican of Aug 26. Gen Kearny left Monterey on May 31st last. There was an escort of 13 of the Mormon btln. We also learn that on arrival at ***Fort Leavenworth*** Col Fremont was arrested by Gen Kearny, & ordered to Washington.

Valuable real estate for sale: by deed of trust executed to me by the late Richd B Mason, dec'd, on Aug 28, 1841, & also a decree of the Circuit Superior Court of Law & Chancery of Alexandria Co, Va, rendered at the last June term of said Court: sale on Oct 15, upon the premises, at public auction, that tract of land known as ***Holmes' Island***, or more recently as ***Jackson City***, lying in Alexandria Co, on the Potomac, immediately opposite Wash, containing, as was computed by its late proprietor, about 500 acres, more or less. Improvements consist of a comfortable dwlg house, with stables & other out-bldgs, & well of good water near the door. -R C Mason, Trustee

FRI SEP 3, 1847
The death of Dr J A Washington, of N Y is announced. He had recently returned from Europe, & was arrested by death in the midst of a bright prospect of higher usefulness than ever before. He was a native of North Carolina, but for 17 years a resident of N Y. [No date-current item.]

Foreign Item: Alfred Tennyson, the poet, has been sojourning at Esher, in bad health. The Queen & Prince, hearing of it, paid their respects to him without delay.

Shakespeare's Birthplace. Prince Albert has contributed the sum of L250, the Queen Dowager has added L100, & the Corp of Stratford another L100, towards purchasing the birthplace of the Bard of Avon.

The children of the Catholic School in James st went on an excursion to New Rochelle yesterday, & Michl McGowan & John Mullin of 59 Bayard st, were drowned. The boys left the main party & went bathing.

Died: on Sep 2, suddenly, of spasms, Clementine, youngest daughter of Benedict & Josephine Jost, aged 8 months & 14 days. Her gentleness while living renders her loss doubly painful to the bereaved parents. Her funeral is this morning at 10 o'clock, from the residence of the parents, 17th st west & Pa ave.

Died: on Aug 25, at Buffalo, Mrs Mary P Wilkeson, w/o Saml Wilkeson, & daughter of the late Gen Absalom Peters, of Connecticut, in her 53rd year.

SAT SEP 4, 1847
Mr Jas Craig, of Bedford Co, Tenn, was fatally wounded at Franklin, Tenn, on Aug 2. A fight occurred near the Planters' Hotel, in which Mr Craig had no concern, but several pistols were discharged & he promiscuously shot. After suffering indescribable torture he died on Wed.

The Boston Transcript: the accomplished Editor of the bijou of a newspaper, Miss Cornelia W Walter, has retired from her long association with its columns, & will be succeeded by Epes Sargent.

$150 reward for runaway negro man Henry Dean, about 30 years of age.
-Wm Swink, living near Prospect Hill, Fairfax Co, Va.

From Europe: Lt Monroe, late of the 2nd Regt of Life Guards, was found guilty of the murder of Col Faucett, whom he killed in a duel about 4 years ago. The verdict caused considerable surprise.

On Wed last week, [says the Amherst Express] there were mowing in the same field in Wendell, four generations of a family named Wilder, consisting of a great grandfather, grandfather, father, & son. The eldest was 96 & the youngest 10 years of age.

Michigan & Wisconsin land for sale: Apply to Dr Chas Collins Parker, Phil, or John D McPherson, Wash. Tracts of land in St Clair Co, Lapier Co, & Sanalac Co, Michigan. Tracts of land in Fond-du-lac Co, Sheboygan Co, Wash Co, & Dane Co, Wisconsin.

Orphans Court of Wash Co, D C. Letters testamentary on the personal estate of Thos Gibson, late of said county, dec'd. -John Holroyd, exc

Whig nomination in Md: for Govn'r-Wm T Goldsborough, of Dorchester Co.

Governess wanted: a gentleman living in Va desires to engage a lady to attend the education of 4 young ladies in Music & French, with the ordinary branches of English. Letters [postage paid] addressed to H J Alexandria, will be attended to.

Here is a chance! Being about to remove to the West, I now offer my Stand & Stock of Groceries for sale. The stand is well established both for river & canal trade.
-Z M P King, Gtwn, D C

Julian Poydras, late of the parish of Pointe Coupee, La, bequeathed to the several parishes in the State, individuals, orphan asylums, & other charitable associations, property of immense value & a large amount of funds. To the parish of Pointe Coupee the dec'd gave $30,000, the interest of this sum to be employed in giving a dowry to all the girls of said parish who may get married; also to West Baton Rouge, $30,000, the interest to be employed in giving a dowry to the girls of the parish when they marry.

Died: on Thu, Maria, youngest daughter of Francis & Anna M Mohun, aged 2 years. Her funeral is today at 3 o'clock.

Died: on Aug 25, in Charlestown, Jefferson Co, Va, suddenly, of apoplexy, Mr Willoughby W Lane, in his 73rd year. He was a native of Westmoreland Co, Va, the son of Col Jos Lane, of that county, but has resided in Charlestown the last 45 years of his life.

Died: on Aug 22, in Hagerstown, Md, [at the residence of her son, Rev Septimus Tustin,] Mrs Susannah Tustin, in her 78th year.

Died: on Jul 31, at Peoria, Ill, Chas Clinton, infant son of Geo C & Mary Jane Beston, aged 3 months.
+
Died: at the same place, on Aug 13, Mrs Mary Jane, w/o Geo C Beston, aged 36, after a protracted illness.

For rent: the rooms over & in the rear of our store, now occupied by the engineers attending to making the avenue. They will suit for a printing ofc or bindery. Apply to Simms & Son.

$5 reward for 4 cows that strayed on Aug 30. -Edw H Edelin, Capitol Hill

MON SEP 6, 1847

John Y Mason, the Sec of the Navy, & acting Sec of War, having been called to Va by the sudden & alarming illness of his father, Mr Appleton, the Chief Clerk, acts as Sec of the Navy pro tem, & Mr Buchanan, Sec of State, acts as Sec of War pro tem.

Died: on Sep 5, at the residence of Matthew St Clair Clarke, in Wash City, Jeanet Clarke, widow of the late Rev John X Clarke, aged 56 years. Her funeral is on Tue at 10 o'clock.

A brakeman, Patrick Hart, attached to the train coming from Grafton to Boston, was killed a few miles above Lowell, on Monday. He had crept along upon the top of the cars to the engine, to procure some matches, & on his return the train reached a bridge, by which he was struck in the head & knocked between the cars on to the track. Nothing was known about the accident until he was missed. The blow received on the head from the bridge had crushed it to have occasioned almost instant death.

Mrd: on Aug 28, in St Paul's Church, in Cincinnati, by Rev R Lewis, Chaplain U S Navy, Cmder J R Sands, U S Navy, of Brooklyn, N Y, to Miss Eleanor Ann Crook, only daughter of the late Geo Crook, of Circleville, Ohio.

Phil: A fatal accident on occurred on Sep 3, near Fairmount, by which a young lady, Miss Caroline Andis, lost her life. She was returning to the city from a picnic excusion, when by some means she slipped & fell into the canal & drowned. Her body was afterwards recovered, & conveyed to her disconsolate friends.

S E Scheel, Teacher of Music, continues to give lessons in Wash & vicinity, at his house or at the private dwlg of his pupils, on the Organ & Piano; also, in Vocal Music & in the principles of thorough Bass, if required. $12 for a course of 24 lessons. Orders may be left at Mrs Anderson's & Mr Fischer's Music Stores, or at the residence of J E Scheel, H st, between 13th & 14th sts.

Orphans Court of Wash Co, D C. Letters testamentary on the personal estate of Fred'k Clitch, late of said county, dec'd. -H H C W Voss, excx

TUE SEP 7, 1847

Clermont Farm, in Fairfax Co, Va, for sale. At my advanced age, it being inconvenient longer to cultivate & manage personally the farm adjoining my residence here, I offer for sale this tract, with the exception of my dwlg-house with its appurtenances & about 20 acres or land adjoining. The farm offered will then contain about 300 acres, of which 160 acres are bottom land upon Cameron run, 40 acres of higher land, & the balance thriving young wood land. The improvements consist of a commodious house for the manager, houses for servants, & all other necessary out-bldgs. Terms will be made accommodating, & be learned from John Mason, jr, Wash, Jas M Mason, Winchester, Va, or the subscriber upon the premises. -John Mason, Clermont, Fairfax Co, Va

Obit-died: on Aug 20, at his residence, Chas Co, Md, Marsham Bowling, in his 81st year. His whole course of life was that of a plain, unostentatious gentleman of the highest integrity. He will long be remembered as one who has sustained so beautifully the interesting relations of a kind husband, an affectionate father, a good master, a charitable neighbor, & a true patriot.

Cmdor Storer on Fri hoisted his broad pennant on board the U S frig **Brandywine**, bound for the Brazil station, on which occasion the usual salutes were fired. She will put to sea with all possible dispatch. List of the ofcrs of the **Brandywine**:
Geo W Storer, cmdor; Thos Crabb, capt
Lts: John A Davis, Luther Stoddard, Saml Larkin, Carter B Poindexter, G Wells, J J Guthrie
Master, John S Taylor
Purser, Jos Terry
Fleet Surgeon, B F Bache
Passed Assist Surgeon, R T Maxwell
Assist Surgeon, Alex'r Robinson
Chaplain, J L Leuhart
2nd lt of Marines, Jas Wiley
Cmdor's sec, Storer
Passed midshipmen, Wm T Truxton, John T Barrand, Simeon S Basseau, T Lee Walker
Midshipmen, John G Sproston & Chas B Smith
Passengers to join the U S ship **Ohio**: Capt Wm V Taylor, Cmder Andrew K Long, Purser Saml Forrest; Capt Marines, Jos L C Hardy; Passed Midshipmen, R L Law, Thos C Eaton, Thos W Brodhead; Midshipmen, John T Wood, Wm H Ward, B C Hand, A B Cummings, Wm Gwinn, David Harmony, J P Baker, John J Cornwall, Jos Miller, E T Chapmen. To join the U S brig **Perry**: Lt Commanding E G Tilton; Passed Midshipmen O C Badger & Asa Sharp.

WED SEP 8, 1847

Foreign Items: Sergent, the Terrorist, Sec of Robespierre, & a member of the French Nat'l Convention, died on Aug 25, at Nice, in his 96th year.

Mrd: on Sep 2, at Oakland, PG Co, Md, by Rev Mr Kepler, Albion Hurdle, of Wash, to Louisa J Jenkins, formerly of Richmond, Va, & daughter of the late Capt Uriah Jenkins.

Died: on Aug 26, at Meades, [the residence of Miss Mary Meade,] Clarke Co, Va, Caroline Rose Gurley, infant daughter of Rev R R Gurley, of Wash City, aged 5 months.

On Mon the boiler of the extract works of the Stanford Manufacturing Co, [Messrs Sandford's,] at the Cove, blew up, destroying the brick bldg & killed were Mr Downing & Mr Aaron Meaker, who were painting the bldgs; Wm Weed, of Darien, & Mr Taylor.

Wash Corp: 1-Cmte of Claims: bill for the relief of John Seitz: passed. 2-Cmte of Claims: asked to be discharged from the further consideration of the ptns of Geo W Hughes & Thos Welch: ptns to lie on the table. Same cmte: bill for the relief of Matilda Radcliff: passed. 3-Ptn from Enoch Ridgway: referred to the Cmte of Claims. 4-Ptn of Jos K Boyd & others, representing the condition of the water course from the termination of the sewer on 11th & C sts: referred to be Cmte on Improvements. 5-Ptn of Garret Flanagan, for remission of a fine: referred to the Cmte of Claims. 6-Cmte of Claims: asked to be discharged from the further consideration of the ptn of Enoch Burnett; ptn of F Hitz; ptn of Danl Knipple; & ptn of P Goings: agreed to.

For rent: the store room now occupied by John Allen as a dry-goods store, on the north side of Pa ave, between 9th & 10th sts. Possession on Sep 14. Inquire of Edwin Green, Pa ave, corner of 11th st.

For rent: 2 new convenient houses, #s 1 & 4, in the block of bldgs on 9th st, between F & G sts; the corner house has in the kitchen one of Stimpson's improved ranges. Apply to J Raymond, 6th st, between Coleman's & Brown's Hotels.

For rent: ***Tiber Mill*** will be unoccupied on Nov 5. It is within the Corporation of Wash, a short distance from the Capitol. Apply at Brentwood, near the Mill, the residence of Mrs Catherine Pearson.

By virtue of 5 writs of fieri facias, to me directed, I will expose at public auction, upon the premises, on Oct 9, 1847, all the right, title, & interest of John Thomas in & to one frame dwlg house, on lots 7 & 8 in square 742, in Wash City, seized & taken in execution to satisfy judgments in favor of Murray & Simms, Saml Lusby, Henry G Murray, use of Murdock & Wright, & Geo Pochelton, & will be sold to satisfy the same.
-Thos Plumsill, Constable

THU SEP 9, 1847

Mrs Catharine Butterworth died at Dubuque, Iowa, on Aug 30, at the advanced age of 114 years. She was a native of Kildare, Ireland.

Mr Wilhelmus Simmons, of Taghkanie, N Y, found a large hornet's nest under the eaves of his barn on Tue. He set fire to the nest, & totally destroyed it. Unfortunately, the barn was also burnt with a loss from $1,200 to $1,500: no insurance.

Lumber! Having rented the yard recently occupied by Mr Geo Collard, on the corner of 6th st & Missouri ave, adjoining that of Mr Wm H Gunnell, have laid in a large supply of all the different kinds of lumber. -Sidney B Webb

Jas B Clarke, Agent, successor of H C Spalding, informs his friends & the public that he is in receipt of considerable supplies of seasonable Dry Goods. -Jas B Clarke, Agent, Pa ave, 2nd door west of 8th st, & opposite Centre Market.

Domestic Dry Goods & Shoe Store, corner of N Y ave & 12th st. -J B Tree & Brother

The powder mill of Messrs Austin, near Xenia, Ohio, was blown up on Aug 30, & Jas Kirkpatrick, a young man employed there, was instantly killed. He was the only person in the bldg at the time.

Mrd: on Sep 7, by Rev G W Sampson, Thos S Burr to Lizzie, daughter of Mr J G Robinson, all of Wash City.

Recent visit to Pitcairn's Island: her Majesty's brig **Spy** arrived off this island on Feb 26, & was boarded by Geo Adams & some more natives shortly after she hove to. Geo Adams is the son of the celebrated John Adams, the father of the colony, the mutineer of the ship **Bounty**. There was a slight disagreement about land, which the natives wished to be brought before Lt Wooldrige, Cmder of the Spy, & who very speedily disposed of it. Mr Nopps is the schoomaster. We were shown the old gun belonging to the **Bounty**, that had been under water for 59 years, & which was now lying near the courthouse. We visited old Adams' house & grave, which is next to his wife's grave, & kept in trim order. We had dinner, pork, yam, & sweet potatoes, at McCoy's house. -Naval & Military Gaz

Mrd: on Sep 7, by Rev Levin Gillis, Mr Jas E Beavin, of Natchez, Miss, to Miss Sarah Ann Richards, of Wash City.

Mrd: on Sep 2, at ***Willow Grove***, Orange Co, Va, the residence of her father, by Rev Martin A Dunn, Col Wm H Caruthers, of Lexington, Va, to Miss Ann H Clark, eldest daughter of Wm D Clark.

Mrd: on Sep 2, in Harrisburg, Pa, by Rev Dr DeWitt, the Rev J H Rittenhouse, of Columbia Co, Pa, to Jane C, daughter of the late Hon Wm Simonton, of Dauphin Co, Pa.

Naval: Lt Palmer, who lately commanded the schnr **Flirt**, has been detached on account of ill health, & the command of the **Flirt** given to Lt E Farrand, who is in daily expectation of sailing for Vera Cruz.

The ship **Isaac Allerton**, Capt Logan, arrived yesterday from Cork, with 160 immigrant passengers on board. They have ship fever on board, about 20 being down with it, & 3 having died coming up the river. The vessel is in quarantine. A relief cmte has taken the subject in hand. May they be encouraged to persevere!

FRI SEP 10, 1847
Wmsport News: on Thu, Thos Stake, aged 9 years, son of Hiram Stake, of that place, while attempting to swim the camal near the basin on a piece of boat rib, accidentally slipped off & was drowned.

Death of a Sister of Charity. One of those angels of mercy, who, for the holy cause of Religion, banish themselves from the gayeties of the world to wait upon the wants of the suffering & the dying, has at last become the martyr of her own charity. On Sat last, Sister Mary Delphina Zeigler died of the yellow fever in the hospital. She was 33 years of age, & was a native of Pa. She had been 2 years in the hospital, & for 8 years a member of the sisterhood. -New Orleans Delta, Aug 31

Accident on the Portage Railroad: from the Hollidaysburg papers. On Sat last, Wm Morgan was caught between 2 trucks & instantly killed. On Tue a section boat Saml L Funk, from Harrisburg, came in contact with a train of cars belonging to the Pa & Ohio line, smashing 2 or 3 or them to atoms. One passenger, Andrew Cassady, from Balt, had his hand crushed. The other passengers escaped injury.

Supreme Court of the U S, Dec Term, 1846. #172. John W Yarborough, trustee, & Henry Shultz, appellants, vs The Bank of the State of Georgia et al. Mr Johnson, of counsel for the appellees, having suggested the death of John W Yarborough, one of the appellants in this cause, moved the Court to dismiss this appeal under the 28th rule of Court. Unless the proper representive of the said John W Yarborough, deceased, shall voluntarily come in within the first 10 days of the ensuing term of this Court, then that the said appellees shall be entitled to have this appeal dismissed. I, Wm Thos Carroll, Clerk of the Supreme Court of the U S, do hereby certify that the above is truly extracted from the minutes of said Supreme Court.

Supreme Court of the U S, Dec Term, 1846. #160: John W Yarborough, trustee, & Henry Shultz, appellants, vs The Bank of the State of Georgia et al. Mr Johnson, of counsel for the appellees, having suggested the death of John W Yarborough, one of the appellants in this cause, moved the Court to dismiss this appeal under the 28th rule of Court. Unless the proper representive of the said John W Yarborough, deceased, shall voluntarily come in within the first 10 days of the ensuing term of this Court, then that the said appellees shall be entitled to have this appeal dismissed. I, Wm Thos Carroll, Clerk of the Supreme Court of the U S, do hereby certify that the above is truly extracted from the minutes of said Supreme Court.

Mrd: on Sep 9, in Wash City, by Rev Mr French, Judge C Neale, of Alexandria, Va, to Miss Virginia Clay, youngest daughter of S F Chapman, of Grafton, Fauquier Co, Va.

Wm B Averett, late teller of the Virginia Bank at Lynchburg, charged with embezzling the funds of said Bank, has been arrested in Tenn, near the Va line, & lodged in jail, to await the requisition of the civil authorities of Va. Green, charged with being an accomplice, is now confined in the jail at Lynchburg.

Supreme Court of the U S, Dec Term, 1846. #180: Geo D Prentiss & others, plntfs in error, vs Platoff Zane. Mr Crittenden, of counsel for the plntfs in error, having suggested the death of Platoff Zane, the dfndnt in error, moved the Court for an order under the 28th rule of Court to make the proper representatives parties. On consideration whereof it is now here ordered by the Court that unless the proper representatives of the said Platoff Zane, dec'd, shall voluntarily become parties within the first 10 days of the ensuing term, the plntf in error shall be entitled to open the record, &, on hearing, have the same reversed if it be erroneous. I, Wm Thos Carroll, Clerk of the Supreme Court of the U S, do hereby certify that the above is truly extracted from the minutes of said Supreme Court.

On Mondy as Mr John Lawson Naylor [brother of Mr F Naylor, of Wash City] was riding in a buggy near the Good Hope Tavern, on the Eastern Branch, the horse attached galloped off at full speed. Mr Naylor, while attempting to jump out of the vehicle, got his leg entangled in the wheel, & the former was snapped in twain between the knee & ankle. He was first under the care of Dr Young, & then sent to the City Infirmary, & his fractured limb was set with the aid of Dr Johnston. He appears to be doing well.

SAT SEP 11, 1847

The French Academy of Sciences. John Fred'k Blumenbach was born at Gotha in 1752. At 17 he left his family & commenced his studies at the Univ of Jena; here he became acquainted with Soemmering. Blumenbach published his 4 principal words, Human Species, Natural History, Physiology, & Comparative Anatomy. All these writings, as M Flourens said, bear the character & stamp of the physiologist. He died on Jan 18, 1840, having lived almost a century. He was of superior mind, & possessed of almost universal knowledge.

Wilmington Chronicle of Wed. Return of Ofcrs. Capt Wm J Price & Geo Williamson, jr, & Lt Tatum, all of the N C Volunteer Regt, arrived here on Thu last, from Gen Taylor's camp, having left there on Jul 26. They have come in on the recruiting service. Mr J B Melvin, of Bladen Co, one of the N C volunteers, of Co I, Capt Kirkpatrick, was discharged on account of sickness. Mr Melvin left Saltillo on Aug 7, & Monterey on the 16th. He informed us that at the time he left about 150 of the regt had died, & about the same number were sick. Lt Beatty, of Co I, has resigned, & is coming home.

Major Clark, commanding the Castle at Vera Cruz, died of the vomito. The health of Vera Cruz was better, & the vomito has decreased.

The new 5th Regt of Ohio Volunteers has been fully organized by the election of Wm Irvin-Colonel, Wm H Latham-Lt Col, & Capt Link-Major.

Mrd: on Sep 8, in the Presbyterian Church, Gtwn, by Rev Thos B Balch, Wm Badger Heiskell, of Phil, to Eliza Jane, daughter of Jas C Wilson, of Gtwn.

Died: on Sep 9, suddenly, Albion Parris, infant son of Z D & Helen P Gilman, aged 8 months & 20 days.

Died: on Aug 27, in his 16th year, Richard, 2nd eldest son of Richd C Bowie, of Belmont, PG Co, Md. A short hour before the fatal accident occurred which terminated his mortal existence, he left in company with a beloved brother & an esteemed friend to enjoy the sports of the field. They has not proceeded far from the home which was so soon to become the house of sorrow, when the gun, which was borne by his friend, was accidentally discharged, & the contents entering through the left eye, were lodged in the brain of the subject of our notice. In a moment his stainless spirit winged its flight to the realms of a happier world. His afflicted parents & friends must look up to Him in whose hands are the destinies of us all.

Orphans Court of Wash Co, D C. Letters testamentary on the personal estate of Wm C Wright, late of Wash Co, D C. -Juliet R Wright, excx

For sale: 1,016 acres of land on Ivy creek, in Albemarle Co, 5 miles from Charlottesville, on the Staunton turnpike. Improvements are a good dwlg house with 8 rooms, a stone barn, & all necessary out bldgs. Also, an estate of 700 acres on James river, in Fluvanna Co, at the junction of Hardware with that stream, which has 100 acres of first rate low grounds. The bldgs consist of a good overseer's house & cabins for 20 negroes, stables for 6 horses, sheds for cows, & other out bldgs. Any communication directed to me at Hardin's tavern, Albemarle Co, Va, will be promptly answered. -W W Gilmer

House to let: the 2 story brick dwlg, with back bldg, on N J ave, now occupied by E B Stelle, with or without stable & coach house. Possession on Oct 1. -John P Ingle, next door to the premises.

For rent: 3 story brick house, owned & recently occupied by Mr E Guttselich, on La ave, near 6th st. Its central position renders it a first rate stand for a tavern or boarding house. Apply to F Mohun.

Very valuable farm, within 1½ miles of the Centre Market, for sale. A Country Seat, in Wash Co, called ***Jacksonville***, containing about 30 acres, with a commodious dwlg-house & out-bldgs thereon. The prospect from the house is beautiful, & the distance from the Capitol is but 1 mile, on the Balt turnpike road, free from toll. This farm was purchased & improved by the owner with the intention of occupying it. Apply to R W Dyer, or the subscrber, Jas Maher, Wash.

MON SEP 13, 1847

Letter received from Assist Adj Gen W H Gray, at Tampico, dated Aug 25, which states that Lt Taneyhill, who was captured by the Mexicans, & taken to Huejutla by the Mexicans, with some other prisoners, that his wounds proved fatal, & he died on Jul 25. The letter closes by stating that he was treated with great kindness by the Mexicans, & had the best of medical skill & care.

The Washington [N C] Whig of Sep 1 announces the decease of Mrs Ann Cambreleng, the mother of the Hon C C Cambreleng, late U S Minister to Russia. [No death date given-current item.]

List of the ofcrs & passengers of the frig **Savannah**, who arrived at N Y from Rio Janeiro: Capt, Wm Mervine
Lts: Robt B Hitchcock, Geo Miner, Robt T Pinkney, W S Schenck, Wm Rockendorff
Surgeon, Chas Chase; Capt of Marines, W Marston; Purser, E D Fauntleroy
Master, Wm F De Jongh; 2nd Lt of Marines, Henry W Queen
Assist Surgeons: M Duvall, & Jos Wilson
Midshipmen:

G E Morgan	J McRoberts	R C Duvall
J V N Phillips	J M Kell	A R Overcrombie
R D Minor	J P Griffin	P G Haywood
A T Byrnes	P J Watmaugh	J H Tilletson

Capt's Clerk, F Goodsell; Boatswain, G Wellmuth; Gunner, J M Cooper
Passengers:

Lt Com Chas Turner	Passed Midshipman, J W A Nicholson
Lt J H Stong	Midshipman, W O Crane,
Capt of Marines, N Waldron	Midshipman, S Gansevoort
Acting Purser, Wm S Hallins	Capt's Clerk, J M Maury
Passed Assist Surgeon, J S Whittle	Purser's Clerk, H Hough
2nd Lt Marines, Geo F Lindsey	Mr Easterbrook

The **Savannah** has been absent from the U S 3 years & nearly 11 months, during which time she has sailed nearly 72,000 miles. She sailed from N Y on Oct 19, 1843; she was the flag-ship of Com Sloat at the taking of Monterey, & has taken an active part in the operations on that coast.

Dr P B Delany, of the U S Navy, died at Laguna, Tucatan, on Aug 10, of yellow fever. The dec'd has but recently entered the navy as an assist surgeon, & died on his first cruise.

Montreal Courier: announces the death, from typhus fever, caught while attending to the faithful discharge of his duties at the emigrant sheds at St John's, the Rev Wm Davis, rector of that parish. He is the second clergyman of the Episcopal Church in the district of Montreal who has fallen a victim to the fever.

Miss Ann Beauchamp, daughter of Mr Edw Beauchamp, of Somerset Co, Md, was killed by lightning on Thu last, while standing near a chimney place.

Mr John Stevenson was almost instantly killed, & a friend of his very seriously hurt, on Sep 9, in Crosscreek township, Pa, by the fall of a tree which they had cut down while on a raccoon hunt.

Unfortunate accident on the Ohio river, lately, by the upsetting of a boat, by which Messrs T B & S C Wood, sons of Mr Silas Wood, of N Y C, were drowned.

Each private in Col Doniphan's regt received about $380, besides land scrip. Col Doniphan received $2,500. New Orleans Mercury [There were upwards of 1,000 men in the above regt, & according to the preceding it required about $400,000 to pay them off. This did not include the cost of their horses, all of which were lost, nor 10 months' forage rations, which were not furnished by the U S, & for which the regt claimed to be paid, but the paymaster here did not settle for either of these items. The Major of the regt informed us that the average amount due the men, including their horses & forage, was about $650 each, besides the land scrip. -New Orleans Bulletin

Several months ago a launch belonging to the U S ship **Warren**, then on the Pacific coast, was dispatched for the mouth of Rio Sacramento, & not having been heard from afterwards but little doubt remained that the boat & all on board were lost, including two of the sons of Cmder Montgomery, of Charlestown, Mass, who commanded the sloop-of-war **Portsmouth**, which vessel was in the vicinity at that time. A letter received by Mrs Montgomery, dated May 31, at Monterey, Calif, from on board the U S ship **Portsmouth**, states that up to that time nothing has been heard of the launch, & there was no doubt it was lost, & all on board perished.

Distressing accident near Claysville, Va, on Aug 22: the house belonging to Mr Isaac Bosely was on that day consumed by fire, together with his 3 little children. The parents had left the children, the eldest 4 years old & the youngest an infant, all of whom being asleep, the parents made fast the doors that they might be interrupted during their absence. The house took fire, originating in the chimney. -Romney [Va] Intel

The house of Maj Saml George, of Seabrook, N H, was destroyed by fire on Mon, & his housekeeper, widow Jane Dow, perished in the flames. She had returned to the house to save her money & papers.

A popular comedian, Thos McCutcheon, attached to the Chatham Theatre, N Y, committed suicide on Wed last by taking laudanum. None of his friends knew that he was in trouble.

John W Miller, a young man, was drowned in North river, Hampshire Co, Va, on Sep 1.

Died: on Sat last, in Wash City, Mrs Mary P Varnum, aged 65 years, relict of the late Hon John Varnum. Her funeral is today at 3:30 o'clock, from her late residence on 8th st.

By deed of trust from Henry Wilson to the subscriber, dated Jun 4, 1842, recorded in Liber W B 94, folios 324 thru 326, Wash Co, D C: to be sold at public auction, on Sep 30, lot 1 in subdivision of square 374, in Wash City: improved by a brick 2 story dwlg-house, fronting on 10th st west, between H & I sts north. -Jas A Kennedy, Trustee
-R W Dyer, auct

For rent: a 2 story brick house, with attic, back bldg, & carriage house, containing 10 rooms, on I st north, between 9th & 10th sts west. Inquire of Mr J B Clarke, the present occupant, or of the subscriber, at Mrs Billings', on 9th st, near E st. -W D Acken

TUE SEP 14, 1847

Lot of ground & premises for sale: on the corner of Mass ave & 4th st, fronting on Mass ave: with a 2 story brick house, new & substantially built. Apply to the subscriber, Md ave & 4½ st, or Walter Lenox, atty at law. -Wm Wise

The English public has been lately startled, [says the N Y American,] by an intimation that Mr Barnum, of the N Y Museum, a dealer in curiosities of various sorts, Thoms Thumb inclusive, was about to purchase Shakespeare's house at Stratford, with the view of conveying it to the U S. [See Sep 3, 1847-Shakespeare.]

The Beau Nash of the West. Cincinnati Commerical: Ohio is the last place in the world that we should have expected such a character to turn up in, & Scotland, his native place, the last country we should have looked to for a dancing master. A letter was received in this city on Sat from Harrodsburg Springs announcing the death of "Uncle Dick Richards," a name familiar to every citizen of Cincinnati. Although in his 72nd year he possessed to the last hour the vivacity of a youth of 20 & maintained with credit to himself his position as a director of balls, & a dancer of more than ordinary grace & ability. [No date-current news item.]

Independence, Sep 1, 1845. Mr Aubry has news from Chihuahua to Jul 3. On Jun 22, Mr Jas Aull, the partner of the late Col S C Owens, in an extensive mercantile business, was killed by 4 Mexicans. They entered his store in Chihuahua, killed him, & took away $5,000. The 3 murderers were arrested & put in prison to await trial. Mr Aull was a gentleman well known in Louisiana, & highly respected.

The scaffolding belonging to the new brick bldg now in process of erection opposite the Navy Dept, on 17th & F sts, gave way yesterday precipitating S H Taylor & Mr Stiff, bricklayers, to the gound, a distance of 15 feet. Mr Taylor was bruised, & Mr Stiff escaped unhurt.

Mrd: on Sep 9, by Rev Mr Sampson, Richd M Downer to Miss Margaret Jane Rugh, both of Wash City.

Died: on Sep 10, at the residence of his son, in Wash City, the Hon Saml Parris, an ofcr of the army of the Revolution, in his 93rd year. He was a native of Plymouth Co, Mass, & joined the American army in Jun, 1775, at Bunker Hill. At the close of the war he removed to Maine, then a part of Mass, where he was for several years a Judge of the Court of Common Pleas, Member of the Legislature, & an Elector of Pres & Vice Pres of the U S at Mr Madison's 2nd election. After appropriate services, his remains were conveyed to Portland, Maine, for interment.

Died: on Sep 12, Miss Sarah R Porter. Her funeral is this morning, at 11 o'clock, from the residence of her brother, on 19th, between I & K sts.

Died: Sep 2, at Smithtown, Long Island, of bilious fever, Robt Lawrence, late of Wash, D C, aged 60 years. Few men were more generally known & respected. For nearly 14 years he resided in Wash & was connected with the Treasury Dept. Since his return to N Y, his former residence, he had been an active member of the American Institute of that city. It seems he applied himself during the summer to hard labor on the farm of his brother; over-worked himself, & was thrown into a fever, & died of it.

Died: on Sep 5, in Newtown, Fred'k Co, Va, James W, infant son & only child of Jas W & Sarah A Barker, of Wash City, aged 13 months.

Died: on Sep 11, Richd Harrison, only child of John H C & Louisa Coffin, aged 1 year & 11 days.

The Hon Geo H Porffitt, formerly a member of Congress from Indiana, & recently Minister to Brazil, died at Louisville, Ky, on Sep 7. He had been afflicted by disease for some time previous to his death, & visited Louisville to obtain medical aid. His political career had been short, but rapid, & he has died comparatively young.

Col Owsley, of Ky, has appointed Manlius V Thompson, Colonel. Thos L Crittenden, Lt Col, & John C Breckenridge, Major, in one the regts of infty called for in the recent requisition of the War Dept from that State. The ofcrs of the other regt have not yet been appointed.

Extensive sale of valuable James River lands & coal property: by decree of the Superior Court of Chancery, for Richmond Circuit, made Jun 29, 1847, the undersigned will offer for sale, on Nov 10, the following estates, on James River & Tuckahoe creek, viz: 1-***Upper Plantation***, adjoining the lands of Thos Mann Randolph, containing 1,250 acres: bldgs are near the centre of the open land. 2-Tract formerly owned by Jas Currie, dec'd, called ***Ellerslie***, adjoining above, containing 765 acres: excellent stuccoed brick dwlg house. 3-***Lower Plantation***, purchased by the late David Meade Randolph, containing 691 acres; dwlg house on this tract. 4-Land bought of Thos Mann Randolph having thereon a grist & saw mill, containing about 195 acres: on about 7½ acres at the s w corner of this tract Mr Randolph has reserved a right to dig coal. Tracts are contiguous to each other. Mr Jenkins, residing on the estate, will show it. -B W Leigh, Wm F Wickham, Com'rs [Before the end of the year the slaves, about 130, & the stock, & crops will for offered for sale.]

Headquarters Army of Occupation. Camp near Monterey, Aug 16, 1847. Capt Fairfax, of the Virginia volunteers, died of fever at Saltillo, on Aug 14. [Sep 15th newspaper: Letter dated at Buena Vista, Aug 15. Capt Fairfax breathed his last on Aug 14: his company-the Gray Guards, is now under the command of 1st Lt Jas Thrift, a brave soldier & a good man. The men are preparing to escort the remains of Capt Fairfax to the grave.]

For sale: property on s e corner of 12th & M sts: with a large new frame dwlg, containing 13 rooms; a stable & carriage-house, bath-house, smoke & poultry-houses, & a pump of pure water but a few feet from the kitchen-door. By the time the last payment is due, in all probability will be worth double the amount now asked for it. -Giles Dyer

Country residence for sale or exchange: farm is at Langley: 54 acres: with a new frame dwlg: in a very populous & wealthy neighborhood. Address, Langley, Fairfax Co, Va. -Lent & Horton

WED SEP 15, 1847

Collector's Ofc, City Hall, Sep 13, 1847. On Dec 8 next, the annexed list of property will be sold by pulbic auction, at the City Hall, Wash City, for taxes due the Corporation of Wash.

Alexander, Chas: 1843 thru 1846
Allen, Mary E: 1842 thru 1846
Adams, Jas: 1843 thru 1846
Acton, Theodore: 1844 thru 1846
Ashton, Henry: 1839 thru 1846
Adams, Wm: 1844 thru 1846
Billing, W W: 1843, 1845 & 1846
Brent, Robt Y: 1843
Barnard, Theodore: 1843 & 1846
Boothe, Edw: 1843 & 1846
Brodeau, Ann: 1844 thru 1846
Bell, Ann: 1841 thru 1846
Bean, Benj: 1842 thru 1846
Bell, Chas: 1842 thru 1846
Bulfinch, Chas: 1844 thru 1846
Burgess, Deborah: 1842 thru 1846
Bowen, Fielder: 1843 thru 1846
Butler, Henry: 1844 thru 1846
Barcroft, John: 1844 thru 1846
Burch, Jos: 1844 thru 1846
Brent, Jas F: 1842 thru 1846
Bangs, John: 1844 thru 1846
Bottemly, John: 1843 thru 1846
Bowen, Jas A: 1844 thru 1846
Bouvet, Matthew: 1841 thru 1846
Burke, Mary P, & S D Anderson: 1843 thru 1846
Bowen, Martha A: 1844 thru 1846
Bradley, Phineas J: 1844 thru 1846
Brown, Robt: 1844 thru 1846
Burdine, Reuben: 1844 thru 1846
Berry, Rhoda L: 1843 thru 1846
Burch, Thos W: 1843 thru 1846

Berry, Wm J: 1843 thru 1846
Burdine, Wm H: 1844 thru 1846
Bohrer, B S: 1843 thru 1846
Bealle, Brooke: 1844 thru 1846
Bealle, Benj B: 1841 thru 1846
Biddle, Clement: 1833 thru 1846
Bliss, Elam: 1842 thru 1846
Burch, Thos: 1842 thru 1846
Berry, Zachariah: 1843 thru 1846
Burch, Jas A: 1844 thru 1846
Birch, Jas H: 1843 thru 1846
Brady, Nathl: 1843, 1845 & 1846
Bradley, Wm A: 1843 thru 1846
Barry, Richd: 1843
Clarke, Ann: 1844 thru 1846
Cross, David G C: 1843 thru 1846
Condict, Henry F: 1844 thru 1846
Callan, John F: 1844 thru 1846
Coombe, Jas G: 1838 thru 1846
Clements, Josias: 1844 thru 1846
Callan, Mich: 1841 thru 1846
Craig, Maria: 1841 thru 1846
Callan, Nicholas, jr: 1844 thru 1846
Culverwell, R L A: 1844 thru 1846
Conley, Thos Y: 1844, 1846
Corcoran, Wm W: 1842 thru 1846
Cripps, Wm M: 1844 thru 1846
Coxe, Wm: 1844 thru 1846
Carroll, Chas, jr: 1824 thru 1846
Cox, Clement: 1844 thru 1846
Chester, Elijah: 1840 thru 1846
Culver, Henry: 1842 thru 1846
Coyle, John: 1836 thru 1846
Carroll, Mary: 1844 thru 1846
Cooper, Robt: 1844 thru 1846
Collins & Smith & B C Smith: 1843 thru 1846
Chandler, Walter S: 1843 thru 1846
Campbell, Wm: 1844 thru 1846
Carroll, Danl: 1843 thru 1846
Davis, Andrew: 1844 thru 1846
Dowson, A R: 1844 thru 1846
Datcher, Francis: 1844 thru 1846
Davis, Geo M, interest: 1843 thru 1846
Deming, Harriet A: 1837 thru 1846
Davidson, Jas: 1845 & 1846

Duedney, John: 1844 thru 1846
Disher, Lewis: 1844 thru 1846
Donn, Thos C: 1843 thru 1846
Dove, Wm T: 1840 thru 1846
Dalton, Catharine: 1834 thru 1846
Dyson, Geo E: 1838 thru 1846
Dewees, Wm: 1836 thru 1846
Donelan, Wm C: 1843 thru 1844
Dunlop, Jas: 1843 thru 1846
Drummond, Noah, in trust: 1842 thru 1846
Dulin, Johm: 1841 thru 1846
Daw, Reuben: 1844 thru 1846
Elliot, Seth A: 1843 thru 1846
Evans, Walter: 1843 thru 1846
Eckel, Chas E: 1843 thru 1846
Eschbach, John: 1844 thru 1846
Franzoni, Jane: 1844 thru 1846
Forrest, Stepney: 1844 thru 1846
Ford, Wm: 1844 thru 1846
Faw, Abraham: 1844 thru 1846
Fisher, John: 1844 thru 1846
Fowler, Job: 1837 thru 1846
Forrest, Richd: 1844 thru 1846
Fletcher, Wm, jr: 1842 thru 1846
Fischer, Wm: 1842 thru 1846
Fletcher, Thos: 1845 & 1846
Glenn, Eliz: 1842 thru 1846
Gibson, Geo, trustee: 1843 thru 1846
Green, Hannah A: 1843 thru 1846
Guest, Jonathan: 1843 thru 1846
Greenleaf, Jas: 1844 thru 1846
Gibson, Joshua: 1844 thru 1846
Goldsborough, L M: 1844 thru 1846
Gatchell, Eliz A: 1841 thru 1846
Givison, Wm: 1843 thru 1846
Grammer, G C: 1843
Hoover, Barbara: 1843 thru 1846
Harkness, Danl S: 1844 thru 1846
Hanley, Edmund: 1844 thru 1846
Hicks, Geo: 1840 thru 1846
Henning, Henry N: 1841 thru 1846
Henshaw, J L: 1843 thru 1846
Hauptman, John W: 1844 thru 1846
Hoover, John: 1844 thru 1846
Holdham, John: 1844 thru 1846

Howard, John T: 1842 thru 1846
Hepburn, Jeremiah: 1845 & 1846
Hodson, John E: 1842 thru 1846
Hoover, Michl: 1842 thru 1846
Hinton, Robt W: 1842 thru 1846
Holme, Sylvanus: 1844 thru 1846
Hamilton, Saml: 1843 thru 1846
Hayman, Wm: 1844 thru 1846
Hazel, Zachariah: 1844 thru 1846
Headley, Eliza: 1844 thru 1846
Hoffman, John: 1844 thru 1846
Haswell, N B: 1844 thru 1846
Hoffman, Peter: 1844 thru 1846
Henley, Robt: 1836 thru 1846
Henley, Wm D: 1844 thru 1846
Jackson, Chaney: 1844 thru 1846
Jones, Chas L: 1844 thru 1846
Jacobs, Harry: 1844 thru 1846
Jardine, Harriet: 1842 thru 1846
Jones, Joel W: 1844 thru 1846
Jeffers, Matthias: 1844 thru 1846
Jones, Richd: 1844 thru 1846
Kennedy & Billing: 1842 thru 1846
Keller, Eliz: 1844 thru 1846
Krofft, Geo: 1845 & 1846
Keating, Geo-[sq 150 lots 7 & 8]: 1842 thru 1846
Kaiser, Herman: 1844 thru 1846
Kerr, Robt E, in trust for heirs of Henry Whetcroft: 1842 thru 1846
Kerr, Robt E: 1844 thru 1846
Keyworth, Robt: 1844 thru 1846
Keane, Stephen: 1844 thru 1846
Kavanagh, Thos: 1843 thru 1846
Key, Ann & others: 1843 thru 1846
King, Geo, of Chas: 1844 thru 1846
Kershner, Martin: 1844 thru 1846
King, Wm: 1843 thru 1846
Klopfer, Chas G: 1843, 1845 & 1846
Leddon, Benj: 1843 thru 1846
Longdon, Chas: 1844 thru 1846
Lydock, Francis: 1843 thru 1846
Landrick, Isaac: 1844 thru 1846
Little, John: 1844 thru 1846
Little, John E: 1844 thru 1846
Lowe, W W: 1844 thru 1846
Lenoir, Wm J: 1844 thru 1846

Linn, Adam: 1835 thru 1846
Little, Warren: 1844
Law, Thos: 1840 thru 1846
Macomb, Alex'r: 1844 thru 1846
Martin, Bernard: 1844 thru 1846
Marshall, Barbara: 1844 thru 1846
Mix, Chas E: 1844 thru 1846
McGlue, G T: 1844 thru 1846
Miller, Geo: 1844 thru 1846
Mattingly, Geo: 1844 thru 1846
Miller, Henry: 1844 thru 1846
Merryman, Horatio R: 1844 thru 1846
Marlow, John W: 1843 thru 1846
McKean, Jas P: 1844 thru 1846
Martin, Jas: 1844 thru 1846
Martin, Jos: 1844 thru 1846
Martin, Jas E: 1844 thru 1846
Murphy, Martin: 1843 thru 1846
Milstead, Mgt N: 1843 thru 1846
Mercer, Rachel: 1844 thru 1846
Milburn, Thos M; 1844 thru 1846
McIntosh, Thos: 1844 thru 1846
Magruder, Wm B, in trust: 1843 thru 1846
Morrow, Wm: 1843 thru 1846
McCormick, W J, in trust: 1843 thru 1846
McGill, Wm: 1844 thru 1846
McWilliams, Clement: 1842 thru 1846
Millard, Joshua: 1844 thru 1846
Maddox, Notley: 1843 thru 1846
Morton, Wm: 1844 thru 1846
McDaniel, Wm: 1844 thru 1846
Maury, J W: 1844 & 1845
Neale, John E: 1844 thru 1846
Nicholson, Peter: 1844 thru 1846
Norris, Wm B: 1843 thru 1846
Nourse, Jos: 1844 thru 1846
Nicholson, Jos H: 1843 thru 1846
Noyes, Wm: 1842 thru 1846
Naylor, Henry & A Rothwell, & L J Denham: 1843 thru 1846
Nash, Michl: 1843 & 1844
Maddox, W A T: 1845 & 1846
O'Conner, Eugene: 1843 thru 1846
Oler, John: 1844 thru 1846
Orme, Wm C: 1844 thru 1846
Orme, T T & Mary Ann: 1844 thru 1846

O'Neale, Wm: 1845 & 1846
Powers, Ann: 1844 thru 1846
Pilling, Jas, jr: 1844 thru 1846
Peck, Jos: 1844 thru 1846
Phillips, Jas B: 1842 thru 1846
Phillips, Overton C: 1843 thru 1846
Prather, O J: 1844 thru 1846
Pollard, Richd: 1843, 1845 & 1846
Parker, Selby: 1844 thru 1846
Phillips, Saml: 1840 thru 1846
Pumphrey, Thos P, Jas W, & F A: 1843 thru 1846
Prout, Wm: 1841 thru 1846
Pearson & Brent: 1844 thru 1846
Peter, David: 1840 thru 1846
Peter, Geo: 1840 thru 1846
Patton, Jas: 1842 thru 1846
Pickrell, John: 1839 thru 1846
Pell, Wm & J B: 1844 thru 1846
Packard, Perez: 1842 thru 1846
Queen, Mgt: 1844 thru 1846
Queen, Nicholas L: 1844 thru 1846
Robinson, Alex'r: 1844 thru 1846
Richards, Alfred: 1844 thru 1846
Ridgway, Enoch: 1842 thru 1846
Roper, Erasmus: 1844 thru 1846
Randal, Emeline W: 1842 thru 1846
Raley, Jas: 1843 thru 1846
Rawlings & Longden: 1842 thru 1846
Robertson, Mary: 1843 thru 1846
Richardson, David: 1843 thru 1846
Robbins, Harriet: 1844 thru 1846
Ringgold, Tench: 1842 thru 1846
Spence, Christopher: 1843 thru 1846
Shirk, Henry & Isaac, & Jos Judith: 1844 thru 1846
Stevens, Jas: 1842 thru 1846
Scrivener, Jas: 1842 thru 1846
Smith, John: 1844 thru 1846
Shiles, J W: 1844 thru 1846
Simms, Mary Ann E: 1843 thru 1846
Sweeney, Mary: 1844 thru 1846
Simpson & Neale: 1844 thru 1846
Sweet, Parker H: 1840 thru 1846
Stevenson, Robt: 1842 thru 1846
Stewart, Wm: 1843 thru 1846
Smith, Archar B: 1839 thru 1846

Scott, Horatio C: 1844 thru 1846
Snowden, John & others: 1843 thru 1846
Somers, Lewis: 1842 thru 1846
Smith, Lewis F: 1835 thru 1846
Smith, Paca: 1843 thru 1846
Sands, R C & Z Hazel: 1844 thru 1846
Sterret, Saml: 1839 thru 1846
Simmons, Wm: 1843 thru 1846
Scott, Jas W: 1824 thru 1846
Sawyer, Jos & Wm: 1843 & 1846
Stott, Saml: 1845 & 1846
Thruston, Buckner, or Jas Frye: 1844 thru 1846
Taylor, John 3rd: 1842 thru 1846
Tompson, Jos: 1844 thru 1846
Thomas, John: 1844 thru 1846
Travis, Levin & wife: 1840 thru 1846
Timberlake, M V: 1844 thru 1846
Taylor, Thos & Josias: 1844 thru 1846
Taylor, Thos: 1844 thru 1846
Tilghman, Frisby: 1844 thru 1846
Thomas, Ann: 1843 & 1845 & 1846
Thomas, Jos & Jas: 1845 & 1846
Venable, Chas: 1843 thru 1846
Venable, Ellen: 1844 thru 1846
Voss, Wm: 1843
Van Ness, J P: 1842 thru 1846
Walker, Dorcas: 1844 thru 1846
Wailes, Dorothea: 1840 thru 1846
Wood, Ferdinand F: 1844 thru 1846
Waters, Henrietta: 1843 thru 1846
Watson, Jas: 1844 thru 1846
Warren, Jos: 1843 thru 1846
Walker, John: 1843 thru 1846
West, John: 1843 thru 1846
Wilson, John A: 1843 thru 1846
Waller, Jas D, [trustee]: 1844 thru 1846
Wood, Mary Ann E: 1844 thru 1846
Welch, Mary Ann: 1844 thru 1846
Wroe, Saml: 1844 thru 1846
Wilson, Wm: 1843 thru 1846
Wheatley, Wm J: 1843 thru 1846
Walker, Wm: 1843 thru 1846
Wheeler, Eliz: 1837 thru 1846
Wescott, Jas D: 1837 thru 1846
Wharton, Franklin: 1844 thru 1846

Winder, Levin H: 1844 thru 1846
West, Richd: 1841 thru 1846
Williams, Sarah B: 1841 thru 1846
Willink, Wm, & Jas & others: 1844 thru 1846
Young, Mgt: 1836 thru 1846
Young, John: 1824 thru 1846
Young, Nicholas: 1844 thru 1846
Wright, Thos: 1836 thru 1846
Young, Notley: 1824 thru 1846
-A Rothwell, collector

Balt, Sep 13-affray in a tavern in Marsh Market space, in which a young man named Wm Perry, journeyman printer, belonging to Balt, was accidentally shot by his friend, Andrew J Scott, a youth now studying medicine here, but a resident of Missioui. A difficulty occurred between Scott & others in the tavern, the ball striking Perry in the groin producing a very serious, if not fatal wound. Perry is a very genteel & inoffensive young man. Scott has been arrested & imprisoned for trial.

Yellow Fever in New Orleans: two of our physicians are down, Drs Carpenter & Eddy. Rev Mr Fay is also down. Another physician, Dr B H Hull, died yesterday. Mr Jno Postlethwaite, of the house of Messrs Crockett, Garland & Co, died. Mr Merrill & Mrs Washington, both teachers, have died.

Mrd: on Sep 11, in Wash City, by Rev Jas B Donelan, Alex'r G Morgan to Mary M McGillicuddy, both of Boston, Mass.

THU SEP 16, 1847

Late victories in Mexico: vast loss of valuable life:

Ofcrs killed-regulars:

Maj Mills, 15th Infty
Capt Hanson, 7th Infty
Capt Thornton, 2nd Dragoons
Capt Burke, 1st Artl
Capt Capron, 1st Artl
Capt Quarles, 15th Infty
Capt Anderson, 2nd Infty
Lt Easly, 2nd Infty
Lt Goodman, 15th Infty
Lt Hoffman, 1st Artl
Lt Irons, 1st Artl, but attached to Gen Cadwalader's staff
Lt Preston Johnson, 1st Artl, but attached to Magruder's battery

Ofcrs killed-volunteers:

Lt Chandler, N Y Regt
Col P M Butler, S C Regt
Lt David Adams, S C Regt
Lt W R Williams, S C Regt

Ofcs Wounded-regulars:

Col Clark, 6th Infty, slightly
Col Morgan, 15th Infty, severely
Maj Wade, 3rd Artl, severely
Maj Bonneville, 6th Infty, slightly
Capt Wessels, 2nd Infty, severely

Capt Phil Kearny, 1st Dragoons, left arm shot off
Capt McReynolds, 3rd Dragoons, severely
Capt Craig, 3rd Infty, severely
Capt Ross, 7th Infty, severely
Capt J R Smith, 2nd Infty, severely
Capt Chapman, 5th Infty, slightly
Capt Johnson, 9th Infty, alightly
Capt Holden, 12th Infty, slightly
Capt Hathaway, 1st Artl, slightly
Capt Hoffman, 6th Infty, slightly
Lt Bacon, 6th Infty, severely
Lt Arnold, 2nd Artl, severely
Lt Hendrickson, 6th Infty, severely
Lt Humber, 7th Infty, severely
Lt Van Buren, of the rifles, slightly
Lt Martin, 1st Artl, right arm shot off
Lt Goodloe, 15th Infty, mortally
Lt Lugenbeel, adj 5th Infty, slightly
Lt Bee, 3rd Infty, slightly
Lt Lovell, 2nd Infty, slightly
Lt Chandler, 3rd Infty, slightly
Lt Collins, 4th Artl, slightly
Lt Tilden, 2nd Infty, slightly
Lt Sprague, adj 9th Infty, slightly
Lt Palmer, 9th Infty, severely
Lt Buckner, 6th Infty, slightly
Lt Cram, 9th Infty, slightly
Lt Simpkins, 12th Infty, slightly
Lt Peternell, 15th Infty, slightly
Lt Bennett, 15th Infty
Lt Schuyler Hamilton, 1st Infty, but attached to Gen Scott's staff, severely
Lt Halloway, 8th Infty, but attached to Smith's light btln, severely
Lt Callender, of the ordnance, but commanding howitzer battery, severely
Lt Herman Thorn, 3rd Dragoons, attached to Col Garland's staff, slightly
Lt Boynton, 1st Artl, but attached to Taylor's battery, slightly
Lt Lorimer Graham, acting with 1st Dragoons, severely
Lt Farelly, 5th Infty, but attached to Smith's light btln, severely

Volunteers-N Y Regt:

Col Burnet, severely
Capt Fairchild, slightly
Capt Dyckman, severely
Lt Sweeney, severely
Lt Jenniss, slightly
Lt Cooper, severely
Lt McCabe, slightly
Lt Potter, severely
Lt Griffin, slightly
Lt Malhowsky, slightly

South Carolina Regt:

Lt Col Dickinson, severely
Capt Jas D Blanding, slightly

Adj Canter, severely
Lt Sumter, slightly
Capt K S Moffatt, slightly
Lt K S Billings, severely
Lt J R Clark, dangerously
Lt J W Steen, slightly
Lt J R Davis, slightly
Capt W D DeSaussure, slightly
Lt Jos Abney, severely

Mr Marion Ward, youngest son of the late Saml Ward, of N Y, & brother of Mr Saml Ward, of Prime, Ward & Co, died at New Orleans on Sep 3 from the prevailing epidemic there.

The Hon P T Jackson, of Boston, died at Beverly on Tue last, in his 73rd year. He was a pioneer in most of the important undertakings which have made Boston what she is, & prepared her for her great future.

Knoxville Tribune of Sep 8: Averett, the Lynchburg defaulter, had, subsequently to his arrest, been brought before the Circuit Court of Grainger Co, under a writ of habeas corpus, & admitted to bail in the sum of $500 for 20 days. The Knoxville Register states that he absconded after being bailed.

Died: on Jun 1, in Monrovia, Africa, Rev Jas Eden, aged 62 years & 16 days, missionary of the Presbyterian Board, & pastor of the 1st Presbyterian Church.

Died: on Aug 27, at the Naval Hospital, Island of Salmandina, aged about 53, of the yellow fever, after a few days' illness, Dr John A Kearney, Fleet Surgeon of the squadron in the Gulf of Mexico, a native of Ireland, & long a resident of this District & Md. By the Navy Register it appears he first entered the service as a surgeon's mate on Mar 3, 1809; present commission bears date of Jul 24, 1813; was a surgeon of the ship **Constitution** during the last war with Great Britain at the time of her successful engagement with the ship **Cyane** & the ship **Levant**; during the same war he was surgeon of the flotilla of gun boats in the harbor of Newport, R I, under command of Com O H Perry, so eminently distinguished on Lake Erie. His family, his wife & several children, mourn their loss.

Reward for runaway negro John Newman, about 40 years old. He has a mother living at Clarke's hotel in Marlborough. $5 if taken in the District, & $10 if taken out of the District. -Edw Mattingly, near the Navy Yard, Wash.

25 cents reward for runaway, an indented apprentice to the tailoring business, Richd Gormley, aged 19. All persons are forbid harboring or employing said apprentice, as the law will certainly be enforced against such offenders. -J Matlock

Huzza! Huzza! Huzza! Great Victory! Thirty-two thousand Mexicans defeated by seven thousand Americans. Gen Santa Anna defeated, whipped, & completely routed. -Sun of Anahuac, Sep 1

N Y Herald: Com A S Mackenzie has been appointed to the command of the steam frig **Mississippi.**

Valuable brick house & lot at auction: on Sep 21, in front of the premises, lot 5 of the subdivision of lots 1 & 2, in square 490, on C st, between 4½ & 6th sts. The property is that belonging to Lt W D Porter. Terms at sale. -A Green, auctioneer

The undersigned, appointed respectively, the three first by Maj Gen Winfield Scott, cmder-in-chief of the armies of the U S, & the two last by his Excellency D Antonio Lopez de Santa Anna, Pres of the Mexican Republic & cmder-in-chief of its armies, met with full powers, in the village of Tacubays, on Aug 22, 1847, to enter into an armistice of receiving propositions for peace from the Com'r appointed by the Pres of the U S, & now with the American army. Signed Aug 23, 1847:
A Quitman, Maj Gen U S A
Persifer F Smith, Brvt Brig Gen U S A
Franklin Pierce, Brig Gen U S A
Ignacio De Mora Y Villamil
Benito Quijano
G W Lay, U S A, Mil Sec to the Genr'l in Chief

Liberal reward for return of lost Dog, brown Terrier Pup. -Edw Stubbs, G st, between 8th & 9th sts.

FRI SEP 17, 1847
Col Jefferson Davis, of Mississippi, has accepted the appointment of U S Senator from that State, to fill the vacancy occasioned by the death of Senator Speight.

The Illinois & Michigan Canal is approaching completion. The balance of the machinery for pumping water upon summit level arrived yesterday from Erie. It is manufactured by Col W J Totten, of Pittsburg, who superintends putting it in place here.

A rencontre took place in the streets of Norfolk on Wed last between Mr Leonard White & Mr Albert Beale, which resulted in the death of the former on Sun. The combatants were brothers-in-law, & the affray grew out of an aggravated assault by the deceased, who was a very intemperate man, on his mother-in-law, Mr Beale's mother, who is blind as well as decrepit from age. The Norfolk Herals says that Mrs Beale was beaten & bruised in a shocking manner, & the assault on White was committed soon after Mr Beale had learned of the brutal manner in which his aged mother had been treated.

Mr E Coleman, well known in Boston as the landlord of the Pavilion, & in Balt as the lessee of the Exchange Hotel, died at the McLean Asylum for the Insane, in Massachusetts, on Fri.

Mrd: on Sep 12, by Rev Alfred H Partridge, Thos H Lane, of Wash, to Ellen H Turk, daughter of the late Jas Turk, of Somers, Wash Co, N Y.

Died: on Sep 16, in Wash City, after an illness of several years, Mrs Eliz Magruder, aged 39 years, w/o Dr Wm B Magruder. Her funeral is on Sat at 10 o'clock.

Fatal railroad accident on Fri last, as the New Haven steamboat train was near Framingham: Jos Jackson, went out upon the locomotive to oil the cylinder, & was not again seen until his mangled body was found upon the track. It is supposed he missed his footing & fell. He was about 23 years old, a single man, & was considered one of the best firemen upon the road. -Boston Traveller

Wash Corp: 1-Bill for the relief of Dorcas Galvin: passed. 2-Ptn of Allison Nailor, in relation to omnibuses, to place the owners of omnibuses residing in Gtwn on the same footing as those residing in any other part of the county & without the limits of the city: referred to the Cmte on Police.

City Ordinances: 1-Act for the relief of Dorcas Galvin: fine for an alleged violation in the erection of frame bldgs, is remitted: said Galvin to pay the costs of prosecution. 2-Act for the relief of Matilda Radcliff: the sum of $3 be returned, this amount being taxes paid upon lot 8 in square 267, for certain improvements erroneously returned at the last general assessment.

Household & kitchen furniture, Philosophical apparatus, electrical machine, school desks, & black boards, at auction: at the residence of Mr Porter, on C, between 3rd & 4½ sts. -A Green, auctioneer

Dr Wm L Fraser, has located himself in the 1st Ward for the practice of his profession: ofc next door to the Six Bldgs, near the West Market.

SAT SEP 18, 1847

Buffalo Commercial Herald: the Hon Chas Townsend, one of the oldest & most estimable residents of the city of Buffalo, died on Mon or Tue last. He spent the Monday about town, & the evening with his family, & retired at the usual hour. On Tue morning early, a servant, on going into the sitting room to light a fire, found him seated in a chair, his head leaning on his hand over a table, dead. His age about 61 years.

Fatal affray on Sat: Capt Jas Wilson, of the Kenton Rangers, Covington, Ky, was shot & killed by Lt Phelps, of the same company. It appears that Phelps had made some remarks about Capt Wilson as an ofcr, at which the latter took offence. Phelps has been arrested. -Cincinnati Atlas

A Naval Genr'l Court Martial was yesterday convened on board the U S ship **North Carolina**, in the harbor of N Y, of which Cmdor John D Sloat is president, Capts Benj Cooper, Wm D Salter, & Hiram Paulding, & Cmder Wm C Nicholson, are members. Purser G R Barry, judge advocate.

Present condition of the South Carolina regt of volunteers: they left their homes 6 months ago about 800 strong; of this number 140 died at Vera Cruz or on the march to Puebla, & 360 were left sick in the various hospitals. About 272 were in a condition to fight in the late battle, & of that number 137 [including their gallant Col, Pierce M Butler] were killed or wounded, leaving a meager remnant of 135, a moiety of whom may yet perhaps fall in battle or perish by disease before the war shall terminate. -Richmond Whig

Assist Surgeon P Benson Delany died at Laguna about Aug 15. Passed Assist Surgeon Chas G Bates died at the Island of Salmedina on Aug 26.

Col Pierce M Butler has been for a long time a conspicuous & prominent citizen of S C: possessed military qualities of the highest order. Alas! Terminated at its very commencement. Col Butler, though twice badly wounded, & weighed down by faintness & loss of blood, maintained his position until a third wound caused his death. Lt Col Dickinson, who was the 1st ofcr wounded at Vera Cruz, also signalized his valor on this occasion, & was again badly wounded. -N O Delta

We learn from a gentleman of the neighborhood, that Mr Jos Fawcett, of Montg Co, Md, had a dght, 7 years of age, drowned in a fish-barrel on Sep 15.

Judge Wm Kent, who was recently appointed to the Royal Professorship of Law in Harvard Univ, has resigned the same. The resignation is caused by imperative duties of a domestic nature, which require his residence in N Y. -N Y Express

Texas Emigration & Land Co: 320 acres of land for $20! 160 acres of land for $10. -Willis Stewart, John J Smith, & W C Peters, Trustees of the Texas Emigration & Land Co. Louisville, Sep 1, 1847

Shocking homicide on a street in Raleigh, N C, on Mon last. Henry Watson, killed with a knife, Lethan Norwood, & both are said to be men of respectability & standing, with large & interesting families. Alcohol was the prime agent in this lamentable & tragic affair.

$200 reward for runaways, negro men Isaac Blackistone, from 38 to 40 years old; & John Fenwick, about 21 years old, a full 6 feet high. They ran away from St Mary's Co, Md. -Wm Coad, Great Mills, Md

John R Wallace, of Fauquier Co, Va, will open an ofc in Wash City for the practice of Law, in Nov.

Lands in Alexandria Co, for sale at Public Auction: by deed of trust from Robt Widdicombe & wife, executed on Mar 25, 1844: sale on Sep 28: tracts of land in Alexandria Co, Va, which is part of the lands formerly belonging to Gen Mason, & by him conveyed to the Bank of Wash, viz: parts of sections 4, 5, & 9, as surveyed & laid off by Lewis Carbery, in 1835 & 1836, containing together about 57 acres. And sections #15, containing about 73 acres & 3 roods. -R W Dyer, auct

John P C Peter wishes to employ immediately an elderly gentleman, of unexceptionable character, capable of teaching all the branches of an English Education, as a Private Tutor in his family. Address, post paid, Montevideo, near Darnestown, Montg Co, Md.

The trustees of the Berryville Academy, Clarke Co, Va, wish to procure the services of an accomplished instructor for the year ensuing. -Richd H Wilmer, Cyrus McCormick, F J Kerfoot, Treadwell Smith, Rand Kownslar

Orphans Court of Wash Co, D C. In the matter of the ptn for the sale of the real estate of Danl H Haskell. The guardian & trustee in this case have reported to this Court: the sale of lot 6 in square 200, & improvements, the real estate of said Haskell, on Apr 6, 1844; at which sale Arthur L McIntire became the purchaser, at the sum of $1,300, & has since paid the purchase money. -Nathl Pope Causin

MON SEP 20, 1847

Meeting of the Exec Cmte of the Chicago Harbor & River Convention, at the Astor House, N Y C, Sep 15, 1847. Present:

Abbott Lawrence, of Mass
Chas King, of N J
John Mills, of Mass
Thos w Williams, of Conn
Philip Ripley, of Conn
Jas Hall, of Ohio
John C Spencer, of N Y
Saml B Ruggles, of N Y
W B Hodgson, of Ga

Killed, wounded & missing, in the battles of Aug 20 & 21. Immense sacrifice at the victories of Gen Scott.

1st Division: commanded by Maj Gen Worth.

Killed: Sgt C W Cobb, Co I, 2nd Artl; Privates Henry Hear, do, John Healy, do; John Sheridan, Co H, 5th Infty; Alex McKenzie, do; Sgt John Farrell, Co C, 2nd Artl; Privates John Daley, do; Wm Landolt, Co I; Jas Wilson, Co G; J L Jordan, Co B, 3rd Artl; Sgt Wm Brown, Co G; Privates Philip Nichols, do; Chas Ray, do; John Ruber, do; Sgt Wm McGuire, Co I; Privates Nicholas Keuniston, do; Wm Johnson, Co A, 4th Infty; Edw Kirwill, Co I; F Pinkerton, do; Cpl T James, Co E, 5th Infty; Privates J C McKinney, Co A; A Vanalstyne, Co E; Saml Wilson, do; B Sirman, Co I; E C Smith, Co K; Porter Hand, Co A, 6th Infty; David Noble, do; D Harnett, Co C; J McKee, Co D; Geo Graham, do; A D Harris, Co F; Wm Bray, Co H; Robt Saddy, do; John Foss, do; Paul Dufour, Co I, 8th Infty; Edw Flemming, do; Caspar Polk, do.

Wounded: Private Jas Reilly, Co A, 2nd Artl; Sgts Philip Wilson, Co K; E Meyn, do; Privates H Acherman, do; John Casey, do; P Dowd, do; W Gravenhart, do; John Stewart, do; Andrew Casey, do; Hugh Casey, do; Jas Davidson, do; Martin Conway, Co I; Patrick Kennedy, do; Wm Lafferty, do; Jos Mills, do; Edw Sullivan, do; Henry Vuchel, do; Sgt Jos Fadding, do; Cpl Wm Sutherland, do; Privates: Jas Donoho, do; Michl Lynch, do; Wm Murray, do; 2nd Lt P Farrally, 5th Infty; Privates: Geo Bishop, Co H; Chas Carner, do; W C Emerson, do; John Francha, do; Peter Flynn, do; Jos Fry, do; J A Hooft, do; Wm Bell, do; Michl Stezer, do; John Shimmel, do; David Wilton, do; Jacob Mayer, do; Danl Rogers, do; Thos Sleck, do; 2nd Lt E B Holloway, Co B, 8th Infty; Privates: Chas Childs,

Co B, 8th Infty; Chas Fitzgerald, do; Michl Hagan, do; John Sawyer, do; 1st Lt Lewis G Arnold, Co F, 2nd Artl; Sgt Chas Wilson, Co C; Cpl Andrew Bell, do; Privates: Chas Carroll, do; Geo Heck, do; Henry Dougalss, do; Powell Oullip, do; Jacob Schriver, do; Jas Gould, Co D; Jas Burgen, do; Richd Birmingham, do; Sgt Thos G Allen, Co F; Privates G W Church, do; John Conner, do; Patrick Gallagher, do; Henry Hatch, do; Hugh Murphy, do; Chas Q Putman, do; Martin Riordan, do; Philip Stevens, do; Lewis Seiter, do; P Zirngrible, do; Church Snyder, do; David Walsh, do; E E Saunders, do; Sgts: Luke Walker, Co G; Jas Chappell, do; Jas H Starr, do; Cpl Simon Stanton; Privates: H Binart, do; P Thornton, do; Lewis Schott, do; John Harper, do; J J Moore, do; Wm Bardon, do; Thos Starr, do; H Levy, do; Jas Hughs, do; D Hagaman, do; Sgts A B Cleveland, Co H; John Walters, do; John Cunningham, do; Cpl J Ric Redman, do; Privates: F Connors,do; Chas Birnan, do; Danl Daly, do; Henry Frank, do; Jas Gourley, do; John King, do; Alex Moore, do; Carles Page, do; Brevet Maj Ward, 3rd Artl; Sgt John H Hick, Co B; Cpls: Wm Young, do; John Hynes, do; E Insworth, do; Jos Akor, do; Privates: John Coogan, do; Adam Deflin, do; Edw Eagan, do; E W Gleason, do; John Hughs, do; F H Lachat, do; G W Smith, do; J Thompson, do; Wm Patton, do; John Morris, Co G; Edw Porter, do; Thos Brady, do; John Mailland, do; Thos Loftis, do; Chas Reis, do; Anthony Sutler, do; V Kenwater, do; Sgt Jas H Hubbard, Co I; Privates: C McClyman, do; Thos McCoy, do; John Naylor, do; John Setser, do; 2nd Lt H Thorn, [A de C.] 3rd Dragoons; Privates: John McLaughlin, Co A, 4th Infty; Danl O'Shea, do; John Alexander, Co B; J Frob, Co I; Jos Shaffa, do; A Hartland, do; E Thompson, Co D; Col N S Clarke, 6th Infty; Adj P Lugenbeel, 5th Infty; Capt W W Chapman, Co G; Maj B L E Bonneville, 6th Infty; Capt W W Hoffman, Co D; 1st Lt T Hendrickson, Co K; 1st Lt J D Baron, Co A; 2nd Lt S B Buckner, [Reg Q M;] Privates: A E Boyer, Co A, 5th Infty; J Connell, do; Peter Frazer, do; M Knott, do; P Mandy, do; D Henry, do; W Weighten, do; F Moreton, do; E M Whitford, do; O Othman, Co B; J Boyle, do; J Jacobson, do; U S Hall, Co E; J McAlthony, do; M O'Brien, do; G Ritner, do; S Seal, do; L Tickelman, do; W Wheeler, do; Sgt Lawrence, Co F; Cpl J Harman, do; Privates: F Mather, do; H Miller, do; D Reim, do; J Rodney, do; P Maloney, do; J Burgen, do; J G Wilmer, do; C Thompson, do; W G Stansbury, Co G; J Rice, do; J L Clark, do; Sgt S Minur, Co I; Privates: G Smith, do; P Barine, do; P Riley, do; G Rung, do; I Mullen, Co K; H Riley, do; L Deray, do; F Knapp, do; Quart Mas Sgt J Mahoney; Cpl W Williams, Co A, 6th Infty; Privates: T Hardy, do; W Williams, do; W Loomis, do; J Hardin, do; W Bowles, do; P Connor, do; W Faley, do; F Schoup, do; Sgts: R McKowen, Co F; J Kronire, do; Mus J O'Neil, do; Privates: A Barker, do; J Connor, do; D Keefe, do; W B Manering, do; H Martineau, do; J McDonough, do; W Lerron, do; J Wilson, do; Cpl R O Shrill, Co B; Privates: W Allen, do; D Dunward, do; D Carroll, do; D Hoss, do; M Hogan, do; Sgts: W Nevins, Co C; F Owens, do; Cpl H Goodwin, do; Mus Jesse Brown, do; Privates: G Christy, do; J Barnes, do; J Lanouer, do; J Tuttle, do; S Madden, do; E McBrehesty, do; D Griffin, do; B Hart, do; M Smith, do; J O'Brien, do; E Langley, do; G R Washington, do; E Jordan, do; F Curtis, Co E; J Draper, do; O Austin, do; R Peples, do; M Stilwell, do; F D C Dye, do; W Biggs, do; M Sailingo, do; P Riner, do; A Stinebaugh, do; H McElvaugh, do; T Owens, do; Sgts: W Linderks, Co H; J Remington, do; Privates: Geo G Fletcher, do; C Perkins, do; S Alcock, do; J McGuire, do; H Costolo, do; O Scofield, do; R Wogan, do; G Stigher, do; H Rudolph, do; Sgt J Craig, Co D; M Keefe, do; Privates: G Baughanan, do; C Burns,

do; J A Eaton, do; G McCarthy, do; H Niehan, do; J Frosk, do; J James, Co K; J Elwater, do; A Sorrel, do; W Reynolds, do; J Misso, W Piercy, Co H; Sgt J Anderson, Co A, 8th Infty; Privates: N Benerlin, do; S Taylor, do; J Curting, do; J D Knipper, do; J Englehart, do; W Hirst, Co C; F Somerhane, do; E Cumberbeach, Co D; E Ashworth, Co E; B G Barret, do; J C Kennedy, do; S Revidon, do; R Russell, do; J White, do; S Johnson, Co F; J Shutz, do; Sgt S Stoeffer, Co I; Privates: C Benner, do; W Delaney, do; M O'Brien, do; Cpl S Hallinan, Co K; E Capon, Co H; Privates: J Bennett, do; J Gordon, do; C Hopkins, do; M Wharton, do; S Donoghaugh, do; W Dunn, Co C.
Missing: Privates John Golden, Co D, 2nd Artl, returned; Stephen Lamb, Co I, 3rd Artl; Michl McGrath, Co F, 4th Infty, wounded; Pat Green, Co F, 4th Infty; Andrew McDonalds, do; Jas Steel, do; John Robertson, Co I; Jos Spencer, Co D, 5th Infty; J R Debaun, Co K; J Smith, Co B, 6th Infty.

2nd Division-Gen Twiggs.

1st Brigade, 2nd Division, in the actions of Aug 19 & 20, 1847, at Contreros & Churubusco:

Killed: Capt E A Capron, Co B, 1st Artl; Capt N J Burke, Co D, 1st Artl; 2nd Lt S Hoffman, Co F, 1st Artl; Sgt John Anderson, Do D, 1st Artl; Privates: M Carr, Co D, M rifles; J Reed, Co E, M rifles; J O'Brien, Co E, M rifles; A Trontfetter, Co F, M rifles; Jos Black, Co B, 1st Artl; Jos Banks, Co D, do; Arthur O'Connor, Co F, do; Chas Taylor, Co F, do; Christopher Wedmayer, Co F, do; Valentine Way, Co H, do; Josh Lutterenger, Co A, 3rd Infty; John L Martin, Co E, do; Geo Fyant, Co F, do; Alex Meister, Co I, do; Thos Crask, Co K, do.

Wounded: Capt J S Hathaway, Co H, 1st Artl, slightly; Capt L S Craig, Co C, 3rd Infty, severely; Capt D T Chandler, Co I, 3rd Infty; 1st Lt & Adj Don Carlos Buell, staff, 3rd Infty, severely; 1st Lt M E Van Buren, Co K, M rifles, slightly; Sgt G L Read, Co C, 3rd Infty; Cpl Jacob Sammons, Co H, 1st Artl, slightly; Capt Henry Buck, Co A, 3rd Infty; Cpl H G Tucker, Co C, do; Cpl J W Kaufman, Co C, do; Privates F Molumby, Co D, rifles, slightly; H Nottage, Co E, M rifles; J Lyons, Co F, do, severely; G H Hough, Co F, do, severely; W S Walker, Co F, do, slightly; J James 1st, Co G, do, slightly; J Hooker, Co G, do, slightly; J McNally, Co H, do, severely; J N Caskey, Co H, do, severely; Wm Shepherd, Co B, 1st Artl, slightly; Francis Buschman, Co B, do, severely; Henry Sheerman, Co D, do, severely; Oliver Snider, Co D, do, severely; John Swan, Co D, do, severely; Thos Billing, Co D, do, severely; Jas Sherry, Co D, do, slightly; Chas Miller, Co D, do, do, slightly; Peter McDermott, Co F, do, severely; Wm B Lambie, Co H, do, slightly; Michl McCormick, Co H, do, slightly; Julius Johnson, Co H, do, slightly; Lemuel Horner, Co G, do, mortally; John Monks, Co G, do, slightly; Henry Perry, Co A, 3rd Infty; Alvin Turner, Co A, do; Jas Hannan, Co A, do; David Burtlett, Co C, do; Nicholas Battendorf, Co C, do; John Quinn, Co C, do; John Madden, Co C, do; Geo W Savory, Co D, do; Diedrick Inergens, Co D, do; Saml Perrin, Co E, do; Wm Leach, Co E, do; Wm Jones, Co F, do; Albert Stimpson, Co H, do; Wm Anderson, Co H, do; Jas McNally, Co H, do; Robt Lennox, Co H, do; Richd Minge, Co I, do; John Halfholden, Co I, do; Chas Rapp, Co I, do; Jas Durham, Co K, do; Henry Sagvier, Co K, do.

Missing: Cpl J O'Connell, Co D, M rifles, since joined; Privates W Wood, Co D, do, since joined; Josh Newhouse, Co E, do, since joined; Geo Karchler, Co B, 1st Artl; Jacob Micar,

Co A, 3rd Infty; Geo Washington, jr, Co B, do; Geo McDonald, Co E, do; Chas Hopkins, Co E, do; Randolph Likens, Co E, do, known to be wounded; Stephen Ferris, Co H, do; John Curry, Co I, do; Saml Davis, Co K, do.

2nd Brigade:

Wounded: Engineer Co: 1st Sgt D D Hastings, slightly; Artificers: W H Bartless, severely; J T Smith, severely; Monell, slightly.

Missing: Engineer Co: Musician Nowoting.

4th Artl: Killed: Sgt Henry D Goodwin, Co G; Privates: John B Shuck, Co E; Wm P White, Co F; Timothy Kelley, Co G. Wounded: 2nd Lt Collins, Co C, severely; Sgt G K Donnelly, Co E, do; Privates: Banks Davis, Co C, do; Jos Athoy, Co C, do; Alex Pierson, Co C, slightly; Enoch Bowles, Co C, severely; Wm G Wharton, Co C, do; John Wymer, Co C, slightly; Wm Wise, Co D, mortally; Benj W Heath, Co D, severely; John T Williams, Co D, do; Wm West, Co D, slightly; Chris Albock, Co E, severely; Jas Egan, Co E, do; Michl Evans, Co E, do; John McHarney, Co E, do; Wm Robinson, Co E, do; John Hutchinson, Co E, slightly; John B Moore, Co F, severely; Wm Gaith, Co F, slightly; Jos W Gavin, Co F, severely; Robt Johnson, Co F, mortally; Wm McCaffery, Co G, severely; August Handler, Co G, slightly; Jos S Hackney, Co G, severely; Jas Fletcher, Co H, mortally; Richd W Allen, Co H, slightly; Luther Whitcombe, Co H, severely; Sgt Danl Wilbro, Co F, severely.

Missing: Privates: Jer Frisbee, Co E; Jas Quinn, do; John McDermott, do.

2nd Infty: Killed: Capt Jas W Anderson, Co H; 2nd Lt Thos Easly, Co K; Privates: Saml G Crawford, Co A; Horace Perry, Co C; Dennis Daily, Co D; John W Arthur, do; David Huston, do; Henrick Reber, Co E; Abraham Clements, Co F; John Boyd, Co H; Lew P Lamontin, do; Danl Stiker, Co K; Francis Gruber, do; Michl Leopold, do; Saml Wilson, do.

Wounded: Capt Jas R Smith, Co B, severely-twice; Capt A W Wessels, Co G, slightly; 1st Lt J Hayden, A D C, slightly; 1st Lt B P Tilden, Co G, slightly-twice; 1st Lt C S Lovell, Co E, slightly-twice; Privates Jas A Taylor, Co A, slightly; Jno Bridgett, do, severely; Malcom Herrington, do, do; Cpl Jas Turney, Co B, slightly; Privates: Wm Hawley, do, do; Wm Stuart, do, severely; Wm Ears, do, do; John Riley, do, slightly; Geo Martin, do, do; W A Malcom, do, do; Hugh Young, do, do; Edw Tierney, do, do; Sgts: Jas Stevenson, Co C, do; John Parks, do, do; Cpls: Jas Knox, do, do; Thos Handley, do, severely; Privates Chas Denpin, do, do; Admand Tallesson, do, do; John Gallagher, do, slightly; Walter Haner, do, severely; Wm Hughes, do, slightly; John D Kelley, do, not severely; Percy Page, do, slightly; Th E Thomas, do, do; Chas Donnelly, Co B, severely; Jas Ferby, do, do; Cpl Henry B Knapp, Co D, slightly; Privates Mont'y Barkholm, do, severely; Frantz Batmas, do, do; Wm Donnoghy, do, slightly; Patrick Dirgen, do, do; Wm H Bobles, do, do; John Kelly, Co E, do; Levi Fisher, do, severely; Howard Sharpless, do, slightly; John Quinn, do, do; Jacob Fry, do, do; Michl Gormily, do, severely; Sgt Jas Mann, Co F, slightly; Privates: E M Bascom, do, do; G A Hornett, do, do; Patrick Linn, do, do; John Hannington, do, severely; D M Fullen, Co G, do; J G McNelly, do, do; M Sheridan, do, severely; S R Thornington, do, do; Cpl P A Taylor, do, slightly; Privates: Wm Mills & Wm Walsh, do, do; Sgt G S Bradley, Co H, slightly; Cpl John Conroy, do, severely; Privates: John Bombard, do, do; Roger McDonough, do, do; Tim Mayon, do, do; Sgt Wm Merrick, Co I, slightly; Cpls H Snow, do, do; John Farley, do, do; Privates: Thos Blake, do, severely;

Danl Clarke, do, do; Thos Dodd, Co K, do; Fras Gruber, do, slightly; Wm Ruket, do, do; Ed Gilligan, do, do; Thos Crawford, do severely; John Peoples, do, do; Geo A Pay, do, do; Cpl Michl Jarauski, do, do; Cpl Jos Lathrop, do, slightly; Private Fras Meyer, do, do.
7th Infty: Killed: Capt Chas Hanson, Co E; Sgt Jas Truman, Co G; Privates: R Stewart, Co G; Wm Webb, Co H.
Wounded: Capt R H Ross, Co D, severely; 1st Lt C W Humber, Co B; Privates: John Sires, Co A, slightly; Francis Brown, Co D, do; Dennis Cardy, do, severely; Saml Benton, Co D, slightly; W Parmentier, do, do; Cpl J Crangle, Co E, severely; Privates: P Mony, do, do; J Walker, do, do; O'Sullivan, do, do; L Clarke, do, slightly; Musician J Mabin, do, do; Cpl J A Roberts, Co G, do; Private Geo Bull, Co H, do; Cpl H Doleman, Co I, severely; Privates: Albert Hart, do, slightly; Peter Maloney, Co K, do; Saml Ratcliffe, do, do; Benj Veny, do, severely.
Missing: Private Rice
Co K, 1st Artl-Light Battery, 2nd Division:
Killed: Privates: Francis Melvin, Harvey Tyng.
Severely wounded: 1st Lt J G Martin, 2nd Lt Edw C Boynton; Sgt Patrick Martin; Sgt Jos McGee; Privates: David Adams, Alex Bruce, Michl Cinchlaw, G W Fish, Alex McCabe, John Jones, Adolphus Shaffer, Patrick Walker, Henry Williams.
Wounded slightly: Cpl John Jones; Privates: John Krahmer, Henry Parrow, John T Prath, Christopher Phillips, Louis Loup, Louis Christian, John Gow; Artificer Ebin F Shedd.
3rd Division-Gen Pillow.
In the actions of Aug 19th & 20th, 1847, near the city of Mexico, of the 1st brigade, 3rd division, commanded by Brig Gen Pierce.
9th Regt Infty, Col T B Ransom. Killed: 1st Sgt L B West; Private, W Thompson.
Wounded severely: Lt W N Newman, Lt A F Palmer, Lt Cranum, 2nd Cpl W E Hoss, Privates: S S Sweet, J B Hale. Wounded slightly: Capt Johnson, 1st Cpl N W Groat; 3rd do W W Page; 4th Sgt J C Stowell; Privates, T A Pratt, W P Haskins, Jas Webber, Geo G Goodman, T Beedle, C Getting, J Moore, S P Hall, W Soule, M Wight, C F Blood, W Traub, H Dixon, J W Bondel, Jas Henderson, G Melville, D K Richmond, A W Brown, D Hogan, B Bearn, J Flinn, W Gould, A T Pike, G W Woods, G Barnes, S F Davis, S D Canfield, J Hosse, D Brown, J F Charterton, W Rhodes, J Scales, J R Higgins, J Linsey, J T Fly.
Killed: Private, B McCluskey.
12th Infty, Lt Col M L Bonham. Killed: 1st Sgt Wm C Oliver; 2nd do Peyton Randolph. Wounded mortally: Private Henry L Dermitt. Wounded severely: 1st Cpl John L Tubbs; Privates: Wm J Enos, Chauncey Howard, Martin Earis, Pinkney Anderson, Levitt, Severs. Wounded slightly: Capt N B Holden; 2nd Lt John C Limpskins; 2nd Sgt, Thos Smithers; 3rd Musician Saml Church; John A G Warneck, Wm M Davis, Fran M Bradley, Beverly Faughn, Warren D Blanton, Jas Calvin, Isaac Baker, John T Bowers, Adam Peyton, Geo Tatnon, Wm Morgan, Elijah Bowlin, Jos Smith.
Missing: Privates: Leander Crutcher, L Sherman.
15th Infty, Col G W Morgan. Killed: Lt John D Goodman; Musician Chester G Andrews; Private Wm Roberts, Saml Carney, Jno Sleath, Peter Hill, & Michl Spelcer
Wounded mortally: Capt Augustus Quarels; Lt Wm H H Goodloe; Privates Jno Glaze, Geo Gouph, Dan P Hanks, Fitch Cornal, Geo White.

Wounded Severely: Col Geo W Morgan; Sgts: Jno Cunningham, J M Camm, Wm Mabee, & Sgt Dan Rodes. Cpls: Isaac W Griffith, Wm B Hopkinson, Jas Healy; Musician Jos Clark; Privates: Jno W Cook, Wm Reed, Henry Widner, Alex Davis, Dorr H Fuller, Hiram Brown, Wm Rogers, Wm G Adams, Francis Fahrm, Jos Francis, Geo Steinman, Jacob Salinger, Jacob Hoger, Cornelius Westfield, Richd Northrup, Jacob J Bartim, Wm Barnett, Lewis Voight, Rupert Whitney, Clark Munson, Napoleon B Perkins, Wm H Miller, Thos Shortall, Peterson Lowry, Robt Linsey, John H Early, Michl Fratenger, & Bedwell Cilley.
Wounded slightly: Lts Chas Peternell, J R Bennell; Sgt Maj Thos McKeen; Sgts Fabian Bydol, Thos French, Fak W Schooner; Capt Horace Hancock; Privates: Westley Gordam, Jas G Corbus, Geo Cooper, Isaac A Smith, Jas Sould, Alva Taylor, Jno McCamm, Jas Hill, Wallace W Wood, Jeremiah Griffith, Mather H Chance, Sam Trask, Edw B Calklin, Martin Klien, & John Witson.
Missing: Maj Fred'k Mills; Sgts: Fred'k Lawbeinheimer, John Smith; Privates: John Hochstetler, Wm Schimyer, Joel Shively, Jasper Matley, John Stall, & Balthaser Happie.
2nd Brigade:
Volunteer Regt, Col T P Andrews. Killed: Sgt Richd S Pullinger. Cpl Robt Enlow.
Wounded: Sgt Robt B Taylor. Privates: Miles K Bell, Richd Brooks, John Fitzsimmons.
14th Regt Infty, Col Trousdale. Killed: Capt John P Miller. Wounded: Privates: Jas G Taliaferro, John J Jones, Theo Martins. Missing: Privates: Timothy A Wooden, John De Barnes.
11th Regt Infty, Lt Col W H Graham. Killed: Private John L Koontz. Wounded: Privates: S S Thompson, Jos Lord, M Hoffman, J Little, J O'Hara, A Harvey, Lyone.
Rocket & Howitzer Battery, Lt F D Callender. Killed: Privates: John Humphries, Robt Douglass, John Ungerer. Wounded: 1st Lt F D Callender, Cpls: Lybanus Rabb, Albert J Borie, John Naglee; Privates: Peter Strassner, Christian Schwartzweller, Ezra Craven, Henry D Perry, Michl Fitzgerald, Michl Farrel, Thos K Folk, Geo Sweekard.
South Carolina Regt, Col P M Butler. Field & Staff: Killed: Col P M Butler.
Wounded severely: Lt Col Dickinson. Wounded slightly: Capt Jas D Blandin, Adj Jas Cantey.
Co A: Killed: Capt C Wilder. Wounded mortally: Thos Black. Wounded severely: 2nd Lt S Sumter, Cpl W T Norton, Privates: B Caughman, J M Smith. Wounded slightly: C H Moody, E Hunt, Jas Dunn.
Co B: Killed: Private W R Davis. Wounded severely: Cpl E C Postell, Privates: Thos Charles, D McHenry, Jas Young, Jas Faucett. Wounded slightly: Sgt G W Curtis, Cpl A J Hood, Privates: T Cahill, J Connor, T E Dallas, T O Estes, J M D Hood, T Robbins, S Terrell.
Co C: Killed: Private Hitton. Wounded severely: 2nd Lt R S Billings; Sgts: Gay, Geo Waters; Cpls: Gaston, Horton; Privates: Bradley, Hunter, Meggs, Stratton, Sidwell, Villipigue. Wounded slightly: Capt R S Moffat; Privates: Ballard, Wooten, Humphreys.
Co D: Killed: 2nd Lt David Adams, Private Thos F Tillman. Wounded severely: 2nd Lt Jos Abney; Cpl W B Brooks; Privates Jas Joff, J Whitaker, J Addison, F Posey, R J Key, W F Unthank. Wounded slightly: Privates J Lark, E Linkins, R Sloman.
Co F: Wounded severely: Sgts: J D Walker, J N Hicks; Cpl J McCollum; Privates: Campson, Hartman, Murken, Valentine, Gilbert, Mackey, Pratt, Weatherby, Vanney, Wagner. Wounded slightly: Cpl J F Quinn; Privates: Miott, Wright.

Co G: Wounded severely: 1st Lt J R Clark; Sgt Row; Cpl McCreight; Privates: M Harper, T H Reynolds, J McNeil, J Cain, W B McCreight, M B Travis, M B Stanley, R J Barber, R J Gladney, S Alexander, Wm Nelson. Wounded slightly: 2nd Lts: J W Steen, J R Davis; Cpl Myers; Privates: S F Bone, S Camack, S Newman, W J Saunders, W M Goodlet, J Romedy.
Co H: Killed: Privates: Timothy Kelly, Shedrick Wiggins. Wounded severely: Privates: J Kennedy, Wm Mooney, R H Corly, W S Johnson, W F Purse, W Devlin, T Price, E Price, J B Cantwell, R Waddall, J F Watts, W Barkslow. Wounded slightly: Capt W D Dessussure; Sgts: H Beard, J L Percival, J M Millet, T Beggs; Privates: M Brown, H J Caughman, J Campbell, J T Lupe, E G Randolph, J D Stanford, D Pollock.
Co D: Killed: 2nd Lt W R Williams; Private John Slattery. Wounded mortally: Privates: Bernard Cregan, J Baughman. Wounded slightly: Cpl W B Eaves.
Co L: Killed: Sgt Jas Denson. Wounded severely: Cpt J A Speers; Privates: W Shephard, C Wood, M B O'Neale, G H Abney, M Clopton. Wounded slightly: Privates B H Mattis, J Warner.
4th Division, Gen Quitman.
Report of the killed & wounded in the 1st Regt of U S Volunteers of N Y:
Col Ward B Burnett, severely wounded; Sgt Maj Jeremiah Reilly, killed.
Co A: Killed: Private Benj Bennett. Wounded severely: 2nd Lt T W Sweeny; 2nd Lt C S Cooper, Cpl Louis Albourg, Privates: Jas M Boyle, John S Drew. Wounded slightly: Private Jas Slacum.
Co B: Killed: Sgt H Von Roman, color-bearer; Sgt Louis Bovet; Privates: David Rathbone, Peter Wilsse. Wounded severely: Sgt Carl Beecher. Wounded dangerously: Private John E Tweedy. Wounded slightly: Cpl H Dardonville; Privates: L Muir, C Pingolt, P Sheon, Geo Doub.
Co D: Wounded: Private G Spalding, slightly.
Co E: Killed: Lt C Chandler; Private Jacob Tuers. Wounded severely: 1st Sgt G Fitzgerald; Privates: Jas Grady, Chas Thompson, John H Leech. Wounded slightly: Privates: Francis Conroy, Munsen, Armstrong, Hoe, Searle, Slowly.
Co F: Wounded severely: Privates: Josh Boyle, D Costello, P McCann. Wounded slightly: Privates: Thos Supple, Wm Tompkins, John Meyer.
Co G: Killed: Privates: Robt Devoe, Bernard Crummy. Wounded slightly: 1st Lt Chas H Innis; 1st Sgt John Wilson; Privates: Nelson Barnes, Albert E Dennis, Bernard De Young, John Shaw, J Smith, Lott Swift; Musician Patt Berry. Wounded severely: Privates: Andrew Kline, Wm Hart, Chas Clapp, Alex E Fisk, Peter Farley, Jas Smith, Jas McGill, Alex Rodney, Edw Carr, Adam Saun, Martin Finney.
Co H: Killed: Private Wm Allison. Wounded slightly: 2nd Lt Jacob Griffin, jr; Cpls: H Moorehead, T W Gray; Privates: Wm Boyd, Alfred Doherty, Edw Fisher, Cornelius Winter. Wounded severely: Privates: Jas Brady, Wm Brumagem, Robt Dyas, John Gower
Co I: Killed: Cpl Smith Harris; Private Jas Murphy. Wounded slightly: Capt Morton Fairchild; Privates: Robt Dooley, Saml Gardner, Harry Lake, Stephen Streeter, John Gardner, Jos Duffin, Richd Orden, Danl Robertson, Jos Franklin, Henry Phillips, Jacob Rielly. Wounded severely: 2nd Lt Jas D Potter; Sgt Edw Cook.

Co K: Killed: Privates: Pat Fagan, Henry Maxlam, Chas Foley. Wounded severely: Capt G Dyckman; Cpl Alex Moran; Privates: Wm Jones, Jas Bowen, Jas Tomkins, Henry S Woods, A Van Allen, Randolph Tuttle.
Wounded slightly: 1st Lt Jas S McCabe. Missing, John Cook.
Dragoons attached to headquarters of Gen Scott:
Capt Thornton, Co F, 2nd Dragoons, killed; Philip Kearney, 1st Dragoons, wounded; Philip McReynolds, 3rd Dragoons, wounded; Lt Graham, wounded; Privates: Cowden, 2nd Dragoons, wounded; Patrick Hart, Co F, 1st Dragoons, killed; John Ritter, do, do, killed; Jas McDonald, do, do, killed; Michl Brophy, do, do, killed; Augustus Deisol, 3rd Dragoons, killed or missing; Edw Curtis, 3rd Dragoons, killed or missing; Geo Duver, 3rd Dragoons, killed.

Article in the St Jos Herald of Aug 27: Mr S L Campbell, late from Oregon, has furnished us with the list of persons supposed to have been murdered by the Indians on the southern route to Oregon. This company left St Joseph under Capt Smith. In this company were: Col Ritchie & family of 11 persons, from Henderson Co, Ill; Mr Tucker & family of 7 persons, from Rock Island, Ill; Job & Jonathan Parr & families of 11 persons, from Lee Co, Iowa; Wm Daniels & family of 4 persons, from Jefferson Co, Iowa; Mr Bothe & family of 6 persons, from Lee Co, Iowa; John Lenox & family of 5 persons, from Indiana; Mr Howell & family of 12 persons, from Hannibal; & John Bowles, from Galena, Ill. [Mr Graves & a family of 7, actually arrived in California.]

In the summer of 1829 Fred'k Kohne, a native of Germany, & for many years a citizen, first of S C, & then of Phil, died at Phil, leaving his wife & Messrs Bohlen & Vaux, of Phil, & Maxwell, of S C, his executors. He was a very wealthy man, strongley attached to the church. The will made ample provisions for his widow, & many private bequests to poor friends, servants, & others. To the House of Refuge, Phil: $100,000; Orphan Asylum, Phil: $60,000; Pa Dead & Dumb Institute: $20,000; Female Prot Epis Asso, Phil: $5,000; Infant School: $5,000; Female Benev So St Jas' Church: $3,000; Gen Epis Theolo Seminary, N Y: $100,000; Prot Epis Ch Sunday School Union: $20,000; Bishop's Fund, Diocese of Pa: $5,000; Prot Epis Ch Dom & For Miss Society: $10,000; Prot Epis So for propagating Christianity in Pa: $5,000. The decease of Mrs Kohne throws the whole of these munificent bequests into the hands of those for whom they were intended by their bestower. Many of them will prove most opportune & useful. -N Y Express
[Sep 24th newspaper: Mrs Kohne is not dead, but is said to be in the enjoyment of excellent health.]

The Hon Richd Henry Wilde, eminent Member of the Bar, successful Belles Bettres scholar, died Sep 10, of the pesticlence at New Orleans, yellow fever. He was about 60 years of age, a widower, since the lost of his wife many years since in Georgia. He leaves to lament his loss 2 sons who have reached manhood.

From the Rio Grande. Brig Gen Hopping died at Mier on Sep 1. His brigade is broken up.

A man & woman were drowned on Thu at Troy, N Y, when a team attached to a barouche became unmanageable, & rushed overboard from the ferry-boat at the foot of Washington st, taking the carriage & 5 passengers & driver with them. Drowned were, Mrs Lyons, who resided in Troy, & has a husband living, but no family. The other, Mr Thos Reynolds, who it is supposed had a wife in Montreal. They were going to attend a funeral at West Troy.

Among the gallant ofcrs who fell in the late battles is Capt Chas Hanson, of the 7th Infty. We sympathize with his father, Mr L K Hanson, of Washington, who has lost in him one of the remaining props of his old age, having already given another gallant son to his country, Capt W K Hanson, who died from disease contracted in a glorious career in the Florida war. -Richmond Republican

Naval: ofcrs attached to the U S sloop-of-war **Jamestown**, now at Norfolk, ready for sea: Cmdor Wm C Bolton; Cmder Saml Mercer; 1st Lt Henry K Thatcher; Purser H M Hieskelt Fleet Surgeon Stephen Rapalie; Lts-3: H N Harrison; W Ross Gardner; Richd L Love Passed Assist Surgeon Morris B Beck; Acting Master Wilmer Shields; Lts of Marines, Israel Greene; Cmdor's Sec, John Carroll Brent; Passed Midshipmen-2: Wm H Murdaugh; Jas Armstrong; Acting Midshipmen-4: A J Barclay; O T Johnston; H Kimberly; O P Allen

Col Fremont arrived in Wash on Thu with his family, but hurried off to Charleston in consequence of information he had received of the illness of his mother.

A little boy, son of Mr Saml Grubb, was trampled upon & bodily injured by a horse, while the little fellow was walking on the commons, near 10th st, Wash. There is a penalty for permitting horses to run at large which ought to be enforced.

Died: on Sep 10, in Wash City, Chas Henry Metteregger, formerly of N Y, in his 26th year.

TUE SEP 21, 1847

The extensive flouring mills of Mr S R Hutchinson, at Cleveland, Ohio, were partially destroyed by fire on Tue last. Loss estimated at $20,000; covered by insurance.

A pretty & cheap farm for sale, in Alexandria Co, Va, containing 100 acres of land: with a small dwlg, stable, smoke-house, & a first rate apple orchard. Inquire of David Munro, 12th st, or the subscriber, on the premises. -F A Tscheffely

Capt Martin Shive, of Cabarrus [N C] company, died in Mexico on Aug 15. -Register

The Flag says that Mr E B Lundy & Mons Montilly, who were taken prisoners some 4 weeks since by Carvajal, have been set at liberty, & arrived at Matamoras on Sep 3. They were liberated by representing that they were not Americans.

Died: on Sep 20, in Wash City, in her 25th year, Lillias M, w/o Chas Stott. Her funeral is Wed at 10 o'clock from her husband's residence, on Missouri ave, between 3rd & 4½ sts.

The Bladensburg Academy will resume on Sep 1. -John Decker, Principal

Household & kitchen furniture at auction: on Sep 28, at the residence of Mr Patrick, on N Y ave, next to 9th st, [Harkness' Row,] an excellent assortment of furniture.
-A Green, auctioneer

Public sale of the real estate of the late Col Henry Gaither: pursuant to a decree of the Chancery Court of the State of Md: sale at Hopkins' Tavern, on Sep 21, the following property: Exchange, 827½ acres, in Montg Co, Md, the seat of the late Col Gaither, 1 mile from Gittings' Tavern: with a spacious mansion house of brick. The Northwest Creek runs through the land. -John Holland, Trustee

WED SEP 22, 1847

Capt Jas Willoughby Anderson, 2nd Regt of U S Infty, who fell in the conflict in Mexico, was a native of Norfolk, Va, & the oldest son of the late Col Wm Anderson, U S Marine Corps, who married into one of our most ancient & respectable families. We believe he graduated from West Point in 1833. -Norfolk Herald

Death of an old soldier named Fugitt, living at Wash City, who was in Washington's army during the Revolution, died on Thu, aged 98 years. Our old friend Fugitt loved to entertain his friends by recounting the stirring incidents of our revolutionary struggle.
-New Orleans National

Maj Gen Wm O Butler, of Ky, has so far recovered from the wounds received at Monterey, that he proposes immediately to join the army in Mexico. -Union

New Orleans Delta of Sep 11: records the death of that brilliant writer, profound jurist, Richd Henry Wilde, who died of the prevailing epidemic yesterday. He was born of Irish parentage, in Balt, Md. He died in this city on Sep 14, after a painfull illness of several months. -Balt Pat

Public sale of valuable real estate on the Potomac River: in pursuance of a decree of Montg Co Court, as a Court of Equity, in the case of French Forrest & others vs Moreau & others, the subscriber will offer on Sep 29, at the dwlg lately occupied by Westley Magruder, near Rushville, all the lands in said county of which the late Jos Forrest was seized & possessed at the time of his death, either in his own right or in the right of his wife. This tract contains about 565 acres, more or less. Improvments consist of a dwlg-house & other our-houses. Also, tract of land called ***Resurvey on Clewerwall***, containing 301 acres, conveyed by Zachariah Gatton & others to Jos Forrest, & part of a tract of land called ***Williamsburg***, conveyed by Benj Dulany & wife, to Eliz Forrest.
-R J Bowie, Trustee

Passengers from & to Europe. From Liverpool: [Name of ship not given.]

Mr Swann
Mr Mason
Mr Mills
D Harvill
Master Harvill
B P Poore, bearer of dispatches
J Oakley
S H Tryon
Hon R C Winthrop & son
S H Thompson
J E Mitchell
Gen Armstrong, J Hall
J A Hall
E G Tuckerman
J J Walworth
H Osginson
Mr Thompson
J Caruther
M Baure
W Sherman
Lt Tryon
John Graveles
H P Cameron
P C Kerr
C O Taurey, lady & 6 children
Mr B Tandy, Delaware
Mrs Blandy
J T White & lady
Mr & Mrs Coolidge
Miss Coolidge & servant
Mr Trist
Mr Kohlsatt & lady
Jos Mackay
Geo Wright & lady
Mr F Patton
T R Lang
Mr R Rodwald
Thos Rowling
Mr Gale
Mr Gunn
Mr Stuart McKechine
G W Chapman
Edw King
Mr C Meandicks
J B Trott
John H Gourlie
J T Fields
Dickson Stewart
W Jackson
Geo Smith
Mr Harris
Chasmon Kidder
F B Gordon
D Pierson
Mr Hamon
Thos Res
J Weddell
P S Chester
P Longary
P S Hogarty
H S Byrs
Robt S Serwell
A Belloe
J McLean
A Anderson
Geo Ross
M Hall
Jos Lawton
J Watersons

In the packet-ship **Baltimore**, at N Y, from Havre:

Col Daingerfield, of Texas
G Tiemans & lady
Mrs Wolkbrabe
Miss A Bishop
Mrs Capt Johnson
John Howard Payne
Capt Carroll, of N Y
L Weddingen, of Bremen
G W Ogrton
John A Hambleton, of Balt

In the packet-ship **Cambridge**, at N Y, from Liverpool:

Mrs Reynolds, child, & servant, of Canada; Mr J Dawson; Henry Lynne, of Liverpool; Arthur Leffer, of Toronto; J H Wakefield, Isaac Wakefield, of London

In the ship **Ocean Monarch**, at Boston, from Liverpool:

Rev Mr Hincks
Wm Hicks, jr
Miss Morris, of London
Cyrus Alger
Henry Bakewell
Wm Welsh
Miss Welsh
Mrs Wooster, of Boston
Henry Clapp, jr, of Lynn
E Gilmoure & lady, of Belfast
G Bech, of Denmark
Capt J R Curtis, of Leeds, Maine
Robt Earp, jr, of Phil
Edw Tyore
Miss Johnson, of England
Mrs Pratt, E H Pratt, 2 Misses Pratt, of New Orleans
Rev T Birmingham, of Charleston
Ellen Kent & Kate McKim, Sisters of Charity
R Frazer, of Alabama
C Lilley, of Lowell
Alfred Tibbs, of N Y
Mr Brimingham
Geo Cetter, of Ireland
S Fletcher Wales
J T Hiltz, of Salem
Martha Phillips, of Scotland
Miss Johnson, of England

In the ship **New York**, from N Y, for Havre.

N K Anthony & lady, N Y
Mr Staples & lady, 4 chldrn, servant-N Y
B H Hutton, N Y
S H Gordon, N Y
F Warden, 4 children, & servant, N Y
Miss Scull, of Phil
Dr Bullock, of Delaware
Geo Lewis & lady, N Y
Master Lewis, N Y
Felix Boudard, N Y
Mrs Felix Boudard, N Y
Mr Spencer & lady, Belgium
Dr C Bertody, Leicester, Mass
E Bloneil Von Cudebroeck, Belgium
Mr Jehl, Belgium
Miss Louisa Virginia, N Y
N F Lassen, N Y
Josephine Lassen, N Y
Charlotte Lassen, N Y
Wm Lassen, N Y
Dr Vanderpoel, of Kinderhook
Jos Bordas, of France
Mrs C J Ruethe, 2 chldrn, servant, N Y
Miss C Davis

Mrd: on Sep 21, by Rev Mr Bean, Y P Page, of Wash City, & Martha E, eldest daughter of R Arnold, of Wash Co, D C.

Died: on Aug 6 last, in camp, near Buena Vista, Chas R West, a native of Fairfax Co, Va, but for a number of years a resident of Wash, aged about 34 years.

Lemuel North, of Chazy, Clinton Co, N Y, died suddenly there on Sep 16. He was seized with apoplexy & died in a few minutes. He was about 60 years of age, of irreproachable character. -Albany Argus

Miss M E Wilson, Fashionable Dress Maker: 10 years experience. South side of Pa ave, between 9th & 10th sts, second story of J B Hill's Variety Store.

Wickliffe Campbell, son of Rev Alex'r Campbell, of Bethany, Brooke Co, Va, was drowned on Sep 4 in a creek near that place. Rev Mr Campbell is now absent in England.

The subscriber, being about to leave Washington, will sell any of his property on terms to suit the times. The House next adjoining the residence of Gen Gratiot, on H, near 18th st. Also, the easternmost of 2 cottages immediately opposite. 2 small houses on 18th st. 2 houses next the Ryland Chapel, on the Island. Also, the School House at present under lease to S Smoot & others, on N Y ave, between 17th & 18th sts, & known as Washington Seminary. Several lots on K st, near 18th. Also, a large lot on 12th & U sts. Inquire of W H Parker, corner of 18th & H sts, First Ward.

For sale or rent: a beautiful & highly finished residence on the heights of Gtwn, opposite Col Robinson's. Inquire of M Duffey, near the premises.

THU SEP 23, 1847

Benj Harrison, the father of Wm Henry, [late President,] was a Delegate to the Continental Congress in 1774-'5-'6. It was between him & John Hancock that the amicable contention took place respecting the Presidency of the Congress. Peyton Randolph & Benj Harrison were brothers-in-law, & upon the decease of Randolph, who was first Pres of Congress, it was the wish of the Southern members that Mr Harrison should be selected to fill the chair vacated by the death of his relatives.

For rent: a 3 story brick house on F st, between 12th & 13th sts. Apply on the premises to Wm Tyson.

Mr Richd Taylor, son of Gen Zachary Taylor, arrived at Balt last night & stopped at Barnum's Hotel. -Balt

Mrd: on Sep 21, by Rev Mr Van Horseigh, Mr M E Bright to Miss Malinda A Grainger, all of Wash City.

Died: on Aug 26, at her residence in Amherst Co, Va, Mrs Mary Phillips, relict of the late Wm Phillips, deceased, in the 104th year of her age.

FRI SEP 24, 1847

Capt White, from Charlestown, Cecil Co, Md, was killed at Perrymansville last week, by being caught by the cow-catcher attached to the locomotive. He was intoxicated at the time, when he met his death.

Distressing suicide in New Orleans on Sep 9. A Frenchman, Jerome Dubois, committed suicide by cutting his throat with a razor. The cause is alleged to have been the death of a beloved sister, a victim of yellow fever, who died a few days ago.

Wash Corp: 1-Ptn of Thos Raleigh: ought not to be granted. 2-Claim of Wm Cooper has no foundation: ought not to be paid. 3-Cmte of Claims: bill for the relief of Christopher C Clements: passed. 4-Cmte of Claims: ptn of John Bohlayer, jr: read twice. 5-Bill for the relief of John Seitz: referred to the Cmte of Claims.

Died: on Sep 23, Jas Davie, aged 28 years. His funeral will take place today at 2 o'clock, from the residence of Mrs Burroughs, 8th & N sts, ***Greenleaf's Point***.

Died: on Sep 21, Henry, infant son of Luther R & Sarah E Smoot, aged 14 months & 2 days.

New Orleans Delta: When the last call for volunteers was made on Indiana, Edgar Derwin was the first to enroll his name. He had not yet crossed manhood's threshold. He got no further than Matamoros with his regt when was seized with a severe fit of sickness. The capt of the company informed his father of his son's illness. Mr Derwin, the father, hurried to his son's side. He reached this city, & was afflicted by the yellow fever: sent to the Charity Hospital, his case a severe one. Skillful medical aid & the nursing of the Sisters of Charity carried through the most violent stage of the disease. On Monday an emaciated youth was carried into the same ward & placed in the bed beside him. The young patient was Edgard Derwin, jr, Indiana. My son, said the father, & fell & expired. The son soon recognized his father. They both died of the same disease & are buried in a stranger's grave, here, not at their homestead in Indiana.

Fatal accident at Cumberland, Md, on Sat last. The coach, driven by Mr Thos Hager-a most skilful driver & manager of horses, upset, injuring Mr Geo C Vincent, of Erie Co, Pa. He died in the course of an hour. He was buried on Sunday & followed to the grave by a very large concourse of our citizens. -Civilian

Jos Palmieri, the celebrated barber, Palmieri of the beard, well known in N Y, Boston, & Wash, died in New Orleans, of yellow fever, on Sep 11. He was an Italian, about 40 years of age. -N Y Comc Adv

Household & kitchen furniture at public auction: on Oct 1, at the residence of Mr Hill, on F st, between 18th & 19th sts. -A Green, auctioneer The houses are for rent: inquire of Wm Wilson.

SAT SEP 25, 1847

Correspondence from England. 1-The London papers will have informed you that Lt Munro, who killed Col Fawcett in a duel, about 4 years ago, has had the sentence of death recorded against him. There has never been the least idea that his sentence would be carried into effect, & there is no doubt an almost universal wish in the public mind that he should receive a free pardon; but it is by no means certain that he will do so. Lt Munro's fate is uncertain; at present he is confined in a condemned cell in Newgate, & placed upon prison allowance. 2-Queen Victoria is rusticating in the Highlands with her husband & 2 oldest children.

City Court of Balt, Thu last. State vs Robt Groober, colored, indicted for the larceny of a $500 note, the property of Messrs Thos J Carson & Saml C Edes, Light st. Groober was found guilty & sentenced to the penitentiary until Aug 30, 1852. -Clipper

A very beautiful impression of the Corporate Seal of the Smithsonian Institution at Washington, has just been finished by Mr E Stabler, of Sandy Spring, Montg Co, Md. It represents a medallion, head of Mr Smithson, through whose liberality the Institution was founded. The likeness is said to be perfect. -Balt American

For rent: 3 story brick house recently occupied by Chauncey, being one of the block of bldgs known as Gadsby's Row, fronting on Pa ave, near 21st st west. Possession immediately. -Alex McIntire

Robbery at the Warm Springs on Fri last. The large iron chest that was kept in one of the front rooms of the hotel belonging to Dr Brockenbrough was carried off & blown to atoms. The Dr's loss is between $4,000 & $5,000.

Sealed proposals for Copper will be received at the Bur of Con, Equip, & Repairs until Oct 4. Class #1: to be delivered at the works of Jabez Couey, Boston, Mass. Class #2: to be delivered at the works of T F Secor & Co, N Y. Class #3: to be delivered at the works of Messrs Murray & Haselhurst, Balt, Md. Class #4: to be delivered at the works of Messrs A Mchaffey & Co, Norfolk, Va.

To let: the 3 story brick house, with large back bldg, fronting on Pa ave, lately occupied by Mrs Patten, opposite Coleman's Hotel. Apply to John P Ingle, Capitol Hill

Wm B Averett, the defaulting teller of the Va Bank at Lynchburg, has been again arrested, & is now in jail in that place.

Died: on Sep 23, in her 19th year, Laura Virginia, daughter of Robt Clements, of Wash City. She was the idol of her parents & sisters.

Died: on Thu, Albert Benjamin, son of Henry L & Julia Cross, aged 17 months. His funeral is this morning at 10 o'clock, from the residence of his father, on Pa ave, near the West Market.

Last offer of a valuable stock farm: the subscriber, having twice before offered for sale his plantation, ***Glenthorn***, [under unfavorable circumstances, however,] without effecting a sale, now offers it for the last time. This place is on the south fork of Rockfish river, Nelson Co, Va, 23 miles from Howardsville: contains about 1,250 acres; improvements are a spacious & handsome brick dwlg & other bldgs usually found on a well-improved place. The subscriber, who will generally be at home, or Mr C T Estes, of Nelson Court-house, will at any time show the lands. A perfect title will be conveyed. Address Jos F Montgomery, Mount Horeb, Nelson Co, Va.

$4 reward for strayed or stolen from the premises on Wed, a Cow & Calf. -J B Clarke, Pa ave, opposite Centre Market

MON SEP 27, 1847
Josiah Barker, for many years in the employment of the Gov't as a Naval Constructor, died at Charlestown, Mass, on Thu last, at the advanced age of 84 years. He was the contractor of the sloop of war **Portsmouth**, said to be the finest vessel of her class in the world.

Gen Worth, in a letter addressed to the Hon A P Bulter, speaks of the gallant Colonel, who fell at Churubusco: "Your brother fell most gloriously in the great battle of the 20th, under the gates of Mexico. In that bloody conflict no man gave higher evidence of valor & patriotism, or exhibited a brighter example. He fell when it was God's will, precisely as he would have desire to die. His body rests here-his memory in the hearts of his countrymen-his spirit, right and pure as his blade, with his God."

The U S steam-transport ship **Massachusetts**, Capt Wood, in 19 days from Vera Cruz, arrived at N Y on Sat. Lt McCorkle brings intelligence of the death of Col Burnett, of the N Y Regt, who was wounded at the battle of Churubusco. The Vera Cruz Sun represents him to have been killed on the spot. Passengers: Dr Baltee, U S A; Lts Clements & Webster, of the Balt Btln, U S A; Lt D P Corkles, U S N.

Among the slain in the battle of Mexico, is the name of Edgar Chandler, a volunteer in Col Burnett's Regt of Infty raised in this city. He was the eldest son of Gen Adoniram Chandler, about 25 years of age. Young Chandler was a gallant fellow, full of military ardor, inherited from his grandfather, a Revolutionary soldier, & his father, a volunteer during the whole of the last war with Great Britain. -N Y Times

The auxiliary steamship **Sarah Sands** arrived at N Y on Thu from Liverpool, having made the passage in 21 days. List of her passengers:
Mr Horace Fuller, lady, 2 children, & 2 servants- N Y
Rev Chas Fox, lady, 2 children, & servant- Mich
Mr & Mrs John Tull, child, & servant, Canada
Matthew J Miller, lady, 3 children, & servant, Phil
Miss Rebecca McDonald & niece, Scotland
Jos Gallier & Miss Gallier, New Orleans
Messrs E O Dominus, N Y
Edw Wetherell, Phil
G H Duncomb, N Y
Miss Maria Sands, Brooklyn
Alex'r McAndrew, England
Mr & Mrs T A Halliday, N Y
Mr & Mrs Moffal, S C
Messrs B Wade, England
Thos Hope, N Y
Geo Cathbert, England
Jas Broadbent, England
M J Andrew, Belfast, Ireland
John Fermally, Ireland
John Grace, England
Jos Morton, Ireland
Miss Clarke, N Y
Miss A Atkin, England
Geo Pooley, England
J Brain, Ohio

Lewis Wagner, addicted to intemperance, was seized last Thu with apoplexy & died almost instantaneously on G st, near the Post Ofc. The Mayor gave an order for the burial of the corpse in the almshouse graveyard, & it was buried accordingly.

Wash Co, D C. I certify that Malachi B Farr, of Wash Co, D C, brought before me as estrays trespassing on his enclosure, a large red cow; also, a red heifer. -J L Smith, Justice of the Peace [Owner to come forward, prove property, pay charges, & taken them away. -M B Farr, near Beale's Bridge]

Orphans Court of Wash Co, D C. In the case of Geo C Morgan, administrator of Maria E Morgan, dec'd. The Court & administrator have appointed Nov 16 next for the settlement of said estate, of the assets in the hands of said administrator. -Ed N Roach, Reg/o Wills

The steamer **Washington** left N Y on Thu, for Bremen & Southampton, with a full cargo, a heavy mail, & the following passengers:

Mr W C Redmond
Mr D D Mocomber
Mr F C Gottleib
Mr E Bernheimer
Mr A Fay
Mr C Lawson
Mr W L Hammond
Mr W H Raines
Mr J T Henry & lady
Mr J Randall, bearer of dispatches to London
Mr J Hunt
Mr S Barker
Mr W Beebe
Mr H E Clark
Mr J Wilson
Mr McCall, lady, & son
Mrs Newmann
Mr Bonick
Mr Sim, N Y
W H Meade, Albany
E V Ashton, Boston
Miss C Runge
H Fredrichs
A Wiegmann
G Dosenbach
J D Bechtel
Mrs Nisse, Germany
Dr Roemer, Berlin
A Cook, West Indies
C Peters, Albany

Trustee's sale of valuable land: by deed of trust from the late Walter Smith, dated Aug 29, 1842, recorded in Liber B S #XI, folios 255, 256, & 257, of the Land Records of Montg Co, Md: land containing 77+ acres, in said county, contiguous to D C: part of the tract called ***Friendship***. It adjoins the lands of Mrs Brooke, Maj W B Scott, [***Dalecarlia***] Mr Shoemaker, & others. -Clement Cox, trustee -Edw S Wright, auctioneer

Constable's sale: by a writ of fieri facias, issued by John H Goddard, a J P for Wash Co, D C, at the suit of Thos Lloyd, against the goods & chattels of John Larcombe, & to me directed. I have seized & taken in execution all the right, title, & interest of said Larcombe in & unto one negro man. Sale on Sep 30, in front of the Centre Market-house, of said negro, to the highest bidder. -Wm Cox, Constable

Household & kitchen furniture at auction: on Sep 28, at the residence of Miss Milligan, on N Y ave, near 15th st. -R W Dyer, auct

TUE SEP 28, 1847
For sale: excellent family horse, well known in town as possessing every good quality & no fault, & to be sold only as the owner has no further use for him. Apply to Gen Towson, Paymaster Gen.

Wash Co, D C, to wit: on Sep 27, 1847, before me, the subscriber, a Justice of the Peace for said county, personally appeared John Waring, & made oath that he mislaid or lost a note drawn by Henry Brooke, of Upper Marlborough, in favor of him, the said John Waring, for $500, & has not used or transferred said note, to the best of his knowledge & belief. -John Waring -Jas Marshall, J P

Information wanted. A man has stopped in Memphis, Tenn, on his way South, with 2 colored boys, named Bristow or Briscoe, who say they are free, & from Wash City. It is suspected they have been kidnapped. Information left with the Mayor of this city will be forwarded to the Head Constable at Memphis, whose inquiries have caused this notice. [Oct 2nd newspaper: the 2 colored boys were left free by the will of their former owner, Mr Harris, of Alexandria; they were subsequently bound to Mr Matthew Thomas, a plasterer of this city. Thomas was held to bail for his appearance at the next term of the Criminal Court. Measures were taken to secure Thos Davis, a negro buyer, who offered the boys for sale as slaves for life.]

Charleston, S C, Sep 24. We regret to learn that Col Fremont did not reach Aiken to see his mother alive. She died but a few hours before his arrival. He accompanied her remains the next day to this city, &, after witnessing the last sad rites, left here, Wed, on his return to Wash. -Mercury

Mrd: on Sep 21, by Rev Mr Morgan, Dr Wm Gray Palmer, of Md, to Eliz Duke, 2nd daughter of Wm B Jackson, of Wash.

Died: on Sep 18, in Roxbury, Mass, aged 54 years, Mrs Amelia Brereton, widow of the late Dr J A Brereton, of the U S Army, & formerly of Wash City, where, as at her late residence, she has left to the public remembrance a most estimable character. A gallant son who has recently distinguished himself in service as an Ofcr in the Army, & other children, survive to mourn their bereavement.

Died: on Sep 26, in Wash City, of consumption, Mark Ferris, in his 26th year. His funeral is from his late residence, on F st, between 1st & 2nd sts, this evening, at 4 o'clock.

Died: on Sep 20, in Boston, Thos Amory, infant son of Thos C Amory & Eliz Marian Dexter, aged 6 months.

The subscriber will sell the bldg he now occupies as a shop on 18th st, between G & Pa ave, very cheap if applied for soon. Also, 2 new one-horse carriages. -Wm Keefe

Notice: by virtue of 7 writs of venditioni exponas, issued by John L Smith, a J P for Wash Co, D C, I will expose to sale at public auction on Sep 11, for cash, all the right, title, & interest of Henry Wilson in one lot with a 2 story brick dwlg-house in Wash City, the east side of 10th st, between H & I sts, late the property of Henry Wilson, & seized & taken in execution at the suit of Wm R Roby. -H R Maryman, constable

For rent or sale: large & elegant house on H, between 9th & 10th sts. Apply to J A M Duncanson.

Orphans Court of Wash Co, D C. Letters of administration on the personal estate of Mary P Varnum, late of Wash Co, dec'd. -Jos B Varnum, adm

Valuable lands for sale: having disposed of only a part of my lands in Orange Co, the remainder is still offered for sale at private bargains. The ***Meadows***: this farm is a tract of 1,005 acres: has a very comfortable dwlg-house containing 6 rooms, thoroughly & newly repaired & painted, with suitable out-bldgs. The ***Winder Tract*** contains 600 acres, adjoining the above, upon ***Mountain Run***: has a small tenement upon it. ***Birchland*** contains 600 acres. The ***Independent Tract*** contains 468 acres, adjoining the ***Meadows***. Further information will be given by my brother Jeremiah Morton, who is fully authorized to act for me. My brother's address is Racoon Ford, Culpeper Co, Va. -Jackson Morton

Important sale of valuable real estate on the Rappannock River, slaves, horses, mules, cattles, farming equipments, & crop. By deed of trust, executed by Jas P Corbin, I shall sell at public auction, on Nov 11 the following: ***Corbin Hall***, an estate of about 1,850 acres of land, in Middlesex Co, between the Rappahannock river & Grange creek: with a comfortable wood dwlg-house of 4 rooms, & all necessary outhouses. Jas P Corbin & his wife will unite in a deed to the purchaser. -Wm N Wellford, trustee

WED SEP 29, 1847

Sgt Moody, of Capt King's Dayton company of Ohio volunteers,was killed by the accidental discharge of a gun, in Mexico, while on the march from Puebla to Vera Cruz.

U S Hotel, Wash. The proprietors have secured the aid of Mr Geo W Yellott as their genr'l agent in refitting the establishment. The services of Mr R R Thompson as caterer, formerly of Colemen's, they trust to render the house every way worthy of patronage.

The U S store ship **Supply**, J D Camp, Lt Commanding, arrived at Sandy Hook anchorage on Sat, after a passage of 25 days from Pensacola. She brings 34 invalids from the Gulf squadron. Lt Robt Emmett Hooe died a few hours after her arrival at the Hock. List of the ofcrs of the ship **Supply**: John D Camp, Lt Commanding; Joel S Kennard, Master; Wm B Fitzgerald & Stephen B Quackenbush, Passed Midshipmen; John Thornley, Passed Assist Surgeon; Jas Y Hudson, Capt's Clerk; Henry Walke, Lt, passenger.

Col John S Stiles, one of the gallant defenders of Balt in 1814, who acted a very conspicuous part during the whole of the war from 1812 to 1815, died on Monday, at his residence in Mulberry, near Paca st. -Paca

Maj Popham died on Sat, at his residence, 122 Waverley Pl, N Y C. He was 95 years old, the oldest commissioned ofcr of the U S, & the Pres of the Society of the Cincinnati. His biography will, it is to be hoped, be undertaken by some competent hand.

Pensacola, Sep 17, 1847. Judge Garnier committed suicide last night [Sep 16] by drowning himself. He assigned as his reason "poverty;" that he had but $120, which was in Mr Hyer's chest, & that it should be used to pay his debts & bury him decently. He laid his clothes in which he wanted to be buried on the bed.

Mr W Smith was killed at the regimental parade on the Saluda side, whilst running a horse-race. He was thrown against a tree & died immediately. He was an excellent carpenter, & has left a wife & 12 children, who were dependent upon him for support. -Abbeville [S C] Banner

Mrs Stead, an English lady, from Yorkshire, in company with her son-in-law, 2 dghts, 2 grandchildren, & a servant, arrived at Rochester, N Y, on Thu last upon the Eastern emigrant train. The son-in-law left the females to make some inquiries about going West. While gone, the person who sweeps the cars went into the one occupied by Mrs Stead & all, & told them to hurry & get upon the other cars. While Mrs Stead was stepping from the platform the engineer started the cars backward, the sudden motion of which threw her across the track between the cars, & before she could rise 2 wheels passed over her, crushing her body, causing her death almost instantly. She was about 48 years of age.

The late battles in Mexico. Letter dated San Augustin on Aug 25. Capt Capron & Capt Burke are with the buried, having been killed dead at the storming of Churubusco, where we lost in 3 hours 700 ofcrs & men. On the 19th our division advanced upon the enemy in position at Contreros, defended by 10,000,000 men, with 22 pieces of artillery. Advanced guard was commanded by Capt Roberts & Capt Porter. In the morning the assault was made. The scene cannot be described: 850 Mexicans were dead upon the field, between 300 & 400 wounded, & 1,500 taken prisoner. Our loss in killed & wounded was less than 200. Capt Hanson, of the 7th infty, & Lt Johnston, of the 1st Artl, were the only ofcrs killed. The Lancers made a stand & continued to fire upon us through the roads & fields up to Cherubusco, where the most terrible battles ever fought on this continent took place. 50 of our ofcrs were killed & wounded. I had eaten nothing but the half of a hard biscuit for 48 hours. Capt Phil Kearny lost an arm here, but he is doing well, & is in no danger. Maj Mills was killed, his horse having run off with him & carried him into the enemy's works, where he was lanced after he had surrendered his sword. -Private letter written by a gentleman of the Army.

Tyler's Hotel, on the north side of Pa ave, near 4½ st, was opened for the reception of visiters & boarders on Sep 20. Mr Tyler is well known to gentlemen in the South, during his long residence in Richmond, & other parts of Va.

The Courrier des Etats Unis contradicts the statement copied into several of our American papers that the eldest son of the Duke de Praslin, aged 17 years, had committed suicide on account of the horrors of the death of his parents. He is only 11 or 12 years old, & was alive & well.

Wash Corp: 1-Act for the relief of Wm P Shedd & others; & act for the relief of Christopher C Clements: referred to the Cmte of Claims. 2-Cmte of Claims: asked to be discharged from the further consideration of the ptn of Thos Welch: discharged accordingly. 3-Ptn of Fred'k Lachmyer, praying remission of a fine: referred to the Cmte of Claims.

New Ky Regts: from the Lexington Observer. Capt John S Williams, of Clarke, who so greatly distinguished himself at Cerro Gordo, has been appointed Col, Wm Preston, of Louisville, Lt Col, & Wm T Ward, of Greensburg, Maj of the 2nd new regt of Ky Volunteers, called for by the recent requistion of the War Dept. Companies which have been accepted & commissioned by the Govn'r for the service of the U S "during the war with Mexico unless sooner discharged, to consititute the 3rd Regt of Ky Volunteer Infty, to be commanded by Col Thomson, are as follows:
Capt A F Caldwell's company, of Laurel Co.
Capt Wm P Chilles' company, of Estill Co.
Capt Thos Todd's Company, of Shelby Co.
Capt Wm E Simms' company, of Bourbon Co.
Capt John R Smith's company, of Scott Co.
Capt Jas Ewing's company, of Bath Co.
Capt Leander M Cox's company, of Fleming Co.
Capt Leonidas Metcalfe's company, of Nicholas Co.
Capt Jas A Pritchard's company, of Boone Co.
Capt Lawrence B Robinson's company, of Fayette Co.
Companies which have been accepted & commissioned by the Govn'r for the same service, which are to consitute the 4th Regt of Ky Volunteer Infty, to be commanded by Col Williams, are as follows:
Capt Jos S Conn's company, of Caldwell Co.
Capt Geo B Cook's company, of Livingston Co.
Capt Decius McCreery's company, of Daviess Co.
Capt P H Gardner's company, of Hart Co.
Capt Timothy Keating's company, of Louisville city.
Capt John C Squires' company, of Adair Co.
Capt John G Lair's company, of Pulaski Co.
Capt Mark R Hardin's company, of Wash Co.
Capt B Rowan Hardin's company, of Nelson Co.
Capt A W Bartlett's company, of Henry Co.

From Chihuahua & Santa Fe. The effects of Jas Hall, who was murdered, were in the hands of the authorities for safe keeping. Six of the prisoners charged with the murder of Lt Brown, Jas McClenahan, & Chas Quisenberry, were hung on Aug 3, under the sentence of a drum-head court martial. Capt Smithson, of the 3rd Regt of Missouri volunteers, was attacked on Aug 1, near Pawnee Fork, by about 400 Indians, in which the latter lost some 6 or 8 killed, & as many wounded. The Indians ran off 24 horses.

The brig **Columiba** sailed from Phil on Fri for Boston, with a cargo of coal, & on Sat, while going down before the wind, when opposite Newcastle, Capt Pierce was struck by the gaff & knocked overboard, &, before the boat could be lowered to his assistance, drowned. His wife & 2 children were on board the vessel at the time, & saw him sinking without being able to render any assistance. The **Columbia** belongs to Belfast, Maine, where Capt Pierce & family resided.

Mr McDermott, foreman in the Globe printing ofc, at N Y, committed suicide by taking laudanum on Fri, which caused his death on Sat. No cause assigned for his unfortunate exit from life.

Mrd: on Sep 27, at Coleman's Hotel, by Rev C M Butler, Mr Wm W Talifour to Miss Virginia E Colman, both of Carolina Co, Va.

Mrd: on Sep 24, by Rev Mr Collier, Mr Robt A Drake, of Wash City, to Miss Ellen P Mann, of N Y.

For rent: 3 story brick house, with back bldgs, at the corner of H & 17th sts. Apply at the first house west of the above, or of Jas L Cathcart.

Household & kitchen furniture at auction: on Sep 29, at the residence of Edw Stubbs, on G st, between 8th & 9th sts. -R W Dyer, auct

THU SEP 30, 1847

The remains of a number of Ky volunteers which were recently brought from the battle-field of Buena Vista were interred at Frankfort on Thu, in the presence of some two or three thousand people.

American Geology ofcrs for the ensuing year elected this past week:

A C Redfield, Chrmn	B Silliman, jr, Treasurer
Prof W R Johnson, Sec	
Standing cmte:	
W C Redfield	Pres E Hitchcock
W R Johnson	Dr S G Morton
B Silliman, jr, ex officio	Lardner Vanuxen
Dr J E Holmbrook	Dr C T Jackson
Prof H D Rogers	Jas D Dana
Prof B Silliman, sen	John L Hayes

Local cmte:

Dr S G Morton, Chrmn
Dr Robt Hare
Prof S S Haldeman
Jas Dundas
Richd C Taylor
Jas B Rogers
Dr J K Mitchell
Wm Hembel
Thos B Wilson
Peter A Browne

-Boston Journal

The U S ship **Decatur** arrived at Pensacola on Sep 20th, last from Tuspan, blockading the port, but was obliged to leave on account of the yellow fever increasing to a serious extent. During 2 weeks at Tuspan, she had 65 cases & 4 deaths. Ofcrs on board when she arrived at Pensacola: Richd S Pinckney, Cmder; Lts-3; Wm H Ball, Edw Carrington Bowers, Napoleon Collins; Purser F Steele; Surgeon, Edw J Rutter; Master Chas W Place

Midshipmen-3: J Malachi Ford, Wm G Hoffman, J H Rochelle

Boatswain, Alfred Hingerty; Gunner, Thos Dewey; Sailmaker, J C Bradford; Carpenter, E B Barnicoat; Capt's Clerk, Wm S Cochrane; Purser's Steward, Thos Gaultney

List of deaths: cause-vomito:

Edw T Carmichael, Mid, Aug 7, 1847
Andrew Gardner, Landsman, Aug 19, 1847
Caspar Grodo, Marine, Aug 18, 1847
John Wilson, boy, Aug 20, 1847
Isbin Schanck, Surgeon's Stewart, Aug 27, 1847
Henry Mansfield, Quartermaster, Sep 8, 1847

Appointments by the Pres: Consuls of the U S: 1-John McPherson, of Va, for the port of Genoa. 2-Hugh Keenan, of Pa, for the port of Dublin. 3-Chas Huffnagle, of Pa, for the port of Calcutta.

The New Orleans packet ship **Auburn**, Capt White, of & for N Y, was wrecked on Long Branch, Barnegat Inlet, during the gale of Sat last, & the capt, 1st mate, & 16 other persons were lost. She sailed from New Orleans about Aug 24.

Farm & an abundance of timber & woodland for sale: in PG Co, Md, near Scaggs' Crossing, on the Balt & Wash Railroad: improvements are a good 2 story dwlg, somewhat out of repair: contains upwards of 350 acres. It is so remote from me that I am anxious to sell. It will be shown by Mr Boteler, the tenent in possession. Apply to me at Leonardtown, Md, or to Jas Biscoe, Commission Agent, 13 Light st wharf, Balt, Md. -H G S Key

By order for distress, & to me directed, I shall expose to public sale for cash, at the house occupied by Jas S Hall, on Pa ave, between 4½ & 6th st, Wash City, the goods & chattels, consisting of furniture, bedding, accessories, bar fixtures & bar, decanters & sundry other articles. -R R Burr, Bailiff -A Green, auctioneer

Alum Springs in Va for sale: in obedience to a decree of the Circuit Superior Court of Law & Chancery for Rockbridge Co, Va, pronounced on Sep 18, 1847, in a cause therein depending, in which Lyleann Robinson, by her next friend, is plntf, & the heirs & reps of Alex'r Campbell & others are dfndnts, the undersigned, as Com'rs appointed by the Court, will sell, on Dec 1, 1847, by public auction, all the lands in the bill, consisting of one tract of about 2,000 acres, upon which the Alum Springs are situated. This tract is in Rockbridge Co, Va, about 17 miles northwest of the ***Warm Springs***: springs were improved about 10 years ago: visited by persons from all parts of the Union.
-John Doyle, J D Davidson, Lexington, Va

Com'rs sale of valuable real estate: by order of the Montg Co Court, [Md] as a Court of Equity, in the case of Chas Offutt et al, vs Horatio Beall et al: the undersigned Com'rs will offer at public vendue, on Oct 21 next, at the late residence of Aaron Offutt, dec'd, all the real estate of which he died seized, lying & being in Montg Co, Md, & divided into 4 lots: Lot #1 being part of the Mansion House Farm, containing 292½ acres. Lot #2, being part of the Mansion House Farm, containing 369½ acres. Lot #3, containing 83 acres. Lot #4, containing 3/4th of an acre of land. Lots 1 & 2 lie in the vicinity of ***Clopper's Mill***, on the high road to Barnesville: with a large 2 story brick dwlg-house, 30 by 40 feet, & all necessary out-bldgs. Lot 3 lies on the public road from Rockville to Darnestown, about 3 miles from the latter. -Otho Magurder, F C Clopper, Lemuel Clements, John T Dezelum, Com'rs

Mrd: on Aug 5, in Wash City, by Rev J W French, Mr Geo Taylor, jr, of Wash, to Miss Mary B Ashton, daughter of J N Ashton, formerly of King Geo Co, Va.

Excellent household & kitchen furniture at auction, on Oct 11, at the residence of Mr Clarke, on 16th st, between G & H sts, which is very good furniture. -R W Dyer, auct

Grocery & Provision Store: Seybolt & Co, [successors of S Holmes,] 7th st, Wash.

For rent: neat & pleasant cottage residence on south C st, near the Smithsonian Institution. Inquire of E Brooke, corner of 11th & B sts, fronting Smithsonian Institution.

Household furniture at auction: on Oct 2, at the residence of Mr W Mann, on Pa ave, between 3rd & 4½ sts: furniture is very good & worthy of the attention of persons furnishing. -R W Dyer, auct

FRI OCT 1, 1847
Capt Landon N Carter, late of Va, of the U S Marine Corps, died at Norfolk on Sep 26. He arrived there on Sep 19 from the Va Springs, in a very feeble condition; entered the hospital that he might have the professional experience of his old & attached friend, Dr Williamson. Capt Carter was a gentleman of accomplished manners, of fine education, amiable temper, & highly respected. -Union

The Winchester Virginian states that Mr John M Elliott, of Clarke Co, Va, was killed on Sunday last in a rencontre with Mr John J Johnson, of Warren, Va.

Maj Wm Popham, whose death at N Y has been lately announced, was born in the town of Bandon, Cork Co, Ireland, on Sep 19, 1752. He was brought to this country at age 9 years, & his parents settled in Newark, Delaware. He was going to enter the ministry, but on the breaking out of the Revolutionary war he was fired with military zeal, & accepted a commission in the army, & raised a company to fight in defence of his country. His first engagement was at the battle of Long Island, where he greatly distinguished himself by taking prisoner the famous Capt Ragg, with 18 men of the enemy. He was then appointed a Capt in the army, & followed the American arms to White Plains, & distinguished himself again. He took part in the battle of Brandywine, & also acted as aid to Gen Clinton in the northern division of the army, & was also the aid of Gen Sullivan in his western expedition among the Indians. After the war he studied law in Albany, N Y; practiced in N Y C for a few years. In 1789 he purchased a farm in Westmoreland Co, resided there many years, & held the Ofc of Clerk of the Court of Exchequer. From 1804 to 1811 he took up his abode in N Y, with attention to the education of his children. He then returned to his farm, & lived there until 1836, when the death of his wife occurred, & returned to N Y where he resided until his own death. At the time of his death he was the only original member of the Society of Cincinnati, of which he was the President. Among his predecessors, as such, was the immortal Washington; but his immediate predecessor was Gen Morgan Lewis. He was a remarkably religious man, & died at age 95, a member of the Episcopal Church. -N Y Express

Mr Milton Boone, of Foundryville, Columbia Co, Pa, was severely wounded by a rifle shot on Tue last. Some persons belonging to the furnace in Foundryville were shooting at a candle in the street, when Mr Boone came out of the store in which he is engaged, & Bartus Johnson accidentally shot him in the thighs.

Ladies with letters in the Post Ofc, Wash, Oct 1, 1847:

Ames, Mrs Eliza J
Atkinson, Miss Julia
Ball, Mrs Jane
Brady, Eliz
Biscoe, Miss Sar A
Barrett, Miss Emily
Busby, Miss Marg't
Blackstone, Miss M
Baker, Miss Eliz
Berry, Mrs Ann
Brawner, Miss E H
Butler, Miss Mary
Butler, Mrs Henry
Butler, Miss M A
Butler, Mrs M
Bell, Miss Catharine
Brooke, Miss Jane C
Brooke, Miss Sus'h E
Brook, Miss Mar'h A
Brown, Miss Mary A
Bryant, Mrs Mary A
Braiden, Miss Eliz
Bogue, Miss Eliz B
Butler, Mrs Charity
Butler, Miss Rebecca
Butler, Mrs Eliz S
Cift, Miss Martha
Clare, Mrs Marg't
Cook, Mrs M
Clarke, Mrs Mary

Callaghan, Mary
Colbert, Mrs Rebec
Colter, Miss M A
Comedore, Lucinda
Chadwick, Mrs A
Carter, Miss Caro M
Curtis, Mrs Eliza
Codrick, Miss Mar'a
Cambell, Miss M A
Dade, Miss Mary
Drake, Miss Eliz
Delany, Miss B J
Duckett, Mrs Lucy
Dorral, Miss Anna L
Dorsey, Mrs Mary M
Ellwood, Mrs Elen'r
Ginnaty, Bridget
Graham, Mrs M G-3
Garner, Miss Martha
Hill, Mrs
Hews, Mrs Sarah
Halliday, Mrs Mary
Hutchins, Mrs Em'a
Hecter, Miss Mary J
Hilry, Miss Lucilla
Henry, Miss Sarah
Jorden, Caroline
James, Mrs Emma F
King, Nancy
Leckron, Mrs Eliz
Lewis, Mgt
Little, Mrs Barbara
Lucas, Miss Hariet
Locke, Mrs Sarah A
Mauds, Miss Alice
Morgan, Mrs Com
Morton, Mrs Siby
Murray, Mrs Geo
Morris, Mrs Ann
Mitchell, Miss Mary
Martell, Mrs Eliz
Magee, Miss Mary
McGurk, Mary C
McGarr, Chloe Ann
Norris, Miss Virg'a
Parsons, Miss H E
Parker, Charlotte
Poole, Mrs Mary M
Poole, Miss Rachel I
Ringgold, Mis E C
Russell, Mrs M E
Ringgold, Mrs L
Richardson, Miss E J
Scott, Mrs Maria
Sturgis, Miss S S
Stewart, Miss E A
Smith, Miss Joannah
Syfax, Miss Eleznor
Seamore, Miss Eliz
Shepard, Catharine
Tone, A Della
Tolson, Miss E B
Townley, Miss S R
Triay, Raphael R
Tenison, Catharine
Thomas, Miss Eliz
Tilley, Miss Sophia
Wise, Miss Sarah
Weisenger, Miss E
Willson, Mary N
Wood, Mrs Matil A
Wilson, Miss Ang R
Wiley, Mrs Virginia
Williams, Miss S C
Wilson, Miss Emma
Young, Miss Mary

The postage on letters & packets directed to foreign Gov'ts must be prepaid, otherwise they cannot be sent, except those addressed to Bremen, in Europe, & places to which they can pass through the Bremen post ofc. The postage on all transient newspapers must be prepaid, three cents. -C K Gardner, P M

Balt, Sep 30. Judge Thos Buchanan, Associate Judge of the Judicial District composed of Alleghany, Wash, & Fred'k Counties, died in his carriage returning from court, as is supposed, of apoplexy. He was about 75 years of age. [No date-current news item.]

Died: on Sep 26, in N Y, Louisa Graham Varnum, in her 17th year, 2nd daughter of Jos B Varnum, of that city.

For rent: 2 story brick dwlg-house, on Capitol Hill, recently occupied by Mr Garinger, & near the residence of John H Houston. Apply to John H Houston, or to Jas Larned, for the owner.

Trustee's sale of real property on ***Greenleaf's Point***: by deed of trust from Wm H Ward, dated Feb 1, 1844, recorded in Liber W M, 106, folio 95, land record of Wash Co, D C: sale on Nov 12, lot 32 & part of lot 31, square 503, fronting 46 feet on Union st, with a brick house. -A B Thruston, trustee -A Green, auct

SAT OCT 2, 1847

Resolutions were adopted at a meeting of the Bar of New Orleans, held there on Sep 18, at which John R Grymes presided; moved by G B Duncan. Recognition of the late Hon Richd Henry Wilde, who died from the invisible pestilence which has taken so many of the fellow citizens.

Drowned: Mr John A Dix, of the Navy, who had left his residence on Tue evening, telling his wife he was going out for a walk, was seen on the East Cambridge bridge, near Boston. The sound of a person falling into the water was heard & a cloth cap was found on the bridge. His body has not been recovered.

Cows, horses, wagons, ploughs, harrows, cultivators, household & kitchen furniture, at auction: on Oct 7, at the residence of Messrs H Mentz & C Schroder, near Logan's Mill, adjoining Mrs Pearson's farm, a little east of North Capitol st. -A Green, auctioneer

Military movements: the N J Btln of Volunteers, recently mustered into the service of the U S, sailed for Vera Cruz on Wed. It consists of 4 companies, & an aggregate of 343 men. The ofcrs are as follows:

Lt Col Dickinson Woodruff
Capt H A Naglee
Capt J Reynolds
Capt d McDowell
Capt D Pierson
Lt J H Stiles
Lt E M Bard
Lt W L Young
Lt J Vanhouten

2nd Lts:

J W Mickle
H C Spillman
A M Law
C Abrams
J McDowell
A McKinley
E Ferris
F Harrison

Lt Bard, who was for a short time a cadet at West Point, was appointed Adj, & Lt Mickle Acting Assist Quartermaster & Commissary.

Rev Dr Leavel, of the Methodist Church, died of the yellow fever at Vicksburg, the theatre of his ministerial labors, a few days since. New Orleans Picayune

London papers announce the death, in Aug, of Gen Sir Geo Cockburn, who died at Shanganah, near Bray, in the county of Dublin, aged 84. He is better known as Admiral Cockburn. He was about 51 years old when, as Admiral & 2nd in command of the British Squadron which visited the waters of Chesapeake Bay under the command of Admiral Cochrane, he volunteered to lead the Detachment of Sailors & Marines that accompanied the British Military force, which, in Aug, 1814, invaded & captured the City of Washington. In that capacity he did the present proprietors of this paper the honor to superintend in person the sacking of the Ofc of the Nat'l Intelligencer, destroying the innocent types, & burning the books found in it; the bldg then occupied by the publishers being saved from the flames only by the representations of distressed females, whose adjoining houses would certainly have perished along with it. They had burned the Capitol & the Pres' House, & the only private property which they took the trouble to destroy was that of the Editors. The Admiral, in full uniform, was mounted upon an old field mare, with a ragged colt at her side; the bluff old Ofcr, haranguing the gathered crowd of non-combatants, chiefly women & children, gathered around him. Well, Well! It was a long time ago. Peace to his ashes!

Trinity College, 8 miles west of Raleigh, N C: Rt Rev L S Ives, D D, Visiter. Rev Fordyce M Hubbard, Rector. The 2nd term will commence on Nov 10, 1847.

Mrs H A Peters proposes to the Young Ladies of Washington to have Evening School, commencing the 1st Mon in Oct at her residence on E st, between 8th & 9th sts.

Notice: I hereby forewarn all persons against purchasing or trading for any note of mine in favor of Chas W Boteler, jr, as I hold notes of his for more than the amount of my obligations to him. -Jas S Hall

The loss of the ship **Auburn** is confirmed. Among the lost were Capt Hoyt; Mr Melbourn, 1st Mate; Mrs Baker, wife of private Baker, of the army; a boy named Henry, of Bridgeport. Saved were: Wm Sutton, seaman; Wm Eccleston, seaman; Thos Chandler, seaman; Richd H Fisby, seaman; Eleanor Fisby, his wife; Mr Fisby, 2nd mate; & Thos Taber, passenger. Sgt Higbee & private Baker, of the U S Army, died on the passage, after leaving New Orleans.

Mrd: on Sep 7, at Col Blanchard's, Rapide Parish, Louisiana, by Rev E Guion, jr, of Natchitoches, Geo Mason Graham, formerly of Wash City, but now of Louisiana, to Miss Mary Eliza Wilkinson, of the latter place, daughter of the late Capt N G Wilkinson, formerly of the U S Army.

Died: at New Orleans, of yellow fever, John Brooks, of Wash City, aged 43 years. The above extract from the list of interments in the cemetery of St Vincent de Paul, of that city, for the 48 hours preceding 6 p m of Sep 20, conveys the sad intelligence to his brothers, sister, & friends of Wash, of the decease of one whose arrival at home they had been daily expecting. The deceased was a member of Capt Corse's company, in the Va regt of volunteers in Mexico; but, on account of sickness contracted in the service, he had received his discharge at Saltillo on Aug 1 last, & was on his return home to this city, when he was stricken down.

Mrd: on Sep 29, in Elizabethtown, N J, by Rev Dr Magie, Wm Chandler, U S N, to Kate, daughter of Jas Crane, of that city.

Died: on Sep 30, after an illness of 7 weeks, Adaline A O'Bryon, aged 4 years & 7 months, daughter of Jas & Adaline O'Bryon.

Dissolution of the partnership between Fred'k Hager & John Henry, by mutual consent. Fred'k Hager calls attention to his Stalls in the West Market #7, & in the Centre Market #s 15 & 17. -Fred'k Hager, John Henry

MON OCT 4, 1847

Genteel furniture at auction: Oct 5, at the residence of R Woodward, in Cox's Row, 1st st. -E S Wright, auct

Died: on Oct 2, in Wash City, Danl Brown, of the War Dept, in his 71st year. Sustained by the Christian hope, he died in peace.

City News. We have had the pleasure of seeing 2 unusually large & fine pomegranates, just cut from a tree raised from seed planted by Mr Jas Maher, the public gardener, on the south side of the Pres' Grounds, in 1839.

St Paul's English Lutheran Church, although in an unfinished state, was open for public worship about 2 years ago, & is undergoing further improvement. Mr Jas B Phillips is doing the stucco work, & with his usual liberality in regard to churches, makes a very considerable deduction from the customary prices. Mr Richd Wroe is employed in erecting pinnacles on the towers of the bldg. Mr A Minnitree is doing the carpenter's work.

Lt Jos McElvain, of the 1st Regt U S Dragoons, died near Santa Fe, on Jul 10, of a wound received on Jul 4.

The Springfield Gaz announces the death of the Rev Caleb J Tenney, D D, an agent of the American Colonization Society, in whose service he has assiduously labored for several years.

Two married women of Nauvoo have recently been shot dead by their husbands, under singular circumstances. A few weeks ago an old Revolutionary pensioner, Hatch, nearly 90 years of age, but a Mormon, killed his wife by mistake in an endeavor to shoot those who were molesting his house. A few days afterwards Mr Tilley killed his wife by shooting her as she entered a rear door of the house at a late hour, supposing her to be a man attached to a body of anti-Mormons.

Two children of Elbridge Tyrrell, of Tyringham, Mass, were instantly killed on Mon by a sand-bank caving in upon them while they were at play near it. The girl was about 11, & the boy about 8.

In a fight between Mr John I Johnston & Mr John M Elliott, in Warren Co, Va, last Sunday, Mr Elliott was killed by a stroke received with a fence rail. Mr Johnston was recently a candidate for the Legislature from Clarke & Warren, & Mr Elliott was one of the wealthiest & most influential citizens in Warren Co. -Va Free Press

Marlboro Gaz: Robt Grierson shot & killed Mr Beverly, in a rencontre at St Leonard's Creek, Calvert Co, Md, on Monday last.

Mr Studiford, a baker of Newark, was killed on the N Y & Phil railroad on Wed. He attempted to jump from the car while at full speed, his foot catching on the step, & being dragged until he was dead. The accident was not known until the body was found the next morning.

TUE OCT 5, 1847

The subscriber desires to sell a lot of young fat Cattle. Also, 70 fat Sheep. Call at my residence, in Chas Co, Md, Nanjemoy, near the Hill-top. -Eliz Gray

Balt, Oct 4. A letter received in Balt today, dated Vera Cruz, Sep 10, announced the death of Lt Murray Winder, of Md. He was wounded in the engagement with Maj Lally's command, at the Nat'l Bridge, & died a few days thereafter at Jalapa. He fought gallantly, & was wounded in the midst of the conflict.

Mrd: on Sep 22, Wyndham Robertson, late of Va, to Miss Judith M Pope, of Memphis, Tenn.

Mrd: on Sep 30, by Rev J W French, at the Church of the Epiphany, D Higgins to Miss Letitia W King, both of this place.

Mrd: on Sep 15, in Waterloo, N Y, by Rev S H Gridley, Mr Chas L Gumaer, of Wash City, to Miss Martha E, eldest daughter of John McAlister, of the former place.

Died: on Sep 13, in New Orleans, of yellow fever, Lewis C Marye, a native of Page Co, Va, aged 26 years.

WED OCT 6, 1847
The fine Rifle Company recently raised here & at Balt, & commanded by Capt F B Shaeffer, late Adj of the Balt Btln, & afterwards in command of Co D of the same btln, is nearly full, & will leave in a few days for Mexico.

Our gallant young townsman, Capt Wm J Clark, of the 12th Regt of U S Infty, has been severely wounded in one of the attacks made by the guerilla parties upon the train under the command of Maj Lally, & to which Capt Clark's company belonged. Maj Lally received a ball, on the 19th, when near Jalapa, through his neck. Capt Calwell of the Voltigeurs, & Capt Cummings, of the 11th Infty, both from Va, & Capt Clark, of N C, were severely wounded, the first in the head, & the second in the leg. -Raleigh Register

Foreign Obituary: among the deaths of eminent men are: Marshl Oudinot, Duke of Reggio, at age 81; M Francis Franzen, Bishop of Hernosand, in Sweden, known as a poet & historian, 65; & Chief Justice Pennefather, of the Queen's Bench in Ireland. He presided at the trial of Mr O'Connell.

Frame shop, & carriages, at auction: on Oct 7, between G & Pa ave, on 18th st, the frame shop occupied by Mr Wm Keele as a coachmaker's shop. -R W Dyer, auct

France: the Duchess of Aumale was safely delivered of a son at the Palace of St Cloud on Sat. The name & title conferred on the young Prince runs thus: "Henri-Leopold-Philippe-Marie d'Orleans, Duc de Guise."

Foreign Items: 1-Sir Walter Scott's grandson has been allowed to change his surname from Lockhart to Scott. 2-On Jan 1 next Poland will officially be incorporated with Russia.

From Pensacola: letter of Sep 23 in the New Orleans Picayune says: the following died of yellow fever on board the ship **Decatur**: Midshipman E F Carmichael; J B Schenck, surgeon's steward; Hy Mansfield, quartermaster; Andrew Gardner, landsman; John Wilson, Z C Boy; Casper Gordon, private marine.

Died: on Sep 25, on board the U S ship **Supply**, off Sandy Hook, of consumption, Lt Robt Emmett Hooe, U S Navy, a native of Va, aged about 37. This sad event, although anticipated, for Mr Hooe had long been suffering under the disease, will be keenly felt by his family & friends. N Y, Sep 29, 1847

Our waters are alive with fish! Three days ago Mr John Turner, who resides near the mouth of Briton's Bay, took 274, at a single sitting, on Tomkins' bar in the Potomac river. -Leonardtown, [St Mary's Co, Md] Beacon

Wanted to rent, for 3 or more months, a well-furnished brick house in a healthy part of Wash City. Inquire of Julius A Peters, Pa ave, near 10th st.

Edwin Bailey & Jos Buchanan were convicted on Fri, in the Brooklyn Oyer & Terminer, of assault with intent to kill Mr Hotchkiss, of South Brooklyn, N Y. They were sentenced to the State prison for life. Mr Hotchkiss was in court, but entirely unconscious of all that was passing. It is feared that his reason is irrecoverably gone.

Meeting of the Philodemic Society of Gtwn College, on Oct 3, consisting of Messrs Allemong, Delacroix, & Higgins, to draught resolutions expressive of the sense of the Society on the death of John Hurd, of Md, for a long time an honorary member of said Society: sympathy to the afflicted relatives of the dec'd.

THU OCT 7, 1847

Boston Daily Times: the late Capt E A Capron, 1st Regt U S Artl, fell in the late action between the American & Mexican forces. He was a native of the State of N Y & a graduate of West Point. He served in Florida for several years, & his first action was at the battle of Withlocoochee. The tears of his young widow, a native of Boston, & a niece of the late Col Fanning, of the U S Army, & the cries of 6 helpless orphans, attest his claim to yet nobler titles, a man of the highest moral worth, a tender husband & father.

U S Flag ship **Germantown**, Vera Cruz, Sep 6, 1847. The Dept announces the death of another valuable ofcr of the squadron: Passed Assist Surgeon J Howard Smith died last evening at the naval hospital. Dr Smith was attached to the steamer **Spitfire**, & volunteered with Dr Hastings, of the ship **Mississippi**, to take charge of the sick at the hospital, when Dr Thorney was taken with the fever. [Letter to the Hon John Y Mason, Sec of the Navy, Wash: from M C Perry, Commanding Home Squadron.]

Pianos, Music, & Fancy Goods: Pa ave. -Richd Davis

Harvard College, Cambridge: Pres Everett, at a recent commencement dinner, singled out the name of the Hon Abbott Lawrence, who has within a few weeks made a donation to the Institution of $50,000-a larger sum than has ever been bestowed in this country, in one gift, by a living benefactor.

Mrd: on Oct 6, by Rev Mr Taylor, Thos B Davis to Miss Catharine S Hudson, all of Gtwn.

Mrd: on Oct 6, at the Convent Chapel, Gtwn, D C, by Rev Mr Flanagan, Mr Henry A Neale, of Chas Co, Md, to Miss Mary A Hammersley, of Gtwn.

$50 reward for runaway, my negro woman Lucy; about 35 years of age. I bought her of Mr John B Magruder, of PG Co, Md, where she has a husband & children living. -Alex'r Lee, Washington

FRI OCT 8, 1847

Rev Jos Henry Allen, of Mass, to become the permanent pastor of the Unitarian Church in Wash City.

The new City Hotel, just rebuilt & enlarged for the owner, B Ogle Taylor, will shortly be occupied by Mr Willard, & ready for the reception of guests. It fronts 140 feet on Pa ave, & 175 feet on 14th st: contains 150 rooms, well arranged into sleeping rooms & suites of rooms for families. The broad stairs, with oak rails & banisters are by the superior workmanship of Mr Harrod. The kitchen is fitted up by Mr Nevett.

Headquarters 5th Infty, Tacubaya, Aug 22, 1847. Operatons of the 5th Regt, under my command, during Sep 20: a number of prisoners were taken, among whom were Brevet Brig Gen Perdigon Gavay, commanding their rear guard, & one lt captured by Lt C S Hamilton-one lt col & 1 lt captured by Lt N B Rossell. A portion of the regt under the command of Capt D Ruggles, with Adj P Lugenbeel & Lt Strong, with the regimental colors, became separated from the main body. My thanks are due to Brevet Lt Col M Scott, second in command, for his valuable assistance, cheerfully tendered me on all occasions. Capt Wm Chapman was slightly wounded early in the action. Capt McPhail, Lts Rossell, Rosencrants, & Hamilton, displayed coolness & courage. Lts Dent, Strong, & J P Smith manifested equal zeal & bravery. I speak highly of the gallantry of Capt Jas L Mason, of the Corps of Engineers: of Sgt John Gollinger, of A; Sgts Dudley, Johnson, & Augustus Whitman, Cpl Geo Wooten, & privates Walter Slingerland, Danl Mahony, Michl McGarvey, Jas Boyle, of B; private Isaac Jacobson, of C; Sgt Jas O'Brien, Capt Francis Smith, privates Thos Hardy, Jas Cox, & Walter Crawford, of E; & Cpl Geo Morley & privates Walter McCormick & Geo Scott, of I, companies 4th Infty. Our total loss during the day was Capt Wm Chapman & 1st Lt & Adj P Lugenbeel slightly wounded, 6 privates killed, 41 non-commissioned ofcrs & privates wounded, & 2 privates missing. -J S McIntosh, Bvt Col U S A: to Col N S Clarke, Commanding 2nd Brig 1st Div U S A

Wash Corp: 1-Ptn of C Gautier: referred to the Cmte of Claims. 2-Ptn of Richd Rice: referred to the Cmte of Claims. 3-Ptn of John Fleming, praying remission of a fine: referred to the Cmte of Claims.

Court Martial is to assemble at ***Fortress Monroe*** [Old Point Comfort] on Nov 2 for the trial of Lt Col Fremont, on charges preferred against him by Gen Kearny, & the following ofcrs are detailed for the Court:

Brevet Brig Gen G M Brooke
Col S Churchill
Col J B Crane
Brevet Col M M Payne
Brevet Lt Col S H Long
Lt Col R E De Russy
Lt Col J P Taylor
Brevet Lt Col H K Craig
Maj R L Baker
Maj J D Graham
Maj R Delafield
Brevet Geo A McCall
Assist Adj Gen, Maj E W Morgan

Capt John F Lee, Ordnance Dept, Judge Advocate of the Court.

The Hon Jos G Kendall, Clerk of the Courts in this county, died on Sat. He was one of our most honored & beloved citizens; he represented the North District of this county for 2 terms in the U S Congress; after which, in 1833, he was appointed Clerk of the Courts. -Worcester [Mass] Transcript

Passengers in the steamer **Hibernia**, at Boston, from Liverpool:

Mr & Mrs Magee
Col Dynely, wife & dght
Mrs Ferguson
Miss Duncan
Miss Paul
Miss Burton
Miss Rifling
Miss Collins
___ Duncan
G E Clark
Mr Paul & son
Wm M Collet
Thos Hall
Lt Lamsden
Geo Martin
C D Dickey
Mr Baker
Mr McIlvain
Mr Penfold
Mr Crowden
Mr Martineau
Mr Letkie
Mr Kinnard
Mr Gray
My Gyetyeus
Mr Aneling
Mr Molen
Mr Brazer
Mr Brines
Mr Sedgwick
Mr Doherty
Mr Craft
Mr Graiffe
Mr Gannen
Mr Jerduns
Mr Stucky
Mr E Tupper
Mr R D Shiperd
Mr Wm Kneale
Mr Joshua Dixon
Mr J Stett
Mr John Mure
Mr Thos Holland
Mr Ireson & wife
Jas A Dow
H Young
Jos Oakes
E R Hoore
R C Anderson
Wm Grange
Thos Valier
Danl Humbert
Hon M McKay
Wm Montgomery
Jotham Carduck
I H Perry
G C McHenry
Wm B Newbury
John Gibson
Wm Platt
I Darsee
J Stuckee
Chs Dobson Pitt
Edw Warburg
Dr W E Weston
G D Borthwick
Jos Lawright
Hy U G Couray
Mrs Dyneley
Col Dyneley
Mrs Addams
Chas Addams
Mr Paul, wife, & dght
Rev E Williams
Elwood Brown
Alex McPherson
Peter Greethill
Hy Knight
O Driscoll
Mr C Thomas, wife & child
Mr H Read, bearer of dispatches
Mrs McKenzie Frazer & female servant
Mr Sturges [Am Consul from Manilla] & family

Mrd: on Oct 6, at the Highlands, near Gtwn, D C, by Rev Mr Shiras, Chas W Forrest, of Wash City, to Louisa Pemberton, daughter of Chas J Nourse.

Died: on Oct 4, in Balt, Jonathan Pinkney, in his 79th year, after a protracted period of ill health. He has a number of years past filled the ofc of Cashier of the Chesapeake Bank.

Died: on Oct 7, at Gtwn, D C, Mrs Jane Eliza Godey, aged 26 years, after a severe illness, which she bore with patience & Christian resignation. Her funeral is today at 2 o'clock, from the residence of her husband, Mr Walter Godey, in Dunbarton, near Wash st.

Died: on Oct 7, in Wash City, after lingering for some months, Irvan, a lovely & interesting child, y/son of Porter & Mary P Robinson, late of Westmoreland Co, Va.

Died: on Sep 21, at Balt, Hannah Ann, the beloved wife of Robt Hull, & daughter of the late Jos Janney.

By 2 writs of fieri facias to me directed, I shall sell at public auction, for cash, on Oct 14, in Wash City, the goods & chattels seized & taken as the property of M S Covell, to satisfy the said judgments due to S S King against Michl Hill, M S Covell, & Saml Walker. -Jas M Wright, Constable

SAT OCT 9, 1847

Household & kitchen furniture at auction: on Oct 13, at the residence of the late Rev Mr Samson, on 9th, between H & I sts. -A Green, auctioneer

Valuable mills & land for sale: subscriber offers Shauck's Mills, on Neuse river, 6 miles from Raleigh: tract contains 210 acres. Address the subscriber, or the Editor of the Register, Raleigh, N C. -Wm N Shauck

Lexington Observer: on Sat, Jas Sutherland killed his father, Rolla Sutherland, who was very intemperature & attempted to whip his wife & cut the throat of his son. Jas Sutherland, his wife, & mother, & others of the Rolla Sutherland's family, fled to the house of Capt Jas Sphar; the whole affair was the result of king alchohol. Rolla Sutherland was a respectable citizen when sober, when drunk, a perfect madman. Jas Sutherland, his son, is a young man of fine moral character, & very much esteemed. He was discharged before an examining court on Mon.

The remains of Louis Bonaparte, Count de Saint Leu, ex-King of Holland, who died a few months ago at Florence & those of his son, who also died in Italy; have arrived at Marseilles, & will be brought to Reuil, & deposited in the tomb of the Empress Josephine & Queen Hortense.

Farm, horses, wagon, carryall, & cart at auction: on Oct 22, on the premises, the farm belonging in & on which Mrs Cummin resides, near Tenallytown, about 2½ miles from Gtwn, containing 60 acres, more or less. -A Green, auctioneer

Headquarters Jalapa, Aug 26, 1847. To Govn'r Wilson, Vera Cruz: My command reached this place on Aug 20. We have been opposed by at least 1,200 or 1,500 guerrillas: they were badly whipped at Cerro Gordo: Fr Jarauta commanded them. At the Nat'l Bridge, Mr Geo D Twiggs, [expecting a commission, & to be A D C to Gen T] was killed while gallantly serving in my staff; Capt J H Calwell, of voltigeurs, & Capt A C Cummings, 11th Infty, were wounded on the 10th, but are doing well now. At the Nat'l Bridge, Lt Jas A Winder, of voltigeurs, & Lt Geo A Adams, of marine corps, were dangerously wounded; also, Capt W J Clark, 12th Infty, in the thigh; 2nd Lt Chas M Crearor, 12th Infty, not severely, in the leg. At Las Animas, on the 19th, Maj F T Lally, 9th Infty, commanding ofcr, was wounded in the neck, not severely, but has for a few days been disabled from command. Col Wynkoop arrived from Perote on the 24th, having heard we were in danger at Cerro Gordo. -F T Lally, Maj 9th Infty, commanding

M Van Berchem, from his researches on vaccination & small pox, concludes that among the vaccinated, the older the individual the greater is the liability to an attack of small pox. Among the unvaccinated it is the reverse, for the younger the person the more he is liable to an attack of small pox.

House for rent & horse & carriages for sale: house #5, Union Row: inquire on the premises, or of Mr Shanks, the proprietor. Also, a valuable horse & carriages: the owner, Mr C M Keller, being about to remove to the North. The horse & carriages can be seen at the stable of Mr Levi Pumphrey.

MON OCT 11, 1847

Mrd: on Oct 7, at St Matthew's Church, by Rev Jas B Donelan, Mr Wm C France, of Cincinnati, to Miss Adele Albert, eldest daughter of Dr A Dorman, of Wash City. Cincinnati papers please copy.

Mrd: on Oct 7, by Rev Jas B Donelan, Mr Valentine Dengel, of Milwaukie, Wisconsin, to Miss Mary A Kurtz, of Wash.

London Spectator: the late Robt Glasgow Dunlop was born at Seafield, near Ayr, in 1815, & was the grandson of the Mrs Dunlop who first patronized Burns. He was educated at the Scottish parochial school, & was a student at the London Univ. In Mar, 1844, he embarked for Central America; where he died, on Jan 1, 1847, of a fever common to the country, the sixth of seven brothers who rest in a foreign soil. His book, which was finished at Guatemala in Dec last, had passed through the press.

Register's Ofc, Wash, Oct 6, 1847. Persons who have taken out licenses under the laws of the Wash Corp during the months of Jul, Aug, & Sep last.

Cart license:

Bitner, W G	Dunlop, Geo	Mills, E B
Brown, Wm	Davis, W W	Mullikin, John
Dunlop, Geo	Herens, Geo	Noble, Martha
Davis, W W	Lindsay, M A	Plant, Nathl

Ridgway, E
Sibley, Wm
Stubbs, W E
Travers, M W

Coal license: Rittenhouse, S F; Stubbs, W E

Concert license: Wash Euterpeans

Confectionary license: Buete, Henry; Thomas, Jacob; Weaver, Jos

Dog license:

Chiseltine, Alex
Chubb, J M
Cosken, John
Campbell, Amel
Collins, Thos
Davy, Jas
Douglass, Chas
Eaton, Richd
Ehlen, J T
Egerton, Jo
Fink, C
Ford, Jas
Green, Jas
Gill, Christ'n
Gregory, Geo
Hutton, Henry
Hollman, Geo
Hall, Eliz
Hickman, Ja
Haines, W T
Jackson, Wm
James, C H
Jones, Henry
Janney, Ann
King, Elijah
Kuhle, Henry
King, Chas
Kingsbury, Thos
Lawrie, Jas
Lowrey, W H
Lepreux, Lewis
Mechlin, J P
Manyett, F
Myers, Sarah
Marsoletti, L E
Norbeck, Wm
Ross, Augustus
Serrin, Wm
Shucking, A
Shaw, Alex
Sinclair, John
Smallwood, D
Storm, Leonard
Smallwood, J, jr
Thompson, C E
Tilghman, H H
Visser, J
Whaley, Martha

Dry Goods license: Beach, Saml B; Hall, R B; Pischer, Aug

Grocery license:

Clarke, Saml
Cook, Matthew
Lancaster, Basil
McKennon, Mary

Hack license: Dent, Bruce

Hardware license: Cochran, G W

Hats & Shoes license: Hall, R B; Wilson, Wm

Huckster license:

Brown, R J
Bayliss & Skidmore-2
Ball, John W
Crampsey, /w
Crowley, Wm
Connor, Michl
Coley, W M
Collins, Geo
Davis, Jas
Eaton, Richd
Fearson, J C-transfer
Goddard, Jas
Hollidge, Thos
Hilton, Alph's
Johnson, W C
Johnson, T J
Kirkham, Wm
Linkins, Walter
Lewis, Benj
Lane, Henry
Moran, W E
Maury, J & C
Murray, Wm A
Plowman, Jesse
Robertson, Danl
Randall, Wm
Sherwood, S
Smith, Sarah
Smallwood, R T
Sherwood, Temple
Soper, Wm
Scroggin, G W
Thomas, Geo
Thacker, Jas
Woolard, Hez
Wallace, Ellen
Yeatman, J H

Lottery license: Maury, J & C, agents; Mattingly, Geo E; Pearce, Thos

Porter license: Conner, John; Holbrook, J H

Retail license:

Barron, W M	Hurdle, Thos	Sekells, T H-transfer
Baumback, A	Lomax, Wm	Thomas, Jacob
Cole, Wm	Lindsley, M S	Vermillian, C A
Gensler, Henry	Nailor, Dickerson	Waring, John
Hutton, Geo	Rosenstock, Saml	

Shop license: Adams, Notley; Burdine, Alfred; Frank, Jos-transfer
Slave license: Hills, J B-2; Jones, R J, ex'r; Lanham, Letitia; Turpin, J S
Stall license: Bell, W D; Gatrell, A M
Stage license: Cruit, Jas
Tavern license: Coleman, S S
Wagon license:

Burr, DeVere	Ledner, Christ'n	Visser, J
Brundbridge, Z	Mullikin, John-2	Wonderlich, John
Goings, Pat	Pettibone, John	Webb, Albert J
Groupe, Wm	Robinson, Ann	
Knott, Geo	Stevenson, Thos	

Wood license: Stubbs, W E; Shadd, B; Travers, J & Son
The following during the months of Jul, Aug, & Sep last, fined for failing to procure their licenses:
Bacon adjoining new market: Shreave, Caleb
Dog license: Brown, O B; Colby, Jas; Peachy, Arch
Dry Goods license: Rosenstock, L
Grocery license: Stoops, Jas
Huckster license: Lucas, Augustus; Lucas, Chas
Less than a pint license: Joyce, John J
Milk cart license: Whitall, Saml:
Retail license: Reeves, R B
Selling liquor license: Nicholson, Jos
Wagon license:

Cook, L O	Conner, John	Hager, C
Cross, A V	Favier, A	Payne, C H

Mrd: on Oct 7, at St Matthew's Church, by Rev Jas B Donelan, Mr Wm C France, of Cincinnati, to Miss Adele Albert, eldest daughter of Dr A Dorman, of Wash City. Cincinnati papers please copy.

Mrd: on Oct 7, by Rev Jas B Donelan, Mr Valentine Dengel, of Milwaukie, Wisconsin, to Miss Mary A Kurtz, of Wash.

For rent: the beautiful residence of D Vermillion, on the Balt road, about 10 or 15 minutes walk from the Capitol. Apply at the place, or to A Provest, in Wash City. -D Vermillion

TUE OCT 12, 1847
Abington, Virginian: a few days ago, in Lee Co, Thos Hamilton, of Claiborne Co, Tenn, was shot & killed by Claiborne Anderson, of Lee. The dispute was over the title of a piece of land claimed by both, but in the possession of Anderson. Hamilton had ordered Anderson & his 3 sons to leave the premises, & a violent altercation ensued, & Hamilton drew a 6 barrelled revolver, &, having cocked it, pointed it at one of the sons of Anderson, who, having a gun in his hand, with which he had been hunting, instantly fired, killing Hamilton on the spot.

Maj Lally's command: killed & wounded while on the way from Vera Cruz to Jalapa:
At Paso Ovijas, Aug 10: Mortally wounded: Private John S Lynch, Co K.
Wounded: Capt Jas H Calwell, voltigeurs; Capt Arthur C Cummings, 11th Infty; Sgt Abis A Selover, Co E 3rd Dragoons, [acting Sgt Maj of this command]; Cpl Cornelius Neighbors, voltiguers; Cpl R J Terrill, Georgia mounted man; Private John Castley, Georgia mounted men; Cpl A W Warein, Co K 4th Infty; Privates John Hubbs & Wm P Campbell, Co K 11th Infty; Musician Peters, Co D voltigeurs.
At the Nat'l Bridge, Aug 12:
Killed: Mr Geo D Twiggs, acting in the staff of the commanding ofcr; Private Casper Beckman, Co K 4th Infty; Private Wm Tomison; Private Henry Sturgey, light artl battery; Private John A Griffin, Co G 12th Infty; Sgt R H Rogers, Co I 12th Infty; Privates A N Crandle & A Miron, Co G 12th Infty; Private Jas S Gove, Co I 12th Infty; Private Chas G Powell, Co I 12th Infty.
Wounded: Capt J W Clark, 12th Infty; Lt Jas A Winder, voltigeurs; Lt Chas W Creamer, 13th Infty, acting assist quartermaster; Lt Geo Adams, Marine Corps; Sgts Ebenezer Legn & Wm Ingles, Co G 15th Infty; Cpl H J Lorens, Co G 15th Infty; Privates J Rice, L Knuht, G P Amidon, F Jackson, N Kendall, H Hulter, & O Stone, Co G 15th Infty; Privates Crider, Harris, & McIntosh, Co C 5th Infty; Privates Geo Secall & Saml Danytesten, Co K voltigeurs; Private Lampten Moon, Co K 4th Infty; Sgt T G Wilkins, Co A Louisiana mounted men; Private Haury, do; Privates Jas M Lauten & Wm S Wood, Co K 11th Infty; Private John Mabury, Georgia mounted men; Private Rick Ford, Co G 12th Infty; Privates Benj Justice, Wm Kirksey, Elijah Kirksey, & Hardy Shandwick, Co I 12th Infty; Privates Rinick & Alpkun, Co D voltiguers; Privates Elijah M Gates, Edw McMillen, Jas H Higgins, Jas W Blassingham, Thos Willson, John T Foster, & Thos Moore, light artl battery.
At Cerro Gordo, Aug 15.
Killed: Privates Fredk'd Notter, Co D 5th Infty, & Saml B Andrews, Co K voltigeurs.
Mortally wounded: Private Geo A Genth, Co I 12th Infty.
Wounded: Privates Danl Jarsell, Co I 12th Infty; Geo W Palmer, Co H 4th Infty; Wm Francis, ___Wilrainish, Jos Tester, & John Ays, Co D 5th Infty; Gamisly Fitzgerald, Co H 4th Infty; Sgts Talbot H Law, Co K 4th Infty; ___ Ruigler, Co F 3rd Infty; Private ___ Jones, Co C 5th Infty.
At Lansanimas:
Killed: Privates Jas Londale & Wm Bell, Co K 4th Infty.
Wounded: Major F T Lally, 9th Infty, commanding; Privates John Sims & Bernard Cowin, Co H 4th Infty; Jas C Reyle, Co K voltigeurs; Jos Shunalt & John Baldwin, light artl batter.

Elsewhere on the road, Aug 9 & 14:
Killed: Privates Edw S Davis, Co H 4th Infty; Antonio Keisenbock, Co K 12th Infty; Jas Davis, Georgia mounted men; Michl Hamlin, Plan del Tio; Bugler Francis Lawerant, Co A Louisiana mounted men.
Wounded: Lt David Griffin, Co H 4th Infty; Sgt Henry Buckly, Co K 12th Infty; Privates Stephen Rotundo, Co C 5th Infty, & Saml Huny.

Orphans Court of Wash Co, D C. Letters of administration on the personal estate of Eliz Summers, late of said county, dec'd. -Jas Crandell, administrator

For rent: the house & lot on Gay st, now in the occupancy of Henry W Tilley, next house but one to Mrs Colonel Humphrey's, with a large lot. Possession will be given on Nov 10. Apply to W S Nichols, Gtwn.

For rent: convenient 3 story brick house near the Capitol square. Rent moderate.
-Geo Watterston

For rent: convenient brick house in Gtwn, on Wash st, above West, containing 11 rooms & backbldgs. Apply to J M Belt, at his store on Bridge st.

Mrd: on Oct 8, at Orange Court House, Va, by Rev Saml T Moorman, Edw M Clark, of Wash City, to Miss Jane S, daughter of the late Marvin Nalle, of Culpeper Co, Va.

Died: on Sep 23, at Contonement Clinch, in Florida, Dr Peyton R Tunstall, a native of Spottsylvania Co, Va, aged 52 years.

Mrs Whitwell has removed from her late residence in Duff Green's Row, Capitol Hill, & has taken the house formerly occupied by Mr Dent, on 4½ st, next door to the First Presbyterian Church, & is now prepared to receive boarders by the week, month, or year.

WED OCT 13, 1847
The Phil Inquirer announces the death of Lt Geo Decatur Twiggs, who until within a few months a resident of this city. He was young, gallant, & gifted. The late Cmdor Stephen Decatur was his uncle by his mother's side, & Gen Twiggs, of the U S Army, his uncle on his father's side. Lt Twiggs was a fine scholar, wrote well, & at the time he left was reading law with a distinguished member of the Bar. He was an only son, & his deeply afflicted mother & sisters are residing at our Navy Yard. The citizens of Phil will deeply sympathize with them in their melancholy bereavement. Maj Twiggs, the father of Lt Twiggs, is with Gen Scott.

Very superior household furniture, plate, wines, & carriages at auction: on Oct 27, at the residence of the late Henry S Fox, late her Britannic Majesty's Minister to the U S, at the corner of K & 24th sts, by order of the Orphans Court. -R W Dyer, auct

Meeting in Abingdon on Sep 27, Gov David Campbell in the chair; & Jacob Lynch acting as Sec: resolutions passed in honor of the memory of Lt John Preston Johnson, of the 1st Artl, who fell mortally wounded while in the discharge of his duty in the battle of Contretos, near the city of Mexico. Lt Johnson was the only son of the late Chas C Johnston, a citizen of Abingdon, a gentleman of great promise, who, in the vigor of manhood, & whilst representing that district in Congress, lost his life by accidentally falling into the Potomac, near Alexandria. The gallant Lt received a military education at West Point, &, after graduating, joined the U S Army. His immediate family, we are told, are all dead, except one devoted sister, Miss Eliza M Johnston. -Richmond Whig

Wash Corp: 1-Ptn of Peter Bergman: referred to the Cmte of Claims. 2-Ptn of Henry Barron: referred to the Cmte of Claims. 3-Ptn of Jos Prather & others: referred to the Cmte on Police. 4-Cmte of Claims: bill for the relief of Michl Shanks: laid on the table. 5-Ptn of Jas H Schreeve & Harrison Taylor, for remission of a fine: referred to the Cmte of Claims. 6-Cmte on Unfinished Business, to which were referred the ptns of Jos Elisha, Jas Gates, Garrett Anderson, Benj Homans, Edw Mead, Antonio Pons, Jos Straub, & of Solomon Hersey, asked to be discharged from the further consideration of the same: ptns postponed. 7-Cmte on Claims: ptn of Saml S Giddings: asked to be discharged from further consideration of the same. 8-Police Magistrates elected for the several wards for the ensuing year:

Saml Drury	Thos Donoho	Jas Crandell
Theodore Kane	B K Morsell	Wm F Purcell
John D Clark	Thos C Donn	Craven Ashford
John P Van Tyne	Jos W Beck	
John L Smith	Jas Marshall	

9-Trustees of the public schools elected:

G J Abbott	Abel G Davis	Peter F Bacon
Geo Watterston	N C Towle	Ignatius Mudd
Robt Farnham	Thos Donoho	J E Morgan
J F Hartley	Valentine Harbaugh	Craven Ashford

Excellent household & kitchen furniture, & piano forte, at auction: on Oct 20, at the residence of the Hon A P Bagby, on C st, between 3rd & 4½ sts. -R W Dyer, auct

THU OCT 14, 1847

The Augusta papers announce the death of Jas Gardner, in his 81st year. He was one of the oldest merchants in Augusta, & the father of the editor of the Georgia Constitutionalist.

The Church of St Sophia at Constantinople, which in 1453 was converted into a mosque, is the oldest Christian temple in existence, [having been built by Justinian,] & is at present undergoing, by order of the Sultan, a complete restoration under the direction of M Fossati, architect. A bed of plaster has been taken off that covered the superb mosaics with which the walls of ***St Sophia*** are decorated.

Marshal Oudinot, Duke de Reggio, & one of the most celebrated of Napoleon's Generals, died at Paris, on Mon, at age 81. He was Govn'r of the Invalides at the time of his death. The Marshal has left a son, the Marquis Oudinot, who is a lt-gen, deputy, & cmder of the Legion of Honor.

Household & kitchen furniture at auction: on Oct 18, at the residence of Mr Aquilla Rickets, on G near 17th st, near the War Ofc, an excellent lot of furniture.
-A Green, auctioneer [The house is for rent or sale.]

The ship **Empire**, bound to Vera Cruz, sailed from N Y on Tue, having on board companies L & M of the 1st, & L & M of the 3rd Regt of Artl, numbering 400 men. She is to call at Charleston to take on board from 500 to 600 men, who are to embark immediately on her arrival. Ofcrs attached to the command of the **Empire**: Capt Van Ness, 1st Artl, commcnding.
Co L, 1st Artl: 1st Lt L B H Hill, 1st Artl, commanding; 2nd Lt L O Morris, 1st Artl; 2nd Lt J J Woods, 1st Artl; 2nd Lt A J Dorn, 3rd Dragoons.
Co M, 1st Artl: 2nd Lt T Talbot, 1st Artl, commanding; 2nd Lt S F Chalfin, 1st Art; 2nd Lt Jas Elder, 11th Infty.
Co L, 3rd Artl: 2nd Lt W Read, 5th Infty, commanding; Brevet 2nd Lt C L Best, 1st Artl; Brevet 2nd Lt S H Neill, 4th Infty.
Co M, 3rd Artl: Brevet 2nd Lt J De Russy, 6th Infty, commanding; 2nd Lt J Q Wilbur, 14th Infty; 2nd Lt Thos Hart, 14th Infty.

Mrd: on Tue, by Rev J C Smith, Mr Geo W Cochran to Miss Sarah E Burns, all of Wash City.

Mrd: on Sep 28, at Jefferson Barracks, by Rev Mr Corbin, Lt F S Mumford, U S Army, to Miss Jane C Callanan, of N Y, adopted dght of Lt Col Staniford, U S Army.

Died: on Sep 25, at the residence of his father, in St Mary's Co, Md, John M Heard, in his 27th year. He has just stepped out upon the arena of the world, the idol of the parent, the pride of the friend, & the delight of the community.

Died: on Oct 10, in Wash City, of inflammation of the lungs, Jane Reynolds, daughter of Valentine & Frances Ann Blanchard, aged 21 months.

Revolutionary Claims: I have authentic documentary evidence of the services & claims of the ofcrs of the Va State Line & Navy to half-pay for life, & bounty lands, & of the ofcrs of the Continental Lines of the several States to pensions, commutation pay, & bounty lands. Letters directed to Gen John P Duval, Atty at law, Tallahassee, Fla, post paid, will be attended to. -John P Duval

Furnished or unfurnished house to rent: the residence of Mrs John Coyle, south B st, Capitol Hill. Apply on the premises.

FRI OCT 15, 1847
Considerable damage was sustained in Martinsburg. The Woollen Factory owned by Mr E Showers, on the Tuscarora, adjoining the town, was swept off the by the torrent of water. Suffers in Winchester of loss property were: Messrs John N Bell, Wm Miller & Co, J B Taylor & Co; Jacob Senseny, & Isaac Paul; among the mechanics, Messrs Sidwell, Brown, & Sherer, the proprietors of the large tanneries in Winchester. One establishment alone, Mr Hartley's, is said to have lost $25,000, & Mr Miller from $5,000 to $10,00. [Oct 19th newspaper: Mr Hartley's loss is not more than $25. -Balt American]

Mr Luther Gould, of Fairfield, Conn, was killed, when, with others, was engaged in blasting rocks, in the vicinity of Black Rock. Fire communicated directly to the powder, & the whole exploded. Mr Gould, about 25 years of age, leaves a wife to mourn his awful death.

Mrd: on Oct 11, by Rev Mr Donelan, Mr John Bates to Mary E, daughter of Geo Savage, all of Wash City.

Died: on Oct 13, in Wash City, Eliz Forrest, daughter of Jonathan & Eliz Forrest, in her 18th year. Her funeral is at 3 o'clock today.

Died; on Oct 8, in Rockville, Montg Co, Md, after a severe & protracted illness, in his 64th year, Col John Cook, one of the oldest members of the Montg Bar, & for many years a highly respected citizen of the village.

$300 reward for runaway negro men: Felix about 23; Arthur, about 24. They went off with another named Henry Berryman. -Edw C Marshall, Richd C Ambler: residing near ***Oak Hill***, Fauquier Co, Va.

Splendid farm for sale: in Chas Co, Md, called ***Glasvar***, on which the subscriber has resided for the last 17 years. The estate contains about 1,200 acres; ample supply of tobacco-houses, stables, granaries, corn-houses, sheep & cow-sheds, negro-houses, & other out-bldgs. -Wm D Merrick

Orphans Court sale of household & kitchens furniture: on Oct 18, the personal estate of the late Jas McVean, dec'd. A sale of the Library will take place at 4 o'clock.
-E S Wright, auct. The house is for rent. Inquire of A Hyde.

SAT OCT 16, 1847
Mrd: on Oct 7, in Gtwn, by Rev Mr Gassaway, Oscar Duncan Thompson, of Pittsburg, to Miss Susan, daughter of the late Clement Smith.

Died: on Oct 4, in New Orleans, of yellow fever, John S Handy, aged 46 years, of Annamessix, Somerset Co, Md, leaving a wife & 6 children to mourn his untimely loss in a strange land.

Died: on Oct 9, at her father's residence near Petersville, Fred'k Co, Md, Miss Mary, 2nd daughter of Mr Mortimer McIlhany, formerly a resident of Loudoun Co, Va. Cut down in the very midst of youth, she has left a father, mother, brothers, sisters, & numerous friends to mourn their irreparable loss.

Died: on Sep 5, in Clarksburg, Montg Co, Md, Dr Horace Willson, in his 55th year. As a physician he ranked high in his profession; as a husband, he was affectionate; as a father, kind & indulgent; & as a master, humane & lenient.

Orphans Court of Wash Co, D C. In the case of Patrick Moran, adm, with the will annexed, of Bernard Kelly, dec'd: the administrator & trustee have appointed Nov 5 next, for the settlement of said estate, so far as the same have been collected & turned into money. -Ed N Roach, Reg o/wills

The Fair in PG Co, Md: held at Upper Marlboro on Thu & yesterday. Competitors in remarkably fine cattles & rare productions of the animal & vegetable kind, we noticed Messrs C B Calvert, Horace Capron, Thos Duckett, W W W Bowie, & Dr John Bayne, of PG Co; Messrs Thos Blagden, Jas Maher, & Mr Pierce, of Wash City & County. Also, noticed John S Skinner, editor of the Farmers' Library.

Notice of copartnership in the butchering business, under the name & firm of Henry & Lewis Walker.

MON OCT 18, 1847

Rt Rev Dr Power, Roman Catholic Bishop of Toronto, Canada West, died in that city on Oct 1. His disease was typhus fever, contracted during his ministration among the sick & dying immigrants. He was about 42 years of age, & was a native of Halifax, Nova Scotia.

Cincinnati, Oct 15, 1847. Violent thunder storm at Nashville & at least 100 houses were destroyed, & loss of life cannot yet be told. Houses owned by the following were either injured or destroyed:

Wm Taylor	Mr Turner	Mr Stephens
Mrs Cleveland	Mr Harris	Mr Chandler
Mr Shevers	Mr Moore	M J L Smith
Mr Reed	Mr Cole	Rev Henry Watch,
Mr Chandler	Mr Stout	
Mr Bang	Mr Deanny	

The new Methodist Church
Household attached to the Church

Mr Geo Jacobs & Mr Harrington, of Boston, were out in a boat on Tue last near that city for the purpose of shooting ducks. Mr Jacobs discharged his gun, which rebounded & threw him back before the muzzle of his comrade's gun, who was also in the act of firing. The contents of the gun entered the back part of Mr Jacobs' head, causing his instant death.

S C papers announce the decease, on Oct 10, of the distinguished citizen of S C, Chancellor Wm Harper.

Mrd: on Sep 20, at Havana, Cuba, Gen Robt B Campbell, Consul of the U S for that port, to Miss Morland, daughter of John Morland, of Havana, formerly of Boston.

Mrd: on Thu last, by Rev Mr Cummings, Lt Edw Bradford, U S Army, to Miss Ann E, 3rd daughter of the Hon Littleton W Tazewell, of Norfolk.

Mrd: on Oct 12, at Phil, by Rev Henry W Ducachet, D D, Lt Wm R Palmer, U S Corps of Topographical Engineers, to Ellen, daughter of the late Geo Blight, of that city.

Circuit Court of D C. Jacob Snider, jr, vs Wm Vaughan, John Merrick & Rebecca his wife, Chas Vaughan, John A Vaughan, & Patsy Vaughan, heirs at law of John Vaughan, dec'd. In Chancery. The bill states that John Vaughan, late of Phil, died in Dec, 1841, having first made his will, by which he bequeathed all his property, subject to the payment of debts & legacies, to the cmplnt, & appointed him executor, that the will was executed in the presence of 2 witnesses; only, & was therefore inoperative to pass real estate in D C; that the complnt, qualified as executor, & has paid all the debts of the estate, except that due to himself, & that the personal estate is exhausted; that certain real estate remains, consisting of lots in squares 583, 585, 598, & 643, in Wash City, for the sale of which the cmplnt prays that a decree may be passed. It further states that the dfndnts do not reside within the Dist of Col, or the jurisdiction of this court. Said dfndnts are to appear on the first Mon of Mar next, & make answer to the said bill. -W Cranch
-Wm Brent, clk

TUE OCT 19, 1847

The jewelry alleged to have been stolen by the servant girl at St Louis, Eliz Reddick, who committed suicide recently, has been found at the house of her former mistress, & in the very spot where it was placed by her accuser, who afterwards forgot the circumstances.

Milton Chronicle: Hon Bedford Brown, who emigrated from N C to Missouri a few years ago, is now returning to this State, with his family. Mr Brown has been unfortunate with his family since his removal, & it is affliction that brings him back among us. -Raleigh Register

On Sat week R D Hardgrave, employed by Thos Watson & Son, bakers, ***Fort Hill*** wharf, Boston, was entrusted with a check for $2,646, to deposit in the Freeman's Bank, but instead he had cashed it at another bank & ran off with the money. He is about 35 years of age. He may pass by the name of Jas Douglas or Jas Delarue, & he has lived in Royalton, Vt. -Boston Post

Cincinnati, Oct 5, 1847. S F R Morris, who was announced to appear at the Theatre this evening, died, book in hand, while studying his part for the evening. -Pittsburg Gaz

Sheriff's sale of the Mount Savage Iron Works, Railroad, & lands. By virtue of 2 writs of venditioni exponas, issued to be by Allegany Co Court against the Md & N Y Iron & Coal Co; one at the suit of John Wright, Robt Saml Palmer, & Chas Weld, trustees for the English bondholders; & the other at the suit of Wm F Cary & John M Forbes. I will sell at the ofc of said Company, Mount Savage, Md, on Nov 11, all the lands of the said Company with improvements thereon, known as the Mount Savage Iron Works, together with the Railroad. These lands are known as follows: ***Mount Savage***, [excepting an immaterial party thereof conveyed by the Company to Harriet Emily Weld,] containing 3,072 1-8 acres; ***Third Addition to Mount Savage***: 212 acres; part of ***Take all That's Left***: 70 acres; ***Sheffield***: 64 acres; ***Billston***: 1¼ acres; ***Dudley***: ½ acre; ***Limestone***: 6 acres; a parcel of land containing 73 acres, described in the deed from Geo Mattingley & others to Lewis Howell, dated Nov 18, 1837; ***Howell***: 875 acres; ***Peter's Patrimony***: 286 15-16 acres; ***Small Addition***: 12 acres; ***Timber Ridge***: 5 acres; ***Three Springs***: 113 acres; ***Straight Hollow***: 55 acres; ***Point Look Out***: 30 acres; ***Nothing Left***: 40 acres; ***Sugar & Wine***: 81 acres; ***Rocky Hollow***: 53 acres; ***Vulcan:*** 254 acres; ***Cedar Ridge***: 140 acres; part of ***Family Inheritance***: 28 acres; ***Walnut Bottom***: several parcels; part of ***Resurvey on Enterprise***: 17 acres, 108 perches; ***Resurvey on Hoffman's Delight***: 2 acres 16 perches; ***Part of the Brothers***: 115 perches; part of ***Resurvey on Mount Pleasant***: 19½ acres; part of ***Mill Seat & Addition to Mill Seat***: 2 acres 96 perches; another part of ***Resurvey on Enterprise***, conveyed to Saml M Semmes in trust for Henry Thomas Weld , by 2 deeds, one from Pierce Byrne & Frances his wife, dated May 25, 1844, & the other from John Black & Lydia his wife, dated May 24, 1844; a parcel of land containing 1 acre 1 rood & 6 perches, being the same that was purchased by the said Company from Aza Beall, described in the agreement between the parties; & lots 34, 35, 46 thru 52, on the east side of Will's Creek, in ***Beall's First Addition*** to the town of Cumberland. -Moses Rawlings, Sheriff of Alleghany Co

Trustee's sale of valuable property: by 2 deeds of trust from Jos Straub, to the subscriber, one dated Jul 15, 1837, recorded in Liber W B 66 folios 164 to 167, the other dated Mar 26, 1839, recorded in Liber W B 75, folios 353 to 357: sale on Nov 19, of lots 9 & 10 in square 450, with the improvements, now occupied by Straub, & at which place he carries on a pottery. This property fronts on 7th st, between L st & N Y ave. Terms of sale cash. -Henry Naylor, trustee -R W Dyer, auct

For rent: a 3 story brick house on N J ave, Capitol Hill. Also, a frame house next door to the house occupied by Mr Robt Bealle. -Jas G Coombe, exc

For sale: the Fred'k City Hotel: main bldg, of 3 stories, fronts 60 feet on Patrick st, the whole affording about 50 rooms. -Nimrod Owings, G M Eichelberger, R Potts, B Norris, Trustees

Died: on Oct 18, after a painful illness of several years, Mrs Mary Rixster, aged about 75 years. Her funeral is this afternoon at 4 o'clock, from her late residence, near the West Market.

Died: at Woodstock, King Geo Co, Va, in her 24th year, Mrs Julia A Dade, consort of Law T Dade. [No date-current item.]

WED OCT 20, 1847

Circuit Court of Wash Co, D C, in Chancery. Easter, Brother & Co, vs Wm Ward et al. The trustee reports he has made sale of the west half of lot 11 in square A, of Wash City, with the appurtenances, to Jos Baugher, for the price of $2,499; & that said Baugher has assigned his purchase to John A Smith, who has complied with the terms of the sale -Wm Brent, clk

Wash Corp: 1-Cmte of Claims: reported a bill for the relief of Enoch Ridgeway: passed. 2-Cmte of Claims: asked to be discharged from the further consideration of the ptns of Wm Allen, Lucian Clavadetacher, & Lawrence Callan: discharged accordingly. Also, from the ptn of R J Pollard: ptn was recommitted. 3-Ptn of Chas Kiernan, for remission of a fine: referred to the Cmte of Claims. 4-Ptn of Moses Lee, for remission of a fine: referred to the Cmte of Claims.

For rent: commodious Boarding House on Pa ave, a few doors east of Coleman's Hotel. Inquire of Mr Ruff, at his shoe store on the premises, or the proprietor at the Wash City Savings bank, opposite. -Lewis Johnson

Mrs Turpin, who formerly resided on 7th st & La ave, has taken that large & commodious house on Pa ave, between 3rd & 4½ sts, opposite Jackson Hall, where she is prepared to accommodate boarders.

THU OCT 21, 1847

New Orleans Delta of Oct 14. The ofcrs thus liberated on parole are: Capts Clay, Heady, & Smith, & Lts Churchill, Davidson, & Barbour, & 16 privates. Ofcrs killed: Maj L Twiggs, Capt A Vanolinda, Col T B Ransom, Brevet Lt Col Martin Scott, Lt Col Wm M Graham, Capt M E Merrill. Ofcrs wounded: Brevet Col J S McIntosh, Majors C A Waite, Geo W Talcott, John H Savage; Brevet Majors G Wright, A Montgomery; Capts R Anderson, A Cady, W H T Walker, L Smith, Thos Glenn, Wm H Irwin, P M Guthrie, E C Williams, Jas Miller, Jas Caldwell; Maj Gen G J Pillow, severely; Maj A H Gladden, Brig Gen Jas Shields, Assist Adj Gen F N Page, A A General M Lovell, Assist Adj Gen W W Mackall, Volunteer Aid-de-camp Geo Wilkins Kendall; Lt Col John Garland, Maj W W Loring, Brevet Col J E Johnston, Capts J H Williams, Jas Barclay, C H Pearson, D E Hungerford, Mitchell Danley, D H McPhail, J S Simenson, J B Bachenstos, S S Tucker, Geo Nauman, Silas Casey, J B Magruder, J M Scantland, Robt G Gale, Moses J Barnard, & Col S M Trousdale.

As the York train was coming in on Tue, the conductor, Mr Dorney, was instantly killed. The coupling bar broke, & Mr Dorney, standing at the time on the platform, was thrown under the cars by the sudden motion. Mr Dorney was from Harford Co, Md, & had been on the road but a few weeks.

The Hon Alex'r H Everett, the American Com'r to China, died in Canton on Jun 29. He had only arrived in that city a few days with his family to take possession of a new house.

Public sale: Nov 6, at the residence of Mrs Martin, near Bladensburg, PG Co, Md: farm implements, horses, cows, feather beds, kitchen stoves, carriage, fodder, hay, & corn. -Hanson Penn, for Mrs Martin

The death of Madame Albertazzi, at London, is announced. She was an eminent vocalist. [No date-late foreign intelligence.]

Nashville Gaz of the 13th: on Oct 12 a powder magazine was struck by lightning, & blown up. Killed instantly were Mrs Marlin, a light dght of Mrs Brownlow, & a Portuguese woman, named Francis. Wounded: Mrs Parker & dght, badly; Mr Armstrong; Mrs Armstrong, arm broken; Mr Caldwell, since dead; Mrs Edmonson; Miss Blake, daughter of N O Blake, badly cut with glass; Susan A Horne, arm badly cut with glass; Petty Reese, arm broken; Mr Murray, badly hurt; a child of Mr Lee, jaw broken; Mrs Ray, severely cut; Mr Lee; Mr Dickson, ribs broken & head cut.

Mrd: Oct 14, at Willow Bank, Flushing, L I, by Rev E S Cornwall, of Conn, Hon Henry Bedinger, of Va, to Caroline B, eldest daughter of John W Lawrence, of the former place.

Died: on Oct 13, at Col Alto, near Lexington, Va, the residence of her husband, Ex-Governor McDowell, in her 48th year, Mrs Susanna Smith McDowell.

FRI OCT 22, 1847

Tacubaya, Sep 9, 1847. I have been enabled to gather a full list of all the killed & wounded ofcrs in Gen Worth's division in the great battle of the Molino del Rey, as also of those in Maj Sumner's company of Dragoons. Gen Worth's Div: Killed: Col Martin Scott, 5th Infty; Capt Merrill, 5th Infty; Capt G W Ayres, 3rd Artl; Lt E B Strong, 5th Infty; Lt W Armstrong, 2nd Artl; Lt W T Burwell, 5th Infty; Lt Farry, 3rd Artl.
Wounded: Col McIntosh, 5th Infty, severely; Maj C A Waite, 8th Infty, badly; Maj G Wright, 8th Infty, slightly; Capt E K Smith, 5th Infty, severely, [since dead;] Capt Cady, 6th Infty, slightly; Capt Larkin Smith, 8th Infty, severely; Capt Walker, 6th Infty, severely; Capt R Anderson, 3rd Artl, severely; Assist Surgeon W Roberts, dangerously; Capt J L Macon, Corps of Engineers, severely; Lt M L Shackelford, 2nd Artl, severely; Lt C S Hamilton, 5th Infty, severely; Lt C B Daniels, 2nd Artl, severely; Lt Ernst, 6th Infty, severely, lost right hand; Lt J G Burbank, 8th Infty, mortally, [since dead;] Lt J Beardsley, 8th Infty, badly; Lt G Wainwright, 8th Infty, severely; Lt H J Hunt, 2nd Artl, slightly; Lt J G S Snelling, 8th Infty, severely; Lt H F Clarke, 2nd Artl, slightly; Lt W Hayes, 2nd Artl, slightly; Lt J G Foster, corps of engineers, severely; Assist Surgeon J Simons, slightly; Lt Dent, 5th Infty, severely; Lt H Prince, 4th Infty, severely; Lt A B Lincoln, 4th Infty, severely; Lt Herman Thorne, 3rd Dragoons, Aid to Col Garland, severely; Lt Montgomery, 8th Infty, slightly; Lt Montgomery, 8th Infty, slightly; Lt Andrews, 3rd Artl, slightly.

Major Sumner's Command: Capt Croghan Ker, 2nd Dragoons, severely; Lt Tree, 2nd Dragoons, severely; Lt Walker, mounted rifles, slightly; Lt Williams, 3rd Dragoons, slightly.
The conduct of all the non-commissioned ofcrs has been gallant & most conspicuous, while several of them behaved so nobly that they have been recommended for immediate promotion to Gen Scott. Their names are: Sgts Benson, Wilson, & Robinson, of the 2nd Artl; Sgt Heck, of the 3rd Artl; Sgts Updegraff, Farmer, Archer, & Dally, of the 5th Infty; Sgt Maj Thompson, of the 6th Infty; Sgt Maj Fink, of the 8th Infty.

Gen Cadwalader's Brigade-killed: Col Wm M Graham, 11th Infty; Lt Dick Johnson, 11th Infty.
Wounded: Maj Savage, 14th Infty, slightly; Maj Talcott, voltigeurs, slightly; Capt Guthrie, 11th Infty, slightly; Capt Irvin, 11th Infty, slightly; Lt Lee, do, do; Lt Kintzing, voltigeurs, slightly; Lt Thos Shields, 14th Infty, slightly; Lt Swan, voltigeurs, slightly.

City of Mexico, Sep 17, 1847. List of the killed & wounded ofcrs in the taking of Chapultepec & the capture of the city. Killed: Col Ransom, 9th Infty; Lt Col Baxter, N Y volunteers; Maj Twiggs, U S Marines; Capt Drum, 4th Artl; Capt Vanolinde, N Y volunteers; Lt Gantt, 7th Infty; Lt Calvin Benjamin, 6th Infty; Lt S B Monague, S C volunteers; Lt A P Rodgers, 4th Infty; Lt J Willis Cantey, S C volunteers; Lt J P Smith, 5th Infty; Lt Sidney Smith, 4th Infty. Wounded: Maj Gen Pillow, slightly; Brig Gen Shields, severely; Col Garland, commanding 1st brigade Worth's division, severely; Col Toursdale, 14th Infty, severely; Lt Col Johnston, voltigeurs, slightly; Lt Col Geary, 2nd Pa volunteers, slightly; Maj Gladden, S C volunteers, severely; Maj Loring, rifles, severely; Capt Pearson, N Y volunteers, severely; Capt Gates, 8th Infty, slightly; Capt C C Danley, volunteer aid to Gen Quitman, slightly; Capt J B Backenstos, rifles, slightly; Capt McPhail, 5th Infty, slightly; Capt E C Williams, 2nd Pa volunteers, slightly; Capt J S Simonson, rifles, slightly; Capt Beauregard, corps engineers, slightly; Capt Magruder, 1st Artl, slightly; Capt Jas Miller, Pa volunteers, severely; Capt M Fairchild, N Y volunteers, slightly; Capt Jas Caldwell, 2nd Pa volunteers, severely; Capt Geo Nauman, artl; Capt S S Tucker, rifles, slightly; Capt Marshall, S C volunteers, slightly; Capt Williams, S C volunteers, slightly; Lt Earl Van Dorn, aid to Gen Smith, slightly; Lt J M Brannan, adj 1st Artl, severely; Lt M Clark, adj S C volunteers, severely; Lt J A Henderson, U S Marines, slightly; Lt Bell, S C volunteers, slightly; Lt Reno, voltigeurs, severely; Lt John Keefe, 2nd Pa volunteers, severely; Lt Martin, voltigeurs, slightly; Lt Maurice Malaney, 4th Infty, slightly; Lt M Lovell, on Gen Quitman's staff, slightly; Lt Selden, 8th Infty, severely; Lt Stevens, corps of Engineers, severely; Lt J W Green, N Y volunteers, slightly; Lt A S Towison, 2nd Pa volunteers, severely; Lt Armistead, 6th Infty, slightly; Lt M Reid, N Y volunteers, severely; Lt Bell__k, S C volunteers, severely; Lt F S K Russell, rifles, slightly; Lt J A Haskin, 1st Artl, severely; Lt D D Baker & Lt J W Steen, S C volunteers, severely; Lt J S Devlin, U S Marines, slightly; Lt Robertson, S C volunteers, severely; Lt C J Kirkland, S C volunteers, slightly; Lt J B Davis, S C volunteers, slightly; Capt J M Scantland, 14th Infty, slightly; Capt King, 15th Infty, slightly; Lt H C Long-ecker, voltigeurs, slightly; Capt R G Beale, 14th Infty, slightly; Lt Richd Stoele, 14th Infty, slightly; Lt Robt Bedford, 14th Infty, slightly; Lt J N Palner, rifles, slightly.

Lt Morris, of the 8th Infty, has died of the wound he received at the hard fought battle of El Molino, & it is extremely doubtful whether Lt Ernst, of the 6th, wounded at the same time, can recover.

SAT OCT 23, 1847

Sep 17. The Mexican loss is impossible to ascertain, but it is immense. Among the killed at Chapultepec were Gen Juan Nepomecuno Perez, Col Juan Cano, a distinguished ofcr of engineers, & Lt Lucian Calve, one of Gen Bravo' aids. Gen Saldana was badly wounded.

Non-commissioned Ofcrs, Musicians, & Privates who were killed & wounded in the late battles at Mexico:

First Division-Maj Gen Worth: in the action of Molino del Rey, Sep 8.

Killed:

Hugh Donahue
Jacobus
Ullenbrook
Brown
Lane
Tansen
Lansing
John Gracie
Saml Grove
Timothy Sullivan
A L Grenier
John Connor
Wm Hanson
Jacob Frank
David Campbel
Jacob Dyas
A B Howe
Wm J Barnhard
John C Elloes
Herman Levy
J F Farry
John Walsh
Simon Margarum
Benj M Harris
B Henry
John Cameron
Stillman Coburn
Patrick Ronnau
John McLoskey
Fred'k Workman
John Gottenger
Augustus Quitman
Stanislaus Minal
Saml Carr
Timothy Howby
Thos Weidman
Fred'k Hobber
Henry Mamark
Francis McKay
Thos S Pole
John P Ronner
Chas Steward
Saml Calhoun
Robt Crawford
Griffith Owens
David Sharpe
Thos Gooding
Peter Henz
Owen Marry
John B Honer
John Koarstoupfads
Peter G Moore
Wm McCloskey
Jas McGlynn
Bernard Althor
Martin Munneman
Michl Sheehan
Mathew Murphy
Victor Durand
John B Hond
Nicholas Ramsey
John Smith
Wm Agol
Wm Fahee
John H Plant
Christian Schuman
Wm Locey
Michl Murphy
John Brodaick
Peter Koite
Isham Canalizo
Edw Bertram
Nicholas Ford
Jas Crogan
John Hughes
Wm Sandys
John Clark
Reuben Brown
Patrick McGrash
Thos Lanson
Geo McGraff
Gabriel Wilson
Patrick Green
Alex'r Prentice
Peter Caffery
Bernard McFarlin
Jacob Neish
Chas Shwarykoryt
Wm Irvin
John A Jackson
Geo H Lightfell
Barthel Mahon
Henry Passor
Lewis Henone
Thos Fles
Saml Clark
Robt Simpson
Sidney W Gunroyer
Henry W Erwin

Geo Johnson	John Sigler	Jas Simpson
Chas Fenner	John Buchanan	Danl Kippy
John McMahon	John Manning	

Wounded: [s-slightly: S-severely: dg-dangerously: m-mortally]]

John Dougherty, s
Sgt McGuire, s
Cpl Slade, s
Cpl Buckley, s
Sgt Murphy, s
Sgt Brooks, s
Pvt Usher, d
Boling, s
Klaws, s
Zink, dg
Sweeney, s
Russell, S
Kerr, s
Wallers, S
Thomas, S
Murphy, S
Porthouse, s
Zalikiwick, S
White, s
Fielding, S
Freeman, s
Kohle, S
Mundeig, S
Westerdelot, S
Drawn, [bugler] s
Pvt Wyatt, s
Pvt Gardener, s
Pvt Fritshe, s
Pvt Hamilton, s
Pvt Paul, s
Pvt Cottrell, s
Pvt Carter, s
Pvt Harris, s
Jacob Price, S
Pvt Richards Boone, s
J M Quick, s
Hugh McCoy, S
Richd Gilmore, s
Jas Witter, s
Geo Wagner, s
Abram Hart, s

Wm Smith, s
Lawrence Dunivan, s
John Forgy, s
Saml Stanley, s
David Wheeler, s
John Murphy, s
Richd Harper, S
Joshua H Corwin, S
JaJas Devine, S
Christoph Yeager, S
Jos Updegraff, S
Thos Johnson, s
Saml Meeker, s
Gilbert G Francher, S
Jacog Nichols, S
Edw Green, S
Darius Ballard, s
Thos Low, S
Patrick Reilly, s
Jas Alexander, s
Geo Barr, S
Wm Conles, S
Herman Knickerbocker, S
Anthony Rounder, S
Thos Sullivan, S
Andrew Casey, S
Alphonso Schaiffer, S [died on the 13th]
Dan Rogers, S
Chas Linder, S
Jas H Brooke, S
Geo Kraffenbaner, S
Augustus Beaver, S
Wm Bell, s
Jos McGarlin, s
Patrick O'Rourke, s
Thos L Sleck, s
Geo W E Sherman, s
Edw Kinneford, S
Elijah J Cain, S
Levi Miles, S
John Kavanagh, s

Timothy Collins, s
Ezra Higgins, s
Michl Leonard, s
Wm Lewis, s
Thos Pardon, s
Thos Joyce, s
Nicholas Seminoff, s
Wm Wright, s
John Flemming, s
Geor Gordon, s
Jas McCormick, s
Henry Balleman, m, [since dead]
Hugh McDonald, S
Thos Clark, s
Wm Shoppe, m, [since dead]
Christi Bower, m, [since dead]
Jas Rochford, S
Chas Hoover, S
Hy Derlin, S
Martin Sharbuck, S
Wm Moore, S
Patrick Kean, s
John Conway, s
John Garrey, s
John Hill, s
Fred'k Blunt, S
Thos Furian, S
Francis Webb, S
Wm Crook, s
Saml R Dickman, s
Archibald McFayden, S, [died on the 11th]
Robt Alexander, S
Jas Montgomery, S
Thos O'Brien, S
Thos Starr, S
Rob Michan, S
John Wiley, s
J D Reynolds, s, [died the 19th]
Wm Sharp, S
Edw Ellsworth, S
Jas Bohanan, S
Jas Heany, S
John McNeil, S
John R Smith, S
Wm Cook, S
Anton Achenback, S, [since dead]
John Matthews, S, [since dead]
John Hynes, s
Jas Walsh, s
Geo Wilcox, s
Wm F Taylor, s
Philip Rouse, s
Julius Martial, S
John Coogan, m, [since dead]
Thos Bloom, S
Saml Brown, S
John Conner, S
Peter Derit, S
Robt McGee, S
Dedrick Deer, S
Wm Parker, S
Watchman, S, [since dead]
Jos Finch, S
John Tornis, S
Marshall Kimball, m, [since dead]
Philip Bacher, s
Wm W Walker, s
Michl Ley, s
John Sullivan, S
Geo W Anderson, S
Wm Quin, S
Jos Holybee, S, [since dead]
John B Weelen, S
Chas Metz, S
Wm Castigan, s
Ephr'm Cain, S
Jas Carrol, S
Oswald Drury, S
Wm Ehrenbaim, S
Jas Keenan, s
Christian Smallbark, s
David Coleman, S
John P Smith, S
Henry Stenoham, S
Jno Clancey, S
Jno Montgomery, S
Martin Rush, S

Wm Allen, S
John Gallagher, s
Lewis Merans, s
Jos L Moody, s
Philip Hady, S, [since dead]
Richd Abercrombie, S
Saml Collier, S
Robt Kuntz, S
Michl Bonet, S
Edw McKeon, S
Peter W Syms, S
Wm C Goddard, s
Danl F McKee, s
Meredith Qualls, s
Levi Leitz, s
John Coyle, S
John Hill, S
Justin O'Brien, S
W Lawrence, m
Martin Meyers, S
E McCready, S
Gilbert Goodrich, m, [since dead]
Lile Barton, s
Alex Miller, s
John T DeHart, s
Jules Gasse, S, [since dead]
John Housiner, s
Lawrence Kenny, s
Adam Beeckel, s
Theo Cranz, s
Wm Wiernest, S
Mich McGuire, s
Jas Steel, m, [since dead]
John P Wirrick, S
Chas Skolinski, s
Edw Kirevin, s
Philip Felby, S, [since dead]
Martin Loughest, S
Alfred Landrage, S
Elisha Buel, s
Henry Farmer, s
Jas O'Brine, s
Alex McClellan, S
David Thompson, s
Jas Eversteine, S, [since dead]
Wm Godfrey, s
J H Haskell, S
Geo Emerick, s
Geo Morely, s
Nicholas Reid, s
John Clarit, s
Wm Babb, s
Dediah Meir, S
Morris Sayers, m, [since dead]
Wm Wotherspoon, S
Wm Goodwin, S
Hugh Frazer, S
Jeremiah Delong, S
S Tiffans, s
J Weight, s
Geo Kingsman, S, [dead]
Isaac Baker, S, [since dead]
Isaac Christman, s
John Lyons, s
Adam Eichstein, S
John Irwing, S
Jas Lollen, S
Jon S Beach, S
Wm A Place, S, [since dead]
Abner Dixson, s
Jno Clark, S
Wm Wheeler, S
Henry Wilkie, S
Moses Papiner, S
Thos McDermott, S
Edw Annison, S
John Coglin, S
Josiah Ettinger, S
Wm Cain, S
Bernard Riley, S
Jas Shepherd, S
Patrick McElroy, S
Wm O Mocht, S
Thos Hogg, S
Josiah Cartwright, S, [since dead]
Edw H Brown, S
John Eisdar, S
Patrick McCue, S
Pat Scanlan, S
Peter Yorick, S

Leonard Johnson, S
Chas Butterling, s
Jas Burns, s
Chas Evans, s
John Hunter, s
John Wrick, s
John Helm S
Matthew Switzer, S
Wm H Morris, S
Wm Schaeffer, S
Michl Coll, S
J M Montgomery, S
Chas Sanders, S
Edw B Conner, s
Peter Bragine, s
Geo McElrie, s
Jos W Brush, s
Jos Wolf, s
Thos Foster, m, [since dead]
Jno Harvey, S, [since dead]
Wm Chapman, S
Wm Curtis, S
John Gorlan, S
John McCameron, S
Cornelius O'Neil, S
Saml Tucker, S
Chester R Tully, S
Thos H Wood, S
Jacob Watson, S
Benj Slater, s
Thos Gloveen, s
Augustus De Lonza, s
Owen Melvin, s
R F Jackson, s
Geo Williams, S
John McIntyre, S
Jas E Dresser, s
John Cummings, S
John Webb, S [since dead]
John Furguson, S
Sylvester Jones, s
Chas Rafferty, m, [since dead]
Michl Eannes, S
Francis Kline, m, [since dead]
Saml Morgan, s
Bennet Keere, s
John Finnerghty, s
Jacob Kennard, s
Richd Wilkinson, s
Jas Bradley, s
J B Johnson, s
Wm Spears, S
Calvin Wells, s
Henry Cropp, s
John Martin, s
John King, S
D Loudensborough, s
Michl McAuley, S, [since dead]
E W Dexter, s
Loreny Flood, s
John McGuire, s
Jas Victory, S
Wm P Moore, S
Jefferson Wells, S
Abraham Riber, S
Henry Bertoled, S
Geo Smith, S
Jos Roland, S, [since dead]
David Bruney, s
Danl Emerson, s
Danl Boghanan, s
Richd Cherry, S
Brian Curry, s
Thos Down, s
Wm C Howe, s
Deobald Snyder, S
Alfred Carlisle, S
John A Reading, S
Jere Ryan, S
Ebenezer Gill, S
Gregory Kepler, S
S P Armtz, S
John Moon, s
Mathew Kols, s
Wm Jones, S, [since dead]
John Fink, S
Thos Muir, s
David Pink, s
Thos Sewell, S
John Robinson, S

Jas H Kearny, S
John Smith, S
Fred'k Backhans, S
Geo Simmons, S
A T Osbourne, s
A C Edson, s
Wm Fairchilds, S
David Lawyer, s
Jos Scanson, s
Caleb Smith, s
David Springham, m, [since dead]
Wm Sheppard, S
L B Hanley, S
Abr'm Fitzpatrick, S
P R Maloed, S
J A Burtyman, S
Sol'on Viedenberg, s
Melon Miller, s
Lyman H Royce, s
Jos Schwager, s
Hy Stevens, s
Hy Jordan, S, [since dead]
E Hamer, S
Anthony Brooks, S
Robt Hawkins, S
Jas Wilson, S
L Kinny, S
John Graves, S
Jas Edmonds, S
Chas Evanson, s
Wm Angel, S
W T Bishop, S
Geo Coffee, S
Chas Hess, S
Michl McEwen, S
Michl Pickett, S
Wm Smith, S
Tho A Wilson, S
Lawrence Fagin, s
Wm Gippard, s
Jas Hannigan, s
Jas B Hill, m
Jas B Kelly, m, [since dead]
Chas Brown, S
Pat'k Cassin, S
David Doace, S
Chester C Kennedy, S
Peter King, S
Patrick McCarty, S
Hy L Snellers, S
Nat Ross, S
Jos Arnold, S
Pat'k Keany, S
Benj Burritt, s
Jas Carroll, s
Jas Gamble, s
Oliver W H Kellogg, s
Patrick Green, m, [since dead]
Aug Bliss, m, [since dead]
H Buckland, S
Wm Collan, S
John K Knock, s
Theo Shinard, s
Jacob Missil, S, [since dead]
Luther Schouts, m
S W Pumroyer, m [since dead]
Wm Shad, S
Wm Looney, S
Th Brennan, S
Th Burke, S
John Cosgrove, S
Ph Cook, S
H Eubank, s
John Gordon, s
Nicholas Hoyt, S
Wm McDonald, S
De Witt McDaniel, S
John McCarthy, S
Bernard Malone, S
Jas Mooney, S
Jno Paul, S
John M Rentor, m
Henry Rumears, m, [since dead]
Oscar F Sweet, S
S Pooler, m, [since dead]
P McMillan, s
Job H McGuire, S
John Bermingham, m, [since dead]
S T Templeman, S
John Weith, S

S A Weller, s
W Wilson, m, [since dead]
John T Blair, s
Wm Sourly, m
Js Raby, m, [since dead]
Chas Daniels, s
Mark Chapple, S
Michl Conrey, s
Wm C Morris, s
H Morinar, s
Wm Thomas, s
Js A Territ, s
Hy Bohan, [since dead]
R Swann, s
Wm J Martin, s
Wash Terrell, s
W B Vertrees, S
C D Weymouth, S
F W Jennings, S
J C Malbon, s
W J Herbert, s
R Harding, s
E R Edwards, s
S Elliott, s
J E Gardiner, s
W S McCorell, s
E D Denson, s
B Ogle, s
J H Walker, s
R H Turner, s
D Graybeer, S
A R Shacklett, S
J Hall, s
J Brown, S
D Wymp, S
A Wamsall, S
J Porter, S
G W Seaton, s
R Simpson, S
J Tompson, s
J Metcalf, s
A Adamson, s
T Davis, S
J Howell, S
J Pugh, S
J Bunger, S
A Fundy, s
T Farish, s
T Pugh, s
J L Knott, s
S A Evans, s
M Conway, s
V Collins, s
____ Holandorf, s
T Clark, s
R Sylvester, s
H Wells, s
H Kilgrove, s
W A Ward, s
J Bean, S
M G Good, S
J L Alverhorn, S
J Malony, s
W Allison, s
D Deavughn, s
J Rowinski, S
J Spencer, s
T C Parish, s
J Donly, s
J J Nickerson, s
M Benton, s
G W Bungeant, S
John Sloan, s
J L Hisse, s
T Evans, s
H Kidwell, s
A W Milbright, s
J McCaslin, s
J Cromley, S
D Davis, S
J V Franklin, s
S Field, S
T Higginson, S
A Idler, s
G Kriner, s
H Keenan, s
R Lemon, s
W S Mendenhall, s
J Massey, s
P Morrel, s

B McCabe, s
J V Perry, s
J Picken, s
J Pierce, s
B J Ross, s
W Jackson, s
O Morton, s
G Spencer, s
J Kock, s
C Eckhart, s
G Beckenschitz, S
F Korse, S
J Rutter, S
T Grooves, s
J Sigmac, s
J F Dentlinger, S
J A Yates, S
G W Jones, S
W H Fitzhue, s
H White, s
W Baldhurst, s
Thos Shields, s
Saml B Davis, s
L Warren, d
Munroe Fliming, s
Thos Pierson, s
Jas M Cox, s
Robt Brenton, s
Fielding Young, S
Jackson W Lowry, s
Asa Sawyer, S
Cayrans Lynch, s
Wm Farrell, s
Louis H Mallerhy, s
David Hall, s
Jas Gillespie, S
Hardy Johnson, s

R Attstin, s
Thos M Hayter, s
Henry Dannigan, s
P M Guthrie, S
John P Weldon, S
___Freeze, sl
Lenox Res, S
J C Handy, s
Chas Barturkey, S
Mil Freeny, S
R Ransch, S
Is'c Mahon, S
U Kitchen, S
John Hayes, m
Jas Rager, s
McCluny Radcliff, S
Robt D Brown, S
Foster R Carson, S
Jas Dilks, S
Wm S Sathall, S
Jas Hight, s
___ Schmidt, s
Wm R Call, s
Jesse Flowers, s
Wm Dorman, s
Isaac Pierce, s
Jas Neshitt, s
Hermine Bickerstine, S
Fred Babe, S
Benj Dickie, s
Simon Pickett, s
John Robering, m
Albert McGill, S
Oscar Wood, S
Jon Wilson, S, [since dead]
Christain Papst, S
Cpl Buston, d

<u>Missing:</u>

Robt McKee
John Jacob Divine
John Coyle
John Gillespie
Thos Hardy
Wm Reynolds
Francis Beer, killed

Jas Smith
Conrad Young
Henry Muilleur
Jackson Adams
Jas Leary
H A Wood

S Vandergriff
J L Hass
David Ayres
Jos G Smith

Isael Barton, killed
Jos Scott, since discovered to have been blown up at Casa del Mata

Non-commissioned Ofcrs, Musicians, & Privates, of the same Division, killed, wounded, & missing in the actions of Sep 13th & 14th

Killed:

Richd Gilmore
John Scar
Jos Cook
Chas Carroll
John Kennedy
Wm O'Neil
Wm Donagan
Geo Blast
Jas Hagan
Conrad Graf
Isaac L Jonson
Alex'r McCoy
Karl Sigmond
Michl Kelley
Wm Billington
Joel Barrom
V E Reed
Jas McLoy
Patrick Hines
Wm Mooney
David Trush
Andrew Leet
Hy Jones

Wounded: [s-slightly: S-severely: dg-dangerously: m-mortally]]

D Hastings, s
P Maguire, s
Davis, S
Edmung Ring, S
Thos Murphy, S
Jos Batemen, s
Wm Smith, s
John Wolf, s
Francis Desmond, s
Jas McCormick, s
Henry Beigle, s
Anthony Baker, m
John Sweeny, S
Herman Von Steen, S
Caro Chapparcan, s
Geo Chiveto_,. S
Fred'k Brugh, s
Jeremiah Cavaugh, s
W Garlick, s
David Rikin, s
Patrick Born, S
John Young, S
Michiael Halloran, S
John Klinz, s
Nathan Randall, s
John Zear, S
Godfrey Piermont, S
Marcus Bain, s
John Haggerty, s
Wm Blaisdell, S
David Toobwill, s
Theodore Gregg, S
Danl Bennet, m, [since dead]
Jos F Cooper, s
Hamilton Sparks, S
John Witnell, s
Wm Grant, S
Patrick Toole, s
___ Lonesee, s
Wm Burton, S
Jas Lawless, s
Stephen Mann, s
Adolphus Schuyer, s
Jacob Shores, s
John M Mallindar, s
Wm Verrel, S
Wm Wilson, s
Mark Spaulding, s
Vernon B West, s
Geo Henry, S
Wm Lawrence, S
Duwilds Myers, s
Thos Collis, s
Wm Cross, S
Jos Peck, S
John C Christie, s
Martonier Crofort, s
Wm Thompson, s
Henry Byrnes, S
Jas Fisher, S
Jas Parker, S
__ Grapincamp, S
Aganus Dowis, m
Henry Farmer, S
Darius Ballard, S
Jos McGartlin, S
Wm O'Shaugnessy, S
John A Schuber, S
Wm Montgomery, s
John Dillon, S
Jas Harny, s
Thos Oats, S
Geo Gill, S
Edw Thompson, s
Geo Ernst, S
Alex'r Maddox, S
Wm Dowley, S
Francis Fox, s
Bernard Lynch, s
Andrew Piper, S
John A Noon, S
J L Fisk, S
Robt Shaw, S
Thos Smith, S
Wm Shaw, s
Jno Hisner, s
John Flummery, s
M Monaghyn, S
Jas C McIntyre, S
Stephen McConnel, S
John McAulay, S
Wm Palmoter, S

John Kibler, S
Alex Reinhart, S
Chas McLosky, S
Wm Fox, s
Nathl Clegg, S
Hanson Palmer, S

Missing:

Chas Quick
Ed Blackman
John Briolon
Valentine Impoff
Victor Whipple
Chas Whitty
Jas Farramier
Jas Leise

Second Division-Brig Gen Twiggs:

Non-commisioned Ofcrs, Musicians, & Privates of the Second Division who were killed, wounded, or missing in the action of Chapultepee & the Garita de Belen on Sep 13th, & in the city of Mexico Sep 14th & 15th, 1847.

First Brigade:

Killed:

Dennis Byrne
Myron Bell
Wm Poruton
C C Arms
Hiram Dengh
John J O'Donnell
Thos D Wheeler
Wm Hagan
Jas Welsh
Geo Town
Wm Finney
John Alexander
Wm Donovan
Jas Harrigan
Walter Scott
Elijah O Pointer
Thos McGlone
Henry Boyle
Jas L Reed
John Bald
Michl O'Loghlin
Jesse James
Jas Huntley
Florence McCarty

Wounded: [s-slightly: S-severely: dg-dangerously: m-mortally]]

Alonzo Stanton, s
Stans Moraski, S
Wm Spear, s
Saml Harp, S
Jos Newhouse, s
M Hamilton, s
Z M P Hand, s
John Harber, S
M Batsner, S
Jas Manly, s
John Richardson, S
Francis Whitebread, S
Wm P Sanders, s
Jos Haban, S
J Hok, S
Hiram Dwyer, s
W F Herrington, s
J Murry, S
D M Frame, s
J C Morton, s
S Young, S
Wm N Winter, S
Geo B Moshers, s
J C Roberts, S
L L Worcester, s
J W Robinson, s
J C Christman, S
Geo Taylor, S
Jos Watson, s
Jos Patterson, S
J M L Addison, s
Levi Grunsby, S
E A B Phelps, s
Rufus Peck, s
Benj Tabbler, S
Robt Williams, s
Jerehiam O'Connell, s
John Dillon, S
Josh Garrison, s
J Freeman, S
John G Myers, S
Josh Debecque, s
J Millard, s
Lindsey Hooker, S
Allen Overly, s
Thos Davis, S
Danl Williams,
Danl Wills, S
Wm P Cook, S
SLewis Copsey, S
Thos Williams, S
Jas Farrell, S
Thos B Brasheno, S
Henry D Silner, s
Edw Allen, s
John Fickle, s
Wm Ferry, s
Chris Linden, s
Lawrence J Filsome, s
Danl B Baker, s
Fred Pilgrim, s
Barth W Wilson, s
John Weins, s
J M Cannon, S
John P Santmyme, s
Richd J Shephaerd, s
A Stickler, s
Clinton Frazer, s
Thos S Perkins, S
Geo W Raymond, S
Wm W Wilson, s
Amos Kingsley, s

Bradly Laud, S	Moses Glesson, S	Edw Zimmerman, s
John McFarne, S	Barns Upton, s	Patrick Moran, s
John Thompson, S	Edw Watson, s	Henry McCamphill, S
Robt Kugan, s	Francis J Shlaihan, s	Thos Pritchard, S
Henry Watts, s	Francis Oestrich, s	Leonard Elias, S
Harvey Gamperd, s	Henry Haldman, S	David Jermon, S
John Miller, s	John O'Brien, S	Eli Gable, s
Lewis Russell, s	Harry Aberlee, S	Chas McKinne, s
Francis Fletcher, s	Amos Barnhart, s	Jacob Varnes, s
Fred'k Wissal, S	Wm Campbell, s	Jos Butterfield, S
Stewart Dougherty, s	John Childer, s	Geo Frank, s
Dixon Ashworth, s	Cornelius Crowley, s	Thos McFarland, s
Orlando B Miles, s	John Hamilton, s	Terry Dale, S
Nelson Chamberlain, S	Wm Myers, s	Chas J Truman, S
John Storm, S	Philip Ryan, s	Fred'k A Collins, s
Wm Adams, s	Timothy Sullivan, s	Elliott Ellmer, s
Jas McNulty, S	Wm Kenny, s	Danl Smith, s
Henry Varner, S	Chas F E Hyer, s	David Wise, s

Missing:-storming party

Edmund Quin	John Witty	John Montgomery
Isaac Tracy	John Venater	Thos Woodbury

Second Brigade:

Killed:

Wm A Morrison	Pat Sheridan	Keyran Temple
Jas Tierney	Lewis Rinhart	Richd Shore
Michl Elwood	Wm Steinson	Neill Donnelly
John M Nash	Jos N Garnett	

Wounded: [s-slightly: S-severely: dg-dangerously: m-mortally]]

Robt Bailey, s	Chris Clarke, s	John Semple, S
Wm Bond, s	Benj Little, S	Danl Lanaham, S
Wm M Evans, s	Asabel H Wells, S	John Lynch, S
F McNally, s	Thos Rose, S	Jas Sullivan, S
John Keely, s	John Brown, S	John Stevier, s
Geo Martin, s	Danl Carr, S	Saml Noble, s
John Wallace, s	Peter Kerr, S	Augustus Walker, s
Cpl Ellis, s	Alex Beebe, s	Wm Anderson, s
Stevenson, s	Pat Gallagher, s	Francis H Fox, S
Wm Feather, s	John Daly, s	John Mclaughlin, s
Thos S Gillow, s	Hiram Shippey, s	Thos Navy, s
Wm Hughes, s	Richd G Martin, s	Robt W Howard, S
Ervin Levin, s	Wm T Ray, s	Richd S Cross, s
Nich C James, s	Thos Graham, S	Jas Lilly, S
Patrick McKenna, s	Lewis Hastings, S	Jos Gillhuly, S
Jacob Miller, s	John Kavenaugh, S	Patrick Murphy, S
Ab'm Sammons, s	Patrick Kelly, S	Chas Howard, S

John Barnes, S
John Hughes, m
Geo F Flagg, S
Patrick Murphy, m

Missing:

Stephen L Rouse
Michl Gilmore
John Pierce
David Mayer

Third Division-Maj Gen Pillow

Return of the Non-commissioned Ofcrs, Musicians, & Privates in the Third Division, who were killed, wounded, & missing during the attack on Chapultepee & the city of Mexico on Sep 13th & 14th, 1847.

First Artl, Co I-Field Battery:

Wounded: [s-slightly: S-severely: dg-dangerously: m-mortally]]

Paul Dalym, S
J Donelly, s
Wm Merrick, s
Edmond Lenergan, S
Antony Kreiss, s

9th Regt Infty:

Killed:

Geo C Spencer
Foster
Geo Ball
John Bailenau
Edson
Geo E Barnes
John Dorsot

Wounded: [s-slightly: S-severely: dg-dangerously: m-mortally]]

Geo W King, s
Robt M Brown, S
John S Lock, s
E T Pike, S
N W King, S
Isaac Ware, s
Chas B Horsewell, S
Benj Osgood, S
A Noyce, s
Clark H Green, S
N G Shett, S
W A Brown, s
Wm March, S
Wm H White, s
J Moody, s
Jas Mohan, S
H B Stone, s
J Bridges, s
Patrick Connars, S
Chas Twist, s
Wm Welsh, S
John Welston, s

14th Regt Infty: Killed:

Benj Hall
H R Manning
Robt Arnold
Jas M Monypenny

Wounded: [s-slightly: S-severely: dg-dangerously: m-mortally]]

Wm M Bledsoe, m
Jas Kennedy, S
A D Aujon, s
H Montgomery, s
Steward White, S
A Chadwick, s
Wm D Pharris, S
John Philand, S
John Wilkinson, s
S Sutzenhizer, S
Bolivar Vincent, S
F Faoball, s
W F Beatty, S
Calvin C Forola, S
J Donnelly, s

Missing:

John Crawford
Jas McDermott
W R Watson
Wm Dearing
John Blair

15th Regt Infty:

Killed:

Jos Grant
John Herrick
Jas D Kensil
John Haviland
Henry W Stoy

Wounded: [s-slightly: S-severely: dg-dangerously: m-mortally]]

Jonathan Jones, S
Wm Koch, m
Jas McGill, m

Harvey Lyon, S
Thos McClaren, S
Jacob Ebeham, S
Seth Millington, S
Jonas Auglemyer, S
Geo Momeney, S
Caleb B Sly, S
Marvin Ward, S
Lewis Anderson, s
Christian Hammel, s
Duncomb McKinsey, s
Frank L Hartinaw, s
Henry Hess, s

Missing:
Private ___ Harkin

Voltigeur Regt:
Killed:
H Frick
E Miller
S Richardson
N Salisbury
S Richardson
[S Richardson listed twice]

Wounded: [s-slightly: S-severely: dg-dangerously: m-mortally]]
W Peat, S
J C Malbon, s
T S Gardner, s
H P Long, s
H E Reed, m
M Finley, m
M Conway, S
J Muldoon, s
R Cooper, s
J McGown, s
A Fair, S
M Bancroft, m
E Brass, m
S McCall, S
W H Fitzhugh, S
W Wood, S
Z Cox, S
J Dwyer, S
T Evans, S
W K Fletcher, S
J Amey, S
J Smith, S
C Redding, S
M Rain, S
G Spencer, S
C Miller, S
J Young, S
P Henry, S
D Haughney, S
J Doitz, S
T Wallace, s
O Russell, s
E T Gooden, s
J H Malbon, s
J M Floyd, s
T H Gill, s
T Trumble, s

Missing: Jas Hall; J Medcalf; J A Maples; G Weygand

Fourth Division-Maj Gen Quitman

Non-commissioned Ofcrs, Musicians, & Privates, in the 4th Division, who were killed, wounded, & missing in the several actions near the city of Mexico, on Sep 14th & 15th, 1847.

Killed:
Wm Carlin
Wm C Bolton
Isaiah Wondus
Chas Stewart
John Street
John Tarn
John McClanahan
Hugh Graham
Anthony E Egbert
Andrew McLoughlin
John Herbert
Mathew Banks
Thos Kelley
Wm Blocker
B F Mattison
T McHenry
L Goode
W B Devlin
J Morwood
C Meyer
D H Tresevant
H Calahan
T Cooper
T Lyles
M Martin
John Patrick
J C Tunison
T Golden
Andrew Jelard
John Wright
John Seaman
Theda Zimmerman
John Homer
Jas Williams
Jos A Dennis
John Shaw
John L Young

Wounded: [s-slightly: S-severely: dg-dangerously: m-mortally]]

Wm Herbert, s
Peter Hogan, s
John Freyman, s
John Miller, s
Jacob Armprister, s
Henry Boyer, s
Thos McGhee, s
Jacob Rapp, s
John Arthur, S
Geo Henry, S
Danl Saul, S
Nathan Martz, dg
Peter Moyer, m, [since dead]
Jno Worthington, s
Wm Humpheys, s
John Brookbank, s
Abraham Rhodes, s
W J Stone, s
John Campbell, s
Hugh Storm, s
John McLoughlin, s
Thos Holland, s
Francis McKee, S
And Dripps, S
Wm H Dietrich, S
Jno Snyder, S
A Patterson, S
E A Downy, S
F C McDermot, S
B F Davis, s
G W Neff, s
David Meckling, s
E McCleland, s
Geo Decker, s
Hugh Fiskil, s
Sgt Chanay, S
F Sergeant, S
Lt A S Towrison, S
Wm H Sogur, s
Thos Humphreys, s
John Vauson, S
Jas T Sample, S
John Betchtel, S

John Copehart, S
Wm Rice, s
Saml E Major, s
Chris Sieh, s
J Palmer, s
M Flaxier, s
P Ward, s
Jacob Meyer, m
R Rodgers, S
J Cosgrove, S
E Moyer, S
A Cummins, s
Henry Rist, s
Saml Morgan, m
Wm Mendenhall, s
Arch Graham, s
I N Hoops, s
Fred Myers, s
W Clements, S
J Horn, S
Jas Bustard, s'
John Solomon, S
Emor M Davis, S
Wm Snyder, s
Wm Smyth, s
M Hasson, s
H Thomas, s
Ed Blain, s
A J Jones, S
Wm Smyth, S
Jos Lutz, s
Thos Davis, s
Chris Malone, s
Jas Stewart, s
Wm Bishop, s
Wm Crabb, s
Joshua Hamilton, S
John Keever, S
David Shine, S
Chas Eplet, S
Benj Shine, s
Lewis Bonnetts, s
Saxfere Heasbly, s
Jas Montgomery, s

Jas Orr, S
John Roach, S
John Curran, s
W J Wilson, S
Grandisen E Tansil, s
___ Seebeck, S
Martin Fogg, S
Hugh Roney, S
John McGuignan, s
Philip Phosoix, s
Saml Williamson, s
___ Biggs, S
___ Connor, s
Francis Quinn, S
Thos B Smith, S
Elhanan Stevens, S
Edw Cooper, s
J Linns, S
Musician McDonald, s
___ Milburn, S
O T Gibbs, s
Thos Gafney, S
R Payan, S
J Dunnogant, D
W Triplett, S
M M Adams, S
J Thomas, S
M Ward, s
Y Muller, S
Y Evans, M
J Only, S
J Hood, s
Y Cahill, s
N R Evans, s
J Ferguson, s
Y Robins, s
C Ingram, s
H Lafferty, s
___ Bennett, s
L B Weaver, s
Y Anderson, s
C H Kenny, s
A Delany, S
R Watson, S

W L Rodgers, S
J H Saxton, S
H J Caughman, S
H Polock, S
J D Stanford, S
Manning Brown, S
J Fitzimmons, S
B Hutchinson, S
J Kelly, S
J G Atkinson, s
J K Parker, m
J Caldbeeth, s
J J Feagle, s
T Chapman, s
J Graham, s
J C Higgins, s
D Brown, s
H Suber, s
A Little, S
R B Lyles, S
A Feagle, S
Private McGennis, S
Private Rowalt, S
Cpl McGowen, s
Pvt Fire, s
Pvt Duncan, s
Pvt Waggoner, s
John Eber, S
John Hunt, S
Jas Kelly, S
John Hal, s
John Keeber, s
Chis Newman, s
S W Peel, s
J White, s
John Russel, s
Jas Saxon, s
C Reymansmyder, S
B Van Deif, S
John Whaley, s
R Anderson, s
John Cassedy, s
Jas Smith, s
Jas Kenneda, s
D Standerwick, s
L Strobill, s
Wm Connell, S
Y Donovan, S
S Calvert, s
J Davis, s
R Jenkin, s
D L McCowen, s
J N Easterby, s
Cpl Bold, s
R Hitchfelt, s
J Martin, s
P S Graham, s
C Rankin, s
C Anderson, s
W L Beadon, s
N Scott, S
D Nolan, S
Jas Walsh, S
J W Shett, s
S Camak, s
E Duke, s
W S Tidwell, s
R J Barker, s
W Claxton, s
J Woodward, s
Jas M Craig, s
C J Gladney, s
J W Brittenham, s
J E Odom, s
A Tunisop, s
J B Glass, s
R S Morrison, s
John T Olneys, s
Jas Burke, S
G Barry, S
M Cohlin, S
H Hardenbrook, S
W Tomkins, S
D Montgomery, s
Chas Thompson, s
Owen Elwood, s
Thos Healey, s
John McKinney, S
John Snyder, S
V Van Slyke, S
Jas Hart, S
John Duffy, s
Pat Roney, s
O Hanzel, s
Michl Butler, m, [since dead]
Sgt Baker, s
Thos L Decker, s
Jas Franklin, s
Geo Pemberton, s
John L Gardner, s
R Headerick, s
Wm Daly, s
O Robertson, S
Geo Thistleton, S
John M Lane, s
Clipolet Everett, s
Alex Cook, S

The Hon Alex'r H Everett died on Jun 28, at the house of Dr P Parker, Sec of Legation, who had been for several years a resident at Canton. He died of a severe & painful chronic disease, under which he had suffered for 2 or 3 years, at the age of 57. During the greater period since his arrival in Canton he resided with his wife at Macao, under the hospitable roof of Mr Forbes, the American Consul. Funeral services were performed on the island by Dr Parker, & his remains were deposited on Dane's island, near Whampos. Where one or more Americans had previously been buried. Mrs Everett remained at the last date at Canton. -Boston Daily Adv

Passengers in the steamship **Cambria**, from Liverpool. Mr & Mrs Blake & servant; Mr Hicks, lady & servant; Mr Rogers, lady & servant; Mr Chadwick & lady; Mr J G Bennett, lady, child & nurse; Mr Leacroft, lady & family; Mr Billings & lady; Mr Glenny & lady; Mrs Sanstead; Misses Jacggi, Iraham, Pratte, Thompson, Green, & maid; Rev Dr Scoresby; Rev Dr Theo Clapp; Rev Atkinson; Rev Mr Campbell; Prof Gibson; Maj Egerton; Surgeon Anderson; Capt Ramsay; Messrs Battersby, Connell, McDowall, Graham, Howard, Walden, Thierman, Hoffman, E R Bill, J C Burnham & servant; Blanchard, Drapman, Wheelwright, C R Green, Wilmot, Johnson, Hopley, Durkin, Segoren, A P Hanford, Alex Walker, H H Williams, Ambrose Lanfear, Schenerhorn, Paul Chandrow, Thos Dixon, Guest, Rouch, Constable, J Drummond, Bradford, E L Loyd, Louis Valz, C T Morey, R Mure, Caleb Barstow, Herkenrath & friend, Chadwick & friend, Sigourney, W H Stoddart, R W Hamilton, A Gordon, W Gordon, Ferguson, Prehu, J L Green, Abbot, J Edwards, A McClure, A Holland, W Baylies, D P Barhydt, J M Esson, Forbes, Dixon, T Metcalf, B Coates, W Laird, J G Ravenal, J H Simpson, C C Thompson, Lo Bruere, J H Hower, Hinshall, E Cachard, J Broom, Andrews, Ross, McHenry, W Quik, A Kinston, De Blaynise, Evans, Palmer, Riara.
[No date-current news item.]

Among the list of the killed in the battles in Mexico is the name of Maj L Twiggs, the father of Lt Twiggs, whose death was recently noticed in this paper. Thus father & son have both fallen in Mexico, fighting in defense of their country. The bereaved family of Maj Twiggs, consisting of his widow & 3 dghts, formerly residents in Wash, now reside in the city of Phil.

The Trustees of the Wash Academy, Somerset Co, Md, desire to engage a competent teacher. He will be required to produce testimonials of good moral character & scholarship. -S W Jones, J H Done, Wm T G Polk, cmte, Princess Anne.

Passengers in the ship **Missouri**, from Cherbourg. Mr Delaporte; Mr & Mrs Mace; Mr Kretz; Miss Ernestine Teinturier; Mr Iselin, sister, & servant; Dr Bodinier & servant; Dr Narbonne; Mr Swift, bearer of dispatches to the American Gov't; Mr Elias Dans; Mr Johnson & son; Mr Perpignan; Mrs Desbordes; Messrs Binoche, Moreau, Marchal, Levois; Mr & Mrs Willemant; Galice; Prady; Mrs Parker & son; Mr Barsalou; Mr Ross; Mr Olombel; Messrs Wilber; Schleicher; Mr & Mrs Bocker; Mr Rodrigues; Mr Henry; Mr Lecesne; Mr Munroe & family, [7 in all;] Mr & Mrs Luis; Mr Cahuzac; Mr Bidault; Mr & Mrs Lentilhon, son, & niece; Mr & Mrs Rossi, vocal artists; Lorenzo Braun; Mr Johnston; Mr Maccarthy; Follain, Benjamin; Poole; Bowman; Livington; Rev Mr Sadler; Weger; Posmantler; Daniel; Bonissant; Bohmer; Chian; Basquin; Mendames les ecclesisastiques Narris & Bure. [No date-current news item.]

N Y, Oct 19: laying of the corner-stone of the N Y Washington Monument, being the anniversary of the surrender of Cornwallis to Washington at Yorktown, the closing scene of the American Revolution. The monument is about 5 miles up from the battery: corner-stone was laid by Govn'r Young, of this State:

Rappahannock estate for sale: on Dec 2, at public auction, at Stony Hill, Richmond Co, my ***Mulberry Island*** estate, lying upon the Rappahannock river: contains 1,795 acres; numerous tenements, the annual rental of which exceed $200. Address the subscriber at Fredericksburg. -Alfred N Bernard

Weston Herald in relation to the arrest of Lt Col Gilpin by Col Wharton, the cmder of ***Fort Leavenworth***: said arrest has been removed, Gilpin making a satisfactory retraction. The true story is as follows: Lt Col Gilpin desired instructions from Col Wharton to go upon an expedition against the Indians on the plains, which the colonel thought was not permitted by the instructions from Washington, & was foreign to the purpose of the command. On his refusing this request, intemperate language was used by Gilpin; such as an inferior ofcr is not, by the rules of the military service, permitted to use to a superior ofcr. The Col twice requested a withdrawal of the offensive expressions, which was refused, & then the arrest ensued. Col Wharton conducted himself as a veteran ofcr in so responsible a situation should have done. -Mo Repub

Mrd: on Oct 20, by Rev Jas B Donelan, Mr Wm M Grant, of Wash City, to Miss Lucinda Cullison, of Balt.

Mrd: on Oct 21, by Rev Mr Finkle, Mr Geo S McElfresh to Miss Eliz M Seafferle, all of Wash City.

Died: on Oct 21, suddently Louisa, infant daughter of Chas & Rowena C Whitman, aged 7 weeks.

Died: on Oct 9, at her residence, near St Marks, Florida, Mrs Mary A Walker, consort of Nathl W Walker, & relict of the late Saml A Spencer, of Port Leon, in her 43rd year. The dec'd was a native of Va & a sister of Alex Moseley, late editor of the Richmond Whig. She removed to Florida many years since, carrying with her an interesting family, several of whom have grown up around her, giving her comfort in her last days. She leaves behind her a devoted husband & 7 doting children.

Died: on Sep 27, in Green Co, Missouri, Lucy Jane, daughter of the Hon Jonn S & Mary Phelps, aged about 3 years. [Jonn is copied as written.]

Mr Saml B Beach, a Clerk in the Post Ofc Dept, properitor of the "Ladies' Furnishing Store," between 4½ & 6th sts, Pa ave, engaged Mrs France as an agent of that establishment. The language used by Beach towards Mrs France was such as no gentleman would utter, & of course she could not continue in the establishment. The friends of Mrs France are merely advised of the above facts. -L H France

The Trustees of the Primary School $48, of Anne Arundel Co, Md, are desirous to procure a teacher in said school. -Benj E Gantt, Rev Henry Aisquith, Wm Sands, M D: Trustees, A A Co, Md.

MON OCT 25, 1847
Mr Webster left Boston on Thu for his farm in Franklin, N H. He has recently had a slight touch of lumbago, which gave rise to a report that he was quite ill.

Among the ofcrs lost to their country in the recent assault upon the city of Mexico was the gallant Lt Col Wm Montrose Graham, of the 11th Regt U S Infty. He was about 47 years of age; entered West Point Military Academy in 1813, & graduated in 1817 as 3rd Lt of Artl. Another brother, Jas D Graham, of the Topographical Engineers, entered & graduated the same year. They were sons of Dr Wm Graham, of Prince Wm Co, Va, who served [as did also other of the family with distinction as ofcrs] in the Revolutionary struggle. Col Graham, who we are now covering, was transfereed to the 4th Regt of Infty, under Col Clinch, which was in Florida, & was placed in command of ***Fort King***, for a long time in the very heart of the troublesome Miscosakies. He was in Florida in 1835 when the Seminole war broke out, & bore the blunt of the first battle at the Withlacoochee, where his final charge upon the Indians with the bayonet dispersed the savages & aided in securing victory. Col Clinch spoke in the highest terms of the conduct of Col [then Capt] Graham. He fell in that charge with 2 severe wounds from the Indian rifles, [one received early in the fight,] & his brother, [Lt Campbell Graham, of the Artl, now Capt of Topographical Engineers] also received at the same time 2 severe wounds, at first believed to be mortal, but from which he recovered. Col Graham was in every battle on the peninsula of much note, & was complimented in the dispatches of his Colonel. His brother, Brevet Maj Lawrence Pike Graham, of the 2nd Dragoons, also served with great credit as a young lt in Twigg's regt, & was severely wounded in 1840, while scouting in the night, being fired upon by a party of militia by mistake.

Mrd: on Oct 21, by Rev Mr French, Mr Cuthbert P Wallach to Annie E, eldest daughter of Richd M Beall, all of Wash City.

Mrd: on Oct 12, at N Y, by Rev Mr Pise, Jas O'Hara, of Wash City, to Leah Maria, daughter of Geo M Grouard, of Wash.

Circuit Court: Sat: Wash. Jos Edmund Law vs Thos Law's Exec & others. Mr Thos Law married Eliz Parke Custis in 1796, & prior to the marriage there was a marriage settlement. Under this settlement the children of Lloyd N Rogers, of Md, claim, &, as this claim would absorb the whole property, the legatees under Mr Law's will are adverse to it. There is also a claim on the part of Wm Blane's reps, of London. The claimants under the will are the grandchildren of Mr Law. Mr R S Cox opened the case on Fri on the part of the children of L N Rogers. Mr Lawrence replied on Sat on the part of Jos Edmund Law.

On May 16 last, John McGarr & his 2 sons, Edmund Jas, aged 14 years, & Owen, 12 years, left Pensacola in the public stage for Mobile. Since that time his distressed helpless family, residing in Wash, have not heard from them. Any information communicated to the care of John Boyle, Wash, will be gratefully received, & impart consolation to hearts now nearly broken by a state of most agonizing suspense.

The Punishment of the Deserters: New Orleans Picayune: Sep 8, court martial, of which Col Riley, of the 2nd Infty, was Pres, tried 29 men for deserton to the enemy. The cases of Thos Riley, Co I, 3rd Infty; Jas Mills, Co H, 3rd Inft; & John Reilly, Co K, 5th Infty: deserted in the early part of Apr, 1846: we were at peace at that time, war was not recognized by the Congress of the U S till May 13: sentence-50 lashes with a rawhide whip, well laid on the bare back of each, & their punishment is commuted accordingly-with the addition that each be branded on the cheek with the letter D, keep a close prisoner as long as this army remains in Mexico, & then be drummed out of the service. No higher punishment could be legally inflicted. So much of the punishment, in the case of Henry Newer, Co D, 4th Artl, as relates to hanging, is, on the recommendation of many members of the court, remitted; & a like remission in the case of Edw McHerron, Co G, 4th Artl, out of consideration for a son, a private in the same company, who has remained faithful to his colors. There being some slight circumstances of mitigation in the cases of Hezekiah Akles, John Bartley, Alex'r McKee, & John Bowers, all of Co H, 3rd Artl, their sentences are commuted as in the cases of T Riley, J Mills, & J Reilly, above. The remainder of the prisoners tried by the same court, & for the same crime, viz: Henry Venator, Co I, 2nd Dragoons; F Rhode, Co I, 2nd Dragoons; W A Wallace, Co C, 3rd Infty; Lawrence Macky, Co K, 3rd Infty; Patrick Dalton, Co B, 2nd Infty; John Sheehan, Co G, 5th Infty; John A Myers, Co G, 5th Infty; Henry Whistler, Co E, 4th Artl; Elizier S Lusk, Co C, 3rd Infty; Jas Spears, Co D, 7th Infty; Dennis Conahan, Co I, 7th Infty; Jas McDowell, Co K, 7th Infty; Martin Lydon, Co D, 7th Infty; Wm H Keeck, Co F, 4th Artl; Wm Oathouse, Co I, 2nd Infty; Henry Octker, Co B, 4th Artl; Wm O'Conner, Co K, 1st Artl; Andrew Nolan, Co G, 4th Artl; Herman Schmidth, Co D, 3rd Infty, R W Garretson, Co H, 3rd Artl, will be hung according to their several sentences, between the hours of 6 & 11 o'clock, in the forenoon next after the receipt of this order, as may be arranged by the cmder of the post or camp where the said prisoners may respectively be found. [The above named men, excepting H Venator, F Rhode, J A Myers, & J Sheehan, were executed at San Angel Sep 10, 1847.] By command of Maj Gen Scott: H L Scott, AAAG Two days subsequently we have further orders, from which we learn that the 4 men named above were not hung on the 10th, as they were passing at the time from Tacubaya to Mixcoac. They were hung on Sep 11, & the sentence was executed at Mixacoac. Thirty-six other prisoners were tried by a court martial over which Col Garland presided. And the court accordingly sentenced the several prisoners-two-thirds of the members in every case concurring in the sentence-each to be hung by the neck till he be dead. Before the same court Martin Miles, Co A, 8th Infty, & Abraham Fitzpatrick, Co A, 8th Infty, were convicted & sentenced each to be shot. Before the same court were duly tried & convicted, upon the charge of desertion, the following named prisoners: Jas Kelly, Co C, 3rd Infty: John Murphy, Co C, 8th Infty: John Little, Co C, 2nd Dragoons: sentence: each to receive 50 lashes, with a raw hide on his bare back, to forfeit all pay & allowance, & to be indelibly marked on the right hip with the letter D, two inches in length; to wear an iron yoke weighing 8 pounds, with 3 prongs, each one foot in length, around his neck, to be confined to hard labor, in charge of the guard, during the time the army remains in Mexico, & then to have his head shaved & be drummed out of the service. Before the same court was tried, upon the charge of desertion, Lewis Preifer, Co C, 4th Infty, whom the court found to be not guilty of desertion, but guilty of absence without leave, &

sentenced him to forfeit all pay & allowances that are or may become due him, & be discharged the service. On the recommendation of the court the sentences of Abraham Fitzpatrick, Co A, 8th Infty; John Brooke, Co F, 6th Infty; & David McElroy, Co E, 6th Infty, are remitted. On account of mitigating circumstances in the cases of Rogers Duhan, Co F, 6th Infty; Saml H Thomas, Co C, 6th Infty; John Daly, rifle regt; Thos Cassady, Co I, 8th Infty; & Martin Miles, Co a, 8th Infty, the sentence of death is commuted to: 50 lashed with a raw hide whip, to be branded on the cheek with the letter D, to be kept in confinement while the army remains in Mexico, & then to be drummed out of the service. The remainder of the prisoners sentenced to death by the court:
Fred'k Fogel, Co K, 2nd Dragoons
Henry Klager, Co K, 2nd Dragoons
Henry Longenhammer, Co F, 2nd Dragoons
Francis O'Conner, 3rd Infty
John Appleby, Co D, 2nd Artl
M T Frantius, Co K, 3rd Infty
Peter Neill, Co B, 4th Infty
Geo W Jackson, Co H, 1st Artl
Kerr Delaney, Co D, 4th Infty
John Price, Co F, 2nd Infty
John Cuttle, Co B, 2nd Infty
Richd Parker, Co K, 5th Infty
Parian Fritz, Co F, 6th Infty
John Benedick, Co F, 6th Infty
Auguste Morstadt, Co I, 7th Infty
John Rose, Co F, 6th Infty
Lachlen McLachlen, Co F, 6th Infty
John Cavanaugh, Co E, 8th Infty
Richd Hanly, Co A, 2nd Artl
Gibson McDowell, Co A, 8th Infty
Lemuel A Wheaton, Co A, 6th Infty
Patrick Casey, Co F, 6th Infty
Patrick Antison, Co E, 4th Infty
Harrison Kenney, Co E, 4th Infty
Roger Hogan, Co I, 4th Infty
Geo Dalwig, Co K, 2nd Artl
Barney Hart, Co K, 2nd Artl
Hugh McClelland, Co A, 8th Infty
Thos Millett, Co D, 3rd Artl
John McDowell, Co A, 8th Infty
Will be hung by the neck until dead, between the hours of 6 & 11 in the forenoon next after the receipt of this order, under the direction of the commanding ofcr of the post at which they may respectively be found.
[Executed Sep 13, 1847, at Mixcoac.]

Valuable tract of heavy wooded land at auction: on Nov 1, at Fowler's Tavern, on the road leading from Wash to Upper Marlborough; 134 acres, adjoining the farms of Richd Young, Robt Marshall, & the late Mathew Wright. -A Green, auctioneer

Circuit Court of Wash Co, D C-Oct Term, 1847: in Chancery. Wm Hayman & Mary Eliz Hayman, cmplnts, vs Anna Hayman, Adelaide Hayman, Julia Hayman, Catharine Hayman, & Saml Hayman, dfndnts. Wm Redin, trustee in the above cause, reports he has sold the following, in Wash City, part of lot 20 in square 254, fronting 20 feet on F st, with frame tenement thereon, & that Joh Byrne was the purchaser at the price of $960, & has complied with the terms of sale. -Wm Brent, clk

City Ordinance-Wash. 1-Act for the relief of Christopher C Clements: fine imposed for an alleged violation of an ordinance relative to stands in the Centre Market, be remitted; provided Clements pay the costs of prosecution. Approved: Oct 23, 1847.

Public sale, under deed of trust from John Sheahan: sale on Nov 26, of lot 17 in square 163, according to Davidson's subdivision, Wash City. -W Redin, trustee
-R W Dyer, auct

Balt, Oct 23. Riot yesterday among the firemen, at a fire that destroyed an ice-house on North Calvert st. Several persons were severely wounded, & John Bond, was shot & died this morning.

For rent: brick dwlg at the corner of 2nd & Fred'k sts, Gtwn. Apply to Wm G Ridgely, at the Navy Dept, or on 1st st, Gtwn.

TUE OCT 26, 1847

The citizens of Troy have presented Gen Wool with a splendid sword, richly engraved with battle scenes, arms, & banners, & the following inscription: "Queenstown, Oct 13, 1812: Plattsburg, Sept 11, 1814: Buena Vista, Feb 22 and 23, 1847."

Rev Jonathan French, of Northampton, N H, has been officiating pastor of the Congregational Church in that town for 46 years. He is nearly 70 years of age, has 11 children, & at least 23 grandchildren; & hitherto no death has occurred in his family or in the family of any of his children. He has occupied the parsonage where he now lives for more than 40 years, & no death has ever occurred in it.

The ship **Mississippi** sailed from ***Fortress Monroe*** for Mexico on Oct 21, with a company of the 4th Artl, [114 strong,] under the following ofcrs: Capt R C Smead, commanding; 2nd Lt J S Garland, & 2nd Lt J A de Lagnel, 2nd Artl. Also, a detachment of U S Voltigeurs, under the command of 2nd Lt Van R Otey, U S Voltigeur Regt.

Two brick houses for sale on D st, between 2nd & 3rd sts. Inquire of A Baldwin, Builder, near the premises.

Excellent household & kitchen furniture at auction: on Oct 29, at the residence of Mr Giles Dyer, at the corner of 12th & M sts. -R W Dyer, auct

Circuit Court of Wash Co, D C-in Chancery. Jas McIntosh, vs Sarah McIntosh, Job P McIntosh, Henry McIntosh, Maddalina McIntosh, Norvel McIntosh, Wm McIntosh, Vernon McIntosh, Jennette McIntosh, heirs at law of Thos McIntosh. This is a creditor's bill of cmplnt, in which the cmplnt in substance charges that Thos McIntosh died intestate, leaving sundry debts; that the personal estate is insufficient to pay his debts; that he was seised in fee at his death of lot 5, in square 725, in Wash City, which has descended to his heirs at law, parties dfndnts, subject to the charge for the payment of his debts, & that the cmplnt is the administrator of his personal estate, & one of his creditors, & the objects of the bill are a sale of the said real estate, in aid of the personalty, for the payment of his debts & general relief. All the dfndnts except Jennette McIntosh reside & are out of D C. Same to appear in Court on the 4th Mon of Mar next. -W Brent, clk

Mrd: on Oct 24, in the Church of the Ascension, by Rev L J Gilliss, Mr Alex'r Saunders to Miss Frances Smith, all of Wash City.

Mrd: on Oct 17, in Alfred, Maine, by Rev John Orr, John H Burney, of N C, to Miss Mary, daughter of Gen Saml Leighton, of the former place.

Sealed proposals will be received in the Engineer's Ofc, at Gordonsville, until Nov 23, for the bridging, masonry, & depots for 14 miles of the Louisa Railroad extension from Gordonsville. Apply at the Engineer's ofc, in Gordonsville. -Wm A Kruper, Chief Engr

WED OCT 27, 1847

Mr Geo Plitt, a resident of Western Pa, was robbed at the Nat'l Theatre in Phil, on Thu, of his pocket-book containing bank notes to the amount of $4,700.

Col Martin Scott, who was killed in one of our battles before the city of Mexico in Gen Worth's division, was a native of Bennington, Vt. He was educated at West Point, & from there entered the army some 30 years ago. In his youth he was famous among the sharp-shooters of the Green Mountains; he never shot game in the body; but, at whatever height or distance, always struck the head. He would drive a nail into a board part way with a hammer, & then, taking the farthest distance at which his eye could distinctly see it, drive it home with his unerring bullet. With a modest income, he has supported his own family & 2 maiden sisters, several nephews, & other relatives, who, with his wife & immediate family, now at Milwaukie, are left to mourn his loss.
-N Y Journal of Commerce

The large & extensive manufactory of Messrs Isaac & Edw Crehore, at Milton Lower Mills, was totally destroyed by fire this morning. This was the only card factory in the New England States.

From Texas: Col Isaac Van Zandt, one of the candidates for Govn'r, & formerly Minister from Texas to this Gov't, died at Houston on Oct 11, of fever-by some physicians said to be yellow fever.

Orphans Court of Wash Co, D C: the matter of Martha Longdon, guardian of Martha Ann, Geo T, Jas D, & Alex'r Longdon, infant children of Chas Longdon, dec'd. The subscriber, as guardian, by order of the Court, passed on Oct 12, 1847, & approved by the Circuit Court of Wash Co, D C, sitting in Chancery, passed Oct 26, 1847, will sell the interest of the said infant, Martha Ann Longdon, being one undivided moiety or half in & to the following parcels in Wash City: piece of ground, being lots 10 & 11 in square 345, on H st north: south line is the property of Michl Sardo. The subscriber will likewise sell the several interests & estates, being one undivided fifth, each, of the said infants, Geo T, Jas D, & Alex'r Longdon, in a parcel of ground beginning on G st north, in square 319: with a good frame house. Those owning the remaining interests in said pieces or parcels of ground will join in the execution of the deed to the purchaser, so that a good title may be given. Apply to Martha Longdon, Guardian, on 10th st, between G & H sts.

Mrd: on Oct 26, in Balt, by Rev J P Donelan, at the Church of St Vincent de Paul, John F Coyle, of Wash City, to Kate, only daughter of the late Robt Hicks Dowson, of Balt.

Mrd: on Oct 26, by Rev T M Reese, Jas L Bond, of Sandy Springs, Md, to Mary Ellen, only daughter of Richd Israel, of Wash City.

Household & kitchen furniture at auction: on Oct 29, at the residence of W H Parker, on H st, between 17th & 18th sts, a good lot of furniture. Also, I shall sell the house & lot above, being in square 127: house contains 8 good rooms. -A Green, auctioneer

Sale of real property: by deed of trust from Wm Bush & Lucy his wife, to the subscriber, dated Sep 22, 1846, recorded the same day in Liber W B 129, of the land records of Wash Co, D C: sale on Nov 3, at public auction, of a parcel of ground, with the bldgs thereon, known on the plat of Wash City as lot 2 in square 734, fronting south on N C ave 64 feet & 4 inches. -John A Linton, Trustee -R W Dyer, auct

I certify that Geo M Duvall brought before me as a stray trespassing on his enclosure, a bay mare, blind in the left eye. -J Crandell, Justice of the Peace

Wash Corp: 1-Ptn from Wm Bush: referred to the Cmte of Claims. 2-Cmte on Finance: referred the ptn of C W Pairo, reported a resolution directing the collector to collect the taxes due upon certain lots: adopted. 3-Nominations from the Mayor for Superintendents of Chimney Sweeps for the ensuing year: John Lewis, Geo T Bowen, Hugh Moffat, Jas Littleton, N V Wilkinson, & Isaac Stoddard. 4-Cmte of Claims: bill for the relief of Enoch Ridgeway: passed.

Positive sale of valuable property on Capitol Hill: On Nov 1, in front of the premises, on the corner of East Capitol & 2nd sts: lots 26 thru 28 in square 729, with a good 2 story frame cottage-house & two 2 story brick houses. -R W Dyer, auct

Public sale of valuable real estate, in Prince Wm & Fauquier Counties, Va, including 3 very desirable fisheries. By virtue of competent authority from the heirs of Alex'r C Bullitt, dec'd, the undersigned, as agent, will offer at public sale, at the market-house square, in Alexandria, Va, on Nov 29, all the lands & real estate of which the said Alex'r C Bullitt, dec'd, died seised & possessed, in Prince Wm Co. This estate is on the Potomac river about 35 miles from Alexandria, & contains about 1,000 acres of land; 3 fisheries attached to this estate, one of which is known as ***Opossum Nose***; they are leased for the year 1848. The bldgs on the shore are new & extensive. Also, sundry houses & lots in & near the town of Dumfries. Also, on Dec 2, at Weaversville, Fauquier Co, the estate, of about 2,500 acres of land, near the town of Weaversville. Prince Wm property will be shown by Mr McEwing, who lives on the estate, & the Fauquier property by Mr Wm H Page, of Weaversville. -Jos R Price

Valuable lots at auction: on Nov 2, in front of the premises, lots 13 & 16 in square 186, one of which is directly in the rear of Mr Ritchie's house, & has the advantage of being near Mr Corcoran's highly-improved grounds; the other fronts on Connecticut ave, back to an alley. -R W Dyer, auct

THU OCT 28, 1847

Nashville Whig: affray recently at Yorkville, Tenn, in which 2 men were killed. A misunderstanding existed between W N Anthony & a family named Reed. Anthony was shot by one of the Reeds, who had concealed himself behind the counter in a store. Anthony discovered another Read in the store & shot him dead. Anthony lived but a few hours. He left a family.

The Founder of the Smithsonian Institution, Jas Smithson, was born in England in 1768; educated at the Univ of Oxford; was a man of amiable disposition, & devoted to science; was the best chemist in Oxford; resided most of the time abroad. He wrote: the best blood of England flows in my veins: on my father's side I am a Northumberland; on my mother's I am related to kings. Smithson died at Genoa in 1829, leaving his property to his nephew, the son of his brother, with a clause in his will leaving it in trust of the U S, for founding an institution for the increase & diffusion of knowledge among men, in case the nephew died without issue. He did so die, & the money, about $500,000, came into possession of our Gov't.

Trustee's sale of a valuable private residence in Philadelphia Row: by deed of trust from Robt P Anderson, recorded in Liber W B 126, folio 28, a land record of Wash Co, D C: public auction on Nov 30, in Wash City: part of lot 3 in square 344, & the improvement, being the centre one of the 3 fine 3 story houses called Phil Row. -Henry Bluner, Saml Tolman, trustees -A Green, auctioneer

Jonathan D Morris, [Dem] has been elected a member of Congress to fill the vacancy occasioned by the death of Gen Hamer, of Ohio. Mr Morris had no opposition, except the Liberty candidate.

Maj Graham, of the Corps of Topographical Engineers, has recently been elected a member of the Historical Society of Maine, as he had previously been of the Historical Societies of Mass & N Y.

Died: on Tue, in Wash City, Mr Lewis Stacom, aged about 35 years, late a member of Capt Bronaugh's company of Md & D C volunteers, leaving a wife & only child. His funeral is from the residence of his sister [Mrs Francis] this evening at 4 o'clock.

Died: on Oct 18, at Pascagoula, Louisiana, near New Orleans, of yellow fever, Theodorick B Skinner, a native of Balt, but for many years a resident of Louisiana. This most estimable young gentleman was a son of John S Skinner, & all who knew him will sympathize most sincerely in the deep distress which his death must inflict on his bereaved parents.

FRI OCT 29, 1847

For rent or sale: large 3 story brick house, with 12 convenient rooms, on 8th st, next to the corner of G st. Possession given immediately. Apply at the subscriber's house, next door, or at his marble yard on D st. -T Berry

For rent: the excellent dwlg house over the Dry Good Store of G F Allen, on the avenue, between 9th & 10th sts, north side, entrance on D st. Apply at the store of Mr Allen.

Mrd: on Sep 12, at Christ's Church, Poughkeepsie, Peter Hulme, of Phil, to Mary C Taylor, daughter of the late Dr Taylor.

Died: on Oct 25, at his residence, near Colesville, Montg Co, Md, Mr Elias Perry, aged 69 years, an old & much respected citizen of said county.

City Ordinance-Wash: Act for the relief of Enoch Ridgeway: that the fine imposed for an alleged violation relative to keeping or harboring of dogs, the same is remitted: provided he pay the costs of prosecution.

My boy having, through mistake, driven from Mr Hilton's neighborhood a cow, & butchered her, supposing her to be the one that I had purchased of Mr Hilton, I feel it my duty to inform the owner of the cow that it will give me pleasure to exchange Mr Hilton's cow for the same or to pay for her. -Jos Prather

+

The above mistake was owing to my colored girl's carelessness in pointing out to Mr Prather's boy the wrong cow, as Mr Prather knew nothing of the mistake that had happened until I had informed him. -John P Hilton

Valuable bldg lot, & pottery, at auction: on Nov 4, on the premises, the lots on which the pottery stands, with appurtenances, being parts of lots 8 & 9 in square 404, at 8th & I sts. The property is well known as ***Butt's pottery***. A deed given & a deed of trust taken. Title indisputable. -A Green, auctioneer

Ray's New Mill is now in operation, & prepared to furnish Corn Meal. An assistant Miller wanted. -A Ross Ray & Bro, Gtwn

SAT OCT 30, 1847

Lost, on Thu last, near Dowson's boarding house, my FREE PAPERS. The finder will greatly oblige a poor man, who will reward him if required according to his ability, by leaving them at the ofc of the Nat'l Intell. -Thos Barton

San Francisco, Apr 1, 1847. I have this moment arrived in Capt Sutter's launch from ***Fort Sacramento***, & drop you a few lines. Mr Read & party were lost in a snow storm & suffered greatly; 11 of the 14 persons who were left by Mr Read were, viz: Mr Brinn, wife, & 5 children, 3 children of Mr Graves, one of which was an infant at the breast, & Mary Donner, a girl about 11 years of age; 3 of the latter children being packed on the backs of Oakley, Stark, & Stone; the other 5 were 3 children of Mr Geo Donner, between the ages of 1 & 4 years, girls; John Baptiste, a Spanish boy, in the employment of Mr Donner, & Simon Murphy, a boy of 6 years of age. The day Mr Read left them the boy Isaac Donner died, & the same night Mrs Graves & one of her children died; the remaining sufferers continued 2 days without food, but on the 3rd day were obliged to resort to the only alternative, that of eating the dead; they commenced on the 2 children, & when my party reached them, which was on the 5th day, they were eating Mrs Graves. The night previous Mary Donner fell into the fire, burning her foot so severely that amputation was necessary in order to save her life. Two of my men, Henry Dan & Chas Cody, had their feet badly frozen. I brought Mary Donner & her brother down for medical aid; the Spanish boy & Howard Oakley came down with them as nurses. When I left they were still remaining at the cabins Mr Kiesbury & Geo Donner, the only 2 men, Mrs Geo Donner, one child & Mrs Murphy. In Bear Valley & on the John River it was yet 20 feet deep on the level. I organized a party consisting of John Rhodes, John Starrs, E Caffemeyer, John Sel, & Danl Tucker, Mr Foster & the son of Mr Graves volunteering to return with them in hopes of saving those remaining: the other 3, Geo Donner, Mrs Murphy, & the child, I do not think can be saved, as it is impossible to remove them, they being so very feeble & ill. I must conclude, S E Woodworth, Passed Midshipman U S Navy, Commanding Expeditions to the Calif Mountains.

In pursuance of an order of the Orphans' Court of Chas Co, Md, notice is given to Teresa Caroline, Teresa, Justin, Wm, & Stanislaus Hills, & the children of ___ Doremus, of the State of Louisiana, next of kin to Chas H Hills, dec'd, late of said county, to appear in said Court either in person or by atty by Mar 1, 1848, to receive their distributive shares of said Chas H Hills' estate. -John W Mitchell, Adm of Chas H Hills

New private Boarding-house, 13th & N Y ave: Mrs E Bryant.

The Union publishes an official correspondence between Com Engle, of the U S ship **Princeton**, & Col Sir Robt Wilson, Govn'r of Gibraltar, relative to an accident which occurred to Thos Dennis, a seaman, whose arms were shot off when firing a salute in honor of the visit on board the **Princeton** of Prince Demedoff, of Russia. The Govnr' tendered the use of the English hospital, & the Prince has assigned him a pension for life of 400 francs. Dennis is a native of Boston, aged 23, & will receive the Prince's pension quarterly, payable in this country.

Shocking murder at Sharpsburg, Bath Co, Ky, on Mon last: Mr J C Robinson, principal teacher of the Academy there, felt compelled, in consequence of a rebellious disregard of the laws of his school, to expel from the school a son of Dr M Q Ashby, 16 or 17 years of age. Young Ashby vowed revenge, & another young man named Crouch, was to aid him. On Tue, while Robinson was locking his school-room door, he was set upon by Ashby & Crouch, & defended himself as best he could with an umbrella, until he saw the opportunity to seize a stone, with which he felled Crouch. Crouch regained his feet, & jointly with Ashby closed on Robinson, cutting his stomach with the knife. A man named Christian ran to catch Robinson, who exclaimed, "I am a dead man,' & instantly expired. The guilty young men made their escape, & on Wed, no efforts had been made to arrest them. -Maysville Eagle

Natham Lampman, of Coxackie, N Y, is now 16 years of age & 7 feet 1 inch in height, bids fair to become a man of higher standing in the world than any man now living, having grown 9 inches during the past year. He weighs 162 pounds. -Worcester Transcript

Died: on Oct 29, in Gtwn, D C, Lewis E Perrie, eldest son of Mr Hugh & Ann Rebecca Perrie, of PG Co, Md, in his 20th year.

Died: on Oct 10, at her mother's [Mrs Buchanan's] residence, in Winchester, Va, after a long & painful illness, Mrs Evelina H Plater, widow of the late Thos Plater, of Md. She has left behind her a mother, son, & brother, besides numberous other relations, who dearly loved her, to deplore her irreparable loss.

MON NOV 1, 1847

Circuit Court of Wash Co, D C-in Chancery. Benj L Jackson & Wm B Jackson, vs Catharine Ledden & Jas B Harvey, adms in the estate of Benj Ledden, dec'd, et al. The trustee reports he has sold all that part of square 353 in Wash City, including a 2 story brick dwlg, to Saml M Edwards, for $785; & that Edwards has assigned his purchase to Jas E Morgan, who has complied with the terms of the sale. -Wm Brent, clk

My new bldg on 11th st, next door to R Farnham's, is in perfect order with new & splendid furniture complete. All who wish such a tenement will call & see. Also, the tenement attached to the store of the Messrs King on Pa ave, can be furnished to please if required. Apply to Jos K Boyd.

The Title of Buckingham. The first who held it was one of the Norman conquerors, Walter Giffard, who was created Earl of Buckingham immediately after the battle of Hastings, in 1066. The title seems to have lapsed in his son; for we find it afterwards merely assumed by the great Earl of Pembroke, Richd de Clare, [commonly known, for his personal prowess, as Strongbow,] who claimed it as sprung from the last Earl's sister. We next find it worn by Thos Plantagenet, Duke of Gloster, the youngest son of Edw III, who was created Earl in 1377. It again became extinct in his son Humphrey. It was revived as a dukedom, in favor of the Earls of Stafford by Ann Plantagenet, sister of Humphrey Plantagenet, [last Earl of B] was created Duke of Buckingham in 1441. It was again extinguished, in 1521, by the attainder & beheading [under Henry 8th] of Humphrey's great-grandson, Edw Stafford, & reverted to the Crown. Then came its fresh resuscitation in favor of that worthless & mischievous favorite of the as worthless Jas I, Geo Villiers. This pestilence minion, the young son of Sir Geo Villiers, knight, seems to have been bred, in France, to all the bodly accomplishments of the times & all the licentiousness of that nation; so that he hardly appeared at Court before he completely captivated James, by the grace of his person & the gayety of his manners. He was stabbed by a mad assassin, Felton, in 1629. To him succeeded his witty, & handsome, but still more profligate son, the Villiers of Pope & the Zimri of Dryden. At the second Villiers' death, in 1687, without male heirs, the dukedom again lapsed. The title was again revived, in 1708, in favor of John Sheffield, Earl Mulgrave, Marquis & then Duke of Normanby as well as Buckingham. The ducal honors failing again in Edmund, the son of John, [1735,] could as little remain in the noble Sheffield as the worthless Villierses. In 1784 the marquisate was revived in favor of Geo Grenville, Earl Temple, father of the present Duke, Richd Grenville, Brydges Chandos; who, marrying Ann Eliza Brydges, dght & heiress of the duke of Chandos, had, in 1822, the double duchy of Buckingham & Chandos revived & conferred upon him. He is also Earl Temple. "So much for Buckingham!"

Railroad accident on Wed last, on the Vt & Mass railroad: known to be killed are Mr Woodbury, the engineer; Mr Wiley, of Baldwinsville; Mr Huntoon, Mr Thompson, & Mr Benj King, all of West Acton. Mr King leaves a wife & 3 children. Mr Whitney, of Chestertown, [since dead,] & Mr A M Reynolds are thought to be dangerously injured. Mr Joshua Lincoln, of Charlestown, had both legs broken, & Mr Alfred A Whittemore was severely injured. The cause of the accident was imperfections in the iron used for rods in the centre of the bridge, causing the bridge to give way. The engine & some cars precipated about 40 feet.

Died: on Oct 25, after a short illness, in her 63rd year, Mary Narden, a native of France, but for the last 38 years a resident of Wash.

Obit: New Orleans Picayune: died-Mr Theodorick Bland Skinner, of this city, who expired on Oct 18, at East Pascagoula, where he had been passing the summer with his family. His disease was congestion of the brain. He was a son of the Hon J S Skinner, formerly of Balt & Wash, & now a resident of N Y, & editor of the Farmers' Library. His son, who had died so prematurely, was a gentleman of elegant accomplishments. Mr Skinner married in Louisiana, &, cut off in the flower of his age, he leaves a wife & 2 children.

Executor's sale of valuable land at auction: on Nov 13, a good tract of land belonging to the estate of Jesse Conn, dec'd, lying in Fairfax Co, Va, near the South Lowell Factory, containing 44 acres. -J N Trook, exc -A Green, auctioneer

By information from Germany & N Y. The Marburgh Institute for the advancement of Sciences has elected Lt Jas M Gilliss, of the U S Navy, a member of their Society.
-C J, Gtwn, Oct 29, 1847

TUE NOV 2, 1847

Household furniture at auction: on Nov 4, at the residence of Mrs Ladd, on 12th st, between F & G sts, part of her household furniture. -R W Dyer, auct

The Naval School at Annapolis. The School is the grand attraction. Cmder Upshur enjoys a high reputation in the city, as do the ofcrs of the School. There are some 60 youths now engaged in several branches of useful education. -Corr Balt Sun
Col David Folson, a highly respectable citizen of the Choctaw Nation, died at his residence in Doaksville on Sep 24. Col Folsom served as a leader of a party of Choctaw warriors against the Creeks during the Creek war, where his bravery & friendship to the U S rendered him a cherished object of Governmental favor. He was also under Gen Jackson at the surrender of Pensacola. -Arkansas Intell, Oct 9

Mr Wm Shaw, an extensive horticulturist in Bloomingdale, N Y, was burnt to death on Fri. His dressing gown took fire, & being somewhat impaired by age, was unable to extinguish the flames.

Lowell Courier: recent explosion of a powder mill belonging to Mr Oliver M Whipple. During the 29 years' occupation in the manufacture of this article, Mr Whipple had lost only some 15 or 20 men.

Household & kitchen furniture at auction: on Nov 4, at the residence of the late Danl Brown, dec'd, on 18th st, between H & I sts. -A Green, auctioneer

A venerable couple-Father Pinson & his family, of Scituate, Mass. Father Pinson has entered his 95th year, his worthy consort her 100th; they have been married 71 years, soon after the battle of Bunker Hill. Young Pinson was among the first to enter into battle. He returned to Scituate where he now resides, in the house in which he was born, built exclusively by his father's hands, where may be seen a rare curiosity in this age, diamond glass for windows, set in lead sash imported from Europe more than a century ago. They have been blest with 5 children, 2 of whom enjoy the sweets of celibacy beneath the paternal roof. The grand, great grand, & great great grandchildren are too munerous & scattered to trace. -Lowell Courier

Mrs Windor's School for Young Ladies, at Walnut Grange, half a mile from the Beltsville depot of the Balt & Wash Railroad, will commence the Winter session of 5 months on Nov 1. Apply to Mrs R S Windsor, Beltsville, PG Co, Md.

A cold-blooded murder was committed at N Y, last Fri, upon the person of Alex'r H Neill, a house & sign painter, residing in Rivington st, & doing business at 43 Ann st. Suspicion rests upon an apprentice as the perpetrator of the act, a lad about 20 years of age. A flat bar of iron was the instrument.

Mrd: on Oct 31, by Rev Mr Donelan, Mr Thos Milburn to Miss Pamela D Sawyer, all of Wash City.

Mrd: on Oct 20, at Alexandria, Va, by Rev Mr Dang, Chas H Rhett, of Charleston, S C, to Matilda, daughter of the late Judge Thomson Mason, of the former place.

Mrd: on Oct 20, at the residence of J H Fitzgerald, in Fauquier Co, Va, Capt W S Shover, U S A, to Felicia, daughter of John S Thornton.

Household & kitchen furniture at auction: on Nov 4, at the residence of the late Danl Brown, dec'd, on 18th st, between H & I sts. -A Green, auctioneer

$1 reward for runaway negro boy John, commonly called Jack, an indented apprentice, about 15 years old. I forwarn all persons from harboring or employing him, as the law will be enforced. -Jno H Clarvoe

$50 reward for my runaway negro woman Rachel Davis. She was purchased by me some 2 years since of a trader in this city & had, then recently been sold out of the estate of Mrs Susannah Campbell, in or near Rockville, Montg Co, Md, where her husband & several children reside. She is about 30 or 35 years of age. -Wm F Butler, Richmond, Va

WED NOV 3, 1847

The Court Martial for the trial of Lt Col Fremont assembled yesterday at the Arsenal in Wash City.
Ofcrs to form the Court:
Gen G M Brooke, Col 5th Infty
Col S Churchill, Inspector Gen
Col I B Crane, 4th Artl
Brevet Col Matthew M Payne, 4th Artl
Brevet Lt Col S H Long, Corps Top Eng
Brevet Col R E DeRussy, Corps Top Eng
Lt Col J P Taylor, Subsistence Dept
Brevet Lt Col H K Craig, Ord Dept
Maj R L Baker, Ord Dept
Maj J D Graham, Corps Top Engineers
Maj R Delafield, Corps Engineers
Brevet Maj G A McCall, Assist Adj Gen
Maj E W Morgan, 11th Infty
Capt John F Lee, Ord Dept, Judge Advocate

The witnesses of Col Fremont were as follows:
Mr J C Davis, of Ohio
Wm Findlay, of Mo
I A Moore, of Ill
Alexis Godey, of Mo
W P Brown, of Ky
T E Breckenridge, of Mo
R T Jacobs, of Louisville, Ky
Col W H Russell, of Mo
W N Loker, of Wash
Lt Geo Minor, U S Navy
Passed Midshipman Edw Beale, U S Navy
Eugene Russell, of Missouri
G W Handy, Master of a Merchantman
The defence expects also the attendance, as witnesses, of Cmdor Robt Stockton; of Lt Gillespie, of the U S Marines; of J W Whitton, of Missouri; of Marion Wise, of Missouri, of L B Vencenthaler, of Ohio; & of Jas Barret, of Missouri. We did not obtain any certain list of the witnesses of the U S. We can only mention as present the following: Brig Gen Kearny; Capt Turner, of the 1st Regt of Dragoons; Maj Swords, of the Quartermaster's Dept; the Hon W P Hall, of Mo; & Edwin Bryant, formerly editor of the Lexington, [Ky,] Reporter.

The new & splendid refectory, on the s w corner of 6th & Pa ave, was opened this past Monday. The design of the bar was furnished by Mr J G Bruff, of Wash City; the carpenter's work was executed by Mr Brown; the Messrs Porter & Pollock painted the bar in a very handsome style.

Obit-died: on Oct 17, in Hartford, Conn, at the residence of his brother, [Rev Thos H Gallaudet,] Edw Gallaudet, of Wash City. To the public he was known as a highly accomplished artist, & to his friends for all those modest & attractive virtues which most win the affections of the human heart.

Died: on Nov 2, suddenly, in her 58th year, Mrs Catharine A Tschiffely, a native of Switzerland, but for the last 40 years a resident of Wash City. Her funeral is on Thu at 11 o'clock, from the residence of Mr Jos A Deeble, on I st, between 9th & 10th sts.

Mrd: on Tue, by Rev John C Smith, Mr Wm H Cooke to Miss Cecilia Ann Caggott, both of Fairfax Co, Va.

Mrd: on Nov 1, by Rev Levi Reese, Mr Wm E Beach to Miss Susan H Devaughan, all of Wash.

Mrd: on Oct 26, by Rev Mr Martin, Alex'r McCormick to Eliz T, daughter of Mr Richd Young, of PG Co, Md.

Mrd: on Oct 31, by Rev Mr Morgan, Mr Thos F Fowler, of N J, to Mrs Eliz Ellis, of Wash City.

The U S Hotel was opened yesterday: it is under the able direction of Mr Geo W Yellott, with whom Mr R R Thompson is associated as caterer. It has been repainted inside & out, & new carpet installed. The new painted floor-cloth in the dining room was made all in one piece, cost $500, & furnished by Mr D Clagett; 3 chandeliers were furnished by Mr Whittlesey; Mr S F Franklin papered the rooms; Mr R Stewart was the carpenter; stoves & grates furnished by Mr F Hill; Mr T Tongue manufactured the copper work & culinary apparatus for the kitchen.

THU NOV 4, 1847

The charges preferred against Col Fremont: mutiny, disobedience of orders of his immediate cmder, & conduct tending to induce a like of disobedience on the part of others. Col Fremont, when informed of the commission from the Gov't as cmder-in-chief with which Gen Kearny arrived in Calif, refused, by written replies, to obey his military orders, & perisited to act as military & civil govn'r of the conquered territory; alleging his own previous appointment as govn'r & cmder by Cmdor Stockton, & the fact that the authority conferred on Gen Kearny had become obsolete by the force of events not looked to by the Gov't as to happen until after the arrival of Gen Kearny in the territory. The chief of these events was the conquest of Calif, already achieved by Cmdor Stockton & Col Fremont, before the coming of Gen Kearny & the troops under his command.

Sam'l Ward, of N J, aged 79 years, committed suicide on Thu by hanging himself with a rope to a beam on the premises of his son, at the corner of Bleecker st & the bowery, N Y. On the top of a trunk in his room were written in chalk: "Tim, take care of yourself, I have trouble enough; this is from your father."

On Sun, as Rev Mr Tappen, the excellent chaplain of the Almshouse, was concluding his opening prayer in the chapel of the institution during Divine service, his voice faltered, & he fell in the pulpit in an apoplectic fit. He sank during the night under universal paralysis. The dec'd has been for 20 years the chaplain of the almshouse, officiating alternately at Bellevue & at Blackwell's island. -N Y Com Adv

The 2 greatest farms in New England are in Vt. Consul Jarvis, upon the Connecticut at Wethersfield, has a giant farm, with 20 barns. Judge Meach has one still larger at Shelburne, on Lake Champlain.

New Confectionary & Ice Cream Saloon, on the north side of Pa ave, between 6th & 7th sts. The subscriber is prepared to supply cake & every kind of sweetmeats & confectionaries. -Geo Krafft

Peach & other fruit trees for sale at the Haddonfield Nursery, N J. -David Roe

Cumberland Coal: at his Lumber & Coal Yard, near the Railroad Depot. -John Purdy

Rev Jos H Towne, of Boston, has been elected Pastor of the First Presbyterian Church, 4½ sts, Wash.

Com'rs sale of land in Va: by decree of the Circuit Superior Court of Law & Chancery of Fauquier Co, Va, pronounced at the Oct term, 1847, in the suit of Hunton vs Tidball, the undersigned, com'rs appointed by the decree, will proceed, on Dec 13, at the tavern of Lewis S Pritchard, at Fairfax Court-house, Va, to sell, at public auction, so much of the tract of land called ***Sudley***, of which the late John Carter, of said county, died seized & possessed, as was allotted in the division of his real estate to his widow, Eliza F Carter, to his children, Wm H Carter, Gustavus A Carter, Fitzhugh H Carter, & to his grandchildren, Harriet Chilton & Douglas Chilton, consisting, agreeably to the survey thereof made: 1,638½ acres. Said land lies upon the waters of Bull & Cub runs, mostly in Fairfax Co, but small portions of it in Loudoun & Prince Wm Counties. I will be shown by Mr Jas Keen, who is in possession of a part of it as tenant, with whom a plat of the land will be left. -Saml Chilton, Wm W Wallace, Com'rs

Died: on Mon last, at Alexandria, Va, Jas Douglas, in his 60th year, for many years a respectable merchant of that town.

Died: on Oct 11, after a short illness, of congestion of the brain, at his residence at Mount Pleasant, Monroe Co, Alabama, Lorman Crawford, a native of Gtwn, D C. He has been for several successive years a member of the House of Reps of the Gen Assembly of Alabama. Cut off in the flower of his age, his memory is embalmed in the hearts of his bereaved relatives & friends.

For rent: 2 story frame dwlg, on 7th st, between G & H sts. Inquire of Alex'r Talburt.

Wash Co, D C: on Dec 27, 1847, personally appears Craven Horton, of Fairfax Co, Va, & makes oath that he has reason to believe that Edmond D Richards, late of Gtwn, D C, took a certain negro girl called Jane, alias Jane Horton, who was free & entitled to her freedom at the time she was taken off by said Richards, out of D C, for the purpose of selling her as a slave for life, into parts unknown; & the said Craven Horton, in manner & form aforesaid, further saith, that the said Edmond D Richards was enjoined by the Circuit Court of Wash Co, D C from removing Jane beyond the jurisdiction of said court, & that Richards knew the said Jane was free. Sworn to before J L Smith, J P. [This is followed by a sworn statement by Craven Horton, that he has reason to believe that Cassius Lay, of Gtwn, did aid & abet Edmond D Richards in taking a certain negro girl called Jane, alias Jane Horton.]

FRI NOV 5, 1847

Valuable property at auction: by deed of trust from R R Goldin to the subscriber, dated Mar 25, 1842, recorded in Liber W B 24, folios 313 through 318, in the land records of Wash Co: sale on Nov 22, parts of lots 15 & 16 in square 453, with improvements thereon, being 4 frame tenements, all of which are under rent. Terms at sale.
-Lewis Johnson, Nich Callan, jr, Trustees -R W Dyer, auct

Jabez W Huntington, one of the U S Senators from Conn, the colleague of Mr Niles, died on Mon, caused by a violent attack of intestinal inflammation. Jabez Williams Huntington, son of Gen Zachariah Huntington, was born at Norwich, Nov 8, 1778; consequently was 59 years of age, wanting 6 days at the time of his decease. Educated at Yale College, where he graduated in 1808; was admitted to the bar in Litchfield Co. In Apr, 1829, elected a Rep in the 21st Congress. In Apr, 1831, elected for the 22nd Congress; & in Apr, 1833, elected for the 3rd time to a seat in the 23rd Congress. He received the appointment of Assoc Judge of the Superior Court & of the Supreme Court of Errors, & resigned his seat in Congress at the close of the first session of the 23rd Congress. In Oct, 1834, he removed to Norwich, where he continued to reside till his death. In May, 1840, he was appointed a Senator in the Congress of the U S for the unexpired term of 6 years from May 4, 1839, to fill the vacancy occasioned by the death of the Hon Thaddeus Betts. He resigned his judicial ofc; & in 1845 he was re-elected to the U S Senate for another term.

The powder mill of Messrs Laflin & Smith, in Greene Co, N Y, exploded on Nov 1, killing 3 workmen: Overbagh, Nescott, & Schribber. Another workman narrowly escaped death.

Mount Vernon: Is it not most unreasonable & unjust, as long as ***Mount Vernon*** is private property, & occupied by a private family, to ask that it should be made public to every body who comes there? Mr Washington is a plain Va farmer, relying upon his crops for his income, & is not a millionaire, with time & means to employ in mere embellishment, or in fancy operatons. All visiters to ***Mount Vernon*** are privileged to go over the grounds & see the tomb of Washington. They are all treated courteously, though courtesy is not always reciprocated on their part. A proposition has been started for the purchase of ***Mount Vernon*** by the Gov't. The terms of the sale have been offered by the proprietor, Mr John Augustine Washington. -Alexandria Gaz

Embarkation of Missionaries. Sailed in the ship **Cato** from Boston for Calcutta, Rev Messrs Stoddard & Danforth, with their wives, for Assan; Rev Mr Brayton & Rev Mr Moore & wife for the Sho Karens; Rev Mr Simmonds for Burmah.

On Sat last, Mr Thos Stevens was in the act of joining 2 cars while they were in slow motion at the depot in Lawrence, Mass, & he was crushed between then, injuring him so severely that he lived but 12 hours after.

Mrd: on Tue last, by Rev Chas A Davis, Mr W C Johnson to Miss Catharine E Moore, all of Wash City.

Mrd: on Thu, by Rev Chas A Davis, Mr John N Crump to Miss Martha A Padgett, both of Fairfax Co, Va.

For rent: 2 story brick house, now occupied by Mr Henry Balmain, near the corner of 18th & I sts. Inquire of Robt Cruit, F st, between 14th & 15th sts.

In the U S District Court in Boston on Sat, Warren Chas Fitz, of Cabotville, who was on trial for the murder of Antonia Silvere, on board schnr **H M Williams**, was acquitted.

Circuit Court of Wash Co, D C-in Chancery: Mar Term, 1847. Edw Plater, cmplnt, vs Wm Plater & others, dfndnts. John Marbury, trustee appointed by the original decree to sell the real estate in the bill of cmplnt, that the proceeds thereof may be divided between & among the parties to said cause, according to their rights as divisees under the last will & testament of John R Plater, dec'd, having reported to the Court that he sold lot 14 in square 256, Wash, D C, to Joel Downer, of said city, for $639.70, & lots 15 thru 17 in square 37, in said city, to Wm G Ridgeley, of Gtwn, D C, for aggregate sum of $178.81. -Wm Brent, clk

Walter S Cox has declined as the collector for the Nat'l Monument for Gtwn, D C, the books are now placed in the hands of Mr Jas Miller as the successor to Mr Cox. -Advocate

Dr John Hubble, of Van Buren Co, Mo, was murdered in the early part of last month. He was engaged in the duty of family worship when he was shot by some person through the window & instantly expired.

Orphans Court of Wash Co, D C: letters testamentary on the personal estate of Thos Burch, late of Wash Co, dec'd. -R J Jones, exc

Jos K Stapleton, 198 Balt st, Balt, Md: manufactures all kind of Brushes, Bellows, & Fishing Rods.

Household & kitchen furniture at auction: on Nov 9, at the residence of Mr Vermillion, on Md ave, on the road leading to the first toll-gate east of the Capitol, a good lot of furniture. -A Green, auctioneer

SAT NOV 6, 1847

Foreign passengers: in the Bremen barque **Alfred**, at N Y from Bremen: H Kothe, & 165 in steerage. In the packet ship **Montezuma**, from N Y for Liverpool: Mr Bruce & Mr McClelland, N Y; Henry Proud & dght, Oswego; Mr S Hardy, Mr W Hardy, Canada; Thos Blakely, England. In the French steamer **Philadelphia**, at N Y from Havre: Mr Lanel, N Y; Messrs Warren, Boston; Peret, Le Baron, Gautherin, & Andorin, Mobile; Mr Laurens, Mrs Laurens, & Miss Laurens, & Mr Darene, Charleston; Messrs Gros, Peschler, Bourkie, & Courvosier, New Orleans; Mr O'Hara, Key West; Messrs De Don Martin, Blackney, Cosier, Montillon, Lampfere, Bernard, Gander, Gandieler, & T A Veonir, France; Messrs Stanton, Girardin, & Bushy, N Y; Mr Boissaulon, Guadaloupe; Messrs Fenley, Nayence, & Troubat, Phil; Mr Strybos, Mexico; Mr Rosey & Mr Mondheiner, Canada.

Mrd: on Nov 2, in Wash City, by Rev J W French, J N Ashton to Miss Margaret M Stuart, both formerly of the State of Va.

We learn from Mr John Alden, of Fairhaven, that the destruction of his carpenter's shop, on Fri last, was probably occasioned by the accidental ignition of a friction match, which may have fallen among the shavings on the floor. Loss of property is about $1,500, of which $800 is insured. -New Bedford Mercury

Mrd: on Nov 4, in the Church of the Ascension, by Rev L J Gilliss, Mr Jas W Plant to Miss Julia Ann Cox, all of Wash City.

Mrd: on Nov 2, in Boston, by Rev Dr Eaton, Lt Henry W Queen, U S Marine Corps, to Abba E Wentworth, daughter of the late Jas Wentworth.

Died: on Nov 5, in Gtwn, at the residence of her mother, Mrs Margaret Chandler, Mrs Lucy Hay, in her 48th year. Her funeral is at 3 o'clock this afternoon.

Capt Wm H Churchill, of the 3rd Artl, Assist Quartermaster, died at Point Isabel on Oct 19, of yellow fever. He graduated at West Point in 1840, & was brevetted captain for his gallant conduct at Resaca de la Palma. Lt Jenkins, of the 1st dragoons, died of yellow fever at Vera Cruz on Oct 18.

MON NOV 8, 1847

Dreadful accident on the Reading railroad on Wed last, caused by the obstruction of coal trains, causing the instant death of Barney McGuire. John Regan is dreadfully crushed & is not expected to survive.

Mr Geo Wilkie, one of the oldest & best farmers in this region, met his death on Thu, when his clothes accidentally caught in the shaft connected with a threshing machine & killed him -N Y Journal of Commerce

Officers of brig **Dolphin**: John Pope, Cmder; L B Avery, S J Shinley, Lts; A Redd, Acting Master; John T Mason, Passed Assist Surgeon; John O'Means, Acting Purser; Wm F Spencer, Passed Midshipman; M C Jones, Chas M Mitchell, Midshipmen.

Roger Kelly, a young man, was murdered in Phil on Fri. He was shot in the face by Saml Cowperthwaite, a prominent actor, it is said, in a lawless gang who call themselves Skinners. The murder was committed deliberately during a general fight. [Nov 11th newspaper: Roger Kelly was 18 years old; his mother reached the scene a short time after he had drawn his last breath. The supposed offender & 7 of his companions have been arrested. -Phil Inquirer, 8th]

Mrd: Nov 2, at Mount Calvert, by Rev Amos Smith, Mr John L Dufief, of Wash, to Miss Catharine A, youngest daughter of Eleazar Talburtt, of PG Co, Md.

Mrd: on Nov 3, in Phil, by Rev R De Charms, Dr Robt Arthur, of Wash, to Miss Mary Hemple, of Phil.

Died: on Oct 29, at Newburg, N Y, Sarah Levater Casey, youngest daughter of Jas K Casey, of N Y C.

On Oct 23, a small boat left the wharf in this village to go to Matilda, at the foot of Point Rockaway, & while descending the Galoo Rapids the boat filled & sunk, & all on board drowned. They were Robt Johnson, Arthur McNevin, Robt Riley, Michl Langhorn, Johnson Aschison, & Geo Darling. -St Lawrence Republican

Groceries & store fixtures at auction: on Nov 10, at the grocery store of Aquila Rickets, on G st, near the War Ofc. -A Green, auctioneer

Trustee's sale of real property in Wash: by decree of the Circuit Court of Wash Co, D C, sitting in Chancery, in the case of Scholfield & others against Scholfield & others: sale on Dec 11, the whole of square 363, on Md ave, between 6th & 7th sts east; & lot 7 in square 576, on Md ave. The former contains a commodious double cottage & the latter 2 small tenements. -Jos Scholfield, trustee -A Green, auct

TUE NOV 9, 1847

Foreign News: 1-The London papers announce the death, at age 55, of the distinguished composer, Wm Michl Rooke, chiefly known by his opera Amilie. He leaves a widow & a large family of children in poverty. 2-Louis Philippe completed his 74th year on Oct 5. 3-The wife of the celebrated Vidocq has committed suicide in Paris.

Circuit Court of Wash Co, D C-in Chancery. Wm P Ingle & others, by next friend, John P Ingle, vs Mary Catharine Ingle. The trustee sold the premises mentioned in the decree of this Court, passed on May 17, 1847: parts of lots 20 & 21 in square 456, in Wash City, & Jacob Gibson was the purchaser for $949.17; & parts of lots 2 & 3 in square 461, in Wash City, & Geo Parker was the purchaser for $11,065.95; & both have complied with the terms of the sale. -W Brent, clk

Through the Charleston Courier we have intelligence of the loss of the U S transport ship **Empire**, Capt Russell, which sailed from N Y on Oct 12, with 15 ofcrs & 370 U S troops, bound for Vera Cruz. She was totally wrecked by running on a coral reef near Abaco, one of the Bahamas, during the night of Oct 17. The only life lost was that of the helmsman, who was badly wounded at the wheel when the vessel struck, & died on the island. The ofcrs & troops remained on the reef for 10 days, & thence shipped for Charleston, at which place the schnr **E A Thompson** had arrived, with Lt Wm Reid, commanding the detachment, Brevet 2nd Lt C L Best, Brevet 2nd Lt H Neil, Brevet 2nd Lt J De Russey, 2nd Lt T Hart, 2nd Lt J O Wilbar, & 129 soldiers. The schnr **Zulma** sailed from the island with a part of the troops on Oct 27, & the brig **Adelaide** was expected to leave with the balance on Nov 2, both for Charleston.

Printing & wrapping paper: Fitzhugh Coyle, near the corner of 8th st & Pa ave.

The Albany papers inform us of the decease, on Thu last, of Crawford Livingston, of the firm of Livingston & Wells, the well known Express Company of that city. He was a young man, & his death has been expected for several months.

Mrd: on Nov 2, by Rev Robt Prout, Henry E Morton, of New Orleans, to Miss Mary C Morton, daughter of Mr Wm Morton, of Calvert Co, Md.

J M Colgan has for rent, over his grocery store, 2 parlors & 2 chambers, furnished or not furnished. Pa ave, between 12th & 13th sts, south side.

The gentleman, for I suppose so he wishes to pass in the world, carried into effect the removal from the premises of the Columbian Hotel, a full sized water color painting [in frame] of the Nat'l Washington Monument-it is requested, without further notice, to restore the stolen property to its rightful owner. -J H Eberbach, Columbian Hotel

WED NOV 10, 1847

Eliz A Leland, daughter of Hon Sherman Leland, Judge of Probate for the county of Norfolk, while returning from a visit on Thu last, fell near the gate of her father's house in a state of insensibility. She was discovered by her brother, & immediately carried into the house. Dr Henry Bartlett was called, but she died within 20 minutes. Miss Leland was a highly accomplished young lady, & leaves a large circle of relatives & friends to mourn her sudden death. -Boston Journal

A stray cow was taken up on ***Greenleaf's Point***, on Nov 9, by Jas R King. The owner can have her by proving property & paying charges.

Chancery sale: by decree of the Circuit Court of Wash Co, D C, sitting in Chancery, made in the cause of Henry B Waring & al, vs John P Waring: I shall offer at auction, on Nov 19, on the premises, all that desirable messuage, with the appurtenances, being the late residence of Mrs Milicent Waring, dec'd, situated at the n w corner of 2nd & Market sts, in Gtwn. This property includes lots 136 & 137, & the south half of lot 149, all of Beatty & Hawkins' addition to Gtwn. The improvements are a commodious 2 story brick dwlg, built in the best manner. -Clement Cox, trustee -E S Wright, auctioneer

The Springfield [Ohio] Republic records the death of Dr John Patton, of that county, by the accidental use of strychnia instead of morphine. He had purchased 2 vials from a drug store, one containing one strychnia & the other morphine, but both supposed to contain morphine. He took a small quantity of strychnia, on the point of a penknife, & did not discover his mistake until he felt the effect of the poison. Strychnia produces death by convulsions & lockjaw in a few hours. It is the alkaloid of nux nomica, the seed of which are called "dog bottons,' & exists in several plants.

Mrd: on Nov 1, by Rev Mr Musgrave, Wm Adkeson to Miss Jane, eldest daughter of Wm Newton, all of Balt, Md.

Louisiana Chronicle: the remains of the Hon Alex'r Barrow, recently removed from this city, reached Bayou Sota on Tue week. The late obsequies in memory of the lamented dead took place on Oct 30, at the residence of Col David Barrow, where his remains were deposited in the family cemetery.

Died: on Oct 16, in Boston, after a long & painful illness, Henry Andrews, youngest daughter of the late Dr J A Brereton, U S Army, aged 12 years.

Mrs Eliz Warren, a widow who kept a small grocery at Lexington, Ky, was murdered by some unknown person on Sun night week. She lived alone & was known to have considerable money in her possession.

By virtue of an order of distrain, to me directed, I shall expose to public sale for cash on Nov 16, the property, to wit; a piano-forte & stool, 1 small sofa, 8 cane-bottom chairs, seized & taken as the property of H W Edwards, to satisfy rent due in arrears to Jos Libbey. -F B Poston, Bailiff

THU NOV 11, 1847

Small colored boy strayed from his home on K st, between 5th & 6th sts; about 8 or 9 years. Name is Peter Dorsey. Information thankfully received by his distressed parents. -Isaac Dorsey, K st, 5th & 6th sts

My new bldg on 11th st, next door to R Farnham's, is in perfect order, with new furniture complete. All who wish such a tenement will call on me, & engage in time. -Jos K Boyd

Catawba Land for sale: tract lying 2 miles from Fincastle, Botetourt Co, Va: contains 2,080 acres. Apply to the subscriber, at Richmond, Va. -Ro W Hughes

For rent: house containing 9 rooms, recently occupied by Alex'r N Zevely, on 6th st, between E & F sts. -Noah Fletcher

U S Patent Ofc, Nov 5,1 847. Ptn of Catharine B Gold, of Washington, Connecticut, excx of the last will & testament of J S Gold, dec'd, praying for the extension of a patent granted to said J S Gold for an improvement in ovens for 7 years from the expiration of said patent, which takes place on Dec 15 next. -Edmund Burke, Com'r of Patents

Mrd: on Nov 8, in Phil, by Rt Rev Bishop Kendrick, Mr Peter Brady, of Wash City, to Miss Sarah Morrison, of the former place.

Died: yesterday, in Wash City, William, only son of Jas & Margaret Francis, aged 3 years & 6 months. His funeral is this afternoon, at 3 o'clock, from the residence of his mother, out 7 st north.

Died: on Nov 9, in Gtwn, D C, Mr Chas King, an old & highly respected citizen of that place, being in the 79th year of his age. His funeral is on Fri, at 9 o'clock, from his late residence, opposite Trinity Church, 1st st, when a solemn service will be offered up in that church for the repose of his soul. Resquiesent in pace!

Died: Nov 1, at ***Wakefield***, Westmoreland Co, Va, the residence of John E Wilson, Major Henry T Garnett, late of Green Co, Ala, in which latter State he resided during the year 1846. He rode over in the morning of Sunday with his brother & a young friend from ***Haywood***, [the residence of his father, Col Henry T Garnett] to visit his neighbor. At 4 o'clock he started with the same company to return home to his father's. Within less than a mile of Mr Wilson's house, while his company was momentarily absent from him, it is supposed his horse fell with him, as he was found prostrate on his face in the road bleeding profusely from the nose & back of the head, speechless & insensible. Several physicians were summoned & he was removed to the house of a friend. His skull was fractured, supposed from the foot of the horse in his efforts to rise. He lingered until next morning, when his spirit took its flight to the God who gave it. He was in his 21st year, full of life & hope. He was kind in all relations to his parents, brothers, & sisters.
[Will the Washington Union, Richmond, & Alabama papers publish this obituary.]

New Millinery: Mrs J B Hills, Pa ave, between 9th & 10th sts, will open on Nov 13.

Railroad accident on Sat, as the passenger train from the Western Railroad was approaching Boston, the second class car was thrown from the tracks. Those killed appeared to be laboring men, one supposed to be Geo Simmons, of Union, Conn; C D Clark, & Keeley. Also killed were Richd Warren, of Jefferson, Maine, & Geo Frye, of Portsmouth, N H. [Information found from wallets & papers in their pockets.]
-Boston Advertiser

Furnished rooms for rent: Pa ave & 10th st, south side. -Mrs M Byrne

To let: the handsome residence of the late Robt Sewall, on the highest part of Capitol Hill, within 250 yards of the n e corner of the Capitol gardens. Inquire of S Scott, on the adjoining premises.

Brick house & lot for sale or rent: C st, between 2nd & 3rd sts. Inquire of W C Choate, La ave & 6th sts.

Wanted, immediately, an active intelligent youth, of strictly moral character, to attend in a fancy dry goods store. Apply at Wm W Carpenter's, Pa ave, between 6th & 7th sts.

FRI NOV 12, 1847

Patrick Toomie, of Wash City, was shot in the knee last Monday, by Harrison Monroe, who objected to Toomie's entering his house, & adopted this method to keep him out. Dr Morgan said the wound is not dangerous.

I certify that Thos J Barclay, of PG Co, Md, brought before me as a stray, trespassing upon his enclosures, a bay horse. -Jno W Scott, J P [Owner is to prove property, pay charges, & take him away. -Thos J Barclay, near Bladensburg, Md.]

The Govn'r of the State of Va has appointed the Hon Wm C Rives one of the Com'rs on the part of that State to settle the boundary line between Va & Ohio. This appointment is to fill the vacancy created by the ineligibility of Richd Kidder Meade, who has been elected to Congress.

The Hon Maturin Livingston died in N Y on Sun, at the residence of Maj Delafield, his son-in-law. Mr Livingston was a highly respectable man, who led an honorable life in the city of his birth, dying at the age of 79 years. He held at one time the ofc of Recorder of N Y. -Evening Post

Official: the following candidates for admission into the Medical Corps of the Navy have been examined by the Board of Surgeons recently at Phil, found qualified, & commissioned as Assist Surgeons, to rank in the following order:

1-Wm Lowber	3-Geo H Howell	5-Ashton Miles
2-D Warren Brickell	4-D P Phillips	6-Phineas J Horwitz

The 3rd Regt of Tenn Volunteers reached New Orleans on Nov 3. They number in all 1,000 men, rank & file, under the command of Col B F Cheatham, Lt Col J W Whitfield, & Maj Solomon. They were immediately transferred on board of vessels destined for Vera Cruz.

Wanted,a youth from 14 to 16 years of age, of good education & unexceptionable character, to attend in the stationery store of Wm Fischer.

Foreign passengers: in the steamship **Washington**, from Southampton:

S R Hobbie, Wash, D C	J M Bull, of Providence, R I
Saml Smith, New Orleans	C H Kutachos, Leipsic
Chas Buloof, of Switzerland	J M Sharp, S L Sharp, of Ky
Mr Follet, N J	C Palmedo, A Palmedo, Hanover
H Von Kaaff, Balt	

Monsieur Picot, lady, child & 2 servants, France.
J H Roberts, lady, & servant, H M Neill, Ireland.
J P Goeop, Geo Heinsohn & lady, Miss Lesette Horstman, Miss Samson, John Droego, T Unckerman, T Rusner, C Scheider, of Germany. Miss Hutteroll, Germany.
U H Levy, M Bates, jr, W P Beecher, F Dellue, J R Crafts, B Tatham & lady, Wm Hurry, Wm Hurry, jr, Miss S Hurry, Miss A E Hurry, W C Hunter, lady, child, & servant, Miss Rankin, Fred'k Victor, lady, 4 children, & servant, M D Brouk, Mr Strange, J Y Westvelt, Mr Hasluck, F M Rice, T O'Sullivan, Mrs O'Sullivan, Geo Spicer, John Spicer, H Bowers, jr, Miss E Low, L Prelaz & lady, John Simpson, Chas Kenigen & lady, N Y.
Smith McCauley, U S Consul at Tripoli, Miss M McCauley, Miss Kate Lovely, Miss Billington, C Ingersoll, Washington Keith, of Phil.

F B Flagg, C D Wade, H B M Consul at Charleston; Mrs C D Wade & servant, C Epping, of Charleston, S C
Mr Fitzmorris & lady, Mr Evitt, Mr Woods, J Richardson, Mrs Meyers, A Solari, Alex'r Brown, H J F Bridges, of England
In ship **Christiana**, from London: Mr C Schulthies, J F Blackman, W H Blackwell, R Hargrave, Mr Hyde, H M Hyde, J Wood, S Hampson, Miss Rachael Hampson, A B How, M C Wearvell, & 127 in the steerage.
In the ship **Bavaria**, from Havre: M Chevalier de Bourman, Sec of Spanish Legation; Rev Ed Mead, lady, & child; J Ahlborn, Jules Rilliet, W C Johnston & lady, Depeyster Dow, Utica; Dr J Y & H Clark, Paris; Mr & Mrs Evans, Phil; W J & F D Reed, Boston.
[No date-the above passenger lists are current news items.]

Mrd: on Nov 3, in N Y, by Rev Dr Skinner, Henry A Mott to Mary J, eldest daughter of Jos B Varnum, all of Wash City.

Died: yesterday, in Wash City, of consumption, Mrs Mary Ann Gatton, w/o Henry Gatton. Her funeral will take place on Sat at 3 o'clock.

Died: yesterday, Mary Alice, 3rd daughter of Jas & Margaret Cornelia Cryer, in her 3rd year. Her funeral is this day, at 3 o'clock, from the residence of her parents, 12th st, between Va ave & C st south.

Died: on Oct 18, at Vera Cruz, Mexico, of yellow fever, 1st Lt Leonidas Jenkins, of the 1st Regt U S Dragoons, aged about 26 years. He was the son-in-law of Maj E V Sumner, 2nd Dragoons, & has left a widow & an orphan.

SAT NOV 13, 1847
North Carolina Times: this is the title of a very handsome paper, the first number of which has reached us from Louisburg, Franklin Co: editor is Mr Chas C Raboteau. -Ral Reg

From Mexico-from the New Orleans Picayune, extra, of Nov 5.
As far back as Oct 14 Generals Pillow & Shields were able to be about.
Gen Smith has been appointed Govn'r of the city of Mexico. Gen Quitman is about to return to the U S.
The train which is to come down will be under the command of Col Harney. Major Gaines, Capt Cassius M Clay, Capt Heady, Maj Borland, Capt Danley, & Midshipman Rogers come home, & we are happy to add our associate, Mr Kendall.
Puebla, Oct 20, 1847. Lt E B Daniels, of the 2nd Artl, has died of his wounds.
We believe, truly, that Capt Walker, of the rifles, was killed in the affair at Huamantla. He had received a lance wound entirely through the body, & also lost a leg by a cannon shot. Capt Layall & 18 men of the rifles, are also known to have been killed in the charge of Capt Walker. A man named Raborg, of Balt, interpreter for Capt Walker, lost a leg from a discharge of artillery.

A duel was fought near Vera Cruz, outside the Gate of Mercy, on Nov 1, between Capts Warrington & White, with muskets, at 60 paces. At first fire Capt Warrington received a ball through the fleshy part of both legs, below the knee.
A duel was fought about Oct 24, between Capt Porter, of the rifles, & Capt Archer, of the voltigeurs. At the 2nd fire Capt Archer was shot in the abdomen-a severe but not a dangerous wound.
Lt Shackleford, of the 2nd Artl, had died of his wounds.
Lt Steen, of the S C Regt, has died of his wounds.
Col Roberts, of the 2nd Pa Regt of Volunteers, died at the capital on Oct 3.
Lt Jos D Bacon, of the 6th Infty, died on the 12th ult, of wounds received at the battle of Churubusco.
Dr Wm Roberts, of the medical staff, & attached to the 5th Infty as surgeon, died on the 12th ult, of a wound received at the King's Mills.
Capt C T Huddleson, of the 14th Infty, died at Mexico on the 11th ult. He was in bad health from the time he left Vera Cruz.
Capt Pierson, of the N Y Regt of Volunteers, died on the 10th ult, of wounds received in the storming of Chapultepec.
Sgt Sutliffe,of the Rifles, was killed on the 15th.
Generals Rincon & Brave has been exchanged for Capts Heady & C M Clay.
The North American says the following ofcrs have leave of absence, & proceed to the U S-those who are not incapacited by wounds or sickness, to recruit for their respective regts:

Brevet Col J Garland, 5th Infty
Col G W Morgan, 14th Infty
Col Ward B Burnett, N Y Volunteers
Col T P Andrews, voltigeurs
Lt Col Saml E Watson, marine corps
Brevet Maj R D A Wade, 3rd Artl
Maj W W Loring, mounted riflemen
Capt Robt Anderson, 4th Artl
Capt Philip Kearny, 1st Dragoons
Capt A F McReynolds, 3rd Dragoons
Capt Jas W Denver, 12th Infty
Capt Julian P Breedlove, 14th Infty
Capt P R Anderson, 14th Infty
Capt Garret Dykeman, N Y Volunteers
Capt Edw A King, 17th Infty
Capt Robt Porter, 2nd Pa Volunteers
Capt Jas Murray, 2nd Pa Volunteers
Capt A P Churchill, Volunteers

<u>Lts:</u>
H Prince, 4th Infty
Wm Moralle, La mounted Volunteers
David Hopkins, 2nd Pa Volunteers
Jas D Potter, N Y Volunteers
Chas A Cooper
Thornton T Brodhead, adj 15th Infty
John T Brown, 3rd Dragoons
H D Codender, ordnance corps
Thos W Sweeney, N Y Volunteers
Lorimer Graham, 10th Infty
Wm A Newham, 9th Infty
Wm H Goodloe, 15th Infty
John W Hathaway, 9th Infty
Henry De Wolf, 9th Infty
Mortimer Rosencrants, 5th Infty
Alphonse F Palmer, 9th Infty
Edw Johnson, 4th Infty
Edw C Brynton, 1st Artl
Chas H Jones, N Y Volunteers
Wm Brown, N Y Volunteers
Llewellyn Jones, mounted rifles
M A Van Bruen, mounted rifles
Henry A M Fillmore, 2nd Pa Volunteers
D D Baker, marine corps
John W Stewart, S C Volunteers
W C Comorsyne, S C Volunteers

G Kinsgin, voltigeurs
G R Kiger, voltigeurs
R H Archer, voltigeurs
F H Larned, voltigeurs
Wm Merrihew, 3rd Dragoons

Later confirmation of the death of Capt Walker: he was shot by a cannon-ball from a masked battery, about 12 miles from the main road. The ball also killed Capt Loyall, of the Georgia mounted company.

Mrd: on Thu last, by Rev John C Smith, Mr Peter Hevener to Miss Virginia Anna, daughter of Mr Geo Cochran, all of Wash City.

Mrd: on Nov 9, by Rev Jas B Donelan, Arthur Clarke to Miss Charlotte A Sears, all of Wash City.

Mrd: on Nov 4, at St Mary's Church, by Rev Matthias Aleg, Mr Patrick Weneble to Miss Margaret Cunningham, both of Wash City.

Died: on Nov 11, in Wash City, Mrs Hannah G Corcoran, w/o the late Michl Corcoran, in her 39th year. Her funeral is on Sat at 2 o'clock, from her late residence, corner of Pa ave & 14th st.

Household & kitchen furniture at auction: on Nov 15, at the residence of Mr Warren, at the corner of 17th & I sts, an excellent lot of furniture. -A Green, auctioneer

Situation wanted. A gentleman competent to instruct in the ordinary English studies & in the French & Latin languages, desires a situation as instructer in a private family in either of the Southern States. Address Rt Rev Thos C Brownell, Hartford, Conn.

MON NOV 15, 1847

For rent: with or without the furniture, the large & convenient residence of the late Saml Humphreys, on Gay st, Gtwn, of easy access to Wash. Apply to the present occupant. -Letitia Humphreys

For rent: 2 story frame dwlg. For terms inquire of Mrs E A Laub, corner of F & 10th sts.

Brick-yard for sale: with 2 kilns for burning, with a great abundance of the finest clay. Also, a frame house with 8 rooms, garden, & fruit trees. Also a lot of ground, at the corner of D & 2nd sts, in the rear of the Railroad Depot. Apply to the subscriber, at Boteler & McGregor's House-furnishing Rooms, between 8th & 9th sts, Pa ave. -N M McGregor

Orphans Court of Wash Co, D C. Letters of administration on the personal estate of Mary Scott, late of said county, deceased. -S S Williams, adm

Capt Babcock, of an Erie canal boat, had a scuffle with the captain of a scow, in the course of which a little son of the Scotsman came up with a gun. Babcock seized the gun & dashed it to the deck, when it went off & shot Babcock dead.

The store-ship **Fredonia** arrived at N Y on Fri, in 34 days from Vera Cruz. Her ofcrs are:
Thos Turner, Lt Commanding
John Hastings, Passed Assist Surgeon
Reginald Fairfax, Acting Master
Thos S Fillebrown, David Coleman, &
L C Sawyer, Midshipmen
Walter Clifton, Capt's Clerk
Passengers in the **Fredonia**:
Lt Henry Moor, Passed Midshipmen Henry H T Arnold & Wm N Jeffers; Midshipman John McLeod Murphy; 3rd Assist Engineer Jos D Alexander, & 90 in the steerage.

Sir Robt Peel is said to possess an estate valued at ninety millions of dollars. His grandfather was in quite ordinary circumstances. His father was a cotton spinner, & accumulated a portion of this immense estate, which the son has since increased by judicious investments. Only 3 generations have sufficed to raise a comparatively obscure family to rank, opulence, & power.

Reuben Sawyer, Chrmn of the Selectmen of Sterling, hung himself on Sat in his paint shop. He began taking laudanum on Sat. He was 40 years old, a man of fine talents, & has left a wife. Embarrassment in business the cause. -Worcester [Mass] Transcript

The body of John Forbes was found upon the track of the Western Railroad, between Springfield & Westfield, Mass, on Sun, with one of the legs cut twice in two, once above & once below the knee. He was intoxicated, as a bottle of rum was found in his pocket; & he bled to death.

The Mount Savage Iron Works, embracing all the land & machinery of the Company, with all the personal property, & the railroad, were sold by the Sheriff of Alleghany Co, Md, on Nov 11. The purchasers were Messrs Corning & Winslow, of Albany, N Y, & Mr J M Forbes, of Boston, Mass. The whole amount of the purchase exceeds $200,000. The company will hereafter be called: Lulworth Iron Company. [Under Balt & the North, Nov 13: The Mount Savage Iron Works sold for $225,000, to Messrs Connolly & Winslow, extensive iron manufacturers of Albany. The sum now paid for the works is not half the first cost. It is estimated a great bargain.]

Mrd: on Oct 16 last, at Preston, England, Francis Seymour Haden, of London, to Deborah Delano, only daughter of Geo W Whistler, late of the U S Army.

Died: on Nov 14, in Wash City, Mrs Elenor Miller, in her 75th year, a native of Anne Arundel Co, Md, but for the last 50 years a resident of this District. Her funeral is from the residence of her son-in-law, John A Cassell, Va ave & 7th st, this afternoon, at 1 o'clock.

Died: on Nov 11, at Oakenbrow, King Geo Co, Va, in his 37th year, Chas Tayloe. He died with the calm serenity of a Christian, not leaving behind him a single enemy.

Headquarters of the Army: Tucubaya, at the Gates of Mexico, Aug 28, 1847. Victory of Contreras achieved: Capt Chas Hanson, 7th Infty, distinguished for gallantry, modesty & piety, killed. Lt J P Johnson, 1st Artl, serving with Magruder's battery, a young ofcr of the highest promise, was killed the evening before. The forcing of San Antonio was the second brilliant event of the day. The third signal triumph of the day were 3 field pieces, 192 prisoners, much ammunition, & two colors, taken in the tete de pont. Lt J F Irons, 1st Artl, aid-de-camp to Brig Gen Cadwalader, a young ofcr of great merit, received, in front of the work, a mortal wound-since dead. Capts E A Capron & M J Bruke, & Lt S Hoffman, all of the 1st Artl, & Capt J W Anderson & Lt Thos Easley, both of the 2nd Infty, 5 ofcrs of great merit, fell gallantly before this work. The capture of the enemy's citadel was the 4th great achievement of our arms in the same day. Brig Gen Pierce, from the hurt of the evening before, under pain & exhaustion, fainted in the action. Col Morgan, being severely wounded, the command of the 15th Infty devolved on Lt Col Howard; Col Burnett receiving a like wound, the command of the N Y volunteers fell to Lt Col Baxter; & on the fall of the lamented Col P M Butler, earlier badly wounded, but continuing to lead nobly in the hottest part of the battle-the command of the S C volunteers devolved, first, on Lt Col Dickinson, who being severely wounded, [as before in the siege of Vera Cruz,] the regt ultimately fell under the orders of Maj Gladden. Lts David Adams & W R Williams, of the same corps; Capt Augustus Quarles & Lt J B Goodman, of the 15th, & Lt E Chandler, N Y volunteers, all gallant ofcrs, nobly fell in the same action. The cavalry charges were headed by Capt Kearney, of the 1st Dragoons. Of the 7 ofcrs of the squadron, Kearney lost his left arm; McReynolds & Lt Lorimer Graham were both severely wounded, & Lt R S Ewell, who succeeded to the command of the escort, had 2 horses killed under him. Maj F D Mills, 15th Infty, a volunteer in this charge, was killed at the gate. -Winfield Scott to Hon Wm L Marcy, Sec of War

Obit-died: on Nov 13, Lt Jos D Bacon, of the 6th Infty, who died of wounds received in the battle of Churubusco. Lt Bacon's first name was John. He was born in Maine, & graduated at West Point in 1840. His regt can bear willing testimony to his noble qualities; he falls without one enemy. -A Friend

TUE NOV 16, 1847
Appointment by the President: Arnold Plumer, of Pa, to be Marshal for the Western District of Pa.

State of N C, Guilford Co: Court of Equity, Oct Term, A D 1847. Thos R Tate & others vs David P Weir & others. Ptn to sell real estate. I shall expose to public sale, in Greensborough, N C, on Feb 21, 1848, the lot of land on which the Cotton Factory stands, erected by the late Henry Humphries: with extensive brick bldg, shops, & store-houses. -J A Mebane, C M E: Greensborough, N C, Nov, 1847.

The Port Tobacco [Md] Times announces the death of John Ferguson, at age 74 years: for many years Chief Judge of the Orphans' Court of Chas Co, Md.

Thompson Burgess, convicted at Richmond of committing a rape, has been sentenced to the penitentiary for life. Jas Benson, who plead guilty to several charges of forgery in the Balt City Court, has been sentenced to the penitentiary for 9 years.

Mrd: on Oct 13, at Belvidere, Warren Co, N J, by Rev Jas Clark, Israel Smith, jr, Civil Engineer, of Detroit, Mich, to Frances E Bell, daughter of Cmder Chas H Bell, U S N.

Died: on Nov 9, at Carlisle Barracks, [Pa,] in his 26th year, Lt Geo S Humphreys, of the 2nd Regt U S Dragoons, son of the Rev Hector Humphreys, Pres of St John's College, Annapolis, MD. This young ofcr was a graduate of West Point in 1846.

Died: on Nov 11, at Rockville, Md, after a short illness, Mrs Maria Nourse, w/o Rev C H Nourse, & 2nd daughter of Wm Robertson. Thus, at the early age of 24 years, has one been cut down who in the midst of usefulness was beloved by all who knew her.

Died: on Wed last, in Richmond, Va, Mrs Mary Cowley, in her 95th year, the oldest inhabitant of the city. She was descended in a right line with the aborigines of this country, & has frequently seen the Father of his Country in the performance of his duty. She knew Richmond when it was nothing more than a country village, & has nursed more than 3,000 different individuals. At the burning of the Richmond theatre her name became memorable for the great number of extraordinary cures which she performed on those who were burned.

WED NOV 17, 1847

Our losses since we arrived in the basin of Mexico: Grand total of losses, 2,703, including 383 ofcrs. -Winfield Scott [to the Hon Wm L Marcy, Sec of War]

Wash Corp: 1-Cmte on Finance, reported resolution in relation to a certain claim made for a portion of the bequest of the late Matthew Wright, dec'd: adopted. 2-Cmte of Unfinished Business: ptns from H M Morfit & others & P Thyson & others: referred to the Cmte on Improvemtments. Same cmte: ptn of Anne R Dermott: postponed. 3-Cmte of Claims: bill for the relief of Ann Wheeler: passed. 4-Ptn of Isaac Selvey, praying to be refunded a sum erroneously paid to the Corp: referred to the Cmte of Claims.
5-Orris S Payne, W N Waters, & Henry L Cross are appointed Com'rs to hold an election on Nov 26, in the 1st Ward, to fill the vacancy occasioned by the resignation of Wm B Magruder: adopted. 6-Ptn from Messrs Ager & Brother & others: referred to the Cmte on Improvements. 7-Ptn of J S Miller & others: referred to the Cmte on the Canal.
8-Cmte of Claims: bill for the relief of Wm A Griffith: rejected. 9-Attention to the fall in battle of Capts Jas Graham, Chas Hanson, & Saml H Walker, 3 Ofcrs of the U S Army: all residents & 2 of them natives of Wash City. [Saml Hamilton Walker was born near Vansville, PG Co, Md, & was age 30 years at the time of his death. He became a citizen of Wash at an early age, & on the breaking out of the Florida war in 1836, he volunteered

for 12 months in that campaign, in the company which was raised in Wash City; he was employed during a great portion of time in scouting, & in the hazardous duty of carrying dispatches to the various posts during active hostilities; he remained in Florida some time, & pursued his business of a carpenter, & accumulated a considerable sum of money, with which he left for New Orleans, in order to locate himself in the South. He took care of sick & penniless old companions in New Orleans, & returned to Wash penniless, in 1840. He soon returned to Florida in the employment of the Tallahassee & St Jos' Railroad Co; in 1842 he left Florida for Galveston, Texas; connected himself as a private in the Texan army; joined Green's celebrated Mier expedition, & was captured & carried into the camp of Gen Ampudia, & there confined. He escaped & was recaptured & sent back to Salado, there to participate in the celebrated "black bean lottery" of Santa Anna, by which every 10th man was slaughtered, but which ordeal he successfully passed. Capt Cameron was shot because he was considered too brave a man for an enemy & his loss would be severely felt by the Texans. He again escaped & returned to Texas; raised a company of volunteers & marched to give his aid, arriving in time to participate in the battles of Palo Alto & Resaca, & rendered important services to Gen Taylor. A regt of Texan Rangers was raised, & he was called to the post of Lt Col, by the voice of his companions, under his old cmder, Capt John Hays, who had charge of the Regt as Col. At Monterey he received the Pres' appointment of Capt in the regt of Mounted Rifles. He repaired to New Orleans, & was sent to Wash by Col P F Smith to give his aid in equipping the regt of mounted riflemen. Some misunderstanding between his Colonel & himself, he was arrested for disobedience of orders: after the arrival of Gen Lane at Perote he was released, & assumed the command of his men, & proceeded in the advance towards Huamantla, & found the place occupied by Santa Anna with about 1,500 men, his own force consisting of about 200. He placed himself at the head of his command, ordered the charge, & received the fire from a masked battery, & with several of his men, fell, mortally wounded. His last words were "Never surrender!" An aged mother & relatives survive him.

Handsome brick dwlg completed, intended as a dwlg for A H Lawrence, on north side of E st, between 6th & 7th sts. The following mechanics were employed upon it: Messrs Berry & Butt, contractors & carpenters; Messrs McCollum & Glasgow, bricklayers; Mr Dougherty, marble cutter; Mills & Siberly, plasterers; & Mr G E Kirk, painter. The front doorway & marble steps are finished in a style of superior workmanship.

Naval: at San Francisco: U S ship **Columbus**, Com Biddle, to sail for the U S on Jul 25, via Valparaiso & Rio de Janiero. The frig **Congress**, Lt John H Livingston, commanding. Jul 27: arrival of razee **Independence**, Cmdor Shubrick, from Mazatlan. Also, the prizes **Malek Adkel**, Lt Schenck, & schnr **Julia**, Lt Selden, to be sold at San Francisco. At Monterey: sloop of war **Warren**, Cmder Hull, unfit for sea. The storeship **Erie**, Lt Com Watson. Prize ship **Admittance**, condemned by Judge Colton as lawful prize to the sloop of war **Portsmouth**. The sloop of war Portsmouth, Com Montgomery, & sloop of war **Cyane**, Com Dupont, at Mazatlan, blockading. The sloop of war **Preble**, Com Shields, at Callao. The storeship **Lexington**, Lt Com Baily, conveying 2 companies of Col Stevenson's Regt to San Jose, Cape St Lucas, Lower Calif, Lt Col Benton commanding.

Army: at Sonoma: Capt Brackett's company, Stevenson's Regt. At San Francisco: Maj Hardin commanding, with 2 companies of Col Stevenson's Regt. At Monterey: Col Mason, Military & Civil Govn'r; Co F, 3rd Regt of Artl, Lts Sherman, Loeson, & Minor. Capts Naglee & Shannon's companies of N Y volunteers, Stevenson's Regt. At Santa Barbara: Capt Lippett's company N Y volunteers. At the Cindad de los Angeles: Col Stevenson & 2 companies of his regt; Co C, 1st Dragoons, Lt Smith, commanding, Lts Davidson & Stevenson, & Assist Surgeon John Griffin. At San Diego: one company of Mormon volunteers: since discharged.

Hon Benj Swift, of St Albans, Vt, died suddenly at that town, last Thu, of an attack of apoplexy. -Express

For sale or rent: or exchange for other city property, the large 3 story brick house, with back bldg, formerly occupied by Mr Hayman, & at present by Mr Gordon. Possession given on Dec 1 next. Apply to Com S Cassin, Gtwn, or to R W Dyer, auct.

Report of Brevet Maj Gen W J Worth: Headquarters 1st Division: Tucubaya, Sep 10, 1847: to Capt Scott, A A Adj Gen, headquarters. Report of the battle of El Molino del Ray, fought & won on Sep 8, 1847. The names of those especially noticed by subordinate cmders, uniting in all they have said, & extending the same testimony to those not named.
Cavalry: the conduct of Capt Harden & Lt & Adj Oakes is noticed with high & deserved commendation.
Light Battery: Lts Hunt, Hays, & Clarke.
Drum's Artl: Lts Benjamin & Porter, 4th Artl.
Ordnance: Lts Hagner & Stone.
Light Btln: Capt Reeve, 8th Infty; Lts Peck, 2nd Artl, & Dent, 5th Infty.
2nd Artl: Lts & Adj Anderson & Lt Sedgwick.
3rd Artl: Capt R Anderson, & Lts Lendrum, Andrews, & Shields.
4th Infty: Brevet Maj Buchanan; Lt & Adj Prince; Lts Gore, Smith, Judah, Lincoln, McConnel, & Jones.
5th Infty: Capts Ruggles & McPhail; Lt & Adj Logenbeel; Lts Rossel, J P Smith, C S Hamilton, & Fowler.
6th Infty: Capt Hoffman; Lts E Johnson, Armistead, Wetmore, Buckner, & Adj Ernst
8th Infty: Brevet Maj Wright; Capts Scriven, L Smith, & Gates; & Lts Selden, Merchant, Morris, Pickett, & particularly Adj Longstreet.
Assaulting Column: Brevet Maj Wright, 8th Infty, commanding, [wounded;] Capt J L Mason, engineers, [wounded;] Capt M E Merriall, 5th Infty, [killed;] Capt A Cady, 6th Infty, [wounded;] Capt W H T Walker, 6th Infty, [wounded;] Capt J V Bomford, 8th Infty; 1st Lt M L Shackleford, 2nd Artl, [wounded;] 1st Lt C B Daniels, 2nd Artl, [wounded;] 1st Lt G O Haller, 4th Infty; 1st Lt J D Clarke, 8th Infty, [wounded;] 2nd Lt J F Farry, 3rd Artl, [killed;] 2nd Lt J G S Snelling, 8th Infty, [wounded;] 2nd Lt M Maloney, 4th Infty; 2nd Lt John G Foster, engineers, [wounded.]

For rent: a very pleasant convenient house, recently occupied by Alex'r N Zevely, on 6th st, between E & F sts. Inquire of Noah Fletcher.

Niagara Suspension Bridge: the contract for this stupendous work has been given to Mr Ellet, of Phil, at $180,000, to be finished by Jul 4, 1849. It is to be 750 feet in length, & be capable of sustaining a weight over & above its own of 450 tons. [Nov 18th newspaper: Chas Ellet, jr, of Phil, was appointed engineer: the entire costs could not exceed $190,000: structure is to have a railway track through the centre so as to pass locomotives & trains to accommodate the two railways that terminate there.]

A young gentleman named Crawford, son of the late Hon W H Crawfrod, of Georgia, & a member of the Jefferson Medical School of Phil, came to his death a few days ago, in that city, from the effects of a slight puncture received in one of his hands while engaged in dissecting.

THU NOV 18, 1847
On Sat week, the dwlg-house of widow Groves, about 1 mile westward from Wiscasset, Maine, was totally destroyed by fire, & the lady owner & her brother, Mr Reuben Young, were both consumed in the flames. They were aged people, upwards of 75 years old, the only ones in the house at the time of the fire.

York [Pa] Pres: 1-Mr Roland Good, 22 years old, was killed on Sat last, by being thrown from his horse whilst racing on the road with other youg men. 2-The daughter of Henry Deibler, of Earl township, aged 10 years, was burnt to death a short time since by her clothes taking fire.

The late Capt Abraham Robinson Johnston, the 2nd son of Col John Johnston, one of the earliest settlers of the State of Ohio, a companion in arms, in his 17th year, of the impetuous Wayne, in his expeditions against the hostile Indians of the then distant frontier of the Northwest, & for many years the Agent for Indian Affairs in Ohio & Indiana, was born at Piqua, Ohio, on May 23, 1815, & entered the Military Academy at West Point as a cadet in 1830, & graduated with distinguished honor. He had a great fondness for the study of the natural sciences, particularly geology & mineralogy, & while in pursuit of this study, he was precipitated into a deep & rugged chasm & fractured his leg, & was compelled to drag himself along, though suffering excruciating agony, until he was found. He was confined to a hospital until after the graduating of his class, but a private examination given him, he was soon appointed to the 1st Regt of Dragoons. On the promotion of Col Kearny to his present rank of brigadier, he was selected by the Gen, having been the adj of his regt, as his aid-de-camp, & accompanied him in his expedition to Calif, until Dec 6 last, when the enemy at San Pascual, Johnston was selected to lead the advance, which he did in the most gallant style, until, receiving a ball in the head, he fell from his horse, & expired without a groan. His bereaved father is solaced by the knowledge that his son was appreciated by the wise & the good. In the words of his General, "he can never be replaced-a loss to his family, to his regt, &, greatest of all, to his country. -Nat'l Intell, Washington, Nov 13.

A machine for making buckles by steam, which will finish 30 in a minute, has been invented by Wm Scarlett, of Newark, N J.

Richmond Examiner: The late 1st Lt Sidney Smith, 4th Infty, son of the late Col Austin Smith, of King Geo Co, Va, was a near & dear connexion of the Hon Wm Smith, Govn'r of the State of Va. In 1839 Lt Smith received the appointment of 2nd Lt of Infty; reported for duty at N Y: ordered to Carlisle Barracks, Pa: ordered to join his regt, then stationed at ***Fort Gibson***, Ark. He desired to go to Florida to participate in the war with the Seminole Indians, & his wishes were complied with. At the close of the war, on his way to Jefferson Barracks, he became acquainted with Sir Wm Drummond Stewart, then in Missouri, with a party on their way to the Rocky Mountains, to obtain information of the natural productions of that region. Lt Smith, with his personal friend, Lt Richd Graham, [who fell in the streets of Monterey, by his side, mortally wounded,] accompanied him. After his return he was ordered from Natchitoches, La, to Corpus Christi, under the command of Gen Taylor. He was in the thickest of the fight in the conflict in the streets of Monterey, where Watson & a host of other gallant souls fell. From Monterey he was ordered to join Gen Scott: landed at Vera Cruz & participated in all the glorious struggles of the American arms until they arrived as conquerors in the city of Mexico, when he fell mortally wounded in the street of that city, from a shot fired by a Mexican assassin from a housetop or window, as the American army was triumphantly marching into the Nat'l Palace & hoisting the star-spangled banner. His form now lies beneath a foreign sod. Peace to his ashes!

Rev Mr Norwood, says the Richmond Times, announced to the congregation of St Paul's Church, on Sun, that Mrs Daniel, the w/o Judge Peter V Daniel, of the U S Supreme Court, had died that morning from the effects of a nervous shock, produced by the fire that occurred near his residence on Sat night.

Circuit Court of Wash Co, D C-in Chancery. Geo Thomas, vs Cornelius F Van Ness, Martin H Hoffman & Gertrude his wife, Edw Van Ness, Eugene Van Ness, Chas W Van Ness, Matilda E Van Ness, & Richd Smith. Bill: John P Van Ness died indebted to the cmplnt by his promissory note, dated Jan 6, 1846, for $500, intestate, leaving the dfndnts [except said Richd Smith] his heirs at law; that the said Cornelius P Van Ness obtained letters of administration, but that the personal estate is insufficient to pay the debts, & the object of the bill is to obtain a sale of so much of the real estate of said John P Van Ness as may be necessary in aid of the personal estate to pay the debt of cmplnt, & the debts of such other creditors as shall choose to come in on the usual terms; & it appearing to the satisfaction of the Court that the said Cornelius P Van Ness, Martin H Hoffman & Gertrude his wife, Eugene Van Ness, & Matilda E Van Ness, & Chas W Van Ness, reside out of this District & beyond the jurisdiction of this Court, therefore, they are to appear in this Court, on or before the first Mon in Apr next. -Wm Brent, clerk -Redin, for cmplnt

Lt W M Walker, U S N, arrived in Wash City on Sat last from Vera Cruz, where he was, at the time of being relieved, in command of the U S schnr **Tampico**. From official papers Lt Spencer C Gist, who succeeded Lt Walker in that command, died on Oct 22. Lt Walker had himself been ill of the fever before he was relieved, but overcame the disease. Through the same channel we learn that Acting Master Frederic W Colly died at Vera Cruz on Nov 3 of the vomito.

Mrd: on Nov 17, in Alexandria, Va, by Rev Mr Johnson, Mr John Dixon to Fanny, daughter of Henry Chatham, all of that place.

By virtue of a writ of fieri facias, at the suit of Jas Wescott against the goods & chattels, lands & tenements of Jas Bush, I have seized & taken into execution, for sale, one hackney carriage, the property of said Jas Bush: sale on Nov 27, opposite the Centre Market-house. -John L Fowler, Constable

Passengers in the French steamship **N Y**, at N Y from Havre. Geo Zimmerman, Carl Gautzel, Doris Gautzel, Anna Melch, Jos Beckel, Geo Funk, Otto Standinger, Jacob Schern Renburger, Peter Eutziger, Rabette Hoff, Louis Hoff, Mary Bilfinger, Ludwig Lauterburg, Adolphe Pohl, Louis Delangle, Eugene & Elenore Fell; Sophia Charity & Hortensia Franenfelder, Antonio Richard, Andra Sternentz, Anna Gorseand, Jaques Bossard, Paul Durand, John Wilson, De Proetre Van Pannel, Casimer Bazil, Mr Fillot & dght, Mr Barbins, Mr Heintzen, Mr Borquet, Dederi Von Hosie, Geo Gohel, Richd Joesfer, Thos Louis, P Longis, Mr Rush & lady, Balli Blanchand & lady, Mr Stucker & lady, Gras Burdet, lady, & son, Jeanne Boudnier, Fanny Le Ballie, Jeanne Gouiss, Alex Morriss, Capt Weeks, Auguste Goerber, Messrs Lampel, De Raigenacher, Kessele, Crischer, Haas, Maugaan, Schans, Mantelard, Gelson, Eugene Vail, Oriduet, Bercoure, Reshen, Camelien, Allison, Amoise, Fremont, Pelisfur La Barbier & son, De Framee-40 in second cabin.

Passengers in the ship **Sir Robert Peel**, at N Y from London. A Rankin & lady, Mrs A M Vanderlop, T D Copp, G Boddington, J Earl, of N Y; J K Robinson, J Walker, H Jergar, Capt P Loury, S Hopkins, Dr C Steane, G Adlard, Mrs M A Wilton, Mrs M Kettle, Mr L Kettle, Miss M Kettle, Miss A Hannegner, J Poole, L Isaacks & lady, J J Smith, R Newbould, A Isaacks, of London, & 80 in the steerage.

FRI NOV 19, 1847

New Orleans Picayune of Nov 11. Among the passenger on the ship **Day** were Maj Iturbide, prisoner of war, & Lt Sears, 2nd Artl, bearer of dispatches to Washington.

Report of the killed & wounded at San Jose, between the commencement & termination of the siege of Puebla. Wounded: [s-slightly: S-severely: dg-dangerously: m-mortally: k-killed: w-wounded]

1st Pa Btln of volunteers: Co A: wounded:

Geo Rusheberger, w/S	David Lindsay, w/s	Jas Bowden, w/s
Jas McCutcheon, w/S	Henry Linch, w/s	R Wilson, w/s
John Hoover, w/s	Mansfield Mason, w/s	John Donlan, w/s

Co C: Wm Eurick, killed; Chas Collison, w; John B Herron, w

Co I: John Preece, K; D W Yarlott, w/s; Jas Ellis, w/s; Sgt Domminick Devanny, w/s; Luke Floyd, w/S

Co K:

Capt E H Jones, k	John H Herrod, k	H Krutzotman, k
John C Gilchrist, k	F B Johns, k	Jas Phillips, k

Wm A Phillips, k
S D Sewell, k
Wm Smitz, k
D S Vernoy, k
F Vandyke, k
Jos Wilson, k
Saml Troyer, k
Capt John Herron, w/s
Thos B Furnam, w/s
A E Marshall, w/s
W C Winebiddle, w/s
R Reed, w/s
Co D: Capt Sylventer Beesly, w/s; John McLellan, w/S; Jas Lamber, w/S
Missing: John Longstaff, Co K; M Stemlar, Co C
Voltigeur Regt: Pvt John H Burgess, killed; John Wilson, Co A, w/s; David Richette, Co F, w/s
Co D: 3rd Dragoons: Eli Stewart, wounded
Quartermaster's dept: A B Duncan, w/s; Wm Waddell, w/s; Wm Johnson, w/S
Gaudalupe: Wm Patterson, Co E, 2nd Artl, w/S; Josiah Blair, mounted rifles, w/S; Saml Houpt, w/s;
Wm Schultz, w/s
Genr'l hospital: J P Hardy, Co G, voltigeurs, w/S; John H Rowney, Co K, 2nd Artl, w/S; T Russell, 2nd Regt light Dragoons, w/S
Field & Staff: Mr A Wengierski, secretary to Govn'r Childs, w/S
Dr Bunting's hospital: Sgt Wm Deal, w/S; John Biers, 2nd Pa volunteers, w/S; Wm Curry, 2nd Artl, w/S.
Sgt Diel's conduct is highly spoken of by Dr Bunting. All the invalids of the hospital capable of firing a musket did good service from the roof of the bldg.
Spy company: Ofcr John Mose, wounded, since killed.
J Gordero, 2 brothers Dominguez & Jose Servezo, wounded
Servant to Col Childs: Danl Sims, wounded
In the battle of Atlizco the enemy are said to have left 200 dead on the road. The Flag give the following as our loss:
Wounded: Bernard Rork, mortally, [since dead]
Mathias Rautter, w/s
Josiah Crowin, w/S
All 3 were attaché to or serving with Capt Ford's Co D, 3rd Dragoons.

Battle of Huamantla-Oct 10, 1847. Killed, Cpl Merriken, privates Hugenen & Tarbox. Wounded, Cpl Glanding, [since died,] Menchem, w/S; Rabor, lost a leg; Welch, Wayne, McGill, Scott, & Myers, slightly. Missing, Sgt Goslin; privates Dement, Darlington, Collins, McCleary, & Richards, of company C, rifles. Capt Lewis' company, private Murry, wounded. Capt Loyall's company, killed, private Richardson; slightly wounded, privates Fornely & Milton. The whole force under Gen Lane returned to camp that night.

The remains of the lamented Capt Walker, & his faithful servant Davis, are now in the Castle of Perote, having been brought from Huamantla by order of Col Wynkoop. They will be forwarded to the U S by a large train, which is shortly expected from Mexico.

Mr Vose, who since 1839 has been a partner in the Providence Journal ofc, is dead. [No date-current news.]

Wanted immediately: 2 young men of character & address, to act as agents for a new magazine, one for Alexandria, & the other for Gtwn. Men of energy can make from $2 to $3 a day, & more. Inquire of Ezra Bauder, corner of F & 12th sts.

The Tenn volunteers: following companies that have been accepted to constitute the regt: Capt Newman, of Knox Co; Capt Bounds, of Hawkins Co; Capt Thomason, of Grainer Co; Capt Reese, of Jefferson Co; Capt Dill, of McMinn Co; Capt Vaughn, of Monroe Co; Capt McKenzie, of Meigs Co; Capt Stuart, of Rhea Co; Capt Fagg, of Blount Co; & Capt McClelland, of Sullivan Co.

Household & kitchen furniture at auction: on Nov 22, at the commission store of W B Lewis, on Pa ave, near 11th st. -A Green, auctioneer

First number of a weekly newspaper, The Family Companion, published in N Y C by Howard F Snowden, & edited by Chas Burdett, was received yesterday.

The Solar Gas Lights prepared by Mr Crutchett for the Capitol, were exhibited last night, for the first time, in the presence of a numerous company of ladies & gentlemen. The blaze of light emitted from the numerous burners in the splendid chandeliers in the Senate & Reps Halls astonished every beholder. After the exhibition in the interiorof the Capitol, the burners in the great Lantern were also ignited, & appeared to yield a magnificent light.

Died: on Nov 9, near the Wash Navy Yard, Lewis Edmund, y/son of Edmond B & Mary Duvall, aged 11 months & 6 days. [Balt Sun]

PG County Court, sitting as a Court of Equity: Nov Term, 1847. Tresa Brooks et al, cmplnts, vs Geo W Dunlop, exc of Jos Dunlop et al, dfndnt. This suit is instituted by the creditors of said Jos Dunlop, dec'd; the object is to procure a decree for the sale of certain real estate of which the dec'd died seized, lying in said county, [Md] to pay the debts of said dec'd. The bill state that said dec'd was indebted to said cmplnts in the amount of $350; that the debts became due & were not paid; that he died in Dec, 1846, insolvent as to his personal estate; that there are heirs at law of said dec'd, namely, Jas Dunlop & Trulove Dunlop, who reside out of the state of Md. Same to appear on or before Jan 10th next. -A C Magruder, Ch J -J B Brooke, clk -S E Williams, for cmplnts

SAT NOV 20, 1847

Died: on Nov 19, after a long & painful illness, Mrs Winifred Margaret Tewell, in her 54th year. Her funeral is from her late residence on 3rd st, between G & H sts, this afternoon, at 3 o'clock.

Mail robbers punished. The U S Circuit Court at Milledgevile, on Nov 11. Two convicted of stealing letters containing money: Jas L Lampkin, driver on the line running from Athens to Gainesville, & Ezekiel Hewett, mail rider on the route from Talbotton to Macon. Lampkin was sentenced to 15, & Hewett to 10 years' confinement in the penitentiary.

Official dispatches: reports of the Cmders of Divisions to the Gen-in-Chief. Report of Maj Gen Pillow. Headquarters 3rd Div U S Army, Mexico, Sep 18, 1847. On Sep 13th, Lt Reid, in command of one company of the N Y regt & one of marines, came forward in advance of the other troops of the command, participated in the assault, & was severely wounded. Though the gallant Col Trousdale was badly wounded by 2 balls which shattered his right arm, still he maintained his position with great firmness. Capt Scantland was shot through the head, & was supposed to have been mortally wounded, but is yet alive, with increasing hopes of his recovery. The command of the 14th Regt devolved upon Lt Col Hebert after Trousdale was wounded. The ladders arrived & efforts were made to scale the walls. Lt Col Johnson received 3 wounds, but they were all slight & did not at all arrest his daring movements. Capt Barnard seized the colors of his regt upon the fall of the color-bearer, scaled the wall with them unfurled, & has the honor of planting the first American standard in the work. Capt Biddle, though so much enfeebled by disease as to be scarce able to walk, left his sick bed on this great occasion & was among the foremost to enter the works. Col Ransom, 9th Infty, fell dead from a shot in the forehead while at the head of his command, waving his sword & leading his splendid regt up the heights to the summit of Chapultepec. I had myself been a witness to his heroic conduct until a moment before, when I was cut down by his side. My heart bleeds with anguish at the loss of so gallant an ofcr. The command of his regt devolved upon Maj Seymour, who faltered not. Lt Selden, of the 8th Infty, of Capt McKenzie's command, one of the first to mount the scaling ladder, fell from its summit severely wounded. Lt Rogers, 4th Infty, & Lt Smith, 5th Infty, of the same party, were both distinguished by their heroic courage & daring, & were both killed while leading on their men. Suffering as I am from my wound, which forces me to write while lying on my back, I trust I shall be pardoned for any omission which may have occurred in this report. Surgeon Slade, of the 15th Regt, was upon the field & in the charge. Among the enemy killed were Gen Perez & Col Cano, of the engineers, & Gen Saldana was wounded on Sep 12. We took about 800 prisoners, among whom were Maj Gen Bravo, Brig Gens Monterde, Nonega, Doramentes, & Saldana. -Gid J Pillow, Maj Gen U S Army -To Capt H L Scott, A A A Gen, Headquarters of the Army

Orphans Court of Wash Co, D C. Letters of administration on the personal estate of Hannah G Corcoran, late of said county, dec'd. -Stan J Murray, adm

On Sat last, as Mr Jas Kendall, of Phil, was standing near the Vt & Mass railroad, in South Royalton, with his horse & wagon, a short distance from him, on the opposite side of the track, he perceived that the horse was becoming frightened at the approach of the gravel train. Mr Kendall started upon the run for the purpose of securing his horse, &, although the bell was rung, & the hands cried to him to stop, he attempted to cross the track in front of the engine, but tripped & fell directly upon the track, the whole train passing over & killing him instantly.

City of Mexico: a letter from Mr Kendall, writes that both Gens Shields & Pillow are out. The wound of the latter is not to have been as severe as was first represented. It was a bruise rather than a wound, & was received in the grove at the foot of Chapultepec.

Report of Brevet Maj Gen Worth: Headquarters 1st Division, City of Mexico, Sep 16, 1847. Lt Jackson, who, although he had lost most of his horses, & many of his men, continued chivalrously at his post, combating with noble courage. On the 14th my troops & heavy guns advanced into the city, & occupied the Alameda to the point where it fronts the palace, Shortly afterwards a straggling assassin-like fire commenced from the house-rops. The first shot struck down Col Garland, badly wounded, & later in the day Lt Sidney Smith was shot down mortally wounded-since dead. I have to make acknowledgments to Cols Garland & Clark, brigade cmders, as also to their respective staffs; to Lt Cols Duncan & Smith; Capt McKenzie, commanding, & the following ofcrs composing the storming party; Lt Simpson, 2nd Artl, & Johnson, 3rd Artl, [light btln;] Lts Rodgers & McConnell, 4th Infty; Capt Ruggles & Lt J P Smith, 5th Infty; Lts Armistead & Morrow, 6th Infty, & Lt Selden, 8th Infty; to Lt Col Belton, 3rd Artl; Maj Lee, 4th; Brevet Maj Montgomery, 8th Infty; to Lt Jackson, 1st Artl, [Magruder's light battery;] Lt Hunt, 2nd Artl, [Duncan's light battery;] 3rd Artl; S Smith, Haller, & Grant, 4th Infty, especially; & Lt Judah, 4th Infty; Lt & Adj Lugenbeel, 5th; & Lt E Johnson, 6th, [much distinguished;] Capts Bomford & Gates, & Lts Merchant & Pickett, [each distinguished for gallantry & zeal;] the young & gallant Rodgers & J P Smith, lts of 4th & 5th Infty, killed with the storming party; Capt Edwards, voltigeurs, & Lt Hagner, ordnance, commanded mounted howitzers, placed upon bldgs, & rendered effective service, well sustained by the intelligent ordnance men. Of the staff: Lts Stephens, Smith, & McClellan, engineers. The first was badly wounded. I must not omit a respectful notice of the very intelligent enlisted men of the sappers & miners, & desire to apply the same remark to Capt Huger & Lt Hagner, & their excellent men. Capt Mackall, Assist Adj Gen, wounded; Capt Pemberton, wounded; Lt Semmes, navy; Lt Wood, aid-de-camp; & Lt Hardcastle, topographical engineers, & Woodbridge, division commissary; Maj Borland & G W Kendall, volunteer aids-de-camp, the latter wounded; each exhibited habitual gallantry, intelligence, & devotion. -W J Worth, Brevet Maj Gen Com'g 1st Division. To Capt Scott, A A A Gen, Headquarters, Mexico

City of Mexico: a letter from Mr Kendall, writes that both Gens Shields & Pillow are out. The wound of the latter is not to have been as severe as was first represented. It was a bruise rather than a wound, & was received in the grove at the foot of Chapultepec.

MON NOV 22, 1847

For rent: well-furnished house entire, or a part of the house only: formerly occupied by Mr H Van Rensselaer, M C, but for the last Congress by Mr Wm S Miller, M C. Located in full view of the Pres' House. Apply to D A Gardner, on G st, near 15th st.

Stage accident on Nov 17 near Brownsville, on the stage from Cumberland, in passing the mountains, was upset over a bank, & W H Gairtray & lady, of N Y, were injured. H G Hearth, of New Orleans, was severely cut in the head. They were removed to a farm house, & all are now doing well.

Mrd: on Nov 16, in St Peter's Church, by Rev Mr Vanhoesigh, Edmund V Rice to Miss Ann Maria McCarthy, all of Wash City.

The late Maj Levi Twiggs was born in Richmond Co, Georgia, on May 21, 1793: was the 6th son of Maj Gen John Twiggs, of Revolutionary memory. The present Maj Gen David E Twiggs is the 5th son of the same illustrious sire. At the declaration of war against Great Britain, in 1812, the subject of the present notice, then just 19, desirous of entering the service, but failing to obtain the sanction of his parents at that time, he continued his studies at the Athens college, in his native State, for some months longer. On learning the news of the capture of the frig **Macedonian** by the ship **Constitution**, under Cmdor Decatur, he immediately left college, & solicited again his parents' consent to apply for an appointment in the marine corps, which was now granted. He entered this corps as 2nd lt, on Nov 10, 1813. In 1822 he united himself in marriage to a dght of the deceased Capt McKnight, of the marine corps, & niece of Cmdor Decatur-the afflicted lady who now deplores his death. On Jun 2, 1847, he sailed for Mexico, having solicited active service. On Jul 16 he left for the interior with Gen Pierce's brigade, & reached Puebla on Aug 6, which place he left with Maj Gen Quitman's division a few days after, & on Sep 13 he fell, at the head of his command, leading them to the assault at the storming of Chapultepec, pierced by a bullet through the heart. The death of his gallant son, Geo Decatur Twiggs, who fell a volunteer in Maj Lally's command at the Nat'l Bridge, on Aug 12, on the way to join his uncle the General, whose aid he was to become, had already excited in our city a deep-felt sympathy for the breaved mother. He had just entered his 20th year, a youth of the finest talents, already distinguished in the walks of literature, & pursuing his legal studies.

A Frenchman, giving his name Casimer Antonious, was arrested in Dayton, Ohio, on Nov 11, charged with passing counterfeit gold eagles, & committed to the county jail. They are so well coined as to deceive the best judges.

Mr Goodman, a citizen of Gibson Co, Tenn, has petitioned the Legislature of that State for permission to sell groceries & liquors without taking out a license, on the ground that he is the father of 22 children, all living.

Masonic Funeral. The remains of the late Robt Coltman, Warden of the U S Penitentiary, who died suddenly last Fri, were interred yesterday evening at Congress Burying Ground. The corpse was drawn to the place of interment on the funeral car of the Franklin Fire Co. 2 bands of music playing solemn dirges formed a part of the funeral procession.

On the morning of Oct 30, Lt Jas R Scott, of the 7th Infty, was found dead in his state-room on board the steamer **James L Day**, on her last voyage from New Orleans to Vera Cruz. He is supposed to have died of apoplexy.

TUE NOV 23, 1847

Interesting relic for sale. The identical PRINTING PRESS at which Dr Benj Franklin worked while in London in 1725-26 is offered for sale. It is now in the U S Patent Ofc at Wash, where it was deposited on its arrival from London in 1842. Address the Hon Edmund Burke, Com'r of Patents, Wash, or John B Murray, 12 Old Slip, N Y.

The service of plate, which was being manufactured at the time of his death, & intended to be presented to the late Silas Wright, as a token of the high respect of the merchants & others of N Y C for his private & public character & services, was on Fri presented, pro forma, to his widow, by the Hon John A Dix, at the Stuyvesant Institute, before a large audience. In dollars & cents it is valued at $18,029, & weighs near 50 pounds, comprising 118 pieces. Gen Dix is to present it in person to Mrs Wright, at her private residence.

Capt Bronaugh, formerly of the Balt btln, was recently killed near Puebla, where he had been acting Postmaster. It appears that, before the siege of that place, 26 of them went on an expedition to retake a number of mules that had been captured by Mexicans. Soon after starting they were surrounded by a large body of lancers, & almost annihilated. 10 were killed on the spot, 2 or 3 were severely wounded, & a few taken prisoners. A son of Capt Nones, of the U S Revenue Service, commanded the party, & was severely wounded, but has since recovered. -Balt Clipper

C P Sengstack was yesterday appointed by the Pres Warden to the U S Penitentiary in Wash City, in place of Robt Coltman, who died on Friday.

A S H White returns his thanks to his fellow-citizens for the assistance rendered on the occasion of the fire at his dwlg on Sunday afternoon.

Mrd: on Oct 28, at Bladensburg, PG Co, Md, Col Saml Hamilton to Miss Anna Maria, a daughter of Elias B Caldwell, dec'd, formerly of Wash City.

Died: on Nov 11, on his birthday, at Millwood, Clark Co, Va, Paul, 2nd son of the Rev W G H & Frances C Jones, aged 15 years.

WED NOV 24, 1847

A daring murder was perpetrated near Camden, N J, on Sat, upon the person of Mr Izry Roberts, an esteemed farmer & citizen, & a leading member of the Society of Friends, in that neighborhood. He had been to market in Phil, with produce, & left for home about 6 o'clock, & about 7:30 his lifeless body, still warm, was found in his wagon, nearly a mile from Camden, covered with a buffalo robe, & his brains dashed almost entirely out. The dec'd was 40 years of age, & leaves a wife & 6 children. A reward of $500 has been offered for the arrest of the murderer.

Bath [Maine] Tribune: 2 French children, Thos Perro, aged 6 years, & Mary Perkett, 4 years] were accidentally shot, on Wed week, at the south part of the city, from a charge fired from a pistol, with intent to kill a dog. The boy died instantly; the girl was severely wounded, but there is hope she will recover.

Wash Corp: 1-Cmte of Claims: bill for the relief of Richd Rice: passed.

Wanted, a Nurse. Inquire at Mrs Ann S Hill's, H st, between 14th & 15th sts.

For rent: the brick house now occupied by Mr J B Moore, on 8th st, between E & F sts; possession given on Dec 5. Apply on the premises, or to A Green, auctioneer, near Brown's Hotel, Pa ave.

For rent: the house at present occupied by Wm Douglass, near the Smithsonian bldgs, corner of 9th & B sts. Inquire on the premises.

$10 reward for the apprehension of Ben, servant of the late Lt John T McLaughlin, who absconded on Nov 20. He is about 16, black, & tall for his age. Information to be sent to the residence of Lt Chas Steedman, corner of F & 21st sts.

Rev Jos Bennett, an orthodox clergyman of the first church in Woburn, Mass, committed suicide on Fri, by cutting his throat. He was about 55 years of age, & had been but recently married to a young lady. He had been subject to fits of melancholy since the death of his first wife.

A dispute about the possession of land in the German colony, in Texas, between Dr Schubert & Mr Spiess, the director of the company. In an attempt to expel Dr Schubert, a melee occurred, in which Capt Sommers, [friend of Schubert,] was killed by a musket ball. A German, named Bostic, fired, but to no effect. One of the assailants, Rohrdoeff, was killed. Mr Spiess has disappeared. Mr Rohrdorff was a landscape painter of superior skill.

J M Gilbert, formerly of the Exchange Hotel, has taken the pleasantly located house on the corner of 4½ st & Pa ave, south side, which he will open, for the accommodation of members of Congress & other boarders, on or before Dec 1.

Passengers going abroad: in the American steamer **Washington** from N Y for Southampton. Thos Achelis, Mrs Achelis, Thos Achelis, jr, Mary Achelis, Anna M Achelis, F Achelis, Geo Achelis, & servant, Melchior Ducker, Mrs Ducker, Henry Ducker, Anna M Ducker, N Y; E Weymann, Mrs E Weymann, Rio; Chas Merle, Oscar Henrichs, Geo T Siemon, H Goslin, S Cutter, jr, Dr Shew, Geo Gibson, John Levy, Isaac Levy, H Arppen, E Beck, S Gueymard, W R Mercer, Mrs Mercer, N Y; Rev R Earp, jr, Mrs Earp, Evan Morris, Phil; Mrs Harrison & child, New Orleans; Fred'k Focke, H G Gerdes, Balt; Mrs Freemantle & child, Otto Tank & dghtr, N Y; Chas M Walcott, Boston; Augustus Helwig, Hesse; W N Nopetsch, Altona; Chas Mogg, England.

In the ship **Fidelia** from N Y for Liverpool: Mr Chas Jerome, New Haven, Conn; Mr Armstrong & lady, Albany; Messrs F S Martine, Wm J Clark, G W Bell, N Y; Col Sherburne, bearer of dispatches to the Legation at London; Mr Albert F Hunt, Mrs Hamilton, England; Mr Hertz, Germany; Mr Budley, Canada.

The Very Rev F Verhagen, Provincial of the Society of Jesus, will preach in St Peter's Church, Capitol Hill, tomorrow, Thanksgiving Day, at 11 o'clock. The public are respectively invited.

St John's Institute, Mount Alban, near Gtwn, will be reopened on Nov 20, under the charge of the Rev A Ten Broeck. Inquiries may be made of the Rev Smith Pyne, Wash, & of Saml J Donalson, or Hugh Davey Evans, Balt, Md.

Mr Isaac Rich, one of the proprietors of the mines of that name, at Pottsville, was instantly killed, on Oct 23, by an explosion of fire-damp. He was at the time observing the progress of the work.

Johnson D May was sentenced to 5 years confinement in the Penitentiary, on Oct 19, in the St Chas [Mo] Circuit Court, for attempting to burn the steamboat **St Croix**, in 1845.

Telegraphic dispatch to the Phil Inquirer, dated at Louisville on Monday night, says: the steamboat **Carolinian**, from Pittsburg bound to Pearl river, burst her boilers on Fri last, when near Shawnestown. Mr Peacock, of Pittsburg, a passenger, was instantly killed, & one of four deck hands scalded, died.

Circuit Court-Wash. Yesterday the Court & jury were engaged the entire day with the cause of W B Bowie, exc of Edmund Coolidge, vs Peter G Washington, which was ably contested by the learned counsel. The jury returned a verdict for the dfndnt on the ground of usury.

THU NOV 25, 1847

The latest accounts from Santa Fe, [to Oct 17,] furnish the annexed list of deaths, from sickness, in the first regt of Illinois volunteers:

Elias Allen
Thos Angell
Felix Ammons
Jas Baker
Wm F Black
David S Blackman
B F Brown
A J Campbell
Jas Carr
Wm A Carr
John W Collins
Robt Easley
Lewis Hiberner
Wm M Hobbs
John Jewett
Wm Jones
Wm N Jones
Dan McArty
F McDaniels
John McDickens
Thos Morrow
Oliver Morton
Capt F Niles
H C Norris
Jacob Penrod
Geo Petra
Isam Pierson
J Posey
Edgar Poole
Spencer Pratt
Wm H Prents
G M Seely
Wm Turner
Harvey Tresner
Jas Vincent
Jos Watkins

For sale or rent: a 2 story fame & 2 new two-story brick dwlgs: all on 4th st west, near I st north. Apply to Matthew Gault at the residence of Wm G Deale, on G near 5th st.

Leesburg [Va] Chronicle of the 18th: the death of the gallant young Capt Calwell, from a letter dated Oct 21, received at the White Sulphur Spings, in which the writer, Geo Cook, who was the servant of Capt Calwell, states that the body of his master was then at Jalapa, & that he would bring it home with him. This is the only intelligence that has been received in regard to his death. -Rich Rep

A shocking accident happened to Govn'r Whitcomb, on Nov 16, on the railroad at Edinburgh. He had stepped off the cars for a few moments, & was about stepping on again while the cars were in motion. His foot slipped, & he fell between the cars & the platform of the depot, the cars whirling him around, & crushing his thighs as they went. The Govn'r was insensible for some time after he was extricated, but finally recovered his consciousness. From what we are told, it will be some time, if ever, before he can recover. -Indiana State Sentinel, Nov 17

Mrd: on Nov 16, at the residence of Z Jacob, in Wheeling, Mr Jas N Montgomery, of Lewisburg, Va, to Miss Ann S Jacob.

Mrd: on Tue, by Rev John C Smith, Mr Jas Hall to Miss Eliz Lacy, both of Fairfax Co, Va.

Died: on Sep 7, at Belleville, Ill, the residence of his son, after a week's illness, Mr John Galbraith, in his 79th year, a native citizen of Rockbridge Co, Va, long known as the proprietor of the Bridge Tavern, on the Valley road, 12 miles above Lexington.

Passengers in the steamship **Acadia** from Liverpool: for Halifax: Hon Francis Brady, Chief Justice of Newfoundland; Hon Edw Palmer, Rev Mr Southerland, Free Church of Scotland; Col Williams, Mrs Baker, Miss Baker, Rev Mr Tompkins, lady, 4 children & servants. For Boston: Mr John Randall, of N Y; Mr Petrie, Miss Petrie, Mrs Randall, & Master Randall, of Phil; Mr Mason, lady & maid, Mrs Sowdon, Mrs Daly, 2 Misses Daly, Dr E M Greenway, lady & servant, Balt; Chas Stoddard & lady, Mobile; Thos Rogers, jr, J Elmer, New Orleans; Mr Redpath & lady, Thos Prosser & lady, N Y; T H Stanley, lady & maid, W Muir, her Birtannic Majesty's Consul at New Orleans; Mr Jones, Dr Daniell, dght & servant, of Georgia; Geo Endicott & lady, N Y; H Andrews, Smithfifeshire, Scotland; Prof Nichol, Univ of Glasgow; A M Forbes, E G Howe, Hartford; Geo H Bicking, Phil; Mr Bowman & lady, B Thorne, J G Stouse, New Orleans; Mr Cook, E P Williams, N Y; Dr Sonsby, Geo Pollock, John Lloyd, Mr Caldwell, John Curell, Mr Leisy, New Orleans; S C Jury, Mobile; J S Ropes, Boston; F Wood, Robt Leslie, Va:; Miss E P Andrews, Miss Andrews, P Bigelow, bearer of dispatches, Boston; Mr Harris, lady & infant, Commissariat Staff; Jas Jones, R C Fuller & lady, J B Toulman & lady, Mobile; Mr Lewis, jr of S C.

Trustee's sale of extensive & valuable real estate on West River, Anne Arundel Co, slaves, horses, cattle, & farming implements. By decree of the Court of Chancery of Md, passed in a cause in said Court, on Oct 28, 1846, wherein Geo Mackubin & Jas Iglehart were cmplnts, & Osborn S Harwood, dfndnt, the subscriber, as trustee, will offer at public sale, on Dec 14 next, the personal estate, ***Cherry Hill***, by survey, 621 acres of land, more or less, in West River: laid off into 4 lots: 197 acres; 175 acres; 120 acres; & the 131 acres, has a comfortable frame dwlg, used as an overseer's house. Also, a large number of valuable slaves for life, of both sexes & all ages. Also, a large number of horses & cattle. Apply to Sprigg Harwood, by mail to West River, Anne Arundel Co, ot to the subscriber. -Frank H Stockett, trustee, Annapolis, Md.

Died: on Nov 8, at Stephentown, N Y, of fever, Arvin Wood. He was in the meridian of life & in the midst of usefulness, leaving a wife & 4 children, besides a large circle of relatives & friends, to mourn his early departure.

SAT NOV 27, 1847

Naval School: Annapolis, Md, Nov 13, 1847. Meeting for the erection of a Monument to the memory of the late Passed Midshipmen H A Clemson & J Ringgold Henson. F G Clarke was called to the chair, & W V Gillis appointed secretary. Ofcrs appointed: F G Clarke, M J Smith, & W H Weaver. That the name of the late Midshipman Wingate Pilsbury, who was drownd while in the execution of his duty off Vera Cruz on Jul 24, 1846, be placed upon one side of the monument. That the name of the late Midshipman T B Shubrick, who was killed while gallantly performing his duty at the navy battery on shore, near Vera Cruz, during its bombardment by our forces, also occupy one side. That the Monument be erected within the limits of the Naval School of Annapolis, by the advice of the Hon Sec of the Navy.

The Times, edited by Duff Green: this paper will be published weekly in Washington. Publication ofc Pa ave, corner 4½ st. Agents: Hugh Latham, Alexandria; Brooke, Shillington & Co, Washington.

The Sat Evening News, edited & published weekly by Wm Thompson, at Wash: now in its 2nd volume.

Sale of valuable property in Phil Row, Wash, by deed of trust, on Nov 30.
-Henry Benner, Saml Tolman, trustees -A Green, auctioneer

The subscriber, being about to resume business as a Restaurateur, offers for rent the House he now resides in. Apply to the subscriber or to Aquilla Ricketts, G st, near the War Dept. -Jos Boulanger

An aged man named Parsons, of Enfield, Conn, was run over & killed by the morning train of cars from Hartford for Springfield, Conn, on Thu. He appeared to notice the approaching train but did get off, as the engineer supposed he would do; the locomotive consequently struck him & killed him instantly.

Mr Peboys has details of the marriage of Lady Jemima Montague, daughter of the first Earl of Sandwich, to Mr Carteret, in 1665, in his diary.

John J Kirkbride, well know as the carrier of the penny papers of Phil, drowned in the canal at Conshohocken on Sat last. We are left entirely to conjectar to account for his untimely end. He was a reputable citizen, & has left a widow & large family to mourn his loss. -Norristown Herald

By a writ of venditioni exponas, at the suit of John Davison, against the goods & chattels, lands & tenements, rights & credits of Barney Barry, I have levied on the interest of said Barry on lot 15 in square 348, Wash City, & will sell the same at public sale on Dec 26. -Horatio R Maryman, constable

Extraordinary surgical operation: performed by Dr Robt Thompson, of Columbus, Ohio, [Surgeon Genr'l of that State] recently in Etna, on Mrs Hugh P Lytle. The entire liver, weighing 29½ pounds, was removed from her body. Without a liver, she survived 12 days. [Post mortem examination disclosed the fact that it was not the liver, but an ovarian tumor, which had occupied the greatly increased concavity of the diaghragm, carrying the liver before it, as well as every other possible part of the abdominal cavity.]

Mrd: on Nov 17, at Charleston, Kanawha Co, Va, by Rev Jas M Brown, Mr Wm Frazier, of Staunton, Va, to Miss Susan Massie Lewis, daughter of Jas A Lewis, of Charleston.

Mrd: on Nov 23, by Rev Smith Pyne, Saml B Elliott, U S Navy, to Juliana Marshall, eldest daughter of J K Randall, of Wash City.

Died: on Nov 12, in Pittsfields, Mass, at the residence of her father, Gen Nathan Willis, after a long illness, Mrs Lucy F Larned, w/o Col Benj F Larned, Assist Paymaster Gen U S Army.

Household & kitchen furniture, & piano forte, at auction: on Dec 1, at the residence of J R Moore, on 8th st, between E & F sts. -A Green, auctioneer

MON NOV 29, 1847

The U S store ship **Supply** sailed on Fri from N Y, under command of Lt Lynch, on a scientific expedition to the Dead Sea. The following are the names of her ofcrs:
Lt Commanding, W F Lynch
1st Lt, A M Pennock
2nd Lt J B Dale
Purser, J T Mason, jr
Passed Assist Surgeon, J Thornby
Acting Master, Bayse N Westcott
Passed Midshipmen, Wm B Fitzgerald, Richmond Aulick, S Quackenbush
Capt's Clerk, F E Lynch

Valuable improved property on Pa ave for sale at Public Auction: on Dec 15, property on Pa ave: part of lots 17 & 18 in square B, with a 3 story brick dwlg & store: dwlg is occupied by Mrs Hipkins as a boarding house. Lots 26 & 27 in square B, with a 3 story brick dwlg & large back bldg & store: occupied by Mrs Hamilton as a boarding house & the store by Mr J H Buthmann as a wine store. -R W Dyer, auct

Passengers to & from Europe.
In the ship **Rajah**, at N Y from Havre: Miss N Signer, Miss C Jeiu, Miss M Desmasier, & 208 in steerage.
In the ship **Huguenot**, at N Y from Liverpool: John Taylor, Mrs Taylor, U S; Miss Taylor, England; Miss Swail; Dr Schaum, Germany; & 196 in steerage.
In the packet ship **Columbia**, at N Y from Liverpool: H Lodge, D Oakley, John Loyd, Jas Ferguson, Capt Hawkins, Mr & Miss Furber; & 390 in steerage.
In the ship **Liberty**, at N Y from Liverpool: Mrs Norton, of Conn; Miss Wilde, of England; Capt W Hope, of British Army; Thos Nutall, England; Wm R Gelderd, Dr Geo Rex, R I; & 270 in steerage.
In the steamship **N Y**, from N Y for Havre: Messrs Laporte, Raymond Gascon, Ant Thibaudier, A M, Della Corre, Fanfernot, John Beck, Jos Amachler, Ernest Peltzer, Jas Keogh, Nicholas Schacler, Mr Hourdequire.

The Marshal of the Russian nobility, Von Witchek Von Cechanowick, a nobleman well known by his extensive travels in Europe & the East, was lately shot by a gamekeeper, who mistook him for a wild beast, on account of his head covering. The dying man fully exculpated the innocent author of his death.

Miles J Rockwood accidentally fell upon a circular saw in his mill, in Brookline, N H, on Nov 12, & was cut in so horrible a manner, that he survived but 4 hours. He had been married only 3 weeks before.

On Sunday last Miss Eliz Whitney, daughter of Theodore Whitney, of this town, was rescued at the foot of Goat Island, when swept away by the sea. A gentleman, seeing her peril, rescued her. -Niagara Falls Iris

For rent: the residence at the corner of G & 22nd sts, recently in the occupancy of Lt Maury, Superintendent of the Observatory. Apply to either of the subscribers, Chas E Eckel, M Adler.

TUE NOV 30, 1847
Trustee's sale: by virtue of a decree of PG Co Court, as Court of Equity, the undersigned will expose to public sale: on Dec 23, at the late residence of John B Beall, dec'd, 2 tracts or parcels of land, late the property of the said Beall, one called ***Snowden's Discovery,*** containing about 68 acres; the other, ***Toaping Castle***, containing about 20 acres; about 2½ miles from Beltsville: with frame dwlg nearly new. Will be shown by Mr Thos Harvey, the tenant thereof. -N C Stephen, Trustee

Col Childs, whose gallant bearing, both in the Florida & Mexican wars, has raised him so high in the estimation of the army & the people, is a native of Pittsfield, Mass, where his widowed mother & a brother, [Dr Henry Childs,] now reside. Timothy Childs, of Rochester, [who is now, for the benefit of his health, in the West Indies,] is also a brother of Col Childs. -Albany Evening Journal

Very excellent household furniture, hogs, & poultry, at auction: on Dec 2, at the Wash Penitentiary, the furniture of the late Robt Coltman. -R W Dyer, auct

In the U S Circuit Court, at Pittsburg, a penalty of $580 has been awarded against Dr Mitchell, of Indiana Co, for enticing a slave from his master. The case was tried under the act of Congress of 1783. The decision in this case goes somewhat farther than the famous Van Zandt case of Ohio. In the Mitchell case, there was no proof of enticing the slaves away from their master, nor was there any proved interference to prevent their return to their owners. He gave them employment, knowing them to be slaves. Judge Grier's charge was pointedly against the dfndnt.

Just received & for sale: 2 new & fashionable family Carriages; from the celebrated manufactory of Wm Dunlap, of Phil, & for sale by Isaac Walton, at Mr Thos Young's.

Chas W Schuermann, Prof of Music, having taught for the last 6 months in this city with sufficient encouragement, has determined to make this city his permanent place of residence. Ofc on Pa ave, south side, between 10th & 11th sts. Notice left for him at Dr A J Schwartz's drug store, 2nd door from 3rd st, will meet with attention.

For rent: the large 3 story brick house with back bldg, opposite the Brewery formerly occupied by the late Wm Hayman. Inquire of Com S Cassin, Gtwn, or of R W Dyer, Auctioneer & Commercial Merchant.

By virtue of an order from Henry Trunnel, Country Collector, I did, on Nov 26, distrain, on the premises occupied by Mr John E Dement, one dark horse, for county taxes due & in arrear, which horse I will offer for sale, for cash, at the Centre Market in Wash City, on Dec 4 next. -John Magar, Bailiff of Henry Trunnel, Collector of Taxes.

Mrd: on Nov 28, at St Patrick's Church, by Rev Wm Matthews, Mr E J Klopfer to Miss Jane F Cole, all of Wash City.

Mrd: on Nov 13, by Rev H B Cunningham, Rev W W Pharr, of Cabarras Co, to Miss Violet Amanda Alexander, of Mecklenburg Co, N C.

Died: Nov 19th, at Columbus, Ga, in his 33rd year, Wm Kerr Moore, son of Jas Moore, [printer,] of Wash City.

WED DEC 1, 1847

For rent: dwlg house on I st, above 17th st. Inquire of me or of J M Moore, adjoining. -C Gordon Also, for rent, the 3 story house adjoining the Union Hotel, Gtwn. Inquire of H Tilley, P M.

Ordered, that Margaret Murphy, the widow of Patrick Murphy, should administer on the estate of Patrick Murphy, on or before Dec 17 next. -Nathl Pope Causin -Ed N Roach, Reg/o wills

The New Orleans Delta publishes a list of our soldiers who died in the general hospital at Perote Castle from Jun 1 to Oct 30. The list is correct, with the exception, probably, of some of the deaths which occurred among members of the Pa regts. Of the total number given, one died of contusion & 6 of gun-shot wounds; remainder died of disease mainly incidental to the climate. In the month of June:

Thos Brewster	Stephen Pervis	L R Sparin
Wm Day	Farley	T L Carr
Wm Noble	Saml Ephraim	R Allen
Wm Meredith	Davis	H Eberlee
Owen D Thomas	J Dobbins	Christson
Effinger	J Proctor	Thos Owens
Simon Repaid	Sharpe	Thos R Staples
John Pop	P Dure	Wm Harriott
Venthiel	Geo Garner	John Warner
Isaac R Baldwin	John Beers	Chas Evans
Warday	H Inks	Henry Peters
Martin	Stephen Brown	Ira White
Robinson	A Beaumont	Benj R Smith
Edw Clark	T Lyons	Edw Groves
David E Gallagher	Brown	Israel Kariker
J Dent	J Smithson	Hill
Pike	Flynn	J C Dubois
Jerome Walker	Mr Mills-citizen	T F Henderson
Drayton Griffin	Williams	Capt Whipple
Wm P Botts	J Myers	Dennis
J Williamson	Wm Walters	H Cook
J Neeley	Peter M Space	Francis R Best
Eli Dowdey	Wm McGee	H Hilburn
John Patterson	Hare	Lindermire
Walker	Watson	Chester

In the month of July:

Geo Wagner	O C Stevens	Wm Banghart
Randolph Ball	Fords	Elam H Bonham
Robt Lyons	H O'Hara	Wm Flanagan
Henry Kariker	A Fifleman	J Siddle
Christian Linderman	Feichtner	John Webster
John Mustard	B F Cook	Thos L Jonesx
Wm Hilburn	W W Reveille	David W Corkle
Jas Bentley	Lt Jacob Brus	M Hood
Edw McCue	H M Ripley	Geo Loomis
McMurry	Joshua Alexander	Wilbert R Gerguson
Pitts	N Robinson	Albert G Morrow
John Hickson	John Sligh	Newton Drummond
Geo Slouth	A Elms	D Burkey
Newell	Jonathan R Saunders	N W Keith

N Stuppick
Lobber
John Cole
Owen Coyle
Robt Welsh
Easinger
Fillman
Shepherd W Guston
Summers
Jos Shaw
J P Smith
Thos Jones
C Sweeney
Simonson
L McNealy
Cpl Leechman
B Wynsers
Benj B Loud
Wm Verdell
Saml Alexander
Rowe
Jesse M Norwood
R Ford
Hicks
Robt Steward
Wm Miller
Wm Conn
John Hammond
Hazel Hardwick
Geo McDonough
John G Judd
David M Cole
Isinghoff
G W Connor
W A Harris
Serj Satterley
Wolfgang Chingers
John Morrison
J Managan
S P Short

J Ridgeley
Leonard
John Dodds
Allen Blane
Willey
Anthony
Wm J Anderson
Alex'r Boyce
Haines
Augustus Lannoy
Wm McDrymer
Hammond
A D Clark
P Poss
J Lowrey
B F Berry
Wm E Rowell
Wm Robinson
Anthony Smith
Rouge
Jas Goodale
Sweet
G W Copeland
Bont
Kinney La Rue
Henry Crook
H McFarland
Saml D Baker
Henry Armour
Farel
Garretson
Jas Rittentein
Wm Walton
R Cooper
Capt Guthrie
Wm Forbes
Thos Crawford
John M Bougher
Baker
Radcliffe

C W Hargrooves
H C Young
C Armstrong
H Meyer
E Rich
N Brown
P Walker
P Coile
M M Price
Philip Rake
John Mehlhorn
Wm Bishop
Wm Robertson
J Flowers
Mansen
Kerr
Baldwin
Wm McCoy
J H Williams
Schmeltz
B W Weathers
Weatherley
R Humphreys
L Reed
Max'n Klinkard
Jas Schaeffer
H M Schenck
Goldman
Eli Shelley
A Franklin
Jas J Hays
J L Cox
J C Trick
John Brown
Jacob Reed
August Kolb
Dinsmore
W H Wassen

<u>In the month of Aug:</u>

A J Gittings
Jas Tinney
R Stephens
Quinn

B Zoller
S Woodward
Wm Robinson
A Smith

Hartman
C E Monday
Harper
Jos L Gandle

R Babcock
P Buchart
A J McConnell
Jacob Hager
A Walker
C Stark
Kenard Cochrane
Chas B Parker
Valintine R Mills
A J Ault
Hare
Walters
H P Robinson
P Hopper
Gibson
John A S Scott
Wm Brown
Wm Crown
Bradley
Kelsey
Henry Whitholm
Benj Grant
Gould
Michl Smith
Wm H Sparrow
Gilbert Ball
Wm D Head
Dennis
Wm H Rogers
Wm A Thruston
Gartegan
John Heilman
Wm Hamilton
H M Horves
Danl Bruner
Jas Church
Taylor
Cole
Geo Myers

Isaac N Shook
J H Corder
W T Baldwin
Thos M Leitch
Chas Williams
Nelson Woodward
John S Dodge
Boyce
Chas A Fowler
Chas Taylor
Abraham Jacobs
John McCollum
Danl Mills
W L Mozier
Henry Mullen
J J Quick
Wm Rose
David Huddleston
Wm Swartz
Jas M Wood
Henry Rhudy
L C Powell
Hiram Hooper
Calvin Ward
Geo Schaeffer
Andrew Blane
Gabriel Niece
Chas Steward
Wm R Miller
Leininger
Danl Ives
J F Staly
Alonzo Blake
Christopher F Lucas
M McClue
A B Cummings
Pierce
Gates McDonald
Jas Adams

Jas Eason
A J Griffin
Abraham Birs
Jas Keeler
Donald Chisolm
Jos Thomas
John Piper
John Hanault
Maurice Tucker
Otto Hahn
A L Charles
A T Zellor
John Russell
Jas Murphy
Saml Cooper
J C Medlin
L Scott
Ross Jones
John Johnson
Von Rheaden
H Gibbons
C Rose
Andrew Hatch
Thos Kennedy
D B Schryver
Jos B Merriett
John A Viney
John F White
Jos Headley
John Cloudsley
N Marbell
Brandstadter
H Boerhurst
Stephen Garber
P McCall
McFarland
Geo Sherwood
John A Lourey
Robt Campbell

<u>In the month of Sep:</u>

Abraham Pratt
E Willingham
Boreson
John Donnelly
J W Davis

Amos Marney
John Pierce
John G St Clair
Saml Sweet
Wm Henry

Saml Firestine
F Triplett
John Butler
Wm Silverthorn
D H Marston

Stephen Cady
N Flaven
John Trenner
John Bradshaw
Robt Kelly
Saml Williams
Oscar Warner
Jas Allen
Wentworth
Summers
Wm Heartie
Abraham Stauffer
Cpl Givins
Andrew Fowler
John McCauley
Warren Freeman
Amasa Whiton
M L Hackler
Preston Dobson
John F Davis
Lewis McFadden
Wm L Duff
Wm Haley
J Rugg
Roberts
Martin Edwards
Wm M Beatty
Jas De Baney
Alex'r Daniels
John Bagley
Trenum
Saml McCartney
Jackson Canada
Hiram Holden
A Murrill
Jacob Dennett
Leavenworth
Abraham Delamaster
Cpl Overmire
Harrison Chase
Albert Peverley
Cpl Corbett

Wm Haylock
Jas Birch
John W Aubrey
L B Smith
John Darragh
Jacog Strobe
Boyle
Beston Hitebens
Finney
Fred'k Magnus
Wm B Edwards
Bigley
Wm Giles
Pritchard
Leonard Fox
John Gaither
Gen Kattler

In the month of Oct:

Jas Boland
Cornelius Frisby
Danl Jarne
Ketler
Benj Tillman
Isaac Fry
Geo Tucker
Warren Elmer
Estis
J B Campbell
Geo Dewell
Wm Blair
Nathl Smith
Robt Newton
John Polly
Fordich
Moses Grunt
Randolph Ruby
McCombs
John Miller
Judson Keen
Adam G Seyfert
John Robinson
Francis Monday

Theodore Conrad
Geo Dooley
John May
John Lndenerg
Walding
Richd E Barrow
Jas Hall
Wm McMurtrey
Chas Harnn
Wm Bakevell
Wm Cochrane
John C Mullins
O H White
Wells
Saml Kelley
Geo Carpar
Wm Foster
McClanighand
Lee
Tyler
McPike
Krass
Lt Doyle
Robt Gavatt
Hiram Smith
Benj Butcher
Jos Linthicam
Wesley Scaggs
Turner Harper
J G Fitzgerald
Geo W Lang
Thos Nelson
Jas O'Conner
Obadiah Purnell
Adolphus Beyer
J Duddleson
Jas Barton
B P Wright
Alex'r Butler
Smith
Van Rensselaer H
French

Valuable city property for sale: the subscriber will sell his valuable brick house, 2 stories, with an elegant lot of ground, on the corner of 20th & E sts, Wash City. Apply to the occupant, Mr M Keller, or to the proprietor, S D Finckel, next door to the German Ev Church, 20th & G sts, 1st Ward.

For sale: a small brick house on 18th st, between H & I sts. Inquire of T Barnard, Pa ave & 11th st, or Jas Kelly, 1st Ward.

Balt, Nov 30. The distinguished American tragedian, Mr Edwin Forrest, has, since his sojourn in this city, presented to his old, well-tried, & faithful friend, our fellow citizen, Jas V Wagner, a splendid carriage & pair of horses.

The St Louis paper states that from 100 to 130 deck passengers lost their lives by the sinking of the steamer **Talisman**. A letter from Rev S H Calhoun gives the only authentic account of the disaster. St Louis, Nov 20, 1847 Yesterday, when near Cape Girardeau, the **Talisman** & the ship **Tempest** came into collision, & our boat immediately sunk. The shrieks & lamentations & cries for help are still ringing in my ears. The deck passengers were unable to get out, so rapidly did the boat sink. It was a scene I hope never to forget.

For rent: the house occupied by W W Corcoran, on H st: possession in 10 days.

The Trustees of the primary school at Mrs Magruder's Mill, PG Co, Md, wish to procure a gentleman to take charge of the same. A salary of $350 can be obtained. Apply to either of the undersigned, through Upper Marlborough post ofc, PG Co, Md. -Wm J Belt, Wm J Berry, Richd W Bowie, Trustees

Mrd: on Nov 25, by Rev T H Reese, Mr Wm T Fisher, of Balt Co, Md, to Miss Ann Rebecca G, youngest daughter of the late Jas Summers.

Died: on Nov 18, at Baton Rouge, La, in his 84th year, Gen Philemon Thomas, well known as a member of the Louisiana Legislature, a member of Congress. We believe he was a native of N C, where, during the Revolutionary war, he was engaged im many skirmishes with the British & tories. He resided some years in Ky, & was a member of the Legislature of that State; he afterwards removed to Louisiana, & in 1810-11 headed the insurrection at Baton Rouge which threw off the yoke of Spain from West Florida. He was an upright man & patriotic citizen. -New Orleans Courier

The U S revenue cutter **Robert J Walker**, built at the ship-yard of Mr Jos Tomlinson, in Pittsburg, was launched last Sat. She is to proceed to New Orleans under command of Capt Evans. This is the 4th iron steamer built by Mr Tomlinson, 3 of which were for the U S service.

THU DEC 2, 1847

Lt John M Gardner, of the U S Navy, died at his residence in Balt on Sun, after an illness of upwards of a year, contracted whilst on duty in the Gulf of Mexico.

The Daily Nat'l Whig is published in Wash City: it speaks the sentiments of the policy of the Whig party of the Union on every question of public policy. It advocates the election to the Presidency of Zachary Taylor, subject to the decision of a Whig Nat'l Convention. -Chas W Fenton, Proprietor of the Nat'l Whig: Wash.

For rent: the house lately occupied by Dr Bode, over the dry goods store of G F Allen, on north side of Pa ave, between 9th & 10th sts. Apply to Mr Allen in the store below, or to S H Hill, on 9th st, near Pa ave.

Trustee's sale of lots: by deed of trust from Chas Hibbs, recorded in liber W B 94, folio 263, at public auction: on Dec 22: lots 17 thru 19, in square 529: on 3rd st west, between G & H sts. -R W Dyer, auct

Trustee's sale of lots: by deed of trust from E H Roper, recorded in liber W B 83, folio 1, at public auction: on Jan 3: lot 9, in square 317: on K st, between 11th & 12th sts. -R W Dyer, auct

Ladies' Furnishing Store, Pa ave, between 4½ & 6th sts. -Mary Alice Murray, agent

Some of the most beautiful specimens of blown glass which we have ever seen, have been shown to us from the glassworks of Mr Hugh Robertson, of Pittsburg, & were blown by Messrs Park & Hannen, of that establishment, for a present to one of our citizens, who desires through us to return his thanks for the compliment.

Mrd: on Nov 23, by Rev Mr Powers, Alfred W Gardiner, of Chas Co, Md, to Miss Mary Ellen, daughter of Wm Gwynn, of PG Co, Md.

Mrd: on Nov 25, by Rev Henry Slicer, Mr Albert H Beach to Miss Evelina B Thorp, all of Wash City.

Died: on Dec 1, of consumption, Edw Lawrence Birch, at age 22 years. His funeral is on Fri, at 3 o'clock, from the residence of his father, on 14th st, between F & G sts.

FRI DEC 3, 1847

Paris, Dec 31, 1846. At the request of the surviving legal reps of the late Maj Gen Baron DeKalb, who are about to renew their position to Congress, I, the undersigned Consul of the U S, do hereby attest & certify the following facts: independently of the amplest evidence of the said reps of their quality as next of kin & sole heirs, their title is matter of notoriety, & recently recognized by the Dept of Foreign Affairs in this capital of the production of notarial proof in the prescribed forms. The widow of Baron Elie de Kalb, son of the Major Gen, & her dght, her only child, married to Viscount d'Abaac, have for many years resided at Milon, where the whole family have been constantly held in cordial esteem. The only surviving grandchild of Maj Gen DeKalb, Luc Geymuller, resides at Versailles, with a wife & several children, & enjoys, as a gentleman & citizen, a like consideration with his relatives at Milon. They possess, & have shown to me, the original certificate of the grant of bounty land in Ohio, which was made by Congress in 1822, to the above mentioned Elie de Kalb & the other heirs, & transmitted to them in that year by Pres Monroe. They have derived no advantage whatever from that grant. In one of his letters to his wife in Paris, at different camps on the Hudson river, 1778, DeKalb narrates how he had been obliged to sell his favorite horses, from economy; & that exclaims, that considering what he left behind him in France, & what he endured in America, he paid dearly, very dearly at the ultimate rewards be what they might. The family papers comprise a copy of the instructions of the French Gov't to Baron de Kalb when, before our declared rupture with the mother company in 1767, he was commissioned to visit Holland for information concerning the rumors of American disaffection, & to repair to the colonies in case of ascertainment. If the Lafayette family had been the petitioners, who can doubt that what they asked, & more, would have been granted without delay, & by acclamation! The Senate, in all likelihood, would redress, to which the attention of that patriotic assembly was not directed in the hurry of that last period of a short session, peculiarly, on the delegations of Md & Delaware, whose gallant troops he commanded, & that of S C, on whose soil he made, "pierced with many wounds," the final sacrifice. He was a German, born at Nuremburg, & signalized himself in the 7 years' war, before he joined the American standard -Robt Walsh

New Orleans Picayune of Nov 24. Ofcrs who came over in the steamship **Alabama**:

Major Gen Quitman
Brig Gen Shields
Surg Gen Lawson
Col Harney, 2nd Dragoons
Col Garland, 4th Infty
Col Andrews, voltigeurs
Col Morgan, 15th Infty
Col Ramsay, 11th Infty
Col Burnett, N Y volunteers
Dr Harney, U S Army
Lt Col Moore, 3rd Dragoons
Maj Smith, engineers
Maj Wade, 3rd Artl
Maj Gwynn, 6th Infty
Maj Bonneville, 6th Infty
Maj Loring, rifles
Maj Borland, Ark volunteers
Maj Bennett, paymaster U S Army
Maj Dykeman, N Y volunteers
Capt Anderson 3rd Artl
Capt Wayne, assist qrtrmstr U S Army
Capt Martin, assist qrtrmstr U S Army
Capt Jones, rifles
Capt McReynolds, 3rd Dragoons
Capt Penrose, 2nd Infty
Capt Kearny, 1st Dragoons
Capt Mason, engineers
Capt Clay, Ky cavalry
Capt Irwin, 11th Infty
Capt Edwards, voltigeurs
Lt G T M Davis, U S Army
Lt Thom, topog engineers
Lt Newman, 9th Infty
Lt Williamson, 3rd Infty
Lt Brodhead, 15th Infty
Lt Potter, N Y volunteers
Lt Sweeny, N Y volunteers
Lt Rosencrantz, 5th Infty
Lt Vernon, voltigeurs
Lt May, rifles
Lt Beardsley, 8th Infty
Lt Maclay, 8th Infty
Lt Hendrickson, 8th Infty
Lt Johnson, 8th Infty
Lt Haskins, 1st Artl
Lt Boynton, 1st Artl
Lt Johnston, 3rd Artl
Lt Judd, 3rd Artl
Lt Thomas, 3rd Artl
Lt Graham, 1st Dragoons

Lt Shields, 14th Infty	Mr David B Pierce
Lt Callender, ordnance	Mr H Marks
Lt Moragne, S C volunteers	Mr R L Doughty
Lt Kiger, voltigeurs	Mr Skirchfield
Lt Semmes, U S Navy	Mr Gibbons
Passed Midshipman Rodgers, U S Navy	Mr Watts
Dr Graves	Mr Foster
Mr Hammond, postmaster, U S Army	Mr Edwards
Mr Geo Wilkins Kendall	Mr N C Davis

The brave Gen Shields, ever in the thickest of the fight, returns disabled from his wounds to recruit his health & gain strength; the same may be said of Cols Garland, Morgan, & Burnett, Majors Wade & Loring, Capts Kearny, Anderson, Irwin, McReynolds, Martin, & Mason, Lts Haskin, Callender, Newman, Hendrickson, Potter, Sweeny, Rosencrantz, Graham, Moragne, Beardsley, Boynton, Shields, & others. The **Alabama** also brought over no less than 210 sick, wounded, & disabled soldiers. Even the Mexican Gov't makes better provisions for its sick, disabled, & wornout soldiers than our own. Three of those who started on the **Alabama**: Henry Kain, 8th U S Infty; Martin Costolow, 2nd U S Artl; & Richd McManns, 2nd Pa volunteers, died on the passage over.

Jas Ross, a distinguished citizen of Pa, died at his residence in Alleghany, near Pittsburg, on Nov 27, in his 86th year. At the commencement of the present century Mr Ross occupied a seat in the U S Senate, & was among the first members of that illustrious body. He was a Washington Federalist, & upon the fall of his party in 1808, bid adieu to the political life.

On Tue, Owen McGee, who resides on Capitol Hill, having had a quarrel with Edmund Hogan, the latter was severely wounded on the head by McGee, who struck Hogan several times with a large screw-driver. McGee's wife interfered in the affray, & was also wounded on the head. McGee was arrested on Wed by Ofcr Cox, & held to bail in the sum of $500 on charge of assaulting with intent to kill.

Yesterday a colored man, Nelson Simms, who has several times been confined in the Penitentiary, was arrested by Capt Goddard, under charge of stealing a silver watch valued at $10. He awaits trial.

<u>Corp of Wash. An act to regulate taverns & ordinaries:</u>
<u>By whom the premises were examined & certified:</u>
<u>By whom recommended:</u>
<u>Job Corson, square 255, 11th & E sts</u>

R Wimsatt	Lewis Thomas	J W Martin
K H Lambell	Thos W Riley	Geo Mattingley
J W Martin	R Wimsatt	Lewis Thomas
Geo Mattingley	K H Lambell	Thos W Riley

<u>Conrad Finkman, square 292, Pa ave</u>

C Eckloff	C P Sengstack	L & A Lepreux

N Travers	C Eckloff	N Travers
John France	C P Sengstack	John France
Jas McColgan	L Lepreux	Jas McColgan
<u>Abraham Butler, square 254, F st</u>		
E Simms	Jos S Wilson	Michl Nourse
McClintock Young	Alison Nailor	Jos S Wilson
Jas Larned	E Simms	Alison Nailor
Michl Nourse	McClintock Young	Jas Larned
<u>Henry M Hannin, square 256, E st</u>		
N Travers	Abraham Butler	Joel Downer
Joel Downer	John C Rives	Jas Larned
Wm Morrow	N Travers	Abraham Butler
Jas Larned	Wm-Morrow	John C Rives
<u>Henry Kuhl, square 291, Pa ave</u>		
C Eckloff	N Travers	John France
C P Sengstack	C Utermuhle	Wm Morrow
John France	C P Sengstack	Nicholas Travers
Wm Morrow	C Eckloff	C Utermuhle
<u>Andrew Hancock, square 292, Pa ave</u>		
John France	L & A Lepreux	C P Sengstack
Joel Downer	Wm Morrow	Geo A W Randall
C P Sengstack	John France	L & A Lepreux
Geo A W Randall	Joel Downer	Wm Morrow
<u>John Hands, square 225, Pa ave</u>		
Thos Miller	Evan Evans	F Burch
S W Handy	N Callan	Jas Anderson
F Burch	Thos Miller	Evan Evans
Jas Anderson	S W Handy	N Callan
<u>P Moran, square 407, 8th & D sts</u>		
B O Sheckell	J H Eberbach	Leonard Harbaugh
Thos Baker	John Foy	Geo Hendley
Leonard Harbaugh	B O Sheckell	J H Eberbach
Geo Hendley	Thos Baker	John Foy
<u>P A De Saules, 7th st</u>		
Michl Talty	John Walker	J D Hendley
Saml Bacon	F Mattingly	John Foy
J D Hendley	Michl Talty	John Walker
John Foy	Thos Bacon	F Mattingly
<u>M Talty, square 432, 7th st</u>		
John A Donoho	Patrick Moran	Wm H Harrover
John Walker	John K Hendley	Thos Baker
Wm H Harrover	John A Donoho	Patrick Moran
Thos Baker	John Walker	John R Hendley
<u>K J Eberbach, square 407, E & 3rd sts</u>		
Thos Baker	Patrick Moran	G W Utermuhle, sr

John R Hendley	Thos Baker	John H Hendley
Wm T Steiger	Patrick Moran	Wm T Steiger
John Foy	G W Utermohle	John Foy

F Stutz, square 408, 9th st

J H Eberbach	F Massi	Raphael Jones
G H Utermohle	Geo Wilner	Thos Cookendorfer
Raphael Jones	J H Eberbach	F Massi
Thos Cookendorfer	G W Utermohle	Geo Wilner

J R Hendley, square 431, 7th & E sts

J D Hendley	Geo Sweeny	Geo Hendley
Thos Baker	Saml Bacon	F Mattingley
F Mattingly	Thos Baker	Geo Sweeny
Geo Hendley	J D Hendley	Saml Bacon

Thos Baker, square 431, D & 8th sts

J H Eberbach	Michl Talty	Patrick Moran
John R Hendley	Saml Bacon	Raphael Jones
Patrick Moran	J H Eberbach	Michl Talty
Raphael Jones	John R Hendley	Saml Bacon

John Foy, square 378, D st

Jos Borrows	Jas E Plant	J C McGuire
C Buckingham	S F Franklin	Thos Donoho
J C McGuire	Jos Borrows	Jas E Plant
Thos Donoho	C Buckingham	S F Franklin

Jas Cuthbert, square 427, 7th st

Geo W Utermuhle	John Williams	J Matlock
J M Pierce	John Shreeve	John Shreeve
Thos Conner	J M Pierce	Gwo W Utermohle
J Matlock	Thos Conner	John Williams

P Dorsey, square 428, I & 7th sts

B F Morsell	T B Brown	J Matlock
Jas H Shreve	D S Waters	B F Morsell
J M Pierce	Jas H Shreve	T B Brown
J Matlock	J M Pierce	D S Waters

Wm H Campbell, square 431, 7th st

J D Hendley	J W Morehead	F Mattingley
Thos Baker	Patrick Moran	Michl Talty
F Mattingley	J D Hendley	J W Morehead
Michl Talty	Thos Baker	Patrick Moran

Jas H Birch, square reservation 10, Pa ave

W H Upperman	Michl McDermott	M Delany
Fred'k Cudlip	R E Simms	Thos Young
M Delany	W H Upperman	Michl McDermott
Thos Young	Fred'k Cudlip	R E Simms

Cotter & Thompson, square reservation 10, Pa ave

J M Johnson	Ed Simms	F Cudlip

W H Upperman	J M Johnson	W H Upperman
Jas Fitzgerald	Ed Simms	Jas Fitzgerald
Alex'r Lee	F Cudlip	Alex'r Lee
Wm Benter, square 491, Pa ave		
Alex'r Lee	R F Middleton	A F Kimmell
J P Pepper	Andrew Small	J M Johnson
A F Kimmell	Alex'r Lee	R F Middleton
J M Johnson	J P Pepper	Andrew Small
B H Shade, square ___, B & 2nd sts		
Wm Greason	Jas Fitzgerald	Nicholas Acker
Jacob Acker	Wm H Upperman	Chas Lee Jones
Nicholas Acker	Wm Greason	Jas Fitzgerald
Chas Lee Jones	Jacob Acker	Wm H Upperman
Jas West, square 461, 7th st		
E D Gilman	A Coyle	Thos Pursell
Jas Long	John H Clarvoe	Jas Long
Thos Pursell	John H Clarvoe	Z D Gilman
T B Brown	T F Brown	A Coyle
Jas Fitzgerald, reservation 10, Pa ave		
W H Upperman	Michl McCarty	R E Simms
Thos Young	Chas Lee Jones	Michl McDermott
R E Simms	W H Upperman	Michl McCarty
Michl McDermott	Thos Young	Chas Lee Jones
Jas Long, square 460, Pa ave & 6th st		
S Hyatt	J M Johnson	T P Brown
Z D Gilman	Jos Beaseley	J M Johnson
Levi Pumphrey	S Hyatt	Levi Pumphrey
Y P Brown	Z D Gilman	R C Weightman
B O Sheckell, square 461, 7th st		
T P Brown	Jas Long	Jos Peck
Jas Kelcher	Z D Gilman	Thos Pursell
Jos Peck	T P Brown	Jas Long
Thos Pursell	Jas Kelcher	Z D Gilman
Wm Samuels, square 458, 7th st		
Wm H Harrover	Jonathan Forrest	Raphael Jones
Raphael Jones	Jos Bradley	Jonathan Forrest
Levi Pumphrey	Levi Pumphrey	Michl Talty
Michl Talty	Wm H Harrover	Jos Beasley
P H King, square B, Pa ave		
S Hyatt	Andrew Small	J M Johnson
R E Simms	Jas Kelcher	A F Kimmell
J M Johnson	S Hyatt	Andrew Small
A F Kimmell	R E Simms	Jas Kelcher
C Casparis, square 688, A st & N J ave		
C K Gardner	W J Wheatly	Simon Brown

Jas T Frye	Robt Brown	Simon Brown
N C Towle	C K Gardner	Jas T Frye
Fred'k May	Wm J Wheatly	N C Towle
L S Roby, square reservation 10, Pa ae		
Edw Simms	Thos Young	W H Upperman
R E Simms	J F Lynch	Jas F Lynch
W H Upperman	Edw Simms	Michl McDermott
Michl McDermott	R E Simms	Thos Young
H W Sweeting, square 490, C st		
Levi Pumphrey	W G W White	J F Pepper
B F Middleton	W A Bradley	Alex'r Lee
J F Pepper	Levi Pumphrey	W G W White
Alex'r Lee	B F Middleton	W A Bradley
Jesse Brown, square 460, Pa ave		
Jas Long	J M Johnson	A Coyle
Jos Bradley	Levi Pumphrey	Z D Gilman
A Coyle	Jas Long	J M Johnson
Z D Gilman	Jos Bradley	Levi Pumphrey
R R Thompson, square reservation 10, Pa ave		
Jas H Birch	J P Pepper	Jas Fitzgerald
W H Upperman	John N Coyle	J M Johnson
Jas Fitzgerald	Jas H Birch	J P Pepper
J M Johnson	W H Upperman	John N Coyle
J S Hall, square B, Pa ave		
S Hyatt	Andrew Small	M McDermott
J M Johnson	Thos Young	J O'Leary
M McDermott	S Hyatt	Andrew Small
J O'Leary	J M Johnson	Thos Young
S S Coleman, square 491, Pa ave & 6th st		
Geo Parker	B F Middleton	B F Middleton
J M Johnson	John W Maury	J P Pepper
J P Pepper	Geo Parker	A F Kimmell
A F Kimmell	J M Johnson	John W Maury
P McGawey & Co, square 575, Pa ave		
Chas Lee Jones	John T Kilmon	W H Upperman
Jas Fitzgerald	John Purdy	Wm Greason
W H Upperman	Chas Lee Jones	John T Kilmon
Wm Greason	Jas Fitzgerald	John Purdy
Jas Casparis, square 688, north A st		
Wm T Wheatley	Simon Brown	Robt Brown
J B Gardner	N C Towle	C K Gardner
Robt Brown	Wm Wheatley	Simon Brown
C K Gardner	J B Gardner	N C Towle
John Donova, square ___		
Jas Fitzgerald	Wm Greason	W H Upperman

Chas Lee Jones	Jas Fitzgerald	Chas Lee Jones
John T Kilmon	Wm Greason	John T Kilmon
Nicholas Acker	W H Upperman	Nicholas Acker
E Rupert, square ___		
E Hazel	D Homans	J Philips
John A Lynch	Vandora Mallion	D Homans
Edmund Reilly	Edmund Reilly	V Mallion
J B Philips	John A Lynch	Z Hazel
Josiah Clements, square 907, L st		
F Otterback	Jacob Small	Geo Hartman
Jas Rhodes	R H Harrington	Adam Gaddis
Geo Hartman	F Otterback	Jacob Small
Adam Gaddis	Jas Rhodes	R H Harrington
John A Golden, square 928, 8th st		
F S Walsh	John Boylayer	R M Combs
Thos Bayne	J R Queen	S Tensh
R McCombs	F S Walsh	John Boylayer
S Tensh	Thos Bayne	J R Queen
R H Harrington, square 930, 8th st		
P Otterback	J M Padgett	Wm M Ellis
Jas Tucker	D E Keally	Thos Kelly
Wm M Ellis	P Otterback	J M Padgett
Thos Kelly	Jas Tucker	D E Keally
Peter Jones, square 356, Water st		
H N Young	Simon Frazer	Lewis Thomas
R Wimsatt	Jas Mitchell	Simon Fraser
J W Martin	J W Martin	Jas Mitchell
Geo Hercus	R Wimsatt	Geo Hercus
Wm Thomas, square 267, M & 14th sts		
P G Howle	John Laskey	J S Harvey
P Cazenave	John Pettibone	Wm H Gunnell
J S Harvey	P G Howle	John Laskey
Wm H Gunnell	P Cazenave	John Pettibone
Job Corson, square 355, 11th & G sts		
Richd Wimsatt	Geo Mattingley	J W Martin
K H Lambell	L Thomas	Thos W Riley
J W Martin	Richd Wimsatt	Geo Mattingley
Thos W Riley	K H Lambell	L Thomas

Cincinnati-Thu: killed while working in a cellar, when the support arch gave way: Robt Patterson, John Alvis, & John Bradford, all of whom were hightly respected mechanics.

Burning of the steamer **Phenix**, & loss of 240 lives: from the Buffalo Commercial Advertiser of Monday. Discovered to be on fire in her hold on Nov 21: about 6 miles from shore, Manitouwac: Mr David Blish, of Southport, took Capt Sweet, the cmder of the propeller, from his berth, where he lay sick, & put him in a small boat, with as many others as the small boat would carry, & it left for the shore, Mr Blish voluntarily remaining behind. The propellar **Delaware** hove in sight but was unable to arrive in time to save those on board from destruction. 150 of the passengers had recently arrived from Holland. Mr Blish perished among the rest. [The Buffalo Express states, on the authority of the mate of the **Phenix**, that there were on board of her some 200 men, women, & children, emigrant passengers, mostly from Holland, besides the crew of about 30 persons, & 40 cabin passengers; of whom only 30 were saved, including 8 of the crew.]

Died: yesterday, after a short illness, of erysipelas, Mrs Martha Pegg, aged 45 years, in the possession of a well founded hope of felicity beyond the grave. Her funeral is today at 10 o'clock, from her late residence on north L st, between 6th & 7th sts. Relatives & friends, & the Dghts of Temperance, are invited to attend.

For rent: 3 story brick house & adjoining 2 story brick back bldg, containing 23 rooms, now occupied by Col Gen Bomford; also, the adjoining house on the west, recently occupied by Capt Chauncey, [now vacant,] being 2 of the block of bldgs known as Gadsby's Row. Apply to Alex McIntire.

Boarding-house for Members of Congress & Families: F Cudlipp, Pa ave, opposite the U S Hotel.

For rent, 3 dwlg houses in the 1st Ward, one in the Six Bldgs, now occupied by Mr Mickum. Also, 2 large brick houses on 21st st, near H, recently occupied by the late Capt Hetzel & Wm Mechlin. Inquire of Mr Mickum, & at the store of Mr Dillow, near the premises.

SAT DEC 4, 1847
Boarding: 1-Mrs Eliza O Robinson, Pa ave, between 6th & 7th sts. 2-J T Frost, boarding: Green's Row, Capitol Hill. 3-Mrs Beall, commodious house adjoining & over the banking rooms of Tyson & Hewlings. 4-Mrs Widdicombe, F st, between 14th & 15th sts. 5-Miss Polk, one door west of Jackson Hall, adjoining Tyler's Hotel.

Trustee's sale of lot: by deed of trust from E H Roper, recorded in Liber W B 83, folio 1: sale on Jan 3, of lot 9 in square 317: fronts on K st between 11th & 12th sts.
-R W Dyer, auct

Mrs Mary Ann Eckman offers her services as NURSE to the ladies of Wash. She had 8 years experience in Phil. Residence at Mr E Pollock's, 6th st, between F & G sts. Unquestionable references as to capability & character can be given.

Switzerland. The only Republic in Europe seems on the threshold of a bloody civil war. The alleged cause of controversy is in a measure religious, namely, the expulsion of the Jesuits from some of the cantons. The real cause, however, is political. The Canton, 22 in number, are very unequal in population. Berne has a population of about 400,000; Zurich, about 230,000; while Zug & Uri have about 14,000 each. The last 2 are almost exclusively Catholic.

Mr House, the engineer of the steamer **Phenix**, lately burnt on Lake Michigan, has furnished the Cleveland Herald with a list of a few of the persons lost by this sad calamity, whom he recollects by name, as follows: Mr West, lady & child, Racine; Mr Fink & lady, Racine; Mrs Heath & sister, ***Little Fort***; Mrs Long & child, Milwaukie; J Burrough, Chicago; D Blish, Southport; 2 Misses Hazleton, Sheboygan. About 25 other cabin passengers, & from 5 to 8 steerage passengers, with 150 Hollanders, were also lost. Of the ofcrs & crew were lost: D W Keller, steward; J C Smith, saloon keeper; N Merrill, 2nd mate; W Owen, 2nd engineer; H Robinson, 1st porter; J Newgent, 1st fireman; T Halsey, T Ferteau, J Murdock, A Murdock, Geo ___, deck hands; H Tisdale, cabin boy; L Southworth, wheelsman; 2 colored cooks. The body of young Tisdale was found floating upon a ladder. He was laying upon his side with his head resting upon his hand. He was evidently not drowned, but died from cold.

The death of Lt Col Saml E Watson, of the Marine Corps, is announced in a late letter from Vera Cruz. He died on Nov 16.

The Lynchburg Virginian recommends that the Legislature take some measures to show the gratitide of the State to her dead & living heroes of the Mexican war. Among those who have fallen by the sword & disease it enumerates: Lt Allen, 2nd Dragoons, who died at Corpus Christi, & Lt A B Botts, who died at Camargo. Lt Geo Mason, of Fairfax, 2nd Dragoons, fell in the first skirmish of the war. Capt Alburtis, of Berkeley, was killed at the siege of Vera Cruz. Of 4 Virginians belonging to the Rifles, 3 were killed at Cerro Gordo, viz: Capt Mason, Lt Ewell, & Lt Davis; & the 4th was severely wounded. In the series of desperate battles fought in the vicinity of Mexico, there fell Capt Seth Thornton, of Stafford; Capt W Anderson, of Norfolk; L P Johnson, of Abingdon; Lt Easley, of Halifax; Lt Col Graham, of Prince William; Lt Gantt, of Loudoun; Lt Burwell, of Petersburg; Lt Sidney Smith, of King George; Lt Shackleford, of Culpeper.

$100 reward for runaway dark mulatto girl, Ellen Ann Stewart, 16 years old, disappeared from the house of her owner about Oct 22. -John Dewdney, constable

A meeting of the descendants of the late Holland Weeks, of Salisbury, Vt, was held on Sep 22: 80 of the family attended, who are all the descendants of John Alden, the first Pilgrim whose feet touched ***Pilgrim Rock***. These meeting have been held occasionally for more than a century; & one of its objects is to keep the genealogy perfect, from the landing of the Pilgrims in New England to the latest posterity. The list, by the way, is soon to be published, & already amounts to more than 4,000 names.

Mrd: on Nov 17, in Batl, by Rev Mr Slicer, Chaplain to the U S Senate, Wm Hayden English, of Indiana, to Mardula Emma, 3rd daughter of Capt John F Jackson, of Fauquier Co, Va.
+
Mrd: on Nov 24, in Balt, by Rev Mr Slicer, Dr Henry Fields to Adelaide Frances, 2nd daughter of Capt John F Jackson, of Fauquier Co, Va.

Mrd: on Nov 18, by Rev Saml L Southard, at Cavalry Church, in N Y C, J Rutsen Schuyler, of Jersey city, N J, to Miss Susanna Haigh, 2nd daughter of Judge Edwards, of the same place.

Died: on Nov 30, in his 22nd year, at the residence of his father, in Fred'k Co, near Winchester, Va, Benj Chew Mason, eldest son of the Hon Jas M Mason.

Died: on Monday last, in N Y, Mr Geo H Colton, aged 29 years, editor of the American Review.

Died: on Nov 26, in Charleston, Benj Allston, of Gtwn, S C, aged 82 years.

Died: on Dec 2, after a short illness, of erysipelas, Mrs Martha Pegg, aged 45 years, in the possession of a well founded hope of felicity beyond the grave. [See newspaper of Dec 3, 1847.]

$5 reward will be given for the detection & conviction of the person who stole from the residence of Mrs Gadsby's, President's Square, 2 joints of Copper Spout, containing about 10 feet.

MON DEC 6, 1847

Fatal fracas at Laurel Factory on Fri last: Sela Smith, Kelly, Marshall, & Miles, came from the railroad with the avowed intention of attacking certain persons employed in the Laurel Factory. Smith, a former workman, has been discharged, & assumed a leadership. During the affray Kelly was struck on the head with a stone by Chas Nickerson. Kelly died during the night. Nickerson gave himself up voluntarily deeming that he acted in self-defence. Smith, at the time, was armed with a loaded pistol. -Sun

Parlor & chambers for rent: the house is on 4½ st, between Pa ave & C st. Inquire of Jas Williams.

We announce with pain the death of our friend, Geo H Colton, Editor & Proprietor of the American Review, after a painful illness of nearly a month. His disease was originally typhus fever, to which congestion of the brain was ultimately superadded. His age was 29 years. -N Y Tribune

Mr Jos K Boyd has now his 2 houses connected, & can accommodate 20 gentlemen with the very best rooms of any in this city. A first-rate cook & servants are in waiting.

Passengers in the steamship **Acadia** for Liverpool: W H Benson, Mrs Benson, 2 servants & 3 children, 2 Misses Price, Mrs Horne & servant, Miss Boxer & servant, C L Bartlett, J Jaffray, C M & Mrs Brockley, S Nichol, H Hitchcock, Mr & Mrs Kepling, K Skerry, H Tyle, B S Welles, A J Kingston, E Ward, John Smith, R Mitchell, F A Grant, A Provon, F A Belle, R E F Powell, Peter Burnett, Benj Shaen, R Gillew, B Carroll, D Mannver, Capt Bradshaw, P Anderson, A G Muney, E W Sergent, Capt Price, I F P Ladd, E Sataillard, W S Mitchell, R Hartshorn, Adam Berry, V Bishop, J H Perry, D A Dickson, J Hall, S Roder, I Cleanley, P Mott, Jas Wier, Andrew Wier, Jas Tottenhalh, John Crudley, R Murphy, John Hancock & lady, J Lumas, Jas Their, C W Steles, Geo Barker.

Furnished house to rent: 2 story dwlg at present occupied by Jas Ferguson, on the corner of 9th & Mass ave, within a few moments' walk of the Depts & the Capitol. Possession will be given immediately.

TUES DEC 7, 1847

Valuable Iron Property at public auction-Dec 14: property known as ***Catharine Furnace***, in Spottsylvania Co, Va: 4,643 acres of land, & numerous shops & houses.
-Wm N Wellford, Fredericksburg, Va.

Jas Patterson Tustin, [son of the Rev Septimus Tustin,] Atty at Law, Hagerstown, Md. [Ad]

Anacostia Fire Co Executive Cmte for the Ball in aid of the Washington Monument.

Hugh F Pritchard	John Ober	Jonas B Ellis
Thos P Tench	Thos Thornley	

M W Galt & Brothers, Watchmakers, Silversmiths, & Jewellers, Pa ave, between 9th & 10th sts. [Ad]

Valuable Farm for sale. I will sell at public or private sale, the Farm adjoining my dwlg, or Mattaponi Place, on the south side of the Mattaponi branch, generally known as my ***Connick's Farm***, containing upwards of 400 acres; with 3 new & very large tobacco houses on this estate; 2 large corn-houses; negro quarters, for the use of the place.
-Robt W Bowie, Mattaponi

Valuable real estate at Trustee's sale: by decree passed in the case in the High Court of Chancery, in which Wm Bryan was cmplnt & Susannah Burch & others were dfndnts, the subscriber, as trustee, will offer at public sale, on Dec 31, all that part of the real estate, containing 263 acres, of which the late Jos N Burch died seized & possessed, lying in PG Co, near Piscataway, which was conveyed by Jos N Burch, sen, to the Jos N Burch, jr, by deed dated about Feb 25, 1826, recorded among the land records of PG Co, Md. Mr Thos Swain now resides upon the land, & will show the same.
-C C Magruder, Trustee, Upper Marlborough

The Trustees of the Upper Marlboro Academy wish to engage, as Assist Teacher, a young competent gentleman. -Jno B Brooke, Pres of Board of Trustees: Upper Marlboro, Md

Valuable Tavern Property for sale: by authority from Capt John Brookes, [the proprietor,] that Tavern Property in Upper Marlboro, now in the occupation of Mr Mason E Clarke, consisting of a very commodious Brick Tavern, large Stable, & Carriage House: also, sale of all the furniture belonging to the Tavern. Public sale on Dec 24.
-C C Magruder, Upper Marlboro

For rent: that large, commodious brick dwlg, on the east side of 8th st, between G & H sts. Inquire at the residence of the subscriber, next door, or at his marble yard & rooms on E st. -Thos Berry

Handsome property at auction: by decree of the Circuit Court of D C, in Chancery, in a case in which Thos Blagden et al are cmplnts & Wm B Jackson, administrator, et al, are dfndnts: sale on Jan 6, the very comfortable frame house & lot on 11th st east, being lot 21, in square 977, near the Navy Yard. The house is a 2 story frame; the lot is 48 feet front by 101 feet in depth, formerly owned by John Little, dec'd.
-S S Williams, Trustee -A Green, auctioneer

Balt, Dec 6. The venerable widow of Alex'r Hamilton is now in this city, sojourning at Barnum's. She purposes remaining in Balt a week or two, when she will proceed to Washington.

For sale: several bldg lots on corner of E & 11th sts, in square 321. Apply to Mrs A Simpson, E & 10th sts.

WED DEC 8, 1847

Died: on Dec 7, aged 85 years, Mr Jas Owner. His funeral is from his late residence on Va ave, near 4th st east, on Thu next, at 2:30 o'clock P M.

Died: on Dec 6, Dr Robt E Kerr, at his residence, 5th & Mass ave. His funeral is this day, at 12 o'clock.

Old-established Drug Store for sale at auction: on Dec 27, in front of the premises, when the large Hotel adjoining it is also to be sold. It is that well-known 3 story brick dwlg house, store, & yard on Patrick st, Fred'k, Md, adjoining the City Hotel. Apply to the subscriber in Washington. -Wm Fischer

In the packet-ship **Isaac Wright**, from N Y for Liverpool: Mr John Platt, Mr Wm Platt, Mr M Noah, N Y; Mr Jerome, New Haven; Mrs Hardie, Ireland; Mr Ebenr Wright, Mr Jas Wright, Boston; Mr Jas Woolley, N Y; Mr Mansfield & lady, Canada; Mr John Bolderstine, England.

Orphans Court of Wash Co, D C. Letters testamentary on the personal estate of Winifred Tuel, late of said county, dec'd. -J Handley, exc

Farm for sale: tract of land belonging to the estate of the late Fielder Ryon, & recently sold by virtue of a decree from the High Court of Chancery, & purchased by the undersigned, is now offered for sale: the tract lies near the ***Long Old Fields***, in PG Co, Md, formerly owned by the late Dr Spencer Mitchell: comfortable dwlg-house on the land. Call on the purchaser, Thos P Ryon, who resides near the ***Long Old Fields***.

Criminal Court-Wash. The following gentlemen constitute the Grand Inquest for the present term:

John Boyle, Foreman	Wm Gunton	Judson Mitchell
John W Maury	Hamilton Luffborough	Andrew Coyle
Peter Force	O M Linthicum	Thos Blagden
John Kurtz	Isaac Clarke	W Doughty
John Mason	Geo W Phillips	B K Morsell
Thos Carbery	G C Grammer	Joshua Peirce
Thos Brown	H C Matthews	Zachariah Walker
Henry Haw	Geo Parker	

Passengers in the packet-ship **Mary Ann**, from Boston to Liverpool: John A Allston, of Lancaster, England; Messrs Grafton Fenne & John Lunt, of Boston; Alfred McKenzie, of North Danvers; & 40 in steerage.

Mrs A V McCormick, corner of 7th & market space, has still 4 or 5 vacant rooms, which she would be happy to fill with permanent boarders.

For rent: that desirable residence on I st north, west of Cmdor Morris', formerly the residence of Mrs Cmdor Stewart, & more recently of Chevalier Hulseman, Charge d'Affaires from Austria. Apply to Richd Smith, Cashier of the Metropolis Bank, who is duly authorized to make the necessary arrangements.

For rent: brick house on L st, near 15th st. Also, a new frame house, on 13th st. Inquire of Alex'r Borland, on the premises.

For rent: with or withour furniture, the large & convenient residence of the late Jos Smoot, on K st, West End, Wash. Apply to Mrs Smoot.

THU DEC 9, 1847

Senate: 1-Ptn from Sarah Hart, asking a pension; also that a balance standing against her late husband, B F Hart, on the books of the Treasury, be cancelled. 2-Ptn from Francis B & Andrew C Dorr, asking that their brother, who they allege was unjustly dismissed from the army while suffering under mental derangement, may be allowed a pension. 3-Ptn from Phebe & Sylvia Ann Wood, asking an extension of patent. 4-Bill for the relief of the heirs of John Paul Jones: considered in Cmte of the Whole, read a 3rd time, & passed.

House of Reps: 1-Nathan Sargent duly elected Sgt-at Arms of the House of Reps: for the 30th Congress. 2-Robt E Hornor, a Member of the Editorial fraternity, from N J, was duly elected Doorkeeper of the House of Reps: for the 30th Congress.

By the accidental discharge of a pistol, J McHenry Boyd, of Balt, was severely wounded, at Phil, on Sat. He arrived on Sat from Balt, with his amiable lady, to whom he had been united on that morning, & his brother-in-law, Rev Mr Brandt. In the attempt to remove the percussion cap from his pistol, Mr Boyd touched the trigger, & the ball entered his abdomen, & was extracted by Dr Motter & Dr King, of the U S A. He is as well as could be expected after so imminent an accident. -North American [Dec 10th newspaper: Mr J McHenry Boyd expired in Phil on Wed of the wound received on Sat by the accidental discharge of his pistol. Mr Boyd was married on Sat morning to an estimable young lady of Harford Co, &, being possessed of wealth, immediately started off to a trip to Europe; but the bridegroom of a few hours is now cold in the embrace of death. -Balt Clipper]

Forewarner: Sole right of the invention of a Self-propelling Engine or Motive Power: John Shannon Gallaher, Winchester, Va.

A late letter from Com Perry confirms the death of Lt Col Saml Edmonston Watson, of the Marine Corps, who died at Vera Cruz on Nov 16. The Boston Journal says that Col Watson was well known in that vicinity. He commenced his services in the Marine Corps in 1812: during the war rendered faithful & efficient services to his country. He was attached to the Portsmouth Navy Yard as commanding ofcr of the Marines for many years, until he, a few years since, succeeded Lt Col Freeman as cmder of the Marines at the Navy Yard in Charlestown. In the battles which preceded the capture of the Mexican capital, he commanded the btln of Marines, which rendered such efficient service. Col Watson has left a large & interesting family, & a numerous circle of warmly attached friends.

Mrd: on Dec 1, at Bowling Green, Caroline Co, Va, by Rev Mr Paris, Mr Chas McGruder, of Richmond, to Miss Ann Hite, daughter of Wm G Maury, of the former place.

Died: on Dec 1, at his residence, ***Hills & Dales***, Montg Co, Md, Maj Thos Gittings, in his 62nd year, esteemed, loved, & respected by all who knew him, & for 10 years a representative of said county in the Legislature of Md.

FRI DEC 10, 1847

Wash Corp: 1-Ptn of Thos Kingsbury, for remission of a fine: referred to the Cmte of Claims.

Rev Septimus Tustin, several years Chaplain to the Senate, was installed Pastor of the Presbyterian Church in Hagerstown on Nov 14, with all the interesting ceremonies-Rev Mr Harper, of Shippensburg, & the Rev Dr Watson, of Gettysburg, Pa, assisting.

We learn of the decease of the Hon Timothy Childs, of Santa Cruz, whither he had recently gone for the benefit of his health. He formerly for several years represented the Rochester district of N Y in Congress.

Cameron Mills, with 190 acres of land adjoining, the property of Mr Richd Windsor, one mile west of Alexandria, was sold last week at private sale, to Reuben Roberts, of N J, for $25,000. It is intended to bring into use the extensive water power at this place for manufacturing purposes. -Alexandria Gaz

Two physicians have died at Boston within a few days past of ship fever, Dr Lane & Dr Jos Moriarty. The latter had charge of the hospital at Deer Island.

Mrd: on Dec 9, in Wash City, by Rev Smith Pyne, Henry K Davenport, of the U S Army, to Jennie Brent, youngest daughter of the late Geo Graham.

John H Harper, of Independence, Jackson Co, Mo, who was charged with the murder of Mr Wm H Meredith, of Balt, a year or two ago, whose trial was procrastinated up to the present time, has just been acquitted. The venue was changed from Jackson to Platte Co. The nature of the defence is not set forth.

Orphans Court of Wash Co, D C. Letters of administration on the personal estate of Catharine Campbell, late of said county, dec'd. -Murry Barker, adm

SAT DEC 11, 1847

Ofcrs & crew that perished in the ill-fated packet ship **Stephen Whitney**, of N Y, which was lately wrecked on the coast of Ireland: Chas W Popham, master, of N Y; Robt Gill, 2nd mate, an Englishman; Thos Bills; Geo Raymond; Wm Brown, New Haven; Chas Brown, N Y; Jas Crawford, N Y; Robt Hope, N Y; Wm Riggs, of Bath, Maine; ___ Cary, of Balt; Wm Hicks, of Mass; Benj Evans, also an American; John Williams, of Carnavaron, Wales; Andrew Deall, of Denmark; Rose McCormack & Ellen Miller, stewardnesses. At the first & second cabin passengers perished, comprising the following persons: Dr Grougney, of Cork, Ireland; Mr Roberts; Mr Fordycy, of Scotland; Mr Robinson, of Liverpool; Mr McCayne, of Ohio; Mrs Thorn, Exeter, England; Jas McClaskey; Mary Connor, Isabella Quinn, David McGrattan, Martha Dunsliffe, & others. So complete was the destruction of the dommed ship that the only vestiges of her to be found were small pieces of timber not more than 4 feet long.

The following ofcrs of the Army arrived at New Orleans on Dec 1, in company with Gen Taylor: Maj J H Eaton, Aid-de-camp; Capt R S Garnett, Aid-de-camp; Col W G Belknap, U S A; Maj G Porter, 4th Artl; Maj W W S Bliss, Assist Adj Gen; & Lt C L Wilburn, 3rd Artl.

Boarding House: Capitol Hill, near the south Capitol gate. -Mrs Sidney Edelin

The President's message was telegraphed on Tue to Pittsburg, Cincinnati, Louisville, & Vincennes, [Indiana,] a distance of nearly 900 miles, in about 12 hours. The Message contains nearly or quite 18,000 words. It is one of the wonders of this wonder-working age, that the Message was most probably printed, in part or entire, on the same day in all the principal papers from Richmond to Boston, & as far West as Louisville. -Phil News

Foreign News: 1-Count Bresson, French Ambassador at the Court of the 2 Sicilies, committed suicide on Nov 2; a short time previous, Count Mortier, also French Ambassador at the Court of Turin, attemped to murder both his children & to cut his own throat, while under a fit of insanity. Dr Felix Mendelssohn Barthody, the eminent composer of Elijah, died suddenly at Leipsic, on Nov 4, in his 39th year.

Mrd: on Dec 9, by Rev Hy Slicer, Thos J Galt to Miss Mary A Hunter, all of Wash City.

Mrd: on Dec 9, at St Paul's Church, in Alexandria, Va, by Rev J T Johnson, Mr John C Wills, of Northumberland Co, Va, to Kate E, eldest daughter of Geo H Duffey, of the former place.

Died: yesterday, of erysipelas, Sarah, consort of Mr Geo Cochrane, aged 48 years. Her funeral is this day at 2 o'clock. [Richmond papers please copy.]

Died: on Aug 3 last, at Puebla, Mexico, Mr Albert G Tschiffely, a native of Wash City, in his 36th year.

MON DEC 13, 1847

Ofcrs of the 2nd Regt of Infty, at the village of Coyoshan, [near the city of Mexico,] Aug 23, 1847, resolutions were adopted of their feelings at the death of Capt J W Anderson & Lt T Easley, the latter killed at the battle of Churubusco on Aug 20, & the former receiving a wound in the neck at the same battle which terminated his life 2 days after. To the wife of Capt Anderson, we tender our deepest sympathy. Lt Easley, though but recently joined in the regt, had evinced ability & energy in his profession tending to merits of high promise. We tender our warmest sympathy to his relatives & friends.

B Riley, Vt Col, 2nd Infty, comm'g
T Morris, Capt 2nd Infty
J J B Kingsbury, Capt 2nd Infty
J R Smith, Capt 2nd Infty
S Casey, Capt 2nd Infty
Jas W Penrose, Capt 2nd Infty
H W Wessells, Capt 2nd Infty
C S Lovell, 1st Lt 2nd Infty
Delosier Davidson, 1st Lt 2nd Infty
G C Westcott, 1st Lt & R M M 2nd Infty
J Hayden, 1st Lt 2nd Infty
Edw R S Canby, A A G
B P Tilden, 1st Lt 2nd Infty
N Lyon, 1st Lt 2nd Infty
Jas W Schureman, 2nd Lt 2nd Infty
Chas E Jarvis, 2nd Lt 2nd Infty
Fred Steele, Lt, 2nd Infty
D R Jones, Adj 2nd Infty
N H Davis, 2nd Lt 2nd Infty
W M Garner, 2nd Lt 2nd Infty

Mrd: on Dec 9, by Rev Dr Wines, Alex'r Loughborough Bohrer to Cornelia, eldest daughter of the late A Fisher, of Montg Co, Md.

Died: on Dec 4, suddenly at May's Landing, Atlantic Co, N J, Elias Boudinot Caldwell, 2nd son of the late Elias B Caldwell, Clerk of the U S Supreme Court. The dec'd was a native of Wash City, a graduate of Columbia College, but studied & practiced law in N J, where he was highly respected & esteemed.

Accident on the Reading Railroad on Fri last, near Pottstown: train thrown off the track by the breaking of an axle: Henry Gallagher, a pedlar of Phil, & Owen M Evans, formerly a conductor, were killed.

Springfield Republican: Mr Bela Rose, a workman in the woolen factory of Mr Henry Terry, at Plymouth Hollow, Conn, accidently had both his hands drawn into the picker machinery, & cut off at the wrists.

Obituary-died: Lt Col Saml E Watson, of the Marine Corps, at Vera Cruz. He was an undisguised, open, & uncompromising Christian, & a true-hearted Catholic churchman. -F C P, Freehold, N J

Commitment of Leeds, the swindler. This man was arrested by Capt Goddard on Thu. On Sat last, Mr F S Anthony, of Petersburg, Va, having arrived & identified the prisoner as the person who passed upon him the counterfeit notes, [$3,600,] Leeds was fully committed to await the requisition of the Govn'r of Va.

For sale: by order of the Orphans Court of Wash Co, D C, the exc of Winifred Tuel, dec'd, the personal estate of said dec'd, for cash, in front of the Centre Market, on Dec 18 next. -John McDevitt, auct

Boarding & Day School on Vt ave & L st, is now in successful operaton. Inquire of the Episcopal Clergy of this city, or of the Principal. -G F Morison

For rent: little 2 story brick house on 9th st, between G & H sts, nearly opposite the Rev John C Smith's Church. Key is with Mr Trutler, next door south. Rent $150 per year.

TUE DEC 14, 1847

Senate: Obit: message was received from the Senate announcing the decease of the Hon Jabez W Huntington; when Mr John A Rockwell, of Conn rose & said: My friend died at his residence, at Norwich, on Nov 2 last, after an illness of a few days, at the age of 59. He was by profession a lawyer. Proceedings in relation to the death of the Hon Huntington be communicated to the family of the dec'd by the Clerk.

Public sale of land & fishing shore: by decree of King Geo Co Court, I shall sell, on Jan 13, 1848, at public auction, the Farm called ***Woodstock***, in said county, between 500 & 600 acres; the dwlg house & other improvements are in good repair.
-Geo Fitzhugh, Com'r

Senate: 1-Mr Robt Beall, having 37 votes, was declared the Sgt-at-Arms & Doorkeeper. Assistant Door-keeper: Mr I Holland, having received 49 votes. 2-Ptn of Jedediah Morse, a Revolutionary soldier, for a pension. 3-Ptn of E Goodrich Smith, for compensation for services. 4-Ptn of Lemuel Cushman, adm of the widow of a Revolutionary soldier. 5-Ptn of Esther Fish, the widow of a Revolutionary soldier, for a pension. 6-Ptn of Robt Roberts, praying for an appropriation under the treaty with Spain in 1819 or with France of 1831, for an indemnity for losses sustained by the capture of the ship **Experiment** in 1805. 7-Ptn that the papers of Wm Culver be taken from the files of the House of the last session, & referred to the Cmte of Claims. 8-Ptn of the heirs of Lt Danl Starr, with accompanying papers, be taken from the files of the House at the last session, & be referred to the Cmte on Revolutionary Pensions. 9-Ptn of Mrs Clark, of Colcester, Conn, for the same. 10-Ptn of Francis Allyer, with the accompanying papers, be taken from the files of the House, & be referred to the Cmte of Claims.

For sale or exchange: a lot of ground at the corner of D & 1st sts, containing 11, 600 feet. Also, square 699, with a comfortable frame dwlg. Apply to the subscriber, at the House-Furnishing Store of Boteler & McGregor. -N M McGregor

Wood for sale: I offer the wood on 300 acres of the estate of my father, Alex'r C Bullett, dec'd, lying on the Potomac river, in Prince Wm Co, Va, on which are the well known fisheries of ***Opossum Nose* & *Timber Branch***. Apply on the premises. I forewarn all person from trespassing in any manner on said estate. -Benj C Bullett [Dec 17th newspaper: Public Warning: Mr Benj C Bullett has no interest whatever in any part of the estate of Alex'r C Bullett, dec'd, whether real, personal, or mixed. Whatever interest Benj C Bullett claimed in this estate, he sold, for value received, & conveyed to the legitimate heirs of the said Alex'r C Bullett, by a regular deed of conveyance, now recorded in Prince Williams. -Philip Otterback, Wm Cockrell]

The Trustees of Cairo City Property, at the confluence of the Ohio & Missouri rivers, Ill, having perfected the titles to the same, under the direction of C Wallace Brooke, of Phil, & John M Krum, of St Louis, now offered for sale, 5,000 shares in the beneficial interest of said property. The declaration of trust has been certified by the written opinion of the Hon John Sergeant, of Phil, Beverly Robinson, of N Y, & ex-Chief Justice Williams, of Boston. -Thos S Taylor 70 Walnut st, Phil; Chas Davis, 58 Merchants' Exchange, N Y, Trustees

Medical Dept of the Army: the candidates who were examined & the following were found qualified for appointment, & were accordingly approved:

Lyman H Stone, of Vt	Wm Hammond, of Mo
John M Haden, of Mis	Henry S Hewit, of Conn
Chas H Crane, of Mass	Thos A McPahlin, of Md

Headquarters of the Marine Corps: Wash, Dec 11, 1847. The Maj & Brevet Lt Col Saml E Watson, who died on with a severe disease, & the gallant Twiggs now occupy the same grave at Vera Cruz. -P G Howle, Adj & Inspector

Mrs John H Gibbs informs her friends & the public that she has commenced the Dress, Cloak, & Mantilla making: Pa ave, beween 9th & 10th sts.

WED DEC 15, 1847

Wed last, at the First Reformed Presbyterian Church of Phil, Rev Dr Wylie, pastor, was presented a piece of plate, & a purse containing $500 in gold. This was the 50th anniversary of Dr Wylie's assumption of his pastoral charge. There stood the noble old man, nearly 75 years of age, deeply affected. -Phil Bulletin

Elected a Board of Directors for the Pittsburg & Connellsville Railroad Co at Pittsburg on Monday last:

Jos Markle	John Gebhert	Geo Hogg
Geo J Ashman	Edw D Gazzam	Wm J Totten
Alex'r M Hill	Wm Larimer, jr	John Fuller
Thos Bakewell	Walter Bryant	J C Plummer

Mrs Mason, of New London, Conn, lost her life last Sunday. Her 2 dghts went to a meeting in the neighborhood, & on their return to the house, they found it enveloped in smoke. The founder their mother, Mrs Mason, some 45 years of age, lying at the foot of the stairway dead-her clothes on fire, & pieces of a spirit gas lamp lying around. It is presumed she slipped on the stairs, breaking the lamp.

On Thu week, says the Phil Christian Observer, the Rev C Baldwin & wife, of Bloomfield, N J; the Rev S Cummings & wife, of N H; the Rev Wm L Richards, son of Mr Richards, of the Sandwich Islands, & Miss Pohlman, a sister of the Rev Mr Pohlman, of Amoy, missionaries of the A B C F M, & the Rev Mr James, M D, & wife, & another young brother of the Am Baptist Board, embarked in the ship **Valparaiso**, Capt Lockwood, from Ohio for Canton.

The venerable Chancellor Kent, of N Y, died at his residence in that city on Sunday, in his 86th year. Mr Kent passed through the various offices of Recorder, Circuit Judge, Justice of the Supreme Court, & Chief Justice & Chancellor.

House of Reps: 1-Ptn of Amzy Judd, praying for a grant of bounty land. 2-Ptn of Anna Giffin, the widow of a Revolutionary soldier, for a pension. 3-Ptn of Geo Hix, of Monroe, Tenn, praying compensation for depredations committed by Lt Fowler & company, in the service of the U S, in the Cherokee nation. 4-Ptn of Elisha H Holmes, with the documents connected therewith, for the renewal of his patent. 5-Ptn of Jos C Delano, & other shipmasters & merchants of New Bedford, Mass, for a beacon-light on Palmer's Island, in the harbor at that port. 6-Memorial of E Sawin & others, of Fairhaven, Mass, praying that the claim of Albora Allen for a balance due him for a revenue boat built by him under a contract with the collector of the port of Nantucket be paid. Mr Grinnell moved that the documents of Mr Allen, be taken from the files & be referred to the Cmte of Claims.

7-Ptn of H D Johnson: referred to the Cmte on Naval Affairs. 8-Ptn & papers of Jacob Gideon, of Caroline Sanders, excs of Wm G Sanders, be referred to the Cmte of Claims. 9-Ptn & papers of the heirs of John Cox: referred to the Cmte of Claims. 10-Ptn of Thos Jenne, praying for bounty land. 11-Ptn of Orange H Dibble, of Buffalo, N Y, praying for the balance of his claim on a contract for bldg a bridge across the Potomac at Washington. 12-Ptn of Sarah Corbin, praying for a pension as the widow of a Revolutionary soldier. 13-Ptn of Sylvia Pond, praying that her pension as widow of a Revolutionary soldier may be continued for life. 14-Ptn of Eunice Goodell, praying for the continuance of her pension as the widow of a Revolutionary soldier. 15-Memorial of Wm Reddin & others, in relation to the collection & disbursement of hospital money on the great lakes. 16-Ptn of Ira Baldwin taken from the files & referred to the Cmte on Private Land Claims. 17-Ptn & papers of Peter Coville taken from the files & referred to the Cmte on Invalid Pensions. 18-Ptn of John R Williams, of Detroit, Mich, for damages. 19-Ptn of the admx of Conrad Teneyck, dec'd, late of Michigan. 20-Ptn of John Gilbert, of Alleghany Co, Pa, asking for an increase of his pension. 21-Ptns of Stephen A Corey, of Saratoga Co; of Saml D Sabine, of Saratoga Co; of Geo Newton, of Fulton Co; of Hugh Riddle, of Schnectady; of Henry R Wendell, of Schnectady; N Y. And the ptn of Ruliff Van Brunt, presented in Dec, 1844. 22-Ptn of J Randolph Clay for compensation as Charge d'Affaires. 23-Ptn of Henry Simpson, surviving administrator of Geo Simpson, dec'd, for a commission for services in obtaining a Gov't loan in 1813. 24-Ptn of J C Maclellan, for additional remuneration for expenses incurred by the funeral from his hotel of a member of the House of Reps. 25-Ptn of J P Skinner & Geo B Green. 26-Memorial of Jas Monroe, of N Y C, praying to be admitted to a seat as a member of the House of Reps for the 13th Congress, in the place of David S Jackson, the sitting member: referred to the Cmte of Elections. 17-Ptn of Hannah Avery, late widow of King Avery, dec'd, of Cornwall, N Y, praying to be restored in the possession, use, & occupation of certain land occupied by her father, Hugh McClannon, in his life time, situated within the tract of land at West Point, claimed by the U S: referred to the Cmte on the Judiciary. 18-Bill from the Senate for the relief of the heirs of John Paul Jones was taken up & read twice by its title. At the last session, it was passed by a large majority of this House, & by the Senate almost unanimously, with a trifling amendment in which this House concurred. On being carried to the Pres' room, it was accidentally dropped, & failed to receive his signature & to become law. Mr Bowlin said, in the passage of this bill, he believed it to be wrong; but he should not now be mad enough to fight against it. One feature was amended on the motion of Mr Daniel, & by that, $900,000 was saved to the country. The amount had been as large as $1,200,000. He found that, contrary to every principle of justice & of right, people from Scotland, of whom we knew nothing, were made the legatees of American seamen & American ofcrs who served with Paul Jones. This Gov't was the residuary legatee of these ofcrs & seamen on the failure of others to appear; & he asked that it might be referred & printed. He had not intention to contest the passage of this bill, but he did desire to see that it was passed in no other shape than that in which it was when, at the close of the last session, it was designed for the Pres' signature. The bill was referred to the Cmte of Claims, & was ordered to be printed.

Trustee's sale: by virtue of 2 deed of trust, executed by the late Chas King, dec'd, to me, one dated Jun 15, 1833, recorded in Liber H S 6, folios 90 thru 94, of the land records of Montg Co, Md; the other dated Dec 12, 1842, recorded in Liber B S 11, files 435 thru 438, of the said land records: auction on Jan 6, on the premises, valuable tract of land in said county, estimated to contain about 300 acres, & embracing parts of ***Friendship & Pritchett's Purchase***, with the appurtenances, being the entire farm in the occupancy & cultivation of the said Chas King at the time of his death. This farm lies on the turnpike leading from Gtwn to Rockville. It has several tenements for residences, with other necessary bldgs. A valid deed of conveyance of the premises sold to such purchasers. -Clement Cox, trustee -E S Wright, auct

Wash Corp: 1-Cmte of Claims: bill for the relief of Isaac Silvy: passed. 2-Ptn of David Hines & others, for a flag footway on 20th st, across Pa ave: referred to the Cmte on Improvements.

The remains of the late Elias B Caldwell, having been brought to Bladensburg, the residence of his brother-in-law, Robt Wright, will be conveyed from thence to the Congressional Burying Ground this morning, at 1 o'clock, where the relatives & friends of the family are respectfully invited to attend.

Criminal Court-Wash: yesterday. 1-Nelson Simms, free negro, [an old offender,] guilty of stealing a silver watch: 2 years in the penitentiary. 2-Richd Bays, free negro, guilty of stealing a coat, property of C Homilier: 1 year in the penitentiary. 3-Georgiana Humphreys, free negress, convicted of grand larceny: 2 gold rings the property of Isaac S Ball: 1 year in the penitentiary. 4-John Henry Butler, free negro, [an old offender,] convicted of larceny: 18 months in the penitentiary. 5-Hannah Turner, free negress, convicted of grand larceny, the property of Hazle Benezet: 15 months in the penitentiary. 6-Jas Digges, free negro, convicted of stealing a horse, saddle, bridle, the property of Richd Mason: 2 years in the penitentiary.

Senate: 1-Ptn from Mary C Kern, asking repayment of money advances by her husband for the use of the Govn't. 2-Ptn from Anne B Cox, asking payment of a balance standing to the credit of her late husband on the books of the Treasury. 3-Ptn from Adelaide Snyder & others, heirs of Jean F Perry, asking confirmation of their claims to certain lands in Ill. 4-Ptn from Sarah Crandall, asking a pension. 5-Ptn from Jas Womsby, a Revolutionary soldier, for a pension. 6-Ptn from Wm Nation & Rachel Davis, asking to be allowed bounty land. 7-Ptn from Evelina Porter, widow of Com Porter, asking to be allowed a pension. 8-Ptn from Saml B Nichols, asking compensation for his services in removing Creek Indians in 1827-28. 9-Ptn from Thos P McBlair, asking that certain payments made by him to acting ofcrs may be allowed in the settlement of his accounts. 10-Bill for the relief of Jos Wilson: introduced. 11-Joint resolution for the relief of David Shaw & Solomon T Corser: introduced.

Mrd: Dec 12, at College Hill, by Rev J S Bacon, Mr Jas Fraser to Miss Salina Broadrup, both of Wash City.

The surviving trustees of the late Mechanics' Bank of Alexandria, have this day declared a 2.50% dividend. -Robt Brockett, Trustee

THU DEC 16, 1847
Columbia Furnace, for rent. Pursuant to a decree of the Circuit Superior Court of Law & Chancery for Shenandoah Co, in a suit therein pending between the Bank of Washington, plntf, & Geo F Hupp & others, dfndnts: sale on Dec 13, upon the premises, proceed to rent at public renting, Columbia Furnace, with the Forge, Mill, & lands attached, lying in said county. -Mark Bird, Com'r

Public sale of valuable fisheries & land on the Potomac River: under authority of a deed of trust from Richd Thompson & wife to Wm Prout, dated Oct 14, 1837, & as substituted Trustee in the place of said Prout, deceased, by the decree of the County Circuit of Fairfax Co, Va, will offer, on Jan 5, all that tract of land in Fairfax Co, Va, which was purchased by the said Richd Thompson from Thomson F Mason, as Trustee of Geo Mason, late of ***Gunston***, in Fairfax Co, dec'd, being part of the ***Gunston estate***, binding on the Potomac river, & embracing several valuable Fisheries, among which are included ***Court's Point*** & ***Hallowing Point***, which tract of land contains 1,081 acres, more or less. -Cassius F Lee, Trustee

Orphans Court of Wash Co, D C. Letters of administration on the personal estate of Mary E Clements, late of said county, dec'd. -W Lenox, administrator de bonis non

FRI DEC 17, 1847
Senate: 1-The Hon Jesse Speight died at his residence, in the State of Mississippi, on May 1 last, after a long & painful illness. He was born in Green Co, N C, a few years anterior to the close of the last century, where he continued uninterruptedly to reside until his removal to the State of Mississippi in 1837. 2-Ptn from Nathl Hoggatt, in relation to confirmation of a land title. 3-Ptn from Wm Pumphrey, asking confirmation of a land title. 4-Ptn from Margaret Carmick, widow of Danl Carmick, asking a pension. 5-Ptn from Eliz Pistole, papers in relation to her pension. 6-Ptn from Mary D Wade, for a pension. 7-Ptn from Henry Washington, asking redress for illegal conduct on the part of the Surveyor Genr'l of the Public Lands in Florida. 8-Ptn from Jas Edwards, asking compensation for property destroyed during the Florida war. Ptn from Eugene Van Ness, Richd Humphreys, Geo Center, & others, in relation to the same subject. 9-Ptn from Maria Caldwell, asking payment of certain outstanding loan ofc certificates lost or destroyed. 10-Ptn from Geo H Lee & others, members of the bar in Va, asking an increase of the salary of the judge of the western district of Va. 11-Ptn from Oliver C Harris, asking an extension of his patent for a paint mill.

Galveston Civilian of Dec 2: yesterday the remains of Capt Saml H Walker were conveyed from the steamer **Palmetto** to the City Hall, followed by a large procession. It will be conveyed to its final resting place at San Antonio, where a spot of great beauty had been selected.

House of Reps: 1-Ptn of F Sumter, adm de bonis non of the late Gen T Sumter, praying payment for money advanced to the colonies by the said T Sumter during the war of the Revolution. 2-Ptn of Nancy Tompkins, with accompanying documents, be taken from the files of the House & referred to the Cmte on Naval Affairs. 3-Ptn of Sally C Wenwood & Eliza S Wenwood. 4-Ptn of Catharine Henrietta C Johnson, widow of Capt Hezekiah Johnson, late of the U S Army, for a pension. 5-Memorial of the heirs of Col David Hopkins, dec'd, with accompanying papers. 6-Ptn of Thos Scott, late register of the land ofc at Chillicothe, praying compensation for extra services connected with the duties of his ofc; heretofore presented Apr 1, 1844. 7-Ptn of Saml Reed, of Pike Co, Ohio, praying payment for part of a tract of land purchased of the U S, the title to which has not been maintained; heretofore presented Jan 21, 1846. 8-Ptn of Jas Morrow, asking payment of certain bills of promise due to him from the Gov't: referred to the Cmte of Claims. 9-Memorial of Jas H Couley, praying for an amendment of the act for his relief, passed & approved on Mar 3, 1847: referred to the Cmte on Naval Affairs. 10-Ptn of Henry Reeks, praying that a special act may be passed to authorize a warrant to be issued to him for the bounty land of his brother, a deceased volunteer: referred to the Cmte on Private Land Claims. 11-Ptn & papers of Lt Jas M Gilliss be withdrawn from the files & referred to the Cmte on Naval Affairs. 12-Ptn of Hall J Kelly, a pioneer in the expiration of Oregon, asking for a grant of land in that Territory. 13-Ptn of Jonathan Moore, of Hadly, Mass, a Revolutionary soldier, asking for a pension. 14-Ptn of the administrator of Geo Brent, praying for commutation pay & pension due said estate. 15-Ptn of the legal reps of Isaac D Taulbee, praying remuneration for a horse lost in the Black Hawk war. 16-Ptn of Mary Patton. 17-Ptn & papers in the case of Danl Wilson, an invalid soldier of the last war: referred. 18-Papers in the case of Geo B Hollenback, Wm Harris, & others, applicants for damages for losses sustained in the Black Hawk war: referred. 19-Ptn of Cornelius Manning & Catharine Hodges, widow of Benj Hodges, praying compensation for a slave taken by the British during the late war. 20-Memorial of Thos Crown, for remuneration for losses sustained by him in consequence of a violation of a contract by the U S. 21-Ptn of Frances Swann, admx of Wm J Swann, for losses sustained during the late war with Great Britain. 22-Ptn of Reynal Hilleary, for remuneration in lieu of bounty land. 23-Ptn of Wm S Dilly, of Trumbull Co, Ohio. Ptn of D Ide & others, of same county. Also, the ptn of Nathan Kinne & others, of same county. 24-Ptn of Hugh B Branch, of Andrew J Kriel, & of Henson Stevens. 25-Memorial of Harriet Burney. 26-Ptn & memorial of Elias Coon, of Connecticut, praying for fishing bounty on the schnr **Congress**, which was wrecked in 1844. 27-Ptn of Jacob Olinger, praying a pension for services in the Revolutionary war. 28-Memorial of Thos L Ross, postmaster at Macon, Ga, setting forth certain inequalities in the operation of the post ofc laws.

Circuit Court of Wash Co, D C. Fred'k Strother, [colored,] insolvent debtor, has applied to be discharged from imprisonment. -Wm Brent, clk

D A Smith has built a new & substantial bridge over the Patispsco river, at Elk Ridge Landing, on the Washington turnpike road, & it is now ready for the traveling public.

Died: on Nov 11, on board the U S ship **John Adams**, at Vera Cruz, of yellow fever, Geo J Marshall, Gunner of that ship. It may be some consolation to his family to be assured of the high esteem in which he was held by myself & every ofcr in the ship. His fellow students at Gtwn College remember him with affection as one among them distinguished for his ever amiable & generous disposition. -S

Mrd: on Tue last, by Rev Mr Van Horsigh, Mr Thos C Boarman to Miss Jannette R, daughter of Maj J Manning.

Mrd: on Tue, by Rev John C Smith, Mr Dangerfield Jones to Miss Mary Jane Boyd, all of Wash City.

Mrd: on Tue last, by Rev Mr Butler, Edwin J McClery to Eliz, daughter of the late Hon Selah R Hobbie.

SAT DEC 18, 1847

Mrd: on Dec 14, in Balt, by Rev John C Backus, Edmund Pendleton, of Va, to Charlotte Ramsay, youngest daughter of the late Alex'r Robinson, of that city.

House of Reps: 1-The Hon Geo C Dromgoole, a late member of this House, died on Apr 27 last, at his residence in Brunswick Co, Va, a few days after he had received intelligence of his re-election. His father, a native of Ireland, was one of the earliest settlers in his district. His was the voluntary duty to publish from his pulpit to his various congregations the declaration of American independence. For more than 50 years he labored to his fellow-man. A few years have elapsed since he left us. The virtue of the father stood as a guaranty for the promises of the son.

Died: Dec 17, Patrick Moran, a native of the county of Wexford, Ireland, in his 34th year, but for the last 20 years a resident of Wash City. His funeral will take place from his late residence on 8th st, today at 3 o'clock.

Died: yesterday, in his 19th year, Wm J Judge, son of Caroline M & the late John Judge, formerly of the Navy Yard. His funeral will taken place at his mother's residence, on 9th st, near E, tomorrow at half past 2 o'clock. The members of the St Matthew's Sunday School & friends & acquaintances are invited to attend.

Furnished parlor & chambers to rent, with or without board. Apply to J L Henshaw, 14th st, between F & G sts, square north of Willard's City Hotel.

MON DEC 20, 1847

House of Reps: 1-Ptn of A Bandouin & A D Robert, of N Y C, praying for remuneration for loss of a flatboat loaded with ice, caused by a collision with the steamer **Col Harney**, a vessel belonging to the U S. 2-Memorial of John Crosby, of New Orleans, administrator of his brother, the late Purser Andrew D Crosby, & on behalf of the children of the dec'd, praying that a pension may be granted them for 5 years. 3-Memorial of Ann H Cox, of

New Orleans, asking payment of an admitted balance due to the late Nathl Cox, formerly Navy Agent at New Orleans. 4-Ptn of Fred'k Durrive, praying to be confirmed in the purchase of a tract of land. 5-Ptn of Mary L Keen, of New Orleans, asking the repayment of a sum of money disbursed by her late husband from his private money whilst attached to the recruiting station at N Y. 6-Ptn of A G Farragut, of New Orleans, a Lt in the U S Navy, praying that he may be promoted to the rank of Capt. 7-Ptn of Anne W Angus, praying to be placed on the pension roll. 8-Ptn of Moses Van Campen for the payment of certain Revolutionary claims. 8-Ptn of Thos Scott, late Register of the Land Ofc at Chillicothe, Ohio, praying for compensation for extra services in discharging the duties of his ofc: heretofore presented. 9-Ptn of Saml Reed, of Pike Co, Ohio, praying compensation for land purchased by him of the U S, the title to which has not been maintained: heretofore presented. 10-Ptn of Thos H Graham, of Daviess Co, Indiana, asking compensation for a flatboat & cargo, lost by being struck & sunk by the Gov't steam frig **Alleghany**, on the Mississippi river, near Memphis. 11-Ptn of Jesse Young, of Hector, Tompkins Co, N Y, a wounded soldier, praying for an increase of pension. 12-Ptn of the heirs of Benj Montagne be taken from the files of the House & referred to the Cmte on Revolutionary Claims. 13-Ptn of Lewis Benedict, asking the passage of a law authorizing him to locate a section of land. 14-Mr Lumpkin withdrew from the files of the Clerk's ofc the ptn & papers of Saml W Bell, a Cherokee Indian, & they were referred to the Cmte on Indian Affairs. 15-Memorial of Thos Ap C Jones, praying to be restored to the list of navy pensioners for partial disabilities by wounds received in battle. 16-Ptn of John Mason, of Va, asking payment for certain cannon manufactured by him for the naval service. 17-Ptn of Phebe Brown, widow of Wm Brown, dec'd, a soldier in the war of the Revolution, for a pension. 18-Ptn of Jas Sloan & others, for an appropriation for the harbor at Buffalo, N Y. 19-Ptn of Ephraim F Gilbert, of Erie Co, N Y, praying for the settlement & payment of his claims against the Gov't. 20-Ptn of Thos Raymond, for a pension. 21-Ptn of Polly Aldrick, for a pension. 22-Ptn of Silas Waterman, for a pension. 23-Ptn of John O Dickey. 24-Ptn of Giles London. 25-Papers of John R Goodenough were taken from the files & referred to the Cmte on Private Land Claims. 26-Ptn of Pierre Choteau, jr, & others, legal reps of Julian Dubuque, dec'd, were withdraw from the files & referred to the Cmte on Private Land Claims. 27-Ptn of Geo R Smith, of Missouri, taken from the files & referred to the Cmte on the Post Ofc & Post Roads. 28-Ptn of Wm B Edwards, praying for a pension, taken from the files & referred to the Cmte in Invalid Pensions. 29-Memorial of Henry M Shreve, praying compensation for the use of the steam snag-boat, patented by him. 30-Ptns of Jos Holmes for bounty for the volunteers **Industry** & **Mary Bee**. 31-The papers in the case of Peter Shaffer were withdrawn from the files & referred to the Cmte of Claims. 32-The papers in the case of John W Hockett were withdrawn & referred to the Cmte of Claims. 33-The ptn & papers of John Moore White, of N J, were withdrawn from the files & referred to the Cmte on Revolutionary Claims. 34-The ptn & papers of John J Adams, of N J, were withdrawn from the files of the House & referred to the Cmte on Patents. 35-The ptn of John Pettibone, with documents, in behalf of himself & the other heirs of Danl Pettibone, praying compensation for the construction & use of the "Patent Rarifying Air Stove," now in use in the Capitol, & for the use of said patent in the public bldgs of the Gov't. 36-Memorial of P J Slaughter, asking for pay & bounty land for services in the army. Memorial of Benj R

Harden, of the same kind. 37-Ptn of Bryan Callaghan, praying compensation for goods destroyed by the U S troops under Col Harney. 38-Ptn of Moses Noyes, with papers, were taken from the files & referred to the Cmte on Revolutionary Claims. 39-Ptn of J W Nye, for an examination of his account & payment of money due him under a contract with the House of Reps. 40-Ptn of Mrs Elvira F Smith, [widow of the late Maj Henry Smith, of Monroe, Michigan,] for a pension. 41-Ptn of Nathan P Bennis, a citizen of Leon Co, Florida, for a grant of land for the purpose of experimenting in the manufacture of turpentine. 42-Memorial of Benj J Cahoone. 43-Ptn & papers of the heirs of Bernard Todd, dec'd, to be taken from the files & referred to the Cmte of Claims.

Army Genr'l Orders: Gen Order 36: War Dept, Adj Genrl's Ofc, Wash, Dec 4, 1847. Promotions & Appointments in the U S Army, made by the Pres, since the publication of Genr'l Orders, #27, of Aug 5, 1847. Promotions:
Quartermaster's Dept:
Capt Osborne Cross, Assist Quartermaster, to be Quartermaster with the rank of Major, Jul 24, 1847, vice Smith, dec'd.
Medical Dept:
Assist Surgeon Wm Hammond, to be Surgeon, Aug 7, 1847, vice Hawkins, dec'd.
5th Regt of Dragoons:
2nd Lt Jos H Whittlesey, to be 1st Lt, Oct 18, 1847, vice Jenkins, dec'd.
Brevet 2nd Lt Geo Stoneman, jr, to be 2nd Lt, Jul 12, 1847, vice McElvain, dec'd.
Brevet 2nd Lt Geo F Evans, to be 2nd Lt, Oct 18, 1847, vice Whittlesey, promoted.
2nd Regt of Dragoons:
1st Lt Ripley A Arnold, to be Capt, Aug 18, 1847, vice Thomas, killed in battle.
2nd Lt Patrick Calhoun, to be 1st Lt, Jul 28, 1847, vice Hill, dec'd.
2nd Lt Elias K Kane, to be 1st Lt, Aug __, 1847, vice Arnold, promoted.
Brevet 2nd Lt Jas Oaken, to be 2nd Lt, Jul 29, 1847, vice Calhoun, promoted.
Brevet 2nd Lt Wm D Smith, to be 2nd Lt, Aug 18, 1847, vice Kane, promoted.
3rd Regt of Dragoons:
1st Lt Walter H Jenifer, to be Capt, Jul 16, 1847, vice Duff, dec'd.
2nd Lt Wm Walker, to be 1st Lt, Jul 16, 1847, vice Jenifer, promoted.
Regt of Mounted Riflemen:
1st Lt Michl E Van Buren, to be Capt, Oct 9, 1847, vice Walker, killed in battle.
2nd Lt Washington L Elliott, to be 1st Lt, Jul 26, 1847, vice Tipton, dec'd.
2nd Lt Geo McLane, to be 1st Lt, Oct 9, 1847, vice Van Buren, promoted.
Brevet 2nd Lt Innis N Palmer, to be 2nd Lt, Jul 20, 1847, vice Elliott, promoted.
Brevet 2nd Lt Jas Stuart, to be 2nd Lt, Oct 9, 1847, vice McLane, promoted.
1st Regt of Artl:
1st Lt Jas L Donaldson, to be Capt, Aug 20, 1847, vice Capron, killed in battle.
1st Lt Wm W Mackall, to be Capt, Aug 20, 1847, vice Donaldson, Assist Quartermaster, who vacates his regimental commission.
2nd Lt Asher R Eddy, to be 1st Lt, Aug 19, 1847, vice Johnstone, killed in battle.
2nd Lt Henry Coppee, to be 1st Lt, Aug 20, 1847, vice Donaldson, promoted.
2nd Lt Edw C Boynton, to be 1st Lt, Aug 20, 1847, vice Mackall, promoted.

2nd Lt Thos J Jackson, to be 1st Lt, Aug 26, 1847, vice Irons, dec'd-of wounds received in battle.
Brevet 2nd Lt John H Dickerson, of the 4th Artl, to be 2nd Lt, Aug 19, 1847, vice Eddy, promoted.
Brevet 2nd Lt Danl T Beltzhoover, to be 2nd Lt, Aug 20, 1847, vice Coppee, promoted.
Brevet 2nd Lt Otis H Tillinghast, of the 3rd Artl, to be 2nd Lt, Aug 20, 1847, vice Boynton, promoted.
Brevet 2nd Lt Jas B Fry, of the 3rd Artl, to be 2nd Lt, Aug 20, 1847, vice Hoffman, killed in battle.
Brevet 2nd Lt Ambrose P Hill, to be 2nd Lt, Aug 26, 1847, vice Jackson, promoted.
2nd Regt of Artillery:
1st Lt Robt Allen, to be Capt, Oct 19, 1847, vice Mackenzie, dec'd.
2nd Lt Henry F Clarke, to be 1st Lt, Sep 8, 1847, vice Armstrong, killed in battle.
2nd Lt Josiah H Carlisle, to b 1st Lt, Oct 12, 1847, vice Shackelford, dec'd-of wounds received in battle.
2nd Lt Geo Edwards, to be 1st Lt, Oct 19, 1847, vice Allen, promoted.
2nd Lt Thos B J Weld, to be 1st Lt, Oct 19, 1847, vice Daniels, dec'd-of wounds received in battle.
Brevet 2nd Lt Anson J Cook, to be 2nd Lt, Sep 8, 1847, vice Clarke, promoted.
Brevet 2nd Lt Chas Griffin, of the 4th Artl, to be 2nd Lt, Oct 12, 1847, vice Carlisle, promoted.
3rd Regt of Artl:
1st Lt Wm Austine, to be Capt, Aug 13, 1847, vice Wall, dec'd.
1st Lt Henry S Burton, to be Capt, Sep 22, 1847, vice Tompkins, resigned.
2nd Lt Louis D Welch, to be 1st Lt, Sep 8, 1847, vice Austine, promoted.
2nd Lt Geo P Andrews, to be 1st Lt, Sep 8, 1847, vice Ayres, killed in battle.
2nd Lt Colville J Minor, to be 1st Lt, Sep 8, 1847, vice Farry, killed in battle.
2nd Lt Hamilton L Shields, to be 1st Lt, Sep 22, 1847, vice Burton, promoted.
2nd Lt Geo T Andrews, to be 1st Lt, Oct 19, 1847, vice Churchill, dec'd.
2nd Lt Benj P McNeil, to be 1st Lt, Dec 4, 1847, vice Welch, promoted.
Brevet 2nd Lt Geo Patten, to be 2nd Lt, Aug 13, 1847, vice Welch, promoted.
Brevet 2nd Lt Horatio G Gibson, of the 2nd Artl, to be 2nd Lt, Sep 8, 1847, vice G P Andrews, promoted.
Brevet 2nd Lt Ambrose E Burnside, of the 2nd Artl, to be 2nd Lt, Sep 8, 1847, vice Minor, promoted.
Brevet 2nd Lt Romeyn B Ayres, of the 4th Artl, to be 2nd Lt, Sep 22, 1847, vice Shields, promoted.
4th Regt of Artl:
1st Lt Wm G Freeman, to be Capt, Sep 13, 1847, vice Drum, killed in battle.
2nd Lt Francis Collins, to be 1st Lt, Sep 13, 1847, vic Freeman, promoted.
2nd Lt Edmond Hayes, to be 1st Lt, Sep 13, 1847, vice Benjamin, killed in battle.
2nd Lt Darius N Couch, to be 1st Lt, Sep 4, 1847, vice Curd, resigned.
Brevet 2nd Lt John Gibbon, of the 3rd Artl, to be 2nd Lt, Sep 13, 1847, vice Collins, promoted.

Brevet 2nd Lt Clermont L Best, of the 1st Artl, to be 2nd Lt, Sep 13, 1847, vice Hayes, promoted.
1st Regt of Infty:
Capt Geo C Hutter, of the 6th Infty, to be Major, vice Clark, dec'd, to date from Feb 16, 1847, & to take place on the list of Majors of Infty next below Major Jouett.
1st Lt Robt S Granger, to be Capt, Sep 8, 1847, vice Abercrombie, promoted to 5th Infty.
2nd Lt Stephen D Carpenter, to be 1st Lt, Sep 8, 1847, vice Granger, promoted.
Brevet 2nd Lt Egbert L Viele, of the 2nd Infty, to be 2nd Lt, Sep 8, 1847, vice Carpenter, promoted.
2nd Regt of Infty:
1st Lt Marsena R Patrick, to be Capt, Aug 20, 1847, vice Anderson, killed in battle.
2nd Lt Edw Murray, to be 1st Lt, Aug 20, 1847, vice Patrick, promoted.
Brevet 2nd Lt Henry B Hendershott, of the 5th Infty, to be 2nd Lt, Aug 20, 1847, vice Murray, promoted.
Brevet 2nd Lt Tredwell Moore, of the 8th Infty, to be 2nd Lt, Aug 20, 1847, vice Easley, killed in battle.
3rd Regt of Infty:
2nd Lt John C McFerran, to be 1st Lt, Oct 22, 1847, vice Johnson, resigned.
4th Regt of Infty:
1st Lt Henry Prince, to be Capt, Sep 26, 1847, vice Morrison, promoted to 8th Infty.
2nd Lt Ulysses S Grant, to be 1st Lt, Sep 16, 1847, vice Smith, dec'd-of wounds received in battle.
2nd Lt Henry M Judah, to be 1st Lt, Sep 26, 1847, vice Prince, promoted.
Brevet 2nd Lt Lewis C Hunt, of the 3rd Infty, to be 2nd Lt, Sep 13, 1847, vice Rodgers, killed in battle.
Brevet 2nd Lt John De Russy, of the 6th Infty, to be 2nd Lt, Sep 16, 1847, vice Grant, promoted.
5th Regt of Infty:
Major Wm G Belknap, of the 8th Infty, to be Lt Col, Sep 26, 1847, vice McIntosh, dec'd-of wounds received in battle.
Capt John J Abercrombie, of the 1st Infty, to be Major, Sep 8, 1847, vice Scott, killed in battle.
1st Lt Nathan B Russell, to be Capt, Sep 8, 1847, vice Merrill, killed in battle.
1stLt John A Whitall, to be Capt, Sep 11, 1847, vice Smith, dec'd-of wounds received in battle.
2nd Lt Henry R Selden, to be 1st Lt, Sep 8, 1847, vice Rossell, promoted.
2nd Lt Fred'k T Dent, to be 1st Lt, Sep 11, 1847, vice Whitall, promoted.
Brevet 2nd Lt Thos H Neill, of the 4th Infty, to be 2nd Lt, Sep 8, 1847, vice Selden, promoted.
Brevet 2nd Lt Wm Burns, of the 3rd Infty, to be 2nd Lt, Sep 8, 1847, vice Strong, killed in battle.
Brevet 2nd Lt Edw F Abbott, of the 6th Infty, to be 2nd Lt, Sep 8, 1847, vice Burwell, killed in battle.
Brevet 2nd Lt Montgomery P Harrison, of the 7th Infty, to be 2nd Lt, Sep 11, 1847, vice Dent, promoted.

Brevet 2nd Lt Augustus H Seward, of 8th Infty, to be 2nd Lt, Sep 13, 1847, vice J P Smith, killed in battle.
6th Regt of Infty:
1st Lt Henry W Wharton, to be Capt, Feb 16, 1847, vice Hutter, promoted to 1st Infty.
2nd Lt Richd B Garnett, to be 1st Lt, Feb 16, 1847, vice Wharton, promoted.
2nd Lt Franklin F Flint, to be 1st Lt, Oct 12, 1847, vice Bacon, dec'd-of wounds received in battle.
Brevet 2nd Lt Henry Heth, of the 1st Infty, to be 2nd Lt, Seo 22, 1847, vice Ernst, dec'd-of wounds received in battle.
7th Regt of Infty:
1st Lt Henry Little, to be Capt, Aug 20, 1847, vice Hanson, killed in battle.
2nd Lt John M Jones, to be 1st Lt, Aug 20, 1847, vice Little, promoted.
2nd Lt Franklin Gardner, to be 1st Lt, Sep 13, 1847, vice Gantt, killed in battle.
2nd Lt Jos H Potter, to be 1st Lt, Oct 30, 1847, vice Scott, dec'd.
Brevet 2nd Lt Henry M Black, of the 4th Infty, to be 2nd Lt, Aug 20, 1847, vice Jones, promoted.
Brevet 2nd Lt Peter W L Plympton, to be 2nd Lt, Sep 13, 1847, vice Gardner, promoted.
8th Regt of Infty:
Capt Pitcairn Morrison, of the 4th Infty, to be Major, Sep 26, 1847, vice Belknap, promoted to 5th Infty.
2nd Lt Jacob J Booker, to be 1st Lt, Sep 10, 1847, vice Burbank, dec'd-of wounds received in battle.
2nd Lt Edmunds B Holloway, to be 1st Lt, Sep 17, 1847, vice Morris, dec'd-of wounds received in battle.
Brevet 2nd Lt Washington P Street, of the 5th Infty, to be 2nd Lt, Sep 10, 1847, vice Booker, promoted.
Brevet 2nd Lt Edw D Blake, of the 2nd Infty, to be 2nd Lt, Sep 17, 1847, vice Holloway, promoted.
9th Regt of Infty:
Lt Col Jones M Withers, of the 13th Infty, to be Colonel, Sep 13, 1847, vice Ransom, killed in battle.
Capt Wm B Taliaferro, of the 11th Infty, to be Major, Aug 12, 1847, vice Seymour, promoted to 12th Infty.
1st Lt Edw H Fitzgerald, to be Capt, Sep 8, 1847, vice Pitman, promoted to 14th Infty.
1st Lt Lyman Bissell, to be Capt, Sep 25, 1847, vice Thompson, dec'd.
1st Lt John S Slocum, to be Capt, Oct 9, 1847, vice Woodman, resigned.
1st Lt Chas J Sprague, to be Capt, Dec 4, 1847, vice Palmer, resigned.
1st Lt Geo Bowers, to be Capt, Dec 4, 1847, vice Johnson, resigned.
1st Lt Danl H Fram, to be 1st Lt Sep 8, 1847, vice Fitzgerald, promoted.
2nd Lt Asa A Stoddard, to be 1st Lt, Sep 25, 1847, vice Bissel, promoted.
2nd Lt Thos P Pierce, to be 1st Lt, Oct 9, 1847, vice Slocum, promoted.
2nd Lt John A Gove, to be 1st Lt, dec 4, 1847, vice Sprague, promoted.
2nd Lt Thompson H Crosby, to be 1st Lt, Dec 4, 1847, vice Bowers, promoted.
2nd Lt Alpheus T Palmer, to be 1st Lt, Dec 4,1 847, vice Crum, resigned
10th Regt of Infty:

1st Lt Geo W Taylor, to be Capt, Sep 13, 1847, vice Pitcher, promoted to 11th Infty.
2nd Lt Edw McGarry, to be 1st Lt, Sep 18, 1847, vice Taylor, promoted.
11th Regt of Infty:
Maj John H Savage, of the 14th Infty, to be Lt Colonel, Sep 8, 1847, vice Graham, killed in battle.
Capt Matthew S Pitcher, of the 10th Infty, to be Major, Sep 13, 1847, vice Morgan, promoted to 13th Infty.
1st Lt Chas T Campbell, to be Capt, Aug 12, 1847, vice Taliaferro, promoted to 9th Infty.
1st Lt John I Gregg, to be Capt, Sep 23, 1847, vice Waddell, dec'd.
2nd Lt Benj F Harley, to be 1st Lt, Aug 12, 1847, vice Campbell, promoted
2nd Lt Horace Haldeman, to be 1st Lt, Sep 23, 1847, vice Gregg, promoted.
2nd Lt Weidman Forster, to be 1st Lt, Dec 4, 1847, vice Hedges, resigned.
12th Regt of Infty:
Lt Col Milledge L Bonham, to be Colonel, Aug 12, 1847, vice Wilson, dec'd.
Major Thos H Seymour, of the 9th Infty, to be Lt Colonel, Aug 12, 1847, vice Bonham, promoted.
13th Regt of Infty:
Major Edwin W Morgan, of the 11th Infty, to be Lt Col, Sep 13, 1847, vice Withers, promoted to 9th Infty.
1st Lt Ely P Howell, to be Capt, Aug 20, 1847, vice Wofford, resigned.
2nd Lt Powhattan R Page, to be 1st Lt, Aug 20, 1847, vice Howell, promoted.
14th Regt of Infty:
Capt Jos S Pitman, of the 9th Infty, to be Major, Sep 8, 1847, vice Savage, promoted to 11th Infty.
1st Lt Jas Blackburn, to be Capt, Oct 1, 1847, vice Huddlestone, dec'd.
1st Lt Thos Shields, to be Capt, Oct 21, 1847, vice Fulton, resigned.
1st Lt Philander A Hickman, to be Capt, Oct 23, 1847, vice Perkins, dec'd.
2nd Lt Richd Steele, to be 1st Lt, Oct 7, 1847, vice Blackburn, promoted.
2nd Lt Richd T Eastlin, to be 1st Lt, Oct 21, 1847, vice Shields, promoted.
2nd Lt Jas G Fitzgerald, to be 1st Lt, Oct 22, 1847, vice Hickman, promoted.
15th Regt of Infty:
Capt Leslie H McKenney, of the 16th Infty, to be Major, Aug 20, 1847, vice Mills, killed in battle.
1st Lt Geo W Bowie, to be Capt, Jul 20, 1847, vice Guthrie, dec'd-of wounds received in battle.
1st Lt Wm S Tanneyhill, to be Capt, Aug 20, 1847, vice Quarles, killed in battle.
1st Lt Thos H Freelon, to be Capt, Dec 4, 1847, vice Toll, resigned.
2nd Lt Danl French, to be 1st Lt, Aug 20, 1847, vice Tanneyhill, promoted.
2nd Lt Chas Peternell, to be 1st Lt, Aug 20, 1847, vice Goodman, killed in battle.
2nd Lt Jas W Wiley, to be 1st Lt, Dec 4, 1847, vice Freelon, promoted.
16th Regt of Infty:
1st Lt Geo W Singleton, to be Capt, Aug 20, 1847, vice McKenney, promoted to 15th Infty.
1st Lt Edw Curd, to be Capt, Oct 12, 1847, vice Bill, dec'd.
2nd Lt Orlando B Griffith, to be 1st Lt, Oct 12, 1847, vice Curd, promoted.

2nd Lt Wm H Slade, to be 1st Lt, Nov 18, 1847, vice Hamer, resigned.
2nd Lt Oliver Dieffendorf, to be 1st Lt, Nov 18, 1847, vice Kellogg, resigned.
Regt of Voltigeurs & Foot Riflemen:
1st Lt Jas C Marriott, to be Capt, Sep 18, 1847, vice Calwell, dec'd-of wounds received in battle.
2nd Lt Chas F Vernon, to be 1st Lt, Sep 18, 1847, vice Marriott, promoted.
Appointments:
Medical Dept:
Nicholas L Campbell, of N Y, to be Assist Surgeon, Aug 23, 1847, vice Hammond, promoted.
Saml L Barbour, of Ga, to be Assist Surgeon, Sep 28, 1847, vice Cuyler, promoted.
Geo E Cooper, of Pa, to be Assist Surgeon, Aug 28, 1847, vice Mills, promoted.
Ebenezer Swift, of Ohio, to be Assist Surgeon, Aug 30, 1847, vice Wickham, dec'd.
John S Battes, of Md, to be Assist Surgeon, Oct 5, 1847, vice Holmes, resigned.
Glover Perin, of Ohio, to be Assist Surgeon, Dec 4, 1847, vice Roberts, dec'd-of wounds received in battle.
Pay Dept:
John R Wallace, of Va, to be Paymaster, Aug 28, 1847, vice Randall, appointed Deputy Paymaster Genr'l.
Henry Hill, of Va, to be Paymaster, Nov 6, 1847, vice Wallace, resigned.
Ordnance Dept:
Wm P Maulsby, of Md, to be Military Storekeeper, Nov 1, 1847, vice Carr, dec'd.
3rd Regt of Dragoons:
Wm H Polk, of Tenn, to be Major, Aug 21, 1847, vice Emory, declined.
Andrew J Dorn, of Missouri, to be 2nd Lt, Aug 28, 1847, vice Walker, promoted.
Elisha E Camp, [Recruit, 2nd Dragoons,] to be 2nd Lt, Aug 28, 1847, vice Wallace, resigned.
Robt J Barnett, of Missouri, to be 2nd Lt, Sep 9, 1847, vice Norment, resigned.
Jas Anderson, of Tenn, to be 2nd Lt, Sep 9, 1847, vice Johnson, resigned.
1st Regt of Artl:
Wm E Aisquith, of Md, late 1st Lt, to be Capt, Nov 20, 1847, vice Burke, killed in battle.
11th Regt of Infty:
Jas W Rhey, of Pa, to be 2nd Lt, Aug 21, 1847, vice Samuels, promoted.
Jas Keenan, jr, of Pa, to be 2nd Lt, Sep 6, 1847, vice Kuhns, resigned.
Junius B Wheeler, [private Co I, 12th Infty,] to be 2nd Lt, Sep 9, 1847, vice Harley, promoted.
13th Regt of Infty:
John C Reese, [Private, Co F,] to be 2nd Lt, Aug 28, 1847, vice Page, promoted.
John J Witherspoon, of Alabama, to be 2nd Lt, Sep 9, 1847, vice Prince, resigned.
Edw F Bagley, of Ala, to be 2nd Lt, Sep 25, 1847, vice Wallace, resigned.
14th Regt of Infty:
Jos Q Wilbar, of Tenn, to be 2nd Lt, Sep 9, 1847, vice Moon, dec'd.
Thos Hart, of Ill, to be 2nd Lt, Sep 9, 1847, vice Helms, declined.
Robt Hagan, of La, to be Assist Surgeon, Nov 9, 1847, vice McGinnis, dec'd.
Regt of Voltigeurs & Foot Riflemen:

Jas H Walker, of Ark [Assist Quartermaster, Volunteer Service,] to be Capt, Sep 9, 1847, vice Cheatham, declined-original vacancy.
Transfers:
The following transfers, made conditionally by Maj Gen Scott, commanding the Army in Mexico, on the mutual application of the parties, are confirmed by the War Dept, viz:
1st Lt Edw H Fitzgerald, 6th Infty, transferred [Aug 26] to the 9th Infty, to take the place on the Army Register next above Lt Bissel.
1st Lt Alex'r Morrow, 9th Infty, transferred [Aug 26] to the 6th Infty, to take place on the Army Register next below Lt Garnett.
2nd Lt Wm M Gardner, 7th Infty, transferred [Jul 13] to the 2nd Infty, to take place on the Army Register next below Lt Davis.
2nd Lt Geo E Pickett, 2nd Infty, transferred [Jul 13] to the 7th Infty, to take place on the Army Register next below Lt Wilcox; & transferred [Jul 18] to the 8th Infty, to stand next below Lt Pitcher.
2nd Lt Saml B Maxey, 8th Infty, transferred [Jul 18] to the 7th Infty, to take place on the Army Register next below Lt Wilcox.
Appointments in the Quartermaster's, Commissary's, & Medical Dept:
Quartermaster's Dept:
Geo V Hebb, of Tenn, to be Quartermaster with the rank of Major, Sep 9, 1847, vice McCullough, resigned.
Geo V Hebb, of Tenn, to be Assist Quartermaster with the rank of Capt, Sep 3, 1847. [Reappointed]
Turney S Gilbert, of Ohio, to be Assist Quartermaster with the rank of Capt, Sep 4, 1847. [Reappointed]
Zebulon C Bishop, of Missouri, to be Assist Quartermaster with the rank of Capt, Sep 8, 1847. [Reappointed]
Hanson G Catlett, of Texas, to be Assist Quartermaster with the rank of Capt, Sep 8, 1847, vice Scott, discharged.
Harry Toulmin, of Ala, to be Assist Quartermaster with the rank of Capt, Sep 8, 1847. [Reappointed.].
John H Young, of Indiana, to be Assist Quartermaster with the rank of Capt, Sep 9, 1847, vice Neff, discharged.
John J Clendenin, of Ark, [late Assist Commissary, to be Assist Quartermaster with the rank of Capt, Sep 10, 1847, vice Walker, appointed Capt of Voltigeurs.
Lyman Mower, of Ill, to be Assist Quartermaster with the rank of Capt, Sep 25, 1847, vice Napier, resigned.
Saml G McClellan, of Tenn, to be Assist Quartermaster with the rank of Capt, Oct 30, 1847, vice Vandever, discharged.
John T Arthur, of Ohio, [late Quartermaster,] to be Assist Quartermaster with the rank of Capt, Nov 10, 1847, vice Gilbert, declined.
Commissary's Dept:
Erastus B Smith, of Ky, to be Commissary with the rank of Major, Sep 9, 1847, vice Boyd, resigned.
Andrew L Potts, of D C, to be Assist Commissary with the rank of Capt, Aug 16, 1847, vice Josselyn, resigned.

Wm P Miller, of Ohio, to be Assist Commissary with the rank of Capt, Sep 8, 1847, vice Stephens, discharged.
Niineveh Berry, of Indiana, to be Assist Commissary with the rank of Capt, Sep 8, 1847, vice Eckels, discharged.
John L Brown, of Tenn, to be Assist Commissary with the rank of Capt, Sep 8, 1847, vice Bunch, discharged.
Reuben L Nance, of Ky, to be Assist Commissary with the rank of Capt, Sep 8, 1847, vice Bunch, discharged.
Robt D Powel, of Tenn, to be Assist Commissary with the rank of Capt, Oct 30, 1847, vice Copeland, discharged.
Wm A Street, of Va, to be Assist Commissary with the rank of Capt, Nov 10, 1847, vice Erskin, dec'd.
Medical Dept:
Wm P Dean, of La, to be Surgeon, Aug 21, 1847, vice Ravanel, declined.
Robt McNeal, of Ohio, [Assist Surgeon,] to be Surgeon, Sep 3, 1847, vice Stone, discharged.
Jas S Athon, of Indian, to be Surgeon, Sep 8, 1847. [Re-appointed.]
John N Esselman, of Tenn, to be Surgeon, Sep 8, 1847, vice McKnight, discharged.
Nathan Gaither, of Ky, to be Surgeon, Sep 8, 1847, vice Holland, discharged.
Jos G Roberts, of Ky, to be Surgeon, Sep 8, 1847, vice Caldwell, discharged.
Jas P Evans, of Tenn, to be Surgeon, Sep 28, 1847, vice Washington, discharged.
John Irwin, of Tenn, to be Surgeon, Sep 28, 1847, vice Esselman, declined.
Saml B Fields, of Ky, to be Surgeon, Oct 8, 1847, vice Gaither, declined.
Minor B Halstead, of N Y, [Assist Surgeon,] to be Surgeon, Oct 20, 1847, vice Hasbrouck, resigned.
J G M Ramsey, of Tenn, to be Surgeon, Oct 30, 1847, vice Mahon, discharged.
Adrian R Terry, of Mich, to be Surgeon, Oct 30, 1847, vice Hensley, discharged.
John Parshall, of Tenn, to be Assist Surgeon, Nov 1, 1847, vice Hale, resigned; & to be Surgeon, Nov 16, 1847, Ramsey, declined.
Alex'r M Cassidy, of Pa, to be Assist Surgeon, Aug 9, 1847, vice Glenn, resigned.
Oliver M Langdon, of Ohio, to be Assist Surgeon, Sep 3, 1847, vice McNeil, appointed Surgeon.
Wm Fosdick, of Indian, to be Assist Surgeon, Sep 8, 1847. [Reappointed.]
Alex'r M Blanton, of Ky, to be Assist Surgeon, Sep 8, 1847. [Reappointed.]
Jas F Bozeman, of Ga, to be Assist Surgeon, Sep 8, 1847, vice Ashe, discharged.
Jas D Caulfield, of Miss, to be Assist Surgeon, Sep 8, 1847, vice Heighway, discharged.
Hugh R Rutledge, of S C, to be Assist Surgeon, Sep 10, 1847, vice Dunn, resigned.
Geo T McDonald, of Ohio, to be Assist Surgeon, Sep 13, 1847, vice Mulvaney, discharged.
John R Steele, of Ky, to be Assist Surgeon, Sep 13, 1847, vice Mathews, discharged.
Jos Malin, of Missouri, to be Assist Surgeon, Sep 17, 1847, vice Sanderson, resigned.
Philip G Jones, of Indiana, to be Assist Surgeon, Sep 22, 1847, vice Fosdick, discharged.
Richd W Gardner, of Tenn, to be Assist Surgeon, Sep 28, 1847, vice Dorris, resigned.
Wm Cromwell, of Ky, to be Assist Surgeon, Sep 28, 1847, vice Blanton, declined.
Wm A Russell, of Tenn, to be Assist Surgeon, Oct 19, 1847, vice Stout, resigned.

John G McKibben, of N Y, to be Assist Surgeon, Oct 20, 1847, vice Halstead, appointed Surgeon.
Henry Lemcke, of Mich, to be Assist Surgeon, Oct 30, 1847, vice Leech, discharged.
Washington L Lyon, of Tenn, to be Assist Surgeon, Nov 16, 1847, vice Parshall, declined.
Eliathah S Gale, of ___, to be Assist Surgeon, Dec 2, 1847, vice Treadwell, discharged.
Casualties:
Resignations:
Capt Christopher Q Tompkins, 3rd Artl, Sep 22, 1847.
Capt John Wofford, 13th Infty, Aug 20, 1847.
Capt Stephen Woodman, 9th Infty, Oct 9, 1847.
Capt Benj F Fulton, 14th Infty, Oct 21, 1847.
Capt Andrew T Palmer, 9th Infty, Dec 4, 1847.
Capt Isaac D Toll, 11th Infty, Dec 4, 1847.
Capt Lorenzo Johnson, 9th Infty, Dec 4, 1847.
1st Lt Bushrod R Johnson, 3rd Infty, Oct 22, 1847.
1st Lt Richd W Johnston, 3rd Artl, Dec 4, 1847.
1st Lt Thos J Curd, 4th Artl, Dec 4, 1847.
1st Lt Jos S Hedges, 11th Infty, Dec 4, 1847.
1st Lt Jos Kellogg, 16th Infty, Nov 18, 1847.
1st Lt Wm Hamer, 16th Infty, Nov 6, 1847.
1st Lt Danl H Cram, 9th Infty, Dec 4, 1847.
2nd Lt Michl O'Sullivan, 3rd Infty, Oct 31, 1847.
2nd Lt Jos C Wallace, 3rd Dragoons, Aug 23, 1847.
2nd Lt Nathl F Swett, 9th Infty, Dec 4, 1847.
2nd Lt Josiah P Chadbourne, 9th Infty, Nov 4, 1847.
2nd Lt Wm W Carr. 16th Infty, Oct 25, 1847.
2nd Lt Langdon C Johnson, 3rd Dragoons, Aug 31, 1847.
2nd Lt Wm H H Goodloe, 15th Infty, Dec 4, 1847.
2nd Lt Oliver H Prince, 13th Infty, Aug 20, 1847.
2nd Lt John P Wallace, 13th Infty, Sep 24, 1847.
2nd Lt Henry B Kuhns, 11th Infty, Sep 4, 1847.
2nd Lt Wm A Morrison, 13th Infty, Oct 9, 1847.
2nd Lt Gaylord H Griswold, 10th Infty, Sep 21, 1847.
2nd Lt John C How, 16th Infty, Nov 6, 1847.
Assist Surgeon Robt S Holmes, Oct 4, 1847.
Assist Surgeon Jas D Stuart, 16th Infty, Nov 6, 1847.
Paymaster John R Wallace, Nov 6, 1847.
Commissions vacated under the provisions of the act of Jun 18, 1846.
Capt Jas L Donaldson, 1st Artl, Assist Quartermaster.
Capt Wm H Shover, Assist Quartermaster, 3rd Artl.
Declined:
1st Lt Wm H Emory, Corps Topographical Engineers, as Major 3rd Dragoons.
2nd Lt John E Helms, 14th Infty.
Deaths:
Brig Gen Enos D Hopping, at Mier, Mexico, Sep 1, 1847.

Bvt Col Jas S McIntosh, 5th Infty, in the city of Mexico, Sep 26, 1847.
Col Louis D Wilson, 12th Infty, at Vera Cruz, Mexico, Aug 12, 1847.
Col Trueman B Ransom, 9th Infty, in assault of Chupultepec, Mexico, Sep 13, 1847.
Bvt Lt Col Martin Scott, 5th Infty, in battle of Molino del rey, Nexico, Sep 8, 1847.
Lt Col Wm M Graham, 11th Infty, in battle Molino del rey, Mexico, Sep 8, 1847.
Maj John B Clark, 1st Infty, at Castle San Juan d'Ulua, Mexico, Aug 23, 1847.
Maj Henry Smith, Quartermaster, at Vera Cruz, Mexico, Jul 24, 1847.
Maj Fred'k D Mills, 15th Infty, in attack of San Antonio Gate, city of Mexico, Aug 20, 1847.
Capt Saml Mackenzie, 2nd Artl, at city of Mexico, Oct 19, 1847.
Capt Moses E Merrill, 5th Infty, in battle Molino del rey, Mexico, Sep 8, 1847.
Capt Ephraim K Smith, 5th Infty, near city of Mexico, Sep 11, 1847.
Capt Wm Wall, 3rd Artl, at Puebla, Mexico, Aug 13, 1847.
Capt Seth B Thornton, 2nd Dragoons, in reconnaissance San Antonio, Mexico, Aug 18, 1847.
Capt Jas W Anderson, 2nd Infty, in battle Churubusco, Mexico, Aug 20, 1847.
Capt Wm H Churchill, Assist Quartermaster, 1st Lt, 3rd Artl, at Point Isabel, Texas, Oct 19, 1847.
Capt Saml H Walker, Mounted Riflemen, in battle Huamantla, Mexico, Oct 9, 1847.
Capt Simon H Drum, 4th Artl, in attack of Belers Gate, City of Mexico, Sep 13, 1847.
Bvt Capt Gep W Ayres, 3rd Artl, in battle Molino Del Rey, Mexico, Sep 8, 1847.
Capt Erastus A Capron, 1st Artl, in battle Churubusco, Mexico, Aug 20, 1847.
Capt Chas Hanson, 7th Infty, in battle Churubusco, Mexico, Aug 19, 1847.
Capt Martin J Burke, 1s Artl, in battle Churubusco, Mexico, Aug 20, 1847.
Capt Wm H Duff, 3rd Dragoons, at Vera Cruz, Mexico, Jul 16, 1847.
Capt Pemberton Waddell, 11th Infty, in city of Mexico, Sep 25, 1847.
Capt Augustus Quarles, 15th Infty, in battle Churubusco, Mexico, Aug 20, 1847.
Capt Edmund B Bill, 16th Infty, at sea, Oct 12, 1847.
Capt Jas W Thompson, 9th Infty, in city of Mexico, Sep 25, 1847.
Capt Has H Calwell, Voltigeurs, at Jalapa, Mexico, Sep 18, 1847.
Capt Jos W Perkins, 14th Infty, in city of Mexico, Oct 22, 1847.
Capt Creed T Huddlestone, 14th Infty, in city of Mexico, Oct 1, 1847.
Capt Edwin Guthrie, 15th Infty, at Perote, Mexico, Jul 20, 1847.
Capt Wm Armstrong, Assist Quartermaster, 1st Lt, 2nd Artl, in battle Molino del Rey, Mexico, Sep 8, 1847.
1st Lt Muscoe L Shackelford, 2nd Artl, in city of Mexico, Oct 27, 1847.
1st Lt John H Hill, 2nd Dragoons, at Puebla, Mexico, Jul 29, 1847.
1st Lt Jas R Scott, 7th Infty, at sea, Oct 30, 1847.
1st Lt John G Burbank, 8th Infty, near city of Mexico, Sep 10, 1847.
1st Lt Sidney Smith, 4th Infty, in city of Mexico, Sep 16, 1847.
1st Lt Spear S Tipton, Mounted Riflemen, at Puebla, Mexico, Jul 20, 1847.
1st Lt John D Bacon, 6th Infty, in city of Mexico, Jul 20, 1847.
1st Lt Chas F Morris, 8th Infty, in city of Mexico, Sep 17, 1847.
1st Lt Leonidas Jenkins, 1st Dragoons, at Vera Cruz, Mexico, Sep 17, 1847.
1st Lt Levi Gantt, 7th Infty, in assault of Chapultepec, Mexico, Sep 13, 1847.

1st Lt Calvin Benjamin, 4th Artl, in attack of Beien Gate, city of Mexico, Sep 13, 1847.
1st Lt Jos F Irons, 1st Artl, in camp near city of Mexico, Aug 26, 1847.
1st Lt John P Johnstone, 1st Artl, in attack of Contreras, Mexico, Aug 19, 1847.
1st Lt Jos F Farry, 3rd Artl, in battle Molino del Rey, Mexico, Sep 8, 1847.
2nd Lt Rudolph F Ernst, 6th Infty, in city of Mexico, Sep 22, 1847.
2nd Lt Wm T Burwell, 5th Infty, in battle Molino del Rey, Mexico, Sep 8, 1847.
2nd Lt Jos P Smith, 5th Infty, in assault of Chapultepec, Mexico, Sep 12, 1847.
2nd Lt Jos McElvain, 1st Dragoons, at Albuquerque, New Mexico, Jul 12, 1847.
2nd Lt Alex'r P Rodgers, 4th Infty, in assault of Chapultepec, Mexico, Sep 13, 1847.
2nd Lt Thos Easley, 2nd Infty, in battles Churubusco, Mexico, Aug 20, 1847.
2nd Lt Benj Yard, 10th Infty, near Matamoros, Mexico, Oct 21, 1847.
2nd Lt A G Moon, 14th Infty, at Vera Cruz, Mexico, Jul 17, 1847.
2nd Lt Washington Meads, 11th Infty, _______
2nd Lt Richd H L Johnston, 11th Infty, in battle of Molino del Rey, Mexico, Sep 8, 1847.
Surgeon Hamilton S Hawkins, at Tampico, Mexico, Aug 7, 1847.
Assist Surgeon Wm Roberts, in city of Mexico, Oct 13, 1847. [Of wounds received Sep 8, in the battle of Molino del Rey.]
Assist Surgeon Robt C Wickham, at Vera Cruz, Mexico, May 13, 1847.
Assist Surgeon Robt H McGinnis, 14th Infty, at Vera Cruz, Mexico, Sep 1, 1847.
Military Storekeeper Saml J Carr, Ordnance Dept, at Pikesville Arsenal, Md, Oct 24, 1847.
Dismissed:
2nd Lt Jas M Smith, 16th Infty, Sep 4, 1847.
Cashiered:
2nd Lt Geo C McClelland, 11th Infty, Oct 13, 1847.
Casualties-Volunteer Service:
Resignations:
Maj Alfred Boyd, Commissary, Aug 20, 1847.
Maj Benj McCullough, Quartermaster, Sep 6, 1847.
Capt Jos Naper, Assist Quartermaster, Sep 25, 1847.
Capt Jas H Walker, Assist Quartermaster, Sep 9, 1847. [Appointed capt Voltigeurs & Foot Riflemen.]
Capt John W Shugert, Assist Commissary, Aug 12, 1847.
Capt Robt Josselyn, Assist Commissary, Aug 16, 1847.
Surgeon E K Chamberlain, Oct 25, 1847.
Surgeon Jos L Hasbrouch, Oct 19, 1847.
Assist Surgeon John G Dunn, Aug 19, 1847.
Assist Surgeon Geo B Sanderson, Aug 31, 1847.
Capt Turney S Gilbert, Assist Quartermaster. [No date.]
Surgeon Edmund Ravanel. [No date.]
Delined:
Surgeon John N Esselman
Surgeon Nathan Gaither
Surgeon Wm P Dean
Surgeon Saml B Fields

Surgeon J G M Ramsey
Assist Surgeon Craven Peyton
Assist Surgeon Alex'r M Blanton
John Parshall, of Tenn, as Assist Surgeon
Deaths:
Capt Robt Fenner, Assist Commissary, at New Orleans Barracks, La, Sep 19, 1847.
Capt Henry Erskin, Assist Commissary, at Monterey, Mexico, Sep 26, 1847.
Capt Solomon Pender, Assist Quartermaster, at Saltillo, Mexico, Sep 2, 1847.
Assist Surgeon Wm Treadwell, at Vera Cruz, Mexico, Oct 24, 1847.
Discharged:
Assist Surgeon Wm Fosdick, Sep 22, 1847.
1st Lt Wm H Emory, Corps of Topographical Engineers, having declined the appointment of Major in the 3rd Regt of Dragoons, the promotions of 2nd Lt Wm R Palmer, to be 1st Lt, & Brevet 2nd Lt Wm G Peck, to be 2nd Lt in the Corps of Topographical Engineers, as announced in Genr'l Orders, #10, Mar 12, 1847, are cancelled; & the named of Lts Emory, Palmer, & Peck are restored to their former places & grades in said corps.
Capt Wm W Mackall, 1st Artl, Assist Adj Gen, & Capts Robt Allen, 2nd Artl, & Edw H Fitzgerald, 9th Infty, Assist Quartermasters, having been promoted to a grade in their regts equal to the commission held by them in the Staff, they will forthwith report, by letter, to the Adj Gen, which of their 2 commissions [Staff or Regimental] they select to vacate. By order: R Jones, Adj Gen

The Springfield Republican announced, with high compliments, the appointment of Lt Oliver Hazard Perry [son of Cmdor Perry, the hero of Lake Erie] to the agency for the Middlesex Mills, at Lowell. It is to be inferred that the Lt has resigned his commission.

Calif: 1-The vessel **Malek Adhel**, captured by the U S sloop-of-war **Warren**, on the southern coast, was sold at auction, for the coast trade, to Capt W D Phelps, for $4,525. 2-The people of San Francisco elected a Town Council to administer their affair, consisting of Wm Glover, Wm D M Howard, Wm A Leidendorff, E P Jones, Robt A Parker, & Wm S Clark, who entered upon their official duties Sep 16. 3-Mr S Brannan, publisher of the Calif Star, after an absence of nearly 6 months, arrived at this place on Fri last, in 28 days from ***Fort Hall***. He informs that the emigration to Oregon was still rolling on; that up to Aug 18, 770 wagons had passed ***Fort Hall***, & more were expected. -Journal of Commerce

Theron Rudd, of the State of N Y, died at St Louis on Dec 2, at the advanced age of 80 years. He leaves a widow & dght in a strange city to mourn his loss.

Wm Von Eichthal, Editor of the Deutsche Schnellpost, of N Y, died there on Wed, after an illness of 2 or 3 days.

Died: on Dec 17, in Balt, of consumption, at the residence of her father, E Guttslich, Mrs Eliz H Broome, w/o Jas Broome, of Wash City.

TUE DEC 21, 1847
A man & his wife, named Hamburg, of Bloomfield, were proceeding in a wagon near Newark, N J, on Sat, when the vehicle overturned. A barrel of flour in the wagon fell on the woman, fracturing her skull & killed her almost instantly. The husband was drunk.

Senate: 1-Bill introduced to compensate John F Moore. 2-Bill for the relief of John R Bryan, administrator of Isaac Garretson, dec'd, late a purser in the navy of the U S: referred. 3-Report of the Solicitor of the Treasury in the case of John Pickett & others, owners of the brig **Albert**, made in pursuance of the directions of the act of Mar 3, 1847: presented.

House of Reps: 1-Ptn of John Mitchell, of the State of Maine, praying a pension for a wound received on board the U S ship **Alabama** while engaged in firing a salute in May last in honor of the victories achieved by Gens Scott & Taylor: referred to the Cmte on Invalid Pensions. 2-Ptn of John P Andrews, of Salem, Mass, praying for an amicable termination of the war with Mexico: referred to the Cmte on Foreign Affairs. 3-Cmte of Claims: bill for the relief of Phineas Capen, administrator of John Cox, dec'd. Also, a bill for the relief of Robt Roberts; which bills were committed. 4-Cmte on Revolutionary Claims: bill for the relief of Mary Brown, widow of Jacob Brown, a Revolutionary pensioner: committed. 5-Bill for the relief of Russell Goss: referred to the Cmte on Invalid Pensions.

The Hon Timothy Pitkin, of Conn, a statesman of the past age, died after a short illness, nearly 80 years of age. He was a Member of the House of Reps from 1805 thru 1819. [No date for his death-current news.]

Capt Alex'r S Hooe, gallant ofcr of the 5th Regt U S Infty, died on Dec 8, at Baton Rouge, from the effects of a severe burn. He was a native of King George's Co, Va, & gained great credit by his conduct upon the field of Palo Alto, the first battles of the Mexican war, where he lost an arm. He graduated in 1827 from the Military Academy. Capt Hooe belonged to a gallant family, & was a brother of Robt Emmett Hooe, of the Navy, who died about 6 months since. We hear that a fond wife & children have been left to mourn the death of a husband & father. -Picayune

Valuable farm for sale: about 300 acres of ***Goose Creek Land***, lying between the subscriber's residence & the estate of the late Dr Francis Neale, & about 5 miles from Port Tobacco. -Chas A Pye

Died: on Dec 20, Miss Joanna M Ruffin, in her 55th year. Her funeral is on Dec 23, from the residence of Mr Thos Pursell, opposite Brown's Hotel, Pa ave, at 10 o'clock. [Dec 22nd newspaper: died on Dec 20, Miss Joanna M Ruff, in her 20th year. Her funeral is on Dec 22, from the residence of Mr Thos Pursell, opposite Brown's Hotel, Pa ave. at 10 o'clock.]

Died: Dec 17, at Harper's Ferry, in her 24th year, Mrs Helen Rebecca Mitterigger, formerly of Wash City.

Died: on Nov 23, in St Louis, Missouri, in her 32nd year, Mrs Ann, wife of Jas Barry, & youngest daughter of C T Coote, of Wash City.

Confectionery, Toys, & Fancy Articles: Wm Grupe, Pa ave, 5 doors west of 4½ st.

For rent: house furnished on Capitol Hill, adjoining the Capitol grounds, near the Dowson Row. Apply to Jos F Brown, on the premises. Also, a small house, not furnished, opposite Judge Cranch's, Delaware ave.

WED DEC 22, 1847

Geo Hunnewell has been convicted at East Cambridge, Mass, of setting fire to the house occupied by his mother, which was entirely destroyed, & with it the life of a brother of the prisoner. The punishment is death. He has been sentenced to be hung.

House of Reps: 1-Ptn of Wm Saunders & Wm R Porter, sureties of Wm Estis, a paymaster in the late war with Great Britain: referred. 2-Ptn of ___ Shiflett, of Va, praying to be placed on the invalid pension roll. 3-Memorial of Geo Taylor, praying indemnity for losses incurred by French spoliations prior to 1800. Memorial of Cassius F Lee, trustee of Hodgson, on the same subject. Also, the memorial of Mary D Adam, atty of Dunlap's heirs, on the same subject. 4-Ptn of Louisa Dascomb & 111 others, of Franklin, Maine: referred. 5-Ptn of Amos Armstrong, a citizen of Summit Co, Ohio, praying for a pension. 6-Memorial of Philip Allen & others, asking payment for depredations on their property committed by the French Gov't prior to 1800. 7-Ptn of Moses E Levy: referred. 8-Ptn of the heirs of Capt Henry Pawling for commutation: referred. 9-Memorial of Catharine Alde, widow of a Revolutionary soldier. 10-Ptn of Calvin Bishop & others, for an appropriation for Buffalo harbor. 11-Memorial of S Morris Waler & Co, asking for a remission of duties. 12-Ptn of Jas W Breedlove, late Collector of the customs for the district of Mississippi, praying to be refunded the amount of counterfeit coin received by the cash clerk of the custom house at New Orleans during his term of ofc.

Selling off at cost for cash: the subscriber, being determined to close his present business, offers his large stock of Dry Goods at cost. -G W Phillips

Stephen Pleasanton, 5th Auditor of the treasury Dept , has been for many years [27 years] at the head of the Lighthouse establishment of the U S, & has made unwearied exertions to improve the character of the lighthouses along the Atlantic coast. The Boston Marine Society tender him their acknowledgments for the same. Signed: Winslow Lewis, John S Sleeper, R B Forbes, Thos B Curtis, Wm A Wellman: Boston, Nov 19, 1847. Reply by Mr Pleasanton: Wash, Dec 3, 1847: "I find the perfecting of lighthouse establishments so delicate and various a subject, that we are always learning, & I trust improving."

The brig **Falconer**, of Belfast, Maine, Capt Jos Robertson, from Sidney for Boston, was wrecked on Ipswich Beach on Sat. The capt, his wife, & son; Mr Tucker, of Phil; Julia Larkin, Margaret Hennessey, & Horace Crobsy, of Albion Maine, cabin passesgers, & 8 steerage passengers died from exposure.

The late fire at Attica, N Y. Among the sufferers are: O Gardner, loss about $500; Wilber & Ellis, $2,000; Dr G Dorrance, $2,000; Scott's Flouring Mills, $7,000; W Sanborn, $500; D & W Scott, $2,000; W B Goodwin, $5,000; A Goodrich, $1,000; Miss Palmer, about $800; & J Civer, $100.

Mrd: on Dec 18, by Rev O B Brown, Mr Henry Bishop, jr, of Wash, to Miss Maria Louisa Mountz, of Gtwn.

Mrd: on Nov 20, at the U S Hotel, by Rev C M Butler, D D, Achille Murat Willis to Miss Florence E Ambler, of Rappahannock Co, Va.

Mrd: on Dec 16, by Rev Mr Reese, Mr Thos H Rawlings to Miss Mary Jane Williams, both of this place.

Senate: 1-Ptn from Chas S Jackson, of the custom-house of Phil, asking for certain allowances. 2-Ptn from Elvira F Smith, asking a pension. 3-Ptn from Timothy B Upham & others, legal reps of John Thomas, deceased, formerly naval agents, asking compensation for acting navy pension agents. 4-Ptn from Jesse Turner, asking confirmation of his title to a tract of land. 5-Ptn from Isaac Varney, jr, praying indemnity for losses sustained in Florida. 6-Ptn from Leslie Combs, asking the payment of certain bonds issued by the late Republic of Texas. 7-Ptn from Susan T E Williamson, asking a pension. 8-Ptn from Joshua Shaw, asking that a balance due him under an act of Congress may be paid. 9-Ptn from Wm M Glendy, an ofcr of the navy, asking compensation for performing duties belonging to a higher grade. 10-Ptn from Sarah Hebbard, widow of a chief engineer in the navy, asking a pension. 11-Ptn from Ann Chase, asking indemnity for losses sustained at Tampico. 12-Ptn from Benj J Cahoone, asking reimbursement of moneys expended in the public service. 13-Ptn from J S Gordon & 500 other citizens, asking the right of pre-emption to the land through which the central Railroad passes. 14-Ptn from Chas L Dell, asking the settlement of his accounts for military services performed in Florida. 15-Ptn from Chas Bradbury, for compensation for losses arising out of French spoliations prior to 1800. 16-Ptn from Mrs Anna J Hassler, widow of Chas A Hassler, of the navy, asking a pension. 17-Ptn from Churchill Gibbs, asking commutation pay. 18-Ptn from Lavinia Taylor, widow of the late Isaac Taylor, of the U S army, asking that the same pension may be granted to her as is allowed to volunteers. 19-Bill for the relief of Susan E Gordon: introduced. 20-Cmte on Military Affairs: bill for the relief of Mary McRea, widow of Col Wm McRea, late of the U S army. 21-Cmte on Naval Affairs: bill for the relief of Jos Wilson. Also, bill for the relief of Walter R Johnson. 22-Cmte of Claims: bill for the relief of Elisha L Keen.

For sale: tract of land of about 780 acres, in Alexandria Co, on the Columbia turnpike. Mr Mills, who resides on the premises, will show the lands. -O Fairfax, exc of Thos Fairfax

For rent: 2 furnished parlors & rooms recently occupied by Mr Crammer, Sec of the Russian Legation, corner of Pa ave & 17th st, opposite the War Dept. -B Jost

House of Reps: 1-Memorial of certain citizens of D C: that the slave trade is now carried on in D C to a large extent. Your petitioners respectfully ask that all laws authorizing or sanctioning such trade within said District may be repealed:

Wm Flaherty	T M Milburn	Jas Handley
Wm Blanchard	Chas C Moore	Martin Buell
Geo Savage	Jos Scholfield	J F Callan
J C Greer	Columbus McLeod	H Taylor
B Milburn	Wm Greer	Thos P Vial
C S Fowler	John T Whitaker	Thos Fitznam

Administrator' s sale: the private property of Chas King, deceased: household & kitchen furniture, & dairy furniture; cattle, sheep, oxen, mules, a wagon, carts, ploughs, & Cider mill. -Clement Cox, adm of Chas King, dec'd. -Edw S Wright, auctioneer

N Y, Dec 17, 1847. Col Burnett & his fellow-ofcrs are in the Govnr's room, at City Hall, today, meeting the salutations of the citizens, several thousands of whom has been calling upon them. Col Burnett & Lt Potter were leaning upon crutches, Maj Kikeman's left hand was in a sling, & Lt Sweeney, having lost his right arm, was giving his left hand to his fellow citizens. Sweeney was a printer in this city, & laid down the "stick" to take up the musket. He has returned now unable to wield either, & must depend on a pension for support.

Grand Firemen's Ball, in honor of Benj Franklin's Birthnight: on Jan 17, 1848, at Jackson Hall. Managers:

J A M Duncanson	Jos Williamson	A Tate
W Durr	W H Fanning	L A Iardella
J Sessford	Richd Abbott	R E Doyle
Jas Stone	John C Donohoo	John Reese
E H Edmonston	John A Donohoo	John T Coumbe
John N Minnix	Grafton Powell	Geo Payne
Jos Reese	Jos Abbott	J C Wise
W Nailor	John H Sessford	A Kirby

Criminal Court-Wash: the trial of Robt Dove, charged with an assault on Jas Johnson, took place on Mon & resulted in the conviction of the accused. He was sentenced to pay a fine of $5 & costs. Richd Jones also charge with an assault upon Jas Johnson, was tried yesterday & acquitted.

THU DEC 23, 1847

Anniversary of the American Colonization Society: Wash, Dec 22, 1847. The Board of Directors will meet on Jan 18, 1848, of which the following Directors for Life will please take notice:

Hon S Wilkeson, N Y
Hon R W Williams, Ct
Rev L Bacon, D D, Ct
Fran Griffin, Miss
Gen John H Cocke, Va
T R Hazzard, R I
Rev E Burgess, D D, Mass
John McDonogh, La
Jona A Coit, Ct
Rev J B Pinney, Pa
Elliot Cresson, Pa
Herman Camp, N Y
Rev W McLain, Wash
A G Phelps, N Y
Ste Duncan, M D, Miss
John Murdock, Miss
Jas Railey, Miss
Alvarez Fish, Miss
David Hunt, Miss
Jas Boorman, N Y
Chas Brewer, Pa

Mrd: Tue, by Rev John S Smith, Mr R B Hall to Miss Susan G Collison, all of Wash City.

A destructive tornado passed over the counties of Perry, Tuscaloosa, & Greene, in Ala, on Dec 10, destroying a large amount of property. The town of Newbern, Greene Co, was entirely demolished, & Sheriff Mr Stokes, of Perry Co, was killed.

$75 reward for runaway, my servant, John Parke: a bright mulatto, a bricklayer by trade, & a good workman. Address to Dr Wm Browne, Fredericksburg, Va.

Wm Nolan, orderly sgt in Co H, 14th U S Infty, Ohio Regt, reached his house in Cincinnati on Thu last, after a journey of 6 weeks from the city of Mexico, & died a few years after his arrival, in the presence of his wife & children. He received a severe wound, which ultimately caused his death, by a fall from a step cliff of rocks shortly after the battle of the city of Mexico, while with others in the pursuit of Santa Anna. He had been 28 years in the U S army, & performed his duty faithfully as a soldier, & received an honorable discharge, with excellent testimonials of character. He leaves a son in the service of his country, who has participated in many of the late battles, among them Monterey & Buena Vista.

Died: at his residence in Greensburg, Green Co, Ky, on Dec 8, the Hon Richd A Buckner, sen, aged about 64 years. His disease was a complaint of the heart, by which he had been confined to his bed some 2 weeks. He was a native of Fauquier Co, Va; removed to Ky whilst a young man, & settled at Greensburg, where he lived until his demise. He was bred to the Bar, & gained considerable reputation as a jurist & advocate. He was appointed Circuit Judge, an ofce he held at his death. Judge Buckner left a large Family, one of whom is a Rep in the present Congress] & numerous relatives & friends to lament his death.

FRI DEC 24, 1847

Senate: 1-Ptn of Eliz Hamilton, widow of Alex'r Hamilton, in relation to papers & documents in her possession. 2-Ptn from Capt Henry M Shreve, in relation to the removal of snags & sawyers, from the great Western rivers, by the use of his patent steam snag-boat. 3-Ptn of David T Brown & 99 other citizens of Pa, asking such an alteration of the laws as will abolish slavery throughout the Territories: laid on the table. 4-Ptn from D A Waterson, asking compensation for his services as a clerk in the Land Ofc in Louisiana. 5-Ptn from Wm B Slaughter, Sec of the Territory of Wisconsin, asking the settlement of his accounts on principles of equity & justice. 6-Ptn from John Black, late Consul at the city of Mexico, asking certain allowances for diplomatic service in that country. 7-Cmte on Naval Affairs: bill for the relief of Capt Foxall A Parker. 8-Cmte on the Post Ofc & Post Roads: bill for the relief of Thos Rhodes. Also, a joint resolution for the relief of Danl Shaw & Solomon T Corson.

House of Reps: 1-Obit-died on Dec 2, 1846, at Monterey, Gen Thos L Hamer, Ohio's favorite son. Gen Hamer was born in Pa, & came to Clermont Co, Ohio, when a lad, without money, without friends, & with no more than a common English education. His first business effort was teaching a common school; next he became a student at law. He was admitted to the bar in 1821, & settled in Gtwn, Brown Co, Ohio, which he made his permanent residence. When our soil had been invaded by Mexico, Gen Hamer was amongst the first who crowded forward; volunteered as a private, & as such entered camp Washington; he was there elected Major of the 1st Ohio Regt, & soon appointed Brig Gen by the Pres, & this last promotion was, on his part, unsolicited. 2-Ptn of Capt Wm P Brady, of Clinton Co, Pa, praying for a pension. 3-Regarding the ptn of Capt Alex'r McEwen, of Northumberland Co, Pa, praying for a pension: to withdraw from the files of the House said ptn & papers.

Persons who took out licenses under the laws of the Wash Corp, during the months of Oct & Nov last: Billards license: Morse, John E; Provost & Wallingsford

Boots & Shoes license:

Barry, Francis
Crandell, Jas
Donoghue, J P
Dodds, Jos
Hall, R B

Cart license:

Adams, Caleb
Adams, Robt
Bean, C W
Choppin, Wm
Cartwright, W
Clements, S M
Dewdney, John
Delany, Levi
Dewers, Lewis
Giddings, Sam
Harshman, Jacob
Hubbard, Solomon
Kibble, Alex
Knight, Wm
Lee, Michl
Lindsay, M S
Lokey, J B
Mulliken, John
Martin, Wm
Maddox, C A M
Newton, Benj
Pulizzi, V
Richards, Thos-2
Raily, Thos
Raily, Jas
Storm, Leonard
Taylor, J H
Tompkins, Richd
Washington, W
Williamson, Thos

Exchange Carts: Cunningham, W

Coal license:

Davis, W W
Deringer, B M
Fugitt, J
Pettibone, J

Confectionary license:

Ager, Jacob
Beute, Hy
Beardsley, S
Columbus, Chas
Gautier, Chas
Horning, John
Knott, Geo
Miller, John
Norbeck, Geo
O'Donnell, John

Dog license:

Going, Pat
Griffith, W A
Ritchie, Thos
Sour, Lewis
Stutz, F
Tench, Stanislaus
Wilcox, E G-2

Dray license: Emery, M G; Wise, Chas J

Dry Goods:

Adams, Sam T
Allen, G R
Allen, John
Beach, S B
Brown & Hyatt-2
Barnes & Mitchell
Briscoe & Clarke
Clavendetcher, L
Carpenter, W W
Carter, Henry
Carter, R W & Co
Combs, R M
Clagett, D & Co
Drury, S T
Duvall & Brother
Egan, W & Son
Galligan, J & Son
Hooe, P H & Co
Hall & Co
Hall, R B
Harper, W & Co
Hills, J B
Hall & Brother
Hitz, John
Johnson, T W & Co
Jennings, W T & Co
Johnson, J W
King, J T & Co
Lusby & Duvall
Lane & Tucker
Perry & Brother
Pursell, Thos
Riley, W R
Rosenstock, Sam
Roby, H W
Shuster, Wm & Co
Shanks & Wall-2
Stettinius, Geo
Stier, P J
Stevens, M H
Tree, J B & Bro
Tucker & Daniel
Visser, J
White & Brother
Wilson, John W
Wall & Donn
Yerby & Bro
Young, A H

Grocery license: Adams, G W

Adams, S T
Caton, John
Duckworth, Marg't
Deveny, Chas
Groupe, Wm
Hines, C & M

Moran, David
Pancoast, W P
Ruff, Geo R
Stewart, G W
Seybolt & Co
Stott, Saml
Westcott, Jas
Williamson, J B

Hack license:

Braxton, Nancy-3
Burrell, John
Becket, Lemuel
Butler, Jas
Chew, Wm
Clarke, Cornelius
Clarke, Thos
Croggan, Isaac
Davis, J R
Dalton, Wm
Dulany, Caleb
Diggs, Judson
Earle, Robt-4
Fleming, John
Foote, Andrew
Fisher, David
Golding, Long
Gothard, Sam
Hensley, Geo
Jameison, Elias
Jeffers, W J
Jones, Isaac
Kelcher, Jas
Kingsbury, Thos
Keiger, Alfred
Kelcher, Jas
Lewis, John
Looby, Terrence
Lawrence, Robt
Magee, R F
Moran, Patrick
Mullen, Basil
Purcell, Thos
Smallwood, Dennis-3
Stewart, Chas
Smith, Richd
Smithson, John H
Turner, Thos
Turner, Gelen
Turner, Henry
Von Essen, Peter
Welch, Thos

Hardware license:

Adams, Wm
Bayly, W F
Berryman, L M
Baden, J W
Bastianelli, T
Campbell & Coyle
Comly, C A
Coyle, Fitzhugh
Cochran, G W
Clitch, Henrietta
Davis, Richd
Eddy, Stephen
Jillard, J & Son
Keyworth, Robt
Lindsley, E
Lewis, Sam
Lawrence, Jas
Morrison, W M
Parke, W
Skirving, Jas
Savage, Geo
Savage, J L & Co
Taylor, Franck
Wheeler, Edw
Woodward, Clem

Hats, Shoes & Boots license:

Bury, Wm
Brown & Hyatt
Bayne, Thos
Cull, Jas
Hoover, A & Son
Knott, J H
Magruder, T J
Mattingly, F

Stevens, M H
Tood, W B
Tree, J B & Bro
Walder, John
Weichman, J C

Huckster license:

Adamson, Richd
Avery & Beach
Addison, W A
Brown, R
Eichorn, Rudd
Henry, Wm
Haines, Wash'n
Jones, Alfred
Klopfer, Benj
Lipscomb, Jesse
Lewis, Washington
Mills, R T
Payne, C H
Potter, T L
Peirce, G E
Quigley, Wm
Quackenboss, Hm

Medicine license:

Chapin, H L
Clarke, D B
Delany, Michl
Elliott, Wallace
Gilman, Z D
Greenleaf, W C
Harbaugh, V
McPherson, H H
Nairn, J W
Patterson, R S
Schwartz, A J
Stott, Chas
Stott, Saml
Walsh, T S
Weatherby & Bates

Retail license:

Ager, J E & Bro
Allen, Wm
Alleir & Thyson
Adams, Washington
Adams, J G
Adams, Alex
Baumback, A
Bright, Rebecca
Brereton, Saml
Bevan, Thos
Beall, R M
Bacon, S & Co
Bush, W W
Bean, Geo
Brashears, W B
Barr, J R
Combs, M R
Callan, Lawrence
Connor, John
Coburn, W A
Dillow, Wm
Dhomas, Jacob
Daly, Jas
Dodds, Jos
Dyer, R W
Donohoo, John A
Duvall, Saml
Donoho, Ellen
Ellis, Henry
Fearson, J C
Fugitt, FJ
Fletcher, Montg
Foller, Thos
Frailer, Chas
Fitzgerald, D
Goddard, Isaac
Greenfield, H C
Green, Owen
Green Jas
Gensler, Henry
Huggins, F B
Hitz, Flor
Harvey, J S & Co
Hurdle, Thos

Humes, Geo
Haisler, John
Henning, Stephen
Harper, W C
Hagerty, Wm
Hutton, Geo
Hagerty, Danl
Horstkamp, H
Hines, David
Handy, S W
Joyce, Michl
Jeffers, W J
Jarboe, benedict
Jackson, Susan
Jackson, B L & Bro
Iardella, L A
Joyce, J J
King, Martin
Killmon, J T
Lord, Wm
Lepreux, L & A-2
Lindsley, M S
Lakemeyer, Fred
Leddy, Owen
Laub, E A
Longdon, Chas
Looby, Patrick
McGenley, Pat
McCarthy, M M
Morsell, B F
McPherson, w S
Marceran, J L
Magee, Pat
Murray, Mary
Murray, Owen
McGill, Thos
McColgan, Jas
Middleton & Beall
Norris, Ann L
Mesmith, Ann
Orme, F M
Ober & Ryon
O'Hare, C S
O'Leary, John
Parker, Geo & Tho
Peters, J A
Pumphrey, S
Peerce, M J
Pilling, Jas
Parsons, M L
Peirce, G E
Redfern, Saml
Randall, G W
Reed, B W
Rosmelle, J C
Rochat, Henry
Ryon, John T
Rigden, Eliz
Ready, John
Robert, John
Simms, E
Stuck, F F
Stoops, Richd
Stewart, Donald
Semmes, T F
Scott, Eliz
Smith, Stewart
Shad, J C
Sweeney, Edw
Trimble, Matthew
Taylor, J H
Tench, Stanislaus
Tench, Thos P
Thornley, Thos
Travers, Elias
Upperman, W H
Wroe, Saml
Wright, Henry
Wallace, W A
Walker, Henry
White, N W
Waring & Brown
Williams, Zad-2
Wilkins, J L

Shop license:
Adams, N L
Bully, A F
Bache, T C
Barnes, Elias

Crane, Michl
Conlan, Peter
Davis, Jas
Fisher, G A
Provost & Wallingsford
Mickum & Turton
Kahl, Henry
Joyce, Susan
Jost, Benedict
Hoffman, Henry-2
Rupp, Wm
Rupert, Eve
Ruppel, Got
Riley, John
Saltzer, G
Turton & Mickum
Todschinder, J A F
Ward, Michl

Slave license:

Bell, Mrs J
Berry, B H
Bell, Jane
Williams, J A
Gettings, Thos
Harper, Mary
Harding, Henry
Jenkins, Mrs
Jones, Chas S
Lightfoot, Lewis
Calvin, Rebecca
Conway, Robt

Stage license:

Elliott, J W
Fowler, W R
Golden, W L
Leckron, D H
Sebastian, Caleb

Tavern license:

Brown, T P & M
Benter, Wm
Butler, Abram
Clarvoe, J H
Corson, Job
Campbell, W H
Casparis, Jas
Dorsey, P W
Eberbach, J H
Golden, John A
Harrington, R H
Hancock, And
Hendly, J R
Jones, Peter
Laskey, L A
McGarvey, Pat
Rand & Williams
Shad, B
Tinkman, Conrad
Topham, Geo
Talty, Michl

Ten Pins license: Casparis, Jas; Farrar, John M; Topham, Geo

Wagon license:

Bowen, J A-2
Barnes, Wm
Choppin, Wm
Filkins, H D
Owner, Jas
Payne, Chas H
Tinney, Chas

Wood license: Kelly, Wm

Persons fined, during Oct & Nov last for failing to procure their license:

Bowen, Jas: wagon
Browning, F W: dry goods
Lipscomb, E B: wagon
McQuay, Benj: huckstering
McKelden, J C: dog
Noerr, Andrew: wagon
Patterson, C W: slut
Raley, Jas: dog
Sawers, Wm: dog
Tenney, Chas: wagon

Wheeler, Ann: slut Whaley, H H: wagon

Adjournment of the Legislature of Indiana: Mr Andrew Kennedy is lying sick at the Palmer House with small-pox. Many members called to see Mr Kennedy previous to the nature of his disease being known, & for that reason it was supposed that it would spread among them so as to prevent legislation, if they remained.

The subscriber has received for sale, from the celebrated manufactory of Gebauhr, [Konigsberg,] 2 magnificent grand Pianos, of rosewood, English action; light enough for the most delicate lady's hand. Apply to O H Berg or Wm Mallinckrodt, 31 South Chas st, Balt, Md.

SAT DEC 25, 1847
Orphans Court of Wash Co, D C. Letters of administration with will annexed, on the personal estate of Martha Morgan, late of said couty, deceased.
-Sarah Washington, admx w a

Extension Dining Tables just received, elegant, fluted columns & patent hinges. Also now on hand, a few more Portable Shower Baths. At Brown's Cheap Furniture Store, Odd-Fellows' Hall, 7th st. -S D Brown

Jeremiah H Hallock died lately at Steubenville, Ohio, much regretted by all who knew him. He was formerly a member of the Legislature: served a term as President Judge of the Court of Common Pleas. He retired to a farm, & devoted himself to farming.
-Cin Gaz [No date-current item.]

Passengers in the ship **Northumberland**, at N Y from London: Doumal, of London; Mrs Macqueen & child, & Miss Macqueen, of Cincinnati; Mr Black, of New Brunswick; Messrs Coleman & O'Brien, British army; Robinson, Kensett, Pratt, Farmer, Maughlin, & Flinn, of N Y; Mr & Mrs Wyatt, Allen, McClery, & Waller, of England, & 170 in steerage.

The communication by **Telegraph** was opened on Thu last between the city of N Y & the city of St Louis, on the Mississippi.

Passengers in the packet-ship **Sheridan**, at N Y from Liverpool: Mr John Burges & lady, Mr Robt Burges, Robt Burges, jr, Isabel Burges, Staffordshire, England; Mr John Dale & lady, Mr Ambrose Dale, Mr Jas Dale, Miss Mary Dale, England; Wm Gaussen, Ireland; John Sniffen, Phil; 36 2nd cabin & 308 in steerage.

Mrd: on Dec 23, in Wash City, by Rev Levi Reese, Rev Saml Keener Cox, of the Methodist Protestant Church, Charleston, S C, to Miss Augusta M Billing, of Wash City.

Mrd: on Nov 28, by Rev Mr Taylor, Mr Solomon L Fowler to Miss Mary Susannah Serrin, both of Wash City.

Mrd: on Dec 2, at Rural Hill, Accomack Co, Va, by Rev J Ufford, Mr Wm P Bayly to Miss Bettie Paramore, youngest daughter of Wm Parramore.

Mrd: on Dec 7, at ***Cedarwood***, the residence of Mrs H Waller, by Rev Mr Billingsley, Dr May Burton, of Madison Co, Va, to Miss Juliet Theresa Szymanski, of Spottsylvania Co.

Died: on Dec 14, at New Orleans, after a short & rather sudden illness, Mrs Charlotte Caroline Johnson, consort of his Excellency Isaac Johnson, Govn'r of Louisiana.

MON DEC 27, 1847

The bridge over the Genesse, near Angelica, fell on Sun last. Mrs Geo B Russell & Miss King were killed.

The Washington [Pa] Reporter announced the death, within a few days past, of two of the oldest citizens of that county-Mr Saml Locock, in his 80th year, & Mr Danl Carter, in his 81st year-both of them having lived on the respective farms where they died for more than half a century.

New Haven, Dec 24: sad affair on the College premises last night. Some rowdies broke open the Lyceum door & proceeded to ring the bell. The noise brought out Tutor Jos Emerson, who called Tutor Wm Goodrich, son of Prof Goodrich, & the 2 sought to arrest the disturbers of the peace. Goodrich was struck on the head with an iron bar, & today much anxiety is felt for him. Emerson was cut in the arm. Two men, Tower, of Phil, & Ewing, of Tenn, were arrested, & each put under $4,000 bonds. -Palladium [Dec 29th newspaper: Emerson is out again: Goodrich was living on Monday morning-hopes for his recovery.]

The Hon Saml Hubbard, one of the Judges of the Supreme Court of Mass, died at Boston on Fri last.

Music for Parties. C Weber & A Ponse will attend Balls, & Parties, with a well organized band of scientific Musicians. Mr Weber has for some years been engaged in the above business. Orders may be left at Mr Gautier's confectionary store; Mr Krafft's, corner of 18th & Pa ave; at Mr Weber's, 2 doors from the Protestant Church, Navy Yard; or at Mr Ponse's, near Gen Henderson's residence, Navy Yard, & at Mr Wm Emmert's, Gtwn.

Died: on Dec 25, after a lingering illness, Mrs Susan Josephine Scott, widow of the late John B Scott, in her 45th year.

Died: on Dec 23, in Wash City, Basil Laman, infant son of the Hon Howell & Mary Ann Cobb, of Georgia.

Died: on Dec 10, at St Louis, Mo, of scarlet fever, Amy Ann Miller, aged 5 years & 10 months, daughter of Willis L & Saram M Williams.

TUE DEC 28, 1847

Mount Hebron for sale: by decree of the Circuit Superior Court of Law & Chancery for Fairfax Co, Va, rendered at the Nov term, 1847, in the suit of John T O Wilbar, cmplnt, vs The Bank of Washington & others, dfndnts, the undersigned, as com'rs therein named will sell, on Mar 1, 1848, at public auction, that valuable tract of land called ***Mount Hebron***, in said county: tract contains about 1,080 acres; the bldgs consist of a 2 story brick dwlg house, 2 cottages, barn, stable, smoke house, & a spring house. -Francis L Smith, Henry W Thomas, A Sidney Tebbs, Henry W Davis, com'rs

Orphans Court of Wash Co, D C. Letters of administration on the personal estate of John Riley, late of said county, dec'd. -Mary Riley, S S Williams, adms

The Hon John Fairfield died at his lodgings in Wash City on Fri last. He was one of the Senators from the State of Maine. His funeral is today, from the Senate Chamber, at 12 o'clock. Govn'r Fairfield was born at Saco, York Co, Maine, Jan 30, 1797. In that place he has ever resided. [He submitted to a surgical operation, to which, with undoubting confidence, he had looked for relief from an infirmity under which he had labored. His physical energies were not equal to his fortitude & courage. His system sank under the unabated anguish which followed, & in full possession of his mind, he breathed his last.

Maj Gen Quitman, with his family, & Brig Gen Shields arrived in town last evening by the Southern boat, & have taken lodgings at Fuller's Hotel.

By 3 writs of fieri facias, at the suits of Geo W Donn, Wm Mann, use of Geo W Adams & Edmund Reilly, against the goods & chattels of Wm Bush, & to me directed, I have seized & taken in execution all the right & title of Wm Bush in one cart, one running gear for hackney carriage, & one lot of cart harness, & one wheelbarrow, to be sold at public auction on Jan 1, 1848, in front of the Centre Market-house, Wash City.
-Horatio R Maryman, constable

The Hon John P Gaines, recently a prisoner in the city of Mexico, & a member elect of the present Congress, reached his home in Covington, Ky, on Thu week, & met with an enthusiastic reception.

The death of Maj E Kirby Barnum, of the U S Army, is announced in the Balt Sun of yesterday. He died in that city on Sunday last, after a lingering illness of many weeks. He has been about 30 years in the army, & served in Florida through the entire campaign. He was about to depart from N Y with his regt, at the commencement of the Mexican war, when he was thrown from his horse & fractured his leg, which laid him up for a long time. After recovering, & again about to leave, he was taken sick at Oswego, N Y, from which place he was removed to Balt a few weeks since, where he died, surrounded by his relatives. -Sun

Port Tobacco Times: Capt Walter H Jenifer, of the 3rd U S Dragoons, arrived in that county a few days since, on a temporary visit for the recovery of his health, which has been much impaired by a recent attack of fever at Vera Cruz.

Trustee's sale of valuable real estate in Calvert Co, Md: by virtue of a decree passed by the High Court of Chancery: sale at the Courthouse, Prince Fred'k, on Jan 7, 1848, the real estate of which Thos Mackall, late of Calvert Co, died seised & possessed, containing 546 acres. Land lies on the Patuxent river: contains a comfortable dwlg house & all necessary outbldgs. -Thos S Alexander, Danl C Digges, trustees

Died: on Dec 26, near Wash City, in his 59th year, Geo Oyster, a native of Pa, but the last 16 years a resident of D C. His funeral is today at 1 o'clock, from his late residence.

WED DEC 29, 1847

Executor's sale of a valuable farm at auction: on Jan 15, on the premises, the farm belonging to the estate of Thos Gibson, deceased, lying on the road leading from Beall's [formerly Benning's] Bridge to Bladensburg, & bounded by the District line, containing 105 acres, more or less, with good frame houses, barn, & stable thereon.
-John Holyrod, exc -A Green, auctioneer

Rev Walter M Lowrie, an American missionary at Ningpo, has been cruelly murdered in the Chinese seas by pirates. The reverend took his passage in a Chinese boat from Shanghae to Ningp, & during the voyage was attacked by a piratical vessel. They threw him into the sea, & he soon sank to rise no more. Mr Sullivan, the English consul at Ningpo, profferd every aid his official station enabled him to render, & steps were being taken to recover the remains if possible. [Mr Lowrie was a son of Hon Walter Lowrie, for many years Sec of the U S Senate, & a graduate of Princton Seminary. He married a daughter of the late Saml Boyd, of the N Y Board, & went to India in the service of the Presbyterian Board of Missions.]

At Savannah, on Dec 22, Mr John M Bell & a black man lost their lives, & Mr Thos Naylor was severely injured, by the falling of a large 4 story brick bldg, used as the reception store for rough rice, which suddenly gave way & fell to the ground.

From Mexico: Capt Jas Smith, 3rd Infty, died at Encero on Dec 4. His disease was congestion of the brain.

Mrd: on Dec 21, at Winchester, Va, by Rev Dr Hill, C W Schuermann, of Wash, to Miss Martha Donohoo, of Balt.

Mrd: on Dec 21, at Balt, by Rev Smith Pyne, rector of St John's Church, Washington, Jas Mandeville Carlisle, of Wash, to Emmeline Sophia, 2nd daughter of Alex'r Norman McLeod, of Scotland.

Senate: 1-Ptn from Thos Thompson, a British subject, asking compensation for rescuing the crew of an American vessel. 2-Ptn from Wm Gitt, asking that the heirs & reps of claimants under the act of Feb 17, 1815, may be allowed to locate certificates on any unappropriated lands. 3-Ptn from Danl McKissick, asking for a patent for lands settled by him in Oregon. 4-Ptn from Jonathan Lewis, asking compensation for depredations committed on his property by Cherokee Indians. 5-Ptn from David Myerlee, asking indemnity for losses sustained in efforts to produce water-rotted hemp for the navy. 6-Ptn from the reps of John G Mackall, asking compensation for property destroyed during the last war with Great Britain. 7-Ptn from the heirs & reps of Geo Gibson, an ofcr in the Revolution, asking to be allowed commutation pay. 8-Cmte on Pensions: asked to be discharged from the further consideration of the memorial of John Crosby, asking a pension for the children of the late Purser Andrew D Crosby, & that it be referred to the Cmte on Naval Affairs. Same on the ptn of Hugh Warmley, & that it be referred to the Cmte on Naval Affairs. 9-Cmte on Finance: adverse report on the memorial of Henry Simpson, adm of Geo Simpson, deceased. 10-Cmte on Military Affairs: asking to be discharged from the further consideration of the ptn of Jas Edwards, adm of Edw M Wanton, & that it be referred to the Cmte of Claims. 11-Cmte of Claims: adverse report on the ptn of Luther Blake, transferee of Lemuel B Nicholls. 12-Cmte on the Judiciary: asking to be discharged from the futher consideration of the ptn of John Bruce, & that it be referred to the Cmte of Claims. Same cmte: bill for the relief of M Hedge Galphin, exc of the last will & testament of Geo Galphin, dec'd. 13-Cmte on Naval Affairs: bill for the relief of Andrew D Crosby. Same cmte: bill for the relief of Wm A Christian. 14-Introduced: bill for the relief of Asa Andrews, of Ipswich, Mass. 15-Resolved: that the Cmte on Military Affairs inquire into the justice of providing for the fulfillment of the contracts entered into by the Sec of War on Mar 12, 1839, under the authority of a joint resolution fo Congress of Feb 13, 1839, to contract with J B & P Ferributt for the purchase of the island at the confluence of the St Peter's & Mississippi rivers. 16-Obit-announcement of the death of Rep Edw Bradley, Rep elect from Michigan: he was born in the town of East Bloomfield, Ontario Co, N Y, in Apr, 1808: at age 26 was appointed an Associate Judge of the Court of Common Pleas in his native county: in Jul, 1839 he removed to Michigan, & located at Marshall, in Calhoun Co: in 1846 he was elected a member of the House of Reps of the 30th Congress. He arrived in N Y C on Jul 31, & on Aug 5 he died. She who came to administer that aid & consolation which his debility required, returned with the lifeless remains of her husband to her stricken family-the widowed to the fatherless.

Mr F Ward [bearer of dispatches from Col Mason, Govn'r of Calif,] met at Cruces, Isthmus of Panama on Nov 23, Com Thos Ap Catesby Jones on his way to the Pacific, accompanied by the following gentlemen, who were all in good health: Capt Geisinger; Cmders Stribling & Glynn; Surgeons Brooke & Barrabine; Passed Midshipman Jones; W Stewart, Com Jones' Sec; Mr Schley, Capt Geisinger's Sec; Mr Stribling, Capt Stribling's Clerk; Mr John J Cornwall, Midshipman; Mr J B Gray, of Fredericksburg, Va; Mr J B Taylor, of N Y; Mr Campbell, of Oregon.

Mrd: on Dec 28, at ***Ivy Hill***, Montg Co, Md, by Rev Orlando Hutton, I Davis Read, of Gtwn, to Martha Eliz, daughter of the late Zadoc Cooke, of the former place.

List of ofcrs of the U S ship-of-the-line **Columbus**, bearing the broad pennant of Com Jas Biddle, which was at Valparaiso on Oct 27, & expected to sail about Nov 1 for the U S. Capt, Thos W Wyman; Lts, Percival Drayton, Henry French, Wm L Maury, Wm B Renshaw, Geo W Chapman; Acting Lts, Louis McLane, Madison Rush; Fleet Surgeon, B Ticknor; Passed Assist Surgeon, C F Guillon; Assist Surgeon, D L Bryan; Purser, Edw T Dunn; Acting Master, J M Wainwright; Chaplain, J W Newton; Prof of Mathematics, M Yarnall; Cmdor's Sec, E St Clair Clarke; passed Midshipmen, A J Drake, John C Febiger, Maurice Simons, G De Douallier, [died at Valapraiso, Oct 28;] Midshipmen, Byrd W Stevenson, Edw A Selden, John B Stewart, C K Graham, N H Van Zandt, Stephen B Luce, Gustavus Harrison, D A McDermot, John G Whitaker, Elliott Johnson, Wm P Toler; Cmdor's Clerk, Jos Lewis; Capt's Clerk, Robt Harris; Cmder's Clerk, John L Keffer; Purser's Clerk, Wm H Needles; Boatswain, V R Hall; Gunner Thos Robinson; Carpenter, Jonas Dibble; Sailmaker, R C Rodman. Marine Ofcrs: Capt H B Tyler, 1st Lt Wm A T Maddox, 2nd Lt John C Cash.

THU DEC 30, 1847
House of Reps: 1-Ptn of Andrew Brien & 110 others, praying for the establishment of an additional post route in Louisiana, & moved its reference to the Cmte on the Post Ofc & Post Roads.

The Mr Cunard named in the following, published in the Halifax Sun, has no connexion with the proprietor of the British Mail steamers. The letter is dated Chatham, Nov 30: Mr Jos Cunard stopped payment on Sat last, & has assigned all his estate & effects to trustees for the benefit of his creditors, & his establishment is closed.

New Confectionary: L A Tarlton's, on 10th st, between E & F sts.

Died: on Dec 28, Bazil Waring, aged 70 years, late of PG Co, Md, & for many years a clerk in the Treasury Dept. His funeral is on Dec 30, at 2 0'clock, from the residence of Mr Willis, F & 13th sts.

Smithsonian Institute: the chief complaint regards the bldg; its unnecessary dimensions & extravagant cost; & it is confidently predicted that it never will be finished, or, if finished, will absorb a third of the funds of the institution. It is not that the Regents are permitted to put up such a bldg; they are required to do so. The act of Congress appropriated the sum of $242,000, together with such other accruing interest as could be spared for the bldg; but, instead of using all that interest, as the Board was expressly authorized to do, the entire bldg will not withdraw from this fund of accumulated interest more than about a $102,000. $140,000 of the accumulated interest will have been saved, to add to the principal. -Wash News

FRI DEC 31, 1847

Concord Academy will commence on Feb 1, 1848: divine services are regularly performed at the Academy by Rev Wm Friend: located in Caroline Co, Va. F W Coleman, A M, Principal: Lewis M Coleman, A M, Assist; Alex Dempster, A M, Assist. References:
*Hon John Y Mason, *Sec of the Navy
*Dr E P Scott, *Speaker of the Senate of Va
*Jas Seddon, *
*Hon Jas M Mason, * Fred'k
*Rt Rev Nicholas Cobbs, D C, * Bishop of Ala
*Judge Saml Chapman, * Alabama
*B W Leigh, Richmond
*Wm R Johnson, Petersburg
*Thos J Randolph, Albemarle
*Andrew Hunter, Jefferson
Gov Reuben Chapman, Alabama
*Gen Bernard Peyton, Richmond
Judge Danl Coleman, Alabama
*Dr Armistead Cook, Portsmouth
Robt C Stanard, Richmond
*Wm H Harrison, PG
*Col Wm Armistead, Ala
*Wm H Tayloe, Mount Airy
*Richd Baylor, Essex
*Clayton G Coleman, Louisa
*Rev Elliott Estes, S C
*John Tabb, Gloucester
*Jas B Thornton, Memphis, Tenn
*Wm H Roy, Gloucester
*Hon Robt M T Hunter, Essex
Hon Thos H Bayly, M C
Rev Wm Friend, Port Royal
*John R Bryan, Gloucester
*Thos S Gholson, Petersburg
*Col John D Morris, Ky
*Wm A Quarles, Ky
*Geo F Wilkins, Northampton
*Alfred C Weeks, Louisiana
*Gentlemen who either have had, or who have at present, sons or wards members of the institution.

Senate: 1-Cmte on Indian Affairs: bill for the relief of Thos Talbot & others: to be printed. 2-Cmte on Public Lands: bill for the relief of Cadwallader Wallace: to be printed. 3-Bill introduced for the relief of Jeanette C Huntington, widow & sole excx of Wm D Cheever, deceased.

Died: on Dec 29, James, youngest son of Isaiah & Ann Catharine Bartley, aged 9 months & 17 days. His funeral is on Fri at 2 o'clock, from the corner of 4½ & G sts south.

The following passengers arrived at New Orleans on Dec 22 in the steamer **Fashion**, from Tampico & Brasos; Maj Forsyth, Paymaster U S army; Lt Col Fauntleroy, 2nd Dragoons; Lt Col Randolph, Va Regt; Capt Barksdale; Lts Mason & Townley; & 60 discharged soldiers & teamsters; also, the remains of the late lamented Capt Churchill. The following gentlemen, passengers from Vera Cuz, have also arrived at New Orleans: Dr Finley, U S army; Capts Wheat & Shepherd, U S army; & Midshipman Scott, U S army.

New Orleans Picayune of Dec 21: in Hancock Co, Miss, an informer named Brown, went out in quest of 2 counterfeiters named Washington Bilbos & Jas Bilbos, brothers, whom they discovered at their infarious business. These men were arrested, & released on bail. Soon after Brown, the informer, & his son-in-law, Wages, sold out their property, & were about to leave Hancock Co, when they were overtaken by the counterfeiters. The counterfeiters were both shot by Wages. One of them was killed on the spot.

Accident on the Ohio river on Wed last: the steamer **A N Johnson**, on her trip from Cincinnati to Wheeling, when near Maysville, burst her boiler, completely destroying the boat, & creating a terrific loss of life. 70 were instantly killed. Messrs Wheat & Pillson, of Balt, were among those scalded.

House of Reps: 1-Cmte of Claims: bill for the relief of Jas Brown: to be printed. Bill for the relief of Danl Robinson: to be printed. 2-Cmte of Claims: adverse reports on the ptns of Wm Brook, Jas Morrow, Patrick Cunningham, & Geo B Hollenback: to be printed. 3-Cmte on Public Lands: adverse report on the ptn of N P Bennet: to be printed. 4-Ptn of Jacob Messersmith & others, citizens of Lordstown, Trumbull Co, Ohio, praying for peace with Mexico. 5-Memorial of Rachel Saltz, widow of an invalid soldier, praying Congress to grant her some relief. 6-Ptn of Elijah Milam, asking pay for a horse lost in the U S ranging service. 7-Ptn of Jane Suller & of Alex'r McDonald, asking a pension. 8-Ptn of Caleb Bell, asking the arrearage of pay of Matthew Bell, who died in the U S army. 9-Ptn of Danl Hart, asking that a land warrant be issued to him as legatee of his father for services in the Revolutionary war.

On Monday some half dozen of the Alabama volunteers now encamped near this city went to the house of Adonice Robeson, a respectable Creole living near the camp, & as reports go, perpetrated various outrages, insulting the female portion of the family, until at length Robeson fired on the crowd with a double-barrelled gun, killing one & wounding 2 or 3 others. The man killed was John Judgins, who belonged to Capt Barr's company from Tuscaloosa. Robeson delivered himself up to the sheriff. -Mobile Advertiser

A

Abbot, 54, 146, 326, 365, 457
Abbott, 16, 26, 63, 227, 258, 300, 336, 433, 540, 553
Abell, 129, 193, 227
Abercrombie, 110, 233, 445, 540
Aberlee, 452
Abernathy, 136
Abert, 105, 116, 181, 281
Abney, 389, 398, 399
Abrams, 311, 419
Academy of the Visitation, 73
Achelis, 500
Achenback, 444
Acherman, 393
Acken, 153, 342, 378
Acker, 517, 519
Ackland, 83
Ackles, 266
Acton, 380
Adair, 45, 79
Adam, 25, 551
Adams, 10, 33, 39, 46, 53, 54, 68, 84, 90, 91, 93, 106, 127, 137, 140, 163, 181, 192, 221, 227, 246, 250, 252, 259, 266, 298, 301, 308, 331, 372, 380, 387, 397, 398, 428, 430, 431, 449, 452, 455, 487, 509, 537, 555, 556, 557, 558, 559, 563
Adamson, 38, 333, 448, 558
Addams, 426
Adde, 194
Addicks, 170
Addison, 72, 96, 266, 267, 274, 331, 398, 451, 558
Addition to Mill Seat, 438
Adkeson, 480
Adkins, 270
Adlard, 493
Adler, 318, 505
Adnet, 342
Affonso, 365
Ager, 488, 556, 558
Agol, 442
Ahlborn, 483
Aigler, 54
Aiken, 72, 182, 259, 288
Ailer, 54
Airs, 142
Aisquith, 130, 458, 543
Aix, 282
Akin, 137
Akles, 460
Akor, 394
Albert, 428, 430
Albertazzi, 440
Albock, 396
Albourg, 399
Albrecht, 14
Alburn, 221
Alburtis, 151, 181, 247, 250, 521
Alcalde, 105
Alcock, 394
Alde, 551
Alden, 14, 16, 94, 477, 521
Aldrick, 537
Aldridge, 30
Aldunante, 316
Aleg, 485
Ales, 181
Alexander, 62, 97, 134, 211, 234, 380, 394, 399, 443, 444, 451, 486, 506, 507, 508, 564
Alexandria, 368
Alexandria Co, 175
Alford, 14
Alger, 54, 100, 404
Alhouse, 278
Alleir, 558
Allemong, 316, 424
Allen, 2, 7, 8, 33, 45, 46, 49, 50, 59, 61, 64, 69, 78, 91, 97, 102, 107, 109, 131, 140, 162, 179, 183, 188, 221, 223, 225, 230, 236, 280, 290, 303, 321, 328, 331, 337, 346, 359, 366, 371,

380, 394, 396, 401, 424, 439, 445, 451, 466, 501, 507, 510, 512, 521, 531, 539, 549, 551, 556, 558, 561
Aller, 267
Allison, 14, 142, 171, 224, 229, 353, 399, 448, 493
Allston, 522, 525
Allyer, 530
Almstedt, 199
Almy, 5
Alpkun, 431
Alsup, 338
Althor, 442
Alum Springs, 416
Alverhorn, 448
Alvis, 519
Alvord, 109
Amable, 209
Amachler, 505
Ambler, 331, 435, 552
Amelia, 366
Ameren, 141
Ames, 192, 333, 417
Amey, 454
Amidon, 431
Ammons, 501
Amoise, 493
Amory, 410
Ampudia, 489
Anderson, 29, 71, 86, 91, 93, 94, 107, 108, 133, 134, 145, 150, 163, 171, 176, 188, 200, 203, 206, 214, 223, 233, 252, 255, 264, 269, 283, 324, 369, 380, 387, 395, 396, 397, 402, 403, 426, 431, 433, 439, 440, 444, 452, 454, 455, 456, 457, 465, 484, 487, 490, 508, 513, 514, 515, 521, 523, 528, 540, 543, 547
Andis, 369
Andorin, 476
Andrade, 152
Andre, 60, 75
Andrew, 408, 525
Andrews, 14, 16, 70, 98, 107, 112, 129, 178, 196, 204, 205, 206, 230, 235, 277, 315, 331, 357, 397, 398, 431, 440, 457, 480, 484, 490, 502, 513, 539, 550, 565
Aneling, 426
Angel, 447
Angell, 501
Angney, 165
Angus, 537
Anlick, 327
Annison, 445
Anonos, 152
Anson, 45, 113, 253, 261, 539
Anthony, 161, 198, 207, 221, 265, 404, 465, 508, 529
Antison, 461
Antonious, 498
Appleby, 461
Applegate, 138
Appleton, 369
Arahood, 223
Archduke Charles, 290
Archer, 87, 153, 195, 204, 205, 208, 441, 484, 485
Archuleta, 171
Archulette, 116
Arguelles, 209
Arlington House, 182
Armfield, 1
Armijo, 116
Armistead, 158, 316, 441, 490, 497, 567
Armour, 508
Armprister, 455
Arms, 451
Armstead, 50
Armstrong, 7, 14, 34, 35, 59, 63, 64, 138, 141, 220, 284, 290, 293, 302, 334, 345, 399, 401, 403, 440, 500, 508, 539, 547, 551
Armtz, 446
Arnold, 60, 114, 140, 141, 221, 279, 315, 388, 394, 404, 447, 453, 486, 538
Arppen, 500
Arter, 138
Arth, 213
Arthur, 4, 339, 396, 455, 478, 544

Aschison, 478
Ash, 337
Ashby, 165, 468
Ashdown, 259
Ashe, 339, 545
Ashford, 96, 433
Ashman, 531
Ashmun, 50
Ashton, 159, 380, 409, 416, 476
Ashworth, 395, 452
Asonos, 128
Astor, 351
Atchison, 46
Atherton, 46, 135
Athon, 545
Athow, 339
Athoy, 396
Athuson, 127
Atkin, 408
Atkins, 91, 92, 96
Atkinson, 117, 135, 270, 417, 456, 457
Atocha, 277
Attstin, 449
Aubert, 316
Aubke, 138
Aubrey, 510
Aubry, 378
Auglemyer, 454
Augur, 247
Aujon, 453
Auldridge, 136
Aulick, 41, 132, 309, 504
Aull, 378
Ault, 509
Austin, 171, 216, 244, 372, 394
Austine, 539
Averett, 327, 373, 389, 407
Avery, 477, 532, 558
Ayers, 110
Ayres, 336, 440, 449, 539, 547
Ays, 431

B

Baare, 76
Babb, 445
Babbitt, 278
Babcock, 486, 509
Babe, 449
Bach, 91
Bache, 32, 187, 219, 370, 559
Bachelder, 195, 207
Bacher, 444
Bachman, 135
Backenstos, 441
Backhans, 447
Backus, 110, 536
Bacon, 47, 226, 258, 388, 430, 433, 484, 487, 515, 516, 533, 541, 547, 554, 558
Bacumlo, 221
Baden, 62, 254, 557
Badger, 46, 79, 345, 370
Baer, 251
Bagby, 188, 257, 303, 312, 433
Baggett, 184
Bagley, 510, 543
Bagman, 121, 231
Bailenau, 453
Bailey, 34, 95, 111, 137, 424, 452
Baily, 71, 317, 489
Bain, 450
Bainbridge, 108, 109
Baines, 121
Baird, 76, 303
Baker, 68, 78, 127, 133, 136, 138, 177, 210, 229, 231, 243, 251, 257, 302, 303, 370, 397, 417, 420, 425, 426, 441, 445, 450, 451, 456, 471, 484, 501, 502, 508, 515, 516
Bakevell, 510
Bakewell, 404, 531
Balch, 353, 374
Bald, 451
Baldhurst, 449
Baldwin, 16, 18, 20, 40, 44, 120, 125, 151, 183, 351, 431, 462, 507, 508, 509, 531, 532
Baleh, 295
Bales, 140
Balis, 270

Ball, 62, 64, 142, 288, 289, 312, 366, 415, 417, 429, 453, 507, 509, 533
Ballard, 139, 311, 328, 360, 398, 443, 450
Balleman, 444
Balmain, 475
<u>Balt Btln</u>, 1
Baltee, 408
Baltimore, 123
Bancroft, 186, 220, 454
Bandorf, 221
Bandouin, 536
Bang, 436
Banghart, 507
Bangs, 380
Bank, 54
Bankhead, 90, 119, 325
Banks, 30, 395, 454
Bannatyne, 153
Banning, 67
Baptiste, 467
Baranda, 209
Barbelin, 38
Barber, 54, 91, 139, 163, 267, 399
Barbins, 493
Barbos, 355
Barbour, 127, 261, 439, 543
Barclay, 230, 258, 401, 439, 482
Barcley, 61
Barcroft, 91, 380
Barculo, 280
Bard, 68, 419, 420
Bardon, 394
Barhydt, 457
Barinds, 236
Barine, 394
Barker, 163, 164, 298, 379, 394, 408, 409, 456, 523, 527
Barkholm, 396
Barksdale, 35, 112, 113, 253, 568
Barkslow, 399
Barlow, 285
Barnard, 101, 142, 204, 207, 380, 496, 511
Barnes, 3, 10, 37, 48, 116, 134, 168, 184, 222, 231, 267, 394, 397, 399, 453, 556, 559, 560
Barnett, 543
Barney, 11, 265
Barnhard, 442
Barnhart, 452
Barnhill, 163
Barnicloe, 191
Barnicoat, 415
Barnum, 108, 378, 405, 524, 563
Baron, 394
barque **Alfred**, 476
barque **Canton**, 79
barque **Catalpa**, 284
barque **Cordelia**, 64, 84
barque **Edith**, 262
barque **Electra**, 324
barque **Iduna**, 349
barque **Pons**, 64, 84
barque **Rothschild**, 58
Barr, 135, 225, 443, 558, 568
Barrabine, 565
Barrand, 370
Barraud, 345
Barret, 395, 472
Barrett, 38, 132, 163, 225, 331, 417
Barrimeria, 215
Barrington, 308
Barrom, 450
Barron, 4, 120, 132, 264, 285, 302, 324, 327, 430, 433
Barrow, 43, 179, 330, 480, 510
Barry, 32, 33, 39, 72, 82, 85, 129, 154, 160, 168, 197, 247, 249, 304, 341, 381, 391, 456, 504, 551, 555
Barsalou, 457
Barstow, 457
Bartheson, 127
Barthody, 528
Bartholomew, 251
Bartin, 183
Bartleson, 135
Bartlett, 11, 138, 139, 164, 302, 413, 479, 523

Bartley, 460, 568
Barton, 32, 96, 129, 193, 227, 236, 313, 445, 450, 467, 510
Bartruff, 81, 145
Barturkey, 449
Basave, 152
Bascom, 396
Basler, 270
Basquin, 457
Bass, 17
Basseau, 370
Basset, 75
Bassett, 80, 91, 256, 345
Bastianelli, 293, 557
Bateman, 225
Batemen, 450
Bates, 11, 37, 54, 58, 79, 225, 226, 242, 305, 313, 346, 392, 435, 482, 558
Batmas, 396
Batsner, 451
Battaile, 41
Battee, 261
Battendorf, 395
Battersby, 457
Battes, 543
Bauch, 223
Bauder, 495
Baughanan, 394
Baugher, 439
Baughman, 399
Baum, 19
Baumback, 430, 558
Baun, 293, 357
Baure, 403
Baxter, 331, 441, 487
Bayard, 50, 335, 342, 367
Baylies, 366, 457
Bayliss, 54, 225, 429
Baylor, 365, 567
Bayly, 49, 117, 163, 231, 286, 332, 557, 562, 567
Bayne, 63, 436, 519, 557
Bays, 346, 533
Bazil, 493
Beach, 202, 244, 429, 445, 458, 472, 512, 556, 558
Beadon, 456
Beagle, 133
Beale, 2, 117, 177, 200, 206, 240, 390, 409, 441, 472
Bealiss, 71
Beall, 10, 19, 91, 106, 120, 239, 252, 267, 348, 416, 438, 459, 505, 520, 530, 558, 559, 564
Beall's First Addition, 438
Bealle, 381, 438
Bean, 58, 191, 225, 267, 380, 404, 448, 555, 558
Bear, 221
Bear Spring Furnace, 327
Beard, 238, 399
Beardsley, 54, 285, 291, 440, 513, 514, 556
Bearn, 397
Beaseley, 517
Beasely, 301
Beasley, 54, 286, 517
Beasly, 50, 54
Beatty, 36, 123, 331, 374, 453, 510
Beaubien, 171
Beaubion, 48
Beauchamp, 376
Beaufort, 314
Beaugrand, 7
Beaumont, 5, 83, 507
Beauregard, 233, 441
Beaver, 443
Beavin, 372
Bech, 404
Bechtel, 409
Beck, 13, 90, 128, 167, 214, 221, 228, 401, 433, 500, 505
Beckel, 493
Beckenschitz, 449
Becker, 7, 223
Becket, 557
Beckett, 122, 202
Beckman, 431
Beckwith, 140, 181

Bede, 93
Bedell, 135
Bedford, 201, 256, 441
Bedine, 111
Bedinger, 117, 440
Bee, 5, 388
Beebe, 409, 452
Beecher, 399, 482
Beeckel, 445
Beedle, 397
Beehler, 95
Beer, 449
Beers, 10, 47, 507
Beesley, 302
Beesly, 494
Begby, 102
Beggs, 399
Begnam, 54, 267
Beham, 170
Behn, 53
Beigle, 450
Belknap, 170, 251, 527, 540, 541
Bell, 20, 30, 43, 54, 61, 63, 67, 78, 92, 94, 113, 133, 214, 221, 225, 253, 261, 342, 380, 393, 394, 398, 417, 430, 431, 435, 441, 443, 451, 488, 500, 537, 560, 564, 568
Bell__k, 441
Belle, 523
Belle Mont, 313
Belloe, 403
Belpark, 41
Belt, 166, 191, 432, 511
Belton, 212, 497
Beltzhoover, 336, 539
Beman, 49
Bender, 149
Benedick, 461
Benedict, 225, 344, 537
Benefiel, 137
Beneget, 58
Benerlin, 395
Benezet, 533
Benguerel, 96
Benham, 132, 133, 311
Benj Ray Tract, 115
Benjamin, 108, 441, 457, 490, 539, 548
Bennell, 398
Benner, 395, 503
Bennet, 217, 450, 568
Bennett, 26, 196, 202, 210, 224, 285, 388, 395, 399, 455, 457, 500, 513
Benning, 27, 564
Bennington, 317
Bennis, 538
Benson, 138, 441, 488, 523
Bent, 105, 131, 144, 165, 171
Bent's Fort, 131
Benter, 19, 91, 163, 517, 560
Bentley, 507
Benton, 49, 58, 85, 89, 94, 102, 106, 110, 114, 118, 157, 247, 284, 305, 306, 397, 448, 489
Berchfield, 328
Bercoure, 493
Berdine, 184
Berg, 561
Bergman, 433
Berkley, 54, 92
Bermingham, 447
Bernard, 168, 458, 476
Bernheimer, 409
Berra, 152
Berrabidas, 209
Berrier, 133
Berrs, 128
Berry, 38, 50, 85, 92, 130, 164, 166, 183, 188, 203, 241, 242, 267, 277, 282, 319, 380, 381, 399, 417, 466, 489, 508, 511, 523, 524, 545, 560
Berryman, 54, 71, 92, 93, 100, 214, 231, 238, 324, 365, 435, 557
Bertody, 404
Bertoled, 446
Bertram, 442
Besancon, 318
Besel, 51
Best, 336, 434, 478, 507, 540
Beston, 369
Bestor, 291

Betchtel, 455
Bethell, 203, 207
Betts, 475
Beute, 556
Beuzenburg, 51
Bevan, 558
Beverage, 267
Beveridge, 267
Beverley, 282
Beverly, 32, 422
Beyer, 510
Bibb, 21, 224
Bichardson, 222
Bickerstine, 449
Bicking, 502
Bickley, 322
Bidault, 457
Biddle, 102, 161, 168, 204, 207, 299, 311, 381, 489, 496, 566
Bideswell, 7
Biers, 494
Bierwith, 222
Big Elk Lick, 115
Bigby, 134
Bigelow, 132, 502
Bigerstaff, 140
Biggs, 394, 455
Bigley, 510
Bignem, 10
Bihler, 54, 267
Bilbos, 568
Bilfinger, 493
Bill, 203, 207, 457, 542, 547
Billing, 329, 380, 395, 561
Billings, 378, 389, 398, 457
Billingsley, 562
Billington, 450, 482
Bills, 14, 527
Billston, 438
Binart, 394
Bingham, 23, 188, 303
Binoche, 457
Birbeck, 94
Birch, 10, 54, 56, 133, 141, 154, 156, 279, 310, 381, 510, 512, 516, 518
Birchland, 411
Birchland Tract, 328
Bird, 3, 93, 136, 173, 267, 534
Birell, 164
Birkley, 93
Birmingham, 394, 404
Birnan, 394
Birs, 509
Birth, 286
Biscoe, 415, 417
Bishey, 301
Bishop, 68, 137, 339, 360, 393, 403, 447, 455, 508, 523, 544, 551, 552
Bishop's, 345
Bisphan, 144
Bissel, 541, 544
Bissell, 93, 169, 195, 541
Bitner, 221, 342, 428
Bitzel, 54
Bixby, 331
Black, 225, 267, 336, 342, 395, 398, 438, 501, 541, 555, 561
Blackburn, 201, 542
Blackford, 28, 274
Blackistone, 392
Blackman, 451, 483, 501
Blackney, 476
Blackstone, 417
Blackwell, 49, 138, 483
Bladen, 299
Blagden, 81, 131, 153, 189, 244, 298, 436, 524, 525
Blagge, 5
Blagrove, 76
Blaiding, 9, 112, 113, 253
Blain, 455
Blaine, 359
Blair, 16, 81, 118, 172, 204, 207, 235, 269, 274, 448, 453, 494, 510
Blaisdell, 354, 450
Blake, 34, 54, 94, 181, 243, 258, 298, 337, 396, 457, 509, 541, 565
Blakely, 134, 476
Blakey, 204
Blakistone, 189

Blakslee, 61
Blalock, 87, 137
Blanchand, 493
Blanchard, 15, 40, 45, 51, 59, 84, 144, 229, 249, 325, 335, 338, 420, 434, 457, 553
Bland, 9, 113, 149, 177, 253, 262
Blandin, 398
Blanding, 199, 388
Blandy, 403
Blane, 459, 508, 509
Blanford, 10
Blanton, 94, 339, 397, 545, 549
Blassingham, 431
Blast, 450
Bleck, 339
Bleckford, 118
Bledsoe, 453
Blight, 437
Blish, 520, 521
Bliss, 7, 127, 170, 175, 284, 381, 447, 527
Blocker, 454
Blondell, 285
Blood, 194, 397
Bloom, 444
Bloss, 23, 63, 67, 78
Blow, 35
Blumenbach, 374
Blunder, 163
Bluner, 465
Blunt, 16, 139, 444
Boardman, 311
Boarman, 45, 91, 163, 316, 341, 536
boat **Sussex**, 191
Boate, 181
Bobbett, 112
Bobles, 396
Bocker, 457
Bocock, 117
Boddington, 493
Bode, 512
Bodfish, 155, 195, 208
Bodinier, 457
Bodisco, 228
Boerhurst, 509
Bogan, 33, 54
Bogard, 140
Bogardus, 207
Bogert, 78
Boggus, 27
Boghanan, 446
Bogue, 417
Bohan, 448
Bohanan, 444
Bohlan, 208
Bohlayer, 54, 91, 92, 267, 307, 405
Bohlen, 400
Bohmer, 457
Bohn, 218
Bohrer, 331, 351, 381, 528
Boissaulon, 476
Boland, 510
Bold, 456
Bolderstine, 524
Boling, 443
Bolio, 221
Bolling, 117
Boln, 221
Bolton, 131, 401, 454
Bolun, 73
bomb ketch **Electra**, 132
bomb ketch **Etna**, 132
bomb ketch **Hecla**, 132
bomb ketch **Stromboli**, 132
bomb ketch **Vesuvius**, 132
Bombard, 396
Bomford, 65, 490, 497, 520
Bonaparte, 121, 287, 292, 427
Bond, 134, 177, 234, 452, 462, 464
Bondel, 397
Bondy, 126
Bone, 399
Bonet, 445
Bonham, 129, 198, 205, 397, 507, 542
Bonick, 409
Bonilla, 128
Bonissant, 457
Bonnaffi, 304
Bonner, 136

Bonnetts, 455
Bonneville, 387, 394, 513
Bont, 508
Booker, 541
Boom, 215
Boon, 37, 183, 345
Boone, 50, 58, 96, 106, 225, 231, 246, 267, 341, 417, 443
Boorman, 554
Booth, 20, 248
Boothe, 380
Boother, 92
Bord, 139
Bordas, 404
Bordaux, 136
Boreson, 509
Borgardus, 201
Borie, 398
Borland, 12, 54, 74, 85, 151, 244, 268, 269, 483, 497, 513, 525
Born, 450
Boronell, 84
Borquet, 493
Borrows, 47, 87, 186, 258, 516
Borth, 139
Borthwick, 426
Bosely, 377
Boss, 42, 91
Bossard, 493
Bostic, 500
Bosworth, 111, 278, 290, 338
Boteler, 10, 26, 32, 65, 116, 162, 185, 232, 415, 420, 485, 530
Bothe, 400
Bottemly, 380
Botts, 44, 114, 117, 182, 507, 521
Boudard, 404
Boudinot, 5
Boudnier, 493
Bougher, 245, 508
Boulanger, 294, 503
Bounds, 495
Bourkie, 476
Bourman, 483
Bouton, 196
Bouvet, 380
Bovet, 399
Bowden, 493
Bowdon, 46
Bowen, 7, 59, 61, 89, 107, 110, 138, 163, 326, 380, 400, 464, 560
Bower, 444
Bowers, 195, 273, 397, 415, 460, 482, 541
Bowie, 38, 54, 97, 141, 142, 162, 183, 202, 204, 206, 213, 239, 249, 361, 375, 402, 436, 501, 511, 523, 542
Bowles, 169, 394, 396, 400
Bowlin, 50, 397, 532
Bowling, 150, 173, 341, 370
Bowman, 236, 457, 502
Bowning, 133
Boxer, 523
Boy, 423
Boyce, 30, 311, 508, 509
Boyd, 21, 38, 79, 91, 153, 184, 224, 252, 300, 321, 339, 354, 371, 396, 399, 468, 480, 522, 526, 536, 544, 548, 564
Boyer, 254, 394, 455
Boylayer, 519
Boyle, 7, 21, 24, 39, 41, 44, 54, 91, 133, 188, 202, 225, 231, 274, 298, 394, 399, 425, 451, 459, 510, 525
Boynton, 107, 388, 397, 513, 514, 538, 539
Bozeman, 545
Bozz, 91
Brackenridge, 281
Brackett, 490
Bracklin, 221
Bradbury, 552
Braddock, 68
Bradey, 54
Bradford, 170, 200, 250, 275, 415, 457, 519
Bradley, 7, 47, 54, 63, 101, 116, 136, 138, 191, 221, 224, 228, 274, 283, 298, 306, 330, 381, 396, 397, 398, 446, 509, 517, 518, 565

Bradshaw, 510, 523
Brady, 95, 141, 163, 259, 294, 298, 357, 381, 394, 399, 417, 480, 502, 555
Bragden, 163
Bragdon, 33
Bragg, 109, 110, 169, 195
Bragine, 446
Braiden, 417
Brain, 408
Bramlette, 25
Branch, 134, 535
Branched, 223
Brand, 137
Brandstadter, 509
Brandt, 526
Branham, 139
Brannan, 107, 441, 549
Branner, 10
Brannon, 203, 323
Branson, 91, 208
Brashear, 236
Brashears, 54, 558
Brasheno, 451
Brass, 454
Braun, 457
Brauner, 98
Brave, 484
Bravo, 442, 496
Brawner, 178, 316, 417
Braxton, 557
Bray, 393
Brayman, 221
Brayton, 475
Brazer, 426
Brazier Tract, 328
Breck, 258
Breckenridge, 153, 316, 379, 472
Bredin, 5
Bree, 5
Breeden, 221
Breedlove, 147, 201, 207, 484, 551
Breese, 32, 132, 187, 217, 219, 331
Brennan, 447
Brenner, 316
Brent, 2, 11, 29, 91, 111, 123, 131, 169, 177, 181, 239, 254, 257, 272, 289, 298, 314, 316, 380, 385, 401, 527, 535
Brenton, 449
Brereton, 106, 163, 410, 480, 558
Bres, 139
Bresson, 528
Brevoort, 309
Brewer, 166, 224, 554
Brewerton, 248
Brewster, 507
Briceland, 320
Brichsler, 92
Brick, 111
Brickell, 482
Bride, 295
Bridge, 345, 360
Bridges, 453, 483
Bridgett, 396
Briel, 91
Brien, 566
brig **Adelaide**, 478
brig **Aetna**, 100
brig **Albert**, 550
brig **Bainbridge**, 327
brig **Belize**, 359
brig **Boxer**, 144
brig **Columiba**, 414
brig **Dolphin**, 477
brig **Elizabeth Ann**, 270
brig **Emilio**, 114
brig **Falconer**, 552
brig **Gen Lamar**, 157
brig **Leveret**, 79
brig **Ocean Queen**, 78, 84
brig of war **Perry**, 132
brig of war **Porpoise**, 132
brig **Paul T Jones**, 273
brig **Perry**, 34, 324, 327, 370
brig **Porpoise**, 58, 158, 160
brig **Saml N Gott**, 87
brig **Somers**, 30, 117
brig **Spy**, 372
brig **Stromboli**, 100
brig **Thetis**, 270

brig **Union**, 278
brig **Washington**, 327
Bright, 71, 86, 138, 317, 405, 558
Brightwell, 6, 71
Brimingham, 404
Brimmer, 179
Brines, 426
Brinn, 467
Briolon, 451
Briscoe, 54, 105, 183, 218, 226, 410, 556
Bristow, 234, 410
Britain, 355
Brito, 152
Britt, 304
Brittenham, 456
Britton, 109, 233
Broadback, 160
Broadbent, 53, 408
Broadrup, 281, 533
Brockenbrough, 407
Brockett, 534
Brockley, 523
Brodaick, 442
Brodbent, 10
Brodeau, 380
Brodhead, 202, 345, 370, 484, 513
Bronaugh, 10, 54, 199, 466, 499
Bronson, 45, 64, 69, 280
Brook, 134, 357, 417, 568
Brookbank, 455
Brooke, 19, 38, 165, 176, 213, 225, 282, 325, 345, 409, 410, 416, 417, 425, 443, 461, 471, 495, 503, 524, 530, 565
Brookes, 239, 335, 524
Brooks, 20, 91, 96, 97, 216, 225, 270, 304, 316, 398, 421, 443, 447, 495
Broom, 357, 457
Broome, 549
Brophy, 400
Brother, 488
Brou, 316
Broughton, 172
Brouk, 482
Brower, 86
Brown, 5, 6, 10, 12, 15, 16, 23, 25, 32, 35, 39, 54, 58, 61, 63, 67, 75, 79, 81, 82, 86, 92, 95, 102, 105, 107, 108, 117, 133, 135, 138, 140, 141, 149, 153, 159, 162, 163, 183, 185, 194, 212, 214, 215, 221, 223, 225, 226, 235, 237, 238, 243, 267, 279, 290, 294, 295, 299, 300, 304, 305, 332, 349, 357, 358, 371, 380, 393, 394, 397, 398, 399, 414, 417, 421, 426, 428, 429, 430, 435, 437, 442, 444, 445, 447, 448, 449, 452, 453, 456, 470, 471, 472, 483, 484, 501, 504, 507, 508, 509, 516, 517, 518, 525, 527, 537, 545, 550, 551, 552, 555, 556, 557, 558, 559, 560, 561, 568
Brownback, 103
Browne, 169, 177, 415, 554
Brownell, 6, 15, 45, 63, 78, 485
Browning, 223, 560
Brownrigg, 272
Brownwell, 59, 66
Brua, 248
Bruce, 29, 58, 64, 84, 115, 225, 397, 476, 565
Bruere, 457
Bruff, 472
Brugh, 450
Bruke, 487
Brum, 33, 84
Brumagem, 399
Brundbridge, 430
Brunel, 145
Bruner, 139, 221, 222, 509
Bruney, 446
Brunner, 218, 339
Bruno, 137, 319, 320
Brunston, 183
Brunton, 127
Brus, 507
Brush, 70, 446
Brusoer, 224
Bruyere, 157, 196, 235
Bryam, 141

Bryan, 8, 29, 133, 161, 169, 217, 229, 258, 523, 550, 566, 567
Bryant, 136, 230, 298, 302, 355, 366, 417, 467, 472, 531
Bryarly, 87
Brydges, 469
Bryding, 221
Brynton, 484
Buchanan, 4, 46, 48, 95, 132, 251, 369, 419, 424, 443, 468, 490
Buchart, 509
Buck, 87, 395
Buckingham, 47, 87, 183, 308, 469, 516
Buckland, 447
Buckley, 54, 61, 92, 124, 128, 246, 443
Buckly, 432
Buckmaster, 136
Buckner, 150, 345, 388, 394, 490, 554
Budd, 221
Budley, 500
Buel, 445
Buell, 365, 395
Buena Vista, 126, 127, 133, 142, 143, 144, 149, 150, 151, 169, 185, 190, 230, 242, 250, 266, 270, 284, 299, 309, 314, 315, 316, 379, 404, 414, 462, 554
Buete, 429
Buffalo Tract, 115
Buford, 106, 246
Buker, 268
Bulfinch, 380
Bulger, 300, 340
Bull, 397, 482
Bullard, 275
Bullett, 530
Bullitt, 465
Bullock, 223, 404
Bullus, 132
Bully, 91, 559
Buloof, 482
Bulow, 51
Bulter, 408
Bunce, 15, 66, 70, 84, 158
Bunch, 339, 545
Bungeant, 448
Bunger, 448
Buntin, 215
Bunting, 253, 261, 494
Burbank, 13, 440, 541, 547
Burch, 27, 54, 62, 90, 104, 121, 212, 298, 380, 381, 476, 515, 523
Burche, 65
Burchstead, 309
Burdet, 493
Burdett, 495
Burdin, 181
Burdine, 270, 380, 381, 430
Burditt, 139
Bure, 457
Burford, 10
Burgen, 394
Burges, 561
Burgess, 28, 170, 380, 488, 494, 554
Burgewin, 183
Burgoyne, 18
Burgwin, 165, 168, 246, 250
Burgwyn, 150
Burkard, 243
Burke, 15, 47, 107, 136, 268, 356, 380, 387, 395, 412, 447, 456, 480, 498, 543, 547
Burkey, 507
Burks, 139
Burn, 222
Burnam, 30
Burnell, 4, 5
Burnet, 136, 221, 267, 388
Burnett, 139, 144, 210, 243, 261, 267, 371, 399, 408, 484, 487, 513, 523, 553
Burney, 463, 535
Burnham, 457
Burnit, 134
Burns, 131, 153, 181, 223, 224, 266, 336, 357, 394, 428, 434, 446, 540
Burnside, 336, 539
Buroughs, 331
Burr, 18, 54, 91, 98, 211, 257, 301, 306, 372, 415, 430
Burrell, 294, 557

Burrh, 135
Burritt, 447
Burrough, 521
Burroughs, 154, 303, 406
Burrows, 354
Burtlett, 395
Burton, 138, 139, 144, 426, 450, 539, 562
Burtyman, 447
Burwell, 358, 440, 521, 540, 548
Bury, 557
Busby, 417
Buschman, 395
Bush, 10, 48, 164, 341, 464, 493, 558, 563
Bushy, 476
Buskirk, 138
Buss, 26
Bustard, 455
Buston, 449
Butcher, 510
Buthmann, 177, 504
Butler, 14, 17, 28, 48, 54, 92, 98, 129, 133, 134, 144, 148, 163, 178, 179, 183, 193, 194, 199, 205, 206, 230, 248, 261, 265, 266, 267, 278, 299, 335, 339, 352, 357, 359, 366, 380, 387, 392, 398, 402, 414, 417, 456, 471, 487, 509, 510, 515, 533, 536, 552, 557, 560
Butt, 61, 149, 489
Butt's pottery, 467
Butterfield, 95, 221, 452
Butterling, 446
Butterworth, 371
Buttner, 349
Bydol, 398
Byer, 184
Byington, 153, 176, 298
Byrd, 316, 351
Byrne, 54, 231, 268, 316, 438, 451, 462, 481
Byrnes, 329, 376, 450
Byrs, 403
Byruirn, 223

C

Cachard, 457
Caden, 54
Cadwalader, 111, 142, 387, 441, 487
Cadwallader, 85
Cady, 202, 267, 280, 439, 440, 490, 510
Caffemeyer, 467
Caffery, 442
Caggott, 472
Cahill, 139, 398, 455
Cahoone, 538, 552
Cahoun, 366
Cahuzac, 457
Cain, 138, 177, 399, 443, 444, 445
Calahan, 454
Calclazer, 99
Caldbeeth, 456
Caldwel, 63
Caldwell, 28, 67, 91, 193, 204, 205, 206, 218, 247, 273, 330, 339, 413, 439, 440, 441, 499, 502, 529, 533, 534, 545
Calfaun, 96
Calhoun, 8, 47, 324, 442, 511, 538
Calkins, 29, 33, 45, 84
Call, 449
Callaghan, 73, 222, 418, 538
Callahan, 141
Callan, 10, 37, 54, 58, 59, 91, 128, 146, 149, 165, 176, 258, 301, 311, 381, 439, 474, 515, 553, 558
Callanan, 434
Callejo, 209
Callender, 94, 106, 388, 398, 514
Calve, 442
Calvert, 54, 257, 268, 436, 456
Calvin, 397, 560
Calwell, 204, 208, 361, 423, 428, 431, 501, 543, 547
Camacho, 209
Camack, 399
Camak, 284, 456
Cambell, 418
Cambreleng, 376
Camelien, 493

Cameron, 270, 271, 274, 357, 403, 442, 489
Camm, 398
Cammack, 93, 97, 122, 254
Camp, 114, 303, 411, 543, 554
Campbel, 442
Campbell, 6, 22, 48, 61, 77, 82, 93, 127, 137, 153, 170, 197, 199, 207, 221, 222, 229, 235, 252, 261, 290, 301, 336, 337, 338, 381, 399, 400, 404, 416, 429, 431, 433, 437, 452, 455, 457, 471, 501, 509, 510, 516, 527, 542, 543, 557, 560, 565
Campben, 91
Camper, 215
Campson, 398
Canada, 510
Canales, 283
Canalizo, 442
Canaught, 135
Canby, 111, 334, 354, 528
Canfield, 28, 116, 122, 397
Cannon, 236, 451
Cano, 442, 496
Canovas, 316
Canter, 365, 389
Cantey, 398, 441
Cantwell, 199, 399
Capella, 8, 45
Capello, 59, 78
Capen, 550
Caperton, 63, 347
Capital of Michigan, 164
Capo, 8, 45, 78
Capon, 395
Capron, 107, 387, 395, 412, 424, 436, 487, 538, 547
Capuchin priest, 232
Carathers, 137
Carbery, 49, 121, 146, 176, 191, 274, 288, 347, 392, 525
Card, 223
Carduck, 426
Cardwell, 290
Cardy, 30, 397
Cariss, 99
Carl, 362
Carleton, 222, 246
Carlin, 130, 139, 202, 454
Carlisle, 16, 32, 162, 182, 228, 446, 539, 564
Carll, 357
Carlshorn, 349
Carlton, 137
Carmichael, 103, 323, 415, 423
Carmick, 534
Carner, 393
Carnes, 5
Carney, 397
Caro, 58
Carothers, 91
Carpar, 510
Carpenter, 131, 221, 291, 387, 481, 540, 556
Carr, 35, 62, 67, 112, 113, 163, 179, 197, 203, 204, 207, 222, 252, 395, 399, 442, 452, 501, 507, 543, 546, 548
Carrere, 97
Carrico, 240
Carrington, 317
Carrol, 444
Carroll, 42, 68, 184, 350, 358, 360, 373, 374, 381, 394, 403, 447, 450, 523
Carson, 134, 224, 269, 278, 335, 353, 406, 449
Carter, 95, 135, 191, 221, 274, 295, 327, 354, 416, 418, 443, 474, 556, 562
Carteret, 503
Carthage, 181
Cartwright, 267, 445, 555
Carty, 140
Carusi, 164
Carusi's Saloon, 164
Caruther, 403
Caruthers, 54, 372
Carvell, 223
Carver, 359
Cary, 18, 340, 438, 527
Casanave, 225, 267
Caseman, 278

Casey, 221, 225, 262, 327, 393, 443, 461, 478, 528
Cash, 161, 566
Caskey, 395
Casparis, 91, 266, 517, 518, 560
Casper, 66
Cass, 16, 46, 50, 187, 193, 205, 219
Cassady, 373, 461
Cassanave, 54
Cassedy, 456
Cassell, 179, 259, 298, 331, 486
Cassidy, 320, 362, 545
Cassin, 447, 490, 506
Caster, 91
Castigan, 444
Castleberrys, 233
Castleman, 191
Castley, 431
Castor, 246
Castro, 11, 51
Catalano, 91
Catharine Furnace, 523
Cathbert, 408
Cathcart, 15, 363, 414
Catholic Church, 278
Catlett, 140, 544
Catlin, 363
Caton, 10, 20, 41, 286, 556
Caughman, 398, 399, 456
Caulfield, 315, 316
Causey, 33, 70, 84
Causin, 20, 87, 162, 240, 274, 351, 393, 506
Caustin, 16
Cavanaugh, 461
Cavaugh, 450
Cayce, 137
Cayen, 127
Cazenave, 519
Cazenove, 150, 185
Cedar Hill, 213
Cedar Ridge, 438
Cedarwood, 562
Celly, 277
Center, 36
Cetter, 404
Chace, 16
Chadbourne, 195, 546
Chaderton, 319
Chadwick, 418, 453, 457
Chalfin, 335, 434
Chalmers, 36, 50, 271, 277
Chaloner, 204, 336, 338
Chamber, 223
Chamberlain, 38, 253, 262, 452, 548
Chambers, 80, 224
Champe, 23, 84, 159
Champion, 52, 78, 84
Champlin, 29, 64
Chanay, 455
Chance, 398
Chandler, 276, 321, 381, 387, 388, 395, 399, 408, 420, 421, 436, 477, 487
Chandos, 469
Chandrow, 457
Chapin, 312, 558
Chapman, 6, 37, 46, 50, 66, 75, 83, 85, 117, 137, 153, 158, 170, 173, 177, 214, 231, 238, 246, 317, 373, 388, 394, 403, 425, 446, 456, 566, 567
Chapmen, 370
Chapparcan, 450
Chappel, 222
Chappell, 99, 394
Chapple, 448
Charity, 493
Charles, 509
Charterton, 397
Chas X, 235
Chase, 5, 73, 202, 206, 248, 290, 376, 510, 552
Chatfield, 33, 42, 84
Chatham, 493
Chaudonia, 33, 39, 85
Chaudowens, 138
Chaulier, 215
Chauncey, 16, 132, 155, 296, 362, 407, 520
Chavez, 116
Chavis, 171

Chaytor, 197, 207
Cheatham, 14, 482, 544
Chedal, 20
Cheek, 136
Cheeson, 224
Cheever, 15, 49, 63, 66, 78, 567
Cheney, 201
Chenoweth, 83, 86
Chenowith, 68
Chenung, 33
Cherry, 249, 250, 446
Cherry Hill, 502
Chesebro, 96
Cheshire, 163
Chesnut, 211
Chester, 201, 291, 381, 403, 507
Chesterman, 72
Chever, 45
Chew, 163, 225, 239, 557
Chian, 457
Chick, 186
Chicks, 311
Chiders, 320
Childer, 452
Childs, 106, 107, 109, 113, 211, 251, 253, 261, 312, 393, 494, 505, 527
Chiles, 50, 277
Chilles, 413
Chilton, 89, 99, 106, 170, 246, 249, 334, 474
Chingers, 508
Chipman, 32, 350
Chiseltine, 429
Chisolm, 509
Chiveto_, 450
Choate, 187, 219, 481
Choiseul, 235
Chopley, 133
Choppin, 91, 555, 560
Choteau, 537
Christ, 278
Christal, 222
Christian, 7, 51, 59, 64, 69, 78, 303, 312, 319, 397, 468, 565
Christianson, 359
Christie, 450
Christman, 445, 451
Christson, 507
Christy, 394
Chubb, 429
Church, 86, 240, 394, 397, 509
Churchill, 111, 170, 204, 206, 252, 263, 425, 439, 471, 477, 484, 539, 547, 568
Churchills, 213
Cift, 417
Cilley, 5, 49, 398
Cillion, 91
Cinchlaw, 397
Cissell, 225
Civer, 552
Clagett, 93, 229, 274, 473, 556
Claiborne, 106, 277, 311
Claibsottle, 135
Clancey, 444
Clap, 18
Clapham, 288
Clapp, 399, 404, 457
Clarage, 136
Clare, 417
Claremont, 17
Claridy, 134
Clarit, 445
Clark, 5, 21, 36, 40, 50, 59, 66, 76, 78, 79, 80, 85, 96, 121, 133, 134, 135, 136, 137, 158, 191, 198, 204, 208, 253, 259, 280, 281, 330, 337, 342, 372, 374, 387, 389, 394, 398, 399, 409, 423, 426, 428, 431, 432, 433, 441, 442, 444, 445, 448, 481, 483, 488, 497, 500, 507, 508, 530, 540, 547, 549
Clarke, 10, 14, 20, 24, 54, 81, 82, 91, 93, 95, 104, 105, 121, 125, 129, 144, 161, 162, 163, 199, 208, 218, 262, 272, 277, 284, 311, 313, 353, 369, 372, 378, 381, 389, 394, 397, 407, 408, 416, 417, 425, 429, 440, 452, 485, 490, 503, 524, 525, 539, 556, 557, 558, 566
Clarvoe, 471, 517, 560

Claude, 148, 166
Clavadetacher, 439
Clavendetcher, 556
Claxton, 20, 40, 456
Clay, 74, 85, 127, 138, 142, 143, 144, 151, 190, 207, 244, 266, 268, 269, 283, 292, 313, 316, 373, 439, 483, 484, 513, 532
Claybrook, 277, 303, 312
Clayton, 33, 45, 50, 84, 224, 261, 342
Cleanley, 523
Cleary, 67, 70
Clegg, 451
Clemants, 8
Clemens, 135, 205, 334
Clement, 214
Clements, 54, 98, 199, 240, 253, 277, 334, 341, 381, 396, 405, 407, 408, 413, 416, 455, 462, 519, 534, 555
Clemson, 503
Clendenin, 544
Clendinin, 339
Clermont Farm, 370
Cleveland, 394, 436
Clifford, 46, 270
Clifton, 486
Clinch, 199, 334, 459
Cline, 221
Clinton, 75, 196, 321, 417
Clitch, 370, 557
Clitz, 54
Clopper, 416
Clopper's Mill, 416
Clopton, 399
Cloud, 224
Cloudsley, 509
Clouth, 130
Clowes, 283
Cluserlan, 140
Clutter, 200
Coad, 73, 392
Coale, 53, 251, 283
Coates, 457
Cobarubiar, 209
Cobb, 5, 48, 50, 393, 562
Cobbs, 45, 113, 253, 261, 567
Coburn, 442, 558
Cochran, 20, 91, 204, 284, 429, 434, 485, 557
Cochrane, 415, 509, 510, 528
Cockburn, 420
Cocke, 554
Cockerille, 156
Cockey, 251
Cockrell, 266, 267, 285, 530
Cockrill, 309
Codender, 484
Codrick, 418
Codwise, 354
Cody, 467
Coe, 16
Coeur, 298
Cofer, 215
Coffee, 111, 127, 136, 143, 170, 229, 447
Coffin, 379
Cogdell, 82, 94
Coglin, 445
Cogswell, 47, 64, 69
Cohen, 91
Cohlin, 456
Coile, 508
Coiron, 316
Coit, 554
Coker, 177, 181
Colbert, 137, 418
Colborn, 181
Colburn, 267
Colby, 430
Cole, 138, 430, 436, 506, 508, 509
Coleman, 10, 36, 42, 49, 80, 146, 156, 256, 285, 335, 371, 390, 407, 414, 430, 439, 444, 486, 518, 561, 567
Colemen, 44, 411
Coley, 429
Colgan, 479
Coll, 446
Collan, 447
Collard, 372
Collet, 235, 426

Collett, 157, 196, 207
Collier, 135, 414, 445
Collings, 163
Collingsworth, 134
Collins, 32, 47, 62, 75, 89, 146, 220, 225, 290, 333, 365, 381, 388, 396, 415, 426, 429, 444, 448, 452, 494, 501, 539
Collis, 450
Collison, 493, 554
Colly, 492
Colquhoun, 188
Colt, 73, 303
Colter, 418
Coltman, 54, 298, 330, 498, 499, 506
Colton, 11, 40, 173, 177, 489, 522
Columbia Furnace, 534
Columbus, 556
Colville, 7, 539
Colvocoressis, 16
Colward, 93
Combs, 7, 9, 54, 75, 142, 519, 552, 556, 558
Comedore, 418
Comegys, 150, 356
Comly, 557
Comorsyne, 484
Compton, 241
Con, 141
Conahan, 460
Conart, 224
Conaway, 138
Condict, 381
Cone, 265
Conger, 129, 196, 235
Congress Burying Ground, 498
Congressional Burial Ground, 183
Congressional Burying Ground, 102, 533
Conian, 54
Conlan, 225, 560
Conles, 443
Conley, 33, 39, 84, 158, 381
Conn, 413, 470, 508
Conn's Island, 345
Connars, 453
Connell, 394, 456, 457
Conner, 3, 127, 136, 137, 169, 267, 384, 394, 429, 430, 444, 446, 460, 510, 516
Connick's Farm, 523
Connington, 311
Connolly, 65, 67, 70, 333, 365, 486
Connor, 40, 300, 394, 395, 398, 429, 442, 455, 508, 527, 558
Connors, 394
Conover, 138
Conrad, 510
Conrey, 448
Conroy, 138, 396, 399
Constable, 457
Contee, 124
Contreras, 487
Converse, 66, 166, 303
Conway, 36, 40, 48, 64, 69, 78, 84, 158, 199, 221, 222, 393, 444, 448, 454, 560
Coody, 28, 75
Coogan, 394, 444
Cook, 91, 136, 163, 184, 194, 223, 267, 271, 336, 399, 400, 409, 413, 417, 429, 430, 435, 444, 447, 450, 451, 456, 501, 502, 507, 567
Cooke, 7, 68, 105, 106, 246, 366, 472, 566
Cookendorfe, 91
Cookendorfer, 516
Coolidge, 97, 403, 501
Coolridge, 277
Coombe, 91, 381, 438
Coombes, 138
Coombs, 66
Coon, 535
Cooney, 171
Cooper, 29, 37, 51, 70, 75, 91, 97, 100, 105, 115, 121, 122, 134, 136, 145, 163, 203, 220, 225, 231, 251, 257, 261, 311, 330, 333, 364, 376, 381, 388, 391, 398, 399, 405, 450, 454, 455, 484, 508, 509, 543
Coote, 359, 551
Copehart, 455
Copeland, 339, 508, 545

Copp, 493
Coppee, 538, 539
Copper, 43
Copps, 224
Copsey, 451
Corbett, 510
Corbin, 411, 434, 532
Corbin Hall, 411
Corbus, 398
Corcoran, 94, 154, 160, 163, 298, 381, 465, 485, 496, 511
Cord, 277
Corder, 509
Corey, 532
Corkle, 507
Corkles, 408
Corly, 399
Cornal, 397
Cornelius, 304
Cornell, 359
Corning, 486
Cornish, 54
Cornwall, 370, 440, 565
Cornwallis, 457
Cornwallis' Neck, 343
Corre, 505
Corse, 242, 289, 421
Corsen, 359
Corser, 78, 533
Corson, 514, 555, 560
Cortez, 171
Corwin, 49, 80, 126, 443
Corwine, 134
Cory, 222
Cosgrove, 447, 455
Cosier, 476
Cosken, 429
Coskrey, 302
Costello, 399
Coster, 289
Costigan, 10
Costin, 54
Costolo, 394
Costolow, 514
Cotter, 230, 516
Cotton, 175
Cottrell, 443
Couch, 108, 134, 169, 539
Couey, 407
Coughenower, 138
Couley, 535
Coulter, 272
Coumbe, 54, 163, 553
Couples, 236
Couray, 426
Court's Point, 534
Court-house in Dooly Co, 234
Courtney, 134, 155, 340
Courvosier, 476
Couts, 246
Couze, 136
Covell, 427
Cover, 263
Covill, 210
Coville, 532
Cowarden, 222
Cowden, 400
Cowin, 431
Cowles, 15, 19
Cowley, 233, 488
Cown, 134
Cowper, 60
Cowperthwaite, 477
Cox, 8, 12, 13, 14, 23, 29, 45, 50, 52, 75, 81, 91, 166, 172, 191, 212, 236, 241, 245, 256, 281, 306, 315, 316, 353, 381, 409, 413, 421, 425, 449, 454, 459, 476, 477, 479, 508, 514, 532, 533, 536, 550, 553, 561
Coxe, 23, 31, 34, 78, 381
Coyeault, 316
Coyle, 40, 54, 81, 129, 179, 241, 361, 381, 434, 445, 449, 464, 479, 508, 517, 518, 525, 557
Crabb, 148, 228, 347, 370, 455
Crabbe, 324
Craft, 292, 426
Crafts, 482

Craig, 3, 25, 110, 140, 170, 211, 290, 303, 312, 367, 381, 388, 394, 395, 425, 456, 471
Craighead, 17
Crain, 27
Cram, 195, 388, 546
Cramer, 128
Crammer, 553
Crampsey, 74, 429
Cranch, 11, 21, 272, 285, 437, 551
Crandall, 533
Crandell, 230, 231, 432, 433, 464, 555
Crandle, 431
Crane, 94, 114, 325, 376, 421, 425, 471, 530, 560
Crangle, 221, 222, 397
Cranston, 46
Cranum, 397
Cranz, 445
Crask, 395
Craven, 398
Crawe, 266
Crawford, 20, 33, 139, 174, 184, 311, 357, 396, 397, 425, 442, 453, 474, 491, 508, 527
Cray, 72
Creamer, 431
Creanor, 199, 334, 335
Crearor, 428
Cregan, 399
Crehore, 463
Cresey, 36
Cresson, 554
Creutzfeldt, 54, 169
Crichton, 153
Crider, 431
Crippers, 136
Cripps, 24, 54, 381
Crips, 184
Crischer, 493
Crispo, 319
Crittenden, 127, 170, 374, 379
Crobsy, 552
Crocker, 238
Crocket, 54
Crockett, 54, 387
Crofort, 450
Crogan, 442
Croggan, 557
Croley, 222
Cromley, 448
Cromwell, 10, 545
Crook, 369, 444, 508
Cropp, 446
Crosby, 7, 21, 51, 59, 61, 64, 69, 78, 195, 335, 536, 541, 565
Crosman, 105
Cross, 14, 15, 71, 93, 104, 121, 128, 149, 189, 221, 225, 381, 407, 430, 450, 452, 488
Cross:, 204
Crossan, 331
Crouch, 468
Crouse, 357
Crowden, 426
Crowin, 494
Crowley, 260, 429, 452
Crown, 509, 535
Crudley, 523
Cruit, 73, 93, 121, 353, 430, 475
Cruitt, 54
Crum, 541
Crummy, 399
Crump, 200, 236, 340, 475
Crursmann, 136
Cruse, 215, 224
Crutcher, 397
Crutchett, 20, 26, 75, 286, 289, 495
Crutchfield, 82, 111
Cruz, 144
Cryer, 225, 483
Cudlip, 516, 517
Cudlipp, 4, 520
Cudney, 224
Cull, 256, 259, 298, 557
Cullen, 96
Cullison, 458
Culver, 14, 165, 381, 530
Culverwell, 340, 381
Cumberbeach, 395

Cummin, 427
Cumming, 85, 110, 114, 157, 160, 223, 247
Cummings, 155, 184, 197, 208, 210, 370, 423, 428, 431, 437, 446, 509, 531
Cummins, 50, 157, 196, 235, 295, 361, 455
Cunard, 566
Cundell, 323
Cunningham, 20, 32, 54, 90, 162, 181, 234, 394, 398, 485, 506, 556, 568
Cunnningham, 103
Curd, 203, 235
Curd, 108, 539, 542, 546
Curell, 502
Curran, 285, 455
Currie, 379
Curry, 160, 396, 446, 494
Curting, 395
Curtis, 117, 120, 144, 330, 362, 394, 398, 400, 404, 418, 446, 551
Cushing, 26, 157, 244, 249, 263
Cushman, 530
Custis, 182, 459
Cuthbert, 54, 180
Cutter, 500
cutter **Ewing**, 132
cutter **Foxward**, 132
cutter **Robert J Walker**, 511
Cuttle, 461
Cutts, 46, 48, 298
Cuvill, 215
Cuyler, 106, 309, 543

D

d'Abaac, 512
d'Lagnel, 112
Dade, 89, 184, 418, 439
Daguerre, 275
Dailey, 220
Daily, 139, 396
Daingerfield, 283, 403
Dale, 16, 44, 63, 185, 452, 504, 561
Dalecarlia, 409
Daley, 393
Dallas, 46, 48, 49, 187, 219, 360, 398
Dally, 441
Dalton, 382, 460, 557
Dalwig, 461
Daly, 31, 49, 269, 394, 452, 456, 461, 502, 558
Dalym, 453
Dameron, 354
Damoiseau, 51
Dan, 467
Dana, 109, 184, 220, 236, 350, 414
Dancey, 184
Dancy, 45, 114, 257
Dandeger, 52
Dandron, 224
Dandy, 135
Danforth, 140, 475
Dang, 471
Dangerfield, 24
Daniel, 66, 457, 492, 532, 556
Daniell, 502
Daniels, 252, 265, 400, 440, 448, 483, 490, 510, 539
Danley, 148, 441, 483
Danner, 215
Dannigan, 449
Dans, 457
Danytesten, 431
Darby, 292, 323
Darden, 68, 304
Dardonville, 399
Darene, 476
Dargan, 50
Darley, 290
Darling, 478
Darlington, 494
Darnold, 348
Darragh, 510
Darsee, 426
Dart, 134
Dascomb, 551
Dashiel, 35, 96, 113, 253, 262
Datcher, 225, 381
Dauby, 42
Davenport, 70, 139, 223, 227, 350, 527

David, 10, 93, 163, 287
Davidge, 233, 241, 260, 324, 326
Davidson, 139, 151, 174, 176, 177, 181, 184, 197, 222, 240, 281, 351, 352, 381, 393, 416, 439, 490, 528
Davie, 406
Davis, 9, 10, 15, 20, 24, 26, 30, 36, 37, 41, 44, 53, 54, 63, 67, 69, 76, 93, 97, 104, 108, 113, 116, 121, 126, 127, 134, 136, 138, 139, 143, 144, 145, 164, 169, 170, 180, 186, 192, 200, 201, 211, 218, 220, 224, 225, 227, 231, 232, 233, 238, 243, 246, 249, 250, 251, 253, 257, 262, 274, 277, 282, 285, 320, 333, 334, 336, 337, 338, 339, 340, 345, 348, 360, 370, 376, 381, 389, 390, 396, 397, 398, 399, 404, 410, 424, 428, 429, 432, 433, 441, 448, 449, 450, 451, 455, 456, 471, 472, 475, 494, 507, 509, 510, 513, 514, 521, 528, 530, 533, 544, 556, 557, 560, 563
Davison, 504
Davy, 291, 429
Daw, 382
Dawd, 173, 302
Dawes, 55
Dawses, 359
Dawson, 29, 43, 47, 99, 288, 316, 403
Day, 225, 267, 507
Daye, 308
De Baney, 510
De Barnes, 398
De Baun, 293, 297
De Blanc, 315
De Blaynise, 457
De Charms, 478
De Framee, 493
De Jongh, 376
de Kalb, 42, 512
De Krafft, 265
de la Houssaye, 64, 69
De la Roche, 84
de Lagnel, 462
De Lonza, 446
De Russey, 321, 478
De Russy, 4, 73, 112, 144, 262, 321, 342, 425, 434, 540
De Saules, 515
De Selden, 290
De Selding, 88, 163, 290
De Vaughan, 146
De Vaughn, 341
De Witt, 196, 237, 286
De Wolf, 195, 484
De Young, 399
Dead Letter, 300
Deakin, 115
Deakins, 115
Deal, 494
Deale, 501
Deall, 527
Dean, 103, 368, 545, 548
Deane, 17
Deanny, 436
Dearborn, 106
Dearing, 453
Dearmar, 224
Deas, 5, 43, 74, 108, 327
Deavughn, 448
Debaun, 395
Debecque, 451
DeCamp, 324
Decatur, 432, 498
Decker, 402, 455, 456
Dedrick, 67, 444
Dee, 5
Deeble, 91, 472
Deering, 52, 89
Deeron, 177
Deflin, 394
Degges, 124, 146, 304, 307
DeGraff, 29
DeHart, 445
DeHaven, 16
Deheid, 223
Deibler, 491
Deisol, 400
DeKalb, 512
Delacarlia, 13

Delacour, 298
Delacroix, 424
Delafield, 425, 471, 482
Delamaster, 510
Delaney, 357, 395, 461
Delangle, 493
Delano, 360, 486, 531
Delany, 91, 93, 130, 225, 376, 392, 418, 455, 516, 555, 558
Delaporte, 457
Delarue, 437
Delavan, 227, 364
Dell, 552
Dellue, 482
Delong, 445
Demarest, 27, 256
Demedoff, 468
Dement, 91, 148, 178, 259, 295, 299, 319, 494, 506
Deming, 381
Dempsey, 136
Dempst, 140
Dempster, 231, 567
Demptster, 121
Deneal, 322
Dengel, 428, 430
Dengh, 451
Denham, 282, 384
Denison, 79, 160, 271
Denman, 334, 335
Dennett, 510
Dennis, 45, 399, 454, 468, 507, 509
Dennison, 8, 85
Denny, 345, 356
Denpin, 396
Denson, 234, 399, 448
Dent, 55, 89, 115, 225, 239, 255, 425, 429, 432, 440, 490, 507, 540
Dentlinger, 449
Denver, 207, 484
Deny, 222
Deppel, 104
Deray, 394
Derby, 211
Dering, 64, 84
Deringer, 74, 299, 556
Derit, 444
Derlin, 444
Dermitt, 397
Dermott, 93, 488
Deroane, 51
Derring, 78
DeRussy, 471
Derwin, 406
DeSaules, 54
DeSaussure, 389
Desbordes, 457
Desha, 190
Deshon, 106
Deslonde, 316
Desmasier, 505
Desmond, 450
DeSoto, 340
Dessussure, 399
Dettro, 10
Devan, 40
Devanny, 493
Devaughan, 472
Deveny, 556
Devers, 225
Devine, 443
Devlin, 47, 64, 95, 399, 441, 454
Devoe, 399
Devore, 185
Dew, 83
Dewdney, 55, 521, 555
Dewees, 382
Dewell, 510
Dewers, 555
Dewey, 50, 59, 415
DeWitt, 372
Dexter, 325, 410, 446
Dezelum, 416
Dhomas, 558
Dial, 198, 335, 338
Dibble, 161, 181, 227, 532, 566
Dick, 42, 225
Dickerson, 11, 90, 92, 93, 336, 430, 539
Dickey, 17, 426, 537
Dickie, 449

Dickinson, 25, 50, 79, 151, 181, 196, 207, 255, 305, 388, 392, 398, 487
Dickman, 444
Dickson, 142, 440, 523
Didlake, 78
Dieffendorf, 543
Dieffendorff, 203
Diel, 494
Dietrich, 455
Digges, 54, 67, 103, 533, 564
Diggs, 58, 85, 184, 557
Dignum, 181
Dilks, 449
Dill, 495
Dillard, 190
Diller, 253
Dillon, 122, 137, 450, 451
Dillow, 520, 558
Dills, 177
Dilly, 535
Dimond, 114, 168, 223, 253
Dingie, 79
Dinsmoor, 288
Dinsmore, 508
Dirgen, 396
Disher, 382
Disney, 278
Divin, 222
Divine, 449
Divorces, 256
Divver, 194
Dix, 39, 170, 419, 499
Dixon, 10, 46, 68, 72, 93, 123, 163, 184, 220, 270, 271, 274, 285, 397, 426, 457, 493
Dixson, 445
Doace, 447
Dobbin, 45, 50, 275
Dobbins, 108, 162, 249, 250, 507
Dobson, 510
Dock, 9, 35, 114
Dockery, 50, 224
Dodd, 225, 309, 397
Dodds, 508, 555, 558
Dodge, 6, 63, 78, 172, 291, 312, 509
Dodson, 310
Doemer, 54
Doherty, 399, 426
Doig, 104
Doitz, 454
Dolan, 304, 323
Dolay, 221
Doleman, 397
Dolen, 221
Dominguez, 494
Dominus, 408
Don Pedro II, 365
Dona, 222
Donagan, 450
Donahue, 442
Donaldson, 7, 110, 111, 169, 234, 269, 538, 546
Donalson, 501
Done, 457
Donegan, 315, 316
Donelan, 31, 41, 45, 169, 178, 188, 244, 263, 289, 340, 341, 343, 382, 387, 428, 430, 435, 458, 464, 471, 485
Donelly, 222, 453
Doniphan, 105, 192, 277, 292, 377
Doniphin, 4
Donlan, 493
Donly, 448
Donn, 65, 99, 124, 176, 279, 311, 382, 433, 556, 563
Donnell, 46, 174, 298
Donnelly, 134, 184, 396, 452, 453, 509
Donner, 467
Donnoghy, 396
Donoghaugh, 395
Donoghue, 555
Donoho, 393, 433, 515, 516, 558
Donohoo, 553, 558, 564
Donova, 518
Donovan, 10, 54, 163, 451, 456
Doohoe, 137
Dooley, 399, 510
Doramentes, 496
Doran, 320
Doremus, 467

Dorly, 163
Dorman, 95, 428, 430, 449
Dorn, 192, 434, 543
Dorney, 439
Dornin, 47, 129, 174
Dorr, 19, 525
Dorral, 418
Dorrance, 552
Dorrell, 70
Dorris, 250, 545
Dorsett, 26, 156
Dorsey, 54, 97, 163, 227, 418, 480, 516, 560
Dorsot, 453
Dosenbach, 409
Douallier, 566
Doub, 399
Doubleday, 107
Dougalss, 394
Dougherty, 102, 303, 443, 452, 489
Doughty, 95, 133, 189, 274, 514, 525
Douglas, 26, 59, 153, 324, 437, 474
Douglass, 26, 45, 46, 48, 78, 83, 91, 96, 162, 225, 398, 429, 500
Doumal, 561
Dove, 23, 54, 220, 294, 382, 553
Dow, 258, 274, 317, 377, 426, 483
Dowd, 393
Dowden, 146
Dowdey, 507
Dowell, 92, 208, 211, 267
Dowis, 450
Dowley, 450
Dowling, 54, 150, 360
Down, 446
Downer, 91, 378, 476, 515
Downes, 35
Downey, 221, 340
Downing, 5, 29, 94, 145, 225, 352, 371
Downs, 91, 222, 266
Downy, 455
Dowson, 180, 231, 381, 464, 467, 551
Dox, 329, 331
Doxier, 137
Doyle, 30, 91, 202, 273, 416, 510, 553
Draine, 267
Drake, 161, 231, 414, 418, 566
Draper, 43, 137, 242, 394
Drapman, 457
Drawn, 443
Drayton, 161, 162, 566
Dresser, 446
Drew, 26, 278, 399
Drinker, 304
Dripps, 455
Driscoll, 426
Droego, 482
Dromgoole, 117, 231, 263, 536
Dromogoole, 183
Drum, 195, 539, 547
Drummond, 382, 457, 507
Drury, 10, 27, 102, 211, 231, 433, 444, 556
Du Pont, 302
Dubois, 405, 507
Duboise, 79
Dubs, 96
Dubuque, 537
Ducachet, 437
Duchess of Aumale, 423
Ducker, 500
Duckett, 38, 91, 212, 418, 436
Duckworth, 10, 556
Duddleson, 510
Dudley, 425, 438
Duedney, 382
Duer, 15
Duerson, 113, 339
Duff, 135, 172, 194, 207, 321, 510, 538, 547
Duffey, 208, 303, 343, 366, 405, 528
Duffin, 399
Duffy, 456
Dufief, 477
Dufour, 393
Dufresne, 47, 64, 82, 84, 316
Dugan, 310
Dugans, 184
Duhan, 461
Duke, 277, 456

Duke de Praslin, 413
Duke of Argyle, 233
Duke of Modena, 51
Duke of Wellington, 233, 297
Dulany, 35, 54, 90, 91, 92, 121, 128, 142, 231, 402, 557
Duley, 122
Dulin, 382
Duling, 27
Duly, 175
Dummer, 157, 191, 196, 235
Dummett, 200
Dumont, 284
Dumphy, 10, 104
Dunbar, 153
Dunblane, 51
Duncan, 66, 72, 75, 147, 153, 184, 208, 303, 355, 360, 419, 426, 456, 494, 497, 554
Duncanson, 63, 91, 411, 553
Duncomb, 408
Dundas, 2, 354, 415
Dunham, 359
Dunighan, 221
Dunivan, 443
Dunlap, 25, 139, 234, 252, 337, 338, 347, 506, 551
Dunlop, 142, 226, 382, 428, 495
Dunn, 161, 222, 253, 262, 372, 395, 398, 545, 548, 566
Dunnington, 93, 188
Dunnogant, 455
Dunsliffe, 527
Dunward, 394
Dunwell, 55
Duperu, 194, 207
Dupont, 173, 489
Dupouchel, 51
Dupre, 14
Durand, 442, 493
Dure, 507
Durfee, 320
Durham, 223, 395
Durievant, 134
Durkee, 18
Durkin, 457
Durock, 136
Durr, 267, 361, 553
Durrine, 29
Durrive, 537
Dusenbery, 105, 170
Dutton, 131, 308
Duval, 17, 434
Duvall, 52, 54, 91, 121, 163, 353, 376, 464, 495, 556, 558
Duver, 400
Dwyer, 136, 222, 267, 451, 454
Dyas, 399, 442
Dyckman, 388, 400
Dye, 200, 237, 394
Dyer, 7, 26, 54, 83, 95, 105, 106, 138, 145, 165, 193, 229, 232, 256, 290, 340, 341, 352, 359, 360, 375, 377, 380, 463, 465, 474, 490, 558
Dyerle, 111
Dykeman, 484, 513
Dyneley, 426
Dynely, 426
Dyson, 54, 382

E

Eaches, 148
Eagan, 394
Eager, 306
Eammons, 184
Eannes, 446
Earis, 397
Earl, 227, 493
Earl of Granville, 51
Earl of Ranfurley, 245
Earle, 55, 557
Early, 136, 398
Earp, 404, 500
Ears, 396
Easby, 2, 3, 226, 240, 258, 292, 298
Easinger, 508
Easley, 487, 501, 521, 528, 540, 548
Easly, 108, 387, 396
Eason, 509
Easter, 256, 439

Easterbrook, 376
Easterby, 456
Eastin, 201, 348
Eastland, 252
Eastlin, 542
Eastman, 202, 247, 249
Easton, 111, 184, 313
Eaton, 3, 55, 88, 94, 110, 170, 345, 370, 395, 429, 477, 527
Eaves, 399
Ebeham, 454
Eber, 456
Eberbach, 91, 479, 515, 516, 560
Eberlee, 507
Ebert, 237
Eccles, 221
Eccleston, 420
Echols, 98, 130, 178, 199, 205, 230
Eckel, 382, 505
Eckels, 339, 545
Eckhardt, 91
Eckhart, 449
Eckington Farm, 176
Eckloff, 55, 514, 515
Eckman, 520
Ecro, 273
Ector, 199, 206
Eddy, 266, 320, 387, 538, 539, 557
Edelen, 28, 34, 282, 316
Edelin, 55, 369, 527
Eden, 389
Edens, 234
Edes, 36, 406
Edgar, 241
Edgerby, 26
Edmond, 350
Edmonds, 274, 280, 447
Edmonson, 349, 440
Edmonston, 55, 126, 553
Edmunds, 36
Edouard, 36
Edouart, 30
Edson, 33, 64, 72, 84, 135, 157, 311, 447, 453
Edward I, 145
Edward VI, 145
Edwards, 14, 15, 27, 37, 40, 91, 134, 139, 179, 204, 206, 276, 280, 287, 312, 326, 351, 361, 448, 457, 468, 480, 497, 510, 513, 514, 522, 534, 537, 539, 565
Effinger, 507
Effonol, 359
Egan, 396, 556
Egbert, 314, 454
Ege, 13
Egerton, 429, 457
Eggleston, 67, 92, 134
Ehlen, 429
Ehninger, 108
Ehrenbaim, 444
Eichelberger, 20, 50, 317, 438
Eichhorn, 220
Eichler, 12
Eichorn, 55, 558
Eichstein, 445
Eickhorn, 162
Eikhorn, 128
Eisdar, 445
Eld, 5
Elder, 335, 434
Eldred, 31, 85, 158
Eldridge, 44, 327
Elias, 452
Elisha, 433
Elk Hill, 175
Elk Island, 175
Elk Ridge, 12
Elkin, 223
Elkinton, 97
Ella, 318
Ellersbee, 244
Ellerslie, 379
Ellett, 50
Ellicott's Mills, 95
Ellie, 91
Ellingwood, 140
Elliot, 25, 26, 61, 63, 91, 94, 212, 285, 382

Elliott, 111, 133, 221, 280, 417, 422, 448, 504, 538, 558
Elliott, J W, 560
Ellis, 29, 47, 85, 92, 160, 223, 231, 298, 309, 452, 473, 493, 519, 523, 552, 558
Ellison, 302
Ellit, 79
Ellmer, 452
Elloes, 442
Ellsworth, 37, 444
Ellwood, 59, 418
Elmer, 327, 502, 510
Elms, 507
Elmwood, 239
Elstner, 284
Elwater, 395
Elwood, 62, 80, 452, 456
Emathala, 67
Embree, 297
Emerick, 445
Emerson, 12, 48, 92, 135, 136, 225, 267, 393, 446, 562
Emert, 55
Emery, 77, 96, 556
Emmerich, 183
Emmerson, 55, 366
Emmert, 160, 323, 562
Emmons, 29, 64, 182, 309
Emory, 193, 205, 240, 293, 543, 546, 549
Empie, 233
Empress Josephine, 427
Endicott, 502
Engels, 63
Engelson, 127
England, 223, 292
Engle, 132, 468
Englehart, 395
Engleman, 136
Engles, 28
English, 5, 210, 266, 267, 277
Engls, 67
Enlow, 398
Ennis, 55, 92, 244
Enos, 252, 397
Entwistle, 215
Ephraim, 507
Eplet, 455
Epperson, 127, 137
Epping, 483
Erb, 255
Erbe, 133
Ericson, 66
Ericsson, 33
Ernst, 440, 450, 490, 541, 548
Erskin, 43, 112, 113, 253, 545, 549
Erskine, 20
Erving, 325
Erwin, 442
Eschbach, 382
Escueno, 215
Eskridge, 298
Eslava, 316
Espy, 37, 64, 69, 78
Esselman, 545, 548
Essex, 122, 341
Esson, 457
Esta, 177
Estas, 14
Estep, 10, 74
Estes, 398, 407, 567
Estis, 20, 510, 551
Etter, 161
Etting, 330
Ettinger, 445
Etzler, 53
Eubank, 447
Eugan, 221
Eunis, 266
Eurick, 493
Eutziger, 493
Evans, 33, 46, 55, 73, 91, 93, 135, 140, 149, 163, 184, 197, 203, 221, 237, 269, 271, 303, 334, 335, 364, 382, 396, 446, 448, 452, 454, 455, 457, 483, 501, 507, 511, 515, 527, 529, 538, 545
Evanson, 447
Everett, 424, 440, 456
Eversfield, 55, 240, 254

Eversteine, 445
Evitt, 483
Ewbank, 181
Ewell, 209, 211, 220, 244, 246, 250, 268, 325, 487, 521
Ewing, 51, 258, 303, 413, 562

F

Fadding, 393
Fagan, 184, 400
Fagans, 214
Fagg, 34, 495
Faggat, 127
Fagin, 447
Fahee, 442
Fahrm, 398
Fair, 184, 454
Fairchild, 117, 388, 399, 441
Fairchilds, 447
Fairfax, 132, 161, 179, 379, 486, 553
Fairfield, 563
Fairlamb, 5
Fairview, 124, 148
Faley, 394
Falkner, 98
Family Inheritance, 438
Famine in Ireland, 124
Fane, 168
Fanfernot, 505
Fanning, 223, 424, 553
Faoball, 453
Faran, 50
Farel, 508
Farelly, 388
Farish, 448
Farland, 29, 116
Farley, 396, 399, 507
Farmer, 136, 445, 450, 561
Farnham, 298, 433, 480
Farnham's, 468
Farqueson, 211
Farquhar, 55, 365
Farquharson, 153, 223
Farr, 40, 87, 295, 409
Farragut, 27, 132, 537
Farrally, 393
Farramier, 451
Farrand, 372
Farrar, 287, 301, 320, 560
Farrel, 184, 398
Farrell, 393, 449, 451
Farris, 137
Farry, 440, 442, 490, 539, 548
Fatio, 328
Faucett, 368, 398
Faughn, 397
Faulkner, 138
Faultleroy, 38
Fauntleroy, 345, 376, 568
Fauquier White Sulphur Springs, 227
Favier, 91, 295, 430
Faw, 382
Fawcett, 392, 406
Fax, 79
Fay, 135, 157, 181, 196, 205, 235, 387, 409
Faysoux, 136
Feagle, 456
Feake, 136
Fearson, 91, 429, 558
Feather, 452
Febiger, 566
Feeks, 63
Feeny, 10
Feichtner, 507
Felameir, 136
Felby, 445
Felch, 198
Fell, 493
Felton, 469
Felts, 134
Fendall, 363
Fenley, 476
Fenne, 525
Fennel, 30
Fenner, 253, 443, 549
Fenton, 36, 47, 124, 135, 512
Fenwick, 81, 208, 238, 301, 341, 392
Ferby, 396

Ferguson, 5, 29, 42, 52, 55, 127, 135, 163, 174, 221, 241, 426, 455, 457, 488, 505, 523
Fermally, 408
Fernandez, 209
Ferributt, 565
Ferris, 396, 410, 419
Ferry, 451
Ferteau, 521
Feslin, 163
Fickle, 451
Fidler, 251
Field, 45, 95, 113, 170, 263, 448
Fielding, 443
Fields, 94, 249, 250, 403, 522, 545, 548
Fifleman, 507
fighting for, 117
Filions, 47
Filkins, 560
Fill, 178
Fillany, 63, 66
Fillebrown, 486
Fillman, 508
Fillmore, 484
Fillot, 493
Filsome, 451
Finch, 444
Finckel, 12, 511
Findlay, 230, 472
Fink, 429, 441, 446, 521
Finkel, 164
Finkle, 458
Finkman, 55, 121, 514
Finley, 14, 167, 454, 568
Finnerghty, 446
Finney, 137, 399, 451, 510
Firbanks, 151
Fire, 456
Firestine, 509
First Baptist Church, 91
Fisby, 420
Fischer, 55, 129, 222, 230, 231, 285, 369, 382, 482, 524
Fiser, 55
Fish, 311, 363, 397, 530, 554
Fisher, 76, 91, 136, 382, 396, 399, 450, 511, 528, 557, 560
Fisk, 133, 399, 450
Fiske, 309
Fiskil, 455
Fister, 55
Fitch, 33, 45, 84, 180, 270
Fitnam, 55
Fitz, 476
Fitzgerald, 93, 198, 201, 266, 267, 289, 334, 394, 398, 399, 411, 431, 471, 504, 510, 517, 518, 519, 541, 542, 544, 549, 558
Fitzhue, 449
Fitzhugh, 40, 54, 89, 210, 251, 351, 361, 454, 529, 557
Fitzimmons, 456
Fitzmorris, 483
Fitznam, 553
Fitzpatrick, 91, 150, 274, 297, 357, 447, 460, 461
Fitzsimmons, 398
Flagg, 453, 483
Flaherty, 553
Flanagan, 258, 371, 424, 507
Flaven, 510
Flaxier, 455
Fleischmann, 125
Fleming, 55, 93, 163, 413, 425, 557
Flemming, 51, 181, 393, 444
Fleniken, 178
Flenner, 266
Flenniken, 19
Fles, 442
Fletcher, 51, 55, 71, 94, 127, 135, 136, 162, 220, 266, 286, 382, 394, 396, 404, 452, 454, 480, 490, 558
Flick, 211
Fliming, 449
Flinn, 146, 397, 561
Flint, 541
Flood, 9, 239, 446
Flores, 355
Flourens, 374
Flournoy, 117

Flowers, 449, 508
Flowery, 225
Floyd, 133, 223, 454, 493
Flummery, 450
Fly, 397
Flynn, 50, 222, 272, 393, 507
Focke, 500
Foering, 279
Fogel, 461
Fogg, 39, 455
Foills, 136
Foley, 221, 308, 400
Folk, 398
Follain, 457
Follansbeel, 55
Foller, 558
Follet, 482
Folsom, 265, 363
Folson, 470
Fontnha, 215
Foote, 10, 24, 176, 557
Forbes, 102, 210, 221, 340, 438, 456, 457, 486, 502, 508, 551
Force, 91, 93, 147, 178, 183, 298, 312, 525
Ford, 1, 10, 16, 55, 75, 120, 184, 190, 194, 207, 221, 225, 226, 254, 308, 382, 415, 429, 431, 442, 494, 508
Fordich, 510
Fords, 507
Fordycy, 527
Fore, 354
Forest, 63
Forgy, 443
Forman, 229
Fornely, 494
Forola, 453
Forrest, 2, 55, 67, 132, 181, 223, 286, 311, 341, 351, 370, 382, 402, 427, 435, 511, 517
Forsher, 267
Forstall, 68, 315, 316
Forster, 349, 542
Forsyth, 204, 309, 568
Fort, 152
Fort Adams, 178
Fort Brown, 109, 141, 227
Fort Conception, 152
Fort Gibson, 2, 492
Fort Hall, 549
Fort Hamilton, 98
Fort Harrison, 151
Fort Jackson, 278
Fort King, 459
Fort Layafette, 98
Fort Leavenworth, 366, 367, 458
Fort McHenry, 304, 307
Fort Mitchell, 175
Fort Monroe, 114, 325
Fort Moultrie, 325
Fort Paredes, 227
Fort Sacramento, 173, 467
Fort Santiago, 152
Fort Scott, 2
Fort Tompkins, 178
Fort Townsend, 293
Fort Wayne, 33, 47, 159
Forteney, 184
Fortress Monroe, 462
Fosdick, 339, 545, 549
Foss, 393
Fossati, 433
Foster, 5, 28, 46, 47, 51, 96, 138, 181, 198, 221, 276, 287, 431, 440, 446, 453, 467, 490, 510, 514
Foulder, 222
Fowle, 257
Fowler, 3, 10, 55, 71, 101, 121, 141, 173, 237, 253, 302, 382, 462, 473, 490, 493, 509, 510, 531, 553, 560, 561
Fox, 130, 134, 140, 181, 182, 215, 260, 268, 325, 327, 408, 432, 450, 451, 452, 510
Foxall, 80, 102
Foy, 47, 146, 515, 516
Frailer, 55, 558
Frailey, 309, 310
Fram, 541
Frame, 451

France, 90, 91, 227, 267, 316, 428, 430, 458, 515
Francewagh, 278
Francha, 393
Francher, 443
Francis, 55, 141, 212, 224, 398, 431, 466, 480
Francis IV, 51
Franenfelder, 493
Frank, 10, 55, 394, 430, 442, 452
Franklin, 1, 42, 47, 166, 170, 181, 258, 399, 448, 456, 473, 498, 508, 516, 553
Frantius, 461
Franzen, 423
Franzoni, 50, 382
Fraser, 173, 256, 263, 347, 391, 533
Fratenger, 398
Frazer, 153, 165, 394, 404, 426, 445, 451, 519
Frazier, 25, 139, 504
Freackind, 137
Fred, 138
Fredell, 322, 323
Frederick the V, 157
Fredrichs, 409
Freelon, 202, 542
Freeman, 105, 221, 247, 271, 341, 443, 451, 510, 526, 539
Freemantle, 500
Freeny, 449
Freeze, 449
Freire, 316
Fremont, 64, 111, 116, 214, 366, 367, 401, 410, 425, 471, 472, 473, 493
French, 41, 73, 107, 118, 126, 133, 155, 161, 169, 171, 186, 188, 189, 202, 233, 237, 241, 279, 303, 310, 312, 339, 373, 398, 416, 422, 459, 462, 476, 510, 542, 566
Freyman, 455
Frick, 155, 454
Friend, 567
Friendship, 409, 533
Fries, 55
frig **Alleghany**, 537
frig **Alliance**, 81
frig **Brandywine**, 159, 324, 370
frig **Congress**, 173, 240, 489
frig **Constitution**, 158
frig **Cumberland**, 4, 297
frig **Java**, 159
frig **Macedonian**, 498
frig **Mississippi**, 356, 390
frig **Potomac**, 132, 168, 309
frig **Raritan**, 132, 216, 311
frig **Savannah**, 376
frig **St Lawrence**, 126
Frisbee, 396
Frisby, 510
Fritshe, 443
Fritz, 461
Frizzell, 298
Frob, 394
Froche, 137
Frohlose, 349
Froman, 223
Frosk, 395
Frost, 8, 45, 48, 59, 84, 106, 126, 204, 520
Frunks, 222
Fry, 42, 169, 170, 204, 266, 336, 345, 393, 396, 510, 539
Frye, 307, 312, 386, 481, 518
Fuentes, 215
Fugett, 259
Fugitt, 266, 267, 333, 402, 556, 558
Fullen, 396
Fuller, 42, 45, 55, 59, 126, 232, 287, 362, 398, 408, 502, 531, 563
Fulmer, 259, 316
Fulton, 58, 200, 206, 542, 546
Fundy, 448
Funk, 55, 58, 136, 309, 373, 493
Fuqua, 257
Furaldo, 96
Furber, 505
Furguson, 446
Furian, 444
Furnace, 103
Furnace Tract, 62, 288

Furnam, 494
Fyant, 395
Fyffe, 7
Fyles, 68

G

Gable, 135, 136, 452
Gaddis, 163, 519
Gadsby, 10, 85, 142, 145, 296, 407, 522
Gadsden, 30
Gafney, 455
Gaiennie, 20, 33, 48, 79, 84, 160
Gaines, 74, 85, 148, 151, 194, 244, 268, 269, 278, 360, 483, 563
Gairtray, 497
Gaith, 396
Gaither, 97, 101, 189, 194, 206, 255, 402, 510, 545, 548
Galbraith, 502
Gale, 403, 546
Gales, 97, 271, 319
Galice, 457
Gallaghan, 72
Gallagher, 8, 394, 396, 445, 452, 507, 529
Gallaher, 526
Gallaudet, 472
Gallegos, 209
Gallier, 408
Galligan, 556
Gallin, 222
Gallozo, 152
Galphin, 20, 63, 67, 78, 565
Galt, 10, 19, 50, 107, 108, 523, 528
Galvin, 333, 391
Gamble, 181, 447
Gamperd, 452
Gander, 476
Gandieler, 476
Gandle, 508
Gannen, 426
Gannon, 91
Ganntt, 94
Gansevoort, 376
Gantt, 16, 94, 109, 130, 149, 331, 441, 458, 521, 541, 547
Garard, 221
Garay, 342
Garber, 222, 509
Garcia, 186, 320
Gardener, 443
Gardiner, 162, 268, 280, 341, 345, 448, 512
Gardner, 37, 47, 55, 108, 110, 184, 230, 241, 247, 259, 291, 298, 342, 399, 401, 413, 415, 418, 423, 433, 454, 456, 497, 511, 517, 541, 544, 545, 552
Garinger, 419
Garland, 23, 48, 64, 69, 78, 109, 112, 309, 387, 388, 439, 440, 441, 460, 462, 484, 497, 513, 514
Garlick, 450
Garner, 226, 267, 418, 507, 528
Garnet, 216, 224
Garnett, 110, 170, 452, 481, 527, 541, 544
Garnier, 412
Garns, 133
Garrard, 113, 114, 203, 207
Garreau, 90
Garretson, 460, 508, 550
Garrett, 92, 134, 203
Garrey, 444
Garrison, 253, 451
Gartegan, 509
Gartland, 59, 310
Gartman, 215
Gascon, 505
Gassaway, 288, 435
Gasse, 445
Gaston, 398
Gatchell, 382
Gates, 18, 27, 109, 431, 433, 441, 490, 497
Gatewood, 131
Gatliff, 318
Gatons, 192
Gatrell, 92, 430
Gatton, 402, 483

Gattrell, 230
Gaul, 36
Gault, 77, 323, 501
Gaultney, 415
Gaussen, 561
Gautherin, 476
Gautier, 425, 556, 562
Gautzel, 493
Gavatt, 510
Gavay, 425
Gavin, 181, 396
Gay, 398
Gazzam, 356, 531
Geary, 441
Gebauhr, 561
Gebhert, 531
Geiger, 255
Geisel, 181
Geisinger, 565
Gelderd, 505
Gelson, 493
Gengeback, 267
Gensler, 430, 558
Genth, 431
George, 112, 252, 345, 377
George III, 18
Georgia Historical Society, 242
Gerdes, 500
Gerguson, 507
Gerhard, 136
German Catholic Church, 12
German Hall, 12
Gerry, 360
Gess, 55, 267
Gessner, 349
Getting, 397
Gettings, 560
Getty, 296
Geymuller, 512
Gherardi, 5
Gholson, 339, 567
Gibb, 126
Gibbon, 5, 336, 539
Gibbons, 509, 514
Gibbs, 10, 69, 130, 134, 199, 208, 220, 455, 531, 552
Gibson, 10, 23, 24, 28, 46, 47, 48, 55, 63, 67, 77, 91, 107, 111, 114, 140, 153, 176, 214, 316, 318, 326, 336, 345, 347, 363, 368, 382, 426, 457, 478, 500, 509, 539, 564, 565
Giddings, 7, 50, 433, 555
Gideon, 66, 72, 87, 121, 158, 181, 214, 274, 298, 532
Giffard, 469
Giffin, 531
Gilbert, 135, 139, 339, 398, 500, 532, 537, 544, 548
Gilbreath, 302
Gilchrist, 150, 493
Giles, 198, 510
Gill, 6, 108, 166, 211, 223, 334, 338, 359, 429, 446, 450, 454, 527
Gillam, 133
Gillaspy, 97
Gillespie, 16, 21, 181, 221, 449, 472
Gillet, 45, 47, 59, 120, 236, 241, 355
Gillett, 8
Gillew, 523
Gillhuly, 452
Gilliam, 157
Gilligan, 397
Gillighin, 222
Gillis, 76, 366, 372, 503
Gilliss, 23, 176, 190, 233, 348, 463, 470, 477, 535
Gillon, 161
Gillott, 55
Gillow, 452
Gilman, 186, 221, 374, 517, 518, 558
Gilmer, 176, 260, 375
Gilmore, 443, 450, 453
Gilmoure, 404
Gilpin, 330, 332, 458
Gin, 177
Ginnaty, 418
Gippard, 447
Girardin, 476
Gist, 492

Gitt, 565
Gittings, 82, 402, 508, 526
Givins, 510
Givison, 382
Givney, 226
Glackin, 195
Gladden, 439, 441, 487
Gladman, 225
Gladney, 399, 456
Glanding, 494
Glasgow, 489
Glass, 456
Glasvar, 435
Glauton, 230
Glaze, 397
Gleason, 337, 394
Glebe, 357
Glendy, 94, 552
Glenn, 147, 201, 207, 253, 262, 339, 382, 439, 545
Glenny, 457
Glenthorn, 407
Glesson, 452
Glocke, 349
Gloveen, 446
Glover, 168, 549
Gluch, 46
Gluok, 65
Glynn, 565
Goathard, 10
Goble, 364
Goddard, 55, 409, 429, 445, 514, 529, 558
Godey, 427, 472
Godfrey, 55, 221, 445
Godwin, 137
Goell, 33
Goen, 137
Goeop, 482
Goerber, 493
Goff, 137
Goforth, 351
Goggin, 30, 117
Gohel, 493
Goin, 117
Going, 556
Goings, 44, 333, 371, 430
Gold, 480
Golden, 10, 181, 214, 395, 454, 519, 560
Goldin, 474
Golding, 91, 92, 557
Goldman, 508
Goldsborough, 5, 47, 48, 55, 368, 382
Goldsby, 50
Gollinger, 425
Gomberlin, 140
Gonzales, 128, 215
Good, 138, 448, 491
Goodale, 136, 508
Goodall, 55
Goodbar, 177
Goode, 454
Goodell, 532
Gooden, 454
Goodenough, 52, 537
Goodier, 189
Gooding, 442
Goodlet, 399
Goodloe, 141, 202, 388, 397, 484, 546
Goodman, 202, 247, 336, 387, 397, 487, 498, 542
Goodparter, 139
Goodrich, 225, 280, 445, 552, 562
Goods, 188
Goodsell, 376
Goodwin, 93, 135, 394, 396, 445, 552
Goodyear, 225
Goose Creek, 358
Goose Creek Land, 550
Gordam, 398
Gordero, 494
Gordon, 6, 12, 15, 28, 37, 44, 45, 55, 59, 63, 66, 78, 84, 153, 176, 222, 296, 306, 395, 403, 404, 423, 444, 447, 457, 490, 506, 552
Gore, 490
Gorgas, 106
Gorham, 79
Gorhon, 269

Gorlan, 446
Gorman, 127, 138, 284, 292, 343
Gormily, 396
Gormley, 389
Gorseand, 493
Gortner, 133
Goshen, 328
Goslin, 221, 494, 500
Goss, 216, 550
Gothard, 557
Gottenger, 442
Gottleib, 409
Gough, 189
Gouiss, 493
Gould, 233, 266, 394, 397, 435, 509
Goulding, 269
Gouph, 397
Gouraud, 275
Gourley, 394
Gourlie, 403
Gouverneur, 46, 48, 112
Gove, 195, 431, 541
Gover, 257
Gow, 397
Gowen, 229
Gower, 399
Grace, 408
Gracie, 442
Grady, 399
Graf, 450
Graff, 156, 222
Graham, 2, 21, 23, 25, 36, 37, 41, 47, 48, 79, 88, 94, 108, 109, 138, 140, 161, 184, 185, 196, 197, 205, 226, 250, 339, 347, 388, 393, 398, 400, 418, 420, 425, 439, 441, 452, 454, 455, 456, 457, 459, 466, 471, 484, 487, 488, 492, 513, 514, 521, 527, 537, 542, 547, 566
Grahan, 108
Graiffe, 426
Graig, 140
Grainger, 91, 267, 405
Gramillion, 29
Grammer, 81, 230, 236, 241, 382, 525
Grange, 426
Granger, 334, 540
Grant, 200, 450, 453, 458, 497, 509, 523, 540
Grapincamp, 450
Grason, 348
Gratiot, 405
Gravel, 30
Graveles, 403
Gravenhart, 393
Graves, 14, 29, 134, 177, 203, 207, 337, 400, 447, 467, 514
Gray, 117, 138, 164, 197, 277, 280, 311, 330, 334, 335, 360, 375, 399, 422, 426, 565
Graybeer, 448
Grayson, 5, 90, 91, 117, 119, 120, 173
Greason, 517, 518
Great triumph, 151
Greeham, 224
Greely, 151
Green, 3, 5, 6, 14, 21, 25, 29, 30, 33, 46, 48, 55, 60, 64, 77, 84, 95, 97, 105, 133, 140, 163, 181, 189, 226, 241, 274, 275, 287, 294, 301, 320, 327, 336, 359, 360, 371, 373, 382, 390, 395, 429, 441, 442, 443, 447, 453, 457, 462, 489, 503, 520, 532, 558
Greene, 18, 49, 401
Greenfield, 558
Greenhow, 95, 283
Greenleaf, 5, 6, 10, 128, 285, 382, 558
Greenleaf's Point, 176, 300, 350, 406, 419
Greenmount Cemetery, 43
Greenough, 150
Greenway, 502
Greenwood, 294
Greer, 28, 82, 553
Greethill, 426
Gregg, 64, 197, 198, 205, 273, 450, 542
Gregory, 139, 224, 257, 349
Greland, 108
Grenier, 442
Grenville, 469

Grey, 91, 200
Gridley, 280, 422
Grier, 181, 506
Grierson, 422
Griffin, 196, 221, 223, 224, 336, 376, 388, 394, 399, 431, 432, 490, 507, 509, 539, 554
Griffith, 27, 34, 91, 170, 203, 214, 215, 227, 398, 488, 542, 556
Griggs, 30
Grimes, 145, 163
Grindall, 244, 306
Gringrich, 138
Grinnell, 163, 531
Griswold, 177, 248, 350, 546
Griswold's, 177
Groat, 397
Grobe, 230
Grodo, 415
Groober, 406
Grooves, 449
Gros, 476
Grouard, 459
Grouchy, 297
Grougney, 527
Group, 55
Groupe, 430, 556
Grove, 160, 442
Grove Wood, 363
Grover, 17, 278
Groves, 212, 491, 507
Grubb, 401
Gruber, 396, 397
Grunsby, 451
Grunt, 510
Grupe, 551
Grymes, 29, 231, 238, 419
Gtwn improvements, 12
Guartney, 304
Guess, 33, 53
Guest, 119, 240, 382, 457
Gueymard, 500
Guillon, 566
Guinea Tract, 328
Guion, 27, 420
Guists, 55
Gumaer, 422
gun-boat **Petrel**, 329
Gunn, 403
Gunnell, 55, 82, 91, 160, 226, 228, 267, 274, 326, 332, 372, 519
Gunroyer, 442
Gunston, 534
Gunston estate, 534
Gunter, 223
Gunthee, 349
Gunton, 55, 81, 94, 525
Gurley, 161, 371
Gustin, 138
Guston, 508
Guthrie, 197, 202, 207, 208, 262, 278, 303, 370, 439, 441, 449, 508, 542, 547
Guttselich, 375
Guttslich, 257, 549
Guxruga, 215
Guy, 282
Guyer, 55, 89, 225, 226
Guzman, 128, 152
Gwinn, 370
Gwynn, 242, 282, 341, 512, 513
Gwynne, 109
Gyetyeus, 426

H

Haas, 493
Haban, 451
Hackelton, 253
Hackets, 287
Hackler, 510
Hackney, 396
Hadden, 170
Haden, 486, 530
Hady, 445
Haffman, 223
Hagaman, 394
Hagan, 67, 194, 208, 394, 450, 451, 543
Hagar, 55, 56, 226, 267
Hager, 267, 406, 421, 430, 509
Hagerty, 226, 559
Haggard, 29

Haggerty, 231, 450
Hagner, 71, 366, 490, 497
Hahn, 509
Haigh, 522
Haile, 201, 247, 248
Haines, 55, 429, 508, 558
Haisler, 559
Haislup, 267
Haitmiller, 226
Haitmiller, Anton, 226
Hal, 456
Haldeman, 197, 415, 542
Haldman, 452
Hale, 45, 84, 200, 211, 215, 250, 344, 360, 397, 545
Haley, 223, 234, 510
Halfholden, 395
Haliday, 55, 258, 298
Halitt, 335
Hall, 5, 7, 34, 40, 43, 55, 69, 79, 86, 91, 93, 94, 97, 101, 117, 120, 123, 128, 161, 184, 230, 289, 291, 294, 302, 303, 327, 342, 357, 366, 393, 394, 397, 403, 414, 415, 420, 426, 429, 448, 449, 453, 454, 472, 502, 510, 518, 523, 554, 555, 556, 566
Haller, 490, 497
Hallett, 5
Halliday, 79, 214, 408, 418
Hallinan, 395
Hallins, 376
Hallock, 561
Halloran, 450
Halloway, 388
Hallowell, 359
Hallowing Point, 534
Halpin, 221
Halse, 60
Halsey, 59, 262, 521
Halstead, 35, 113, 253, 261, 545, 546
Halzinger, 210
Ham, 209, 235, 245
Hambleton, 97, 180, 403
Hamburg, 550
Hamer, 7, 28, 62, 203, 287, 447, 466, 543, 546, 555
Hamilton, 6, 7, 61, 62, 87, 91, 106, 119, 120, 136, 139, 140, 196, 198, 205, 206, 211, 264, 266, 271, 285, 301, 309, 316, 329, 334, 335, 340, 343, 383, 388, 425, 431, 440, 443, 451, 452, 455, 457, 490, 499, 500, 504, 509, 524, 548, 554
Hamlet, 338
Hamlett, 50, 197, 334
Hamlin, 221, 432
Hammel, 454
Hammerly, 221
Hammersley, 424
Hammersly, 181
Hammond, 96, 111, 134, 184, 223, 233, 246, 250, 270, 278, 335, 338, 409, 508, 514, 530, 538, 543
Hamner, 360
Hamon, 403
Hampson, 234, 483
Hampton, 265
Hamtramck, 261
Hanault, 509
Hancock, 239, 398, 405, 515, 523, 560
Hand, 280, 370, 393, 451
Handler, 396
Handley, 396, 525, 553
Hands, 126, 226, 232, 267, 515
Handshy, 223
Handy, 5, 91, 145, 181, 214, 279, 326, 332, 435, 449, 472, 515, 559
Haner, 396
Hanford, 457
Hanger, 55
Hanks, 397
Hanley, 382, 447
Hanly, 55, 461
Hanna, 277
Hannams, 133
Hannan, 395
Hannegan, 46, 48, 50
Hannegner, 493
Hannell, 360

Hannen, 512
Hanner, 222
Hannigan, 447
Hannin, 515
Hannington, 396
Hanover, 267
Hans, 224
Hansford, 222
Hanson, 18, 109, 111, 112, 119, 130, 197, 234, 247, 334, 338, 387, 397, 401, 412, 442, 487, 488, 541, 547
Hanzel, 456
Happie, 398
Harbaugh, 22, 87, 145, 170, 231, 329, 363, 433, 515, 558
Harber, 451
Harbert, 275
Harbison, 220
Hardbottle, 329
Hardcastle, 497
Harden, 490, 538
Hardenbrook, 456
Hardey, 303
Hardgrave, 437
Hardie, 107, 144, 524
Hardin, 127, 135, 137, 143, 144, 168, 190, 260, 299, 306, 316, 375, 394, 413, 490
Harding, 99, 288, 356, 448, 560
Hardwick, 508
Hardy, 95, 366, 370, 394, 425, 449, 476, 494
Hare, 260, 415, 507, 509
Hargrave, 483
Hargrooves, 508
Haristene, 216
Harkin, 454
Harkins, 139, 181
Harkness, 10, 81, 266, 298, 307, 308, 325, 382, 402
Harlan, 223
Harley, 197, 221, 542, 543
Harman, 306, 394
Harmell, 7
Harmer, 245
Harmon, 139
Harmony, 370
Harnett, 393
Harney, 73, 74, 181, 211, 220, 483, 513, 538
Harnn, 510
Harny, 450
Harp, 451
Harper, 10, 55, 147, 150, 212, 218, 222, 257, 291, 394, 399, 437, 443, 508, 510, 526, 527, 556, 559, 560
Harrel, 309
Harrigan, 48, 451
Harrington, 55, 164, 436, 519, 560
Harriott, 507
Harris, 46, 64, 83, 86, 91, 93, 96, 140, 181, 184, 191, 203, 216, 280, 314, 331, 334, 345, 393, 403, 410, 431, 436, 442, 443, 502, 508, 534, 535, 566
Harrison, 10, 33, 37, 42, 55, 60, 64, 69, 90, 134, 135, 138, 161, 170, 175, 179, 184, 194, 226, 230, 240, 243, 301, 336, 363, 379, 401, 405, 419, 500, 540, 566, 567
Harrod, 425
Harrover, 47, 515, 517
Harrvell, 32
Harry, 213
Harshamn, 26
Harshman, 555
Hart, 35, 73, 114, 224, 273, 276, 277, 324, 369, 394, 397, 399, 400, 434, 443, 456, 461, 478, 525, 543, 568
Harte, 126, 196
Hartinaw, 454
Hartland, 394
Hartley, 433, 435
Hartman, 259, 398, 508, 519
Hartshorn, 523
Hartstene, 224
Hartzman, 221
Harvey, 91, 127, 226, 227, 231, 267, 290, 326, 327, 398, 446, 468, 505, 519, 558
Harvill, 403

Harvimeah, 171
Harwood, 171, 296, 502
Hasbrouch, 548
Hasbrouck, 35, 113, 253, 261, 545
Haselhurst, 407
Haskell, 39, 84, 158, 176, 209, 211, 229, 393, 445
Haskin, 441, 514
Haskins, 2, 397, 513
Hasley, 253
Hasluck, 482
Haslup, 81
Hass, 449
Hassel, 50
Hassler, 32, 279, 552
Hasson, 455
Hastings, 79, 396, 424, 450, 452, 486
Hastins, 46
Haswell, 354, 383
Hatch, 246, 255, 394, 422, 509
Hatcher, 177
Hatfield, 171
Hathaway, 148, 177, 195, 388, 395, 484
Hatheway, 246
Hatton, 223
Haugh, 14
Haughey, 166
Haughney, 454
Haughton, 127
Hauptman, 25, 382
Haury, 431
Hauseman, 40
Haven, 73, 166, 271
Havener, 299
Havenner, 226, 259, 360
Haviland, 194, 335, 453
Havritt, 137
Haw, 81, 525
Hawes, 96
Hawk, 199, 334
Hawke, 25, 174
Hawkins, 52, 55, 84, 108, 109, 123, 162, 203, 246, 277, 352, 447, 505, 538, 548
Hawks, 325
Hawley, 23, 24, 187, 219, 362, 363, 396
Hawse, 89
Hay, 14, 47, 87, 118, 303, 477
Hayden, 10, 181, 216, 253, 326, 396, 522, 528
Hayes, 108, 119, 137, 414, 440, 449, 539, 540
Hayfroon, 349
Haylock, 510
Haymam, 306
Hayman, 109, 231, 247, 383, 462, 490, 506
Haynes, 201, 312
Hays, 1, 107, 201, 256, 262, 296, 297, 489, 490, 508
Hayter, 449
Hayward, 200
Haywood, 376, 481
Hazel, 383, 386, 519
Hazell, 66
Hazen, 268
Hazleton, 521
Hazzard, 335, 554
Head, 171, 213, 509
Head of Frazier, 32
Headerick, 456
Headley, 264, 383, 509
Headon, 260
Heady, 85, 151, 439, 483, 484
Healey, 456
Healy, 37, 64, 69, 78, 222, 393, 398
Heaney, 59
Heany, 191, 444
Hear, 393
Heard, 315, 434
Hearth, 497
Heartie, 510
Heasbly, 455
Heath, 18, 141, 396, 521
Hebb, 19, 339, 544
Hebbard, 552
Hebert, 200, 205, 496
Heck, 278, 394, 441
Hecter, 418
Hedges, 197, 542, 546
Hedgman, 35

Hedspeth, 134
Heidelberg, 83
Heighway, 339, 545
Heilman, 184, 509
Heiner, 299
Heinsohn, 482
Heintzen, 493
Heiskell, 374
Heisler, 57
Heiss, 94, 155, 298
Heister, 40
Heiter, 267
Heitmiler, 55
Heitre, 226
Helan, 277
Hellen, 74
Helm, 203, 446
Helms, 336, 543, 546
Help, 141
Helwig, 500
Heman, 223
Hembel, 415
Hemple, 478
Hempstead, 96
Henck, 163
Hendershott, 336, 540
Henderson, 16, 23, 39, 117, 141, 144, 153, 181, 240, 282, 344, 355, 397, 441, 507, 562
Hendley, 515, 516
Hendly, 560
Hendren, 304, 312
Hendrick, 223
Hendricks, 203, 206, 334, 338
Hendrickson, 115, 388, 394, 513, 514
Hendron, 139
Henkler, 136
Henley, 165, 383
Henly, 18
Hennessey, 552
Henning, 56, 382, 559
Hennon, 210
Henone, 442
Henrichs, 500
Henrie, 85, 193, 304
Henry, 27, 56, 61, 89, 94, 141, 187, 194, 219, 248, 267, 316, 345, 394, 409, 418, 421, 442, 450, 454, 455, 457, 509, 558
Henshaw, 5, 193, 231, 245, 247, 305, 309, 382, 536
Hensley, 336, 339, 545, 557
Henson, 58, 181, 503
Henz, 442
Hepburn, 3, 163, 383
Herbert, 55, 141, 308, 448, 454, 455
Hercus, 34, 519
Herd, 18
Herens, 428
Hereran, 223
Herkenrath, 457
Hermes, 314
Hermitage, 361
Herndon, 96, 140
Herold, 55
Herrera, 152
Herreta, 213
Herrick, 253, 262, 286, 337, 339, 453
Herring, 16
Herrington, 396, 451
Herrity, 279
Herrod, 493
Herron, 284, 493, 494
Hersey, 433
Hershman, 278
Hersman, 72
Hertz, 500
Hervey, 138, 303
Heslin, 9
Hess, 55, 177, 447, 454
Hesse Darmstadt, 172
Hessey, 223
Hester, 221
Heston, 13
Heth, 337, 541
Hetzel, 313, 334, 338, 363, 520
Hevener, 485
Hevner, 285
Hewe, 340
Hewett, 97, 495

Hewit, 530
Hewlings, 322, 520
Hews, 418
Heyden, 55
Heynes, 221
Hibbs, 136, 512
Hiberner, 501
Hick, 394
Hickerson, 55
Hickey, 18, 181, 310
Hickman, 55, 56, 201, 316, 429, 542
Hicks, 14, 56, 226, 365, 382, 398, 404, 457, 508, 527
Hickson, 507
Hieskelt, 401
Higany, 134
Higbee, 420
Higgin, 221
Higgins, 102, 140, 199, 207, 240, 397, 422, 424, 431, 444, 456
Higginson, 448
Hight, 449
Hilburn, 507
Hildreth, 77, 79, 80
Hill, 38, 50, 87, 91, 97, 108, 136, 166, 181, 184, 212, 220, 221, 225, 226, 241, 250, 258, 265, 267, 269, 274, 278, 298, 300, 303, 311, 336, 337, 360, 397, 398, 404, 406, 418, 427, 434, 444, 445, 447, 473, 499, 507, 512, 531, 538, 539, 543, 547, 564
Hilleary, 121, 130, 251, 257, 535
Hillen, 88
Hilliard, 187, 219
Hills, 93, 147, 430, 467, 481, 556
Hills & Dales, 526
Hill-Side, 150
Hillyard, 10
Hilry, 418
Hilton, 173, 218, 302, 429, 466
Hiltonan, 136
Hiltz, 404
Hilyard, 93
Hincks, 404
Hind, 138
Hines, 226, 357, 450, 533, 556, 559
Hingerty, 415
Hinkle, 138
Hinshall, 457
Hinton, 383
Hipkins, 504
Hirst, 395
Hisner, 450
Hisse, 448
Hitchcock, 90, 119, 133, 161, 170, 190, 376, 414, 523
Hitchfelt, 456
Hitebens, 510
Hitton, 398
Hitz, 91, 371, 556, 558
Hix, 531
Hoagland, 202, 208
Hoban, 8, 301
Hobb, 179
Hobber, 442
Hobbie, 55, 214, 241, 482, 536
Hobbs, 501
Hochstetler, 398
Hockett, 537
Hodgden, 222
Hodge, 195, 311, 348
Hodges, 52, 213, 535
Hodgson, 303, 393, 551
Hodson, 383
Hoe, 399
Hoenhorsen, 357
Hoff, 493
Hoffman, 50, 111, 349, 383, 387, 388, 394, 395, 398, 415, 457, 487, 490, 492, 539, 560
Hogan, 7, 16, 79, 136, 140, 222, 394, 397, 455, 461, 514
Hogarty, 403
Hoge, 136, 167
Hoger, 398
Hogg, 16, 445, 531
Hoggart, 79
Hoggatt, 534
Hok, 451
Hoke, 198, 334

Hola, 67
Holandorf, 448
Holbrook, 429
Holden, 36, 198, 206, 221, 388, 397, 510
Holder, 139
Holdham, 382
Holdridge, 118
Holeman, 309
Holland, 25, 35, 55, 112, 113, 138, 146, 339, 363, 402, 426, 455, 457, 530, 545
Holle, 225
Hollenback, 535, 568
Holley, 133
Hollidge, 91, 429
Hollingsworth, 134
Hollister, 365
Hollman, 429
Holloway, 133, 154, 393, 541
Hollyday, 171
Holmbrook, 414
Holme, 383
Holmead, 126, 190
Holmes, 10, 14, 21, 38, 46, 50, 61, 64, 93, 110, 239, 266, 327, 363, 416, 531, 537, 543, 546
Holmes' Island, 367
Holroyd, 28, 368
Holt, 45
Holton, 79
Holtzman, 80
Holybee, 444
Holyrod, 564
Holzinger, 168
Homans, 20, 55, 122, 145, 184, 209, 231, 252, 257, 265, 281, 321, 433, 519
Homer, 454
Homilier, 533
Homiller, 55
Hond, 442
Honer, 442
Hongsage, 82
Hood, 398, 455, 507
Hooe, 10, 34, 74, 146, 162, 259, 411, 423, 550, 556
Hooft, 393
Hooker, 7, 110, 111, 221, 395, 451
Hooper, 91, 205, 336, 509
Hoops, 455
Hoore, 426
Hoover, 55, 92, 184, 191, 239, 267, 382, 383, 444, 493, 557
Hope, 408, 505, 527
Hopkins, 23, 26, 31, 85, 167, 181, 195, 266, 309, 395, 396, 402, 484, 493, 535
Hopkinson, 398
Hopley, 457
Hopner, 222
Hopper, 509
Hopping, 85, 111, 400, 546
Hoppock, 359
Horine, 349
Horn, 176, 224, 455
Horne, 275, 440, 523
Horneller, 346
Horner, 96, 395
Hornett, 396
Horning, 91, 226, 556
Hornor, 526
Hornsby, 198, 208
Horsewell, 453
Horstkamp, 55, 559
Horstman, 482
Horton, 71, 380, 398, 474
Horves, 509
Horwitz, 482
Hoskins, 2
Hoss, 394, 397
Hosse, 397
Hotchkiss, 192, 424
Hotons, 273
Houck, 265
Hough, 28, 187, 219, 376, 395
Houghton, 135, 306
Houk, 139
Houpt, 494
Hourdequire, 505
Houseman, 52
Housiner, 445
Houssaye, 84

Houston, 46, 50, 105, 220, 419
Hovey, 146
How, 336, 483, 546
Howard, 20, 55, 73, 93, 97, 130, 131, 132, 140, 168, 170, 177, 178, 186, 196, 198, 201, 204, 205, 207, 230, 252, 253, 267, 337, 338, 359, 383, 452, 457, 487, 549
Howards, 126
Howby, 442
Howe, 10, 18, 212, 218, 270, 343, 442, 446, 502
Howell, 50, 55, 200, 355, 400, 438, 448, 482, 542, 562
Howels, 359
Hower, 457
Howison, 191, 319
Howland, 294
Howle, 91, 117, 120, 519, 530
Howlett, 149
Hoxey, 114
Hoye, 185
Hoyle, 339
Hoyt, 33, 45, 84, 113, 138, 253, 261, 280, 420, 447
Huan, 270
Hubard, 48
Hubbard, 93, 95, 138, 181, 267, 394, 420, 555, 562
Hubble, 179, 476
Hubbs, 431
Huchison, 287
Huddleson, 484
Huddleston, 256, 509
Huddlestone, 201, 208, 542, 547
Hudnut, 14
Hudson, 133, 135, 201, 277, 308, 350, 411, 424
Hueston, 138
Huffnagle, 415
Hugenen, 494
Hugennin, 173, 302
Huger, 90, 119, 497
Huggins, 93, 558
Hughes, 139, 203, 209, 226, 277, 293, 304, 305, 317, 341, 365, 371, 396, 442, 452, 453, 480
Hughs, 394
Hughtway, 277
Huhn, 237
Hulbert, 88
Hull, 279, 302, 387, 427, 489
Hulme, 466
Hulse, 200
Hulseman, 525
Hulter, 431
Humber, 388, 397
Humbert, 426
Hume, 345
Humes, 559
Humpheys, 455
Humphrey, 350, 359, 432
Humphreys, 68, 166, 201, 227, 256, 279, 310, 340, 350, 398, 455, 485, 488, 508, 533, 534
Humphries, 398, 487
Hungerford, 439
Hunn, 212
Hunnewell, 551
Hunt, 68, 94, 132, 181, 224, 227, 324, 329, 336, 398, 409, 440, 456, 490, 497, 500, 540, 554
Hunter, 55, 65, 82, 132, 138, 139, 148, 179, 180, 184, 197, 200, 206, 217, 240, 282, 309, 345, 357, 365, 398, 446, 482, 528, 567
Huntingdon, 13, 78
Huntington, 30, 32, 45, 63, 66, 118, 173, 221, 312, 475, 529, 567
Huntley, 451
Hunton, 474
Huntoon, 469
Huny, 432
Hupp, 534
Hurd, 424
Hurdle, 231, 370, 430, 558
Hurlbut, 280
Hurry, 482
Hurst, 131

Hussey, 69
Huston, 396
Hutchings, 136
Hutchins, 184, 330, 355, 418
Hutchinson, 309, 396, 401, 456
Hutchison, 184
Hutter, 249, 540, 541
Hutteroll, 482
Hutton, 35, 96, 97, 112, 113, 253, 404, 429, 430, 559, 566
Hyatt, 216, 225, 349, 517, 518, 556, 557
Hyde, 11, 47, 435, 483
Hyer, 412, 452
Hynes, 394, 444
Hystop, 42

I

Iardella, 553, 559
Ide, 535
Idler, 14, 448
Iglehart, 502
Ijams, 238
Immigrants, 293
Impoff, 451
Independent Tract, 328, 411
Inergens, 395
Ingalls, 246
Inge, 50
Ingersoll, 16, 50, 83, 125, 482
Ingle, 56, 137, 230, 263, 274, 375, 407, 478
Ingles, 431
Ingraham, 120, 225, 226
Ingram, 134, 224, 455
Inks, 507
Inman, 87
Innis, 399
Inskeep, 138
Insworth, 394
Iraham, 457
Ireson, 426
Iron Ore Lot, 288
Irons, 107, 387, 487, 539, 548
Irriges, 136
Irvan, 203
Irvin, 185, 343, 374, 441, 442
Irving, 117
Irwin, 19, 25, 28, 43, 164, 165, 168, 197, 206, 292, 439, 513, 545
Irwing, 445
Isaacks, 226, 493
Isaacs, 91, 201
Ischam, 222
Iselin, 457
Isinghoff, 508
Isler, 78, 224
Israel, 464
Iturbide, 493
Ives, 96, 154, 337, 420, 509
Ivy Hill, 566
Izard, 32

J

Jacggi, 457
Jack, 67, 212, 266
Jackson, 10, 27, 33, 49, 56, 68, 107, 141, 143, 163, 195, 223, 226, 229, 241, 256, 260, 266, 277, 298, 326, 331, 344, 345, 362, 383, 389, 391, 403, 410, 414, 429, 431, 442, 446, 449, 461, 468, 470, 497, 522, 524, 532, 539, 552, 559
Jackson City, 362, 367
Jacksonville, 375
Jacob, 502
Jacobs, 18, 243, 267, 383, 436, 472, 509
Jacobsen, 149
Jacobson, 425
Jacobus, 442
Jaffray, 523
Jameison, 91, 557
James, 61, 77, 89, 189, 280, 304, 324, 393, 395, 418, 429, 451, 452, 531
James Dick, 235
Jamesson, 297
Jamieson, 259
Jamison, 123, 236, 316
Janney, 67, 167, 257, 427, 429
January, 33
Jarauski, 397

Jarauta, 428
Jarboe, 27, 559
Jardine, 301, 383
Jareno, 209
Jarero, 209
Jarnagin, 45
Jarne, 510
Jarsell, 431
Jarvis, 24, 208, 222, 473, 528
Javelli, 44
Javis, 303
Jeff, 168
Jeffers, 216, 260, 383, 486, 557, 559
Jefferson, 183, 308, 331
Jefferson House, 313
Jeffries, 313
Jehl, 404
Jeiu, 505
Jelard, 454
Jenifer, 91, 194, 538, 564
Jenkin, 456
Jenkins, 10, 32, 56, 58, 91, 136, 137, 265, 310, 341, 370, 379, 477, 483, 538, 547, 560
Jenne, 532
Jennings, 56, 89, 148, 448, 556
Jenniss, 388
Jennisson, 140
Jerduns, 426
Jergar, 493
Jermon, 452
Jerome, 500, 524
Jesuits, 521
Jesup, 118, 162
Jewell, 142, 265, 353
Jewett, 61, 187, 219, 280, 501
Jicotercal, 152
Jillard, 56, 91, 241, 557
Joesfer, 493
Joff, 398
John, 68
Johns, 19, 20, 63, 67, 78, 83, 84, 158, 185, 493
Johnson, 5, 6, 16, 22, 26, 27, 30, 33, 36, 39, 43, 46, 49, 50, 56, 61, 63, 67, 78, 79, 85, 91, 93, 102, 105, 133, 134, 139, 140, 144, 145, 150, 161, 166, 177, 181, 194, 195, 197, 208, 213, 222, 223, 224, 226, 245, 258, 259, 268, 269, 280, 283, 290, 294, 298, 303, 308, 332, 341, 354, 373, 387, 388, 393, 395, 396, 397, 399, 403, 404, 414, 417, 425, 429, 433, 439, 441, 443, 446, 449, 457, 474, 475, 478, 484, 487, 490, 493, 494, 496, 497, 509, 513, 516, 517, 518, 521, 528, 532, 535, 540, 541, 543, 546, 552, 553, 556, 562, 566, 567
Johnston, 70, 94, 111, 198, 199, 204, 205, 206, 210, 211, 222, 246, 250, 374, 401, 412, 422, 433, 439, 441, 457, 483, 491, 513, 546, 548
Johnstone, 56, 246, 538, 548
Joice, 222
Joline, 185
Jolly, 267
Jones, 3, 5, 7, 20, 29, 31, 33, 36, 38, 52, 56, 58, 61, 63, 66, 69, 77, 80, 81, 82, 83, 84, 85, 87, 89, 91, 95, 98, 99, 107, 113, 114, 116, 117, 118, 123, 130, 132, 134, 136, 139, 140, 147, 173, 174, 177, 181, 184, 198, 202, 204, 206, 208, 213, 214, 215, 221, 224, 225, 226, 230, 232, 248, 249, 250, 253, 254, 259, 262, 269, 280, 292, 298, 305, 309, 315, 317, 325, 334, 336, 337, 339, 345, 358, 366, 383, 395, 397, 398, 400, 429, 430, 431, 446, 449, 450, 453, 455, 457, 476, 477, 484, 490, 493, 499, 501, 502, 507, 508, 509, 513, 516, 517, 518, 519, 525, 528, 532, 536, 537, 541, 545, 549, 553, 557, 558, 560, 565
Jonson, 450
Jordan, 23, 56, 67, 101, 109, 111, 130, 200, 393, 394, 447
Jorden, 418
Josselyn, 35, 112, 113, 253, 544, 548
Jost, 56, 367, 553, 560
Jouett, 540

Joyce, 134, 190, 236, 360, 444, 559, 560
Judah, 490, 497, 540
Judd, 508, 513, 531
Judge, 536
Judgins, 568
Juffer, 357
Jullien, 244, 268
Jury, 502
Justice, 431
Justinian, 433

K

Kahl, 560
Kain, 514
Kaiser, 225, 349, 383
Kallmyer, 222
Kammar, 278
Kane, 80, 221, 433, 538
Kapuscinski, 364
Karchler, 395
Kariker, 507
Kaseburg, 349
Kattler, 510
Kaufman, 91, 395
Kavanagh, 383, 443
Kavenaugh, 452
Kealing, 221
Keally, 519
Kean, 444
Keane, 383
Keany, 447
Kearney, 184, 266, 389, 400, 487
Kearny, 106, 214, 240, 246, 270, 302, 366, 367, 388, 412, 425, 447, 472, 473, 484, 491, 513
Keating, 56, 64, 313, 319, 383, 413
Kedglie, 302, 358
Keeber, 456
Keeck, 460
Keef, 163
Keefe, 273, 310, 394, 411, 441
Keegan, 221
Keele, 423
Keeler, 509
Keeley, 481
Keely, 452
Keen, 474, 510, 537, 552
Keenan, 415, 444, 448, 543
Keene, 31, 34, 67, 82, 84
Keeny, 223
Keere, 446
Keever, 455
Keezee, 177
Keffer, 566
Keiger, 557
Keisenbock, 432
Keiser, 12
Keith, 224, 482, 507
Kelcher, 517, 557
Kell, 136, 228, 376
Keller, 251, 383, 428, 511, 521
Kelley, 30, 63, 98, 135, 136, 138, 140, 396, 450, 454, 510
Kellogg, 193, 203, 447, 543, 546
Kellum, 96
Kelly, 12, 23, 73, 84, 119, 201, 236, 291, 365, 396, 399, 436, 447, 452, 456, 460, 477, 510, 511, 519, 522, 535, 560
Kelse, 137
Kelsey, 133, 509
Kemp, 133
Kemper, 43, 45, 112, 113, 252, 341
Kendall, 7, 208, 220, 244, 360, 362, 425, 431, 439, 483, 496, 497, 514
Kendrick, 66, 480
Keneday, 134
Kenigen, 482
Kenly, 307
Kennard, 411, 446
Kennaugh, 20
Kenneda, 456
Kennedy, 47, 66, 148, 188, 214, 228, 377, 383, 393, 395, 399, 447, 450, 453, 509, 561
Kennerly, 252
Kennett, 235
Kenney, 10, 222, 461
Kennon, 5, 324
Kenny, 322, 445, 452, 455
Kensett, 561

Kensil, 453
Kent, 224, 316, 392, 404, 531
Kenwater, 394
Kenyon, 136
Keogh, 505
Kepler, 91, 133, 370, 446
Kepling, 523
Ker, 147, 234, 441
Kerby, 148, 353
Kerfoot, 332, 393
Kern, 11, 72, 173, 347, 533
Kernan, 211
Kerney, 234
Kernochan, 323
Kerr, 16, 40, 188, 222, 383, 403, 443, 452, 508, 524
Kerrow, 351
Kershaw, 135
Kershner, 383
Kessele, 493
Kessinger, 245
Ketchum, 202
Ketler, 510
Ketter, 136
Kettle, 493
Keuniston, 393
Key, 34, 40, 47, 226, 232, 331, 344, 383, 398, 415, 476
Keyser, 224
Keyworth, 91, 93, 383, 557
Kibble, 555
Kibler, 451
Kidd, 7
Kidder, 403
Kidwell, 56, 448
Kierman, 223
Kiernan, 439
Kiersted, 135
Kiesbury, 467
Kiger, 204, 235, 485, 514
Kigler, 357
Kikeman, 553
Kilburn, 107, 169
Kilchula, 3
Kilgore, 312
Kilgour, 209
Kilgrove, 448
Killmon, 559
Kilmiste, 10, 56, 93, 163
Kilmon, 518
Kilpatrick, 87
Kim, 218
Kimball, 195, 207, 444
Kimberly, 401
Kimmel, 80
Kimmell, 63, 517, 518
Kinchloe, 249, 253, 262
Kinckle, 274
Kinder, 127, 137
King, 5, 10, 29, 34, 46, 48, 50, 91, 137, 163, 177, 181, 202, 207, 226, 235, 269, 289, 291, 302, 303, 316, 320, 368, 383, 393, 394, 403, 418, 422, 427, 429, 441, 446, 447, 453, 468, 469, 479, 481, 484, 517, 526, 533, 553, 556, 559, 562
King of Sardinia, 185
Kingman, 56
Kingsbury, 106, 170, 429, 526, 528, 557
Kingsley, 451
Kingsman, 445
Kingston, 523
Kinks, 133
Kinman, 135
Kinnard, 426
Kinne, 535
Kinneford, 443
Kinney, 222, 277
Kinny, 447
Kinsey, 136
Kinsgin, 485
Kinston, 457
Kintzing, 204, 441
Kip, 300
Kippy, 443
Kirby, 56, 90, 119, 553
Kirevin, 445
Kirk, 50, 218, 359, 489
Kirkbride, 503
Kirkham, 429

Kirkland, 441
Kirkpatrick, 192, 200, 372, 374
Kirksey, 431
Kirkwood, 251
Kirwill, 393
Kisote, 60
Kitchen, 224, 449
Kizer, 136
Klaener, 40
Klager, 461
Klaws, 443
Klengden, 304
Klieber, 307
Kline, 7, 399, 446
Klinge, 137
Klinkard, 508
Klinz, 450
Klopfer, 231, 329, 383, 506, 558
Knaneally, 7
Knapp, 68, 394, 396
Kneale, 426
Kneeland, 78
Kneller, 7
Knickerbocker, 443
Knife, 27
Knight, 14, 138, 349, 426, 555
Knipe, 79
Knipper, 395
Knipple, 325, 371
Knock, 447
Knott, 10, 33, 56, 58, 84, 125, 394, 430, 448, 556, 557
Knoulton, 18
Knox, 38, 214, 331, 396
Knuht, 431
Koarstoupfads, 442
Koch, 453
Kochreiser, 7
Kock, 221, 449
Kohle, 443
Kohlsatt, 403
Kohne, 400
Koite, 442
Kolb, 508
Kolisher, 133
Kols, 446
Konigsberg, 561
Konover, 196
Koontz, 353, 398
Kopp, 324
Korse, 449
Kothe, 476
Kotzebue, 51
Kownslar, 393
Kraff, 10
Kraffenbaner, 443
Krafft, 39, 56, 91, 286, 473, 562
Kraft, 267
Krahmer, 397
Krass, 510
Krauth, 40
Kreamer, 263
Kreiss, 453
Kretz, 457
Kriecht, 7
Kriel, 535
Krimpe, 181
Kriner, 448
Kring, 139
Krips, 279
Krofft, 383
Kronire, 394
Krouse, 275
Krum, 530
Krumer, 181
Kruper, 463
Krusenstern, 51
Krutzotman, 493
Kugan, 452
Kuhl, 56, 164, 515
Kuhle, 429
Kuhn, 198
Kuhns, 353, 543, 546
Kuntz, 220, 445
Kurtz, 13, 81, 91, 216, 306, 357, 428, 430, 525
Kutachos, 482
Kuykendall, 6, 45, 59, 78
Ky volunteers, 414

L

L'Infant, 358
La Barbier, 493
La Francis, 8
La Housaye, 37
La Reintree, 33, 39, 84, 158
La Rue, 508
La Vega, 25, 209, 210
Lacey, 46, 48
Lachat, 394
Lachmyer, 413
Lackett, 67
Lacy, 42, 502
Ladd, 96, 173, 302, 470, 523
Ladira, 215
Lafayette, 238, 513
Lafferty, 137, 393, 455
Lafleche, 37
Laflin, 475
Lafollet, 138
Lafon, 274
Laidley, 106
Lain, 138
Lair, 413
Laird, 134, 142, 457
Lake, 399
Lakemeyer, 176, 225, 307, 559
Lalanne, 273
Lally, 46, 194, 206, 353, 361, 422, 423, 428, 431, 498
Laman, 562
Lamar, 130, 199
Lamb, 343, 395
Lambell, 56, 514, 519
Lamber, 494
Lambert, 152
Lambie, 395
Lamkin, 184
Lamontin, 396
Lamotte, 110
Lampel, 493
Lampfere, 476
Lampkin, 495
Lampman, 468
Lamright, 56
Lamsden, 426
Lanaham, 452
Lanbeck, 181
Lancaster, 53, 56, 316, 429
Land, 304, 312
Lander, 223
Landero, 152
Landolt, 393
Landon, 274, 361
Landrage, 445
Landrick, 56, 226, 383
Landry, 316
Lane, 56, 127, 137, 169, 170, 173, 181, 269, 339, 368, 390, 429, 442, 456, 489, 494, 527, 556
Lanel, 135, 476
Lanfear, 457
Lang, 221, 403, 510
Langdon, 545
Langfit, 184
Langford, 134
Langhorn, 478
Langley, 188, 394
Langston, 224
Langwell, 222
Lanham, 282, 430
Lannes, 290
Lanning, 133
Lannoy, 508
Lanouer, 394
Lanphier, 79
Lansburg, 137
Lansdale, 75, 97
Lansing, 35, 111, 442
Lanson, 84, 442
Laporte, 505
Larado, 215
Larcombe, 19, 409
Largston, 137
Larig, 137
Larimer, 531
Lark, 398
Larkden, 349
Larkin, 94, 349, 370, 552

Larned, 56, 68, 111, 205, 230, 260, 270, 335, 419, 485, 504, 515
Larner, 124
Larnes, 324
Laselle, 33
Laskey, 56, 92, 519, 560
Lasley, 25
Lasselle, 53, 84
Lassen, 404
Lassent, 404
Latham, 90, 93, 94, 140, 141, 374, 503
Lathrop, 141, 397
Latimer, 95
Latour, 86
Laub, 43, 56, 93, 146, 147, 271, 485, 559
Lauck, 245
Laud, 452
Lauderdale, 1, 223
Laughan, 82
Laughrey, 29
Lauman, 252, 338
Laurel Hill Cemetery, 279
Laurens, 476
Laurie, 23, 39, 101, 104, 105, 130
Lausen, 349
Lauson, 157
Lauten, 431
Lauterburg, 493
Lauxman, 91
Lavalette, 279
Lavender, 56
Law, 56, 216, 258, 345, 358, 370, 384, 419, 431, 459
Lawbeinheimer, 398
Lawerant, 432
Lawless, 450
Lawrence, 28, 101, 124, 129, 132, 134, 181, 259, 303, 379, 393, 394, 424, 440, 445, 450, 489, 557
Lawrie, 429
Lawright, 426
Lawson, 33, 90, 119, 323, 409, 513
Lawton, 221, 403
Lawyer, 447
Lay, 90, 110, 119, 390, 474
Layall, 483
Layne, 201
Layton, 139
Lazenby, 325
Le Ballie, 493
Le Baron, 476
Le Roy, 363
Lea, 196
Leach, 184, 395
Leacroft, 457
Leake, 117
Leal, 105, 171
Lear, 23, 68, 112, 136
Leary, 10, 125, 128, 363, 449, 518
Leatham, 317
Leaumont, 316
Leavel, 420
Leavenworth, 75, 510
Leborio, 48
Lecesne, 457
Leckron, 418, 560
Ledden, 468
Leddon, 241, 260, 326, 383
Leddy, 56, 226, 559
Ledergerber, 136
Ledner, 430
Lee, 10, 11, 31, 47, 51, 68, 85, 92, 105, 106, 108, 109, 131, 136, 137, 159, 162, 163, 166, 171, 173, 184, 197, 222, 223, 233, 234, 235, 277, 302, 327, 340, 355, 357, 424, 425, 439, 440, 441, 471, 497, 510, 517, 518, 519, 534, 551, 555
Leech, 155, 225, 339, 399, 546
Leechman, 221, 508
Leeds, 529
Leet, 450
Leffer, 403
Leffler, 79
Lefler, 56
Legar, 79
Legget, 17
Leggit, 62
Legn, 431

Leidendorff, 549
Leigh, 204, 379, 567
Leight, 245
Leighton, 463
Leigle, 40
Leininger, 509
Leise, 451
Leisy, 502
Leitch, 509
Leitz, 445
Leland, 479
Lemcke, 546
Lemington, 15
Lemon, 448
Lendrum, 112, 490
Lenergan, 453
Lenhart, 94
Lenman, 53, 267
Lennox, 395
Lenoir, 383
Lenox, 47, 83, 97, 185, 256, 285, 298, 301, 378, 400, 534
Lent, 380
Lentilhon, 457
Lenzing, 184
Leonard, 444, 508
Leonhard, 127, 137
Leopold, 396
Lepretre, 316
Lepreux, 225, 429, 514, 515, 559
Lerasy, 141
Lerron, 394
Lescure, 364
Lesette, 482
Leslie, 111, 248, 250, 298, 502
Letkie, 426
Leuhart, 370
Levering, 167
Levier, 133
Levin, 452
Levitt, 397
Levo, 138
Levois, 457
Levy, 72, 126, 168, 394, 442, 482, 500, 551
Lewis, 15, 30, 47, 56, 68, 93, 127, 137, 177, 227, 242, 266, 269, 279, 309, 318, 327, 330, 347, 369, 404, 417, 418, 429, 444, 464, 494, 495, 502, 504, 551, 557, 558, 565, 566
Ley, 444
Libbey, 480
Liberty, 308
Lighter, 86
Lightfell, 442
Lightfoot, 560
Ligon, 50
Likens, 396
Lillard, 139, 140
Lilley, 404
Lilly, 140, 452
Lillybridge, 20, 159
Limestone, 438
Limpskins, 397
Linch, 493
Lincoln, 95, 109, 126, 127, 133, 143, 247, 250, 264, 266, 304, 308, 312, 314, 440, 469, 490
Linden, 451
Lindenberger, 88
Linder, 443
Linderks, 394
Linderman, 507
Lindermire, 507
Lindsay, 70, 95, 117, 122, 224, 428, 493, 555
Lindsey, 376
Lindsley, 20, 34, 93, 265, 430, 557, 559
Lindstron, 349
Link, 374
Linkins, 92, 226, 266, 398, 429
Linn, 199, 354, 384, 396
Linnard, 170
Linns, 455
Linsey, 397, 398
Linthicam, 510
Linthicum, 175, 274, 315, 357, 525
Linton, 26, 40, 64, 78, 84, 232, 464
Linwood, 366
Lipp, 221

Lippett, 490
Lippincott, 320, 359
Lipscomb, 50, 558, 560
Lisha, 56
Lisles, 163
List, 51
Lithner, 349
Little, 22, 56, 64, 92, 142, 163, 213, 240, 256, 266, 356, 383, 384, 398, 418, 452, 456, 460, 524, 541
Little Fort, 521
Littlebrand, 221
Littledeer, 3
Littlejohn, 40
Littleton, 464
Livingood, 133
Livingston, 18, 32, 61, 310, 311, 479, 482, 489
Livington, 457
Lizardo, 217, 346
Lloyd, 259, 267, 319, 409, 502
Lndenerg, 510
Lobber, 508
Locey, 442
Lock, 453
Locke, 134, 418
Lockey, 266
Lockhart, 423
Lockwood, 210, 531
Locock, 562
Lodge, 5, 184, 505
Loeser, 107
Loeson, 490
Lofland, 248
Loftis, 394
Logan, 140, 266, 372, 419
Logenbeel, 490
Loker, 472
Lokey, 555
Lollen, 445
Lomax, 430
Lombardini, 128
Lombardino, 152
Londale, 431
London, 537
Lonesee, 450
Long, 7, 28, 131, 292, 299, 305, 335, 349, 370, 425, 454, 471, 517, 518, 521
Long Old Fields, 525
Longary, 403
Longdon, 227, 383, 464, 559
Long-ecker, 441
Longenhammer, 461
Longis, 493
Longley, 7
Longnecker, 204
Longstaff, 494
Longstreet, 247, 490
Longstreth, 315, 316
Looby, 557, 559
Loomis, 79, 394, 507
Looney, 447
Looper, 177
Lord, 47, 56, 76, 169, 226, 252, 297, 398, 559
Lorens, 431
Loring, 5, 73, 106, 198, 211, 439, 441, 484, 513, 514
Lorman, 357
Lortz, 136
Loud, 508
Loudensborough, 446
Loughborough, 19, 81
Loughest, 445
Louis, 493
Louis XVIII, 235
Loup, 397
Lourey, 509
Loury, 493
Love, 45, 113, 201, 253, 256, 262, 298, 345, 401
Lovejoy, 13, 304, 312, 347
Loveless, 226, 266
Lovell, 103, 108, 259, 388, 396, 439, 441, 528
Lovely, 482
Lovier, 224
Low, 181, 195, 443, 482
Lowallen, 140
Lowber, 482

Lowd, 109
Lowden, 82, 147
Lowe, 56, 259, 383
Lowell, 200, 248, 250
Lower Plantation, 379
Lown, 141
Lowndes, 70, 245
Lowrey, 429, 508
Lowrie, 564
Lowry, 20, 111, 226, 257, 274, 299, 398, 449
Loyall, 315, 485, 494
Loyd, 22, 457, 505
Lucas, 10, 39, 102, 226, 248, 418, 430, 509
Luce, 23, 161, 566
Lucker, 15
Ludlam, 118
Ludlow, 124
Luffborough, 525
Lugenbeel, 388, 394, 425, 497
Luis, 457
Lumas, 523
Lumpkin, 537
Lundy, 401
Lunt, 525
Lupe, 399
Lusby, 92, 226, 371, 556
Lusk, 460
Luther, 107
Lutterenger, 395
Lutz, 455
Luyando, 152
Luyundo, 128
Lydock, 383
Lydon, 460
Lykins, 61
Lyles, 47, 229, 454, 456
Lynch, 5, 37, 115, 177, 221, 317, 393, 431, 433, 449, 450, 452, 504, 518, 519
Lyndhurst, 224
Lyne, 345
Lynes, 221
Lynne, 403
Lyon, 108, 355, 454, 528, 546
Lyone, 398
Lyons, 221, 226, 310, 395, 401, 445, 507
Lytle, 504

M

Mabee, 398
Mabin, 397
Mabury, 431
Macaulay, 153
Maccarthy, 457
Maccubbin, 63
Macdaniel, 49
Mace, 138, 364, 457
Mackae, 113
Mackall, 43, 74, 188, 439, 497, 538, 549, 564, 565
Mackay, 403
Mackenzie, 224, 232, 324, 390, 539, 547
Mackey, 259, 398
Mackle, 250
Mackubin, 502
Macky, 460
Maclay, 259, 513
Maclellan, 532
Macleod, 263
Macomb, 94, 141, 142, 143, 155, 281, 384
Macon, 440
Macown, 5
Macqueen, 561
Macrae, 253, 261
MacRae, 45
Madden, 394, 395
Maddox, 27, 95, 194, 259, 384, 450, 555, 566
Madigan, 222
Madison, 72, 74, 151, 234, 331, 378
Maffitt, 122
Magar, 25, 162, 506
Magee, 10, 184, 196, 225, 226, 331, 418, 426, 557, 559
Magie, 421
Magill, 194, 245, 309
Magilton, 108

Magnum, 50
Magnus, 510
Magruder, 25, 38, 43, 51, 56, 61, 62, 69, 92, 97, 99, 132, 153, 186, 199, 212, 218, 223, 229, 230, 263, 266, 267, 282, 365, 384, 387, 391, 402, 424, 439, 441, 487, 488, 495, 497, 523, 524, 557
Maguire, 56, 93, 450
Magurder, 416
Mahaffy, 334
Mahan, 259
Maher, 39, 286, 310, 364, 375, 421, 436
Mahnhort, 349
Mahon, 339, 442, 449, 545
Mahoney, 394
Mahony, 425
Mailland, 394
Major, 124, 280, 455
Malaney, 441
Malbon, 448, 454
Malcoln, 153
Malcom, 396
Malhowsky, 388
Malin, 545
Mallerhy, 449
Mallinckrodt, 561
Mallindar, 450
Mallion, 519
Mallory, 328
Maloed, 447
Malone, 125, 130, 134, 199, 447, 455
Maloney, 7, 222, 394, 397, 490
Malony, 448
Malsen, 223
Malthy, 223
Mamark, 442
Mamlouk, 360
Managan, 508
Manahan, 141
Manaker, 136
Mandy, 394
Manering, 394
Maney, 194
Mangham, 200
Manigault, 198, 206, 334
Mankin, 56, 292
Mankins, 56
Manly, 451
Mann, 10, 172, 324, 396, 414, 416, 450, 563
Manne, 235
Manning, 83, 271, 340, 443, 453, 535, 536
Mannver, 523
man-of war **Greyhound**, 18
Manouvrier, 82, 96
Mansen, 508
Mansfield, 108, 110, 170, 177, 415, 423, 524
Manson, 221
Mantelard, 493
Mantz, 227
Manyett, 429
Maples, 279, 454
Marbell, 509
Marbury, 52, 122, 123, 175, 191, 218, 255, 315, 318, 343, 476
Marceran, 559
Marceron, 10, 214, 342
March, 119, 170, 311, 453
Marchal, 457
Marchand, 5, 31
Marcy, 211, 253, 487, 488
Margarum, 442
Marguard, 16
Marin, 311
Markle, 531
Markley, 204
Marks, 56, 277, 514
Markward, 306, 365
Marlin, 440
Marlow, 136, 384
Marney, 509
Marr, 92
Marrast, 200
Marrin, 140
Marriott, 204, 543
Marron, 345
Marry, 442

Marsh, 46, 51, 221, 222, 281
Marshall, 25, 56, 116, 122, 127, 143, 145, 149, 153, 154, 163, 169, 171, 180, 181, 190, 202, 212, 229, 258, 280, 281, 299, 323, 384, 410, 433, 435, 441, 462, 494, 504, 522, 536
Marsoletti, 429
Marston, 376, 509
Martell, 418
Marteni, 59
Martial, 444
Martin, 4, 5, 7, 14, 22, 28, 46, 56, 63, 92, 107, 110, 125, 135, 140, 162, 163, 184, 198, 201, 204, 206, 224, 249, 250, 253, 263, 266, 334, 335, 384, 388, 395, 396, 397, 398, 426, 440, 441, 446, 448, 452, 454, 456, 472, 476, 507, 513, 514, 519, 553, 555, 559
Martine, 500
Martineau, 394, 426
Martins, 398
Martz, 455
Marvin, 29, 64, 69, 95, 205, 280
Marye, 422
Maryman, 15, 65, 66, 88, 91, 92, 160, 231, 236, 257, 332, 411, 504, 563
Masi, 56, 147
Mason, 26, 31, 32, 46, 48, 56, 65, 81, 88, 100, 112, 121, 123, 141, 154, 209, 211, 220, 236, 246, 256, 271, 280, 298, 331, 334, 335, 338, 339, 346, 349, 355, 366, 367, 369, 370, 392, 403, 424, 425, 471, 477, 490, 493, 502, 504, 513, 521, 522, 525, 531, 533, 534, 537, 565, 567, 568
Maspule, 215
Massey, 137, 448
Massi, 516
Massie, 337, 347
Massoletti, 11, 186
Masten, 111
Masters, 357
Masterten, 360
Mather, 394
Mathews, 24, 41, 52, 284, 289, 339, 351, 545
Mathias, 215, 322, 359
Mathis, 138
Matley, 398
Matlock, 96, 389, 516
Matten, 222
Matthews, 6, 18, 24, 41, 81, 137, 154, 216, 218, 251, 310, 360, 444, 506, 525
Mattingley, 514, 519
Mattingly, 86, 169, 225, 384, 389, 429, 515, 516, 557
Mattis, 399
Mattison, 454
Mattocks, 356
Matz, 209
Matzell, 260
Mauds, 418
Maugaan, 493
Maughlin, 561
Maulding, 223
Maule, 67
Maulsby, 89, 543
Maury, 3, 47, 81, 146, 163, 208, 220, 258, 335, 376, 384, 429, 505, 518, 525, 526, 566
Maxey, 247, 544
Maxlam, 400
Maxwell, 10, 133, 136, 184, 240, 370, 400
May, 16, 35, 71, 133, 169, 190, 195, 205, 213, 225, 230, 248, 255, 262, 289, 298, 304, 308, 311, 316, 319, 501, 510, 513, 518
Mayer, 393, 453
Mayhall, 140
Maynard, 280
Mayo, 22, 23, 35, 269, 331
Mayon, 396
Mays, 135
McAdams, 343
McAdde, 224
McAfee, 103
McAlister, 422
McAllen, 201

McAllister, 335
McAllon, 247, 248
McAlwee, 212
McAndrew, 408
McAninch, 320
McArthur, 102
McArty, 501
McAulay, 450
McAuley, 446
McBlair, 10, 52, 58, 259, 342, 533
McBrehesty, 394
McCabe, 222, 388, 397, 400, 449
McCabny, 184
McCaffery, 396
McCaffrey, 301
McCall, 409, 425, 454, 471, 509
McCalla, 47
McCallaster, 148
McCamant, 21
McCameron, 446
McCamm, 398
McCamphill, 452
McCandless, 356
McCann, 224, 399
McCardle, 116, 122
McCarter, 7
McCarthy, 366, 395, 447, 497, 559
McCartney, 510
McCarty, 196, 206, 447, 451, 517
McCaslin, 448
McCaudlin, 253
McCauley, 17, 47, 95, 184, 482, 510
McCauly, 221
McCayne, 527
McCeney, 102
McCenvill, 222
McChesney, 4
McClanahan, 134, 454
McClanighand, 510
McClannahan, 201
McClannon, 532
McClaren, 454
McClaskey, 527
McClean, 30, 118
McCleary, 56, 202, 336, 338, 494
McCleland, 455
McClellan, 73, 216, 246, 445, 497, 544
McClelland, 197, 461, 476, 495, 548
McClenahan, 349, 414
McClernand, 50
McClery, 536, 561
McClintic, 39
McClintock, 140
McCloskey, 442
McClosky, 168
McClue, 509
McCluney, 132, 311
McClung, 143, 164, 248
McClure, 457
McCluskey, 397
McClyman, 394
McColgan, 257, 515, 559
McColgin, 121, 128
McColgon, 251
McCollan, 345
McCollum, 223, 398, 489, 509
McComas, 197, 206
McComb, 68
McCombs, 510, 519
McConnel, 450, 490
McConnell, 108, 127, 135, 497, 509
McCook, 331
McCool, 140
McCorell, 448
McCorkle, 408
McCormack, 527
McCormick, 56, 221, 241, 332, 384, 393, 395, 425, 444, 450, 472, 525
McCoun, 280
McCowen, 456
McCoy, 50, 56, 197, 284, 372, 394, 443, 450, 508
McCrae, 74, 222
McCray, 133
McCrea, 48
McCready, 445
McCreery, 413
McCreight, 399
McCrory, 224
McCrury, 136

McCrystal, 221
McCue, 445, 507
McCullar, 139
McCullen, 224
McCulloch, 47, 170
McCullough, 50, 222, 252, 342, 544, 548
McCurdy, 139
McCutchan, 302
McCutcheon, 267, 377, 493
McDaniel, 384, 447
McDaniel's Resurvey, 282
McDaniels, 177, 501
McDerby, 221
McDermot, 244, 455, 566
McDermott, 75, 85, 163, 365, 395, 396, 414, 445, 453, 516, 517, 518
McDevitt, 56, 62, 93, 168, 281, 296, 314, 529
McDickens, 501
McDonald, 92, 106, 121, 137, 153, 173, 181, 220, 231, 248, 269, 298, 302, 396, 400, 408, 444, 447, 455, 509, 545, 568
McDonalds, 395
McDonnell, 133
McDonogh, 554
McDonough, 394, 396, 508
McDougall, 18
McDowall, 457
McDowell, 31, 50, 89, 117, 170, 247, 347, 419, 440, 460, 461
McDrymer, 508
McDuell, 303
McElfresh, 458
McElrie, 446
McElroy, 362, 445, 461
McElvain, 421, 538, 548
McElvaugh, 394
McEwen, 447, 555
McEwing, 465
McFadden, 510
McFadgen, 181
McFarlan, 99, 153
McFarland, 312, 452, 508, 509
McFarlane, 249, 253, 261, 277
McFarley, 62
McFarlin, 442
McFarne, 452
McFaul, 329
McFayden, 444
McFerran, 540
McGarlin, 443
McGarr, 418, 459
McGarry, 196, 542
McGartlin, 450
McGarvey, 138, 267, 300, 425, 560
McGawey, 518
McGawley, 163
McGee, 220, 397, 444, 507, 514
McGenley, 559
McGennis, 456
McGhee, 455
McGill, 122, 184, 384, 399, 449, 453, 494, 559
McGillicuddy, 387
McGinnis, 130, 200, 277, 543, 548
McGlone, 451
McGlue, 384
McGlynn, 442
McGowan, 9, 85, 112, 113, 221, 252, 367
McGowen, 456
McGown, 454
McGraff, 442
McGrash, 442
McGrath, 395
McGrattan, 527
McGregor, 10, 65, 485, 530
McGruder, 140, 526
McGuignan, 455
McGuire, 393, 394, 443, 445, 446, 447, 477, 516
McGurk, 418
Mchaffey, 407
McHarney, 396
McHenarie, 235
McHenry, 398, 426, 454, 457
McHerron, 460
McIlhany, 436

McIlvain, 277, 426
McIlvaine, 153
McIlver, 68
McIntire, 56, 296, 393, 407, 520
McIntosh, 26, 63, 67, 78, 141, 204, 218, 384, 425, 431, 439, 440, 463, 540, 547
McIntyre, 446, 450
McJilton, 186
McKany, 273
McKay, 154, 426, 442
McKean, 384
McKechine, 403
McKee, 127, 138, 142, 143, 144, 266, 283, 316, 393, 445, 449, 455, 460
McKeen, 398
McKelden, 560
McKenna, 312, 452
McKenney, 114, 203, 206, 274, 542
McKennon, 429
McKenny, 27
McKenzie, 277, 393, 495, 496, 497, 525
McKeon, 445
McKibben, 546
McKim, 153, 404
McKinley, 419
McKinne, 452
McKinney, 94, 134, 236, 393, 456
McKinsey, 454
McKinstry, 111
McKissick, 565
McKnight, 2, 10, 58, 137, 141, 184, 339, 498, 545
McKowen, 394
McKown, 196, 286
McKutcheons, 322
McLachlen, 461
McLain, 136, 554
McLane, 209, 220, 309, 342, 538, 566
Mclaughlin, 452
McLaughlin, 27, 49, 132, 135, 154, 162, 293, 326, 394, 500
McLaws, 109
McLean, 50, 99, 132, 135, 137, 185, 279, 310, 361, 390, 403
McLellan, 236, 494
McLeod, 162, 189, 486, 553, 564
McLoskey, 442
McLosky, 451
McLoughlin, 454, 455
McLoy, 450
McMahan, 222
McMahon, 443
McMann, 265
McManns, 514
McMichel, 136
McMillan, 337, 447
McMillen, 165, 431
McMillion, 200
McMilton, 137
McMordie, 203
McMullen, 117, 322
McMullin, 26, 188
McMurry, 507
McMurtrey, 510
McMurty, 136
McNabb, 335
McNair, 93, 214, 313
McNally, 395, 452
McNamara, 11
McNeal, 545
McNealy, 508
McNeil, 253, 310, 399, 444, 539, 545
McNeill, 262
McNeir, 294
McNelly, 396
McNemar, 115
McNevin, 478
McNiel, 112
McNorton, 92
McNulty, 126, 134, 452
McNutt, 106
McPahlin, 530
McPhail, 425, 441, 490
McPheeters, 172
McPherson, 45, 75, 81, 146, 194, 346, 368, 415, 426, 558, 559
McPike, 510
McQuay, 266, 267, 560
McRae, 8, 19, 95
McRee, 90, 119

McReynolds, 194, 208, 388, 400, 484, 487, 513, 514
McRoberts, 376
McSorley, 269
McTaviss, 317
McVean, 142, 296, 435
McVicker, 178
McWilliams, 145, 384
Meach, 473
Mead, 264, 433, 483
Meade, 96, 110, 162, 176, 198, 309, 371, 409, 482
Meadows, 328, 411
Meads, 548
Meaker, 371
Meandicks, 403
Meashrell, 93
Mebane, 487
Mechan, 360
Mechlin, 351, 429, 520
Meckling, 455
Meckum, 188
Medburg, 349
Medcalf, 454
Medill, 47
Medlin, 509
Meehan, 56
Meek, 138
Meeker, 443
Meem, 297
Meggs, 398
Mehaffy, 197, 338
Mehan, 135
Mehlhorn, 508
Meigle, 92
Meihle, 181
Meir, 445
Meister, 395
Melbourn, 420
Melch, 493
Meldron, 257
Mellen, 136
Melling, 188
Mellish, 222
Melton, 223
Melville, 42, 397
Melvin, 221, 374, 397, 446
Menchem, 494
Mendenhall, 448, 455
Meneely, 176
Mengs, 287
Mentz, 419
Mentzer, 163
Merans, 445
Mercer, 18, 47, 295, 322, 329, 384, 401, 500
Merchant, 92, 112, 227, 497
Meredith, 507, 527
Merelesh, 56
Meridian Hill, 75, 172
Merland, 93
Merle, 500
Merriall, 490
Merriam, 321
Merrick, 168, 173, 194, 207, 331, 396, 435, 437, 453
Merriett, 509
Merrifield, 141, 202, 277, 335, 338
Merrihew, 194, 485
Merriken, 119, 494
Merrill, 138, 297, 387, 439, 440, 521, 540, 547
Merritt, 10, 223
Merryfield, 194
Merryman, 384
Merton, 324
Meruende, 215
Mervin, 11
Mervine, 11, 376
Mesheral, 93
Mesmith, 559
Messenger, 136
Messersmith, 568
Messick, 320
Metamora, 306
Metayer, 20, 48, 79
Metcalf, 51, 240, 448, 457
Metcalfe, 413
Metherall, 145
Methodist Church, 12

Metoyer, 33, 84, 160
Metteregger, 401
Metz, 444
Mexican names, 315
Mexico, 1, 4, 7, 12, 16, 17, 27, 29, 34, 36, 44, 80, 87, 110, 112, 114, 117, 130, 131, 132, 144, 155, 162, 165, 168, 171, 175, 178, 182, 183, 192, 193, 214, 218, 228, 230, 235, 242, 244, 249, 250, 251, 256, 259, 261, 266, 268, 269, 270, 273, 289, 297, 301, 307, 314, 317, 333, 338, 339, 352, 360, 387, 389, 397, 401, 402, 408, 411, 412, 413, 421, 423, 433, 441, 442, 451, 453, 454, 457, 459, 460, 462, 463, 476, 483, 484, 487, 488, 492, 494, 496, 497, 498, 511, 521, 528, 544, 546, 547, 548, 549, 550, 554, 555, 563, 564, 568
Meyer, 397, 399, 454, 455, 508
Meyers, 445, 483
Meyn, 393
Micar, 395
Michan, 444
Mickle, 29, 419, 420
Mickum, 520, 560
Middleton, 10, 100, 103, 211, 225, 231, 267, 274, 291, 293, 348, 517, 518, 559
Mifflin, 68
Migginbotham, 137
Milam, 568
Milbright, 448
Milburn, 30, 77, 226, 384, 455, 471, 553
Miles, 79, 108, 109, 110, 264, 300, 337, 443, 452, 460, 461, 482, 522
Miley, 364
Mill Seat, 438
Millard, 303, 384, 451
Millburn, 223
Milledge, 20
Miller, 5, 7, 29, 35, 37, 52, 56, 73, 74, 76, 80, 92, 108, 110, 113, 121, 134, 137, 138, 140, 166, 168, 177, 181, 184, 199, 202, 221, 222, 224, 225, 226, 230, 235, 252, 253, 261, 266, 267, 269, 286, 298, 317, 324, 337, 339, 340, 347, 359, 370, 377, 384, 394, 395, 398, 408, 435, 439, 441, 445, 447, 452, 454, 455, 476, 486, 488, 497, 508, 509, 510, 515, 527, 545, 556, 562
Milles, 106
Millet, 399
Millett, 79, 461
Milligan, 12, 171, 337, 410
Millington, 454
Millis, 151
Mills, 21, 83, 92, 128, 184, 187, 196, 201, 205, 220, 298, 299, 303, 307, 325, 387, 393, 396, 398, 403, 412, 428, 460, 487, 489, 507, 509, 542, 543, 547, 553, 558
Milroy, 354
Milstead, 101, 384
Milton, 494
Minal, 442
Miner, 376
Minge, 395
Minix, 229
Minnick, 6
Minnitree, 421
Minnix, 553
Minon, 169
Minor, 30, 107, 240, 309, 356, 366, 376, 472, 490, 539
Minton, 112, 139
Minur, 394
Mioton, 35, 113, 253
Miott, 398
Mirick, 46
Miron, 431
Missil, 447
Misso, 395
Missroon, 240
Mitchell, 42, 81, 82, 99, 122, 142, 144, 180, 269, 340, 341, 343, 344, 346, 357, 403, 415, 418, 467, 477, 506, 519, 523, 525, 550, 556
Mitterigger, 551
Mix, 83, 131, 160, 304, 384

Mizner, 290
Moberg, 349
Mocht, 445
Mockabee, 224
Mocomber, 409
Moenster, 101
Moffal, 408
Moffat, 398, 464
Moffatt, 389
Moffett, 133
Moffitt, 19, 139
Mogg, 500
Mohan, 453
Mohler, 56
Mohttohon, 349
Mohun, 101, 147, 266, 368, 375
Moil, 221
Molen, 426
Molumby, 395
Momeney, 454
Monaghyn, 450
Monague, 441
Monday, 508, 510
Mondheiner, 476
Monell, 396
Monks, 395
Monroe, 90, 119, 222, 224, 331, 345, 368, 481, 532
Montage, 136
Montagne, 537
Montague, 296, 503
Monterde, 496
Monterdeoca, 152
Montford, 34
Montgomery, 9, 71, 109, 112, 113, 136, 139, 140, 173, 217, 247, 249, 252, 290, 302, 377, 407, 426, 439, 440, 444, 446, 450, 452, 453, 455, 456, 489, 497, 502
Montillon, 476
Montilly, 401
Montoya, 165, 171
Mony, 397
Monypenny, 453
Moody, 277, 398, 411, 445, 453
Mooklar, 277
Moon, 196, 201, 273, 431, 446, 543, 548
Mooney, 252, 399, 447, 450
Moor, 486
Moore, 7, 14, 37, 42, 56, 64, 69, 84, 96, 126, 132, 134, 163, 168, 175, 193, 194, 197, 205, 218, 246, 250, 267, 277, 302, 316, 330, 331, 334, 336, 337, 394, 396, 397, 431, 436, 442, 444, 446, 472, 475, 500, 504, 506, 513, 535, 540, 550, 553
Moorefield, 115
Moorehead, 399
Moorhead, 19, 124, 226, 258, 267, 298, 305
Moorman, 432
Moragne, 514
Moralle, 484
Moran, 92, 93, 121, 125, 329, 400, 429, 436, 452, 515, 516, 536, 557
Moraski, 451
Morders, 25
More, 59
Moreau, 402, 457
Morehead, 303, 359, 516
Morehouse, 280
Moreland, 143
Morelia, 128
Morely, 445
Moren, 11
Moreno, 209
Moreton, 394
Morey, 457
Morfit, 124, 145, 488
Morgan, 40, 56, 58, 88, 98, 106, 119, 127, 129, 133, 140, 171, 178, 185, 191, 196, 197, 201, 205, 230, 237, 245, 258, 298, 299, 318, 325, 361, 373, 376, 387, 397, 398, 409, 410, 418, 425, 433, 446, 455, 468, 471, 473, 484, 487, 513, 542, 561
Moriarty, 214, 527
Morin, 349
Morinar, 448

Morison, 529
Morland, 437
Morley, 425
Mormon Temple, 278
Morrel, 448
Morris, 4, 16, 25, 32, 68, 94, 109, 111, 134, 135, 139, 153, 184, 223, 234, 236, 258, 268, 318, 331, 359, 363, 394, 404, 418, 434, 437, 442, 446, 448, 466, 490, 500, 525, 528, 541, 547, 567
Morrison, 17, 59, 78, 84, 170, 200, 252, 452, 456, 480, 508, 540, 541, 546, 557
Morriss, 493
Morrow, 195, 384, 497, 501, 507, 515, 535, 544, 568
Morse, 10, 46, 127, 224, 280, 320, 530, 555
Morsell, 81, 164, 193, 279, 307, 433, 516, 525, 559
Morstadt, 461
Mortier, 528
Mortimer, 56, 71, 93, 120
Morton, 79, 253, 262, 328, 384, 408, 411, 414, 415, 418, 449, 451, 479, 501
Morwood, 454
Mose, 494
Moseley, 68, 248, 348, 458
Mosely, 240, 276
Moses, 35, 111, 148, 163
Moshers, 451
Mosier, 127
Moss, 152, 277, 278
Mossop, 15
Mott, 197, 483, 523
Motter, 526
Motz, 197, 334
Moulder, 27
Moulon, 8, 45, 59
Mount, 189
Mount Hebron, 563
Mount Pleasant, 263
Mount Repose, 45
Mount Savage, 438
Mount Savage Iron Works, 340
Mount Vernon, 68, 183, 229, 350
Mount View, 340
Mount Willow, 75
Mountain Run, 411
Mountaineer, 9
Mountz, 552
Mower, 544
Mowett, 292
Mowry, 224
Moxley, 90
Moye, 304
Moyer, 455
Mozier, 509
Mt Ararat, 281
Mudd, 56, 99, 259, 336, 433
Muddy Branch, 281
Muhlemberg, 9
Muhlenberg, 113, 249, 250
Muilleur, 449
Muir, 224, 399, 446, 502
Muldoon, 454
Mullany, 327
Mulledy, 6
Mullen, 11, 364, 394, 509, 557
Muller, 56, 92, 455
Mullett, 280
Mulliken, 555
Mullikin, 93, 278, 428, 430
Mullin, 118, 367
Mullins, 510
Mullowny, 23
Mulvaney, 339, 545
Mulvany, 137
Mumford, 434
Muncaster, 63
Mundeig, 443
Muney, 523
Munneman, 442
Munro, 311, 349, 401, 406
Munroe, 49, 110, 142, 153, 170, 457
Munsch, 222
Munsen, 399
Munson, 398
Murdaugh, 345, 401
Murdoch, 153

Murdock, 371, 521, 554
Mure, 426, 457
Murken, 398
Murmert, 136
Murphy, 5, 92, 140, 166, 177, 184, 223, 239, 243, 266, 346, 384, 394, 399, 442, 443, 450, 452, 453, 460, 467, 486, 506, 509, 523
Murpy, 163
Murray, 40, 83, 87, 131, 166, 201, 211, 239, 371, 393, 407, 418, 429, 440, 484, 496, 498, 512, 540, 559
Murrill, 510
Murry, 223, 451, 494
Mury, 198
Muse, 56
Musgrave, 480
Musick, 71
Mustard, 507
Mustin, 163
Myerlee, 80, 565
Myers, 95, 108, 221, 247, 249, 399, 429, 450, 451, 452, 455, 460, 494, 507, 509

N

Naglee, 398, 419, 490
Nailor, 11, 90, 92, 93, 121, 231, 254, 391, 430, 515, 553
Nairn, 558
Nalle, 309, 432
Nally, 176
Nance, 545
Nano, 155
Naper, 252, 548
Naphew, 179
Napier, 122, 139, 544
Napoleon, 287, 290, 297, 434
Narbonne, 457
Narden, 469
Narris, 457
Nash, 242, 384, 452
Nat'l Monument, 238
Nation, 533
Nauman, 441
Navy, 452
Nayence, 476
Naylor, 58, 65, 115, 177, 191, 293, 301, 347, 374, 384, 394, 438, 564
Neal, 181, 267, 295, 307
Neale, 92, 266, 316, 373, 384, 385, 424, 550
Needles, 566
Neeley, 507
Neely, 134, 361
Neeper, 211
Neff, 339, 455, 544
Neighbors, 431
Neil, 478
Neill, 151, 181, 246, 336, 434, 461, 471, 482, 540
Neilson, 363
Neish, 442
Nelligan, 297
Nelson, 6, 26, 52, 68, 96, 138, 211, 223, 268, 279, 399, 510
Nesbit, 156
Nescott, 475
Neshitt, 449
Neuman, 223
Nevins, 196, 394
New Design, 281
Newbould, 493
Newbury, 426
Newby, 234
Newcomb, 84, 119, 158
Newcomer, 245
Newell, 33, 39, 84, 159, 507
Newer, 460
Newgent, 521
Newham, 484
Newhouse, 395, 451
Newland, 323
Newlin, 357
Newman, 4, 134, 135, 156, 195, 223, 328, 389, 397, 399, 456, 495, 513, 514
Newmann, 409
Newton, 13, 92, 117, 161, 331, 480, 510, 532, 555, 566
Niagara Suspension Bridge, 491
Nichol, 502, 523

Nicholas, 110, 198
Nicholl, 4
Nicholls, 248, 249, 276, 565
Nichols, 56, 74, 200, 206, 227, 308, 357, 393, 432, 443, 533
Nicholson, 42, 47, 48, 71, 117, 120, 140, 181, 376, 384, 391, 430
Nickerson, 448, 522
Nicolson, 17, 88, 94
Niece, 509
Niehan, 395
Niel, 324
Niles, 204, 234, 359, 475, 501
Nipp, 92
Nisbet, 153
Nisse, 409
Nixon, 179
No Gain, 142
Noah, 524
Noble, 23, 63, 67, 106, 225, 226, 246, 303, 393, 428, 452, 507
Noe, 130, 203, 336, 338
Noerr, 92, 560
Nokes, 92
Nolan, 456, 460, 554
Noland, 92, 93, 94
Noles, 277
Nolland, 136
Nonega, 496
Nones, 132, 499
Noon, 450
Nopetsch, 500
Nopps, 372
Norbeck, 56, 429, 556
Norison, 224
Normandie, 309
Norment, 194, 338, 543
Norris, 66, 155, 258, 384, 418, 438, 501, 559
North, 241, 309, 364, 404
North Carolina, 391
Northerman, 151
Northern Market, 23
Northrup, 21, 398
Northup, 21, 128
Norton, 227, 398, 505
Norval, 273
Norvell, 24, 95, 203, 205, 277
Norwood, 140, 392, 492, 508
Nothing Left, 438
Nottage, 395
Notter, 431
Nottingham, 215
Nourse, 28, 56, 63, 67, 301, 302, 384, 427, 488, 515
Nowlen, 278
Nowoting, 396
Noyce, 453
Noyes, 123, 384, 538
Nugent, 56, 92
Nunez, 209
Nunn, 304, 312
Nurse, 179
Nutall, 505
Nutman, 279
Nutwell, 27
Nye, 14, 82, 538

O

O'Blennis, 7
O'Brien, 5, 14, 35, 38, 111, 121, 126, 128, 133, 169, 191, 226, 331, 360, 394, 395, 425, 444, 445, 452, 561
O'Brine, 445
O'Bryon, 421
O'Connell, 271, 280, 311, 364, 395, 423, 451
O'Conner, 461
O'Donnell, 46, 97, 252, 451, 556
O'Donoghue, 92, 226, 316
O'Hara, 252, 398, 459, 476, 507
O'Hare, 559
O'Harrs, 224
O'Leary, 559
O'Loghlin, 451
O'Means, 477
O'Neal, 366
O'Neale, 227, 385, 399
O'Neall, 214
O'Neil, 33, 394, 446, 450

O'Neill, 84, 157, 221
O'Rourke, 443
O'Shaugnessy, 450
O'Shea, 394
O'Sheets, 245
O'Sullivan, 546
Oak, 139
Oak Grove, 318
Oak Hill, 435
Oak Lodge, 274
Oaken, 538
Oakes, 426, 490
Oakland, 7
Oakley, 403, 467, 505
Oathouse, 460
Oats, 450
Obando, 209
Ober, 56, 226, 523, 559
Octker, 460
Odell, 269, 360
Odom, 456
Oestrich, 452
Officer, 177
Offley, 34
Offutt, 4, 243, 416
Ogden, 132
Ogg, 221
Ogle, 448
Ogrton, 403
Okill, 363
Oldham, 16
Olds, 304
Olen, 269
Oler, 384
Olinger, 535
Oliver, 50, 71, 185, 269, 397
Olmstead, 363
Olneys, 456
Olombel, 457
Olsted, 222
Onate, 152
Only, 455
Opossum Nose, 465, 530
Orchard, 138
Orden, 399
Oriduet, 493
Orme, 3, 256, 298, 384, 559
Ormsby, 218
Orndorff, 97
Orr, 56, 455, 463
Ortis, 171
Ortiz, 116
Ortobus, 131
Osborn, 127, 137, 146, 213
Osborne, 329, 538
Osbourne, 447
Osginson, 403
Osgodby, 47
Osgood, 68, 453
Otey, 204, 462
Othman, 394
Otterback, 56, 266, 267, 290, 298, 519, 530
Otterson, 199
Oudinot, 423, 434
Ouijano, 152
Ould, 20, 60, 274, 325
Oullip, 394
Oury, 26
Ousley, 149
Overbagh, 475
Overcrombie, 376
Overly, 451
Overmire, 510
Owen, 29, 50, 75, 172, 187, 203, 206, 219, 521
Owens, 34, 92, 138, 163, 192, 341, 349, 378, 394, 442, 507
Owings, 34, 90, 438
Owner, 56, 524, 560
Owsley, 379
Oyster, 56, 564

P

Pack, 339
Packard, 98, 385
packet ship **Auburn**, 415
packet ship **Prince Albert**, 126
packet-ship **Baltimore**, 403
packet-ship **Cambridge**, 403

packet-ship **Isaac Wright**, 524
packet-ship **Liverpool**, 178
packet-ship **Mary Ann**, 525
Padgett, 475, 519
Page, 35, 92, 109, 181, 186, 200, 247, 303, 394, 396, 397, 404, 439, 465, 542, 543
Pageland, 89
Pageot, 164, 191
Paige, 280
Pain, 29
Paine, 34, 184, 261, 266, 350
Pairo, 22, 321, 464
Paixhan, 132
Pakenham, 156
Palen, 27, 28, 86, 101
Palm, 211
Palmedo, 482
Palmer, 87, 93, 163, 195, 207, 340, 372, 388, 397, 410, 431, 437, 438, 451, 455, 457, 484, 502, 538, 541, 546, 549, 552
Palmieri, 406
Palmoter, 450
Palner, 441
Pancoast, 557
Papiner, 445
Papst, 449
Paramore, 562
Pardon, 444
Parin, 261
Paris, 58, 526
Parish, 448
Park, 139, 512
Parke, 554, 557
Parker, 9, 16, 58, 81, 83, 92, 102, 103, 140, 141, 146, 190, 216, 224, 244, 248, 249, 253, 261, 262, 263, 267, 268, 274, 280, 311, 346, 356, 368, 385, 405, 418, 440, 444, 450, 456, 457, 461, 464, 478, 509, 518, 525, 549, 555, 559
Parkes, 11
Parkins, 177
Parks, 5, 254, 396
Parmentier, 397
Parr, 127, 134, 137, 400
Parris, 163, 216, 378
Parrish, 43
Parrott, 310
Parrow, 397
Parshall, 545, 546, 549
Parson, 17
Parsons, 23, 102, 225, 232, 270, 277, 418, 503, 559
Part of Carpenter's Square, 343
Part of Green Spring, 343
Part of St Matthew, 343
Part of the Brothers, 438
Partridge, 390
Pascoe, 19, 103
Passor, 442
Passover, 360
Pasteur, 50
Pate, 136
Patrick, 17, 35, 111, 248, 249, 402, 454, 540
Patten, 146, 211, 336, 349, 359, 407, 539
Patterson, 9, 47, 48, 138, 146, 181, 211, 229, 233, 298, 316, 335, 451, 455, 494, 507, 519, 558, 560
Patton, 71, 136, 157, 197, 199, 216, 235, 385, 394, 403, 479, 535
Pattridge, 111
Paul, 257, 426, 435, 443, 447
Paulding, 141, 391
Pawling, 302
Paxon, 245
Paxton, 57
Pay, 397
Payan, 455
Payne, 45, 77, 78, 85, 299, 403, 425, 430, 471, 488, 553, 558, 560
Peabody, 149, 255
Peach Island, 288
Peachy, 156, 176, 430
Peacock, 350, 501
Peale, 52, 61
Pearce, 132, 187, 209, 219, 429

Pearson, 21, 35, 223, 264, 371, 385, 419, 439, 441
Pease, 134, 365
Peat, 454
Pebo, 278
Peboys, 503
Peck, 13, 57, 58, 107, 232, 311, 385, 450, 451, 490, 517, 549
Peddicord, 294
Peel, 225, 456, 486
Peerce, 121, 231, 238, 559
Pegg, 520, 522
Peirce, 57, 525, 558, 559
Peixoto, 268
Pelham, 140, 190, 365
Pell, 385
Peltzer, 505
Pemberton, 110, 197, 207, 208, 304, 427, 456, 497
Pena, 128, 152
Pender, 112, 113, 252, 549
Pendergast, 316
Pendergrast, 160
Pendleton, 45, 117, 536
Penfold, 426
Penn, 123, 183, 245, 253, 262, 293, 337, 338, 343, 440
Pennefather, 423
Pennington, 5, 127, 137, 177
Pennock, 504
Pennoyer, 58, 66, 68, 84, 160
Pennybacker, 16, 31
Penrod, 501
Penrose, 513, 528
Penser, 135
Penter, 140
Pentz, 117
Peoples, 397
Peples, 394
Pepper, 57, 180, 298, 517, 518
Percival, 399
Peret, 476
Perez, 442, 496
Perin, 543
Perkett, 499
Perkins, 14, 184, 185, 200, 201, 208, 231, 394, 398, 451, 542, 547
Perpignan, 457
Perrie, 468
Perrin, 199, 395
Perro, 499
Perrod, 221
Perrry, 217
Perry, 47, 61, 77, 95, 108, 132, 139, 154, 165, 179, 202, 207, 216, 232, 235, 244, 250, 253, 261, 273, 308, 319, 329, 331, 346, 387, 389, 395, 396, 398, 424, 426, 449, 466, 523, 533, 549, 556
Pervis, 507
Peschler, 476
Pestorias, 93
Peter, 50, 385, 393
Peter's Patrimony, 438
Peternell, 202, 388, 398, 542
Peters, 39, 168, 189, 221, 241, 367, 392, 409, 420, 423, 431, 507, 559
Peterson, 57, 190, 226
Petigru, 162, 194
Petra, 501
Petriken, 101
Pettibone, 92, 115, 430, 519, 537, 556
Petticord, 174
Pettigrew, 11
Pettis, 332
Pettit, 92, 319
Petty, 70
Peverley, 510
Peyrouse, 122
Peyton, 12, 66, 188, 209, 337, 397, 549, 567
Pharr, 506
Pharris, 453
Phelan, 184
Phelps, 46, 78, 95, 96, 296, 391, 451, 458, 549, 554
Philand, 453
Philippe, 356, 478
Philips, 134, 135, 519

Phillips, 11, 57, 81, 141, 181, 188, 236, 238, 257, 269, 376, 385, 397, 399, 404, 405, 421, 482, 493, 494, 525, 551
Phipps, 140
Phister, 277
Phosoix, 455
Pickell, 283
Picken, 449
Picket, 312
Pickett, 33, 60, 84, 127, 136, 247, 277, 447, 449, 490, 497, 544, 550
Pickrell, 385
Picot, 482
Pierce, 20, 60, 70, 85, 96, 110, 122, 141, 191, 195, 245, 274, 326, 360, 390, 397, 414, 436, 449, 453, 487, 498, 509, 514, 516, 541
Piercey, 304, 306
Piercy, 304, 395
Piermont, 450
Pierpont, 174, 312
Pierson, 396, 403, 419, 449, 484, 501
Pigeon, 193
Pike, 79, 85, 148, 169, 170, 185, 186, 190, 453, 507
Pile, 193
Pilgrim, 451
Pilgrim Rock, 521
Pilgrims, 183
Pilling, 385, 559
Pillow, 152, 157, 209, 223, 232, 233, 247, 249, 251, 352, 397, 439, 441, 453, 483, 496, 497
Pillows, 211
Pillson, 568
Pilsbury, 503
Pinckney, 132, 415
Pingolt, 399
Pink, 446
Pinkerton, 393
Pinkney, 94, 97, 331, 376, 427
Pinney, 554
Pino, 116
Pinson, 209, 470
Piolet, 286
Pioletti, 278
Piollet, 335
Piper, 47, 126, 450, 509
Pischer, 429
Pise, 316, 459
Pistole, 23, 63, 67, 78, 534
Pitcher, 196, 206, 542, 544
Pitkin, 550
Pitman, 195, 206, 541, 542
Pitson, 135
Pitt, 426
Pittibone, 92
Pittman, 11, 298
Pitts, 27, 295, 507
Place, 49, 415, 445
Plains, 282
Plant, 56, 69, 359, 362, 428, 442, 477, 516
Planta Place, 6
Plantagenet, 469
Plater, 191, 468, 476
Platt, 100, 426, 524
Pleasanton, 109, 551
Pleasants, 57, 80, 97, 313
Plitt, 463
Plowden, 208
Plowman, 429
Plumbe, 75
Plumer, 487
Plummer, 531
Plumsell, 163, 333
Plumsill, 253, 371
Plunket, 224, 269
Plunkitt, 358
Plympton, 337, 541
Plymton, 211
Pocahontas, 183
Pochelton, 371
Pohl, 493
Pohlman, 531
Poindexter, 370
Point Look Out, 438
Point Pleasant, 38
Pointer, 220, 451
Pole, 442

Poletti, 123
Polk, 1, 187, 219, 241, 254, 276, 289, 316, 333, 348, 393, 457, 520, 543
Pollard, 304, 312, 385, 439
Pollock, 222, 357, 399, 472, 502, 520
Polly, 510
Polock, 456
Pomeroy, 140
Pomery, 96
Pond, 532
Pons, 433
Ponse, 562
Pool, 117, 269
Poole, 418, 457, 493, 501
Pooler, 447
Pooley, 408
Poore, 314, 403
Pop, 507
Pope, 110, 170, 232, 278, 358, 422, 477
Pope Gregory XVI, 51
<u>Pope's Nuncio</u>, 306
Popham, 412, 417, 527
Poplin, 140
Porffitt, 379
Porter, 46, 107, 127, 140, 172, 180, 181, 190, 241, 248, 298, 299, 317, 320, 334, 336, 338, 379, 390, 391, 394, 412, 448, 472, 484, 490, 527, 533, 551
Porterfield, 58, 64
Porthouse, 443
Portillo, 215
Portsmouth, 489
Poruton, 451
Posey, 134, 344, 398, 501
Posmantler, 457
Poss, 508
Post, 339
Postell, 398
Postlethwaite, 387
Postley, 196, 207
Poston, 92, 480
Potter, 30, 42, 80, 118, 388, 399, 484, 513, 514, 541, 553, 558
Potts, 46, 126, 137, 170, 438, 544
Powel, 188, 545
Powell, 11, 50, 57, 87, 96, 252, 266, 431, 509, 523, 553
Power, 310, 311, 436
Powers, 30, 196, 385, 512
Poydras, 368
Poynor, 276
Pozey, 126
Prady, 457
Prath, 397
Prather, 37, 42, 51, 57, 92, 174, 225, 226, 385, 433, 466
Pratt, 98, 133, 280, 330, 397, 398, 404, 501, 509, 561
Pratte, 457
Preece, 493
Prehu, 457
Preifer, 460
Prelaz, 482
Prentice, 442
Prentiss, 23, 40, 43, 44, 67, 79, 374
Prents, 501
Prescott, 224, 355
Presgraves, 156
Preston, 2, 17, 87, 89, 92, 117, 134, 187, 219, 221, 267, 331, 413
Prettyman, 119, 291
Prevost, 288
Prewit, 165
Price, 11, 21, 35, 66, 85, 87, 113, 127, 135, 137, 165, 171, 182, 200, 223, 252, 253, 333, 337, 338, 345, 374, 399, 443, 461, 465, 508, 523
Prigg, 60
Prim, 277
Primeau, 66, 75, 85, 158
Prince, 130, 440, 484, 490, 540, 543, 546
Prince Albert, 367
Prince de Polignac, 235
Prince Louis, 51
Prince:, 200
<u>PRINTING PRESS</u>, 498
Pritchard, 12, 316, 413, 452, 474, 510, 523
Pritchartt, 303

Pritchett's Purchase, 533
Prive, 112
Prize Money, 180
Procter, 36, 348
Proctor, 507
Pronoz, 128
propellar **Delaware**, 520
propellar **James Cage**, 73
propeller **Independence**, 272
Prosser, 502
Proud, 97, 476
Prout, 81, 385, 479, 534
Prouty, 272
Provest, 430
Providence Enlarged, 282
Provon, 523
Provost, 555, 560
Puckett, 134
Puffer, 133
Pugh, 14, 448
Pulizze, 92
Pulizzi, 555
Pullim, 138
Pullinger, 398
Pumphrey, 57, 163, 184, 225, 226, 385, 428, 517, 518, 534, 559
Pumroyer, 447
Purcell, 139, 433, 557
Purdom, 288
Purdy, 105, 180, 226, 259, 264, 366, 473, 518
Purkis, 20, 63, 67
Purkitt, 237
Purnell, 27, 510
Purse, 399
Pursell, 57, 122, 267, 517, 550, 556
Pursivall, 245
Purviance, 86
Putman, 394
Putnam, 17
Pyne, 9, 188, 501, 504, 527, 564
Pywell, 226

Q

Quackenboss, 558
Quackenbush, 411, 504
Qualls, 445
Quarels, 397
Quarles, 202, 207, 387, 487, 542, 547, 567
Quarrier, 265
Queen, 44, 133, 137, 259, 298, 333, 340, 341, 376, 385, 477, 519
Queen Dowager, 367
Queen Hortense, 427
Queen Victoria, 406
Quenaudon, 299
Quesenbury, 190
Quevillion, 254
Quick, 443, 451, 509
Quigley, 167, 558
Quijano, 390
Quik, 457
Quill, 222
Quin, 444, 452
Quinby, 107
Quincy, 323
Quinn, 27, 61, 135, 278, 337, 338, 395, 396, 398, 455, 508, 527
Quirk, 93
Quisenberry, 349, 414
Quitman, 7, 157, 247, 249, 251, 390, 399, 441, 442, 454, 483, 498, 513, 563

R

Rabb, 398
Rabor, 494
Raborg, 483
Raboteau, 483
Raby, 448
Radcliff, 11, 27, 104, 163, 180, 371, 391, 449
Radcliffe, 508
Radd, 222
Radford, 366
Radzimiski, 194
Rafferty, 446
Rager, 449
Ragg, 417
Ragland, 136

Ragnet, 334
Raguet, 338
Raidy, 226
Raigenacher, 493
Railey, 554
Raily, 555
Rain, 454
Raines, 409
Rains, 108, 233
Rainy, 136
Rake, 508
Raleigh, 299, 405
Raleo, 135
Raley, 385, 560
Ralston, 252
Ramage, 179
Ramer, 179
Ramey, 33, 84, 140
Ramsay, 94, 457, 513, 536
Ramsey, 21, 33, 98, 136, 178, 197, 203, 205, 230, 334, 336, 442, 545, 549
Rancliffe, 235
Randal, 184, 385
Randall, 57, 149, 166, 198, 248, 335, 338, 409, 429, 450, 502, 504, 515, 543, 559
Randebaugh, 139
Randle, 253
Randolph, 90, 96, 128, 134, 161, 181, 186, 220, 243, 311, 358, 379, 397, 399, 405, 567, 568
Raney, 221
Rankin, 86, 456, 482, 493
Ranneberg, 136
Ransch, 449
Ransom, 16, 194, 439, 441, 496, 541, 547
Ranson, 70, 129, 178, 205, 230
Rapalie, 401
Raper, 125
Rapp, 344, 348, 395, 455
Rariden, 134
Ratcliff, 121, 236, 255
Ratcliffe, 33, 222, 397
Rathbone, 71, 399
Rautter, 494
Ravanel, 337, 545, 548
Ravel, 44
Ravenal, 457
Rawlings, 57, 92, 243, 263, 267, 340, 385, 438, 552
Rawlins, 137
Ray, 25, 140, 393, 440, 452, 467
Raymond, 31, 79, 371, 451, 527, 537
Raynor, 88
razee **Independence**, 489
Razor Tract, 288
Read, 14, 95, 181, 226, 268, 395, 426, 434, 467, 566
Reader, 140
Reading, 446
Reads, 342
Ready, 559
Reardon, 279
Reber, 396
Recruiting Service, 13
Recruiting Sgts, 81
Rector, 354, 355
Redd, 477
Redder, 127
Reddick, 437
Redding, 454
Reddish, 140
Reddy, 163
Redfern, 49, 57, 226, 244, 559
Redfield, 414
Redin, 145, 209, 226, 231, 245, 462
Redman, 139, 394
Redmond, 409
Redpath, 502
Reed, 17, 29, 62, 92, 140, 222, 234, 330, 357, 395, 398, 436, 450, 451, 454, 465, 483, 494, 508, 535, 537, 559
Reeder, 14, 92
Reeks, 535
Reese, 6, 119, 199, 227, 249, 329, 335, 341, 357, 440, 464, 472, 495, 511, 543, 552, 553, 561
Reeve, 490
Reeves, 11, 277, 430

Regan, 477
registry of births, 332
Reid, 270, 277, 441, 445, 478, 496
Reidel, 193
Reilly, 393, 399, 443, 460, 519, 563
Reily, 267, 345
Reim, 394
Reinhart, 451
Reip, 181
Reis, 394
Rekow, 135
Rema, 181
Remes, 365
Remington, 394
Renburger, 493
Renehan, 43, 70
Rennard, 16
Rennison, 221
Reno, 106, 441
Renshaw, 5, 94, 240, 566
Rentor, 447
Renwick, 187, 219, 270
Repaid, 507
Rermante, 215
Res, 403, 449
Reshen, 493
Resin, 226
Resurvey on Clewerwall, 402
Resurvey on Enterprise, 438
Resurvey on Hoffman's Delight, 438
Resurvey on Mount Pleasant, 438
Retter, 185
Reubens, 287
Reveille, 507
revenue cutter **Hamilton**, 128
Revere, 11, 210, 240, 242
Revidon, 395
Reville, 134
Rex, 505
Rey, 162
Reyle, 431
Reymansmyder, 456
Reynolds, 16, 32, 33, 45, 84, 95, 107, 111, 112, 114, 139, 169, 218, 235, 253, 261, 334, 364, 395, 399, 401, 403, 419, 434, 444, 449, 469
Reys, 325
Rham, 139
Rhea, 108, 114
Rhett, 246, 471
Rhey, 543
Rhinehart, 25
Rhoads, 202, 334, 338
Rhode, 460
Rhodes, 6, 45, 57, 59, 85, 92, 235, 266, 267, 397, 455, 467, 519, 555
Rhudy, 509
Riara, 457
Riber, 446
Ricard, 295
Rice, 20, 92, 191, 199, 207, 223, 284, 394, 425, 431, 455, 482, 497, 499
Rich, 145, 214, 501, 508
Richard, 81, 493
Richards, 93, 207, 279, 287, 292, 318, 320, 334, 338, 372, 378, 385, 474, 494, 531, 555
Richardson, 12, 35, 57, 114, 135, 137, 143, 154, 226, 306, 385, 418, 451, 454, 483, 494
Riche, 121
Riches, 272
Richette, 494
Richey, 47, 87, 114, 183
Richie, 31
Richley, 72
Richmond, 397
Rickets, 276, 434, 478
Ricketts, 14, 39, 57, 131, 136, 357, 503
Riddall, 57
Riddle, 218, 532
Ridge, 160
Ridgeley, 164, 476, 508
Ridgely, 12, 21, 41, 43, 52, 108, 331, 462
Ridgeway, 439, 464, 466
Ridgley, 191, 342
Ridgway, 233, 371, 385, 429
Ridley, 173

Rielly, 399
Rifling, 426
Rigault, 4
Rigden, 559
Riggles, 43, 141
Riggs, 23, 58, 97, 129, 160, 245, 330, 527
Riker, 138
Rikin, 450
Riley, 11, 83, 136, 222, 226, 269, 315, 360, 362, 394, 396, 445, 460, 478, 514, 519, 528, 556, 560, 563
Rilliet, 483
Rincon, 484
Riner, 394
Ring, 450
Ringgold, 38, 106, 132, 335, 353, 385, 418
Rinhart, 452
Rinick, 431
Rining, 225, 226
Riordan, 57, 394
Rios, 152
Ripley, 6, 50, 107, 200, 303, 334, 336, 393, 507
Rist, 455
Ritchie, 44, 46, 48, 50, 70, 74, 129, 198, 296, 400, 465, 556
Ritner, 394
Rittenhouse, 181, 226, 267, 372, 429
Rittentein, 508
Ritter, 57, 60, 400
Rived, 57
Rives, 11, 47, 57, 81, 274, 298, 336, 482, 515
Rixster, 438
Roach, 62, 87, 141, 171, 240, 260, 270, 281, 301, 351, 353, 409, 455, 506
Roane, 12, 92, 170, 190, 253, 262
Robb, 153
Robbins, 135, 385, 398
Robering, 449
Roberson, 224
Robert, 14, 171, 244, 536, 559
Roberts, 14, 57, 58, 79, 87, 106, 220, 233, 261, 355, 357, 397, 412, 440, 451, 482, 484, 499, 510, 527, 530, 543, 545, 548, 550
Robertson, 57, 87, 129, 174, 193, 254, 288, 302, 385, 395, 399, 422, 429, 441, 456, 488, 508, 512, 552
Robeson, 568
Robey, 93, 103, 267
Robins, 135, 136, 455
Robinson, 5, 32, 49, 57, 80, 134, 136, 137, 140, 161, 168, 170, 171, 193, 215, 218, 221, 222, 245, 277, 281, 288, 337, 342, 343, 356, 370, 372, 385, 396, 405, 413, 416, 427, 430, 441, 446, 451, 468, 493, 507, 508, 509, 510, 520, 521, 527, 530, 536, 561, 566, 568
Robles, 152
Robosson, 17
Roby, 284, 332, 411, 518, 556
Rocha, 152
Rochambeau, 66
Rochat, 11, 57, 138, 559
Roche, 15, 160, 282
Rochelle, 415
Rochester, 44
Rochford, 315, 444
Rock, 68
Rockendorff, 376
Rockwell, 93, 529
Rockwood, 505
Rocky Hollow, 438
Roddy, 343
Roder, 523
Rodes, 398
Rodgers, 25, 156, 244, 296, 441, 455, 456, 497, 514, 540, 548
Rodier, 296
Rodman, 106, 161, 173, 302, 566
Rodney, 342, 394, 399
Rodrigues, 457
Rodwald, 403
Roe, 135, 223, 473
Roemer, 409

Rogers, 11, 106, 140, 142, 144, 149, 268, 269, 277, 307, 330, 332, 360, 393, 398, 414, 415, 431, 443, 457, 459, 483, 496, 502, 509
Rohanon, 223
Rohr, 349
Rohrdoeff, 500
Rohshuber, 349
Roland, 107, 110, 224, 446
Rolland, 185
Rollins, 127
Roman, 252
Rome, 358
Romedy, 399
Romes, 316
Roney, 345, 455, 456
Ronnau, 442
Ronner, 442
Rooke, 478
Rooker, 331
Rooney, 221
Roosevelt, 53
Root, 222, 271, 321
Roots, 311
Roper, 385, 512, 520
Ropes, 502
Rork, 494
Rose, 28, 70, 79, 122, 153, 452, 461, 509, 529
Rose Hill, 166
Rosencrants, 425, 484
Rosencrantz, 513
Rosenstock, 430, 556
Rosenthal, 226
Rosey, 476
Rosmelle, 559
Ross, 8, 14, 29, 36, 92, 125, 126, 140, 163, 198, 221, 224, 248, 250, 251, 309, 356, 388, 397, 403, 429, 447, 449, 457, 514, 535
Rossel, 490
Rossell, 425, 540
Rosset, 79
Rossett, 25
Rossi, 457
Rossiter, 9
Roszel, 119
Roth, 57
Rothschilds, 126
Rothwell, 318, 352, 384, 387
Rotundo, 432
Rotundo of the Capitol, 9
Rouch, 457
Rouge, 508
Roulin, 140
Rounder, 443
Roundtree, 135
Rourke, 308
Rouse, 444, 453
Roush, 26, 63, 67, 78, 84
Rouston, 140
Row, 399
Rowalt, 456
Rowe, 195, 206, 508
Rowell, 508
Rowinski, 448
Rowland, 140, 177
Rowles, 97
Rowling, 403
Rowney, 494
Rows, 314
Roy, 567
Royce, 447
Rozer, 316
Ruber, 393
Ruby, 510
Rucker, 111, 170, 246, 334, 338
Rudd, 132, 549, 558
Rude, 297
Rudolph, 394
Ruethe, 404
Ruff, 149, 439, 550, 557
Ruffin, 550
Rufus, 314
Rugg, 510
Ruggles, 40, 280, 303, 393, 425, 490, 497
Rugh, 378
Ruigler, 431
Ruillinan, 328

Ruket, 397
Rumears, 447
Rumley, 137
Rumney, 8
Rung, 394
Runge, 409
Runner, 245
Runyan, 184
Rupert, 92, 162, 220, 307, 519, 560
Rupp, 164, 225, 560
Ruppel, 225, 560
Ruppert, 15
Rush, 40, 83, 107, 161, 187, 219, 265, 444, 493, 566
Rusheberger, 493
Rusk, 49
Rusner, 482
Ruson, 140
Russ, 32
Russel, 456
Russell, 26, 33, 75, 109, 160, 184, 196, 222, 224, 247, 252, 309, 355, 362, 395, 418, 441, 443, 452, 454, 472, 478, 494, 509, 540, 545, 562
Russy, 337
Rust, 340
Rutherford, 57, 302, 343, 363
Rutledge, 545
Rutter, 415, 449
Ryan, 221, 222, 446, 452
Rydal Mount, 328
Ryer, 261
Ryland, 94
Ryon, 56, 226, 525, 559

S

Sabine, 532
Saddler, 184
Saddy, 393
Sadler, 457
Saffold, 82
Sagvier, 395
Sailingo, 394
Saldana, 442, 496
Salinas, 96
Salinger, 398
Salisbury, 454
Saloman, 20
Salter, 8, 391
Saltmarsh, 45, 59
Saltz, 568
Saltzer, 267, 560
Sammons, 395, 452
Sample, 455
Sampson, 31, 34, 61, 221, 223, 372, 378
Samson, 4, 19, 118, 221, 427, 482
Samuel, 51
Samuels, 31, 197, 334, 517, 543
Sanborn, 552
Sander, 140, 234
Sanders, 57, 110, 140, 162, 217, 234, 346, 356, 446, 451, 532
Sanderson, 30, 90, 92, 104, 137, 251, 253, 257, 262, 366, 545, 548
Sandford, 69, 184, 371
Sandiford, 229
Sands, 130, 132, 166, 184, 232, 327, 369, 386, 458
Sandys, 442
Sanford, 16, 201
Sanger, 15, 84, 160
Sanstead, 457
Santa Anna, 118, 124, 127, 152, 164, 243, 244, 251, 389, 390, 489, 554
Santangelo, 34
Santmyme, 451
Santo, 215
Sardel, 226
Sardo, 464
Sargent, 368, 526
Sarpy, 37
Sartori, 66, 158
Sataillard, 523
Sathall, 449
Satori, 72, 84
Satterley, 508
Saul, 455
Saun, 399

Saunders, 7, 116, 127, 130, 132, 199, 218, 263, 288, 314, 394, 399, 463, 507, 551
Savage, 34, 200, 205, 256, 273, 435, 439, 441, 542, 553, 557
Savory, 395
Sawers, 560
Sawin, 531
Sawyer, 77, 263, 276, 301, 344, 386, 394, 449, 471, 486
Saxon, 456
Saxton, 456
Sayers, 445
Sayward, 79
Scaggs, 92, 415, 510
Scahill, 139
Scales, 397
Scammon, 90, 119
Scandlett, 140
Scanlan, 445
Scanson, 447
Scantland, 201, 207, 441, 496
Scar, 450
Scarlett, 491
Scarritt, 110
Schacler, 505
Schaeffer, 42, 155, 446, 508, 509
Schaiffer, 443
Schall, 339
Schanck, 415
Schans, 493
Schaum, 505
Schaumburg, 7, 8
Scheder, 221
Scheel, 369
Scheider, 482
Schelbecker, 349
Schelinger, 285
Schenck, 376, 423, 489, 508
Schenecke, 222
Schenerhorn, 457
Schimyer, 398
Schleicher, 457
Schleigh, 273
Schley, 251, 283, 565
Schmeltz, 508
Schmidt, 279, 449
Schmidth, 460
Schnebly, 19, 268
Schneider, 135
schnr **Congress**, 535
schnr **E A Thompson**, 478
schnr **Eleanor Ann**, 320
schnr **Flirt**, 372
schnr **Gen Patterson**, 266
schnr **George M Bache**, 292
schnr **H M Williams**, 476
schnr **Harrison**, 87
schnr **J F Porter**, 265
schnr **John Y Mason**, 240
schnr **Julia**, 489
schnr **Millington**, 238
schnr of war **Bonita**, 132
schnr of war **Petrel**, 132
schnr of war **Reefer**, 132
schnr of war **Tampico**, 132
schnr **On-ka-hy-e**, 324
schnr **On-Ka-Hy-e**, 100
schnr **Phoenix**, 229
schnr **Reefer**, 331
schnr **Robinson Crusoe**, 270
schnr **Sally**, 25
schnr **Shark**, 319
schnr **Spitfire**, 225
schnr **Tampico**, 492
schnr **Valante**, 322
schnr **Velasco**, 330
schnr **Wasp**, 270
schnr **Zulma**, 478
Scholfield, 167, 478, 553
Schoolcraft, 136, 355
Schooley, 252
Schooner, 398
Schoonover, 194
Schott, 29, 47, 394
Schoup, 394
Schouts, 447
Schramm, 221
Schreeve, 433
Schribber, 475

Schriver, 394
Schroder, 419
Schroeder, 59, 218, 273
Schryver, 509
Schuber, 450
Schubert, 500
Schuermann, 506, 564
Schulthies, 483
Schultz, 494
Schuman, 442
Schureman, 528
Schuster, 163
Schuyer, 450
Schuyler, 522
Schwager, 447
Schwartz, 163, 340, 506, 558
Schwartzweller, 398
Schwettzer, 92
Scofield, 394
Scooley, 141
Scoresby, 457
Scott, 34, 47, 57, 74, 86, 89, 90, 92, 109, 110, 115, 119, 135, 136, 144, 152, 167, 168, 177, 181, 197, 198, 203, 206, 210, 211, 222, 223, 225, 226, 233, 235, 237, 241, 243, 244, 247, 258, 262, 270, 277, 298, 305, 309, 313, 314, 334, 338, 339, 346, 360, 386, 387, 388, 390, 400, 409, 418, 423, 425, 432, 439, 440, 450, 451, 456, 460, 463, 481, 482, 485, 487, 488, 490, 492, 494, 496, 497, 498, 509, 535, 537, 540, 541, 544, 547, 550, 552, 559, 562, 567, 568
Scott:, 199
Scouten, 248
Scovell, 181
Scriven, 490
Scrivener, 221, 385
Scroggin, 429
Scull, 404
Scurry, 278
Seafferle, 458
Seal, 394
Seaman, 454
Seamore, 418
Searcy, 140, 190
Searey, 140
Searle, 289, 399
Sears, 10, 107, 485, 493
Seaton, 46, 47, 50, 57, 59, 97, 118, 187, 219, 221, 243, 282, 298, 448
Seavey, 34
Seawell, 109, 201, 247, 273
Seay, 134
Sebastian, 227, 560
Secall, 431
Secor, 407
Seddon, 117, 197, 248, 249, 567
Sedgwick, 350, 426, 490
Seebeck, 455
Seely, 501
Segar, 85, 160
Segoren, 457
Segui, 64, 69
Seidurbergh, 215
Seifert, 277
Seifferly, 92, 93
Seiter, 394
Seitz, 225, 371, 405
Sekells, 430
Sel, 467
Selby, 226
Selden, 100, 161, 162, 172, 345, 441, 490, 496, 497, 540, 566
Selding, 90
Seldon, 280
Selfridge, 161
Selkirk Settlement, 347
Sellers, 134
Selover, 431
Selvey, 488
Seminoff, 444
Semmes, 32, 88, 131, 141, 241, 316, 322, 333, 340, 341, 438, 497, 514, 559
Semple, 452
Senancourt, 51
Senelan, 11
Sengstack, 57, 499, 514, 515
Senseny, 435

Serbrau, 215
Sergeant, 455, 530
Sergent, 370, 523
Serrin, 429, 561
Servezo, 494
Serwell, 403
Sessford, 47, 153, 324, 553
Seston, 140
Seton, 310
Setser, 394
Settle, 140
Setz, 349
Severance, 50
Severs, 397
Sevier, 46
Sewall, 57, 82, 108, 119, 180, 481
Sewall, 57
Sewalls, 17
Seward, 336, 353, 541
Sewell, 31, 64, 69, 239, 446, 494
Sexton, 342
Seybolt, 416, 557
Seyfert, 510
Seymour, 107, 115, 194, 205, 272, 496, 541, 542
Seytes, 226
Shackelford, 440, 539, 547
Shackleford, 484, 490, 521
Shacklett, 448
Shad, 57, 447, 559, 560
Shadd, 430
Shade, 517
Shaeffer, 423
Shaen, 523
Shaffa, 394
Shaffer, 52, 57, 397, 537
Shakespeare, 367, 378
Shandwick, 431
Shane, 133
Shankland, 280
Shanks, 116, 319, 323, 428, 433, 556
Shannon, 141, 490
Shannondale Springs, 66, 227
Sharbuck, 444
Sharp, 112, 134, 223, 233, 250, 311, 345, 370, 444, 482
Sharpe, 126, 170, 442, 507
Sharpless, 396
Shaub, 267
Shauck, 427
Shaw, 23, 57, 63, 78, 84, 132, 157, 224, 267, 399, 429, 450, 454, 470, 508, 533, 552, 555
Sheahan, 462
Shearer, 7
Shebling, 223
Sheckell, 57, 225, 515, 517
Sheckells, 270
Shedd, 57, 92, 230, 267, 319, 397, 413
Sheehan, 222, 442, 460
Sheele, 272
Sheerman, 395
Sheffield, 331, 438, 469
Shekell, 17
Sheldon, 11, 33, 64, 69
Sheleen, 224
Shelley, 508
Sheon, 399
Shepard, 325, 418
Shephaerd, 451
Shephard, 399
Shepherd, 57, 79, 115, 141, 147, 185, 218, 223, 226, 264, 269, 312, 395, 445, 568
Sheppard, 177, 247, 273, 447
Sherburne, 81, 500
Sherer, 435
Sheridan, 222, 310, 393, 396, 452
Sheriff, 309, 348
Sherman, 18, 68, 169, 277, 311, 397, 403, 443, 479, 490
Sherrard, 24
Sherrick, 245
Sherrill, 241
Sherrod, 133
Sherry, 395
Sherwood, 93, 429, 509
Shett, 453, 456
Shevers, 436

Shew, 500
Shields, 84, 86, 107, 159, 201, 209, 210, 211, 222, 223, 233, 236, 251, 255, 319, 401, 439, 441, 449, 483, 489, 490, 496, 497, 513, 514, 539, 542, 563
Shiflett, 551
Shiles, 385
Shilling, 357
Shillingburg, 115
Shimmel, 393
Shinard, 447
Shine, 455
Shinley, 477
Shinn, 57
ship **Adams**, 26
ship **Admittance**, 489
ship **Alabama**, 550
ship **Alexandria**, 304, 307
ship **Appollo**, 319
ship **Arago**, 284
ship **Atlantic**, 214
ship **Auburn**, 420
ship **Baltimore**, 237
ship **Bavaria**, 483
ship **Borden**, 275
ship **Boston**, 8, 160
ship **Bounty**, 372
ship **Catharine**, 73
ship **Cato**, 475
ship **Charles**, 214
ship **Charleston**, 273
ship **Christiana**, 483
ship **Columbia**, 71, 505
ship **Columbus**, 161, 489
ship **Constitution**, 389, 498
ship **Cornelia**, 297
ship **Cyane**, 173, 302, 389
ship **Day**, 493
ship **Decatur**, 415, 423
ship **Diadem**, 147
ship **Dutchesse d'Orleans**, 265
ship **Eliza Warwick**, 73
ship **Empire**, 434, 478
ship **Esther**, 270
ship **Euphrasia**, 215
ship **Experiment**, 530
ship **Fidelia**, 500
ship **Flying Fish**, 270
ship **Fredonia**, 16, 486
ship **Germantown**, 424
ship **Huguenot**, 505
ship **Independence**, 161
ship **Isaac Allerton**, 372
ship **Jamestown**, 102, 210
ship **Jas Hewitt**, 50
ship **John Adams**, 216, 308, 536
ship **Levant**, 161, 389
ship **Liberty**, 505
ship **Mamlouk**, 359
ship **Massachusetts**, 278, 408
ship **Mississippi**, 21, 217, 224, 308, 319, 346, 424, 462
ship **Missouri**, 457
ship **Monongahela**, 290
ship **Montezuma**, 476
ship **Napier**, 307
ship **New Orleans**, 217
ship **New York**, 404
ship **Northumberland**, 561
ship **Ocean Monarch**, 404
ship **Ohio**, 5, 132, 216, 370
ship **Ondiaka**, 73
ship **Ontario**, 7
ship **Oswego**, 147
ship **Pennsylvania**, 8, 35
ship **Potomac**, 216
ship **Princeton**, 52, 468
ship **Rajah**, 505
ship **Raritan**, 311
ship **Remittance**, 263
ship **Scorpion**, 308, 320
ship **Shanunga**, 349
ship **Sheridan**, 561
ship **Sir Robert Peel**, 493
ship **Sisters**, 319
ship **St Paul**, 73
ship **Stephen Whitney**, 527
ship **Supply**, 324, 411, 423, 504
ship **Tempest**, 511
ship **Union**, 81

ship **Valparaiso**, 531
ship **Vesta**, 245
ship **Vesuvius**, 308
ship **Vixen**, 21
ship **Wakona**, 278
ship **Warren**, 302, 377
ship **Yazoo**, 147
Shiperd, 426
Shipley, 123
ship-of-the-line **Columbus**, 566
Shippey, 452
ships **Etna**, **Bonita**, **Petrel & Reefer**, 216
ships **Germantown**, **Decatur**, **Spitfire**, **Vixen**, 216
ships **Princeton & Porpoise**, 329
ships **Scourge**, **Vesuvius**, **Hecla**, 216
ships **Statesman**, **Prentice**, 73
Shiras, 50, 108, 243, 268, 427
Shirk, 385
Shirley, 92, 100
Shive, 401
Shively, 105, 133, 398
Shlaihan, 452
Shock, 331
Shoemaker, 409
Shoenberger, 356
Shonnard, 279
Shook, 134, 509
Shoppe, 444
Shore, 452
Shores, 450
Short, 335, 508
Shortall, 398
Shorter, 57, 184
Shortridge, 293
Shoultz, 137
Shounand, 100
Shover, 35, 110, 111, 169, 247, 471, 546
Showers, 435
Shreave, 430
Shreeve, 516
Shreve, 38, 57, 226, 288, 516, 537, 554
Shrill, 394
Shroder, 266
Shryock, 147
Shubrick, 23, 151, 161, 331, 489, 503
Shuck, 396
Shucking, 429
Shugart, 9, 112, 113, 253
Shugert, 548
Shultz, 224, 349, 373
Shunalt, 431
Shunk, 237
Shurtzenback, 181
Shuster, 556
Shutt, 135
Shuttleworth, 117, 120
Shutz, 395
Shwarykoryt, 442
Siberly, 489
Sibley, 106, 170, 266, 429
Siddle, 507
Sidwell, 398, 435
Sieh, 455
Siemon, 500
Sietz, 307
Sigerson, 74
Sigler, 443
Sigmac, 449
Sigmond, 450
Signer, 505
Sigourney, 457
Sill, 280
Sillan, 215
Silliman, 414
Silner, 451
Silvere, 476
Silverthorn, 509
Silvy, 533
Sim, 409
Simkins, 248
Simm, 35
Simmerman, 21
Simmonds, 475
Simmons, 12, 22, 23, 84, 96, 109, 139, 195, 226, 371, 386, 447, 481
Simms, 57, 71, 92, 226, 266, 274, 369, 371, 385, 413, 514, 515, 516, 517, 518, 533, 559

Simons, 39, 224, 440, 566
Simonson, 441, 508
Simonton, 372
Simpkins, 388
Simpson, 5, 50, 71, 93, 107, 134, 226, 258, 269, 309, 385, 442, 443, 448, 457, 482, 497, 524, 532, 565
Sims, 6, 15, 200, 231, 263, 298, 431, 494
Sinclair, 16, 135, 184, 327, 429
Singer, 111
Singleton, 203, 216, 542
Sinsel, 136
Sioussa, 41, 291, 362
Sioussi, 57
Sires, 397
Sirman, 393
Siscoe, 14
Sisson, 57
Sister Ann Barrilia, 317
Sister Mary Agatha, 308
Sister Mary Delphina, 373
Sister Mary Simplecia, 258
Sister of Charity, 373
Sisterhood of Charity, 317
Sisters of Charity, 310, 404, 406
Sisters of the Visitation, 23, 131, 308
Sitgreaves, 170, 194, 207, 273
Skerry, 523
Skidmore, 54, 86, 429
Skinner, 8, 29, 45, 221, 236, 239, 344, 436, 466, 469, 483, 532
Skirchfield, 514
Skirving, 72, 87, 267, 314, 557
Skolinski, 445
Slack, 95, 135
Slacum, 8, 45, 59, 78, 399
Slade, 130, 175, 201, 203, 210, 226, 443, 496, 543
Sladen, 137
Slamm, 32
Slate Cabin Tract, 115
Slater, 446
Slatter, 340
Slattery, 399
Slaughter, 205, 537, 555
Slaughters, 233
slave trade, 553
Sleath, 397
Sleck, 393, 443
Sleep, 127, 138
Sleeper, 551
Sleight, 153, 303
Slicer, 28, 119, 133, 185, 227, 237, 341, 512, 522, 528
Sligh, 507
Slight, 92
Slingerland, 425
Sloan, 221, 448, 537
Sloat, 376, 391
Slocum, 36, 195, 541
Sloman, 398
sloop **Mariner**, 132
sloop of war **Albany**, 132, 216
sloop of war **Cyane**, 489
sloop of war **Decatur**, 132
sloop of war **Germantown**, 132
sloop of war **John Adams**, 132
sloop of war **Portsmouth**, 408, 489
sloop of war **Preble**, 489
sloop of war **Saratoga**, 132
sloop of war **St Mary's**, 132
sloop of war **Vincennes**, 141
sloop of war **Warren**, 489
sloop **Portsmouth**, 173, 302
sloop-of-war **Albany**, 331
sloop-of-war **Jamestown**, 322, 401
sloop-of-war **Levant**, 181
sloop-of-war **Portsmouth**, 377
sloop-of-war **Warren**, 173, 549
Slouth, 507
Slowly, 399
Slubb, 357
Slummer, 15
Sly, 454
Small, 153, 260, 517, 519
Small Addition, 438
Smallbark, 444
Smallwood, 104, 231, 237, 259, 429, 557

Smart, 241
Smead, 7, 462
Smedes, 154
Smedley, 140
Smith, 2, 3, 5, 6, 11, 16, 17, 23, 24, 25, 29, 32, 36, 37, 46, 47, 49, 57, 58, 61, 62, 63, 66, 68, 77, 79, 87, 89, 92, 94, 95, 99, 100, 101, 109, 110, 111, 113, 115, 116, 120, 121, 122, 133, 135, 136, 137, 138, 153, 163, 174, 177, 180, 181, 182, 183, 184, 185, 190, 191, 201, 203, 205, 207, 209, 210, 212, 213, 222, 224, 239, 246, 250, 256, 257, 259, 261, 268, 270, 271, 272, 273, 278, 279, 283, 289, 291, 294, 298, 301, 304, 308, 309, 310, 312, 314, 315, 318, 326, 328, 330, 331, 332, 339, 341, 347, 348, 350, 351, 353, 357, 358, 364, 370, 381, 385, 386, 388, 390, 392, 393, 394, 395, 396, 397, 398, 399, 400, 403, 409, 411, 412, 413, 418, 424, 425, 429, 433, 434, 435, 436, 439, 440, 441, 442, 443, 444, 446, 447, 449, 450, 452, 454, 455, 456, 463, 472, 474, 475, 477, 482, 483, 485, 488, 489, 490, 492, 493, 496, 497, 502, 503, 507, 508, 509, 510, 513, 521, 522, 523, 525, 528, 529, 530, 535, 536, 537, 538, 540, 541, 544, 547, 548, 552, 554, 557, 559, 563, 564
Smith T, 8, 20, 66, 85
Smithers, 397
Smithson, 218, 407, 414, 465, 507, 557
Smithsonian, 218
Smithsonian Institute, 237, 566
Smithsonian Institution, 76, 181, 183, 186, 270
Smitson, 163
Smitz, 494
Smoot, 92, 226, 236, 257, 312, 405, 406, 525
Smyth, 126, 455
Smythe, 205
Smyzer, 341
Snail, 253, 262
Snellers, 447
Snelling, 440, 490
Snider, 395, 437
Sniffen, 271, 561
Snively, 87
Snodgrass, 141
Snow, 139, 396
Snowden, 141, 153, 386, 495
Snowden's Discovery, 505
Snyder, 203, 230, 394, 446, 455, 456, 533
Society of Friends, 29
Society of Jesus, 162
Soderlann, 349
Sogur, 455
solar gas lights, 82
Solar Gas Lights, 495
Solari, 483
Soller, 209
Solomon, 455, 482
Somerhane, 395
Somers, 224, 386
Somerville, 345
Sommerauer, 84
Sommers, 500
Son, 222
Sonop, 137
Sonsby, 502
Soper, 184, 429
Sorneo, 316
Sorrel, 395
Sorvera, 217
Sothoron, 34, 48, 69, 80, 82, 229
Sothron, 64
Soto, 346
Sould, 398
Soule, 43, 397
Soulouque, 129
Sour, 556
Sourly, 448
Southall, 46, 268, 313
Southard, 522
Southerland, 502
Southworth, 521

Soutter, 172
Sowdon, 502
Space, 507
Spalding, 65, 75, 85, 123, 138, 171, 372, 399
Spangler, 255
Sparin, 507
Spark, 111
Sparks, 450
Sparrow, 509
Spaulding, 33, 66, 159, 450
Speakes, 182
Speakman, 84, 158
Speaks, 92
Spear, 451
Spears, 102, 446, 460
Spedden, 318
Speers, 399
Speiden, 240
Speight, 228, 390, 534
Speir, 150
Speiser, 266, 267
Speisser, 142
Spelcer, 397
Spence, 17, 65, 153, 335, 385
Spencer, 8, 33, 47, 114, 129, 140, 159, 163, 181, 189, 196, 221, 248, 250, 290, 303, 314, 393, 395, 404, 448, 449, 453, 454, 458, 477
Sphar, 427
Spicer, 57, 163, 482
Spiess, 500
Spignal, 57
Spignall, 57
Spillman, 419
Sprague, 24, 195, 222, 388, 541
Sprigg, 92, 166
Sprigman, 92
Spring Grove, 243
Spring Hill, 80
Springer, 230
Springham, 447
Springman, 163
Sprole, 27, 34, 62, 115, 126, 133, 147
Sproston, 181, 370
Sprotson, 45
Squibb, 327
Squires, 136, 413
Srough, 139
Sryoch, 191
St Clair, 184, 509
St Elizabeth, 131
St George, 328
St John, 76
St Marks, Florida, 241
St Osyth, 149
St Real, 76
St Sophia, 433
St Vrain, 165
Stabler, 407
Stacey, 222
Stacker, 327
Stackpole, 308, 312
Stacom, 466
Stacy, 111
Stafford, 202, 334, 336, 469
Stake, 373
Staley, 13
Stall, 398
Stallings, 121, 145, 162, 220
Staly, 509
Stanard, 185, 567
Standerwick, 456
Standinger, 493
Stanford, 399, 456
Staniford, 109, 312, 325, 434
Stanley, 67, 92, 94, 211, 341, 399, 443, 502
Stansberry, 259
Stansbury, 83, 394
Stanton, 47, 167, 246, 394, 451, 476
Stanwood, 278
Staples, 301, 404, 507
Stapleton, 476
Stark, 117, 120, 467, 509
Starr, 234, 394, 444, 530
Starret, 75
Starrs, 467
Stauffer, 510
Stead, 412

Steager, 269
stealing cartridges, 344
steamboat **Atlantic**, 32
steamboat **Atlantic's Bell**, 83
steamboat **Carolinian**, 501
steamboat **Defiance**, 306
steamboat **Eureka**, 228
steamboat **George Washington**, 235
steamboat **Jewess**, 294
steamboat **Joseph Johnson**, 359
steamboat **Mingo Chief**, 346
steamboat **New Hampshire**, 236
steamboat **Osceola**, 180
steamboat **Saranac**, 235
steamboat **St Croix**, 501
steamboat **Talma**, 235
steamboat **Tuscaloosa**, 265
steamboat **Tuskaloosa**, 50
steamer **A N Johnson**, 568
steamer **Admiral**, 269
steamer **Alabama**, 21, 162, 346
steamer **Alleghany**, 132
steamer **Ann Chase**, 323
steamer **Chesapeake**, 265
steamer **Col Harney**, 536
steamer **Col Yell**, 273
steamer **Duchess of Kent**, 364
steamer **Edna**, 269
steamer **Fashion**, 568
steamer **Hibernia**, 122, 125, 331, 426
steamer **Hunter**, 132, 154
steamer **James Hewitt**, 265
steamer **James L Day**, 498
steamer **John Bunn**, 125
steamer **Louisiana**, 273
steamer **Lucy Walker**, 295
steamer **Lune**, 235
steamer **Mississippi**, 132, 154, 216
steamer **Mountaineer**, 179
steamer **New Orleans**, 277
steamer **Newark**, 179
steamer **Old Hickory**, 352
steamer **Palmetto**, 534
steamer **Petrita**, 132
steamer **Phenix**, 520, 521
steamer **Philadelphia**, 476
steamer **Pike No 8**, 235
steamer **Polk**, 132
steamer **Pontiac**, 273
steamer **Princeton**, 7, 132
steamer **Scorpion**, 132
steamer **Scourge**, 132, 179, 217
steamer **Spitfire**, 132, 319, 320, 362, 424
steamer **Talisman**, 511
steamer **Telegraph**, 213
steamer **Tweed**, 114, 130, 215
steamer **Union**, 132
steamer **United States**, 281
steamer **Vixen**, 132, 232, 329
steamer **Washington**, 409, 500
steamer **Water-Witch**, 360
Steamers, 223
steamship **Acadia**, 502, 523
steamship **Alabama**, 24, 513
steamship **Cambria**, 457
steamship **Giraffe**, 44
steamship **Mary Kingsland**, 365
steamship **Massachusetts**, 365
steamship **N Y**, 493, 505
steamship **New Orleans**, 365
steamship **Princeton**, 158
steamship **Sarah Sands**, 408
steamship **Washington**, 482
Steane, 493
Stearns, 60, 80, 292
Stedman, 299
Steedman, 500
Steel, 127, 135, 269, 395, 445
Steele, 119, 201, 364, 415, 528, 542, 545
Steen, 133, 169, 199, 389, 399, 441, 450, 484
Steer, 11, 324, 364
Steiger, 225, 310, 516
Stein, 126
Steinbrook, 346
Steiner, 111
Steinman, 398
Steinson, 452

Steles, 523
Stelle, 358, 375
Stem, 89
Stemlar, 494
Stenoham, 444
Stenson, 240
Stephen, 11, 181
Stephens, 6, 96, 137, 339, 436, 497, 508, 545
Stephenson, 45, 117, 226
Stepper, 11, 57, 226
Stepter, 269
Steptoe, 107
Sterling, 18
Sterne, 96
Sternentz, 493
Sterret, 386
Sterrett, 62
Stetson, 36
Stett, 426
Stettinius, 62, 87, 93, 243, 273, 556
Steuart, 314
Steuben, 17
Stevens, 129, 134, 137, 163, 181, 182, 184, 194, 237, 385, 394, 441, 447, 455, 475, 507, 535, 556, 558
Stevenson, 29, 33, 63, 84, 109, 135, 161, 261, 277, 334, 376, 385, 396, 430, 452, 489, 490, 566
Stever, 198
Stevier, 452
Steward, 442, 508, 509
Stewart, 3, 33, 35, 48, 53, 57, 59, 68, 73, 84, 92, 135, 140, 158, 161, 163, 184, 189, 218, 258, 266, 267, 296, 330, 385, 392, 393, 397, 403, 418, 454, 455, 473, 484, 492, 494, 521, 525, 557, 559, 565, 566
Stezer, 393
Stickler, 451
Stickney, 304
Stier, 556
Stiff, 378
Stigher, 394
Stiker, 396
Stiles, 412, 419
Stille, 233
Stillings, 99, 163
Stilwell, 60, 394
Stimpson, 395
Stinebaugh, 394
Stirling, 15
Stiver, 223
Stober, 214
Stockaw, 134
Stockett, 502
Stockton, 33, 42, 69, 84, 85, 126, 157, 160, 214, 472, 473
Stoddard, 195, 230, 370, 464, 475, 502, 541
Stoddart, 457
Stoddert, 101
Stoeffer, 395
Stoekl, 48
Stoele, 441
Stokes, 33, 34, 85, 160, 554
Stone, 23, 29, 33, 34, 106, 114, 192, 249, 260, 278, 303, 339, 431, 453, 455, 467, 490, 530, 545, 553
Stoneman, 538
Stoner, 209, 245
Stonestreet, 50
Stong, 376
Stoops, 57, 60, 306, 430, 559
store ship **Fredonia**, 132
store ship **Relief**, 132
store ship **Supply**, 132
Storer, 35, 311, 370
storeship **Erie**, 489
storeship **Lexington**, 489
store-ship **Lexington**, 181
storeship **Relief**, 324
store-ship **Relief**, 147
Storm, 224, 429, 452, 455, 555
Story, 342
Stott, 42, 44, 57, 101, 146, 226, 258, 386, 402, 557, 558
Stouse, 502
Stout, 14, 41, 138, 250, 436, 545
Stover, 13

Stowell, 397
Stoy, 453
Straight Hollow, 438
Strange, 482
Strassner, 398
Stratton, 398
Straub, 267, 433, 438
Straw, 21
Street, 71, 336, 454, 541, 545
Streeter, 399
Stribling, 565
Strickland, 45
Stringer, 139, 269
Stringfellow, 125, 300
Stringham, 5, 132
Strobe, 510
Strobel, 166
Strobill, 456
Strong, 136, 161, 280, 344, 425, 440, 540
Strongbow, 469
Strother, 535
Stroud, 86, 288
Struthers, 279
Strybos, 476
Stuart, 5, 138, 153, 245, 248, 336, 396, 476, 495, 538, 546
Stubblefield, 134
Stubbs, 92, 256, 332, 390, 414, 429, 430
Stuck, 559
Stuckee, 426
Stucker, 493
Stucky, 426
Studds, 19
Studiford, 422
Stuppick, 508
Sturgeon, 276, 278, 335, 338
Sturges, 71, 426
Sturgey, 431
Sturgis, 79, 128, 246, 418
Stutz, 516, 556
Stuyvesant, 351, 352, 363
Suber, 456
Sudley, 474
Sugar & Wine, 438
Suit, 135
Suller, 568
Sullivan, 18, 46, 68, 93, 134, 140, 221, 325, 393, 397, 417, 442, 443, 444, 452, 482, 564
Sully, 169, 247, 293, 297
Summeraner, 45, 59, 78
Summers, 31, 261, 432, 508, 510, 511
Summerville, 184
Summuraner, 8
Sumner, 208, 211, 214, 220, 440, 441, 483
Sumter, 389, 398, 535
Supple, 399
Supreme Court, 72
Suter, 3, 290
Sutherland, 211, 223, 265, 393, 427
Sutler, 394
Sutliffe, 484
Sutter, 11, 467
Sutter's Fort, 11
Sutton, 202, 224, 237, 294, 420
Sutzenhizer, 453
Swail, 505
Swain, 137, 279, 523
Swan, 204, 395, 441
Swann, 78, 87, 97, 148, 403, 448, 535
Swartwout, 141, 162, 354, 355
Swartz, 509
Sweekard, 398
Sweeney, 385, 388, 443, 484, 508, 553, 559
Sweeny, 30, 57, 224, 255, 258, 274, 298, 399, 450, 513, 514, 516
Sweet, 133, 385, 397, 447, 508, 509, 520
Sweet Springs, 347
Sweeting, 57, 153, 273, 275, 518
Swegert, 309
Swett, 195, 546
Swift, 47, 48, 192, 246, 250, 261, 399, 457, 490, 543
Swink, 368
Switzer, 269, 446
Swords, 366, 472

Syberg, 197, 208
Syfax, 418
Sykes, 50
Sylvester, 173, 302, 448
Symmes, 335
Syms, 445
Szymanski, 562

T

Tabb, 567
Tabbler, 451
Taber, 420
Taff, 27
Tafoya, 171
Tagart, 251
Taggart, 138
Tait, 92
Take all That's Left, 438
Talbert, 92
Talbot, 26, 152, 248, 315, 434, 567
Talbott, 191, 203, 206
Talburt, 163, 474
Talburtt, 477
Talbut, 136
Talcott, 106, 204, 205, 439, 441
Taliaferro, 166, 197, 206, 398, 541, 542
Talifour, 414
Tallesson, 396
Talty, 27, 104, 231, 251, 257, 515, 516, 517, 560
Tams, 191
Tandy, 403
Taney, 187, 219
Taneyhill, 375
Tank, 500
Tannehill, 50
Tanner, 92, 323
Tanneyhill, 202, 342, 542
Tansen, 442
Tansil, 455
Tansill, 117, 120
Taplin, 198
Tappen, 473
Tarbonny, 293
Tarbox, 494
Tarlton, 566
Tarn, 454
Tarring, 99
Tastet, 57, 251
Tatam, 53
Tate, 19, 186, 275, 364, 487, 553
Tatham, 482
Tatnall, 132, 216, 224, 259
Tatnon, 397
Tatum, 374
Taulbee, 535
Taulor, 290
Taurey, 403
Tavenner, 290
Tayloe, 4, 487, 567
Taylor, 5, 8, 16, 19, 23, 42, 45, 57, 64, 69, 70, 74, 85, 92, 93, 95, 107, 118, 119, 123, 124, 127, 140, 143, 148, 150, 151, 157, 164, 169, 170, 175, 181, 185, 196, 229, 230, 233, 235, 246, 262, 264, 266, 273, 277, 297, 304, 312, 317, 319, 343, 346, 360, 361, 370, 371, 374, 378, 386, 388, 395, 396, 398, 405, 415, 416, 424, 425, 433, 435, 436, 444, 451, 466, 471, 489, 492, 505, 509, 512, 527, 530, 542, 550, 551, 552, 553, 555, 557, 559, 561, 565
Tchiffely, 57
Teague, 140
Teahan, 221
Teasley, 137
Tebbs, 563
Teinturier, 457
Telegraph, 561
Teluns, 181
Temple, 98, 129, 178, 196, 205, 230, 452, 469
Templeman, 115, 447
Templeton, 202, 235
Ten Broeck, 261, 363, 501
Ten Eyck, 16, 79, 117
Tenant, 57
Tenatt, 222
Tench, 523, 556, 559

Teneyck, 532
Tenison, 418
Tennent, 287
Tenney, 223, 296, 421, 560
Tennison, 340
Tennyson, 367
Tensh, 519
Terhune, 53
Terrell, 398, 448
Terrett, 117, 120, 172, 205, 352
Terrill, 235, 431
Territ, 448
Terry, 370, 529, 545
Tester, 431
Tete, 316
Tevarts, 140
Tevis, 7
Tewell, 495
Thacker, 429
Tharman, 133
Thatcher, 322, 401
Thayer, 351
Their, 523
Therman, 67, 136
Thibaudier, 505
Thierman, 457
Thiess, 181
Third Addition to Mount Savage, 438
Thistleton, 456
Thom, 48, 314, 513
Thomas, 3, 5, 6, 11, 14, 21, 29, 43, 49, 57, 61, 77, 87, 89, 92, 110, 137, 156, 169, 226, 229, 233, 247, 250, 267, 274, 281, 298, 303, 309, 345, 350, 371, 386, 396, 410, 418, 426, 429, 430, 443, 448, 455, 461, 492, 507, 509, 511, 513, 514, 519, 538, 552, 563
Thomason, 495
Thomasson, 223
Thomkins, 93
Thompsn, 309
Thompson, 3, 6, 11, 18, 39, 46, 47, 70, 92, 100, 103, 117, 134, 135, 146, 163, 194, 195, 205, 207, 222, 225, 240, 242, 253, 262, 269, 275, 295, 308, 310, 334, 337, 338, 340, 341, 346, 355, 394, 397, 398, 399, 403, 411, 429, 435, 441, 445, 450, 452, 456, 457, 469, 473, 503, 504, 516, 518, 534, 541, 547, 565
Thoms, 57, 226
Thomson, 140, 186, 413
Thorburn, 129, 174
Thorn, 20, 108, 139, 194, 248, 266, 267, 336, 355, 388, 394, 527
Thornburgh, 45
Thornby, 504
Thorne, 440
Thorney, 424
Thornington, 396
Thornley, 274, 298, 348, 356, 411, 523, 559
Thornton, 97, 166, 345, 348, 387, 394, 400, 471, 521, 547, 567
Thorp, 62, 512
Thouron, 79
Three Springs, 438
Thrift, 275, 379
Throckmorton, 19
Throop, 326
Thruston, 386, 419, 509
Thucker, 139
Thumb, 150, 226, 378
Thunley, 223
Thurger, 61
Thurston, 39
Thyson, 54, 180, 488, 558
Tibbatts, 46, 98, 130, 148, 178, 203, 205, 230, 277
Tibbs, 404
Tiber, 358
Tiber Creek, 124
Tiber Mill, 371
Tickelman, 394
Ticknor, 161, 566
Tidball, 246, 474
Tidd, 136
Tidwell, 456
Tiemans, 403
Tierney, 177, 396, 452

Tiffans, 445
Tilden, 62, 108, 388, 396, 528
Tilghman, 171, 225, 240, 386, 429
Tilletson, 376
Tilley, 418, 422, 432, 506
Tillinghast, 336, 539
Tillman, 398, 510
Tilton, 202, 204, 235, 370
Timber Branch, 530
Timber Ridge, 438
Timberlake, 386
Tims, 259, 281, 289, 298
Tinkler, 226
Tinkman, 560
Tinney, 57, 508, 560
Tippett, 86
Tippin, 198
Tipton, 538, 547
Tirley, 134
Tischer, 133
Tisdale, 521
Titus, 202
Toaping Castle, 505
Tobias, 314
Tod, 83
Todd, 79, 128, 212, 223, 413, 538
Todschinder, 560
Toler, 566
Toll, 202, 207, 542, 546
Tolman, 465, 503
Tolque, 171
Tolson, 184, 267, 418
Tomas, 165, 171
Tomison, 431
Tomkins, 400, 423, 456
Tomlinson, 511
Tompkins, 6, 45, 64, 83, 84, 157, 196, 208, 352, 399, 502, 535, 539, 546, 555
Tompson, 386, 448
Tone, 418
Tonge, 11, 57, 323
Tongue, 473
Toobwill, 450
Tood, 558
Tool, 192
Toole, 450
Toomie, 481
Tooten, 360
Topham, 560
Tornis, 444
Torowny, 269
Torpete, 215
Torrance, 138
Totten, 23, 48, 90, 107, 112, 119, 152, 187, 219, 390, 531
Tottenhalh, 523
Touge, 47
Toulman, 502
Toulmin, 339, 544
Toursdale, 441
towboat **Porpoise**, 278
Tower, 246, 562
Tower of London, 145
Towers, 47, 298, 319
Towison, 441
Towle, 17, 433, 518
Town, 131, 451
Towne, 474
Townley, 418, 568
Townsend, 7, 103, 224, 391
Towrison, 455
Towson, 410
Tracy, 14, 79, 195, 350, 452
Traenkle, 136
Trafton, 36
Trail, 170
transport **Sophia Walker**, 87
Trapier, 94
Trapnall, 77
Trapnell, 77
Trask, 398
Traub, 397
Travers, 92, 429, 430, 515, 559
Travet, 273
Travis, 386, 399
Treadwell, 546, 549
Tredway, 117
Tree, 248, 258, 267, 372, 441, 556, 558
Trenchard, 94, 238
Trenner, 510

Trenor, 70, 106, 114
Trenum, 510
Tresevant, 454
Tresner, 501
Trevitt, 253, 262
Trevor, 41
Triay, 418
Trick, 508
Tricon, 316
Trimble, 252, 559
Triplet, 61
Triplett, 93, 455, 509
Triplitt, 3
Trist, 47, 48, 403
Trontfetter, 395
Trook, 470
Trott, 403
Trotter, 134, 139, 266, 283
Troubat, 476
Trousdale, 98, 130, 178, 200, 205, 230, 398, 439, 496
Troyer, 494
Trubush, 171
Truman, 397, 452
Trumble, 454
Trumbull, 18
Trunnel, 3, 506
Trush, 450
Trutler, 529
Truxton, 370
Truxtun, 345
Tryon, 73, 403
Tscheffely, 401
Tschiffely, 154, 472, 528
Tubbs, 397
Tucker, 23, 42, 44, 57, 76, 92, 133, 141, 163, 183, 186, 221, 237, 253, 262, 279, 395, 400, 439, 441, 446, 467, 509, 510, 519, 552, 556
Tuckerman, 403
Tuel, 525, 529
Tuers, 399
Tulip Hill, 293
Tull, 408
Tully, 446
Tuner, 58
Tunison, 454
Tunisop, 456
Tunnecliff, 358
Tunstall, 432
Tupper, 426
Turberville, 134
Turfley, 75
Turk, 390
Turley, 171
Turnbull, 90, 119
Turner, 11, 27, 35, 97, 119, 122, 140, 143, 153, 173, 222, 234, 302, 366, 376, 395, 423, 436, 448, 472, 486, 501, 533, 552, 557
Turney, 138, 253, 262, 337, 396
Turpin, 182, 332, 430, 439
Turrentine, 237
Turton, 254, 560
Tustin, 369, 523, 526
Tuttle, 26, 394, 400
Tweedy, 399
Twigg, 459
Twiggs, 208, 220, 251, 395, 428, 431, 432, 439, 441, 451, 457, 498, 530
Twin island, 87
Twist, 453
Twrouski, 140
Tyant, 222
Tyle, 523
Tyler, 96, 109, 129, 161, 163, 204, 206, 226, 235, 296, 334, 337, 360, 413, 510, 520, 566
Tyler, 199
Tyng, 284, 397
Tyore, 404
Typhoya, 165
Tyrrell, 422
Tyson, 93, 322, 405, 520

U

Ufford, 562
Ullenbrook, 442
Ulman, 269
Umberfield, 329

Unckerman, 482
Underwood, 40, 60, 241, 328
Ungerer, 398
Unisck, 226
Unthank, 48, 398
Uoriaga, 209
Updegraff, 441, 443
Updike, 138
Upfold, 28
Upham, 552
Upman, 202
Upper Plantation, 379
Upperman, 57, 267, 516, 517, 518, 519, 559
Uppman, 136
Upsher, 57
Upshur, 8, 94, 470
Upton, 452
Urquhart, 103
Urrea, 144
Ursery, 288
Usher, 83, 213, 443
Utermohle, 516
Utermuhle, 515, 516
Uttermuhle, 92

V

Vail, 493
Val, 277
Valentine, 398
Valier, 426
Valliers, 185
Valz, 457
Van Alen, 197
Van Allen, 400
Van Amburgh, 226
Van Berchem, 428
Van Bokkelen, 259, 321
Van Bruen, 484
Van Brunt, 100, 132, 532
Van Buren, 37, 177, 237, 335, 388, 395, 538
Van Camp, 136
Van Campen, 29, 537
Van Court, 306
Van de Venter, 202, 206
Van Deif, 456
Van Deusen, 166
Van Doren, 265
Van Dorn, 247, 441
Van Dyke, 236, 342
Van Horn, 276
Van Horseigh, 42, 101, 167, 213, 405
Van Horsigh, 536
Van Loan, 237
Van Ness, 2, 3, 288, 318, 346, 348, 357, 386, 434, 492, 534
Van Pannel, 493
Van Patten, 79
Van Rensselaer, 497
Van Reswick, 92, 226, 231
Van Slyck, 33, 70, 84
Van Slyke, 456
Van Tassel, 222
Van Tyne, 433
Van Valkenberg, 79
Van Vliet, 162, 334
Van Wycke, 324
Van Zandt, 57, 99, 161, 310, 360, 464, 506, 566
Vanalstyne, 393
Vance, 39, 84, 158, 194
Vancoble, 130
Vandenbeck, 181
Vandergriff, 449
Vanderier, 139
Vanderlop, 493
Vanderpoel, 404
Vandever, 339, 544
Vandevere, 7
Vanduden, 310
Vandyke, 494
Vanfleet, 139
Vanhoesigh, 497
Vanhook, 141
Vanhorne, 263
Vanhouten, 419
Vankleek, 156
Vankleharker, 135
Vann, 29, 181

Vanney, 398
Vanolinda, 439
Vanolinde, 441
Vantine, 72
Vanuxem, 36
Vanuxen, 414
Varden, 20
Varick, 11
Varner, 452
Varnes, 452
Varney, 552
Varnum, 46, 215, 377, 411, 419, 483
Vasquez, 152, 210
Vaughan, 126, 140, 252, 266, 283, 316, 437
Vaughn, 112, 113, 142, 495
Vauson, 455
Vaux, 400
Vean, 48
Vega, 209
Vela, 168
Velez, 209
Venable, 11, 169, 231, 386
Venater, 452
Venator, 460
Vencenthaler, 472
Venthiel, 507
Veny, 397
Veonir, 476
Verdell, 508
Vergano, 51
Verhaegan, 59
Verhagen, 41, 500
Vermillian, 430
Vermillion, 430, 476
Vernon, 16, 204, 235, 513, 543
Vernoy, 494
Verrel, 450
Vertrees, 448
vessel **Cambria**, 76
vessel **Malek Adhel**, 549
vessel **Shannon**, 124
Vest, 139
Vestal, 137
Vial, 553
Vice, 14
Vickers, 222
Victor, 482
Victory, 446
Vidocq, 478
Viedenberg, 447
Viele, 336, 540
Vigil, 171
Villamil, 390
Villanueva, 152
Villiers, 310, 469
Villipigue, 398
Vincent, 406, 453, 501
Viney, 509
Vinson, 99, 134
Vinton, 106, 110, 151, 168, 181, 247, 250
Virginia, 404
Virtu, 321
Vischer, 7
Visser, 429, 430, 556
Vivan, 268
Vivans, 146
Vivings, 215
Vizers, 221
Vodery, 184
Vogle, 221
Voight, 138, 398
Voiturat, 181
volunteers **Industry** & **Mary Bee**, 537
Von Cechanowick, 505
Von Cudebroeck, 404
Von Eichthal, 549
Von Essen, 557
Von Hosie, 493
Von Kaaff, 482
Von Rheaden, 509
Von Roman, 399
Von Schmidt, 37, 52, 60, 169
Von-Albade, 283
Voorhees, 143, 155, 166
Voorhies, 181
Voort, 137
Vose, 494
Voss, 241, 269, 287, 289, 370, 386

Warein, 431
Warfield, 5
Warford, 139, 141
Waring, 166, 227, 238, 244, 263, 410, 430, 479, 559, 566
Warker, 184
Warm Springs, 416
Warmley, 565
Warneck, 397
Warner, 213, 265, 399, 507, 510
Warren, 31, 88, 140, 170, 386, 449, 476, 480, 481, 485
Warring, 225, 321
Warrington, 5, 47, 48, 58, 484
Warsea, 181
Washburn, 58, 122
Washington, 5, 18, 23, 32, 36, 60, 66, 68, 107, 108, 135, 169, 183, 184, 187, 238, 293, 339, 358, 367, 387, 394, 396, 457, 475, 501, 534, 545, 555, 561
Wassen, 508
Watch, 436
Watchman, 444
Waterman, 79, 89, 537
Waters, 11, 35, 90, 97, 122, 130, 167, 184, 188, 202, 210, 226, 242, 274, 299, 310, 338, 386, 398, 488, 516
Waterson, 555
Watersons, 403
Watkins, 33, 142, 501
Watmaugh, 376
Watmough, 240
Watson, 4, 6, 15, 21, 41, 43, 47, 48, 52, 64, 69, 95, 139, 199, 201, 207, 240, 260, 269, 280, 284, 288, 294, 309, 311, 336, 338, 386, 392, 437, 446, 451, 452, 453, 455, 484, 489, 492, 507, 521, 526, 529, 530
Watterston, 92, 182, 274, 358, 432, 433
Watts, 117, 399, 452, 514
Waugh, 118, 134
Way, 395
Wayles, 261
Wayne, 491, 494, 513
Waynflete, 314
Wearvell, 483
Weatherby, 11, 58, 233, 398, 558
Weatherford, 169, 170
Weatherley, 508
Weatherly, 303
Weathers, 508
Weaver, 58, 92, 272, 331, 429, 455, 503
Webb, 17, 171, 195, 203, 205, 207, 233, 235, 304, 312, 339, 372, 397, 430, 444, 446
Webber, 221, 397
Weber, 58, 562
Webster, 7, 35, 46, 48, 50, 102, 110, 112, 227, 252, 263, 274, 286, 343, 408, 459, 507
Weddel, 138
Weddell, 403
Weddingen, 403
Wedmayer, 395
Weed, 371
Weeden, 93
Weekly, 133
Weeks, 75, 493, 521, 567
Weelen, 444
Weems, 163
Weger, 457
Weichman, 558
Weidman, 442
Weight, 445
Weighten, 394
Weightman, 47, 274, 277, 292, 298, 311, 517
Weins, 451
Weir, 129, 137, 197, 273, 487
Weisenger, 418
Weith, 447
Welch, 95, 125, 227, 325, 371, 386, 413, 494, 539, 557
Weld, 89, 96, 107, 340, 438, 539
Weldon, 449
Wellborne, 200
Weller, 448
Welles, 280, 523
Wellford, 103, 411, 523
Wellington, 139, 357

Wellman, 551
Wellmuth, 376
Wells, 163, 198, 207, 261, 278, 370, 446, 448, 452, 479, 510
Welsh, 11, 58, 139, 222, 364, 404, 451, 453, 508
Welston, 453
Welton, 115
Wendell, 532
Wenderlich, 92
Weneble, 485
Wengierski, 494
Wentworth, 50, 477, 510
Wenwood, 535
Wenzel, 349
Werden, 94, 331
Werner, 58
Werster, 349
Wescott, 386, 493
Wesley, 231
Wessells, 108, 528
Wessels, 387, 396
West, 22, 127, 136, 141, 163, 221, 314, 345, 386, 387, 396, 397, 404, 450, 476, 517, 521
Westcott, 46, 98, 101, 504, 528, 557
Westerdelot, 443
Westerfield, 230
Westfield, 398
Westly, 77
Weston, 301, 339, 426
Westvelt, 482
Wetherall, 251
Wethered, 251
Wetherell, 408
Wetmore, 94, 490
Wetten, 62
Weyer, 133
Weygand, 454
Weymann, 500
Weymouth, 448
Weyrich, 92
Whaley, 429, 456, 561
Wharton, 386, 395, 396, 458, 541
Wheat, 39, 58, 115, 568
Wheatley, 139, 267, 281, 386, 518
Wheatly, 517
Wheaton, 129, 194, 237, 461
Whedbee, 106
Wheeden, 199
Wheeler, 11, 130, 162, 166, 184, 224, 234, 239, 361, 386, 394, 443, 445, 451, 488, 543, 557, 561
Wheelwright, 457
Whelan, 302
Whelply, 79
Whetcroft, 383
Whipple, 89, 195, 222, 321, 334, 338, 346, 451, 470, 507
Whipples, 76
Whippo, 283
Whistler, 108, 252, 325, 460, 486
Whitaker, 45, 112, 113, 253, 351, 398, 553, 566
Whitall, 430, 540
Whitcomb, 248, 287, 313, 502
Whitcombe, 396
White, 7, 11, 37, 38, 47, 50, 64, 66, 69, 82, 84, 85, 103, 134, 135, 136, 158, 163, 165, 191, 200, 213, 214, 218, 221, 223, 224, 227, 259, 260, 274, 305, 360, 390, 395, 396, 397, 403, 405, 415, 443, 449, 453, 456, 484, 499, 507, 509, 510, 518, 537, 556, 559
Whitebread, 451
Whiteman, 230
Whiteside, 29, 127, 136, 170
Whitesides, 5, 365
Whitfield, 482
Whitford, 394
Whitholm, 509
Whiting, 108, 169, 170, 181, 305, 340
Whitman, 425, 458
Whitney, 5, 29, 47, 318, 398, 469, 505
Whiton, 510
Whitson, 33, 84, 157
Whittaker, 337, 339
Whittal, 162
Whittel, 224
Whittemore, 469

Whitten, 195, 335, 338
Whittingham, 77
Whittington, 224
Whittle, 5, 36, 216, 376
Whittlesey, 57, 238, 473, 538
Whitton, 472
Whitty, 451
Whitwell, 58, 172, 294, 432
Whyte, 225
Wiberg, 349
Wick, 14, 211
Wickes, 35
Wickham, 7, 14, 16, 111, 379, 543, 548
Wickliffe, 203, 206
Widdicomb, 121
Widdicombe, 22, 392, 520
Widdicombe's, 22
Wiegmann, 409
Wier, 523
Wiernest, 445
Wiey, 136
Wiggins, 399
Wight, 397
Wightman, 89
Wilbar, 478, 543, 563
Wilber, 457, 552
Wilbro, 396
Wilbur, 434
Wilburn, 527
Wilcox, 109, 163, 335, 444, 544, 556
Wilde, 400, 402, 419, 505
Wilder, 196, 206, 249, 368, 398
Wildman, 344
Wilds, 200
Wiley, 202, 370, 418, 444, 469, 542
Wilhart, 137
Wilhelm, 224
Wilkes, 48, 136, 345
Wilkeson, 367, 554
Wilkie, 445, 477
Wilkin, 157, 196, 208
Wilkins, 202, 235, 362, 431, 559, 567
Wilkinson, 8, 134, 203, 233, 234, 283, 327, 420, 446, 453, 464
Willard, 95, 280, 425
Willcox, 345
Willemant, 457
Willet, 189, 255, 299
Willett, 58, 362
Willey, 508
Williams, 24, 33, 47, 57, 58, 85, 90, 92, 94, 100, 101, 107, 119, 139, 140, 159, 163, 166, 167, 177, 184, 194, 209, 211, 221, 224, 225, 226, 233, 235, 237, 239, 240, 264, 266, 269, 294, 303, 326, 327, 342, 353, 387, 393, 394, 396, 397, 399, 413, 418, 426, 439, 441, 446, 451, 454, 457, 485, 487, 495, 502, 507, 508, 509, 510, 516, 522, 524, 527, 530, 532, 552, 554, 559, 560, 562, 563
Williamsburg, 402
Williamson, 108, 141, 153, 181, 374, 416, 455, 507, 513, 552, 553, 555, 557
Willingham, 509
Willink, 387
Willis, 127, 138, 142, 143, 164, 220, 223, 266, 283, 316, 504, 552, 566
Willliams, 64
Willock, 349
Willow Grove, 372
Wills, 14, 451, 528
Willson, 185, 291, 341, 418, 431, 436
Wilmer, 41, 176, 393, 394
Wilmot, 457
Wilmouth, 140
Wilner, 93, 516
Wilrainish, 431
Wilson, 6, 11, 31, 45, 57, 58, 59, 61, 62, 79, 98, 99, 106, 110, 121, 137, 138, 141, 154, 172, 188, 198, 205, 222, 225, 226, 230, 231, 246, 258, 263, 267, 285, 289, 303, 311, 315, 332, 333, 346, 349, 353, 354, 362, 374, 376, 377, 386, 391, 393, 394, 396, 399, 404, 406, 409, 411, 415, 418, 423, 428, 429, 441, 442, 447, 448, 449, 450, 451, 455, 468, 481, 493, 494, 515, 533, 535, 542, 547, 552, 556
Wilsse, 399

Wiltberger, 4, 11, 164
Wilton, 393, 493
Wimsatt, 514, 519
Winans, 28, 33, 45, 84, 202, 207
Winchester, 92
Winder, 204, 240, 330, 351, 387, 422, 428, 431
Winder Tract, 328, 411
Windle, 221, 346
Windor, 470
Windsor, 527
Winebiddle, 494
Wines, 528
Wingerd, 283
Winlock, 139
Winn, 218, 313
Winship, 233, 330
Winslow, 24, 327, 343, 486
Winston, 50, 58, 248, 273, 277
Winter, 298, 399, 451
Winthrop, 323, 363, 403
Wirrans, 134
Wirrick, 445
Wirt, 163
Wise, 57, 65, 83, 94, 184, 230, 231, 259, 298, 313, 321, 378, 396, 418, 452, 472, 553, 556
Wishart, 33, 66
Wisner, 24
Wisniowski, 364
Wissal, 452
Wiswall, 53
Witbeck, 300
Withers, 90, 127, 139, 199, 205, 541, 542
Witherspoon, 162, 543
Witnell, 450
Witter, 443
Witty, 452
Wm the Conqueror, 145
Wofford, 199, 206, 542, 546
Wogan, 394
Wolbert, 229
Wolf, 446, 450
Wolfe, 133
Wolkbrabe, 403
Wolke, 139
Wollard, 30, 360, 361
Womsby, 533
Wonderlich, 226, 430
Wondus, 454
Wood, 42, 58, 67, 80, 96, 98, 104, 110, 111, 164, 180, 184, 198, 200, 206, 211, 213, 221, 224, 239, 246, 288, 326, 329, 370, 376, 386, 395, 398, 399, 408, 418, 431, 446, 449, 454, 483, 497, 502, 503, 509, 525
Woodbridge, 497
Woodbury, 99, 452, 469
Woodcock, 63
Wooden, 398
Woodhouse, 195
Woodling, 136
Woodlot #6, 288
Woodly, 181
Woodman, 195, 303, 541, 546
Woodriff, 287
Woodruff, 199, 306, 419
Woods, 137, 177, 201, 205, 226, 267, 327, 335, 400, 434, 483
Woodside, 317
Woodson, 66, 206
Woodstock, 529
Woodville, 347
Woodward, 46, 47, 96, 127, 135, 242, 279, 421, 456, 508, 509, 557
Woodworth, 32, 46, 467
Wool, 12, 74, 170, 264, 462
Woolard, 429
Wooldrige, 372
Wooley, 181
Woolf, 278
Woolfolk, 101
Woolford, 126, 204
Woolley, 221, 524
Wooster, 290, 404
Wooten, 398, 425
Wootton, 209
Worcester, 451
Worden, 32

Wordsworth, 328
Workman, 221, 442
Wormstead, 96
Worster, 83
Worth, 73, 74, 110, 152, 408, 440, 441, 463, 490, 497
Wortherspoon, 237
Worthington, 251, 455
Wotherspoon, 445
Wrick, 446
Wright, 10, 13, 15, 26, 46, 48, 58, 88, 102, 121, 123, 136, 140, 152, 184, 202, 210, 221, 233, 239, 245, 252, 280, 301, 311, 318, 329, 340, 349, 361, 371, 375, 387, 398, 403, 409, 421, 427, 435, 438, 439, 440, 444, 454, 462, 479, 488, 490, 499, 510, 524, 533, 553, 559
Wroe, 310, 386, 421, 559
Wurts, 94
Wyatt, 97, 137, 443, 561
Wyche, 199, 334, 335
Wylie, 531
Wyman, 161, 566
Wymer, 396
Wymp, 448
Wynkoop, 261, 428, 494
Wynn, 140
Wynsers, 508
Wyse, 107, 141

Y

Yarborough, 373
Yard, 157, 196, 207, 235, 548
Yarlott, 493
Yarnall, 161, 566
Yates, 331, 449
Yeabower, 58
Yeager, 443
Yearwood, 211
Yeates, 316
Yeatman, 118, 429
Yeats, 284
Yeawon, 223
Yell, 12, 127, 140, 143, 144, 170, 190, 299, 316
Yellott, 411, 473
Yelton, 139
Yerby, 34, 58, 556
Yorick, 445
York, 265
Yost, 66
Young, 11, 45, 52, 58, 65, 86, 92, 161, 163, 171, 181, 212, 214, 226, 230, 231, 241, 244, 245, 259, 261, 274, 286, 314, 316, 350, 355, 358, 364, 374, 387, 394, 396, 398, 418, 419, 426, 449, 450, 451, 454, 457, 462, 472, 491, 506, 508, 515, 516, 517, 518, 537, 544, 556
Youngs, 133
Ypsilanti, 51
Yurchanote, 215

Z

Zabriskie, 127, 135, 299
Zalikiwick, 443
Zane, 374
Zear, 450
Zeigler, 373
Zeilin, 240
Zell, 237
Zellor, 509
Zevely, 480, 490
Zimmerman, 103, 175, 221, 452, 454, 493
Zink, 443
Zirngrible, 394
Zoller, 508

Other Heritage Books by the author:

National Intelligencer *Newspaper Abstracts, Special Edition: The Civil War Years, 1861-1863*

National Intelligencer *Newspaper Abstracts 1848*

National Intelligencer *Newspaper Abstracts 1847*

National Intelligencer *Newspaper Abstracts 1846*

National Intelligencer *Newspaper Abstracts 1845*

National Intelligencer *Newspaper Abstracts 1844*

National Intelligencer *Newspaper Abstracts 1843*

National Intelligencer *Newspaper Abstracts 1842*

National Intelligencer *Newspaper Abstracts 1841*

National Intelligencer *Newspaper Abstracts 1840*

National Intelligencer *Newspaper Abstracts, 1838-1839*

National Intelligencer *Newspaper Abstracts, 1836-1837*

National Intelligencer *Newspaper Abstracts, 1834-1835*

National Intelligencer *Newspaper Abstracts, 1832-1833*

National Intelligencer *Newspaper Abstracts, 1830-1831*

National Intelligencer *Newspaper Abstracts, 1827-1829*

National Intelligencer *Newspaper Abstracts, 1824-1826*

National Intelligencer *Newspaper Abstracts, 1821-1823*

National Intelligencer *Newspaper Abstracts, 1818-1820*

National Intelligencer *Newspaper Abstracts, 1814-1817*

National Intelligencer *Newspaper Abstracts, 1811-1813*

National Intelligencer *Newspaper Abstracts, 1806-1810*

National Intelligencer *Newspaper Abstracts, 1800-1805*

www.ingramcontent.com/pod-product-compliance
Lightning Source LLC
Chambersburg PA
CBHW070802020526
44116CB00030B/976

9780788444753